# HOLLYWOOD  SONGSTERS

Garland Reference Library of the Humanities
*(Vol. 1164)*

# Also of Interest from Garland

*Hollywood Baby Boomers: A Biographical Dictionary*
by James Robert Parish and Don Stanke

*Encyclopedia of American War Films*
by Larry Langman and Edgar Borg

*Encyclopedia of American Spy Films*
by Larry Langman and David Ebner

*Black Arts Annual*
edited by Donald Bogle

*Blacks in American Films and Television: An Illustrated Encyclopedia*
by Donald Bogle

*Encyclopedia of American Film Comedy*
by Larry Langman

# HOLLYWOOD SONGSTERS

*by*
James Robert Parish
*and*
Michael R. Pitts

GARLAND PUBLISHING, INC.

*New York & London* 1991

**Library of Congress Cataloging-in-Publication Data**

Parish, James Robert.
    Hollywood Songsters / by James Robert Parish and Michael R. Pitts.
       p.   cm. — (Garland reference library of the humanities : vol. 1164)
    Includes index.
    ISBN 0-8240-3444-9 (alk. paper)
    1. Singers—United States—Biography. 2. Motion picture
actors and actresses—United States—Biography. I. Pitts, Michael
R. II. Title. III. Series.
ML400.P295   1991
782'.0092'2—dc20
[B]                             90-41110
                                 CIP
                                 MN

Book design: Barbara Bergeron
Cover design: John Röblin

Printed on acid-free, 250-year-life paper
Manufactured in the United States of America

for

Kate Smith (1907–1986)

*The Songbird of the South*

# CONTENTS

# Contents

# AUTHORS' NOTE

AS INDICATED BY THE TITLE, *HOLLYWOOD SONGSTERS* INCLUDES performers who have had success both as singers *and* as film stars. In compiling this volume, we have tried to include a variety of personalities who have been popular since the introduction of sound to movies in the late 1920s. Naturally, some of those included have had more success than others and some are associated more with singing than acting, or vice versa, but all have had an impact in both media.

While we have included over one hundred performers in this volume, we realize that not every singer who has worked successfully in motion pictures has been included. If you find that your favorite is missing, drop us a note (in care of the publisher) and tell us so. Also, we welcome additions and corrections for this book. Given the space limitations, we could not give minute details on all aspects of the lives and careers of the people included here, but we hope we have provided well-rounded coverage of their show business activities, especially in relation to their music and films.

James Robert Parish
Michael R. Pitts

JAMES ROBERT PARISH, a Los Angeles–based direct marketing consultant and freelance writer, was born in Cambridge, Massachusetts. He attended the University of Pennsylvania and graduated Phi Beta Kappa with a degree in English. A graduate of the University of Pennsylvania Law School, he is a member of the New York Bar. As president of Entertainment Copyright Research Co., Inc., he headed a major research facility for the film and television industries. Later he was a film reviewer–interviewer for the trade newspapers *Motion Picture Daily* and *Variety*. He is the author of over seventy-five volumes, including *Prison Pictures from Hollywood, The Fox Girls, Good Dames, The Slapstick Queens, The RKO Gals, The Tough Guys, The Jeanette MacDonald Story, The Elvis Presley Scrapbook, The Hollywood Beauties, The Great Combat Pictures*, and *The Great Cop Pictures*. Among those he has co-written are *The MGM Stock Company, The Debonairs, Liza!, Hollywood Character Actors, The Hollywood Reliables, The Funsters, The Best of MGM, Black Action Pictures from Hollywood*, and his ongoing series, *Complete Actors Television Credits* with Vincent Terrace. With Michael R. Pitts, he has co-written such books as *Hollywood on Hollywood, The Great Western Pictures* (base and companion volumes), *The Great Gangster Pictures* (base and companion volumes), *The Great Spy Pictures* (base and companion volumes), *The Great Science Fiction Pictures* (base and companion volumes), *The Great Detective Pictures*, and *Great Hollywood Musicals*. Mr. Parish's entertainment research collection is archived at Kent State University Library in Kent, Ohio.

MICHAEL R. PITTS is a freelance writer who has written or co-authored numerous books on entertainment, including *Kate Smith: A Bio-Bibliography, Western Movies, Hollywood and American History, Horror Film Stars, Famous Movie Detectives, Hollywood on Record, The Bible on Film*, and two editions of *Radio Soundtracks*.

With Mr. Parish he has written *The Great . . . Pictures* series and its companion volumes. In addition, he has contributed to several other published books and his magazine articles have been published both here and abroad. With degrees in history and journalism, Mr. Pitts writes columns on record collecting for *The Big Reel* and *Classic Images* magazines. He has written record album liner notes and lectures on film history and entertainment. Mr. Pitts resides in Indiana with his wife, Carolyn, and daughter, Angela.

# KEYS TO ABBREVIATIONS

## *Filmography Key*

| | |
|---|---|
| AA | Allied Artists |
| ABC-TV | American Broadcasting Corporation |
| AIP | American International Pictures |
| Aus | Austrian |
| Avco Emb | Avco Embassy Pictures |
| Br | British |
| Braz | Brazilian |
| BV | Buena Vista |
| Can | Canadian |
| CBN | Christian Broadcasting Network (Family Channel) |
| CBS-TV | Columbia Broadcasting System |
| Cin | Cinerama Releasing Corporation |
| Col | Columbia Pictures |
| Emb | Embassy Pictures Corporation |
| FBO | Film Booking Offices of America |
| FN | First National Pictures (Warner Bros.) |
| Fox | Fox Film Corporation |
| Fr | French |
| Ger | German |
| GN | Grand National Pictures |
| Ir | Iranian |
| It | Italian |
| Lip | Lippert Films |
| MGM | Metro-Goldwyn-Mayer Pictures |
| MGM/UA | Metro-Goldwyn-Mayer/United Artists Pictures |
| Mon | Monogram Pictures |
| NBC-TV | National Broadcasting Corporation |
| NG | National General Pictures |
| NTA | National Television Associates |
| Par | Paramount Pictures |
| PRC | Producers Releasing Corporation |
| Rep | Republic Pictures Corporation |
| RKO | RKO Radio Pictures |
| (s) | Short Subject |
| Soundies | Soundies Distributing Corporation of America (SDCA) |
| Sp | Spanish |

| | |
|---|---|
| Synd | Syndicated TV |
| Tif | Tiffany Film Corporation |
| 20th–Fox | 20th Century–Fox Film Corporation |
| UA | United Artists Pictures |
| UI | Universal–International Pictures |
| Univ | Universal Pictures |
| Unk | Unknown Distributor |
| Vita | Vitaphone Corporation (Warner Bros.) |
| WB | Warner Bros. Pictures |
| WB–7 Arts | Warner Bros.–Seven Arts Pictures |

### Notes

- A film title in brackets following a listing is the alternate release, reissue, or British release title for the given film.
- Made-for-television feature films (telefilms) broadcast originally on one or two nights are listed as part of the filmography; miniseries of three or more parts are listed under television series.

## Television Series Key

| | |
|---|---|
| ABC | American Broadcasting Corporation |
| CBN | Christian Broadcasting Network (Family Channel) |
| CBS | Columbia Broadcasting System |
| NBC | National Broadcasting Corporation |
| NN | Non-Network |
| Synd | Syndicated |
| TNN | The Nashville Network |

## Album Discography Key

| | |
|---|---|
| Cap | Capitol Records |
| CIF | Classic International Filmusicals Records |
| Col | Columbia Records |
| Har | Harmony Records |
| Mer | Mercury Records |
| MGM | Metro-Goldwyn-Mayer Records |
| OC | Original Cast |
| Par | Paramount Records |
| SRO | Standing Room Only Records |
| ST | Soundtrack (film) |
| ST/R | Soundtrack (radio) |
| ST/TV | Soundtrack (television) |
| UA | United Artists Records |
| WB | Warner Bros. Records |

*Notes*
- The listing 10" in front of the company name refers to a ten-inch long playing record; all others are twelve-inch LPs. We have NOT included 78s, 45s, EPs, 8-tracks, cassettes, or CDs.
- When two catalogue numbers are given for a recording, the first is for the Monaural release; the second for Stereo.
- Regarding reissues: the original issue company and catalogue number are listed first, followed by any reissues; the one exception is some of the soundtracks from MGM musical films, which have had as many as a half-dozen reissues. In such cases, we have listed the first issue only. When a title was first issued on a ten-inch LP, we listed it, followed by the first twelve-inch LP release (if any).
- We had to draw the line on some LPs where one of the Hollywood Songsters does *not* do the entire record. In general, if a performer does at least one side of the LP or is given substantial billing on the jacket, we listed it, and tried to include the names of other performers on the record.
- In the record listings, Amalgamated Records is an umbrella title for a host of small, independent labels. We have used the Amalgamated catalogue numbers for such releases.

# ACKNOWLEDGMENTS

Academy of Motion Picture Arts &
  Sciences Library
Beverly Hills Public Library
Stephen Bourne
Beverly B. Buehrer
Diana Canova
Grace A. Catalano
John Cocchi
Howard Davis
George Dean
Dennis Deas
Philip R. Evans
Film Favorites (Karen Martin)
Sharon R. Fox
Charlene George
Kim Holston
Barbara Hoover
Dr. Tom Joyce
Larry Edmunds Bookshop (Peter Bateman)
Bruce R. Leiby
Frank Lenger
Doug McClelland
Alvin H. Marill

Lee Mattson
Mrs. Earl Meisinger
Jim Meyer
Peter Miglierini
Music & Memories Record Shop (Dan Alvino)
Ron Parker
Joe Pike
Barry Rivadue
Dr. Tom Royce
Margie Schultz
Arleen Schwartz
Les Schwartz
Jimmy Short
Steve Skjelstad
Mark Speck
Les Spindle
Connie Stein
Tom J. Studo
Charles K. Stumpf
Kevin Sweeney
Vincent Terrace
Tinseltown Titles (Ann V. McKee)
Ray White

*Special Editorial Consultant*: T. Allan Taylor

# JUNE ALLYSON

PORTRAYING THE TWINKLY-EYED GIRL NEXT DOOR BECAME JUNE Allyson's movie forte. During the 1940s she was America's idealized image of the wholesome young woman left behind. On screen she was always one step away from a tear, with that telling catch in her husky voice belying her brave smile. Fans (if not always the critics) liked her best when she teamed in romantic fluff with bobby-soxer idol Van Johnson (he was 6' 2", she was 5' 1"; and he had even more freckles than she). Infrequently, she was permitted to sing and dance in pictures. On these occasions she radiated such verve that she stole the limelight from better-known musical performers. But then it would be back to the Peter Pan collars and more saccharine, sappy roles for this petite miss, who demonstrated a surprising dramatic flair in THE SHRIKE (1955). It is off camera that June Allyson has proven what a gritty lady she really is, overcoming several personal tragedies, and always reemerging in the public eye in one aspect or another of show business.

She was born Ella Geisman in a three-room tenement on 143rd Street and Third Avenue in New York's South Bronx on October 7, 1917. (Later, MGM publicists would subtract as much as a decade from her real age.) She was the second child of Clara and Robert Geisman. She was six months old when her father, a building janitor, left her mother, taking her older brother, Henry, to live with his mother. Clara Geisman went to work in a print shop, while Ella was sent to stay with her maternal grandparents. Whenever enough money was scraped together, Clara would rent a cheap railroad flat apartment so she and Ella could be together. Then, when money ran out again, Ella would be shipped back to her grandparents or passed around to other relatives. One day, when Ella was eight, she was racing down the neighborhood street one Sunday with a little wire-haired terrier. They stopped beneath a tree to rest. A large limb came loose, landing on Ella and the animal. The dog was killed while Ella suffered a fractured skull and a broken back. She was injured so badly that she had to wear a heavy steel brace from her neck to her hips for four years.

"My whole youth was a nightmare," the actress would recall. "I grew up wanting to escape from everyone and everything that had made it so." Thus she would concoct an elaborate story that she had been born in tree-lined Lucerne, New York; that in high school (after her injury from running down a hillside and tripping over a concealed log) she had become a swimming star; and that her home life had been rosy. In retrospect, she rationalized, "I told myself that movie audiences wouldn't respect a girl from the tenement side of New York City."

Part of her escape from her precarious childhood was going to the movies; she especially thrived on the screen magic of Fred Astaire and Ginger Rogers. She dreamed of becoming an entertainer and this strong determination—plus exercise—helped her to regain her strength. By the time Ella entered Theodore Roosevelt High School her mother had remarried (to Arthur Peters) and she had a half brother named Arthur. With the household finances more stable, Ella took lessons at Ned Wayburn Dancing Academy. As Elaine Peters she entered neighborhood amateur night contests in the Bronx. Although she never won, she enthusiastically continued dancing. When her stepfather died, Ella quit high school (after only two and a half years), determined to enter the world of professional show business.

She managed, eventually, to get a $60 per week tap-dance job at the Lido Club in Montreal and later appeared inconspicuously in several short subjects for Vitaphone (Warner Bros.) and Educational that were filmed in New York. Then came Broadway. She landed a chorus job in Harold Rome's musical revue *Sing Out the News* (1938). That show closed after 105 performances, and ultra-aggressive Ella (already billing herself as June Allyson) joined the Copacabana Club chorus line. Always auditioning, she next was cast in *Very Warm for May* (1939), a Jerome Kern–Oscar Hammerstein II musical, in which she hoofed in the chorus line. Although this show folded after fifty-nine performances, it led to June's being hired for Rodgers and Hart's *Higher and Higher* (1940). "I've been in more flops than you can imagine. I couldn't dance, and Lord knows I couldn't sing, but I got by somehow. It was Richard Rodgers who was always keeping them from firing me, as every dance director wanted to do." Next came Cole Porter's *Panama Hattie* (1940), starring Ethel Merman. June was in the chorus along with roommate Betsy Blair (who married Gene Kelly). The latter would recall, "She was the smallest girl and the last in the line—and on our exit, she would pretend to trip. When she picked herself up, everyone would applaud out of sympathy, which was just what she wanted." Chorine June also understudied bombastic ingenue Betty Hutton. When Hutton was ill with the measles, June went on for five performances and in the audience one of those nights was Broadway director George Abbott, who cast her in the musical *Best Foot Forward* (1941). June was earning $125 a week and had by now moved into the American Women's Club in Manhattan and was dating singer Tommy Mitchell (who had been in *Sing Out the News*). *Best Foot Forward* closed after a 326-performance run, with June and Nancy Walker being among those cast members contracted by Metro-Goldwyn-Mayer for the film version.

According to Allyson, it was producer Joe Pasternak who convinced MGM studio head Louis B. Mayer to look at her screen test. Pasternak urged, "Please look at this test and do just two things. Look at her eyes and listen to her voice. Don't pay any attention to anything else about her. These are distractions we can iron out." In the Technicolor BEST FOOT FORWARD (1943), which starred Lucille Ball as a movie star visiting a military academy as a publicity stunt, June repeated her role as Ethel who, along with Nancy Walker and Gloria De Haven, is on campus for the big prom. She joined in the numbers "The Three B's" and "Buckle Down Winsocki." This film proved an adequate feature debut for June, a perky redhead with an unexpectedly husky voice (due to recurrent bronchitis and enlarged vocal cords). Next she did a specialty number in the musical GIRL CRAZY (1943), in which she sang "Treat Me Rough" in a Manhattan nightclub scene while manhandling a bewildered Mickey Rooney. In THOUSANDS CHEER (1943) the trio of June, Gloria De Haven, and deadpan Virginia O'Brien performed "Spanish Town" to the accompaniment of Bob Crosby and His BobCats Band.

June's professional turning point was TWO GIRLS AND A SAILOR (1944), which boasted a bevy of guest stars: José Iturbi, Lena Horne, Gracie Allen, Xavier Cugat's Orchestra, and Harry James's Orchestra. It showcased June and Gloria De Haven as song-and-dance sisters performing at a posh New York club. Until this picture, it was a toss-up at MGM whether the studio would promote Allyson *or* De Haven as their newest ingenue star. Oddsmakers would have favored more conventionally attractive De Haven, but in TWO GIRLS AND A SAILOR it was June (originally cast in the other role) who stole the show and won the on-camera love of leading man Van Johnson. This star-making assignment was preceded by a supporting part in MEET THE PEOPLE (1944), starring Lucille Ball and Dick Powell. During the making of this film she renewed her acquaintance with crooner/ actor Powell, who had seen one of her Broadway performances and met her backstage after the show. Allyson and the older Powell (who was ending his marriage to movie star Joan Blondell) became a Hollywood item and they were wed on August 19, 1945, despite the strong objections of Louis B. Mayer, who feared it might interrupt June's promising movie career. The bitterness Blondell felt over losing Powell to Allyson would translate into a nasty portrayal of her rival in Blondell's thinly veiled autobiographical fiction, *Center Door Fancy* (1972).

June was pushed into three 1945 releases. She was the weepy orchestra cellist whose husband is away at war in MUSIC FOR MILLIONS, outsobbed only by Margaret O'Brien as her little sister. Allyson cried her way through HER HIGHNESS AND THE BELLBOY as the invalid who adores bellhop Robert Walker who, in turn, is overwhelmed by the beauty of visiting royalty (Hedy Lamarr). She and Walker reteamed for THE SAILOR TAKES A WIFE. June and Kathryn Grayson were TWO SISTERS FROM BOSTON (1946), in a musical con-coction that corraled Lauritz Melchior, Jimmy Durante, and Peter Lawford into the same film! In the star-crowded TILL THE CLOUDS ROLL BY (1946), June was seen demurely dueting the title tune with Ray McDonald, was noticeably spirited in her rendition of "Leave It to Jane," and was downright spunky in her singing and cavorting to "Cleopatterer."

MGM, which frequently used June as a "threat" to recalcitrant Judy Garland, was now insistent that Allyson belonged in romantic fabrications, especially those co-starring Van Johnson. The sweetheart team made HIGH BARBAREE (1947), a failed wartime fan-tasy, followed by the madcap comedy THE BRIDE GOES WILD (1948). In between these, June actually starred in a musical, a reworking of the 1920s campus romp GOOD NEWS (1947), matched with Peter Lawford. She was already thirty, but she came across on camera as a high-spirited, much younger woman. Her last musical assignment under contract to the studio was singing a sparkling "Thou Swell" in WORDS AND MUSIC (1948). Also in this year, and much against her will (she hated the idea of parading in period costumes), she played Lady Constance opposite Gene Kelly in THE THREE MUSKETEERS, while domestically she and Powell adopted a baby girl they named Pamela. Powell's children (Ellen, Norman) by Joan Blondell sometimes lived with him and June.

After assuming Katharine Hepburn's role of Jo in a remake of LITTLE WOMEN (1949), June was in THE STRATTON STORY (1949) as the spunky miss who encourages her baseball-playing husband (James Stewart) after he loses a leg in a hunting accident. It was Powell who urged her to take the stereotyped assignment, which proved to be one of her most popular parts. Powell wanted to borrow his wife to co-star in United Artists' MRS. MIKE (1949), but Metro said no. Instead, they signed the actor to co-star with June in two mild home-lot productions: THE REFORMER AND THE REDHEAD (1949) and RIGHT CROSS (1950). It was also this year (on December 25) that she gave birth to Richard, Jr.; because of her pregnancy, she was replaced by Jane Powell opposite Fred Astaire in the musical ROYAL WEDDING (1951).

With her continuing popularity, June should have been getting better assignments. Instead, she was rematched with Van Johnson (already becoming passé) in TOO YOUNG TO KISS (1951), posing as a child prodigy pianist. In the tepid THE GIRL IN WHITE (1952) she was a dedicated female doctor, and in the absurd Korean War romance BATTLE CIR-CUS (1953) she replaced Shelley Winters as an Army nurse in love with Dr. Humphrey Bogart. Her final big-screen appearance with Johnson was in REMAINS TO BE SEEN (1953), a whodunit that played on the wrong half of double bills. When MGM, now run by Dore Schary, gave the promised lead comedienne role in THE LONG, LONG TRAILER (1954) to Lucille Ball and asked Allyson to take a pay cut, Allyson announced she would leave the studio.

June Allyson and Peter Lawford in GOOD NEWS (1947)

Her first freelance picture was the extremely popular THE GLENN MILLER STORY (1954), which again teamed June with Jimmy Stewart and capitalized effectively on her image as the weepy, loving wife. She was supposed to do THE GIBSON GIRL for Dick Powell, but the project did not jell, and it was Jane Russell not Allyson who played opposite Jeff Chandler in FOXFIRE (1955) at Universal. Instead, Allyson was among the all-star gathering in MGM's EXECUTIVE SUITE (1954); here she was William Holden's loyal spouse. More fun for her was 20th Century–Fox's CinemaScope comedy WOMAN'S WORLD (1954), in which she excelled as Cornel Wilde's well-meaning helpmate. Paramount cast her opposite Jimmy Stewart yet again for STRATEGIC AIR COMMAND (1955) and she was with equally short Alan Ladd in THE McCONNELL STORY (1955) at Warner Bros. Herein, on camera, she was the wife of a stressed-out jet pilot; off camera she and Ladd had a very personal relationship. Meanwhile, she wangled the title role in THE SHRIKE (1955) opposite José Ferrer; it was an acting stretch for June that came across more as a credible exercise than as good dramatics.

What followed was a period of being Hollywood's Queen of Remakes. At a $150,000 salary, she had the Norma Shearer role in MGM's musical rehash of THE WOMEN (1939), now known as THE OPPOSITE SEX (1956—in which her husband's ex-wife, Joan Blondell, had a featured role). She took over Claudette Colbert's Oscar-winning assignment from IT HAPPENED ONE NIGHT (1934) in the poor revamping, YOU CAN'T RUN AWAY FROM IT (1956). She was the lead in INTERLUDE (1957), a tearjerker revision of Irene Dunne's WHEN TOMORROW COMES (1939), and in MY MAN GODFREY (1957), opposite David Niven, she inherited Carole Lombard's classic screwball comedy lead from 1936. Thereafter, it was two years before she was back on camera, now as the woman who defies *all* for Jeff Chandler in Universal's STRANGER IN MY ARMS. It was her finale as a motion picture leading lady.

Like others before her, most notably Loretta Young, June turned to television to revive her career. (Dick Powell had already become a major force in the TV industry as an actor/director/producer.) As Allyson gained national media exposure for her anthology series, "The DuPont Show with June Allyson" (CBS-TV, 1959–61) she became more candid in her career observations. "I want to be me. During all those years at MGM, everything was done for me. The publicity department told me what to say on every interview. They stuck my neck into a Peter Pan collar, and Peter Pan and I were stuck together like glue. . . . I have a temper like everybody else and I get mad sometimes. But as June Allyson I wasn't allowed to get mad. . . . I see a camera, any kind of camera, and I automatically smile. . . ."

In 1961 she underwent a kidney operation and later throat surgery (which for a time left her with a soprano voice). She and Powell, who had a see-sawing marriage with separations (because he was *too* busy with his Four Star Productions), reconciled. By then he had developed cancer and he died on January 2, 1963, leaving a $2 million estate. Ten months later (October 12, 1963) she married Glenn Maxwell in Florida. He owned barber shops and had been Powell's hair stylist. They divorced in 1965, were re-wed in 1966, and divorced yet again (but still lived together). The latter divorce was prompted by the terms of Powell's will: she would receive $4,000 monthly if she was not married, $700 monthly if she was.

In the early 1960s June had appeared frequently on her husband's teleseries ("The Dick Powell Show" and "Zane Grey Theatre") and was a guest on pal Judy Garland's variety series in 1963. In 1967 Allyson attempted a nightclub act comeback with Donald O'Connor in Las Vegas, and in 1968 she and Van Johnson were reunited in the "High on a Rainbow" episode of the teleseries "Name of the Game." She was scheduled to star in a duo of Spanish Westerns in 1969 which did not materialize, and in 1970 she was among those who succeeded Julie Harris in the long-running Broadway romantic comedy *Forty Carats*. She went on national tour in 1972 with Judy Canova and Dennis Day in the revival of the old musical *No, No Nanette*. There was heightened media attention when June returned to MGM to appear in the James Garner detective thriller THEY ONLY KILL THEIR MASTERS (1972); she was cast as a lesbian. Two years later she was among the MGM alumni promoting the studio's documentary THAT'S ENTERTAINMENT! That same year she toured (as she had in 1968) with Dick Powell, Jr., in the comedy *My Daughter, Your Son*.

In the 1980s June, still looking youthful and trim, cropped up in telefeatures (THE KID WITH THE BROKEN HALO, 1982) and in episodes of such teleseries as "Love Boat" (1983) and "Murder, She Wrote" (1985). Her greater notice came in the mid-1980s when she became spokesperson for an adult diaper product. Wed to Dr. David Ashrow since October 1976, she has authored her autobiography, *June Allyson* (1982), written with Frances Spatz Leighton, in which she admits, "Today I am a woman. I'm not the scared little girl anymore. . . . Peace."

## Filmography

Swing for Sale (Vita, 1937) (s)
Pixilated (Educational, 1937) (s)
Dime a Dance (Educational, 1937) (s)
Dates and Nuts (Educational, 1938) (s)
The Prisoner of Swing (Vita, 1938) (s)
Sing for Sweetie (Educational, 1938) (s)
Rollin' in Rhythm (Vita, 1939) (s)
Best Foot Forward (MGM, 1943)
Girl Crazy (MGM, 1943)
Thousands Cheer (MGM, 1943)
Meet the People (MGM, 1944)
Two Girls and a Sailor (MGM, 1944)
Music for Millions (MGM, 1945)
Her Highness and the Bellboy (MGM, 1945)
The Sailor Takes a Wife (MGM, 1945)
Two Sisters from Boston (MGM, 1946)
Till the Clouds Roll By (MGM, 1946)
The Secret Heart (MGM, 1946)

High Barbaree (MGM, 1947)
Good News (MGM, 1947)
The Bride Goes Wild (MGM, 1948)
The Three Musketeers (MGM, 1948)
Words and Music (MGM, 1948)
Little Women (MGM, 1949)
The Stratton Story (MGM, 1949)
The Reformer and the Redhead (MGM, 1949)
Right Cross (MGM, 1950)
Too Young to Kiss (MGM, 1951)
The Girl in White [So Bright the Flame]
   (MGM, 1952)
Battle Circus (MGM, 1953)
Remains to Be Seen (MGM, 1953)
The Glenn Miller Story (Univ, 1954)
Executive Suite (MGM, 1954)
Woman's World (20th–Fox, 1954)
Strategic Air Command (Par, 1955)

The McConnell Story [Tiger in the Sky] (WB, 1955)
The Shrike (Univ, 1955)
The Opposite Sex (MGM, 1956)
You Can't Run Away from It (Col, 1956)
Interlude (Univ, 1957)
My Man Godfrey (Univ, 1957)
Stranger in My Arms (Univ, 1959)
See the Man Run (NBC-TV, 12/11/71)

They Only Kill Their Masters (MGM, 1972)
Letters from Three Lovers (ABC-TV, 10/3/73)
Curse of the Black Widow (ABC-TV, 9/16/77)
Vegas (ABC-TV, 4/25/78)
Blackout (New World, 1978)
Three on a Date (ABC-TV, 2/17/78)
The Kid with the Broken Halo (NBC-TV, 4/5/82)

## Broadway Plays

Sing Out the News (1938)
Very Warm for May (1939)
Higher and Higher (1940)

Panama Hattie (1940)
Best Foot Forward (1941)
Forty Carats (1970) (replacement)

## TV Series

The DuPont Show with June Allyson (CBS, 1959–61)

## Album Discography

Best Foot Forward (Caliban 6039) [ST]
Girl Crazy (Curtain Calls 100/9-10) [ST]
Good News (MGM E-3229, Sountrak 111, Vertinge 2001) [ST]
Judy Garland & Friends (Minerva MIN LP-6JG-FNJ) [ST/TV] w. Steve Lawrence
Thousands Cheer (Amalgamated 232, Hollywood Soundstage 409) [ST]

Till the Clouds Roll By (10" MGM E-501, MGM E-3231, Metro M/S-578, Sountrak 115, Vertinge 2000) [ST]
Two Girls and a Sailor (Sound Stage 2307) [ST]
Very Warm for May (AEI 1156) [OC]
Words and Music (MGM E-3233, Metro M/S-580) [ST]

# DON AMECHE

DON AMECHE CELEBRATED MORE THAN A HALF-CENTURY IN SHOW business by making one of filmdom's biggest comebacks when he won an Academy Award for his performance in the science-fiction hit COCOON (1985). For years, although he had remained professionally active, Ameche had been considered a figure from Hollywood's nostalgic past, a personality best known for (and teased about) his title role in THE STORY OF ALEXANDER GRAHAM BELL (1939). In his seventies, his reemergence on the movie scene as a major box-office figure brought the actor a new generation of followers. In addition to appearing in some fifty feature films, Ameche has had a very diverse career, which has also included radio, Broadway, and television. In the 1930s and early 1940s, the dapper and droll Ameche was also a movie crooner who sang in many of his films. While he had a more than passable singing voice, vocalizing was to be only one of his screen accomplishments, for he was equally adept, or better, as a light comedian and a dramatic performer. In retrospect, the breezy, very polished leading man should have fought harder for showcase vehicles during his prime starring years during World War II.

Don Ameche was born Dominic Felix Amici in Kenosha, Wisconsin, on May 31, 1908, the son of an Italian immigrant father and a German-Irish mother; he was the second of eight children. He was educated in Catholic schools and at Columbia Academy in Dubuque, Iowa, where he was to meet his future wife, Honore Prendergast. After earning his school diploma, the young man acceded to his father's wishes and studied law at Washington, D.C.'s Georgetown University, but later transferred to the University of Wisconsin, where he became interested in dramatics. Thanks to his impressive work in college plays he won a part in the touring show *Excess Baggage*. He dropped out of school and went to New York City, where he obtained a small part in the Broadway show *Jerry for Short* (1929), billing himself as Don Ameche, the phonetic pronunciation of his name.

After the Broadway experience, Ameche became a singer in Texas Guinan's traveling vaudeville show. She disliked his stage presence and he was let go in Chicago, but got a part in the play *Illegal Practice* and then headed back to Manhattan where he landed radio work. In the next few years he acted in such radio programs as "The Empire Builder," "Betty and Bob," "Foreign Legion," "The Little Theatre Off Times Square," "Grand Hotel," and "Rin-Tin-Tin." However, his best-known role was as the host of the NBC series "The First Nighter" in the early 1930s. Don's brother Jim also became a radio announcer and performer and stayed with the medium to become one of its best-known voices in the next two decades. Meanwhile, Don Ameche was doing so well financially that he and Honore Prendergast were wed in 1932 and over the next several years they had five children. In 1933 he made his film debut in the short subject BEAUTY AT THE WORLD'S FAIR.

Ameche made a Hollywood screen test for MGM in 1935 which did not impress the studio. However, Darryl F. Zanuck at the newly formed 20th Century–Fox saw the test and offered the radio actor a seven-year contract. His first major appearance was as one of Jean Hersholt's sons in SINS OF MAN (1936). He made such a favorable impression that he was cast as the male lead in the remake of RAMONA (1936), as the Indian who weds a half-breed girl (Loretta Young) only to have them both suffer racial prejudice; it was in Technicolor. Ameche was one of a trio of suitors in LADIES IN LOVE (1936) and first displayed his trademark thin mustache when he co-starred with Sonja Henie in her film debut, ONE IN A MILLION (1937). In this delightful musical comedy he is the newsman who tumbles romantically for Henie and croons to her during the proceedings.

By now 20th Century–Fox realized that Don Ameche's handsome features, able singing voice, and likable personality were definite pluses for the studio. He would be used by his employer in a diverse number of roles (several of them thankless) in the next few years, always providing the studio with good box-office returns. In his first thirty-three motion pictures, he was loaned out on only three occasions. His five features for the studio in 1937 fairly well exemplify the tone of his career for his tenure with the Zanuck organization, which always favored its blondized female stars over contract leading men. ONE IN A MILLION and YOU CAN'T HAVE EVERYTHING (the first of a half-dozen screen pairings with Alice Faye) were tuneful musicals which offered him dashing, if one-dimensional, leading man roles with a chance to croon a bit; LOVE IS NEWS had him as a romantic contender who loses Loretta Young to handsome Tyrone Power; FIFTY ROADS TO TOWN had him winning the girl in a light comedy; and LOVE UNDER FIRE presented him in a basically dramatic role (although he does sing a song!) as a Scotland Yard detective caught in Spain during its civil war. In 1937 Ameche also began one of his best-known assignments, that of host of NBC radio's "The Chase and Sanborn Hour" with Edgar Bergen and Charlie McCarthy. Even after he became one of the top two dozen stars in Hollywood, he retained this post into the early 1940s, and was often a part of the famous radio duels between McCarthy and W. C. Fields.

The year 1938 offered congenial Ameche five more feature film parts at 20th Century–Fox and helped solidify his growing Hollywood popularity. The period melodrama IN OLD CHICAGO had him as a crusader at odds with crooked brother Tyrone Power over politics and Alice Faye, while HAPPY LANDING reteamed him with Sonja Henie. JOSETTE was a delightful comedy about brothers (Ameche, Robert Young) both pursuing Simone Simon while the Irving Berlin songfest ALEXANDER'S RAGTIME BAND had him as a pianist who wins singer Alice Faye only to lose her to bandsman Tyrone Power. The latter film provided Ameche and Faye with a good duet on "Now It Can Be Told." GATEWAY was a programmer that cast him as a war correspondent. The next year, 1939, again offered five features and it was his peak movie year. THE THREE MUSKETEERS was a delightful rendition of the Dumas swashbuckling classic with Ameche as D'Artagnan to the Ritz Brothers' musketeers, while in his first loanout he was a Paris cab driver who finds love with a beautiful woman (Claudette Colbert) in Paramount's grand comedy MIDNIGHT. Next came Ameche's most enduring film role, the title assignment in the contrived biography THE STORY OF ALEXANDER GRAHAM BELL. So completely identified was Ameche with Bell that it became a national joke that it was Don Ameche who actually invented the telephone! Dramatically he was just as good as the D. W. Griffith–like film director in HOLLYWOOD CAVALCADE (starring Alice Faye), and in SWANEE RIVER he portrayed the famous nineteenth-century American composer Stephen Foster. This film gave Ameche occasion to sing some of Foster's famous songs (although most were done by Al Jolson as E. P. Christie). Although Ameche intermittently sang in films, he never recorded commercially at the time because studio mogul Darryl F. Zanuck had a prohibition against studio stars making records, except for Alice Faye. Ameche and Faye were teamed for the fifth occasion in LILLIAN RUSSELL in 1940, in which he portrayed the famous star's first spouse. Later that year, in FOUR SONS (1940), he had a strong dramatic role as the scion of a Czech family persecuted by the Nazis. He closed out 1940 with the sprightly Technicolor musical DOWN ARGENTINE WAY in which he was a horse-breeder who carries a torch for Betty Grable in South America.

Despite going on suspension for refusing to go over to Paramount for the unimportant whodunit THE NIGHT OF JANUARY 16TH (1941), five more screen vehicles came Don Ameche's way in 1941. He began the year with another colorful song-and-dance entry, THAT NIGHT IN RIO, in which he was involved in a mistaken identity case as a singer *and*

Leonid Kinskey, Don Ameche, and S. Z. Sakall in THAT NIGHT IN RIO (1941)

a bank president; he and Alice Faye performed "Chica, Chica, Boom Chic," but the song was cut in deference to Carmen Miranda's exotic south-of-the-border version. MOON OVER MIAMI found Ameche being stalked by one of a trio of husband-hunting women, and he was a film director again in Paramount's comedy KISS THE BOYS GOODBYE, opposite Mary Martin. At MGM he was a college professor/writer whose wife (Rosalind Russell) gets jealous of his chic editor (Kay Francis) in THE FEMININE TOUCH while CONFIRM OR DENY had him back in the dramatic vein as a reporter who uncovers a Nazi plan to invade England. THE MAGNIFICENT DOPE (1942) offered Ameche a good part as a con artist, while he was a playboy romancing an heiress (Joan Bennett) in GIRL TROUBLE (1942). Ameche's favorite film role came in 1943 in the classic HEAVEN CAN WAIT, Ernst Lubitsch's wry period comedy which cast him as a droll sinner reliving his zesty life. HAPPY LAND (1943) found Ameche as the father of a typical middle-American family facing the war problem, and then it was back to musicals for the star in SOMETHING TO SHOUT ABOUT in 1943. Ameche had another solid dramatic role as an Air Force officer in the fine war drama WING AND A PRAYER (1944), and, in a lighter vein, he was a composer who finds love with Vivian Blaine in the unstellar musical GREENWICH VILLAGE (1944), his last contract feature for 20th. At United Artists he made a guest appearance as a comic singing waiter in the Fred Allen farce IT'S IN THE BAG (1945). Freelancing (and as a financial investor), the actor again co-starred with Claudette Colbert as a war correspondent in the comedy GUEST WIFE (1945) while at Universal he was a loony inventor in SO GOES MY LOVE (1946). In another comedy—more strained than amusing—THAT'S MY MAN (1947), he was a bookkeeper who becomes a horse-race fanatic, while in the modestly budgeted thriller SLEEP, MY LOVE (1948) he attempts to drive wife Claudette Colbert mad. In SLIGHTLY FRENCH (1949) he was a con man again.

Ameche had benefitted professionally during the World War II years from not being called into active service. However, his film career faded in the late 1940s as demobilized stars and younger players claimed the spotlight. Moreover, in the public's eye Ameche had been too typecast in frothy musicals, which were drifting out of fashion in the postwar years. Ameche again returned to radio, guesting on programs like Mutual's "Mother's Day Special" in 1947 and "Mail Call" and "The Spike Jones Show" in 1949. During the 1946–47 season he co-starred with Frances Langford and Pinky Lee on NBC's "The Dreme Program" on which he and Langford did their famous "The Bickersons" (feuding husband-and-wife characters created originally on "The Chase and Sanborn Hour") and in 1947–48 they starred as "The Bickersons" on CBS radio.

In 1950 Don Ameche and his family moved to New York City where he became actively involved in television. From October to December 1950 he emceed the NBC-TV quiz show "Take a Chance" and from 1950 to 1951 he was the hotel manager in ABC-TV's "Holiday Hotel," later called "Don Ameche's Musical Playhouse." He starred in the religious film THE TRIUMPHANT HOUR in 1950 and in the summer of 1951 he and Frances Langford reprised "The Bickersons" on CBS radio. The year 1953 found him a regular on NBC-TV's "Coke Time with Eddie Fisher." In 1954 he starred in two early TV movies, PHANTOM CARAVAN and FIRE ONE.

Don Ameche successfully made his leading man debut on Broadway in *Silk Stock-ings* (1955), Cole Porter's sophisticated musical version of the film NINOTCHKA (1939). The hit show cast Ameche as a hedonistic Frenchman in love with a beautiful Communist (Hildegarde Neff); he sang the title song and "All of You," and the play ran for a year; Fred Astaire did the screen version in 1957. On TV Ameche starred with Nanette Fabray in the NBC-TV special of "High Button Shoes" in 1956, and the next year he reappeared on Broadway in the middling comedy *Holiday for Lovers* as well as starred with Joan Bennett in a version of "Junior Miss" on CBS-TV's "DuPont Show of the Month." In 1958 he played Albert Anastasia on CBS-TV's "Climax" and hosted the syndicated TV series "Don Ameche Theatre." He also returned again to Broadway in a musical about early movie making, *Goldilocks*, with Elaine Stritch and Margaret Hamilton. This show had a good run, but Ameche was less successful with the Hawaii-set musical *13 Daughters* (1961). He co-starred with Joan Bennett in the short-lived 1959 NBC-TV comedy series "Too Young to Go Steady," and he was a frequent panelist on the CBS-TV quiz program "To Tell the Truth" in 1960–61.

In 1961 Ameche relocated to California and appeared as a senator in the political thriller A FEVER IN THE BLOOD and narrated an episode of NBC-TV's "Our American Heritage" before commencing a five-season run as the urbane host of that network's Friday night series "International Showtime." This successful series had him traveling in Europe to film the various circus acts he introduced. Back home he and Frances Langford were reunited on Columbia Records for two best-selling LPs about their Bickerson characters. Following the "International Showtime" run, Ameche guest-starred on such TV series as "The Greatest Show on Earth" and "Burke's Law." He returned to films in RINGS AROUND THE WORLD (1966), a film repeating his circus introductions, and in the tawdry murder mystery PICTURE MOMMY DEAD (1966) he was a father whose daughter (Susan Gordon) is supposedly haunted by the specter of her murdered mother (Zsa Zsa Gabor). He was back on Broadway in 1967's *Henry, Sweet Henry*, a failed musical version of Peter Sellers' popular film comedy THE WORLD OF HENRY ORIENT (1964). After that it was back to TV for guest shots on programs like "Alias Smith and Jones," "Julia," "Columbo," and TV movies such as SHADOW OVER ELVERON (1968) and GIDGET GETS MARRIED (1972), as well as featured roles in two 1970 theatrical comedies: SUPPOSE THEY GAVE A WAR AND NOBODY CAME and THE BOATNIKS, in both of which he played a military officer. He was on stage in 1974 for a tour with Evelyn Keyes in *No, No Nanette* and then another tour in the same show with Ruby Keeler. The next year he and Alice Faye reunited for a very successful road revival of *Good News* and Ameche guest-starred on the "McCloud" and "Ellery Queen" teleseries.

Outside of sporadic TV guest shots in such series as "The Love Boat," "Quincy," "Fantasy Island," "Mr. Smith," "Not in Front of the Kids," and "Detective in the House," Ameche remained fairly inactive until 1983, when he co-starred in the Eddie Murphy comedy TRADING PLACES and nearly stole the movie with his deft, underplayed humor. As a result he was cast as one of the Florida retirees who has his youth restored mystically in

COCOON (1985), the film netting him an Academy Award as Best Supporting Actor. He then co-starred with Bob Hope in the feckless TV-movie comedy A MASTERPIECE OF MURDER (1986) and had a featured part in the good-natured HARRY AND THE HENDER-SONS (1987), about a family trying to domesticate a Big Foot monster. In the TV-movie PALS (1987) he and another retiree (George C. Scott), living in a trailer park, stumble across hidden cash (drug-related proceeds) and discover money is not everything, especially when it brings such problems. The next year brought Ameche his second-favorite movie role, that of Italian immigrant Gino who goes to prison for the Mafia after having his dream of owning a fishing boat fulfilled, in THINGS CHANGE, directed by playwright David Mamet. "Working with David Mamet and Ernst Lubitsch are the only two great, great joys I've ever had," Ameche said. (In the fall of 1988 Ameche shared the Venice Film Festival's Best Actor Award with Joe Mantegna for their performances in THINGS CHANGE.) He closed out the year repeating his Oscar-winning role in COCOON: THE RETURN and early 1989 found him on Broadway taking over the role of the Stage Manager in yet another revival of *Our Town*.

Today Don Ameche credits his good health and lengthy, successful career to his religious faith. "I'm a deeply religious man, a Catholic—and without my religion I don't think I could have handled this business. More than once I've been at the pinnacle of success—and plunged into the depths. . . . For many people, to have climbed those mountains and then fallen so far would have created such bitterness they couldn't have survived. But I always had my God for comfort. In the good years I said an awful lot of prayers that helped keep my feet on the ground. And in the bad times, I always felt God was there watching over me."

Regarding his discipline in keeping himself mentally and physically active, he pointed out not long ago, "How many actors in their twenties and thirties have two pictures being released by major studios right now?"

## Filmography

Beauty at the World's Fair (Unk, 1933) (s)
Clive of India (Fox, 1935)
Dante's Inferno (Fox, 1935)
Sins of Man (20th–Fox, 1936)
Ramona (20th–Fox, 1936)
Ladies in Love (20th–Fox, 1936)
One in a Million (20th–Fox, 1937)
Love Is News (20th–Fox, 1937)
Fifty Roads to Town (20th–Fox, 1937)
You Can't Have Everything (20th–Fox, 1937)
Love Under Fire (20th–Fox, 1937)
Screen Snapshots #8 (Col, 1937) (s)
In Old Chicago (20th–Fox, 1938)
Happy Landing (20th–Fox, 1938)

Josette (20th–Fox, 1938)
Alexander's Ragtime Band (20th–Fox, 1938)
Gateway (20th–Fox, 1938)
The Three Musketeers [The Singing Musketeer] (20th–Fox, 1939)
Midnight (Par, 1939)
The Story of Alexander Graham Bell [The Modern Miracle] (20th–Fox, 1939)
Hollywood Cavalcade (20th–Fox, 1939)
Swanee River (20th–Fox, 1939)
Lillian Russell (20th–Fox, 1940)
Four Sons (20th–Fox, 1940)
Down Argentine Way (20th–Fox, 1940)
That Night in Rio (20th–Fox, 1941)

Moon over Miami (20th–Fox, 1941)
Kiss the Boys Goodbye (Par, 1941)
The Feminine Touch (MGM, 1941)
Confirm or Deny (20th–Fox, 1941)
The Magnificent Dope (20th–Fox, 1942)
Girl Trouble (20th–Fox, 1942)
Heaven Can Wait (20th–Fox, 1943)
Happy Land (20th–Fox, 1943)
Something to Shout About (20th–Fox, 1943)
Wing and a Prayer (20th–Fox, 1944)
Greenwich Village (20th–Fox, 1944)
It's in the Bag! [The Fifth Chair] (UA, 1945)
Guest Wife (UA, 1945)
So Goes My Love [A Genius in the Family] (Univ, 1946)
That's My Man [Will Tomorrow Ever Come?] (Rep, 1947)
Sleep, My Love (UA, 1948)
Slightly French (Col, 1949)
The Triumphant Hour (Peyton, 1950)
Hollywood Night at 21 Club (Col, 1952) (s)

Phantom Caravan (Princess, 1954)
Fire One (Princess, 1954)
A Fever in the Blood (WB, 1961)
Rings Around the World (Col, 1966)
Picture Mommy Dead (Emb, 1966)
Shadow over Elveron (NBC-TV, 3/5/68)
Suppose They Gave a War and Nobody Came (UA, 1970)
The Boatniks (BV, 1970)
Gidget Gets Married (ABC-TV, 1/4/72)
Won Ton Ton, the Dog Who Saved Hollywood (Par, 1976)
Trading Places (Par, 1983)
Cocoon (20th–Fox, 1985)
A Masterpiece of Murder (NBC-TV, 1/26/86)
Harry and the Hendersons (Univ, 1987)
Pals (CBS-TV 2/28/87)
Coming to America (Par, 1988)
Things Change (Tri-Star, 1988)
Cocoon: The Return (20th–Fox, 1988)

## Broadway Plays

Jerry for Short (1929)
Silk Stockings (1955)
Holiday for Lovers (1957)
Goldilocks (1958)

13 Daughters (1961)
Henry, Sweet Henry (1967)
Our Town (1989) (revival) (replacement)

## Radio Series

The First Nighter (NBC, ca. 1931–35)
The Chase and Sanborn Hour (NBC, ca. 1937–40s)

The Bickersons (NBC, 1946–47; CBS, 1947–48; CBS, 1951)

## TV Series

Holiday Hotel (ABC, 1950–51)
Take a Chance (ABC, 1950)
Star Time (Dumont, 1950–51)
Don Ameche's Musical Playhouse (ABC, 1951)
The Frances Langford–Don Ameche Show (ABC, 1951–52)

Coke Time with Eddie Fisher (NBC, 1953)
Don Ameche Theatre (CBS, 1958)
Too Young to Go Steady (NBC, 1959)
To Tell the Truth (CBS, ca. 1960–61)
International Showtime (NBC, 1961–65)

## Album Discography

Alexander's Ragtime Band (Hollywood Soundstage 406) [ST]

The Bickersons (Col CL-1692/CS-8492) w. Frances Langford

The Bickersons (Radiola 115) w. Frances Langford

The Bickersons Fight Back (Col CL-1883/CS-8683) w. Frances Langford

The Bickersons Rematch (Col G-30523) w. Frances Langford

Don Ameche—Co-Star (Co-Star 112)

Down Argentine Way (Caliban 6003, Hollywood Soundstage 5012) [ST]

The Further Radio Adventures of Larson E. Whipsnade and Other Taradiddles (Col KC-33240) w. W. C. Fields

Goldilocks (Col OL-5340/OS-2007) [OC]

The Great Radio Feuds (Col KC-33241) w. W. C. Fields

Greenwich Village (Caliban 6026) [ST]

Lillian Russell (Caliban 6016) [ST]

Mae West—Original Radio Broadcasts (Mark 56 643)

Mae West on the Chase and Sanborn Hour (Radiola 126)

Moon over Miami (Caliban 6001) [ST]

The Return of the Bickersons! (Radiola 3MR-4) w. Frances Langford

Silk Stockings (RCA OC-1016, RCA LOC/LSO-1102) [OC]

You Can't Have Everything (Titania 508) [ST]

# JULIE ANDREWS

AT THE HEIGHT OF HER TREMENDOUS POPULARITY IN THE MID-1960S, *Time* magazine effused, "To grown men, Julie Andrews is a lady; to housewives, she's the girl next door; to little children, the most huggable aunt of all. She is a Christmas carol in the snow, a companion by the fire, a laughing clown at charades, and a girl to read poetry to on a cold winter's night." Such high praise was not unusual then for this perfect-pitch soprano from England who had sung winningly on Broadway in *The Boy Friend, My Fair Lady,* and *Camelot.* She had gone on to claim an Oscar as the screen's MARY POPPINS (1964) and followed it with the enormously commercial THE SOUND OF MUSIC (1965) and the very successful THOROUGHLY MODERN MILLIE (1967). However, within a few years, as big-budget movie musicals proved unsalable, she became a star in desperate search of a proper vehicle. She attempted a TV variety series and a return to films, but they were typically comedies or dramas and her presence—while still welcome—was a case of nepotism since her filmmaker husband (Blake Edwards) was making the project.

Much of the career backlash was not Julie Andrews' fault. It was an instance of an overly successful personality being overhyped by the press. The public eventually grew weary of this "perfect" person who apparently had everything. (And so did Julie, who, more recently, has admitted she spent years in therapy adjusting to her image, her fame, and her career crises.)

When she toppled from her throne Julie chose, for a time, to devote herself to family life and other pursuits rather than fight the odds. Despite her continued professionalism, she has never quite made that anticipated return to the top. Ironically, today she is a more satisfying performer than in her glory years. She has expanded her acting range and with her mature warmth and strength she registers far truer as a person and as less of a manufactured star. Her looks remain intact as does her crystal-clear, beautiful voice with its superb diction.

She was born Julia Elizabeth Wells on October 1, 1935, in Walton-on-Thames in Surrey, England. Her father (Edward C. "Ted" Wells) was a metalcraft teacher, and her mother (Barbara Morris) was an amateur pianist who acted as rehearsal and performance accompanist in her sister Joan's dance school. Because Barbara could not afford a babysitter, Julie, as she became known, was taken along to the dance classes, thus developing an affinity for song and dance early in her life. When she was two, Julie began taking ballet and tap classes from Joan and was soon participating in the school's musical presentations. At age four, Julie's parents divorced, with her younger brother John going to live with her father. Her mother married Canadian-born tenor Ted Andrews (who billed himself as

"The Canadian Troubadour: Songs and a Guitar"), and the Andrews family moved to London. They began touring the provinces with their act and in 1943 the family relocated to Beckenham, Kent. The Andrewses would have two sons of their own: Donald and Christopher.

Ted Andrews was convinced that young Julie, with her four-and-one-half octave soprano range, had a calling in show business. He arranged for concert singer Madame Lilian Stiles-Allen to train the girl and later for Julie to enroll in a London performing arts school. By 1946, the family had moved back to Walton-on-Thames and Julie was appearing occasionally with her parents' vaudeville act and also with them on radio. In 1947 Ted Andrews introduced Julie to Val Parnell, head of the important Moss Empire theatrical booking circuit. That October she made her professional debut singing the "I Am Titania" aria from the opera *Mignon* in the *Starlight Roof* revue at London's Hippodrome Theatre. As a result of her excellent reviews, Julie came to the attention of MGM producer Joe Pasternak, who considered testing her for a screen career in Hollywood, then had second thoughts. She also met theatrical manager Charles Tucker during the show's run; he would have a strong influence on her budding career. More important, she was asked to appear in a Royal Command Performance (November 1, 1948) at the London Palladium for which Danny Kaye headlined the bill. It was also in 1948 that fifteen-year-old Julie met fourteen-year-old Tony Walton (her future husband). She was appearing in *Humpty Dumpty* at the London Casino and he was in the audience.

In 1950 she became a regular performer on the British Broadcasting Company's radio comedy series "Educating Archie." The show gained instant popularity for her throughout England and she stayed with it through 1952. Meanwhile, Julie continued concert appearances (with and without her parents) and was much in demand for an array of holiday pantomime productions: *Little Red Riding Hood* (1950), *Jack and the Beanstalk* (1952), and *Cinderella* (1953). It was during the latter—at the London Palladium—that Vida Hope, the director of the hit London musical spoof *The Boy Friend*, visited her backstage and offered her the lead of Polly Browne in the Broadway edition. She rejected the offer initially, despite the protests of her family and Charles Tucker. Instead, she accepted the role of a ruined southern belle in *Mountain Fire*, which played the provinces in the spring of 1954. When the show closed in August of that year, Julie accepted the New York City assignment reluctantly, insisting that her contract be for one year only. Meanwhile, her parents had separated and her own romance with Tony Walton had faltered, due to her infatuation with her *Mountain Fire* co-star, Neil McCallum.

The Americanized *The Boy Friend* opened on Broadway on September 30, 1954, the evening before Julie's nineteenth birthday. The infectious musical caught on immediately and its ingenue (being paid $400 weekly) became a Broadway figure. It led to television and radio guest appearances for her. Because of her short-term *Boy Friend* contract she was sought to audition for upcoming Broadway musicals. She was rejected for Rodgers and Hammerstein's *Pipe Dream* (1955), but won the interest of Alan Jay Lerner and Frederick Loewe, who were preparing a musical (*My Fair Lady*) based on George Bernard Shaw's *Pygmalion*. Less than a month before Julie was scheduled to return to England, she was contracted to play the lead female role of Eliza Doolittle opposite Rex Harrison as Professor Henry Higgins. After leaving *The Boy Friend* she joined Bing Crosby in a television musical special of Maxwell Anderson's fanciful *High Tor* (CBS-TV, March 10, 1956).

Much has been written about the pre-Broadway hazards of transforming *My Fair Lady* into a magical show, and of how Julie Andrews was *almost* discharged for not bringing conviction to her role of the Cockney flower girl who is transformed into an aristocratic lady. Director Moss Hart devoted a full weekend to a crash course of coaching and practice. The drilling worked. *My Fair Lady* opened on March 15, 1956, at the Mark Hellinger Theatre. The show was a smash hit and Julie was the new toast of Broadway. The *New York Times* enthusiastically noted, "Miss Andrews acts her part triumphantly," and a few weeks later she was on the cover of *Life* magazine. During the show's run Julie's weekly salary escalated from $1,000 to $1,250. While in *My Fair Lady* she finally worked with Rodgers and Hammerstein, in their original TV musical, "Cinderella" (CBS-TV, March 31, 1957) with Jon Cypher as the Prince. On April 30, 1958, *My Fair Lady* bowed at the Drury Lane Theatre with Julie and Rex Harrison recreating their star assignments. Once again they and the show were a major hit. On May 10, 1959, Julie and Tony Walton (now a magazine art director) were married in Outlander, Waybridge, England, and that August she left the British cast of *My Fair Lady*.

Julie had rejected a small featured role in the film version of George Bernard Shaw's THE DEVIL'S DISCIPLE (1959), wanting a more major assignment for her screen debut. Instead, she agreed to star in Lerner and Loewe's new Broadway musical, based on T. H. White's classic of King Arthur, *The Once and Future King*. *Camelot* was to be a big, lavish production with Richard Burton as the wistful King Arthur and Julie as his Queen Guinevere. The expensively mounted costume show opened on December 3, 1960, to mixed reviews but to a solid ($3 million) advance sale. She again enjoyed impressive reviews. Meanwhile, her husband, Tony Walton, was being successful as the set and costume designer for the 1962 Broadway musical comedy hit *A Funny Thing Happened on the Way to the Forum*. One of Julie's most engaging performances occurred when she teamed with friend Carol Burnett in the CBS-TV special "Julie and Carol at Carnegie Hall" (June 11, 1962). Each played delightfully against type and they worked extremely well together. The show received an Emmy as Best Musical Program. On November 27, 1962, in London, Julie gave birth to Emma Kate Walton.

Julie Andrews' first major career setback occurred when Warner Bros. studio head Jack L. Warner hired Audrey Hepburn (a nonsinger) to star in MY FAIR LADY (1964) on film. Walt Disney was wise enough, however, to sign Andrews to play the lovable flying nanny in MARY POPPINS (1964), his screen musical based on the series of children's books by Pamela (P. L.) Travers. It caught filmgoers' fancy and became an enormous box-office champion. (The LP soundtrack of MARY POPPINS won a Grammy Award as Best Album for Children.) More important, in the Oscar race, Julie won the Best Actress Award. When she received the Golden Globe Award as Best Actress for the same movie, she said, "My thanks to Jack L. Warner for making all this possible." By now she had already signed for two additional pictures. THE AMERICANIZATION OF EMILY (1964) was a stark, satirical antiwar entry which cast Andrews in a dramatic role opposite flippant James Garner. Neither she (being too stiff) nor the picture was liked by the public. Fortunately, her next film was a commercial bonanza. Robert Wise's THE SOUND OF MUSIC (1965) was an expansion of Rodgers and Hammerstein's Broadway megahit, which had starred Mary Martin. Julie was just right as the irrepressible Sister Maria caught up in romance and strife in World War II Austria while tending a flock of motherless children. Her renditions of "The Sound of Music" and "My Favorite Things" helped to make the film the highest-grossing feature up to that time and its film soundtrack became the best-selling LP to that date, surpassing the Broadway cast recording of My *Fair Lady*.

Hoping to break her mold as the screen's prim miss, Julie made TORN CURTAIN (1966), an Alfred Hitchcock cold war thriller. It is most noteworthy for the scene which finds Andrews in bed with co-star Paul Newman. For HAWAII (1967), based on portions of James Michener's historical epic novel, Julie was the 1820s New England girl who weds a religious fundamentalist (Max Von Sydow) and sails for Hawaii. She sang the Academy Award–nominated song "My Wishing Doll" in the course of the melodrama. Neither project lived up to expectations. By this time she was separated from her husband, and was dating producer/director Blake Edwards. In addition, she had begun work on her third screen musical, Ross Hunter's THOROUGHLY MODERN MILLIE (1967). In this 1920s lark, she sang, danced, and performed slapstick, abetted by Carol Channing, Beatrice Lillie, and Mary Tyler Moore. The picture was a big earner and for the third year in a row, Julie Andrews was named the top box-office attraction in the United States. Unknown to her, her career had peaked.

Julie reunited with THE SOUND OF MUSIC director Robert Wise for STAR! (1968) at 20th Century–Fox. But the magic was gone, and this $12 million biography of British stage star Gertrude Lawrence

Julie Andrews and Christopher Plummer in THE SOUND OF MUSIC (1965)

failed to recoup its costs. It was later reedited to remove many of the musical numbers. Matters were not improved by Blake Edwards' DARLING LILI (1970), a $16.7 million spoof of World War I espionage with Rock Hudson as Julie's vis-à-vis. Edwards blamed its failure on the studio's massive editing; the truth was, the public had tired of musicals. In the interim, Julie married Edwards on November 12, 1969, in Beverly Hills. He had two children by a prior marriage.

Movie musicals and Julie on screen were passé and MGM shelved plans to star Julie in SHE LOVES ME (based on the Broadway show) and SAY IT WITH MUSIC. However, there was still television. She was seen on "An Evening with Julie Andrews and Harry Belafonte" (NBC-TV, November 9, 1969) and then enjoyed a return matching with Burnett in "Julie and Carol at Lincoln Center" (CBS-TV, December 7, 1971). Less popular was her "The Julie Andrews Hour," a variety-format teleseries produced by England's Sir Lew Grade. The show debuted on ABC-TV in September 1972, but despite a roster of top guest stars, good reviews, and several Emmy Awards, the program was cancelled after one season. As part of her deal with Grade she starred in THE TAMARIND SEED (1974), a tepid spy romance with Omar Sharif. By now Julie and Edwards had relocated to Switzerland, with a London house as well. They would adopt two Vietnamese children, Amy and Joanne. She authored two children's books—*Mandy* (1971) and *The Last of the Really Great Whangdoodles* (1974)—which traded more on her star reputation than on their contents. There were a series of specials and in 1976 she had a popular concert stand at the London Palladium, followed by a not-so-well-liked cabaret engagement in Las Vegas the same year. A 1977 concert tour took her across the U.S. and to Japan.

Apart from providing the off-camera voice for the song "Until You Love Me" for a sequence in Blake Edwards' THE PINK PANTHER STRIKES AGAIN (1976)—she was billed as Ainsley Jarvis—Julie had been away from the screen for five years. She returned in her husband's comedy hit "10" (1979). Charming as she was, it was co-stars Dudley Moore and Bo Derek who received most of the attention. In the fourth screen version of LITTLE MISS MARKER (1980) she was in definite support of Walter Matthau and moppet actress Sara Stimson, and for a change *not* directed by her husband. S.O.B. (1981) was Edwards' long-festering attack against Hollywood for the fate of DARLING LILI. It was biting, bitter, and sometimes hilarious. Its plot required Julie to bare her breasts on screen. Much more popular was VICTOR/VICTORIA (1982), in which she played an actress masquerading as a man who plays a woman on stage. She sang "The Shady Dame from Seville," "Le Jazz Hot," and "Crazy World," and dueted "You and Me" with Robert Preston. She received a Best Actress Academy Award nomination and it seemed that her career was on an upturn. However, this judgment was premature. She was a patient psychiatrist in Burt Reynolds' THE MAN WHO LOVED WOMEN (1983) and was again under Edwards' aegis in the overlooked THAT'S LIFE! (1986), in which she sparkled as the patient wife of self-centered Jack Lemmon. (Both her daughter Emma and her stepchild Jennifer appeared in the picture.) She was reunited with HAWAII co-star Max Von Sydow in DUET FOR ONE (1986), stark theatrics about a woman cellist suffering from multiple sclerosis. Nothing seemed to revive her star impetus. In 1987 she made another concert tour of major U.S. cities and continued to appear on TV in occasional specials (her 1987 Christmas outing won an Emmy) and guest appearances (such as the American Film Institute Salute to Jack Lemmon in 1988). Plans to translate VICTOR/VICTORIA to the stage fell through, while talk of a London revival of *Lady in the Dark* continued to surface. In 1985 she hoped to make a film on the story of Yvette Pierppaoli, the French woman who helped war-torn children in 1966 Cambodia. More recently Julie cut an album, *Love, Julie*, in which critics found a new sexiness to her voice as she sang such standards as "Tea for Two," "How Deep Is the Ocean," and "Come Rain or Come Shine." In the spring of 1989 she recorded a special Christmas album for Hallmark Cards with the London Symphony Orchestra as well as taped a new holiday special. In Los Angeles in June 1989 she and Carol Burnett taped a new special for ABC-TV and Julie then embarked on a six-week series of concerts. The *Love, Julie* tour (which was taped for a PBS-TV telecast in early 1990) included a two-night engagement at Hollywood's Greek Theatre in late July 1989. It was her first Los Angeles solo concert in a decade. She told the press, "Now, I can't do the coloratura any more. But my voice was so quiet and thin then [as a young performer]—now it's mature, and I can do more varied things with it."

With her husband and children as major priorities, Julie and the Edwards family continue to reside at their villa in Gstaad, Switzerland. Her standard still remains to be "an original, to be myself and not a pale copy of anyone else." She stated in mid-1989, "Hopefully, one never stops growing and learning. I'd like to lose certain restrictions I put on myself when I work, be able to loosen up a little bit more, be a little bit easier in my skin at times. My passion all my life has been to do as much that is varied as possible. So, inasmuch as there's a lot out there that I haven't tried, I guess you could say that's my goal."

## Filmography

Mary Poppins (BV, 1964)
The Americanization of Emily (MGM, 1964)
The Sound of Music (20th–Fox, 1965)
Torn Curtain (Univ, 1966)
Hawaii (UA, 1967)
The Singing Princess [La Rosa di Bagdad] (Trans National, 1967) (voice only)
Thoroughly Modern Millie (Univ, 1967)
Star! (20th–Fox, 1968)
Darling Lili (Par, 1970)

The Tamarind Seed (Avco Emb, 1974)
The Pink Panther Strikes Again (UA, 1976) (voice only)
"10" (Orion, 1979)
Little Miss Marker (Univ, 1980)
S.O.B. (Par, 1981)
Victor/Victoria (MGM, 1982)
The Man Who Loved Women (Col, 1983)
That's Life! (Col, 1986)
Duet for One (Cannon, 1986)

## Broadway Plays

The Boy Friend (1954)                          Camelot (1960)
My Fair Lady (1956)

## TV Series

The Julie Andrews Hour (ABC, 1972–73)

## Album Discography

An Evening with Julie Andrews (RCA SX-281)
   (released in Japan only)
The Boy Friend (RCA LOC-1018) [OC]
Broadway's Fair Julie (Col CL/CS-1712)
Camelot (Col KOL/KOS-5620) [OC]
Christmas Treasure (RCA LPM/LSP-3829)
Christmas with Julie Andrews (RCA PRS-290)
Cinderella (Col OL/OS-2005) [ST/TV]
Darling Lili (RCA LSPX-1000) [ST]
Don't Go into the Lion's Cage Tonight (Col
   CL/CS-8686)
Firestone Presents Your Favorite Christmas
   Carols, Starring Julie Andrews (Firestone
   SLP-7012/MLP-7012)
Hawaii (UA UA-LA283) [ST]
High Tor (Decca DL-8272) [ST/TV]
Julie and Carol at Carnegie Hall (Col OL-5840)
   w. Carol Burnett [ST/TV]
Julie and Carol at Lincoln Center (Col S3115)
   w. Carol Burnett [ST/TV]
Julie Andrews (RCA ANL1-1098)
Julie Andrews Sings (RCA LPM/LSP-1681)
The Lass with the Delicate Air (RCA LPM/LSP-
   1403)

A Little Bit in Love (Har H-30021)
Love, Julie (USA JA)
Love Me Tender (Julie 1)
Mary Poppins (Buena Vista 4026) [ST]
My Fair Lady (Col OL-5090/OS-2015) [OC]
The Pink Panther Strikes Again (UA UA-LA-
   694-G) [ST] (Billed as Ainsley Jarvis)
Rose Marie (RCA LOP/LSO-1001)
Secret of Christmas (Embassy 31237/31522)
Songs the Whole World Loves (Suffolk
   Marketing/RCA DVL 1-09779/CBS)
The Sound of Music (RCA LSOD/LSPD-2005)
   [ST]
Star! (20th Century–Fox 5102) [ST]
The Story Behind "My Fair Lady" (Radiola
   1122)
Tell It Again (Angel 65041) w. Martyn Green
"10" (WB BSK-3399) [ST]
Thoroughly Modern Millie (Decca DL-71500,
   MCA 1723) [ST]
TV's Fair Julie (Har KH-31958)
Victor/Victoria (MGM MG-1-5407) [ST]
The World of Julie Andrews (Col KG-31970)

# THE ANDREWS SISTERS

SISTER ACTS HAVE LONG BEEN AN INTRIGUING SHOW BUSINESS staple. There were the Cherry Sisters, the Dolly Sisters, and the Duncan Sisters in vaudeville; the sisters Boswell, Dinning, King, and DeMarco on radio; and on television, the Lennons and McGuires. But when harmonizing siblings are discussed, the group that comes to mind immediately is The Andrews Sisters. During the Swing Era (late 1930s to mid-1940s) they were the reigning jive Queens of Song. They were natural singers, solid musicians, and always fun. They performed in many media: radio, cabarets, recordings, and several motion pictures, becoming an indelible symbol of the World War II years.

Viewing their mostly low-budget feature films today may be an experience in true camp, but despite their unstylish outfits, frizzy coiffures, and naive dramatics, The Andrews Sisters' gusto and harmonics remain supreme. Their distinctive vocal blend carried them through years of tremendous popularity and when, in the early 1970s, Bette Midler recorded their famous "Boogie Woogie Bugle Boy of Company B," a whole new generation developed a fascination with the distinctive singing sisters. Here was a group who really knew how to sell a song. As Maxene once detailed, "Until we came along, all harmony groups put their heads together to get a blend, and because music was such a part of our lives, we had to move! We were the first harmony group that ever moved on stage. Other groups just sang."

The Andrews Sisters came of immigrant stock. Their Greek father (Peter) and Norwegian mother (Olga "Ollie" Sollie) operated the Pure Food Cafe on Hennepin Avenue in Minneapolis, Minnesota. LaVerne was born on July 6, 1911; Maxene on January 3, 1916; and Patricia (Patty) on February 16, 1918. A vaudeville theater close by the restaurant was where the little girls spent a great deal of time while their parents worked at the Cafe. Mrs. Andrews came from a musical background and instilled a love of song and dance into her daughters. It was LaVerne, learning to play the piano, who paid for the sisters' dancing lessons by playing for the sessions. (Over the years, only LaVerne of the sisters could read music.) It was from listening to the Boswell Sisters (with Bing Crosby) on the radio that LaVerne picked up songs which she then taught to her sisters. The girls entered kiddie talent contests. Among their several wins was a first prize at Minneapolis's Orpheum Theatre on the same bill with a then-unknown ventriloquist named Edgar Bergen. In the audience one night was bandleader Larry Rich who, months later, hired the girls to perform with his troupe. They toured with his orchestra, performing on the vaudeville circuit and living in cheap theater hotels, and although they were paid next to nothing, they learned the art of putting over a song and winning audiences' enthusiastic attention. After eighteen months with Larry Rich, they joined Joe E. Howard's vaudeville act and later sang with Ted Mack's band. While singing in Chicago at nightclubs like the High Hat, they were heard at the Royal Frolics by Leon Belasco, who signed the trio, at $225 a week, to sing with his band. With the Belasco unit The Andrews Sisters made their first recordings on Brunswick Records on March 18, 1937, singing "Jammin'," "There's a Lull in My Life," "Turn Off the Moon," and "Wake Up and Live." Later, while performing at the Mayfair Hotel in Kansas City, a fire backstage destroyed the band's equipment, costumes, and arrangements. Belasco quit the band business and became a character actor in films. The girls, in turn, decided to try New York City. Their father sold the family restaurant to finance the expedition and the parents soon relocated to Manhattan to be with their ambitious daughters.

Accepting any and every play date they could muster, the Sisters managed a radio assignment at $15 weekly with the Billy Swanson Band, broadcast from the Hotel Edison. They were fired after two air dates. However, two men had heard them performing "Sleepy Time Down South": Dave Kapp (who along with his brother Jack owned Decca Records) and struggling booking agent Lou Levy. It was Levy who brought the Sisters to Decca Records where they were signed to a recording contract ($50 per record with *no* royalties). Their initial Decca session on October 18, 1937, produced "Just a Simple Melody" and "Why Talk About Love?" The results were negligible, but the next session proved to be their breakthrough. Levy, who by now had abandoned his other clients, taught the girls the lyrics to an old Yiddish song, "Bei Mir Bist Du Schoen," and convinced the Kapp brothers to record it with "Joseph, Joseph" on the flip side. That 78 recording was *not* released, because the Kapps wanted a more universal approach to the lead song. Sammy Cahn was hired to prepare English lyrics for "Bei Mir Bist Du Schoen" and on November 24, 1937, they cut the record for Decca with "Nice Work If You Can Get It" as the new flip side. "Bei Mir Bist Du Schoen" made the team an overnight hit and the sisters were given a new Decca contract which paid them from two to five cents royalty on each disc sold. The Andrews Sisters would remain with Decca Records for almost seventeen years. They would record over four hundred songs, and would collectively sell over eighty million records. (For the record, LaVerne was the tall, quiet redhead on the right; Patty was the blonde lead singer in the center, who belted out the tunes and provided the barrelhouse comedy; and Maxene, on the left, was the snappy brunette, considered the prettiest of the group.)

Lou Levy continued to pick hits for his sensational client team. With Vic Schoen providing customized (brassy) arrangements, The Andrews Sisters turned out pop hit after hit for Decca, including "The Beer Barrel Polka," "Hold Tight, Hold Tight," and "Well, All Right." They were guest performers on several of the major radio programs and quickly became an American institution.

As America moved closer to World War II, Hollywood began a resurgence of diversionary musical movies. The studio that churned out the most—even though in low-budget, assembly-line fashion—was Universal (which later absorbed Decca Records). Through Decca's Jack Kapp, who was friendly with Universal Pictures head Nate Blum-berg, The Andrews Sisters were hired by the studio where Deanna Durbin reigned as singing star. Without any preparation, they were tossed into their debut picture, ARGEN-TINE NIGHTS (1940). They were the impoverished singing trio who, abetted by their managers (the Ritz Brothers), head south-of-the-border to avoid their creditors. The quickie production was trite and pretty awful (Argentina banned the film and the *Harvard Lampoon* named it the most frightening movie of the year), but The Andrews Sisters were sensational in their singing. They performed "Hit the Road," "Oh, He Loves Me," and "Rhumboogie," which they later recorded for Decca. Giving audiences the chance to see the fun sisters on film certainly boosted their record sales. Later in the year they had top recordings of "Beat Me Daddy, Eight to the Bar," "I'll Be with You in Apple Blossom Time" (which became their signature song), and "Mean to Me."

BUCK PRIVATES (1941) was the movie that made the comedy team of Bud Abbott and Lou Costello a big success. In this laugh fest, The Andrews Sisters provided musical interludes, singing "Bounce Brother, with a Solid Four," "You're a Lucky Fellow, Mr. Smith," and one of the Sisters' greatest hits, "Boogie Woogie Bugle Boy from Company B." After recording all these tunes for Decca, the trio joined Abbott and Costello for IN THE NAVY (1941), along with crooner Dick Powell, and sang three undistinguished numbers, including "Hula Ba Lua." Their next assignment with Abbott and Costello was HOLD THAT GHOST (1941), in which they delivered zesty renditions of "Aurora" and "Sleepy Serenade."

With Patty singing the leads, LaVerne reading their music for the group, and Maxene explaining, "We sing what we feel—from the heart," their professional momentum continued unabated. There were more guest-starring assignments on radio variety shows, record-breaking engagements at New York's Paramount Theatre, personal appearances throughout the United States, and in March 1941, Maxene married the trio's manager, Lou Levy.

Their lively, if unsophisticated, film romps continued. WHAT'S COOKIN'? (1942) was hubba hubba nonsense about youngsters wanting to break into show business, with the Sisters doing "What to Do?" PRIVATE BUCKAROO (1942) was a celluloid jam session uniting the singing team with Harry James and His Music Makers, giving The Andrews Sisters occasion to harmonize on "Three Little Sisters" and "Don't Sit Under the Apple Tree with Anyone Else But Me" (which became one of their quintessential theme songs). GIVE OUT, SISTERS (1942) crammed a lot of talent (including Donald O'Connor, Peggy Ryan, the Jivin' Jacks and Jills, and Grace McDonald) into sixty-five minutes, with the snappy girls posing as wealthy socialites. They harmonized four ditties, including one of their prime hits, "The Pennsylvania Polka."

Between performing at military bases both in the United States and, later, in France and Italy, and embarking on war bond tours, they made two 1943 releases. They were singing elevator operators in a building full of music publishers in HOW'S ABOUT IT? and between floor stops socked across "The Beer Barrel Polka." In ALWAYS A BRIDESMAID they were club hostesses involved innocently in a lonely hearts club scam. In 1944 they were at their most prolific with four releases. They guested in Universal's all-star salute FOLLOW THE BOYS singing "Shoo-Shoo Baby." For Warner Bros.' celebrity-packed HOLLYWOOD CAN-

TEEN they delivered the humorous "I'm Getting Corns for My Country." SWINGTIME JOHNNY (1944) found the three misses working on the swing shift in a shell-casing factory, reprising "Boogie Woogie Bugle Boy from Company B" with Mitch Ayres and His Orchestra. In the tuneful mini-Western MOONLIGHT AND CACTUS they wore cowgirl garb and put across such numbers as "Send Me a Man, Amen." For HER LUCKY NIGHT (1945), a box-office dud, the threesome were nightclub entertainers and offered five numbers to their audience, the best of which was "Dance with a Dolly with a Hole in Her Stocking."

World War II ended in 1945 and so did The Andrews Sisters' contract with Universal. The studio had never figured out how to use them effectively on screen—their costuming, makeup, and hair styles were generally atrocious. Having exploited them, the company now dropped them. (According to the team, *they* dropped the studio, finding a loophole in their contract and getting even for the studio's refusal to let them move over to 20th Century–Fox.) Despite their movie interlude, The Andrews Sisters remained extremely popular through their recordings and their radio series, the "Eight-to-the-Bar Ranch." The latter had begun airing over the ABC network in 1944 and moved to CBS for the 1945–46 season. Back in 1944 they had recorded vocal backing ("Johnny Fedora and Alice Blue Bonnet") for the "A Love Story" segment of Walt Disney's cartoon feature MAKE MINE MUSIC! which was finally released in 1946. The next year they were featured, attractively photographed, in a shipboard sequence of Paramount's ROAD TO RIO (1947). They sang "You Don't Have to Know the Language." Their songmate was crooner Bing Crosby, with whom they had first teamed on Decca Records on September 20, 1939, singing "Cirbiribin" and "Yodelin' Jive" backed by Joe Venuti's orchestra. Despite the success of that hit record it was not until late 1943 that the four disparate song

The Andrews Sisters (Maxene, LaVerne, and Patty) in FOLLOW THE BOYS (1944)

stylists were reunited for "Pistol Packin' Mama." Thereafter, they were heard together frequently on radio and on records, with their final waxing sessions being "Cool Water" and "South Rampart Street Parade" on September 5, 1952. (The Andrews Sisters would perform often in the 1940s with Dick Haymes and with Guy Lombardo and His Orchestra.)

In 1948 The Andrews Sisters repeated their voice-over chores for Walt Disney in his animated MELODY TIME, this time singing "Little Toot" in the segment about a little tugboat heroically saving a big steamer from a heavy storm. That year LaVerne married Lou Rogers and their mother, Ollie Andrews, died (followed shortly thereafter by their father's passing). Meanwhile, they and arranger Vic Schoen split. In 1949, Patty had a solo record hit with "I Can Dream Can't I." It was also in 1949 (August) that Patty separated from agent Martin Melcher, whom she had wed in October 1947. They would divorce in 1950 and the next year he would wed Doris Day. In 1950 The Andrews Sisters went to London for a successful Palladium engagement. Maxene and Lou Levy divorced, with Maxene being awarded custody of their children, Peter and Aleda Ann. When Maxene underwent major surgery in 1951, Patty and LaVerne completed their prearranged bookings, appearing as a duo for the first time. Lou Levy continued as their agent, with Maxene explaining, "We love our work too much to break up, and each of us has too great an investment to sacrifice it. We sisters are a corporation, with Lou and each of us owning an equal amount of stock." On Christmas Day, 1951, Patty wed Walter Wescheler, the group's accompanist, and that same week the Sisters played Las Vegas.

There had been rumors of strife between The Andrews Sisters for years, and in 1954 Patty devised her own act with Wescheler. She signed with Capitol Records. That fall Patty brought legal action against her sisters demanding a proper settlement of their mother's estate. On December 21, Maxene was in the headlines for an apparent suicide attempt brought on by the family discord. Maxene denied it and LaVerne insisted, "She loves life too much to want to end it!"

Thereafter, the Sisters reunited, broke up, and reunited for recording, club, and television sessions, but their popularity had peaked. When LaVerne developed cancer, Patty and Maxene performed as a duo (sometimes as a trio using Joyce DeYoung) and on May 8, 1967, LaVerne died, survived by her husband, Lou Rogers. The next year Maxene retired to teach in the drama and speech department of Nevada's Tahoe Paradise College, becoming Dean of Women there. Patty continued in show business, explaining, "Show business is my life. I'll never leave it!" She teamed with Lucille Ball and Lucie Arnaz to make a new singing trio on an episode of the "Here's Lucy" show and she was among the veteran personalities trapped in THE PHYNX (1970), concocted as part of the nostalgia craze by Warner Bros. In 1971, Patty was contracted for the stage musical *Victory Canteen*, which opened at Hollywood's Ivar Theatre on January 27, 1971. "I've never done a book show before," she told the press. "It's one phase of show business we promised each other we'd never do. I'm not worried about it, though. I was always the one doing the talking when the sisters worked and that was like doing a show. Musically too, I'm right at home. This is a play about the 40s and canteen life. Well, let me tell you, we lived it." The show soon folded.

It was in the early 1970s that Bette Midler's dynamic renditions (on stage and on record) of "Boogie Woogie Bugle Boy from Company B" and "In the Mood" refocused American audiences—including the younger set—on the unique talent that was The Andrews Sisters. Their recordings received new popularity in yet more reissues and Kenneth Waissman and Maxine Fox, who had produced *Victory Canteen,* developed a new book show (by Will Holt) entitled *Over Here!* Both Maxene and Patty joined the musical comedy which had a long shakedown on the road and opened on Broadway on March 6, 1974. Looking a bit plumper than in their heyday, but still peppy and in wonderful voice, they trucked, boogied, and harmonized through numbers like "The Big Beat," "We Got It!" and "Wartime Wedding." However, the highlight of the evening came after the final curtain when the two sisters appeared onstage in shimmering gowns and Patty bubbled to the audience, "Do you want to hear some of the old ones?" *Over Here!* closed in January 1975 and a projected road tour of the musical hit was cancelled because the two sisters were feuding with the producers. Later they agreed to recreate the show for summer stock. They announced plans to do a book about their career, but it never appeared.

In the mid-1970s both Maxene and Patty were living in Encino, California, but neither sister was speaking to the other, although neither one would admit the exact nature of the rift. Patty and her husband (Wescheler) began working on their own act again, and Maxene thought—once more—that she would retire. However, in 1979 she thought again about having a solo career and began experimenting in the recording studios again. She tested her solo club act at Reno Sweeney's in New York and began concertizing. In August 1982 she had a near-fatal heart attack and underwent quadruple bypass surgery. Five weeks later she was performing in Denver. "I had a desire to continue singing," she said. "It's the only thing I know how to do. Singing is my whole life." Maxene's solo album, *Maxene: An Andrews Sister,* appeared in 1985 and thereafter the two surviving sisters—singly, *never* together—were seen occasionally on TV nostalgia documentaries syndicated on the PBS network. In early 1989 Maxene sold her Encino home and moved closer to Nevada.

Once, when asked to define the phenomenon of their 40s' fame, Patty offered, "We were such a part of everybody's life in the Second World War. We represented something overseas and at home—a sort of security."

## Filmography

Argentine Nights (Univ, 1940)
Buck Privates (Univ, 1941)
In the Navy (Univ, 1941)
Hold That Ghost (Univ, 1941)
What's Cookin'? [Wake Up and Dream] (Univ, 1942)
Private Buckaroo (Univ, 1942)
Give Out, Sisters (Univ, 1942)
Always a Bridesmaid (Univ, 1943)
How's About It? (Univ, 1943)

Swingtime Johnny (Univ, 1944)
Follow the Boys (Univ, 1944)
Hollywood Canteen (WB, 1944)
Moonlight and Cactus (Univ, 1944)
Her Lucky Night (Univ, 1945)
Make Mine Music! (RKO, 1946) (voices only)
Road to Rio (Par, 1947)
Melody Time (RKO, 1948) (voices only)
The Phynx (WB, 1970) (Patty only)

## Broadway Plays

Over Here! (1974) (Maxene and Patty only)

## Radio Series

Eight-to-the-Bar Ranch [The Andrews Sisters
Show] (ABC, 1944–45; CBS, 1945–46)

## Album Discography

### Patty, Maxene, and LaVerne Andrews:

The Andrews Sisters (Decca DL-8360)
The Andrews Sisters (EEC DMC 42-796)
The Andrews Sisters (Rediffusion ZS153)
The Andrews Sisters at Their Very Best (Pair
 PDL2-1159)
The Andrews Sisters Go Hawaiian (Dot 3632/
 25362)
The Andrews Sisters Greatest Hits (Decca DL-
 4919)
The Andrews Sisters Greatest Hits (Dot 3406/
 25406)
The Andrews Sisters Greatest Hits, Vol. 2 (Dot
 3543/25543)
The Andrews Sisters in Hi-Fi (Cap W-790)
The Andrews Sisters Live (Amalgamated 210)
The Andrews Sisters Live (Andros 4566)
The Andrews Sisters on Radio (Radiola 1033)
The Andrews Sisters on the Air (Pelican 123)
The Andrews Sisters Present (Dot 3529/25529)
The Andrews Sisters Show (Radiola MR-1033)
 w. Bing Crosby, Gabby Hayes
The Andrews Sisters Sing World War II . . . And
 Win! (Official 12008)
At the Microphone (Take Two TT-305)
Beat Me Daddy, Eight to the Bar (Music for
 Pleasure 50556)
The Best of The Andrews Sisters (MCA 2-4024)
The Best of The Andrews Sisters, Vol. 2 (MCA
 4093)
Bing Crosby and The Andrews Sisters, Vols. 1–3
 (Coral 80, 91, 112)
Bing Crosby and The Andrews Sisters (MCA
 Coral 804)
Boogie Woogie Bugle Girls (Par 6075)
Collection of Favorites (10" Decca 5120)

The Dancing Twenties (Cap T-973, EMI 417)
Dick Tracy in B-Flat (Curtain Calls 100/1) [ST/
 R]
Don't Sit Under the Apple Tree (Pickwick
 3904)
The Early Years 1937–42 (Official 12005)
The Early Years (Vol. II), 1938–41 (Official
 12011)
Favorite Hymns (Hamilton 154/12154)
Follow the Boys (Hollywood Soundstage 5012)
 [ST]
Fresh and Fancy Free (Cap T-860)
Give Out, Sisters (Vertinge 2004) [ST]
Great Country Hits (Dot 3567/25567)
Great Golden Hits (Contour 2870-169)
Great Performers (Dot 3807/25807)
Greatest Golden Hits (Dot DLP-3452D/DLP-
 25452)
The Greatest of The Andrews Sisters, Vols. 1–2
 (Telehouse TH-2-164 SLB-6935)
Hits (Cap T/DT-1924)
I Love to Tell the Story (10" Decca DL-5306)
In the Mood (Par 1002)
Irving Berlin Tunes (Decca DL-5263)
Jingle Bells (Decca DL-8354)
The Jumpin' Jive (MCA 1789)
More Hits of The Andrews Sisters (MCA Coral
 8030)
My Isle of Golden Dreams (Decca DL-5423)
Near You (Vocalion 3611)
Pennsylvania Polka (Hamilton 24/12124)
Rarities (MCA 908)
Says My Heart (Conifer Happy Days CHD
 161)
Sing, Sing, Sing (Decca DL-5438)

Sing, Sing, Sing (Music for Pleasure 5841)
Sing, Sing, Sing (Pickwick 3382)
Sixteen Great Performances (ABC 4003)
Stage Door Canteen/Hollywood Canteen
(Curtain Calls 100/11-12) [ST]

Tropical Songs (10" Decca DL-5065)
The Very Best of The Andrews Sisters (MCA
1635)
Worth Remembering (Magic 4)

## Patty and Maxene Andrews:

Over Here! (Col KS-32961) [OC]

## Maxene Andrews:

Maxene: An Andrews Sister (Bainbridge BT
6258)

# ANN-MARGRET

TO SUCCESSFULLY MAKE THE TRANSITION FROM SEX KITTEN TO POL-ished cabaret performer and dramatic actress is a far greater career jump than most sex symbols ever contemplate, let alone accomplish.

Curvaceous Ann-Margret burst into show business prominence in the early 1960s as Hollywood's latest sex bomb. She was a 5' 4 ³/₄" whispery reddish brunette with a breathy voice described as "feathers falling on whipped cream." By the mid-1960s she was labeled a "lewd mechanical doll" who had passed the peak of her fad. However, through a sharp career shift (sponsored by her agents and her husband, Roger Smith) she made an impressive professional turnabout. Gradually, she emerged as a respected screen performer and a strong cabaret attraction. In clubs she became an electric personality whose dancing, singing, and rapport with her audience drew customers in droves.

In the early 1970s Ann-Margret survived a near-fatal on-stage accident; thereafter she coped with her husband's ongoing medical problems with great dignity. These struggles gave added dimension to her persona as she pushed into middle age. More recently, in films and on television, she has proved repeatedly that noteworthy performances in CARNAL KNOWLEDGE (1971) and TOMMY (1975) were *not* flukes from a sex bomb. In the 1980s she emerged as one of Hollywood's most accomplished dramatic actresses. Today she remains one of show business's most magnetic club stars.

She was born Ann-Margret Olsson on April 28, 1941, in Valsjobyn, Sweden, some 185 miles north of Stockholm. She was the only child of Gustav and Anna (Aronsson) Olsson. Her electrician father had spent fourteen years in the United States and returned to America when his daughter was just a year old. He settled near Chicago where he obtained work with the Johnson Electrical Company, hoping to save enough money to send for his family. Because Mrs. Olsson was hesitant to leave her homeland, several years passed.

At the age of four Ann-Margret discovered music and rhythm. Her uncle played the accordion and she would dance around and sing; her mother taught her Swedish children's songs. In 1946, Mrs. Olsson and Ann-Margret, neither of whom could speak English, came to America to be united with Mr. Olsson. The family settled in Fox Lake, forty miles northwest of Chicago. Even though funds were low, Mrs. Olsson insisted that her daughter have the dancing, singing, and piano lessons she could never afford for herself back in Sweden. At one point, when Gustav Olsson fell two stories at work and was disabled, Mrs. Olsson got a job as a receptionist at a mortuary in Wilmette. Part of her salary included free living quarters for the family. For a time, Ann-Margret slept on a convertible couch in the mourners' room and for years was haunted by memories of the big rats that ran through the building at night. Later, Ann-Margret was enrolled in New Trier High School in nearby Winnetka.

By now she was singing in class plays, at churches, at charity functions, at socials, and at clubs. Having won $75 in a talent contest she competed on "Don McNeil's Breakfast Club" on a Chicago radio station. Ted Mack was the substitute host that day and she sang "Them There Eyes." She lost to a boy who made music by blowing through a leaf. However, Mack invited her to guest on his New York–based "The Original Amateur Hour" (ABC-TV). During the summer of 1957, after her sophomore year in high school, she made the rounds of Chicago talent agents. Finally she won a month's engagement as a vocalist with Danny Ferguson's band at the Muehlebach Hotel in Kansas City. During 1959 she made her recording debut on *Lagniappe 1959*, an LP produced by the Boys' Tri-Ship Club of New Trier High School. She sang "Heat Wave." After graduating from high school in 1959 she enrolled at Northwestern University as a speech major, with a minor in dramatics. During her first college year she joined with three male classmates in a group called The Suttletones. On weekends they performed at Chicago-area clubs. That June they drove to Las Vegas, hoping for a summer's booking/vacation at the Nevada Club. Their attempt failed and they drove on to Los Angeles where they made the rounds of agents. They finally obtained a three-week engagement at the Villa Marina Club in Newport Beach, California. Their new agent (Bobby Roberts) helped them find additional bookings (in Reno and Elko, Nevada) and then it was time to return to college. Ann-Margret decided to remain on the coast.

In November 1960, after she finished singing in the lounge show of the Dunes Hotel in Las Vegas, Roberts and his partner, Pierre Cossette, took Ann-Margret to meet George Burns back in Los Angeles.

> Burns: Why did you want to meet me?
> Ann-Margret: Because I've read in the papers that you did a lot for Bobby Darin.
> Burns: Can you sing as good as Bobby?
> Ann-Margret: I don't know if I sing as well as Bobby Darin, but when I sing, I feel as good as Bobby Darin.

She auditioned for the comedian by singing "Mack the Knife" and "Bill Bailey, Won't You Please Come Home." He hired her for his Christmas 1960 show at the Sahara Hotel, paying her $100 nightly for the ten-evening gig. From that exposure she was hired to guest with Burns on "The Jack Benny Program" (CBS-TV, April 2, 1961) and signed a recording contract with RCA Victor. (Her song "I Just Don't Understand" reached number seventeen on the charts in the autumn of 1961.) Meanwhile, she came to the attention of Twentieth Century–Fox, which screentested her, as did filmmaker Frank Capra.

Capra used Ann-Margret to play the demure, convent-bred daughter of a Manhattan bag lady (Bette Davis) in his Damon Runyon fable, POCKETFUL OF MIRACLES (1961). *Variety* acknowledged, "Ann-Margret emotes with feeling." Far more audience-grabbing was Ann-Margret's role in STATE FAIR (1962), Twentieth Century–Fox's third rendering piece of Americana. In a cast that featured Bobby Darin, Alice Faye, and Pamela Tiffin, Ann-Margret was the high-voltage showgirl with whom farm boy Pat Boone falls wildly in love. (Originally she had been scheduled for the docile role of Boone's sister, played by Tiffin.) She soloed "Isn't It Kind of Fun?" and dueted with Boone on "Willing and Eager." With her long dark brown hair changed to red and her electric presence, Ann-Margret was the film's main attraction.

In 1961 Ann-Margret had earned $18,000; but by the next year her career was zooming and she was grossing $200,000. Her agents orchestrated an intensive publicity campaign to transform their client into a very recognizable personality. This campaign's crescendo came on April 19, 1962, when she sang the Oscar-nominated song "Bachelor in Paradise" on the Academy Awards telecast. She recalls, "I was standing in the wings, petrified. Perspiring terribly. I heard Mr. [Bob] Hope introduce me and suddenly found myself standing there. I started to snap my fingers, and I remember saying to myself, 'I'll show them. I'll show them!' Then the music got to me and I just went." That sizzling performance, filled with bumps and grinds, made her Hollywood's hottest commodity.

She was already under a nonexclusive seven-year (one picture a year) contract with Fox, starting at $500 per week. She now signed a three-picture deal with Columbia, which would escalate to $100,000 per movie. For Columbia she co-starred in the musical BYE BYE BIRDIE (1963), easily stealing the limelight from Dick Van Dyke and Janet Leigh as the small town high schooler who develops a wild crush on a visiting rock 'n' roll star. She sang "One Boy" with Bobby Rydell, but her highlight was performing "How Lovely to Be a Woman." *Variety*, enraptured, noted, "this is one of the most exciting fresh personalities to take the cinematic stage in some time. The magnetism of

Ann-Margret and Bobby Rydell in BYE BYE BIRDIE (1963)

early-vintage Judy Garland is here." That soundtrack album sold well, better than had her two earlier LPs (*And Here She Is—Ann-Margret* and *On the Way Up*). She was among the entertainers performing in 1963 at President John F. Kennedy's forty-fifth birthday celebration in New York. (The next year she would sing at President Lyndon Johnson's Inaugural Gala.) She provided an off-camera voice in one episode of "The Flintstones" (ABC-TV, September 19, 1963) cartoon series. It seemed Ann-Margret could do no wrong, even if she was given the Sour Apple Award in both 1962 and 1963 for being uncooperative with the Hollywood Women's Press Club in detailing matters about her private life. Off camera she dated Frankie Avalon, Vince Edwards, Eddie Fisher, and Hugh O'Brian and then announced (and later broke off) her engagement to businessman Burt Sugarman. She made headlines when she began dating Elvis Presley, the co-star of her next musical picture, VIVA LAS VEGAS! (1964). It was the start of a long-standing friendship which led to her attending his funeral in Memphis in 1977 and to her later being hostess of a TV tribute to Presley.

Most of her mid-1960s motion pictures were claptrap, exploiting her sex star image. Nevertheless, she was twice named Star of the Year by the Theatre Owners of America. It would be years before she could live down KITTEN WITH A WHIP (1964), a horrendously shrill melodrama co-starring John Forsythe. In it she was cast as a reformatory escapee. Advertisements of a slinky Ann-Margret provocatively snapping a whip made her a figure of mirth in the industry. Distinguished playwright William Inge had written the screenplay for BUS RILEY'S BACK IN TOWN (1965), but there were so many problems with the production, which co-starred Ann-Margret with Michael Parks, that it was held up for a year to do retakes. It was released in a severely edited, badly received version and with Inge's name removed from the credits. By contrast, she was among the star lineup in MGM's superior THE CINCINNATI KID (1965) as Rip Torn's wife who has an affair with stud poker champ Steve McQueen. She inherited Claire Trevor's old role of dance hall girl Dallas in a bad remake of STAGECOACH (1966) with Alex Cord as the new Ringo Kid. The Western was a flop. The nadir of her career was THE SWINGER (1966), which cast her as writer Kelly Olsson who pretends to be a mod "swinger" to convince her publisher that she can write lurid prose. She shimmied, sang, and simpered through the trash. One reviewer said of her appearance that she is a "pale-faced creature with streaming red hair and over-inflated mammary glands who emits strange sounds through her nose." Another reviewer wrote that for New Year's he wished "Ann-Margret would stop acting like Everyman's Erotica, blow her nose and get back to being a girl."

By 1967 Ann-Margret had earned $3 million but had $117,000 in debts. She had worn out her show business welcome. At this juncture she began to listen seriously to the career advice of actor/producer Roger Smith, whom she had met in 1961 and whom she had been seriously dating since 1964. He suggested that he and his talent agency partner, Allan Carr, become her managers. She agreed. She also agreed to become Smith's wife. They were married at the Riviera Hotel in Las Vegas on May 8, 1967. He had three children by a prior marriage. As part of her professional revamping, she made her debut at the Riviera Hotel in July 1967 as a headliner. She went to Italy to co-star with Rossano

Brazzi in a film, SETTE UOMINI E UN CERVELLO (Criminal Symphony) (1968), produced by Smith and Carr. Then she starred in "The Ann-Margret Show" (CBS-TV, December 11, 1968), the first of several hour specials she would do for television, teamed with the likes of Lucille Ball, Dean Martin, Bob Hope, and Jack Benny. In each of these lucrative, high-tech outings she exploited her growing versatility as a singer and dancer and sought to soften and sweeten her image. In December 1968 she returned to Vietnam (to which she had gone in 1966) to entertain the troops with a USO show, this time headlined with Bob Hope.

Her agents turned down roles for Ann-Margret in THE MALTESE BIPPY (1969), VIVA MAX! (1969), and SONG OF NORWAY (1970), but agreed to her starring in the action melodrama C. C. AND COMPANY (1970), in which she sang and rode a motorcycle (as she did in real life). She guest-starred on a segment of Lucille Ball's "Here's Lucy" (CBS-TV, February 2, 1970). She joined with Anthony Quinn in the embarrassing R.P.M. (1970), a college revolution drama produced and directed by the once esteemed Stanley Kramer. The film was a bust but she received respectable reviews as the grad student who falls in love with a zealous professor (Quinn) and has a nude scene. The turning point of her career was winning (over Dyan Cannon, Jane Fonda, Raquel Welch, and Natalie Wood) a key role in the Mike Nichols–directed CARNAL KNOWLEDGE (1971). She was love-hungry Bobbie Templeton, the blowsy and busty neurotic whom Jack Nicholson eventually dumps. Critics and moviegoers alike were amazed by her serious dramatics and she was Oscar-nominated. (She lost the Best Supporting Actress Oscar to Cloris Leachman of THE LAST PICTURE SHOW, but she did win the Golden Globe Award for Best Supporting Actress.) *Time* magazine noted that because of this film "her body got a degree and quality of exposure that made her overnight what for eleven years she had clumsily tried to be: a sex symbol." She was again on the cover of *Life* magazine. In 1971 she earned $2,000,000, part of that income from appearing in the musical spoof "Dames at Sea" (NBC-TV, November 15, 1971), in which she co-starred with Ann Miller.

Ann-Margret had had accidents before. She had spilled off her motorcycle in 1968; she had fallen in Las Vegas in 1971 and required twenty-four stitches. But these were nothing like what occurred at the Sahara Hotel in Lake Tahoe on September 10, 1972. She was performing a Carnival in Rio number for the midnight show when she tumbled from a faulty platform. She fell twenty-two feet, and would most likely have died had not a stagehand heard her screams and rushed in her direction to break her fall. As it was, besides suffering a concussion, she broke her jaw, facial bones in five places (pieces of which were driven up into her sinuses), and her left arm. After she was rushed to a local hospital, her husband flew her in their private jet to UCLA Medical Center where a team of five doctors, including a plastic surgeon who had done wonders on comedienne Phyllis Diller, operated on her for two hours. Her jaw was wired from the inside; it was a very painful procedure, but one which ensured there would be no scars. Scarcely ten weeks later, she was back performing. (Part of her drive to recover was to prove to her dying father that she was okay.) When asked what drove her, Ann-Margret explained, "If I don't work I climb the walls. You see, entertaining is what I do. I've been doing it since I was four, and I don't do anything else. If I stop, the world might not come apart. But I would." When she played on the Las Vegas stage she now had a specialty number, "Return of the Kitten with a Whip," which teased her former sex cat image. She ended the show with a teary rendition of "When You're Smiling." On April 4, 1973, she had another television special, "Ann-Margret: When You're Smiling" (NBC-TV). On her TV studio dressing room door was posted the sign "Nothin' Stops the Champ!"

She had made THE TRAIN ROBBERS (1973) with John Wayne before her accident, and on January 23, 1975, she was back with another NBC-TV special: "Ann-Margret Olsson," which included tributes to Marilyn Monroe, Betty Grable, Rita Hayworth, and Esther Williams. In the bizarre, vulgar Ken Russell–directed rock opera TOMMY (1975) Ann-Margret played the mother of Roger Daltrey (of the rock group The Who). Even though musically Elton John (with "Pinball Wizard") and Tina Turner (with "Acid Queen") were more outrageous, Ann-Margret was Oscar-nominated for her (over)strong dramatics. (She lost the Best Actress Academy Award to Louise Fletcher of ONE FLEW OVER THE CUCK-OO'S NEST.) Also in England she co-starred in JOSEPH ANDREWS (1976), a rowdy eighteenth-century sex adventure, playing the earthy Lady Booby.

Her films at home and abroad continued to be a mixed bag, ranging from the failed adventure satire THE LAST REMAKE OF BEAU GESTE (1977) to Neil Simon's commercial private-eye spoof THE CHEAP DETECTIVE (1978) to the ignored Western burlesque THE VILLAIN (1979). They were stopgaps in her career, which also included annual club tours and more TV specials, such as "Ann-Margret . . . Rhinestone Cowgirl" (NBC-TV, April 26, 1977), on which Perry Como, Bob Hope, Minnie Pearl, and Chet Atkins were guests. Much more substantial was the film MIDDLE AGE CRAZY (1980), in which she was the wife of a Houston building contractor (Bruce Dern) undergoing male menopause on his fortieth birthday. (Ann-Margret had co-starred previously with Dern in the confusing Claude Chabrol–directed FOLIES BOURGEOISES, 1976.)

Now in her forties, Ann-Margret played a succession of understanding women on screen. She was Walter Matthau's thoughtful girlfriend in the underrated I OUGHT TO BE IN PICTURES (1982). In LOOKIN' TO GET OUT (1982; shot in 1980), co-produced and co-written by co-star Jon Voight, Ann-Margret was seen as an ex-hooker now living with a wealthy Las Vegas hotel owner who is sympathetic to her old lover/loser (Voight). She was tremendously effective as the terminally ill (with cancer) mother of ten in the telefeature WHO WILL LOVE MY CHILDREN? (1983) and the next year, she was hand-picked by playwright Tennessee Williams to play Blanche Dubois opposite Treat Williams' Stanley in the telefilm A STREETCAR NAMED DESIRE. Some critics compared her favorably to Vivien Leigh's benchmark performance. For TWICE IN A LIFETIME (1985) she was the striking barmaid who falls in love with Seattle steelworker Gene Hackman, who is suffering the blues from his thirty-year marriage to Ellen Burstyn. The picture and Ann-Margret's resilient performance received much critical attention, but insufficient public response. For every artistic appearance Ann-Margret made, there was a calculated commercial effort, such as THE TWO MRS. GRENVILLES (NBC-TV, February 8–9, 1987), based on Dominick Dunne's best-seller. In this slick four-hour miniseries, she played the Kansan from the wrong side of the tracks who marries a handsome sailor (Stephen Collins) only to be rebuffed by her upper-crust East Coast in-laws and to end up a drunk after shooting her husband. Although Ann-Margret was Emmy-nominated for her role, it was Claudette Colbert who stole the notices as the blue-blooded matriarch. In the May–September romance A TIGER'S TALE (1988), she was the warm-blooded older woman who attracts much younger C. Thomas Howell. In A NEW LIFE (1988), written and directed by and co-starring Alan Alda, she was his overly patient spouse who, after twenty-six years of marriage, strikes out on her own. Said the *Los Angeles Times*, "As always, it is a special pleasure to watch Ann-Margret, who has become that rarity in American films, a glamorous star who is also an impeccable ensemble player."

Since 1980 her husband, Roger Smith, had been suffering from myasthenia gravis (a nerve disease that weakens the muscles) and much of Ann-Margret's career had been subordinated to accommodating his illness, as she had devoted time to raising her stepchildren. The Smiths resided (and still do) on a Benedict Canyon (Beverly Hills) estate once owned by Humphrey Bogart and Lauren Bacall. In October 1988 Ann-Margret returned to performing on stage in Las Vegas, after a five-year absence. The spectacular floor show at Caesars Palace was successfully geared to remind audiences why Ann-Margret had been known as "Queen of the Strip" for many years. She informed the opening night audience that George Burns remained her inspiration and that it was he who advised her to continue doing "all that dramatic [movie] stuff but get back on stage." It was the beginning of a new club pact which saw her performing in Las Vegas, Atlantic City, and Lake Tahoe. In October 1988 the Thalians' 33rd anniversary ball in Los Angeles honored Ann-Margret and raised $600,000 for charity. Debbie Reynolds was co-hostess of the event and June Haver, the previous year's honoree, made the presentation to Ann-Margret. In December 1988, Ann-Margret was among four Southern Californians awarded the Swedish Royal Order of the Polar Star for their efforts to promote Sweden in the United States.

Regarding her career thus far, Ann-Margret has said, "No one gets everything he or she wants, but I'm really a very lucky lady."

## Filmography

Pocketful of Miracles (UA, 1961)
State Fair (20th–Fox, 1962)
Bye Bye Birdie (Col, 1963)
Kitten with a Whip (Univ, 1964)
Viva Las Vegas! [Love in Las Vegas] (MGM, 1964)
The Pleasure Seekers (20th–Fox, 1964)
Bus Riley's Back in Town (Univ, 1965)
Once a Thief (MGM, 1965)
The Cincinnati Kid (MGM, 1965)
Made in Paris (MGM, 1966)

The Swinger (Par, 1966)
Stagecoach (20th–Fox, 1966)
Murderers' Row (Col, 1966)
The Tiger and the Pussycat [Il Tigre] (Emb, 1967)
Il Profeta [The Prophet/Mr. Kinky] (It, 1967) (released in U.S. in 1976)
Sette Uomini e un Cervello [Criminal Affair/ Criminal Symphony] (It/Arg, 1968)
Rebus [The Puzzle] (It/Sp/Ger, 1968)
C. C. and Company (Avco Emb, 1970)

R.P.M. (Col, 1970)
Carnal Knowledge (Avco Emb, 1971)
The Train Robbers (WB, 1973)
The Outside Man [Un Homme Est Mort] (UA, 1973)
Tommy (Col, 1975)
Joseph Andrews (Par, 1976)
Folies Bourgeoises [The Twist] (Fr, 1976)
The Last Remake of Beau Geste (Univ, 1977)
The Cheap Detective (Col, 1978)
Magic (Avco Emb, 1978)
The Villain [Cactus Jack] (Col, 1979)
Ken Murray Shooting Stars (Royal Oaks, 1979) (documentary)

Middle Age Crazy (20th–Fox, 1980)
I Ought to Be in Pictures (20th–Fox, 1982)
Lookin' to Get Out (Par, 1982) (made in 1980)
Who Will Love My Children? (ABC-TV, 2/14/83)
A Streetcar Named Desire (ABC-TV, 3/4/84)
Twice in a Lifetime (Yorkin, 1985)
The Return of the Soldier (European Classics, 1985) (made in 1982)
52 Pick-Up (Cannon, 1986)
The Two Mrs. Grenvilles (NBC-TV, 2/8/87–2/9/87)
A Tiger's Tale (Atlantic Releasing, 1988)
A New Life (Par, 1988)

## Album Discography

And Here She Is—Ann-Margret (RCA LPK/LSP-2399)
Ann-Margret (MCA 3226)
Ann-Margret and John Gary Sing David Merrick's Hits from Broadway Shows (RCA LPM/LSP-2947)
Bachelors' Paradise (RCA LPM/LSP-2659)
Beauty and the Beard (RCA LPM/LSP-2690) w. Al Hirt
Bye Bye Birdie (RCA LOC/LSO-1081) [ST]
The Cowboy and the Lady (LHI 12007) w. Lee Hazelwood
Dames at Sea (Bell System K-4900) [ST/TV]
It's the Most Happy Sound (WB 1285) w. The Ja-Da Quartet

The Many Moods of Ann-Margret (Raven RVLP 1009)
On the Way Up (RCA LPM/LSP-2453)
The Pleasure Seekers (RCA LOC/LSO-1101) [ST]
Songs from "The Swinger" and Other Swing Songs (RCA LPM/LSP-3710)
State Fair (Dot DLP-29011) [ST]
The Swinger (RCA LPM/LSP-3710) [ST]
Three Great Girls (RCA LPM/LSP-2724) w. Kitty Kallen, Della Reese
Tommy (Polydor 2-9502) [ST]
Va-Va Voom (Rhino RNTA 1999)
Viva Las Vegas! (Lucky LR-711) [ST]
The Vivacious One (RCA LPM/LSP-2551)

# FRED ASTAIRE

A SHOW BUSINESS LEGEND, FRED ASTAIRE MADE MOVIE DANCING BOX-office with his elegant style and aristocratic, smooth personality. While everything he accomplished on screen, and in other facets of show business, appeared to be performed with the maximum of ease, in reality he was a tremendously hard-working craftsman who toiled long and hard to make his work appear so natural. In addition to becoming the movies' best-known dancer, Astaire was also a fine actor and a more than fair vocalist who had a distinctive knack for lyric phrasing. Because of his ten screen teamings with vivacious Ginger Rogers, Fred Astaire is always thought of in context with the blonde actress, although most of his screen endeavors were without her. Astaire was beloved by audiences and co-workers alike, and in 1949 the Academy of Motion Picture Arts and Sciences presented him with a special Oscar for his "unique artistry and his contributions to the technique of musical pictures."

The future dancing star was born Frederick Austerlitz in Omaha, Nebraska, on May 10, 1899. He was the son of a beer salesman. His sister, Adele, was a year and a half older than he, and when she began taking dancing lessons, he accompanied her and also took up the art. As children they performed locally and in 1906 their mother enrolled them in the Ned Wayburn School of Dance in New York City. When Fred was five he and Adele made their vaudeville debut in Paterson, New Jersey; their dancing act was so good they obtained steady work and began using the surname Astaire.

After five years on the road, with their only academic schooling being their mother's tutoring, the brother-and-sister act was booked into New York City and their notices were so gilt-edged they landed a part in the Broadway musical *Over the Top* (1917) the next year. This was followed by such Great White Way productions as *The Passing Show of 1918* (1918), *Apple Blossoms* (1919), and *The Love Letter* (1921); *For Goodness Sake* was written for them in 1922. This was followed by Jerome Kern's *The Bunch and Judy* the same year and in 1924 they starred in George Gershwin's sensational musical *Lady Be Good* (Gershwin had done the additional music for *For Goodness Sake*). In the interim, between the Kern and Gershwin shows, the Astaires took *The Bunch and Judy* to London as *Stop Flirting* in 1923 and they became the toast of the British capital. They returned to London in 1926 for a run there in *Lady Be Good* and in 1927 they headlined still another Broadway triumph that George Gershwin wrote for them, *Funny Face*.

While in England in 1923 Fred and Adele made their recording debuts doing two songs from *Stop Flirting* on HMV (His Master's Voice) Records. In 1926, accompanied by George Gershwin on the piano, they recorded two *Lady Be Good* selections for Columbia:

"Hang on to Me" and "Fascinatin' Rhythm." At the same time Fred did his first solo record vocal on "The Half of It Dearie Blues," also from the Gershwin show. In 1928 they recorded a quartet of tunes from *Funny Face* in London for Columbia.

In 1930 the Astaires returned to America to headline the Broadway musical *Smiles* and the next year they co-starred in *The Band Wagon*. Also in 1931 they made their screen debuts in a Vitaphone short doing songs from *Funny Face*, which the studio (Warner Bros.) considered filming with them as the stars. This all came to a sudden halt, however, in 1932 when Adele Astaire married Lord Charles Cavendish, the second son of the Duke of Devonshire, and retired from show business. Going it alone, Fred took the lead in the musical *The Gay Divorce* in 1932, introducing Cole Porter's song "Night and Day"; after a 248-performance run, he took the show to London.

After filmmaker Samuel Goldwyn signed Fred Astaire to and then released him from a screen contract, Astaire was hired by RKO to star in a new musical. However, that project was slow in developing and he was loaned to MGM where he made his feature debut in the 1933 Joan Crawford musical DANCING LADY. The *New York Times* commented, "The dancing of Fred Astaire and Miss Crawford is most graceful and charming. The photographic effects of their scenes are an impressive achievement." By now RKO had its project, FLYING DOWN TO RIO (1933), ready and he was teamed with Ginger Rogers (a replacement for Dorothy Jordan) as featured dancers in the elaborate picture starring Dolores Del Rio and Gene Raymond. The duo caused a sensation dancing the "Carioca." Realizing there was money to be made from their teaming, the studio quickly starred them in THE GAY DIVORCEE (1934), a screen version of Astaire's stage musical *The Gay Divorce*. This light and elegant story of an American dancer romancing a pretty young woman in London introduced the dance "The Continental," and Astaire and Rogers (despite the fact that Fred never wanted to be teamed with anyone) were a hot box-office property.

In 1935 they co-starred with Irene Dunne and Randolph Scott in ROBERTA, in which they were essentially wasted, but this was remedied by TOP HAT the same year, in which they were again romancing in London and executing such beautiful songs as "No Strings," "Isn't This a Lovely Day," "Cheek to Cheek," "The Piccolino," and "Top Hat, White Tie and Tails." The picture grossed over $3 million at the box office. Astaire and Rogers opened 1936 with FOLLOW THE FLEET with Fred as a sailor romancing dance hall girl Ginger; the movie contained Irving Berlin's song "Let's Face the Music and Dance." Next came SWING TIME (1936), perhaps their best screen pairing, with its songs "A Fine Romance" and "The Way You Look Tonight" and Fred's solo on "Bojangles of Harlem" and his hoofing on "Never Gonna Dance." While the plot of SHALL WE DANCE? (1937) appeared to be mostly warmed-over leftovers from some of their earlier scripts, the film was alive with great George Gershwin songs like the title tune, "Let's Call the Whole Thing Off," "They All Laughed," and "They Can't Take That Away from Me," plus a delightful roller-skating sequence. In 1937, Astaire went solo *without* Ginger Rogers in A DAMSEL IN DISTRESS, which cast him as a composer in love with a pretty British lass (Joan Fontaine), and which sported such good Gershwin songs as "A Foggy Day" and "Nice Work If You Can Get It." However, the public did not react favorably to Fred without

Ginger and in 1938 they were matched for the eighth time in CAREFREE with Astaire as a psychiatrist who finds himself in love with his patient (Rogers). It contained the song "Change Partners," but its nearly $2 million budget was not recouped at the box office. The couple's final RKO pairing was in the biopic THE STORY OF VERNON AND IRENE CASTLE (1939), tracing the lives of the famous husband-and-wife ballroom dancing team of the pre–World War I era, but it lacked a good score and again failed to return its production costs. At this point Astaire, then earning $150,000 per film, and RKO came to a parting.

During the period of the Astaire-Rogers musicals in the 1930s, Fred recorded many of the songs from their films for Brunswick records and, in addition, the duo performed most of their joint films in radio versions. Astaire also headlined the one-hour "The Fred Astaire Show" on NBC radio from 1936 to 1937. On a personal note, Astaire had one of the happiest marriages in Hollywood, having wed New York socialite divorcee Phyllis Baker Potter in 1933. They later had two children: Fred, Jr. (born in 1941) and Ava (born in 1942).

Fred Astaire's first real dancing partner after Ginger Rogers was tap dancer Eleanor Powell in MGM's BROADWAY MELODY OF 1940 (1940). She proved more than a match for Astaire. He next danced with Paulette Goddard in Paramount's SECOND CHORUS (1941), in which Fred and Burgess Meredith, the latter as an Artie Shaw bandsman, both romanced the leading lady. At Columbia, Astaire was teamed with Rita Hayworth and Cole Porter music for YOU'LL NEVER GET RICH (1941). The two stars worked well together, plus the film offered the song "So Near and Yet So Far." After vying with Bing Crosby for Marjorie Reynolds in Paramount's expensive HOLIDAY INN (1942), Astaire reteamed with Rita Hayworth for YOU WERE NEVER LOVELIER in 1942; this time the duo had a screen romance against the backdrop of such Jerome Kern songs as "I'm Old Fashioned" and "Dearly Beloved," both of which Astaire recorded for Decca Records. He then returned to RKO for the unremarkable THE SKY'S THE LIMIT (1943), which cast him as a service pilot on leave in Manhattan and falling for a pretty magazine photographer (Joan Leslie). It offered the Harold Arlen songs "One for My Baby," "I've Got a Lot in Common with You," and "My Shining Hour." It was not popular at the box office.

In 1944 the much-matured Astaire thought his film career was over, but MGM's Arthur Freed unit urged that he be signed with the studio for more musicals. He inaugurated the association with ZIEGFELD FOLLIES (not released until 1946) in which he danced the "Limehouse Blues" with Lucille Bremer and teamed with Gene Kelly for "The Babbitt and the Bromide" number; the latter dance vehicle found the two very disparate dancers blending their unique styles surprisingly well. In the bland whimsical fantasy musical YOLANDA AND THE THIEF (1945), Astaire again danced with Lucille Bremer. He reteamed with Bing Crosby in 1946 for BLUE SKIES at Paramount, which cast them as two rival performers who were once partners; they did the number "A Couple of Song and Dance Men" while Astaire soloed on "Puttin' on the Ritz." As in their last joint offering, it was Crosby who won the heart of the film's leading lady (this time, Joan Caulfield). Since MGM could not smooth out a script of THE BELLE OF NEW YORK for Astaire and Judy

Garland, he decided now was the right time to retire. Two years later he was wooed back to MGM to replace Gene Kelly, who had broken his ankle, in EASTER PARADE (1948). The Irving Berlin songfest cast him as a dancer who is lovelorn over a stage star (Ann Miller) but teams with a new singer (Judy Garland). He soloed on "Steppin' Out with My Baby" and he and Garland performed a duo on the novelty number "A Couple of Swells." The result was a smash hit. When Garland was unable to take the lead in THE BARKLEYS OF BROADWAY in 1949, Ginger Rogers replaced her and the vehicle, while not one of their best, was a pleasant, nostalgic reunion for the performers. The reprised song "They Can't Take That Away from Me" was better than the thin plot about feuding husband-and-wife performers.

In the late 1940s and early 1950s Fred Astaire guest-starred on radio shows which starred Bing Crosby and Bob Hope and he kicked off the 1950s with the MGM musical THREE LITTLE WORDS (1950) co-starring Vera-Ellen. This biopic of songwriters Bert Kalmar and Harry Ruby had Fred singing the title song and dancing with Vera-Ellen.

Fred Astaire and Judy Garland in EASTER PARADE (1948)

Next he went to Paramount for the over-long LET'S DANCE (1950), which mismatched the elegant Astaire with the rambunctious Betty Hutton. In ROYAL WEDDING (1951), back at MGM, his dancing on the ceiling highlighted this tale of a dancer (Astaire) and his sister (Jane Powell) each finding love in London at the time of Queen Elizabeth II's coronation. Next Astaire finally made THE BELLE OF NEW YORK (1952) with Vera-Ellen, but this mundane period fantasy was unpopular. By contrast, the Vincente Minnelli–directed musical THE BAND WAGON (1953) proved to be his best film in some time with its story of washed-up movie actor Astaire hoping for success on Broadway. It featured songs like "That's Entertainment" and "Dancing in the Dark" plus the Mike Hammer spoof "The Girl Hunt" which he performed with his favorite screen partner, Cyd Charisse. As a result of THE BAND WAGON's popularity, he signed a new contract with MGM for three more films at $100,000 per picture, but when nothing developed he thought again of retiring and then moved over to Paramount. He rejected a co-starring role (which went to Danny Kaye) with Bing Crosby in WHITE CHRISTMAS (1954) and turned down PAPA'S DELICATE CONDITION (later made with Jackie Gleason).

Meanwhile, his wife Phyllis died in 1954 and as therapy he did a musical remake of DADDY LONG LEGS (1955) at 20th Century–Fox with Leslie Caron. Made on a modest budget, it was a profitable picture and had the hit tune "Something's Gotta Give." He made another May-September musical romance in Paramount's FUNNY FACE (1956), a top-notch production which cast him as a chic fashion photographer who makes a star out of a young model (Audrey Hepburn) against a Parisian setting. For his final MGM musical he teamed with Cyd Charisse for Cole Porter's SILK STOCKINGS (1957), a musical version of NINOTCHKA (1939); Astaire performed the role done by Don Ameche in the Cole Porter musical on Broadway. Astaire and Charisse danced well together but the story line was worn and the score essentially mediocre.

His screen dancing seemingly behind him, Astaire accepted a dramatic (supporting) role in the science fiction film ON THE BEACH (1959) about several Australians awaiting the end of the world following a nuclear holocaust. As the veteran race car driver, he proved adept in a telling straight acting assignment. In 1961 he was urbane and light-hearted when he co-starred in Paramount's drawing-room comedy THE PLEASURE OF HIS COMPANY as a man who returns to visit his grown daughter (Debbie Reynolds) and causes family havoc. At Columbia he was wasted in the Kim Novak–Jack Lemmon British-set comedy THE NOTORIOUS LANDLADY (1962).

Fred Astaire came to TV in 1957 in a dramatic role on "General Electric Theatre" and he did another episode of the CBS series in 1959. His biggest TV splash, however, was in 1958 in the special "An Evening with Fred Astaire" on NBC-TV, which won nine Emmy Awards. Beautiful Barrie Chase was his astute dancing partner in the special, as she would be in the two equally good follow-ups, "Another Evening with Fred Astaire," in 1959, and 1960's "Astaire Time." In 1961–63 he hosted ABC-TV's anthology dramatic series "Alcoa Premiere" and during the decade made guest appearances on "The Bob Hope Chrysler Theatre," "Dr. Kildare," and "It Takes a Thief," the latter on ABC-TV in 1969. In 1970 he took a regular role on the international intrigue series "It Takes a Thief" as Robert Wagner's debonair detective father. He made his TV movie debut late in 1970 with ABC's THE OVER-THE-HILL GANG RIDES AGAIN, about a group of old lawmen who reteam to take on an outlaw gang. In 1971 he did a voiceover on the ABC-TV special "Santa Claus Is Coming to Town."

In 1968 Fred Astaire returned to the screen in FINIAN'S RAINBOW, an overlong musical with Petula Clark, but it proved a good singing and dancing showcase for him as an energetic leprechaun. It was certainly superior to the British-made MIDAS RUN (1969), which had him plotting a big bank heist; his son had a brief role as an aviator in this feature.

Over the years, Astaire continued to make records and in the 1950s and 1960s he made LPs for such labels as MGM, Kapp, and Verve. In the 1970s he cut two albums for United Artists and he and Bing Crosby did a duet album for that label called *A Couple of Song and Dance Men.*

In 1974 Astaire was one of several on-screen hosts of the excellent compilation film THAT'S ENTERTAINMENT!, made up of footage from vintage MGM musicals, and two years later he and Gene Kelly teamed to repeat the chore in the sequel, THAT'S ENTERTAINMENT, PART 2 (1976). In 1977 he went to Ireland to star in the international production PURPLE TAXI, playing a local doctor who drives a purple auto. In 1978 he and Helen Hayes co-starred in the telefeature A FAMILY UPSIDE DOWN on NBC-TV, about how the elderly can become overly dependent on their children. The next year he guest-starred on ABC-TV's "Battlestar Galactica" science fiction series and later that year he was in the NBC-TV movie THE MAN IN THE SANTA CLAUS SUIT playing seven (!) different roles in this film about Santa Claus's affecting the lives of various people; he also sang the title song. His final film appearance came in GHOST STORY (1981), in which he was one of four elderly men who is haunted in revenge by the spirit of the girl they used and murdered a half century before. That year he also received the American Film Institute's Life Achievement Award.

Phyllis Astaire had died in the fall of 1954 and Astaire did not remarry until the summer of 1980 when he wed thirty-five-year-old jockey Robyn Smith. Despite the age difference (which caused much media speculation), they led a quiet, happy life together in Astaire's Beverly Hills home. Adele Astaire died in the early 1980s. Fred, who once claimed he would live to be one hundred, remained in fairly good health until he was stricken with pneumonia and died on June 22, 1987. He was buried on June 24, 1987, seven years to the day after his second marriage. In June 1989 he was elected posthumously to the Hall of Fame of the Academy of Television Arts & Sciences.

## Filmography

Municipal Bandwagon (Vita, 1933) (s)
Dancing Lady (MGM, 1933)
Flying Down to Rio (RKO, 1933)
The Gay Divorcee [The Gay Divorce] (RKO, 1934)
Roberta (RKO, 1935)
Top Hat (RKO, 1935)
Follow the Fleet (RKO, 1936)
Swing Time (RKO, 1936)
Shall We Dance? (RKO, 1937)
A Damsel in Distress (RKO, 1937)
Carefree (RKO, 1938)

The Story of Vernon and Irene Castle (RKO, 1939)
Broadway Melody of 1940 (MGM, 1940)
Second Chorus (Par, 1941)
You'll Never Get Rich (Col, 1941)
Holiday Inn (Par, 1942)
You Were Never Lovelier (Col, 1942)
The Sky's the Limit (RKO, 1943)
Yolanda and the Thief (MGM, 1945)
Blue Skies (Par, 1946)
Ziegfeld Follies of 1946 (MGM, 1946)
Easter Parade (MGM, 1948)

The Barkleys of Broadway (MGM, 1949)
Three Little Words (MGM, 1950)
Let's Dance (Par, 1950)
Royal Wedding [Wedding Bells] (MGM, 1951)
The Belle of New York (MGM, 1952)
The Band Wagon (MGM, 1953)
Daddy Long-Legs (20th–Fox, 1954)
Funny Face (Par, 1956)
Silk Stockings (MGM, 1957)
On the Beach (UA, 1959)
The Pleasure of His Company (Par, 1961)
The Notorious Landlady (Col, 1962)
Paris When It Sizzles (Par, 1964) (voice only)
Finian's Rainbow (WB–7 Arts, 1968)

Midas Run [A Run on Gold] (Cin, 1969)
The Over-the-Hill Gang Rides Again (ABC-TV, 11/17/70)
The Towering Inferno (20th–Fox, 1974)
That's Entertainment! (MGM, 1974) (co-host)
That's Entertainment, Part 2 (MGM, 1976) (co-host)
Taxi Mauve [Purple Taxi] (Fr/It/Irish, 1977)
The Amazing Dobermans (Golden, 1977)
A Family Upside Down (NBC-TV, 4/9/78)
The Man in the Santa Claus Suit (NBC-TV, 12/23/79)
Ghost Story (Univ, 1981)

## Broadway Plays

Over the Top (1917)
The Passing Show of 1918 (1918)
Apple Blossoms (1919)
The Love Letter (1921)
For Goodness Sake (1922)
The Bunch and Judy (1922)

Lady Be Good (1924)
Funny Face (1927)
Smiles (1930)
The Band Wagon (1931)
The Gay Divorce (1932)

## Radio Series

The Fred Astaire Show (NBC, 1936–37)

## TV Series

Alcoa Premiere (ABC, 1961–63)
It Takes a Thief (ABC, 1969–70)

## Album Discography

Another Evening with Fred Astaire (Chrysler Corp K80P-1087-8) [ST/TV]
The Astaire Story (DRG 1102)
Astaireable Fred (DRG 911)
Attitude Dancing (UA LA-580-G)
The Band Wagon (X LVA-1001) [OC]
The Band Wagon (MGM E-3051) [ST]
The Barkleys of Broadway (MGM SES-51ST) [ST]

The Belle of New York (10" MGM E-108, Stet 15004) [ST]
The Best of Fred Astaire (Epic LN-3137)
Blue Skies (Sountrak 104) [ST]
Blue Skies (10" Decca DL-5042, Decca DL-4259) w. Bing Crosby
Broadway Melody of 1940 (CIF 3002) [ST]
Cavalcade of Dance (Coral CRL-57008)

A Couple of Song and Dance Men (UA LA-588-G) w. Bing Crosby

Crazy Feet! (ASV 5021)

Daddy Long Legs (Caliban 6000) [ST]

Damsel in Distress/The Sky's the Limit (Curtain Calls 100/19) [ST]

Easter Parade (10" MGM E-402, MGM E-3227) [ST]

Easy to Dance With (Verve 2114)

An Evening with Fred Astaire (Chrysler Corp) [ST/TV]

Finian's Rainbow (WB 2550) [ST]

Flying Down to Rio/Carefree (CIF 30040) [ST]

Follow the Fleet (Caliban 6024) [ST]

Follow the Fleet/Damsel in Distress (Scarce Rarities 5505) [ST]

Fred Astaire (Lion 70121)

Fred Astaire (Vocalion 3716)

Fred Astaire (VSP 23-24)

Fred Astaire Live! (Pye 5542) [ST/TV]

Fred Astaire Now! (Kapp 1165/3049)

Fred Astaire Sings (MCA 1552)

Fred Astaire Sings Gershwin "Nice Work" (Saville 199)

The Fred Astaire Story (Clef 1001-04)

From Classic MGM Films (MCA 25985) [ST]

Funny Face (Monmouth-Evergreen 7037) [OC]

Funny Face (Verve 15001, Stet 15001) [ST]

The Gay Divorcee/Top Hat (Sountrak 105) [ST]

The Golden Age of Fred Astaire (Music for Pleasure 5827)

Holiday Inn (Decca DL-4256) w. Bing Crosby

Holiday Inn (Sountrak 112) [ST]

Lady Be Good (Monmouth-Evergreen 7036) [OC]

The Legendary Fred Astaire (Murray Hill 15532)

Let's Dance (Caliban 6017)

Mr. Top Hat (Verve 2010)

Never Before—The Songs from Original Soundtracks 1933–48 (Oxford 3038) [ST]

Nothing Thrilled Us Half as Much (Epic FLM-13103/FLS-15103)

Original Recordings 1935–40 (CBS 66316)

Roberta (Amalgamated 218) [ST]

Roberta/Top Hat (Star-Tone 204) [ST/R]

Royal Wedding (10" MGM E-543, MGM E-3235) [ST]

Santa Claus Is Comin' to Town (MGM E/SDE-4732)

Second Chorus (Hollywood Soundstage 404) [ST]

A Shine on Your Shoes (MGM 2353-112)

Shoes with Wings On (MGM E-3413)

Silk Stockings (MGM E-3542) [ST]

The Special Magic of Fred Astaire (MGM 2317-082)

Starring Fred Astaire (Col SG-34272, Col C2-44233)

The Story of Vernon and Irene Castle (Caliban 6000) [ST]

Swing Time/The Gay Divorcee (EMI 1010) [ST]

Swing Time/The Gay Divorcee/Top Hat/Shall We Dance? (Pathé 184-95807- 08) [ST]

Swing Time/Shall We Dance? (Sountrak 106) [ST]

They Can't Take That Away from Me (UA 29918)

They Can't Take These Away from Me (UA 29941)

Three Evenings with Fred Astaire (Ava 1, Choreo 1, DRG 518) [ST/TV]

Three Little Words (10" MGM E-516, MGM E-3229, Metro M/S-615) [ST]

Top Hat/Shall We Dance? (EMI 102) [ST]

Top Hat, White Tie and Golf Shoes (Facit 142) w. Bing Crosby, Ginger Rogers

Top Hat, White Tie and Tails (Saville 184)

You Were Never Lovelier (Curtain Calls 10/24) [ST]

You'll Never Get Rich (Hollywood Soundstage 5001) [ST]

Ziegfeld Follies of 1946 (Curtain Calls 100/15-16) [ST]

# GENE AUSTIN

FOREVER ASSOCIATED WITH THE SONG "MY BLUE HEAVEN," GENE AUS-
tin was a smooth-sounding crooner whose phonograph records sold some eighty-six
million copies during the 1920s and early 1930s. With his pleasing tenor voice, a
propensity for hitting high notes, and an easy-going musical style, Gene Austin was the
antithesis of the Jazz Age which spawned him. Starting out as a country singer, he changed
his style under the guidance of Nathaniel Shilkret at Victor Records and, along with his
close friend Nick Lucas, he made crooning a vogue. His success paved the way for Rudy
Vallee, Bing Crosby, Dick Powell, and other romantic songsters. In addition to his
singing, Austin composed many songs and also found success in other media. Although he
sang of "a little nest that nestles where the roses bloom," he was a vagabond who kept on
the move throughout his life, often claiming "I never want to nest anywhere."

He was born Eugene Lucas in Gainesville, Texas, on June 24, 1900, but he grew up
in Yellow Pine and Minden, Louisiana. His father died when he was small and Gene's
mother remarried later, to Jim Austin. Music came easy to the youth, and by the time he
was a teenager he had the urge to roam. At age fifteen he ran away from home with a circus
and while traveling with the aggregation he learned to play the calliope. Lying about his
age, he joined the Army in 1916 and saw service with General John J. Pershing in the
Mexican Punitive Expedition; during World War I he was stationed in France. After the
war he returned home to study both dentistry and law and for a time he was enrolled at the
University of Baltimore. However, his love of music became the driving force behind his
career efforts and he began working as a professional singer.

In the early 1920s Gene Lucas changed his name to Gene Austin to avoid confusion
with another rising music performer, Nick Lucas. At this time Austin teamed with Roy
Bergere and, billed as Austin & Bergere, they performed a comedy duet in vaudeville in the
East and Midwest. In the spring of 1924 they made their recording debut on Vocalion
Records performing "A Thousand Miles from Here." The duo also composed the song
"How Come You Do Me Like You Do?" which became a national favorite in 1924. While
working at Vocalion, Austin was asked to team with George Reneau, "The Blind Musician
of the Smoky Mountains." Together they cut a series of successful records for that label as
well as for Edison while Austin also continued working with Roy Bergere.

Early in 1925 popular Victor recording star Aileen Stanley waxed Gene Austin's
tune "When My Sugar Walks Down the Street" and she insisted he accompany her on the
record. The label next teamed him with Carson Robison on a duet of "Way Down
Home." In the spring of 1926 Gene Austin had his first solo Victor best-seller, "Yearning,"

and he was to remain with the label for six more years, developing into one of the top two (the other was Nick Lucas) record sellers in the nation. His Victor best-sellers included such numbers as "Yes Sir, That's My Baby," "Five Foot Two, Eyes of Blue," "Bye Bye Blackbird," "One Sweet Letter from You," "The Sweetheart of Sigma Chi," "Carolina Moon," "I Can't Give You Anything But Love," and "Ain't Misbehavin'." His two biggest sellers for Victor were "My Blue Heaven" and "Ramona." The former was waxed in 1927 and eventually sold over eight million copies, while "Ramona" came out the next year and had sales in excess of three million platters.

Like most popular recording artists of the day, Gene Austin toured in vaudeville, plugging his latest records and making a good living from the stage. In 1927 he also had a successful stand in London and during the rest of the 1920s he became a very wealthy man from his vaudeville appearances and record royalties. He and Nathaniel Shilkret composed the song "The Lonesome Road" in 1927 and it was a best-seller for Austin on Victor Records. In 1929 the composition was used in the Universal film SHOW BOAT.

The Roaring Twenties brought Gene Austin his greatest success, but the bubble burst with the coming of the Depression. As his career began to fade as record sales dwindled, he turned to radio but was unable to obtain a sustaining network series. In 1931 he began cutting records for the American Record Company, which sold its product on a variety of labels (Banner, Conqueror, Oriole, Perfect) in dime stores. In the early 1930s he was a vocalist on the "California Melodies" radio show before touring in musical revues like *Broadway Rhapsody* and *Going Places*. In the mid-1930s he teamed with bass player Candy Candido and guitarist Otto "Coco" Heimel, who were billed as Candy and Coco, and he had a career resurgence. He returned to Victor in 1934 to record his own "Ridin' Around in the Rain" and it sold well.

It was in 1934 that he made his film debut with Candy and Coco in the Joan

Gene Austin in 1932

Crawford starrer SADIE McKEE at MGM. During a cabaret sequence Austin offers a hot rendition of "After You've Gone." That year also found him with Candy and Coco in the Universal musical THE GIFT OF GAB performing "Blue Sky Avenue," which failed in its attempt to repeat the success of his "My Blue Heaven." He also appeared briefly in Mae West's ribald BELLE OF THE NINETIES (1934) singing "My American Beauty"; one of his compositions, "When a St. Louis Woman Comes Down to New Orleans," was performed by Miss West. That same year he appeared in the first of four short subjects he would star in for RKO, beginning with FERRY-GO-ROUND in which he crooned "My Blue Heaven," "Pretty Lady," "Baby, Won't You Please Come Home," "Dear Old Southland," and "Nobody Loves Me No More." In the 1935 RKO short NIGHT LIFE he performed a number of songs including "My Melancholy Baby" and his signature, "My Blue Heaven."

Mae West had taken a shine to Austin and she hired him to write the songs for her sassy KLONDIKE ANNIE (1936); he created such tunes as "I'm an Occidental Woman in an Oriental Mood for Love," "Little Bar Fly," and "Mr. Deep Blue Sea." He also had a featured role in this Paramount release; playing a singing evangelist, he performed "You'll Feel Better in the Morning" and "It's Better to Give Than to Receive." He also made two additional RKO shorts, BAD MEDICINE (1936) and TRAILING ALONG (1937). In the former he sang "Smoke Rings," "When My Sugar Walks Down the Street," "Sweet Sue," and "Git Along," while TRAILING ALONG found him doing numbers like "Trailing Down the Highway" and "You've Got to Get That Mellow Jive." By now Russell Hall had replaced Candy Candido in the Candy and Coco backup act for Gene.

The quickie SONGS AND SADDLES (1938) was Austin's only Western feature. It was made to cash in on the popularity of the Gene Autry musical cowboy pictures. Austin played himself as he and his musical troupe attempted to stop a gang of land grabbers. He handled the rugged role surprisingly well and he also composed a number of the tunes he sang in the feature including "Song of the Saddle," "I Fell Down and Broke My Heart," "I'm Comin' Home," and "That Rootin' Tootin' Shootin' Man from Texas." To help the box-office grosses on the picture, Austin and his touring company appeared with the film when it was roadshown in the South. Meanwhile, from early in 1937 until late in 1938, Gene Austin was the featured vocalist on comedian Joe Penner's CBS radio program.

By the late 1930s, Gene Austin's greatest following was in the South, and during this period he had a group, including Candy and Coco and Joan Brooks, which toured with a musical revue financed by Mae West. Late in the decade, though, his fortunes had fallen so far that for a time he broadcast from a Mexican border station at Del Rio using the name Bob Roberts. Mae West, however, brought him back to Hollywood in 1940 for a brief appearance as himself leading a band, including Candy and Coco, as she sang "Willy of the Valley" in MY LITTLE CHICKADEE (1940).

In the early 1940s Gene Austin starred in a batch of three-minute musical shorts for Soundies Distributing Corporation of America and Murray Hollywood Productions; several of these featured singer Doris Sherrell, to whom he was married at the time. He also sang "My Blue Heaven" in the inconsequential Universal musical MOON OVER LAS VEGAS (1944) starring Anne Gwynne, and in the East Side Kids comedy FOLLOW THE LEADER (1944) he performed his composition "Now and Then." He reprised "My Blue Heaven" yet again in the Universal short PAGLIACCI SWINGS IT (1944) and in the 1945 Soundies musical MY BLUE HEAVEN.

During the late 1930s Austin had recorded for Decca Records as well as for Standard and Thesaurus Transcriptions. In the mid-1940s he resumed his recording career for the Four Star and Universal labels and also formed his own record firm, Gene Austin Records. (During the 1920s and early 1930s he had also operated Gene Austin,

Inc., a music publishing company.) He made guest appearances on such radio shows as those of The Andrews Sisters and on "Philco Radio Hall of Fame." Another aspect of his activities was Austin's penchant for purchasing a nightclub, starring himself as its main attraction, and then selling the business at a profit. It was a practice he would continue on and off throughout the remainder of his career. In the late 1940s Austin ceased performing for a time after he was reported missing at sea and a memorial service was conducted for him—the incident disturbed him greatly.

The early 1950s found Austin resuming his career, and in 1954 he cut a long-playing album, *Blue Heaven*, for RCA Victor. His career really rebounded in 1957 after NBC-TV aired "The Gene Austin Story" on "The Goodyear Television Playhouse" (April 20, 1957), with George Grizzard playing the title role and Austin dubbing the vocals. At the end of the hour show Austin appeared and sang his latest composition, "Too Late"; his RCA single of it put him on the record charts for the first time in a quarter of a century. After that he appeared on such TV shows as those of Ed Sullivan, Jimmy Dean, Red Skelton, and Dave Garroway, "The Woolworth Hour," and Patti Page's "The Big Record." In 1958, he returned to London for a successful engagement. He also cut albums for RCA and Dot and toured the nation with his club act. Gene Austin entered politics in 1962 when he opposed Nevada Governor Grant Sawyer in the Democratic primary (he had been a Las Vegas resident since the 1940s and had operated a gambling casino called "My Blue Heaven" there); but he and his running mate, Eddie Jackson (of Clayton-Jackson-Durante fame), lost to Sawyer and his running mate, former film star Rex Bell. After that Austin moved to Florida where he operated still another "My Blue Heaven" club, and in the late 1960s he settled in California.

Gene Austin's last years were spent like his previous ones, traveling with his club act and writing songs. Early in 1971 he appeared on Merv Griffin's CBS-TV tribute to popular composers and later in the year he assisted in establishing the Museum of Jazz in New Orleans. By now, however, he was suffering from cancer. His final appearance was at the Jack London Club in Palm Springs where he brought in the year 1972 performing his old favorites. Three weeks later, on January 24, 1972, at the age of seventy-one, he died in a Palm Springs hospital. He was survived by his fifth wife, Gigi; two daughters from previous marriages, Charlotte (who as Charlotte Austin starred in several 1950s movies) and Ann; and three grandchildren. It is ironic that although Gene Austin wanted originally to become a country singer, his godson (David Houston) and cousin (Tommy Overstreet) both became popular country singing stars in the 1960s and 1970s.

## Filmography

Show Boat (Univ, 1929) (song only)
Sadie McKee (MGM, 1934)
Ferry-Go-Round (RKO, 1934) (s)
The Gift of Gab (Univ, 1934)
Belle of the Nineties (Par, 1934) (also song)
Night Life (RKO, 1935) (s)
Klondike Annie (Par, 1936) (also songs)
Bad Medicine (RKO, 1936) (s)
Trailing Along (RKO, 1937) (s)
Songs and Saddles (Colony, 1938) (also songs)
My Little Chickadee (Univ, 1940)
One Dozen Roses (Soundies, 1942) (s)
That Rootin' Tootin' Shootin' Man from Texas
    (Soundies, 1942) (s)
I Hear You Knockin' But You Can't Come In
    (Soundies, 1942) (s)

Take Your Shoes Off Daddy (Murray Holly-
    wood Productions, 1943) (s)
I Hear You Knockin' But You Can't Come In
    (Murray Hollywood Productions, 1943) (s)
You're Marvellous (Murray Hollywood
    Productions, 1943) (s)
Boogie Woogie Wedding (Murray Hollywood
    Productions, 1943) (s)
My Melancholy Baby (Murray Hollywood
    Productions, 1943) (s)
I Want to Be Bad (Soundies, 1944) (s)
I Want to Lead a Band (Soundies, 1944) (s)
Moon over Las Vegas (Univ, 1944)
Imagine (Soundies, 1944) (s)
Follow the Leader (Mon, 1944) (also song)
Pagliacci Swings It (Univ, 1944) (s)
My Blue Heaven (Soundies, 1945) (s)

## Radio Series

California Melodies (CBS, 1932–34)
The Joe Penner Show (CBS, 1937–38)

## Album Discography

All-Time Favorites by Gene Austin (Vik LX-
    998, X LVA-1007)
Blue Heaven (10" RCA LPM-3200)
Gene Austin and His Lonesome Road (Fraterni-
    ty 1006)
Gene Austin's Great Hits (Dot 3300/25300)

My Blue Heaven (Decca DL-8433)
My Blue Heaven (RCA LPM-2490)
Old Pals Are the Best Pals (Sunbeam 507)
Restless Heart (RCA LPM-1547)
This Is Gene Austin (RCA VPM-6056)

# GENE AUTRY

GENE AUTRY STARTED THE CRAZE OF THE SINGING MOVIE COWBOY IN the mid-1930s and he utilized his enormous popularity with the public to develop a number of lucrative business interests. In 1988 *Forbes* magazine named him one of the richest people in America with assets of $230 million. While many critics insist Autry was a less than mediocre actor (he was) and only a mediocre singer (he was actually a *very* good vocalist), the performer was so consistently popular, especially in the South and Midwest, that he singlehandedly changed the image of the American cowboy forever. He devised a Cowboy Code of Clean Living as a model for the country's youth and he forever espoused the American dream. Gene Autry's tremendous show business success encompassed not only motion pictures but also radio, personal appearances, records, television, songwriting, and all types of merchandising. Long retired as a performer, Autry is today a man of business and baseball, but his fans still remember him fondly as the cleancut cowboy who crooned the songs of the plains.

The future cowboy hero was born Orvon Gene Autry on September 29, 1907, in Tioga, Texas, the son of Delbert and Elnora Ozmont Autry. He was the eldest of four children, with two younger sisters and a brother. His grandfather, a minister, taught young Autry to sing at age five and, thereafter, the boy sang in the local church choir. At the age of twelve Autry received his first guitar, and while a teenager he worked one summer in a medicine show. After high school he became a telegraph operator in Chelsea, Oklahoma, for the Frisco Line, but show business had become his passion. He developed his guitar technique after coming under the influence of popular singer-guitarist Nick Lucas' recordings, and he practiced singing while on the job during the day and also wrote songs with fellow telegrapher Jimmie Long. One evening Will Rogers stopped by Autry's office to send his syndicated newspaper column; he heard Autry singing and suggested he perform on radio. This led to work on station KVOO in Tulsa as "The Oklahoma Yodeling Cowboy," for no pay. He cut a single for Paramount Records in 1927 but the company went bankrupt before it was issued. Autry then relocated to New York City where he looked up two Oklahoma men: Johnny and Frankie Marvin. Johnny Marvin had been very successful on stage and with recordings in the mid- to late 1920s and had a vaudeville act with his brother Frankie. They befriended young Autry and tried to get him bookings as well as a recording contract. In the fall of 1929 he managed a session with Victor Records and recorded two tunes, "My Dreaming of You" and "My Alabama Home," the latter written by Johnny Marvin. Autry then began recording for a number of dime-store labels like Champion, Clarion, Conqueror, Diva, Harmony, Perfect, and

Velvet Tone, under his own name as well as such pseudonyms as Bob Clayton, Johnny Dodds, John Hardy, Overton Hatfield, Sam Hill, Gene Johnson, Tom Long, and Jimmie Smith.

In 1930 Autry signed with Art Satherley's new American Record Corporation (ARC) and the next year he and Jimmie Long had a best-selling record of "That Silver Haired Daddy of Mine," a tune they had written. The next spring (1931) Autry married Long's niece, Ina Mae Spivey. The song also changed Autry's singing style, as his earlier recordings showed the influence of then-popular country singer Jimmie Rodgers. The year 1930 also found Autry working in Chicago on the "National Barn Dance" radio show on WLS, a clear-channel station which reached most of the Midwest. As a result of the radio program, personal appearances, and more best-selling records (like "Mexicali Rose"), Gene Autry quickly became a household name in the Midwest. In 1932 Sears-Roebuck began marketing the Gene Autry Guitar, and Autry was being featured on sheet music and songbooks.

In 1934, Autry, Smiley Burnette, and Frankie Marvin came to Hollywood where they appeared in the barn dance sequence in the Ken Maynard Western IN OLD SANTA FE for Mascot Pictures. Autry was especially impressive in his brief singing appearance and landed a small acting part in another Maynard Mascot production, the serial MYSTERY MOUNTAIN (1934). When Ken Maynard quit Mascot in 1935, studio chief Nat Levine took a chance and toplined Autry in the science fiction/Western cliffhanger THE PHAN-TOM EMPIRE (1935). It proved a great success. That year Mascot merged with Monogram and several other studios to form Republic Pictures and Autry was signed to star in the Western feature TUMBLING TUMBLEWEEDS (1935) with Smiley Burnette as his pal Frog Millhouse. Despite Autry's lack of acting acumen, he proved a sensation in the film and quickly became Republic's most popular action film star. From 1936 to 1954 he was in the *Motion Picture Herald*'s poll of Top Ten Money-Making Western Stars, except for 1943–45 when he was off the screen, and he topped the poll from 1937 to 1942. From 1940 to 1942 he was also ranked in the poll's Top Ten Money-Making Stars, the only "B" Western star to make the chart in those years.

Gene Autry's Republic pictures were slickly made standardized affairs, with Autry as the hero who saves the heroine from the villains and sings a number of songs along the way. His movies were particularly popular with rural audiences and youngsters. Although his movies were consistent moneymakers, he was paid very little by Republic, his initial contract calling for a salary of only $150 per week. In the late 1930s Autry walked out on Republic and the studio threatened to replace him with Roy Rogers; his new contract had him making $12,500 per picture. More lucrative, however, were personal appearances, and Autry was popular on the rodeo circuit. When he toured the British Isles in 1939, some 750,000 people showed up in Dublin, Ireland, to see him in a parade. By now Autry was recording for Okeh Records and he had many best-sellers, some from his films, like "Tumbling Tumbleweeds," "Nobody's Darlin' But Mine," "There's a Gold Mine in the Sky," "You Are My Sunshine," "Rainbow on the Rio Colorado," "Have I Told You Lately That I Love You," "South of the Border," "Amapola," and "That Little Kid Sister of

Mine," in addition to his theme song, "Back in the Saddle Again," written with Ray Whitley. In 1940 Autry came to network radio with his "Melody Ranch" program on CBS; it was one of his few media activities which did not include his beautiful horse, Champion. That year also found him the subject of the newspaper comic strip "Gene Autry Rides"; late in 1941 the first Gene Autry comic book appeared and comics about him were on the newsstands until 1959. In the 1930s and 1940s he was also the subject of Whitman Publishing's fictional Better Little Books for Children and in the 1950s he was featured in the company's Little Golden and Tell-A-Tale books. In addition, from 1944 to 1957 he was featured in eight novels published by Whitman.

Late in 1941 a town in Oklahoma was named for Gene Autry, and as the year ended he volunteered for military service and was inducted on a "Melody Ranch" radio broadcast. At first he entertained troops and sold war bonds, but after earning his pilot's license he flew cargo and men in North Africa and the Far East for the duration of World War II. After the war, Autry returned home to resume his film career, but found that his number one cowboy status had been usurped by Roy Rogers (of Republic Pictures) in his absence. In 1946 Autry returned to the screen in SIOUX CITY SUE, but he was no longer happy at Republic and left the studio in 1947 to produce his own pictures at Columbia. He also continued on radio, made personal appearances, and had several best-selling records for Columbia, including the children's favorites "Here Comes Santa Claus," "Peter Cottontail,"

Judith Allen and Gene Autry in BOOTS AND SADDLES (1937)

and "Rudolph, the Red-Nosed Reindeer" (which sold over ten million records).

In 1950 Gene Autry came to television with "The Gene Autry Show," which ran on CBS-TV for over ninety episodes through 1956. Co-starring with him on the program was Pat Buttram, with whom he had worked at WLS in the 1930s. In fact, Autry was instrumental in bringing many of his WLS co-workers to Hollywood, including Lulu Belle and Scotty Wiseman, Patsy Montana, Max Terhune, The Cass County Boys, and the Maple City Four. Smiley Burnette was Autry's co-star in scores of films and Frankie Marvin appeared in nearly all of his pictures as well as wrote songs for them. In addition, Johnny Marvin composed many songs for Autry's movies and handled some of his business affairs until his death in 1944.

Although more portly, Gene Autry continued to make feature films until 1953 when he left the screen after THE LAST OF THE PONY RIDERS. He had starred in eighty-nine feature films and one serial in addition to appearing in the two Ken Maynard productions. In 1958 Autry appeared on NBC-TV's "Wide, Wide World" program in a tribute to Western movies. The show was telecast in part from Gene Autry's Melody Ranch Movie Location in Newhall, California. He had purchased the ranch in 1940 (and it would burn down in 1962). In 1959 Autry returned to the screen for the last time for a guest bit in Bob Hope's ALIAS JESSE JAMES. (Contrary to reports, Autry did *not* appear in the unreleased 1969 film THE SILENT TREATMENT.) Autry continued to record for Columbia Records well into the 1950s and then he formed his own company, Republic Records, which also owned Challenge Records. He recorded for both labels. In 1962 he cut his final album, *Gene Autry's Golden Hits*, for RCA. In 1956 his radio show, "Melody Ranch," left the air after sixteen years. The show returned to TV from 1961 to 1972 over Autry's Los Angeles TV station, KTLA, and was hosted by his radio co-star, Johnny Bond. Autry made occasional appearances on the program, which was also syndicated.

Around 1960 Gene Autry began to ease himself out of show business in deference to his many other lucrative financial activities. Since the mid-1940s he had been involved in broadcasting through his Golden West Broadcasting Corporation, and he controlled several radio and television stations throughout the country. Moreover, he owned several hotels, including Palm Springs's Gene Autry Hotel. During the 1950s, in addition to his own TV series, Gene Autry's company produced a number of TV Western series, including "The Adventures of Champion, the Wonder Horse," "Buffalo Bill Jr.," "Annie Oakley," "The Range Rider," and the first season of "Death Valley Days." Perhaps his most noted enterprise was his purchase of the California Angels baseball team late in 1960. In 1966 the team moved to a new stadium in Anaheim. In 1969 Gene Autry was inducted into the Country Music Hall of Fame.

During the 1970s Gene Autry made occasional guest appearances on TV shows like "Hee Haw" and "The Tonight Show," but he was primarily involved in his assorted commercial activities. Nevertheless, he was always available for interviews, happily and openly talking about the past and his long career. During that decade his record label, Republic, was revived and several albums by Autry made up of "Melody Ranch" radio songs were issued and sold well. In 1977 some of his recordings were used in the feature film SEMI-TOUGH and in 1978 his autobiography, *Back in the Saddle Again*, written with Mickey Hershowitz, was published by Doubleday. The next year Henry Crowell, Jr. portrayed Autry in the television tribute "Gene Autry, An American Hero." In 1980 he was inducted into the Cowboy Hall of Fame of Great Westerners in Oklahoma City, Oklahoma, but in the spring of that year his wife of forty-nine years, Ina Mae, died. In accordance with her will, Autry sold several of his properties, including KTLA.

The 1980s found Gene Autry making a somewhat surprising return to the limelight. On July 19, 1981, he wed thirty-nine-year-old banking executive Jackie Ellam, whom he had known through various business transactions since 1964. He received plenty of publicity when the California Angels won the baseball pennant in the mid-1980s and in 1987 Autry returned to television, with Pat Buttram, hosting "Melody Ranch Theatre" on The Nashville Network. On the show, the two partners showed Autry's old films and discussed various aspects of his career. Late in 1988 the Gene Autry Western Heritage Museum in Los Angeles's Griffith Park was opened, to much fanfare. The museum is designed as a permanent shrine for Gene Autry memorabilia and to the heritage of the American frontier.

Despite all the success and wealth Gene Autry attained as a businessman, he will always be best remembered as the singing cowboy hero. It is to this image that he owes his success, but despite all it has brought him, he never took it too seriously. He summed up his successful film career by stating, "We had to have a decent story, good music, comic relief, enough action with chases and gunfights, and a little romance. But we had to treat that love angle *real* careful. Almost no clinches or embraces. I could put my arm around the girl only if it was necessary to stop her falling off a cliff."

## Filmography

In Old Santa Fe (Mascot, 1934)
Mystery Mountain (Mascot, 1934) (serial)
The Phantom Empire (Mascot, 1935) (serial)
Tumbling Tumbleweeds (Rep, 1935)
Melody Trail (Rep, 1935)
Sagebrush Troubador (Rep, 1935)
The Singing Vagabond (Rep, 1935)
Red River Valley (Rep, 1936)
Comin' Round the Mountain (Rep, 1936)
The Singing Cowboy (Rep, 1936)
Guns and Guitars (Rep, 1936)
Oh, Susannah! (Rep, 1936)
Ride, Ranger, Ride (Rep, 1936)
The Old Corral (Rep, 1936)
Round-Up Time in Texas (Rep, 1937)
Git Along, Little Dogies [Serenade of the West] (Rep, 1937)

Rootin' Tootin' Rhythm [Rhythm on the Ranch] (Rep, 1937)
Yodelin' Kid from Pine Ridge [The Hero of Pine Ridge] (Rep, 1937)
Public Cowboy No. 1 (Rep, 1937)
Holiday Greetings (Unk, 1937) (s)
Boots and Saddles (Rep, 1937)
Manhattan Merry-Go-Round [Manhattan Music Box] (Rep, 1937)
The Old Barn Dance (Rep, 1938)
Gold Mine in the Sky (Rep, 1938)
Man from Music Mountain (Rep, 1938)
Prairie Moon (Rep, 1938)
Rhythm of the Saddle (Rep, 1938)
Western Jamboree (Rep, 1939)
Home on the Prairie (Rep, 1939)
Mexicali Rose (Rep, 1939)

Blue Montana Skies (Rep, 1939)
Mountain Rhythm (Rep, 1939)
Colorado Sunset (Rep, 1939)
In Old Monterey (Rep, 1939)
Rovin' Tumbleweeds (Rep, 1939)
South of the Border (Rep, 1939)
Rancho Grande (Rep, 1940)
Shooting High (20th–Fox, 1940)
Gaucho Serenade (Rep, 1940)
Carolina Moon (Rep, 1940)
Rodeo Dough (MGM, 1940) (s)
Ride, Tenderfoot, Ride (Rep, 1940)
Melody Ranch (Rep, 1940)
Meet Roy Rogers (Rep, 1941) (s)
Ridin' on a Rainbow (Rep, 1941)
Back in the Saddle (Rep, 1941)
The Singing Hills (Rep, 1941)
Sunset in Wyoming (Rep, 1941)
Under Fiesta Stars (Rep, 1941)
Down Mexico Way (Rep, 1941)
Sierra Sue (Rep, 1941)
Cowboy Serenade [Serenade of the West] (Rep, 1942)
Heart of the Rio Grande (Rep, 1942)
Home in Wyomin' (Rep, 1942)
Stardust on the Sage (Rep, 1942)
Call of the Canyon (Rep, 1942)
Bell of Capistrano (Rep, 1942)
Screen Snapshots #108 (Col, 1942) (s)
Sioux City Sue (Rep, 1946)
Trail to San Antone (Rep, 1947)
Twilight on the Rio Grande (Rep, 1947)
Saddle Pals (Rep, 1947)
Robin Hood of Texas (Rep, 1947)
The Last Round-Up (Rep, 1947)

The Strawberry Roan [Fools Awake] (Col, 1948)
Loaded Pistols (Col, 1949)
The Big Sombrero (Col, 1949)
Riders of the Whistling Pines (Col, 1949)
Rim of the Canyon (Col, 1949)
Screen Snapshots #129 (Col, 1949) (s)
The Cowboy and the Indians (Col, 1949)
Riders in the Sky (Col, 1949)
Sons of New Mexico [The Brat] (Col, 1949)
Mule Train (Col, 1950)
Beyond the Purple Hills (Col, 1950)
Cow Town [Barbed Wire] (Col, 1950)
Indian Territory (Col, 1950)
The Blazing Sun (Col, 1951)
Gene Autry and the Mounties (Col, 1951)
Texans Never Cry (Col, 1951)
Whirlwind (Col, 1951)
Silver Canyon (Col, 1951)
Hills of Utah (Col, 1951)
Valley of Fire (Col, 1951)
The Old West (Col, 1952)
Night Stage to Galveston (Col, 1952)
Apache Country (Col, 1952)
Wagon Team (Col, 1952)
Blue Canadian Rockies (Col, 1952)
Barbed Wire [False News] (Col, 1952)
Winning of the West (Col, 1953)
On Top of Old Smoky (Col, 1953)
Goldtown Ghost Riders (Col, 1953)
Pack Train (Col, 1953)
Memories in Uniform (Col, 1953) (s)
Saginaw Trail (Col, 1953)
The Last of the Pony Riders (Col, 1953)
Hollywood Cowboy Stars (Col, 1954) (s)
Alias Jesse James (UA, 1959)

## Radio Series

National Barn Dance (WLS, 1930–34)
Gene Autry's Melody Ranch (CBS, 1940–56)

## TV Series

The Gene Autry Show (CBS, 1950–56)
Melody Ranch Theatre (TNN, 1987– )

## Album Discography

Back in the Saddle Again (Encore P-14380)

Back in the Saddle Again (Har HL-7399/HS-11276)

Christmas Favorites (Col Special Products P-15766)

Christmas with Gene Autry (Challenge 600, Republic 6018)

Christmastime with Gene Autry (Mistletoe 1207)

Country and Western Memories (Cattle CAT-8008)

Country Music Hall of Fame (Col CL-1035)

Cowboy Hall of Fame (Republic 6012)

Everyone's a Child at Christmas (Col Special Products P-15767)

Famous Favorites/His Golden Hits (Suffolk Marketing)

Gene Autry and Champion Western Adventures (Col CL-677, Har HL-9505)

Gene Autry at the Rodeo (Col JL-8001)

Gene Autry Classics, Vol. 1 (Republic 6021)

The Gene Autry Collection (Murray Hill 17079)

Gene Autry—Columbia Historic Edition (Col FD-37465)

Gene Autry Favorites (Republic 6013, Birchmont 562)

Gene Autry Favorites/Live from Madison Square Garden (Republic 1968/69)

Gene Autry—50th Anniversary (Republic 6022)

Gene Autry Live (Amalgamated 118)

Gene Autry Sings (Hallmark HM-582)

Gene Autry Sings (Har HL-7399/HS-11199)

Gene Autry's Christmas Classics (Starday SD-1038)

Gene Autry's Golden Hits (RCA LPM/LSP-2623)

Great Western Hits (Har HL-7332)

Greatest Hits (Col CL-1575)

Holiday Time with Gene Autry (Republic 1966)

Little Johnny Pilgrim & Guffy the Goofy Gobbler (10" Col MJV-83)

Live from Madison Square Garden (Republic 6014, Bulldog 1024)

Melody Ranch (Golden Age 5012)

Melody Ranch (Melody Ranch 101) w. Johnny Bond

Melody Ranch (Radiola 1048)

The Melody Ranch Show (Murray Hill 897296)

Merry Christmas with Gene Autry (10" Col CL-2547)

Peter Cottontail (10" Col CL-2568, Har HL-9555)

Rudolph the Red-Nosed Reindeer (Design DLPX-5, Grand Prix KSX-11, Hurrah HX-11)

Rudolph the Red-Nosed Reindeer and Other Children's Christmas Favorites (Har HL-9550)

Rusty the Rocking Horse & Bucky, the Bucking Bronco (10" Col MVJ-94)

The Singing Cowboy (Republic 1967)

Songs of Faith (Republic 6107)

Sounds like Jimmie Rodgers, Vol. 2 (Anthology of Country Music AMC-19)

South of the Border (Republic 6001, Bulldog 1021)

South of the Border/All American Cowboy (Republic 6011)

Stampede (10" Col JL-8009)

The Story of the Nativity (10" Col MJV-82)

20 Golden Pieces (Bulldog 2013)

Twenty-Two All-Time Favorites (GRT 2103-720)

The Very Rarest of Young Autry (Peace Maker 01)

Western Classics (10" Col CL-6020)

Western Classics (10" Col HL-9001)

Western Classics, Vol. 2 (10" Col HL-9002)

The Yellow Rose of Texas (Bear Family 15204)

The Young Gene Autry (Six Gun Singers 69)

The Young Gene Autry, Vol. 2 (Prairie Justice 70)

The Young Gene Autry, Vol. 3 (Prairie Justice 71)

# FRANKIE AVALON

IN THE LATE 1950S THERE WERE (APPARENTLY) THREE REQUISITES TO becoming a teenie bopper rock 'n' roll star: (1) be born in South Philadelphia; (2) have clean-cut good looks; and (3) be able to carry a tune—just barely. Frankie Avalon, like two of his pals (Fabian and Bobby Rydell), fulfilled these qualifications and then some.

Avalon was an instinctive musician whose goal had been to become a professional trumpeter, so he had studied music and understood it. Singing was a lark which he fell into and did not take seriously (he used to sing in a nasal twang as a joke) until he had become a national rage with a series of hot-selling pop tunes. Like Ricky Nelson, Connie Francis, Tommy Sands, and Fabian, he became part of the Hollywood cycle drawing upon "American Bandstand" stars as film "talent." The film factories counted on these adolescents to draw millions of their enthusiastic fans into movie theaters. The gimmick had worked with Elvis Presley and Pat Boone and it did with Frankie Avalon— for a while.

Just when it appeared his career was burning out in the early 1960s, Avalon was teamed with ex-Mousketeer star Annette Funicello in a batch of low-budget beach party musicals which found box-office favor. They were examples of sunny foolishness which, over the years, have become tremendously important escapist memories for a great many moviegoers of that generation. On the strength of those sand-and-song flicks the very aggressive Avalon carried his career through subsequent decades of nostalgia revivals, including a very well-liked BACK TO THE BEACH (1987). However, as with most of his confreres yanked into premature stardom, it was not all sugar and spice. THE IDOLMAKER (1980), loosely based on the rise and . . . of Frankie Avalon and Fabian-like personalities, made all that painfully clear.

He was born Francis Thomas Avallone on September 18, 1939, in South Philadelphia, the son of Nicholas and Mary Avallone. His father was a machinist and his mother was a tailor shop seamstress. There were two other children: two sisters. From his earliest days, Frankie wanted to be a somebody. After he won a red scooter in a talent contest for singing "Give Me Five Minutes More," he thought show business would be his entrée to a better life. Then he became intrigued with boxing. However, after seeing the Kirk Douglas– Doris Day movie YOUNG MAN WITH A HORN (1950), he was determined to become a trumpeter. Avalon remembers, "It inspired me so much. I asked my father if I could get a trumpet. He was elated, being a frustrated musician himself. So not having money to buy me a horn, he borrowed the money and went to a pawn shop, where he bought my first trumpet for $15." After four hours of self-teaching, Frankie could play "Music, Music,

Music." Later he took lessons from Seymour Rosenfeld, a member of the Philadelphia Symphony Orchestra.

By the time he was twelve, Frankie and his family had aspirations for him to become a professional musician. Performing for singer Al Martino at a neighborhood block party opened career doors that led to Frankie's doing instrumental recordings for X Records, one of RCA Victor's budget labels. Frankie appeared on the Philadelphia-based "Paul Whiteman's TV Teen Club" (ABC-TV), where neighborhood pal Bobby Rydell was already a regular. It was Whiteman who suggested Avalon as a new surname for the boy. Later, Frankie was taken to New York where he was snuck into a midnight penthouse audition for Jackie Gleason. The Great One was so impressed by the boy's trumpeting that he hired him to guest on "The Jackie Gleason Show" (CBS-TV). Other TV variety show appearances (Pinky Lee, The Dorsey Brothers) followed.

Avalon attended Vare Junior High School in South Philadelphia and during summer vacations was the trumpeter for Bobby Boyd and the Jazz Bums. He also formed Frankie Avalon's Teen and Twenty Club, sponsored by two older businessmen (Bob Marcucci and Peter DeAngelis) from the neighborhood. During the academic year Frankie was a member of the band Rocco and the Saints, led by one of his schoolteachers, Rocco de Laurentis. They occasionally had gigs at Murray's Inn in South Camden, New Jersey. Although the group had two vocalists, Avalon typically sang at least one number per session. One day Bob Marcucci called Avalon and told him he was forming a record label (Chancellor Records) and needed new talent. Did Avalon know of any? "I told him that I was in a band and a couple of guys sang. So he came in one night to hear us. I did a couple of songs, and after the set, he said he wanted to make a record with the band doing an instrumental on one side and me singing on the other. That's how it got started."

At the time Avalon was determined to promote his trumpet playing, not his "singing." But, recalls Marcucci, with whom Avalon would have a long-standing love-hate relationship, "Frankie never understood that trumpet prodigies sound better at eleven than they do at seventeen." Marcucci signed Rocco and the Saints to record "Cupid"/ "Jivin' with the Saints." Marcucci also negotiated for Rocco and the Saints to be among the teen groups hired by Warner Bros. for JAMBOREE (1957). In eighty-five minutes of inglorious black-and-white, this quickie film trotted out twenty-one disc jockeys (including Dick Clark) and an amazing array of recording artists ranging from Count Basie and His Orchestra to Fats Domino, Jerry Lee Lewis, and Connie Francis. Avalon's solo was "Teacher's Pet." As a single, neither that nor "Cupid" made any chart marks, but at local record hops, Avalon proved he had charisma with the gals. This was not lost on Marcucci.

Marcucci continued to record Avalon (as he was doing with Fabian and others). Marcucci and Peter DeAngelis had written a song which they insisted Frankie should record. If it failed, he could go back to his trumpet playing. Frankie was not impressed by the song's beat and, as a lark, began holding his nose as he rehearsed the lyrics. Marcucci and DeAngelis recorded Avalon singing like that, and the result was the nasal "Dede Dinah." It was on the charts for eleven weeks, rising to number seven in early 1958. "Ginger Bread," sung in the same twangy way, rose to number nine that summer. "I'll

Wait for You" was a more conventional ballad—and was sung more romantically. It rose to number fifteen that fall. Avalon went on tour to Australia with The Platters and Tommy Sands.

By now song writers were coming to Frankie with new numbers to record. One of them, Ed Marshall, brought him an item which Al Martino had been considering for an album. Avalon was drawn to the song and three days later recorded it. A short time later, when he was doing a live telephone interview with Dick Clark ("American Bandstand"—ABC-TV), he said he had just recorded a new song which he was sure would be a hit. The song was "Venus" and in early 1959 it rose to number one on the charts, staying there for five weeks. It would become the song most closely associated with Frankie Avalon. Throughout 1959 he created juke box magic with "Bobby Sox to Stockings," "A Boy Without a Girl," and "Just Ask Your Heart."

Now his manager, Marcucci engineered several film deals for his hot young talent who was now taking acting and voice lessons. Avalon was hired for Alan Ladd's GUNS OF THE TIMBERLAND (1960). It was a modestly conceived actioner about northwestern lumbering camps, produced by the star and featuring the actor's real-life daughter, Alana. Frankie was the wholesome young man drawn to her. Three song numbers (including "Gee Whizz Whillikens Golly Gee") were forced into the screenplay to appease Avalon's fans. Said *Variety,* "Avalon turns in some respectable work."

While Avalon's song "Why?"—his last really big song hit—began rising to number one on the charts in December 1959, he was on four months' location in Racketville, Texas, for John Wayne's THE ALAMO (1960). It was a $15 million spectacle about Colonel Davy Crockett (Wayne), Colonel James Bowie (Richard Widmark), and the defenders of The Alamo, Texans who for thirteen days in 1836 staved off General Santa Anna (Ruben Padilla) and his Mexican troops, before succumbing. Avalon was cast as Smitty, the exuberant young friend of Bowie. The picture was disliked by the critics but it made money eventually. For Avalon, it was an important career boost to be in a major production.

In quick order (and without any career direction or particular studio backing) Frankie Avalon supplied one of the off-camera voices in the Japanese cartoon ALAKAZAM THE GREAT! (1961), supported Robert Wagner and Ernie Kovacs in the service comedy SAIL A CROOKED SHIP (1961—Avalon sang "Opposites Attract"), was among the underwater crew in VOYAGE TO THE BOTTOM OF THE SEA (1961), and played one of Ray Milland's teenaged children in the science fiction entry PANIC IN THE YEAR ZERO (1962).

While Frankie Avalon's screen career and television guesting (ranging from a "Shirley Temple Theatre" to an "Eleventh Hour" to a "Jack Benny Program") was exploring and exploiting his popularity, his record successes were winding down. In 1960 he had hit songs with "Swingin' on a Rainbow" (from his only top forty album, *Swingin' on a Rainbow*), "Don't Throw Away All Those Teardrops," "Where Are You," and "Togetherness." He had no charted hits in 1961 and in mid-1962 he had his final best-selling single, "You Are Mine." Meanwhile, he had passed the age of twenty-one. In teen parlance, "He was over the hill."

He went to Spain to film a dreary costume picture, THE CASTILIAN (1963—which worked in a few Bob Marcucci songs for its youthful co-star). This was followed by the inept jungle actioner DRUMS OF AFRICA (1963—in which he sang "The River Love" by Marcucci and Russell Faith), and a slight tale of a World War II underwater demolition team called OPERATION BIKINI (1963—in which he vocalized "The Girl Back Home" by Marcucci and Faith).

By 1963 Avalon was twenty-four years old. He was *supposed* to have $250,000 in trust fund accounts. However, through a series of bad investments, owing back taxes, and a subsequent mid-1960s breakup with Marcucci (which cost him an estimated $100,000 to sever the relationship), Frankie Avalon had exhausted most of his financial resources. That year he guested on several TV shows ("Rawhide," "Burke's Law," and "Mr. Novak") and married dental technician Kay Deibel. They would have eight children.

Just as overexposure and the coming of the British Invasion (The Beatles, and others) combined to make Avalon and his peers passé, he suddenly got another show business break. It was American International's BEACH PARTY (1963), made on a $500,000 budget. Avalon had already made several pictures for the economy company, and no one had any particular expectations for this project when he and Annette Funicello (still under Walt Disney contract) were signed to be the youthful love interest in a hack account of an anthropologist (Bob Cummings) studying the mating habits of the Southern California surf set. With Avalon, Annette, Dick Dale, and the Del-Tones delivering the bubble-brained songs ("Promise Me Anything," "Treat Him Nicely," "Don't Stop Now"), Harvey Lembeck and crew doing a Three Stooges–like version of a motorcycle gang, and the presence of healthy young adults frolicking on the beach doing the rest, BEACH PARTY was a surprise hit. *Variety* perceived, "*Beach Party* has the kind of direct, simple-minded cheeriness which should prove well nigh irresistible to those teenagers who have no desire to escape the emptiness of their lives."

With the formula so bankable, American International turned out a slew of these beach party romps. They all had the same formula: a mix of forgettable pop rock tunes, a bevy of shapely young women, a few old-timers for the adult segment, and always Frankie (known as surfing champ "Big Kahuna") pursuing Annette (who always insisted virtuously, "Not without a ring."). They would surf (against a process screen), her hair would be sprayed frozen to offset her decorous bathing suit, and Avalon would realize, at the last moment, that waiting for Annette was far better than succumbing to the wiles of the latest seductive siren of the sands. Most of these mini-films were shot in ten days, and Avalon received $30,000 per film.

Sometimes American International teamed him with another co-star in a new setting, such as Deborah Walley in SKI PARTY (1965), or starred him in a different genre: the service comedy SERGEANT DEADHEAD (1965), also with Walley, or the science fiction farce DR. GOLDFOOT AND THE BIKINI MACHINE (1965—with Susan Hart). However, Avalon was always the same: convivial, wholesome, and usually spouting a song now and again. Occasionally he would be cast in a major production, such as United Artists' I'LL TAKE SWEDEN (1965), a lesser Bob Hope comedy in which guitar-strumming Frankie romanced hyperactive teenager Tuesday Weld. By 1966 he and Funicello had made their last joint teen outing, FIREBALL 500. Having exhausted the beach scene, they were in a race track environment with Fabian tossed in for good measure. The cycle had run its course.

Avalon had a growing family to support and he took his jobs where he could. He had no recording contract so he continued testing a club act, trying to cross over into the adult marketplace with his "hat and cane" routine. He would recall of this struggle, "I'd been leading a man's life since I was sixteen. When I was twenty-five or twenty-six, I was still playing nineteen-year-old kids. It's a long struggle. . . ." In the summer of 1966 he co-starred with Yvonne De Carlo in a stock version of *Pal Joey* and in 1967 he was back in court dealing with suits and countersuits on his disagreement with Marcucci. He still had his American International Pictures contract, and the studio used him for the exotic THE MILLION EYES OF SU-MURU (1967) and HORROR HOUSE (1970). For Paramount, he was in Otto Preminger's big-budgeted comedy misfire SKIDOO (1968) in a cast that included Groucho Marx, Carol Channing, and Avalon's one-time booster, Jackie Gleason. Off camera, family man Avalon was noted as a great golfing advocate and seemed to be low-key about his show business career. However, since he had no other trade, he was determined to survive financially in the business.

Fabian, Annette Funicello, and Frankie Avalon in FIREBALL 500 (1966)

There were occasional TV guest spots ("Love, American Style," "Here's Lucy") and a syndicated minor television special ("Frankie Avalon's Easter Special," 1969). He hoped to star in a biopic of THE WILLIE PEP STORY but the project's backer died; he auditioned for Sean Connery's THE ANDERSON TAPES (1971) but director Sidney Lumet rejected him for this caper film. In his early thirties, Avalon was considered a congenial carryover from a past era. He was always good for a quote. In 1970 he said, "It isn't like the old days. There isn't the excitement. Nobody has it today. People come in, go out in thirty days." In 1974 he showed up in a police melodrama (THE TAKE) starring Billy Dee Williams. Avalon was the shifty-eyed stoolie and in his three scenes gave a resourceful account of himself.

In the mid-1970s several artists from the 1950s (Frankie Valli, Neil Sedaka, Paul Anka, Bobby Vinton) were making nostalgic comebacks. Fourteen other record companies had already turned Avalon down when De-Lite Records signed him. Since disco was the current rhythm fad, they decided on a disco version of "Venus," which was popular briefly in late 1975. It was enough to convince Avalon to abandon plans to move with his family to Hawaii to take a permanent singing job at a hotel there. He was on a segment of "The Sonny and Cher Comedy Hour" (CBS-TV) in March 1976. Things seemed to be improving, even if someone wrote to the *Los Angeles Times* that year and asked, "I would like to know if Frankie Avalon is dead or alive." He recorded a few other singles ("Daydream Sunday") but they made no impact.

At the urging of long-time friend Dick Clark, CBS-TV took a chance on Avalon for a comeback in "Easy Does It . . . Starring Frankie Avalon." Debuting on August 25, 1976, the four-week half-hour series co-starred him with Annette Funicello. Together they sang, did skits, and joked about their old images. Two years later Frankie and Annette (for their fans, first names always sufficed) shot a Dick Clark–produced comedy pilot, "Frankie and Annette: The Second Time Around." It aired November 18, 1978, on NBC-TV but the series did not sell (nor did an earlier NBC-TV pilot, "The Beach Girls," which was aired early in 1978). Much more important to his career was his appearance in the blockbuster nostalgia musical movie GREASE (1978). John Travolta and Olivia Newton-John were the stars, but Avalon made a strong impression with his "Beauty School Dropout" number which, from the soundtrack album, earned him a Grammy nomination.

Avalon was still playing the club circuits in 1980 when United Artists released THE IDOLMAKER. It was a thinly veiled account of record producer/agent Bob Marcucci (played by Ray Sharkey) and his discovery/promotion of Philadelphia-sound talent, especially two rival rock 'n' roll stars whose looks and career moves paralleled those of Frankie Avalon and Fabian Forte. It led to a round of fresh interest in Fabian and Avalon. Frankie said of his on-camera act-alike, "So the character that was supposed to be me made me out a real heel. . . . That's the movies. They went strictly for a Hollywood-type cliché story, and that's exactly what came out."

Throughout the years, Avalon was constantly promoting new ventures (music publishing companies, film projects). He wanted to film ROCK GARDEN, about young rock and rollers, back in 1958–59, but could find no backing. In 1981 he toured with Dick Clark and his nostalgia rock 'n' roll show. In 1982 Avalon traveled with a fourteen-piece band, starred in a low-budget splatter movie called BLOOD SONG in which he was an ax-murderer, guested on TV's "Happy Days," and was in the syndicated TV special "Rock 'n' Roll: The First 25 Years." He organized a touring act with Fabian and Bobby Rydell called "Golden Boys of Bandstand" and continued to boost a project which he had had in mind for years—another reunion of the Beach Party gang, with himself and Annette as middle-aged marrieds. The concept kept cropping up for years and finally, in 1987, it became a reality. At a cost of $9 million and an eight-and-a-half-week shooting schedule, BACK TO THE BEACH had Avalon as an Ohio car dealer who with his wife (Annette) and their fourteen-year-old son fly to Los Angeles to track down their daughter, who is living in Malibu with a surfer. With Connie Stevens as the femme fatale, a guest appearance by Pee-wee Herman, and lots of light-hearted digs about the stars' pedigree (the son says, "A long time ago my parents were the most popular teenagers in the world"), the musical comedy had surprising appeal for the public.

Since BACK TO THE BEACH, Avalon continues to play eighty one-nighters yearly. He, Fabian, and Bobby Rydell reunited for the "Bandstand Boogie" number on the "All-Star Salute to the President" (ABC-TV, January 19, 1989). In the spring of 1989 he hosted the two-part syndicated special "Frankie Avalon Presents Surfs Up." The oldest of Frankie and Kay Avalon's eight children (four girls, four boys), Diana, was married in May 1987 and the Avalons continue to live in a six-bedroom house in Malibu Canyon.

Reflecting on his career, Avalon insists, "Sure, the average Joe probably thinks of us as these pretty boys who were turned into marketable packages, but I'll tell you something. There weren't that many of us guys who happened to hit and become successful in a business that is very difficult to become successful in."

## Filmography

Jamboree [Disc Jockey Jamboree] (WB, 1957)
Guns of the Timberland (WB, 1960)
The Alamo (UA, 1960)
Alakazam the Great! (AIP, 1961) (voice only)
Sail a Crooked Ship (Col, 1961)
Voyage to the Bottom of the Sea (20th–Fox, 1961)
Panic in the Year Zero! [End of the World, Survival] (AIP, 1962)
The Castilian [Valley of the Sword] (WB, 1963)
Operation Bikini (AIP, 1963)
Drums of Africa (MGM, 1963)
Beach Party (AIP, 1963)
Muscle Beach Party (AIP, 1964)
Dr. Goldfoot and the Bikini Machine [Dr G. and the Bikini Machine] (AIP, 1965)

Beach Blanket Bingo [Malibu Beach] (AIP, 1965)
Ski Party (AIP, 1965)
How to Stuff a Wild Bikini (AIP, 1965)
Sergeant Deadhead (AIP, 1965)
I'll Take Sweden (UA, 1965)
Fireball 500 (AIP, 1966)
The Million Eyes of Su-Muru [Sumuru] (AIP, 1967)
Skidoo (Par, 1968)
Horror House (AIP, 1970)
The Take (Col, 1974)
Grease (Par, 1978)
Blood Song (Summa Vista/Allstate/Mountain High, 1982)
Back to the Beach (Par, 1987)

## TV Series

Easy Does It . . . Starring Frankie Avalon (CBS, 1976)

## Album Discography

Alakazam the Great! (Vee Jay 6000) [ST]
And Now Mr. Avalon (Chancellor 5022)
Avalon Italiano (Chancellor 5025)
Back to the Beach (Col SC 40892) [ST]
Christmas Album (Chancellor 5031)
Fabian & Frankie Avalon: The Hit Makers
   (Chancellor 5009)
Facade (Chancellor 68901)
Fifteen Greatest Hits (UA 6382)
Frankie Avalon (Chancellor 5001)
Frankie Avalon Sings "Cleopatra" Plus 13 Other
   Great Hits (Chancellor 5032)
Grease (RS RS-2-4002) [ST]
The Greatest of Frankie Avalon and Fabian
   (MCA 27097)

I'll Take Sweden (UA 4121) [ST]
More Frankie Avalon (Sunset 5244)
Muscle Beach Party and Other Motion Picture
   Songs (UA 3371)
Sixteen Greatest Hits (ABC X-805)
Summer Scene (Chancellor 5011)
Swingin' on a Rainbow (Chancellor 5004)
Venus (De-Lite 2020)
The Very Best of Frankie Avalon (UA LA-450)
Whole Lotta Frankie (Chancellor 5018)
You Are Mine (Chancellor 5027)
The Young Frankie Avalon (Chancellor 5002)
You're My Life (De-Lite 9504)

# HARRY BELAFONTE

HARRY BELAFONTE FIRST CAME TO MUSICAL PROMINENCE THROUGH the mid-1950s calypso craze with such favorites as "Matilda," "Jamaica Farewell," and "Banana Boat." But he is really a folksinger. Along with Pete Seeger and The Weavers, Belafonte helped to carry folk music into the popular arena of American musical taste. His particular brand of folk music combines West Indian African, American pop gospel, and folk strains into a warm universal blend. As a velvety song interpreter Belafonte was one of the first folksingers to discard the guitar to use his hands for expression. His trademark open-necked (to the navel) silk performance shirts became a symbol for the trend away from formal attire in concert performance. It is in the concert arena that he has made his greatest dramatic impact, merging purpose, dramatic intensity, and imagination into his performances. A critic once noted of his sexy stage presence, "Like a cat, he is never caught in an ungraceful posture."

Belafonte's impact goes beyond his decades of successful concertizing and recording. He has starred in Broadway shows and has performed as a dramatic actor and variety entertainer on television. Unlike his friend Sidney Poitier, who persevered to find suitable roles for a black man in white Hollywood, Belafonte has acted in only eight theatrical motion pictures. Under other circumstances, this handsome 6' 2" performer might have continued in filmmaking. Instead, he has chosen to devote a great deal of his time and concern to issues of integration (as an entertainer he broke several "color lines") and to other humanitarian causes.

He was born Harold George Belafonte in the Harlem section of New York on March 1, 1927. His father (Harold George Belafonte, Sr.) was a cook in the British Royal Navy. His mother (Melvine [Love] Belafonte) was a dressmaker/domestic. His father, from Martinique in the French West Indies, became a British subject during World War I. His mother was from Jamaica, British West Indies. Belafonte's paternal grandfather and his maternal grandmother were white. There would be a younger brother, Dennis. Before Harry was six, his father had deserted the family. Belafonte was a troubled youth, greatly upset about the racial tension in his neighborhood and angry that he was poor. When he was nine, Mrs. Belafonte moved with her two sons to Kingston, Jamaica. By the time he was thirteen, his mother, who had remarried, moved her family back to Harlem. He was in his second year of high school (at George Washington High in the Bronx) in 1944 when he enlisted in the Navy, believing that serving in World War II (even as a black man) would be better than continuing with the frustrations at home. He received training at the Navy's Storekeeper School at Hampton, Virginia, and was later transferred to the West Coast. Without ever going overseas, he was discharged in 1945 at war's end.

By late 1945 Belafonte was living in Harlem again and working as a maintenance man for his stepfather. It was in December 1945 that he saw his first play, *Home Is the Hunter*, presented by the American Negro Theatre in Harlem. He suddenly realized he wanted to become a performer and he began to hang around the American Negro Theatre, first as a volunteer stagehand, then as an actor and singer. In *On Striver's Row* he had the juvenile lead. To improve his craft, he used his G.I. Bill of Rights to pay for a drama workshop at the New School for Social Research in downtown New York City. Among his fellow students were Marlon Brando and Sidney Poitier (who had been at the American Negro Theatre). Meanwhile, Belafonte began dating Frances Marguerite Bryd, whom he had met initially when he was in the Navy and she was a student at Hampton Institute in Newport News. She had since come to New York to attend New York University, where she would later teach child psychology. She and Belafonte were married on June 18, 1948.

After working at a summer camp in Pennsylvania and briefly in Manhattan's garment district, Belafonte stopped in one night at the Royal Roost, a midtown jazz club. Its owner, Monte Kay (who later married Diahann Carroll), had heard Belafonte sing before when he was at the New School. Kay had been impressed then and now auditioned him live in front of the club audience. The test was successful and Belafonte was hired to sing for a week at $70. This was in January 1949. He was so popular that he stayed at the Royal Roost for nineteen additional weeks. During this period Kay became his manager and Belafonte was among the jazz musicians who appeared in a Carnegie Hall concert. He made his first recordings, "Lean on Me" and "Recognition" (which he had written), which were distributed by a local record company without much impact. By now, the Belafontes' first daughter, Adrienne, had been born.

Belafonte and Sidney Poitier thought briefly of forming a comedy team and rehearsed an act. They both concluded they were not born comedians. Meanwhile, Kay promoted his client as the new Billy Eckstine and Belafonte performed as a jazz and/or pop singer in clubs around the country. Although he did not enjoy singing this type of music, he hoped the exposure would lead to acting assignments. In 1949 he was signed to a contract by Capitol Records and recorded "They Didn't Believe Me" and "How Green Was My Valley." Neither these numbers, nor a later session at the end of December (in which he sang such songs as "Sometimes I Feel Like a Motherless Child"), created much of an impression. He was dropped by the label. Among the club engagements Kay arranged for him was a month's stay at Cafe Society Downtown in Greenwich Village. *Variety* ranked Belafonte as "a vocalist of promise." From September 13 to October 20, 1949, he appeared with Timmy Rogers and The Jubileers in a half-hour CBS-TV series, "Sugar Hill Times" ("Uptown Jubilee"), a variety show featuring black entertainers. By Christmas of 1950, Belafonte's frustration at singing a type of music that was not meant for him culminated in his walking out of his contract at Martha Raye's Five O'Clock Club in Miami Beach. He was then earning $350 a week.

To help support his family (his wife was still teaching), he opened a Greenwich Village restaurant with two friends. Eight months later The Sage failed. Meanwhile,

Belafonte had used the restaurant as a bohemian mecca for musicians, folksingers in particular. By now his interest in folk music had expanded tremendously, and on weekends he would travel to the Library of Congress in Washington, D.C., to do research in their folk music archives and to listen to folk records. Belafonte's friends, novelist Bill Attaway (who collaborated on many of Belafonte's later folk adaptations) and guitarist Millard Thomas (who later became his accompanist), worked together to build a repertoire of old and new folk ballads. By 1951 Belafonte had polished his performing as a folksinger and was booked into the Village Vanguard. He remained there for fourteen weeks at $225 weekly. From there he moved uptown to the Blue Angel where he stayed for sixteen weeks at $300 weekly. Millard Thomas had become his official accompanist, leaving Belafonte free to use his hands for "dramatic treatment" while performing. After an engagement in Philadelphia, Belafonte returned to the Village Vanguard in June 1952.

An MGM talent scout had seen Harry Belafonte perform and he was brought to Hollywood to be screentested. He was hired for BRIGHT ROAD (1953), a sensitive but slight tale of a fourth-grade student helped by his understanding teacher (Dorothy Dandridge) to acclimate to his academic routine. Belafonte had the subordinate role of the school principal. Within the sixty-eight-minute film he sang "Suzanne," a song he and Millard Thomas had written. Neither the movie nor Belafonte received much attention. Said *Variety*, "Harry Belafonte is satisfactory as school principal." While on the West Coast he appeared at the Mocambo Club in Beverly Hills and at the Thunderbird Hotel in Las Vegas. Throughout this period he experienced a great deal of racial discrimination.

By 1953 Belafonte had signed a recording contract with RCA Victor and by his third session, his songs ("Shenandoah" and "Scarlet Ribbons") began meeting with commercial success. It was his recording of the Japanese folk-style song "Gomen-Nasai" that made a mark in record sales; RCA renewed his contract. He had a successful stand at The Black Orchid Club in Chicago as well as a popular return engagement at The Boulevard Club in Queens. *Billboard* magazine chose Belafonte for their prestigious "Talent Showcase of 1954." He was also signed to appear with Hermione Gingold, Billy De Wolfe, and others in *John Murray Anderson's Almanac*, which opened on Broadway on December 10, 1953. Within the revue he sang "Acorn in the Meadow" and "Hold 'Em Joe," but his most dramatic number was a song rendering of "Mark Twain." The show lasted for 229 performances and he won both the Tony and Donaldson Awards as Best Supporting Actor. While performing in the show he also appeared at the East Side Manhattan club La Vie en Rose.

Filmmaker Otto Preminger saw Belafonte in *Almanac* and hired him for the role of the soldier Joe in the all-black film musical CARMEN JONES (1954). Like co-star Dorothy Dandridge's, Belafonte's singing voice was dubbed (his by Levern Hutcherson), but at least he had the opportunity to express his dramatic talent. When released, the CinemaScope production was considered heavy-handed, yet he received good reviews. "Harry Belafonte's Joe is a clean-cut American youth, handsome and guileless" (*New York Herald-Tribune*). While on the West Coast he made his second appearance at the Cocoanut Grove

Club, his most popular number being "Noah." The Belafontes became parents for a second time in September 1954, with the birth of Shari (who would become a film and TV actress).

In early 1955 Belafonte, with Marge and Gower Champion, toured for three months for ninety-four one-night engagements of the pre-Broadway production of *3 for Tonight*. The show opened in New York on April 17, 1955. Belafonte performed fourteen numbers (folk songs and spirituals) in the revue and the *New York Times* reported that he "sings every song with the fierce conviction of an evangelist." The show itself lasted only eighty-five performances but was transformed into a CBS-TV special (June 25, 1955). That year he also played club engagements in Los Angeles, Las Vegas, Chicago, San Francisco, and at the Empire Room of the Waldorf-Astoria. He began expanding the size and range of his backup musicians and did further research into folk music around the country. He continued recording for RCA, and on television he made the first of five appearances on NBC-TV's "Colgate Variety Hour." On November 6, 1955, he co-starred with Ethel Waters in "Winner by Decision," a drama of a young fighter on "G.E. Theatre" (CBS-TV). He earned $350,000 in 1955.

In 1956 Belafonte worked on *Sing, Man, Sing*, a musical in which he played Everyman from the Garden of Eden to contemporary times. The show was performed a few times at the Academy of Music in Brooklyn in April 1956 and later at the Shubert Theatre in Chicago, but it did not reach Broadway. It was in this year that his recordings broke into the mainstream. In the first half of 1956 he had three albums in the top ten: *"Mark Twain" and Other Folk Favorites, Belafonte*, and *Calypso*. The latter contained "Banana Boat (Day-O)," which in early 1957 rose to number five on the charts. Later in 1956, such songs as "Jamaica Farewell" and "Mary's Boy Child" were in the top fifteen on the singles chart. He also appeared (June 1956) at a sold-out open-air concert at Lewisohn Stadium in the Bronx. In July 1956 he appeared at the Greek Theatre in Los Angeles, bringing in $145,000 in two weeks—$30,000 more than the old records. He reportedly turned down a ten-year TV contract that would have brought him $200,000 in salary because he did not like the terms; he also rejected a role in a new Tennessee Williams play. By late 1956 he and his wife ended their troublesome marriage and they were divorced early in 1957. His companion of recent years, Julie Robinson (a white, Jewish dancer), became his wife in March 1957 in Mexico. (They would have two children, David and Gina.) The interracial marriage caused a great deal of controversy.

Because of the huge success of the *Calypso* album (it remained number one for thirty-one weeks), Belafonte was concerned that he would be caught in a mold (which he would be, to a degree, as the King of Calypso). He tried to diversify. He was hired by 20th Century–Fox to co-star in ISLAND IN THE SUN (1957), a tawdry, multi-storied drama of the Caribbean in which he had a controversial interracial romance with Joan Fontaine. He sang two songs in the picture, "Island in the Sun" and "Lead Man Holler," both of which appeared on his album *Belafonte Sings of the Caribbean* (1957). Although the exploitative film was popular, neither it nor Belafonte (now considered a "matinee idol") received many favorable reviews.

In 1958 he underwent three corrective eye operations, made his first European tour, and turned down a leading role in PORGY AND BESS (1959) because he felt the movie would compromise his race. He had formed his own production company (Harbel) and hoped to do a film biography of Martin Luther King, Jr.; however, neither this nor a project called THE BROTHERS materialized. In 1959, in a deal between his company and United Artists, he starred in the low-budget ($1.4 million) science fiction–morality tale THE WORLD, THE FLESH AND THE DEVIL, set in post-holocaust New York. He was the Pennsylvania coal miner who is tempted by a white woman (Inger Stevens) and pitted against a bigoted seaman (Mel Ferrer). In the course of the picture he sang the ballad "Fifteen." The movie received more attention for its stridently handled interracial issues than for its effectiveness as a film. Also in 1959 he appeared successfully in two one-man concerts at Carnegie Hall (which led to a live album), recorded a version of *Porgy and Bess* with Lena Horne, and starred in a variety special, "Tonight with Belafonte" (CBS-TV, December 10, 1959), on which Bonnie McGee, Odetta (one of his idols), and Sonny Terry were his guests. For this program Belafonte won an Emmy Award.

During this time, he was also producer of ODDS AGAINST TOMORROW (1959). It was another racially themed picture, but also a superior crime caper. It co-starred Robert Ryan and Shelley Winters, and gave Belafonte a part as a member of a disparate trio robbing an upstate New York bank of $150,000 with ironic results. Despite the fine performances, this *film noir* was not popular and it was the actor's last movie for a decade. (Plans to star in a Western, THE LAST NOTCH, or the life of Russian poet Pushkin did not work out.) Also in 1959, he produced on Broadway the short-lived French comedy *Moonbirds*, starring Wally Cox.

He had another TV special on November 20, 1960, "Belafonte, New York" (CBS-TV) with Gloria Lynne as his guest. He continued to record for RCA, never able to get away from the calypso beat in his folk albums. His *Belafonte Returns to Carnegie Hall* (1960), one of his "live" albums, featured such guest artists as Miriam Makeba, Odetta, and the Chad Mitchell Trio. Throughout the years Belafonte did much to foster new talent, especially artists from South Africa. He performed frequently in tandem with Makeba, and later Lette Mbulu, Nana Mouskouri, Hugh Masekela, and Falumi Prince. His album *Swing Dat Hammer* (1961) won a Grammy, as did his later *An Evening with Harry Belafonte and Miriam Makeba* (1965). The last time Belafonte made the top forty album charts was in 1964 with his album *Belafonte at the Greek Theatre*. After his three 1966 albums (*An Evening with Harry Belafonte and Nana Mouskouri, In My Quiet Room*, and *Calypso in Brass*) he did not record an album until 1970. But always, both here and abroad, there were his extensive club engagements. On November 9, 1969, he starred in an NBC-TV special, "An Evening with Julie Andrews and Harry Belafonte," and the next year he reunited with friend Lena Horne for "Harry and Lena" (ABC-TV, March 22, 1970).

In the 1950s Belafonte had been accused frequently of trying to overacclimate to the white world. In the 1960s he became a strong advocate of racial integration and a great supporter of the work of Dr. Martin Luther King, Jr. After the latter's assassination and its discouraging aftermath for race relations, Belafonte was among the personalities featured in the documentary KING: A FILMED RECORD . . . MONTGOMERY TO MEMPHIS (1970). In the symbolic fantasy THE ANGEL LEVINE (1970), Belafonte played an angel, the soul of a black street hustler, who is sent to earth by God to help an elderly Orthodox Jewish tailor (Zero Mostel) regain his failing faith. It was another Belafonte production, more noteworthy for its message than its entertainment value.

Far more commercial was Belafonte's participation in BUCK AND THE PREACHER (1972), a Western co-produced and directed by Sidney Poitier. With a cast that included Ruby Dee, BUCK AND THE PREACHER was a high-grade entry in Hollywood's cycle of black action pictures. Belafonte excelled as the bogus preacher in post-Civil War days who claimed to be of the High and Low Orders of the Holiness Persuasion Church. The Western was hugely successful (with the public, not the critics) and, as the rollicking rogue, Belafonte stole the show. *Variety* noted, "Never let it be said that Sidney Poitier and Harry Belafonte will sit still for being typecast." Two years later the duo reteamed for another buddy picture, UPTOWN SATURDAY NIGHT (1974), this time a comedy also featuring Bill Cosby, Flip Wilson, Richard Pryor, and Roscoe Lee Browne. In the course of the shenanigans, Poitier and Cosby must recover a stolen winning lottery ticket. They appeal to ghetto ganglord Geechie Dan (Belafonte) for help. Once again, with his boisterous performance (this time in a gruff-voiced, puff-cheeked imitation of Marlon

Harry Belafonte, Ruby Dee, and Sidney Poitier in BUCK AND THE PREACHER (1972)

Brando in THE GODFATHER), Belafonte was the comic focus of the very successful film. Belafonte did not participate when Poitier and Cosby combined for their next joint outing, LET'S DO IT AGAIN (1976).

Since he could earn a million dollars with one of his frequent European tours, Belafonte abandoned filmmaking once again. In 1980 he and Sidney Poitier planned to make a film together in Africa but that did not happen. Also that year he received the Sixth Annual Paul Robeson Award for Humanitarianism from the Actors' Equity Association. On October 4, 1981, he co-starred in the NBC telefeature GRAMBLING'S WHITE TIGER, based on a true story. Belafonte was Eddie Robinson, football coach at Grambling College in Louisiana, who trains quarterback Jim Gregory (Bruce Jenner), the only white student at the all-black college. Although he received good reviews, it was his last such effort to date. He explained, "Anyone who does it [TV movies] is masochistic and anyone who continues to do them is sadistic." In 1982 he received the Tenth Annual Martin Luther King Nonviolent Peace Prize.

In the mid-1970s Belafonte had ended his recording association with RCA and then, after a six-year hiatus, returned on other labels, including CBS Records. But for him, recording was now an exception, not the rule. He insisted, "I've been on enough charts and played that game. But I wasn't won over by the game. I haven't lost the vitality because I haven't been burned out by the industry. I haven't played their game." On May 2, 1983, he was among the *Parade of Stars Playing the Palace*, a benefit staged at New York's Palace Theatre for the Actors' Fund of America; it was televised in abbreviated form as an ABC-TV special. When asked in 1983 why he was not acting in more films, he said, "To be very honest, those who make movies and TV decisions nowadays are not aware of my existence, nor do they care. We have nothing in common." In 1984 he co-produced BEAT STREET, a musical film starring Rae Dawn Chong that exploited the rap and break-dancing craze. Plans to produce a docudrama film on Nelson Mandela have remained unrealized.

In 1985 Belafonte was part of the USA for Africa delegation that went on a sixteen-day tour of the famine-stricken continent, and the next year he considered (but decided against) running for U.S. Senator from New York on the Democratic ticket. In April 1987 he was co-producer of *Asinamali!*, a stage drama set in a prison cell at Leeuwkop Prison near Johannesburg, South Africa. The play lasted only twenty-nine performances on Broadway. He continued with an abbreviated concert schedule, which included his traditional annual appearance at the Greek Theatre in Los Angeles. On September 14, 1988, he was a singing guest on "Live! Dick Clark Presents" (CBS-TV). Also in 1988 his song "Banana Boat" was featured in the Michael Keaton comedy film BEETLEJUICE, which gave him a fresh audience with the new generation. While his wife Julie (a former Katherine Dunham dancer) was planning to produce THE KATHERINE DUNHAM STORY for Home Box Office, both she and Belafonte were active in mid-1989 in trying to start a new film festival in Cuba.

When he made his return to Los Angeles's Greek Theatre in July 1989, *Daily Variety* reported, "Musically, Belafonte remains in excellent voice . . . the rich vibrant tone that made him a hit three decades ago is still there, seemingly as resilient as ever and able to take full advantage of any vocal line." Regarding his singing of such politically oriented songs as "We Are the Wave," "Global Carnival," and "Paradise in Gazankula," the trade paper noted, "There are few entertainers who can deliver this message with as much sincerity and good fellowship as Belafonte." Thus, several decades after making his performing debut, Harry Belafonte remains an outspoken advocate of integration and equality.

## Filmography

Bright Road (MGM, 1953)
Carmen Jones (20th–Fox, 1954)
Island in the Sun (20th–Fox, 1957)
The World, the Flesh and the Devil (UA, 1959) (also co-producer)
Odds Against Tomorrow (UA, 1959) (also producer)
The Angel Levine (UA, 1970) (also producer)

King: A Filmed Record . . . Montgomery to Memphis (Commonwealth, 1970) (documentary)
Buck and the Preacher (Col, 1972) (also co-producer)
Uptown Saturday Night (WB, 1974)
Grambling's White Tiger (NBC-TV, 10/4/81)
Beat Street (Orion, 1984) (co-producer/co-songs only)

## Broadway Plays

John Murray Anderson's Almanac (1953)
3 for Tonight (1955)

Moonbirds (1959) (producer only)
Asinamali! (1987) (co-producer only)

## TV Series

Sugar Hill Times (CBS, 1949)

## Album Discography

Abraham, Martin and John (Camden ACL1-0502)
Ballads, Blues and Boasters (RCA LPM-LSP-2953)
Belafonte (RCA LPM-1150)
Belafonte at Carnegie Hall (RCA LOC/LSO-6006)
Belafonte at the Greek Theatre (RCA LOC/LSO-6009)
Belafonte Live (RCA VPSX-6077)
Belafonte on Campus (RCA LPM/LSP-3779)
Belafonte Returns to Carnegie Hall (RCA LOC/LSP-6007)

Belafonte Sings Five Early Songs (Coronet CX-CSX-115)
Belafonte Sings of Love (RCA LPM/LSP-3938)
Belafonte Sings of the Caribbean (RCA LPM-1505)
Belafonte Sings the Blues (RCA LOP-1006/LPM-1972)
By Request (RCA LSP-4301)
Calypso (RCA LPM-1248)
Calypso Carnival (RCA LSP-4521)
Calypso in Brass (RCA LPM/LSP-3658)
An Evening with Harry Belafonte (RCA LPM/LSP-1402, RCA ANL1-1434)

An Evening with Harry Belafonte and Miriam Makeba (RCA LPM/LSP-3420)

An Evening with Harry Belafonte and Nana Mouskouri (RCA LPM/LSP-3415)

Fabergé Presents Harry and Lena (RCA PRS-295) [ST/TV] w. Lena Horne

Harry (Camden CAS-2599)

Homeward Bound (RCA LSP-4255)

In My Quiet Room (RCA LPM/LSP-3571)

Jump Up Calypso (RCA LPM/LSP-2388)

Love Is a Gentle Thing (RCA LPM/LSP-1927)

Loving You Is Where I Belong (Col FC-37489)

The Many Moods of Belafonte (RCA LPM/LSP-2574)

"Mark Twain" and Other Folk Favorites (RCA LPM-1022)

The Midnight Special (RCA LPM/LSP-2449)

My Lord, What a Morning (RCA LPM/LSP-2022)

Play Me (RCA ANL1-0094)

Porgy and Bess (RCA LOP/LSOL-1507) w. Lena Horne

Pure Gold (RCA ANL1-0979)

Streets I Have Walked (RCA LPM/LSP-2695)

Swing Dat Hammer (RCA LPM/LSP-2194)

This Is Harry Belafonte (RCA VPS-6024)

To Wish You a Merry Christmas (RCA LPM/LSP-1887)

The Warm Touch (RCA LSP-4481)

# ANN BLYTH

BEAUTIFUL, TALENTED ANN BLYTH—PROFICIENT AS BOTH A DRAMATIC actress and a singer—has had a rather checkered career during her many years as an entertainer. Her show business achievements range from Universal Pictures programmers at the start of her screen years in the mid-1940s, to an Academy Award nomination in 1945 for MILDRED PIERCE, to a succession of more standard film roles (although she was notable in a strong dramatic assignment in ANOTHER PART OF THE FOREST, 1948). Then she settled down to a series of glossy MGM musicals in the mid-1950s in which she proved to be a sweet soubrette. But movie musicals were going out of vogue and her career came to a near halt. Since then she has been mostly retired, choosing a family over fame. However, it has been a busy retirement, and for an actress who has not made a film in over three decades her face is still a very familiar one through a variety of television work.

Ann Marie Blyth was born in Mt. Kisco, New York, on August 16, 1928. Her parents separated when she was still an infant, and her mother took her and her older sister, Dorothy, to live in New York City. The family lived in a walk-up flat on New York's east side and Mrs. Blyth earned a meager living by doing ironing for the Park Avenue elite. As a little girl Ann, a child prodigy, dreamed of a show business career, and despite the financial difficulty, her mother always managed to have the necessary money for her singing, dancing, and dramatic lessons. While older sister Dorothy worked as a secretary, Ann, at age eight, wound up singing on radio station WJZ while attending Catholic schools and the New York Professional Children's School. Ann also did dramatic work on radio and undertook opera at the San Carlo Opera Company. At age thirteen she received her first solid break when she was cast as Babette, the daughter of a freedom fighter (Paul Lukas), in the Broadway production of Lillian Hellman's *Watch on the Rhine* (1941) and she remained with the hit drama for nearly a year before going on tour with the patriotic melodrama. In the interim she had dinner at the White House. While she was on tour, a Universal Pictures talent scout saw Ann and signed her to a seven-year studio contract. Ann made her motion picture debut as a society snob who vies with Peggy Ryan for Donald O'Connor's affections in the musical comedy CHIP OFF THE OLD BLOCK (1944). This vehicle was quickly followed by another musical with Ryan and O'Connor, THE MERRY MONAHANS (1944). This low-budget imitation of the Judy Garland–Mickey Rooney MGM musicals cast Ann as the daughter of a singer (Rosemary De Camp) who meets her former lover (Jack Oakie), who has two grown children (O'Connor, Ryan). Next Ann and Peggy Ryan co-starred as two teenagers staging a benefit show in BABES ON SWING STREET (1944), followed by the studio's all-star musical BOWERY TO BROADWAY (1944). This quartet of innocuous fluff proved she was not destined to be the replacement for the studio's now adult Deanna Durbin. Ann was loaned to Warner Bros. for the most telling role of her screen career, that of self-centered teenager Veda, the willful daughter of a restaurateur (Joan Crawford) who murders her mother's lover (Zachary Scott) after having an affair with him, in MILDRED PIERCE (1945). James Agee (*The Nation*) found Ann's performance "as good an embodiment of all that is most terrifying about native contemporary adolescence as I ever hope to see." Ann earned an Academy Award nomination for the part and her motion picture career was on its way.

Following the completion of MILDRED PIERCE, Ann and Zachary Scott were reunited for HER KIND OF MAN (1946). However, after two weeks of shooting, Ann was involved in a toboggan accident at Snow Valley in the San Bernardino Mountains. It left her with a broken back and what appeared to be the end of her career. While in a body cast she worked at graduating from high school with her studio class. She also found spiritual reward from the accident. She wrote later, "The busy exciting world I had known faded away and my life slowed down to little things. But even here I found myself blessed, for a new sense of prayer began to unfold to me. Now there were not the busy times of telling Him what I needed but rather, times of listening communion, of gathering strength, when my human strength and courage seemed to ebb away." After seven months in the cast, Ann was told she *would* be able to walk again, but there were seven more months in and out of a wheelchair before she was able to swim, attend a preview of MILDRED PIERCE, and play golf.

In her first film after the accident Ann was cast by Universal as a small town girl in love with a newly arrived con man (Sonny Tufts) in SWELL GUY (1946). This programmer was followed by a guest role as a young adult who loves a convict (Howard Duff) in the taut prison melodrama BRUTE FORCE (1947). Between these assignments, her mother died. A loanout to MGM followed with the role of boxer Mickey Rooney's romantic interest in KILLER McCOY (1947) followed by Universal's A WOMAN'S VENGEANCE (1947) in which she portrayed a shop girl whose lover (Charles Boyer) is tried for poisoning his wife. Next the studio gave her a strong dramatic role, that of young Regina Hubbard in Lillian Hellman's ANOTHER PART OF THE FOREST (1948), which examined the early years of the ruthless southern clan Ms. Hellman had made famous in her play *The Little Foxes*. The role Ann played was done in the earlier play by Tallulah Bankhead on stage and by Bette Davis in the 1941 screen version of THE LITTLE FOXES. Unfortunately, Regina Hubbard was to be Ann's last substantial screen part, although she was to make more than twenty feature films in the next decade.

In 1948 Ann Blyth garnered lots of publicity as the aquatic object of William Powell's affections in the pleasant comedy-fantasy MR. PEABODY AND THE MERMAID, but this was followed by such conventional studio fare as the Western RED CANYON (1949), the arch comedy FREE FOR ALL (1949), and the small town doings of KATIE DID IT (1951). Bing Crosby chose her as his leading lady in the pedestrian TOP O' THE MORNING (1949) and Samuel Goldwyn borrowed her for the soap opera OUR VERY OWN (1950). Her career received a tremendous boost when she was cast as Mario Lanza's leading lady in THE GREAT CARUSO (1951) at MGM, a part that would have gone to Metro's own Kathryn Grayson had she not so much despised being co-starred with the boorish Lanza. Complete with new makeup, Ann made a strong impression in this colorful biographical musical and got to sing the film's best song, "The Loveliest Night of the Year." Universal provided Ann with a good role as a convicted murderess who takes refuge in a convent during a storm in THUNDER ON THE HILL (1951) and whose innocence is believed in by one of the nuns (Claudette Colbert).

At this time the actress also worked on radio, being heard on such series as "Guest Star" and "The Louella Parsons Show," as well as in the "Ultimately Yours" segment of the 1950 syndicated program "Voice of the Army." On January 11, 1951, she and Jeff Chandler starred in the CBS radio adaptation of "Shadow of a Doubt" on "Hollywood Soundstage." Filmwise, Ann's early 1950s movies were a motley assortment, like Universal's THE GOLDEN HORDE (1951) and, on loan to 20th Century–Fox, I'LL NEVER FORGET YOU (1951) opposite Tyrone Power. She was Gregory Peck's love interest in THE WORLD IN HIS ARMS (1952), and then joined Edmund Gwenn in the light comedy SALLY AND SAINT ANNE (1952). When Claudette Colbert bowed out of the Korean War melodrama ONE MINUTE TO ZERO (1952) at RKO, Ann Blyth replaced her.

In 1952 Ann's Universal contract expired and she signed with MGM, which had long wanted her on their roster. They promised to star her in the type of screen fare she longed to do—musicals. Instead, her initial Metro contract outing was the rugged seafaring actioner ALL THE BROTHERS WERE VALIANT (1953). Then she was given the Jeanette MacDonald part in the widescreen remake of ROSE MARIE (1954) opposite Howard Keel in the Nelson Eddy role. The film was colorful and glossy but hardly up to the well-remembered 1936 version, as Ann sang "Free to Be Free" and dueted with Fernando Lamas on "Indian Love Call." Next she replaced Jane Powell as the barmaid loved by a prince (Edmund Purdom) in the operetta THE STUDENT PRINCE (1954) with the over-weight Mario Lanza (originally set for the lead) dubbing Purdom's singing. Ann was then thrust into the bland swashbuckler THE KING'S THIEF (1955), also with Purdom, and she and Howard Keel were reunited for a color remake of KISMET (1955), which was well produced but surprisingly vapid. Ann soloed on "Baubles, Bangles and Beads" and performed duets with Keel and Vic Damone. By now MGM was abandoning musicals and going in a new direction. She closed out her MGM tenure with the smut magazine exposé SLANDER (1956). At Paramount she was reunited with Donald O'Connor, who had the title role in THE BUSTER KEATON STORY (1957) with Ann playing the loyal Mrs. Keaton. In her final film to date, she had the title role in THE HELEN MORGAN STORY (1957), in which she gave a fine performance as the torch singer who sinks into alcoholism. Although Ann's natural singing voice was very much like Helen Morgan's, Warner Bros. decided to have the songs dubbed on the film's soundtrack by full-voiced Gogi Grant. The movie was not popular.

In 1953 Ann had married Dr. James McNulty, the brother of Irish tenor/comedian Dennis Day, and it was on the latter's program, "The RCA Victor Show," that the actress made her television debut in June 1953. The next year she appeared on CBS's "Video Theatre" and then took a hiatus from TV work while making her MGM features. In 1959 she came back to TV for a "Wagon Train" segment and in the next four years would guest-star three additional times on the program. She also guested on such programs as "Dick Powell Theatre," "Twilight Zone," "Burke's Law," "Kraft Suspense Theatre," and "The Name of the Game." In 1960 she starred in the ABC-TV production of "The Citadel" and in 1963 she guest-starred in an interesting segment of NBC-TV's "Saints and Sinners" show called "The Year Joan Crawford Won the Oscar." More important than her career, however, was Ann's family. She has five children: Timothy Patrick (born in 1954), Maureen Ann (born in 1955), Kathleen Mary (born in 1957), Terence Grady (born in 1960), and Eileen Alana (born in 1963). The McNultys live in a large home in Toluca Lake and in addition to her family and charity work, Ann is a devout and very active Catholic. In 1973 she and her husband were invested with the rank of Lady and Knight of the Holy Sepulchre by Cardinal Cooke in New York City.

During the 1970s Ann Blyth was seen frequently on television promoting Hostess cupcakes and other Hostess products; her three youngest children often appeared in the commercials with their still-famous mother. In 1974 she did the one-minute CBS-TV spot detailing the history of Santa Claus in the network's "200 Years Ago Today" series and late in 1975 she did a guest-starring role in that network's series "Switch." During the decade she also performed yearly tours with various Light Opera companies in musicals such as *Bittersweet, The King and I, South Pacific*, and *The Sound of Music*. For *South Pacific*

Ann Blyth in THE HELEN MORGAN STORY (1957)

in 1973 she was given the coveted "Show Stopper Plaque" because all the show's performances were SRO ("standing room only") in every city where it was staged. In 1978 she guest-starred on the NBC-TV series "Quincy" and in 1983 she returned again to the detective show. In 1985 she made an appearance on the CBS-TV show "Murder, She Wrote." In 1988 Ann was given the "Angel Award" for her work with St. Anne's Maternity Home.

Although Ann Blyth never reached the screen heights suggested by her performances in MILDRED PIERCE and ANOTHER PART OF THE FOREST, she did have a well-rounded and satisfactory show business career. Unlike many of her contemporaries, she has no bitterness toward the film capital. She has said, "Hollywood has been very good to me. I was never hurt by the town or the profession." Still, personal happiness far outweighed a career in Ann Blyth's mind, and because of her husband and children she can contentedly say, "I consider myself a blessed woman."

## Filmography

Chip Off the Old Block (Univ, 1944)
The Merry Monahans (Univ, 1944)
Babes on Swing Street (Univ, 1944)
Bowery to Broadway (Univ, 1944)
Mildred Pierce (WB, 1945)
Swell Guy (Univ, 1946)
Brute Force (Univ, 1947)
Killer McCoy (MGM, 1947)
A Woman's Vengeance (Univ, 1947)
Another Part of the Forest (Univ, 1948)
Mr. Peabody and the Mermaid (Univ, 1948)
Red Canyon (Univ, 1949)
Once More, My Darling (Univ, 1949)
Top o' the Morning (Par, 1949)
Free for All (Univ, 1949)
Our Very Own (RKO, 1950)
The Triumphant Hour (Peyton, 1950)
The Great Caruso (MGM, 1951)

Katie Did It (Univ, 1951)
The Golden Horde (Univ, 1951)
Thunder on the Hill [Bonaventure] (Univ, 1951)
I'll Never Forget You (20th-Fox, 1951)
The World in His Arms (Univ, 1952)
Sally and Saint Anne (Univ, 1952)
One Minute to Zero (RKO, 1952)
All the Brothers Were Valiant (MGM, 1953)
Rose Marie (MGM, 1954)
The Student Prince (MGM, 1954)
Kismet (MGM, 1955)
The King's Thief (MGM, 1955)
Slander (MGM, 1956)
The Buster Keaton Story (Par, 1957)
The Helen Morgan Story [Both Ends of the Candle] (WB, 1957)

## Broadway Plays

Watch on the Rhine (1941)

## Album Discography

Hail, Mary (Everest 5113/1113)
Kismet (MGM E-3281, Metro M/S-526) [ST]

Rose Marie (10" MGM E-229, MGM E-3228, Metro M/S-616) [ST]

# JOHN BOLES

AT THE TIME, THE LATE 1920s, JOHN BOLES SEEMED EVERYTHING THAT a film matinee idol could or should be: he was tall, good-looking, and an understated actor. When talkies swamped Hollywood he demonstrated a fine, cultivated speaking voice for the screen, and he could sing admirably as well! Therefore, in the studios' crush to churn out all-talking, all-singing, all-dancing pictures he was a tremendous asset, especially in operettas. Even before the musical genre craze died out, industry executives had concluded that he (like George Brent) was the perfect type of leading man to play opposite strong screen actresses: he never overshadowed them, but provided a well-bred vis-à-vis who allowed *the* star the full limelight. Thus he was in great demand to appear with the likes of Irene Dunne, Gloria Swanson, Loretta Young, Rosalind Russell, and Barbara Stanwyck, and even survived several pictures with that ace scene-stealer Shirley Temple. Granted, some critics did not succumb to his southern gentility and well-modulated voice; they found his movie persona banal, artificial, and passive. However, John Boles was a trouper (four decades on the screen), who proved himself repeatedly on stage, on screen, and off (during World War I he was a U.S. spy in Germany, Bulgaria, and Turkey).

John Boles was born October 28, 1895, in Greenville, Texas. During his childhood, he spent summers in a neighboring town with his grandparents, who encouraged him to sing. Throughout his school years he was an avid vocalist and was often the lead performer at Friday afternoon "entertainments." Planning on either joining the family banking business or becoming a surgeon, he attended the University of Texas at Austin and graduated in June 1917. Two days later he wed his college sweetheart, Marceline Dobbs; it was a union which would last fifty-two years. Not long thereafter, he was detailed to the Criminal Investigation Department of the American Expeditionary Force where his mastery of French and German (learned during childhood from a Greenville matron) made him useful in secret missions on the Continent during World War I. After the Armistice, he attended the Peace Conference in Paris.

Returning to Greenville from his eighteen months overseas, Boles abandoned the idea of a medical career and turned to the cotton industry. When vocal coach/performer Oscar Seagle was passing through Austin on a concert tour, Boles managed a private audition. Seagle was so impressed he encouraged the young man to become his student back in upstate New York. With a $1,000 loan from his father, Boles and his wife relocated to Schroon Lake in the Adirondacks. When funds ran out, Boles taught French and music at a nearby high school to pay for his singing lessons and to support his wife. When his mentor urged him to pursue his study in Paris, he organized a band of musical students. Serving as their business manager, Boles paid for his passage to France, accompanied by his wife and young daughter (Frances). He studied for two years with renowned operatic tenor Jean de Reszke.

Returning to New York City, Boles tried Broadway. After three months of bad luck, he auditioned for producer L. Lawrence Weber and was assigned to replace Jay Velie in the Broadway musical hit *Little Jessie James* (1923), which featured Miriam Hopkins. Boles sang "I Love You" and dueted with Louise Allen on "Little Jack Horner." It was no small feat to be a leading man in his debut professional appearance. After *Little Jessie James* closed, Boles made his screen bow in Metro-Goldwyn's comedy drama SO THIS IS MAR-RIAGE? (1924) starring Eleanor Boardman, Conrad Nagel, and Lew Cody, and boasting Technicolor sequences. For the same studio, he was the fifth lead in the farce EXCUSE ME (1925), featuring Norma Shearer, Conrad Nagel, and Renée Adorée, and also filmed in New York. He was back on Broadway in *Mercenary Mary* (April 13, 1925), which lasted for thirty-two performances. Next he was signed to play opposite the legendary Geraldine Farrar in her operetta debut in Franz Lehár's *Romany Love*, which opened and closed in November 1926 in New Haven, Connecticut, as *The Love Spell*. Years later, Boles admitted, "She was, possibly, the grandest personality I shall ever encounter!"

Boles reappeared on Broadway in *Kitty's Kisses* (May 6, 1926), a musical with a book by Otto Harbach and lyrics by Con Conrad and Gus Kahn. Film superstar Gloria Swanson attended one of the show's forty-six performances and chose Boles to be her leading man in her first United Artists production. The exotic feature, THE LOVE OF SU-NYA (1927), which opened New York City's Roxy Theatre, was a showcase for Miss Swanson, but the New York–lensed feature allowed room for Boles to shine as the man she eventually marries.

Impressed by his screen presence, Universal signed Boles to a term contract. Boles and his family (which now included a second daughter, Janet) moved westward. He was cast initially by the studio in a supporting role in the society drama WE AMERICANS (1928) which starred Patsy Ruth Miller. Then he made several 1928 loanouts, including FAZIL at Fox, in which he was in support of Charles Farrell and Greta Nissen; Paramount's Zane Grey Western THE WATER HOLE, starring Jack Holt and Nancy Carroll, in which his screen character goes crazy in the desert heat; and Pathé's MAN-MADE WOMAN as Leatrice Joy's husband. In First National's THE SHEPHERD OF THE HILLS, based on Harold Bell Wright's oft-filmed melodrama, he was Young Matt.

With so many varied picture assignments to his credit, Boles next did two 1929 part-talking features (THE LAST WARNING, SCANDAL), both starring Laura La Plante, for Universal. But the film that was to change his screen future was made on loan to Warner Bros. THE DESERT SONG cast him as Pierre Birbeau who masquerades as "The Red Shadow," the masked leader of the Riffs. It was Hollywood's first sound operetta. With a score by Sigmund Romberg, a bright leading lady (Carlotta King), and Technicolor sequences, the musical was a big hit. The *New York Times* wrote, "John Boles . . . has a voice that is quite pleasing." Universal announced that Boles would star in MOONLIGHT MADNESS and THE SONG OF PASSION, but instead he went to RKO for their plush screen operetta RIO RITA (1929), starring Bebe Daniels and featuring the frantic comedy of Wheeler and Woolsey. At Warner Bros. Boles starred in SONG OF THE WEST (1930), based on the Broadway musical *Rainbow* and dealing with 1840s California. Vivienne Segal made her screen debut in this Technicolor feature, with Boles as her manly hero. In November 1929 he recorded this movie's three songs (by Vincent Youmans–Oscar Hammerstein II, Grant Clarke, and Harry Akst) for Victor Records.

Finally, Universal utilized its valuable singing star in a home-lot musical, originally to be titled LA MARSEILLAISE. It was started by director Paul Fejos, but completed by John Stuart Robertson and released as CAPTAIN OF THE GUARD (1930) with Boles singing love songs to Laura La Plante against a Louis XVI France setting. He recorded two of the film's songs ("You, You, Alone" and "For You") for the Victor label. Following the example of the other Hollywood studios, Universal produced an extravagant Hollywood revue in Technicolor, called THE KING OF JAZZ (1930). It boasted Paul Whiteman and His Orchestra, Bing Crosby and The Rhythm Boys, many vaudeville artists, and Boles teamed yet again with Laura La Plante. He sang the film's big hit song ("It Happened in Monterey") and, because Bing Crosby was in jail for drunken driving when "The Song of the Dawn" was due to be lensed, Boles took over that spotlight number as well. He recorded both these songs for Victor. Meanwhile, Boles was loaned to United Artists to appear opposite English actress Evelyn Laye in her U.S. film debut, ONE HEAVENLY NIGHT (1930).

By the end of 1930 Hollywood had oversaturated moviegoers with song and dance pictures and Boles's singing talents were no longer wanted. However, he was an established screen name so Universal starred him in a remake of Leo Tolstoy's story RESURRECTION (1931). Neither he nor his South American co-star, Lupe Velez, was credible as a doomed Russian. The studio promoted the idea that Boles would have the lead in Preston Sturges' STRICTLY DISHONORABLE (1931), but Paul Lukas was borrowed for that assignment and instead Boles appeared in SEED (1931). Here he was seen to advantage as the average American male frustrated by the marriage trap. *Variety* reported, "John Boles emerges here much more finished in camera bearing and extremely the better actor than when seen before." It opened a new career vista for the handsome leading man. Also at the studio he appeared as the loyal friend of Dr. Frankenstein (Colin Clive) in the classic FRANKENSTEIN (1931) and then moved over to Fox for two bread-and-butter features.

Producer Carl Laemmle, Jr. realized Fannie Hurst's enduring soap opera BACK STREET (1932) required a top production. He borrowed Irene Dunne from RKO to star as the self-sacrificing heroine and cast Boles as the upper-crust married man Walter Saxel, who keeps a mistress (Dunne) on the side. Under John Stahl's direction, Dunne shone in this woman's picture and Boles was serviceable in his cardboard subordinate role. The mold was set for Boles. After joining Nancy Carroll in Columbia's CHILD OF MANHATTAN (1933) and Lillian Harvey in Fox's MY LIPS BETRAY (1933), Universal put him in another tearjerker, ONLY YESTERDAY (1934), in which he played Margaret Sullavan's lover.

Fox's I BELIEVED IN YOU (1934) was intended to launch Rosemary Ames as a star, but it failed. And the same studio's expensive MUSIC IN THE AIR (1934) did no better. The latter was based on Jerome Kern's stage hit and reteamed Boles with Gloria Swanson in her movie comeback. The operetta won no plaudits from critics or moviegoers. For Universal's BELOVED (1934) he was a Viennese baron singing and romancing Gloria Stuart and in Fox's BOTTOMS UP (1934) with Spencer Tracy it was drink-happy Boles who sang "Waiting at the Gate for Katie." In Fox's revue STAND UP AND CHEER (1934), Boles played himself in support of the studio's moppet star, Shirley Temple, whom he joined again in CURLY TOP (1935; he sang the title song to her) and THE LITTLEST REBEL (1935). Diplomatic Boles insisted, "I'd rather work with Shirley than anyone I know." Meanwhile, he was doing BACK STREET–type chores yet again, this time opposite Ann Harding in RKO's THE LIFE OF VERGIE WINTERS (1934). Then he was among 1870s New York socialites in Irene Dunne's THE AGE OF INNOCENCE (1934), also at RKO. During this period Boles was a constant guest star on radio shows, performing scenes from well-known plays and movies.

He was paid $50,000 by Paramount to portray the undercover federal agent in the musical ROSE OF THE RANCHO (1936) with Metropolitan Opera diva Gladys Swarthout. He enthusiastically admitted his preference for the genre: "And now musicals have begun to come back and I've had a chance to do some first-class singing in ROSE OF THE RANCHO." Paramount intended to co-star the two singers in MADAME BUTTERFLY, but the mild reception for ROSE OF THE RANCHO quashed those expansive plans.

If Boles was ill at ease in the Twentieth Century–Fox action drama A MESSAGE TO GARCIA (1936) with Wallace Beery and Barbara Stanwyck, he was adequate (some critics called him "dismal") as the henpecked husband in CRAIG'S WIFE (1936). This landmark film, directed by Dorothy Arzner and starring Rosalind Russell as the shrewish spouse, left little room for audience sympathy for Boles as the milquetoast man who finally rebels. He was back in form as Stephen Dallas in Samuel Goldwyn's elaborate remake of STELLA DALLAS (1937) in which Barbara Stanwyck (as the self-sacrificing mother) and Anne Shirley (as the daughter) shone. The star trio repeated their assignment for "Lux Radio Theatre" on October 11, 1937.

John Boles in 1932

After more than a decade in Hollywood, Boles's career ground down. His three 1938 releases were programmers at best, including ROMANCE IN THE DARK, which reteamed him in infelicitous comedy with Gladys Swarthout and in which Boles's attempts at broad farce were almost embarrassing.

By the summer of 1939, forty-three-year-old Boles was performing "in person" at assorted theaters around the country, singing such career-associated songs as "Rio Rita," "One Alone," and "I See Your Face Before Me." He continued such appearances during the next three years. Meanwhile, in the summer of 1940 he was dashing as Gaylord Ravenal in a revival of *Show Boat* which played Los Angeles and San Francisco. Norma Terris recreated her Broadway role as Magnolia, Paul Robeson was Joe, Guy Kibbee was Cap'n Andy, and, for the Los Angeles engagement, Helen Morgan was Julie.

It was quite a comedown for Boles when he reemerged on screen in Monogram's ROAD TO HAPPINESS (1942). In this poverty-row entry he was the divorced dad overcoming obstacles to make a home for his son (Billy Lee). He was in support of chic Kay Francis in Universal's BETWEEN US GIRLS (1942), which spotlighted Diana Barrymore, and he was properly charming as Kathryn Grayson's Army colonel father in MGM's star-filled THOUSANDS CHEER (1943).

Back on Broadway John Boles co-starred with fellow Texan Mary Martin and Kenny Baker in *One Touch of Venus* (1943), directed by Elia Kazan. In this Kurt Weill musical, he sang "West Wind" and several other numbers. After the show closed in February 1944, Boles and Martin took the hit on the road for a year. In 1948 he was appearing at London's Palladium in a musical revue, *Sky High*, and later made a concert tour of the British Isles.

In September 1950 he returned to the legitimate stage in the West Coast production of *Gentlemen Prefer Blondes*, starring Gertrude Niesen. What proved to be his cinema farewell was the low-budget United Artists release BABES IN BAGDAD (1952), shot in Spain. It was an embarrassing costume satire starring the aging Paulette Goddard and Gypsy Rose Lee. Boles would admit later that anyone who failed to see it certainly "didn't miss much."

Seeing the handwriting on the wall, Boles wisely chose to retire, returning home to San Angelo in Texas, becoming involved in the oil business. In late 1954 he was a founder of the Pipecote Service Co., Inc., which serviced pipelines. As he explained in the mid-1950s, "When my career started to slow down, I didn't want to sit around. So when the opportunity came to get into the oil business, I jumped at it. All the fun appears to have gone out of making movies. In the old days, we used to enjoy ourselves!" Boles did make one final return to Hollywood in 1961 when his old studio remade BACK STREET yet again and asked the veteran star to publicize the picture.

On February 27, 1969, Boles died of a heart attack in San Angelo, Texas, at the age of seventy-three. He was survived by his wife, Marceline, by his daughters, Frances (Mrs. Daniel Queen) and Janet (Mrs. Robert Fullerton), and by seven grandchildren. His autobiography, which he had been working on, was never completed or published.

It was a typically candid Boles who had said years before about his chosen profession, "Why attempt to kid the public? When a screen actor tells you his art, business, profession, or whatever he chooses to call it, is a serious, dignified pursuit, he is either spouting 'poppycock' or just taking himself too seriously."

## Filmography

So This Is Marriage? (Metro-Goldwyn, 1924)
Excuse Me (Metro-Goldwyn, 1925)
The Love of Sunya (UA, 1927)
We Americans [The Heart of a Nation] (Univ, 1928)
The Shepherd of the Hills (FN, 1928)
The Bride of the Colorado (Pathé, 1928)
Fazil (Fox, 1928)
The Water Hole (Par, 1928)
Virgin Lips (Col, 1928)
Man-Made Woman (Pathé, 1928)
Romance of the Underworld (Fox, 1928)
The Last Warning (Univ, 1929)
The Desert Song (WB, 1929)
Scandal (Univ, 1929)
Rio Rita (RKO, 1929)
Voice of Hollywood #1 (Tif, 1929) (s)
Song of the West (WB, 1930)
The King of Jazz (Univ, 1930)
One Heavenly Night (UA, 1930)
Captain of the Guard (Univ, 1930)
Queen of Scandal (UA, 1930)
Resurrection (Univ, 1931)
Seed (Univ, 1931)
Frankenstein (Univ, 1931)
Good Sport (Fox, 1931)
Voice of Hollywood #6 (Tif, 1931) (s)
Careless Lady (Fox, 1932)
Back Street (Univ, 1932)
Six Hours to Live (Fox, 1932)
Hollywood on Parade #2 (Par, 1932) (s)
Child of Manhattan (Col, 1933)

My Lips Betray (Fox, 1933)
Hollywood on Parade #9 (Par, 1933) (s)
Only Yesterday (Univ, 1933)
I Believed in You (Fox, 1934)
Music in the Air (Fox, 1934)
Beloved (Univ, 1934)
Bottoms Up (Fox, 1934)
Stand Up and Cheer (Fox, 1934)
The Life of Vergie Winters (RKO, 1934)
Wild Gold (Fox, 1934)
The Age of Innocence (RKO, 1934)
The White Parade (Fox, 1934)
Orchids to You (Fox, 1935)
Curly Top (Fox, 1935)
Redheads on Parade (Fox, 1935)
The Littlest Rebel (Fox, 1935)
Screen Snapshots #8 (Col, 1935) (s)
Rose of the Rancho (Par, 1936)
A Message to Garcia (20th–Fox, 1936)
Craig's Wife (Col, 1936)
Screen Snapshots #13 (Col, 1936) (s)
As Good as Married (Univ, 1937)
Stella Dallas (UA, 1937)
Fight for Your Lady (RKO, 1937)
Holiday Greetings (Unk, 1937) (s)
She Married an Artist (Col, 1938)
Romance in the Dark (Par, 1938)
Sinners in Paradise (Univ, 1938)
The Road to Happiness (Mon, 1942)
Between Us Girls (Univ, 1942)
Thousands Cheer (MGM, 1943)
Babes in Bagdad (UA, 1952)

## Broadway Plays

Little Jessie James (1923)
Mercenary Mary (1925)

Kitty's Kisses (1926)
One Touch of Venus (1943)

## Album Discography

Jerome Kern 1934–38 (Box Office Productions 19747)
The King of Jazz (Caliban 6025) [ST]

Stars of the Silver Screen 1929–30 (RCA LPV-538)

# PAT BOONE

PAT BOONE WILL FOREVER BE TYPECAST AS THE CLEAN-CUT SINGER
wearing white buck shoes who provided an alternative to Elvis Presley at the dawn of the
mid-1950s rock 'n' roll era. While still in his twenties, Pat Boone became the idol of
millions, both teenagers and adults, and he sold over twenty million records, starred in
several successful films, and was a TV star and best-selling author. Yet by the time he was
thirty, Pat Boone's popularity had begun to erode and he never recaptured his legion of
followers. Still, his career has been a steadily successful one, although since the 1970s he
has worked in show business mainly as a spokesman for Fundamentalist Christianity
through his music. Today many chroniclers of rock music are reluctant to allow Pat Boone
his due credit as one of the founders of the genre, declaring that much of his early
recording success was founded on making "white," gentler versions of songs originally
recorded by black artists which many radio stations refused to play. In actuality, while
many (especially adults) were turned off by Elvis and his ilk, the good looks and fine
baritone voice of Pat Boone made many a convert to the rock 'n' roll movement, paving
the way for several of the stars who were to follow. Without Pat Boone, rock music might
never have found the mainstream following it needed to succeed.

Pat Boone was born Charles Eugene Boone, the son of Archie and Margaret Boone,
in Jacksonville, Florida, on June 1, 1934, one of four children (he had two sisters and a
younger brother named Nick). His family traced its lineage to pioneer Daniel Boone;
Archie Boone was a building contractor while Margaret was a registered nurse. When
Boone was six, the family moved to Nashville and by the time he was ten, the young man
was performing in public. Always devout, he was baptized in the Church of Christ not
long after he turned thirteen. He attended David Lipscomb High School where he excelled
in sports and worked on the school newspaper as a reporter and a cartoonist. He also
appeared in school dramatics, was elected president of the student body, and was voted the
"most popular boy" in school. During his junior year he met and fell in love with Shirley
Foley, daughter of country music star Red Foley. After high school Pat, as he had been
called since he was a small boy, attended David Lipscomb College and had his own radio
show, "Youth on Parade," on Nashville station WSIX. He also made his television debut
on "The Original Amateur Hour" with Ted Mack on ABC-TV; he was one of the show's
few three-time winners and became a semi-finalist in its big contest. However, when he
appeared on "Arthur Godfrey's Talent Scouts" on CBS-TV and won, he was disqualified
from being a finalist on the "Amateur Hour" because he was now a professional. Meanwhile,
he and Shirley eloped and were married on November 7, 1953.

After that Boone accepted a job at WBAP-TV in Fort Worth, Texas, and he enrolled at North Texas State College in Denton, intending to become a school teacher. When Arthur Godfrey fired Julius LaRosa from his TV show, Boone was hired as his replacement on "Arthur Godfrey and His Friends." Boone had already been signed by record producer Randy Wood for his Dot Records label, for which he would record for thirteen years. (His brother, Nick, would later record on Dot under the name Nick Todd.) Boone's first single for Dot, "Two Hearts," did well and in the summer of 1955 he had his first big seller, the rocker "Ain't That a Shame," followed by "At My Front Door." Moving to New York City to appear on the Godfrey program, Boone enrolled at Columbia University as a junior. However, he soon had to take a leave of absence as 20th Century–Fox Pictures production chief Buddy Adler (who predicted he would be the biggest star in Hollywood since James Stewart) had signed him to a contract, at the studio where Elvis Presley had already made his screen debut in LOVE ME TENDER (1956).

Pat Boone had best-selling single records of "Friendly Persuasion," "Chains of Love," "Don't Forbid Me," "I Almost Lost My Mind," "I'll Be Home," and "Anastasia" in 1956, but the year 1957 proved to be the high water mark of his career with several hit records, two big money-making movies, and his own network TV show. His hit records that year included "I'm Just Waiting for You," "Love Letters in the Sand" (which sold over a million copies and remains Boone's most successful single), "Remember You're Mine," "There's a Goldmine in the Sky," "Why Baby Why," and the themes to his hit movies BERNADINE and APRIL LOVE. The former cast Boone as a teenager facing life's problems; it brought Oscar winner Janet Gaynor back to the screen. The project was conceived as a nonmusical and only belatedly did the studio decide that its hit vocalist/leading man should have songs in the picture. So two were added: "Bernadine" and "Love Letters in the Sand." APRIL LOVE provided the star with a meatier role, that of a juvenile delinquent who is placed in the custody of his aunt (Jeanette Nolan) and uncle (Arthur O'Connell). Thanks to his winning way with horses, he not only redeems himself with his relatives, but also finds love with pretty farm girl Shirley Jones. In the wholesome movie Boone sang "Clover in the Meadow," "Give Me a Gentle Girl," and the title song, while he and Shirley Jones dueted on "Do It Yourself" and "The Bentonville Fair." During the shooting of APRIL LOVE, Pat Boone received a great deal of fan magazine copy by refusing (for religious reasons) to kiss Shirley Jones on screen. In addition, due to his attractive family (he and his wife, Shirley, would have four daughters: Cheryl, Linda, Debby, and Laura) he was one of the most written-about of stars both in fan and family-type magazines. Boone left the Arthur Godfrey television show in 1957, and in the fall of that year, his "The Pat Boone–Chevy Showroom" debuted on ABC-TV as a prime-time variety show on Thursday nights. The series featured Boone and guest performers singing without expensive production trimmings, with each program typically closing with an inspiration number. While a *TV Guide* critic complained that the show was "about as exciting as a milkshake with two straws," it found an immediate audience which sustained it for three seasons.

Although Boone was extremely active during this period, he turned down many lucrative offers in order to continue his education. In 1958 he graduated from Columbia

University *magna cum laude* with a Bachelor of Science degree. At the time he explained, "Too many teenagers want to quit school. I can't set a bad example. Besides, I'll need an education to support my family if this bubble ever bursts." At the time there was no need to worry because in 1958 Boone continued his string of hit records for Dot (by now he was the label's top-selling artist) with "Cherie, I Love You," "For My Good Fortune," "I'll Remember Tonight," "It's Too Soon to Know," "That's How Much I Love You," and another million seller, "A Wonderful Time Up There."

Boone's movie and TV contracts called for him to be paid one million dollars annually, he was involved in product endorsements (such as Pat Boone shoes, wristwatches, etc.), and he had many investments such as oil wells, two music publishing companies, a restaurant in Denton, Texas, and two radio stations. The year 1958 saw the publication of his first book, the best-selling *Twixt Twelve and Twenty* (which remained a good seller well into the 1970s), and he starred in his third 20th Century–Fox feature, MARDI GRAS, that year. He played a military school cadet who wins a raffle, the prize being a date with film star Christine Carère. The next year he was top billed as Alec McEwen in the Technicolor adventure film JOURNEY TO THE CENTER OF THE EARTH (1959), adapted from the Jules Verne novel, which exploited Boone's physique in scanty clothing. That year he continued to churn out hit records for Dot with "Beyond the Sunset," "Fool's Hall of Fame," "Good Rockin' Tonight," "Twixt Twelve and Twenty," and "With the Wind and Rain in Your Hair." His top-selling long playing albums for the company

Pat Boone, Diane Baker, Arlene Dahl, and James Mason in JOURNEY TO THE CENTER OF THE EARTH (1959)

included *Howdy!*, *Pat*, *Star Dust*, *Pat Boone Sings*, and *Tenderly*.

Buddy Adler, Pat Boone's movie mentor at 20th Century–Fox, died in the summer of 1960 and that was the beginning of the end of Boone's superstardom. He made no movies that year and his TV show had already ended. However, he still had chart records (albeit not at the top) such as "Alabam," "Candy Sweet," "Dear John," "New Lovers," "Spring Rain," and "Walkin' the Floor over You," along with the album *Moonglow*. In 1961 his pop recording of "Moody River" and the album of the same title were big sellers while his other single sellers that year included "Big Cold Wind," "The Exodus (Theme) Song," and "Johnny Will." That year also found him back on screen for 20th Century–Fox as he and Buddy Hackett played two sailors out to find romance in the breezy service comedy ALL HANDS ON DECK, and the next year he starred as farm boy Wayne who journeys with his family to the local STATE FAIR (1962) where he finds the girl of his dreams (Ann-Margret). Unfortunately, this pale remake did little to bolster Boone's screen career.

In 1962 he did have a good-selling record for Dot with "Speedy Gonzales," but his other releases—"I'll See You in My Dreams," "Pictures in the Fire," and "Ten Lonely Guys"—did not have long chart stays. In an attempt to change his clean-cut image Boone starred in THE YELLOW CANARY for Fox in 1963 as a self-centered pop singer who changes his ways when his child is kidnapped, and in the British-made THE MAIN ATTRACTION as a drifter who finds trouble and romance with a traveling circus. Neither film caused much of a box-office stir. While in England he also starred in the horror comedy entry THE HORROR OF IT ALL (1964) as an American tourist trapped in a spooky old house. But by now his marquee allure was so tepid the movie ended up on the lower half of a double bill. Receiving even less release was another programmer he made in London for Allied Artists called NEVER PUT IT IN WRITING (1964), in which he played a man out to retrieve an embarrassing letter which could cost him his job. Back in Hollywood, Boone ended his 20th Century–Fox contract by co-starring in the abysmal farce GOODBYE CHARLIE about a murdered gangster who is reincarnated as a beautiful woman (Debbie Reynolds).

During the 1960s the maturing Pat Boone suffered the low point of his career. His records rarely made the charts, with only "Wish You Were Here Buddy" in 1966 doing well, and he attempted to become a nightclub star. But as he later admitted, he looked "like a choirboy imitating Liberace." He did well by his cameo role as the Young Man at the Tomb in the United Artists release THE GREATEST STORY EVER TOLD (1965), and in 1967 a TV pilot he made was expanded into a theatrical film called THE PERILS OF PAULINE, in which he played a globetrotter out to find his lost sweetheart (Pamela Austin). In 1969 he guest-starred on the TV series "The Beverly Hillbillies" and "That Girl" and that year he was in the TV movie THE PIGEON for ABC-TV as a man involved with a detective (Sammy Davis, Jr.) on a complicated case. In 1971 Boone was on TV's "Night Gallery" and two years later he was in an "Owen Marshall" segment.

The 1970s brought a distinct change in Pat Boone and in his show business career. He gave up "trying to round myself out as an actor" and began to devote most of his energies to religious-oriented entertainment. In 1970 he made his last feature film to date, THE CROSS AND THE SWITCHBLADE, directed by Don Murray, a biography in which he portrayed country minister David Wilkerson who comes to Manhattan to combat gang wars, drugs, and racial disharmony. The production proved successful not only in theaters but also on the religious circuit, where it continues to be shown. Boone also formed his own record company, Lamb & Lion (which in 1988 filed for protection in the U.S. Bankruptcy Court), and he recorded a number of religious albums, some with his wife and daughters, as well as produced LPs with such performers as Stuart Hamblen, Del Wood, and Johnny Bond. Although he sometimes performed at rock festivals, Boone mostly confined his personal appearances to religious congregations. He also recorded for various labels such as Motown, Word, MGM, Tetragrammaton (co-owned by Bill Cosby), Thistle, and Hitsville. He returned to the record charts in the 1970s, but now in country music, with "I'll Do It." Recorded in 1975 for Melodyland Records, the song was followed by two 1976 singles for Hitsville, "Oklahoma Sunshine" and "Texas Woman"; in 1980 for Warner Bros./Curb he charted a single with "Colorado Country Morning." In addition, Boone, already a published author (*Between You, Me and the Gatepost*, 1960; *The Care and Feeding of Parents*, 1967), wrote a number of other books, most of them on religious topics, like *The Real Christmas* (1972), *Joy* (1973), *A Miracle a Day Keeps the Devil Away* (1974), *Dr. Balaam's Talking Mule* (1975), *Get Your Life Together* (1978), *Pray to Win* (1980), and *A New Song* (1981). *The Honeymoon's Over* (1977) and *The Marriage Game* (1984) were both co-authored with his wife. In the late 1970s Boone made a number of joint appearances with his daughter Debby, who won a Grammy Award as Best New Artist of the Year in 1977 for the song "You Light Up My Life." In the early 1980s, the still youthful-looking Boone resumed hosting a television program on the Christian Broadcasting Network (CBN) with the weekly "Together with Pat and Shirley Boone," and today he is still a frequent television personality, guesting on religious programs and charity telethons. In 1989, now a grandfather, he produces *Gospel America*, a touring show of rock gospel singers. He is also co-founder/co-owner and host of Shop Television Network on cable TV, as well as part owner of a TV station in Anaheim, California.

## Filmography

Bernadine (20th–Fox, 1957)
April Love (20th–Fox, 1957)
Mardi Gras (20th–Fox, 1958)
Journey to the Center of the Earth (20th–Fox, 1959)
All Hands on Deck (20th–Fox, 1961)
State Fair (20th–Fox, 1962)
The Yellow Canary (20th–Fox, 1963)
The Main Attraction (20th–Fox, 1963)

The Horror of It All (20th–Fox, 1964)
Never Put It in Writing (AA, 1964)
Goodbye Charlie (20th–Fox, 1964)
The Greatest Story Ever Told (UA, 1965)
The Perils of Pauline (Univ, 1967)
The Pigeon (ABC-TV, 11/4/69)
The Cross and the Switchblade (Gateway, 1970)
Seven Alone (Doty-Dayton, 1974) (voice only)

## TV Series

Arthur Godfrey and His Friends (CBS, 1955–57)
The Pat Boone–Chevy Showroom (ABC, 1957–60)

The Pat Boone Show (NBC, 1966–67)
Together with Pat and Shirley Boone (CBN, 1982)

## Album Discography

Ain't That a Shame (Dot 3573/25573)
All in the Boone Family (Lamb & Lion 1008)
April Love (Dot 9000) [ST]
Blest Be the Tie (Dot 3601/25601)
Born Again (Lamb & Lion 1007)
Boss Beat (Dot 3594/25594)
Canadian Sunset (Pickwick 3123)
Christian People (Lamb & Lion 1005)
Christmas Is a Comin' (Dot 25770)
The Country Side of Pat Boone (Motown 6-501)
The Cross and the Switchblade (Light 5550) [ST]
Departure (Tetragrammaton 118)
The Family Who Prays (Lamb & Lion 1006)
Favorite Hymns (Pickwick 3145)
First Nashville Jesus Band (Lamb & Lion 1004)
The General Motors Fiftieth Anniversary Show (RCA LOC-1037) [ST/TV]
Golden Era of Country Hits (Dot 3626/25626)
Golden Hits (Dot 3455/25455)
Golden Hits—15 Hits (Dot 3814/25814)
Great, Great, Great! (Dot 3346/25346)
Great Hits (Pickwick 3597)
Greatest Hits (Paramount 1043)
Greatest Hits of 1965 (Dot 3685/25685)
Greatest Hymns (Paramount 1024)
He Leadeth Me (Dot 3234/25234)
How Great Thou Art (Dot 3798/25798)
Howdy! (Dot 3030)
Hymns We Love (Dot 3068/25068)
Hymns We Love (Word 8664)
I Love You More and More (MGM SE-4899)
I Was Kaiser Bill's Batman (Dot 3805/25805)
I'll See You in My Dreams (Dot 3399/25399)
In the Holy Land (Lamb & Lion 5000)
Jivin' Pat (Bear Family BFX-15230)
Just the Way I Am (Lamb & Lion 1039)
Look Ahead (Dot 25876)
The Lord's Prayer (Dot 3582/25582)
Love Me Tender (Pickwick 3101)
Memories (Dot 3748/25748)
Moody River (Dot 3384/25384)
Moonglow (Dot 3270/25270)
My God and I (Dot 3386/25386)

Near You (Dot 3606/25606)
1965 (Hamilton 153/12153)
The Old Rugged Cross (Pickwick 3568)
Pat (Dot 3050)
Pat Boone (Dot 3012)
Pat Boone (MCA 2-6020)
The Pat Boone Family (Word 8536)
Pat Boone Reads from the Bible (Dot 3402)
Pat Boone Sings (Dot 3158/25158)
Pat Boone Sings Golden Hymns (Lamb & Lion 1001)
Pat Boone Sings Irving Berlin (Dot 3077/25077)
Pat Boone Sings the New Songs of the Jesus People (Lamb & Lion 1002)
Pat's Great Hits (Dot 3071/25071)
Pat's Great Hits, Vol. 2 (Dot 3261/25261)
A Pocketful of Hope (Thistle 1005)
Rapture (Supreme 2060)
The Romantic Pat Boone (Pickwick 2006)
S-A-V-E-D (Lamb & Lion 1013)
Side by Side (Dot 319/25199) w. Shirley Boone
Sing Along with Pat Boone (Dot 3513)
Sixteen Great Performances (ABC 4006, MCA AB-4006)
Something Supernatural (Lamb & Lion 1017)
Songs from the Inner Court (Lamb & Lion 1016)
Speedy Gonzales (Dot 3455/25455)
Star Dust (Dot 3118/25118)
The Star Spangled Banner (Word 8725)
State Fair (Dot 9011) [ST]
Tenderly (Dot 3180/25180)
Tenth Anniversary with Dot (Dot 3650/25650)
Texas Woman (Hitsville 40551)
This and That (Dot 3285/25285)
The Touch of Your Lips (Dot 3546/25546)
True Love (Pickwick 3079)
Twelve Great Hits (Hamilton 118/12118)
White Christmas (Dot 3222/25222)
Winners of the Reader's Digest Poll (Dot 3667/25667)
Wish You Were Here, Buddy (Dot 3764/25764)
Yes, Indeed (Dot 3121/25121)

# BOBBY BREEN

FOR A TIME IN THE LATE 1930s ONE CHILD STAR RIVALED SHIRLEY Temple in popularity. He was Bobby Breen, a Canadian youth who appeared with extraordinary success in a series of mawkish RKO low-budget musicals, all showcasing his amazingly cultivated soprano voice. These wafer-thin scenarios displayed curly-haired little Bobby coping with life's vagaries, always singing and always finding happiness by the picture's finale. Detractors insisted he presented a very syrupy, sissified image. In real life, his voice changed in 1939 and his movie career faded immediately, and he has since devoted decades to avoiding and/or capitalizing on his tremendous childhood fame.

Bobby Breen was born in Montreal, Canada, on November 4, 1927, the son of Hyman and Rebeccah Borsuch [Borsuk] who had fled from Kiev, Russia, during one of the many anti-Jewish pogroms of the 1910s. (Mrs. Borsuch's father, a violinist/cellist, had been killed in the Bolshevik gun fighting.) The Borsuchs arrived penniless in western Canada, first living in Regina, Saskatchewan, and then resettling in Montreal. There were already three older children (Gertrude, seventeen; Michael, fifteen; and Sally, nine) when Bobby was born. Hoping for better, the Borsuch family moved to Toronto where they operated a tiny candy store, with the family packed into crowded living quarters in the back. Hyman Borsuch was a garment cutter usually too sick to work.

Young Michael Borsuch had already displayed a fine singing voice, but it paled in comparison to little Bobby's. When Bobby was still a tyke, his doting sister Sally took him to amateur contests. The sight of this precocious child with light yellow curly hair singing in a surprisingly mature lyrical treble quickly won him a series of first prizes. When Sally was fourteen she called the Silver Slipper, a Toronto restaurant, and bargained for a waitress job for herself. After she had worked there for a while, she asked whether she could bring her little brother in for the Silver Slipper's Wednesday night radio amateur programs. Bobby won a prize. Thereafter she escorted him to the restaurant weekly for this event and for nearly two years he sang on the program. Little Bobby also performed at the Savarin Restaurant for nearly a year. By now Sally had changed the family name to Borene and then to Breen. In the summertime, Sally (who also sang and danced) and Bobby toured the outskirts of Toronto, entertaining at estate parties. At the Canadian National Exposition, Bobby Breen sang and Sally modeled.

Sally, who had assumed the role of Bobby's devout stage mother, dreamed of transforming her little brother into a stellar show business attraction. With money saved from various jobs, she (now sixteen) took Bobby to Chicago. Through a man who had managed brother Mickey as a "concert singer" she was given an entrée to stage producer Louis Lipstone of the Balaban and Katz Theatre circuit. He auditioned the boy and hired him to sing at the Oriental Theatre in the same variety revue as Milton Berle, with Bobby being promoted as Berle's nephew. Next Breen appeared at the Chicago Theatre where he was on the same bill as Gloria Swanson. During this six-month period in late 1933/early 1934, Bobby was heard also on Chicago radio programs.

Wanting greater opportunities for Bobby, Sally determined to move to New York City. Lipstone provided her with a letter of introduction to Boris Morros, then in Manhattan in charge of the Paramount Theatres' stage prologues. Morros was so impressed with the youngster's abilities that he went to a great deal of trouble (obtaining a special work permit for the young boy) to employ him for two weeks at the flagship Paramount Theatre. Meanwhile, Sally—who had a job as a cigarette girl at the Hotel Edison— enrolled Bobby at the New York Professional Children's School. When vocalist/actor Harry Richman was preparing the Broadway musical *Say When* (November 1934), he contacted the school to send over some kids to audition for a small role in the show. Bobby was among the seventy-six who tried out and he was hired to be the newsboy son of a drunk (Bob Hope). *Say When* lasted for only seventy-six performances. Later, there was an appearance on Alexander Woollcott's radio program.

More determined than ever for Bobby's success, Sally led her brother on endless rounds of calls to casting agents, including Ben Holtzman, then Eddie Cantor's manager. Bobby auditioned for Cantor, who was impressed but did not hire Bobby for his network radio show as Sally had hoped. The steadfast girl prophetically advised the superstar, "Some day, Mr. Cantor, you will ask this little boy to sing with you."

Now reduced to living on $7 a week, Sally and Bobby moved from one boarding house to another, each move always a step down. At one theatrical lodging, a neighbor led Sally to showman Arthur Levy who, in turn, called in agent William Shapiro who signed the talented boy (now seven) to a three-month trial contract. Sally and Bobby moved to Hollywood. Near the end of the three months, Mike Hoffman of Pathé suggested that Sally take Bobby to audition for Sol Lesser, a former movie exhibitor, who in the 1930s turned to producing low-budget films and serials. More important, Lesser had experience in promoting/exploiting child performers (such as Baby Peggy Montgomery).

Lesser was impressed by Bobby's voice, presence, and wholesome youthfulness. To confirm his hunch, he had young Breen perform for famed vocal coach Dr. Mario Marafioti (he numbered Grace Moore among his clients) who endorsed the boy's potential. Lesser next arranged for Bobby to perform in an outdoor program at the Uplifters Club in suburban Los Angeles. Eddie Cantor was at the concert and he now hired Bobby to sing on his NBC network radio program. Bobby had just turned eight. For Cantor's Christmas show, Bobby sang "Santa, Bring My Mommy Back to Me." Audience response was so enthusiastic that Cantor hired Bobby to be a permanent member of his radio troupe, along with another Canadian prodigy, Deanna Durbin. On the air Bobby referred to Cantor as "Uncle Eddie" and listeners were convinced the two were indeed relatives.

Meanwhile, Sol Lesser, through his Principal Pictures, which released its product through RKO Pictures, rushed Bobby into his first feature, LET'S SING AGAIN (1936). It contained every saccharine ingredient that would become standard for Breen vehicles. Here he is a supposed orphan who runs away from the orphanage to join a circus, ending in New York City and being reunited with his long-lost tenor father (George Houston). Besides the title tune, there were such items as "Lullaby," "Farmer in the Dell," and "La Donna è Mobile." *Variety* decided, "Young Breen makes a decidedly promising shove off. He has a voice which is sweet. . . . He reads his lines naturally. . . ." The *New York Times* dubbed him "the most curious voice in a generation of vocal curiosities" and reported, "Bobby's dwarf tenor also appears to excite rapturous feminine murmurs in his audience."

The die was cast and Bobby Breen was now a movie star. His next vehicle—a period piece—was his most popular. RAINBOW ON THE RIVER (1936) finds the winsome boy in short pants melting the cold heart of his grandmother (May Robson) and being reunited with his loving mammy (Louise Beavers). The maudlin movie contained Breen's signature tune, "Rainbow on the River," and the low-budget musical featured the Hall Johnson Choir.

As a moppet star, Breen was earning $50,000 a year just from testimonials, plus the income from films and radio and up to $500 weekly for personal appearances. Sister Sally was on Sol Lesser's payroll at $75 per week and Bobby was attending Los Angeles's Black Foxe Military Academy, along with such fellow students as Charlie Chaplin's two boys and Paul Whiteman's son. By now Bobby's awestruck parents had moved to Hollywood where their youngest child was supporting them. (The father died in 1954 and the mother in 1957, at which time there was a squabble as to which offspring deserved the $60,000 estate.)

MAKE A WISH (1937) was set at a boys' summer camp with smiley Bobby acting as matchmaker between his mother (Marion Claire) and a

Bobby Breen and Henry Armetta in LET'S SING AGAIN (1936)

Broadway composer (Basil Rathbone) who is writing a new operetta. Among the musical interludes were "Make a Wish," "Music in My Heart," and "Old Man Rip." HAWAII CALLS (1938) boasted exotic settings (via process photography) with stowaway bootblack Breen on a vessel headed for the tropical paradise, with such tunes as "Hawaii Calls," "That's the Hawaiian in Me," and "Down Where the Trade Winds Blow." BREAKING THE ICE (1938) displayed sensitive Bobby running away from home yet again—this time to Philadelphia where he performs in an ice-skating show, his co-performer being precocious Irene Dare (touted as the world's youngest skater). The songs this go-round included "Telling My Troubles to a Mule," "Put Your Heart in a Song," "The Sunny Side of Things," and "Happy as a Lark."

The year 1939 was Bobby Breen's busiest on camera; he was in three releases. FISHERMAN'S WHARF used San Francisco as a backdrop, and had the support of such stalwarts as Leo Carrillo, Henry Armetta, and Slick the Seal. When not running away from home yet again, Breen was busy singing "Sell Your Cares for a Song," "Songs of Italy," and "Fisherman's Chantie." WAY DOWN SOUTH was laid in the pre–Civil War South with Louisiana youth Breen almost fleeced of his inheritance, but aided by a kindly New Orleans innkeeper (Alan Mowbray) and a happy (!) slave (Clarence Muse). The Hall Johnson Choir supported Bobby in two of his numbers: "Louisiana" and "Good Ground." Breen's finale film for the year was ESCAPE TO PARADISE (1939), a meandering study of a South American port youth who convinces a lazy playboy (Kent Taylor) that getting a job is the best way to win a beautiful local woman (Marta Shelton). The lackluster songs were "Tra-La-La" ("youngster's soprano warbling is shrill on the high notes," *Variety* alerted), "Ay, Ay, Ay," and "Rhythm of the Rio."

By now, twelve-year-old Bobby Breen was undergoing a severe career crisis. His voice was changing. At the first signs of his vocal maturity (in late 1938), he had been dropped from Eddie Cantor's radio program and as 1939 concluded, Sol Lesser announced gravely, "Bob's voice is changing, and he has been warned to do no more singing for at least two years." Breen had just had his tonsils and adenoids removed, a surgical procedure much delayed for fear of what it would do to his voice. After graduating from high school he attended UCLA where he studied music and drama. (Later, he reflected, "I suppose I should have learned something else, business, for instance, but I was waiting for my voice to settle down so I could get started again.") He became the California State oratorical champ six successive times and had a brief flurry as guest pianist with the NBC (radio) Symphony Orchestra.

Meanwhile, Breen's career eclipse ended briefly in 1943 when he appeared with several other one-time child stars (Jane Withers, Carl "Alfalfa" Switzer, Spanky McFarland, Cora Sue Collins) in a mini-musical at Republic Pictures. In this entry, JOHNNY DOUGHBOY, Bobby was given no songs to sing.

During World War II, Breen served in the Army, sometimes in the infantry and sometimes appearing in jeep shows to entertain Allied troops in Europe, often appearing with Mickey Rooney. In February 1946 he was demobilized and entered the American Academy of Dramatic Arts in New York City. He later had a local fifteen-minute variety

TV show and began playing nightclub engagements. He was much in the national news in November 1948 when he and a pilot/hunter friend were traveling from Waukesha to Haywood, Wisconsin, in a small plane that was reported missing. After a massive twenty-four-hour search, Breen and his pal were found to be safely resting in a Glidding, Wisconsin, hotel, unharmed. The search party sheriff suggested the entire episode might have been a publicity gimmick dreamed up by the former child star.

In the 1950s, Breen, now a full-bodied tenor who was finding decent engagements hard to find, was the first to admit, "Thank God my folks put away some of the money I made as a kid. I've never been hungry. I'm trying to prove to producers and agency people that I still have talent as a grownup. That child star label never stops haunting me. The notion is that a child star isn't supposed to have talent when he grows up." In November 1952, he and Brooklyn model Jocelyn Lesh were married. They would have a son, Keith, separate in 1958, and be divorced in 1961.

Breen spent much of the 1950s in and out of show business. "I wasn't getting ahead fast enough. I was insecure in an insecure business." When he was not performing his club act (based on the old style of entertainment), he was selling real estate or producing TV commercials. To continue performing he had to go far from home, sometimes overseas. Regarding his audiences, he admitted, "They expect me to come on stage still wearing short pants. It takes a lot of work out there to make them believe I'm grown up. They resent it somehow. It's something I have to fight every single performance."

By the early 1960s Breen had relocated to Miami, Florida, and was signed to Thunderbird Recordings to do albums. Later he would make a pact with Motown Records, but it also failed to revive his career. There were occasional club engagements, but more often Breen was occupied as a talent booker. He had a nostalgic reunion with Eddie Cantor in 1964, shortly before the latter's death. Cantor's advice to the one-time star was, "No matter what happens, keep going." Breen did.

In 1971 Breen appeared at the London nitery "The Plough" and that same year, when beginning a New Jersey club engagement, he badly scratched his eyes with defective contact lenses and was nearly blinded. Later in the 1970s, Breen, now re-wed (to Audra, who had two sons, Paul and Ronald, by a prior marriage), was performing a mini-musical stage version of *The Jazz Singer* doing the numbers in the Al Jolson style. According to his wife, it was she who helped Breen change his stage image. "I made him put on sports clothes and throw away his elevator shoes."

Even in the 1980s, Florida-based club booker Bobby Breen (head of Bobby Breen Enterprises) had mixed feelings about his long ago successes. "As a child I had pretty nearly everything—except a childhood. The demands of a career—the practicing, rehearsals, and appearances on radio and film—just didn't allow for it." When interviewed by TV's "Entertainment Tonight" (December 1985) from his Fort Lauderdale home, Breen commented, "If I couldn't make it really big again, super big, like I was when I was a kid, I'd rather go into other businesses." He ended his brief appearance on the television show by singing "The Best of Times."

## Filmography

Let's Sing Again (RKO, 1936)
Rainbow on the River (RKO, 1936)
Make a Wish (RKO, 1937)
Hawaii Calls (RKO, 1938)
Breaking the Ice (RKO, 1938)

Fisherman's Wharf (RKO, 1939)
Way Down South (RKO, 1939)
Escape to Paradise (RKO, 1939)
Johnny Doughboy (Rep, 1943)

## Broadway Plays

Say When (1934)

## Radio Series

The Eddie Cantor Show (NBC, ca. 1935–38)

## Album Discography

Bobby Breen: Songs at Yuletide (London 270)
Radio Memories, Number 3 (Bergen 1476-69)

Those Wonderful Thirties, Vol. 1 (Decca DEA-7-1)

# JUDY CANOVA

DECADES BEFORE SUCH POPULAR TV SHOWS AS "THE BEVERLY HILLBIL-lies," "Petticoat Junction," "Green Acres," or "Hee Haw," there was Judy Canova. Long before country and western's Minnie Pearl became a U.S. institution, there was Judy Canova. It was Judy Canova, in the 1930s–50s, who made hillbilly humor a national pastime through her successful work on the Broadway stage, in films, on recordings, and especially on radio. As the energetic country hick spouting good-natured humor she became an entertainment landmark. Yet beneath her trademark braided pigtails, oafish ankle boots, sloppy socks, and checkered blouse was a far more versatile performer than her public (or even she) would allow. Fans remember her best for that bellowing (yet melodic) voice which seemed forever geared to yodeling and guffawing. When Judy sang, her public expected to hear a countrified ballad like "Wabash Blues" or "Tons of Love." However, Judy Canova had an operatic-trained voice that was professionally adept at all types of music. And when given that rare opportunity, the "canyon-mouthed, pigtailed girl" could be a wow at dramatics.

She was born Juliette Canova in Starke, Florida, on November 20, 1916, the daughter of Joe (a cotton broker) and Henrietta Perry Canova (a former concert singer). There were three older Canova children: Anne, Zeke, and Pete. In the 1920s, Anne, Zeke, and Judy would be heard as the Canova Cracker Trio on WJAX in Jacksonville, Florida. Meanwhile, Judy, the most effervescent of the trio, was performing in talent shows and in any other avenue she could find for her show business ambitions. Coming to terms with her plain looks, she admitted later, "I got smart and not only accepted my lack of glamour, but made the most of it." Both Anne and Zeke had attended the Cincinnati Conservatory of Music and Judy had hoped to study there as well. But her father died in 1930, and there was no money for tuition. Instead, Judy and her mother went to New York City where Judy studied tap dancing with Tommy Nip. Later she returned to Florida where she taught contortion dancing at Orlando's Ebsen School.

Determined to prosper as an entertainer, Judy saved her money and returned to New York. Joined by Anne and Zeke, she won a job at Jimmie Kelly's Club and later at the Village Barn. It was during these engagements that she introduced her cornpone character to audiences. It was a successful novelty in Gotham and she expanded the rubber-faced comedy aspect of her act. Rudy Vallee used her in a spot on his radio show, which led to a regular assignment on orchestra leader Paul Whiteman's NBC radio program. This gave her a much wider audience for her developing brand of country humor and singing. In time away from her radio commitments, she toured the country in vaudeville.

Judy made her Broadway debut in *Calling All Stars*, which opened at the Hollywood Theatre on December 13, 1934. Besides Martha Raye, Mitzi Mayfair, and Phil Baker, the revue featured Anne, Pete, and Zeke Canova. Judy's best moment was a sketch entitled "Last of the Hillbillies" in which she sang "If It's Love." Unfortunately, the show ran for only thirty-six performances.

*Calling All Stars* had been financed by Warner Bros. Pictures and when it folded, the studio contracted the Canovas to come to California. Judy's screen debut proved to be her most memorable film appearance. IN CALIENTE (1935) was a musical potpourri with choreography by Busby Berkeley and songs by Harry Warren, Al Dubin, Mort Dixon, and Allie Wrubel. In the film's elaborate production number, "The Lady in Red," Winifred Shaw sings the lead. From the midst of an ensemble of shapely chorines, angular Judy Canova suddenly pops up to yodel her nasal variation of the lilting torch song. Later in the movie, the Canova quartet had a hillbilly musical spot, but it was Judy's superb burlesque of "The Lady in Red" that grabbed audience attention. In BROADWAY GONDOLIER (1935) the Canovas performed a brief specialty number, while in GOING HIGHBROW (1935), Judy was cast without her family and played a dumb waitress. When the studio allowed their contract to lapse, the Canovas returned to New York City.

Without her family, Judy was hired to play in *The Ziegfeld Follies of 1936*, which opened at the Winter Garden Theatre on January 30, 1936. The Lee Shubert production had Ira Gershwin lyrics and an ensemble that included Fanny Brice, Bob Hope, Josephine Baker, and Eve Arden. The revue ran for 115 performances before closing for the summer, and Judy received solid reviews for her antics and parodies. However, when the show reopened that fall she was no longer part of the production. She had negotiated a radio contract with NBC/WJZ radio for the "Rippling Rhythm Revue," which gave her family parts in the show. The program was on the airwaves for the 1936–37 season.

Paramount now offered the Canovas a film contract and the group (minus Pete, who had entered business management) reported back to Hollywood. In ARTISTS AND MODELS (1937) Anne and Zeke were part of the Canova act, but it was Judy who had a featured role and a specialty number, "Pop Goes the Bubble" (a send-up of bubble bath songs). It was also during this "new" Hollywood period that Judy gained much publicity with her (staged) fracas with Edgar Bergen, the ventriloquist, who, in tandem with dummy Charlie McCarthy, was starring on radio's "Chase and Sanborn Hour." Judy confessed publicly that she and Bergen were no longer an item (she could not compete with the dummy). Bergen retorted that he had never met Canova. Unpublicized was the fact that Judy was already wed, having married New York insurance man Robert Burns in Maryland in 1936.

In THRILL OF A LIFETIME (1937), Paramount cast Judy as the sex-starved, clumsy sister of Eleanore Whitney and Johnny Downs who is courted by Ben Blue. She, Anne, and Zeke sang a hillbilly song. Paramount dropped its option, which ended the Canovas' $6,000 weekly paycheck. Judy assessed later, "I would have done better getting eighteen bucks a week and a good part."

The Canovas returned to vaudeville, where they had developed an enthusiastic following, and played a two-week engagement at London's Café de Paris. They then joined Edgar Bergen on his NBC radio "Chase and Sanborn Hour" for thirteen weeks in 1938, for which they received $4,300 weekly for their efforts. On May 3, 1939, the Canova clan appeared on an experimental NBC-TV program, making them the first hillbilly act ever seen on television.

It was on Broadway in *Yokel Boy* (July 6, 1939) that Judy Canova reached a career peak. The comedy featured Phil Silvers, Buddy Ebsen, Dixie Dunbar, and Anne and Zeke Canova. Judy starred as the hillbilly who becomes an "overnight" movie star. The *New York Times* enthused about Judy: "A rowdy mixture of Beatrice Lillie and other comediennes along parallel lines in the general direction of Fannie [sic] Brice. . . . Quite a girl on the whole." *Yokel Boy* ran for 208 performances and Hollywood took notice of Judy Canova for the *third* time.

It was Herbert J. Yates, head of Republic Pictures, who offered Judy a contract. She reasoned that her rustic bumpkin specialty would be better utilized at a studio noted for its horse opry stars (Gene Autry and Roy Rogers) and that here, without glamorous leading ladies to compete with, she would shine. Her Republic debut was SCATTERBRAIN (1940), in which she was a hillbilly who is transformed into a movie starlet. She performed slapstick (washing her kitchen floor on roller skates with brushes tied to them) and sang "Benny the Beaver (You Better Be Like That, Yeah, Yeah)." The *New York Daily News* reported, "The gags are good, the situations funny, and Judy Canova herself a riot in her first starring role for the screen."

As part of her five-year Republic pact (which called for three films annually) Judy made SIS HOPKINS (1941), featuring Charles Butterworth, Jerry Colonna, and a rising newcomer, Susan Hayward. This movie, more than any of her other pictures, displays Judy's vocal virtuosity. She did selections ranging from an operatic aria from *La Traviata* to Frank Loesser–Jule Styne's "It Ain't Hay (It's the U.S.A)," and on to "Cracker Barrel County," showing that she could handle a swing number (with Bob Crosby's band) admirably. The film produced her trademark expression, "You're telling I."

Judy Canova was now a star of sorts. Republic had bought the screen rights to *Yokel Boy* as a Canova vehicle, but she and the studio had a disagreement and she was replaced in the screen version (1942) by Joan Davis. MGM asked to borrow her services and Judy responded, "I don't want any more big studios for a while. You get lost." Instead, Judy and Republic renegotiated her contract, which now provided she be part owner of her features for them. Meanwhile, Judy, divorced since 1939, made headlines in June 1941 while on a Honolulu vacation. On June 10, she and a hometown Florida friend, Army corporal James H. Ripley, became engaged, and they were wed on June 14. That evening he was arrested for being A.W.O.L. Judy soon returned to the mainland and on October 8, 1941, she had the marriage annulled.

PUDDIN'HEAD (1941) was more of the same profitable Judy Canova bucolic shenanigans. She sang "Minnie Hotcha," "Hey, Junior!," "Manhattan Holiday," and "You're Telling I" (a duet with Eddie Foy, Jr.). Her busiest screen year was 1942 with three releases. In Republic's SLEEPYTIME GAL she was a cake decorator at a Miami hotel and sang

"Barrelhouse Bessie," "I Don't Want Anybody at All," "Sleepytime Gal," and "The Cat's Away." On loan to Paramount for TRUE TO THE ARMY, she was a circus tightrope walker who witnesses a killing and flees to Fort Bragg, where her boyfriend (Jerry Colonna) is a G.I. Judy did her stock-in-trade hillbilly gambits, while Ann Miller tap danced and Allan Jones crooned. Back at Republic she was paired with equally big-mouthed funster Joe E. Brown in JOAN OF OZARK, a spy farce, and she got to warble "Backwood Barbecue," "The Lady at Lockheed," and "Wabash Blues." Judy and Brown would recreate their roles for radio's "Screen Guild Playhouse" in February 1945.

By now Judy had guested on most of the top radio variety programs, and on July 6, 1943, she began "The Judy Canova Show" on the CBS network. The humor remained strictly hillbilly, with Judy braying forth with backwoods jokes. ("Is this a room with bath?" "Hoo," Judy replies, "the only thing we got here is a room with a path.") *Variety* reported, "Miss Canova, when given to songs, spreads her style from scat to rhythm to plain hog calling, but it was all entertaining." Her show was a big hit. Earlier in the year, on March 14, 1943, Judy wed Chester B. England in Newton, New Jersey. She had met England in London during her 1938 club engagement there.

CHATTERBOX (1943) rematched her with Joe E. Brown in a satire of the radio industry and Western movies. The Mills Brothers and Spade Cooley performed musical

Judy Canova in PUDDIN'HEAD (1941)

specialties and Judy sang "Why Can't I Sing a Love Song?" In SLEEPY LAGOON (1943) Judy is a radio singer who is made mayor of her home town and must endure the hazards of an amusement park's fun house. She vocalized "I'm Not Myself Anymore" and, with Joe Sawyer, harmonized "You're the Fondest Thing I Am Of." It was her last film at Republic for several years because she and the studio were in constant disagreement over properties and budgets for her pictures.

During the World War II years Judy was active in war bond tours and entertaining at Army camps. On August 24, 1944, she gave birth to her first child, Julieta. Two weeks later, her husband went overseas for active military duty. That month also marked her first Columbia Pictures effort, LOUISIANA HAYRIDE. She was a hillbilly debutante and got to vocalize "You Gotta Go Where the Train Goes," "Rainbow Road," "I'm a Woman of the World," "Put Your Arms Around Me Honey," and a smattering of "Short'nin' Bread." If her Republic properties had been economy-conscious, Judy's three Columbia projects were shoddy programmers tossed out to rural audiences to exploit the popular Canova image. HIT THE HAY (1945) presented Judy in dual roles. Besides belting out "Old MacDonald Had a Farm" and "No Other Love," the versatile songstress provided arias from such operas as *Rigoletto, The Barber of Seville,* and *La Traviata.* In SINGIN' IN THE CORN (1946), she is a carnival fortune-teller who inherits a fortune and must deal with a ghost town. Her numbers included "Pepita Chiquita," "I'm a Gal of Property," "Ma, He's Making Eyes at Me," and "An Old Love Is a True Love."

If her films were mired in an uncreative rut, Judy was faring far better on radio. Having been off the air since June 1944, she returned to the airwaves on January 6, 1945, for NBC with a new Saturday night program. The lineup included a host of talented players: Verna Felton, Joe Kerns, Ruby Dandridge, and Mel Blanc. Using a comedy-variety format she continued to garner howls as the back-country miss from Unadella, Georgia, who had relatives out west in Cactus Junction and who had a rich Aunt Agatha in the big city. Judy would regale audiences with humorous tales of her cousin Ureenus who fancied chopped liver ice cream and with her nonsensical interchanges with Pedro the gardener. She would close each show by singing "Go to Sleepy Little Baby." As with her films, Judy's production company owned a percentage of her show.

Judy's mother died on August 30, 1949, at the age of eighty. In the following years (until 1952), radio was her primary medium. She made a nightclub tour of Latin America in 1947 (the same year her brother Pete died). In February 1950 she divorced Chester B. England and in July 1950 married Filiberto [Philip] Rivero, a Cuban musician and ardent Cuban nationalist who had had a band in Havana. (It would prove to be a stormy marriage; they divorced in 1964 and Rivero died in 1971). She made personal appearances at large fairs throughout the southwest. One of her biggest career disappointments was not being considered seriously by MGM for the lead in the musical ANNIE GET YOUR GUN (1950). (She had been considered for the lead in the Broadway production, but at the time she was making movies at Columbia Pictures.)

In 1951 Herbert J. Yates lured Judy Canova back to Republic Pictures for more films. Her first, in Trucolor, was HONEYCHILE (1951) and her singing ranged from an operatic version of "Rag Mop" to "Tutti Frutti." OKLAHOMA ANNIE (1952) could have been a half-hour TV Western, with Canova at her best singing "Blow the Whistle." THE WAC FROM WALLA WALLA (1952) was a service comedy and her four songs included "If Only Dreams Came True." Also in 1952, on November 2, she made her major television debut on "The Colgate Comedy Hour" (NBC) along with Anne and Zeke Canova. She was off the screen in 1953 due to the birth of her daughter Diana (June 1). Plans for a "Judy Canova Show" TV series did not materialize but she was back on screen in the black-and-white UNTAMED HEIRESS (1954), singing, among others, "A Dream for Sale." It was a family affair, for Canova's daughter Julieta played Judy as a youngster and five-month-old Diana had a bit in this caper. CAROLINA CANNONBALL (1955) was very thinly produced, with Judy singing the title song, and LAY THAT RIFLE DOWN (1955) had such novelty tunes as "I'm Glad I Was Born on My Birthday." Because Republic was moving out of theatrical filmmaking, Judy and the studio ended their contract.

The late 1950s were a fallow period for the country star. She guest-starred occasionally on TV, in such shows as "The Danny Thomas Show" (March 17, 1958), and in July 1958 Tops Records released *Judy Canova in Hi-Fi,* an LP compilation of such Canova singles as "Blow Whistle Blow," "Butcher Boy," and "Ain't Gonna Grieve My Lord." On May 29, 1960, she returned to television, making her dramatic TV debut on "Alfred Hitchcock Presents" in the episode "Party Line." She proved that she was far more than a comedienne. In the feature film THE ADVENTURES OF HUCKLEBERRY FINN (1960) she had a brief scene as the sheriff's wife. She was also among the cast in the low-budget HILLBILLY JAMBOREE (1960).

Canova, whose slapstick talents should have made her a rival to television's Lucille Ball, unfortunately could not gain a foothold in the medium. She made several unsold pilots for TV series—"Cap'n Ahab" (1965), "Li'l Abner" (1967), and "The Murdocks and the McClays" (1970)—as well as doing commercials. However, she could not regain the momentum of her star years, an ironic situation since country and western was becoming so fashionable in the United States. In late December 1971, Judy, still suffering from emphysema, returned to the stage, taking the maid's role in the national touring company of the revived *No, No Nanette.* Her co-stars were June Allyson and Dennis Day and she mugged to full audience approval. Later there were more TV commercials, a role as the mom of a buffoonish country and western singer in CANNONBALL (1976), and guest appearances on "Police Woman" (1974) and "Love Boat" (1977). A planned cookbook and autobiography never materialized. In 1980 her brother Zeke died. Judy's last public appearance was at a showing of a trio of her films at a Hollywood revival theater in September 1982.

Judy Canova died of cancer on August 5, 1983, at age sixty-six. She was survived by her daughters Julieta, in the mortage business, and Diana, an actress who has starred in several teleseries: "Soap," "I'm a Big Girl Now," "Foot in the Door," and "Throb."

## Filmography

In Caliente (WB, 1935)
Going Highbrow (WB, 1935)
Broadway Gondolier (WB, 1935)
Artists and Models (Par, 1937)
Thrill of a Lifetime (Par, 1937)
Scatterbrain (Rep, 1940)
Sis Hopkins (Rep, 1941)
Puddin'head [Judy Goes to Town] (Rep, 1941)
Meet Roy Rogers (Rep, 1941) (s)
Joan of Ozark (Rep, 1942)
True to the Army (Par, 1942)
Sleepytime Gal (Rep, 1942)
Chatterbox (Rep, 1943)
Sleepy Lagoon (Rep, 1943)
Louisiana Hayride (Col, 1944)

Hit the Hay (Col, 1945)
Singin' in the Corn (Col, 1946)
Famous Hollywood Mothers (Col, 1946) (s)
Radio Characters of 1946 (Col, 1946) (s)
Honeychile (Rep, 1951)
Oklahoma Annie (Rep, 1952)
The WAC from Walla Walla [Army Capers] (Rep, 1952)
Untamed Heiress (Rep, 1954)
Carolina Cannonball (Rep, 1955)
Lay That Rifle Down (Rep, 1956)
The Adventures of Huckleberry Finn (MGM, 1960)
Hillbilly Jamboree (Ronnie Ashcroft, 1960)
Cannonball [Carquake] (New World, 1976)

## Broadway Plays

Calling All Stars (1934)
The Ziegfeld Follies of 1936 (1936)

Yokel Boy (1939)

## Radio Series

The Kraft Music Hall (NBC, ca. 1933–34)
Rippling Rhythm Revue (NBC, 1936–37)
The Chase and Sanborn Hour (NBC, 1938)

The Judy Canova Show (CBS, 1943–44; NBC, 1945–52)

## Album Discography

Country Cousin Sings (Coronet CX/CSX-239)
Favorite Songs (10" Royale 6108)
Featuring Judy Canova (Viking 8802)
Judy Canova (Camden CAL-662)

Judy Canova/Esmeraldy (Sutton SSU-296)
Judy Canova in Hi-Fi (Tops L-1613)
Miss Country, U.S.A. (Craftsmen 8062)

# EDDIE CANTOR

EDDIE CANTOR IS ONE OF THE MORE FABULOUS SHOW BUSINESS phenomena of the first half of the twentieth century. Honing his craft in vaudeville, he rose to stardom on Broadway, in motion pictures, on radio, on television, and in recordings. Often appearing in blackface (like fellow star Al Jolson) the dapper 5' 7" Cantor was known as Banjo Eyes, an endearing term referring to his oversized brown orbs, which gazed in perpetual surprise at life's perplexing realities. The hyperenergetic performer was a sight to behold; prancing about on stage, with arms akimbo or hands clasped in bemusement. His singing of such ditties as "Ida," "If You Knew Susie," "Dinah," "Mandy," "My Baby Just Cares for Me," "You'd Be Surprised" (his top seller), "Ma, He's Making Eyes at Me," or his indelible "Making Whoopie" were unforgettable moments of entertainment. His professional guise was often seemingly ineffective and boyish, but his heart was always set on winning the ingenue and outmaneuvering his city-slicker opponents. Like equally beloved comedians Al Jolson and Jack Benny, Cantor traded heavily on his Jewish background and made lighthearted ethnic remarks a part of the national vocabulary. His trademark song became "I'd Love to Spend This Hour with You," and throughout five decades as a performing star, he introduced and guided such new talent as Deanna Durbin, Bobby Breen, Dinah Shore, and Eddie Fisher.

He was born January 31, 1892, to Russian immigrants Michael and Maite (Minnie) Iskowitch in a crowded tenement flat over a Russian tearoom on New York's Lower East Side. A year later, Minnie died in childbirth; the violin-playing Michael died in 1894 of pneumonia. The orphaned Isidor Iskowitch was raised by his maternal grandmother, Esther Kantrowitz. She was sixty-two years old and supported both of them by peddling wares door to door and, later, by running her own employment agency.

Izzy had a sparse formal education, and he never completed grade school. When he won a $5 (top) prize as Edward Cantor while impersonating current show business greats at Miner's Bowery Theatre Amateur Night, his career was decided. He made his professional vaudeville bow in 1907 at the Clinton Music Hall teamed with Dan Lipsky. The latter, Cantor's lifelong friend, would later become vice president of Manufacturers Trust Company in New York City.

Cantor's fledgling stage years were erratic. He was stranded in Shenandoah, Pennsylvania, on Christmas Eve 1908, when Frank B. Carr's burlesque unit, *Indian Maidens*, folded there. At Carey Walsh's Coney Island saloon he worked as a singing waiter, accompanied by a big-nosed, ragtime piano player named Jimmy Durante. He played for sixteen weeks, at $20 weekly, in the four-house vaudeville circuit owned by Adolph Zukor,

Marcus Loew, and Joseph and Nicholas Schenck (all future film magnates). This People's Vaudeville Company circuit offered Cantor additional bookings if he would revamp his act. His stratagem was to blacken his face with burnt cork as done in the minstrel shows and to heighten his performance with more physical comedy and ad libs. The gimmicks succeeded and he soon became the featured "stooge" with the popular team of Bedini and Arthur and was performing at Hammerstein's Victoria Theatre on Broadway.

Concluding nearly two years with Bedini and Arthur, Cantor next signed with promoter Gus Edwards and was featured in his *Kid Kabaret* touring show in 1912. Fellow performers included Lila Lee, Eddie Buzzell (later a film director), and George Jessel. Cantor would recall, "It was not first class vaudeville, but the best and only acting school of its kind, where poor young boys and girls could learn the art of entertainment in all its forms and get paid for learning." He stayed with this popular act for two years, playing a black butler. Cantor left the show to wed his childhood sweetheart, Ida Tobias. They were married in Brooklyn on June 9, 1914, and sailed to England for their honeymoon. Shortly after arriving in London, Cantor paired with Sam Kessler for a week's engagement at the Oxford Theatre and then joined André Charlot's revue *Not Likely* at the Alhambra, where he sang the show-stopping tune "I Love the Ladies."

Back in the United States, Cantor teamed in a vaudeville act, *Master and Man*, with straight man Al Lee and for almost two years they played the circuits. The pair split when Cantor was hired for *Canary Cottage*, which opened its tour in the spring of 1916 in San Diego, California. He had the supporting role of a black chauffeur, but built up his role with ad libs. By now the Cantors had two children: Marjorie (born in 1915) and Natalie (born in 1916). Returning to New York, Cantor extended a one-night tryout in Florenz Ziegfeld's *Midnight Frolics* (atop the New Amsterdam Theatre) into a twenty-seven-week turn. The delighted Ziegfeld cast him in his new *Follies* at $400 weekly. The revue opened on June 12, 1917, and lasted 111 performances with a star-studded roster including Will Rogers, W. C. Fields, Bert Williams, Fanny Brice, and Cantor. He remained with various editions of the *Follies* through 1919, during which period his grandmother died (on his birthday, January 31, 1917) and he and Ida had a third daughter, Edna (born in 1919). It was in the 1919 *Follies* that the team of Van and Schenck introduced the song "Mandy," which Cantor adopted later as his own.

Cantor and Ziegfeld had a falling out when the former supported the great Actors' Equity strike (which began August 6, 1919). Thus he went to work for the Shubert Brothers in *Broadway Brevities of 1920* and starred for the same producers on the road in *The Midnight Rounders* (1921). The Cantors' fourth daughter, Marilyn, was born in September 1921. After touring with *The Midnight Rounders* (which featured a sketch of an enterprising Jewish tailor) Cantor revamped much of the material into the revue *Make It Snappy*, which bowed on Broadway on April 13, 1922. He was also busy recording for Brunswick Records under a new pact (signed in 1920) which paid him a total of $220,000. It was reportedly the biggest such contract to that date. When Cantor opened a new vaudeville tour at the Orpheum Theatre in Brooklyn (June 1923), *Variety* noted, "Eddie Cantor is an entertainer with a capital 'E.' He is value received for vaudeville."

A chastened Ziegfeld petitioned Cantor to return to the fold by offering him a "book" show in which he would have the lead as a Florida golf caddie/club bootlegger. *Kid Boots* debuted on New Year's Eve 1923 and played on Broadway and on tour well into 1926. By this time, Paramount Pictures had acquired the screen rights to the hit production, along with Cantor's services as star.

Cantor had already made his motion picture debut in 1911 when he and George Jessel appeared in an experimental talking picture, WIDOW AT THE RACES, for Thomas Edison. Then, in 1925, he made a short subject for the DeForrest Photofilm Company.

For the silent KID BOOTS (1926), which co-starred Billie Dove and Clara Bow (with whom he became infatuated), Cantor was paid $3,000 weekly. Audience response to Cantor was positive and the studio contracted him for SPECIAL DELIVERY (1927), directed by William Goodrich (better known as Roscoe "Fatty" Arbuckle). Because this comedy was unsuccessful, Paramount abandoned plans to feature Cantor in picture versions of Rodgers and Hart's *The Girl Friend* or a comedy to be called HELP.

Cantor returned to Broadway for his last *Follies* (1927) and that same year his fifth and final daughter, Janet, was born. *Whoopee!* (1928), based on the stage hit comedy *The Nervous Wreck*, co-starred Ruth Etting and ran for a resounding 379 performances on Broadway. The stock market crash of 1929 wiped out most of Cantor's savings; he recounted his bad luck in the amusing book *Caught Short*, which was made into a 1930 MGM movie comedy with Marie Dresser and Polly Moran. It was just one of several humorous books and autobiographies the comedian wrote during this period. In other venues, Cantor continued to tax his physical endurance. He was appearing on stage, making talkie short subjects for Paramount at its Astoria, Long Island, studio, and repeating his antic tailor shop sketch in Ziegfeld's Technicolor film GLORIFYING THE AMERICAN GIRL (1929).

In mid-1930 Eddie Cantor announced his retirement from the stage. He reasoned, "I've enough money and I've reached the peak of a theatrical career. Why shouldn't my family and children enjoy my companionship? . . . What does a performer work for? Only two things—money and applause. If I still want to remain before the public, how long does it take to make a picture. In two or three months I can make one and then I'm through for the rest of the year to do as I darn please."

Cantor went to Hollywood to star in the Samuel Goldwyn–Florenz Ziegfeld production of WHOOPEE! (1930), filmed in two-strip Technicolor. The *New York Times* enthused, "It is a picture in which one never tires of Mr. Cantor . . . one looks forward to another chance to chuckle and giggle at the ludicrous conduct of the 'nervous wreck.'" Cantor negotiated a profitable contract with Goldwyn to star in five additional United Artists releases. First came PALMY DAYS (1931), a gangster farce set in a candy factory. It was co-written by Cantor and co-starred angular, high-kicking comedienne Charlotte Greenwood. *Time* magazine analyzed, "Eddie Cantor belongs to the school of clowns whose humor derives from ineffectuality; a certain eccentric excitability makes him sometimes hilariously funny. . . . He is a culprit from a comic strip and no one would be surprised if, when something hit him on the head, it gave the sound of 'plop' or 'zowie!'"

In PALMY DAYS (1931), which boasted the by-now-obligatory Goldwyn chorus girls and Busby Berkeley's geometric choreography, Cantor sang "My Baby Says Yes, Yes" (which became part of his repertoire) and "There's Nothing Too Good for My Baby" (which he co-composed). On October 31, 1931, Cantor was reunited with George Jessel on Broadway at the Palace Theatre in a bill that included Burns and Allen. Originally scheduled to last two weeks, the hugely popular engagement was extended through New Year's Eve. Cantor was paid $8,000 weekly.

Goldwyn lavished a $1 million budget on THE KID FROM SPAIN (1932), directed by Leo McCarey, in which Cantor was an ersatz bullfighter on the lam from the law. Then the setting was ancient Rome for ROMAN SCANDALS (1933), an extravaganza featuring Cantor with the likes of Ruth Etting, Gloria Stuart, and Edward Arnold. In this show, stuffed with hokum, low comedy, and very scantily clad chorines, Cantor put across such numbers as "Build a Little Home." Because the star "tampered" with the film's story and dialogue, authors George S. Kaufman and Robert Sherwood brought legal action and won a judgment against producer Goldwyn.

For KID MILLIONS (1934) Cantor was a Brooklyn dock worker who inherits $77 million and sails to Egypt to claim his rewards. Ethel Merman and Warren Hymer were the preying con artists while Ann Sothern and George Murphy (in his film bow) played the young lovers. The nonsense plotline worked in a blackface number ("I Want to Be a Minstrel Man") for the star. He also got to sing Irving Berlin's "Mandy" and the Brooklyn ice cream factory finale was in Technicolor. STRIKE ME PINK (1936) was Eddie Cantor's sixth and final Goldwyn motion picture. Despite a horde of scripters, it proved pretty thin stuff about a tailor who takes over an amusement park and must deal with greedy gangsters out to control the slot machine concession. The Harold Arlen–Lew Brown score was unremarkable, with Cantor dueting "Calabash Pipe" with Ethel Merman and leading "The Lady Dances" with the Goldwyn Girls and Rita Rio. Since Cantor's performing style (which he was not about to change) was now considered out of sync with Hollywood's new wave of musicals, he and Goldwyn parted company.

If he was no longer a king of movie musicals, Cantor was still very much a star of radio. He had begun in the medium on January 6, 1929, on CBS's "Majestic Theatre of the Air" with Ruth Etting. After guesting on Rudy Vallee's radio program in February 1931, Cantor started a long-running show on NBC network radio (September 13, 1931) which would stretch almost unbroken to 1954, with a year (1938–39) on CBS. (He was taken off the air in 1939 for his outspoken remarks at the New York World's Fair accusing particular government officials of being "fascists," but he returned to NBC in 1940, thanks to the intervention of his pal Jack Benny.) Cantor was one of the first to have a live audience for his shows; in fact, he had a habit of previewing the new script in a dress rehearsal for the studio audience and leaving in the jokes they liked best. His enormous appeal on the airwaves was reflected by the $7,000 per show salary he earned from Texaco when he began a new season under their sponsorship in September 1936.

20th Century–Fox, hoping to duplicate Goldwyn's box-office successes with Cantor, hired him for the high-budgeted ALI BABA GOES TO TOWN (1937), in which he was a tramp who falls asleep on an Oriental movie set and dreams that he is the savior of old Baghdad, using "New Deal" know-how to succeed. He pranced, sang ("Swing Is Here to Stay"), cavorted with Gypsy Rose Lee—one of the Sultan's (Roland Young) 865 wives—and played nursemaid to the romantic lead (Tony Martin). For too many, the merriment seemed a watered-down version of ROMAN SCANDALS and Fox lost interest in pursuing more films with Cantor. Movie offers became scarce. In 1939 MGM announced it would team Eleanor Powell and Cantor in GIRL CRAZY, but court battles over the screen rights delayed production. (The musical was finally made in 1943 with Mickey Rooney and Judy Garland.) Instead, the studio put Cantor into a mild, sentimental comedy, FORTY LITTLE MOTHERS (1940), playing a college professor protecting an abandoned baby. Busby Berkeley directed this tepidly received quasi-drama.

Cantor again returned to Broadway, this time to star in a musical version of the old comedy hit *Three Men on a Horse*. As *Banjo Eyes*, the show bowed on December 25, 1941, with the star cast as a meek greeting-card writer who is a wow at selecting winning race horses. He performed his usual schtick of singing and prancing about in blackface, straw hat, and white-rimmed spectacles. This seemed amazing bravado to a new generation of theatergoers, but despite glowing reviews, the show lasted only 126 performances. Meanwhile, with America involved in World War II, Cantor repeated his volunteer efforts of

George Murphy, Constance Moore, Eddie Cantor, and Joan Davis in SHOW BUSINESS (1944)

World War I by entertaining troops and raising enormous funds through selling war bonds. During one twenty-four-hour radio marathon he hosted in 1944, the war cause netted $41 million in sales of war bonds.

In 1943 Cantor was the focal point of THANK YOUR LUCK STARS, an all-star musical concocted by Warner Bros. for its stable of luminaries. In the plot ploy tying together the sketches, he was featured as both studio tour guide Joe Simpson and as himself, and sang "We're Staying Home Tonight." For many viewers, such a double dose of Cantor was too much for one picture. In the same studio's personality-filled HOLLYWOOD CANTEEN (1944) he dueted "We're Having a Baby" with Nora Martin. That same year, with his very good friend, slapstick comedienne Joan Davis, Cantor co-starred in RKO's SHOW BUSINESS, a modestly budgeted picture he produced. It was a clichéd but fond tribute to vaudeville and showcased the leads well, especially in their burlesque of Antony and Cleopatra. In the finale, Cantor reprised his trademark "Makin' Whoopee" number.

After financing a failed Broadway musical, *Nellie Bly* (1945) with Marilyn Maxwell and Victor Moore, Cantor returned to the silver screen, producing RKO's IF YOU KNEW SUSIE (1948), a benign comedy with zany Joan Davis co-starring as his effervescent screen spouse. Cantor rolled his eyes, mugged, and sang the title tune and other standards. *Variety* warned, "There's little here that Cantor hasn't done in one form or another for many years, whether it's been in radio, musicomedy or pictures." The picture failed at the box office.

Ever since Columbia's profitable THE JOLSON STORY (1946) and JOLSON SINGS AGAIN (1949), Hollywood had been in a cycle of screen biographies of show business legends. Warner Bros. induced Cantor to appear as himself in the uninspired THE STORY OF WILL ROGERS (1952), starring the late legend's lookalike son. The next year, the studio paid Cantor a reported $1 million (over a ten-year period) for the rights to make THE EDDIE CANTOR STORY. The unimaginative biography featured Keefe Brasselle as the legendary star with Cantor dubbing the singing. Eddie, along with his wife, Ida, appeared in a brief epilogue to the picture, in which, having just seen a screening of the film, he turns to the movie audience and says, "I never looked better!"

Milton Berle may have been dubbed "The King of Television," but many other ex-vaudeville and burlesque stars became mainstays of the new medium as well—including Eddie Cantor. "I didn't jump into TV," he would explain, "I waited until 1950, the year five million more television sets were sold. . . . After all, Cantor likes to play to full houses." He had a four-year engagement (1950–54) as one of the revolving hosts of the popular NBC network variety show "The Colgate Comedy Hour." It afforded him ample opportunity to dust off many of his old routines and to sing all of the songs that had become associated with him throughout his lengthy show business career. It was, as the *New York Times's* Jack Gould termed it, "a sort of Cavalcade of Cantor." In 1955 he hosted the Ziv Television Programs Company's syndicated half-hour show "The Eddie Cantor Comedy Theatre," performing sketches and songs in some of the offerings. In one of his rare dramatic appearances on TV, he starred with Farley Granger on CBS's "Playhouse 90" (October 18, 1956) in "Seidman and Son."

Cantor's final stage appearances were at New York's Carnegie Hall on March 21 and September 30, 1950, in *My Forty Years in Show Business* and in 1951 and 1952 with *An Evening with Eddie Cantor*. As a show business luminary, he received a constant flood of testimonials and awards. On January 31, 1952, the State of Israel Bond Committee hosted a gala Eddie Cantor Sixtieth Birthday Party in the grand ballroom of New York's Hotel Commodore, at which 1,800 guests honored his remarkable efforts in selling $60 million worth of bonds for Israel. He dealt with the event in his published booklet *I'm Glad I Spent Those Sixty Years*. (Previously he had written, among other books, *My Life Is in Your Hands*, 1928; and *Take My Life*, 1957.) At the 1956 Academy Awards he was given a special honorary Oscar for his distinguished service to the film industry, including his work as head of the Screen Actors Guild. (He had been a founder of Actors' Equity and the American Federation of Radio Artists [later: AFTRA].)

Eddie and Ida Cantor celebrated their thirty-ninth wedding anniversary on national TV on Sunday, June 7, 1953, reenacting their marriage vows. Cantor's protégée Dinah Shore served as matron of honor, with Jack Benny, Ralph Edwards, and George Jessel as ushers. In August of 1962, two years before their golden anniversary, Ida died of a heart attack. This, combined with the earlier death (1959) of daughter Marjorie, took its toll on Cantor, who had first been stricken with a heart ailment himself in September 1952.

The State of Israel awarded Cantor the Medallion of Valor in 1962 for his many "extraordinary achievements" on behalf of that country and in 1964 he was given the U.S. Service Medal from President Lyndon Johnson for his devotion to the United States and to humanity (he was the creator of the March of Dimes charity).

On October 10, 1964, seventy-two-year-old Eddie Cantor died of a sudden coronary occlusion at his Beverly Hills home. What this energetic and beloved comedian once said of his career as a funster personified him as an entertainer: "Laughter is the world's oxygen tank."

## Filmography

Widow at the Races (Edison, 1911) (s)
Short Subject (DeForrest Photofilm Company, 1925) (s)
Kid Boots (Par, 1926)
The Speed Hound (Bray Studios, 1927) (s)
Special Delivery (Par, 1927)
Glorifying the American Girl (Par, 1929)
Midnite Frolics (Par, 1929) (s)
That Party in Person (Par, 1929) (s)
Whoopee! (UA, 1930)
The Cockeyed News #1 (Par, 1930) (s)
Getting a Ticket (Par, 1930) (s)
Insurance (Par, 1930) (s)
Palmy Days (UA, 1931) (also co-script, co-song)
The Kid from Spain (UA, 1932)

Roman Scandals (UA, 1933)
Kid Millions (UA, 1934)
Hollywood Cavalcade (Unk, 1934) (s)
Screen Snapshots #11 (Col, 1934) (s)
Strike Me Pink (UA, 1936)
Ali Baba Goes to Town (20th–Fox, 1937)
Forty Little Mothers (MGM, 1940)
Thank Your Lucky Stars (WB, 1943)
Hollywood Canteen (WB, 1944)
Show Business (RKO, 1944) (also producer)
Screen Snapshots #10 (Col, 1946) (s)
If You Knew Susie (RKO, 1948) (also producer)
The Story of Will Rogers (WB, 1952)
The Eddie Cantor Story (WB, 1953)

## Broadway Plays

The Ziegfeld Follies (1917)
The Ziegfeld Follies (1918)
The Ziegfeld Follies (1919)
Broadway Brevities of 1920 (1920)
Make It Snappy (1922)

Kid Boots (1923)
The Ziegfeld Follies (1927)
Whoopee! (1928)
Banjo Eyes (1941)
Nellie Bly (1945) (producer only)

## Radio Series

The Eddie Cantor Show (NBC, 1931–38; CBS, 1938–39; NBC, 1940–49, 1951–54)

## TV Series

The Colgate Comedy Hour (NBC, 1950–54)
The Eddie Cantor Comedy Theatre (Synd, 1955)

## Album Discography

The Best of Eddie Cantor (Vik LX-1119, Camden CAL/CAS-531)
A Date with Eddie Cantor—The Carnegie Hall Concert (Audio Fidelity 702)
The Eddie Cantor Album (Top Ten 5)
Eddie Cantor on the Silver Screen, 1934–35 (Sandy Hook 2039)
The Eddie Cantor Show, Vols. 1–2 (Memorabilia 702-03)
Eddie Cantor Sings (10" Decca DL-5504)
Eddie Cantor Sings Ida, Sweet as Apple Cider (Camden CAL/CAS-870)
The Eddie Cantor Story (10" Cap L-467) [ST]
Harry Richman and Eddie Cantor Live (Amalgamated 127)
Hollywood Canteen (Curtain Calls 100/11-12) [ST]
Immortals: Al Jolson and Eddie Cantor (Epic LN-1128)
Jimmy Durante/Eddie Cantor Sings (Ace of Hearts 25)

Kid Millions/Roman Scandals (CIF 3007) [ST]
The Legends of Al Jolson, Jimmy Durante and Eddie Cantor (Ambassador Artists 1003-3)
The Living Legend (Show Biz 1004)
Memories (MCA 1506)
Ol' Banjo Eyes Is Back (Pelican 134)
Rare Early Recordings, 1919–21 (Biograph 12054)
Show Business (Caliban 6034) [ST]
Songs He Made Famous (Decca DL-4431)
Thank Your Lucky Stars (Curtain Calls 100/8) [ST]
Tweedle De Dee and Tweedle De Dum (Heidi Ho 5501)
Whoopee! (Smithsonian 0349, Meet Patti 1930) [ST]
The Ziegfeld Follies of 1919 (Smithsonian R009/P14272) [OC]

# DIAHANN CARROLL

THERE HAS LONG BEEN A GILT-EDGED QUALITY ABOUT SHOW BUSINESS veteran Diahann Carroll, even years before she gained renewed popularity as the chic bitch Dominique Devereaux on TV's "Dynasty." For years, whether singing on Broadway, in clubs, or on the air, this svelte 5' 6" entertainer came across as an aloof, sophisticated chanteuse. She always seemed more comfortable interpreting old standards than performing contemporary pop or rock music. Like Lena Horne, she is a superior technician. But also like that performer, her mixed reactions to becoming a leading black star (and role model) in the white world of show business, caused her to erect an invisible shield between herself and audiences. (Both dropped the protection, to varying degrees, as they reached middle-age.)

The multi-talented Diahann Carroll, long noted for her elegant living style, can also be quite outspoken. When, in the 1960s, she became the first black actress to star in a major TV sitcom, "Julia," she used her position to speak out against racial inequity. She was quite direct in assessing her token status in the "new" Hollywood. Today, far removed from her unclassy childhood, she is a leading cabaret attraction, teamed with her long-time friend and, more recently, husband, singer Vic Damone.

She was born Carol Diahann Johnson on July 17, 1935, in the Bronx, New York. She was the older daughter of subway conductor John Johnson and his wife, Mabel, a nurse. There would be a younger sister, Lydia. As a child she was musically inclined and by the age of six was performing in school plays. As a child she became a member of the Tiny Tots choir at Adam Clayton Powell's Abyssinian Baptist Church. She was ten years old when she won a music scholarship from the Metropolitan Opera, but she abandoned the singing lessons because they interfered with her being a normal little girl on her ghetto block. She went to Public School 46 and to a local junior high (which she has referred to as "my own blackboard jungle"). However, the High School of Music and Art was "a wonderful, beautiful oasis." When she was fifteen, she began a career modeling clothes for Johnson Publications, which distributed black-oriented magazines. She also made an appearance on "Arthur Godfrey's Talent Scouts" (CBS-TV) and was heard on the radio version as well.

To appease her parents, who wanted her to attend Howard University, she enrolled at New York University, planning to become a psychiatric social worker. However, she continued her singing and dancing lessons—and modeling—while attending school. She understood that show business could open doors and offer a new lifestyle for her in racially segregated America. But this realization caused intellectual friction within her. She knew her career path would separate her from her ethnic roots. "The conflict first took the form of music. The music we all listened and danced to, rhythm and blues . . . I never sang that kind of music. I never had a jazz feeling, a blues feeling, and I still don't. I had a very strong resistance to that kind of music because it was racial. I saw the other kind, my kind, as a move to *assimilation*." To balance her growing attraction to the mainstream, she became a modest spokeswoman for black causes, allying herself with SNICK (Student Nonviolent Coordinating Committee). Later in her career, she would testify before a U.S. Congressional hearing that she was proof of discrimination in America and in show business.

While still a college freshman she auditioned for Lou Walters' all-black revue *Jazz Train*, but the show never came to be. However, Walters (father of TV interviewer Barbara) got her an audition for Dennis James's talent show "Chance of a Lifetime" (ABC-TV). She won three weeks in a row, earning $1,000 in prize money. By now she was known professionally as Diahann Carroll. She quit college, promising her parents that if she did not become a successful entertainer within two years, she would return to the university. Walters booked her into the Latin Quarter, where, despite an extreme case of stage fright, she was successful. Later he negotiated for her to sing at Ciro's and The Cloister in Los Angeles, and got her club dates in Chicago, Miami, Philadelphia, Paris, and at New York's Persian Room (Plaza Hotel) and the Waldorf-Astoria Hotel.

Her film debut came in CARMEN JONES (1954), the all-black version of Bizet's opera *Carmen* as adapted by Oscar Hammerstein II. On film, as in the 1943 Broadway version, the characters were one-dimensional. Making the movie even more artificial were director Otto Preminger's heavy-handed touches. Because he demanded a certain look and yet a different sound, most of the main players (including Dorothy Dandridge, Harry Belafonte, and Joe Adams), but excluding Pearl Bailey, had their voices dubbed. Bernice Peterson provided the singing voice for Diahann's character of Myrt. Diahann recalls that as one of her costumes she was given a hand-me-down red fringed gown once worn on screen by Bonita Granville. It was not an auspicious screen beginning for Carroll.

Much more successful was her Broadway bow. On December 30, 1954, at the Alvin Theatre, she joined Pearl Bailey, Juanita Hall, Ray Walston, and Frederick O'Neal in *House of Flowers*, a Harold Arlen–composed musical based on a Truman Capote story and set in the West Indies. As Ottilie, the innocent bordello girl, she sang such numbers as "House of Flowers" and "A Sleepin' Bee" and earned a warm critical reception, despite the show's mixed reviews. The *New York Herald-Tribune* judged her "a plaintive and extraordinarily appealing ingenue." While the show lasted only 165 performances, she had made a favorable debut both on stage and on the original cast album released by Columbia Records. She returned to club work and began making guest appearances on TV variety shows both in the U.S. ("The Red Skelton Show," "The Jack Paar Show," "The Steve Allen Show") and abroad. In September 1956 Diahann married Monte Kay, the white casting director of *House of Flowers* who later became manager for the Modern Jazz Quartet, other jazz musicians, and then Flip Wilson. Their daughter, Suzanne Patricia Ottilie, would be born in 1961. Meanwhile, on September 27, 1957, Diahann, along with Louis Armstrong, Peggy Lee, Ethel Merman, Carol Channing, and others, was featured on the

Rex Harrison TV special "Crescendo" (CBS-TV).

Composer Richard Rodgers had been delighted with Diahann's abilities in *House of Flowers* and had promised her that he would create a role for her in one of his next Broadway shows. He attempted to cast her in *Flower Drum Song* (1958), but no matter what makeup and costuming effects they tried, she did not look Oriental. They abandoned the effort. Thereafter, for producer Samuel Goldwyn, Diahann return to moviemaking in PORGY AND BESS (1959), based on the classic Broadway operetta with songs by George and Ira Gershwin and DuBose Heyward. The film was plagued with problems ranging from the July 1958 studio fire which razed all the sets to the firing of director Rouben Mamoulian and the hiring of Otto Preminger. The cast included several holdovers from CARMEN JONES, with Dorothy Dandridge as Bess and Pearl Bailey as Maria, and Sidney Poitier as Porgy and Sammy Davis, Jr. as Sportin' Life. The story was set in the early 1900s on Catfish Row in Charleston, and Diahann played Clara, the wife of a fisherman who is lost at sea. Once again, the decision was made to dub the singing of many of the film's leads, from Poitier to Dandridge to Carroll. Despite Diahann's reputation as a songstress, her vocal range was deemed too low to handle the character's big number, "Summertime." Thus Caucasian soprano Loulie Jean Norman provided her singing voice. PORGY AND BESS, which cost over $6 million to make, met with lukewarm reviews and did not recoup its costs. Although Diahann did not sing on the soundtrack album, she later recorded a United Artists LP on which she sang *Porgy and Bess* numbers, backed by the André Previn Trio.

It was during the making of PORGY AND BESS that Diahann and Sidney Poitier, both married, began an affair which lasted off and on for nine years. In his autobiography, *This Life* (1980), Poitier describes Diahann as "an independent woman who shifted emotional gears quickly." When their relationship finally terminated, Poitier wrote, "Regrets? Yes, I'll have a few." Diahann would comment of her famous beau, "I think he felt confounded by what actually happened. Unfortunately, there's no way for me to be confounded." Carroll's marriage to Monte Kay, who was informed about the affair by Diahann, ended in divorce in 1963. (He died of a heart attack in May 1988 at the age of sixty-three.)

In 1961 Sidney Poitier joined with Paul Newman in making PARIS BLUES, a study of two jazz musician expatriates living in post–World War II Paris. Saxophonist Poitier falls in love with American tourist Diahann, as Newman does with Carroll's pal Joanne Woodward. Before the conclusion of this somber romantic film, Diahann convinces Poitier to return to the United States to marry her and to confront the racial bigotry which drove him away originally. The Duke Ellington score and Louis Armstrong's exuberant if brief appearance playing jazz received better notices than the actors. While on location in Paris for this feature, Diahann made a cameo appearance in another United Artists release, GOODBYE AGAIN (1961). She was the chic club chanteuse attracted to Anthony Perkins and she sang "Say No More, It's Goodbye" and "Love Is Just a Word."

According to Diahann it was seeing her guest appearance on a "Jack Paar Show" in 1961 that led Richard Rodgers to remember his original promise to build a show around

Carroll. When they lunched and talked about the project, she suggested doing a musical in which the leading character, a black woman, falls in love with a white man, and they play through the usual boy-girl situations without skin color's being a stated problem. Thus came about *No Strings*, which opened at the 54th Street Theatre in New York on March 15, 1962. The story was set in Paris, and she played Barbara Woodruff, a high fashion model who falls in love with an ambivalent Pulitzer Prize–winning novelist (Richard Kiley) from Maine. What made the intimate show special was not Samuel Taylor's mundane book, but the staging, which established the musicians behind a scrim curtain upstage (sometimes they strolled into the action), and the personal messages of the touching songs. The *New York Times* said of the star, "Miss Carroll brings glowing personal beauty to the role of the model, and her singing captures many moods." Critics were quick to notice the special attention she gave to interpreting the lyrics (a trademark quality of her showmanship). "To do justice to a song," she explained, "a singer should have a feeling for dramatic interpretation as well as an ear for musical sound. You must be able to create a mood, to make the audience feel that the words have meaning to the singer. . . ." The show lasted 580 performances. For Diahann, who had already been named Entertainer of the Year in the late 1950s as a club singer, it brought new tributes. She won a Tony Award.

After *No Strings*, which was mentioned for some time as a possible film project for Frank Sinatra (and maybe Diahann), she returned to club work and to television guesting.

She made several dramatic appearances on the small screen, on "Peter Gunn" (NBC-TV, March 7, 1960) and "Eleventh Hour" (NBC-TV, October 23, 1963). For her performance on the "A Horse Has a Big-Head—Let Him Worry" segment of "Naked City" (ABC-TV, November 21, 1962) she was Emmy-nominated. On "ABC Stage '67" she was in "A Time for Laughter" (April 6, 1967), a review of black humor in America that co-starred Harry Belafonte, Sidney Poitier, Redd Foxx, Richard Pryor, and others. She returned to Hollywood to appear in Otto Preminger's tasteless, steamy tale of the contemporary South, HURRY SUNDOWN (1967). Carroll was the prim Georgia schoolmarm who helps fellow black Robert Hooks to prove his ownership of a piece of property

Diahann Carroll in PARIS BLUES (1961)

coveted by grasping, bigoted Michael Caine. The movie was specious trash, more noted for the disturbing acts of racism by Louisiana locals during the filming and for co-star Jane Fonda's fondling of a saxophone in one of the picture's more lurid moments. The next year she and The 5th Dimension were Sinatra's guests on his special "Francis Albert Sinatra Does His Thing" (CBS-TV, November 25, 1968). Also during that year Diahann co-starred with Jim Brown (the ex-football player turned movie-hunk-of-the-year) in a robbery caper called THE SPLIT, one of the first black action pictures. She played the ex-wife of ex-convict Brown who is killed by her lust-driven landlord (James Whitmore). It was an earthy role for the songstress.

In a mid-1960s article about frequent television guest artist Diahann Carroll, TV Guide reported, "She is Negro first and Diahann Carroll second." This individuality-numbing description of the singer was certainly not unusual for a black performer—then or even now. However, it reflected Carroll's continual struggle between being regarded as a voice for her people and being thought of as a talented vocalist who just happened to be black. The conflict was not eased when she was cast in a TV sitcom to play Julia Baker, the twenty-six-year-old widow of an Air Force captain killed in Vietnam. As a nurse, she attempts to make a new life for herself and her six-year-old son. Produced by 20th Century–Fox, "Julia" debuted on September 24, 1968. The program was highly touted as "a new experience in television," the first weekly series built around a contemporary black character. During its popular three-season run, Carroll existed in a no-person's land: criticized by many in the black community for not reflecting black life accurately, and yet discriminated against by whites for daring to be a success in their world. Trying to balance these ironies, she told the press candidly, "The moneyed people, the managers, know they can deal with me. I'm 'acceptable.' In fact I'm sure that's why I got the part of Julia. I'm a black woman with a white image. I'm as close as they can get to having the best of both worlds. The audience can accept me in the same way, and for the same reason. I don't scare them."

In 1970 Diahann was dating black actor Don Marshall (of "Land of the Giants") and was on the international best-dressed list for the second time. She continued playing the cabaret circuit globally and was the star of "The Diahann Carroll Show" (NBC-TV, April 5, 1971) in which her guest stars were Harry Belafonte, Tom Jones, and Donald Sutherland. For two years in the early 1970s she dated British show business figure David Frost and then, in 1973, married Las Vegas businessman Freddie Glusman. She described her three-month marriage as "another mistake." She then had her best feature film role to date, in 20th Century–Fox's CLAUDINE (1974). She played a down-to-earth single mother of six children trying to keep everything going in her working-class environment. She is romanced by robust garbage collector James Earl Jones who eventually overcomes his fear of a long-term commitment. Coming in the midst of the blaxploitation craze, CLAUDINE was praised for its range of wholesome, respectful, and loving characters. Diahann was Oscar-nominated, but lost the Best Actress Award to Ellen Burstyn (of ALICE DOESN'T LIVE HERE ANYMORE).

In 1975, Diahann married Robert DeLeon, managing editor of *Jet* magazine. (In retrospect she assessed, "I set about finding a relationship that would punish me for being successful.") She was forty; he was twenty-four. Because he had business interests in Oakland, they moved there. The marriage was stormy and depleted much of her savings. Meanwhile, with her career taking a back seat to her personal life, she appeared in the telefeature DEATH SCREAM (ABC, September 26, 1975) as Betty May, one of fifteen neighbors who witness a young woman's murder. She had a four-week variety series on CBS-TV, "The Diahann Carroll Show," an hour-long program which debuted on August 14, 1976. She allowed her husband to produce the series; his inexperience, she says, caused the shows to be an embarrassment. DeLeon died in an auto crash on Mulholland Drive in Los Angeles in March 1977. As therapy after his death, she co-starred with Cleavon Little in June 1977 in the comedy *Same Time, Next Year* at the Huntington Hartford Theatre in Los Angeles.

The next few years found Diahann Carroll at a low ebb. She admits the industry had come to regard her as risky, believing she had not taken her career seriously enough during the 1970s. Producers were unwilling to take a chance on her; besides, she was over forty. She was on the February 23, 1979, segment of the mini-series "Roots: The Next Generations" (ABC-TV) playing Zeona, the wife of Simon Haley (Dorian Harewood). In the telefeature I KNOW WHY THE CAGED BIRD SINGS (CBS, April 28, 1979) she joined with Ruby Dee, Roger E. Mosley, Paul Benjamin, Esther Rolle, and Madge Sinclair in an eloquent study of a gifted youngster (Constance Good) growing up in the 1930s South. Diahann had appeared on several Bob Hope television specials, and in September 1980 she played with him in a concert opening the new Amphitheatre at Universal Studios in California. She credits Hope as one of the few to take a chance on her when she needed it. John Berry had already directed Carroll in CLAUDINE, and in 1979 he cast her in the telefeature SISTER, SISTER, filmed largely in Montgomery, Alabama. It was not shown on NBC until June 7, 1982. Diahann was one of three sisters (with Rosalind Cash and Irene Cara) who reunite to sell the family home. She was the inflexible spinster loved by local club owner Paul Winfield. For a week in the fall of 1982 she replaced Elizabeth Ashley as Dr. Livingston in the Broadway drama *Agnes of God*. It was a rewarding dramatic stretch for Carroll. Because she thrived on the New York lifestyle, she moved back to Manhattan.

Not since "Julia" had Diahann Carroll enjoyed so much professional exposure as she did in her next stint, portraying the velvet vixen, Dominique Devereaux. She first showed up on the "New Lady in Town" segment (ABC-TV, May 2, 1984) of "Dynasty." In future installments of this plush prime-time soap opera, it was revealed that her character, a black singer who had arrived in Denver with her record mogul husband (Billy Dee Williams), was actually the illegitimate half sister of patriarch Blake Harrington (John Forsythe). She remained with the hit series until 1987 and also made crossover appearances in late 1985 and early 1986, again as the scheming Dominique, on the spinoff series, "The Colbys" (ABC).

In 1980 Carroll had been commissioned to write her memoirs, but it was not until 1986 that *Diahann!*, written with Ross Firestone, appeared. She confessed to problems in preparing the book: "It has meant digging up a lot of painful things as part of the process of trying to tell the truth about my life, its struggles and what it's been like as a single working woman raising a child." *People* magazine called it "a spicy read" and the trade journal *Publishers Weekly* judged it "engrossing and frank." She dedicated her autobiography "To my mother, Mabel, and my daughter, Suzanne. From where it came, to where it is going." In 1989 she turned up as the mother of one of the college girls on the "Different World" (NBC-TV) series, and in the two-part Grand Guignol suspense telefeature, FROM THE DEAD OF NIGHT (NBC, February 27–28, 1989), starring Lindsay Wagner. She was Maggie, who runs the fashion house in which Lindsay Wagner is the chief designer.

Diahann and singer Vic Damone had met several years earlier, but it was in 1984 that she and the singer renewed their acquaintance while performing in a Palm Springs show. They were married on January 3, 1987, in Las Vegas and since then have been performing together frequently in a cabaret show throughout the country. He continues to record, and has tried to persuade her to do likewise. However, she insists, "I've always considered myself primarily a visual artist. I just don't like to listen to my records." Of marriage the fourth time around (for both of them) she says, "This business of learning how to be married is taking up a great deal of my time; no one told me that. Once I learn how to handle it, without feeling like I'm juggling five balls at the same time, I'd like to move toward producing." Regarding her next career move, she says, "I want to do the 1990 version of KLUTE [a 1971 movie with Jane Fonda]. I want something to test me, to make me want to jump out of bed in the morning."

## Filmography

Carmen Jones (20th–Fox, 1954)
Porgy and Bess (UA, 1959)
Goodbye Again (UA, 1961)
Paris Blues (UA, 1961)
Hurry Sundown (Par, 1967)
The Split (MGM, 1968)
Claudine (20th–Fox, 1974)

Death Scream [The Woman Who Cried Murder] (ABC-TV, 9/26/75)
I Know Why the Caged Bird Sings (CBS-TV, 4/28/79)
Sister, Sister (NBC-TV, 6/7/82)
From the Dead of Night (NBC-TV, 2/27/89–2/28/89)

## Broadway Plays

House of Flowers (1954)
No Strings (1962)

Agnes of God (1982) (replacement)

## TV Series

Julia (NBC, 1968–71)
The Diahann Carroll Show (CBS, 1976)

Roots: The Next Generation (ABC, 1979) (miniseries)
Dynasty (ABC, 1984–87)

## Album Discography

"A" You're Adorable (Disque 398-2)

Best Beat Forward (Vik LX-1131)

Cole Porter in Paris (Bell Telephone 36508)
[ST/TV]

Diahann Carroll (Har HS-11347)

Diahann Carroll (Motown 805)

Diahann Carroll Accompanied by the André
Previn Trio (Sunset 5293)

Diahann Carroll and André Previn (UA 6069)

The Fabulous Diahann Carroll (UA UAL-3229/
UAS-6229)

Fun Life (Atlantic 8048)

Goodbye Again (UA UAL-4091/UAS-5091)
[ST]

Harold Arlen Songs (RCA LPM-1467)

House of Flowers (Col OL-4969/OC-2320)
[OC]

Love Songs for Children (Golden 141)

No Strings (Cap O/SO-1695) [OC]

Nobody Sees Me Cry (Col CL-2571/CS-9371)

The Persian Room Presents Diahann Carroll
(UA 6080)

Porgy and Bess (UA UAL-4021/UAS-5021)

Showstopper! (Camden CAL/CAS-695)

# JOHNNY CASH

ONE OF THE LEGENDS OF COUNTRY MUSIC, DEEP-VOICED JOHNNY Cash has had sustained popularity for more than three and a half decades and a successful career that has encompassed not only music but also films and television. The composer of scores of country songs, Cash has also delved into movie production with his self-conceived religious feature GOSPEL ROAD (1973). To many, this famous man in black is the epitome of a country music star. Ironically, Cash is held in higher regard by non-country fans than by followers of this type of music. Around 1970, when Cash's national popularity was at its height due to his ABC-TV program and several top-selling singles and LPs, a poll was taken in the Nashville area to determine the most popular country music performer. The winner was Marty Robbins, not Johnny Cash. When Cash was inducted into the Country Music Hall of Fame in 1980, there was some grumbling around Nashville that many pioneer country performers had been overlooked in favor of Cash. He has been somewhat resented in Music City due to his association with country rock and the "Country Jesus" crowds. Still, Johnny Cash's accomplishments have been many; in 1969, for example, he was the first performer to receive six awards from the Country Music Association. Although he has participated in various capacities in more than a dozen feature films, acting is certainly one of the least of his many abilities.

Born John R. Cash in Kingsland, Arkansas, he was the son of poor cotton share-croppers, Ray and Carrie Cash. With his brothers and sisters Cash worked in the fields when he was old enough, but he was also attracted to music, especially the country sounds he heard over the radio (the only form of entertainment available to the family). When he was three the family moved to the Dyess Colony, a government resettlement community, and by 1940 the Cash family included seven children with the birth of son Tom (who as Tommy Cash later became a popular country singer).

As a boy Johnny Cash started writing poems and songs and in high school he sang over a local radio station while his older brother Roy Cash formed a band called The Delta Rhythm Ramblers. Cash graduated from high school in 1950 and moved to Detroit to work in an auto plant. He also took other manual labor jobs before enlisting in the Air Force that summer and spending the next four years in West Germany. While in the military, Cash learned to play the guitar and he composed a number of songs. In 1954, after leaving the Air Force as a staff sergeant, Cash wed Vivian Liberto (who was part Italian; in later years, she was branded a mulatto by the Ku Klux Klan, who boycotted Cash's performances) and they moved to Memphis where he sold electrical appliances. In Memphis, Cash met musicians Luther Perkins (guitar) and Marshall Grant (bass), and along with brother Roy Cash, the four began performing together, mostly Hank Snow songs and religious numbers. This led to some unpaid radio work and an audition for Sam Phillips, who had just launched Elvis Presley, at Sun Records.

Signing with Sun Records proved to be the professional launching pad for Johnny Cash and The Tennessee Two (made up of Luther Perkins and Marshall Grant). Their first single, Cash's compositions of "Cry, Cry, Cry"/"Hey Porter," sold well and was followed by the even more popular "Folsom Prison Blues" and the gold disc "I Walk the Line." Thereafter Cash had a string of best-sellers, becoming Sun's most popular recording star, and he began his round of seemingly endless one-night stands. He also became a regular on "Louisiana Hayride" in 1955 and the "Grand Ole Opry" in 1957. Next, Hollywood called and Johnny Cash starred in his first feature film, FIVE MINUTES TO LIVE, a poverty-row effort for Sutton Pictures which was filmed in 1958 but not issued until 1961. In it Cash was a third-rate country singer who joins a gang of crooks in abducting a woman (Cay Forester) in order to get ransom money from her rich husband (Donald Woods). In the feature, Cash sang the title song and "I've Come to Kill," both of which he co-composed with Gene Kauer. In the mid-1960s new footage was added to this exploitation thriller (by this time Cash had lost so much weight due to amphetamine addiction that the new footage did not match the old) and American International reissued it as DOOR-TO-DOOR MANIAC in 1966.

Next, Cash and his group successfully toured Australia and Canada, and in 1958, they switched to the Columbia label, where Cash would remain for three decades. His singles and albums for the company sold well and he did a number of theme LPs for the label like the pro-Indian *Bitter Tears*, his narration of the "Grand Canyon Suite" with André Kostelanetz, and a tribute to the railroad, *Ride This Train*. By 1960 drummer W. S. Holland had been added to his backup group, now called The Tennessee Three, and they began playing clubs in addition to some three hundred one-nighters each year. The grind of constant travel became so great that Cash began using prescription drugs to keep going and, within a few years, he was hopelessly addicted to pills. In 1961 June Carter joined the Cash troupe and the next year his heavy schedule included a month in Korea and a failed Carnegie Hall concert. He also starred in the Western featurette THE NIGHT RIDER (1962) with Eddie Dean, Merle Travis, Johnny Western, and Gordon Terry, the latter two often a part of his touring shows.

In 1963 he performed in the undistinguished low-budget MGM feature HOOTE-NANNY HOOT, directed by ex-dancer/singer Gene Nelson and also featuring Sheb Wooley and The Brothers Four. Cash expanded his musical horizons by appearing with Bob Dylan at the Newport Folk Festival in 1964, but by the next year Cash was in trouble with the law. He received a suspended sentence and a fine for narcotics violations and in 1965 he was arrested in Georgia for carrying illegal drugs. When Carl Perkins (who had problems with alcohol and with whom Cash had toured along with Elvis Presley in 1954 when all three were on the Sun label) joined his troupe in 1966, both Cash and Perkins agreed to seek medical help for their addictions. Cash was able to kick his pill habit and resume his career, but his wife, Vivian, divorced him in 1966; they had two daughters, one of whom,

Rosanne, later toured with her dad and then became a country star in her own right in the 1970s.

Despite his health problems, Johnny Cash continued to have hit records for Columbia like "Ring of Fire," "The Ballad of Ira Hayes," "I Got Stripes," "In the Jailhouse Now," "It Ain't Me, Babe," and "Understand Your Man." From 1959 to 1962 Cash was heard singing the title theme, "The Ballad of Johnny Yuma" (also a hit for him on record), for the ABC-TV series "The Rebel" and early in 1960 he guest-starred in a segment of that series, followed by an appearance on NBC-TV's "The Deputy" in 1961. In 1967 Johnny Cash and June Carter won a Grammy for their duet on the song "Jackson" and the next year (March 1968) they were married. (June daughter's Carlene, by a previous marriage to country singer Carl Smith, would also have a singing career.)

Following highly successful albums recorded during his group's appearances at Folsom Prison in 1968 and at San Quentin Prison in 1969, the singer came to national television with the very popular "The Johnny Cash Show" on ABC-TV, which ran from 1969 to 1971. As a result of the popularity of the program, he was the subject of the documentary film JOHNNY CASH! THE MAN, HIS WORLD, HIS MUSIC (1969). (He had

The Brothers Four, Johnny Cash (center), and Pam Austin
in HOOTENANNY HOOT (1963)

"HOOTENANNY HOOT"
M-G-M presents a Four-Leaf Production

appeared briefly in the 1966 country music feature THE ROAD TO NASHVILLE singing "I Walk the Line.") In 1970 he appeared on the "NET Playhouse" production of "The Trail of Tears" and had a guest shot on the ABC-TV series "The Partridge Family." For his first major Hollywood film Cash was cast as an old-time gunman who agrees to shoot it out with a rival (Kirk Douglas), with an admission charged for the deadly event, in A GUNFIGHT (1971). The less said about Cash's performance the better.

Following the demise of his teleseries in 1971, Cash resumed his heavy touring schedule, although by now he and his wife had a son, John Carter Cash, to care for. Besides the Tennessee Three, Carl Perkins, and Gordon Terry, the package tour group with Cash included not only his wife but also her mother, Maybelle Carter, and her sisters Anita and Helen—all of whom had worked with Cash since the early 1960s and had performed on his TV variety show. In 1970 Cash provided the songs and sang many of them on the soundtracks of the features I WALK THE LINE and LITTLE FAUSS AND BIG HALSY, and he began performing at Billy Graham religious crusades.

A visit to the Holy Land in 1972 resulted in the feature film THE GOSPEL ROAD (1973), the script of which Cash co-wrote. In addition, he co-produced the movie with his wife (who played Mary Magdalene), sang its songs, and served as on-screen narrator. While this motion picture was a very personal statement on religion by the star, it did not do well in theaters and finished as a roadshow for church viewing.

Cash made a guest appearance on the network TV program "Columbo" in 1974 and starred in a well-regarded TV "documusical," "Ridin' the Rails—The Great American Train Story," for which he wrote songs. He was a guest on the TV series "Little House on the Prairie" in 1976 and that year he came back with four episodes of the CBS-TV music show "Johnny Cash and Friends."

By the mid-1970s, however, Cash's records were no longer selling well, except for an occasional duet with more currently popular sellers like Waylon Jennings. Nevertheless, Cash was much in evidence, appearing with frequency on his own TV specials (usually celebrating Christmas and always with June and other members of his entourage), in addition to his regular touring schedule. In 1978, Cash and Bo Hopkins played two vagabonds in the CBS telefeature THADDEUS ROSE AND EDDIE, in which June Carter Cash also appeared. It was the first of several made-for-television features he has done to date. He hosted the ninety-minute CBS-TV special (May 8, 1980) "Johnny Cash: The First 25 Years," a salute to his twenty-five years in show business. In 1981, after a London concert (later released on videocassette), he starred as an illiterate who wants an education in THE PRIDE OF JESSE HALLAN for CBS-TV with Cash and his wife singing the telefeature's songs. MURDER IN COWETA COUNTY, for CBS-TV in 1983, offered Cash the part of a stubborn southern lawman determined to prove a murder charge against a powerful businessman (Andy Griffith), with June cast as an eccentric soothsayer. THE BARON AND THE KID (1984) for the same network showcased Cash as a pool hustler who meets the son (Greg Webb) he has never known; the TV movie provided the star with a moderate record seller, "The Baron." Health problems arose for Cash again in 1984 when ulcer surgery led to problems with morphine. Again overcoming a near drug addiction, he resumed his career activities. It was also in 1984 that the documentary videocassette *The Other Side of Nashville* was issued by MGM-UA. The 118-minute tape contained old performance clips and interviews with Johnny Cash, Kris Kristofferson, Chet Atkins, Carl Perkins, Willie Nelson, Hank Williams, Jr., and others.

In 1986 Cash, by now very portly and leather-faced, starred in two TV Western features, THE LAST DAYS OF FRANK AND JESSE JAMES and STAGECOACH. In the former he was Frank James to Kris Kristofferson's Jesse, while June Carter Cash portrayed their mother! In the third feature-length version of STAGECOACH, Cash was the least impressive of a bevy of country singers (Willie Nelson, Kris Kristofferson, Waylon Jennings, John Schneider) in dramatic roles; Cash played a lawman while wife June and son John had brief assignments as waystation owners. In 1988 Cash appeared as Davy Crockett in the NBC Disney telefilm RAINBOW IN THE THUNDER. That year he also participated in the Rob Lowe comedy feature ILLEGALLY YOURS, which was so poorly received it was not released theatrically but was distributed directly to video stores. *Daily Variety* noted, "Johnny Cash warbles several nothing songs (co-written by [director Peter] Bogdanovich) over the action." He also resumed acting in feature films in 1988 with a part in TENNESSEE WALTZ, set for late 1989 release.

Late in 1988 Johnny Cash blacked out while en route to Bristol, Virginia, for a charity concert. He was diagnosed as having a blocked heart artery. He underwent successful surgery, but complications sidelined him for several weeks. Ironically, his country singer friend Roy Orbison had died of a heart attack just a few days before and Waylon Jennings (a one-time roommate of Cash in Nashville in the 1960s), who was also on the Bristol bill, had undergone surgery after suffering a heart attack en route to the same concert. After a long recuperation, Cash resumed his activities, saying, "It's a wonderful life and I'm not going to miss a second of it. I want to enjoy every precious moment with my family."

## Filmography

Five Minutes to Live [Door-to-Door Maniac] (Sutton Pictures/Astor Pictures/AIP, 1961) (also co-songs)

The Night Rider (Parallel, 1962) (s)

Hootenanny Hoot (MGM, 1963)

The Sons of Katie Elder (Par, 1965) (voice only)

The Road to Nashville (Crown International, 1966)

Johnny Cash! The Man, His World, His Music (Continental, 1969)

Johnny Cash All-Star Extra (Road Show, 1969) (s)

I Walk the Line (Col, 1970) (voice, songs only)

Little Fauss and Big Halsy (Par, 1970) (voice, songs only)

A Gunfight (Par, 1971)

The Nashville Sound (John F. Bradford, 1972)

The Gospel Road (20th–Fox, 1973) (co-producer, co-script, co-songs, narrator only)

Thaddeus Rose and Eddie (CBS-TV, 2/24/78)

The Pride of Jesse Hallan (CBS-TV, 3/3/81)

Murder in Coweta County (CBS-TV, 2/15/83)

The Baron and the Kid (CBS-TV, 12/21/84)

The Last Days of Frank and Jesse James (NBC-TV, 2/16/86)

Stagecoach (CBS-TV, 5/18/86)

Illegally Yours (MGM/UA, 1988) (voice, co-songs only)

Rainbow in the Thunder (NBC-TV, 11/20/88)

Tennessee Waltz (Condor, 1989)

## Radio Series

Louisiana Hayride (Synd, 1955)
Grand Ole Opry (Synd, 1957)

## TV Series

The Johnny Cash Show (ABC, 1969–71)
Johnny Cash and Friends (CBS, 1976)

## Album Discography

Adventures of Johnny Cash (Col FC-38094)
All Aboard the Blue Train (Sun 1270)
America: A 200 Year Salute in Story and Song
  (Col KC-31645)
Any Old Wind That Blows (Col KC-32091)
Ballads of the American Indian (Har KH-32388)
Ballads of the True West (Col C2L-28/2CS-
  838, CBS Embassy 31520)
Baron (Col FC-37179)
Believe in Him (Word 8333)
A Believer Sings the Truth (Cachet CL3-9001,
  Priority 38074)
The Best of Johnny Cash (Trip 8500)
Big River (Hilltop 6118)
Biggest Hits (Col FC-38317)
Bitter Tears (Col CL-2248/CS-9048, Bear
  Family BFX-15127)
Blood, Sweat and Tears (Col CL-1930/CS-
  8730)
The Blue Train (Share 5002)
Carryin' on (Col CS-9528) w. June Carter
The Children's Album (Col C-32898)
Christmas Spirit (Col CS-8917)
Christmas with the Johnny Cash Family (Col C-
  31754)
The Class of '55 (Mer/Polygram 830-002-1) w.
  Jerry Lee Lewis, Carl Perkins, Roy Orbison
Classic Cash (Mer/Polygram 834-526-1)
Classic Christmas (Col JC-36866)
Columbia Records 1958–86 (Col C2-40637)
Country Classics (Col Special Products P-
  16915)
Country Gold (Power Pak 246)
Country's Round-Up (Hilltop 6010) w. Billy
  Grammer, The Wilburn Brothers

Encore (Col FC-37355)
Everlasting (Out of Town Distributors 8019)
Everybody Loves a Nut (Col CS-9292)
The Fabulous Johnny Cash (Col CL-1253/CS-
  8122)
The First Years (Allegiance 5017)
Five Feet High and Rising (Col CS-32951)
Folsom Prison Blues (Hilltop 5001)
Folsom Prison Blues (Share 6114)
Friend to Friend (Album Globe 2360) w.
  Jeannie C. Riley
From Sea to Shining Sea (Col CS-9447)
Get Rhythm (Sun 105)
Give My Love to Rose (Har KH-31256) w. June
  Carter
Golden Sounds of Country Music (Har HS-
  11249)
Gone Girl (Col KC-35646)
The Gospel Road (Col KG-32253, Priority
  32253) [ST]
Gospel Singer (Priority 38503)
Grand Canyon Suite (Col MS-7425) w. Andre
  Kostelanetz
Greatest! (Sun 1240)
Greatest Hits, Vols. 1–3 (Col CS-9478, PC-
  30887, KC-35637)
The Greatest Hits (Share 5003)
Happiness Is You (Col CS-9337)
The Heart of Johnny Cash (Col STS-2004)
Hello, I'm Johnny Cash (Col KCS-9943)
Heroes (Col 40327) w. Waylon Jennings
Highwayman (Col 40056) w. Willie Nelson,
  Waylon Jennings, Kris Kristofferson
The Holy Land (Col KCS-9766)
Hot and Blue Guitar (Charity CRM-2013)

Hot and Blue Guitar (Sun 1220)

Hymns by Johnny Cash (Col CL-1284/CS-8125)

Hymns from the Heart (Col CL-1722/CS-8522)

I Love Country (CBS 54938)

I Walk the Line (Accord 7134)

I Walk the Line (Album Globe 9206)

I Walk the Line (Col CL-2190/CS-8490)

I Walk the Line (Col S-30397) [ST]

I Walk the Line (Hilltop 6097)

I Walk the Line (Nashville 2108)

I Walk the Line (Share 5000)

I Would Like to See You Again (Col KC-35313)

Inside a Swedish Prison (Bear Family BFX-15092)

John R. Cash (Col KC-33370)

Johnny and June (Bear Family BFX-15030) w. June Carter Cash

Johnny Cash (Everest S-278)

Johnny Cash and His Woman (Col KC-32443) w. June Carter Cash

Johnny Cash and Jerry Lee Lewis Sing Hank Williams (Sun 125)

Johnny Cash at Folsom Prison (Col CS-9639)

Johnny Cash at Folsom Prison and San Quentin (Col CG-33639)

Johnny Cash at San Quentin (Col CS-9827)

Johnny Cash Is Coming to Town (Mer/Polygram 837-031-1)

The Johnny Cash Scrapbook (Har KH-31602)

The Johnny Cash Show (Col KC-30100)

Johnny Cash Sings Hank Williams (Sun 1245)

Johnny 99 (Col FC-38696)

The Junkie and the Juicehead Minus Me (Col KC-33086)

The King and Queen (Col Musical Treasury P2S-5418) w. Tammy Wynette

The Last Gunfighter Ballad (Col KC-34314)

Legends and Love Songs (Col DS-363)

Little Fauss and Big Halsy (Col S-30285) [ST]

Look at Them Beans (Col KC-33814)

The Lure of the Grand Canyon (Col CL-1622/CS-8422) w. André Kostelanetz

The Man in Black (Col C-30550)

The Man, the World, His Music (Sun 2-216)

Mean as Hell (Col CS-9246)

More of Old Golden Throat (Bear Family BFX-15073)

Now Here's Johnny Cash (Sun 1255)

One Piece at a Time (Col PC-34193)

Old Golden Throat (Bear Family BFX-15072)

Old Golden Throat (Charly CR-30005)

Orange Blossom Special (Col CL-2309/CS-9109)

Original Hits, Vols. 1–3 (Sun 100, 101, 127)

The Original Johnny Cash (Charly CR-30113)

Previous Memories (Col C-33087, Priority 33087)

Ragged Old Flag (Col KC-32917)

Rainbow (Col 39951-4)

The Rambler (Col KC-34883)

Ride This Train (Col CL-1464/CS-8255)

Ring of Fire (Col CL-2053/CS-8255)

Rock Island Line (Hilltop 6101)

Rockabilly Blues (Col 36779)

The Rough Cut of Country Music (Sun 122)

Show Time (Sun 106)

Silver (Col JC-36086)

The Singing Story Teller (Sun 115)

Songs of Our Soil (Col CL-1339/CS-8148)

The Songs That Made Him Famous (Sun 1235)

The Sons of Katie Elder (Col OL/OS/6420) [ST]

The Sound Behind Johnny Cash (Col C-30220) w. The Tennessee Three

The Sound of Johnny Cash (Col CL-1802/CS-8602)

Story Songs of Trains and Rivers (Sun 104)

Strawberry Cake (Col KC-34088)

The Sun Years (Charly 103)

Sunday Down South (Sun 119) w. Jerry Lee Lewis, Charlie Rich

Sunday Morning Coming Down (Col KC-32240)

Superbilly (Sun 1002)

The Survivors (Col FC-37961) w. Jerry Lee Lewis, Carl Perkins

A Thing Called Love (Col KC-31332)

This Is Johnny Cash (Har HS-11342)

Understand Your Man (Har KH-30916)

The Unissued Johnny Cash (Bear Family BFX-15016)

The Vintage Cash (Rhino 70229)

The Walls of Prison (Har KH-30138)

Water from the Wells of Home (Mer/Polygram 834-778-1)

The World of Johnny Cash (Col GP-29)

Years Gone By (Accord 7208)

# CHER

THE OUTRAGEOUS CHER HAS GONE THROUGH MANY DRAMATIC
career stages in her transformation from the trash queen to queen of class. She was first a
teenaged backup singer; then the prettier half of the androgynous pop team of Sonny and
Cher, noted for their sweet harmony. By the 1970s she had become an exotic (self-
satirizing) sex symbol on TV, famed for her glamorous costumes, zany exhibitionism
(especially the display of her navel), and sly humor. Then, having split from Sonny Bono
in private life, she became a solo contralto singing act. She amazed the public when she
moved her career into a new direction as a dramatic performer. After her solid emoting in
SILKWOOD (1983) and MASK (1985), she struck gold with her Oscar-winning starring role
in the romantic comedy MOONSTRUCK (1987).

The blatantly direct Cher is far closer in temperament to the "me" generation of
today's hard rock stars than to any sultry vocalist of bygone eras. Once emancipated from
Sonny, Cher became a brash solo attraction insisting on a self-sufficient lifestyle. These
days there seem to be two Chers. There is the energetic middle-aged woman (still
displaying miles of bare skin and tattoos), vying to remain contemporary in her singing
and to out-trash the trashier of today's rock stars in her performance style. Equally
dominant is the other Cher, whose self-determination has shaped her into a charismatic
screen presence. Tying together these wildly divergent personalities is the off-stage,
rebellious Cher. She is filled with excessive frankness, hyper emotions (ranging from super
toughness to charming vulnerability), and an ever-present overpowering belief in herself.

She was born Cherilyn Sarkisian on May 20, 1946, the daughter of truck driver
George Sarkisian and his teenaged wife, Jackie Jean (Crouch) Sarkisian. He was of
Armenian descent; she was part Cherokee Indian. George Sarkisian was scarcely around
when Cherilyn was a little child and he and Jackie eventually divorced (they would marry
and divorce twice more over the years). With her next husband, Jackie had another
daughter, named Georgeanne; by then the family was living in Los Angeles. Jackie was
pursuing an acting career (while working as a waitress) and changed her name to Georgia
Holt. As Georgia Holt she earned small roles in films and on television. (Some accounts
have it that she obtained work for her young daughters as extras in such TV shows as "The
Adventures of Ozzie and Harriet.") As Jackie married and divorced, the family moved
from place to place (including New York City, Texas, and Bel Air, California). The girls
also transferred from school to school, including a stay at Mother Cabrini's High School in
the San Fernando Valley of California. It was Georgia's fifth husband, Gilbert LaPiere,
who adopted both Cherilyn and Georgeanne. (Georgia would marry three more times.)

He was a wealthy banker and the girls attended private school. But in 1962, at age sixteen, Cher dropped out of school. She would recall, "I was never really in school. I was always thinking about when I was grown up and famous. . . ." (In recent years she admitted she is dyslexic.) Cher moved out of her mother's house and in with a girlfriend in Hollywood, supporting herself with menial jobs.

With her long black hair, pronounced nose, and very thin legs, the bohemian Cher was more exotic than intriguing when she first met Sonny Bono in November 1962 at a Hollywood coffee shop. Born Salvatore Philip Bono in Detroit, Michigan, in 1935, he had been married (and was now separated) and had a four-year-old daughter (Christy). He was a struggling songwriter/singer/promoter who could not make a success of the various recording company ventures he had begun. He was then existing as a subordinate to pop music entrepreneur Phil Spector of Gold Star (Recording) Studios in Hollywood. It was not long before the 5' 6" Sonny and the 5' 7" Cher were living together. Cher began hanging around at Gold Star and Phil Spector used her eventually to sing backup vocals for several of his performers, including The Ronettes, The Crystals, and Darlene Love. In some of these sessions Sonny played percussion.

When Georgia Holt learned of Cher's new living arrangement, she demanded that her daughter return home. As a compromise Cher moved to a women's residence and later, for a time, stayed in Arkansas with her mother and Georgeanne. Throughout this period, Cher continued dating Sonny and being part of the pop music scene. In early 1964, deep-voiced Cher recorded the song "Ringo, I Love You" for Phil Spector's Annette Records. However, Sonny, who had become her controlling influence, demanded that she use an alias for this recording (which he thought atrocious). Thus the record was released as a (novelty) single featuring "Bonnie Jo Mason." Soon thereafter, Sonny, now divorced, began moving away from Spector's influence. Elsewhere, he and Cher (billed as Caesar and Cleo) recorded such singles as "The Letter" and "Love Is Strange," which received some air play. On October 27, 1964, Sonny and Cher were married in Tijuana, Mexico. (It later developed this was an unofficial ceremony and they reportedly rewed on December 13, 1965. Other sources state they were not married legally until 1969, just before the birth of their child.)

In November 1964 Sonny and Cher were hired as the opening act (for Ike and Tina Turner) at Hollywood's Purple Onion Club. Soon thereafter, Sonny arranged a recording contract for Cher with Imperial Records. In early 1965 Sonny and Cher were on concert tour, playing mostly one-night stands for $350 weekly. For Reprise, the team of Sonny and Cher sang "Baby Don't Go," a song he had written. It would rise to number eight on the charts by the fall of 1965. Meanwhile, in mid-1965, Sonny negotiated a joint contract for the singing team of Sonny and Cher with Atco Records, a division of Atlantic Records. Their first Atco hit single was "I Got You Babe" (written by Bono). It rose to number one on the charts in the summer of 1965, beating out the latest songs of The Rolling Stones, Tom Jones, and Herman's Hermits for the top spot.

Suddenly the warm harmony and smooth sound of Sonny and Cher was in, and competing successfully with the British Invasion of The Beatles and the Motown Sound of

The Supremes and others. Sonny and Cher had hits with the singles "But You're Mine" (1965) "What Now My Love" (1966), and "Little Man" (1966). Their joint album *Look at Us* (1965) was number two on the charts. Meanwhile, as a single performer on the Imperial label, Cher had a top twenty hit with "All I Really Want to Do" (1965—the album of the same title was also in the top twenty) and her "Bang Bang (My Baby Shot Me Down)" was number two on the scoreboard in the spring of 1966. As a result of their prosperity Sonny and Cher moved from a shabby Hollywood apartment to a $75,000 model home in Encino and thereafter to a thirty-one-room Holmby Hills mansion with fancy cars and motorcycles.

Then came "The Beat Goes On," which rose to number six on the charts in early 1967. Along with "I Got You Babe," it was one of the two songs most associated with Sonny and Cher. The team made several appearances on "Hullabaloo" (NBC-TV) and "Shindig" (ABC-TV). They guested, along with Mitzi Gaynor and Jim Nabors, on Danny Thomas' NBC-TV special in January 1966. They were now instant celebrities adored by their young fans and invited to participate in jet-set partying. Cher expanded her range by designing a line of marketed wardrobe.

In 1965, Cher had sung the theme song for the Michael Caine movie ALFIE. Together with Sonny, she had made a fleeting appearance in the independently produced WILD ON THE BEACH, released by 20th Century–Fox. In this minor sand-and-music flick, Sonny and Cher sang "It's Gonna Rain," written by Bono. This movie and their performance had gone so unnoticed that when they starred in Columbia's GOOD TIMES in the spring of 1967, it was promoted as their screen debut. In GOOD TIMES they played themselves, with Sonny's character more interested than Cher's in expanding themselves into screen careers. In the scenario, they have several fantasy sequences as they imagine themselves starring in a variety of movie genres. The film was the first feature directed by William Friedkin, who made a name for himself later with THE FRENCH CONNECTION (1971) and THE EXORCIST (1973). *Variety* reported, "Sonny and Cher are natural enough in their acting, but expectedly excel in their song numbers which they sock over in their customary style." Among their nine numbers were "I Got You Babe," "Good Times," and "I'm Gonna Love You." The movie was a flop, as was the soundtrack album.

Before GOOD TIMES was released, Sonny and Cher undertook a European concert tour. After the movie failed, they attempted to resurrect their recording/concertizing career in the U.S., which had been on hold during the many months of planning and filming their feature. The duo's "Plastic Man" (1967) never got beyond seventy-fourth position on the charts, while Cher's solo "You Better Sit Down Kids" (1967—written by Bono) reached number nine in the winter of 1967. It was her last single hit for four years. Almost as fast as they had risen to popularity, Sonny and Cher became passé in 1968. Their records were no longer selling and their club dates and concert bookings began to come from the bottom of the barrel. To reverse their career decline (and their overextended finances), Sonny wrote a screenplay to star Cher. When no Hollywood studio showed interest in the project, he mortgaged everything to raise the $300,000-plus needed to finance the venture. American International Pictures agreed to distribute it. The film,

CHASTITY (1969), with music by Sonny, traced the maturation of an unhappy young woman (Cher) who takes to the roads in the Southwest. Despite meeting a succession of men, she remains chaste, always haunted by her troubled childhood. The arty movie, shot in Phoenix, Arizona, was a commercial dud that put the couple $190,000 in debt for back taxes. However, a few critics noted that deadpan Cher demonstrated traces of good, instinctive acting. It was also in 1969 that Cher gave birth to their child, Chastity.

At a low professional ebb, Sonny determined they should try nightclubs, complete with a new image that moved away from their hippie gear into more mainstream costumes. By 1970 the couple was booked into the Empire Room of the Waldorf-Astoria Hotel in New York City and a good part of the act was focused on Cher's sexy gowns and her put-down wisecracks to her partner. In April 1971, as one of their frequent TV guest performances, they were substitute hosts on "The Merv Griffin Show" (CBS-TV). Network officials were sufficiently impressed by the duo to offer them a contract to star in "The Sonny and Cher Comedy Hour." The summer replacement show debuted on August 1, 1971, and ran for six episodes. Because the show's ratings were decent, the couple returned that December with a regularly scheduled show, which enjoyed a three-season run. The weekly sixty minutes were filled typically with blackout skits, a recurring visit to "Sonny's Pizzeria," a stopover at the laundromat where housewife Cher chatted with her friend (Teri Garr), a satirical newscast portion, and a segment devoted to Cher portraying assorted "vamps" throughout history. And, of course, the couple sang a wide assortment of songs, always ending their show with "I've Got You Babe." As contrasting images, Sonny was blithely optimistic and energetic, Cher—in her increasingly ridiculous, outré fashions (by Bob Mackie)—was constantly putting her mate down with sardonic humor.

Now recording for MCA, the team's joint albums (including 1971's *All I Ever Need Is You* and 1972's *A Cowboy's Work Is Never Done*) did well. As a solo Cher had number one hits with "Half-Breed" (1973) and "Dark Lady" (1974). Her solo album *Gypsys, Tramps & Thieves* (1971—the title song had been a number one single) reached number sixteen on the charts. Sonny and Cher played Las Vegas clubs successfully.

Since the fall of 1972 Sonny and Cher had been separated and she dated, among others, record producer David Geffen. In February 1974 Sonny filed for a legal separation from his wife of nine years. Fifty-eight hours later (February 22, 1974) they did their last series show together. That summer the now single Cher explained that when she first met Sonny, "I was lonely. I was shy. I had absolutely no confidence. Sonny brought me up with a whole new set of values. . . . He was more of a mother to me than my own mother. But," she added, "now I have to break out. And Sonny's not willing to make the transition with me." Meanwhile, her ex-spouse sued her for contractual default.

Sonny floundered both on television ("The Sonny Comedy Revue" flopped on ABC in the fall of 1974) and as an actor. Cher continued to record for Warner Bros. with unspectacular results. She also became the star of her own variety series, "Cher," which debuted on February 16, 1975, on CBS. Somehow the magic was missing in her solo effort. Her daughter, Chastity, frequently appeared on the show, as did Sonny. One month after her show left the air in January 1976, "The Sonny and Cher Show" began and would survive through mid-1977. But things were not the same. Cher had married rock singer Gregg Allman (a year her junior) three days after her divorce (June 27, 1975) from Sonny became final. She was soon involved in highly publicized separations and reconciliations with her new husband, who had a much-discussed drug problem. She had his child (Elijah Blue) in July 1976 and thereafter their relationship was very much on-again, off-again. They were termed one of show business's strangest married couples until their union finally ended in 1978. All this adverse publicity, added to Cher's much-reported high style of living, had created a public backlash which contributed a great deal to the failure of the revived Sonny and Cher teaming.

By now Cher had developed renewed interest in acting. She was among those considered for the lead role in the remake of A STAR IS BORN (1976). However, once Barbra Streisand expressed a desire for the part, Cher (as well as nearly everyone else) was out of the running. In the late 1970s Cher dated Gene Simmons of the rock group Kiss. She signed with Casablanca Records and in 1979 her song "Take Me Home" was number eight on the charts. The album of the same title, which contained some rock numbers, rose to number five. A later LP that year, *Prisoner*, featured an album cover photo of a nude Cher bound in chains. She had reached her peak of outlandishness. She sang in the major clubs of Las Vegas. (One of her routines used two female impersonators to team Cher with "Diana Ross" and "Bette Midler.") She had begun making music videos, such as "Hell on Wheels," a single from the *Prisoner* LP. Her friendship with Gene Simmons ended and he began a romance with Cher's pal Diana Ross. She had a relationship with rock guitarist Les Dudek, with whom she performed in the group Black Rose and with whom she made an album (which failed) in 1980. During this period, she starred in three TV specials (1978, 1979, 1983).

Tiring of being "just" a splashy Las Vegas star (at $320,000 weekly) noted for high fashion costumes and exotic living, Cher tried stage acting. She auditioned for and was signed by producer/director Robert Altman (whose wife was a friend of Cher's mother) for the Broadway stage production of *Come Back to the 5 & Dime, Jimmy Dean, Jimmy Dean* (1982). It dealt with five former members of a James Dean fan club having their twentieth anniversary reunion in a rundown Texas town in 1975. She played Sissy, the dime store waitress with a broken heart. The show ran for sixty performances and shortly after it closed Altman filmed a shoe-string movie of it, featuring Cher and members of the original cast (including Sandy Dennis and Karen Black). Like the play, it was considered an arty failure, more interesting for its oddball cast than for its dramatic content. Cher received a Golden Globe nomination for her on-camera performance.

One of those who had seen Cher on stage in *Jimmy Dean* was director Mike Nichols, who offered her the part (at $150,000) of Meryl Streep's lesbian friend and plant co-worker in the controversial motion picture SILKWOOD (1983). For her intense, unvarnished performance, Cher was Oscar-nominated but lost the Best Supporting Actress Award to Linda Hunt (of THE YEAR OF LIVING DANGEROUSLY). She did win a Golden Globe for her performance. It was two years before she returned to the screen, this time in the sensitive drama MASK (1985) in which she was a pill-popping biker who has a lover

(Sam Elliott) and is coping with her teenaged son (Eric Stoltz) who is suffering from a severe head deformity. There were as many conflicts between Cher and director Peter Bogdanovich as there were between Bogdanovich and Universal, which released the hard-to-position-drama. Many felt (including Cher) that because she was so anti-Establishment, the industry bypassed her in the Oscar nominations. To show her scorn for the "system," she showed up at the Academy Awards ceremony that year in one of her most outlandish (tarantula-like) costumes. She did win the Cannes Film Festival Award as Best Actress.

Now based mostly in New York City and receiving as much attention for her health spa commercials as for her still controversial lifestyle, Cher returned to the screen three times in 1987. She was the star of SUSPECT, playing a dedicated public defender who is both helped and romanced by one of the jurors (Dennis Quaid) in the homicide case she is handling. Along with Susan Sarandon and Michelle Pfeiffer, she was one of three divorcees involved with Jack Nicholson, the mysterious rich visitor (from Hell) who comes to a small New England town in THE WITCHES OF EASTWICK. This horror comedy earned $31,800,000 in domestic film rentals. Even better was MOONSTRUCK, a joyously romantic comedy set in Brooklyn in which an Italian widow falls in love with her fiancé's headstrong younger brother (Nicolas Cage). As the focal point of this Italian-American set

Cher in SILKWOOD (1983)

piece, Cher was spunky and radiant as the blossoming bookkeeper who responds so enthusiastically to her passionate young lover. This time she was Oscar-nominated and won. The movie earned $34,393,000 in domestic film rentals. She had broken her frustrating mold as part of Sonny and Cher and proved her point that "I refuse to accept other people's limitations." With her new sleek look, she made a "comeback" album for Geffen Records. *Cher* contained the hit song "I Found Someone," which was popular in both audio and music video versions.

Now taken seriously as a dramatic actress and

a bankable star (commanding $1 million per film when and if she chooses one), Cher set up her own movie production firm, Isis Productions. She received a great deal of attention in 1988 for her romance with Rob Camilletti, a former doorman/bartender nearly twenty years her junior. He appeared in a rock video that she directed—tied in with one of her new LP albums. (The highly documented romance dissolved in mid-1989 and she soon began a new romance with another younger man—a musician.) Meanwhile, in April 1988, she appeared on "Late Night with David Letterman" in a reunion with Sonny (who had recently remarried and who would soon become mayor of Palm Springs, California). They did an impromptu harmonizing of "I Got You Babe." Besides making a concert and nightclub tour, she promoted a new line of perfume called Uninhibited. She has written a nutrition book with Robert Haas (author of *Eat to Win*), is set to star in a new film comedy (MERMAIDS), and continues to record.

The Cher of today, who over the years has had her nose, breasts, and teeth restructured, admits, "I do keep wondering about how much longer I'll be able to dress the way I want to dress and get away with it." She also says, "I'm not a role model, but trust me: if I could accomplish this thing [career success] that seemed impossible, you can accomplish anything you want to do. It's not me, it's just people need symbols along the way to remind them, Yes, I can do this."

## Filmography

### Sonny and Cher:

Wild on the Beach (20th–Fox, 1965) (also songs by Sonny)
Good Times (Par, 1967) (also songs by Sonny)

Chastity (AIP, 1969) (also producer, script, and songs by Sonny, who did not appear in this feature)

### Cher:

Alfie (Par, 1965) (voice only)
Come Back to the 5 & Dime, Jimmy Dean, Jimmy Dean (Cinecom International, 1982)
Silkwood (Par, 1983)

Mask (Univ, 1985)
Suspect (Tri-Star, 1987)
The Witches of Eastwick (WB, 1987)
Moonstruck (MGM/UA, 1987)

## Broadway Plays

Come Back to the 5 & Dime, Jimmy Dean, Jimmy Dean (1982)

## TV Series

The Sonny and Cher Comedy Hour (CBS, 1971–74)
Cher (CBS, 1975–76)

The Sonny and Cher Show (CBS, 1976–77)

## Album Discography

### Cher:

All I Really Want to Do (Imperial 12292)
Backstage (Imperial 12373)
The Best of Cher, Vols. 1–2 (Liberty 10110/11)
Bittersweet White Light (MCA 2101)
Black Rose (Casablanca NBLP-7234) w. Les Dudek
Chastity (Atco 302) [ST]
Cher (Geffen 6HS-24164)
Cher (Imperial 12320)
Cher Backstage (Imperial 12373)
Cher Superpak, Vols. 1–2 (UA 88, 94)
Cherished (WB 3046)
Dark Lady (MCA 2113)
Foxy Lady (Kapp 5514)
Golden Greats (Imperial 12406)
Greatest Hits (MCA 2127)

Gypsys, Tramps & Thieves (Kapp 3649)
Half-Breed (MCA 2104)
Heart of Stone (Geffen GHS-24239)
I Paralyze (CBS 38096)
I'd Rather Believe in You (WB 2898)
Prisoner (Casablanca 7184)
The Sonny Side of Cher (Imperial 9301/12301)
Stars (WB 2850)
Take Me Home (Casablanca 7133)
3614 Jackson Highway (Atco SD-33-298)
This Is Cher (Sunset 5276)
Two the Hard Way (WB K-3120) w. Gregg Allman [Cher billed as Woman]
The Very Best of Cher (UA 377)
With Love (Imperial 12358)

### Sonny and Cher:

All I Ever Need Is You (Kapp 3660, MCA 2021)
Baby Don't Go (Reprise 6177)
The Beat Goes On (Atco 11000)
The Best of Sonny and Cher (Atco 233-219)
A Cowboy's Work Is Never Done (Kapp)
Good Times (Atco 33-214) [ST]
Greatest Hits (Atco A2S-5178, MCA 2117)
In Case You're in Love (Atco SD-33-203)

Look at Us (Atco SD-33-177)
Sonny and Cher Live (Kapp 3654)
Sonny and Cher Live in Las Vegas, Vol. 2 (MCA 2-8004)
The Two of Us (Atco SD-2-804)
The Wondrous World of Sonny and Cher (Atco SD-33-183)

# MAURICE CHEVALIER

THE WORD "CHARMER" HAS BEEN USED TO CHARACTERIZE MANY
entertainers, but perhaps no one exemplified its meaning better than boulevardier Maurice
Chevalier. With his bright smile, Gallic charm, and straw hat he charmed generations of
theater and moviegoers for the most of the twentieth century. Although Chevalier freely
admitted he was a man of limited talents, he used his distinctive abilities to their utmost
and he hewed his act to perfection. He presented a picture of a happy-go-lucky Parisian
who never took life seriously and always found romance. It was an image that remained
with him throughout his life. Chevalier chronicler R. A. Israel summed it up, "The ease,
the charm, the droll insights, the physical dexterity, the incredible ability to create
meaningful characters in a seemingly effortless manner was astonishing, but not accidental."

The perennial entertainer was born Maurice August Chevalier on September 12,
1888, in Paris, the son of a house painter and his Flemish wife. The family was quite poor
and several of the ten offspring (Maurice was the next to youngest child) died at an early
age. When Chevalier was eight his father left the family; Maurice did not see the man again
for nearly two decades. Life was miserable for the Chevaliers, and after only brief
schooling, young Maurice had to go to work at a variety of jobs, always losing them
because of his daydreaming about becoming either an acrobat or a singer. In 1900 he
began working as an amateur singer and he became a professional the next year, billed as
"Le Petit Chevalier," singing in cafés around Paris and its suburbs. He eventually toured
the provinces and performed in Belgium. Thus he grew to manhood through the vagabond
life of a cabaret entertainer and in 1907 he became the head singer at Paris's Eldorado
Club, which led to three seasons of work with the prestigious Folies-Bergère. By now he
also danced and used comedy in his act, in addition to songs, and he was much in demand.
In 1909 he met the esteemed French star Mistinguett, who took the much younger man as
her stage partner and lover; they worked together adroitly for a decade. During this period
Chevalier also began making films, the first being TROP CREDULE in 1908. Starting in 1910
he appeared in a trio of movie shorts with the noted French film comedian Max Linder.

The year 1913 found Chevalier joining the French army, although he continued to
appear in tandem with Mistinguett and they filmed their act in a 1914 short, LA VALSE
RENVERSANTE. When France joined the Allies in World War I, Chevalier's 31st Infantry
regiment was sent to Germany; during an assault on a small village he was wounded and
taken prisoner. He spent the remainder of the war in a prisoner-of-war camp at Alten
Grabow, where he worked as a pharmacist's assistant and learned English from a British

prisoner. When the Red Cross obtained an exchange-of-prisoners pact, Chevalier returned home in 1916; the next year he was awarded the Croix de Guerre. In Paris he returned to the Folies-Bergère with Mistinguett and the duo made a second film, UNE SOIREE MONDAINE (1917). Two years later he appeared in London with Elsie Janis in the revue *Hullo, America*, and came back home to do the same show as *Hullo, Paris*. By now he had split with Mistinguett and had become the headliner at the Casino de Paris, and was also starring successfully in the operetta *Dede*. He then came to America, planning to produce the show in the United States, but the plans came to naught and the star suffered a nervous breakdown. During his recuperation back in France, he became attached to dancer Yvonne Vallee and during the 1920s he toured the provinces and made several feature films, most of which he also produced. He and Yvonne were wed in 1926 and the next year they went to London to headline the *White Birds* revue. While Chevalier was performing at the Casino de Paris, MGM's Irving Thalberg saw him and had him test for the movies, but no studio contract was forthcoming. However, Jesse L. Lasky also saw the test and the Frenchman was signed by Paramount, the most cosmopolitan of the Hollywood studios, to appear in talkies.

Maurice Chevalier made his sound film debut in the travelogue short subject BONJOUR, NEW YORK!, in 1928, directed by Robert Florey. By now his image of the debonair Frenchman, in a tuxedo and straw hat (which was suggested by cabaret star Gaby Deslys), with a carefree manner, was well established, as was his singing of the song favorite "Valentine." Hollywood would not alter the basic Chevalier image, but his half-dozen years in the film capital would greatly expand his song catalogue. This extension of his repertory would be inaugurated by his initial English-language feature film, INNOCENTS OF PARIS (1929), in which he sang his most famous song, "Louise." Although modestly mounted, the sentimental musical proved to be a good showcase for Chevalier and he appealed immediately to moviegoers in America and elsewhere. THE LOVE PARADE (1929), the first of a quartet of very sophisticated features with Jeanette MacDonald, followed; in it he sang the title song. In the studio's all-star revue, PARAMOUNT ON PARADE (1930), he performed "All I Want Is Just One Girl," but his biggest hit came at the film's finale when he sang "Sweeping the Clouds Away." He also headlined the French-language version of the movie. In 1930 he co-starred with Claudette Colbert in the English and French editions of THE BIG POND (a frou-frou about the manufacture of liquor-flavored gum), singing "You Brought a New Kind of Love to Me." That same year, with a new contract (four films for $1 million), he starred in the English and French versions of PLAYBOY OF PARIS, with Frances Dee, performing "My Ideal."

He did "One More Hour of Love" in THE SMILING LIEUTENANT in 1931, which again paired him with Claudette Colbert in English and French versions. Off camera he was romancing Paramount leading ladies Kay Francis and Marlene Dietrich. Next he was with Jeanette MacDonald for the second time in the urbane ONE HOUR WITH YOU (1932), which gave him the popular title tune plus "Oh, That Mitzi!"; the two (whose strong egos clashed off screen) also made the French version. Chevalier did a guest bit as himself in Paramount's MAKE ME A STAR (1932) as well as a cameo in the Masquers Club all-star detective spoof short THE SLIPPERY PEARLS (1932). The same year, after a visit to Paris, he was seen as himself in BATTLING GEORGES [TOBAGGAN], which starred his close friend, boxing champion Georges Carpentier.

Back in Hollywood, Chevalier, who was tiring of his successful but limited one-dimensional charming playboy screen roles, co-starred with Jeanette MacDonald for the third time in LOVE ME TONIGHT (1932), which gave him the songs "Mimi" and "Isn't It Romantic?" By 1933 the stereotyping was affecting his box-office appeal. Neither A BED-TIME STORY nor THE WAY TO LOVE (also issued in a French version as L'AMOUR GUIDE) gave him any memorable songs to sing. Audiences were tiring of seeing him in a succession of fake Paris tales which were all too similar. Chevalier and Paramount ended their contract and he moved over to MGM at the suggestion of second-in-command Irving Thalberg.

The first Metro-Goldwyn-Mayer project was to be THE MERRY WIDOW. Ernst Lubitsch, who had directed Chevalier's most successful Paramount vehicles, was to direct the operetta and opera diva Grace Moore was to co-star. But after a billing dispute she withdrew, and much against Chevalier's will, Jeanette MacDonald was substituted. The glittery production was extremely expensive to produce, and neither it nor its French-language edition, LA VEUVE JOYEUSE, could recoup the enormous expense. Chevalier was loaned to United Artists for FOLIES BERGERE (1935) with Merle Oberon and Ann Sothern and he had a trio of memorable tunes: "I Was Lucky," "The Rhythm of the Rain," and "I Don't Stand a Ghost of a Chance with You." Once again, neither it nor its French-language version, LES HOMMES DES FOLIES BERGERE, was particularly popular. Back at MGM, the executives decided to try to team Chevalier with Grace Moore, but he preferred MacDonald. When she declined the offer and he could not decide upon a proper vehicle, the MGM contract was dissolved. He now left Hollywood and again returned to Paris. His wife had left him in the early 1930s (their only child died just after birth in 1927) because she did not appreciate Hollywood life, and they were divorced in 1939. During the time he was in Hollywood Chevalier recorded most of his popular movie numbers for Victor Records, plus other songs such as "Hello Beautiful," "There Ought to Be a Moonlight Saving Time," and "Walking My Baby Back Home." Chevalier had been recording since 1919, and after returning to Paris he continued to record for Victor's British label HMV (His Master's Voice) through 1941.

Upon his return to his homeland, Chevalier appeared in two 1936 French releases, L'HOMME DU JOUR and AVEC LE SOURIRE, and then went to England where he topped the cast in THE BELOVED VAGABOND (1936) and BREAK THE NEWS (1938), the former of which was also produced in a French-language version. He continued to work in music halls and in 1939 starred in Robert Siodmak's PIEGES, his last film for the duration of World War II.

By now France was involved in the war and Chevalier remained inactive professionally, except for occasional appearances. One of these was at the German prisoner-of-war camp Alten Grabow, where he had been a prisoner in the previous war. He entertained French prisoners there and worked for the exchange of several of his incarcerated countrymen. For his efforts he was branded a collaborator and in 1944 published reports insisted he had been killed. When the war was over, Chevalier was exonerated of charges of aiding the

Nazis but the stigma stayed with him for a long time.

In 1947 Maurice Chevalier returned to filmmaking in René Clair's comedy LE SI-
LENCE EST D'OR which found him in a new persona, that of the older man who loses the
girl to someone her own age; in the United States it was shown as MAN ABOUT TOWN. That
year also saw him make a triumphant return to the United States, taking his one-man show
to New York City. It was his first Gotham appearance since he had worked in vaudeville
there a dozen years before. While in the U.S. he newly recorded his standards "Louise" and
"Valentine" for RCA Victor with Henri René and His Orchestra and he also appeared on
several network radio shows such as "Philco Radio Time" with Bing Crosby. In 1949 he
starred in the Mutual radio series "This Is Paris," and for the next several years he made
films in France; performed his one-man show throughout Europe, England, and the U.S.;
and recorded for labels like Pathé, Vox, and London.

It was in 1955 that the star came to American TV with "The Maurice Chevalier
Show," a special on NBC-TV, and in 1957, he did the documentary "Maurice Chevalier's
Paris." That year also saw his return to American films in Billy Wilder's bittersweet
comedy LOVE IN THE AFTERNOON, which found him as an engaging detective whose
pretty daughter (Audrey Hepburn) becomes attracted to an older American (Gary Cooper).
This film gave Chevalier a good song—its theme, "Fascination." In 1958, seventy-year-old

Michael Connors, Eleanor Parker, and Maurice Chevalier in PANIC BUTTON (1964)

Maurice Chevalier had one of the biggest successes of his career, the role of the roué playboy uncle in GIGI, which provided him with two additional trademark songs—"Thank Heaven for Little Girls" and "I'm Glad I'm Not Young Anymore"—plus a poignant duet with Hermione Gingold on "I Remember It Well." The MGM musical's success (and multi-Oscars) catapulted Chevalier into the kind of stardom he had enjoyed after his U.S. film debut nearly three decades earlier. As a result, he made a string of long-playing record albums for MGM Records, and appeared on a variety of TV shows such as "The Lucille Ball–Desi Arnaz Comedy Hour," a CBS-TV presentation of his one-man show (February 4, 1960), "The Bing Crosby Show," "The World of Maurice Chevalier," "April in Paris," "The Bell Telephone Hour," "The Ed Sullivan Show," "The Hollywood Palace," and "Music by Cole Porter." On February 23, 1967, he starred on the ABC-TV special "C'est la Vie," the first American-French program from Paris in color.

GIGI also revitalized Maurice Chevalier's movie career, although now he mainly acted in films as a character star. For MGM he did the comedy COUNT YOUR BLESSINGS (1959) followed by the gaudy musical CAN-CAN (1960) with Shirley MacLaine and Frank Sinatra, in which he sang "Just One of Those Things" and "I Love Paris." He provided support to Sophia Loren and John Gavin in A BREATH OF SCANDAL (1960) and appeared as himself in PEPE (1960). He had a fine acting assignment in FANNY (1961) as the older man who marries the young daughter (Leslie Caron) of his friend (Charles Boyer) so her unborn child will have a father. Chevalier enthused about the part: "In FANNY for the first time I've done a character far away from Maurice Chevalier. I found it enjoyable to create a man with a personality not my own." JESSICA (1962) gave him the opportunity to both sing and act as a priest who advises the curvacious title character (Angie Dickinson) on the dangers of lust. For Walt Disney he made the well-executed IN SEARCH OF THE CAST-AWAYS (1962) as a scientist searching for a missing sea captain, and he appeared as himself in the Paul Newman–Joanne Woodward romantic comedy A NEW KIND OF LOVE (1963). In the very mediocre comedy PANIC BUTTON (1964) he was a divorced man romancing a younger woman (Jayne Mansfield), while in I'D RATHER BE RICH (1964) he inherited an old Charles Laughton role as Sandra Dee's grandfather who pretends to be terminally ill in order to see her married. This well-mounted but mostly overlooked film reteamed him with Hermione Gingold. His final two features were for Walt Disney: MONKEYS, GO HOME! (1967) cast him as a priest who aids a young American (Dean Jones) who has inherited an olive farm and plans to use monkeys to harvest the crop; in the cartoon feature THE ARISTOCATS (1970) he sang the title song.

After numerous "farewell tours" Maurice Chevalier retired from the stage in the late 1960s and spent the remainder of his life on his country estate outside Paris, with his companion, Odette Meslier-Junet, and her young mute daughter, Pascale. He died January 1, 1972, at the age of eighty-three, of a kidney ailment. The entertainer left an estate valued at $20 million and many awards, including France's Legion d'Honneur and Ordre Mérite National, Belgium's Order of Leopold, and a special 1959 Academy Award. He also left behind three engaging volumes of published memoirs, *The Man in the Straw Hat* (1949), *With Love* (1960), and *I Remember It Well* (1970).

## Filmography

Trop Crédule (Fr, 1908) (s)

Un Marié Qui Se Fait Attendre (Fr, 1911) (s)

La Mariée Récalcitrante (Fr, 1911) (s)

Par Habitude (Fr, 1911) (s)

La Valse Renversante (Fr, 1914) (s)

Une Soirée Mondaine (Fr, 1917) (s)

Le Mauvais Garçon (Fr, 1922)

Le Match Criqui-Ledoux (Fr, 1922)

Gonzague (Fr, 1923)

L'Affaire de la Rue de Lourcine (Fr, 1923)

Jim Bougne, Boxeur (Fr, 1923)

Par Habitude (Fr, 1924)

Bonjour, New York! (Fr, 1928) (travelogue)

Innocents of Paris (Par, 1929)*

The Love Parade (Par, 1929)*

Paramount on Parade (Par, 1930)*

The Big Pond (Par, 1930)*

Playboy of Paris (Par, 1930)*

The Smiling Lieutenant (Par, 1931)*

El Cliente Seductor (Sp, 1931) (s)

One Hour with You (Par, 1932)*

Make Me a Star (Par, 1932)

Battling Georges [Toboggan] (Fr, 1932)

Love Me Tonight (Par, 1932)

Hollywood on Parade #5 (Par, 1932) (s)

The Stolen Jools [The Slippery Pearls] (Masquers Club, 1932) (s)

Stopping the Show (Par, 1932) (s) (voice only)

A Bedtime Story (Par, 1933)

The Way to Love (Par, 1933)*

The Merry Widow (MGM, 1934)*

Folies Bergère [The Man from Folies Bergère]
(UA, 1935)*

L'Homme du Jour [The Man of the Hour] (Fr,
1936)

Avec le Sourire [With a Smile] (Fr, 1936)

The Beloved Vagabond (Br, 1936)*

Break the News (Br, 1938)

Pièges [Personal Column] (Fr, 1939)

Paris 1900 (Fr, 1946) (documentary)

Le Silence Est d'Or [Man About Town] (Fr,
1947)

Le Roi [A Royal Affair] (Fr, 1949)

Ma Pomme [Just Me] (Fr, 1950)

Schlager-Parade (Ger, 1953)

Jouons le Jeu . . . l'Avarice (Fr, 1953) (s)

Chevalier de Menilmontant (Fr, 1953) (s)

Caf'Conc (Fr, 1953) (s)

Cento Anni d'Amore [A Hundred Years of Love]
(It, 1954)

Sur Toute la Gamme (Fr, 1954) (s) (narrator)

J'Avais Sept Filles [My Seven Little Sins] (Br,
1955)

Rendez-Vous avec Maurice Chevalier (Fr, 1956)
(documentary)

The Heart of Show Business (Col, 1956) (s)

Love in the Afternoon (AA, 1957)

The Happy Road (MGM, 1957) (voice only)

Gigi (MGM, 1958)

Count Your Blessings (MGM, 1959)

Can-Can (20th–Fox, 1960)

Un, Deux, Trois, Quatre! [Black Tights] (Fr,
1960) (narrator)

A Breath of Scandal (Par, 1960)

Pepe (Col, 1960)

Fanny (WB, 1961)

Jessica (UA, 1962)

In Search of the Castaways (BV, 1962)

A New Kind of Love (Par, 1963)

Panic Button (Gorton Associates, 1964)

I'd Rather Be Rich (Univ, 1964)

Monkeys, Go Home! (1967)

The Aristocats (BV, 1970) (voice only)

Le Chagrin et la Pitié [The Sorrow and the Pity]
(Fr, 1972) (documentary)

---

*Also starred in the French-language version*

## Radio Series

This Is Paris (Mutual, 1949)

## Album Discography

A la Chevalier (AEI 2125)

The Art of Maurice Chevalier (London International 91183)

Bing Crosby, Groucho Marx and Maurice Chevalier—Live (Amalgamated 221)

Black Tights (RCA FOC/FSO-3) [ST]

Bravo Maurice! (ASV 5034)

A Breath of Scandal (Imperial 9132) [ST]

Can-Can (Cap W/SW-1301) [ST]

Chevalier Chante Paris (RCA 540-036)

Chevalier's Paris (Col CL-1049)

Deux Fois Vingt Ans (EMI/Pathé 240-356)

The Early Years (World Record Club SH-120)

Encore Maurice! (ASV 5016)

Franco-American Hits (9CBS 63447)

Gigi (MGM/E-SE-3641) [ST]

Gigi (Col WL-158) [ST—French]

Hollywood, 1929–32 (EMI/Pathé 240-639)

In Search of the Castaways (Disneyland 3916) [ST]

Jessica (UA UAL-4097/UAS-5096) [ST]

Lerner and Loewe and Chevalier (MGM E/SE-4015)

Life Is Just a Bowl of Cherries (MGM E/SE-3801)

Love Me Tonight (Caliban 6047) [ST]

Love Parade/One Hour with You/Love Me Tonight (Ariel CMF 23) [ST]

Maurice (EMI/Pathé C162-1186/9)

Maurice Chevalier (Col CL-568)

Maurice Chevalier (Emidsic CO48-50656)

Maurice Chevalier (Pickwick 3161) w. Paul Mauriat

Maurice Chevalier (10" RCA LPT-3042)

Maurice Chevalier (Time S/2072)

Maurice Chevalier, Vol. 1 (RCA LPV-564)

Maurice Chevalier at 80 (Epic FXS-15117)

Maurice Chevalier Sings (Metro M/S-533)

Maurice Chevalier Sings (Vox 30020)

Maurice Chevalier Sings Broadway (MGM E/SE-3738)

Maurice Chevalier Sings Early Movie Hits (World Record Club SH-156)

The Merry Widow (Hollywood Soundstage 5015) [ST]

The Merry Widow/The Love Parade (Amalgamated 240) [ST]

A Musical Tour of France (Disneyland 3940)

One Hour with You (Caliban 6011) [ST]

Originals, 1935–47 (10" HMV CLP-1640)

Paramount on Parade (Caliban 6044) [ST]

Paris Je T'Aime (10" Vox 3180)

Paris to Broadway (MGM E/SE-4120)

Pepe (Colpix 507) [ST]

Playboy of Paris/The Way to Love/The Beloved Vagabond (Caliban 6013) [ST]

Poèmes de Jehan Rictus (London International 91065)

Quatre Fois Vingt Ans (EMI/Pathé 240-732)

Rendezvous à Paris, Vols. 1–3 (London International 91078-80)

A Royal Affair (10" Audio Archives 0026) [ST]

A Salute to Al Jolson (Metro M/S-595)

Sixty Years of Song (London 56001-4)

Souvenir, 1928–48 (Cap SPBO-10549)

Teen Street (Buena Vista 3313) w. Hayley Mills

Thank Heaven for Girls (MGM E/SE-3835)

Thank Heaven for Maurice Chevalier (RCA LPM-2076)

This Is Maurice Chevalier (RCA VPM-6055)

Today (MGM E/SE-3703)

Toujours Maurice (Camden CAL-579)

A Tribute to Al Jolson (MGM E/SE-3773)

Trois Fois Vingt Ans (EMI/Pathé 240-170)

The Very Best of Maurice Chevalier (MGM E/SE-4205)

We Remember Him Well (MGM 2353-055)

Yesterday (MGM E/SE-3702)

Yesterday and Today (MGM 2E/2SE-5)

You Brought a New Kind of Love to Me (Monmouth Evergreen 7028)

The Young Maurice Chevalier (Cap T-10360)

# ROSEMARY CLOONEY

IN THE EARLY 1950s ATTRACTIVE BAND SINGER ROSEMARY CLOONEY rose to "overnight" stardom with a string of novelty tune hits ("Come on-a My House," "Mambo Italiano," "This Old House") recorded in her husky, bouncy manner. Music lovers wondered if that was her limit. But as the star of TV and radio variety programs—and other types of recordings—she demonstrated a versatility and musicianship that soon ranked her as a top female vocalist of the period, along with Patti Page, Peggy Lee, and Jo Stafford. In her brief film career (Paramount envisioned her as Betty Hutton's successor), Rosemary Clooney was comely, pert, and direct. A few more picture assignments and her acting stiffness would certainly have evaporated. But her private life intervened: she was coping with raising a large family and dealing with a troublesome marriage. When she could no longer cope she had a severe nervous breakdown. As part of her therapy, which included a revealing autobiography and a telefeature based on the book, she made it all public.

When the "new" Rosemary Clooney emerged professionally—boosted by her long-time friend Bing Crosby—she was no longer svelte. And her singing was not the same—it had improved! There was a smoky edge to her remarkable voice that enhanced her expert phrasing. Critics ranked her with Ella Fitzgerald, Frank Sinatra, and Mel Tormé at their jazz peak. More recently, in a series of highly regarded albums for a small label, she has taken familiar material by great songwriters (Cole Porter, Irving Berlin, Ira Gershwin) and, without distortion, given it fresh meaning. It was Bing Crosby who said, "To me, Rosemary Clooney is a unique lady in many respects. She combines the ability to deliver a song with an unquenchable sense of humor."

She was born May 23, 1928, in Maysville, Kentucky, the daughter of Andrew and Frances (Guilfoyle) Clooney. He was a house painter and a heavy drinker. There was a brother (Nick), a half brother (Andrew—who drowned in an accident after World War II), and a sister (Betty). When Rosemary was very young, her parents began a pattern of separations and reconciliations. Frances Clooney went to Lexington where she worked in a dress shop. The Clooney children were farmed out to various relatives, sometimes living with their paternal grandfather, Andrew J. Clooney. When he was campaigning for reelection as mayor of their small Ohio river town, Rosemary and Betty (three years younger than Rosemary) would sing frequently at his political rallies. They also sang in amateur contests. Grandmother Clooney died when Rosemary was nine, and they were sent to live with the widowed Grandmother Guilfoyle. Later, when Frances Clooney married a sailor and left for California, Andy Clooney tried to make a home for his children, but it did not work out. Thereafter, the kids were shunted from relative to relative, and Rosemary attended four different schools. The only consistency in her life was her love of music, and during their high school years Rosemary and Betty sang with a local band.

When Rosemary was sixteen, she learned that Cincinnati radio station WLW was holding auditions to discover new talent. Rosemary and Betty responded and were hired to sing on a nightly local show at $20 each per week. They continued singing (as The Clooney Sisters) at the station for nearly two years. In the interim, Cincinnati bandleader Barney Rapp (with whom Doris Day had once sung) hired the girls to sing with his group. The summer after Rosemary graduated from Our Lady of Mercy Convent, Rapp introduced the sisters to bandleader Tony Pastor who was passing through town on tour. He hired them to join his band. It was 1945. Their uncle George Guilfoyle went with them on the tour; Pastor's star singer (Dolly Dawn) taught the girls how to put on stage makeup. In the post–big band boom Pastor and his group had to settle for mostly one-night stands as they played across the country: in theaters, at proms, in hotel ballrooms, at barn dances. In July 1946 they were performing at the Steel Pier in Atlantic City. Because Rosemary had the better middle-range voice, she sang solos for the sister team.

Rosemary's first recording with the Pastor group was "I'm Sorry I Didn't Say I'm Sorry When I Made You Cry Last Night" (Columbia Records). Disc jockeys took note of her "revolutionary" styling (she was so scared she was whispering) and predicted a good future for her. Rosemary admitted later that recording so frightened her that she avoided many more terror sessions for a long time. (Other recordings she and Betty made with Pastor's group were "Saturday Night Mood," "Bread and Butter Woman," and "The Secretary Song.") In the spring of 1949, Betty got fed up with the pressures of the business. During intermission one night in Elkhart, Indiana, she quit, packed her bag, and went home. Now on her own, Rosemary blossomed into a more polished, assertive songstress, enhancing her industry reputation. Later in 1949, Rosemary decided it was time to leave Pastor and go out on her own. Through Joe Shribman, then manager for Tony Pastor (and soon to become Rosemary's), Clooney gained an entrée to Mannie Sacks of Columbia Records in New York City. He signed her to a recording contract. Its terms guaranteed her only eight sides a year at $50 per side.

Between recording dates, she made club, radio (especially with Vaughn Monroe on the "Camel Caravan"), and television appearances. She was on "Arthur Godfrey's Talent Scouts" (CBS-TV) in early 1950 and won first prize. This led to her being hired for "Songs for Sale" (CBS-TV), which debuted on July 7, 1950. The program was a showcase for aspiring songwriters and there were two permanent show vocalists: Rosemary and Tony Bennett (who soon left and was replaced by Richard Hayes). The show was simulcast on radio and television. During late January 1951 she was also on the short-lived daily variety program "The Johnny Johnston Show" (CBS-TV). Meanwhile, her singles of "The Kid's a Dreamer" and especially "Beautiful Brown Eyes" gained her recognition at Columbia Records, where Doris Day and Dinah Shore were the top contract recording artists.

One of Rosemary's (known as Rosie) biggest boosters at Columbia Records was artist and repertoire man Mitch Miller, who insisted, "Rosie can sing anything and in any style. Then she always sings as if she's singing just to you. But her most important asset springs straight from the girl's character. To Rosie, everything is rosy." To prove her versatility, Miller asked her to record a novelty number that William Saroyan and Ross Bagdasarian had adapted from an old Armenian folk song. She refused. He insisted. The song was "Come on-a My House" and it became a huge hit, selling over a million copies. It was followed by such pop hits as "Botcha Me" and "Suzy Snowflake." She made the ballad "Tenderly" a big seller. And she began to record children's records ("Little Johnny Chickadee," "Me and My Teddy Bear") which had a distinct appeal because she understood "the arrangements can be cute, but your diction has to be perfect. Kids have to understand every single word." Clooney also continued to perform on radio and TV.

On a TV talk show in 1950 Rosemary Clooney had met stage and film actor José Ferrer, a man much acclaimed for his talent, his acerbic wit, and his ego. He was then separated from his stage actress wife, Phyllis Hill. Since then Ferrer had won an Academy Award (for CYRANO DE BERGERAC) and had been divorced. On July 13, 1953, he and Rosemary Clooney were married in Durant, Oklahoma, which was near Dallas where Ferrer was starring in *Kiss Me Kate* at the State Fair. They bought a house in Beverly Hills—it had once belonged to Russ Colombo (he died in the den there) and later to George Gershwin, and then to singer Ginny Simms. Meanwhile, Bing Crosby had become a big fan of Clooney's straightforward song style and it was he who recommended to Paramount production head Don Hartman that she be screentested. The studio was having problems with their blonde bombshell star, Betty Hutton, and was looking for a backup/replacement. Paramount contracted Clooney. She made her screen debut in THE STARS ARE SINGING, which premiered in her hometown of Maysville, Kentucky, in early 1953. Clooney was cast as a New York vaudevillian who, with the help of her neighbor (Lauritz Melchior) and others, hides an illegal alien (Anna Maria Alberghetti). The Technicolor film was slim going, but it was a strong showcase for peppy Rosemary, who reprised her hit "Come on-a My House," among other numbers. *Variety* reported that she "bounces about with considerable gusto in a part that doesn't allow for much show of histrionic talent." More zesty was HERE COME THE GIRLS (1953), one of Bob Hope's best 1950s vehicles. Set in a theater environment where the comedian/singer is being stalked by a slasher, it featured Arlene Dahl as the leading lady of the show-within-the-movie and Tony Martin and Clooney (once again refreshingly attractive) as the production's singing leads. Rosemary sang "When You Love Someone" and the more frantic "Ali Baba Be My Baby" as well as dueted with Hope on "Ya Got Class."

The studio had high hopes for its satirical musical Western RED GARTERS (1954), a project originally planned for Betty Hutton. There were stylistic flat sets and garish costumes, and all the expected genre conventions were overturned (the hero does *not* always win the gunfights, etc.). Clooney was the saloon owner who takes advantage of cowpoke Guy Mitchell to make her lawyer boyfriend (Jack Carson) jealous. She sang "Red Garters" and dueted "Man and Woman" with Mitchell. The picture was a flop. In contrast, WHITE CHRISTMAS (1954), shot in widescreen VistaVision and co-starring Bing

Crosby, Danny Kaye, and Vera-Ellen, was an enormous hit. Its show business story was a loose reworking of Crosby's HOLIDAY INN (1942) and Crosby not only reprised his megahit "White Christmas" but also scored well with "Count Your Blessings." Clooney's solo number was "Love, You Didn't Do Right by Me," and she was praised for a relaxed presence and her improved dramatics. This film is now a holiday perennial, telecast every yuletide. Coming at year's end was DEEP IN MY HEART, made on loan-out to MGM. The picture was an overproduced biopic of Sigmund Romberg, with José Ferrer in the title role. Among the horde of guest stars paraded forth was Rosemary Clooney, who joined Ferrer in a rendition of "Mr. and Mrs." During this period (October 7, 1954) she had begun "The Rosemary Clooney Show" on CBS radio, which lasted for a season.

In February 1955, Rosemary gave birth to her first child, Miguel José, and on March 11, 1955, she was the subject of "Person to Person" (CBS-TV). She did not return to the screen but instead pursued her recording career, with such hits as "Hey There" and "Tenderly." With her husband she recorded "A Bunch of Bananas" and "Woman" and with her good friend Marlene Dietrich she dueted on "Too Old to Cut the Mustard" and "That's a Nice, Don't Fight." She was a frequent TV guest on variety shows such as "The Ed Sullivan Show," "The Perry Como Show," and "The Steve Allen Show." She played at

Rosemary Clooney (second from left) in RED GARTERS (1954)

the London Palladium and at the Sands Hotel in Las Vegas. That December she announced she had been granted her release (at her own request) from her Paramount film contract. She planned, she said, to freelance in pictures thereafter. She made no further theatrical films.

In January 1956 she was contracted by Music Corporation of America (MCA) to star in the syndicated half-hour television show "The Rosemary Clooney Show." The well-received, intimate program featured Nelson Riddle's Orchestra and The Hi-Los. With The Hi-Los, she recorded the Columbia LP album *Now Hear This,* which rose to number nineteen on the charts in the fall of 1957. She had her own top ten single, "Mangos," which was on the charts for nine weeks in the spring of 1957. That fall, on September 26, 1957, she began a new half-hour variety series on NBC-TV, "The Lux Show Starring Rosemary Clooney," which featured Paula Kelly & the Modernaires and Frank DeVol and His Orchestra. It remained on the air for a season. By now Rosemary's divorced-again mother and her twelve-year-old stepsister Gail were living with the Ferrers (and their three children: Miguel, Maria, and Gabriel), as was José's daughter, Letty, by his first marriage. Because Mitch Miller at Columbia Records and José Ferrer did not get along at all, Miller's working relationship with Clooney suffered. She had no more big hits with the label and in 1958 left Columbia to join RCA. By now her entire career was subordinated to her family's needs and to her husband's whims. The Ferrers' fourth child, Monsita, was born in October 1958. When Ferrer decided California was no longer congenial to his talents, he ordered that they move to New York City. As Clooney's career petered out, she became more intrigued with politics, especially with the rising careers of the Kennedys. Later the Ferrers moved back to California and in March 1960 her fifth child, Rafael, was born. After his birth, she became active in John F. Kennedy's presidential campaign. On radio (a dying medium) she starred in "The Ford Road Show," which alternated daily with Bing Crosby's program. It lasted until 1962.

In September 1961 Clooney learned she was not the only woman in her husband's life. Over the next five years the couple separated, divorced, remarried, and divorced again. She had the responsibility of bringing up the children. She guested on "The Losers" episode (NBC-TV, January 15, 1963) of "The Dick Powell Show" and was on Bing Crosby's CBS-TV special that February, along with Frank Sinatra, Dean Martin, and Bob Hope. She continued to play the cabaret circuit.

The year 1968 was disastrous for Rosemary Clooney. That January she ended a two-year romantic relationship with a drummer fifteen years her junior. She had been relying heavily on pills for years, and this dependence increased on her pressured concert tour of the Far East, the Continent, and Brazil. Back in New York she contacted Robert Kennedy in California, a pal since the 1960 elections, and volunteered to work on his presidential primary campaign on the west coast. With all else in her world failing, politicking for Kennedy became *the* cause in her life. She was on the election trail for him in Oakland and San Diego, California. She flew back with Kennedy and his family from San Diego to Los Angeles in early June and was with the party at the Ambassador Hotel rally the night of June 5 when he was assassinated. She could not deal with the horrible reality of his death, was hospitalized briefly, but talked her way out of the situation as she would over the next weeks. In early July she was performing at Harold's Club in Reno when singer Jerry Vale showed her the *Life* magazine cover story on Robert Kennedy's murder. At her performance that night she told a stunned audience, "You can't imagine the price I've paid to be here to sing a bunch of dumb songs for you." Later, she hysterically tore up her hotel room and then fled to her Lake Tahoe apartment. Her physicians admitted her to a local hospital and later she was flown to Los Angeles where she managed to get released from one hospital before relatives, friends, and her priest convinced her to check into Mount Sinai Hospital, where she remained for several weeks. She underwent extensive therapy for the next eight years.

Less than six months after her crack-up she returned to performing, but several years of care and therapy were required before she regained the confidence necessary to make her performing nonmechanical. Meanwhile, rock had taken over the music business and she was considered a has-been. In December 1973 her mother died (as Clooney referred to it, "One of the great conflicts in my life ended") and in August 1974 her father died. In 1975 she and Bing Crosby made several performing tours together (including playing the London Palladium), which did a great deal to reestablish her both in the industry and with the public. She began recording again. Then, in August 1976, her sister, Betty (who had been in and out of show business over the years), died of a brain aneurysm. Then Bing Crosby died of a heart attack in October 1977. A month before Crosby died, he wrote the foreword to Rosemary's straightforward autobiography, *This for Remembrance*, written with Raymond Strait. Clooney said of this therapeutic experience, "It turned out to be the best thing I could do: Tell all and learn to live with it."

A much happier, much heavier Rosemary Clooney emerged in the 1980s. She played the nightclub circuit (especially Las Vegas) and in 1982 began touring with a theatrical revue, *Four Girls Four*, which at various times featured Margaret Whiting, Helen O'Connell, Rose Marie, Martha Raye, and Kay Starr. When CBS bought the screen rights to her autobiography, it was friend Merv Griffin who suggested that Sondra Locke would be ideal for the lead in ROSIE: THE ROSEMARY CLOONEY STORY (December 8, 1982). Clooney provided the soundtrack singing voices for both her character and that of her sister. In 1986 she turned up on an episode of "Hardcastle & McCormick" (ABC-TV) and on January 17, 1987, she was seen in the telefeature SISTER MARGARET AND THE SATUR-DAY NIGHT LADIES. In this CBS-TV film about a nun (Bonnie Franklin) who operates a halfway house for ex-convicts, she was a Bible-toting murderess. In 1988, when the gangster spoof MARRIED TO THE MOB was released, a recording of Rosemary's "Mambo Italiano" was featured in the film. Said Clooney, "I put that one to bed thirty years ago and I thought it would stay there." In April 1989 she and her brother, Nick, hosted the fourth annual *Singers' Salute to the Songwriter* in Los Angeles. It was a benefit for the Betty Clooney Foundation for Persons with Brain Injury, an organization founded by Rosemary. Currently she concertizes on tours for forty weeks a year.

Tremendously family-oriented, Clooney has a large clan, which now includes grandchildren and a rapport with Ferrer. ("José and I are friendly now. With five children we have to be.") Her painter son Gabriel is married to singer Pat Boone's daughter Debby. Daughter Maria is a painter, Monsita is married to a producer for the Christian Broadcasting Network, and both Miguel and Rafael are actors. Clooney's brother, Nick, is a TV anchorman in Cincinnati and host of the syndicated show "On Trial." His son is actor George Clooney. In recent years, Clooney's companion has been Dante DiPalolo, a dance coordinator whom she met at Paramount during the making of RED GARTERS.

During Clooney's tours with Bing Crosby in the 1970s, their drummer was Jake Hanna, who was the house drummer for Concord Jazz records. By the end of the 1980s she had recorded thirteen albums for the label, typically using small jazz groups for the LPs, although one album united her with Woody Herman's Orchestra. She has been consistently praised as one of this country's leading jazz vocalists for her phrasing. As she explains her craftsmanship, "You know, an awful lot of very good jazz singers do things with a melodic line within the chord, the improvisation. I don't have that ability. But I can read a lyric well, and I understand it. As Crosby used to say, 'You have three minutes as an actor to create that mood and tell your story, and that's all the time you've got.'"

## Filmography

The Stars Are Singing (Par, 1953)
Here Come the Girls (Par, 1953)
Red Garters (Par, 1954)
White Christmas (Par, 1954)
Deep in My Heart (MGM, 1954)

Rosie: The Rosemary Clooney Story (CBS-TV, 12/8/82) (voice only)
Sister Margaret and the Saturday Night Ladies (CBS-TV, 1/17/87)

## Radio Series

Songs for Sale (CBS, 1950–51)
The Rosemary Clooney Show (CBS, 1954–55)

The Ford Road Show with Bing Crosby & Rosemary Clooney (CBS, 1958–62)

## TV Series

Songs for Sale (CBS, 1950–51)
The Johnny Johnston Show (CBS, 1951)
The Rosemary Clooney Show (Synd, 1956–57)

The Lux Show Starring Rosemary Clooney (NBC, 1957–58)

## Album Discography

Blue Rose (Col CL-872, Col Special Products EN-13085) w. Duke Ellington
Children's Favorites (Col CL/2569)
Clap Hands, Here Comes Rosie (RCA LPM/ LSP-2212, RCA International 89315)

The Clooney Sisters (Epic LN-3160) w. Betty Clooney
Clooney Tunes (Col CL-969)
Come on-a My House (Col Special Products 14382)

Country Hits from the Heart (RCA LPM/LSP-2565)

A Date with the King (10" Col CL-2572) w. Benny Goodman

Deep in My Heart (MGM E-3153) [ST]

Everything's Coming up Rosie (Concord Jazz CJ-47)

Fancy Meeting You Here (RCA LPM/LSP-1854, RCA International 89461)

The Ferrers Sing Selections from "Oh Captain!" (MGM E-3687) w. José Ferrer

Greatest Hits (CBS 32263)

Greatest Hits (Embassy 31389)

Here's to My Lady (Concord Jazz CJ-81)

Hollywood Hits (Har HL-7213) w. Harry James

Hollywood's Best (10" Col CL-6224, Col CL-585, Col Special Products EN-13083) w. Harry James

Hymns from the Heart (MGM E/SE-3782)

Look My Way (UA 29918)

Love (Reprise 6088)

Mixed Emotions (Har HL-7454/HS-11254)

Now Hear This (Col CL-1023) w. The Hi-Los

Red Garters (10" Col CL-6282, Phillips B07652R) [ST]

Rendezvous (Camden CAS-2330) w. Bing Crosby

Ring Around Rosie (Col CL-1006) w. The Hi-Los

Rosemary Clooney and Dick Haymes (Exact 232)

Rosemary Clooney in High Fidelity (Har HL-7123)

Rosemary Clooney on Stage (Col CL-2581)

Rosemary Clooney Sings Ballads (Concord Jazz CJ-282)

Rosemary Clooney Sings the Lyrics of Ira Gershwin (Concord Jazz CJ-112)

Rosemary Clooney Sings the Lyrics of Johnny Mercer (Concord Jazz CJ-333)

Rosemary Clooney Sings the Music of Cole Porter (Concord Jazz CJ-195)

Rosemary Clooney Sings the Music of Harold Arlen (Concord Jazz CJ-210)

Rosemary Clooney Sings the Music of Irving Berlin (Concord Jazz CJ- 255)

Rosemary Clooney Sings the Music of Jimmy Van Heusen (Concord Jazz CJ-308)

Rosemary Clooney Swings Softly (MGM E/SE-3834)

Rosie Sings Bing (Concord Jazz CJ-60)

Rosie Solves the Swingin' Riddle (RCA LPM/LSP-2265)

Rosie's Greatest Hits (Col CL-1230)

Show Tunes (Concord Jazz CJ-364)

Songs for Children (Har HL-9501)

The Story of Celeste (MGM E-3709, MGM CH-111, Leo the Lion CH-104)

Swing Around Rosie (Coral 57266, Jasmine 1502)

Tenderly (10" Col CL-2525)

Thanks for Nothing (Reprise 6108)

That Travelin' Two Beat (Cap T/ST-2300) w. Bing Crosby

A Touch of Tabasco (RCA LPM/LSP-2133) w. Perez Prado

The Uncollected Rosemary Clooney (Hindsight HSR-234)

While We're Young (10" Col Cl-6297)

White Christmas (10" Col CL-6338)

With Love (Concord Jazz CJ-144)

Young at Heart (Har HL-7236)

# RUSS COLUMBO

RUSS COLUMBO'S IMAGE AS A ROMANTIC CROONER—HE IS PER-
haps the epitome of the word—has lived on although he has been dead for more than half
a century, and his memory has been retained in only a handful of recordings and films. Yet
even today his name conjures up the impression of the handsome, dark, velvet-voiced
crooner who made women swoon at the height of the Depression. In 1931 Al Dubin and
Joe Burke wrote a popular novelty song which pinpointed correctly the three top singing
idols of the day; it was called "Crosby, Columbo and Vallee." While Bing Crosby and
Rudy Vallee went on to become show business immortals, Russ Columbo's tragic death in
1934 made him a legend. Once called "Radio's Valentino," Russ Columbo, like Rudolph
Valentino, has lingered on in the public memory because of his untimely demise, which
cut short a career of tremendous promise.

Ruggiero Eugenio di Rodolfo Columbo was born in San Francisco, California, on
January 14, 1908, allegedly the twelfth child of a twelfth child of a twelfth child. When he
was five, Columbo's family moved to Philadelphia, where his father had a low-paying job
in a private bank in the Italian ghetto. A next-door neighbor taught young Columbo to
play the guitar; later, after the family returned to the West Coast, where the elder
Columbo now worked in the construction field, the boy took up the violin and opera
studies. While still in high school, Russ Columbo earned money as a violinist and he found
jobs playing background music during the making of silent films. In this capacity he came
to the attention of screen siren Pola Negri, who thought he resembled Rudolph Valentino.
She got him more music work as well as bits and extra work in motion pictures. After
graduating from Belmont High School in Los Angeles, where he was the school band's first
violinist, Columbo obtained work with George Eckhart and His Orchestra at the Mayfair
Hotel in Los Angeles. Next he worked with Slim Martin's Band at the Pantages Theatre
and then took a job at the Roosevelt Hotel in Hollywood with Professor Moore and His
Orchestra. He played violin in all these groups but with Moore he also was a substitute
singer and in that capacity sang on a nationwide hookup on CBS radio.

Russ Columbo's first substantial show business break occurred in 1928 when he
signed with Gus Arnheim and His Orchestra at the Cocoanut Grove Club in Los Angeles.
Again Columbo played violin and was backup vocalist to Bing Crosby, although the two
future singing idols often sang together. This exposure with Arnheim led to Columbo's
getting small parts in sound films, beginning with STREET GIRL in 1929 in which he appeared with the Arnheim aggregation. This was followed by a straight acting role as a Latin
type in WOLF SONG (1929). Next came WONDER OF WOMEN (1929), in which he sang

"Ich Liebe Dich," popularized that year by Nick Lucas on Brunswick Records. In Cecil B. De Mille's first talkie, DYNAMITE (1929), Columbo was cast as a Mexican prisoner, and he introduced the popular Dorothy Parker–Jack King song "How Am I to Know?" which Gene Austin made popular on Victor Records. In 1930 Columbo made his recording debut with Gus Arnheim on Okeh Records, and sang "Back in Your Own Backyard" and "A Peach of a Pair" for Victor Records. He then went on a tour of the East with the band but left in the summer of 1930 to return to Hollywood for roles in more films: HELLO, SISTER (1930), in which he had a small part in addition to composing the film's background music; THE TEXAN (1930), in which he played a cowboy singing around a campfire; and HELLBOUND (1931).

Columbo next formed his own band. After a brief tour the band played the Silver Slipper Club in Los Angeles, but when it closed he opened his own night spot, the Club Pyramid on Santa Monica Boulevard. It was there that he came to the attention of songwriter Con Conrad, who believed that Columbo had a real future as a singing star. In the summer of 1931 he cut a test record for Victor of "Out of Nowhere" with Conrad at the piano. After much trying in New York City, Conrad landed Columbo a fifteen-minute, four-week show on NBC radio, after Rudy Vallee introduced Columbo to network executives. When the month was up, Columbo was dropped, but after failing in its attempt to sign Bing Crosby for a series, NBC rehired Columbo and put him on the NBC Blue network. Within a matter of weeks his fan mail soared and he was soon dubbed "The Romeo of Radio." In September 1931, he began recording for Victor Records and he had several best-sellers, including "You Call It Madness (But I Call It Love)," which became his theme song, and "Prisoner of Love," both of which he wrote with Con Conrad. There were also such hits as "You Try Somebody Else," "Time on My Hands," "Save the Last Dance for Me," "Just Friends," and "Paradise." Columbo also composed such songs as "Let's Pretend There's a Moon," "Too Beautiful for Words," "My Love," "Just Another Dream of You," and "When You're in Love."

Columbo's success on radio and records soon spilled over into vaudeville and personal appearances, including a ten-week run at the Brooklyn Paramount Theatre. Con Conrad constantly churned out publicity for the new star, including accounts of alleged romances with Pola Negri and Greta Garbo. In reality, he did date actresses Dorothy Dell, Sally Blane, and Carole Lombard and was said to be particularly close to the latter two. Within a year of becoming associated with Con Conrad, Russ Columbo was able to command as much as $7,500 per week. During this period the musicians who worked in Columbo's band included Benny Goodman, Gene Krupa, Joe Sullivan, Babe Russin, Jimmy McPartland, Perry Botkin, and Leo Arnaud.

While performing in New York City, Columbo returned to moviemaking, starring in the Vitaphone/Warner Bros. two-reeler THAT GOES DOUBLE (1933), in which he portrayed himself and his lookalike, an office employee whom he hires to take his place at hectic personal appearances. In the short Columbo sang "My Love," "Prisoner of Love," and "You Call It Madness." Columbo then went to Hollywood to star in the United Artists feature BROADWAY THRU A KEYHOLE (1933). In this, his first major role, he was a crooner whose girlfriend is kidnapped; the case is solved with the aid of a Walter Winchell radio broadcast. Not only did Columbo receive solid reviews, but the feature gave him an opportunity to sing a song thereafter closely associated with him, "You Are My Past, Present and Future." Next Columbo was featured with The Boswell Sisters in the musical numbers for the Constance Bennett marital comedy MOULIN ROUGE (1934), for 20th Century Pictures and United Artists release. While Bennett sang "Boulevard of Broken Dreams," Columbo pleasingly crooned "Coffee in the Morning and Kisses at Night."

With his new-found success in motion pictures, in addition to radio, records, and personal appearances, Russ Columbo had become one of the most popular singers of the Depression era. He and Con Conrad formed a music publishing company, Rusco, Inc., and after Columbo returned to Hollywood he began starring on a Sunday night NBC radio program, hosted by gossip columnist Jimmy Fidler. In 1934 Russ Columbo signed a long-term, lucrative contract with Universal Pictures to star in a series of musicals for the studio (including James Whale's production of SHOW BOAT) but he was to make only one film for the studio, WAKE UP AND DREAM. Here Columbo was top-featured as Paul Scotti, a singer who forms a vaudeville act with two partners (Roger Pryor, June Knight) that becomes a star act. Columbo co-wrote the trio of songs he performed in the film—"When You're in Love," "Too Beautiful for Words," and "Let's Pretend There's a Moon"—all of

Russ Columbo and June Knight in WAKE UP AND DREAM (1934)

which he also recorded for Brunswick Records. He told interviewers at the time, "I find that I have just about everything I want from life and am pretty happy about the way things have worked out for me." The much-anticipated musical was released to affirmative reviews in October 1934, but by that time, twenty-six-year-old Russ Columbo was dead.

On September 2, 1934, Russ Columbo was visiting a close friend, Hollywood portrait photographer Lansing V. Brown, Jr., in the latter's home. The two were talking and looking at Brown's collection of Civil War dueling pistols when Brown struck a match on one of the weapons. A long-forgotten charge in the pistol exploded from the barrel, ricochetted off a table, and hit Columbo in the left eye. The corroded ball lodged in his brain. He was rushed to Los Angeles's Good Samaritan Hospital where he died without regaining consciousness. Sally Blane was at the hospital when he died. Columbo was buried in Los Angeles, and among his pallbearers were Bing Crosby, Gilbert Roland, Zeppo Marx, Carole Lombard's brother Stuart, Walter Lang, and Lowell Sherman (who had directed him in BROADWAY THRU A KEYHOLE).

Columbo's mother was never told of his death by his seven surviving brothers and sisters. Mrs. Columbo had suffered a heart attack two days before her son's tragic death and she was nearly blind. The family was afraid the shock of hearing about his death would kill her. They concocted a story about Columbo's being on a five-year tour abroad, and money from his life insurance policy was used to support her; they even made up letters to their mother written allegedly by the singer. The loving deception was continued for a decade, until her death. In her will she bequeathed part of her estate to Russ Columbo.

Over the years there have been a number of tribute albums to Russ Columbo, including those of Jerry Vale, Steve Mason, Gordon Lewis, and Paul Bruno, and several singers—including Johnny Desmond, Tony Martin, Perry Como, and Don Cornell—have been considered for the leading role in a yet-to-be-made movie based on the life of Russ Columbo. A TV drama with Tony Curtis playing the crooner also failed to materialize in the 1950s.

Because Russ Columbo developed into Bing Crosby's biggest 1930s rival, it is interesting that in the 1950s singer Rosemary Clooney purchased the home where Columbo was shot. In the very room where the shooting took place, she and Bing Crosby recorded several of their network radio shows in 1956.

Over the years it has been argued whether or not Russ Columbo would have remained as popular as Bing Crosby did, or even have eclipsed him. In the final analysis, however, it does not really matter since Russ Columbo continues to be fondly remembered for what he accomplished during his too-short, but successful, life.

## Filmography

Wolf Song (Par, 1929)
Street Girl (Radio, 1929)
Wonder of Women (MGM, 1929)
Dynamite (MGM, 1929)
The Texan (Par, 1930)
Hello, Sister (Sono Art–World Wide, 1930)

Hellbound (Tif, 1931)
Broadway Thru a Keyhole (UA, 1933)
That Goes Double (Vita, 1933) (s)
Moulin Rouge (UA, 1934)
Wake Up and Dream (Univ, 1934)

## Radio Series

The Russ Columbo Show (NBC, 1931–33)
The Jimmy Fidler Show (NBC, 1934)

## Album Discography

Crosby, Sinatra and Columbo (10" RCA LPT-5)
   w. Bing Crosby, Frank Sinatra
The Films of Russ Columbo (Golden Legends
   2000/2) [ST]
A Legendary Performer (RCA CPL1-1756)
The Long Lost 1932 Broadcasts (Broncoli
   Gegend 32134)

Love Songs by Russ Columbo (X LVA-1002,
   RCA LPM-2072)
Prisoner of Love (Pelican 141)
Russ Columbo 1930–34 (Sandy Hook 2006)
Russ Columbo on the Air (Totem 1031)
Russ Columbo on the Air—The Romeo of
   Radio 1933–34 (Sandy Hook 2038)

# PERRY COMO

THE ART OF CROONING ORIGINATED IN THE 1920s WITH NICK LUCAS and Gene Austin, who sold millions of records, and it reached its apex in 1929 with the romantic song stylings of Rudy Vallee, who was followed by Bing Crosby, Russ Columbo, Dick Powell, and many others. In the 1940s Frank Sinatra was still regarded as a crooner, but the vogue came to a halt as the decade waned and the last major exponent of the art of crooning was extremely clean-cut, supercongenial Perry Como. From his beginnings as a band singer, through his many years on radio and TV, plus his assorted hit records and a brief motion picture interlude, Como retained his ultra-relaxed crooning style as well as the reputation of being one of the nicest people ever to find success in show business.

Born Pierino Ronald Como on May 18, 1912, in Canonsburg, Pennsylvania, and called Perry, the future star was the son of Pietro and Lucia Como and the first of their thirteen children to be born an American citizen; he was the seventh son of a seventh son. Canonsburg was a mill and mining town and Como's father was a mill hand, but with fifteen mouths to feed, all the siblings who were old enough had to go to work. So young Perry, at age eleven, began an apprenticeship in a barber shop for fifty cents a week. His duties included opening the shop, lighting the stoves, and keeping the floors and mirrors constantly cleaned; the owner also taught him how to cut hair. When Como was fourteen, his father developed a debilitating heart condition so he set his son up in his own barber shop and the young man began earning his own living cutting hair. When business was slow, he picked up a guitar and sang. Within six years he was making $40 a week as a barber and he married his blonde childhood sweetheart, Roselle Belline, on July 31, 1933.

While they were vacationing in Cleveland, Ohio, Roselle talked her husband into auditioning as a singer for bandleader Freddy Carlone. The bandsman liked what he heard and offered the young man $25 per week to sing with his group. Como would recall later, "That was the end of my making an honest living. But it began seven years of one-night stands, climbing on and off buses, living in fleabag hotels."

Como began working with Freddy Carlone in 1933, mostly touring southwestern Pennsylvania. One night in 1936 while Como was performing in a casino in Warren, Ohio, bandleader Ted Weems came in to gamble and, upon hearing Como croon, offered him a job. Como accepted on the spot. In the spring of that year, in Chicago, Como made his recording debut with Weems on Decca Records vocalizing "You Can't Pull the Wool Over My Eyes" and dueting with Elmo Tanner on "Lazy Weather." For the next six years the younger singer continued to tour and record with the Weems Orchestra; among their Decca recordings were "Picture Me Without You," "Rainbow on the River," "Simple and

Sweet," "May I Never Love Again," and "Angeline." In 1939 Como sang the vocal on Weems's best-seller for Decca, "I Wonder Who's Kissing Her Now?" From 1940 to 1941 Como was the featured singer with Ted Weems and His Orchestra on the NBC radio program "Beat the Band." By the time the Weems group disbanded in 1942 after several members were drafted into World War II service, Como was making $125 a week. However, he was tired of the touring grind and wanted to settle down, especially since he and Roselle were expecting their first child (their son, Ronnie, was born that year). Como decided to return to Canonsburg and open another barber shop, but he received a call from General Artist Corporation in New York City offering him $76 a week to star in his own program on radio, and his wife convinced him that he should accept the job.

"The Perry Como Show" debuted on CBS radio on Sunday nights in 1943 and was an immediate hit. As a result he was given a singing engagement at the Copacabana in New York where he was a big success. The *New York World-Telegram* judged that Como was "darkly handsome, pleasantly wholesome and mercifully unaffected. His voice is a clear, full-throated baritone, and when he sings he appears to be suffering no pain at all." In 1943 he also began recording for RCA Victor with the song "Goodbye Sue," but sales were minimal. As he continued to record, RCA producer Eli Oberstein urged Como to put more volume into his singing and the result was his hit recording "Till the End of Time"; it would become the biggest-selling single record of the year (1945).

By this time, Hollywood had latched onto Como, hoping to repeat his singing success on film as with Frank Sinatra and Dick Haymes. In the next three years he would appear in a trio of 20th Century–Fox musicals with Vivian Blaine and Carmen Miranda, all directed by Lewis Seiler, but they failed to establish him as a popular screen crooner. (He was too mild a personality to make a vivid impression.) The first of the three films was SOMETHING FOR THE BOYS (1944), a watered-down movie version of Cole Porter's popular stage musical. This was followed in 1945 by DOLL FACE, based on a Gypsy Rose Lee play. In it he sang "Here Comes Heaven Again" and "Dig You Later (A Hubba-Hubba-Hubba)," which he also recorded successfully for RCA Victor. While Como's debut movie was in Technicolor, the second one was in economy black and white as was his final Fox musical, IF I'M LUCKY (1946), a mild remake of THANKS A MILLION (1935), which had starred Dick Powell and Ann Dvorak. Here Como crooned the title tune and "One More Kiss"; that number also featured Harry James and his band. In 1948 Como, who had still to develop a screen persona, made his final movie appearance, a brief song cameo (singing "With a Song in My Heart") in MGM's WORDS AND MUSIC, a specious screen biography of composers Richard Rodgers (Tom Drake) and Lorenz Hart (Mickey Rooney).

In 1944 Como and Jo Stafford became co-hosts of the weeknight radio series "The Chesterfield Supper Club" on NBC; they continued this chore until 1949 when the series became a half-hour Thursday night offering with Peggy Lee as Como's new co-host. During this period Como reigned as RCA Victor's top recording star with hits like "Prisoner of Love," "Temptation," "If I'm Lucky," "Because," "Some Enchanted Evening," "You Call It Madness," and "More Than You Know." Both "Prisoner of Love" and "You

Call It Madness" were associated with the late crooner Russ Columbo, whom Como had once met in Cleveland. Columbo greatly impressed Como, but his real idol was Bing Crosby. In fact, he guest-starred on Crosby's radio program in 1950 as well as on such other series as "Guard Session" and "Guest Star."

In 1948 Perry Como brought his radio show to TV, but in the early days he made little concession to the camera, which was simply planted in front of the microphone as the star and his guests performed. The fifteen-minute NBC-TV show ran in various time slots through 1950, when "The Perry Como Show" moved to CBS-TV and was seen for a quarter-hour on Monday, Wednesday, and Friday nights at 7:45 P.M. The series kept this format for five seasons; his radio show, meanwhile, was broadcast on Mutual in 1953 and 1954 and then simulcast with the TV show on CBS during the 1954–55 season. In 1954 Como won the first of his several Emmy Awards as a television musical show star. In 1955 Como's easygoing TV program became an hour-long variety outing on NBC each Saturday night and he was now one of the most popular singers on TV, famed for his unrufflability and his smooth singing of middle-of-the-road ballads. He also continued to be one of RCA's biggest sellers (often vying for top position with Tony Martin and Vaughn Monroe) with records like "A Bushel and a Peck" (with Betty Hutton), "Catch a Falling Star," "Caterina," "Don't Let the Stars Get in Your Eyes," "Hoop-Dee-Do," "Hot Diggity," "If," "Just Born," "Kewpie Doll," "Love Makes the World Go 'Round," "Magic

Harry James, Vivian Blaine, and Perry Como in IF I'M LUCKY (1946)

Moments," "Mandolins in the Moonlight," "Maybe" (with Eddie Fisher), "Moon Talk," "More," "No Other Love," "Papa Loves Mambo," "Round and Round" (a number one hit on the charts), "Tina Marie," "Wanted," "You're Just in Love" (with the Fontane Sisters), and "Zing, Zing—Zoom, Zoom." Como also continued to make lucrative personal appearances, and, on the domestic front, he and his wife adopted two children: son David and daughter Terri.

Perry Como's TV show moved to Wednesday nights on NBC-TV in 1959, and the one-hour program remained an audience favorite (especially because he showcased a wide variety of new, popular performers) until the 1962–63 season, when it was overwhelmed in the ratings by CBS-TV's "The Beverly Hillbillies"; it left the air in the spring of 1963. After that Como continued to appear on television every six to eight weeks in specials, but as the years progressed these outings came further and further apart until, by the end of the decade, he was making only yearly appearances on the small screen, although his ratings remained strong. Como's record sales also began to slip, although his 1963 album, *The Songs I Love*, sold well. In the fall of 1970, however, Como received his fourteenth gold record, for "It's Impossible," and he followed it up with a best-selling album of the same title; in 1973 he had the best-seller "And I Love You," which again produced a charted LP. He continued with his TV specials, most of them aired at various holiday times, and did good business in personal appearances at places like the Hilton Hotel in Las Vegas and Harrah's in Lake Tahoe. In the 1980s Como appeared in a PBS-TV special with the Boston Pops orchestra. On June 21, 1983, RCA hosted a special dinner at the Rainbow Grill at New York's Rockefeller Center to honor Como's fortieth year with RCA Victor Records and his fiftieth anniversary as a performer. (Como's last RCA album was issued in the fall of 1987.) In June 1989 he was elected to the Academy of Television Arts & Sciences Hall of Fame.

A religious man, Como is happiest spending time with his family and fishing and playing golf at his Florida home. While he never succeeded as a movie crooner, he certainly achieved great success on radio, on TV, and in recordings, making him one of the richest and most beloved of pop singers. Como maintains that religion has been the foundation for his continuing success. He said once, "Everything that's ever happened to me has been the result of faith. The faith I found in my father's house, and now find in my own house, and in my world. Sure, there are different beliefs, but as long as men believe, they believe basically the same thing. The lyrics may be different, but the music is always the same."

## Filmography

Something for the Boys (20th–Fox, 1944)  
Doll Face (20th–Fox, 1945)

If I'm Lucky (20th–Fox, 1946)  
Words and Music (MGM, 1948)

## Radio Series

Beat the Band (NBC, 1940–41)
The Perry Como Show (CBS, 1943–44)
The Chesterfield Supper Club (NBC, 1944–49)

The Perry Como Show (Mutual, 1953–54; CBS, 1954–55)

## TV Series

The Chesterfield Supper Club (NBC, 1948–50)
The Perry Como Show (CBS, 1950–55)

The Perry Como Show (NBC, 1955–61)
The Kraft Music Hall (NBC, 1961–63)

## Album Discography

And I Love You So (RCA APL1-0100)
The Best of Irving Berlin's Songs from "Mr. President" (RCA LPM/LSP- 2630) w. Sandy Stewart
The Best of Perry Como (Reader's Digest/RCA RDA-167-A)
Bing Crosby and Perry Como (Broadway Intermission 123)
Blue Skies (Pair 2-1112)
Broadway Shows (RCA LPM-1191)
By Request (RCA LPM/LSP-2567)
By Special Request (RCA Special Products DPL1-0193)
Como Swings (RCA LPM/LSP-2010)
Como's Golden Records (RCA LOP-1007, RCA LPM/LSP-1981)
Dream Along with Me (Camden CAL/CAS-403)
Dream on Little Dreamer (Camden CAS-2609)
Dreamer's Holiday (Camden CAL-582)
Easy Listening (Camden CXS-9002)
Easy Listening (Pair 2-1001)
An Evening with Perry Como (Camden CAL-742)
For the Young at Heart (RCA LPM/LSP-2343)
Greatest Hits (RCA International 89019)
Greatest Hits, Vol. 2 (RCA International 89020)
Hello Young Lovers (Camden CAS-2122)
I Believe (RCA LPM/LSP-4539)
It's Impossible (RCA LSP-4473)
Just (RCA AFL1-0863)
Just for You (Camden CAL/CAS-440)
Just for You (RCA Special Products DPL1-0153)

Just Out of Reach (RCA 1-0863)
A Legendary Performer (RCA CPL1-1752)
Lightly Latin (RCA LPM/LSP-3552)
Live on Tour (RCA AQL1-3826)
Look to Your Heart (RCA LSP-4052)
The Lord's Prayer (Camden CAS-2299)
Love Makes the World Go 'Round (Camden CAL/CAS-805)
Love Moods (Pair 2-10384)
Love You So (RCA AYL1-3672)
Make Someone Happy (Camden CAL-694)
Merry Christmas (RCA LPM-51)
No Other Love (Camden CAL/CAS-941)
Over the Rainbow (RCA ANL1-2969)
Perry (RCA AFL1-0585)
Perry at His Best (RCA PR/PRS-138)
Perry Como (RCA LPC-160)
Perry Como in Italy (RCA LSP-3608)
Perry Como in Nashville (RCA 1009)
Perry Como Sings Broadway Shows (RCA LPM-1191)
Perry Como Sings Christmas Music (Camden CAL/CAS-660)
Perry Como Today (RCA 6368)
Perry Como's Wednesday Night Music Hall (Camden CAL-511)
Pop Singers on the Air! (Radiola 1149) w. Vic Damone, Eddie Fisher, Dick Haymes
Pure Gold (RCA ANL1-0972)
Relaxing with Perry Como (RCA LPM-1176)
Saturday Night with Mr. C (RCA LOP/LSO-1004, RCA LPM/LSP-1971)
Season's Greetings from Perry Como (RCA LPM/LSP-2066)

Seattle (RCA LSP-4183)
The Scene Changes (RCA LPM/LSP-3396)
Sentimental Date (RCA LPM-3035)
A Sentimental Date with Perry Como (RCA
    LPC-187, RCA LPM-1177)
The Shadow of Your Smile (Camden CAS-
    2547)
Sing to Me, Mr. C (RCA LPM/LSP-2390)
So Smooth (RCA LPM-1085)
Somebody Loves Me (Camden CAL/CAS-858)
Something for the Boys (Caliban 6030) [ST]
The Songs I Love (RCA LPM/LSP-2708)
The Sweetest Sounds (Camden ACL-0444)
This Is Perry Como (RCA VSP-6026)

This Is Perry Como, Vol. 2 (RCA VSP-6067)
Till the End of Time (RCA LPC-109)
TV Favorites (RCA LPM-3013)
We Get Letters (RCA LPM-1463)
When You Come to the End of the Day (RCA
    LPM/LSP-1885)
Where You're Concerned (RCA AFL1-2641)
With Love (Family 149)
Words and Music (10" MGM E-501, MGM E-
    3231, Metro M/S-578, Sountrak 115) [ST]
You Are Never Far Away (Camden CAS-2201)
The Young Perry Como (MCA 1805) w. Ted
    Weems

# BING CROSBY

BING CROSBY, THE MOST FAMOUS OF ALL CROONERS, IS CONSIDERED by many critics and fans alike to be the most popular entertainer of all time. Certainly he was one of the most consistently active of twenthieth-century performers and he achieved monumental success in practically all aspects of show business in which he chose to participate; only Broadway eluded him, as he never ventured onto the stage in a play. Bing Crosby appeared in more than one hundred films, winning one Academy Award, and he is one of the all-time best record-sellers, with disc sales exceeding 200 million copies. His recording of "White Christmas," with sales of over ten million, is the champion best-selling seasonal disc. In addition, he was a star of radio for over three decades, he mastered television in a series of specials, and he was a big star in vaudeville and made numerous personal appearances throughout his more than half a century as an entertainer. Crosby's popularity seems to have been fostered equally by his many talents and his likable personality, although the latter has come under fire in recent years in books such as *Bing Crosby: The Hollow Man* (1981) by Donald Shepherd and Robert F. Slatzer and son Gary's *Going My Own Way* (1983). Nevertheless, troubadour Bing Crosby will always be thought of as the easygoing warbler who magically captivated a nation for some fifty years. In the early days Crosby's singing style was sincere with emotion and vocal clarity. By the mid-1930s, however, he adapted the easygoing, relaxed manner which included his famous "bo-bo-ba-bo" style (because he was said to have a poor memory for lyrics) as well as a penchant for whistling the chorus.

Harry Lillis Crosby was born in Tacoma, Washington, on May 2, 1901, the son of Harry Lowe and Catherine Helen (Harrigan) Crosby; the fourth of seven children, he had four brothers (one of whom, Bob, became a bandleader and occasional film player) and two sisters. He earned the nickname Bing because of his childhood addiction to the comic strip "The Bingville Bugle." In school he played football and baseball and won medals as a swimmer. He continued his athletic pursuits at Gonzaga University, where he studied law, but he was more interested in singing and playing the drums than in either his major or sports. He dropped out of college in 1921, and he and friend Al Rinker went to Los Angeles where the latter's sister, Mildred Bailey, was a successful singer at various night spots. The duo, "Two Boys and a Piano—Singing Songs Their Own Way," got vaudeville bookings. In 1926 they joined Paul Whiteman's band unit and the same year Crosby and Riker recorded "I've Got the Girl" for Columbia. Crosby's first solo record was "Muddy Water" for Victor in March 1927. Thereafter Whiteman added pianist Harry Barris to their act and the trio became known as Paul Whiteman's Rhythm Boys. Under that name they recorded many sides with the famed bandleader on Victor through 1930, with Crosby sometimes performing vocal solos.

In 1930 Whiteman and His Orchestra appeared in the Universal color musical THE KING OF JAZZ. Crosby was supposed to be spotlighted on the tune "Song of the Dawn," but a drunk-driving charge landed him in jail. The song went instead to John Boles, although Crosby and the Rhythm Boys did appear in the musical, performing a quartet of songs. The Rhythm Boys then left Whiteman in March 1930, to join Gus Arnheim's orchestra at the Cocoanut Grove where Crosby did many vocal solos (and some duets with the band's violin player, Russ Columbo) and got national exposure on the Grove's radio broadcasts. Crosby also began recording vocals with Arnheim on Victor and continued to do so until the spring of 1931 when the boys broke with Arnheim. At that point the trio dissolved, and Crosby went solo. Also in 1930 he married film starlet Dixie Lee, and starred in two Pathé film shorts, RIPSTITCH THE TAILOR and TWO PLUS FOURS. As a solo, Crosby landed singing bits in two 1931 features, REACHING FOR THE MOON and CONFESSIONS OF A CO-ED.

The breakthrough year for Bing Crosby, the one which sent him on his way to superstardom, was 1931. By now Bing's older brother Everett was managing his career. He maneuvered him into a job singing for CBS radio as well as starring in a series of comedy shorts for Mack Sennett in which Bing sang songs he recorded under his new pact with Brunswick Records and featured on the air. The radio show debuted in the late summer of 1931; Bing and Kate Smith became the network's two most popular radio singers. He played for twenty weeks at the Paramount Theatre in New York City, earning $2,500 per week for the first half of the vaudeville booking and $4,000 per week for the rest of the enormously popular stand. His Brunswick discs also began selling well, despite the Depression, and he had success with "Just One More Chance," "I Found a Million Dollar Baby," "I'm Through with Love," "Dinah," and his radio theme, "When the Blue of the Night Meets the Gold of the Day." Crosby quickly became Brunswick's biggest seller, eclipsing its former champions, Nick Lucas (after whom Bing patterned his crooning style) and The Mills Brothers.

Bing had become so popular that in 1932 he signed a deal with Paramount to appear in five feature films in three years for $300,000. The first film (in which he insisted on second billing to Stuart Erwin) was THE BIG BROADCAST (1932), the first of many features interpolating radio personalities into its plot; Bing sang one of his biggest hits, "Please," in the picture. After that Crosby was top billed in a series of pleasant musicals: COLLEGE HUMOR (1933), TOO MUCH HARMONY (1933), WE'RE NOT DRESSING (1934), HERE IS MY HEART (1934), SHE LOVES ME NOT (1934), plus a loanout to MGM to appear with and serenade Marion Davies in GOING HOLLYWOOD (1933). By 1934, Crosby was one of the film capital's top ten box-office draws and his 1934 CBS radio contract called for him to make $6,000 per week for thirty-nine weekly broadcasts. Also that year he became the first singer to sign with Jack Kapp's newly formed Decca Records, where he would remain for two decades. At Decca, and on radio, Bing Crosby's singing style began to change from strong-voiced, romantic crooning (a style at which he was the best) to easygoing "groaning," in a style that seemed to solidify his popularity with the American public, as did his being an all-around family man and the father of four sons: Gary (born in 1933), twins Philip and Dennis (born in 1934), and Lindsay (born in 1937).

In 1935 Bing joined NBC radio as host of the "Kraft Music Hall" and stayed with the show (later renamed "The Bing Crosby Show") for eleven years. He continued to make popular films for Paramount, such as MISSISSIPPI (1935) with W. C. Fields, THE BIG BROADCAST OF 1936 (1935) with George Burns and Gracie Allen, ANYTHING GOES (1936) with Ethel Merman, and RHYTHM ON THE RANGE (1936) with Frances Farmer and Martha Raye. He was loaned to Columbia Pictures for PENNIES FROM HEAVEN (1936) and returned to his home lot to star in such frothy Paramount entries as WAIKIKI WEDDING (1937) with Martha Raye and SING YOU SINNERS (1938). Then he was again loaned to Universal for EAST SIDE OF HEAVEN (1939) with Joan Blondell and returned to Paramount to play vaudeville impresario Gus Edwards in THE STAR MAKER (1939). For Decca Records he began turning out a host of best-selling platters like "The Very Thought of You," "With Every Breath I Take," "Love Is Just Around the Corner," "Soon," "It's Easy to Remember," "Without a Word of Warning," "I Wished on the Moon," "Red Sails in the Sunset," "Boots and Saddles," "Pennies from Heaven," "Small Fry," "You Must Have Been a Beautiful Baby," "Maybe," and "Too Romantic," among many others. Often he successfully waxed songs he sang in his Paramount features. In 1936 Bing and his wife, Dixie Lee, recorded duets on "The Way You Look Tonight" and "A Fine Romance."

In 1940 Bing Crosby's screen image began to change when he co-starred with funster Bob Hope in the first of their "Road" movie comedies, ROAD TO SINGAPORE. Instead of the crooning leading man, Bing became a wisecracking comedian as he and Hope made fast work of the film scripts. They peppered them liberally with their own topical ad libs, among exotic locales, music, and pretty girls, most specifically Dorothy Lamour, who appeared with them in all the "Road" entries. Crosby and Hope had a percentage deal on the series and made a bundle from the movies' immense profits. In addition to the "Road" comedies, which kept him in the top ten at the box office, Bing continued to appear in musicals such as IF I HAD MY WAY (1940) with Gloria Jean at Universal, BIRTH OF THE BLUES (1941) with Mary Martin, and in the yuletide classic HOLIDAY INN (1942) in which Crosby, co-starred with Fred Astaire, introduced Irving Berlin's "White Christmas" (which became Bing's top-selling single recording). During this World War II period, Bing Crosby was also a tireless worker for the war effort, entertaining both in the U.S. and overseas with the USO; he also appeared on scores of patriotic radio shows such as "Command Performance" and "Mail Call." In 1944 he won an Oscar for his portrayal of down-to-earth Father O'Malley in Paramount's GOING MY WAY and repeated the winning portrayal the next year for RKO's equally good THE BELLS OF ST. MARY'S with Ingrid Bergman. In the mid-1940s, Crosby turned to film production, but the two efforts he backed, THE GREAT JOHN L. (1945) and a remake of ABIE'S IRISH ROSE (1946), were not successful. However, he could afford the losses since it was estimated that he had earned $868,000 in 1946 alone.

After World War II, Bing continued to make movies and be heard on radio. He also resumed making records following the end of the union ban on recording ASCAP songs in 1945. His platters continued to sell well for the rest of the decade and included hits like "If I Loved You," "All My Life," "Day by Day," "Personality," "Golden Earrings," "But Beautiful," "Now Is the Hour," "Tallahassee" (one of a number of duets he did with The Andrews Sisters), "Memories," "So in Love," and "Dear Hearts and Gentle People." Wanting more free time, Crosby terminated his NBC contract and began recording his radio shows on tape with "Philco Radio Time" for ABC. He reteamed with Fred Astaire for the very buoyant BLUE SKIES (1946) and he also starred in an amusing version of A CONNECTICUT YANKEE IN KING ARTHUR'S COURT (1949), along with other musicals and the continuing "Road" series with Bob Hope.

In 1949 Chesterfield Cigarettes took over the sponsorship of Bing's CBS radio show, which became "The Bing Crosby Show" and ran until 1956. On camera he and Jane Wyman sang Hoagy Carmichael's "In the Cool, Cool, Cool of the Evening" in HERE COMES THE GROOM (1951). Increasingly, Bing was turning to dramatic roles in films such as JUST FOR YOU (1952), also with Wyman; LITTLE BOY LOST (1953); and, probably one of his most inspired roles, as the drunken former stage star in THE COUNTRY GIRL (1954), which earned him an Oscar nomination opposite Academy Award–winning Grace Kelly. He and Bob Hope made ROAD TO BALI (1952), their penultimate "Road" entry. By the mid-

Bing Crosby and Jane Wyman in HERE COMES THE GROOM (1951)

1950s, the inroads of television had greatly cut into his radio audience and the coming of rock 'n' roll eclipsed Bing's record sales. In the late 1950s he left Decca but continued to be an active recording artist for companies like Capitol, RCA Victor, Warner Bros., and Reprise well into the 1960s.

Although Bing had always photographed well on film, like many big-time performers he had been leery of television and he did not make his debut in the medium until June 1952 (at the age of fifty-one), when he and pal Bob Hope hosted a telethon for the Olympic Fund. Later that year Dixie Lee died of cancer. Two years later Bing starred in the musical comedy WHITE CHRISTMAS (1954) with Danny Kaye and Rosemary Clooney and ended his long association with Paramount with 1956's ANYTHING GOES as a faded stage star trying for a comeback. That year he teamed with Grace Kelly and Frank Sinatra (who had been Crosby's biggest rival as a crooner in the 1940s) for HIGH SOCIETY (1956), MGM's musical remake of THE PHILADELPHIA STORY (1940). The bright proceedings featured long-time Crosby musical friend Louis Armstrong, and the hit movie had Crosby and Kelly dueting "True Love," which became a very popular single. Bing played basically dramatic roles in MAN ON FIRE (1957) and SAY ONE FOR ME (1959), which found him again as a priest, though there were a few songs scattered among the drama. He produced the latter film at 20th Century–Fox as he also did the later college-set shenanigans of HIGH TIME (1960).

In 1958 Bing returned to network radio for CBS's "The Ford Road Show" with Rosemary Clooney; it ran until 1962. By now Bing was more active in television and had guested on Joan Davis's comedy series "I Married Joan" in 1953. In 1956 he co-starred with Julie Andrews in CBS-TV's elaborate production of "High Tor" on "Ford Star Jubilee," followed by a guest spot on "The Phil Silvers Show" the next year. He also began appearing on variety shows like those of Jackie Gleason, Bob Hope, and Perry Como. In 1957 he married actress Kathryn Grant; they had three children: Harry (born in 1958), Mary Frances (born in 1959), and Nathaniel (born in 1961).

In 1962 Crosby and Bob Hope did their last "Road" picture, THE ROAD TO HONG KONG (with only a guest bit by Dorothy Lamour) and he had his final dramatic role in feature films, that of the drunken doctor in the disappointing remake of STAGECOACH in 1966. He also starred on the unsuccessful TV sitcom "The Bing Crosby Show" for ABC in the 1964–65 season. By this time his recordings were only sporadic, although his older vinyl material was being reissued constantly. Crosby turned down the lead role (which went to Lee Marvin) in the film version of the Broadway hit PAINT YOUR WAGON (1969) because he did not want to go on location.

During the 1970s Bing Crosby, now head of Bing Crosby Productions, which produced film and television projects, appeared in DR. COOK'S GARDEN as the kindly doctor who practices euthanasia on dying patients, a part played by Burl Ives on Broadway. He was offered the lead in the "Columbo" detective teleseries, but did not want a long-term commitment. Bing appeared in a number of well-mounted television specials in tandem with his wife and three youngest children, and as a group they made personal appearances, both in the U.S. and abroad. Most fans seemed to agree that Crosby's voice had continued to season into a fine timber, and he recorded for labels like Pickwick, Amos and Daybreak. For the latter he and Count Basie did an album in 1972. Bing was always popular in England; in the mid-1970s he waxed two LPs there for United Artists, one with Fred Astaire, and his single of "Tie a Yellow Ribbon 'Round the Old Oak Tree" was a best-seller there.

On March 3, 1977, Bing finished taping a TV special saluting his half century in show business, then fell into the orchestra pit and was sidelined for months with a ruptured disc. Despite that fall, he and his family taped his annual Christmas program and they appeared for two weeks before SRO crowds at the London Palladium. He also recorded his final album, *Seasons*, for Polydor Records. There was serious talk of Crosby and Hope's making yet another "Road" picture. After the London engagement, Bing went to Spain for a golfing holiday (he was a near fanatical enthusiast of the sport) and on October 14, 1977, at age seventy-six, he collapsed and died from a heart attack on a golf course near Madrid, Spain.

Once, when asked about his extraordinarily successful career, Crosby said, "I wouldn't change a thing. I would do it just exactly the same way—by singing. I had a wonderful time. I would want everything to be the same."

## Filmography

Ripstitch the Tailor (Pathé, 1930) (s)
Two Plus Fours (Pathé, 1930) (s)
King of Jazz (Univ, 1930)
Check and Double Check (RKO, 1930)
I Surrender Dear (Educational, 1931) (s)
One More Chance (Educational, 1931) (s)
At Your Command (Educational, 1931) (s)
Reaching for the Moon (UA, 1931)
Confessions of a Co-ed [Her Dilemma] (Par, 1931)
The Billboard Girl (Educational, 1932) (s)
Hollywood on Parade #2 (Par, 1932) (s)
Dream House (Educational, 1932) (s)
Hollywood on Parade #4 (Par, 1932) (s)
The Big Broadcast (Par 1932)
Blue of the Night (Par, 1933) (s)
Please (Par, 1933) (s)
Sing, Bing, Sing (Par, 1933) (s)
College Humor (Par, 1933)
Too Much Harmony (Par, 1933)
Going Hollywood (MGM, 1933)
Just an Echo (Par, 1934) (s)
We're Not Dressing (Par, 1934)
Here Is My Heart (Par, 1934)
She Loves Me Not (Par, 1934)

Star Night at the Cocoanut Grove (MGM, 1935) (s)
Mississippi (Par, 1935)
Two for Tonight (Par, 1935)
The Big Broadcast of 1936 (Par, 1935)
Anything Goes (Par, 1936)
Rhythm on the Range (Par, 1936)
Pennies from Heaven (Col, 1936)
Waikiki Wedding (Par, 1937)
Screen Snapshots #5 (Col, 1937) (s)
Double or Nothing (Par, 1937)
Sing You Sinners (Par, 1938)
Don't Hook Now (Par, 1938) (s)
Dr. Rhythm (Par, 1938)
Paris Honeymoon (Par, 1938)
The Star Maker (Par, 1938)
East Side of Heaven (Univ, 1939)
Swing with Bing (Univ, 1940) (s)
Rhythm on the River (Par, 1940)
Picture People #1 (RKO, 1940) (s)
Road to Singapore (Par, 1940)
If I Had My Way (Univ, 1940)
Birth of the Blues (Par, 1941)
Road to Zanzibar (Par, 1941)
My Favorite Blonde (Par, 1942) (guest)

Holiday Inn (Par, 1942)
Angel of Mercy (MGM, 1942) (s)
Road to Morocco (Par, 1942)
Star Spangled Rhythm (Par, 1942)
Dixie (Par, 1943)
The Road to Victory (WB, 1943) (s)
Show Business at War (20th–Fox, 1943) (s)
The Princess and the Pirate (RKO, 1943) (guest)
The Shining Future (WB, 1944) (s)
Going My Way (Par, 1944)
Here Comes the Waves (Par, 1944)
Road to Utopia (Par, 1945)
All Star Bond Rally (20th–Fox, 1945) (s)
Hollywood Victory Caravan (Par, 1945) (s)
State Fair (20th–Fox, 1945) (voice only)
Duffy's Tavern (Par, 1945)
Out of This World (Par, 1945) (voice only)
The Bells of St. Mary's (RKO, 1945)
Monsieur Beaucaire (Par, 1946) (guest)
Blue Skies (Par, 1946)
Screen Snapshots #9 (Col, 1946) (s)
Road to Hollywood (Astor, 1946)
Welcome Stranger (Par, 1947)
My Favorite Brunette (Par, 1947) (guest)
Road to Rio (Par, 1947)
Variety Girl (Par, 1947)
The Emperor Waltz (Par, 1948)
Rough But Hopeful (Unk, 1948) (s)
A Connecticut Yankee in King Arthur's Court
  [A Yankee in King Arthur's Court] (Par,
  1949)
The Road to Peace (Unk, 1949) (s)
It's in the Groove (Unk, 1949) (s)
Honor Caddie (Unk, 1949) (s)
You Can Change the World (Unk, 1949) (s)
The Adventures of Ichabod and Mr. Toad
  (RKO, 1949) (narrator)
Down Memory Lane (Eagle–Lion, 1949)
Top o' the Morning (Par, 1950)
Riding High (Par, 1950)
Mr. Music (Par, 1950)
Here Comes the Groom (Par, 1951)
Angels in the Outfield [Angels and the Pirates]
  (MGM, 1951) (guest)

A Millionaire for Christy (20th–Fox, 1951)
  (voice only)
The Greatest Show on Earth (Par, 1952) (guest)
Son of Paleface (Par, 1952) (guest)
Just for You (Par, 1952)
Road to Bali (Par, 1952)
Little Boy Lost (Par, 1953)
Faith, Hope and Hogan (Unk, 1953) (s) (guest)
Off Limits [Military Policemen] (Par, 1953)
  (guest)
Scared Stiff (Par, 1953) (guest)
White Christmas (Par, 1954)
The Country Girl (Par, 1954)
Bing Presents Oreste (Par, 1955) (s)
Hollywood Fathers (Col, 1955) (s)
Anything Goes (Par, 1956)
High Society (MGM, 1956)
The Heart of Show Business (Col, 1956) (s)
  (narrator)
Man on Fire (MGM, 1957)
Showdown at Ulcer Gulch (Saturday Evening
  Post, 1958) (s)
Alias Jesse James (UA, 1959) (guest)
Say One for Me (20th–Fox, 1959)
This Game of Golf (Unk, 1959) (s)
Your Caddy Sir (Unk, 1959) (s)
Let's Make Love (20th–Fox, 1960) (guest)
High Time (20th–Fox, 1960)
Pepe (Col, 1960)
Kitty Caddy (Unk, 1961) (s) (voice only)
The Road to Hong Kong (UA, 1962)
The Sound of Laughter (Union, 1963)
Robin and the Seven Hoods (WB–7 Arts, 1964)
Bing Crosby's Cinerama Adventures [Cinerama's
  Russian Adventure] (Cin, 1964) (narrator)
Stagecoach (20th–Fox, 1966)
Bing Crosby's Washington State (Cinecrest,
  1968) (s)
Golf's Golden Years (Unk, 1970) (s) (narrator)
Dr. Cook's Garden (ABC-TV, 1/19/71)
Cancel My Reservation (WB, 1972) (guest)
That's Entertainment! (MGM, 1974) (co-host)

## Radio Series

Fifteen Minutes with Crosby (CBS, 1931)
The Bing Crosby Show (CBS, 1931–35)
Kraft Music Hall (NBC, 1935–40)
The Bing Crosby Show (NBC, 1940–46)

Philco Radio Time with Bing Crosby (ABC, 1946–49)
The Bing Crosby Show (CBS, 1949–56)
The Ford Road Show with Bing Crosby and Rosemary Clooney (CBS, 1958–62)

## TV Series

The Bing Crosby Show (ABC, 1964–65)

## Album Discography

Accentuate the Positive (Decca DL-4258)
Ali Baba and the 40 Thieves (Golden 20)
All the Way (Blue & Gold 1)
All-Time Hit Parade (Longines 224)
America, I Hear You Singing (Reprise 2020) w. Frank Sinatra, Fred Waring
Anything Goes (Caliban 6043) [ST] (1936 version)
Anything Goes (Decca DL-8318) [ST] (1956 version)
Anything Goes (Decca DL-4264)
Around the World with Bing (Decca DL-8687)
At My Time of Life (UA 29956)
Auld Lang Syne (10" Decca DL-5028)
Beloved Hymns (10" Decca DL-5351)
The Best of Bing (Decca DXB-184/DXS-7184, MCA 4045)
The Big Broadcast (Sountrak 101) [ST]
The Big Broadcast of 1935 (Kasha King 1935) [ST/R]
Bing—A Musical Autobiography (Decca DX-151)
Bing—A Musical Autobiography, Vols. 1–5 (Decca DL-9054, 9064, 9067, 9077, 9078)
Bing and Al, Vols. 1–6 (Totem 1003, 1007, 1013, 1015, 1016, 1017) w. Al Jolson
Bing and Bob Hope (Spokane 22)
Bing and Connee (10" Decca Dl-5390) w. Connee Boswell
Bing and Connee Boswell (Spokane 18)
Bing and Dinah Shore (Spokane 32)
Bing and Hoppy (Critter 8901) w. William Boyd

Bing and Louis (Metro M/S-591) w. Louis Armstrong
Bing and Mary—Rhythm on the Radio (Star-Tone 225) w. Mary Martin
Bing and Satchmo (MGM E/SE-3882) w. Louis Armstrong
Bing and the Music Maids (Spokane 21)
Bing and the Dixieland Bands (10" Decca DL-5323, Decca DL-8493)
Bing and Trudy Erwin (Spokane 23)
Bing at His Extra Special (Avenue International 1018)
Bing, Bob and Judy (Totem 1009) w. Bob Hope, Judy Garland
Bing Crosby (Going Hollywood [No Number])
Bing Crosby (Metro M/S-523)
Bing Crosby and Al Jolson Duets (Amalgamated 0003)
Bing Crosby and Bob Hope (Radiola 1044) w. Dorothy Lamour
Bing Crosby and Dorothy Lamour—Live (Amalgamated 237)
Bing Crosby and Friends (Magic 3)
Bing Crosby and Friends, Vol. 2 (Magic 10)
Bing Crosby and Perry Como (Broadway Intermission 123)
Bing Crosby and Red Nichols—Together Again (Broadway Intermission 142)
Bing Crosby and The Andrews Sisters (MCA Coral 804)
Bing Crosby and The Andrews Sisters, Vols. 1–3 (Coral 80, 91, 112)
Bing Crosby and The Rhythm Boys (Arcadia 5001)

Bing Crosby at the Music Hall (Joyce 1117)

Bing Crosby Classics, Vols. 1–3 (Cap SM 11738-40)

A Bing Crosby Collection, Vols. 1–3 (Col C-35093, C-35094, C-35748)

Bing Crosby, Duke Ellington and Nat (King) Cole (Amalgamated 253)

Bing Crosby/Glenn Miller—Rare Radio (Broadway Intermission 114)

Bing Crosby, Groucho Marx and Maurice Chevalier—Live (Amalgamated 221)

Bing Crosby—His Greatest Hits (Musidisc 30CV1356)

Bing Crosby in Hollywood (Col C2L-43)

Bing Crosby in the Thirties, Vols. 1–3 (JSP 1076, 1084, 1104)

Bing Crosby Live at the London Palladium (K-Tel 951)

Bing Crosby, Lucille Ball and Spike Jones—Live (Amalgamated 239)

Bing Crosby on the Air (Sandy Hook 2002)

Bing Crosby on the Air (Spokane 1)

Bing Crosby on the Air (Totem 1008) w. The Boswell Sisters

Bing Crosby Reads Tom Sawyer (Argo 561-63)

The Bing Crosby Show (Memorabilia 705)

Bing Crosby Sings (Vocalion 3603)

Bing Crosby Sings for Children (Vocalion 73769)

Bing Crosby Sings the Great Songs (MCA 2721)

Bing Crosby Sings the Great Standards (Verve 4129)

Bing Crosby Sings the Hits (10" Decca DL-5520)

The Bing Crosby Story, Vol. 1 (Col Special Products 201)

The Bing Crosby Story, Vol. 1—The Early Jazz Years (Epic E2E-201)

Bing Crosby—The Best (Music for Pleasure 5814)

Bing Crosby Treasury (Longines 344)

Bing Crosby with Special Guests (Amalgamated 1007)

Bing Goes Latin (MGM 2354-028)

Bing in Paris (Decca DL-8780)

Bing in the Thirties, Vols. 1–8 (Spokane 12, 14, 24, 25, 26, 27, 28, 29)

Bing Is Back (Totem 1002)

Bing 'n Basie (Daybreak 2014) w. Count Basie

Bing 1932–34 (Col Special Products 14369)

Bing Sings (Reader's Digest 127)

Bing Sings Broadway (MCA 173)

Bing Sings Crosby (Broadway Intermission 139)

Bing Sings While Bregman Swings (Verve 2020) w. Buddy Bregman

Bing with a Beat (RCA LPM-1473)

Bingo Viejo (Anahuac International ANC-3901)

Bing's Beaus (Amalgamated 805) w. Tallulah Bankhead, Marlene Dietrich

Bing's Music (Magic 1)

Bing's Party (Artistic 001)

Birth of the Blues (Spokane 9) [STR]

Bix 'n Bing (ASV 5005) w. Bix Beiderbecke, Paul Whiteman

Blue Hawaii (Decca DL-8269)

Blue of the Night (10" Decca DL-5105)

Blue Skies (10" Decca DL-5042, Decca DL-4259) w. Fred Astaire

Blue Skies (Sountrak 104) [ST]

Both Sides of Bing Crosby (Curtain Calls 100/2)

But Beautiful (Decca DL-4260)

The Chesterfield Show, Vols. 1–2 (Joyce 1133, 6050)

Christmas Greetings (10" Decca DL-502)

Christmas Sing with Bing (Decca-8419)

Christmas with Bing Crosby, Nat (King) Cole & Dean Martin (Cap SL-6925)

The Chronological Bing Crosby, Vols. 1–11 (Jonzo 1–11)

The Classic Years (BBC 648)

Cole Porter Songs (10" Decca DL-5064)

Collection of Early Recordings, Vols. 1–2 (10" Brunswick BL-5800-1)

Collector's Classics, Vols. 1–8 (10" Decca DL-6088-6015)

Command Performance, U.S.A. (Tulip 108)

The Complete Bing Crosby (Silver Eagle)

Cool of the Evening (Decca DL-4262)

Country Style (10" Decca DL-5321)

A Couple of Song and Dance Men (UA LA-588-G) w. Fred Astaire

Cowboy Songs, Vols. 1–2 (Decca DL-5107, 5129)

The Crooner (Col C4X-44229)

Crosby Classics, Vols. 1–2 (10" Col CL-6027, CL-6105)

Crosby, Columbo and Sinatra (10" RCA LPT-5) w. Russ Columbo, Frank Sinatra

Crosbyana, Vols. 1–2 (Broadway Intermission 111, 116)

Day Dreaming (Coral 113)

Der Bingle (10" Col CL-2502)

Der Bingle, Vols. 1–5 (Spokane 5, 10, 20, 30, 32)

Dick Powell–Bing Crosby (Amalgamated 162)

The Dinah Shore–Bing Crosby Show (Sunbeam 309)

Distinctively Bing (Sunbeam 502) w. Guy Lombardo

Don't Fence Me In (10" Decca DL-5063)

Down Memory Lane, Vols. 1–2 (10" Decca DL-5340, 5343)

Drifting and Dreaming (10" Decca DL-5119)

The Early Bing Crosby (Ajazz 526)

Early Film Soundtracks (Biograph BLP-M-1) [ST]

Early Gold (Col Special Products P4-13153)

The Early Thirties, Vols. 1–2 (Ace of Hearts 40, 88)

East Side of Heaven (Decca DL-4253)

Easy to Remember (Saville 190)

El Bingo (10" Decca DL-5011)

El Senor Bingo (MGM E/SE-3890)

The Emperor's New Clothes (Golden 79)

Fancy Meeting You Here (RCA LPM/LSP-1854, RCA International 89315) w. Rosemary Clooney

Favorite Hawiian Songs, Vols. 1–2 (10" Decca DL-5122, 5299)

51 Good Time Songs (WB 1435)

Forever (RCA International 89535)

From Bing's Collection, Vols. 1–2 (Broadway Intermission 135, 136)

From the Forties (Joyce 6052)

George Gershwin Songs (10" Decca DL-5081)

Go West Young Man (10" Decca Dl-5302)

Going My Way/The Bells of St. Mary's (10" Decca DL-5052)

Golden Memories (Col Special Products P614370)

Goldilocks (Decca DL-3511) [ST/TV]

Great Country Hits (Cap T/ST-2346, Cap SM-11737)

The Greatest Christmas Show (Music for Pleasure 210)

The Greatest Hits of Bing Crosby (M.F./MCA 7007)

Happy Holiday (Spokane 6)

The Happy Prince/The Small One (10" Decca DL-6000)

Havin' Fun (Sounds Rare 5009) w. Louis Armstrong

Hawaiian Gold/Island Magic! (Good Music/ MCA MSM-35082)

Here Is My Heart (Caliban 6042) [ST]

Here Lies Love (ASV 5043)

Hey Bing! (MCA 915)

Hey Jude—Hey Bing! (Amos 7001, Springboard SP-4003)

High Society (Cap W/SW-750) [ST]

High Tor (Decca DL-8272) [ST/TV]

Holiday in Europe (Decca DL-4281)

Holiday Inn (10" Decca DL-5092, Decca DL-4256, MCA 25205) w. Fred Astaire

Holiday Inn (Sountrak 112) [ST]

Holiday Inn/The Bells of St. Mary's (Spokane 15) [ST/R]

Home on the Range (Decca DL-8210)

How Lovely Is Christmas (Golden 121)

I Love You Truly (Coral 79)

I'll Sing You a Song of the Islands (Coral 90)

In a Little Spanish Town (Decca DL-8846)

Jack Be Nimble (Golden 23)

The Jazzin' Bing Crosby (Top Classic Historia 622)

Jerome Kern Songs (10" Decca DL-5001)

Join Bing in a Gang Song Sing Along (WB 1422)

Judy and Bing Together (Legend 1973) w. Judy Garland

Just Breezin' Along—A Tenth Anniversary Momento (EMI 1274)

Just for Fun, Vols. 1–2 (Broadway Intermission 134, 138)

Just for You (10" Decca Dl-5417)

King of Jazz (Caliban 6025) [ST]

Kraft Music Hall, Vols. 1–7 (Spokane 2, 3, 4, 7, 11, 13, 17)

Le Bing (10" Decca DL-5499)

A Legendary Performer (RCA CPL1-2086)

Lullaby Time (Decca DL-8110) w. Fred Waring

A Man Without a Country/So Proudly We Hail (Decca DL-89020)

Many Happy Returns (Vocalion 1)

Merry Christmas (10" Decca DL-5019, Decca DL-8128/78128, MCA 167)

Mr. Crosby and Mr. Mercer (MCA Coral 8025, Music for Pleasure 50554) w. Johnny Mercer

Mr. Music (10" Decca DL-5284)

More Fun! (Sounds Rare 5010) w. Louis Armstrong

Music! (Grappenhauser 1001)

Music Hall Highlights, Vols. 1–2 (Spokane 16, 19)

My Golden Favorites (Decca DL-4086)

Never Be Afraid (Golden 22)

New Tricks (Decca DL-8575)

New Tricks (Memoir 202)

Old Masters (Decca DX-152)

On the Happy Side (WB 1482)

101 Gang Songs (WB 1401)

Only Forever (Decca DL-4255)

Original Radio Broadcasts (Mark 56 762)

Paris Holiday (UA 40001) [ST]

Pennies from Heaven (Decca DL-4251)

Pepe (Colpix 507) [ST]

Pocketful of Dreams (Decca DL-4252)

Les Poupées de Paris (RCA LOC/LSO-1090) [OC]

Radio Cavalcade of 1936 (Amalgamated 252) [ST/R]

Rare Early Recordings, 1929–33 (Biograph 13)

Rare 1930–31 Brunswick Records (MCA 1502)

The Rare Ones (Broadway Intermission 128)

Rare Style (Ace of Hearts 164)

Remembering (Happy Days 123)

Rendezvous (Camden CAS-2330) w. Rosemary Clooney

Return to Paradise Island (Reprise 6106)

Rhythm on the Range (Coral 81)

Rip Van Winkle (10" Decca DL-6001)

The Road Begins (Decca DL-4254)

The Road to Bali (10" Decca DL-5444) [ST]

The Road to Hong Kong (Liberty 16002) [ST]

Robin and the Seven Hoods (Reprise 2021) [ST]

St. Patrick's Day (10" Decca DL-5037)

St. Valentine's Day (10" Decca DL-05039)

The San Francisco Experience (S.F.E. 101)

Say One for Me (Col CL-1337/CS-8147) [ST]

Seasons (Polydor PD-1 6128)

Selections from "The Country Girl" and "Little Boy Lost" (10" Decca DL-5556)

She Loves Me Not (Caliban 6042) [ST]

She Loves Me Not (Totem 1004) [ST/R]

Shhh! Bing (Crosbyana LLM-02)

Shillelagh and Shamrocks (Decca DL-8207)

Show Hit Tunes (10" Decca DL-5298)

Sing, You Sinners (Spokane 8) [ST/R]

Singularly Bing (Broadway Intermission 137)

The Small One/The Happy Prince (Decca DL-4283/74283)

Soft Lights and Sweet Music (Pelican 104)

Some Fine Old Chestnuts (10" Decca DL-5508)

Song Hits from Hit Musicals (10" Decca DL-5000)

Songs Everybody Knows (Decca DL-4415/74415)

Songs I Wish I Had Sung the First Time Around (Decca DL-8352)

The Special Magic of Bing (MGM 2353-101)

The Special Magic of Bing and Satchmo (MGM 2353-084) w. Louis Armstrong

Star Spangled Rhythm (Curtain Calls 100/20, Sandy Hook 2045) [ST]

Stardust (10" Decca DL-5126)

State Fair (Box Office Productions 19761, CIF 2009, CIF 3007, Sound/Stage 2310) [ST]

Stephen Foster Songs (10" Decca DL-5010X)

Sunshine Cake (Decca DL-4261)

Swinging on a Star (Decca DL-4257)

That Christmas Feeling (Decca DL-8781/78781)

That Travelin' Two-Beat (Cap T/ST-2300) w. Rosemary Clooney

That's What Life Is All About (UA LA-554-G)

Themes and Songs from "The Quiet Man" (10" Decca DL-5411)

This Is Bing Crosby (RCA DPS-2066)

Thoroughly Modern Bing (Pickwick International 6802)

Three Billion Millionaires (UA UXl-4/UXS-4) [ST]

A Time to Be Jolly (Daybreak 2006)

Too Much Harmony/Going Hollywood (Caliban 6039) [ST]

Top Hat, White Tie and Golf Shoes (Facit 124) w. Fred Astaire, Ginger Rogers

Top of the Morning/The Emperor Waltz (10" Decca DL-5272)

Traditional Carols (WLSM 1170) w. The Bonaventura Choir

Twelve Songs of Christmas (Reprise 2022) w. Frank Sinatra

20th Anniversary in Show Business (Joyce 1128)

Twilight on the Trail (Decca DL-8365)
Variety Girl (Caliban 6007) [ST]
The Very Best of Bing Crosby (MGM E/SE-4203)
The Very Best of Bing Crosby (World Record Club SHB-291-96)
The Very First Radio Broadcast (Frogbien 6309)
Victor Herbert Songs (10" Decca DL-5355)
The Voice of Bing in the Thirties (Brunswick BL-54005)
The War Years (Broadway Intermission 129)
Way Back Home (10" Decca DL-5310)
When Irish Eyes Are Smiling (10" Decca DL-5403)

Where the Blue of the Night Meets the Gold of the Day (Music for Pleasure 50249)
White Christmas (Decca DL-8083)
White Christmas (MCA 1777) w. Danny Kaye, Peggy Lee
Wrap Your Troubles in Dreams (RCA LPV-584)
The Young Bing Crosby (X LVA-1000, RCA LPM-2071)
Yours Is My Heart Alone (10" Decca DL-5326)
Zing a Little Zong (Decca DL-4263)

# VIC DAMONE

OVER THE PAST FORTY YEARS, HANDSOME VIC DAMONE HAS CARVED
for himself a respectable position in show business with his fine voice and easygoing
singing style. While he has had success on radio, recordings, and television, the mainstay of
Damone's career has been his steady nightclub engagements. For nearly all of his career
Vic Damone has been a popular club attraction both in the United States and abroad.
With his laid-back vocalizing and pleasant personality, Vic Damone has never really made
a big career splash. Instead, his success is a result of continuous hard work over the decades.
In the early and mid-1950s Metro-Goldwyn-Mayer attempted to make a movie star of the
singer, but although he crooned in a handful of big-budget screen musicals, he never
caught on with filmgoers. His intimate brand of entertaining is far better geared to the
more personal atmosphere of clubs.

Vic Damone's family migrated to America from Italy after World War I and settled
in Brooklyn, where he was born Vito Farinola on June 12, 1928. His family was musically
inclined: his mother played the piano and the boy learned Italian folk songs from his dad.
While in school he sang in amateur contests and in the school glee club. When he was
fifteen the teenager made his professional singing debut on radio station WOR's "Rainbow
House" program and then found a job as an usher at New York City's Paramount Theatre,
where he saw the finest entertainers of the day at work. His next job was as an elevator
operator. Legend has it that one day one of his passengers was Perry Como, for whom
Damone auditioned on the spot. Como urged the young man to continue with his
singing, and Vic auditioned for "Arthur Godfrey's Talent Scouts" radio show where he
was heard by Milton Berle. The comedian, too, was impressed by the young man's singing
and told him if he won the Godfrey show contest, he would help him get a club audition.
Damone won the amateur contest and, true to his word, Berle got him an audition at La
Martinique. As a result, Vic Damone (his professional name by now) had a stay of eleven
weeks to critical and audience acclaim.

Vic Damone's hard work at USO canteens, church socials, and small clubs had paid
off, and he was soon signed to star at the Paramount Theatre, where only a short time
before he had been an usher. As a result of these winning appearances, he was signed by
Mercury Records in 1948. He also contracted for his own radio series, "The Pet Milk
Program," which was heard on NBC. During the 1948–49 season the show was on
Saturday nights, while in 1949–50 it was broadcast on Sundays. He also guested on such
radio programs as those of Spike Jones and Louella Parsons, and on "Guest Star." His
Mercury singles established him as a solid song plugger with such items as "Vagabond
Shoes," "Tzena, Tzena, Tzena," "Just Say I Love Her," "My Truly, Truly Fair," "Longing

for You," "My Heart Cries for You," "Calla Calla," "Por Favor," and "April in Portugal." He headlined clubs like the Copacabana and the Riviera, plus the Roxy Theatre, Gotham's Waldorf-Astoria, and the Mocambo in Hollywood.

Following his success on stage, radio, and recordings, Hollywood called on Vic Damone and he signed with MGM, making his screen debut in the Technicolor musical RICH, YOUNG AND PRETTY (1951) as André Milan, a Parisian who romances American Jane Powell who is on a French holiday. The *New York Times* assessed, "Vic Damone, idol of the bobby soxers, is somewhat stiff and callow in his screen debut," while *Variety* admitted, "Vocally, Damone knows his way around a tune." Next he was cast in THE STRIP (1951), a low-budget drama about a drummer (Mickey Rooney) who fends off mobsters while trying to get Sally Forrest a movie contract. Damone was on hand as a guest star who sings "Don't Blame Me."

Before Damone's screen career could gain any momentum, he was drafted into military service and served two years in the U.S. Army in Europe. Back in civilian life, he resumed radio and club work and returned to MGM—which was coming apart at the seams by this time—playing the part of singer Johnny Nyle in the musical ATHENA (1954), a satire on health fads. It had him romancing Debbie Reynolds on camera and performing tunes like "Imagine," "Venezia" (a pretentious production number), and "The

Wendell Corey, Vic Damone, Jane Powell, and Fernando Lamas in
RICH, YOUNG AND PRETTY (1951)

Girl Next Door." He then made a guest appearance in the Sigmund Romberg biopic DEEP IN MY HEART (1954) singing "Road to Paradise" and dueting with Jane Powell on "Will You Remember."

In 1955 Damone and Tony Martin played two sailors on shore leave looking for romance, and finding it with Jane Powell and Debbie Reynolds in HIT THE DECK. Damone and Jane Powell sang "I Know That You Know" and with Tony Martin, Russ Tamblyn, and the Jubilaires he performed "Hallelujah!" If any of his studio pictures could be considered a starring vehicle, it was the Technicolor musical KISMET (1955), in which he played a Caliph in ancient Mesopotamia who romances the beautiful Marsinah (Ann Blyth), the daughter of poet/beggar Jaaj (Howard Keel). Looking stiff and very uncomfortable, Damone warbled "Night of My Nights," dueted with Ann Blyth on "Stranger in Paradise," and with Keel and Blyth sang "This Is My Beloved." *Variety* observed of the Damone–Blyth love team: "their romantic pairing does not come off." It did not matter, for by now MGM was phasing out its musicals and Damone, along with many other singing personalities, was let go by the studio. It was two years before he was involved in filmmaking again. He was heard, singing over the opening credits, the exceedingly popular title song of AN AFFAIR TO REMEMBER (1957); the next year, for the same studio (20th Century–Fox), he performed similar chores for THE GIFT OF LOVE.

In the mid-1950s, Vic Damone signed with Columbia Records, and had best-selling single records such as "On the Street Where You Live," "An Affair to Remember," and "Gigi." His LPs for the label also sold well, particularly *That Towering Feeling!* (1956), which reached number eight on the *Billboard* charts. On December 23, 1956, he appeared in the NBC-TV special "The Stingiest Man in Town" with Johnny Desmond, Basil Rathbone (as Ebenezer Scrooge), Patrice Munsel, and The Four Lads. The previous summer he had begun his "The Vic Damone Show" on CBS-TV, which served as a summer replacement for "December Bride." It was a half-hour experimental show which dealt with Damone's "personal" life, his friends, and various guests. The next summer the program returned on CBS-TV, but as a one-hour musical variety show with Damone backed by The Spellbinders. Damone also continued to be a top nightclub attraction. In 1960 he did a dramatic role on "The June Allyson Show."

It was also in 1960 that Damone returned to movies, starring in the wartime drama HELL TO ETERNITY for Allied Artists. In it he was soldier Pete involved in the U.S. action in the South Pacific during World War II with his two buddies, played by Jeffrey Hunter and David Janssen. Continuing his dramatic work, he guest-starred in the ABC-TV Western "The Rebel" as well as in episodes of the comedy series "The Dick Van Dyke Show" and "The Joey Bishop Show." In the early 1960s he signed with Capitol Records and had a best-selling album called *Linger Awhile*. From July to September 1962 he starred in the half-hour NBC-TV musical program "The Lively Ones"; Joan Staley and Shirley Yelm co-hosted the show with Damone. When it returned for a second season on NBC-TV in the summer of 1963, Quinn O'Hara and Gloria Neil co-hosted with Damone.

In 1965, Vic Damone began recording with Warner Bros. Records and had good selling singles with "You Were Only Fooling" and "Why Don't You Believe Me?" as well as the album *You Were Only Fooling*. He was also one of the first contemporary pop singers to record an entire LP of country tunes, with *Country Love Songs*. On November 11, 1965, he starred in the ABC-TV special "The Dangerous Christmas of Red Riding Hood" with Cyril Ritchard, Liza Minnelli, and The Animals. He did a dramatic role on "Jericho" on CBS-TV in 1966 and guested on such comedy and variety programs as those of Danny Thomas, John Gary, Johnny Carson, Mike Douglas, and Merv Griffin. From June to September 1967 Damone headlined the NBC-TV off-season series "The Dean Martin Summer Show Starring Your Host Vic Damone." The one-hour musical show also featured Carol Lawrence, Don Cherry, and Gail Martin (Dean's daughter). He was also back on screen in 1967 in the independent feature SPREE, a junk entry which spliced in portions of his nightclub act in Las Vegas. Neither he nor the film's other unhappily included stars (Juliet Prowse, Jayne Mansfield, Mickey Hargitay, The Clara Ward Singers) received billing—they sought a court order to have their names removed. In the late 1960s he cut a series of record albums for RCA. During the summer of 1971 Damone was back on TV in NBC-TV's "The Vic Damone Show." However, the shows were composed of segments of the 1967 outing he had done for the network, not new material.

In the past two decades Vic Damone has remained a headliner through his constant club work, TV appearances, and recordings, although the latter have been for minor labels (Applause, Rebecca, West Coast, and others). While his career has continued to flow like a strong and steady stream, his personal life has been an emotional see-saw. On November 24, 1954, Damone married beautiful Italian actress Pier Angeli, also under MGM contract, in what appeared to be a storybook love story. Their son, Perry Rocco Luigi (named in honor of singer Perry Como), was born the following August. Thereafter there were a series of much-publicized emotional separations and reconciliations with Damone insisting that his mother-in-law was the cause of their domestic problems. They were divorced in 1959, but spent the next six years in court battles over the custody of their son, each accusing the other of kidnapping the child. They finally reached a settlement in 1965. In September of 1971 Pier Angeli committed suicide by taking barbiturates; three years later, Damone's second wife, Judy Rawlins, with whom he had three daughters and from whom he was divorced, killed herself in the same manner. Later he married and divorced for a third time. For many years, Damone and songstress Diahann Carroll had been dating. On January 8, 1987, the black star and Damone were married in Las Vegas and that same weekend sang together in the showroom at the Golden Nugget Hotel. It was the fourth marriage for each, and generated a great deal of publicity. They took up residence in Beverly Hills and began performing together on the nightclub circuit throughout the country. *Variety* reported of one of their joint engagements at Harrah's in Reno, Nevada, "few evenings can offer so much fine singing and pleasant personality. . . . It's what can be expected from Damone, who has always been one of the more underrated of the saloon singers." For Damone, who has long had an unsettling personal life, tragedy struck again in 1987 when his younger sister, Sandy Boucher, was shot and killed in Miami Beach by her ex-husband, Avrum Cohen, who also killed himself.

While Vic Damone has never achieved the superstar status of Bing Crosby, Frank Sinatra, or Dean Martin, or become a singing idol like Perry Como, he has established himself as one of the entertainment world's most reliable songsters. Although his greatest popularity came in the 1950s, he still has a solid coterie of fans who insist that Damone is, as one of his record album titles puts it, *The Best Damn Singer in the World.*

## Filmography

Rich, Young and Pretty (MGM, 1951)
The Strip (MGM, 1951)
Athena (MGM, 1954)
Deep in My Heart (MGM, 1954)
Hit the Deck (MGM, 1955)
Kismet (MGM, 1955)

Meet Me in Las Vegas (MGM, 1956)
An Affair to Remember (20th–Fox, 1957) (voice only)
The Gift of Love (20th–Fox, 1958) (voice only)
Hell to Eternity (AA, 1960)
Spree (United Producers, 1967)

## Radio Series

The Pet Milk Program (NBC, 1948–50)

## TV Series

The Vic Damone Show (CBS, 1956, 1957)
The Lively Ones (NBC, 1962, 1963)

The Dean Martin Summer Show Starring Your Host Vic Damone (NBC, 1967)
The Vic Damone Show (NBC, 1971)

## Album Discography

An Affair to Remember (Col CL-1013) [ST]
America's Favorites (10" Mer MG-25045)
Amor (10" Mer MG-25174)
Angela Mia (Columbia CL-1088/CS-6046)
Athena (10" Mer MG-25202, M.P.T. 2) [ST]
The Best Damn Singer in the World (West Coast 14001)
The Best of Vic Damone (Har HL-7328)
Born to Sing (Wing PKW-2-117)
Closer Than a Kiss (Col CL-1174/CS-8019)
Country Love Songs (WB 1607)
The Damone Type of Thing (RCA LPM/LSP-3916, RCA International 89261)
Damone's Best (RCA International 89170)
Damone's Feelings (Rebecca 1212)
Damone's Inspiration (Rebecca 1213)

The Dangerous Christmas of Red Riding Hood (ABC ABC/ABCS-536) [ST/TV]
Deep in My Heart (MGM E-31530) [ST]
Ebb Tide (10" Mer MG-25194)
The Gift of Love (Col CL-1113) [ST]
Hit the Deck (MGM E-3163) [ST]
I'll Sing for You (Wing 12113/16113)
In My Own Way (Ember 5051)
Judy and Vic (Minerva 6JG-TVD) w. Judy Garland
Kismet (MGM E-3281, Metro M/S-526) [ST]
Linger Awhile (Cap T/ST-1646, EMI/Cap 186741)
The Liveliest (Cap T/ST-1944)
The Lively Ones (Cap T/ST-1748, EMI/Pathé 260414)

Make Someone Happy (RCA International 5125)

Melody Parade (Mer MG-20041) w. Vincent Lopez, Lanny Ross

My Baby Loves to Swing (Cap T/ST-1811, EMI/Cap 1151)

The Night Has a Thousand Eyes (10" Mer MG-25131)

Now and Forever (RCA International 5234)

On the South Side of Chicago (RCA LPM/LSP-3765, RCA International 89263)

On the Street Where She Lives (Col Special Products 11128)

On the Street Where You Live (Cap T/ST-2133)

On the Swingin' Side (Col CL-1573/CS-8373)

Over the Rainbow (Applause 1018)

Pop Singers on the Air! (Radiola 1149) w. Perry Como, Eddie Fisher, Dick Haymes

Starring Vic Damone (Premiere 9013) w. Johnny Desmond, The Stradivari Strings

Stay with Me (RCA LPM/LSP-3671, RCA International 89262)

The Stingiest Man in Town (Col CL-950) [ST/TV]

Strange Enchantment (Cap T/ST-1691, EMI/Cap 260003)

Take Me in Your Arms (10" Mer MG-25132)

Tenderly (Wing 12157)

That Towering Feeling! (Col CL-900)

This Game of Love (Col CL-1368/CS-8169)

20 Golden Pieces (Bulldog 2001)

Vic Damone (10" Mer MG-25028)

Vic Damone (CBS 32371)

Vic Damone Favorites (Mer MG-20194)

Vic Damone in San Francisco (Rebecca 1214)

Vic Damone Now (RCA International 5080)

Vic Damone Sings (Har HL-7431/HS-11231)

Vic Damone Sings (Manhattan 521)

Vic Damone Sings the Great Songs (CBS 32261)

The Voice of Vic Damone (Mer MG-20194)

Why Can't I Walk Away (RCA LSP-3984, RCA International 89264)

You Were Only Fooling (WB 1602)

Young and Lively (Col CL-1912/CS-8712)

# BOBBY DARIN

FEW PERFORMERS HAVE BEEN AS BLATANTLY AMBITIOUS, DRIVEN, AND egotistical as Bobby Darin, who earned the nickname of show business's "Angry Young Man." But then few performers have been as talented as this aggressive New Yorker. He was determined to make it big and he did. Within a few short years in the late 1950s to early 1960s he rose from teenaged singing idol to respected nightclub attraction to an Oscar-nominated screen performer. While he had charisma and sex appeal, he was not a handsome man: his face was chubby, his hairline receding and his profile far from classic. Nor was he a melodious singer in the traditional manner. He typically thrust out lyrics from the side of his mouth, punctuating them by his snapping fingers and bolstering them by his flippant demeanor. Darin was the first to admit, "Vic Damone is a singer, I'm a performer. Even on records, what I'm saying is far more important than how well I'm singing." A *TV Guide* magazine interviewer in 1961 summed it up, "All in all, Darin has little working in his favor—except that vast, imperious finger-snapping, self-confidence—and for some reason . . . this makes people stand and cheer him."

Bobby Darin's craftsmanship as a vocalist extended to song writing, and went far beyond the songs most closely associated with him: "Splish Splash," "Mack the Knife," and "Beyond the Sea." Politically he was an ardent follower of John F. and Robert F. Kennedy. Romantically he was loved by singing peer Connie Francis but he married movie star Sandra Dee instead. In retrospect, a good deal of his brash, self-assertive behavior was attributed to his long-standing hunch that he would have a short life (he died at age thirty-seven).

He was born Walden Robert Cassotto on May 14, 1936, in New York's East Harlem, the son of Saverio "Sam" Anthony Cassotto and Vivian "Polly" Fern (Walden) Cassotto. (Mrs. Cassotto had been in vaudeville and had been twice previously married.) There was already an older child, Vanina (Nina), born fourteen years earlier. (According to Connie Francis in her autobiography, *Who's Sorry Now* [1984], Darin would learn shortly before his own death that Nina was actually his mother, having given birth to him out of wedlock.) Cassotto, a gambler with many shady connections, died in prison from narcotics withdrawal seven months before Walden was born. He was a sickly baby and from the age of eight until thirteen suffered recurring attacks of rheumatic fever. It was this constant illness (and pampering from his mother and married sister who fostered his love of show business) that later drove him in his obsession to become a star by the age of twenty-five or earlier. (As he remarked in 1972, "For thirty years I expected to die.")

Growing up in the tough part of the Bronx, where any illness was considered a sign of weakness, he very quickly developed a swaggering demeanor. Because of his poor health, he was bedridden much of his early life and his doting mother served as his teacher. He read a great deal and by the time he entered junior high school he was an excellent student, albeit with a chip on his shoulder. It was this excellence that led to his being recommended for admission to the respected Bronx High School of Science. By then he had learned to play the drums, piano, guitar, vibraharp, and bass, none of which was appreciated by his classmates at the science-oriented high school. He admitted later, "All the arrogance you read about stems from those days in high school. It all stems from a desire to be nobody's fool again."

After graduating from high school in June 1952 he entered Hunter College, planning to become an actor. But after a semester he rebelled at the regimen and competition of the New York college scene and quit. By now he had been spending his summers at Catskill resorts, serving as a singing waiter and also as a drummer in a local band there. Sometimes during these gigs he filled in as singer, master of ceremonies, or general entertainer, sometimes doing imitations of Donald O'Connor or Jerry Lewis. Back in the city he held a variety of odd jobs, from sweeping up scrap in a metal factory to cleaning guns for the Navy at the Navy Yard in Brooklyn. He met a thirty-one-year-old dancer (and the mother of a ten year old) who hired him to play drums for her on tour. Eighteen months later she had fired him and rejected him as a lover. ("Before I met her I said 'I want to.' Afterwards I said 'I'm going to.'") By now he was Bobby Darin (having selected his new surname at random from the telephone book; other sources say that it derived from his taking part of a word from a Chinese restaurant sign which flashed the word "mandarin"—only the first three letters were burned out). He was living in a tenement apartment with another struggling show business hopeful, Richard Behrke, and was collaborating with Don Kirschner (a fellow Bronx Science classmate and later a music publisher). Together they wrote radio commercials which they sometimes sang. They used their salaries to make demonstration records of their own songs.

Kirschner took one of these records (which featured Darin singing) to George Scheck (Connie Francis' manager) who, in turn, brought it to Decca Records. Decca was sufficiently impressed to sign Darin to a year's contract. Darin recorded four songs and to plug them he was put on the Dorsey Brothers' TV variety show "Stage Show" (CBS-TV). According to Darin, "I went on 'cold,' scared to death, and sang 'Rock Island Line.' It bombed." So did the three other ballads he had recorded, as well as four subsequent recordings. Decca dropped him. And Connie Francis' father, fearful of losing control over his daughter, broke up her relationship with Darin and forced Scheck to break off his working relationship with Bobby.

Darin went on the road, singing at third-rate clubs. In Nashville, he paid for his own session to record "Million Dollar Baby." Through Kirschner's connections, the demo record was heard by executives at Atco Records (a subsidiary of Atlantic Recording Company). They signed him but kept him sidelined for several months.

In 1957 Darin earned $1,600 singing; but 1958 was far different: he earned $40,000. Among the several numbers he wrote (he would sing them on a tape recorder and someone else would transcribe them) was a rock 'n' roll item called "Splish Splash." That June he sang it on "The Bob Crosby Show" (NBC-TV) and also on Dick Clark's "American Bandstand" (ABC-TV). It became an immediate hit with teenagers, selling 100,000 copies in three weeks and rising to number three on the record charts over a thirteen-week period. Meanwhile, Darin, who thought he would be dropped from Atco as he had been from Decca, had recorded "Early in the Morning" for Brunswick Records using a different singing group name, The Rinky Dinks. After "Splish Splash" became a runaway hit, Brunswick released their Darin item. Atco legally forced Brunswick to withdraw the single, and that company rerecorded it with Buddy Holly. Meanwhile, Darin had made his acting debut on television, appearing on the "Way of the West" segment of "Schlitz Playhouse of Stars" (CBS-TV, June 6, 1958).

Unlike many other young singers of the day, Darin had an astute sense of the record business. "It's tough these days. The kids are fickle. They do more flipping over the songs than they do over any one singer." While he continued to write rock songs such as "Queen of the Hop" (which rose to number nine on the charts in October 1958), he wanted to reach beyond this category into the more secure adult market. "It's the only way to build a future," he said. He used his popularity to work in nightclubs and began to expand his repertoire. In his act he sang a hip version of "Mack the Knife" from Bertolt Brecht and Kurt Weill's *The Threepenny Opera*. With profits from "Splish Splash" and his first LP (*Bobby Darin*) Darin financed his next album, *That's All*. "Mack the Knife" was among the numbers he recorded. Atco insisted on releasing the song first as a single and it became a smash hit, selling over two million copies. When *That's All* was released a short time later, it sold over 450,000 copies. As a result Darin won two Grammy Awards that year, including Best New Artist of 1959.

There were a lot of changes for Bobby Darin in 1959. Polly Cassotto (actually his grandmother), who had remarried and had three children, died of a stroke that February, not living to see Bobby become a star. After his "Mack the Knife" phenomenon, he signed two seven-year performing contracts with two different studios (Paramount and Universal) while turning down an offer from NBC-TV. Among his many television appearances he had been on "The Ed Sullivan Show" twice, sung "Mack the Knife" on an NBC-TV special in November, guested on an episode of the comedy series "Hennessey" (CBS-TV), been one of the guest artists on "The Big Party" (NBC), and on December 2, 1959, was the subject of "This Is Your Life" (NBC-TV). On the NBC-TV special "George Burns in the Big Time" (November 17, 1959) he joined such superstars as Jack Benny, Eddie Cantor, and George Jessel. Darin was now earning $40,000 per TV appearance; was starring at such clubs as Los Angeles's The Cloister (which gave him exposure to the film industry), Chicago's Chez Paree, and New York City's Copacabana; and had appeared at the Sahara Hotel with George Burns (who became one of his mentors). Darin owned a recording company (Direction) and two music publishing companies and it was estimated he was currently earning $250,000 a year. (In 1960 he earned $500,000 and in 1961 he had a gross income of over $1 million.)

Describing one of his performances at the Copacabana, the *New York World-Tele-*

*gram and Sun* reviewer noted, "He has a driving, pulsating style, which, combined with an impish, small boy smile, made him irresistible to his fans." Most critics chose to review his impudence rather than his voice. It led one columnist to insist: "When Will Rogers wrote he never met a man he didn't like, he had never met Bobby Darin." Darin had his own theory: "Cocky is my favorite word. . . . I want a battle. If it's a battle, I have a chance to change people's minds." Darin was the type of club performer who, when a record company executive (who once said he had no talent) showed up in the audience, had him removed. When a party became overly boisterous, he had their table and drinks taken away. When a drunk stumbled up and put his arm around him, the star attraction left the stage. Because he was "the newest singing rage," he could get away with such behavior.

After his relationship with Connie Francis ended, Darin began dating blonde songstress Jo-Ann Campbell and they became engaged in 1960. But then, while in Rome making the feature film (COME SEPTEMBER), Darin fell in love with his eighteen-year-old blonde co-star, Sandra Dee. The singer confessed, "I've finally found someone more important to me than myself." They were married on December 1, 1960, on the spur of the moment in Newark, New Jersey. Their son, Dodd Mitchell Cassotto, was born on December 16, 1961.

Despite having signed long-term film commitments in 1959, Darin had not rushed into making his first picture, reasoning, "I don't think I'm mature enough yet to see what one role it is I want to play but I don't want to be billed as 'Bobby Darin in Rock around the Rumble Hall.'" In the interim he had turned down a co-starring role in Columbia's CRY FOR HAPPY (1961) because he was contracted to perform with George Burns at the Sahara Hotel in 1960. His screen debut came casually in the star-studded PEPE (1960), in which he played himself and sang "That's How It Went All Right" with Mickey Callan, Shirley Jones, and Matt Mattox. However, he made his motion picture acting debut in COME SEPTEMBER (1961), a lighthearted sex comedy starring Rock Hudson and Gina Lollobrigida, with Darin and Sandra Dee as the young romantic leads. He was brash and cheeky and sang "Multiplication" (which he wrote, as he did the wordless title tune). *Variety* reported, "Darin does a workmanlike job, and gives evidence he'll have more to show when the parts provide him with wider opportunity." For Paramount he was in John Cassavetes' somber TOO LATE BLUES (1961). He played a troubled jazz musician who endures angst to keep his band and his girlfriend (Stella Stevens). Darin gave a low-keyed, thoughtful performance.

His most productive year on camera was 1962, with four releases. He was in the third version of 20th Century–Fox's STATE FAIR, inheriting the Dana Andrews role as the cynical media man who falls in love with the wholesome farm girl (Pamela Tiffin). His solo was "This Isn't Heaven," which summarized the picture. For Paramount, he was one of the begrimed G.I.s coping with World War II warfare in HELL IS FOR HEROES (1962). Steve McQueen was the star in a diverse cast that included Bob Newhart (!), Fess Parker, and James Coburn. Universal chose to exploit the Darin–Dee marriage by reteaming them in IF A MAN ANSWERS, a featherweight comedy of newlyweds who overcome marital discord and become parents-to-be. Darin wrote/sang the title song as well as wrote "Chantal's

Theme." While most of his prior films traded on the drawing power of his singing career, PRESSURE POINT was different. This Stanley Kramer production for United Artists allowed Darin an opportunity to demonstrate his acting prowess. He gave a strong portrayal of a highly disturbed young man who is imprisoned during World War II as a Nazi sympathizer. Despite the efforts of a black psychiatrist (Sidney Poitier) to treat Darin, he is released only to later kill an innocent old man and be executed for the crime. This film role brought Darin tremendous recognition as a dramatic performer and should have garnered him an Oscar bid. The film itself was a box-office dud.

Darin had had top twenty albums in 1960 (*This Is Darin, Bobby Darin at the Copa*) and 1961 (*The Bobby Darin Story*), and he continued with top ten hits: "You Must Have Been a Beautiful Baby" (1961), "Things" (1962), and "You're the Reason I'm Living" (1963). He switched from Atco to Capitol Records in 1962 (but would return to Atlantic in 1966). However, his focus was on his movie career. He co-starred with Gregory Peck and Tony Curtis in CAPTAIN NEWMAN, M.D. (1963), another glossy World War II study. He played the much decorated Corporal Jim Tompkins who is being treated by psychiatrist Peck for a huge guilt complex built from believing he deserted a pal in the midst of combat. This time he was Oscar-nominated, but lost to Melvyn Douglas of HUD. It was the pinnacle of Darin's relatively brief film career. He wrote the songs for Universal's teen romance THE LIVELY SET (1964) starring singer James Darren (who sang Darin's numbers), and the next year the studio milked whatever box-office magic was left in the Darin–Dee team by pairing them in the strained comedy THAT FUNNY FEELING with Donald O'Connor.

Sandra Dee and Bobby Darin in THAT FUNNY FEELING (1965)

Darin wrote and sang the title song. For Walt Disney's THAT DARN CAT (1965) he wrote and sang the title tune. Darin was now telling the press, "I am an investor. I invest in me, because it's the only thing I'm absolutely sure of. Since childhood, I've always prepared for the success that I knew was going to come."

By 1966 Darin and Sandra Dee had separated, and in March of 1967 they were divorced. He began dating Diana Hartford who had been married to multi-millionaire Huntington Hartford since 1962. He showed up in Universal's low-budget Western GUNFIGHT IN ABILENE (1967), a remake of a 1957 film (SHOWDOWN AT ABILENE), as an ex-Confederate soldier who cannot avoid a climactic shootout. He also wrote the score for this ignored genre piece. In the little-seen, British-filmed COP-OUT (1967), a murder mystery starring James Mason, he was a sinister ship's steward.

In the mid-1960s Darin, while still pushing hard to become Mr. Show Business and the "new" Frank Sinatra, became politically active, being especially drawn to the ideology of Robert Kennedy. As part of his new awareness, he started to appear in his club act wearing scruffy blue jeans (instead of his usual tuxedo), sometimes moustached, usually without his toupee, and singing very politically liberal, anti–Vietnam War songs. He now called himself Bob Darin. His last big hit was "If I Were a Carpenter," which rose to number eight on the charts in October 1966, and his last top forty hit was "Lovin' You" in February 1967. On March 2, 1967, he joined with Diana Ross and the Supremes, The Mamas and the Papas, and Count Basie and His Band for the special "Rodgers and Hart Today" (ABC-TV). Later in 1967 Darin was booed from the stage of Las Vegas's Sahara Hotel when his program consisted of political diatribes against Richard Nixon and others, freedom songs, and protest ballads. At this time he did two folk albums, which failed.

When presidential candidate Robert Kennedy, whom the singer knew slightly and for whom he had campaigned, was assassinated in June 1968, Darin went into shock. He attended the funeral at Arlington Cemetery and his life was never the same thereafter. "With him in the ground, part of me went, too," Darin said. "Most people took four days to get over his death. It took me almost four years." He sold his music publishing company (in a very unfavorable financial deal that he regretted later), got rid of his possessions, bought a trailer, and relocated to the Big Sur area of northern California. He claimed he needed time to re-align his values and to find a new perspective. In the midst of this retrenchment he made one movie, United Artists' HAPPY ENDING (1969), playing a very subordinate role as a gigolo who attempts to fleece an unhappily married woman (Jean Simmons). He also produced an album on his own label of soulful, thoughtful songs. It was not a big seller.

By 1971 Darin began to reemerge in show business, no longer angry and no longer young. Now wearing his toupee again, he was a guest on "Ironside" (NBC-TV) and "Cade's County" (CBS-TV) and returned to nightclubs. Soon he was back performing in Las Vegas, but after closing there on February 8, 1971, he checked into a hospital for treatment of heart fibrillations. He underwent open-heart surgery, which took nine hours. Two plastic valves were implanted in his heart, and the recovery required a month. He continued to perform in clubs and guest on TV (including an episode of NBC's "Night

Gallery"), and in July 1972 he became the summer replacement for Dean Martin on NBC. The hour-long variety show, "Dean Martin Presents The Bobby Darin Amusement Company," was relatively popular. Besides singing, Darin developed comedy skits in which he was Dusty John the hippie poet, Angie the tenement dweller, Groucho, and the Godmother. Socially, his constant companion was now legal secretary Andrea Yaeger about whom he said, "I think I've been married for the past two years. We've just dispensed with the bureaucratic involvement." (They would marry on June 26, 1973, but would separate a few months later.)

In early 1973 NBC-TV scheduled him as a mid-season replacement. "The Bobby Darin Show" bowed on January 19, 1973, and lasted through the end of April. It was a continuation of the format he had used the prior summer. With very little fanfare the low-budget movie HAPPY MOTHER'S DAY . . . LOVE, GEORGE was released in September 1973. It was directed by actor Darren McGavin on location in Nova Scotia, with a cast including Patricia Neal, Cloris Leachman, Ron Howard, and Darin in a very abbreviated role as Leachman's new boyfriend who sadistically beats Howard. It was a confused tale of sin, mystery, and gore in a small town and quickly disappeared.

In 1972 Darin had joined with Motown Records and was attempting to reestablish himself yet again as a recording artist. He signed a $2 million, three-year contract with the MGM Grand Hotel in Las Vegas. But poor health continued to plague him. On December 10, 1973, he summoned an ambulance to take him to Cedars-Sinai Medical Center in Los Angeles. He was suffering from congestive heart failure (the implanted valves were malfunctioning), and he slipped into a coma on December 18. He died two days later following surgery. There was no funeral as he donated his body to UCLA for research.

That long-time purveyor of the pop music scene, Dick Clark, who saw the full spectrum of the Bobby Darin phenomenon firsthand, would assess, "I used to laugh when people told me how Bobby was an arrogant little son-of-a-bitch. But if you knew him, he was the kindest and gentlest person I knew. He had a great native intellect and if he were only healthy physically, he probably could have gone on to be a legend."

For years there has been talk of a biopic, THE BOBBY DARIN STORY, but it has yet to happen.

## Filmography

Pepe (Col, 1960)
Come September (Univ, 1961) (also songs)
Too Late Blues (Par, 1961)
State Fair (20th–Fox, 1962)
Hell Is for Heroes (Par, 1962)
If a Man Answers (Univ, 1962) (also songs)
Pressure Point (UA, 1962)
Captain Newman, M.D. (Univ, 1963)
The Lively Set (Univ, 1964) (songs only)

That Funny Feeling (Univ, 1965) (also music, song)
That Darn Cat (BV, 1965) (voice, song only)
Gunfight in Abilene (Univ, 1967) (also music)
Cop-Out [Stranger in the House] (MGM, 1967)
The Happy Ending (UA, 1969)
Happy Mother's Day . . . Love, George [Run Stranger Run] (Cinema 5, 1973)

## TV Series

Dean Martin Presents The Bobby Darin Amusement Company (NBC, 1972)

The Bobby Darin Show (NBC, 1973)

## Album Discography

As Long as I'm Singin' (Jass 9)

The Best of Bobby Darin (Cap T/ST-2571)

Bobby Darin (Atco 33-102)

Bobby Darin (Motown 753)

Bobby Darin at the Copa (Atco 33-122)

Bobby Darin Born Walden Robert Cassotto (Direction 1936, Bell MBLL 112/SBLL 112)

Bobby Darin Sings Ray Charles (Atco 33-140)

The Bobby Darin Story (Atco 33-131)

Bobby Darin—The Star Collection (Midi 20-031)

Clementine (Clarion 603)

Commitment (Direction 1937)

Darin 1936–1973 (Motown 813VI)

Doctor Dolittle (Atlantic 8154)

Dream Lover (Leedon 5026)

Earthy (Cap T/ST-1826)

Eighteen Yellow Roses (Cap T/ST-1942)

For Teenagers Only (Atco 1001)

From "Hello Dolly" to "Goodbye Charlie" (Cap T/ST-2914)

Golden Folk Hits (Cap T/ST-2007)

If I Were a Carpenter (Atlantic 8135)

In a Broadway Bag (Atlantic 8126)

Inside Out (Atlantic 8142)

It's You or No One (Atco 33-124)

The Legendary Bobby Darin (Candelite CMI-1959)

The Lively Set (Decca DL-9119) [ST]

Love Swings (Atco 33-134)

Multiplication and Irresistible You (Atco 33-115)

Oh! Look at Me Now (W/SW-1791)

Or No One (Atco 33-124)

Pepe (Colpix 507) [ST]

The Shadow of Your Smile (Atlantic 8121)

Something Special (Atlantic 557073)

Stardust (Arista 5000)

State Fair (Dot 9011/290112) [ST]

That's All (Atco 33-104)

Things and Other Things (Atco 33-146)

This Is Darin (Atco 33-115)

25th Day of December (Atco 33-125)

Twist with Bobby Darin (Atco 33-138)

Two of a Kind (Atco 33-126) w. Johnny Mercer

Venice Blue [I Wanna Be Around] (Cap T/ST-2322)

The Versatile Bobby Darin (EMI 671)

The Very Best of Bobby Darin (Imperial House NU-9380)

Winners (Atco 33-167)

You're the Reason I'm Living (Cap T/ST-1866)

# SAMMY DAVIS, JR.

ONE OF THE MOST VERSATILE AND BOUNDLESSLY ENERGETIC OF ALL
entertainers (in the true vaudevillian sense), Sammy Davis, Jr. has been a professional
performer since 1927, when he was two years old. Today he is still a headliner, terming
himself a complete entertainer (not a complete singer). Whether tap dancing nimbly,
singing in his throaty baritone, or going heavily dramatic in movies, he always makes a
strong impression. He has long been identified with such show-stopping numbers as "Mr.
Bojangles," "The Candy Man," and "What Kind of Fool Am I."

In his formative years, lantern-jawed Davis rose to distinction as a member of the
Will Mastin Trio. In later years, he was an on-again–off-again member of Frank Sinatra's
Rat Pack and more recently has functioned as part of the globe-trotting Sinatra–Liza
Minnelli–Sammy Davis, Jr. cabaret trio. However, through all these cycles, the 5' 6" Davis
has displayed a strong individualistic drive. Some have described this trait as egocentric,
while others have termed his nonstop career efforts as a manic push for self-identity. (A
standing joke of the 1960s had it that if Davis merely opened a refrigerator and its light
went on, he would start performing.)

As a black man who suffered racial persecution in his earlier years, Davis was
accused later of abandoning his race (by marrying a white woman and joining the Rat
Pack). He then suffered a backlash when he championed the causes of integration. Davis is
the first to admit it has never been easy being a multi-minority figure: i.e., black, Jewish
(his adopted religion), and handicapped (he lost his left eye in an auto accident years ago).
Nor have his past excesses (decades of ostentatious flash, heavy drug use, and drinking)
made life simple for him or those surrounding him. Nevertheless, through all these highly
publicized phases, his remarkable talent has survived. With his ability to blow hot trumpet
licks, display solid drum rhythm, dance, sing, and act, Davis is regarded by many as one of
the last surviving major variety performers—a Renaissance man of show business.

Sammy Davis, Jr. was born in Harlem, in New York City, on December 8, 1925.
His vaudevillian father was a lead dancer in Will Mastin's "Holiday in Dixieland" troupe;
his mother—Elvera (Sanchez) Davis—was the act's leading chorus girl. When Sammy, Jr.
was two, his sister Ramona was born. While their parents were on the road, Ramona was
brought up by maternal relatives, and he was placed in the care of his paternal grandmother,
Rosa B. "Mama" Davis. When he was two and a half, his parents split up and Sammy, Jr.
was put in his father's care. He began traveling with the Will Mastin show and soon
became part of the twelve-member vaudeville act. (Although Sammy, Jr. would always call
Mastin "uncle," he was not a relative.) At first Sammy, Jr. just mimicked the older

performers, but gradually he became an accomplished singing and dancing member of the group. In 1933 he made his film debut in two short subjects filmed at the Warner Bros.–Vitaphone studios in Brooklyn. The first, RUFUS JONES FOR PRESIDENT (1933), cast him as Ethel Waters' son who dreams he becomes the chief executive of the United States. In the second, SEASON'S GREETINGS (1933), he was featured with Lita Grey.

As the effects of the Depression and competition from motion pictures caused vaudeville to fade, the Will Mastin troupe was reduced gradually to the Will Mastin Trio. During the 1930s the Trio continued to perform around the country, with Sammy, Jr. befriended and tutored at one point by Bill "Bojangles" Robinson in the art of tap dancing. In the early 1940s Davis first met Frank Sinatra, who was then performing with Tommy Dorsey and His Band.

In late 1943 the eighteen-year-old Davis was drafted into World War II service. During his basic training in Cheyenne, Wyoming, a black master sergeant taught him to read. He also learned how to deal with discrimination in the service—using his fists. As a member of the Special Services he wrote and directed Army camp shows around the country. He was discharged from the Army in late 1945 and he rejoined the Will Mastin Trio. Bookings were very slim, and they often found themselves playing rundown burlesque houses or seedy clubs in Los Angeles, Chicago, and elsewhere. During the many lean periods, Davis continued to expand his repertoire of impressions, his musical ability (including piano and vibes), and his flashy dancing (his father and "uncle" were now mostly background performers in the act). In 1946 his show business connections brought him to Capitol Records where his recording of "The Way You Look Tonight" won recognition and led *Metronome* magazine to name him 1946's "Most Outstanding New Personality." Other friends introduced the Will Mastin Trio to Mickey Rooney, who was performing a stage revue in Boston, and they became his opening act for several weeks on the road. Later the Trio was booked into Slapsie Maxie Rosenbloom's Hollywood cabaret and began playing Las Vegas (where they could not get a room except in the black part of town). They performed with Frank Sinatra at the Capitol Theatre in New York in 1947 and played Ciro's in Hollywood (supporting Janis Paige). Soon the Trio was making $1,250 a week on tour with Jack Benny's stage revue, and later they appeared on "The Colgate Comedy Hour" (NBC-TV), hosted by Eddie Cantor. The Trio would be frequent guests on the summer 1954 "Comedy Hour." They also played the Copacabana Club in New York City and the Apollo Theatre in Harlem. For each success, there were steps backwards due to racial discrimination.

In June 1954 Davis signed a recording contract with Decca Records, and that November the Will Mastin Trio was performing at the New Frontier Hotel in Las Vegas at $7,500 weekly. On November 19, 1954, Davis was in an auto accident that nearly cost him his life and did cost him his left eye. It was during this ordeal that, inspired by Jewish friends (Eddie Cantor and Jeff Chandler), Davis converted to Judaism. When he recovered from the accident, he at first wore a patch over his eye; later he had a plastic eye inserted. The accident had focused a great deal of attention on him and he was now much in demand as a performer. He returned to entertaining with the Will Mastin Trio at Ciro's in

Hollywood and at other clubs nationwide. He also was enjoying healthy record sales with his Decca LPs. His album *Starring Sammy Davis, Jr.* rose to number one on the charts and *Just for Lovers* rose to number eight in mid- to late 1955. That same year he appeared briefly as musician Fletcher Henderson in THE BENNY GOODMAN STORY at Universal and had top twenty singles hits with "Something's Gotta Give," "Love Me or Leave Me," and "That Old Black Magic." By now, Davis was a flashy member of Sinatra's high-living Rat Pack, which included—at different periods—Humphrey Bogart, Lauren Bacall, Dean Martin, Joey Bishop, Henry Silva, and Peter Lawford.

The only thing wonderful about the Broadway musical comedy *Mr. Wonderful* was Sammy Davis, Jr. as the energetic club performer who overcomes racial obstacles to succeed. The show opened on March 22, 1956, and also featured Sammy Davis, Sr. and Will Mastin. It ran for 383 performances. By early 1957 Davis was back performing in clubs, where he was happiest, and was regularly singing his custom-written song, "Give Me a Saloon Every Time." Due to insurmountable friction among the partners, the Will Mastin Trio disbanded and Davis was left to perform solo successfully.

The year 1958 marked Davis' debut performance in a TV drama on the "Auf Wiedersehen" episode of "G.E. Theatre" (CBS-TV, October 5, 1958). He also had a substantial feature film assignment. He was to have been in THE DEFIANT ONES (1958), a project Davis' friend Elvis Presley wanted to co-star in with Davis. However, Presley and his manager backed out of the interracial melodrama, fearing it might have repercussions on Presley's singing career. Instead, Davis went into the all-black ANNA LUCASTA (1958). He was the grasping, jive-talking Danny Johnson who lusts for a streetwalker (Eartha Kitt) and almost spoils her marriage to another man. *Variety* noted, "Sammy Davis, Jr. lives his role as the cocky little fellow. . . . He brings to the character a good deal of understanding and balance." The next year Davis campaigned for and won (after Cab Calloway turned down the part) the role of the dope-dealing Sportin' Life in the all-black operetta PORGY AND BESS (1959). Unlike many of the film's other stars (Sidney Poitier, Dorothy Dandridge, Diahann Carroll), Davis did his own singing ("It Ain't Necessarily So"). However, ironically, on the soundtrack album it was Calloway who sang the role of Sportin' Life because Davis was then signed to a rival recording label. Davis would later make an album of PORGY AND BESS for Decca. It was also in 1959 that Davis was briefly married to black chorus girl Loray White. Harry Belafonte was best man at the ceremony.

In the early 1960s hip Davis was at the height of his Rat Pack (and gaudy chain-wearing) period. He appeared in a trio of Frank Sinatra movies: OCEAN'S ELEVEN (1960), SERGEANTS THREE (1962), and ROBIN AND THE SEVEN HOODS (1964), all of which were undisciplined celluloid larks. (He had been scheduled to appear in the earlier NEVER SO FEW [1959], but he and Sinatra had a spat and Steve McQueen inherited the Davis role.) Much more solid were Davis' performances as Wino the Halloween Bandit in the prison tale CONVICTS FOUR (1962); as Educated in the crime drama JOHNNY COOL (1963); and as The Ballad Singer (who performs "Mack the Knife") in THE THREEPENNY OPERA (1963). He had the leading role of a self-defeated jazz musician in A MAN CALLED ADAM (1966), as the trumpet player who blames himself for the death of his family in an automobile accident. It was a solid dramatic performance (as were those by Cicely Tyson, Ossie Davis, and Louis Armstrong). However, the New York City–lensed film was marred by weak performances by several of the supporting cast, which included pals and associates Mel Tormé, Peter Lawford, and Frank Sinatra, Jr. In 1968 he and Rat Pack-er Peter Lawford co-starred in the spy spoof SALT AND PEPPER, which was popular enough, but the embarrassing sequel, ONE MORE TIME (1970), directed by Jerry Lewis, was a bust. In Shirley MacLaine's inflated musical SWEET CHARITY (1968), Davis was thrown in as Big Daddy, the hippie religious cult leader who sings "Rhythm of Life."

On television the hard-driving Davis guested on a variety of programs from "The Dick Powell Show" (1962) to "The Rifleman" (1962) to "Ben Casey" (1963) and "The Patty Duke Show" (1965). He headlined his own specials, "Sammy Davis and the Wonderful World of Children" (ABC-TV, November 25, 1963) and "The Sammy Davis, Jr. Special" (NBC-TV, February 18, 1965). From January to April 1966 he had his own NBC-TV variety series, "The Sammy Davis, Jr. Show," which tried too hard to make the spontaneous performer conform to a regimented formula. (Moreover, after the first segment, he was not allowed to be on his own show for four weeks due to a contract with another network.) Davis seemed to be everywhere on the small screen: "Batman" (1966), "I Dream of Jeannie" (1967), "The Beverly Hillbillies" (1969), and "The Mod Squad"

Peter Lawford and Sammy Davis, Jr. in SALT AND PEPPER (1968)

(1969). He also filled in for Johnny Carson several times as host of "The Tonight Show." On November 4, 1969, he made his telefeature debut, starring in THE PIGEON (ABC-TV) as a black private detective based in San Francisco. It was an early example of the black action cycle then enveloping Hollywood. However, the lighthearted show, which featured Pat Boone and Ricardo Montalban, failed to sell as a series.

Besides films, television, and continuous club work, Davis also returned to Broadway, starring in a musical version of Clifford Odets' *Golden Boy*. He was the black musician who abandoned his craft for the fast bucks of the boxing world and the love of a white woman (Paula Wayne). The show opened on October 20, 1964, to mixed reviews, but on the strength of Davis' acting, it ran for 569 performances. He had top twenty albums with *What Kind of Fool Am I* (1962), *The Shelter of Your Arms* (1964), and *I've Gotta Be Me* (1969), and among his single hits in the top forty was "Don't Blame the Children" (1967), a spoken disc. Through much of the 1960s he was recording for Reprise Records, a label owned by Frank Sinatra. Before his first marriage in 1959, Davis had been "linked" with Ava Gardner and later with Kim Novak, but it was Swedish actress May Britt whom he married in 1960. Together they had a daughter (Tracey) and adopted two sons (Mark and Jeff). In 1968 they were divorced. In 1965 his autobiography *Yes I Can* (written with Jane and Burt Boyar) was published, becoming a best-seller with its candid account of how Davis overcame many discriminatory odds on his road to success.

In 1970 Davis married black dancer Altovise Gore, who was once a member of his dancing troupe. Two years later he bought an eight-percent interest in Las Vegas's Tropicana Hotel, where he was being paid $100,000 a week to perform. He grossed $3 million in 1972. It was also that year that he had his last big hit single, "The Candy Man," which rose to number one on the charts. He continued to star in TV specials ("Old Faithful," 1973), to guest on teleseries ("The Courtship of Eddie's Father" and "All in the Family" in 1972), and to appear in telefeatures: THE TRACKERS (1971) and POOR DEVIL (1973). He and Mickey Rooney were on almost every episode of "NBC Follies," a variety show that ran from September to December 1973 on NBC-TV. He had his own "Sammy and Company," a syndicated ninety-minute variety show that began its two-season run in September 1975. He sang the theme song on the "Baretta" detective series (1975–78) and he appeared as a guest star on two network soap operas: "Love of Life" (1975) and "One Life to Live" (1979–80). Politically, the man who had endorsed John F. Kennedy and Robert F. Kennedy in the 1960s had become a supporter of Richard Nixon in the early 1970s, which caused much consternation. Having been accused in past decades of ignoring his own race, Davis exercised social consciousness in the 1960s as a follower of Dr. Martin Luther King, Jr. In the musical documentary SAVE THE CHILDREN (1973) he was among the black performers (Marvin Gaye, Isaac Hayes, the Staple Singers, Roberta Flack) singing at a charity concert.

Having dealt with liver and kidney trouble and chest pains in 1974 (which curtailed his assorted addictions), he appeared in a stage revue, *Sammy on Broadway*, at the Uris Theatre in April 1974. Four years later (August 1978) he starred in his own version of the Anthony Newley–Leslie Bricusse musical *Stop the World, I Want to Get Off* at the New York

State Theatre at Lincoln Center. It was this 1960s hit show that had provided Davis with his trademark song, "What Kind of Fool Am I." A specially taped version of the new stage production received limited distribution as the film SAMMY STOPS THE WORLD (1978).

Davis was among the guest stars in Burt Reynolds' comedy travesty THE CAN-NONBALL RUN (1981). Said Davis, "It was a horrible picture, I guess, but a terrific giggle." He also appeared in the sequel, CANNONBALL RUN II (1984—which featured Frank Si-natra in a cameo), and was one of the co-hosts of the documentary THAT'S DANCING! (1985). After a second and more serious bout with liver disease in 1983, he publicly swore off liquor in November 1983, and cut down (at least by his own hectic standards) his performance schedule. Nevertheless, he still appeared in clubs and guested on television. On TV he was on "Fantasy Island" (1983 and 1984), "The Jeffersons" (1984), and in the syndicated special "Dancing in the Wings" (1985). He played The Caterpillar and Father William in the four-hour version of ALICE IN WONDERLAND (CBS-TV, 1985). In 1986 he gave a concert at the Hollywood Bowl which showed a new, toned-down Sammy Davis, Jr. Afterwards, he continued to guest on a spectrum of TV outings: "The Kennedy Center Honors: A Celebration of the Arts" (1987—he was a Life Achievement medalist that year), "Evening at Pops" (1988), "A Whole Lotta Fun" (1988), "An Evening with Sammy Davis, Jr. and Jerry Lewis" (1988—taped during their joint Las Vegas club act), and "Motown Returns to the Apollo" (1988). He turned up on episodes of "Hunter" (1989) and "The Cosby Show" (1989) as well as on assorted talk shows and telethons.

Having turned down a role in BEETLEJUICE (1988), Davis returned to dramatic acting with TAP (1989), a heavy dance drama starring Gregory Hines and a host of tap dancing greats from the past. Davis was cast as Little Mo, the father of the woman (Suzanne Douglas) that ex-convict Hines adores. While the movie met with tepid audience response, Davis received uniformly solid reviews ("[he] does a nice, unshowbizzy turn as an old hoofer," wrote *Newsweek* magazine). Davis' nonchalant reaction to his revived movie career was, "I'm a saloon entertainer who happens to make pictures."

In the late 1980s Davis began performing again in cabarets with Frank Sinatra and they planned an extensive international tour with Dean Martin (who dropped out and was replaced by Liza Minnelli). Of the three veteran singers, Davis received the best reviews as they criss-crossed the U.S. and went around the world, leading to a cable network taping of their club act, "Frank, Liza & Sammy: The Ultimate Event" (Showtime, May 20, 1989). In 1988 Davis underwent extensive reconstructive hip surgery, and his father died. In 1989 he continued performing in tandem with Sinatra and Minnelli, and did a Las Vegas club act with Jerry Lewis. Also in 1989 his new autobiography, *Why Me?*, was published. He admitted that writing the new book was painful. "The guy from twenty-five years ago doesn't exist anymore. The guy from ten years ago doesn't exist anymore. And I hope ten years from now I'll be able to say that this guy doesn't exist anymore. He's a better human being, a more caring person."

No longer pushed by a need to prove something, Davis is nonetheless driven by a desire to maintain his lifestyle. Regarding his philosophy of life, he claims, "You have to be able to look back at your life and say, 'Yeah, that was fun.' The only person I ever hurt was myself and even that I did to the minimum. If you can do that and you're still functioning, you're the luckiest person in the world."

*[On May 17, 1990, Sammy Davis, Jr., aged sixty-four, died of cancer at his Beverly Hills, California, home. He was buried on May 18, 1990, at Forest Lawn Cemetery in Glendale, California, in a family burial plot next to his father, Sammy Davis, and his adopted uncle, Will Mastin.]*

## Filmography

Rufus Jones for President (Vita, 1933) (s)
Season's Greetings (Vita, 1933) (s)
The Benny Goodman Story (Univ, 1955)
Meet Me in Las Vegas (MGM, 1956) (voice only)
Anna Lucasta (UA, 1958)
Porgy and Bess (Col, 1959)
Ocean's Eleven (WB, 1960)
Pepe (Col, 1960)
Convicts Four [Reprieve!] (AA, 1962)
Of Love and Desire (20th–Fox, 1962) (voice only)
Sergeants Three (UA, 1962)
The Threepenny Opera [Der Dreigroschenoper] (Emb, 1963)
Johnny Cool (UA, 1963)
Robin and the Seven Hoods (WB, 1964)
Nightmare in the Sun (Zodiak, 1965)
A Man Called Adam (Emb, 1966)
Salt and Pepper (UA, 1968)
Sweet Charity (Univ, 1968)

The Pigeon (ABC-TV, 11/4/69)
One More Time (UA, 1970) (also executive producer)
The Trackers (ABC-TV, 12/14/71)
Poor Devil (NBC-TV, 2/14/73)
Save the Children (Par, 1973)
Sammy Stops the World [Stop the World—I Want to Get Off] (Special Event Entertainment, 1978)
Man Without Mercy [Gone with the West/Little Moon and Jud McGraw] (International Cine Corp, 1979) (made in 1969)
The Cannonball Run (20th–Fox, 1981)
Heidi's Song (Par, 1982) (voice only)
Cannonball Run II (WB, 1984)
That's Dancing! (MGM, 1985) (co-host)
Alice in Wonderland (CBS-TV, 12/9/85–12/10/85)
Moon over Parador (Univ, 1988)
Tap (Tri-Star, 1989)

## Broadway Plays

Mr. Wonderful (1956)
Golden Boy (1964)

Stop the World, I Want to Get Off (1978) (revival)

## TV Series

The Sammy Davis, Jr. Show (NBC, 1966)
NBC Follies (NBC, 1973)

Sammy and Company (Synd, 1975–77)
Baretta (ABC, 1975–78) (voice only)

## Album Discography

All the Way and Then Some (Decca DL-8779)
Back on Broadway (Reprise 6169)
The Best of Broadway (Reprise 2010)
The Best of Sammy Davis, Jr. (Decca DX-192/ DXS-7192)
Big Ones for Young Lovers (Reprise 6131)
Boy Meets Girl (Decca DL-8490) w. Carmen McRae
California Suite (Reprise 6126)
Closest of Friends (Applause 1016)
Doctor Dolittle (Reprise 6264)
Forget-Me-Nots for First Nighters (Decca DL-4381/74381)
The Goin's Great (Reprise 6339)
Golden Boy (Cap VAS/SVAS-2124) [OC]
Great (Har HS-11299)
Greatest Hits (Reprise 6291)
Here's Lookin' at You (Decca DL-8351)
Hey There! It's Sammy Davis, Jr. at His Dynamite Best (MCA 4109)
I Gotta Right to Swing (Decca DL-8981/78981)
If I Ruled the World (Reprise 6159)
It's All Over But the Swingin' (Decca DL-8641)
I've Gotta Be Me (Reprise 6324)
Just for Lovers ((Decca DL-8170)
Let There Be Love (Har HS-11365)
A Live Performance of His Greatest Hits (WB BSK-3128)
Lonely Is the Name (Reprise 6308)
A Man Called Adam (Reprise 6180) [ST]
The Many Faces of Sammy (Pickwick 3002)
The Men in My Life (Three Cherries TC 44411) w. Lena Horne, Joe Williams
Mr. Entertainment (Decca DL-4153/74153)
Mr. Wonderful (Decca DL-9032) [OC]
Mood to Be Wooed (Decca DL8676)
The Nat "King" Cole Songbook (Reprise 6164)
Now (MGM SE-4832)
Of Love and Desire (20th Century–Fox 5014) [ST]
Our Shining Hour (Verve 8605/68605) w. Count Basie
Pepe (Colpix 507) [ST]
Porgy and Bess (Decca DL-8854/78854)

Robin and the Seven Hoods (Reprise 2021) [ST]
A Salute to Nat (King) Cole (Reprise PRO-212) w. Frank Sinatra
Sammy (MGM SE-4914) [ST/TV]
Sammy Davis, Jr. (Design 146)
Sammy Davis, Jr. (Vocalion 3827/73827)
Sammy Davis, Jr. and Count Basie (MGM SE-4825)
Sammy Davis, Jr. at the Cocoanut Grove (Reprise 6063)
Sammy Davis, Jr. at Town Hall (Decca DL-8841)
Sammy Davis, Jr. Now (MGM 4832)
Sammy Davis, Jr. Salutes the Stars of the London Palladium (Reprise 6236)
The Sammy Davis, Jr. Show (Reprise 6188)
Sammy Davis, Jr. Swings (Decca DL-8486)
Sammy Davis Swings—Laurindo Almeida Plays (Reprise 6236)
Sammy Jumps with Joya (Design 22)
Sammy Steps Out (Reprise 6410)
The Shelter of Your Arms (Reprise 6114)
Something for Everyone (Motown 710)
The Sound of Sammy (WB 1501)
Sounds of '66 (Reprise 6214)
Spotlight on Sammy Davis, Jr. (Spectrum DLP-146)
Starring Sammy Davis, Jr. (Decca DL-8118)
Summit Meeting at the 500 (Souvenir 247-17) w. Frank Sinatra, Dean Martin
Sweet Charity (Decca DL-71502) [ST]
That's All (Reprise 6237)
That's Entertainment (MGM SE-4965)
Three Billion Millionaires (UA UXL-4/UXS-4) [ST]
The Threepenny Opera (RCA LOC/LSO-1086) [ST]
Try a Little Tenderness (Decca DL-4582/74582)
The Wham of Sam (Reprise 2003/92003)
What Kind of Fool Am I (Har H-30568)
What Kind of Fool Am I (Reprise 6051/96051)
When the Feeling Hits You (Reprise 6144)

# DORIS DAY

FEW PERFORMERS HAVE PERPETUATED AN IMAGE LONGER OR MORE successfully than Doris Day. From the start of her cinema career in the late 1940s, she was labeled as the freckle-faced, sunny girl-next-door and for the next several decades maintained this (not always flattering) identification in films and on television. Occasionally, in her string of hit pictures, she was allowed to be spunky (CALAMITY JANE, 1953), to go dramatic (THE MAN WHO KNEW TOO MUCH, 1956), or to be slightly risqué (MOVE OVER, DARLING, 1963). However, the public preferred her as the perennial screen virgin and she obliged.

But there has always been more dimension to Doris Day as a performer than just a Miss Goody Two-Shoes actress. She was a popular big band vocalist who made a smooth transition to become a leading recording artist on her own. Her voice displayed a freshness and intimate directness that overcame the cotton candy arrangements of her singing sessions. When Day sang, the listener always felt enlivened and refreshed. Many of the numbers she recorded from her movies became hits, none so enduringly popular as "Que Sera, Sera." There was also a deeper emotional side to the singing star than being Miss Apple Pie would allow. When her therapeutic autobiography *Doris Day: Her Own Story*, written with A. E. Hotchner, was published in 1975, no one was more surprised than Day herself at the various tragedies she had been faced with and, more importantly, had survived.

She was born Doris von Kappelhoff on April 3, 1924, in Cincinnati, Ohio, the third child of Frederick Wilhelm and Alma Sophia von Kappelhoff, both of German descent. There was a three-year-older brother, Paul; another child (Richard) had died at the age of two before Doris was born. Her father, a Catholic church organist/choir master, was a stern taskmaster, a tyrant about other people's morals. In sharp contrast was her outgoing, amiable mother, who had named Doris after a favorite screen star, Doris Kenyon. At the age of four, Doris made her performing debut singing her rendition of "I's Gwine Down to the Cushville Hop" at a Cincinnati Masonic hall. Her mother enrolled Doris at Pep Golden's Dance School (and at several other dance/singing schools thereafter), hoping to foster the child's interest in show business. By 1936 the von Kappelhoffs were divorced, Frederick having been caught in an affair with Alma's best friend. Doris, her brother, and mother moved to College Hill. There Mrs. von Kappelhoff worked in a bakery and Doris attended Our Lady of the Angels School.

When Doris become intrigued with a cute teenager named Jerry Doherty, this infatuation led to their teaming as Doherty and Kappelhoff. They won a $500 prize in a dance contest sponsored by a Cincinnati department store. Inspired by this success, their mothers took the children to Hollywood for professional dance lessons and, they hoped, to get them into motion pictures. Once they arrived on the coast and settled in a Glendale, California, apartment, Doris and Jerry were enrolled in classes given by Louis DaPron, a leading tap dance teacher. The young dancers garnered a few professional appearances, but despite the mothers' taking on part-time jobs, the two families ran out of funds. They returned to Ohio to convince Mr. Doherty, a dairyman, to relocate to California. He was agreeable. Meanwhile, the team of Doherty and Kappelhoff was hired to perform for a few weeks with a touring edition of the Fanchon and Marco stage show. The night before the two families were to leave for California, Doris was injured in an automobile accident in Hamilton, Ohio. Her right leg was crushed and she was hospitalized for fourteen months. With professional dancing now out of the question, she began vocalizing. Her mother fastened on this new opportunity and took in sewing to pay for her daughter's singing lessons with Grace Raine.

Doris was hired to sing at the Shanghai Inn and later appeared on "Karlin's Karnival," a local radio show over WCPO. She received no salary for her radio chores, but she was heard by bandleader Barney Rapp, who was preparing to open his own nightclub. He hired her in 1940 and suggested her new surname, taking it from a song, "Day After Day," that she had sung over the airwaves. Later, she sang with Bob Crosby and His BobCats at $75 weekly and, thereafter, sang with Fred Waring's band. By the summer of 1940, she was with Les Brown and his group. *Metronome* magazine, reviewing the Brown band in 1940, noted, "And there's Doris Day, who for combined looks and voice has no apparent equal: she's pretty and fresh-looking, handles herself with unusual grace, and what's most important of all, sings with much natural feeling and in tune."

Meanwhile, Doris had met Al Jorden, a trombone player with Barney Rapp, who later joined Gene Krupa's band. They were married in April 1941 at New York's city hall, while Doris was between shows at Radio City Music Hall. Their son, Terry (named after the radio show "Terry and the Pirates"), was born February 8, 1942. A year later, she and Jorden were divorced. (She would later term him a "psychopathic sadist"; he would commit suicide in July 1967.) Doris and her baby returned to Cincinnati where she sang briefly over a local radio station. Leaving her child with her mother, she then returned to singing with Les Brown and His Band of Renown at $350 weekly.

Doris remained with Brown's group for three years. During this period she recorded many singles with his band, including "Sentimental Journey" (November 1944) for Okeh Records. It became a huge hit, as did such other tunes as "My Dreams Are Getting Better All the Time" (February 1945). On March 30, 1946, in Mount Vernon, New York, she married George Weidler (brother of child actress Virginia Weidler) who was the temporary first saxophonist with Brown's band. When the first saxophonist returned from World War II, Weidler was demoted back to third alto saxophonist and he quit. Weidler decided to try his luck in California, and the couple moved to the West Coast, living in a mobile home (due to a housing shortage) on Sepulveda Boulevard in Santa Monica. Doris, who had sung previously for twenty weeks on "Your Hit Parade" (CBS) in New York, was hired as vocalist for the Bob Sweeney–Hal March CBS radio show. Later, she replaced Frances Langford as vocalist on Bob Hope's NBC radio program from 1948 to 1950.

In March 1947, Doris' agent got her a job singing at Billy Reed's Little Club in New York. *Variety* reported, "Miss Day does justice by her pop chores . . . she's more than the adequate ex-band singer. She's a fetching personality and will more than hold her own in class or mass nighteries." While performing there as a soloist, she received a letter from her husband asking for a divorce, insisting he did not want to stand in the way of her career. They were divorced in 1949. Meanwhile, Doris had recorded "Love Somebody" with Buddy Clark for Columbia Records, and it had become a big hit. When she returned to Los Angeles, her agent, Al Levy, took her to meet filmmaker Michael Curtiz. He was seeking a replacement for Paramount's Betty Hutton (then pregnant) and MGM's Judy Garland (whose studio would not release her) to star in a Warner Bros. musical called ROMANCE ON THE HIGH SEAS (1948). Despite Day's being tremendously depressed about her pending divorce (and crying through the entire interview), Curtiz was sufficiently impressed both to hire her for the picture and to sign her to a personal contract (starting at $500 weekly) with his own production company.

ROMANCE ON THE HIGH SEAS was a nonsense story about an aggressive wife (Janis Paige) hiring a stand-in (Day) to take her place on a South American cruise so she can snoop on her spouse (Don DeFore) at home. Meanwhile, the husband hires a private detective (Jack Carson) to trail the wife on shipboard. For the million dollar Technicolor production, Busby Berkeley provided the choreography, with Sammy Cahn and Jule Styne writing eight songs. Unlike many big band vocalists, Doris was very photogenic and even in her screen debut displayed sufficient comedy timing and adequate dramatics to carry her through the snappy production. *Film Daily* observed, "The whole show has been draped around Miss Day and she not only looks good in it but she is good." *Variety* concurred, "Pop numbers are given strong selling by Doris Day. . . . [She] clicks in her story character and should draw nifty fan response." She sang five of the eight songs, and one of them, "It's Magic," was Oscar-nominated (but lost to "Buttons and Bows").

Warner Bros., which lacked its own female singing stars (the studio borrowed June Haver twice from 20th Century–Fox in 1949), saw the box-office potential in Doris and bought her contract from Curtiz. The studio reteamed her twice (MY DREAM IS YOURS, IT'S A GREAT FEELING) with Jack Carson, whom she dated briefly in private life. The focal point of the dramatic YOUNG MAN WITH A HORN (1950) was an obsessed musician (Kirk Douglas) who is distracted from his career by a selfish playgirl (Lauren Bacall), but is redeemed by friends, including band vocalist Jo Jordan (Doris Day). The movie was a distortion of Dorothy Baker's fine novel, but it provided Day with several standards to sing ("Marvelous," "The Very Thought of You") and offered her an opportunity to extend her dramatic range on camera. *The New York Times* lauded her for her "complete naturalness."

TEA FOR TWO (1950), an updating of *No, No Nanette*, was her first screen teaming with Gordon MacRae. They were as wholesome together as Van Johnson and June Allyson at MGM. Warner Bros. would reteam Doris and Gordon four times. In THE WEST POINT STORY (1950) they supported James Cagney, who starred as the egocentric Broadway director hired to stage a show at the military academy. The screen team were among the Warner Bros. star lineup caught in STARLIFT (1951). They came into their own in ON MOONLIGHT BAY (1951), which featured them as citizens of small town Indiana circa 1917. They were so successful in this homey musical that the studio created a sequel, BY THE LIGHT OF THE SILVERY MOON (1953), which followed their ingenuous path to matrimony in post–World War I days. In the interim, Day went heavily dramatic in STORM WARN-ING (1950), an exposé of the Ku Klux Klan in the deep South. *Photoplay* magazine judged, "Songster Doris Day . . . has her first crack at dramatic acting in this violent melodrama and comes off remarkably well." LULLABY OF BROADWAY (1951), originally to have starred June Haver, matched her with dancer Gene Nelson and scene-stealing Gladys George (as her mother), while I'LL SEE YOU IN MY DREAMS (1951) united her with Danny Thomas in a specious biography of composer Gus Kahn. Day's most unlikely leading man was dancer Ray Bolger in APRIL IN PARIS (1952). The original songs by Sammy Cahn and Vernon Duke were a bad lot, especially in contrast to the title tune by E. Y. Harburg and Duke. In THE WINNING TEAM (1952), a stale interpretation of the life of baseball great Grover Cleveland Alexander, she played opposite Ronald Reagan, whom she had dated briefly in the early 1950s after he divorced Jane Wyman. By 1952 Day was earning $2,500 weekly at Warner Bros. and had surpassed Betty Grable as the U.S.'s most popular female box-office attraction.

On April 3, 1951 (her twenty-seventh birthday), at Burbank City Hall, Doris wed her new agent, Marty Melcher. He had been married previously to Patty Andrews of The Andrews Sisters. He now took complete control of her career, in addition to adopting Doris' son, Terry, in 1952. The best of her Warner Bros. films was the rollicking CALAMITY JANE (1953), the studio's answer to MGM's ANNIE GET YOUR GUN (1950). In fact, that picture's co-star, Howard Keel, was borrowed from Metro to play Wild Bill Hickok to Doris' boisterous tomboy. The *New York Times* argued, "As for Miss Day's performance, it is tempestuous to the point of becoming just a bit frightening. . . ." However, if her emoting was overblown, her singing was on the mark. She was raucous in performing "The Deadwood Stage" and was magical in stylizing "Secret Love." The latter received an Academy Award as the year's Best Song, but the movie was not the box-office bonanza anticipated. By now Day had become one of the top recording artists for Columbia Records.

LUCKY ME (1954) was Doris' first widescreen musical, a comedy set in Miami and teaming her with Bob Cummings (replacing Gordon MacRae), Nancy Walker, and Phil Silvers. She was zippy in this outing, but turned teary as the brave sister in YOUNG AT HEART (1954) who copes with a brash songwriter loser (Frank Sinatra). He did most of the crooning in that tearjerker, but she provided a lively rendition of "Ready, Willing and Able."

Doris had made seventeen pictures in a row for Warner Bros. when she and the studio parted company. (She had signed a new pact with the lot in 1954 before LUCKY ME, but they could not agree on future projects and she was displeased that Warner Bros. was using rival vocalist Peggy Lee in feature films.) Day went to MGM for $150,000, plus a percentage of the profits, to take over the role once planned for Ava Gardner in LOVE ME OR LEAVE ME (1955). This twisted version of the Ruth Etting story reteamed her with James Cagney, who stole her thunder as the possessive, gimpy-legged gangster. She tried to be brassy but there was still an air of innocence clinging to her; fortunately her song renditions of 1920s favorites were stylish. The Columbia soundtrack album rose to number one on the charts, where it stayed for seventeen weeks. (Her single "I'll Never Stop Loving You," also from the film, rose to number thirteen on the charts in the summer of 1955.) MGM signed her to a long-term pact. There was talk of Day and Howard Keel reteaming for Metro's THE OPPOSITE SEX (1956), but instead her next feature was for esteemed director Alfred Hitchcock at Paramount. She was cast as James Stewart's distraught mate in the suspense yarn THE MAN WHO KNEW TOO MUCH (1956), and her singing of "Que Sera, Sera (Whatever Will Be, Will Be)" rose to number two on the charts in the summer of 1956. She had thought the song "would never get out of the nursery."

JULIE (1956), back at MGM, tested her emotional mettle as a flight attendant who must be "talked down" when she takes over piloting a disabled aircraft. She returned to Warner Bros. at a $250,000 salary to star in THE PAJAMA GAME (1957), reprising the Broadway role done so memorably by another ex-Warner Bros. singing star, Janis Paige. Day was zesty as the determined union worker. Thereafter, she jumped around from studio to studio, now, however, focusing on comedy. (Musicals were out, but she worked a bouncy title tune into each picture.) She turned down AN AFFAIR TO REMEMBER (1957—Deborah Kerr replaced her), but she was Clark Gable's young nemesis in TEACHER'S PET (1958). Next, under

Doris Day and James Cagney in LOVE ME OR LEAVE ME (1955)

Gene Kelly's direction, she was Richard Widmark's spouse in the suburban sex farce THE TUNNEL OF LOVE (1958). At Columbia she matched comic double takes with Jack Lemmon and Ernie Kovacs in IT HAPPENED TO JANE (1959), which, like THE TUNNEL OF LOVE, was not well received.

At this juncture of what seemed to be a sagging career, glamour producer Ross Hunter was inspired to team Doris with Rock Hudson in PILLOW TALK (1959) at Universal. The *New York Times* termed it "One of the most lively and up-to-date comedy-romances of the year." The screenplay won an Oscar, the film did great business, and the project brought both Day and Hudson (back) to the top as box-office favorites. They would star in two additional sex farces, LOVER COME BACK (1961) and the far less successful SEND ME NO FLOWERS (1964). Meanwhile, Doris' last charted single, "Everybody Loves a Lover," rose to number six position in the summer of 1958, and she had two more popular Columbia LPs: *Day by Day* (1957) and *Listen to Day* (1960). (In the mid-1950s she had signed a new $1 million recording contract with Columbia.)

Day claimed that the demands of the stylish murder mystery MIDNIGHT LACE (1960), opposite Rex Harrison, drained her; thereafter, she chose to do only comedies or musicals. She had wanted the lead in SOUTH PACIFIC (1958), but it was the less-expensive Mitzi Gaynor who got the plum assignment. BILLY ROSE'S JUMBO (1962) was a leaden musical with Stephen Boyd, Jimmy Durante, and Martha Raye. Its financial failure cost her the starring roles in THE UNSINKABLE MOLLY BROWN (1964) and THE SOUND OF MUSIC (1965), parts she wanted badly. She traded double-takes with David Niven in PLEASE DON'T EAT THE DAISIES (1960) and was both innocent and insouciant in THAT TOUCH OF MINK (1962), opposite Cary Grant. She and James Garner responded so well to each other's barbs and cooing in THE THRILL OF IT ALL (1963) that when Twentieth Century–Fox fired Marilyn Monroe (and also lost Dean Martin's services), the studio hired Day and Garner to reteam in the Monroe vehicle, now titled MOVE OVER, DARLING (1963). It was her last really successful feature film. The recurrent Doris Day formula was wearing thin—and she was past forty—as she teamed twice with beefy Rod Taylor in DO NOT DISTURB (1965) and THE GLASS BOTTOM BOAT (1966), neither of which was much liked. She rejected the role of Mrs. Robinson (played by Anne Bancroft) in THE GRADUATE (1967) because "it offended my sense of values." She went mod in the spy spoof CAPRICE (1967) with Richard Harris, and seemed too mature for the shenanigans of WHERE WERE YOU WHEN THE LIGHTS WENT OUT? (1968). THE BALLAD OF JOSIE (1968) was a program Western, and by the time she made the weak comedy WITH SIX YOU GET EGG ROLL (1968), Doris Day had exhausted her screen welcome. The *New York Times* carped that Day's comic talents had, "over the years, become hermetically sealed inside a lacquered personality, like a butterfly in a Mason jar."

In November 1962, Doris and Marty Melcher had tried a separation. Later, they came to an understanding that they would live together in name only, largely to protect their several joint business holdings. On April 20, 1968, at age fifty-two, Melcher died. It would be many months before she learned the ramifications of the business decisions he had made regarding her. However, she discovered right away that she had been committed (without her knowledge) to star in a sitcom for CBS-TV. Both as therapy and to bolster her assets (Melcher and her attorney had wiped out her $20 million in savings and she found that she owed $500,000 in back taxes), she began "The Doris Day Show" (CBS-TV). It debuted on September 24, 1968, and during its five-season run, the setting changed from the family ranch to urban San Francisco. Initially she had been cast as a widow with two sons, but by the fourth season she was, in "The Mary Tyler Moore Show" mold, a carefree magazine staff writer. She had done her first special, "The Doris Mary Anne Kappelhoff Special" (CBS-TV, March 14, 1971), with Rock Hudson as her guest star; her second special, "Doris Day Today" (CBS-TV, February 19, 1975), featured Rich Little and Tim Conway.

In 1974 she became spokesperson for Studio Girl Cosmetics, a division of Helene Curtis, and began working on her 1975 autobiography. Among the book's many revelations was the subject's blunt statement, "After twenty-seven years in show business my public image is that of America's la-di-da happy-go-lucky virgin, carefree and brimming with happiness. An image, I can assure you, more make-believe than any film part I ever played." She explained why in 362 pages. On April 14, 1976, she married Barry Comden, an eastern restaurant host eleven years her junior. They separated in 1979 and were divorced in 1981. Upset by the dissolution of her fourth marriage, she built a house near Carmel where she lives at present. With more open space, she nurtured her caring for animals. She had been president of Actors and Others for Animals, and in 1977 she started the Doris Day Pet Foundation ("I'm trying with all my heart to make this world a better place for the animals."). In 1985 she was encouraged to return to television with a talk show focusing on animals, "Doris Day's Best Friends," which aired over cable's Christian Broadcasting Network for a season. Her first guest was old friend Rock Hudson; his gaunt appearance on the show brought to public knowledge that he was dying of AIDS. Day owns the Cypress Inn Hotel on the Monterey Peninsula, and her record-producer son, Terry, and his second wife (Jacqueline) made her a grandmother. She insists she has no further interest in recordings.

In 1989 she made one of her rare public appearances to accept the Cecil B. De Mille Award, given by the Hollywood Foreign Press Association. This Golden Globe tribute was televised on January 28, 1989. A radiantly beautiful Day received a tremendous ovation as she stepped to the dais and commented, "I've been in the country and I've got to come to town more often. It's been a wonderful life and I'm not finished yet. I want to do some more. I think the best is yet to come. I really do!"

## Filmography

Romance on the High Seas [It's Magic] (WB, 1948)

My Dream Is Yours (WB, 1949)

It's a Great Feeling (WB, 1949)

Young Man with a Horn [Young Man of Music] (WB, 1950)

Tea for Two (WB, 1950)

The West Point Story [Fine and Dandy] (WB, 1950)

Storm Warning (WB, 1950)
Lullaby of Broadway (WB, 1951)
Starlift (WB, 1951)
On Moonlight Bay (WB, 1951)
I'll See You in My Dreams (WB, 1951)
The Winning Team (WB, 1952)
Screen Snapshots #206 (Col, 1952) (s)
April in Paris (WB, 1952)
By the Light of the Silvery Moon (WB, 1953)
Calamity Jane (WB, 1953)
So You Want a Television Set (Vita, 1953) (s)
Lucky Me (WB, 1954)
Young at Heart (WB, 1954)
Love Me or Leave Me (MGM, 1955)
The Man Who Knew Too Much (Par, 1956)
Julie (MGM, 1956)
The Pajama Game (WB, 1957)
Teacher's Pet (Par, 1958)
The Tunnel of Love (MGM, 1958)

It Happened to Jane [Twinkle and Shine] (Col, 1959)
Pillow Talk (Univ, 1959)
Midnight Lace (Univ, 1960)
Please Don't Eat the Daisies (MGM, 1960)
Lover Come Back (Univ, 1961)
That Touch of Mink (Univ, 1962)
Billy Rose's Jumbo (MGM, 1962)
The Thrill of It All (Univ, 1963)
Move Over, Darling (20th–Fox, 1963)
Send Me No Flowers (Univ, 1964)
Do Not Disturb (20th–Fox, 1965)
The Glass Bottom Boat (MGM, 1966)
Caprice (20th–Fox, 1967)
The Ballad of Josie (Univ, 1968)
Where Were You When the Lights Went Out? (MGM, 1968)
With Six You Get Egg Roll (NG, 1968)

## Radio Series

Moon River (WLW, 1943)
Your Hit Parade (CBS, ca. 1945)
The Bob Sweeney–Hal March Show (CBS, 1946)

The Bob Hope Show (NBC, ca. 1948–50)
The Doris Day Show (CBS, 1952–53)

## TV Series

The Doris Day Show (CBS, 1968–73)
Doris Day's Best Friends (CBN, 1985–86)

## Album Discography

Annie Get Your Gun (Col OL-5960/OS-2360, Har KH-30396)
The Best of Doris Day (Spot 8533)
Bright and Shiny (Col CL-1614/CS-8414)
By the Light of the Silvery Moon (10" Col CL-6248, Caliban 6019) [ST]
By the Light of the Silvery Moon/Lullaby of Broadway (Col Special Products 18421) [ST]
Calamity Jane (10" Col CL-6273)
Christmas Album (Col CS-9026, Har H-30016)
Cuttin' Capers (Col CL-1232/CS-8078)
Day by Day (Col CL-942)

Day by Night (Col CL-1053/CS-8089)
Day Dreams (10" Col CL-6071, Col CL-624)
Diamond Horseshoe (Caliban 6028) [ST/R]
Doris Day (Joyce 6013) w. Les Brown and Harry James
Doris Day (Lots LOP 14132)
Doris Day, Vols. 1–2 (Hindsight 200, 226)
Doris Day 1940–41 (Joyce 6004)
Doris Day 1944–45 (Joyce 6005)
Doris Day Sings Do-Re-Mi, Que Sera, Sera & Other Children's Favourites (Hallmark HM 534)

Duets (Col CL-1752, DRG 601) w. André Previn

Great Movie Hits (Har HL-7392/HS-11192)

Greatest Hits (Col CL-1210)

Heart Full of Love (Memoir MOIR 511)

Hooray for Hollywood (Col C2L-5/CS-8006-7, Col Special Products 5)

I Have Dreamed (Col CL-1660/CS-8460)

I'll See You in My Dreams (10" Col CL-6198) [ST]

I'll See You in My Dreams/Calamity Jane (Col Special Products 19611) [ST]

It's Magic (Har HS-11382)

Jumbo (Col OL-5860/OS-2260) [ST]

Latin for Lovers (Col CL-2310/CS-9110)

Lights! Camera! Action! (10" Col Cl-2518)

Listen to Day (Col DDS-1)

Love Him (Col CL-2131/CS-8931)

Love Me or Leave Me (Col CL-710/CS-H773) [ST]

Lucky Me (Athena LMIB-9) [ST]

Lullaby of Broadway (10" Col CL-6168) [ST]

Lullaby of Broadway/I'll See You in My Dreams (Caliban 6008) [ST]

My Dream Is Yours/The West Point Story (Titania 501) [ST]

On Moonlight Bay (10" Col CL-6186, Caliban 6006) [ST]

One Night Stand (Joyce 1020)

One Night Stand (Sandy Hook 2011)

One Night Stand with Les Brown 1940–45 (Sandy Hook 2078)

The Pajama Game (Col OL-5210) [ST]

Radio Soundtracks (Caliban 6047)

Romance on the High Seas/It's a Great Feeling (Caliban 6015) [ST]

Sentimental Journey (Cameo 32257)

Sentimental Journey (Col CL-2360/CS-9160)

Show Time (Col CL-1470/CS-8261)

Softly as I Leave You (Har H-31498)

Starlift (Titania 510)

Stars of Hollywood (Avenue International AV INT 1011) w. Frank Sinatra

Tea for Two (10" Col CL-6149, Caliban 6031) [ST]

Tea for Two/On Moonlight Bay (Col Special Products 17660) [ST]

Through the Eyes of Love (Memoir 123)

The Uncollected Doris Day, Vol. 1: 1953 (Hindsight HSR-200)

The Uncollected Doris Day, Vol. 2: 1952–53 (Hindsight HSR-226) w. Page Cavanaugh Trio

The Uncollected Les Brown & His Orchestra 1944–46 (Hindsight HSR-103)

What Every Girl Should Know (Col CL-1438/CS-8234)

What Will Be, Will Be (Har HS-11282)

With a Smile and a Song (Col CL-2266/CS-9066)

Wonderful Day (Col Special Products 82021)

You'll Never Walk Alone (Col CL-1904/CS-8704)

Young at Heart (10" Col CL-6106, Col CL-582, Col Special Products 582) [ST]

Young at Heart/April in Paris (Titania 500)

You're My Thrill (10" Col CL-6071)

# MARLENE DIETRICH

ONE OF THE SCREEN'S GREATEST SEX SYMBOLS, SOPHISTICATED AND
sensual Marlene Dietrich held sway in the world of entertainment for over half a century.
In the process she became an exotic living legend; the mere mention of either of her names
alone was sufficient for identification. She was a friend of the famous and an intellectual
soulmate of some of the world's best minds. She retained her image of the inveterate
femme fatale long after most of her contemporaries had chosen retirement. When her film
career slackened, she continued to appear around the world as an elegant, alluring
chanteuse in her one-woman showcase. It is as a singer, as well as an actress, that Marlene
Dietrich established her screen siren presence, and through the years she translated this
appeal successfully not only on film but also on radio, recordings, and the stage. While in
many ways limited in range as an actress and performer, Marlene Dietrich coaxed the most
out of her public persona, thanks to her innate intelligence, Prussian fastidiousness, and
her uncanny ability to retain her striking beauty well into her seventies.

Marlene Dietrich's early years are almost as enshrouded in mystery as were the
characters she later played on celluloid. Her year of birth is reported to be anywhere
between 1901 and 1908. It has been reported that her birth certificate was found in East
Berlin and that she was born Maria Magdalena Dietrich on December 27, 1907, the
daughter of Prussian policeman Louis Erich Otto Dietrich and Wilhelmina Elisabeth
Josephine Felsing. After her father's death, while Marlene was quite young, her mother
married Edouard von Losch, an officer in the German army. At an early age she took to the
violin and planned a career in music, but this was cut short by a wrist injury. In 1921 she
studied drama with the renowned Max Reinhardt in Berlin and had small roles in several
of his Shakespearean productions. She remained with Reinhardt for two years and then
began seeking work at the German movie studios. It was there she caught the eye of
assistant director Rudolf Sieber, who gained for her a small role in DIE TRAGÖDIE DER LIEBE
(1923), directed by Joe May, and starring Emil Jannings. Marlene continued to get small
roles in films, and in 1924 she and Sieber were married. In 1925 she had a bit part in DIE
FREUDLOSE GASSE, directed by G. W. Pabst, which brought Greta Garbo to the attention
of American filmmakers when it was issued in the United States as THE STREET OF SOR-
ROW in 1927. In 1926 she was billed on screen as Marlene Dietrich for the first time in
EINE DUBARRY VON HEUTE [A Modern Du Barry].

Dietrich left the entertainment field for a time in the mid-1920s after the birth of
her daughter, Maria. She then returned to Max Reinhardt's company and won the lead in
a stage production of *Broadway* followed by *Es Liegt in der Luft* [Something in the Air]. In

1928 she was a member of the chorus *Ensemble des Nelson-Revue* and in that capacity made her first records, for the Electradisk label in Berlin. She also continued to do small roles in German movies, and in 1929 she appeared with Hans Albers in the stage production *Misalliance*, followed by the revue *Zwei Kravetten* [Two Neckties]. While appearing in this show she came to the attention of Josef von Sternberg, who had come to Berlin in 1929 at the behest of Emil Jannings to direct the German star's first sound film, DER BLAUE ENGEL (1930). Marlene was one of many actresses he tested for the lead of Lola Lola, the cabaret singer, and she won the part even though she did not believe she photographed well.

Still plumpish, Marlene Dietrich caused a sensation as the low-class cabaret trollop who seduces and marries a much older professor (Emil Jannings) and then casually casts him aside like her previous lovers. In the film she sang "Falling in Love Again" and "Lola," which she recorded in Berlin for HMV [His Master's Voice] Records. THE BLUE ANGEL was made in German, French, and English versions and as soon as it premiered in her homeland, she left with Josef von Sternberg for Hollywood, where they had been signed to make MOROCCO (1930) for Paramount. Before facing the American camera, she underwent a transformation that removed the hausfrau in her and accentuated her exotic beauty. She was again cast as a cabaret singer, this time with a tainted past. Her character, Amy Jolly, wore a tuxedo when she performed such numbers as "Give Me the Man" and the provocative "What Am I Bid for My Apples." In this stylistic romance she rejects a jaded, rich roué (Adolphe Menjou) for the love of a French legionnaire (Gary Cooper). At the finale she joins with the other camp followers in plodding across the desert sands to follow her man. When the movie was released, Dietrich took Depression-weary America by storm. (She was Oscar-nominated, but lost the Best Actress award to Marie Dressler of MIN AND BILL.) Soon the English-language version of THE BLUE ANGEL was also issued. The two movies established the ultimate Dietrich icon, that of an incredibly beautiful woman who is physically, but rarely emotionally, attainable.

Eager to rival MGM's foreign-bred star Greta Garbo, Paramount offered Dietrich $125,000 a picture plus artistic concessions on her productions. Marlene's now-established screen character was perpetuated by director Josef von Sternberg in the other five features he and Dietrich made for Paramount between 1931 and 1935. Their relationship took on the aura of a Svengali–Trilby pairing, which eventually took its toll on both their careers. After THE BLUE ANGEL and MOROCCO, though, Dietrich was acknowledged to be in the same league as two others of filmdom's swank sex symbols: Garbo and Constance Bennett.

Dietrich's screen popularity reached its peak in the spring of 1931 when DISHON-ORED was released. She played a prostitute who becomes an Austrian spy during World War I and sacrifices her life to save the Russian agent (Victor McLaglen) she loves. Following its making, Marlene returned to Berlin and reappeared in Hollywood with her husband and daughter; the revelation of their existence failed to make a dent in her enormous screen popularity. Dietrich and her husband would live mostly apart; he became a chicken farmer.

She next did SHANGHAI EXPRESS (1932) with von Sternberg, a stylishly photographed thriller in which she was cast as the notorious "China Coaster," another woman with a shady past. She is reunited with an old lover (Clive Brook) aboard the title train during a revolution. The result did little to help her box-office drawing power, which slipped even further with the overlong BLONDE VENUS (1932), in which she portrayed a nightclub entertainer who sells herself to a playboy (Cary Grant) to obtain funds to help her ailing husband (Herbert Marshall) get well. The otherwise lachrymose film contains a wild "Hot Voodoo" production number in which she appears on stage in a gorilla outfit. She broke temporarily from working with von Sternberg to make SONG OF SONGS (1933) with director Rouben Mamoulian. She gave a solid performance in an unbelievable story about a poor young woman who finds brief happiness with an artist (Brian Aherne) and misery with a cruel lecher (Lionel Atwill). The film allowed her the occasion to sing "Johnny," a song associated with her since she first recorded it in Berlin in 1931. However, the most famous aspect of SONG OF SONGS was the nude life-size statue of Dietrich displayed in the film and as an advertising gimmick.

Marlene was reunited with von Sternberg for the stifling THE SCARLET EMPRESS (1934), in which she was the shy young girl who becomes the scheming Catherine the Great of Russia. The movie was lavish in period detail but vapid in plot. Her final production with von Sternberg was THE DEVIL IS A WOMAN (1935); in it she was strik-

Marlene Dietrich and Clive Brook in SHANGHAI EXPRESS (1932)

ingly photographed as a Spanish courtesan who romances both a younger man (Cesar Romero) and a wealthy older one (Lionel Atwill). Despite the stellar production trappings and a fine performance by Atwill as the love-smitten elder suitor, the film was sterile. The Spanish government requested that the picture be withdrawn from distribution because of its "misrepresentations," and Paramount did so. It was the end of the teaming of Dietrich and von Sternberg, the latter claiming he had done as much as he could for her. Despite its many shortcomings, the picture remained a favorite with Dietrich "because I looked more lovely in that film than in any other of my whole career."

In Paramount's DESIRE (1936) for director Frank Borzage, she was quite good as a jewel thief who falls in love with a vacationing American (Gary Cooper) after hiding in his suit a valuable pearl necklace she has just stolen. For Paramount she began working on I LOVE A SOLDIER with Charles Boyer, but after disputes with studio producer Ernst Lubitsch she left the production. Starmaker David O. Selznick thought he knew better how to showcase Marlene. He paid her $200,000 to replace Merle Oberon in his Technicolor THE GARDEN OF ALLAH (1936) for United Artists, which cost over $2 million to produce. She was seen as a siren who seduces a Trappist monk (Charles Boyer). She earned a mammoth $375,000 for starring in the British-lensed KNIGHT WITHOUT ARMOUR (1937), which cost almost as much as the previous film. Alexander Korda produced this lavish melodrama of the Russian Revolution with Marlene as a countess who is saved from a Bolshevik firing squad by her British spy lover (Robert Donat). The film was not popular at the box office. She was again at Paramount for Ernst Lubitsch's ANGEL (1937), a confection about a titled woman (Marlene) leaving her spouse (Herbert Marshall) for a harmless fling with another man (Melvyn Douglas). It did nothing to bring back her former marquee glory. By the end of 1937 she had joined the group (which included Katharine Hepburn) labeled "box-office poison." Because of this and her recurring conflicts with the Paramount filmmakers, plans for her to star in FRENCH WITHOUT TEARS (1939) and MIDNIGHT (1939) came to nothing. Instead, Paramount paid her $200,000–$250,000 not to make her final film for the studio.

If the public seemed tired of her, the studios were not. Both Columbia and Warner Bros. signed her for one-picture deals. She was to make the life of George Sand for the former, and do a remake of ONE WAY PASSAGE for the latter. Neither project happened with Dietrich, and she would later substitute other pictures to fulfill her commitments. Meanwhile, the French cinema beckoned and it was rumored she would star in DÉDÉE D'ANVERS with Raimu. However, the escalation of World War II prevented her doing the project.

What did bring Dietrich back as a movie draw was DESTRY RIDES AGAIN (1939), which cast her as earthy Frenchy, a western saloon singer who helps a gawky young man (James Stewart) tame a corrupt town. Her saloon fight with Una Merkel and her throaty singing of "The Boys in the Backroom" and "You've Got That Look" (recorded for Decca Records) were the highlights of this entertaining Western. She had done this comeback vehicle for Universal at a very reduced rate and now signed a contract with the studio. None of her next films would match DESTRY RIDES AGAIN. She turned down MY LITTLE

CHICKADEE (which Mae West did) and instead made SEVEN SINNERS (1940), the first of a trio of films with John Wayne (with whom she had an off-screen affair). It cast her as a South Seas trollop bewitched by a Navy lieutenant (Wayne). She sang "I've Been in Love Before." Less enjoyable was the period piece THE FLAME OF NEW ORLEANS (1941), directed by Frenchman René Clair in his American film debut, with Marlene as a French adventuress who ends up with a poor boatman (Bruce Cabot) instead of a rich banker (Roland Young). George Raft and Edward G. Robinson next co-starred with Dietrich in MANPOWER (1941) for Warner Bros., a melodrama which did well by them as electric wire workers but wasted Marlene as a clip-joint hostess and the object of their heated affections. She was better served by the light comedy THE LADY IS WILLING (1942), for Columbia, which cast her as a singing star who wants to adopt a baby and seeks the aid of a pediatrician (Fred MacMurray). Back at Universal she made two rough-and-tumble melodramas with John Wayne and Randolph Scott, both movies benefitting the two male stars more than Dietrich. THE SPOILERS (1942) was the third remake of the famous 1914 classic with William Farnum (who was also in this version) and Tom Santschi; Dietrich was cast as Alaskan saloon hostess Cherry Mallotte. PITTSBURGH (1942) had Dietrich out of place as the girl coveted by coalmining businessmen Scott and Wayne; the film boasted the beautiful "Garden in the Rain" as its theme, but Marlene did not sing it.

Marlene Dietrich had become an American citizen in 1938, and when the United States entered World War II, she was one of the most active of Hollywood entertainers in the war effort. She worked at the Hollywood Canteen, joined war bond drives, made radio broadcasts in various languages for the government to send to Europe, made records (including her noteworthy "Lili Marlene") in German, which were dropped behind enemy lines, and tirelessly entertained servicemen at the USO. After the war she received the U.S. Defense Department's Medal of Freedom for uplifting the spirits of Allied fighting men during World War II.

She also worked on radio. In the 1930s she had appeared on Rudy Vallee's "The Fleishmann's Hour"; in 1940 she and Fred MacMurray did a radio adaptation of "Desire" for CBS's "Gulf Screen Guild Theatre," and she and Clark Gable were heard on "Lux Radio Theatre" in "Legionnaire and the Lady," a radio version of MOROCCO. She also did radio editions of "Grand Hotel" and "Pittsburgh," the latter with John Wayne and Randolph Scott. Moreover, she guest-starred on such radio shows as Fred Allen's "Texaco Star Theatre," "The Jack Benny Program," and "Hollywood Open House." Having turned down the lead in Broadway's *One Touch of Venus* (1943—Mary Martin took the part), she made a brief guest appearance in Universal's FOLLOW THE BOYS (1944)—being sawed in half in a magic act performed by her off-screen friend Orson Welles—and then starred in MGM's lavish adaptation of KISMET (1944) as Jamilla. The highlight of the latter film was the scene in which, painted in gold, she performed an exotic dance number.

After the war, Dietrich went to France where she and her off-screen romance, Jean Gabin, were to star in LES PORTES DE LA NUIT. She changed her mind and instead the two made MARTIN ROUMAGNAC (1946), about a tart (Marlene) who is murdered by the man (Gabin) who loves her, after he learns about her many affairs. In the U.S. a censored version was released as THE ROOM UPSTAIRS. Now in her forties, Marlene found it harder to compete for starring roles in postwar Hollywood. At Paramount she was a gypsy fortune teller who helps a Britisher (Ray Milland) escape from Nazi Germany in GOLDEN EAR-RINGS (1947). Far more popular, and helpful for her career, was Billy Wilder's A FOREIGN AFFAIR (1948). Although Jean Arthur was the top-billed star, it was Dietrich who stole the show as the seductive German songstress with a Nazi past in postwar Berlin. She sang "Illusions" and "Black Market," both by her favorite and faithful composer Friedrich Hollander. In Alfred Hitchcock's STAGE FRIGHT (1950), filmed largely in London, she was a self-centered singing star engulfed in murder. In it she sang two of her most famous songs: "La Vie en Rose" and "The Laziest Gal in Town." In between these two assignments, she did a guest bit in JIGSAW (1949) and performed on radio in "The Lady from the Sea" on CBS's "The Philip Morris Playhouse" in 1949. By this time Marlene's married daughter, Maria (who as Maria Riva would be a star of early television), had a child, and Dietrich was being promoted as "The World's Most Glamorous Grandmother."

In 1951 Marlene appeared at the Academy Awards presentation and performed "Anna Karenina" on radio's "MGM Theatre of the Air." That year she also co-starred (again) with James Stewart in the British-made NO HIGHWAY IN THE SKY, as an actress aboard a plane that may fall apart. Because she asked for "too much" money ($150,000), the female lead in MGM's THE MAN WITH THE CLOAK (1951) went to Barbara Stanwyck. Instead she headlined the psychological Western RANCHO NOTORIOUS (1952) for direc-tor Fritz Lang. She was the bawdy mistress of the outlaw hangout in this unpopular entry. In 1952 she guested on Bing Crosby's CBS radio show and then starred in her own ABC series, "Cafe Istanbul," a program about international intrigue. When it failed to catch on with listeners, she switched to CBS, changed the format, and retitled her program "Time for Love"; it ran until 1954. After that Marlene began her long-running one-woman show, which she performed around the world for the next two decades, both in concerts and nightclubs. (Her frequent conductor and arranger was Burt Bacharach.) The outings were noteworthy for elegance, precision, and the star's meticulous devotion to detail, which always created the most glamorous mystique for her viewers. The patter between songs perpetuated the myths she had chosen to create, which were also part of her grand illusion.

In 1956 she played a cabaret singer in a cameo in AROUND THE WORLD IN 80 DAYS and in 1957 she starred with Vittorio De Sica in THE MONTE CARLO STORY as a noble-woman who cannot give up gambling but finds love with a penniless count (De Sica) in the European gaming capital. She landed another plum film role in 1957 as the loyal wife in Billy Wilder's outstanding production of Agatha Christie's WITNESS FOR THE PROSE-CUTION. The next year she was a black-wigged fortune teller in Orson Welles's underrated TOUCH OF EVIL. She made a triumphant return to West Germany with her one-woman show in 1960 and the next year had her last good screen role, that of Mme. Berthholt, a German general's wife, in the all-star JUDGMENT AT NUREMBERG.

Throughout the 1950s and 1960s she turned out a steady stream of single and long-playing records for such labels as Capitol, Columbia, Dot, Liberty, and Vox. Her record-ing of "Where Have All the Flowers Gone?" was especially noteworthy. She commanded high fees for her one-woman act; for example, in 1953, Las Vegas's Sahara Hotel paid her $30,000 a week for three weeks' work. In 1961 her book, *Marlene Dietrich's ABC,* was published; it was in dictionary format and contained her comments on a number of subjects. In 1967 she finally brought her act to Broadway for a successful engagement, followed by another the next year. In the 1960s she did two more films, as narrator of a documentary about Adolf Hitler called THE BLACK FOX (1962) and a guest bit in PARIS WHEN IT SIZZLES (1964). She was persuaded to do her club act as a special for CBS-TV in 1973. While it earned good reviews, it was too sophisticated to gain high ratings, thus negating the possibility of any future major TV outings. She continued to tour with her stage act until sidelined by a leg injury in the mid-1970s. In 1979 she returned to films for the role of a heavily veiled madam in post–World War I Germany in JUST A GIGOLO, singing the title song, which she also recorded.

Since then Marlene has led a reclusive life in Paris, although she has made it known she is available for voice-over work. In the early 1980s her long-anticipated autobiography was rejected as not being spicy enough, but was later published anyway. She did grant an interview to actor Maximilian Schell, which he interpolated into his film tribute to her, the 1984 documentary MARLENE. It further enshrined her image as an enigmatic, disciplined soul who shrewdly manipulated her charisma into decades of international popularity.

It was Ernest Hemingway who once said of his friend Marlene Dietrich, "If she had nothing more than her voice, she could break your heart with it. But she also has that beautiful body and the timeless loveliness of her face."

## Filmography

Die Tragödie der Liebe [Tragedy of Love] (Ger, 1923)

So sind die Männer [Der kleine Napoleon] (Ger, 1923)

Der Mensch am Wege [Man by the Roadside] (Ger, 1923)

Der Sprung ins Leben [The Leap into Life] (Ger, 1923)

Die freudlose Gasse [The Street(s) of Sorrow/ Joyless Street] (Ger, 1925)

Eine Dubarry von heute [A Modern Du Barry] (Ger, 1926)

Manon Lescaut (Ger, 1926)

Kopf hoch Charly! [Heads Up, Charly!] (Ger, 1926)

Madame wünscht keine Kinder [Madame Wants No Children] (Ger, 1926)

Der Juxbaron [The Imaginary Baron] (Ger, 1927)

Sein grösster Bluff [His Greatest Bluff] (Ger, 1927)

Cafe Electric [Wenn ein Weib den Weg verliert/ Die Liebesbörse] (Aus/Ger, 1927)

Prinzessin Olala [The Art of Love] (Ger, 1928)

Die glückliche Mutter (Ger, 1928) (s)

Ich küsse ihre Hand, Madame [I Kiss Your Hand, Madame] (Ger, 1929)

Die Frau, nach der man sich sehnt [Three Loves] (Ger, 1929)

Das Schiff der verlorenen Menschen [The Ship of Lost Men] (Ger/Fr, 1929)

Gefahren der Brautzeit [Dangers of the Engagement Period] (Ger, 1929)

Der Blaue Engel [The Blue Angel] (Par, 1930) (also English- and French-language versions)

Morocco (Par, 1930)

Dishonored (Par, 1931)

Shanghai Express (Par, 1932)

Blonde Venus (Par, 1932)

Song of Songs (Par, 1933)

The Scarlet Empress (Par, 1934)

The Devil Is a Woman (Par, 1935)

Desire (Par, 1936)
The Garden of Allah (UA, 1936)
Knight Without Armour (UA, 1937)
Angel (Par, 1937)
Destry Rides Again (Univ, 1939)
Seven Sinners (Univ, 1940)
Manpower (WB, 1941)
The Flame of New Orleans (Univ, 1941)
The Lady Is Willing (Col, 1942)
The Spoilers (Univ, 1942)
Pittsburgh (Univ, 1942)
Screen Snapshots #103 (Col, 1943) (s)
Show Business at War (20th–Fox, 1943) (s)
Follow the Boys (Univ, 1944)
Kismet (MGM, 1944)
Martin Roumagnac [The Room Upstairs] (Fr, 1946)

Golden Earrings (Par, 1947)
A Foreign Affair (Par, 1948)
Jigsaw (UA, 1949)
Stage Fright (WB, 1950)
No Highway in the Sky [No Highway] (20th–Fox, 1951)
Rancho Notorious (RKO, 1952)
Around the World in 80 Days (UA, 1956)
The Monte Carlo Story (UA, 1957)
Witness for the Prosecution (UA, 1957)
Touch of Evil (Univ, 1958)
Judgment at Nuremberg (UA, 1961)
The Black Fox (MGM, 1962) (narrator)
Paris When It Sizzles (Par, 1964)
Just a Gigolo (UA, 1979)
Marlene (Zev Braun Pictures, 1984) (documentary)

## Radio Series

Cafe Istanbul (ABC, 1952–53)
Time for Love (CBS, 1953–54)

## Album Discography

Ann Sheridan and Marlene Dietrich—Live (Amalgamated 249)
The Best of Marlene Dietrich (Col C-32245)
Bing's Beaus (Amalgamated 805) w. Tallulah Bankhead and Bing Crosby
The Blue Angel (Caliban 6046) [ST]
The Fabulous Marlene Dietrich (Hallmark 834)
Falling in Love Again (Regal 1078)
German Popular Songs (10" Vox 3040)
Grand Hotel (Caliban 6040) [ST]
Her Complete Decca Recordings (MCA 1501)
The Legendary, Lovely Marlene (MCA 1685)
Lili Marlene (Col CL-1275, Col Special Products 1275)
Lili Marlene (MCA Coral 8002)
Magic Marlene (Cap TCL/DTCL-300)
The Magic of Marlene Dietrich (Music for Pleasure 5790)
Marlene (ASV 5039)
Marlene (Cap T/ST-10397)

Marlene (Stanyan SR-10124)
Marlene Dietrich (Decca DL-8465/DL-78465)
Marlene Dietrich and Clark Gable in "Morocco" (Amalgamated 257) [ST/R]
Marlene Dietrich at the Café de Paris (Col ML-4975)
The Marlene Dietrich Collection—20 Golden Greats (Dejavu 2098)
Marlene Dietrich in London (Col OL-6430/OS-2830)
Marlene Dietrich in Rio (Col WL-164/WS-316, Col Special Products 316)
Marlene Dietrich: Lili Marlene (Nostalgia 22005)
Marlene Dietrich Live (Malcon 5290)
Marlene Dietrich Overseas (10" Col ML-2615)
Marlene Dietrich's Berlin (Cap T/ST-10443)
Souvenir Album (10" Decca DL-5100)
Wiedersehen mit Marlene (Cap T-10282)

# THE DINNING SISTERS

THE DINNING SISTERS WERE ONE OF THE MOST POPULAR FEMALE vocal groups of the 1940s thanks to their appearances on radio, their Capitol recordings, and a series of motion pictures. In an era when female trio harmony was extremely popular and the field was crowded, the talented sister act managed to climb to the very top by beating out the long-popular Andrews Sisters not only in a 1946 *Billboard* magazine award poll of jukebox operators but also for the *Cashbox* magazine award that same year. All three of The Dinning Sisters were very attractive; Lou a blonde and the twins dark-haired. The Dinning Sisters were more beautiful than either of their predecessors: the Boswell Sisters or The Andrews Sisters.

Success for The Dinning Sisters first came while they were still teenagers. As they grew older, they married and eventually separated as an act. Their music's appeal faded with the coming of rock 'n' roll in the mid-1950s. In the 1980s, however, thanks to the reissue of their older recordings, a new generation began listening to and appreciating the melodious harmony of "The Sweethearts of Sunbonnet Swing."

The Dinning Sisters were the daughters of farmer John Dinning and his wife, Bertha; they had nine children in all: five girls and four boys. During the 1920s and 1930s times were tough for farm folk and the family moved several times, to farms in Kentucky, Kansas, and Oklahoma. The oldest of the singing trio, Ella Lucille "Lou" Dinning, was born September 29, 1920, in Auburn, Kentucky, while her twin sisters, Virginia (called Ginger) and Eugenia (nicknamed Jean) were born March 29, 1924, in Braman, Oklahoma. Since their father was a church choir director and their mother sang in the choir, it was only natural for the girls to gain an appreciation of music. At an early age they joined their mother in the church choir, and the trio also began singing together, first at home and then at social events and amateur shows. At the latter, they frequently won first prize, the money going to help feed the growing Dinning family.

By the time the girls were teenagers they had their own noontime daily radio show over station KCRC in Enid, Oklahoma, where they were billed as "The McCormick/Deering Sisters," to accommodate their sponsors. Their fan mail was the most ever received by the station, and since their older sister, Marvis Dinning, was now a successful vocalist with Freddy Owen's orchestra, the three young ladies determined to try for the big time. Their older brother Wade drove them to Chicago in 1939 where they got a few singing jobs before having a successful audition at NBC Radio. The network executives were so impressed with the trio that they were signed to a five-year contract as NBC staff singers. They were assigned immediately to a variety of daily shows like "Don McNeil's

Breakfast Club," "Garry Moore's Club Matinee," "The Roy Shields' Review," and the Saturday night favorite "The National Barn Dance," which had already spawned stars like Gene Autry, Patsy Montana, Max Terhune, George Gobel, The Cass County Boys, Lulu Belle and Scotty, The Hoosier Hot Shots, and many more. Because the young performers were so outstanding, NBC also gave them their own daytime "The Dinning Sisters Show" on which they were billed as "The Loreleis of the Airwaves." Thanks to all this air exposure, the trio gained national popularity quickly, and as a consequence, in 1942 they made their recording debuts waxing a series of discs for Standard Transcriptions.

While working in Chicago, the sisters met NBC staff musician Jack Fascinato, who became their pianist and arranger. They credit him with polishing their music and harmony work and helping them develop the smooth sound that was to make them the nation's favorite girl trio. While in Chicago they also had successful stands at the Chicago Theatre and several Windy City night spots.

In 1942 they filmed two shorts for the Soundies Corporation of America (they would do eight more for the company in 1945–46). Also that year they made their feature film debut at Universal, which had a profitable policy during the war years of churning out budget musicals spotlighting the likes of The Andrews Sisters, Donald O'Connor, Peggy Ryan, Gloria Jean, Robert Paige, and others. The fifty-eight-minute STRICTLY IN THE GROOVE was double-bill fodder peopled with Ozzie Nelson and His Band, Mary Healy, Martha Tilton, The Jimmy Wakely Trio, Leon Errol, and Shemp Howard. In a dude ranch setting The Dinning Sisters sang three of the sixteen songs: "A Pretty Girl Milking Her Cow," "Be Honest with Me," and "Elmer's Tune." *Variety* noted that the trio "with similar style and delivery to the Andrews Sisters are a bright spot in their brief appearance." It was two years before they returned to feature filmmaking.

In 1944 they came to Hollywood with the cast of their Saturday night radio show to lens the low-budget THE NATIONAL BARN DANCE for Paramount; they portrayed themselves and sang "Angels Never Leave Heaven," "Swing Little Indian," and "The Barn Dance Polka." Their contract with NBC ended in 1945, at which time they were signed by Johnny Mercer to record on Capitol Records. They were the premier vocal group to be contracted by the label and they became the first performers ever to make their commercial record debut with an entire LP. The album, an immediate success, was on the charts for eighteen weeks. As a result they were given the Award for Achievement by *Orchestra World* magazine and *Song Hits* magazine's Award of Merit as "The Outstanding Vocal Trio of 1945."

The late 1940s was the busiest and most fruitful period in The Dinning Sisters' career as they guested on such top radio programs as "The Kate Smith Hour," "The Chesterfield Supper Club" with Perry Como, "The Kraft Music Hall," "The Carnation Hour," "The Nat (King) Cole Show," "The Alec Templeton Show," "The Grand Ole Opry," and "The Eddy Arnold Show." They were in constant demand for personal appearances, and in 1946 they appeared in the Universal Pictures short film TAKIN' THE BREAKS with Russ Morgan and His Orchestra, singing "Mary Lee" and "Pin Marin." That year also saw them as the featured headliners of two minor Columbia musical features:

THROW A SADDLE ON A STAR and THAT TEXAS JAMBOREE, both with Ken Curtis, Jeff Donnell, and Guinn "Big Boy" Williams. Director Ray Nazarro filmed both of these economy items simultaneously. In the first entry the girls had one acting scene and sang "Mary Lee" and "Once in Awhile," while in THAT TEXAS JAMBOREE they had their largest screen assignment, portraying the owners of a small western town's bar and restaurant who become involved with the town's politics. In the latter film they sang "I Still Remember" and "Valley of the Sun." Next Walt Disney used The Dinning Sisters to provide voices for two of his animated feature films at RKO. That proved to be their final movie work. In FUN AND FANCY FREE (1947) they did the song "Lazy Countryside" while in MELODY TIME (1948) they sang "Blame It on the Samba." Ironically, The Andrews Sisters, their biggest rivals, who also could never harness a strong filmmaking career, sang the story of "Little Toot" in the latter feature.

In 1948 The Dinning Sisters enjoyed their strongest commercial recording success with "Buttons and Bows" for Capitol; the disc sold over one million copies. Among their other Capitol best-sellers were "Love on a Greyhound Bus," "And Then It's Heaven," "Years and Years Ago," "My Adobe Hacienda," "Lolita Lopez," "Once in Awhile," "Brazil," "Beg Your Pardon," "I Love My Love," "San Antonio Rose," "Melancholy," "Oh

The Dinning Sisters (Jean, Lou, and Ginger) in THAT TEXAS JAMBOREE (1946)

Monah," and "Harlem Sandman." During the 1949–50 season, the trio were regulars on CBS Radio's "The Spike Jones Spotlight Revue."

By 1950, The Dinning Sisters were tiring of the show business grind. In addition, each had a distinct personal life of her own. Ginger Dinning recalled later, "We didn't work as hard as the Andrews Sisters. We were also more centered around our husbands and raising families." Older sister Lou, who sang alto in the trio to Ginger's lead and Jean's soprano, started recording solo for Capitol, and she left the group in early 1946 after marrying singer/songwriter Don Robertson; she was replaced for three years by Jayne Bundesen. Lou later co-starred on radio with Tennessee Ernie Ford. For a time in 1949, the family's youngest sister, Dolores, joined the trio, and in 1952 The Dinning Sisters filmed a half-dozen TV short subjects for Snader Telescriptions: "Winter Wonderland," "Brazil," "Mornin' on the Farm," "Pig Foot Pete," "You're a Character, Dear," and "Ma, He's Makin' Eyes at Me." In the mid-1950s Jean Dinning cut a series of singles for Essex Records; she sang all three parts on the discs, which were issued as being by The Dinning Sisters, "Featuring Jean Dinning." In the late 1950s a budget label, Somerset, released an album by "The Dinning Sisters" made up of Jean's Essex recordings.

The Dinning Sisters ceased to appear professionally in the 1950s, although they remained very close-knit as a family. Jean, who moved to Tennessee, wrote the song "Teen Angel" which the girls' younger brother, Mark, recorded for MGM Records, resulting in a best-selling platter. Lou remained in California where she ceased to perform but continued to write songs, while Ginger settled in Sussex, New Jersey. In 1983 EMI Records of France issued an album of the trio's vintage Capitol recordings; it was so successful that another followed in 1985. A West German label, Cattle Records, distributed an LP in 1986 made up of the Dinnings' Standard Transcription material. More albums are planned as there has been a marked renewed interest by the public in the singing sisters. In addition they have reunited for occasional personal appearances, such as a tribute to them in the Ozarks in the fall of 1987, followed by a TV appearance on "Nashville Now" and their singing at the "Grand Ole Opry" for the first time in over thirty-five years. In an age of acid rock and outlandish music videos, The Dinning Sisters and their consistently pleasing harmony are again in the spotlight.

## Filmography

By the Light of the Silvery Moon (Soundies, 1942) (s)

Ho-Hum (Soundies, 1942) (s)

Strictly in the Groove (Univ, 1942)

The National Barn Dance (Par, 1944)

Clancy (Soundies, 1945) (s)

Pig Foot Pete (Soundies, 1945) (s)

No Can Do (Soundies, 1945) (s)

Winter Wonderland (Soundies, 1945) (s)

Takin' the Breaks (Univ, 1946) (s)

Mary Lee (Soundies, 1946) (s)

Valley of the Sun (Soundies, 1946) (s)

I Still Remember (Soundies, 1946) (s)

Pin Marin (Soundies, 1946) (s)

Throw a Saddle on a Star (Col, 1946)

That Texas Jamboree (Col, 1946)

Fun and Fancy Free (RKO, 1947) (voice only)

Melody Time (RKO, 1948) (voice only)

## Radio Series

The Dinning Sisters Show (NBC, ca. 1940–41)
The National Barn Dance (NBC, 1940–45)

The Spike Jones Spotlight Revue (CBS, 1949–50)

## Album Discography

At the Barn Dance (Cattle LP-120)
Buttons and Bows (Official Records)
The Dinning Sisters (10" Cap H-318)
The Dinning Sisters (Pathé Marconi/EMI/Cap PM 231-2068-54572)
The Dinning Sisters, Vol. 2 (Pathé Marconi/EMI/Cap PM 231-1566261)

The Dinning Sisters and Friends (Cattle LP-116)
Songs by The Dinning Sisters (Somerset P-3800) featuring Jean Dinning
Songs We Sang at the National Barn Dance (Cattle LP-96)
Swingin' at the Barn Dance (Cattle)

# IRENE DUNNE

HER SINGING IS SWEET AND CLEAR, HER COMEDY TIMING SUPERB. Her approach to dramatics is direct and understated. Because she was so versatile and excelled so effortlessly at so many screen forms, audiences frequently took beautiful Irene Dunne for granted. They enjoyed her wide range of talents, but remembered her best for her comedy roles. Thus it is for light comedies like THEODORA GOES WILD (1936), THE AWFUL TRUTH (1937), and LIFE WITH FATHER (1947) that durable Irene Dunne is best remembered. And with good reason: with a twinkle in her eyes, a mere tilt of her head, or the slightest inflection in her voice, she could imply so much. However, she also starred successfully in the epic Western CIMARRON (1931); sang the lead in musicals such as ROBERTA (1935) and SHOW BOAT (1936); was the dignified heroine of tearjerkers like BACK STREET (1932), MAGNIFICENT OBSESSION (1935), and PENNY SERENADE (1940); and was a regal elderly Queen Victoria in THE MUDLARK (1950). When screen roles were no longer plentiful in the 1950s, Irene turned to politics. With her humanitarian interests she became active at the United Nations. Of the major singing stars of Hollywood's Golden Era, it is gifted Irene Dunne whose productive career requires reassessment. For a long time many of her films (which often inspired inferior remakes) were unavailable due to copyright problems. But now cable TV and videocassettes have remedied that situation. She is a natural treasure to be rediscovered.

She was born Irene Marie Dunn (she added the final "e" to her surname after entering show business) on December 20, 1898 (some sources list 1901, 1904, or 1907 as her birth year) in Louisville, Kentucky. She was the older child (there was a younger brother, Charles) of Joseph John Dunn and Adelaide Antoinette (Henry) Dunn. Her father built and operated Mississippi riverboats and later became a ship inspector for the federal government. Irene received a Catholic education at Saint Benedict's Academy in Louisville. When Irene was eight her father died and Mrs. Dunn took her two children to Madison, Indiana, to live with her parents. There Mrs. Dunn, herself an accomplished pianist, had her daughter begin lessons in voice and dance. Irene eventually entered the Conservatory Division of the Chicago Musical College in 1918, planning an opera career.

In 1920 Irene went to New York City to audition for the Metropolitan Opera. She failed the test but on a lark (so she insists) tried out for the lead in the road company of the musical comedy *Irene*. She was hired to tour the midwest for four months. When no further offers developed, Irene thought of teaching music in the Chicago public schools, but her mother persuaded her to return to New York. She won a tiny role on Broadway in *The Clinging Vine* (1922), starring Peggy Wood, and when the latter became ill on the show's later road tour, Irene got to star. Later, she took over the ingenue role in another musical, *Lollipops* (1924) on Broadway and was a replacement in *Sweetheart Time* (1926). She finally created a leading role in *Luckee Girl* (1928), but that musical comedy lasted only eighty-one performances.

By this time Irene had already wed Manhattan-based Dr. Francis J. Griffin and had thought of retiring. But fate, according to the star, interceded. She was in the crowded elevator of a theatrical office building in midtown New York City. One of the other passengers was producer Florenz Ziegfeld, who was entranced by her beauty and arranged a conference. She was offered the role of Magnolia in Ziegfeld's road company of *Show Boat*. During the Chicago engagement she won solid reviews for her singing and came to the attention of RKO Radio Pictures, which, like the other Hollywood studios, was turning out a rash of musical comedies.

She was signed for the screen version of the Broadway musical *Present Arms*. However, by the time the film reached the screen in 1930, it had been retitled LEATHERNECKING and, because the song-and-dance picture craze had passed, it was shorn of its musical side and turned into a straight service comedy. Plans to star Irene in a version of Victor Herbert's *Babes in Toyland* were dropped. Instead she won the lead in the expansive (131 minutes) screen adaptation of Edna Ferber's CIMARRON (1931). For her role as the spunky Sabra Cravat—who copes with a husband afflicted with wanderlust (Richard Dix) in 1880s Oklahoma—she was nominated for an Oscar. The studio then pushed her into an urbane comedy, BACHELOR APARTMENT (1931), which showed she could handle that genre quite well.

It was not her home lot, but MGM, which took advantage of Irene's vocal talents. She was borrowed to play the opera singer in THE GREAT LOVER (1931), and *Variety* reported, "Part calls for quiet and persuasive grace, which this young actress possesses abundantly." Then it was back to romantic drama in RKO's CONSOLATION MARRIAGE (1931) opposite Pat O'Brien. This effort demonstrated that Irene could play the same weepy roles that had been the province of Ann Harding, the contract star of Pathé Pictures, which had now merged with RKO. SYMPHONY OF SIX MILLION (1932) was a slick reworking of a Fannie Hurst tale with Irene as the crippled schoolteacher who falls in love with, and is cured by, a Jewish doctor (Ricardo Cortez). But of her 1932 releases, the most important was BACK STREET, made on loan to Universal. It was a tearjerker of classical proportions with Irene as the quintessential suffering woman who cannot wed the married man (John Boles) she loves over the decades. She thought the film "trash" but it made her the first lady of screen soap opera and a major cinema star. After the completion of each of her films, Irene always returned to New York where her husband still practiced medicine.

For the 1933 season, RKO had her suffering nobly on camera for four pictures, including a loanout to MGM (THE SECRET OF MADAME BLANCHE). She was at her flintiest in ANN VICKERS, the adaptation of Sinclair Lewis' novel. Irene was showcased as the feminist social worker who adores a salty judge (Walter Huston). By now Oscar-winning Katharine Hepburn was queen of the RKO lot, although Irene was still more popular with filmgoers. The titles of Irene's next films (IF I WERE FREE, 1933, and THIS MAN IS MINE,

1934) say all that is necessary about these celluloid exercises of noble suffering by the love-hungry heroine. She was supposed to star in MY GAL SAL, a Gay Nineties musical, but instead was reunited with Richard Dix (as a roguish outlaw) in STINGAREE (1934), a tale of 1874 Australia—in which she interpolated a bit of operatic singing. When Hepburn rejected THE AGE OF INNOCENCE (1934), based on Edith Wharton's satire of 1870s New York society, Irene was handed the role, again teamed with John Boles.

Eventually Irene sang again on screen when Warner Bros. borrowed her to play the lead in SWEET ADELINE (1935), based on the Jerome Kern—Oscar Hammerstein II stage musical that had starred Helen Morgan. With her cool, high soprano, Irene sang "Don't Ever Leave Me" and "Why Was I Born?" and with an Irish tenor dueted "We Were So Young." For some, Irene's gentility clashed with her role as the innocent daughter of a beer garden owner. RKO finally used its singing star to headline ROBERTA (1935), which co-featured Fred Astaire and Ginger Rogers in their third screen teaming. Dunne was the Russian princess working in a Paris dressmaking shop who is courted by a young American football player (Randolph Scott). Astaire and Rogers shone in their four dance numbers, but it was Irene who sang "Smoke Gets in Your Eyes," "Lovely to Look At," and "Yesterdays."

By the time the popular ROBERTA was in release, Irene had left RKO. She rejected Paramount's offers to join with Ann Harding in THE OLD MAID or to make PETER IB-BETSON (Harding did so instead). Dunne chose to join Universal on a short-time basis, with MAGNIFICENT OBSESSION (1935) as her first vehicle. "Heavy dramatic roles are essential for an actress of my type," Irene reasoned. "I know definitely that the status I have achieved has been achieved through tears. So for my career I cry." MAGNIFICENT OBSES-SION, like BACK STREET (1932), IMITATION OF LIFE (1934), and STELLA DALLAS (1937), remains a key tearjerker of the 1930s. MAGNIFICENT OBSESSION featured Irene as the widow whose blindness is cured by a physician (Robert Taylor), the former playboy who accidentally caused her husband's death.

Universal had already filmed an earlier version of SHOW BOAT in 1929, removing most of the Jerome Kern—Oscar Hammerstein II score. This was remedied for the 1936 edition, which starred Irene Dunne as Magnolia Hawks and Allan Jones as dashing riverboat gambler Gaylord Ravenal. Helen Morgan recreated her stage role as the mulatto torch singer and Paul Robeson was the muscular dock worker. With Jones Irene sang "You Are Love," "I Have the Room Above," "Why Do I Love You?" (cut from the film), and the enchanting "Make Believe." On her own she shuffled and trucked through a vibrant "Can't Help Lovin' Dat Man." The picture was a huge moneymaker and boosted Irene's stock with the public. However, Irene, who was paid $100,000 for the film, was very unhappy with the movie's director (James Whale). "There were lots of interpolations that we didn't need at all and I think the ending was stupid."

At this point Irene chose to join Columbia Pictures on a nonexclusive basis. Studio head Harry Cohn decreed her first project should be a comedy. Irene was dubious and fled to Europe for six weeks with her husband. When she returned, she was forced to report for work on THEODORA GOES WILD (1936). Her concerns to one side, she shone in this wacky screwball comedy as the small town miss who writes a racy novel and is courted by an urbane book illustrator (Melvyn Douglas). "She surprises with a spirited gift for clowning," insisted the *New York Daily News*. She won her second Oscar nomination for this farce. Also in 1936, Dr. Griffin gave up his New York City practice to move to Los Angeles and on March 17, 1936, the Griffins adopted four-year-old Anna Mary Bush. On December 17, Irene's mother, who was her constant companion, died of a cerebral hemorrhage.

For Paramount's HIGH, WIDE AND HANDSOME (1937) Irene was the amorous daughter of a medicine sideshow proprietor who becomes enraptured with a farmer (Randolph Scott). The plot is complex, the artiness of director Rouben Mamoulian excessive, and the cast ranges from Dorothy Lamour to Charles Bickford. Irene sang "Can I Forget You?," "The Folk Who Live on the Hill," and "Allegheny Lil." Critics made comparisons to the way MGM's diva Jeanette MacDonald *might* have handled the role and *Variety* noted tactfully that Irene (now in her late thirties) was "perhaps a shade too mature" for the ingenue role. Far more successful was Columbia's THE AWFUL TRUTH

Allan Jones and Irene Dunne in SHOW BOAT (1936)

(1937), which matched her with another top farceur, Cary Grant, in a merry story of marital strife and reunion. She was Oscar-nominated for the third time, but lost (for the second time) to Luise Rainer (on this occasion for THE GOOD EARTH).

Irene returned to RKO to play a musical comedy star in JOY OF LIVING (1938) with Douglas Fairbanks, Jr. as her madcap playboy suitor and Lucille Ball as her parasitic sister. Perhaps the film's greatest ingenuity was in creating offbeat settings in which Irene could sing: "Just Let Me Look at You" (done at the play-within-the-movie finale and elsewhere), "You Couldn't Be Cuter" (sung in a nursery), "What's Good About

Good Night?" (performed at a radio station broadcast), and "A Heavenly Party" (sung into a 25-cent recording device at the carnival). Sadly, JOY OF LIVING was Irene's final musical.

RKO's LOVE AFFAIR (1939) was a sophisticated romance with Irene paired with Charles Boyer. It allowed her a chance to sing "Just Keep on Wishing." She was Oscar-nominated and would recall it as her favorite film, "not only because it was so well done, but also because we had such a good time making it." Far less felicitous was Paramount's INVITATION TO HAPPINESS (1939) with Fred MacMurray as a dumb prizefighter she comes to love. WHEN TOMORROW COMES (1939) reunited her with Boyer in a persuasive love tale.

Irene rejected a bid to return to Broadway in *Lady in the Dark* and instead remained in Hollywood to make MY FAVORITE WIFE (1940) with Cary Grant. Like so many of her features, this joyous comedy would be remade, but with far lesser results, with Doris Day and James Garner as MOVE OVER, DARLING (1963). Again with Grant, Dunne was the maudlin but effective leading lady of PENNY SERENADE (1940), about a couple whose adoption of a baby re-cements their love. She would comment, "I don't think I've ever felt as close to any picture. It's very much the scheme of my personal life."

After two mundane comedies (UNFINISHED BUSINESS, 1941, and LADY IN A JAM, 1942) at Universal, Irene performed as guest artist with the Chicago Symphony Orchestra in the 1941–42 season and then moved over to MGM where her former RKO rival, Katharine Hepburn, was enjoying a new vogue as co-star with Spencer Tracy. Irene's first assignment was A GUY NAMED JOE (1943), a patriotic war fantasy in which a deceased American pilot (Tracy) returns to "life" to help his fiancée (Dunne) fly a vital military mission. When co-star Van Johnson was injured in a motorcycle accident during filming of A GUY NAMED JOE and shooting was temporarily halted, Irene began work on the elaborate THE WHITE CLIFFS OF DOVER (1944). It was saccharine, full of blatant Anglo-American propaganda, but very well liked at the time.

In the mid-1940s Irene's screen career tapered off to one picture a year. She was with Charles Boyer a third and final time for the romantic TOGETHER AGAIN (1944) and starred in Ruth Gordon's frivolous stage hit OVER 21 (1945). In March 1945 she received an honorary degree of Doctor of Music from the Chicago Musical College and learned that MGM had decided that having Greer Garson on the payroll to play noble heroines was sufficient. Irene starred at 20th Century–Fox with Rex Harrison in ANNA AND THE KING OF SIAM (1946), a sumptuously mounted costume feature which would later be transformed into the musical *The King and I*.

On the new wave of popularity that resulted from ANNA AND THE KING OF SIAM, Irene joined with William Powell in bringing the long-running Broadway comedy hit LIFE WITH FATHER (1947) to the screen. In her first color feature she was the ever-patient but addled wife, Vinnie, in 1890s New York. Dunne rejoined her alma mater, RKO, for I REMEMBER MAMA (1948) as the Norwegian mother battling adversities in 1910s San Francisco. She was Oscar-nominated for her fifth and final time, but lost to Jane Wyman (JOHNNY BELINDA).

Irene was off the screen in 1949; during that year she was named the outstanding member of the American Catholic laity by the University of Notre Dame. In 1950 she made a tepid comedy with Fred MacMurray, NEVER A DULL MOMENT. She underwent vigorous makeup changes to play the dowdy old matron Queen Victoria in THE MUDLARK (1950), but despite her noteworthy impersonation, the film was unsuccessful. Her last feature was Universal's IT GROWS ON TREES (1952), a whimsical tale full of forced gaiety.

Irene surprised many by accepting the post of hostess on CBS-TV's anthology series "Schlitz Playhouse of Stars" for a year (1952–53). Thereafter, she was seen only infrequently on television, in such shows as "A Touch of Spring" on "Ford Theatre" (NBC, 1955), "The Opening Door" segment of "The June Allyson Show" (CBS, 1959), and the "Go Fight City Hall" episode of "G.E. Theatre" (CBS, 1962). On "The Perry Como Show" (NBC, 1956) she sang selections from *Show Boat*. She turned down suggestions of doing a TV series, feeling she could not do her best if she had to perform week after week.

More important for Irene in the 1950s were her political attachments. She was a staunch Republican and a supporter of General Dwight Eisenhower who as President appointed her in 1957 as an alternate delegate to the Twelfth General Assembly of the United Nations in New York. She confided, "I've played many parts, but this offers the greater challenge." After a year she returned to Hollywood, where her married daughter gave birth to her first child in 1958.

Irene's doctor husband, a shrewd real estate investor who also was a partner in his family's Griffin Equipment Company (of New York), died on October 15, 1965. Thereafter, Irene made even fewer public appearances, preferring to continue her philanthropic work (for St. John's Hospital in particular), to supervise her vast real estate holdings, and, for a time, to serve on the California Arts Commission. She was elected to the Board of Directors of Technicolor, Inc. in 1965, and in 1967 was at the televised Oscarcast to present an award. In 1970 she was the subject of a major tribute program sponsored by the Los Angeles County Museum and the California Palace of the Legion of Honor (in San Francisco), at which festival she sang a few refrains of her LOVE AFFAIR song. In December 1985 she was among the six recipients (along with Bob Hope and Beverly Sills) of the eighth annual Kennedy Center Honors for lifetime achievement.

Reminiscing, Irene Dunne once claimed she never missed being a movie star. "I knew all along acting was not everything there was." Of her peak years of fame, she admitted, "I never really had time to enjoy my success. Time! All my mother wanted was me and my time. I could buy her a new car, but I couldn't go around to the shops with her. I didn't have time."

## Filmography

Leathernecking [Present Arms] (RKO, 1930)
Consolation Marriage [Married in Haste] (RKO, 1931)
Cimarron (RKO, 1931)
Bachelor Apartment (RKO, 1931)

The Great Lover (MGM, 1931)
Symphony of Six Million [Melody of Life] (RKO, 1932)
The Stolen Jools [The Slippery Pearls] (Masquers Club, 1932) (s)

Back Street (Univ, 1932)
Thirteen Women (RKO, 1932)
The Secret of Madame Blanche (MGM, 1933)
No Other Woman (RKO, 1933)
The Silver Cord (RKO, 1933)
Ann Vickers (RKO, 1933)
If I Were Free [Behold We Live] (RKO, 1933)
This Man Is Mine (RKO, 1934)
Stingaree (RKO, 1934)
The Age of Innocence (RKO, 1934)
Sweet Adeline (WB, 1935)
Roberta (RKO, 1935)
Magnificent Obsession (Univ, 1935)
Show Boat (Univ, 1936)
Theodora Goes Wild (Col, 1936)
High, Wide and Handsome (Par, 1937)
The Awful Truth (Col, 1937)
Joy of Living (RKO, 1938)

Invitation to Happiness (Par, 1939)
Love Affair (RKO, 1939)
When Tomorrow Comes (Univ, 1939)
My Favorite Wife (RKO, 1940)
Penny Serenade (Col, 1940)
Unfinished Business (Univ, 1941)
Lady in a Jam (Univ, 1942)
Show Business at War (20th–Fox, 1943) (s)
A Guy Named Joe (MGM, 1943)
Together Again (Col, 1944)
The White Cliffs of Dover (MGM, 1944)
Over 21 (Col, 1945)
Anna and the King of Siam (20th–Fox, 1946)
Life with Father (WB, 1947)
I Remember Mama (RKO, 1948)
Never a Dull Moment (RKO, 1950)
The Mudlark (20th–Fox, 1950)
It Grows on Trees (Univ, 1952)

## Broadway Plays

The Clinging Vine (1922)
Lollipops (1924) (replacement)
The City Chap (1925)
Sweetheart Time (1926) (replacement)

Yours Truly (1927)
She's My Baby (1928)
Luckee Girl (1928)

## TV Series

Schlitz Playhouse of Stars (CBS, 1952–53)

## Album Discography

Anna and the King of Siam (Sandpiper 3) [ST/
R]
Christmas Stories from Guideposts (Guideposts)
w. Dick Van Dyke
High, Wide and Handsome/Sweet Adeline
(Titania 506) [ST]

Roberta (CIF 3011) [ST]
Roberta (Star-Tone 204) [ST/R]
Show Boat (Vertinge 2004, Xeno 251) [ST]
Show Boat (Sunbeam 501) [ST/R]

# DEANNA DURBIN

CRITICS AND FILM HISTORIANS HAVE LONG BEEN PERPLEXED BY THE popularity of Deanna Durbin, which, at its height in the late 1930s, is credited with singlehandedly saving Universal Pictures from bankruptcy. When looking objectively at the typical Deanna Durbin screen persona, it is difficult to see what all the fuss was about. She usually portrayed overly precious and very meddlesome teenagers who were prone to fib and to get mired in all types of sticky situations. Further, she was apt to burst out in song—operatic, no less—at any time, which would hardly seem to make her popular with her peers. Yet, despite all, this sprightly miss captured the hearts of moviegoers who watched her mature from an awkward teenager into an attractive young woman in twenty-one Universal feature films—all of them moneymakers. In addition, the mystique remains since Deanna Durbin retired from the screen at age twenty-seven and has since lived in seclusion in France, permitting few interviews.

Deanna was born Edna Mae Durbin in Winnipeg, Canada, on December 4, 1921, the second daughter (her sister, Edith, was eleven years her senior) of British parents, James and Ada Read Durbin. The family had moved to Canada in 1912 and in 1922 they migrated to California because of Mr. Durbin's poor health. There they lived near Los Angeles and James Durbin became a real estate salesman. Little Edna showed a proclivity for music at a young age, but the family was unable to afford voice lessons until after her older sister, Edith, became a teacher and helped provide the funds. She studied voice at Ralph Thomas' Academy in Los Angeles and sang for clubs and churches in the city.

In 1935 she auditioned for MGM casting director Rufus LeMaire for the role of the young Ernestine Schumann-Heink in a biopic to be made about the famous opera singer. She impressed not only LeMaire but also MGM voice teacher Andres DeSegurola, who judged her voice to be that of a fully matured soprano. When Louis B. Mayer heard Edna sing, he signed her to a contract and her name was changed to Deanna Durbin. MGM maneuvered their new charge a guest spot on "The Los Angeles Breakfast Club" radio show for three appearances, and then cast her opposite another new contractee, Judy Garland, in the two-reel short EVERY SUNDAY (1936), in which they played teenagers who try to save their small town's local weekly park concerts. She sang "Il Bacio" and dueted with Garland on "Americana." When the studio dropped the Schumann-Heink project, MGM did not renew her contract (much to its later regret).

At this time Rufus LeMaire moved to Universal. He placed Deanna under personal contract to him at a $300 weekly salary and retained Andres DeSegurola as her vocal coach. At LeMaire's urging, producer Joe Pasternak and director Henry Koster—both

recently arrived from the company's Berlin studios—cast Deanna in the comedy THREE
SMART GIRLS (1936). She was the youngest of three sisters (Nan Grey and Barbara Reed
played the older siblings) who try to reconcile their mother (Nella Walker) and father
(Charles Winninger), the latter being hotly pursued by a golddigger (Binnie Barnes) and
her ambitious mother (Alice Brady). Deanna sang "Il Bacio," "Someone to Care for Me"
(both recorded for Decca Records), and "My Heart Is Singing." During the filming
Deanna became a regular on Eddie Cantor's weekly NBC radio show and on it she
popularized "Someone to Care for Me." Also on the program was another moppet star,
Bobby Breen. THREE SMART GIRLS was a huge success (especially in England) and salvaged
Universal's falling stock. Deanna Durbin was the nation's new sweetheart, with a large fan
club, "The Deanna Durbin Devotees," and a merchandising campaign to equal that of
Shirley Temple's with all kinds of Deanna Durbin items on the market for young people.
She negotiated a new contract with Universal which would escalate her weekly salary from
$1,500 to $3,000 and provide her a $10,000 bonus per film.

Her next film, ONE HUNDRED MEN AND A GIRL (1937), was even more successful
than her first, and continued her association with Joe Pasternak and Henry Koster. Here
she puts together a symphony orchestra and even gets Leopold Stokowski to conduct it, all

Binnie Barnes, Barbara Reed, Charles Winninger, Nan Grey, and Deanna Durbin
in THREE SMART GIRLS (1936)

so her unemployed musician father (Adolphe Menjou) will have a job. In the feature Deanna sang classical (Mozart's "Alleluia" and "Libiamo" from Verdi's opera *La Traviata*) plus pop tunes ("It's Raining Moonbeams" and "A Heart That's Free"). In 1938 she was given a special Academy Award, and she became the first female to be sworn into the Boy Scouts.

Her first 1938 film, MAD ABOUT MUSIC, cast her as a schoolgirl who persuades a dapper composer (Herbert Marshall) to pose as her father, thus instigating a romance with her mother (Gail Patrick). She performed "Chapel Bells," "Serenade to the Stars," "There Isn't a Day Goes By," "I Love to Whistle," and Bach's "Ave Maria," the latter backed up by the Vienna Boys Choir. She recorded "Ave Maria" for Decca Records, the company she would work with for the rest of her film career, often waxing songs from her pictures. THAT CERTAIN AGE (1938) found teenager Deanna with a crush on droll war correspondent Melvyn Douglas, who has a fiancée (Nancy Carroll). This lighthearted exercise offered her a half-dozen musical outings, including "My Own" (which became a best-seller on Decca) and "Les Filles de Cadiz."

Henry Koster directed both of Deanna's 1939 pictures, THREE SMART GIRLS GROW UP, a sequel to her debut feature, which had the teenager guiding the romances of her two sisters (Nan Grey, Helen Parrish) and their boyfriends (William Lundigan, Robert Cummings) and singing a quartet of songs, including "Because" and "The Last Rose of Summer." FIRST LOVE generated a great deal of hoopla because in it Deanna received her first screen kiss, from Robert Stack. The plot had her and nasty stepsister Helen Parrish both in love with handsome Stack. This time Deanna performed seven songs, including "Amapola," "Sympathy," and Puccini's "One Fine Day" ("Un Bel Dì" from the opera *Madama Butterfly*).

Deanna Durbin opened the decade of the 1940s with a new studio contract that allowed her over $300,000 per film. IT'S A DATE (1940) found her as a young singer who gets the stage role coveted by her chic mother (Kay Francis). Her quartet of numbers included "Love Is All," "Loch Lomond," and Schubert's "Ave Maria." By this time Deanna had graduated from high school and was nixing popular rumors that she planned to desert films for grand opera. SPRING PARADE (1940) had Deanna as a Viennese peasant girl in love with a nobleman (Robert Cummings); this pleasant confection had her doing a variety of songs including "When April Sings," "Waltzing in the Clouds," "It's Foolish, But It's Fun," and "Blue Danube Dream," whose music derived from Johann Strauss' "Blue Danube Waltz." NICE GIRL? (1941) cast the actress as a scientist's daughter who is engulfed in a scandal with her father's rival (Franchot Tone), but who really loves her boyfriend (Robert Stack). Her songs included "Perhaps," "Love at Last," Stephen Foster's "Old Folks at Home," and the patriotic "Thank You America." (For British release prints she also sang "There'll Always Be an England," as she was the most popular box-office star in that country.) After completing the picture, Deanna was a guest at the White House for President Franklin D. Roosevelt's birthday; she also performed at various military installations. In the spring of 1941 she married Vaughn Paul in a lavish ceremony in Hollywood. By now, Deanna's screen popularity had not only generated rivals at other studios, such as

Kathryn Grayson at MGM, but Universal also kept a roster of teenaged girls on hand, the most successful being Gloria Jean.

Deanna culminated her association with Joe Pasternak and Henry Koster with the delightful comedy IT STARTED WITH EVE (1941), in which she and Charles Laughton proved to be a most amiable screen team. Laughton is a dying millionaire who wants to meet his son's (Robert Cummings) fiancée; since the girl is unavailable, Deanna substitutes. She and Laughton performed a hilarious conga dance and Deanna sang "The Lord's Prayer," "Going Home," and "When I Sing," none of which she recorded. Instead she began recording other tunes for Decca, such as "Kiss Me Again," "My Hero," "Poor Butterfly," "God Bless America," and "The Star-Spangled Banner," along with the holiday carols "Adeste Fideles" and "Silent Night."

Deanna Durbin made no films during 1942. Her mentor, Joe Pasternak, had left Universal in a dispute and moved over to MGM, and the studio was not sure how to guide Durbin into adult roles. She refused the lead in BOY MEETS BABY and went on suspension. She kept active singing for soldiers at USO clubs and appeared on patriotic radio shows like "Command Performance." Amid many production problems and the departure of French director Jean Renoir, she made THE AMAZING MRS. HOLLIDAY, about a missionary trying to get nine Chinese orphans into the U.S. She sang only a trio of songs, "Vissi d'Arte" from Puccini's opera *Tosca*, "Mighty Lak' a Rose," and a Chinese lullaby. By now Universal was forcing her into a standardized adult glamour mold, but her strong individuality kept her screen personality unique and appealing.

Producer Felix Jackson began managing Deanna's career and he chose for her the wartime drama HERS TO HOLD (1943), in which she played a factory worker who is attracted to a dashing pilot (Joseph Cotten). Her songs included the patriotic "Say a Prayer for the Boys Over There," Cole Porter's "Begin the Beguine," and "The Kashmiri Song." For director Frank Borzage, she starred in HIS BUTLER'S SISTER (1943) as a young lady involved with a self-centered composer (Franchot Tone), and she offered a good rendition of the aria "Nessum Dorma" from Puccini's opera *Turandot* and "When You're Away."

Durbin was bent on becoming a "dramatic" actress and pressured the studio into allowing her to star in Somerset Maugham's CHRISTMAS HOLIDAY (1944), which, even when watered down, was a very adult story about a young woman marrying a killer (Gene Kelly) and forced to perform in a New Orleans dive. She did sing "Always," "Spring Will Be a Little Late This Year," and "Ave Maria" (in a tearful church sequence), but her loyal fans did not care for this change of pace, despite Durbin's solid emoting. The reaction soured Durbin on moviemaking.

If Universal could not afford to buy the rights to the big Broadway hit *Oklahoma!*, it could create its own. The studio starred her in her only color film, CAN'T HELP SINGING (1944), filmed in Utah. Here she was a plucky young lady who goes West to locate her wayward boyfriend (Robert Paige); the film's Jerome Kern songs were lifeless, except for the title tune.

Having divorced Vaughn Paul (much to her fans' dismay), Deanna married Felix Jackson in the summer of 1945 in Las Vegas and then starred in the comedy/murder mystery LADY ON A TRAIN (1945). It was a deft combination of the *film noir* and hard-boiled detective genres interpolated with crazy hijinks. She played a devout murder mystery fan who observes a killing from her train window. In trying to convince the authorities that there was a murder, she becomes a potential prey for the killer. She also got to sing "Night and Day," "Silent Night," and the Jazz Age favorite "Give Me a Little Kiss." The star reteamed with Charles Laughton and Franchot Tone for the amusing comedy BECAUSE OF HIM (1946), which offered her as a waitress who wants to be an actress with support from old-timer Laughton and doubts from author Tone. She did a delightful version of Tosti's "Goodbye," "Danny Boy," and "Lover," but the film was only a moderate success. Following its completion, Deanna became a mother early in 1946 with the birth of a daughter, Jessica. Back on the screen she starred in a middling remake of THE GOOD FAIRY (1935), now called I'LL BE YOURS (1947), as a young woman who aids a lawyer (Tom Drake) while trying to fend off millionaire Adolphe Menjou. Despite the raggedness of the plot, Deanna was in fine voice in songs like "Granada" and "It's Dream Time." The movie was her last to be produced by husband Felix Jackson. Universal was now undergoing extreme corporate changes and the new regime decided to cut the budgets of her future films, as a way to improve the profit margin on her projects. In both 1945 and 1947 Deanna was the highest-paid Hollywood female star.

Deanna Durbin was to star in only three more movies, beginning with SOMETHING IN THE WIND (1947), where she was a disc jockey (!) who is abducted by a millionaire's (John Dall) screwy family who think she is his golddigging girlfriend. Although she and Jan Peerce (in a jail scene!) dueted "Miserere" from Verdi's opera *Il Trovatore*, her quartet of pop selections was mediocre. Sigmund Romberg's UP IN CENTRAL PARK (1948) had been a big Broadway hit in 1945 and it deserved a well-mounted screen production, but Universal cut corners. Deanna was a young woman involved with corrupt Gotham Mayor Boss Tweed (Vincent Price) and sang "Ave, Pace, Mio Dio" from Verdi's *La Forza del Destino*. Her screen finale was the mediocre comedy FOR THE LOVE OF MARY (1948), in which she played a White House telephone operator who involves government officials, including the President, in her romantic troubles. Its only asset was Deanna's rendering of such songs as "On Moonlight Bay," "Let Me Call You Sweetheart," "I'll Take You Home Again Kathleen," and a comical "Largo al Factotum" from Rossini's *The Barber of Seville*. With no further worthwhile scripts forthcoming, Deanna Durbin and Universal called it quits. (They paid her for not making three final pictures under her contract.) She and Felix Jackson were divorced that year, having been separated since 1948. At the end of 1950 she wed for the third time, to Pathé Films executive Charles David, and moved to Normandy. In 1951, Deanna gave birth to her second child, a son, Peter.

Deanna Durbin had long wanted to abandon her career and told her former mentor Eddie Cantor, "I don't want to have anything to do with show business ever." She insisted she hated the dieting, the fabricated screen image (which she claimed had no relationship to the private Deanna Durbin), and everything that accompanied being a screen star. With her money wisely invested, she could and did enjoy the quiet life in France.

Though she has been off the screen for four decades, Deanna Durbin still retains some of her popularity, thanks to reshowings of her Universal films and the steady reissues of her Decca recordings on both sides of the Atlantic. Unlike some of her contemporaries, Deanna Durbin saw the handwriting on the wall when she left films, realizing that her favored screen persona had vanished as she matured and grew plumper. She was able to forsake filmdom with the satisfaction that she had had a successful career and had helped to enrich America's culture by introducing its youth to classical music.

## Filmography

Every Sunday (MGM, 1936) (s)
Three Smart Girls (Univ, 1936)
One Hundred Men and a Girl (Univ, 1937)
That Certain Age (Univ, 1938)
Mad About Music (Univ, 1938)
Three Smart Girls Grow Up (Univ, 1939)
First Love (Univ, 1939)
Spring Parade (Univ, 1940)
It's a Date (Univ, 1941)
Nice Girl? (Univ, 1941)
It Started with Eve (Univ, 1941)
The Amazing Mrs. Holliday (Univ, 1943)

Hers to Hold (Univ, 1943)
His Butler's Sister (Univ, 1943)
Show Business at War (20th–Fox, 1943) (s)
Christmas Holiday (Univ, 1944)
The Shining Future (WB, 1944) (s)
Can't Help Singing (Univ, 1944)
Lady on a Train (Univ, 1945)
Because of Him (Univ, 1945)
I'll Be Yours (Univ, 1947)
Something in the Wind (Univ, 1947)
Up in Central Park (Univ, 1948)
For the Love of Mary (Univ, 1948)

## Radio Series

The Eddie Cantor Show (NBC, ca. 1936–37)

## Album Discography

All-Time Favorites (Suffolk Marketing/MCA MSM-35050)
The Best of Deanna Durbin (MCA 1634)
The Best of Deanna Durbin, Vol. 2 (MCA 1729)
Can't Help Singing (Coral 43)
Can't Help Singing (Music for Pleasure 50559)
A Date with Deanna Durbin (Coral 64)
Deanna Durbin (Decca DL-8785)
Deanna Durbin Favorites (Memoir 206)

It's a Date (Coral 23)
Memories (MCA 1514)
Movie Songs (MCA 1668)
Original Voice Tracks (Decca DL-75289) [ST]
Radio Broadcast Follies of 1935 (Amalgamated 227) [ST/R]
Souvenir Album (10" Decca DL-5099)
Spring Parade (Caliban 6005) [ST]
Sweetheart of Song (MCA 2579)
Three Smart Girls (Caliban 6006) [ST]

# NELSON EDDY

ALTHOUGH PERENNIALLY LINKED WITH JEANETTE MacDONALD IN THE public's mind, Nelson Eddy had a long and illustrious career which encompassed opera, concert work, films, radio, records, television, and nightclubs. He is said to have earned over $5 million from his movie career alone, which included only nineteen feature films, and some two decades after his film career faded, he was still able to command $5,000 a week for club engagements. Perhaps the ultimate romantic male lead of film operetta (an image which would be made fun of by later generations), Nelson Eddy was the heartthrob of millions of women who swooned to his blond good looks and baritone voice, while he was also popular with men, who liked his singing and somewhat self-effacing manner.

It is not surprising that Nelson Eddy took up music as a career since his father, William Eddy, was a choir singer and drum major of the Rhode Island National Guard's First Regimental Band. His mother, Isabel Kendrick Eddy, was also a choir singer and her mother (Caroline Kendrick) had sung opera with some success. Eddy was born June 29, 1901, in Providence, Rhode Island. He learned to play the drums from his father, and he sang in his church choir and later did solo church work as he grew older. In 1915 Nelson's parents separated and he went with his mother to Philadelphia, where he quit school to go to work. Later he earned his equivalency degree through night school. He worked many odd jobs, from drummer to newspaperman (selling classified ads), but by the early 1920s he was determined to make singing his career. Lacking money for music lessons, the young man studied voice by listening to opera records. He made his stage debut in 1922 in Philadelphia in *The Marriage Tax* and then won the lead in the Gilbert and Sullivan operetta *Iolanthe*. This led to work with both the Philadelphia Civic Opera (his first role being Amonasro in *Aïda*) and the Philadelphia Operatic Society, where he especially enjoyed singing Wagner.

In the mid-1920s, Eddy, sponsored by veteran opera singer/coach Dr. Edouard Lippe, journeyed to Europe to study voice in Paris and Dresden. However, he rejected offers to work there in opera, instead opting for success in America. Back in the United States he sang Tonio in *Pagliacci* at the Metropolitan Opera in New York City—as a guest artist with the Philadelphia Civic Opera Company—and his repertoire included over thirty roles in a half-dozen languages. In the late 1920s, out of financial necessity, he left opera for concertizing, teaming with pianist Theodore Paxson, who worked with him for the rest of his life. For the next several years Nelson Eddy eked out a living doing concerts, with an occasional foray into opera, as in 1931 when he returned to the Metropolitan Opera to be the Drum Major in Alban Berg's modern opera *Wozzeck*, which was conducted by Leopold Stokowski.

In 1933, Eddy was working in San Diego and was chosen as a last-minute substitute for famed singer Lotte Lehmann, who had become ill, and he drew a warm reception when he sang at the Philharmonic Auditorium in Los Angeles. Ida Koverman, Louis B. Mayer's secretary, was in the audience, and the six-foot blond so impressed her with his vocalizing and stage presence that she urged Mayer to place him under MGM contract. He did so when he found that other studios were also vying for the handsome baritone. Then, in typical manner, the studio could not decide what to do with Eddy and used him in a wasteful manner to perform guest song stints in BROADWAY TO HOLLYWOOD (1933), DANCING LADY (1933), and STUDENT TOUR (1934). By now, the studio had lost interest in him, and Eddy returned to concert work.

In 1935 MGM was planning to produce NAUGHTY MARIETTA as a vehicle for its singing star Jeanette MacDonald. Upon the urging of Ida Koverman, Nelson Eddy was tested and assigned the male lead. (Allan Jones had been an earlier choice but was contracted for conflicting stage work at the time.) This slick production, set in pioneer Louisiana, with Eddy as the dashing Yankee military man who comes to the aid of a princess (MacDonald), was a huge success. Eddy scored with audiences (particularly women) as he sang "Ah, Sweet Mystery of Life," "Tramp, Tramp, Tramp," "'Neath the Southern Moon," and "I'm Falling in Love with Someone." The first of eight screen teamings of Jeanette MacDonald and Nelson Eddy, NAUGHTY MARIETTA was followed the next year by ROSE MARIE, which was originally to have teamed Eddy with Metropolitan Opera star Grace Moore. Herein, he was the handsome Mountie who sang the title song and "The Mounties," while he and Jeanette MacDonald attained screen immortality with their duet of "Indian Love Call." They recorded the song for Victor at the time and in 1959 it was designated a gold record, having sold over one million copies.

The third screen teaming of Eddy and MacDonald in MAYTIME (1937) almost did not happen. Once again he was to have been paired on camera with Grace Moore, but when she was unavailable, Jeanette was substituted. Part way through production, MGM production executive Irving Thalberg died and the color filming was halted and scrapped. Later, with a revised script, new supporting players, and now in black and white, shooting started over. MAYTIME is indeed a schmaltzy Sigmund Romberg romance, set in Europe. The two stars appeared as young singers in love; however, Jeanette is promised to her older music teacher/sponsor (John Barrymore). The film provided them with two good songs, "Will You Remember?" and "Farewell to Dreams." The same year, 1937, found Eddy in his first solo starring vehicle, ROSALIE, with Nelson as a West Point football hero who romances a princess (Eleanor Powell). The title song became one of the most requested in his repertoire.

By now Nelson Eddy was getting over six thousand fan letters per week, mostly from women, and he was in big demand for personal appearances. From 1937 to 1939 he was a regular on NBC Radio's "The Chase and Sanborn Hour" and in 1937 and 1938 he headlined that program's summer shows.

It was no secret on the MGM lot that Nelson Eddy and Jeanette MacDonald did not care for one another professionally, but there was money for all concerned in their continued screen teaming. In 1938 they made two more operettas: THE GIRL OF THE

GOLDEN WEST and SWEETHEARTS. The former showcased them as lovers, with saloon girl Jeanette playing cards with a sheriff (Walter Pidgeon) to win Eddy's freedom from the law. SWEETHEARTS was MGM's first Technicolor production and the contemporary plot had the two stars as stage singing partners who feud, break up, and then reunite. Neither picture provided the duo with noteworthy songs, but the latter was far more popular. Throughout this period and later, Eddy and MacDonald would frequently recreate their landmark operetta roles for radio editions.

To appease Eddy and MacDonald, who each wanted solo star billing (and to market their popularity to the maximum), MGM agreed to star each of them in separate vehicles. In 1939 Eddy starred in two productions without MacDonald and proved he could definitely carry a vehicle solo. Over the years it has been fashionable with writers to poke fun at Eddy's acting, but a closer look at his pictures shows he was a more than adequate thespian who, on several occasions, was simply overpowered by ponderous scripts. This was *not* the case with LET FREEDOM RING (1939), in which he was excellent as the scion of a rich family who sides with homesteaders against a corrupt land baron (Edward Arnold). A highlight of the production was his singing of "America." Next came the glossy but top-

Edward Arnold, Nelson Eddy, Charles Butterworth, and Virginia Bruce
in LET FREEDOM RING (1939)

heavy BALALAIKA, with Eddy as a Russian Cossack prince in love with a beautiful singer (Ilona Massey) whose father (Lionel Atwill) is a Bolshevik, all on the eve of the Russian Revolution. This overlong production did allow Eddy the opportunity to sing "The Volga Boatman" and "At the Balalaika," which was a good-selling record for him on Columbia Records. He had joined that company in 1938 and would continue to record for Columbia well into the 1950s, doing a variety of projects which ranged from popular songs to opera to Stephen Foster melodies to Gilbert and Sullivan patter songs. Despite rumors that he and Jeanette MacDonald were lovers off camera, Eddy married Ann Denitz Franklin, the ex-wife of MGM film director Sidney Franklin, early in 1939, and they remained together for the rest of his life. She was three years his senior and had a son by her prior marriage.

NEW MOON, the first of two 1940 pairings of MacDonald and Eddy, breathed fresh life into their popularity. It was a tale set in colonial Louisiana with French political prisoner Eddy harbored by MacDonald, the daughter of a wealthy businessman. A quartet of Sigmund Romberg standards highlighted the story: "Stout-Hearted Men," "Softly, as in a Morning Sunrise," "Wanting You," and "Lover, Come Back to Me." Not so good was the songsters' next entry, BITTER SWEET. With the stars as lovers in eighteenth-century Vienna, its prime asset was their dueting of "I'll See You Again." Not much better was Nelson's teaming with Metropolitan Opera diva Risë Stevens for THE CHOCOLATE SOLDIER in 1941, with the star pretending to be a Cossack to test the love of his wife (Stevens). The star performed the title song, "My Hero," and "Sympathy." Jeanette MacDonald and Nelson Eddy were teamed for an eighth and final time in the long-delayed I MARRIED AN ANGEL (1942), with Jeanette in the title role romancing a wealthy count (Eddy). His recording of the title song was very successful, but the movie was vapid. Eddy would explain, "Everybody on the lot told us it was either going to be the best picture we ever did, or the worst. It was the worst. It took the studio years to figure out how to present it without offending anybody and then they slashed it to pieces. When we finally finished it, it was a horrible mess."

While the MacDonald–Eddy productions were still profitable ventures for MGM, the studio was having great difficulty finding additional properties congenial to both stars; it was obvious on camera that the two luminaries were no longer young, and World War II had shut out much of the lucrative overseas market. Both stars soon left MGM.

In 1943 Eddy went to Universal to star in the studio's remake of THE PHANTOM OF THE OPERA. A posh production, it gave him the opportunity to sing several operatic sequences as well as to romance beautiful Susanna Foster, who was lusted after by the Phantom (Claude Rains). Next he headlined KNICKERBOCKER HOLIDAY (1944) for United Artists, a disappointing film version of the Kurt Weill–Maxwell Anderson play. Eddy was a rebellious newsman in Dutch New Amsterdam at odds with Peter Stuyvesant (Charles Coburn) over politics and Constance Dowling. There was talk of RKO's producing a new MacDonald–Eddy songfest but that came to naught and it was two years before he was heard on the screen again. He supplied the voice of the singing whale in Walt Disney's MAKE MINE MUSIC (1946). Eddy, in fact, did all the voices in the film's final sequence,

"The Whale Who Wanted to Sing at the Met." The star's final film appearance came in NORTHWEST OUTPOST (1947) for Republic, with an original screen score by Rudolf Friml, who had done the music for ROSE MARIE. The film was ponderous at best in its telling of frontier ranger Eddy fighting corrupt nobleman Joseph Schildkraut and winning the love of the latter's wife (Ilona Massey).

Nelson Eddy never again appeared on the silver screen, although he continued to receive movie offers, both solo and in tandem with Jeanette MacDonald. In the 1940s he earned up to $15,000 a week for concertizing and he continued to be quite active on radio. Not only was he a guest star on many musical programs, but during the summers of 1947 and 1948 he also headlined "The Nelson Eddy Show" on NBC as a summer replacement for the "Kraft Music Hall." In his September 16, 1948, program he reteamed with guest Jeanette MacDonald.

In the early 1950s Nelson Eddy filmed a pilot for a TV series which did not sell. Then he joined with beautiful actress/soprano Gale Sherwood to do a nightclub act which made them worldwide popular attractions; they did the act forty weeks of every year for the remainder of Eddy's life. On May 7, 1955, he had the starring role in NBC-TV's production of "The Desert Song" with Gale Sherwood, and he recorded the score for Columbia Records. On that label Eddy did duets with Jo Stafford. He also made guest appearances on TV's "The Danny Thomas Show" and "The Gordon MacRae Show," the latter appearance reuniting him in song with Jeanette MacDonald. In 1958 Jeanette and Nelson recorded the album *Jeanette MacDonald and Nelson Eddy Favorites,* which became a best-seller for RCA and went gold in 1967. When MacDonald died in 1965, Eddy sang "Ah, Sweet Mystery of Life" at her funeral. She willed him a print of ROSE MARIE as he had never saved any memorabilia from his lengthy career.

Throughout the 1960s Nelson Eddy and Gale Sherwood continued their club touring, commanding $5,000 per week in salary. In the early 1960s he cut three LPs for Everest Records, one a duet with Gale Sherwood. In 1965 they appeared on ABC-TV's "The Hollywood Palace," and Eddy's popularity was such that he was still receiving an average of one hundred fan letters weekly. Early in 1967 the duo had a successful Australian tour and returned to the U.S. to fulfill their year's bookings. They brought in 1967 by appearing on Guy Lombardo's New Year's Eve program, and Eddy was in top voice as he sang many of the songs associated with his long career. On March 6, 1967, Nelson Eddy and Gale Sherwood were appearing at a Miami Beach Hotel when Eddy became ill on stage and his singing partner helped him to his dressing room; he had suffered a stroke. He died the next day as Gale Sherwood held his hand. Nelson Eddy was survived by his wife and was buried next to his mother's grave in Hollywood's Memorial Park Cemetery.

Unlike many singers of his day, Nelson Eddy continues to be popular through the reshowing of his movies theatrically, on television, and on videocassette; through the constant reissuing of his recordings on a variety of labels; and through the devoted efforts of the Jeanette MacDonald and Nelson Eddy International Fan Club.

## Filmography

Broadway to Hollywood [Ring Up the Curtain] (MGM, 1933)
Dancing Lady (MGM, 1933)
Student Tour (MGM, 1934)
Naughty Marietta (MGM, 1935)
Rose Marie (MGM, 1936)
Maytime (MGM, 1937)
Rosalie (MGM, 1937)
The Girl of the Golden West (MGM, 1938)
Sweethearts (MGM, 1938)
Let Freedom Ring (MGM, 1939)

Balalaika (MGM, 1939)
New Moon (MGM, 1940)
Bitter Sweet (MGM, 1940)
The Chocolate Soldier (MGM, 1941)
I Married an Angel (MGM, 1942)
The Phantom of the Opera (Univ, 1943)
Knickerbocker Holiday (UA, 1944)
Make Mine Music (RKO, 1946) (voice only)
Northwest Outpost [End of the Rainbow] (Rep, 1947)

## Radio Series

The Chase and Sanborn Hour (NBC, 1936–39)
The Charlie McCarthy Summer Show (NBC, 1937, 1938)

The Nelson Eddy Show (CBS, 1942–43; NBC, 1947, 1948)

## Album Discography

The Artistry of Nelson Eddy (Everest 3292)
Balalaika (Caliban 6004) [ST]
Because (Har HL-7151)
The Best Loved Carols of Christmas (Har HL-7201)
Bitter Sweet (Amalgamated 200) [ST/R]
By Request (10" Col ML-2037)
The Chocolate Soldier/Naughty Marietta (Col Special Products P-13707)
Christmas Songs (Col ML-4442)
The Desert Song (Col ML-4636, Col CL-831, Col Special Products ACL-831) w. Doretta Morrow
The Desert Song (Mac/Eddy JN 116) [ST/TV] w. Gale Sherwood
Gilbert and Sullivan Patter Songs (Col ML-4027)
Great Songs of Faith (10" Col ML-2166)
Greatest Hits (Col CL-2681/CS-9481, CBS 32312)
I Married an Angel (Caliban 6004) [ST]
Jeanette MacDonald and Nelson Eddy (Mac/Eddy JN 111)
Jeanette MacDonald and Nelson Eddy (Murray Hill X14078)

Jeanette MacDonald and Nelson Eddy (RCA LPV-526)
Jeanette MacDonald and Nelson Eddy Favorites (RCA LPM/LSP-1738, RCA ANL1-1075)
Jeanette MacDonald and Nelson Eddy—Legendary Performers (RCA CPL1- 2468)
Jeanette MacDonald and Nelson Eddy: The Early Years (Mac/Eddy JN 110)
Jeanette MacDonald and Nelson Eddy—Together Again (Sandy Hook 2101)
The Lord's Prayer (Har HL-7254)
Love Songs (Everest FS-354) w. Gale Sherwood
Love Songs from Foreign Lands (10" Col ML-2130)
Maytime (Pelican 121, Sandy Hook 2008) [ST/R]
Naughty Marietta (10" Col ML-2094)
Naughty Marietta (Hollywood Soundstage 413) [ST]
Naughty Marietta (Pelican 117) [ST/R]
Nelson and the Ladies (Sounds Rare 5002) w. Jeanette MacDonald, Risë Stevens, Anne Jamison
Nelson Eddy (Empire 806)
Nelson Eddy (Scala 887) w. Gale Sherwood

Nelson Eddy and Gale Sherwood (Everest 9002/8002)

Nelson Eddy and Jeanette MacDonald (Nostalgia LPF 222009)

Nelson Eddy and Jeanette MacDonald—America's Singing Sweethearts (RCA/Suffolk Marketing DVM1-0301)

Nelson Eddy and Jeanette MacDonald Sing Patriotic Songs (Mac/Eddy JN 118)

Nelson Eddy Favorites (Camden CAL-492)

Nelson Eddy on the Air (Totem 1035) w. Jeanette MacDonald

Nelson Eddy Selections from Chase and Sanborn Hour (Mac/Eddy JN 113)

The Nelson Eddy Show (Mac/Eddy JN 101, JN 102, JN 103, JN 106, JN 107)

Nelson Eddy Sings (Col CL-812)

Nelson Eddy Sings the Songs of Stephen Foster (Col ML-4090)

Nelson Eddy with Isabel Eddy and Caroline Kendrick (Mac/Eddy JN 121)

Nelson Eddy with Shirley Temple, Jane Powell, Kathryn Grayson, Lois Butler and Norma Nelson (Mac/Eddy JN 128)

New Moon (10" Col ML-2164)

New Moon/I Married an Angel (Pelican 103) [ST/R]

New Moon/Rose Marie (Col Special Products P-13878)

Of Girls I Sing (Everest 9006/8006)

Oklahoma! (Col ML-4598, Col CL-828/CS-8739, Har HL-7364/HS-1164)

Operatic and Song Recital (OASI 610)

Operatic Recital: 1938–48 (Mac/Eddy JN 105) w. Dorothy Kirsten, Anne Jamison, Nadine Connor

Operatic Recitals II (Mac/Eddy JN 114)

Operatic Recitals III (Mac/Eddy JN 123) w. Jeanette MacDonald

Operetta Favorites by Jeanette MacDonald and Nelson Eddy (10" RCA LCT-16)

Our Love (Sunset 11276/5176) w. Gale Sherwood

Phantom of the Opera (Mac/Eddy 124) [ST/R]

The Phantom of the Opera (Sountrak 114) [ST]

Rose Marie (10" Col ML-2178)

Rose Marie (Hollywood Soundstage 414) [ST]

Rose Marie/Naughty Marietta/I Married an Angel/Bitter Sweet (Sandy Hook 3-SH-1) [ST]

Rose Marie/New Moon/Naughty Marietta (Col GB-3)

Russian Songs and Arias (Mac/Eddy JN 108)

Song Jamboree (10" Col ML-2091)

Songs We Love (Col ML-4343)

The Story of a Starry Night (Everest 9004/8004)

Stout-Hearted Men (Har HL-7142/HS-11246)

The Student Prince/The Chocolate Soldier (Col ML-4060) w. Risë Stevens

Sweethearts (Pelican 143, Sandy Hook 2025) [ST/R]

Till the End of Time (Sunset 1143/5143)

The Torch Singer and the Mountie (Amalgamated 205) w. Helen Morgan, Gale Sherwood, Guy Lombardo

The World's Favorite Love Songs (Sunset 50261) w. Jan Peerce

# CLIFF "UKULELE IKE" EDWARDS

WHEN CLIFF EDWARDS DIED IN THE SUMMER OF 1971, HE WAS A welfare patient whose body went unclaimed. This was the same jovial, wide-eyed man who was so proficient as a high, clear tenor singer, ukulele player, and actor that he starred on Broadway, in films, radio, television, and vaudeville, and as a recording artist sold over seventy million records. With the coming of sound, Cliff Edwards came to Hollywood movies as a singing star and developed into a fine comic character performer, appearing in nearly a hundred movies.

Clifton A. Edwards was born in Hannibal, Missouri, on June 14, 1895, the son of railroad worker Edward Edwards and Nellie Farnus Edwards. He quit school while still a boy to support his family, which included three younger siblings, after his father became too ill to work. He held a variety of jobs, including several years' work in a shoe factory. During this period he began entertaining and later worked in a St. Louis movie house, singing to lantern-slide-illustrated song programs. He also learned to make sound effects for the silent films, effects he would later use in his singing act. From St. Louis, Cliff joined a carnival and then got by with singing in saloons for loose change. It was here he took up the ukulele for accompaniment and acquired his professional nickname. The story goes that a waiter could not remember his name and just called him Ike and, since he strummed the uke, he became known as Ukulele Ike.

By the late 1910s, Edwards was working in Chicago, singing at the Arsonia. There he met songwriter Bob Carleton and he introduced the latter's new novelty tune "Ja Da," which soon swept the nation and gave some prestige to Cliff Edwards, although he did not record the song until 1956. Next Edwards teamed with comic Joe Frisco for a vaudeville engagement at New York City's Palace Theatre, after which the pair was among those joining in the *Ziegfeld Follies* of 1918. When that run ended, Edwards returned alone to Chicago where he joined with singer/dancer Pierce Keegan in an act they called "Jazz as Is." The duo appeared in Ziegfeld's new *Midnight Frolics* (atop the New Amsterdam Theatre in Manhattan), and when the late evening revue closed in 1920 they toured in vaudeville, even making several unissued records for the Columbia label. Next Edwards teamed with Lou Clayton (later better known as a partner in the team of Clayton–Jackson–Durante) for a short time and in 1922 he began making records for Gennett, a label owned by the Starr Piano Company. He also made his film debut in the silent picture SUNFLOWER SUE (1924), but it was never issued.

Late in 1923 Cliff Edwards began recording for the Pathé Phonography and Radio Company in New York City; during his four years with the firm he developed into one of the biggest-selling recording artists in popular music. Among his best-sellers, issued both on the Pathé and Perfect labels, were "Where the Lazy Daisies Grow," "Who's the Meanest Gal in Town, Josephine," "It Had to Be You," "When My Sweetie Puts Her Lovin' On," "June Night" (which sold over three million copies), "Charley, My Boy," "Who Takes Care of the Caretaker's Daughter," "Clap Hands, Here Comes Charley," "Meadowlark," and "I Can't Believe That You're in Love with Me."

In addition to his new-found success on records, Cliff Edwards took Broadway by storm when he appeared with Walter Catlett and Fred and Adele Astaire in George Gershwin's musical *Lady Be Good,* singing "Fascinatin' Rhythm." The show debuted in December 1924 at the Liberty Theatre and ran for 330 performances. Edwards next appeared with Marilyn Miller and Clifton Webb in *Sunny* (1925), by the team of Otto Harbach–Oscar Hammerstein II–Jerome Kern, singing "I'm Moving Away." This was followed in August 1927 by the new edition of *The Ziegfeld Follies,* which featured Edwards performing "Shakin' the Blues Away" (also done in the revue by Ruth Etting) and "Everybody Loves My Girl."

Following his Broadway prosperity, Edwards returned to vaudeville, earning several thousand dollars per week with his act. In 1928, while appearing in Los Angeles, he was signed by Metro-Goldwyn-Mayer to make two film shorts in which he performed two songs each. MGM, caught up in turning out a rash of sound musical features, signed him to a contract, and the stocky performer made his feature film debut in Marion Davies' MARIANNE (1929) as a doughboy in World War I France, singing four songs, including "Hang on to Me" and "Just You, Just Me." Edwards' biggest screen success came in THE HOLLYWOOD REVUE OF 1929, in which he sang "Singin' in the Rain." He had a best-selling recording of the song on Columbia Records, a label he signed with late in 1927 after leaving Pathé. He continued to have hit records for Columbia, including "Mary Ann," "That's My Weakness Now," "Half-Way to Heaven," "My Old Girl's My New Girl Now," "Hang on to Me," "Reaching for Someone," "I'll See You in My Dreams," and "Singing a Song to the Stars."

Cliff Edwards continued to appear in movies at MGM throughout the 1930s, but surprisingly, despite his musical talent, he was cast primarily in dramatic assignments. In most instances he played comical characters, although he occasionally won sympathetic parts, like that of Joan Crawford's newspaperman friend who is shot in the gangster tale DANCE, FOOLS, DANCE (1931). *Variety* endorsed, "Cliff is good all the way and in a likable role with sentiment attached." In 1930, Edwards' second wife (he had been married to Gertrude Benson from 1919 to 1921; they had a son, Clifton, Jr.), Irene Wylie, sued him for divorce. After a headline-making trial, she was awarded *all* their property and one-half of Cliff's income for life. Undaunted, in 1932 he wed actress Nancy Dover, but they were divorced in 1936. For the rest of his working days, he would be plagued with financial problems, filing for bankruptcy on three occasions. (Edwards was noted for spending huge sums on gambling, alcohol, and cocaine.)

Despite his persistent financial woes, Edwards continued to be professionally in demand. Although his Columbia recording contract concluded in 1930, he resumed making singles in 1932 for the American Record Corporation, which distributed its discs on the Brunswick label, and Edwards made regular appearances on Rudy Vallee's radio program, "The Fleischmann's Hour." In the summer of 1932, he hosted his own fifteen-minute radio show on CBS and around this time he signed with talent producer Ted Collins, who also managed Kate Smith. Together he and Smith appeared in the vaudeville presentation *Kate Smith and Her Swanee Music Revue* at the Palace Theatre. When "Kate Smith's Matinee Hour" debuted on CBS Radio in the fall of 1934, Cliff Edwards was a show regular. The previous spring he had worked in London, where he recorded for English Brunswick, and in October 1934, he resumed recording for the American Record Corporation, which now issued his discs on a variety of dimestore labels such as Melotone, Oriole, Perfect, Banner, and Rex. By 1936 his record fortunes had sunk so low that—without billing—he made a series of risqué party records for Novelty Record Distributors in Hollywood.

Late in 1935 Cliff Edwards made his final Broadway bow in *George White's Scandals of 1936* (he had previously had good roles in the movie musicals GEORGE WHITE'S SCANDALS [1934] and GEORGE WHITE'S 1935 SCANDALS [1935]). However, Edwards' leading role was short-lived since, upon the request of producer White, he was replaced in

Russell Hopton and Cliff Edwards in DANCE, FOOLS, DANCE (1931)

the lead assignment by Rudy Vallee, with Cliff taking a lesser role in the show. A few weeks later Vallee and White had a fistfight backstage; during the arbitration hearing, Edwards testified against Vallee, who had quit the production. As a result Edwards returned to his leading part, but the show quickly folded. He continued to make films, mostly at MGM, with good roles in SARATOGA (1937), BAD MAN OF BRIMSTONE (1938), MAISIE (1939), and HIS GIRL FRIDAY (1940), but his part as the reminiscing soldier in GONE WITH THE WIND (1939) was so tiny he was only heard and not seen. Another voice-only characterization, however, somewhat renewed his popularity when he supplied the voice of antic Jiminy Cricket in Walt Disney's animated feature PINOCCHIO (1940), singing the Oscar-winning song "When You Wish upon a Star." Edwards' film career was relaunched as a result, and he appeared in numerous films, even having sidekick parts in "B" Westerns opposite Charles Starrett at Columbia and Tim Holt at RKO Radio. One of his best-remembered performances was another voice-over, that of the crow singing "When I See an Elephant Fly" in DUMBO (1941).

Edwards continued to make records, for Decca in 1936 and 1939, and in 1940–41 he recorded the various songs he sang in the Disney productions for Victor. In 1943 he began recording radio transcriptions (noncommercial records sold directly to radio stations) for C. P. MacGregor and Lang-Worth, and in 1944 he had a five-minute weekday morning show on the Mutual radio network. In 1944 he also recorded thirty programs called "The Cliff Edwards Show" for Tower Transcriptions; these were syndicated to radio stations throughout the country. From March to September 1946 he starred on the weekly "The Cliff Edwards Show" on ABC. During the late 1940s work became less frequent for him, although he had a brief recording session with Mercury in 1949 and he recorded children's records for Victor in 1950. In the spring of 1949 he began a run on network television in the fifteen-minute "The Cliff Edwards Show" on CBS-TV, telecast three evenings a week. At the same time he was a regular on another CBS show, "The 54th Street Revue," and he made guest appearances on network TV with Ken Murray and Kate Smith. Late in 1951 he embarked on a brief but successful tour of Australia; while there he recorded two songs for the Fidelity record label.

In the mid-1950s Cliff Edwards had a marked resurgence in his career thanks to Walt Disney's television program, which used his recording of "When You Wish upon a Star" as its theme song. As a result he became the voice of Jiminy Cricket again in numerous animated shorts and he worked on "The Mickey Mouse Club" TV show as well as appeared in the Disney feature THE LITTLEST OUTLAW (1955). In 1956 he recorded an album for Disneyland Records called *Ukulele Ike Sings Again*. He continued to work until the mid-1960s, when his alcohol addiction made him unemployable. In the late 1960s he lived in a small apartment on Hollywood Boulevard and suffered leg problems. In 1969 he was moved to a nursing home as a relief patient of the Actor's Fund. He died there penniless on July 21, 1971, of heart failure. No one claimed his body and the destitute one-time star was buried in North Hollywood.

Like most people who exist purely for the moment, Cliff Edwards, in later life, claimed to have no regrets.

## Filmography

Sunflower Sue (Unissued, 1924)
Ukulele Ike (MGM, 1928) (s)
Ukulele Ike #2 (MGM, 1928) (s)
Marianne (MGM, 1929)
The Hollywood Revue of 1929 (MGM, 1929)
So This Is College (MGM, 1929)
Dough Boys (MGM, 1930)
Good News (MGM, 1930)
Lord Byron of Broadway (MGM, 1930)
Montana Moon (MGM, 1930)
The Voice of Hollywood #10 (Tif, 1930) (s)
Dogway Melody (MGM, 1930) (s) (voice only)
Great Day (Unfinished, 1930)
Those Three French Girls (MGM, 1930)
Way Out West (MGM, 1930)
Dance, Fools, Dance (MGM, 1931)
The Great Lover (MGM, 1931)
Laughing Sinners (MGM, 1931)
Stepping Out (MGM, 1931)
Parlor, Bedroom and Bath (MGM, 1931)
The Prodigal (MGM, 1931)
Shipmates (MGM, 1931)
Sidewalks of New York (MGM, 1931)
The Sin of Madelon Claudet (MGM, 1931)
Fast Life (MGM, 1932)
Hell Divers (MGM, 1932)
Stepping Out (MGM, 1932)
Paramount Pictorial #3 (Par, 1932) (s)
The World at Large (UM & M Pictorial, 1932) (s)
Young Bride (MGM, 1932)
Hollywood on Parade #12 (Par, 1933) (s)
Flying Devils (MGM, 1933)
Strange Case of Hennessy (RKO, 1933) (s)
Take a Chance (Par, 1933)
George White's Scandals (Fox, 1934)
George White's 1935 Scandals (Fox, 1935)
Red Salute (Fox, 1935)
The Man I Marry (Univ, 1936)
Bad Guy (MGM, 1937)
Between Two Women (MGM, 1937)
Saratoga (MGM, 1937)
They Gave Him a Gun (MGM, 1937)
The Women Men Marry (MGM, 1937)
Bad Man of Brimstone (MGM, 1938)
The Girl of the Golden West (MGM, 1938)

Little Adventuress (Col, 1938)
Maisie (MGM, 1939)
Royal Rodeo (Vita, 1939) (s)
Smuggled Cargo (Rep, 1939)
Ride Cowboy Ride (Vita, 1939) (s)
Gone with the Wind (MGM, 1939)
Flowing Gold (WB, 1940)
Cliff Edwards and His Musical Buckaroos (Vita, 1940) (s)
Friendly Neighbors (Rep, 1940)
Just a Cute Kid (Vita, 1940) (s)
High School (20th–Fox, 1940)
His Girl Friday (Col, 1940)
Millionaires in Prison (RKO, 1940)
Pinocchio (RKO, 1940) (voice only)
Dumbo (RKO, 1941) (voice only)
Jeannie with the Light Brown Hair (Soundies, 1941) (s)
International Squadron (WB, 1941)
Knockout (WB, 1941)
Thunder over the Prairie (Col, 1941)
Riders of the Badlands (Col, 1941)
The Monster and the Girl (Par, 1941)
Power Dive (Par, 1941)
Prairie Stranger (Col, 1941)
She Couldn't Say No (WB, 1941)
The New Spirit (RKO, 1942) (s)
American Empire (UA, 1942)
Bandit Ranger (RKO, 1942)
Pirates of the Prairie (RKO, 1942)
Red River Robin Hood (RKO, 1942)
Bad Men of the Hills (Col, 1942)
Lawless Plainsmen (Col, 1942)
Riders of the Northland (Col, 1942)
Seven Miles from Alcatraz (RKO, 1942)
Picture People #12 (RKO, 1942) (s)
Overland to Deadwood (Col, 1942)
Sundown Jim (20th–Fox, 1942)
West of Tombstone (Col, 1942)
The Falcon Strikes Back (RKO, 1943)
Sagebrush Law (RKO, 1943)
The Avenging Rider (RKO, 1943)
Minnie, My Mountain Moocher (Soundies, 1943) (s)
Paddlin' Madeline Home (Soundies, 1943) (s)
Fighting Frontier (RKO, 1943)

Salute for Three (Par, 1943)
Between the Devil and the Deep Blue Sea
    (Soundies, 1944) (s)
Movieland Magic (Vita, 1945) (s)

Fun and Fancy Free (RKO, 1947) (voice only)
The Littlest Outlaw (BV, 1955)
The Man from Button Willow (United Screen
    Arts, 1964) (voice only)

## Broadway Plays

The Ziegfeld Follies (1918)
Lady Be Good (1924)
Sunny (1925)

The Ziegfeld Follies (1927)
George White's Scandals of 1936 (1935)

## Radio Series

Cliff Edwards, Ukulele Ike (NBC, 1932)
The Cliff Edwards Show (CBS, 1932, 1934)
Variety Hour (CBS, 1934)

Kate Smith's Matinee Hour (CBS, 1934)
The Cliff Edwards Show (Mutual, 1944; Synd,
    1944; ABC, 1946)

## TV Series

The Cliff Edwards Show (CBS, 1949)
The 54th Street Revue (CBS, 1949)

## Album Discography

Cliff Edwards (10" Bateau Chinois A-1)
Cliff Edwards, Vols. 1–2 (10" Ristic 39, 42)
Cliff Edwards and His Hot Combination 1925–
    26 (Fountain LFV-203)
Dumbo (Disneyland 1204) [ST]
Fascinatin' Rhythm (Totem 1045)
I Want a Girl (Totem 1014)
I'm a Bear in a Lady's Boudoir (Yazoo 1047)

Pinocchio (Disneyland 1202) [ST]
Remember (Blue Heaven 8-807)
Shakin' the Blues Away (Totem 1005)
Ukulele Ike (Glendale 6011)
Ukulele Ike Happens Again (Buena Vista 4043)
Ukulele Ike Sings Again (Disneyland 3003)
The Vintage Recordings of Cliff Edwards (Take
    Two TT-205)

# RUTH ETTING

RUTH ETTING WAS PROBABLY THE MOST POPULAR FEMALE VOCALIST of the Roaring Twenties. Her high, clear voice and precise phrasing made her a natural for the popular tunes of the day and, with her good looks, made her the epitome of the mature flapper of the Jazz Age. Her Columbia recordings in the last half of the 1920s sold in the millions and she became a favorite Broadway attraction as well. In the 1930s she also starred on radio and made dozens of appearances on the silver screen, but only a trio of these were in feature films. Lacking thespian abilities, Ruth Etting mainly headlined short subjects, which showcased her good looks and sterling voice.

Sources vary on Ruth Etting's year of birth, reporting it as from 1896 to 1907, but most likely November 23, 1896, is correct. Her parents, Alfred and Winifred (Kleinhen) Etting, were farm folk and she was born on their farm near David City, Nebraska. When she was five, her mother became ill and Ruth accompanied her mother to San Diego, California, where Mrs. Etting's family attempted in vain to nurse Winifred back to health. After her mother died, Ruth was brought back to live with her paternal grandparents in David City, where George Etting owned the Etting Roller Mill.

Ruth was not academically inclined, much preferring the world of show business. (Her grandfather had built the David City Opera House and she loved to mingle with the circus and tent show players who pitched camp on the vacant lot near the Etting Roller Mill. She sang in the Congregational Church choir, later recalling, "I sang in a high, squeaky soprano. It sounded terrible, but I didn't know I could sing in any other range.") After she graduated (barely) from high school, she worked for a time in Omaha, Nebraska, in a department store and then went to Chicago to begin studies at the Academy of Fine Arts, planning to study costume design. She was interviewed by the manager of the Marigold Gardens nightclub about designing costumes for the show there, but ended by joining the chorus. She was soon featured as a singer at the Gardens. At this time, she met Moe "The Gimp" Snyder, an arrogant gangster who fell in love with her. Snyder immediately set about making her a star, and thanks to his connections, she soon was getting good bookings and salaries—which would not have continued if she had not possessed sufficient talent of her own. She also began singing on radio, winning the title of "Chicago's Sweetheart." She married Snyder on July 12, 1922, in Crown Point, Indiana, and raised his two children from a previous marriage. Although her relationship with the hot-headed Snyder was constantly stormy, Ruth had a good rapport with her stepchildren and remained close to them throughout her life.

After the Marigold Gardens, Ruth began performing in the revue at the Rainbo

Gardens and later at a variety of Chicago clubs: the Green Mill, the Granada, the Terrace Gardens, and the Montmartre Café. She was heard on the Windy City's KYW radio in 1924 and began touring on the midwestern vaudeville circuit. In the spring of 1924 Ruth made a test record for Victor in Chicago and, early in 1926, had her first commercial record release on Columbia, "Let's Talk About My Sweetie"/"Nothing Else to Do."

By 1927 Snyder had moved Ruth's base of operations to New York City. Years later, Ruth would say of her increasingly troublesome relationship with the obsessive Snyder: "My sad story is that my first marriage wasn't a marriage at all. It was a mistake." Her recording career got into full swing in Gotham. For the next half-dozen years she recorded with Columbia and was soon known as "The Sweetheart of Columbia Records."

At first she used only a piano accompanist on record, usually Rube Bloom or Arthur Shutt, but as her recordings grew in popularity her arrangements became more elaborate. As the 1920s progressed her background musicians included such jazz greats as violinist Joe Venuti, guitarist Eddie Lang, trumpeter Manny Klein, Tommy and Jimmy Dorsey, Andy Sanella, Charlie Spivak, Joe Tarto, and Charlie Butterfield. Ruth always came to recording sessions well prepared and these jazz musicians loved to work with her, not only because of her professionalism but also because the sessions usually finished early, giving them time to record their own specialty numbers. Ruth Etting had dozens of Columbia best-sellers from 1926 to 1932, including "Sleepy Baby," "My Blackbirds Are Bluebirds Now," "Love Me or Leave Me," "You're the Cream in My Coffee," "Mean to Me," "What Wouldn't I Do for That Man," "The Right Kind of Man," "Ten Cents a Dance," "At Sundown," "Shaking the Blues Away," "Dancing with Tears in My Eyes," "Happy Days and Lonely Nights," and "A Faded Summer Love." She also helped compose some of her own popular songs, like "Wistful and Blue," "When You're with Somebody Else," and "Maybe, Who Knows?"

In 1927 Ruth was appearing with Paul Whiteman and His Orchestra at the Paramount Theater in New York City. After hearing some of her recordings, Irving Berlin introduced her to Florenz Ziegfeld who hired her at $400 weekly to appear in his new edition of the Ziegfeld Follies, for which Berlin was to do the music. In the show she sang "Shaking the Blues Away" and was a sensation. She kept her age a secret. "I fooled New Yorkers for a long time," she would recall years later. "They thought I was a kid. I was little and slim and blonde. Very few people knew I'd been working around Chicago for almost ten years. Even Ziegfeld didn't have any idea of my age." After her success in the Follies she made personal appearances in Chicago (at $8,000 weekly) and on the West Coast (at $1,000 plus a percentage of the box-office receipts). The next year she was featured in a new version of the Ziegfeld Follies and during the same season she appeared with Eddie Cantor in *Whoopee!*, popularizing the song "Love Me or Leave Me." Next came 1929's Ziegfeld Follies followed by *Simple Simon* with Ed Wynn in 1930. In the latter show she made famous the Richard Rodgers–Lorenz Hart song "Ten Cents a Dance," which the composers rewrote for her. Next came the brief-running *The Nine-Fifteen Revue* in 1930 and 1931's Ziegfeld Follies, in which she revived the old Jack Norworth–Nora Bayes standard "Shine On, Harvest Moon."

While appearing in *Whoopee!* in 1928, Ruth Etting made her film debut in the Paramount one-reel talkie RUTH ETTING, singing "Roses of Yesterday" and "Because My Baby Don't Mean 'Maybe' Now." She photographed well and sounded great, even given the primitive recording techniques of the time, and quickly followed it with another short, PARAMOUNT MOVIETONE, also shot in 1928 at the company's Astoria, Long Island, studio. In 1929 Warner Bros.–Vitaphone signed Ruth to a film contract and over the next five years she starred in a host of one- and two-reel musical shorts for the studio. Typical of these cheaply made films is the 1930 two-reeler ROSELAND, directed by Roy Mack and lensed at the Vitaphone Studios in Brooklyn. Here Ruth is cast as a pretty dancehall girl, whose ordeals, before finding true love at the finale, permit her to sing two popular tunes, "Let Me Sing and I'm Happy" and "Dancing with Tears in My Eyes." ARTISTIC TEMPERAMENT (1932), also directed by Mack, has Ruth as a kitchen maid who becomes a big Broadway singing star only to abandon it all and become a housewife for the man she adores. Along the way she warbles "That's What Heaven Means to Me," "What a Life," and "Loveable."

Coupled with her success on stage, records, and movies, Ruth Etting ventured into radio in 1930, appearing with Walter Winchell on his first broadcast that year as well as on Rudy Vallee's "The Fleischmann's Hour." From 1932 to 1933 she headlined the "Chesterfield Satisfies" program on CBS and in the summer of 1934 she appeared with Gus Arnheim and His Orchestra in "The Demi-Tasse Revue." From 1934 to 1935 she was the featured attraction on another musical series on the NBC Blue network. She continued to guest-star on programs such as "The Majestic Hour," "The Chase and Sanborn Hour," "The Oldsmobile Show," and "Kellogg's College Prom."

In 1932 Ruth ended her association with Columbia Records and cut several singles for the American Record Corporation, which issued its product to various dimestore chains on labels like Melotone, Conqueror, Perfect, and Romeo. In 1933 she recorded with Brunswick and after more sessions with that label the next year, she returned to Columbia where she remained through 1935.

Ruth Etting made her feature film debut in the 1933 Samuel Goldwyn musical extravaganza ROMAN SCANDALS, starring Eddie Cantor. She was featured in the role of Olga (which required very little acting) and was the centerpiece of a posh production number (filled with Goldwyn chorines) singing "No More Love." A second number was cut, however, after Cantor extended the film's running time with too many comedy bits. *Variety* thought Ruth's handling of the Busby Berkeley–choreographed number was "socko." Two more feature films followed for Ruth, but again she was showcased in production numbers and not given dramatic parts. In HIPS, HIPS HOORAY (1934), one of the zany Bert Wheeler–Robert Woolsey comedies for RKO, she performed "Keeping Romance Alive." The same year she played herself in Universal's all-star radio tribute GIFT OF GAB, singing "Talking to Myself" and "Tomorrow, Who Cares?" She was scheduled to be in RKO's STRICTLY DYNAMITE (1934) starring Lupe Velez, but by the time production began, her role had been written out of the scenario.

By the mid-1930s, Ruth Etting was being dubbed "Queen of the Torch Singers" (a title she won in a national poll) and "America's Radio Sweetheart." In 1933 she signed with RKO Radio Pictures and through 1936 appeared in more than a dozen two-reelers for the studio (while continuing to appear in other companies' short subjects). Like her previous Vitaphone shorts they were quite thin on plot but highlighted the star in musical renditions. Still, there was repetition as Ruth sang "Shine On, Harvest Moon" in CALIFORNIA WEATHER (1933), A TORCH TANGO (1934), and TUNED OUT (1935), as well as in two return trips to Warner Bros.: THE SONG OF FAME (1934) and NO CONTEST (1935). By the time the RKO series was winding down with MELODY IN MAY (1936), forty-year-old Ruth was cast as herself but was no longer the love interest; here she sang "St. Louis Blues" and "It Had to Be You" and played cupid to a couple of teenagers. In 1936 Ruth went to London and on October 1 of that year she debuted in the production *Transatlantic Rhythm* at the Adelphi Theatre. While in London, during the run of the unsuccessful show, she recorded for the Rex label.

Upon her return to the United States late in 1936, Ruth recorded for Decca Records in New York City. At that time she and her husband separated, and in 1937 Ruth moved to Hollywood where she met musician/accompanist/arranger Myrl Alderman, who worked for various film studios. Ruth had filed for divorce from Moe Snyder and did not know he had followed her to the West Coast. She and Alderman fell in love and planned to marry. Snyder forced Alderman to take him to Ruth one evening and then shot the musician while Ruth and Snyder's daughter both threatened the gangster with a gun. Snyder was arrested for kidnapping and attempted murder while Alderman recovered from his minor wounds. A sensational trial followed, and Snyder was sentenced to prison. Not long after, in December 1938, Ruth married Alderman in Las Vegas and they moved to a ranch near Colorado Springs, Colorado. Because of the scandal, Ruth remained out of the limelight for several years, but in the late 1940s she returned to radio as a guest on Rudy Vallee's variety program and this led to her own "The Ruth Etting Show" for WOR in New York City in 1947. Her comeback was short-lived, however, as Ruth and Alderman, who were financially secure, preferred their private life to any kind of public life. They alternated their home life in Colorado with winters in Florida.

Ruth Etting in 1935

In 1955 a great deal of interest in Ruth Etting was generated when MGM filmed a version of her life story as LOVE ME OR LEAVE ME with Doris Day as Ruth, James Cagney as Moe "The Gimp" Snyder, and Cameron Mitchell as Myrl Alderman. Highlighted by top-notch renditions of Ruth's many song hits, the film was a treasure trove of misinformation about Ruth's stormy life, even picturing her as a dance hall girl—something that was totally false. (Years later, she would say, "Oh what a _____ mess that was. . . . They took a lot of liberties with my life, but I guess they usually do with that kind of thing.") Following the movie's great success, however, Columbia Records issued an LP of Ruth's old recordings called *Love Me or Leave Me* and she was offered a five-figure sum to sing in Las Vegas, an offer she declined. She said, "I'm never going to go out there to have people in the audience say, 'Gee, I remember her when she was really something.'"

Myrl Alderman died in November 1966 and Ruth soon moved to an apartment in Colorado Springs where she remained for the rest of her life. She kept up correspondence with fans and wrote the liner notes for a reissue album of some of her old records, *Hello, Baby*, in 1973. Although she was always available for interviews, Ruth Etting refused all requests to sing in public—those close to her insist her voice was gone. Ruth Etting died on September 24, 1978, following a long illness. In recent years a number of record albums and cassette tapes have appeared containing reissues of her vintage recordings and her old films have been popular items on videotape.

## Filmography

Ruth Etting (Par, 1928) (s)
Paramount Movietone (Par, 1928) (s)
Favorite Melodies (Par, 1929) (s)
Melancholy Dame (Par, 1929) (s)
The Book of Lovers (Illustrated, 1929) (s) (voice only)
Glorifying the Popular Song (Vita, 1929) (s)
Ruth Etting (Vita, 1929) (s)
One Good Turn (Vita, 1930) (s)
Broadway's Like That (Vita, 1930) (s)
Roseland (Vita, 1930) (s)
Ruth Etting in Broadway's Like This (Vita, 1930) (s)
Old Lace (Vita, 1931) (s)
Freshman Love (Vita, 1931) (s)
Words and Music (Vita, 1931) (s)
Stage Struck (Vita, 1931) (s)
Radio Salutes (Par, 1931) (s)
Seasons Greeting (Vita, 1931) (s)
A Modern Cinderella (Vita, 1932) (s)
A Mail Bride (Vita, 1932) (s)
A Regular Trouper (Vita, 1932) (s)
Artistic Temperament (Vita, 1932) (s)

Bye-Gones (Vita, 1933) (s)
Along Came Ruth (Vita, 1933) (s)
California Weather (RKO, 1933) (s)
Crashing the Gate (Vita, 1933) (s)
I Know Everybody and Everybody's Racket (Univ, 1933) (s)
Knee Deep in Music (RKO, 1933) (s)
Roman Scandals (UA, 1933)
Gift of Gab (Univ, 1934)
Hips, Hips, Hooray (RKO, 1934)
Bandits and Ballads (RKO, 1934) (s)
Derby Decade (RKO, 1934) (s)
The Song of Fame (Vita, 1934) (s)
Southern Style (RKO, 1934) (s)
A Torch Tango (RKO, 1934) (s)
Hollywood on Parade (Par, 1934) (s)
No Contest (Vita, 1935) (s)
An Old Spanish Onion (RKO, 1935) (s)
Ticket or Leave It (RKO, 1935) (s)
Tuned Out (RKO, 1935) (s)
Aladdin from Manhattan (RKO, 1936) (s)
Melody in May (RKO, 1936) (s)
Sleepy Time (RKO, 1936) (s)

## Broadway Plays

The Ziegfeld Follies (1927)
Whoopee! (1928)
The Ziegfeld Follies (1928)
The Ziegfeld Follies (1929)

Simple Simon (1930)
The Nine-Fifteen Revue (1930)
The Ziegfeld Follies (1931)

## Radio Series

Chesterfield Satisfies (CBS, 1932–33)
The Demi-Tasse Revue (NBC, 1934)
The Ruth Etting Show (NBC Blue, 1934–35)

The Ruth Etting Show (WOR, 1947) (New York City)

## Album Discography

America's Radio Sweetheart (Totem 1018, Sandy Hook 2033)
The Big Broadcast of 1935 (Kasha King 1935) [ST/R]
Encores (Take Two TT-211)
Fanny Brice, Helen Kane and Ruth Etting (Amalgamated 250)
Hello, Baby (Biograph 11)
Let Me Call You Sweetheart (Take Two TT-224)

Love Me or Leave Me (Col ML-5050)
The Original Torch Singers (Take Two TT-207) w. Fanny Brice, Libby Holman
Queen of the Torch Singers (Broadway Intermission 143)
Reflections (Take Two TT-203)
Roman Scandals (CIF 3007) [ST]
Ruth Etting Sings Again (Jay 3011)
Ten Cents a Dance (ASV 5008)

# DALE EVANS

DALE EVANS, BILLED AS "THE QUEEN OF THE WEST," IS ALMOST ALWAYS considered as part of a team with her husband, Roy Rogers, "The King of the Cowboys." While their personal and professional relationship has lasted for over four decades, Dale Evans has carved for herself a distinctive and separate career in a diverse number of fields including radio, films, recordings, television, concerts, author of more than two dozen best-selling books, and songwriter. Religion has made the main difference in Dale Evans' life; despite many personal tribulations, she has always considered her firm faith the main reason for her enduring career success. She has stated often that she would have preferred to be an evangelist but that she has best carried her Christian message as an entertainer and author.

A native of Uvalde, Texas, and christened Frances Octavia Smith, she was the daughter of Walter Hillman, a cotton farmer and hardware store owner, and Betty Sue Smith, who imbued her daughter with a strong Baptist heritage. Frances was born October 31, 1912, and a few years later she had a younger brother, Walter. She attended high school in Osceola, Arkansas, and it was there at age fourteen that she met and eloped with a young man named Tom Fox. Within a year she was the mother of a son, Tom Fox, Jr., but her husband soon deserted her and the teenaged mother supported herself and her son by working as a secretary for an insurance firm in Memphis, Tennessee. (Later, when she was first in movies, she would introduce her son as her young brother, on the advice of her agent who insisted that an actress with a teenaged child would not be accepted by filmgoers.) When her employers discovered she was a good singer, they put her on the company-owned radio station, WMC, as a vocalist. Next she went to work for WHAS in Louisville, Kentucky, where the station's program director changed her name to Dale Evans. From there she went to WFAA in Dallas where she became very popular and began working with touring bands, including those of Jay Mills and Herman Waldman. This activity led to an engagement with Anson Weeks and His Orchestra at the Chez Paree in Chicago in 1939. The next year she made her recording debut dueting with Lucio Garcia on "Help Me" with Abe Lyman and His Californians on Bluebird Records.

Besides working in Chicago nightclubs, Dale began performing on radio in the Windy City, mostly with Caesar Petrillo's Orchestra. She became so popular that her picture was often featured on the sheet music of songs she had sung. During this period she met and married pianist Dale Butts and the two wrote a number of songs, including "Will You Marry Me, Mr. Laramie?" The song brought her to the attention of Joe Rivkin, a Hollywood talent agent, who got her a screen test for Paramount's HOLIDAY INN (1942), but instead she ended with a twelve-month pact with 20th Century–Fox.

When nothing materialized for Dale in the movies, she was heard for a season on "The Chase and Sanborn Hour" on radio with Edgar Bergen and Charlie McCarthy, and then was a vocalist with Roy Noble and His Orchestra on his radio show in 1943. The next season she performed the same chore on "The Jack Carson Show." She was also cast in small roles in two 20th Century–Fox musicals, GIRL TROUBLE and ORCHESTRA WIVES, both 1942 releases, before her contract option was dropped. By now her manager was Art Rush, also the manager for Roy Rogers, and he got her work at Republic Pictures where she did five feature films, the best being the John Wayne production IN OLD OKLAHOMA (1943), in which she sang "Put Your Arms Around Me, Honey." She continued to work on radio as a regular on "The Jimmy Durante–Garry Moore Show" and she cut four sides for Bel-Tone Records as well as appeared at Hollywood clubs like the Mocambo and the Trocadero. Dale also worked tirelessly as an entertainer at Army camps and she appeared on a number of Armed Forces Radio programs like "Personal Album," "Showtime," "Mail Call," and "Radio Hall of Fame." Her marriage to Dale Butts, now an orchestrator at Republic, ended during this period. Dale Evans also had a renewal of her Christian faith at this time.

In 1944 Dale was cast as the second female lead in the Roy Rogers Western THE COWBOY AND THE SENORITA, in the part of Ysebel Martinez, singing the popular tune

Dale Evans and Roy Rogers in THE YELLOW ROSE OF TEXAS (1944)

"Besame Mucho." She was so successful teaming with Rogers that in the next three years she was to do nineteen more formula Westerns with him. In 1947 she was voted the first (and only!) woman to appear in the *Motion Picture Herald*'s poll of top money-making Western stars. Perhaps the main reason for her popularity in these action-packed and glossy Western-musicals, apart from her good looks and ability to act and sing, was the fact that her characters were not in the traditional mold of the helpless Western heroine. Dale's characters were independent females who were full of life and had minds of their own. Thus women and girls could empathize with Dale on the screen, while she also appealed to the men and boys in the audience.

Roy Rogers' wife, Arlene, died in 1946, following complications from the birth of their second child, and after a time, Roy and Dale, who had gotten along well as co-stars, became involved romantically and were married in 1947. Republic, however, then removed her from the Rogers pictures and instead cast her in a tepid remake of Gloria Swanson's THE TRESPASSER (1947), which gave her a chance to sing Swanson's standard, "Love, Your Magic Spell Is Everywhere." Next came a remake of a Colleen Moore picture, SLIPPY McGEE (1948), which co-starred her with another Republic Western star, Don "Red" Barry. However, Dale then rejected the role of a bad girl in another Barry feature, MADONNA OF THE DESERT (1948). She continued to guest-star on radio shows like "All-Star Western Theatre," "Here's to Veterans," "Hollywood Tour," and "Treasury Song Parade." She also recorded for Majestic Records, waxing such Western tunes as "When the Roses Bloom in Red River Valley," "Under a Texas Moon," "I'm the Rage of the Sage," "Loaded Pistols," "The Guitar Song," and her self-penned "Aha San Antone."

Dale, now billed as "Queen of the West," was finally allowed to reteam with her spouse on camera in 1949 in Republic's SUSANNA PASS. She did five more films with Roy through 1950 and then took a hiatus from the series, returning in 1951 for his final two starring "B" Westerns: SOUTH OF CALIENTE and PALS OF THE GOLDEN WEST. In 1949 Dale also began recording with RCA Victor Records (Roy had been on the label since 1945) and she would remain with the powerful label through 1952, recording solo (often children's songs) and dueting with her husband. In 1950 the duo cut the first of several religious albums, *Hymns of Faith*, for RCA. From 1950 to 1952 Dale returned to the top money-making Western stars poll of the *Motion Picture Herald.* In 1950 Dale gave birth to her second child, a daughter, Robin. The infant, however, had Down syndrome, but Roy and Dale did not institutionalize the child. Instead they raised her at home where she died two days before her second birthday. Out of the traumatic experience Dale wrote the book *Angel Unaware* (1953), which became a best-seller with its proceeds going to the National Association for Retarded Persons. The loss of their child further cemented Roy and Dale's religious activities and they worked closely with Norman Vincent Peale and Billy Graham. When the screen team made a successful tour of Britain in 1954, they also appeared as part of Billy Graham's London crusade.

Dale Evans had co-starred with Rogers on radio since 1948, when "The Roy Rogers Show" was broadcast on Mutual. The show moved to NBC in 1951 when General Foods took over its sponsorship. Late in 1951 the Western duo came to television with the half-hour "The Roy Rogers Show" on NBC. Like the radio program, which ran on NBC through 1955, the TV show was set in a Western locale with Dale operating a café and teaming with Roy to fight assorted villains, aided by Pat Brady and his trusty Jeep "Nellybelle," along with Roy's horse, Trigger, and dog, Bullet. The action-packed, but cheaply produced, series ran for nearly one hundred episodes through 1957. Its theme was "Happy Trails to You," a song written by Dale and one she and Roy recorded for RCA Victor in 1952.

During the 1950s the Rogerses guest-starred on a number of TV programs, like those of Perry Como and Milton Berle, and they were extremely active in personal appearances and on the rodeo circuit. In 1957 they cut another religious album for RCA, *Sweet Hour of Prayer*, and the next year they recorded still another one for RCA's subsidiary label, Bluebird, called *Jesus Loves Me*. Heard with them on this LP were their children: Linda, Dusty, Sandy, Dodie, and Debbie, the last three of whom were adopted. In the 1950s Roy and Dale also made many recordings for Golden Records, most of them for children. In 1958 the Rogerses were at Billy Graham's Washington, D.C., crusade and attended Easter services with the President and Mrs. Dwight D. Eisenhower. In the late 1950s Roy and Dale headlined two TV specials, and in 1962 they starred in the hour-long variety program "The Roy Rogers and Dale Evans Show" on ABC-TV. It ran for only three months due to heavy competition from Jackie Gleason on CBS-TV. That year also found them recording for Capitol Records with the duet album *The Bible Tells Me So*. In 1967 Dale recorded a gospel album for Capitol called *It's Real* and she and Roy did a Christmas LP, *Christmas Is Always* (Dale composed the title tune). In 1970 she and The Jordanaires did still another gospel LP for Capitol, *Get to Know the Lord.*

Tragedy again struck the Rogers family when their nine-year-old adopted daughter, Debbie, was killed in a church bus accident near San Clemente, California, in the summer of 1964. The next year Dale wrote the book *Dearest Debbie* as a remembrance to her daughter. Among Dale's other best-selling books have been *My Spiritual Diary* (1955), *Christmas Is Always* (1958), and her autobiography, *The Woman at the Well* (1970), which sold over 275,000 copies in hard cover. In 1965, a third Rogers child, adopted son Sandy, died in Germany of alcohol poisoning; Dale wrote the book *Salute to Sandy* in 1965. As a tribute to Sandy, she and Roy entertained servicemen in Vietnam in 1966 and the same year Dale was declared "The Texan of the Year" by the Texas Press Association. The next year Dale was named California's "Mother of the Year" and she and Roy opened a museum centered around their careers near their Apple Valley home. In the 1970s the museum was moved permanently to Victorville.

By the late 1960s Roy and Dale had settled into a life of both domestic happiness as well as joint/separate careers. Together they appeared on such TV shows as "The Hollywood Palace" and "Hee Haw" and made many personal appearances together. On her own, Dale continued to write such books as *Time Out Ladies!* (1966), *Where He Leads* (1974), *Let Freedom Ring* (1975), and *Grandparents Can* (1983). In the early 1970s she began recording for Word Records in Waco, Texas, and for the rest of the decade she was featured on LPs like *Faith, Hope and Charity*, *Heart of the Country*, *Country Dale*, and *Totally Free*, plus two duet albums with Roy: *In the Sweet By and By* and *The Good Life*. During the decade the Rogerses also hosted and were heard many times on the radio program "Country Crossroads," sponsored by the Southern Baptist Convention.

The 1980s proved to be an active decade for the seemingly indefatigable Dale Evans, now in her seventies. She has maintained an active schedule of concerts along with church visitations. In 1984 she and Roy and their son Roy, Jr. (Dusty) recorded a two-record set for Teletex Records called *Many Happy Trails*, which highlighted music from their careers with Dale doing Western, religious, and big band numbers. Earlier in the decade, in 1981, she cut a religious album for the Manna label called *Reflections of Life*. The year 1984 also found her returning to films for the first time in thirty years in the religious feature GOD IN HARD TIMES, made by Word Pictures and based on her book of the same title. In 1985 she and Roy began their television series "Happy Trails Theatre" on the Nashville Network; on the show they screened their old Westerns and discussed them with guest stars. The same year she began appearing on her own syndicated TV program, "The Dale Evans Show," for Trinity Broadcasting in Santa Ana, California. On the show Dale discusses religious topics and interviews guests, including members of her own family. In 1988 Word Books published her twenty-fifth volume, *The Only Star*.

Today Dale Evans is a happy and fulfilled woman who has found success in both her private and professional life. Her son Tom is a minister and she and Roy Rogers have a large family, which includes grandchildren and great-grandchildren. Perhaps she best summed up her feelings toward life and her deep faith in her book *Where He Leads*: "He has led me in Galilee and Judea and New York and California and everywhere I go. . . . I find the light of His countenance going before me on the common roads of home as I found it leading me there, and it lightens my journey . . . and gives me peace. . . ."

## Filmography

Orchestra Wives (20th–Fox, 1942)
Girl Trouble (20th–Fox, 1942)
Here Comes Elmer (Rep, 1943)
Hoosier Holiday [Farmyard Follies] (Rep, 1943)
Swing Your Partner (Rep, 1943)
The West Side Kid (Rep, 1943)
In Old Oklahoma [War of the Wildcats] (Rep, 1943)
The Cowboy and the Senorita (Rep, 1944)
Casanova in Burlesque (Rep, 1944)
San Fernando Valley (Rep, 1944)
The Yellow Rose of Texas (Rep, 1944)
Song of Nevada (Rep, 1944)
Utah (Rep, 1945)
Lights of Old Santa Fe (Rep, 1945)
The Big Show-Off (Rep, 1945)

The Man from Oklahoma (Rep, 1945)
Don't Fence Me In (Rep, 1945)
Hitchhike to Happiness (Rep, 1945)
Bells of Rosarita (Rep, 1945)
Sunset in El Dorado (Rep, 1945)
Along the Navajo Trail (Rep, 1945)
Song of Arizona (Rep, 1946)
My Pal Trigger (Rep, 1946)
Under Nevada Skies (Rep, 1946)
Roll On, Texas Moon (Rep, 1946)
Home in Oklahoma (Rep, 1946)
Rainbow over Texas (Rep, 1946)
Out California Way (Rep, 1946)
Heldorado (Rep, 1946)
Apache Rose (Rep, 1947)
Bells of San Angelo (Rep, 1947)

The Trespasser (Rep, 1947)
Slippy McGee (Rep, 1948)
The Golden Stallion (Rep, 1949)
Susanna Pass (Rep, 1949)
Twilight in the Sierras (Rep, 1950)
Bells of Coronado (Rep, 1950)

Trigger, Jr. (Rep, 1950)
South of Caliente (Rep, 1951)
Pals of the Golden West (Rep, 1951)
Screen Snapshots #24 (Col, 1954) (s)
God in Hard Times (Word Pictures, 1984)

## Radio Series

The Chase and Sanborn Hour (NBC, 1941–42)
Ray Noble and His Orchestra (NBC, 1943)
The Jack Carson Show (CBS, 1944)

The Jimmy Durante–Garry Moore Show (CBS, 1945–46)
The Roy Rogers Show (Mutual, 1948–51; NBC, 1951–55)

## TV Series

The Roy Rogers Show (NBC, 1951–57)
The Roy Rogers and Dale Evans Show (ABC, 1962)

The Happy Trails Theatre (TNN, 1985– )
The Dale Evans Show (Synd, 1985– )

## Album Discography

The Bible Tells Me So (Cap TST-1745, Cap SM-1745) w. Roy Rogers
A Child's Introduction to the West (Golden 7) w. Roy Rogers
Christmas Is Always (Cap ST-2818) w. Roy Rogers
Country Dale (Word 8611)
Dale Evans Sings (10" Allegro 4116)
Faith, Hope and Charity (Word 8566)
Favorite Gospel Songs (Sacred Sounds 4505)
Get to Know the Lord (Cap ST-399) w. The Jordanaires
The Good Life (Word 8761) w. Roy Rogers
Heart of the Country (Word 8658)
Hymns of Faith (10" RCA LPM-3168) w. Roy Rogers

In the Sweet By and By (Word 8589) w. Roy Rogers
It's Real (Cap T/ST-2772, Word 8546)
Jesus Loves Me (Bluebird LBY-1022, Camden CAL/CAS-1022, Camden/ Pickwick ACL-7021) w. Roy Rogers & Family
Many Happy Trails (Teletex C-7702) w. Roy Rogers, Roy Rogers, Jr.
Reflections of Life (Manna MS-2075)
16 Great Songs of the West (Golden 198:7) w. Roy Rogers
Sweet Hour of Prayer (RCA LPM-1439, Stetson HAT-3088) w. Roy Rogers
Sweeter as the Years Go By (Word 8583)
Totally Free (Word 8803)
Western Favorites (Evon 336)

# ALICE FAYE

ALICE FAYE FIRST CAME TO HOLLYWOOD AT AGE NINETEEN. SHE WAS glamourized immediately into a platinum blonde similar to Jean Harlow. When Darryl F. Zanuck took over Fox Pictures in the mid-1930s, he perceived more potential in Alice and showcased her natural beauty and infectious, warm personality. As a result, she became 20th Century–Fox's top money-making star and her vogue lasted well into the 1940s. She was the adorable heroine who could deliver a ballad in a tender contralto voice and make the audience really care about her yielding character. Eventually she tired of the competition and pressures of the movie star routine and chose instead to focus on her family life. (Betty Grable inherited her mantle as the blonde singing queen of the studio.) Although Faye has never retired, her most successful years encompassed the thirty feature films she made from 1934 to 1943, most of which had show business motifs, fluffy plots, pretty songs, and—best of all—the good looks and talent of Alice to put them across.

Alice Faye was born Alice Jeanne Leppert in the Hell's Kitchen section (on Tenth Avenue; she always referred to it jokingly as "Double Fifth Avenue") of New York City on May 5, 1915, the daughter of city patrolman Charley and Alice (Moffat) Leppert. She was the youngest of three children, having two older brothers (Charles and William). Early in life she loved to dance and was encouraged in such activities by her maternal grandmother, who resided with the family. When she was thirteen she quit school and tried to win a job with the Ziegfeld Follies, but failed. However, a year later she obtained employment with Chester Hale's dancers at the Capitol Theatre and other nightspots. She was in the chorus of *George White's Scandals of 1931*; at a cast party one of the production's stars, Rudy Vallee, was impressed with her singing. He began featuring her on his popular variety radio show "The Fleischmann's Hour." When the sponsor would not pay Alice's salary, Vallee did so himself; he also took her on a tour of New England with his band. During a storm the two were in a car wreck and Alice missed several broadcasts. The NBC radio network was swamped with letters asking for her, and when she recovered, the sponsor agreed to pay her radio salary. It was during this period that Vallee's second wife, Fay Webb, sued him for divorce, charging that he was involved with Alice. (Vallee won the divorce settlement.) In the fall of 1933 Alice Faye (she had taken the surname not, as legend has it, because of entertainer Frank Fay, but because she thought it was pretty and that it suited her) made her recording debut with Rudy Vallee and His Connecticut Yankees doing a trio of vocals for Bluebird Records. One of the songs, "Happy Boy, Happy Girl," was a duet with Vallee. Later that year Vallee signed with Fox Pictures to star in GEORGE WHITE'S SCANDALS (1934) and he made sure Alice obtained a part in the musical. When his co-star, European Lillian Harvey, walked out over a dispute about the size of her role, Vallee convinced the studio to substitute Alice, who got to sing the song "Nasty Man." The *New York Herald Tribune* enthused, "Miss Faye reveals, in addition to considerable personal allure, a talent for projecting a hot song number that is extremely helpful to the work." Because she had done so well in her screen debut, the studio signed her to a long-term contract.

At the beginning of her Fox tenure, Alice was the leading lady in comedies with the overbearing comedy team of Mitchell and Durant for a trio of programmers: SHE LEARNED ABOUT SAILORS (1934), in which she sang "Here's the Key to My Heart"; 365 NIGHTS IN HOLLYWOOD (1934), which had her performing "Yes to You" and "My Future Star"; and MUSIC IS MAGIC (1935), in which she had a decent dramatic role as an aspiring actress who sings "Honey Chile." She was also featured in the gangster melodrama NOW I'LL TELL (1934) singing "Foolin' with Other Women's Men" and she played a vaudevillian in GEORGE WHITE'S 1935 SCANDALS (1935), singing "According to the Moonlight" and "Oh, I Didn't Know," which she recorded for the American Record Corporation (ARC). On loan to Paramount, Alice co-starred with Frances Langford and Patsy Kelly as a trio of singers seeking radio stardom in EVERY NIGHT AT EIGHT (1935). In this bouncy musical she vocalized "Speaking Confidentially" and "I Feel a Song Coming On." She also made the elaborate backstage musical KING OF BURLESQUE (1936) with Warner Baxter, singing "I'm Shooting High," "Spreadin' Rhythm Around," "I Love to Ride Horses," and "I've Got My Fingers Crossed" (all recorded for ARC). It was at this point that Zanuck began softening her brassy screen image. As a result, she was cast in the Shirley Temple opus POOR LITTLE RICH GIRL (1936) as a singer who becomes a star with her partner (Jack Haley) *after* they add orphan Shirley to their act. Alice sang "Military Man" and "But Definitely," and joined Temple on "You Gotta Eat Your Spinach." With the slight change in her looks, Alice became far more down to earth and thus easier to cast in girl-next-door parts. It did a great deal to heighten her appeal to moviegoers.

SING, BABY, SING (1936) was Faye's tenth movie and the one in which she received her first star billing, as an actress in love with a has-been performer (Adolphe Menjou). She sang the catchy title song, "Love Will Tell," and "You Turned the Tables on Me." This film also featured another studio hopeful, singer Tony Martin. She then returned to supporting Shirley Temple in STOWAWAY (1936), which gave Faye one of her most memorable screen songs, "Goodnight, My Love" (which she recorded for Brunswick Records). For Brunswick she also waxed a trio of songs: "I've Got My Love to Keep Me Warm," "This Year's Kisses," and "Slumming on Park Avenue," from her next 20th Century–Fox film, ON THE AVENUE (1937). This film matched her with another blonde (Madeleine Carroll) and another crooner (Dick Powell). The delightful radio satire WAKE UP AND LIVE (1937) provided Faye with a rich score, including "Never in a Million Years," "It's Swell of You," "There's a Lull in My Life," and "Wake Up and Live," all of which were recorded for Brunswick. Because Darryl Zanuck decided he wanted to focus the talents of his singing stars on camera, he dictated that all studio stars refrain from making commercial records. As a result, Faye would not make another recording for more than a decade.

Alice Faye was now earning $2,000 weekly at Fox. She closed out 1937 in YOU CAN'T HAVE EVERYTHING as a playwright who makes her show a success. In it she and Tony Martin dueted on "Afraid to Dream" while Alice sang the title song, "Pardon Us We're in Love," and "Danger, Love at Work!" In YOU'RE A SWEETHEART, made on loan to Universal, she was the showgirl who warbled "My Fine Feathered Friend" (wearing feathers and crouched in a tree!), "So It's Love," and the enduring "You're a Sweetheart." In July 1937 Alice joined Hal Kemp and His Orchestra on his half-hour CBS radio show, "Music from Hollywood." Zanuck was annoyed and bought out her contract on the series by year's end; he had decided that she should be available professionally only to 20th Century–Fox. On September 3, 1937, she and Tony Martin were married in Yuma, Arizona.

Tony Martin was her co-star in the weak show business musical SALLY, IRENE AND MARY (1938), with Faye singing "Who Stole the Jam?," "Got My Mind on Music," and "This Is Where I Came In," and dueting with Martin on the forgettable "Half Moon on the Hudson." Cut from the final print were her song "Think Twice" and her dance to "Minuet in Jazz." Indicating her value to the studio, Alice's last two 1938 features were big-budget productions and helped to put her in the top ten at the box office (as she would be the next year too). IN OLD CHICAGO and ALEXANDER'S RAGTIME BAND, both with Tyrone Power and Don Ameche, established her as one of filmdom's most popular female stars. In the former, a historical drama set in the 1870s, she played a cabaret singer who performed "Carry Me Back to Old Virginny" and "I've Taken a Fancy to You." The $750,000 sequence of the burning of Chicago was the movie's highlight. (Before starting IN OLD CHICAGO, Faye had said of Zanuck, "he has given me a type of role which I had not expected for at least a couple more years. It is my one big chance, and I'm just in a jittery state of nerves and elation.") ALEXANDER'S RAGTIME BAND was also a period piece (spanning 1911–38) in which, as a musical comedy star, she performed such Irving Berlin tunes as "Now It Can Be Told" (written for the film), the title song, "When the Midnight Choo-Choo Leaves for Alabam'," "Everybody's Doing It," "What'll I Do," and "All Alone." Almost lost in the shuffle of twenty-six Berlin melodies was Ethel Merman in a secondary role.

After two such well-received projects, it was a waste that 20th Century–Fox cast Alice as a flyer (!) in the mediocre TAIL SPIN (1939), in which she sang "Are You in the Mood for Mischief?" and "Go in and out the Window," the latter of which was cut from release prints. Far better was her Fanny Brice imitation in the delightful ROSE OF WASHINGTON SQUARE (1939), in which she sang the title song, "My Man," and "I Never Knew Heaven Could Speak." However, her renditions of "I'll See You in My Dreams," "Avalon," and "I'm Always Chasing Rainbows" were deleted from the final print. Fanny Brice sued the studio over this thinly veiled account of her life, which led to curtailed distribution of the musical. HOLLYWOOD CAVALCADE (1939) was Alice's first Technicolor movie. It was a fast-paced look at the history of filmmaking as seen through the career of a once-great director (Don Ameche) who was patterned on D. W. Griffith and Mack Sennett. Alice played Molly Adair, the girl he makes a star. (The character was based on Mabel Normand.) Fox had Alice close out the year in a mishmash called BARRICADE (1939), which had begun two years before as THE GIRL FROM BROOKLYN. It was a straight drama in which she was the woman falsely accused of murder. Her one song ("There'll Be Other Nights") was filmed but not used.

During the period from 1940 (the year she divorced Tony Martin) to 1943, Alice Faye starred in eight pictures for 20th Century–Fox and these are the movies for which she is best remembered. Mostly in Technicolor, they were breezy romantic comedies with flashy musical numbers, and her co-stars included Don Ameche, Betty Grable, John Payne, Cesar Romero, Carmen Miranda, and Jack Oakie. The first of these, LITTLE OLD NEW YORK (1940), a biopic about steamboat inventor Robert Fulton (Richard Greene), was the least memorable; romantic lead Alice sang only "Who Is the Beau of the Belle of New York." Far more indelible was her work in the title role of LILLIAN RUSSELL (1940), an entertaining look at the Gay Nineties entertainer and her romances with Edward Solomon (Don Ameche), Alexander Moore (Henry Fonda), and Diamond Jim Brady (Edward Arnold). Alice sang "Come Down Ma' Evening Star," "Ma' Blushin' Rosie," and "Blue Lovebird." Then she and Betty Grable, who became her close friend, were teamed in TIN PAN ALLEY (1940) as a sister act in the World War I era; this was also her first vehicle with John Payne. Among her numbers were the "Sheik of Araby" routine with Grable and "You Say the Sweetest Things Baby" with Payne and Jack Oakie. Alice appeared with Don Ameche for the sixth and last time, while working with Carmen Miranda for the first time, in the Technicolor musical THAT NIGHT IN RIO (1941), with the star singing "They Met in Rio" and "Boa Noite." A history of radio broadcasting was the plot crux of THE GREAT AMERICAN BROADCAST (1941) with Alice cast as speakeasy singer Vicki Adams who weds radio pioneer Rix Martin (John Payne) and becomes a big star in the medium. She sang "Where Are You," "I Take to You," and "Long Ago Last Night."

On May 12, 1941, in Endenado, Mexico, Alice married bandleader-actor Phil Harris, whom she had met when she was with Rudy Vallee's musical group. When it was discovered that Harris' divorce from his first wife was not final, the couple remarried on September 22, 1941—this time in Galveston, Texas. Faye said prophetically, "My career for the first time in my life doesn't mean a thing to me. . . . I hung onto my job because I always had an idea I was going to need it some time. But now I know I'll always be taken care of as a wife should be." WEEKEND IN HAVANA (1941) had Faye again working with John Payne and Carmen Miranda in the grandeur of Technicolor in which she performed "Tropical Magic" (a well-staged production number) and "Romance and Rhumba." However, another routine, "The Man with the Lollipop Song," was snipped out. On May 19, 1942, Alice gave birth to her first child, Alice. In this period she was replaced by Gene Tierney in BELLE STARR (1941), by Rita Hayworth in MY GAL SAL (1942), and by Betty Grable in SPRINGTIME IN THE ROCKIES (1942). Faye explained her priorities: "I have always felt that motherhood is infinitely more important than any career."

The studio eventually persuaded her to return to films. She was again paired with John Payne and Jack Oakie in HELLO, FRISCO, HELLO (1943), a gaudy Technicolor opus set on the Barbary Coast of the early 1900s. The movie provided Alice with another memorable song, "You'll Never Know," which won an Oscar. She also performed "Why Do They Pick on Me?" and "By the Light of the Silvery Moon." Alice repeated her role of Trudy Evans on "Lux Radio Theatre" and "Showtime." The film grossed $3.4 million. Faye went contemporary in THE GANG'S ALL HERE, issued at Christmas 1943. She and Carmen Miranda were showgirls out for romance with Alice singing "No Love, No Nothin'," "A Journey to a Star," and "The Polka Dot Polka." In the spring of 1944 Alice became a mother again with the birth of a second daughter, Phyllis, and she dropped out of THE DOLLY SISTERS (1945) with Betty Grable and was replaced by June Haver. Alice did appear as herself entertaining soldiers in FOUR JILLS IN A JEEP in 1944, reprising "You'll Never Know"; the black-and-white picture proved to be her last musical while under contract to the studio.

"I became tired of playing those big musicals. . . . I felt if I could make pictures I'd be proud to show my kids some day, that would be different. . . . I wear simple dresses and tailored knits and, above all, I'm a real person—a human being—a woman with a heart.

John Payne, Alice Faye, Betty Grable, and Jack Oakie in TIN PAN ALLEY (1940)

Not just a painted, doll-like dummy." So commented Alice Faye to columnist Hedda Hopper about her role in the star melodrama FALLEN ANGEL (1945), geared by the studio as a successor to its LAURA (1944). It was the first film under her new 20th Century–Fox contract. She was the wealthy woman romanced and married by a heel (Dana Andrews) who really craves a slatternly waitress (Linda Darnell). Alice was simply too young and attractive for the heavily dramatic part and her only song, "Slowly," was deleted from the film. The brooding *film noir* picture was not a success. Faye later reflected, "I had some great scenes in it, but they ended up on the cutting-room floor. That was when they were building up Linda Darnell, and they threw the picture to her."

Having come to a parting with Fox—she never forgave Darryl Zanuck for his "betrayal"—Alice withdrew from picturemaking. (Over the years, 20th Century–Fox offered her roles in such films as STATE FAIR [1945], A TREE GROWS IN BROOKLYN [1945], GREENWICH VILLAGE [1945], SWEET ROSIE O'GRADY [1945], THE RAZOR'S EDGE [1946], A LETTER TO THREE WIVES [1949], WABASH AVENUE [1950], and I'LL NEVER FORGET YOU [1951], but she was not interested.) From 1946 to 1954 Alice co-starred with her husband on the popular Sunday night radio comedy "The Phil Harris–Alice Faye Show" on NBC with Alice sometimes singing on the broadcasts. She and Harris also guested on such programs as "American Red Cross," "The Bob Hope Show," and the twentieth anniversary episode of "One Man's Family" in the spring of 1952. She and Phil also cut a record for RCA Victor, "The Letter."

Apart from her radio show, Alice made only occasional public appearances, such as one on her husband's TV program in 1959. However, in 1962, with her children grown, she returned to films, playing the mother in 20th Century–Fox's mundane remake of STATE FAIR. She sang "Never Say No to a Man," "Our State Fair," and "It's the Little Things in Texas," all of which appeared on the Dot Records soundtrack album. *Time* magazine observed of her comeback, "[she] looks refreshingly real—she is middle-aged now, and she doesn't try to hide it." That year she also recorded an LP for Reprise called *Alice Faye Sings Her Famous Movie Hits* on which she did a dozen songs from her films. (The LP was reissued in the 1970s by Stanyan Records as *Alice Faye's Greatest Hits*.)

During the 1960s Alice appeared on such TV shows as "The Red Skelton Show" and "The Hollywood Palace" and late in 1973 she returned to the stage with John Payne in the nostalgic revival of *Good News*. After a lengthy pre-Broadway engagement, the show opened in New York in December 1974, with Gene Nelson as her new co-star. The next summer she toured with Don Ameche in the musical. Her Reprise recording of "You'll Never Know" was used in the movie ALICE DOESN'T LIVE HERE ANYMORE (1975) and in 1976 she was among the many former luminaries who did a cameo in Paramount's WON TON TON, THE DOG WHO SAVED HOLLYWOOD—she was a studio gate secretary. In 1978 she was seen in the family film THE MAGIC OF LASSIE as a waitress. Said Alice, "It was fun to put on the eyelashes again."

In 1980 Alice guested on the ABC-TV show "The Love Boat" and during the 1980s she became a spokesperson for Pfizer Inc.'s "Help Yourself to Good Health" program, lecturing to senior citizens about staying fit. As a part of her talk she appeared in the Pfizer short film WE STILL ARE (1988), which examined her career and used clips from WAKE UP AND LIVE and WEEKEND IN HAVANA. In 1989 her memoirs, *Growing Older-Staying Young*, were published. On June 3, 1989, she received an honorary degree from Vincennes University in Indiana where, along with Phil Harris, she was a given a Doctorate in the Performing Arts.

## Filmography

George White's Scandals (Fox, 1934)
She Learned About Sailors (Fox, 1934)
Now I'll Tell [When New York Sleeps] (Fox, 1934)
365 Nights in Hollywood (Fox, 1934)
George White's 1935 Scandals (Fox, 1935)
Music Is Magic (Fox, 1935)
Every Night at Eight (Par, 1935)
Poor Little Rich Girl (20th–Fox, 1936)
Sing, Baby, Sing (20th–Fox, 1936)
King of Burlesque (20th–Fox, 1936)
Stowaway (20th–Fox, 1936)
On the Avenue (20th–Fox, 1937)
Wake Up and Live (20th–Fox, 1937)
You Can't Have Everything (20th–Fox, 1937)
You're a Sweetheart (Univ, 1937)
In Old Chicago (20th–Fox, 1938)
Sally, Irene and Mary (20th–Fox, 1938)
Alexander's Ragtime Band (20th–Fox, 1938)
Tail Spin (20th–Fox, 1939)
Hollywood Cavalcade (20th–Fox, 1939)

Rose of Washington Square (20th–Fox, 1939)
Barricade (20th–Fox, 1939)
Lillian Russell (20th–Fox, 1940)
Little Old New York (20th–Fox, 1940)
Tin Pan Alley (20th–Fox, 1940)
That Night in Rio (20th–Fox, 1941)
The Great American Broadcast (20th–Fox, 1941)
Weekend in Havana (20th–Fox, 1941)
Hello, Frisco, Hello (20th–Fox, 1943)
The Gang's All Here [The Girls He Left Behind] (20th–Fox, 1943)
Four Jills in a Jeep (20th–Fox, 1944)
Fallen Angel (20th–Fox, 1945)
State Fair (20th–Fox, 1962)
Won Ton Ton, The Dog Who Saved Hollywood (Par, 1976)
The Magic of Lassie (International Picture Show, 1978)
Every Girl Should Have One (Unk, 1979)
We Still Are (Pfizer, 1988) (s)

## Broadway Plays

George White's Scandals of 1931 (1931)
Good News (1974) (revival)

## Radio Series

The Fleischmann's Hour (NBC, 1931–34)
Music from Hollywood (CBS, 1937)

The Phil Harris–Alice Faye Show (NBC, 1946–54)

## Album Discography

Alexander's Ragtime Band (Hollywood
Soundstage 406) [ST]

Alexander's Ragtime Band (Pelican 132) [ST/R]

Alice Faye (Curtain Calls 100/3)

Alice Faye and Phil Harris (Radio Archives 101)

Alice Faye in Hollywood, 1934–37 (Col CL-
3068, Col Special Products 3068)

Alice Faye on the Air (Totem 1011)

Alice Faye on the Air, Vol. 2 (Totem 1032)

Alice Faye on the Air—Rare Radio Recordings
(Sandy Hook 2020)

Alice Faye: Outtakes and Alternates, Vol. 1
(Limited Edition, AF-1)

Alice Faye: Outtakes and Alternates, Vol. 2
(Limited Edition, AF-2)

Alice Faye Sings Her Famous Movie Hits
(Reprise 6029/96029)

The Alice Faye Songbook (Amalgamated 146)

Alice Faye's Greatest Hits (Stanyon 10072)

Every Night at Eight (Caliban 6043)

The Gang's All Here (CIF 3003) [ST]

The Gang's All Here (Sandy Hook 2009)
[ST/R]

Good News (SA 101-104) [OC]

Hello, Frisco, Hello (Caliban 6005, Hollywood
Soundstage 5015) [ST]

Hello, Frisco, Hello (Pelican 126) [ST/R]

Lillian Russell (Caliban 6016) [ST]

Music Is Magic (Caliban 6047) [ST]

Music, Music, Music (Take Two TT-302)

On the Avenue (Hollywood Soundstage 401)
[ST]

Rose of Washington Square (Caliban 6002) [ST]

Sally, Irene and Mary (Caliban 6031) [ST]

Sing, Baby, Sing (Caliban 6029) [ST]

The Songs of Harry Warren (Citadel 6004)

State Fair (Dot 9011/29011) [ST]

Tin Pan Alley (Caliban 6003) [ST]

Wake Up and Live (Hollywood Soundstage 403)
[ST]

Weekend in Havana/That Night in Rio (Curtain
Calls 100/14) [ST]

You Can't Have Everything (Titania 508) [ST]

You're a Sweetheart (Scarce Rarities 5502) [ST]

# SUSANNA FOSTER

HOLLYWOOD IS A WORLD WHERE THE "HAS-BEEN" IS NOTORIOUSLY prevalent. Hundreds of pretty ingenues have been thrust aside by the studios and their production mills after their box-office potential either faded or failed to be exploited. During the late 1930s and early 1940s, blonde Susanna Foster was a very bright light on the Hollywood scene. The star of a dozen films, she not only possessed good looks but was also an accomplished actress and a very fine soprano. However, it was Foster who turned her back on Hollywood, and *not* vice versa. When her studio contract ended in 1945, she soon left the film capital for good, never wanting to return. She said, "I want to do what I want to do and that has nothing to do with show business."

Born Susanna DeLee Flanders Larson in Chicago, Illinois, on December 6, 1924, she was still an infant when her family moved to Minneapolis, where she went to school. Gifted as a singer and quite bright in school, young Susanna began to be heard on local radio programs, as well as to sing at theaters and conventions in the Minneapolis–St. Paul area. Her idol was Jeanette MacDonald and she practiced imitating that famed songstress. Susanna was impressive enough that Merle Potter, drama editor of the *Minneapolis Star*, and orchestra leader Carl Johnson persuaded her to make test recordings (including "Italian Street Song" and "Ah, Sweet Mystery of Life") which were dispatched to Metro-Goldwyn-Mayer studios. Without seeing her in person, the studio signed her to a one-year contract. Susanna and her family, which included two younger sisters, moved to Hollywood in 1935, but an intended starring vehicle for Susanna, B ABOVE HIGH C, never materialized. When her year's contract was up, the studio dropped her. (She had refused their offer to star in a planned production of NATIONAL VELVET because the story did not allow her to sing.)

It was at this point that Susanna's parents separated, and the children and their mother had to struggle to survive financially. Nevertheless, Susanna studied voice with Gilda Marchetti, who helped her student strengthen her lower tones. Through Marchetti's brother Milo, Susanna later earned an audition at Paramount Pictures, where she was signed to a contract. Milo Marchetti became her agent.

In her three years at Paramount, Susanna Foster, as she was now called, appeared in only four feature films, beginning with THE GREAT VICTOR HERBERT, produced in 1939, when she was fifteen. Her screen debut, however, was a good one, for the project provided her the opportunity to sing "Kiss Me Again" (hitting B flat above high C). In this biography of the great operetta composer, played by Walter Connolly, she was cast as the daughter of Allan Jones and Mary Martin. The *New York Times* predicted: "a charming juvenile songstress, Susanna Foster, is a newcomer who is going to be very bearable to watch." On the other hand, Susanna, who was very mature for her age, was unimpressed with her noteworthy screen debut. She would recall, "When I did see THE GREAT VICTOR HERBERT, and finally saw myself on the screen, all I could think was, 'My God! I'm not Jeanette MacDonald!'"

Allan Jones was also her co-star in Susanna's second picture, THE HARD-BOILED CANARY (later retitled THERE'S MAGIC IN MUSIC) (1941), in which she portrayed a hard-boiled little burlesque chirp whom Jones takes to a children's recreational camp. In 1941 Paramount released a follow-up to the decade-old success SKIPPY called GLAMOUR BOY. The star of the earlier film, Jackie Cooper, recreated his most famous role, and Skippy, now a soda jerk, romanced Susanna. "Love Is Such an Old Fashioned Thing," "The Magic of Magnolias," and "Sempre Libera" from Verdi's *La Traviata* were sung by Susanna in the movie. Her Paramount finale was a guest bit in STAR SPANGLED RHYTHM in 1942. The studio simply did not know what to do with her, and much of her last year under contract was spent in idleness. Susanna, always very outspoken (she was dubbed Paramount's "Impulsive Rebel" by one fan magazine), asked for her studio release.

After leaving Paramount, Susanna, who now had Myron Selznick as her agent, was quickly hired by Universal, which was the home of much musical talent in the early 1940s. Moreover, Universal viewed Susanna as a good weapon to keep their reigning soprano star (Deanna Durbin) in line. Susanna would appear in eight productions for the studio and they showcased her far better than had Paramount. THE PHANTOM OF THE OPERA (1943), the expensive remake of the famous 1925 Lon Chaney silent classic, was her initial Universal feature and the best film of her career. Filmed in gorgeous Technicolor with handsome production values, this Academy Award–winning opus presented her as Christine Dubois, a beautiful Parisian opera singer who is lusted after by the Phantom (Claude Rains) and romanced by her handsome leading man (Nelson Eddy). The film allowed both Susanna and Eddy ample occasion to sing opera (based on the music of Chopin and Tchaikovsky) and both were in top form in these musical sequences. Overall, though, the remake was not up to the standards of the Chaney version in the terror department. But the production won very favorable reviews for Rains, Eddy, and Susanna Foster. She was soon known as "the Universal Nightingale." However, the studio did not know how to follow up on Susanna's success in THE PHANTOM OF THE OPERA. Said Susanna, "They had a leading woman in me after PHANTOM, and most of what they gave me to do had no more to do with my PHANTOM role than the man in the moon."

Universal had the notion of teaming Susanna with Donald O'Connor, turning them into a road company version of MGM's Mickey Rooney and Judy Garland. Thus she was cast in TOP MAN (1943), about a teenager (Donald O'Connor) who takes over the leadership of his family when his father (Richard Dix) is recalled to active duty. To aid the war effort he and girlfriend Susanna put on a talent show at a nearby factory. The film gave her the chance to sing the popular tune "Wrap Your Troubles in Dreams" and it also brought Lillian Gish back to the screen as O'Connor's mother. Of this project, the *Los Angeles Examiner* observed, "Susanna Foster . . . is a pretty fancy dish to be high schooling around in an O'Connor film. From Nelson Eddy to Donald is quite a thing, if you know what we mean. . . ."

For her third Universal excursion, Susanna was co-starred with Boris Karloff in THE CLIMAX (1944), which deliberately paralleled THE PHANTOM OF THE OPERA. Here she is pretty opera singer Angela, who resembles another performer, killed years before by mad doctor Hohner (Karloff). Again the production was in color with posh sets and Susanna enjoyed many opera sequences, plus singing "Some Day I'll Know" and "Now at Last." Turhan Bey played her romantic interest and *Variety* reported that she "is in good voice with the several numbers handed her for delivery." Susanna was then third-billed as singer Peggy Fleming in BOWERY TO BROADWAY (1944), a musical drama about rival beergarden owners (Jack Oakie, Donald Cook) joining forces to produce Broadway musicals. Susanna was featured singing "There'll Always Be a Moon." Next she had a cameo as herself in the Hollywood Victory Committee scene in FOLLOW THE BOYS (1944). For her fourth and final release of 1944 she was paired again with Donald O'Connor in THIS IS THE LIFE, actually made in the summer of 1943. But this time she had a substantial role as fickle

Jonathan Hale, Susanna Foster, Donald O'Connor, and Dorothy Peterson in
THIS IS THE LIFE (1944)

Angela, the singer who deserts her boyfriend (O'Connor) when she becomes attracted to a mature rival (Patric Knowles). She sang "With a Song in My Heart" and "L'Amour, Toujours, l'Amour." Increasingly, Susanna was unhappy about the quality of her screen assignments and, being vocal about it, became unpopular with the studio hierarchy. She also, following the advice of Universal peer Maria Montez, demanded a raise from the front office, which agreed reluctantly to give her a $5,000 bonus for each picture she made thereafter.

Universal casually thrust Susanna into the "B" Western FRISCO SAL (1945), playing a young woman who goes West to locate her brother's killer. She sang "Beloved," "Good Little Bad Little Lady," and "I Just Go In," but the Technicolor trappings promised originally when the film was announced as FRISCO KATE failed to materialize. Her final Universal feature—and what proved to be her last film—was THAT NIGHT WITH YOU (1945), a screwball comedy which cast Susanna as a bubbly, ambitious singer who informs a producer (Franchot Tone) that she is his offspring from a one-day marriage. In it she performed five numbers, including "Once upon a Dream" (the film's working title) and a distaff version of arias from *The Barber of Seville*. The story ends happily with her succeeding on Broadway, wedding her boyfriend (David Bruce), and having many children. Off camera, Susanna was very unhappy with her role in THAT NIGHT WITH YOU. "Imagine—singing a female version of *The Barber of Seville*! And that makeup—my eyebrows all plucked out and pencilled on, a toupee widow's peak on me, a lipstick mouth that went all over my face. I looked like a made-up doll."

While working at Universal, the practical (and unhappy) Susanna had trained as a nurse's aide at the Los Angeles County Hospital and graduated with an aide's license. She then borrowed nearly $20,000 from Universal and went to New York and then to Europe to study voice. Upon her return, she repaid the loan. By now, however, Susanna—always pushed by her parents to further a show business career she did not want—was totally sick of studio politics. She refused to be cast in any of the roles offered her, including that of the maid in the Sonja Henie vehicle THE COUNTESS OF MONTE CRISTO (1948); she was replaced by Olga San Juan (who also replaced her in ONE TOUCH OF VENUS, 1948, starring Ava Gardner). Said the sharp-tongued Susanna, "It was the same old thing. They wanted me to sing while Sonja Henie skated . . . she comes up to here on me. She should have been the maid!" Universal, which had undergone corporate changes, gladly terminated her contract.

Now at liberty, Susanna appeared in the West Coast production of *Naughty Marietta* and fell in love with her co-star, Wilbur Evans. The two were married on October 23, 1948, in Evans' home town (Philadelphia) at the city hall and honeymooned in Atlantic City. Evans was nineteen years older than his twenty-four-year-old bride. Eventually they had two sons, Michael David (born in 1950) and Philip (born in 1952), and together they appeared in operetta with the Cleveland Light Opera Company and headed a touring company of *The Merry Widow*. Their publicity billed the husband-and-wife duo as "The Singing Lunts" and "America's Singing Sweethearts." They relocated to England when Evans was signed to appear opposite Mary Martin (and later Julie Wilson) in the London production of *South Pacific*. They returned to America when Evans was hired to play opposite Shirley Booth in the unsuccessful Broadway musical *By the Beautiful Sea* (1954). In 1955 Susanna sang the leads in *Brigadoon* and *Show Boat* at the Valley Forge Music Fair in Pennsylvania where her husband was the director. The next year the couple went through a bitter, much publicized divorce.

To support her sons, Susanna held a variety of low-paying jobs in New York City, where she had settled. She even was heard on radio asking listeners for the whereabouts of her ex-spouse and for a part-time position to supplement her daytime employment at the brokerage firm of Merrill, Lynch, Pierce, Fenner & Smith. The feud was still in the news in April 1962 when Evans informed a court that his ex-wife had turned "beatnik," that she had squandered a $25,000 trust fund and that her apartment was "slovenly, slipshod." Things continued to spiral downhill for Susanna, who insisted, "I want to do what I want to do and that does not include anything in show business." She added, "I made a dozen pictures in Hollywood . . . and only in one did I approach—even remotely approach—being in the least satisfied. That was PHANTOM OF THE OPERA. . . . It, at least, had some taste." By the mid-1970s, Susanna, who had been reduced to being (temporarily) a check-in attendant at a Manhattan Turkish bath, returned to Hollywood—this time by bus. There was no welcoming committee to greet her. She later resided in North Hollywood and worked at a non–show business job.

In the spring of 1989, just as a version of Broadway's *The Phantom of the Opera* was opening in Los Angeles, there were newspaper accounts of how the ex-co-star of 1943's THE PHANTOM OF THE OPERA was impoverished and forced to live in her car. When ex-child stars Jane Withers and Margaret O'Brien read of this, they came to Susanna Foster's financial rescue.

## Filmography

The Great Victor Herbert (Par, 1939)
The Hard-Boiled Canary [There's Magic in Music] (Par, 1941)
Glamour Boy (Par, 1941)
Star Spangled Rhythm (Par, 1942)
The Phantom of the Opera (Univ, 1943)
Top Man (Univ, 1943)

The Climax (Univ, 1944)
Bowery to Broadway (Univ, 1944)
Follow the Boys (Univ, 1944)
This Is the Life (Univ, 1944)
Frisco Sal (Univ, 1945)
That Night with You (Univ, 1945)

## Album Discography

The Phantom of the Opera (Sountrak 114) [ST]

The Phantom of the Opera (Mac/Eddy JN 124) [ST/R]

# CONNIE FRANCIS

WITH OVER EIGHTY-EIGHT MILLION RECORDS SOLD GLOBALLY, Connie Francis was long one of the world's most popular recording artists. In the late 1950s and early 1960s she reflected the youth pop music scene, belting out in her trademark contralto vibrato such hits as "Stupid Cupid," "Lipstick on Your Collar," "My Heart Has a Mind of Its Own," "Breakin' in a Brand New Broken Heart," and "Don't Break the Heart That Loves You." She first rose to popularity with an old standard, "Who's Sorry Now," and for five years was never off the charts. Of the hundreds of songs she recorded, she is most closely associated with "Where the Boys Are." The latter was the theme song of her first MGM movie (1960), in which she demonstrated a wonderful sense of comedy (like Judy Garland, whose successor she was proclaimed to be). It was a talent her subsequent films never capitalized on.

A songstress can be a teen queen for only so many years before maturity, changing musical styles, and—most of all—new talent crowds her from the throne. Connie Francis initially made a successful transition to the major cabaret circles and, if her recordings were no longer chart-breakers, she was certainly not forgotten. But then a series of highly publicized tragedies (her beloved Bobby Darin died; she was raped; her brother was murdered gangland style; she lost her voice temporarily) in the 1970s and 1980s transformed her into a figure warranting grand sympathy rather than high adulation. These experiences led to emotional breakdowns, followed by several comeback attempts, many of which were engineered by her long-time mentor and friend, Dick "American Bandstand" Clark. Each new emotional milestone in her seesawing life made her fans (now middle-aged) more aware how much time had elapsed since she and they were teenagers rocking at the hop.

She was born Concetta Constance Franconero on December 12, 1938, at St. James Hospital in Newark, New Jersey, the daughter of George Franconero and Ida (Ferrara) Franconero. Her father, the son of Italian immigrants, was a former dockworker turned roofing contractor. Two years later her brother, George, was born. Connie was brought up in Belleville, New Jersey, and later in Bloomfield. Because her father enjoyed playing the concertina, he had his daughter take lessons on a miniature accordion when she was three and a half years old. By the age of five she made her debut singing "O Sole Mio" at a school recital, and was soon singing and playing the accordion at community gatherings. When she was twelve, she was 4' 11" and weighed 135 pounds. As she recalls, "I played the accordion then and it was a good place to hide behind."

She had already appeared on Paul Whiteman's "TV Teen Club" (ABC-TV) which originated in Philadelphia. In December 1950 her father took her to New York to appear on "Arthur Godfrey's Talent Scouts" where, at Godfrey's suggestion, she adopted her stage name of Connie Francis. She won first prize that night. Later her father brought her to the attention of George Scheck, who produced a New York City–based TV show called "Star Time," which featured young talent. He was not interested in more kid singers but he was intrigued that she played the accordion. He hired her to be on his show, the start of a four-year run. Very soon after starting with Scheck, she happily dropped the accordion and concentrated on singing. (She would recall, "in 1967 there was a big flood in my basement and the accordion died.") During summers she performed in entertainments at Catskill resorts, sometimes working backstage as well. Having had a strict Catholic upbringing and an overprotective father, she was at a loss how to cope with her new, more permissive environment. "I never mixed socially with these other kids. I just sat around by myself and ate. . . ."

In June 1955 she graduated from high school (where she was an overachiever). George Scheck, now her manager, negotiated a contract for her with MGM Records after she had been rejected by several labels and had spent years making demos for music publishers. In a two-year period with MGM she recorded ten singles (including "Freddy"), but none of them became hits. Unconvinced that her career would ever become substantial, she enrolled at New York University, where she had a four-year scholarship. She quit after four months when she decided that show business must be her life. She auditioned for Broadway musicals (including *West Side Story*), clubs, and television, but no one was interested. She sang in cocktail lounges and second-rate clubs, usually chaperoned by one of her parents.

Through George Scheck, Connie had become acquainted with rising young singer Bobby Darin, when he and his partner tried to sell songs to Scheck for Connie to record. A deep romance developed between Francis and the arrogant, confident, talented Darin, but always her father stood between the two. It was the first time she had ever rebelled against parental control. Connie was torn between these two strong loyalties. Her father won out. In her autobiography, written many years later, she asks, "Why didn't my father want a relationship for me with someone he knew was going to be a winner?" Because she abided by her father's wishes, Darin finally broke with her. To ensure the tie was cut, her manipulative father pressured George Scheck, who was not only Darin's agent but also a father figure for the young man, to sever his bonds with the singer—which he did. Francis' abiding love for Darin would carry through his two marriages and his untimely death in 1973 and be an unresolved matter for her even today.

Meanwhile, Scheck finally negotiated some Hollywood interest in his client. However, because of her weight, Connie was not considered screen material and therefore made her film debut as the off-camera singing voice of Tuesday Weld in ROCK! ROCK! ROCK! (1956). It was a slapdash independent picture about a teenaged girl (Weld) wanting a new gown for the school prom and needing to raise money for the big purchase. Of the rock 'n' roll talent involved, which included The Moonglows and Alan Freed, *Variety* thought

LaVern Baker, Chuck Berry, and Frankie Lymon and The Teenagers were okay. The trade paper added, "Talent runs out of class after that, except for maybe Connie Francis, who does the off-screen vocalling for Tuesday Weld."

Alan Freed (of ROCK! ROCK! ROCK!) was more successful as a New York City radio disc jockey, and in the summer of 1957, he began a four-week series called "The Big Beat" on ABC-TV. Connie was on the first show (July 12, 1957), along with the Everly Brothers, the Billy Williams Quartet, Ferlin Husky, and others. (Later guests included Bobby Darin.) For her final MGM recording session, her father convinced her to sing one of his favorite old songs, "Who's Sorry Now," using a contemporary beat. Released in November 1957, the song went nowhere until it was plugged by Dick Clark on his "American Bandstand" TV show in January 1958. It moved onto the charts in March and remained there for fifteen weeks in 1958, climbing to fourth position. It sold over a million copies. Meanwhile, Connie had returned to Hollywood for another movie quickie, JAMBOREE (1957), made by the producers of ROCK! ROCK! ROCK! This time, however, she was in front of the black-and-white cameras, along with a horde of other new rock 'n' roll talent (including Frankie Avalon, whom she had once briefly dated, Carl Perkins, and The Four Coins) and assorted disc jockeys (including Dick Clark). For 20th Century–Fox's Western movie spoof THE SHERIFF OF FRACTURED JAW (1958), starring Jayne Mansfield and Kenneth More, Connie provided the vocals for a few song numbers which buxomy Mansfield lip-synched.

Connie recorded more hits, using such young song writers as Jack Keller, Neil Sedaka, and Howard Greenfield. She was on the charts in 1958 with several numbers: "I'm Sorry I Made You Cry," "Fallin'," and "My Happiness." She was a frequent guest on "American Bandstand" and soon began crossing over into adult variety TV programming ("The Ed Sullivan Show," teamed on one occasion with Bobby Darin; "The Perry Como Show"; and others) as a guest performer. She was a regular on "The Jimmie Rodgers Show" (NBC-TV) during its March to September 1959 run. In addition, she continued to play nightclubs; she performed at Carnegie Hall that November; and, as her record sales increased, she began concert tours around the world, including Australia, the Continent, and the Far East. Meanwhile, she had been refining her figure, profile, and coiffure.

Her song "Mama" rose to number nine on the charts in the spring of 1960, but it was "My Heart Has a Mind of Its Own" that was her first number one hit (in September 1960), supplanting Chubby Checker's "The Twist" from the top spot. It also made her the first female singer to have two consecutive singles (the other was "Everybody's Somebody's Fool") reach the first position on the charts. By then, another division of MGM, MGM Pictures, and producer Joe Pasternak had cast her in WHERE THE BOYS ARE (1960), a youth comedy focusing on the annual college student invasion of Fort Lauderdale, Florida, during Easter break. Filled with popular and attractive young performers (George Hamilton, Yvette Mimieux, Dolores Hart), the film featured Connie as a practical-minded whiz, full of self-deprecating humor and thrilled to be wanted by myopic Frank Gorshin. The picture was bright, topical, and entertaining and, even if conventionally executed, was very popular with young moviegoers. One of the picture's highlights was Connie's singing of the title tune, a song she had persuaded Pasternak could be written in four days by her New York friends Neil Sedaka and Howard Greenfield. *Variety* decided she sang her two numbers (title tune and "Turn on the Sunshine") with "zip and style."

Having become more sophisticated in her wardrobe and makeup, Connie was now a top club attraction globally, earning about $1 million in 1961. She was the subject of "Person to Person" (CBS-TV) and "This Is Your Life" (NBC-TV), and on September 13, 1961, she starred in her own TV special on ABC. Her managers merchandised her image in every conceivable outlet from sweaters to diaries and charm bracelets. Although now over twenty-one, she still lived at home (in Bloomfield, New Jersey) with her parents. Her father, retired from the roofing business, controlled the four music publishing companies she owned. She won a variety of awards, from being named Most Programmed Vocalist of the Year by *Billboard* magazine to being dubbed Best Female Singer of the Year by *Cashbox* magazine. Four years in a row she was named Best Female Singer of the Year by "American Bandstand." She was a rarity in a field dominated by young male singers (Elvis Presley, Bobby Darin, Rick Nelson, Frankie Avalon, Tommy Sands).

Paula Prentiss, Janis Paige, Dany Robin, and Connie Francis in
FOLLOW THE BOYS (1963)

One of the most clever merchandising gambits used by Connie Francis was to record a number of singles and albums of songs in foreign languages. In 1960 her albums *Italian Favorites* and *More Italian Favorites* were in the top ten on the charts. She soon produced a string of multilingual albums with assorted ethnic themes; each one featured an album cover photograph of her in appropriate native garb. The ploy sold lots of records and made her an international favorite. These records did much more for her than her paltry feature films for MGM. FOLLOW THE BOYS (1963) attempted to duplicate WHERE THE BOYS ARE, but this time set on the Riviera. It was an anemic romance and an unfunny comedy. Besides performing the title tune (which rose to number seventeen on the charts), she sang "Italian Lullabye." LOOKING FOR LOVE (1964), produced by Joe Pasternak, cast her as a switchboard operator with her heart set on capturing Jim Hutton's affections. Johnny Carson, Danny Thomas, George Hamilton, and others made pointless cameo appearances. Her best number was the title tune, and with Thomas she dueted "I Can't Believe That You're in Love with Me." The next year, she showed up in an impoverished remake of the Judy Garland–Mickey Rooney GIRL CRAZY (1943), refurbished as WHEN THE BOYS MEET THE GIRLS (1965). As always she shone when doing comedy dialogue, but there was no chemistry between Francis and her leading man (Harve Presnell). The guest star roster included Louis Armstrong, Liberace, and Herman's Hermits. Besides the title song (by Jack Keller and Howard Greenfield), she sang George and Ira Gershwin's "But Not for Me" and harmonized "I Got Rhythm" with Presnell and Louis Armstrong. It was the inglorious end of her movie career.

By the mid-1960s the British invasion of singers had changed the American musical scene. Connie's last charted song was "Be Anything" in the late spring of 1964. She performed for several years at the Sahara Hotel in Las Vegas (in 1967 she was named Best Female Entertainer in Las Vegas). During 1967 she had cosmetic nasal surgery that left her with the side effect that she could not sing in air-conditioned facilities. She underwent another operation. Thereafter, as she recalls, "I went into a recording studio and panicked. It sounded like someone else's voice. I had a range of seven notes. I had no vibrato. I felt like a surgeon who had his hands cut off." She had a nervous breakdown.

In subsequent years she was twice married and twice divorced. She made unspectacular comeback attempts. She was championed by Dick Clark, who invited her to guest on his special "Dick Clark Presents the Rock 'n' Roll Years" (ABC-TV, September 27, 1973). By 1974 she was married to Joseph Garzilli, who was in the travel business. She had suffered three miscarriages and was seeking to adopt a baby. On November 7, 1974, she was performing at the Westbury Music Fair (Westbury, Long Island). She had just learned that there was a baby boy available for adoption and she intended to become the child's mother. After singing on stage that night she returned to her motel room where in the early morning hours of November 8 she was held at knife point for two-and-a-half hours and raped. The felony received worldwide attention and resulted in Francis' $5 million suit against the motel which was reduced to $2.5 million in court and which she settled for $1.5 million. Her attacker was never found. The trauma of that event and its aftermath halted Connie's career yet again. She adopted that little boy, named Joey, who became the focus of her life, especially after her separation, reconciliation, and eventual divorce from Garzilli.

Living on past earnings and record royalties, she remained mostly out of the limelight. In the fall of 1978 she was a much-heralded guest on "Dick Clark's Live Wednesday" (NBC-TV), singing a medley of her hits. Unknown to viewers, her performance "was all tricks" done in the engineer's booth. Because of her severe vocalizing problems, she had prerecorded the songs and then lip-synched them on the air. She did not know how else to get through the ordeal. In 1980 she made a new album in England. She claimed the songs were "done four bars at a time." In November 1981, she was again at the Westbury Music Fair singing her old hits ("Stupid Cupid," "Who's Sorry Now," "Where the Boys Are") and such personally meaningful newer songs as "I Will Survive" and "I've Made It Through the Rain." She brought seven-year-old Joey on stage and she told the audience, "I'm rusty. I'm klutzy. You forget a lot in seven years. I'm an amateur. I have to start all over again." This time she was not staying at a motel, but was being driven back to her Essex Falls, New Jersey, home nightly.

On March 6, 1981, her forty-year-old brother, George, a former law partner of New Jersey Governor Brendan Byrne, was gunned down in front of his home. Having endured criminal charges of racketeering himself, he had been aiding a federal investigation of mob infiltration into the state's banking industry. From that tragedy, Francis claimed she gained new strength. For her, it was "the turning point. Suddenly I had a whole family I was responsible for. My mother and father were basket cases. I had to get my sister-in-law's house in order." It led her to realize, "I'm not a teen-age idol anymore and I'm not a child. I'm a woman with a story to tell." And she did just that in *Who's Sorry Now* (1984), her best-selling autobiography. After writing the book, she stated, "It helped me analyze my relationship with my father, which I really had never done fully before. It helped me put to bed my fear about the rape—it helped me to confront my brother's death."

In October 1985 she gave an elaborate two-performance concert in Los Angeles which included singing her old hits, new songs, clips from her movies and TV appearances, and a tribute to Bobby Darin. Once she overcame her initial mike fright, she was in excellent voice. She announced she was going to make new record albums. Instead, a few weeks later, she began a series of much-reported scenes of extravagant behavior and hysterical outbursts (on airplanes and in other public places) which led to her being committed for psychiatric evaluation in Los Angeles and, later, in Miami. In March 1989 she admitted to the media, as she began a singing engagement at the Diplomat Hotel in Hollywood, Florida, "For the last four years I've been in and out of mental institutions. It has been by far the most distressing experience of my life." She stated that for several of those years she had refused to take the medication prescribed by her doctors and that the resulting chemical imbalance had made her manic depressive. She then set out on her latest comeback bid, which included a successful engagement at the Aladdin Hotel in Las Vegas. The *Las Vegas Review-Journal* reported, "Her voice was powerful and clear, riding lyrical waves to those high, crisp tones . . . it was immediately obvious that the love and affection the crowd was showing her with a standing ovation would permit acceptance of whatever she chose to do onstage." During her act, she told her audience, "You've always let me know you were there, in good times and bad, and for that I'll always love you."

## Filmography

Rock! Rock! Rock! (Distributors Corp. of America, 1956) (voice only)
Jamboree (Col, 1957)
The Sheriff of Fractured Jaw (20th–Fox, 1958) (voice only)

Where the Boys Are (MGM, 1960)
Follow the Boys (MGM, 1963)
Looking for Love (MGM, 1964)
When the Boys Meet the Girls (MGM, 1965)

## TV Series

Star Time (NN, ca. 1951–55)
The Big Beat (ABC, 1957)

The Jimmie Rodgers Show (NBC, 1959)

## Album Discography

All Time International Hits (MGM E/SE-4298)
Award Winning Motion Pictures (MGM E/SE-4048)
Brylcream Presents Sing Along with Connie Francis and the Jordanaires (Mati-Mor 8002)
Christmas in My Heart (MGM E/SE-3792)
Connie and Clyde (MGM E/SE-4573)
Connie Francis (Metro M/S-519)
Connie Francis and the Kids Next Door (Leo the Lion 935)
Connie Francis Live at the Copa (MGM E/SE-3913)
Connie Francis Live at the Sahara in Las Vegas (MGM E/SE-4411)
Connie Francis Sings (MGM E/SE-4049)
Connie Francis Sings Bacharach and David (MGM E/SE-4584)
Connie Francis Sings Favorites (MGM E/SE-3869)
Connie Francis Sings Jewish Favorites (MGM E/SE 3869)
A Connie Francis Spectacular (MGM E6PS-2)
Connie, Italiano (Laurie House LH-8019; CBS Special Products LV-8098)
Connie's Christmas (MGM E/SE-4399)

Connie's Greatest Hits (MGM E/SE-3793)
Country and Western Golden Hits (MGM E/SE-3795)
Country Greats (MGM E/SE-4251) w. Hank Williams, Jr.
Country Music Connie Style (MGM E/SE-4079)
Do the Twist with Connie Francis (MGM E/SE-4022)
The Exciting Connie Francis (MGM E/SE-3761)
Folk Favorites (Metro M/S-538)
Follow the Boys (MGM E/SE-4123) [ST]
For Mama (MGM E/SE-4294)
Fun Songs for Children (Leo the Lion 70126)
German Favorites (MGM E/SE-4124)
Grandes Exitos del Cine de Los Años 60 (MGM E/SE-4474)
Greatest American Waltzes (MGM E/SE-4145)
Greatest Golden Groovie Goodies (MGM GAS-109)
Greatest Hits (Mer/Polygram 827-582-1)
Greatest Hits Vol. 2 (Mer/Polygram 831-699-1)
Happiness: Connie Francis on Broadway Today (MGM E/SE-4472)

Hawaii: Connie (MGM E/SE-4522)
I'm Me Again (MGM E/SE-5406)
In the Summer of His Years (MGM E/SE-4210)
The Incomparable Connie Francis (Metro M/S-603)
Irish Favorites (MGM E/SE-4013)
Italian Favorites (MGM E/SE-3791)
Jealous Heart (MGM E/SE-4355)
Looking for Love (MGM E/SE-4229) [ST]
Love, Italian Style (MGM E/SE-4448)
Mala Femmena (Evil Woman) (MGM E/SE-4161)
Merry Christmas: Connie Francis (Sessions ARI-1023)
Modern Italian Hits (MGM E/SE-4102)
More Greatest Hits (MGM E/SE-3942)
More Italian Favorites (MGM E/SE-3871)
Movie Greats of the Sixties (MGM E/SE-4382)
My Best to You (Cap Record Club 91145)
My Heart Cries for You (MGM E/SE-4487)
My Special Favorites/More Great Love Songs (Suffolk Marketing)
My Thanks to You (MGM E/SE-3776)

Never on Sunday (MGM E/SE-3965)
A New Kind of Connie (MGM E/SE-4253)
Noah's Ark and Other Wondrous Bible Stories (Leo the Lion 1035)
Rock 'n Roll Million Sellers (MGM E/SE-3794)
Rocksides (1957–64) (Mer/Polygram 831-698-1)
Second Hand Love (MGM E/SE 4049)
Sessions Presents Connie Francis (Sessions SG-60)
The Songs of Les Reed (MGM E/SE-4655)
Songs of Love (Metro M/S-571)
Songs to a Swinging Band (MGM E/SE-3893)
Spanish and Latin American Favorites (MGM E/SE-3853)
Treasury of Love Songs/Sentimental Favorites (Suffolk Marketing SM-1-50, SM-1-51)
The Very Best of Connie Francis (MGM E/SE-4167)
The Wedding Cake (MGM E/SE-4637)
When the Boys Meet the Girls (MGM E/SE-4334) [ST]
Who's Sorry Now (MGM E/SE-3686)

# ANNETTE FUNICELLO

THROUGH THE MEDIUM OF TELEVISION, AMERICA SAW ANNETTE Funicello grow from an ingratiating little girl on "The Mickey Mouse Club" into a beautiful young woman. Thanks to her support from the Walt Disney organization, Annette not only developed into a popular film and TV star and role model, but also had a successful recording career. As she left childhood and became a voluptuous young woman, Annette embarked on a series of highly successful beach party movies for American International. They forever typed her in the minds of the public as delightfully filling out a (decorous) bathing suit while passing away the hours on the California sands rocking and rolling and being romanced by Frankie Avalon. As the 1960s ended, the actress opted for marriage and a family rather than a career, although she has remained in the public eye with occasional appearances, mostly on the small screen (promoting peanut butter), which launched her in the first place.

Annette Funicello was born on October 22, 1942, in Utica, New York. When she was four her family moved to California. The next year she took dancing lessons in hopes of becoming a ballerina. At the age of nine she won the "Miss Willow Lake" beauty contest and began a modeling career. While appearing in the outdoor production "Ballet vs. Jive," Annette was spotted by Walt Disney, who signed her to appear as one of the original Mouseketeers on "The Mickey Mouse Club" on ABC-TV in 1955. As a result of her cute looks and pleasing personality, Annette was an immediate hit on the children's program and quickly became the most recognizable of the Mouseketeer children, remaining with the program through its four-season run. During that time she also appeared in several Disney multipart stories on ABC-TV: "Adventure in Dairyland," "The Further Adventures of Spin and Marty," "The New Adventures of Spin and Marty," and her own starring serial, "Annette," which aired early in 1958. For Disney she also did guest roles in three episodes of the "Zorro" series. In 1958, Annette (as she was now simply billed) made her recording debut on the Disneyland label and she had chart singles with "How Will I Know My Love" and "Tall Paul"; the latter reached the top ten. In the spring of 1959 Annette became a regular on "The Danny Thomas Show" on CBS-TV, appearing in several episodes in the recurring role of Gina. That year she also made her movie debut for Disney, playing Tommy Kirk's girlfriend, Alison, in the comedy THE SHAGGY DOG.

By 1960 avuncular Walt Disney realized that Annette Funicello—like fellow contractee Hayley Mills—was a valuable star for his studio: a growing and attractive teenager who was popular on both the big and small screens and on records. In the latter medium, Disney switched Annette to the Buena Vista label. In 1959 she scored well with

"Jo-Jo the Dog Faced Boy," "Lonely Guitar," and "First Name Initial," while in 1960 she had hits with "O Dio Mio," "Train of Love," and "Pineapple Princess" along with the charted albums *Annette Sings Anka* and *Hawaiiannette*.

In films, she was also kept busy by singing the title song, with Tommy Sands, for THE PARENT TRAP (1961) and that year a now grownup Annette played Mary Contrary, who is about to marry Tom Piper (Tommy Sands), in Disney's remake of the children's fantasy BABES IN TOYLAND. In the movie Annette sang "I Can't Do Sums" and was serenaded by Ray Bolger in the "Castle in Spain" sequence. She also starred in several segments of "The Wonderful World of Disney" on NBC-TV. Four of these were issued theatrically in Europe: THE HORSEMASTERS (1961), filmed in England, teamed her with Tommy Kirk as fellow students at a school who teach young people to become expert riders; with Louis Armstrong, Bobby Rydell, the Osmond Brothers, and Kid Ory, she was part of a tour of Disneyland called DISNEYLAND AFTER DARK (1962); and with Ed Wynn she co-starred in THE GOLDEN HORSESHOE REVUE (1962). The fourth "telefeature" was called ESCAPADE IN FLORENCE (1962) and in it she and Tommy Kirk portrayed American teenagers who meet on holiday in Italy and try to stop a count (Nino Castelnuovo) from stealing a classic work of art. By now Annette's popularity was such that she was a prime feature of fan and teenage magazines, her name was on a diverse line of merchandise, and, in the early 1960s, she was the subject of a quartet of fiction books published by Whitman: *The Desert Inn Mystery, The Mystery at Moonstone Bay, The Mystery at Smugglers' Cove*, and *Sierra Summer*.

Now billed as Annette Funicello, the twenty-one-year-old star became an established film player in 1963 when she appeared with Tommy Kirk in Disney's THE MISADVEN-TURES OF MERLIN JONES. This crazy comedy's title character (Kirk) can read minds and, with his girlfriend, Jennifer (Annette), he tries to prevent a judge (Leon Ames) from carrying out a big robbery. Even more successful with the public were the six "Beach Party" movies Annette starred in for American International, all directed by William Asher. The first one, BEACH PARTY (1963), set the trend for the airy series in that the movies offered a lot of fun-loving teenagers romping on the beach (with the nubile teenaged girls—except decorous Annette—wearing as little as the censor allowed) with lots of rock 'n' roll music but no violence, sex, profanity, alcohol, or tobacco. The initial outing had an anthropology professor (Bob Cummings) and his bemused secretary (Dorothy Malone) on the California sands studying the sex habits of teens with Annette and Frankie Avalon playing teenagers in love. *Variety* endorsed, "It's a bouncy bit of lightweight fluff, attractively cast . . . beautifully set . . . and scored throughout . . . with a big twist beat."

MUSCLE BEACH PARTY (1964) followed, with Annette becoming jealous when a beautiful contessa (Luciana Paluzzi) pursues her boyfriend (Frankie Avalon) after dumping muscleman Rock Stevens (Peter Lupus). In BIKINI BEACH (1964) Annette finds herself attracted not only to boyfriend Frankie Avalon but to long-haired British rocker the Potato Bug (also played by Avalon). In 1964 enterprising American International also reteamed Tommy Kirk and Annette for a spin-off called PAJAMA PARTY, a silly science fiction comedy about a Martian (Kirk) coming to Earth and lusting for Annette, who sang

"Where Did I Go Wrong." During this period Annette found herself back on the record charts thanks to the successful sales of the soundtrack albums of BEACH PARTY and MUSCLE BEACH PARTY on the Buena Vista label. The actress also made guest appearances on such TV fare as "Wagon Train," "Burke's Law," and "The Greatest Show on Earth" and in the fall of 1964 she guested on Bob Hope's NBC-TV special.

In the mid-1960s Annette Funicello continued her reign as queen of the surf and sand movies when she and Frankie Avalon became involved with other peers in saving a kidnapped singer (Paul Lynde) from a motorcycle gang in BEACH BLANKET BINGO (1965). She and Avalon also starred in the last of the "Beach" series, HOW TO STUFF A WILD BIKINI (1965), which found Frankie in the military service based in the South Seas. He hires a witch doctor (Buster Keaton) to make sure Annette remains faithful to him. In it Annette sang "Better Ready" and "The Perfect Boy."

The year 1965 also found Annette reteamed yet again with Tommy Kirk (as Merlin Jones) for Disney in a sequel to the very popular THE MISADVENTURES OF MERLIN JONES called THE MONKEY'S UNCLE, in which she again played Jones's girlfriend, Jennifer. Herein the addled young genius attempts to use sleep-learning on a monkey and constructs a one-man flying craft. Annette and the Beach Boys sang the film's title theme. She also made a guest appearance in American International's DR. GOLDFOOT AND THE BI-

Annette Funicello on the set of THE MISADVENTURES OF MERLIN JONES (1963)

KINI MACHINE (1965) as a girl trapped in a wooden stock. Getting off the beach (which was wearing thin with young moviegoers), Annette and Avalon made FIREBALL 500 (1966) for American International, along with singer Fabian. This proved to be a frail drama about race car driver Frankie taking part in a cross-country spin, not realizing he is hauling whiskey for bootleggers. For her last American International outing, THUNDER ALLEY (1967), Annette co-starred with Fabian in a tawdry race car melodrama as the daughter of thrill circus owner Jan Murray. Her boyfriend (Warren Berlinger) throws her over for a fling with new driver Fabian's gal (Diane McBain). Annette closed out the 1960s by making a guest appearance as Minnie in the freaked-out mod/nostalgia comedy HEAD (1968), starring The Monkees. Little appreciated when first released, it now has a solid cult following.

Marrying her agent Jack Gilardi, Annette Funicello pretty much deserted show business in the 1970s to raise her family. In 1971 she did make a guest appearance on ABC-TV's "Love, American Style" and the next year headlined the syndicated special "The Mouse Factory." She and Frankie Avalon were reteamed in the late summer of 1976 for a brief CBS-TV variety series called "Easy Does It . . . Starring Frankie Avalon" and the next year she reemerged for ABC's "Dick Clark's Good Old Days: From Bobby Sox to Bikinis" and "The Mouseketeers at Walt Disney World" on NBC-TV's "The World of Disney." Late in 1978, at Avalon's urging, she joined with him in the NBC-TV pilot "Frankie and Annette: The Second Time Around" and in 1979 she guested on "Fantasy Island." She was also visible on television and in print ads in a nine-year series of commercials for Skippy peanut butter.

In 1980 Annette Funicello had a flurry of small-screen activity, guesting again on "Fantasy Island," appearing on the CBS special "Disneyland's 25th Anniversary," and on two NBC specials, "Men Who Rate a '10'" and "The Mouseketeers Reunion." She then did roles on "The Love Boat" and "Fantasy Island" before returning to Disney for the cable TV movie LOTS OF LUCK in 1985. She starred as a housewife coping with the inconveniences that arise when she wins a big lottery. Theatrically, Annette and Frankie Avalon reprised their "Beach" roles in the delightful Paramount comedy BACK TO THE BEACH (1987). Now the two are wed with teenagers of their own, and Annette is forced to use her sex appeal to get Frankie back after he strays with her rival Connie Stevens. This mini-musical not only generated a profit but it did much to reestablish Funicello and Avalon in the minds of viewers. Late in 1988 Annette appeared on the CBS-TV program "Pee-wee's Playhouse Special" with Pee-wee Herman, who was a guest star in BACK TO THE BEACH.

Although Annette made an effort in 1984 to break into the country music field with the Starview Record LP *Annette Funicello Country Album*, the actress appears content with her home life and an occasional foray into TV, such as a few segments of ABC's "Growing Pains" in 1986. She insists she owes all her success to the late Walt Disney: "I don't think that I would have gone on to do anything else had it not been for my association with Disney. I was the only Mouseketeer to remain under contract. Walt starred me in films, television, and recording. He really did a lot for me." Having divorced Jack Gilardi (they had three children) she married Bakersfield rancher–horse breeder Glen Holt in the spring of 1987.

## Filmography

The Shaggy Dog (BV, 1959)
Babes in Toyland (BV, 1961)
The Parent Trap (BV, 1961) (voice only)
The Misadventures of Merlin Jones (BV, 1963)
Beach Party (AIP, 1963)
Muscle Beach Party (AIP, 1964)
Bikini Beach (AIP, 1964)
Pajama Party (AIP, 1964)
Dr. Goldfoot and the Bikini Machine [Dr. G and the Bikini Machine] (AIP, 1965)

The Monkey's Uncle (BV, 1965)
Beach Blanket Bingo [Malibu Beach] (AIP, 1965)
How to Stuff a Wild Bikini (AIP, 1965)
Fireball 500 (AIP, 1966)
Thunder Alley (AIP, 1967)
Head (Col, 1968)
Lots of Luck (The Disney Channel [TV], 1985)
Back to the Beach (Par, 1987)

## TV Series

The Mickey Mouse Club (ABC, 1955–59)
The Danny Thomas Show (CBS, 1959)

Easy Does It . . . Starring Frankie Avalon (CBS, 1976)

## Album Discography

Annette (Buena Vista 3301)
Annette and Hayley Mills (Buena Vista 3508)
Annette Funicello Country Album (Starview 4001)
Annette Sings Anka (Buena Vista 3302)
Babes in Toyland (Buena Vista 4022) [ST]
Back to the Beach (Col SC 40892) [ST]
Beach Party (Buena Vista 3316) [ST]
The Best of Broadway (Disneyland 1267)
Bikini Beach (Buena Vista 3324)
Dance Annette (Buena Vista 3305)
Golden Surfin' Hits (Buena Vista 3327)
Hawaiiannette (Buena Vista 3303)
How to Stuff a Wild Bikini (Wand 671) [ST]

Italiannette (Buena Vista 3304)
Muscle Beach Party (Buena Vista 3314) [ST]
Pajama Party (Buena Vista 3325) [ST]
Snow White and the Seven Dwarfs (Disneyland 3906)
Something Borrowed, Something Blue (Buena Vista 3328)
Songs from Annette (Disneyland 24)
State and College Songs (Disneyland 1293)
The Story of My Teens (Buena Vista 3312)
Thunder Alley (Sidewalk 5902) [ST]
Tubby the Tuba (Disney 1928) w. Jimmie Dodd

# JUDY GARLAND

WHEN SHE DIED IN 1969, *NEWSWEEK* MAGAZINE OBSERVED, "JUDY Garland was the single great musical entertainer who developed within the Hollywood studio system." Her best movie musicals remain classics: THE WIZARD OF OZ (1939), MEET ME IN ST. LOUIS (1944), THE HARVEY GIRLS (1945), and A STAR IS BORN (1954). In addition, there were her song-and-dance romps with Mickey Rooney, her celluloid teamings with Gene Kelly (including the complex THE PIRATE, 1948) and her pairing with Fred Astaire (EASTER PARADE, 1948). But there was more to "Miss Show Business" (as she was known affectionately) than her activities as an active recording, radio, and TV artist. There was also the "in person—live on stage" Judy Garland. Of twentieth-century American performers who consistently captivated audiences with their own magic—not relying on lighting and sound effects to do the trick—Judy Garland stands at the pinnacle, with perhaps Al Jolson as her closest rival. Anyone who ever experienced one of her concerts witnessed and was part of the tremendous emotional control she exuded over audiences as she sang, joked, and toyed with her much-publicized image of Miss Vulnerability. (She said once, "If I'm such a legend, then why am I so lonely?") Like Marilyn Monroe, Garland drew power from audiences' tremendous love of her. It eased the torment of her well-documented insecurities and woes, harrowing pain that liquor and drugs could not touch.

She was born on June 10, 1922, in Grand Rapids, Minnesota, the third daughter of Frank Avent Gumm and Ethel Marion (Milne) Gumm. He was a struggling Irish tenor and she was a vaudeville house pianist. After their marriage, they toured the lesser circuits as "Jack and Virginia Lee, the Sweet Southern Singers." Later, they settled in Grand Rapids where Gumm managed the New Grand Theatre and Ethel played the piano. Sometimes their two elder daughters, Mary Jane (Suzanne) and Virginia (Jimmy), joined their parents in reviving their act. Their third daughter was named Frances Ethel. She was born with scoliosis, a curvature of the spine which would lead to a lifelong insecurity about her figure. (She had long legs but a short, almost dwarflike torso and was not quite 5' tall.)

When she was two and a half, Frances (known as "Babe" or "Baby" to her family) made an impromptu show business debut by running onto the stage and joining her parents in singing "Jingle Bells." Immediately she became part of their act. Because Ethel Gumm was so intent on getting her children—especially Frances—into the movies, the family moved to California, settling in Lancaster, seventy miles north of Los Angeles. Gumm took over management of a movie theater and Ethel made the rounds of the studios and booking agents with her three girls. These visits led, eventually, to their signing with the Meglin Kiddies, a specialty agency which handled child acts in and around Los Angeles. Soon there were scattered bookings and work in at least four film short subjects. By now the Gumms had moved to Lomita, far closer to Hollywood. While Frank managed another cinema, the unwavering Ethel chaperoned her three daughters whenever they had road engagements. (The girls were never very good as a singing team and their bookings were always second-rate at best.) The girls were enrolled at Mrs. Lawler's Professional School, where Joe Yule, Jr.—later Mickey Rooney—was a student. In 1934, the trio performed on the midway at the Chicago World's Fair, but were left stranded when they were not paid for their work. They managed a booking at Chicago's Oriental Theatre. When they arrived for the play date, they found that the theater marquee listed them as "The Glum Sisters." It was headliner George Jessel who renamed them the Garland Sisters, and it would be Frances who chose the new name of Judy for herself.

It was while the Garland Sisters were on a working vacation at the Cal-Neva Lodge at Lake Tahoe that songwriter Harry Akst and his friends—Columbia Pictures casting agent Lew Brown and talent agent Al Rosen—heard Judy perform. They agreed that Judy was the real talent of the family and they gave her introductions to the movie studios. Eventually their contacts led to an audition for Judy at MGM with that studio's musical arranger, Roger Edens (who became a lifelong friend and mentor). He, in turn, had Garland audition for Ida Koverman, executive secretary to studio head Louis B. Mayer. Koverman was so impressed with Judy's singing of "Dinah" that she called in her boss. Two weeks later Judy Garland was under MGM contract and the mogul was proclaiming, "We have just signed a baby Nora Bayes." Years later Garland claimed, "I was very thrilled by it, though I actually didn't sign the contract. Nobody asked me. That should be the title of my life: *Nobody Asked Me.*"

Soon after Judy joined MGM in 1935, her father died of meningitis and the family had to depend on Garland's $150 weekly salary. The studio was not sure how to use the plump teenager with the glorious voice. They had her perform at assorted studio functions and then, as a throwaway, teamed her with equally young contractee Deanna Durbin in a two-reeler, EVERY SUNDAY (1936). The gimmick of the short was to have Deanna sing "sweet" while Judy sang "hot." MGM still pondered, and meanwhile Universal Pictures snatched Deanna away and turned her into a major star. But still Mayer could not decide what to do with Garland. Instead, she guested on radio shows (such as "The Shell Chateau Hour") and made recordings for Decca Records. Then, to hedge his bets, Mayer loaned Judy to 20th Century–Fox for PIGSKIN PARADE (1936), in which she made her feature film debut singing the swinging "Balboa" number. *Variety* reported, "She's a cute, not too pretty but pleasingly fetching personality, who certainly knows how to sell a pop [tune]."

Roger Edens made a special arrangement of "You Made Me Love You" which he entitled "Dear Mr. Gable." Judy sang the lyrics at Gable's thirty-sixth birthday party (February 1, 1937) at the studio. Mayer was so enthralled that he ordered the number to be incorporated into BROADWAY MELODY OF 1938 (1937), then in pre-production. In that musical Judy played Sophie Tucker's daughter and sang the song as she sat writing Gable a fan note. The *New York Times* insisted this solo was "probably the greatest tour de force in recent screen history." Of her next four releases, LOVE FINDS ANDY HARDY (1938) was the most important. It was her first screen teaming with her old pal Mickey Rooney and it demonstrated that Judy, besides singing, could deliver comedy lines with a delicious tartness.

MGM had hoped to borrow Shirley Temple for their upcoming musical fantasy THE WIZARD OF OZ (1939), but when that proved impossible, they settled on Judy for the lead. With the help of corsets, pigtails, and makeup, the seventeen-year-old Judy looked the innocent young Dorothy from Kansas who discovers in the Land of Oz that there is no place like home. The tremendously expensive color production turned a profit eventually, became a classic through annual TV showings, earned Judy a special Oscar, and provided her with her signature song, "Over the Rainbow."

Judy was number ten at the box office in 1940 as she continued making musicals with and without her peer, Mickey Rooney. Already she was engulfed in a regimen of dieting and pill taking (to suppress her appetite, to keep her peppy) while continuing her hectic routine of filmmaking, recordings, and radio and personal appearances. All of this dieting/pill taking was with the encouragement of the stuido, which cared only about maximizing their investment in this big moneymaker. In July 1941—much to the annoyance of her mother and the studio—she married composer/musician David Rose (twelve years her senior), who had recently been divorced from Martha Raye.

In FOR ME AND MY GAL (1942) Judy first received star billing and sang the memorable "After You've Gone." It was the first of her several musicals with movie newcomer Gene Kelly. It was also in 1942 that Judy, with the encouragement of MGM scriptwriter Joseph L. Mankiewicz, began seeking psychiatric help. When her mother found out and, in turn, told Louis B. Mayer, a battle royal ensued. Mankiewicz left the studio, Mayer was furious with Garland, and Judy never forgave her mother. (Garland would later refer to Ethel as "the real-life Wicked Witch of the West" and always blamed her for the unhappy/abnormal childhood she endured. They were still feuding when Mrs. Gumm died in 1953.)

Judy sang "The Joint Is Really Jumpin' at Carnegie Hall" in the all-star THOUSANDS CHEER (1943) and gave memorable interpretations to "But Not for Me," "Embraceable You," and "Bidin' My Time" in GIRL CRAZY (1943)—teamed yet again with Mickey Rooney. In PRESENTING LILY MARS (1943), originally conceived as a dramatic vehicle for Lana Turner, Judy was the small town girl who finds love (with Van Heflin) and show business success on Broadway. Also in 1943, Garland played her debut concert engagement on July 1 in Philadelphia, made an extended USO tour, and ended her marriage to David Rose, much to the relief of Louis B. Mayer who had never approved of the union. (Mayer the mogul had forced Judy to have an abortion during her marriage to Rose.) During this period there were brief romances with Artie Shaw and Tyrone Power.

MEET ME IN ST. LOUIS (1944) was a joyous excursion into Americana set in 1903–4. It allowed Judy to pine vocally over "The Boy Next Door" with whom she fell in love while "Clang, Clang, Clang, Went the Trolley" ("The Trolley Song"). This warm-hearted family study was directed by Vincente Minnelli who understood Judy very well and who smartly handled her next film, THE CLOCK (1945). This touching dramatic study of her love for a young G.I. (Robert Walker) led James Agee (*The Nation* magazine) to judge, "She can handle any emotion in sight, in any shape or size, and the audience along with it." Judy and Minnelli were married on June 15, 1945, and their daughter, Liza May, was born on May 12, 1946. Judy was back to what the public wanted in the musical THE HARVEY GIRLS (1946), as the resourceful restaurant worker in the Old West who sang the electric "On the Atchison, Topeka and the Santa Fe." She did a sharp mock send-up of the archetypical lofty movie star in "The Interview" segment of ZIEGFELD FOLLIES OF 1946 (1946) and, as Broadway's Marilyn Miller in TILL THE CLOUDS ROLL BY (1946), she was wistfully effective vocalizing "Who?" and "Look for the Silver Lining."

Judy's ever-mounting insecurities caused production delays on THE PIRATE (1948), a fanciful costume musical with Gene Kelly, directed by Minnelli. It was too sophisticated to be a box-office hit. In WORDS AND MUSIC (1948) she was edgy, drawn and thin, playing herself and singing "Johnny One Note" and dueting with pal Mickey Rooney on "I Wish I Were in Love Again." She was set to reteam with Gene Kelly in Irving Berlin's EASTER

Judy Garland and Margaret O'Brien in MEET ME IN ST. LOUIS (1944)

PARADE (1948), but he broke his ankle during rehearsals and was replaced by Fred Astaire. The latter proved to be an admirable song-and-dance partner for Garland. Together they performed the indelible "A Couple of Swells," a tramp routine that she would use frequently in years to come. MGM set Astaire to be with her in THE BARKLEYS OF BROADWAY (1949), but Judy was too distraught so the studio used Ginger Rogers instead.

Judy substituted for a pregnant June Allyson in IN THE GOOD OLD SUMMERTIME (1949), but there was little chemistry between her and Van Johnson. Again there were production delays because Judy was ill and unhappy. MGM had acquired the screen rights to Broadway's *Annie Get Your Gun* as a Garland vehicle. Filming began in May 1949, after Judy had prerecorded the score. Director George Sidney finally had to acknowledge that Judy was unable to proceed and the studio suspended her. Shipped to a Boston sanatorium for a "rest cure," she underwent shock treatments. The studio replaced her in ANNIE GET YOUR GUN (1950) with Paramount's Betty Hutton.

When Judy returned to Hollywood she required an on-the-set psychiatrist during SUMMER STOCK (1950). The tormented Judy fluctuated between chunky and thin during filming, but still shone in the lustrous "Get Happy" finale (shot months after the original footage). The increasingly exasperated studio ordered her to replace the pregnant (again) June Allyson in ROYAL WEDDING (1951) but Judy instead collapsed. Jane Powell eventually appeared in that film, opposite Fred Astaire.

Unable to cope with her domestic and professional problems, Judy attempted suicide on June 20, 1950, by slashing her throat with a bit of glass. Co-Metro-worker Katharine Hepburn was among those who gave Garland a pep talk, advising her, "Now listen, you're one of the three greatest talents in the world. And your ass has hit the gutter. There's no place to go but up. Now, goddamit, do it!" But Judy could not and MGM ended her over $5,000 weekly contract, with a planned role as Julie in SHOW BOAT (1951) going to Ava Gardner. She and Minnelli, two highly artistic individuals unable to cope with each other further, divorced in 1951.

At this crisis, Michael Sidney Luft, former secretary to Eleanor Powell and ex-husband of screen actress Lynn Bari, entered Judy's life. He was an ambitious promoter who understood how to manage Judy—both on stage and off. He realized she still had value as a stage attraction and channeled her into performing at the London Palladium in 1951, where she was a sensation. That October, albeit stocky, she was at the Palace Theatre in New York, gloriously reviving the two-a-day vaudeville policy. Her engagement was extended for nineteen weeks, grossed $750,000, and won Garland a special Tony Award. Despite the pressures of her schedule, Judy relaxed for the first time in her career. She and Luft wed in June 1952 and that November she gave birth to daughter Lorna. (Their other child, Joseph Wiley, was born in March 1955.)

How A STAR IS BORN (1954) was conceived and executed has been documented meticulously in Ronald Haver's book *A Star Is Born* (1988). The battles of wills between Judy and Luft on the one hand and Warner Bros. studio head Jack L. Warner on the other, while director George Cukor and co-star James Mason served as intermediaries, are legendary. Despite the production delays (primarily due to Judy's emotional instability), the widescreen musical was released in October 1954. And, despite the severe editing the picture underwent after roadshow engagements, Judy was Oscar-nominated for playing the movie extra who becomes a major screen attraction. The autobiographical "Born in a Trunk" number is one of filmdom's longest production exercises, and "The Man Who Got Away" presented Garland at her chanteuse best. The picture was her career zenith.

Her downhill slide required fifteen years to complete. She debuted on TV on NBC's "Ford Star Jubilee" in a ninety-minute special on September 24, 1955, the first of several such outings in which she sang, danced, and joked. She was among the many who enthusiastically supported John F. Kennedy in his presidential bid and she labeled him "one of the best friends I ever had." On April 23, 1961, she appeared at Carnegie Hall in a magnificent show-stopping performance that drew raves. The two-record live recording has sold over two million copies to date and won two Grammy Awards (Best Album and Best Female Solo Vocal). Despite all these successes, she still yearned for a movie return and for $50,000 accepted a small role—as a plump, distraught German hausfrau—in Stanley Kramer's JUDGMENT AT NUREMBERG (1961). It won her an Oscar nomination as Best Supporting Actress.

She was at her most hyperactive in 1963 with two additional movies. She played a music teacher at an institution for mentally retarded children in A CHILD IS WAITING, for which director John Cassavetes channeled her nervous energy effectively. For the British-made I COULD GO ON SINGING she was chic in an autobiographical role which required her to sing energetically. CBS-TV thought they could succeed, where MGM and everyone else had failed, in making Judy a disciplined performer. She was the star of a weekly network musical program, "The Judy Garland Show," which debuted on September 29, 1963. Unfortunately it competed in a time slot against the medium's then most popular show ("Bonanza"), and after twenty-six weeks Judy was off the air. Mel Tormé, Judy's musical writer/advisor on the series, told his version of working with such a tormented person in *The Other Side of the Rainbow with Judy Garland on the Dawn Patrol* (1971). Meanwhile, she returned to the concert stage, where her entrances and banter were often the most polished parts of the evening.

In 1965 Judy and Luft divorced and she married (briefly) young actor Mark Herron. She was replaced by Ginger Rogers in a quickie biography film, HARLOW (1965), and after prerecording two songs for Jacqueline Susann's VALLEY OF THE DOLLS (1967) she withdrew from the project; Susan Hayward substituted as the aging Ethel Merman–type Broadway star. In 1968 it was thought that Judy Garland would take over for Angela Lansbury in the Broadway musical *Mame*, but it was Janis Paige who did. In 1969, Judy wed discotheque manager Mickey Deans, twelve years her junior. At London's Talk of the Town Club she made yet another comeback. As was typical in her last years, there were media accounts of her lateness on stage and of fuming audiences. On June 22, 1969, Judy Garland was found dead in the bathroom of her London apartment by her husband. The death was ruled as from an "accidental" overdose of barbiturates. The funeral was held in New York. A hysterical gathering of over twenty thousand crowded the funeral home to mourn and to pay their final respects.

Following Judy Garland's death there were many LP album reissues of her performances in many media and several books by ex-husbands and friends analyzing the "real" Judy. Perhaps the most understanding explanation of this enigmatic legend was provided by daughter Liza, herself a show business phenomenon:

> Mama had this great thing. She was different with everyone. . . . She tuned in to individuals on their own wave length. . . . She was all things to all people. . . . I think mama got everything she ever wanted. . . . Do you know anyone in show business who ever made more comebacks?

## Filmography

The Meglin Kiddie Revue (Vita, 1929) (s)
Holiday in Storyland (Vita, 1930) (s)
The Wedding of Jack and Jill (Vita, 1930) (s)
The Old Lady in the Shoe (Vita, 1931) (s)
La Fiesta de Santa Barbara (MGM, 1935) (s)
Every Sunday (MGM, 1936) (s)
Pigskin Parade [The Harmony Parade] (20th–Fox, 1936)
Broadway Melody of 1938 (MGM, 1937)
Thoroughbreds Don't Cry (MGM, 1937)
Everybody Sing (MGM, 1938)
Love Finds Andy Hardy (MGM, 1938)
Listen, Darling (MGM, 1938)
The Wizard of Oz (MGM, 1939)
Babes in Arms (MGM, 1939)
Andy Hardy Meets Debutante (MGM, 1940)
Strike Up the Band (MGM, 1940)
Little Nellie Kelly (MGM, 1940)
Life Begins for Andy Hardy (MGM, 1941)
Ziegfeld Girl (MGM, 1941)
Babes on Broadway (MGM, 1941)
Meet the Stars #4 (Rep, 1941) (s)
Cavalcade of the Academy Awards (Vita, 1941) (s)

For Me and My Gal [For Me and My Girl] (MGM, 1942)
We Must Have Music (MGM, 1943) (s)
Presenting Lily Mars (MGM, 1943)
Girl Crazy (MGM, 1943)
Thousands Cheer (MGM, 1943)
Meet Me in St. Louis (MGM, 1944)
The Clock [Under the Clock] (MGM, 1945)
The Harvey Girls (MGM, 1946)
Ziegfeld Follies of 1946 (MGM, 1946)
Till the Clouds Roll By (MGM, 1946)
The Pirate (MGM, 1948)
Words and Music (MGM, 1948)
Easter Parade (MGM, 1948)
In the Good Old Summertime (MGM, 1949)
Summer Stock [If You Feel Like Singing] (MGM, 1950)
A Star Is Born (WB, 1954)
Pepe (Col, 1960) (voice only)
Judgment at Nuremberg (UA, 1961)
Gay Purr-ee (WB, 1962) (voice only)
A Child Is Waiting (UA, 1963)
I Could Go On Singing (UA, 1963)

## TV Series

The Judy Garland Show (CBS, 1963–64)

## Album Discography

The ABC Collection (ABC 620)

All of Judy (Telebrity 1228)

Alone (Cap T-835)

Annie Get Your Gun (Sound/Stage 2302, Sandy Hook 2053) [ST]

Babes in Arms/Babes on Broadway (Curtain Calls 100/6-7) [ST]

The Beginning (DRG 5187)

Behind the Scenes at the Making of *The Wizard of Oz*—The Complete "Maxwell House Good News" Radio Broadcast of June 29, 1939 (Jass 17) [ST/R]

The Best of Judy Garland (Decca DX-172/7172, MCA 4003, MCA 1630)

Bing, Bob and Judy (Totem 1009) w. Bing Crosby, Bob Hope

Born in a Trunk (Col CL-762)

Born in a Trunk, Vols. 1–3 (AEI 2108–10)

Broadway Melody of 1938 (Motion Picture Tracks MPT-3) [ST]

By Myself (Sears SP-430)

Christmas with Judy (Minerva MIN 6JG-XST) w. Liza Minnelli, Lorna Luft, Jack Jones

Collector's Items (Decca DEA-7-5, MCA 4046)

Dean Martin, Judy Garland & Frank Sinatra (Jocklo International 1007)

Deluxe Set (Cap TCL-STCL-2988)

Dick Tracy in B-Flat (Curtain Calls 100/1) [ST/R]

Drive-In (Command Performance 8) [ST/R]

Easter Parade (10" MGM E-502, MGM E-3227) [ST]

For Collectors Only (Paragon 1002)

For Me and My Gal (Sountrak 107) [ST]

Forever Judy (MGM PX-102)

From MGM Classic Films (MCA 25165) [ST]

From the Decca Vaults (MCA 907)

Garland at the Grove (Cap T/ST-1118)

The Garland Touch (Cap W/SW-1710)

Gay Purr-ee (WB 1479) [ST]

Girl Crazy (10" Decca DL-5412) w. Mickey Rooney

Girl Crazy/Strike Up the Band (Curtain Calls 100/9-10) [ST]

The Golden Years at MGM (MGM SDP-1-2)

The Great Garland Duets (Paragon 1001)

Greatest Hits (Decca DL-75150)

Greatest Hits (Radiant 711-0104) [ST/TV]

Greatest Performances (Decca DL-8190)

The Harvey Girls (Hollywood Soundstage 5002) [ST]

The Harvey Girls/Meet Me in St. Louis (Decca DL-8498)

I Could Go On Singing (Cap W/SW-1861, EMI 1288) [ST]

I Could Go On Singing Forever (Longines SY-52222)

I Feel a Song Coming On (Pickwick 3053)

If You Feel Like Singing (MGM E-3149)

In the Good Old Summertime (MGM E-3232) [ST]

Judy (Cap T-734)

Judy (Radiant 711-0101) [ST/TV]

Judy All Alone (Take One! TLP 201)

Judy and Bing Together (Legend 1973) w. Bing Crosby

Judy and Her Partners in Rhythm and Rhyme (Star-Tone ST-213)

Judy and Vic (Minerva MIN 6JG-TVD) w. Vic Damone

Judy Garland (Metro M/S-505)

Judy Garland (MGM GAS-113)

Judy Garland—The Long Lost Holland Concert (Amalgamated 160)

Judy Garland, 1935–51 (Star Tone ST201)

Judy Garland and Friends (Minerva MIN 6JG-FNJ) w. June Allyson, Steve Lawrence, Jerry Van Dyke

Judy Garland at Carnegie Hall (Cap WBO/SWBO-1569)

Judy Garland at Home at the Palace (ABC 620)

Judy Garland at the Grove (EMI 26007)

Judy Garland at the Palace (10" Decca DL-6020)

The Judy Garland Deluxe Set (Cap STCL 2988)

Judy Garland Duets (Broadcast 003)

Judy Garland in Concert (Trophy 2145)

Judy Garland in Concert in San Francisco (Mark 56 632)

Judy Garland in Holland, Vols. 2–3 (Amalgamated 195, 208)

Judy Garland in Hollywood (Radiant 711-0102)

Judy Garland Live (Amalgamated 145)

Judy Garland Live (Cap C2-92343)

Judy Garland Live at the Palace (CIT 2001)
Judy Garland on Radio (Radiola 1040)
Judy Garland Sings (10" MGM E-82)
The Judy Garland Story (MGM E-4005)
The Judy Garland Story, Vol. 2 (MGM E-4005P)
Judy in Love (Cap T/ST-1036)
Judy in Love (EMI/Pathé 54573)
Judy! Judy! Judy! (Star-Tone 224)
Judy! That's Entertainment (Cap T/ST-1467)
Judy the Legend (Radiant 711-0103)
Judy's Greatest Hits (Radiant 711-0104)
Judy's Portrait in Song (Radiant 711-0106)
Just for Openers (Cap W/DW-2062)
Lady in the Dark (Command Performance 10) [ST/R]
The Last Concert: 7/20/68 (Paragon 1003)
The Last Performance—London, 1969 (Juno 1000)
The Legend (Radiant 711-0103)
The Letter (Cap TAO-STAO-1188, EMI 602) w. John Ireland
Little Nellie Kelly/Thousands Cheer (Amalgamated 323) [ST]
Live at the London Palladium (Cap WBO-SWBO-2295, Cap ST-11191) w. Liza Minnelli
The Magic of Judy Garland (Decca DL 4199, DNFR 7632)
Meet Me in St. Louis (Pelican 118) [ST/R]
Meet Me in St. Louis/The Harvey Girls (AEI 3101) [ST]
Merton of the Movies (Pelican 139) [ST/R]
Miss Show Business (Cap W-676)
More Than a Memory (Stanyan 10095)
Musical Scrapbook (Star-Tone 208)
Mutual Admiration Society (Minerva MIN 6JG-FST) w. Mickey Rooney, Jerry Van Dyke
Our Love Letter (Cap T/ST-1941) w. John Ireland
Over the Rainbow (Music for Pleasure 50555)
Over the Rainbow (Pickwick 3078)
Over the Rainbow (Radiant 711-0107)

Over the Rainbow (Springboard 4054)
Pepe (Colpix 507) [ST]
Pigskin Parade/Everybody Sing (Amalgamated 231) [ST]
The Pirate (10" MGM E-21, MGM E-3234) [ST]
Presenting Lily Mars (Caliban 6033, Sountrak 117) [ST]
Radio Broadcast Follies of 1936 (Amalgamated 227) [ST/R]
Rare Performance (Windmill 258)
Sixteen Greatest Hits (Trip 16-9)
A Star Is Born (Col BL-1201, Col CL-1101/CS-8740, Har HS-11366) [ST]
The Star Years (MGM E-3989)
Summer Stock (10" E-519, MGM E-3234) [ST]
That Old Song and Dance (Minerva MIN 6JG-FSS) w. Donald O'Connor, Jerry Van Dyke
That's Entertainment (Cap SM-11876)
Thousands Cheer (Amalgamated 232, Hollywood Soundstage 49) [ST]
Three Billion Millionaires (UA UXL-4/UXS-54)
Till the Clouds Roll By (10" MGM E-501, MGM E-3231, Metro M/S-578, Sountrak 115, Vertinge 2000) [ST]
Twelve Hits (Oxford 3030)
The Uncollected Judy Garland (Stanyan 10095)
The Unforgettable Judy Garland (Radiant 711-0105)
The Very Best of Judy Garland (MGM E/SE-4204)
The Wit and Wonder (DRG 5179)
The Wizard of Oz (MGM E-34640) [ST]
The Wizard of Oz (10" Decca DL-51520)
The Wizard of Oz (Decca DL-8387/78387, MCA 521)
The Wizard of Oz (Radiola 1109) [ST/R]
Words and Music (10" MGM E-505, MGM E-3233, Metro M/S-580) [ST]
The Young Judy Garland (Amalgamated 251)
Ziegfeld Follies of 1946 (Curtain Calls 100/15-16) [ST]
Ziegfeld Girl (CIF 3006) [ST]

# MITZI GAYNOR

IN MANY CASES, BEING TALENTED, PRETTY, AND AMBITIOUS HAS LITTLE
to do with retaining screen stardom. Sometimes it is a case of being in the right place at the
wrong time. Such was the situation with gifted, curvacious, and dedicated Mitzi Gaynor.
She made her screen debut, in 1950, in a Betty Grable musical at 20th Century–Fox just as
the musical genre was again peaking. She was touted by the industry as the vivacious
successor to Betty Grable and June Haver. However, song-and-dance pictures were
waning by the 1950s and she did her best work after leaving Fox. Her movie career seemed
revived when she was showcased in SOUTH PACIFIC (1958), but the momentum did not
last long. Musicals had died again. She was only in her early thirties when she abandoned
the "new" Hollywood and turned to TV specials and the nightclub stage. There she not
only displayed musical versatility and glamour, but she exhibited a refreshing comic verve
which enhanced her entertainment value to her public. She has been a highly paid star for
decades.

She was born on September 4, 1931 (some sources say 1930; she insists 1932), in
Chicago, as Francesca Mitzi Marlene De Charney von Gerber. Of Austro-Hungarian
descent, her father was a cellist/music director and her mother was an exhibition ballroom
dancer. Mitzi made her first stage appearance at the age of three in one of her mother's
recitals and by the next year was taking dance classes. By the time she began high school
the family had moved to Detroit. When her dance instructor, Mme. Katherine Etienne,
moved to Hollywood, Mitzi followed her teacher to the coast and was enrolled in a
professional school in Los Angeles. During the World War II years she was part of a troupe
which entertained at armed services camps; one of her specialties was her imitation of
Carmen Miranda. By the late 1940s she was in the corps de ballet of the Los Angeles Light
Opera Company, appearing in *The Great Waltz* (with Walter Slezak), and in such other
shows as *Song of Norway, Louisiana Purchase,* and *Naughty Marietta.* Producer/actor/ra-
conteur George Jessel saw her in one of these productions and had her screen-tested at
20th Century–Fox. She was signed to a term contract.

MY BLUE HEAVEN (1950) was the third of four screen teamings of Betty Grable and
Dan Dailey. It was all about a husband-and-wife song-and-dance team who plan to adopt
a baby after the Mrs. suffers a miscarriage. What gave this backstage tale some novelty was
that it was set in the TV industry and the leads were stars of a musical variety program.
This twist aside, the best surprise of the film was hazel-eyed, brunette Mitzi Gaynor as
Gloria Adams. Not only did she perform several amusing send-ups of TV cosmetic
commercials, but she sparkled in the song number "Live Hard, Work Hard, Love Hard."
*Variety* lauded this vivacious newcomer: "In addition to a pert and saucy face and the kind

of figure boys don't forget, she's long on terping and vocalizing."

Fox was not sure how best to use Gaynor on camera. It cast her as Jeanne Crain's no-nonsense campus friend in TAKE CARE OF MY LITTLE GIRL (1951), an indictment of the college sorority system. Mitzi's next release, GOLDEN GIRL (1951), remains her favorite motion picture. Produced by George Jessel, it featured Mitzi in a fictionalized account of stage performer Lotta Crabtree, who rose to renown in the 1860s California gold rush days. Dale Robertson was her gambler/Confederate spy beau and Dennis Day (Jack Benny's sidekick) was the shy troupe member who adores her. It was traditional hokum saved by Gaynor's verve. Her best number was "Dixie." The GOLDEN GIRL lead was the type of part Paramount's Betty Hutton would have given her own or anyone's eyeteeth for.

Betty Grable and the younger June Haver were still the queens of musical comedy at 20th Century–Fox. However, another young blonde starlet, named Marilyn Monroe, was rising fast at the studio and she was the one who stood out among the new crowd peppering WE'RE NOT MARRIED (1952). The episodic comedy dealt with five couples who discover they are not really married: the judge (Victor Moore) who wed them had allowed his license to expire. In one of the film's most contrived segments, Gaynor (whose hair shade kept being lightened) played a pregnant wife whose G.I. "husband" (Eddie Bracken) is being shipped overseas during the Korean War. If WE'RE NOT MARRIED was an "A" production, BLOODHOUNDS OF BROADWAY (1952) was a "B" picture. It was another George Jessel–produced musical comedy, this time based on a Damon Runyon yarn about a New York bookie (Scott Brady) meeting an attractive Georgia yokel (Mitzi Gaynor). She persuades Brady to help her become a Broadway name. The picture's choreographer, Bob Sydney, would later become Mitzi's dance director on her TV specials.

George Jessel not only produced THE 'I DON'T CARE' GIRL (1953), he also played himself in the Technicolor picture. He was the movie producer attempting to learn the facts about the life of vaudeville star Eva Tanguay (Mitzi Gaynor) so he can make a movie about her. The scripting was abysmal and the direction was helter-skelter in its attempt to cover the story's inadequacies. Gaynor was vivacious (one might say frantic) in the title role, but she could not breathe life into this hodgepodge of flashbacks and hackneyed set pieces. She tap danced with David Wayne, traded quips with acerbic pianist/manic humorist Oscar Levant, and sang such numbers as "I Don't Care" and "Hello, Frisco, Hello." Jack Cole staged the three production numbers and Seymour Felix choreographed the tap routines. Moviegoers were now weary of such sugary, unbelievable musical biopics.

Back in 1951 studio head Darryl F. Zanuck had begun pre-production on a musical called DOWN AMONG THE SHELTERING PALMS (1953), intending it as a June Haver vehicle. She refused to be in it, claiming the storyline was immoral. Those who were corralled into the project, including Jane Greer, Gloria De Haven, and Mitzi, wished they had not been. This group also included director Edmund Goulding, who peevishly did his best to sabotage the production. At the end of World War II an Army captain (William Lundigan) and his troop command are stationed on the South Pacific isle of Midi. The order of the day is nonfraternization with the natives. Mitzi is the luscious Rozouila, daughter of the island king (Billy Gilbert). She is offered as a good-will gesture to Lundigan. When the film was finally released, it was considered naive foolishness by critics and public alike. Zanuck never forgave any of the cast involved in the mishmash. However, the *New York Times* pointed out, "Miss Gaynor supplements her adroit inquiry, 'What Makes De Diff'rence?' with a couple of electric feats of tribal choreography, stopping the show cold, or hot, as usual."

By 1954 June Haver had left Fox and Betty Grable was on her way out; so were musicals. The studio was banking heavily on Marilyn Monroe at the box office and would soon have Sheree North and Jayne Mansfield as back-ups to that sexpot star. Mitzi Gaynor was caught in midstream. She was considered too talented to be wasted as screen fluff and yet too wholesome (of the Doris Day girl-next-door variety) to make a reputation as a sex goddess of musical comedy. She floundered at the studio, finally being cast in an independent "B" Western, THREE YOUNG TEXANS (1954), which Fox released in early 1954. It was a pedestrian effort that wasted its three young performers: Mitzi, Keefe Brasselle, and Jeffrey Hunter. She was hardy in her cliched role, but it was Vivian Marshall who sang the saloon song "Just Let Me Love You." Then Fox had second thoughts, for the studio cast her in the splashy Irving Berlin musical THERE'S NO BUSINESS LIKE SHOW BUSINESS (1954). It was a major production boasting CinemaScope, Ethel Merman, Dan Dailey, Donald O'Connor, Johnnie Ray, Marilyn Monroe, and Mitzi Gaynor (sixth billed!). It was all about a vaudeville family and their talented offspring. Long-legged Gaynor was the spunky (and sometimes quite sexy) daughter who falls in love with Hugh O'Brian. All the stars had their share of production numbers, but between Merman's belting, O'Connor's soft-shoeing, Ray's wailing, and especially Monroe's sensuous "Heat Wave" number, Gaynor was nearly lost in the shuffle. During production Fox announced that the studio was not picking up Gaynor's option.

In the early 1950s Mitzi had been dating corporate attorney Richard Coyle, eleven years her senior. However, her constant escort was Jack Bean, an MCA talent agent whom she had met in 1952 when he tried unsuccessfully to sign her for his agency. On December 2, 1954, they were married in San Francisco. He later left the industry and went into real estate, as well as became his wife's business manager.

During her Fox period, Richard Rodgers and Oscar Hammerstein II had voiced interest in having Mitzi play the ingenue role in a stage revival of Irving Berlin's *Annie Get Your Gun*. When their OKLAHOMA! (1955) went into production, Gaynor (like Betty Hutton) was considered for the part of Ado Annie, but when Fox would not loan her, Gloria Grahame was signed for the role of the girl who just can't say no. Looking back on her contract years Gaynor would admit in her kidding way, "I went through a very sexy period. Boy, I was full of attitudes. Even my ears were sexy, I thought, and lips—did I have lips! Practically used to put my lipstick up inside my nose, and I'd shave my eyebrows until I looked smolderingly hot. But I knew that the whole thing was kind of ridiculous, too."

More realistically and with the advice of her husband, she went about making herself more marketable as a freelance movie personality. She streamlined her figure, sharpened her singing/dancing techniques, adopted a more sensual persona, and became more blonde. She was off the screen all through 1955. However, at $100,000 she was hired to play opposite Bing Crosby in ANYTHING GOES (1956) at Paramount. She was the crooner's shipboard romance who wins a role in his new Broadway musical. In the proceedings there was quite a contrast between the ballet dancing of Zizi Jeanmaire and Gaynor's more provocative terpsichorean display. Mitzi had another shipboard romance in RKO's THE BIRDS AND THE BEES (1956), an unsatisfactory remake of the comedy classic THE LADY EVE (1941). RKO was a dying studio by this time and THE BIRDS AND THE BEES, despite the valiant efforts of Gaynor, David Niven, and George Gobel, helped to sink the lot.

20th Century–Fox had wanted Mitzi to return to co-star in THE BEST THINGS IN LIFE ARE FREE (1956), but she declined (the role went to Sheree North). Instead she co-starred with Frank Sinatra in THE JOKER IS WILD (1957), again at Paramount. It was a version of the life and times (the Roaring Twenties) of nightclub singer-turned-comedian Joe E. Lewis (Sinatra), who loves socialite Jeanne Crain but instead marries leggy chorine Mitzi, only to succumb later to booze. Sinatra sang effectively (the song "All the Way" won an Academy Award), Gaynor was gammy and sexy, and Sophie Tucker appeared as herself. In this, her best year on screen, Mitzi next co-starred with Gene Kelly in MGM's sophisticated LES GIRLS (1957), directed by George Cukor. It was a stylish Cole Porter original that had Gene Kelly doing what he did best—dancing, singing, and playing a heel. Here he was a stage trouper on the Continent who acts fast and loose with his three stage partners: Mitzi, Kay Kendall, and Taina Elg. Gaynor was the one he married and with whom he danced "Why Am I So Gone (About That Gal)?" With Kendall and Elg, Mitzi performed several routines, including the saucy boudoir spoof "Ladies in Waiting." Unfortunately, the movie was too chic for most moviegoers' tastes.

In the late 1950s Hollywood had almost abandoned the traditional musical (except for rock 'n' roll efforts). Occasionally, in the case of a sure-fire Broadway hit, the studios would take a risk. SOUTH PACIFIC had begun on Broadway in 1949 and nearly a decade later was finally being translated to the screen. It was "the" role of the year. Mary Martin, who had originated the part, was now considered too mature to play frolicking nurse Nellie Forbush on screen. Thus, such talent as Doris Day, Elizabeth Taylor, Susan Hayward, Ginger Rogers, and Jean Simmons campaigned for the part. Mitzi Gaynor was among those tested by the show's authors, Rodgers and Hammerstein. She auditioned for Hammerstein at the Crystal Ballroom of the Beverly Hills Hotel. As she recalls, "while I was singing, Oscar, who was a little deaf, kept moving farther and farther back. He wanted me to project, as if I were auditioning for the theatre! . . . When I was finished, I put my shoes back on and asked, 'How was I?' and he said, 'Thank you, Miss Gaynor, you're a very good sport!'" He was still not sure if she had the box-office allure required for the highly budgeted musical. She then did a secret screen test (the other competitors were jumpy about anyone's getting the edge) for director Joshua Logan at 20th Century–Fox, the distributor of this Magna production. Gaynor won out and was hired at double her past salary. Shot on location in Hawaii in a super widescreen process, SOUTH PACIFIC *should* have been a milestone screen musical—but it was not. Logan's direction was heavy-handed and gimmicky (the multicolored gassy sky effects); the singing of co-stars Rosanno Brazzi (as the plantation owner who loves Gaynor) and John Kerr (the second male lead) was dubbed; and the film was a too lengthy 171 minutes. Nevertheless, Gaynor cavorted energetically in this $5 million production, acting gamine-like as she admitted to being "A Cockeyed Optimist," that "I'm in Love with a Wonderful Guy," and that "I'm Gonna Wash That Man Right Outa My Hair." She and Brazzi (and his voice double) dueted "Some Enchanted Evening" and with Ray Walston (the brightest personality in the picture) she performed the lively "Honey Bun." Because of the hoopla involved, the picture earned $17,500,000 in domestic film rentals. However, it was generally not liked and damaged Mitzi Gaynor's standing in Hollywood. It was said she had no sex appeal on screen.

Thereafter she turned to another genre, screen comedy. She was vivacious with David Niven in the domestic comedy HAPPY ANNIVERSARY (1959), did her best to buoy a leaden SURPRISE PACKAGE (1960) opposite Yul Brynner, and was one of the few bright ingredients in FOR LOVE OR MONEY (1963), in which she was paired with Kirk Douglas. By now her film career was over. "The movie musical thing was finished, the contract players were flooding the streets, and I was just part of the backwash," she said.

Meanwhile, she had been testing the waters in other entertainment media. She was the only female guest on "The Frank Sinatra Show" (ABC-TV, October 9, 1959), shining

Mitzi Gaynor and Rossano Brazzi in SOUTH PACIFIC (1958)

out in an array of talent that included Bing Crosby, Jimmy Durante, and Dean Martin. More important, in 1961 she began performing in Las Vegas. The gambling capital catered to a Southern California crowd and anyone with a film name was considered potential marquee bait. Morris Landsberg, the owner of the Flamingo Hotel, urged her to star in a cabaret act for him. She claims she was very uncertain about the venture. When Landsberg invited her and her husband to a Las Vegas middleweight prize fight (Sugar Ray Robinson versus Gene Fullmer), Gaynor said, "If Fullmer wins, I'm going to do the act." He did and she did. It was Mitzi who pioneered the original (and soon to become standard) Las Vegas production ensemble show: glitzy costumes and sets, high-tech lighting and sound, superb male dancers, and, for its focal point, a singing star who could vocalize, dance, and even clown. She was a pre–Carol Burnett type, only a lot prettier. She tested the act in Hot Springs, Arkansas, and it opened in Vegas in July 1961. She has been performing in clubs ever since.

In 1964 she finally appeared on "The Ed Sullivan Show" (CBS-TV), once Sullivan agreed to the proviso that she have at least a fifteen-minute segment. She shared the spotlight that night with The Beatles and some viewers thought her act was too suggestive. By 1968 she was earning $45,000 a week in Las Vegas. In her club act she did skits that kidded her sexy screen image and demonstrated her versatility as a performer. That she could frolic as a leggy dancer, be a stylish chanteuse, and excel as a comedienne with perfect timing made her a great audience-pleaser. Among her comedy alter egos were Mitzi Goodglove, Nancy Neat, and Betty Bath. She continued demonstrating the independence that had marked (marred) her Fox contract years. She insisted, "I'd rather work in-person than in a movie I don't like. . . . If I told you the [Broadway] hits I've turned down—but something just has to strike me." She wowed the audience with her show-stopping dance number on the April 11, 1967, Academy Award telecast, proving that her reputation as a perfectionist paid dividends.

For her first starring TV special, "Mitzi" (NBC-TV, October 14, 1968), produced by her husband, her guests included George Hamilton and Phil Harris. It received good ratings and led to "Mitzi's Second Special" (NBC-TV, October 20, 1969). She did an hour-long show with Perry Como on NBC-TV on December 9, 1971. This was followed by such annual entries as "Mitzi . . . The First Time" (CBS-TV, March 28, 1973), "Mitzi and a Hundred Guys" (CBS-TV, March 24, 1975), "Mitzi . . . Roarin' in the 20s" (CBS-TV, March 14, 1976, with guests Linda Hopkins and Ken Berry), "Mitzi . . . Zings into Spring" (CBS-TV, March 29, 1977, with Roy Clark), and "Mitzi . . . What's Hot, What's Not" (CBS-TV, April 6, 1978). Her most elaborate outing was "Mitzi and a Hundred Guys," which had an array of guest performers, ranging from Michael Landon to Bill Bixby, Andy Griffith, Monte Hall, and Bob Hope.

Meanwhile, she continued her club engagements. She played three to four months on the road (earning $80,000 weekly) and then devoted the rest of the year to perfecting a new act. When she was at Harrah's in Lake Tahoe in 1971, *Variety* reported of the typical Gaynor production, "Gaynor herself is an excellent comedienne. In baby pink fluff, she camps 'My Heart Belongs to Daddy' and dressed in hokey hick bloomer outfit worn for

'Doin' What Comes Naturally' she sits on the stage and sings 'Look to the Rainbow,' and comes off superbly." There had been talk in 1972 of her doing a musical picture called HOLLYWOOD! HOLLYWOOD! with Carol Burnett, but the plans were never realized. "I have no desire to do films any more," Gaynor insisted. "My [annual] television special is my movie. . . . I love television because it's fast. All that waiting around on movie sets while they change the set or the lights isn't for me any more. . . . When people ask me why I work so hard and when am I going to retire, I think they're crazy." When asked about her old films, she said, "I see pictures I've done and I say, 'Ugh, Mitzi, don't act so much.' I'm all eyebrows, teeth, and hair. Reaction upon reaction! . . . But Virgo people are hard on themselves."

When Mitzi was at the Westbury Music Fair in October 1979, *Newsday* reminded readers, "She's not just a straight hoofer and singer, but a first-rate musical comedienne, injecting wit and humor into her act that comes out charmingly." By 1982 she was netting $250,000 annually from her club engagements and had done ten network specials. On November 10, 1986, she was honored by the Friars Club as one of the great song-and-dance stars of her generation. Throughout the rest of the 1980s she continued her cabaret appearances, wearing Bob Mackie costumes, celebrating and satirizing theme subjects, and dancing up a storm. Her 1987–88 national tour was a salute to Irving Berlin and was produced at a cost of $350,000. Now in her late fifties, she continues unabated, with an eleven-month, thirty-six-city national tour of the classic musical *Anything Goes* set for the 1989–90 season. "I got my Social Security card when I was twelve and I haven't been out of work a single day since then."

## Filmography

My Blue Heaven (20th–Fox, 1950)
Take Care of My Little Girl (20th–Fox, 1951)
Golden Girl (20th–Fox, 1951)
We're Not Married (20th–Fox, 1952)
Bloodhounds of Broadway (20th–Fox, 1952)
The 'I Don't Care' Girl (20th–Fox, 1953)
Down Among the Sheltering Palms (20th–Fox, 1953)
Three Young Texans (20th–Fox, 1954)

There's No Business Like Show Business (20th–Fox, 1954)
Anything Goes (Par, 1956)
The Birds and the Bees (RKO, 1956)
The Joker Is Wild [All the Way] (Par, 1957)
Les Girls (MGM, 1957)
South Pacific (Magna, 1958)
Happy Anniversary (MGM, 1959)
Surprise Package (UA, 1960)
For Love or Money (Univ, 1963)

## Album Discography

Anything Goes (Decca DL-8318) [ST]
Golden Girl (Caliban 6037) [ST]
The Joker Is Wild (Caliban 6024) [ST]
Les Girls (MGM E-3590) [ST]
Mitzi (Verve 2110)
Mitzi Gaynor Sings the Lyrics of Ira Gershwin (Verve 2115)

Mitzi Zings into Spring (Armstrong ICPR 3-77) [ST/TV]
My Blue Heaven (Titania 503) [ST]
South Pacific (RCA LOC/LSO-1032) [ST]
There's No Business Like Show Business (Decca DL-8091, MCA 1723) [ST]

# BETTY GRABLE

AN ICON IN AMERICAN CULTURAL HISTORY, BLUE-EYED BETTY
Grable will forever be remembered as the most celebrated of all pin-up girls. The famous
World War II poster shot of her in a form-fitting bathing suit looking seductively over her
shoulder is embedded in the minds of many Americans—it is just as much a part of the war
effort as rationing or helping to retake the beaches at Normandy. Her legs (like those of
Marlene Dietrich) were insured for a million dollars, her vital statistics (34-23-35) were
legendary, and her spunky personality made her all the more enticing. Although she was
one of the top money-making stars (in the top ten at the box office for a decade!), she was
quite down-to-earth and unaffected by her enormous star status. "As a dancer I couldn't
outdance Ginger Rogers or Eleanor Powell. As a singer I'm no rival to Doris Day. As an
actress I don't take myself seriously." On another occasion she said, "I am what I wanted to
be. Just give me the lines that lead into a song-and-dance routine. I'm the girl the truck
drivers love."

Grable was the blonde bombshell link between the 1930s' Jean Harlow and the
1950s' Marilyn Monroe. Her peaches-and-cream good looks were highlighted superbly
when filmed in splashy color, and her typical film backstage stories were a marvelous
excuse for her to parade in abbreviated, revealing costumes. She captivated the moviegoing
public during the war years with her ingratiating personality and fluffy screen vehicles. It is
somewhat ironic that although she is typed as a movie singer, Betty Grable was a mediocre
vocalist at best.

She was born Elizabeth Ruth Grable in South St. Louis, Missouri, on December 18,
1916, the daughter of bookkeeper/truck driver Conn Grable and ambitious Lillian Rose
(Hoffman) Grable. The younger of two girls, she had an older sister, Marjorie. Her mother
was insistent that her younger daughter become a show business success, and at an early
age Betty took ballet and acrobatic lessons in addition to playing the ukulele and singing.
By the time she was seven she was adept enough to appear in local talent shows booked by
Jack Haley and Frank Fay. While hardly in her teens, Betty fell in love with Hollywood
when the family vacationed there. Against her father's will, Betty and her mother remained
in the film capital where she attended the Hollywood Professional School and did a
vaudeville act with Emlyn Pique (Mitzi Mayfair).

At thirteen (but claiming she was two years older), Betty was in the ensemble of
HAPPY DAYS (1929), landed a blackface chorus bit in Fox's LET'S GO PLACES (1930), and
was also in the chorus of the NEW MOVIETONE FOLLIES OF 1930 (1930). When the musical
movie craze faded, she auditioned for and was signed by producer Samuel Goldwyn to be

a "Goldwyn Girl" and appeared in a string of features for the producer, including three Eddie Cantor opuses, WHOOPEE! (1930), PALMY DAYS (1931), where she met her future lover, George Raft, and THE KID FROM SPAIN (1932). During this time her grasping mother put her in a series of Educational shorts directed by Fatty Arbuckle (as William Goodrich) and she used the name Frances Dean. When her Goldwyn contract was terminated ("I had that girl under contract once. I wonder why I never did anything with her," Goldwyn would say), she appeared in the revue *Tattle Tales* with Barbara Stanwyck and Frank Fay in 1933, but left the show during its pre-Broadway tryout in San Francisco. Then she did an eight-month tour as the vocalist with Ted Fio Rito and his band. (The candid Grable would admit of her stint as a band singer, "The trouble was, I couldn't sing!") With Fio Rito she appeared in THE SWEETHEART OF SIGMA CHI (1933) and she was in a variety of other Hollywood products, several of which, like PROBATION (1932) and WHAT PRICE INNOCENCE? (1933), were made on poverty row.

Betty was the ingenue in the studio's Bert Wheeler–Robert Woolsey comedy HOLD 'EM JAIL (1932) and later toured with the comedy team, as well as appeared with them in THE NITWITS (1935). After she gained some attention singing "Let's K-nock K-neez" in THE GAY DIVORCEE (1934) with Edward Everett Horton, RKO signed her to a contract. But as with her Goldwyn tenure, not much happened. When her RKO contract ended, she went to Fox (again) for a co-lead in PIGSKIN PARADE (1936). However, it was Judy Garland (in her first feature picture) and Stuart Erwin (who was Oscar-nominated) who received the most attention. Grable's big number, "It's Love I'm After," was cut from the final release print. She was part of a vaudeville tour with ex-child star Jackie Coogan and on her birthday (December 18, 1937) they were married. She had already begun her "Betty Co-ed" type of role at Paramount with COLLEGIATE (1936) and was soon signed by that studio to a contract. Despite the promise of a big build-up she continued to play the same type of collegiate roles in a string of "B" features, including COLLEGE SWING (1938), CAMPUS CONFESSIONS (1938), and MILLION DOLLAR LEGS (1939). She was voted "America's Ideal Girl" by the Hollywood Artists and Local Chamber of Commerce. Then she made newspaper headlines by standing by Coogan during his famous court battle to obtain his screen earnings from his mother and stepfather. She was earning $500 weekly when Paramount dropped her option in 1939. It was yet another crisis in her seesawing career and she later admitted, "something had to be done or I would be a promising youngster until I was a grandmother."

She returned once more to vaudeville, where she earned up to $1,500 weekly. After appearing for two weeks with Jack Haley at the San Francisco Exposition, Buddy DeSylva (who had co-written the book for a new Cole Porter musical) saw her and hired her for this Broadway vehicle, *DuBarry Was a Lady* (1939). Ethel Merman was the star, but Betty, in the second lead, got good notices for her dance number "Well, Did You Evah." She appeared on the cover of *Life* magazine. Meanwhile, 20th Century–Fox mogul Darryl F. Zanuck noticed the Grable hoopla and signed her to a contract, admitting, "This girl has qualities we missed here."

Grable returned to Hollywood in June 1940. Her marriage to Coogan was over. Her romance with bandleader Artie Shaw had ended when he married Lana Turner in February 1940. She began dating George Raft. For her first role under her new 20th Century–Fox contract she replaced Alice Faye, the studio's top musical star, when the latter became ill. The vehicle was the Technicolor DOWN ARGENTINE WAY (1940) and Betty scored well as the heiress who is mad about horse racing and is romanced by Don Ameche. She and Faye, who became lifelong friends, were co-starred as dancing sisters in TIN PAN ALLEY (1940), a delightful period musical which highlighted Betty in a very sexy rendition of "The Sheik of Araby" in a harem-girl outfit. The film also allowed her to sing "Honeysuckle Rose" and "Moonlight and Roses." She and Don Ameche were paired again in still another Technicolor musical, MOON OVER MIAMI (1941), in which she sang "Kindergarten Conga."

Although she always insisted she was not a good actress, her next two features—both in black and white—belied that notion as she handled drama well in A YANK IN THE RAF and I WAKE UP SCREAMING, both in 1941. But exhibitors and moviegoers liked her best in Technicolor fluff such as SONG OF THE ISLANDS (1942), in which she was matched with studio beefcake contractee Victor Mature. She was now receiving more than a thousand fan letters a week and within a year was to be among the top ten money-making Hollywood stars. Her brand of snap and sparkle was definitely in vogue. In 1942, replacing pregnant Alice Faye, she starred in SPRINGTIME IN THE ROCKIES and this color opus had her appearing with bandleader Harry James. James soon replaced George Raft in Grable's love life and they were wed on July 5, 1943, in Las Vegas. Meanwhile, Betty churned out more musicals. She was a chorus girl performing "I Heard the Birdies Sing" in FOOTLIGHT SERENADE (1942—her final black-and-white starring vehicle) and CONEY ISLAND (1943) had her singing "Cuddle Up a Little Closer" and "Take It from There." She was a Brooklyn chirp who becomes a British music hall star in SWEET ROSIE O'GRADY (1943), in which she performed "Waitin' at the Church." She had a guest bit as herself in FOUR JILLS IN A JEEP (1944) and then romanced a sailor (John Harvey) in PIN-UP GIRL (1944), a lame musical designed to exploit her title as the Queen of the G.I.s. On March 3, 1944, she gave birth to her first child, Victoria. (Her second child, Jessica, would be born on May 20, 1947.) Said the ever-candid Grable, "It isn't difficult to be a good mother and a movie star at the same time. It just calls for planning. . . . My family always comes first."

Betty returned to the screen in 1945 in BILLY ROSE'S DIAMOND HORSESHOE, singing "Welcome to the Diamond Horseshoe" and "Acapulco" in this slight tale of chorine Grable falling for medical student Dick Haymes. Fox had wanted Betty to reteam with Alice Faye in THE DOLLY SISTERS (1945), but the latter had retired from the screen so it was newcomer June Haver who was paired with Grable in this entertaining production. Grable sang "I Can't Begin to Tell You." Her only 1946 feature film appearance was a guest bit at the finale of DO YOU LOVE ME?, which co-starred her husband, Harry James. During the 1940s Grable appeared on radio in such shows as "Gulf Screen Guild Theatre," "Lux Radio Theatre," "Philco Radio Time," and "Suspense." Although she was known as a singer, she cut no records. 20th Century–Fox studio chief Darryl F. Zanuck refused to let most of his stars record and Betty was one of them. However, she did one commercial record in 1945 for Columbia Records called "I Can't Begin to Tell You" with Harry James, but on the record she was billed as Ruth Haag.

By now Grable was the studio's chief moneymaker and was earning some $300,000 yearly. But in 1947, her period comedy THE SHOCKING MISS PILGRIM, which did not reveal her fabulous legs, lost money. The studio wisely returned her to form in MOTHER WORE TIGHTS (1947), in which she sang "Kokomo, Indiana," "Burlington Bertie from Bow," and "You Do." She missed again in THAT LADY IN ERMINE (1948), a musical fantasy production fraught with problems when director Ernst Lubitsch died in the middle of its filming and was replaced by Otto Preminger. She and Dan Dailey had scored as a team in MOTHER WORE TIGHTS and they were reunited in WHEN MY BABY SMILES AT ME (1948), a remake of the earlier DANCE OF LIFE (1929) and SWING HIGH, SWING LOW (1937).

The bottom really fell out from under Betty Grable's film career when she starred in Preston Sturges' THE BEAUTIFUL BLONDE FROM BASHFUL BEND (1949). Grable never looked lovelier on film, but the movie itself was a vulgar, turgid Western which cast the star as a gun-slinging school marm in the Old West romanced by slick crook Cesar

Rudy Vallee and Betty Grable in THE BEAUTIFUL BLONDE FROM BASHFUL BEND (1949)

Romero and stuffy millionaire Rudy Vallee. She was back with Dan Dailey for MY BLUE HEAVEN in 1950. However, this marital comedy about radio stars wanting to adopt a baby was mediocre and young contractee Mitzi Gaynor received the best notices. Much better was a remake of CONEY ISLAND called WABASH AVENUE (1950) in which saloon singer Betty (who warbled "I Wish I Could Shimmy Like My Sister Kate") was romanced by her boss (Phil Harris) and a gambler (Victor Mature). She and Mature repeated their roles on "Lux Radio Theatre" on CBS on November 13, 1950.

Betty and Dan Dailey were teamed for the final time in CALL ME MISTER (1951), about a show business couple doing a USO tour in Japan. For producer George Jessel she headlined MEET ME AFTER THE SHOW (1951), which was reminiscent of the star's musicals from the 1940s. Grable was suspended for refusing to do yet another song-and-dance with Dailey (THE GIRL NEXT DOOR, 1953) and June Haver did the part. Betty also turned down a dramatic role in PICKUP ON SOUTH STREET (1953), which Jean Peters performed. (Her rationale was, "I don't go in for that dramatic stuff; I'm no actress.") Instead she went on suspension and then returned to the studio to make THE FARMER TAKES A WIFE (1953). However, it was a weak musical and fared poorly. With musicals (and Grable) on the wane, studio plans to star Betty in remakes of HEAVEN CAN WAIT and BAD GIRL were dropped. Fox had a new blonde sexpot named Marilyn Monroe who won the lead away from Grable in GENTLEMEN PREFER BLONDES (1953). It was Monroe who received top billing in HOW TO MARRY A MILLIONAIRE (1953) over Grable and Lauren Bacall. Ever the professional, Grable turned in a deft comedy performance as the showgirl determined to wed a rich businessman (Fred Clark). Fox loaned Grable to Columbia Pictures for a remake of the 1940 film TOO MANY HUSBANDS, a clumsy musical named THREE FOR THE SHOW (1955). Although Grable was good as the show business star who thinks her husband (Jack Lemmon) has died and marries a dancer (Gower Champion), the picture proved to be a lumbering mess. Her final picture at 20th, HOW TO BE VERY, VERY POPULAR (1955), teamed her with Sheree North. The studio was grooming the latter as a Marilyn Monroe replacement, just as it had groomed Monroe to replace Grable. The two blondes did a fine job in this CinemaScope comedy as burlesque dancers who hide in a men's dormitory after witnessing a murder. But it was considered old hat and did poor business. Grable and Fox ended their contract. Reportedly, Grable, typically good natured, told Marilyn Monroe (who inherited her star dressing room), "Honey, I've had it. Go get yours. It's your turn now."

There were plans for Grable to make films for United Artists, but they did not gel, nor did negotiations for her to star in GUYS AND DOLLS (1955) for her old boss Samuel Goldwyn; she was replaced by another ex-Fox musical star, Vivian Blaine. Following the demise of her film career, Grable worked for a time in television. In 1956 she appeared as "Cleopatra Collins" on NBC-TV's "Stage Door" and the same year played with Orson Welles, Keenan Wynn, and Ray Collins in the "Ford Star Jubilee" presentation of "Twentieth Century" on CBS-TV, plus guesting on a TV special with Mario Lanza. On the 1957 Academy Awards telecast she and Harry James performed "Lullaby of Broadway" and the duo guest-starred the next year on CBS's "The Lucy-Desi Comedy Hour." She and James also appeared together in Las Vegas and she toured with her revue, *Memories*. However, she had no great desire to continue working hard. In fact she admitted, "I never really had any great drive for my career; it was my mother who wanted it. Even now she's mad at me for not working any more. . . . Once in a while my agents call me, but I couldn't care less."

In the late 1950s Grable and James moved their family to Las Vegas where his musical activities were centered and they moved into a new $100,000 home located behind the Tropicana Hotel. Never having been happy in Hollywood, Betty found more personal contentment in Las Vegas, although by now her marriage to the heavy-drinking and gambling Harry James was a rocky one.

Late in 1962, Grable and Dan Dailey reteamed for a condensed version of *Guys and Dolls* at the Dunes Hotel in Las Vegas and they would continue with the show, on and off, both in Vegas and in stock productions. In 1965 Betty and Harry James were divorced. Betty sold their home and moved into a smaller house. That same year Betty took on one of her most successful roles, that of Dolly Levi in one of the many touring editions of *Hello, Dolly!* After opening in Las Vegas, she undertook a sixteen-month tour, which culminated in her return to Broadway in the role in the summer of 1967. After a successful run, she returned to Las Vegas and did road tours with productions like *Plaza Suite*, *High Button Shoes*, and *Guys and Dolls*. She needed money badly as she was again friendly with Harry James (who had remarried) and she loaned him more than a million dollars to pay off gambling debts.

In 1969 she went to London to star in the expensive musical Western *Belle Starr*, but it flopped, closing after only sixteen performances. In 1971 she and her old pal Dorothy Lamour co-starred in the summer theater revue *That's Show Business* in St. Louis. She also made appearances on Carol Burnett's TV variety program and became a TV spokesperson for Geritol. In 1972 Betty worked twice on TV with her movies co-star Dick Haymes: first on a TV special and then at the 1972 Academy Awards show. In 1972 it was announced that Grable would take over for Yvonne De Carlo in the Australian company of *No, No Nanette*, but illness intervened as tests showed Betty had cancer. Despite deteriorating health, Grable went to Jacksonville, Florida, early in 1973 to appear in *Born Yesterday*. After the show's run, she returned to Las Vegas and was hospitalized. She died there on July 2, 1973; one of her last visitors was Alice Faye. Grable had earned $5 million from her career, but she died nearly broke. Attending her funeral on July 5, 1973, was Harry James, who had married her exactly forty years before. (He died on July 5, 1983.)

In 1986 Betty Grable was the subject of a revealing biography, *Pin-Up: The Tragedy of Betty Grable* by Spero Pastos. The book revealed that Grable was a woman of many facets. It detailed how she had been victimized by her ambitious mother and had, in turn, been a poor mother herself. Betty's main appeal was revealed by the book's dust jacket; both sides boasted the picture of this glamourous star in her famous World War II pin-up.

## Filmography

Happy Days (Fox, 1929)

Let's Go Places [Mirth and Melody] (Fox, 1930)

Fox Movietone Follies of 1930 [New Movietone
Follies of 1930] (Fox, 1930)

Whoopee! (UA, 1930)

Kiki (UA, 1931)

Palmy Days (UA, 1931)

Ex-Sweeties (Educational, 1931) (s)

Crashing Hollywood (Educational, 1931) (s)*

Hollywood Luck (Educational, 1932) (s)*

Hollywood Lights (Educational, 1932) (s)*

Lady, Please (Educational, 1932) (s)

Over the Counter (MGM, 1932) (s)

The Flirty Sleepwalker (Educational, 1932) (s)

The Greeks Had a Word for Them (UA, 1932)

Child of Manhattan (Col, 1932)

Probation [Second Chances] (Chesterfield,
1932)

Hold 'Em Jail (RKO, 1932)

The Kid from Spain (UA, 1932)

Cavalcade (Fox, 1932)

Air Tonic (RKO, 1933) (s)

The Sweetheart of Sigma Chi [Girl of My
Dreams] (Mon, 1933)

Melody Cruise (RKO, 1933)

What Price Innocence? [Shall the Children Pay?]
(Col, 1933)

Susie's Affairs (Col, 1934) (s)

The Gay Divorcee [The Gay Divorce] (RKO,
1934)

Student Tour (MGM, 1934)

Hips, Hips, Hooray! (RKO, 1934)

By Your Leave (RKO, 1934)

Love Detectives (Col, 1934) (s)

Business Is a Pleasure (Vita, 1934) (s)

The Nitwits (RKO, 1935)

Old Man Rhythm (RKO, 1935)

A Quiet Fourth (RKO, 1935) (s)

A Night at the Biltmore Bowl (RKO, 1935) (s)

Drawing Rumors (RKO, 1935) (s)

The Spirit of '76 (RKO, 1935) (s)

Pigskin Parade [The Harmony Parade] (20th–
Fox, 1936)

Follow the Fleet (RKO, 1936)

Don't Turn 'Em Loose (RKO, 1936)

Collegiate [The Charm School] (Par, 1936)

This Way Please (Par, 1937)

Thrill of a Lifetime (Par, 1937)

College Swing [Swing, Teacher, Swing] (Par,
1938)

Give Me a Sailor (Par, 1938)

Campus Confessions [Fast Play] (Par, 1938)

Man About Town (Par, 1939)

Million Dollar Legs (Par, 1939)

The Day the Bookies Wept (RKO, 1939)

Down Argentine Way (20th–Fox, 1940)

Tin Pan Alley (20th–Fox, 1940)

A Yank in the RAF (20th–Fox, 1941)

Hedda Hopper's Hollywood (Par, 1941) (s)

I Wake Up Screaming [Hot Spot] (20th–Fox,
1941)

Moon over Miami (20th–Fox, 1941)

Footlight Serenade (20th–Fox, 1942)

Song of the Islands (20th–Fox, 1942)

Springtime in the Rockies (20th–Fox, 1942)

Coney Island (20th–Fox, 1943)

Sweet Rosie O'Grady (20th–Fox, 1943)

Four Jills in a Jeep (20th–Fox, 1944)

Pin-Up Girl (20th–Fox, 1944)

Billy Rose's Diamond Horseshoe [Diamond
Horseshoe] (20th–Fox, 1945)

The Dolly Sisters (20th–Fox, 1945)

All Star Bond Rally (20th–Fox, 1945) (s)

Do You Love Me? (20th–Fox, 1946)

Hollywood Park (Unk, 1946) (s)

The Shocking Miss Pilgrim (20th–Fox, 1947)

Mother Wore Tights (20th–Fox, 1947)

Hollywood Bound (Unk, 1947) (s)

That Lady in Ermine (20th–Fox, 1948)

When My Baby Smiles at Me (20th–Fox, 1948)

The Beautiful Blonde from Bashful Bend (20th–
Fox, 1949)

Wabash Avenue (20th–Fox, 1950)

My Blue Heaven (20th–Fox, 1950)

Call Me Mister (20th–Fox, 1951)

Meet Me After the Show (20th–Fox, 1951)

The Farmer Takes a Wife (20th–Fox, 1953)

How to Marry a Millionaire (20th–Fox, 1953)

Three for the Show (Col, 1955)

How to Be Very, Very Popular (20th–Fox,
1955)

---

*As Frances Dean

## Broadway Plays

DuBarry Was a Lady (1939)
Hello, Dolly! (1967) (replacement)

## Album Discography

Betty Grable (Curtain Calls 100/5, Scarce
    Rarities 5501)
Betty Grable (Sandy Hook 2014)
Betty Grable, 1934–60 (Star-Tone 219)
Billy Rose's Diamond Horseshoe (Caliban 6028)
    [ST]
Call Me Mister (Titania 510) [ST]
Collegiate (Caliban 6042) [ST]
Coney Island/Moon over Miami (Caliban 6001)
    [ST]
The Dolly Sisters (CIF 3010) [ST]
Down Argentine Way (Hollywood Soundstage
    5012) [ST]
Down Argentine Way/Tin Pan Alley (Caliban
    6003) [ST]
Footlight Serenade (Caliban 6002) [ST]

Four Jills in a Jeep (Hollywood Soundstage 407)
    [ST]
The Gay Divorcee (EMI 101, Sountrak 105)
    [ST]
Meet Me After the Show (Caliban 6012) [ST]
Mother Wore Tights/The Shocking Miss
    Pilgrim (CIF 3008) [ST]
My Blue Heaven (Titania 503) [ST]
Pigskin Parade (Pilgrim 4000) [ST]
Pin-Up Girl/Song of the Islands (Caliban 6009)
    [ST]
Springtime in the Rockies (Pelican 128) [ST/R]
Sweet Rosie O'Grady (Titania 507) [ST]
Three for the Show (10" Mer MG-25204) [ST]
Wabash Avenue (Caliban 6029) [ST]

# KATHRYN GRAYSON

KATHRYN GRAYSON WAS GROOMED BY MGM AS THAT STUDIO'S answer to Universal's Deanna Durbin. However, despite good looks, acting ability, and a fair coloratura operatic voice, she never really was in competition with Durbin, nor did she ever become a top singing star even at her home studio. Usually she was more ornamental than versatile, because of script limitations and because on camera, she was too often coy and mannered. It was not until the 1950s that she blossomed as a star of movie operettas. However, by then that genre was in its twilight and her film career ended when that type of light screen fare became passé. In the years since, Kathryn Grayson has carved for herself a career in nightclubs and on stage, doing her movie songs and operettas, sometimes in tandem with screen co-star Howard Keel. The star admits she was never sufficiently ambitious about her movie career and was content to appear in whatever MGM offered her, preferring financial security to superstardom. Her initial goal had always been to be an opera diva and when that did not happen, being a movie star was always second best. After she retired from films she said, "I want to do something intelligent, and movie musicals don't classify."

Kathryn Grayson was born Zelma Kathryn Hedrick on February 9, 1922, in Winston-Salem, North Carolina, the daughter of a building contractor–realtor. For most of her childhood the family moved frequently, but they lived for some years in St. Louis. Her interest in music was evident from an early age. At St. Louis's Municipal Opera she performed for Chicago Civic Opera star Frances Marshall, who told Kathryn and her family to continue with her music lessons. While she was a teenager, Kathryn's family moved to Hollywood and she went to Manual Arts High School and took vocal training from Minna Letha White. Louis B. Mayer heard Kathryn sing at a city festival and offered her an MGM contract without even a screen test. Much to White's chagrin, the young lady accepted the lucrative studio offer, and in 1940 she began a year's training in drama, elocution, and voice. To provide her with actual show business experience, the studio negotiated for her a steady job singing on "The Eddie Cantor Show" on NBC Radio.

Like many MGM starlets of the period, Kathryn made her screen debut in an "Andy Hardy" feature, ANDY HARDY'S PRIVATE SECRETARY (1941). She played an aspiring singer whom Andy (Mickey Rooney) engages to be his secretary and get his mixed-up affairs at high school in order. In her pleasing film bow, Kathryn not only emoted well, but she also provided pleasing vocals to "Voci de Primavera" and a scene from Donizetti's famous opera *Lucia di Lammermoor. Variety* observed of the pretty miss with the heart-shaped face and dimpled cheeks, "Looks like Metro has a name nugget in Miss Grayson." She did even better in THE VANISHING VIRGINIAN (1941) as the daughter of a small town Southern public servant (Frank Morgan) and in it she sang "The World Was Made for You." In 1940 Kathryn married another MGM player, John Shelton. Their marriage would be plagued with separations, reconciliations, a miscarriage, and more partings. They finally divorced in 1946. Shelton died in May 1972.

For her first starring role, MGM cast the singer opposite Bud Abbott and Lou Costello in RIO RITA (1942), a remake of the 1929 Radio Picture which had starred John Boles, Bebe Daniels, and the comedy team of Bert Wheeler and Robert Woolsey. Kathryn was cast as the sweetheart of radio star John Carroll, and her ranch was invaded by Abbott and Costello *and* Nazi spies. A fairly bright effort, it gave Grayson the new Harold Arlen– E. Y. Harburg song "Long Before You Came Along." In 1942 she also did well in the overly cute comedy SEVEN SWEETHEARTS as the oldest of seven daughters, none of whom can marry until she weds; here Kathryn sang "You and the Waltz and I." The star's operatic training was again on display in the all-star THOUSANDS CHEER (1943), in which she was romanced by Army private Gene Kelly and sang the aria "Sempre Libera" from Verdi's *La Traviata* and the novelty tune "I Dug a Ditch in Wichita." In the big-budget affair she played the daughter of John Boles and Mary Astor. She commented later, "there's so much one can learn from people like them." Kathryn was then off the screen for two years but in the interim she did war-effort entertaining and appeared on radio programs like Paul Whiteman's "Radio Hall of Fame" on NBC in 1943. After recurring battles in the early 1940s with studio head Louis B. Mayer about her wanting to return to her operatic studies (he called her an "ungrateful little bitch"), she gave in to his will about her movie career. (Some insist her studio career was perpetuated by a mentor in the Metro hierarchy.)

She returned to the screen in 1945 in MGM's ANCHORS AWEIGH in which Navy men Gene Kelly and Frank Sinatra romanced her but the singer was more intent on dropping her film extra jobs and auditioning for José Iturbi. She sang "My Heart Sings." Next she and studio rival June Allyson co-starred in the title roles of TWO SISTERS FROM BOSTON (1946), a period musical with a mediocre score. Its fair plot had Kathryn becoming the singing star at a Bowery saloon run by Jimmy Durante and being romanced by Peter Lawford. Once again her screen image was too lofty for broad audience acceptance. The singer's last two films of 1946 were guest appearances in the all-star musicals ZIEGFELD FOLLIES OF 1946 and TILL THE CLOUDS ROLL BY. In the former (filmed in 1944) she was stuck with the dud production number "There's Beauty Everywhere," while in the second outing, a biopic of Jerome Kern, she had a well-staged sequence from *Show Boat* in which she and Tony Martin did a splendid, if stagey, duet on "Make Believe." Five years later she would portray Magnolia in MGM's remake of SHOW BOAT, and in 1953 she and Tony Martin would reteam on RCA Victor Records for a very fine rendering of the score to *The Desert Song.*

MGM unwisely teamed Kathryn Grayson and Frank Sinatra for two glossy feature films, neither of which helped their careers. IT HAPPENED IN BROOKLYN (1947) had them as part of a theatrical group out to stage a musical show. Kathryn got a chance to perform from the opera *Lakmé*, but the results were less than satisfying. Next she was the object of outlaw Sinatra's affections in the hokey Western THE KISSING BANDIT (1948), which was so badly received it was almost laughed off the screen. Its only attraction for Kathryn was that if offered her the chance to sing "Love Is Where You Find It." Far better for the songstress were her two teamings with Mario Lanza, in THAT MIDNIGHT KISS (1949) and THE TOAST OF NEW ORLEANS (1950). Lanza made his screen debut in the former as a singing truck driver and he and Grayson made an attractive screen pair. In THE TOAST OF NEW ORLEANS he was a singing fisherman who becomes an opera star and the film gave Kathryn the chance to perform excerpts from Puccini's *Madama Butterfly* as Cho-Cho-San (her favorite operatic part). Following the film's release, she and Lanza went on a successful cross-country tour with the picture and she became close to the tenor and his family and would remain so even after his tragic death in 1959 and his wife's demise the following year. (When Grayson's daughter, Patricia, married in 1969, the maid of honor was Colleen Lanza, Mario's daughter and Kathryn's best friend.) On screen she was cast as an opera star in the comedy GROUNDS FOR MARRIAGE (1950) but most of its footage was devoted to the effort to get her and her ex-husband doctor (Van Johnson) to reconcile.

Kathryn Grayson, Agnes Moorehead, and Frances Williams in SHOW BOAT (1951)

In her personal life, Kathryn had wed actor Johnny Johnston in 1947 and on October 7, 1948, she gave birth to her only child, Patricia Kathryn. She and Johnston would divorce in 1951 and she never remarried, although she would be seen frequently on the Los Angeles social scene with attractive escorts. (In the late 1950s actor Robert Evans was her frequent escort.) Grayson would say of tinseltown social life, "You can never tell what a man has in mind when he asks you for a date in this town. He may be thinking of romance or he may just want his name in the papers."

After a decade on the screen, Kathryn Grayson finally came into her own when MGM teamed her with Howard Keel for its color remake of SHOW BOAT and top-billed Kathryn in the role of Magnolia. In it she and baritone Keel did beautiful duets on "Make Believe," "You Are Love," and "Why Do I Love You?" The musical grossed over $5 million at the box office and she and Keel were reteamed in a thin remake of ROBERTA (1935) entitled LOVELY TO LOOK AT (1952); neither star wanted to do this lavish but bland production. After it was completed Kathryn, earning $4,000 weekly, went on loan to Warner Bros. (That same year Metro's Jane Powell also went on loan to that studio.) Grayson was set initially to make a quartet of musicals with Warners, but only two materialized: THE DESERT SONG and SO THIS IS LOVE, both in 1953. Cast as Margot in THE DESERT SONG, she and co-star Gordon MacRae battled valiantly with the mildewed script about the Riffs in North Africa as they dueted on "One Alone" and Kathryn soloed with "Romance." The color musical proved only that Sigmund Romberg's score was more suited to the stage than to the screen, although this was its third movie rendering. While at MGM Kathryn had wanted to portray opera star Grace Moore on screen; she had the chance at Warners in SO THIS IS LOVE but she was defeated by a mundane script and a moviegoing audience already tiring of musicals and little interested in operatic arias.

Warner Bros. and Grayson concluded their joint ventures and the star returned to MGM to star in the delightful KISS ME KATE (1953), reteamed with Howard Keel. In the dual roles of Lili and Katherine she made a fine shrew. She soloed on "I Hate Men" and dueted spiritedly with Keel on "So in Love," "We Open in Venice" (with Ann Miller and Tommy Rall), "Wunderbar," and the title song. MGM then announced that Kathryn would star in musical versions of TRILBY and CAMILLE but they never came about and her planned role in BRIGADOON (1954) went to Cyd Charisse. Grayson especially wanted the role of the disabled opera singer in INTERRUPTED MELODY (1955), but it went to Eleanor Parker (whose singing voice had to be dubbed).

In the fall of 1955 she made her dramatic television debut on CBS-TV's "General Electric Theatre" in the segment "Shadows of the Heart," for which she was nominated for an Emmy Award. She did another segment of the anthology series the next year. Her final screen role came also in 1956 in THE VAGABOND KING, which was supposed to have reunited her with Mario Lanza. However, he lost the role due to health problems and it was assumed by a little-known opera singer named Oreste, who played François Villon to Grayson's Catherine. They both handled the film score nicely, especially their duet of "Only a Rose," but the age of the screen operetta was over. Kathryn then returned to television for roles in two CBS-TV programs, "Playhouse 90" in 1957 and "Lux Playhouse" the following year.

Although regarded primarily as a singer, Kathryn Grayson did very little recording during her career. While at MGM she did perform some of her movie songs—"My Heart Sings," "Love Is Where You Find It," and "You Are Love"—for the company's label, MGM Records. In the mid-1950s she cut an album for MGM called *Kathryn Grayson Sings.* Since she had done concert work in the early 1950s, both in Hollywood and London, Kathryn returned to such chores following the end of her screen career. (She was offered low-budget film properties, which she rejected, as she did a 1958 offer for $1 million over five years to be the television spokeswoman for Revlon Cosmetics.) In 1960 she was on stage in productions of the operas *Madama Butterfly, La Bohème,* and *La Traviata.* In 1961 she starred in stage productions of *The Merry Widow, Rosalinda,* and *Naughty Marietta.* She toured in 1963 with an elaborate production of *Camelot* with Louis Hayward but plans for her to replace Julie Andrews as Queen Guenevere in the Broadway edition fell through. She continued to be active in cabaret work and on stage, and in 1969 she and Howard Keel reteamed for a club act. During their run at the Fremont Hotel in Las Vegas in 1969 *Variety* commented, "Miss Grayson is earnest in her soprano scalings, which occasionally have a metallic edge at the top. . . . Identified with melodies of limpid nostalgia, Miss Grayson, nevertheless, gives a very good accounting of the strong modern ballad, 'Both Sides Now.'" She and Keel would continue their club act together, on and off, through the 1970s and during that decade they also appeared together to advantage in the stage production of *Man of La Mancha.* A much-heavier Kathryn Grayson occasionally appeared on television in the 1980s; late in the decade she and Gloria DeHaven were guests on another ex-MGM-er's (Angela Lansbury) teleseries, "Murder, She Wrote."

A level-headed woman, Kathryn Grayson never took her stardom too seriously. Regarding her screen vehicles she once admitted, "well, most of them were big-budgeted and seemed to take forever to make. I didn't have very good directors on most of them."

## Filmography

Andy Hardy's Private Secretary (MGM, 1941)
The Vanishing Virginian (MGM, 1941)
Rio Rita (MGM, 1942)
Seven Sweethearts (MGM, 1942)
Thousands Cheer (MGM, 1943)
Anchors Aweigh (MGM, 1945)
Two Sisters from Boston (MGM, 1946)
Ziegfeld Follies of 1946 (MGM, 1946)
Till the Clouds Roll By (MGM, 1946)
It Happened in Brooklyn (MGM, 1947)
The Kissing Bandit (MGM, 1948)

That Midnight Kiss (MGM, 1949)
The Toast of New Orleans (MGM, 1950)
Grounds for Marriage (MGM, 1950)
Show Boat (MGM, 1951)
Lovely to Look At (MGM, 1952)
The Desert Song (WB, 1953)
So This Is Love [The Grace Moore Story] (WB, 1953)
Kiss Me Kate (MGM, 1953)
The Vagabond King (Par, 1956)

## Radio Series

The Eddie Cantor Show (NBC, 1940)

## Album Discography

Always (A.Z. 105)

Anchors Aweigh (Curtain Calls 100/17, Sandy Hook 2024) [ST]

The Desert Song (10" RCA LPM-3105) w. Tony Martin

Grounds for Marriage (10" MGM E-536) [ST]

Kathryn Grayson (Lion 70055)

Kathryn Grayson Sings (10" MGM E-551, MGM E-3257)

Kiss Me Kate (MGM 3-077, Metro M/S-525) [ST]

The Kissing Bandit (Motion Picture Tracks MPT-7) [ST]

Let There Be Music (A.Z. 102)

Lovely to Look At (10" MGM E-150, MGM E-3230) [ST]

Make Believe (A.Z. 101)

Nelson Eddy with Shirley Temple, Jane Powell, Kathryn Grayson, Lois Butler and Norma Nelson (Mac/Eddy JN 128)

Show Boat (10" MGM E-559, MGM E-3230, Metro M/S-527) [ST]

So This Is Love (10" RCA LOC-3000) [ST]

Thousands Cheer (Hollywood Soundstage 409) [ST]

Till the Clouds Roll By (10" MGM E-501, MGM E-3231, Metro M/S-578, Sountrak 115, Vertinge 2000) [ST]

Toast of New Orleans (A.Z. 104) [ST]

20 Golden Favorites (Bulldog 3034)

Ziegfeld Follies of 1946 (Curtain Calls 100/15-16) [ST]

# JUNE HAVER

PRETTY AND TALENTED JUNE HAVER STARRED IN A DOZEN FEATURES
for 20th Century–Fox in the 1940s and early 1950s, the bulk of them in Technicolor. The
studio groomed her as a rival and possible successor to Betty Grable. In turn, Marilyn
Monroe, who was in two of Haver's features, was brought in to succeed June. Like most of
Darryl F. Zanuck's blonde stars of the period, June Haver was "a film personality"—a
movie player who had little experience on stage, radio, or television. As was true with most
Fox stars, she was not permitted to make recordings.

Ironically, June Haver first came to the attention of the film industry through her
vocalizing in the big band era. However, it was as a singer, dancer, and actress that she
made her mark on the musicals of post–World War II vintage. Being a close lookalike for
Betty Grable, June rarely earned plum screen assignments at Fox—they went to the
reigning Pin-Up Queen. Thus Haver rarely had occasion to display her full potential on
camera. Always deeply religious, June Haver tired of Hollywood eventually and for a time
in the early 1950s entered a convent. Later she resumed her acting career briefly and then
settled down to raise a family after her marriage to Fred MacMurray.

June Haver was born June Stovenour in Rock Island, Illinois, on June 10, 1926. A
precocious child, guided by a very determined mother, she showed an interest in music as
well as singing, dancing, and oratory. At the age of eight she won the Cincinnati (Ohio)
Conservatory of Music's Post Music Contest and then played piano (as a guest artist) with
the Cincinnati Symphony Orchestra. As a teenager she studied dramatics, dance, and
vocalizing and she landed a job singing with bandleader Dick Jurgens. This led to a brief
association with Freddy Martin's band and then, with her mother chaperoning, she
embarked on a tour with Ted Fio Rito's musical group. (Betty Grable had also been a band
vocalist with Fio Rito.) June made her screen debut with the bandleader in the Universal
musical short SWING'S THE THING (1942) and then appeared with Tommy Dorsey and
His Orchestra in another Universal short musical, TRUMPET SERENADE (1942).

Now living in Beverly Hills with her family, June Haver (as she was now billed)
attended high school there. While appearing in community theater she came to the
attention of 20th Century–Fox, which screen-tested her and soon placed the 5' 2" blue-
eyed blonde under contract, starting at $75 weekly. Both June and Jeanne Crain, with
whom she would work later at Fox, made their feature film debuts in the Alice Faye
musical THE GANG'S ALL HERE (1943), with June on camera briefly at the beginning of the
proceedings as hat-check girl Maybelle. Seeing potential in her looks and screen presence,
Darryl F. Zanuck groomed June as a possible replacement for Betty Grable, the studio's

top moneymaking star. Haver was cast as little sister Cri-Cri in HOME IN INDIANA (1944), whose plot concerned a farm youth (Lon McCallister) who becomes a successful small town jockey while finding love with a local girl (Jeanne Crain). At this time June became a protégé of studio producer George Jessel, who personally cast her in the role that was to bring her stardom, in THE DOLLY SISTERS (1945).

Prior to THE DOLLY SISTERS, June was given the female lead in IRISH EYES ARE SMILING (1944), the biopic of Irish composer Ernest R. Ball (Dick Haymes). She was a chorus girl whom Ball follows to Manhattan where both of them achieve stardom. Next she had the supporting role of Lucilla in the fantasy WHERE DO WE GO FROM HERE? (1945) in which her future real-life husband, Fred MacMurray, starred. He was a 4-F salvage depot guard who finds an old lamp whose genie (Gene Shelton) gives him three wishes, which allow him to be a hero at three different periods in American history. Then came THE DOLLY SISTERS, in which she and Betty Grable were the two show business siblings whose act brings them stardom at the turn of the century. This colorful production offered lots of the era's peppy tunes and it really boosted June's career, although (understandably) she and her co-star were personally cool to each other during its filming.

June was top-billed for the first time in THREE LITTLE GIRLS IN BLUE (1946) as she co-starred with Vivian Blaine and Vera-Ellen as one of three sisters hunting for rich husbands in 1902 in Atlantic City. The musical, which offered such songs as "Somewhere in the Night" and "This Is Always," grossed over $3 million at the box office. It was a remake of THREE BLIND MICE (1938) and MOON OVER MIAMI (1941) and would be re-worked yet again as HOW TO MARRY A MILLIONAIRE (1953). For her next two vehicles, June was guided by veteran director Lloyd Bacon. The dramatic WAKE UP AND DREAM (1946) cast her as a young woman seeking her missing brother. She sang the song "Give Me the Simple Life." One critic said of her in this failed patriotic fantasy, "June Haver . . . looks good in Technicolor, but never comes to fair grips with the script." She was back at her forte with the musical I WONDER WHO'S KISSING HER NOW? (1947), the fictional biography of 1890s composer Joseph E. "Joe" Howard (Mark Stevens). June was the entertainer who performed many of Howard's tunes ("Honeymoon," "I Wonder Who's Kissing Her Now?," and "What's the Use of Dreaming"). The feature was June's sole 1947 release. That year she married childhood boyfriend trumpeter Jimmy Zito. They eloped to Las Vegas on March 9 and were wed in a civil ceremony; they were then remarried in a Catholic Church service on March 26. The marriage was not a happy one: it ended in divorce two years later, with the actress then dating dentist Dr. John Duzik (who had been her fiancé before her marriage to Zito). Duzik's sudden death in October 1949 was a sobering experience for the once exuberant and carefree June.

In 1948 Fox reteamed June Haver with Lon McCallister in another bucolic love story, SCUDDA-HOO! SCUDDA-HAY! in which he played a Hoosier farm boy who trains a pair of mules that, by accident, help him win the young woman (Haver) he adores. Then she was cast in another composer screen biography, this time that of Fred Fisher (S. Z. Sakall) in OH, YOU BEAUTIFUL DOLL! (1949). It was set in the colorful 1890s with serious composer Fisher having his works made into popular melodies by a song plugger (Mark

Stevens). June was showcased as singer Doris and she performed many of the Tin Pan Alley standards of the day.

Her home studio apparently considering June more profitable as a loanout star, Zanuck made an agreement with Warner Bros. whereby June was to be borrowed by that studio for four movies. (This was in contrast to Betty Grable, who was *never* loaned out during her fourteen-year rule at Fox.) At Warner Bros. June had what was probably her best screen assignment, that of musical comedy star Marilyn Miller. LOOK FOR THE SILVER LINING (1949) told of Miller's rise to Broadway stardom and it offered well-staged production numbers built around such songs as "Who," "Time on My Hands," "A Kiss in the Dark," "Sunny," and the title tune. It pleased undemanding filmgoers, but not severe film critic Bosley Crowther (*New York Times*) who snipped, "Her lack of vitality is a volume of blonde inconsequence in a shimmering void." Also at Warner Bros. June starred in THE DAUGHTER OF ROSIE O'GRADY (Grable had starred in SWEET ROSIE O'GRADY at Fox in 1943), another turn-of-the-century musical in which her screen father (James Barton) forbids her to have a movie career. In it she performed the title song and "As We Are Today." There was discussion at Warner Bros. of starring June in THE WEST POINT STORY (1950) and LULLABY OF BROADWAY (1951), but it was that studio's rising blonde singing

William Frawley, Martha Stewart, June Haver, and Mark Stevens in
I WONDER WHO'S KISSING HER NOW? (1947)

star Doris Day who snared the leads. At this point June and Warner Bros. came to a professional impasse.

Back at Fox, June showed a disinterest in her career. She turned down a lead in WHEN WILLIE COMES MARCHING HOME (1950; Colleen Townsend was featured). She refused to appear in FRIENDLY ISLAND and went on suspension. "I don't think people would like me in the picture because of several objectionable elements in the story." (The film was eventually made as the unsuccessful DOWN AMONG THE SHELTERING PALMS [1953], starring Jane Greer, Mitzi Gaynor, and Gloria DeHaven.) She did agree to appear in I'LL GET BY (1950), an updated version of Alice Faye's TIN PAN ALLEY (1940). It was a thin tale of a songwriter (William Lundigan) who finds success and his lady love (Haver). Gloria DeHaven, as June's screen sister, got the better notices. Off screen, with 1950 being a Holy Year, June made a pilgrimage to Rome and to the Vatican.

Fox felt her box-office draw was dwindling, so June's next, the comedy LOVE NEST (1951), was shot in economical black-and-white. It was nevertheless an amusing affair in which she was the wife of a former soldier (William Lundigan). Together they purchase an apartment building and must deal with its zany denizens, including an ex-WAC played by Marilyn Monroe (who had a bit part in Haver's SCUDDA-HOO! SCUDDA-HAY!).

In 1952 June Haver was given another Betty Grable castoff, THE GIRL NEXT DOOR (1953), teamed with Dan Dailey who had become Grable's frequent co-star. June was the musical comedy star who moves next door to a widowed cartoonist (Dailey) and his young son. While shooting an athletic dance routine involving gyrating tables, June fell off one of the tables and suffered a concussion. By the time she had recovered from the injury, her co-stars (Dailey and Dennis Day) were busy elsewhere and production was not completed until the next year.

Meanwhile, June began withdrawing further from the filmmaking world. Although her studio contract would not expire until February 20, 1953—she was earning $3,500 weekly—she continued to refuse offers. (Columbia Pictures wanted to borrow her for the musical remake of MY SISTER EILEEN—Janet Leigh was eventually used in this 1955 picture.) In February 1952 June announced that she planned to become a nun. She told the press, "I know what I want to do. But what I want must also be what God wants. May His will be done." She entered St. Mary's Academy in Leavenworth, Kansas, as a novice in the Order of the Sisters of Charity. She remained at the convent for several months, but was forced to leave for reasons of health. Her always very vocal mother had her own interpretation of the events: "I think Junie realized almost from the start she had made a mistake. All her life she has been devoted to her family—a real home girl. You can understand this made it difficult to readjust to a religious life."

By this point June's THE GIRL NEXT DOOR had been released to less than stellar results. Her studio contract was not renewed. Fox was also ending its association with Betty Grable and was preoccupied with promoting Marilyn Monroe as its new blonde star. (Fox also would soon have Sheree North as its back-up blonde singing/dancing starlet.) As her performance comeback, June starred (February 13, 1954) in a "Lux Radio Theatre" adaptation of "Trouble Along the Way" with Jack Carson as her co-star. June explained, "I decided to go back to acting after I received letters from all over the world—thousands of them. They wanted to know when I was going back. They said they were happy I was contemplating it and wanted to see me, especially in happy stories."

In the spring of 1954 she attended a birthday party for John Wayne and there she became reacquainted with Fred MacMurray, whose wife, Lillian, had died eleven months before. June and MacMurray began dating and a month later, on June 28, 1954, they were married in Ojai, California. She was twenty-eight; he was forty-five. Late in 1956 the couple adopted two baby girls, twins Katie and Laurie. Early in 1958 (January 3) the MacMurrays made their second and last professional acting appearance together in a segment of "The Lucy-Desi Comedy Hour" on CBS-TV called "Lucy Hunts Uranium." (A month later Betty Grable and her husband Harry James would appear on the Ball-Arnaz series.) After that television outing June announced, "You can say definitely that I have retired." June opted for the life of a wife and mother in her Brentwood home with Fred MacMurray and their girls, although she did do volunteer work as a nurse's aide at Los Angeles' St. John's Hospital. Today the MacMurray children are grown and June is a grandmother. MacMurray, who has had bouts with cancer in recent years, rarely performs. Together, the extremely wealthy (through real estate investments) MacMurrays lead a quiet but satisfying life.

## Filmography

Swing's the Thing (Univ, 1942) (s)
Trumpet Serenade (Univ, 1942) (s)
The Gang's All Here [The Girls He Left Behind] (20th–Fox, 1943)
Home in Indiana (20th–Fox, 1944)
Irish Eyes Are Smiling (20th–Fox, 1944)
Where Do We Go from Here? (20th–Fox, 1945)
The Dolly Sisters (20th–Fox, 1945)
Three Little Girls in Blue (20th–Fox, 1946)
Wake Up and Dream (20th–Fox, 1946)

I Wonder Who's Kissing Her Now? (20th–Fox, 1947)
Scudda-Hoo! Scudda-Hay! [Summer Lightning] (20th–Fox, 1948)
Oh, You Beautiful Doll! (20th–Fox, 1949)
Look for the Silver Lining (WB, 1949)
The Daughter of Rosie O'Grady (WB, 1950)
I'll Get By (20th–Fox, 1950)
Love Nest (20th–Fox, 1951)
The Girl Next Door (20th–Fox, 1953)

## Album Discography

The Dolly Sisters (CIF 3010) [ST]
I'll Get By/Look for the Silver Lining (Titania 604) [ST]

Kurt Weill in Hollywood [Where Do We Go from Here?] (Ariel KWH 10) [ST]
Oh, You Beautiful Doll/I Wonder Who's Kissing Her Now? (Titania 502) [ST]

# DICK HAYMES

LIKE FRANK SINATRA, DICK HAYMES WAS A PRODUCT OF THE BIG BAND era, and for a time their careers had other parallels, with both starting off as band vocalists to be catapulted to stardom via Gotham clubs and then records, radio, and motion pictures. In fact, of the two, Dick Haymes probably had the better voice. He certainly was more handsome, even if his acting style was too antiseptic for any enduring popularity. Somewhere along the way Haymes's career fizzled, mostly as a result of his personal excesses. He was forced to spend the remainder of his life eking out a living while Sinatra became so wealthy he worked only when he wished. Nevertheless, talented Dick Haymes had a varied and, at times, successful career. During the 1940s he was one of the most popular singers of his day, and was known as "The King of the Juke Boxes."

He was born Richard Benjamin Haymes in Buenos Aires, on September 13, 1916, the son of Argentinian cattleman Benjamin Haymes and his wife, Margaret, a musical comedy singer. When Dick was a small boy, the family ranch folded due to a drought. Subsequently, his parents separated and he and younger brother Robert (later known as actor Bob Stanton) went with their mother to Rio de Janeiro. The boys were educated in Europe and in 1936 the family settled in Connecticut. Dick later enrolled at Montreal's Loyola University.

Since his mother was a fine vocal coach, she taught Haymes how to sing at an early age. (She once admitted that as a child Dick was "a little ham running around the house.") After Haymes quit college, he sang for a time in New Jersey before working as a vocalist for bandsmen Johnnie Johnston and Bunny Berigan at $25 weekly. Engagements then came with Orin Tucker, Freddy Martin, and Carl Hoff, with Haymes eventually forming his own group, The Katzenjammers. He also worked as a radio announcer and had hopes of becoming a pop composer as well.

Wanting to better himself, he hitchhiked to Hollywood where he wrote songs and did stunt and extra work in the movies, even getting a small role in MGM's DRAMATIC SCHOOL (1938). A fall from a horse ended his stunt career, and in 1940 he was back East in New York City. He attempted to peddle his songs to bandleader Harry James, who was not impressed with the tunes but thought Haymes such a good singer that he hired him for his band. This was the break the young man required; during his stay with James, the singer recorded a number of good-selling records, including the ballads "You've Changed" and "I'll Get By." Leaving the James organization late in 1941, he went to work for Benny Goodman and again scored on Columbia Records with Goodman on "Idaho"/"Take Me" and "Serenade in Blue"/"I've Got a Gal in Kalamazoo." Also in 1942 Haymes hired Bill

Burton as his agent and maneuvered a two-week singing engagement at La Martinique in New York City. He was such a sensation he stayed for three months. He was signed by Decca Records and by the end of July 1943 this smooth vocalist had three singles simultaneously on the Hit Parade. "You'll Never Know" was number one, "It Can't Be Wrong" was number two, and "In My Arms" was in the number ten position. Later, during the course of a nine-week job with Tommy Dorsey and His Band (after Sinatra had left the group), Haymes returned with them to California to join the group in appearing at MGM in DU BARRY WAS A LADY (1943). In this costume musical, Haymes, disguised in a powdered wig, was barely noticeable. He then replaced Buddy Clark on the CBS radio program "Here's to Romance."

Haymes's most popular recording in the mid-1940s was "Little White Lies," which sold over 2.25 million copies and earned him $75,000. 20th Century–Fox studio head Darryl F. Zanuck was so impressed by Haymes's impact as a vocalist that he signed him to a seven-year contract. By now Dick Haymes was the father of a son, Dick, Jr., from his September 1941 marriage to dancer Joanne Marshall (later known as actress Joanne Dru). It was his second marriage, for he had been wed briefly to singer Edith Harper in 1939.

Haymes's first 20th Century–Fox film was FOUR JILLS IN A JEEP (1944), in which he portrayed a lieutenant romantically interested in one of the title characters (Mitzi Mayfair). He sang "How Blue the Night," "You Send Me," and "How Many Times Do I Have to Tell You." Next he played Irish composer Ernest R. Ball in IRISH EYES ARE SMILING (1944). Thanks to this film, plus his records and radio work, Dick Haymes was fast becoming a serious rival to Bing Crosby and Frank Sinatra (and certainly surpassing Perry Como, who was also making musicals at Fox). In 1944 Haymes also co-starred with Helen Forrest on the popular NBC radio show "Everything for the Boys" and he and Forrest cut several successful duets on Decca Records, the best-selling being "I'm Always Chasing Rainbows."

Probably Haymes's best-remembered film role came as the farmer's son in Rodgers and Hammerstein's STATE FAIR (1945), filmed in color. He sang "It's a Grand Night for Singing" and also recorded (although he did not sing it in the film) "It Might as Well Be Spring." His film acting of the hayseed young lover in STATE FAIR was earnest but wooden. Nevertheless, his performance was a distinct improvement over the work of Norman Foster in the initial screen version (in 1933) and better than that of Pat Boone in the tattered remake (of 1962). With his boyish genuineness Haymes was a proper leading man for Betty Grable in BILLY ROSE'S DIAMOND HORSESHOE (1945), one of her lesser musicals. He was the medical intern who thinks he wants to follow in the show business footsteps of his father (William Gaxton) but has a change of heart after marrying a sensible chorine (Grable). He had a hit recording with "The More I See You," one of his DIAMOND HORSESHOE numbers. Much to his disappointment, the studio would not give him the role of the downtrodden Irish drunk Johnny Nolan in A TREE GROWS IN BROOKLYN (1945), but Fox considered him too young and too inexperienced as a dramatic actor. The role went instead to James Dunn, who won an Academy Award as Best Supporting Actor.

The next year Haymes had a reunion with Harry James, playing a big band vocalist in DO YOU LOVE ME? (1946). This time he was teamed with Maureen O'Hara who was the fiery college dean he romances. The picture provided him with the title tune and "I Didn't Mean a Word I Said." He and Grable were rematched in THE SHOCKING MISS PILGRIM (1947), set in turn-of-the-century Boston and boasting a George and Ira Gershwin score. He sang "For You, for Me, for Ever More," which was popular with audiences; the period film, however, was not. He was top-billed for the first time in CARNIVAL IN COSTA RICA (1947) and he crooned "Mi Vida." The picture itself was mundane in its tale of newlyweds (Haymes, Vera-Ellen) coping with bickering in-laws. The authentic color footage of Costa Rica received better reviews than Haymes's emoting.

20th Century–Fox sold Haymes's contract to Universal Pictures and here he did two musicals, UP IN CENTRAL PARK (1948), a trite piece of historical froth about Deanna Durbin and newsman Haymes uncovering the corruption of Boss Tweed (Vincent Price). His second and last Universal feature, ONE TOUCH OF VENUS (1948), was a fantasy in which Robert Walker and Ava Gardner had the leads and he had a throwaway part as the hero's best friend. He crooned "Speak Low."

Although Haymes's movie career had sputtered out by the late 1940s, he was still very much in vogue thanks to his radio and Decca recording work, plus his many personal appearances. On radio he starred in "The Dick Haymes Show" on NBC from 1944 to

Dick Haymes and Betty Grable in BILLY ROSE'S DIAMOND HORSESHOE (1945)

1945 and on CBS from 1945 to 1947. In 1947 he joined with Bob Crosby on CBS's "Club 15" and that year also found him on CBS's "Your Hit Parade." In addition, he guest-starred on such radio shows as "Command Performance," "Guest Star," "The Jack Benny Program," "Philco Radio Time," and "Showtime." On the latter he appeared in a radio adaptation of "Alexander's Ragtime Band" with Tyrone Power, Al Jolson, Dinah Shore, and Margaret Whiting, and on December 23, 1946, on CBS's "Lux Radio Theatre," he and Maureen O'Hara recreated their DO YOU LOVE ME? roles.

In 1949 Dick Haymes and Joanne Dru divorced and she received $350,000 from him in alimony over the next seven years, as well as support for their three children. In July that year, Haymes wed Nora Eddington, the ex-wife of Errol Flynn. Their marriage proved, however, to be a brief, stormy one, due mainly to Haymes's excessive drinking. His career, on the other hand, continued. He returned to films as a crook in ST. BENNY THE DIP (1951), a low-budget entry that received surprisingly good reviews. *Variety* noted that Haymes, "as the youngest of the con men, surprises with a smooth performance." He sang "I Believe" in the film. He made his musical comedy debut that year in Dallas in *Miss Liberty*, in the role Eddie Albert had originated on Broadway. He also starred in 1951 in the ABC radio series "I Fly Anything" as aviator Dockery Crane; the show ran for one season. At the time he also began doing dramatic work on television, appearing in such series as "Ford Theatre," "Lux Video Theatre," and "Suspense."

In 1952 Haymes became enamored with Rita Hayworth and they became a much-reported item in the national press. It was through her efforts that her home studio, Columbia Pictures, provided Haymes with screen assignments. He supported Mickey Rooney in ALL ASHORE and starred in CRUISIN' DOWN THE RIVER. Both were 1953 "B" movies and proved to be Haymes's last significant big-screen appearances. Trouble developed for Haymes when he visited Hayworth on location in Hawaii on the set of MISS SADIE THOMPSON (1953) and it was revealed/announced that Haymes was not a U.S. citizen. Further, it was stated that he had intentionally avoided military service during World War II by keeping his Argentine citizenship. The singer was declared an alien who had left the United States without government permission, since Hawaii was not yet a state. Not until the U.S. Supreme Court had ruled was it decreed that he could remain in the United States. Meanwhile, on September 24, 1953, he and Rita Hayworth were married in Las Vegas, where he was singing at the Sands Hotel. Since he had married a U.S. citizen, he was assured legal residence. Nevertheless, court battles still ensued, but eventually he won the right to remain. The effort cost him a great deal in legal fees. Plans to co-star him with Rita in the biblical film JOSEPH AND HIS BRETHREN (he was to play Joseph!) fizzled despite a $50,000 personal loan from Columbia boss Harry Cohn, which was based on the prospect of Hayworth's and Haymes's starring in the epic. The marriage splintered and she claimed he beat her. They were divorced in 1954, with Hayworth receiving $1 million in alimony.

Haymes wed singer Fran Jeffries in 1955 and they had a winning nightclub act together while he also appeared on such TV programs as "Screen Directors Playhouse" and "Producers Showcase." He also cut several well-received albums for Capitol Records. In

1956, however, he lost the lead in a stage production of *The Tender Trap* because he was still an alien without U.S. citizenship and in 1960 he and Fran Jeffries were divorced; the marriage had produced a daughter, Stephanie. That year Haymes also declared bankruptcy.

During the 1960s Haymes worked mostly in Europe and in the early 1960s he married British model Wendy Smith, with whom he had two children, Sean and Samantha. He quit drinking in 1965 and made a living by appearing in clubs in England, Australia, Africa, Europe, and Ireland, where he became a citizen in 1965. He also made a guest appearance on the British teleseries "The Saint" with Roger Moore; it was aired in the U.S. in 1965. In 1969 he was hospitalized in England with tuberculosis but recovered within the year. Things began to pick up for the singer, despite another bankruptcy in 1971, when in 1972 he made his first U.S. appearance in a decade on the NBC-TV special "The Fabulous Fordies" hosted by Tennessee Ernie Ford. Also on the show were his former Fox screen co-stars Betty Grable and Maureen O'Hara. Haymes sang "It Might as Well Be Spring" and "The More I See You" and "showed that the ravages of time had taken very little from what was always conceded as the best voice of his pop era" (*Variety*). This comeback led to successful nightclub engagements in New York City, Los Angeles, and Las Vegas. The *Los Angeles Times* commented, "Dick proved that time hasn't dimmed his smooth voice or ingratiating style of projection. . . . He has returned to headline status." Daybreak Records issued his Los Angeles Cocoanut Grove performance on the LP album *Dick Haymes Comes Home!* He also acted on such TV series as "McMillan and Wife," "Hec Ramsey," "Adam-12," and "Eddie Capra Mysteries" as well as co-starred in the TV suspense movie BETRAYAL (1974). Mostly, though, he made his living working in nightclubs and by cutting several albums for Audiophile Records. He was among the horde of faded stars paraded forth in WON TON TON, THE DOG WHO SAVED HOLLYWOOD (1976). He admitted, "When I see myself on the late show in an old musical, I think: That person is no longer—he's been reborn."

Despite his professional resurgence throughout the 1970s, Dick Haymes did not look well, and as the 1970s progressed, his health deteriorated. On March 28, 1980, he died from lung cancer in Los Angeles.

Blessed with a superior singing voice and an ingratiating personality, Dick Haymes might well have become the premier singing star of the twentieth century had he not succumbed so quickly to his own hedonistic ways, and had he been able to concentrate more fully on furthering and building his career.

## Filmography

Dramatic School (MGM, 1938)
Du Barry Was a Lady (MGM, 1943)
Four Jills in a Jeep (20th–Fox, 1944)
Irish Eyes Are Smiling (20th–Fox, 1944)
State Fair (20th–Fox, 1945)
Billy Rose's Diamond Horseshoe [Diamond Horseshoe] (20th–Fox, 1945)

Do You Love Me? (20th–Fox, 1946)
Carnival in Costa Rica (20th–Fox, 1947)
The Shocking Miss Pilgrim (20th–Fox, 1947)
Up in Central Park (Univ, 1948)
One Touch of Venus (Univ, 1948)
St. Benny the Dip [Escape If You Can] (UA, 1951)

All Ashore (Col, 1953)
Cruisin' Down the River (Col, 1953)
Betrayal (ABC-TV, 12/3/74)

Won Ton Ton, the Dog Who Saved Hollywood (Par, 1976)

## Radio Series

Here's to Romance (CBS, 1943)
Everything for the Boys (NBC, 1944)
The Dick Haymes Show (NBC, 1944–45; CBS, 1945–47)

Club 15 (CBS, 1947–53)
Your Hit Parade (CBS, ca. 1947–48)
I Fly Anything (ABC, 1951)

## Album Discography

As Time Goes By (Audiophile 170, Ballad 6)
The Best of Dick Haymes (MCA 2720, MCA 1651)
Billy Rose's Diamond Horseshoe (Caliban 6028) [ST]
Christmas Songs (10" Decca DL-5022)
Dick Haymes (Glendale 9006)
Dick Haymes (Vocalion 3616)
Dick Haymes and The Andrews Sisters—Club 15 (Sounds Rare 5004)
Dick Haymes Comes Home! (Daybreak 2016)
Dick Haymes 1940–41 (Joyce 6006)
Dick Haymes 1941 (Joyce 6009) w. Benny Goodman, Harry James
The Dick Haymes Show (Joyce PIX-3)
The Dick Haymes Show: 1945–47 (Take Two TT-303)
Dick Haymes Sings Irving Berlin (MCA 1773)
Dick Haymes with Harry James (Joyce 6001)
Dick Haymes with Harry James and His Orchestra (Harlequin 2008)
Dick Haymes with Helen Forrest, Vols. 1–2 (10" Decca DL-5243/4)
Do You Love Me? (Caliban 6011) [ST]
Du Barry Was a Lady (Titania 509) [ST]
Easy (Coral CB-20016)
Featuring Dick Haymes (Viking 1035)
For You, for Me, for Everyone (Audiophile 130)
Four Jills in a Jeep (Hollywood Soundstage 407) [ST]
Great Song Stylists: Vol. 1: Dick Haymes (Apex SAX 4)
Haymes in Hollywood 1944–48 (Vedette 8701)
Helen Forrest and Dick Haymes—Long Ago and Far Away (MCA 1546)
Imagination (Audiophile 79)
James and Haymes (Circle 5) w. Harry James

Keep It Simple (Audiophile 200)
Kurt Weill in Hollywood [One Touch of Venus] (Ariel KWH 10) [ST]
The Last Goodbye (Ballad 7)
Little Shamrocks (10" Decca DL-5038)
Little White Lies (Decca DL-8773)
Look at Me Now! (Hollywood 138)
Love Letters (Memoir 107)
Moondreams (Cap T-787, EMI/Pathé 81989)
The Name's Haymes (Hallmark 301)
Polka Dots and Moonbeams (Memoir 120)
Pop Singers on the Air! (Radiola 1149) w. Perry Como, Vic Damone, Eddie Fisher
Rain or Shine (Cap T-713, Cap 1019)
The Rare Dick Haymes (Ballad 8)
Rare Early Broadcast Performances (Starcast 1002)
The Rarest Cuts (Amalgamated 254)
Richard the Lion-Hearted (Warwick 2023)
Rosemary Clooney and Dick Haymes (Exact 232)
Sentimental Songs (10" Decca DL-5291)
Serenade (10" Decca DL-5341)
The Shocking Miss Pilgrim (CIF 3008) [ST]
Songs for Romance (Presto 636)
Souvenir Album (10" Decca DL-5012)
The Special Magic of Dick Haymes (SRO 1002)
Spotlight on Dick Haymes (Tiara 513/7513) w. Johnny King
State Fair (Box Office Productions 19761, CIF 2009, CIF 3007, Sound/Stage 2310) [ST]
State Fair/I Fly Everything (EOH 99603) [ST/R]
Sweethearts (10" Decca DL-5335)
The Unreleased Dick Haymes (Amalgamated 255)
The V-Disc Years (SRO 1001)

# LENA HORNE

"I WAS THE FIRST BLACK SEX SYMBOL, THE FIRST BLACK MOVIE STAR, and the first black to integrate saloons. . . . I had to take a lot of flak from my own people, and everybody else's people." So spoke the very outspoken 5' 5" Lena Horne, a musician's singer who overcame a great deal of prejudice to establish herself professionally. No study of her lengthy career can avoid the adversities with which she coped as a black entertainer in a white-dominated show business environment. Bitterly recalling her tenure as a Metro-Goldwyn-Mayer specialty performer, she has said, "I was always told to remember I was the first of my race to be given a chance in the movies, and I had to be careful not to step out of line, not to make a fuss. It was all a lie. The only thing that wasn't a lie was that I did make money; if I didn't, they wouldn't have kept me."

In her several decades as a major singer, the exotic and stunning Lena Horne developed her own rich contralto style, noted for its crisp diction and its perfection of sensual phrasing. Whether performing a sultry romantic ballad or a haunting blues number, she balanced her natural style with professionalism, giving her song interpretations their uniqueness. These special vocal qualities are as basic to Lena Horne the performer as the many career steps which led the star through segregation to integration and to her present black self-identity.

Lena Mary Calhoun Horne was born June 30, 1917, in Brooklyn, New York. Her grandmother, Cora Calhoun Horne, had graduated from Atlanta University in 1881, in an era when few women attended college. She had been a suffragette and had married a magazine editor and schoolmaster, Edwin Horn (who later added an "e" to his name). They were both active in the newly formed National Association for the Advancement of Colored People (NAACP). Her maternal grandfather was the first black member of the Brooklyn Board of Education, and an uncle (Dr. Frank Smith Horne) was an educator and government administrator who would be an occasional unofficial adviser on race relations to President Franklin D. Roosevelt. Her father (Edwin F. "Teddy" Horne) was both a servant and a numbers runner/gambler. Lena was three when he left home. Her mother (Edna Scottron) was stagestruck and soon left Brooklyn to tour the East Coast with the black Lafayette Players. Much of Lena's childhood was spent living in foster homes or with her Uncle Frank in Ft. Valley, Georgia.

At age twelve Lena returned to Brooklyn to live with her grandmother and later with her mother, now married to a Cuban (Michael Rodriguez). She attended a variety of schools in Brooklyn and the South, and sometimes traveled with her mother on her stock company tours. Because Lena was so light-skinned and considered such a "smarty pants," she was regarded as an outsider by her own race. "I never let myself love anybody, because I knew I couldn't stay around." This mixture of independence and hurt shaped her personality and became an integral part of her performing persona.

In the fall of 1933, at the age of sixteen, she left school to help support her parents. Through family contacts, she got a $25 weekly job at Harlem's Cotton Club, which was operated by white gangsters. She appeared in the chorus line there, in shows featuring such entertainers as Cab Calloway, Ethel Waters, and Avon Long. Later she was given her own dance numbers in these revues. Lena would remember, "My mother didn't want me in that atmosphere, and she'd come with me every night—or my stepfather. One night they pushed his head in the toilet because they didn't want him coming around." Producer Laurence Schwab saw her performing at the Cotton Club and hired her to play a quadroon in *Dance with Your Gods*, which opened at the Mansfield Theatre on October 6, 1934. The play, about a skeptic who invokes an ancient voodoo curse, lasted a scant nine performances. Then, hired more for her looks than her talents, she joined Noble Sissle's Society Orchestra—where she was a dancer, occasional singer, and, using the name Helena Horne, even took over as the orchestra's temporary leader when Sissle was injured in an accident.

By 1936 Lena had become reconciled with her father, who had remarried and who owned the Hotel Belmont in Pittsburgh. It was he who introduced her to his friend Louis J. Jones, a minister's son who was active in politics (as a Democrat) in Pittsburgh. Prompted by her desire to get away from show business and her mother and stepfather, Lena married Jones in January 1937. Their daughter, Gail, was born in December 1937. Because Jones found it difficult to obtain steady work during the Depression, Lena had to continue performing. She made money singing at private parties in the Pittsburgh vicinity. In 1938 she made her film debut in THE DUKE IS TOPS, a very low-budget effort starring Ralph Cooper, a former emcee at Harlem's Apollo Theatre. Filmed in ten days in Hollywood, the independently produced musical film cast Lena as the star of a small town revue who moves to New York to win show business success. Looking slightly chubby, she sang "I Know You Remember." *Variety* recorded that Lena "is a rather inept actress, but something to look at and hear." She was in the cast of Lew Leslie's Broadway revue *Blackbirds of 1939*, but the show was short-lived. Her son, Edwin (Teddy), was born in 1940 and thereafter Lena and Jones separated (and would be divorced in 1944). She returned to New York in the fall of 1940 and, after months of rejection because she did not fit the usual racial stereotypes, she joined Charlie Barnet's Orchestra, becoming one of the first black entertainers to sing with a leading white band. While with the group she recorded "Good for Nothing Joe," which became a hit single. In March 1941 she began a seven-month engagement singing at the Cafe Society Downtown in Greenwich Village, at $75 weekly. She became noted for her singing of blues numbers. During this period she recorded with Teddy Wilson and his band (who were at the Cafe Society Downtown), with Henry Levine's Dixieland Jazz Group, and with Artie Shaw (with whom she waxed "Love Me a Little, Little"). Later in 1941 she recorded, for the RCA Victor label, songs including "Moanin' Low" and "I Gotta Right to Sing the Blues." She was also a featured vocalist on several radio shows, and made occasional film appearances.

Along with Katherine Dunham's dancers and others, Horne was hired to perform at the Little Troc Club in Los Angeles. Among those attending the well-received show was George Raft, who arranged a screen test for her at Universal. Nothing came of it. However, another ringsider was MGM staff arranger/composer Roger Edens. He organized an audition for her with producer Arthur Freed and other MGM executives. When it came time to negotiate terms, her unimpressed father and her agents (who took forty percent instead of the customary ten percent) represented her interests with MGM. Lena had reservations about having a film career at a major studio, considering the lot of black artists at that time. However, NAACP executive secretary Walter White, bandleader Count Basie, and actor Paul Robeson, among others, encouraged her to accept the contract, insisting it would help make things easier for other black performers. She signed a seven-year contract, which began at $200 weekly.

Lena made it clear from the start that she did not intend to portray maids on screen, and rejected the suggestion that she play one in Jeanette MacDonald's CAIRO (1942). (Ethel Waters took the assignment.) She also refused to go along with publicity that would suggest she was Latin American. The studio devised a special "Light Egyptian" pancake makeup to further lighten Lena's skin tones, and she agreed to use it. She made her MGM bow in PANAMA HATTIE (1942). She sang "Just One of Those Things" and was given a rumba routine to sing called "The Sping." Her segments were so situated in the film that they could be easily snipped out of release prints in the South. (Lena remembers, "Once I stopped at a train counter for something to eat. The lady behind the counter refused to serve me, but she did want my autograph because I'd just made my first film.") One of her closer friends off camera was Oscar-winning black actress Hattie McDaniel who explained the political game necessary to succeed in a segregated film industry. It was also in this period that she dated married championship boxer Joe Louis, who in 1943 enlisted in the Army.

Lena was auditioned to play opposite Eddie "Rochester" Anderson in a specialty number in Warner Bros.' THANK YOUR LUCKY STARS (1943), but it was decided she looked too white next to Anderson. During her extended periods of free time, she returned to café work in New York City. Finally, MGM cast her in the role for which the studio had hired her, as the chanteuse in the all-black CABIN IN THE SKY (1943). She gave a heady performance as the temptress Georgia Brown dispatched by the devil to pull Eddie "Rochester" Anderson away from his wife (Ethel Waters). Lena, who had an off-camera feud with Waters (who felt threatened by the young, slim newcomer), offered a strong, naughty rendering of the song "Honey in the Honeycomb" and dueted with Anderson on "Life's Full of Consequences." Under other circumstances, this would have led to further meaty roles at the studio. But not at MGM, which had already developed a love-hate relationship with its determined contractee. She was loaned to 20th Century–Fox for the all-black STORMY WEATHER (1943), a musical based loosely on the career of Bill "Bojangles" Robinson. She soloed "Stormy Weather" and "Digga Digga Doo," dueted with Robinson on "I Can't Give You Anything But Love, Baby," and was with Robinson and Cab

Calloway on "There's No Two Ways About Love." (One scene, in which she took a bubble bath, was deleted by the censors.) The *New York Times* enthused that the film was "a joy to the ear, especially when Miss Horne digs deep into the depths of romantic despair to put across the classic blues number . . . in a manner that is distinctive and refreshing." The song "Stormy Weather," which she had sung previously in clubs and on record, would be closely linked with Horne throughout her career.

Despite excellent notices for her two major film roles, Lena's screen career stagnated. MGM could envision her only in stereotypical ethnic roles and was quite concerned that blacks did not accept her because she was so fair-skinned and fine-featured. ("I just couldn't be my own person . . . the only other black person at MGM was the shoeshine man.") Thus Metro, which had an agreement that called for Lena's services only a few months per year, used her merely as an added attraction in some of its musical features. Usually she would be seen on screen leaning seductively against a pillar and singing a number or two. In THOUSANDS CHEER (1943) she performed "Honeysuckle Rose," and in a brief interlude in Red Skelton's I DOOD IT (1943), she was paired with black pianist-singer Hazel Scott for a heated rendering of "Jericho." She sang "You're So Indifferent" in SWING FEVER (1943) and in BROADWAY RHYTHM (1944—where she actually had a character name, Fernway De La Fer) she performed "Somebody Loves Me" and "Brazilian Boogie." For TWO GIRLS AND A SAILOR (1944) she crooned "Paper Doll" and in a West Indies club setting for ZIEGFELD FOL-LIES OF 1946 (1946) she sang "Love." When she vocalized "Can't Help Lovin' Dat Man" and "Why Was I Born?" as Julie in the *Show Boat* segment of TILL THE CLOUDS ROLL BY (1946) it was clear she should be the one to play the troubled mulatto when the studio filmed that musical. (However, even in TILL THE CLOUDS ROLL BY the studio had excised her few lines of dialogue with Kathryn Grayson's Magnolia, fearful of racists' repercussions. By 1951 when SHOW BOAT was made, Horne and MGM were at loggerheads and the part of Julie went to Ava Gardner.) Lena was the most sophisticated ingredient of WORDS AND MUSIC (1948), singing "The Lady Is a Tramp" and "Where or When." Her last studio assignment was a cameo in Esther Williams' DUCHESS OF IDAHO (1950), performing "Baby, Come out of the Clouds."

Lena Horne in 1946

During the war years she became one of the nation's top black entertainers (earning $1,000 weekly at MGM and $6,500+ weekly in nightclubs). She performed regularly at the Hollywood Canteen and frequently toured with the USO to entertain at armed forces bases around the country. She became a favorite pin-up girl for black soldiers. There was much press coverage when she complained publicly while entertaining at Fort Riley, Kansas. She found that several German prisoners-of-war were seated in the front rows, while black American G.I.s were seated behind. Meanwhile, Lena continued her cabaret work, becoming the first black entertainer to perform at the Savoy-Plaza Hotel and the Copacabana Club in New York. In 1948 *Life* magazine labeled her "the season's top nightclub attraction." Others noted the icy, aloof style that had become the singer's trademark posture. Years later Lena reasoned, "The image I chose to give is of a woman the audience can't reach and therefore can't hurt. They were not getting me, just a singer."

In 1947 Lena performed in London and Paris and, on a later trip to England, was presented to the royal family. In December 1947 in Paris she married a white man, Lennie Hayton, an MGM musical director (who later served as her arranger and conductor). The marriage remained a near secret for three years. In the interval, Lena continued feuding with MGM, which kept her on salary only fifteen weeks a year. She asked to be loaned to 20th Century–Fox to play the light-skinned black in PINKY (1949), but the studio refused. She nearly begged to play Julie in SHOW BOAT (1951), but the hierarchy said no. They were still punishing her for refusing in the mid-1940s to appear in a Broadway musical (*St. Louis Woman*) the studio was interested in backing. (Pearl Bailey played the role when *St. Louis Woman* was produced in 1946.) The studio did not renew Horne's contract in 1950. Lena returned to cabarets and was soon earning $12,500 weekly. Of her movie years, she would say, "I never considered myself a movie star. Mostly, I just sang songs in other people's movies."

Constantly outspoken and at times bitter, Lena was in the headlines in 1950 when she commented about black entertainer Josephine Baker's spat at the Stork Club. (She later apologized, and she and the French-based chanteuse became friends.) More damaging were the aftereffects of Senator Joseph McCarthy's anti-communist hearings of the early 1950s. Lena Horne was cited for her friendship with Paul Robeson and for her membership in assorted "leftist" organizations. She was then blacklisted in films, TV, radio, and recordings. She would say of this period, "Sure it hurt me but it educated me to a lot of things. I began to grow as a person. . . ." Eventually, by the mid-1950s, she reestablished herself in television and mainstream club work. She made a cameo appearance in MGM's MEET ME IN LAS VEGAS (1956), as a favor to her husband, singing "If You Can Dream." She signed a new recording contract with RCA Victor. Her single of "Love Me or Leave Me" was number nineteen on the charts in July 1955. Her live LP *Lena Horne at the Waldorf-Astoria* (1957) became a huge seller (the best-selling LP by a female singer in RCA's history to that date). She appeared frequently as a guest artist on the TV variety shows of Peggy Como, Ed Sullivan, and Steve Allen. Her RCA albums *Give the Lady What She Wants* (1958) and *Porgy and Bess* (1959—with Harry Belafonte) also became best-sellers, and the latter LP won a Grammy. (She would also win a Grammy for her 1962 album, *Lena—Lovely and Alive.*)

On Broadway Lena headlined the Harold Arlen–E. Y. Harburg musical *Jamaica*, which opened October 31, 1957. Her co-star was another ex-MGMer, Ricardo Montalban. The *New York Post* enthused, "she is one of the incomparable performers of our time." The exotic show ran for 555 performances. She did *Jamaica* largely because she hoped it would set a precedent for more minority-oriented shows on Broadway. To her regret, it did not. Her next stage venture, *Lena Horne in Her Nine O'Clock Revue* (1961), never reached Broadway, closing in New Haven after a Toronto tryout.

During much of the 1960s Lena Horne was a strong civil rights activist. In 1960, when a patron made a slurring remark to her at the Luau Restaurant in Beverly Hills, she threw anything and everything at hand at the harasser. She became a very visible advocate for integration and frequently spoke/sang at rallies and began including message songs in her club act repertoire. In 1966 she participated in the round-table discussions sponsored by the National Council of Negro Women and its affiliated Lambda Kappa Mu sorority. She explained to the press, "Now I have a lot more ease with myself." Meanwhile, in 1965 her autobiography, *Lena*, written with Richard Schickel, was published. Never happy performing in cabaret, she reduced the number of her live appearances in the late 1960s. She insisted that before 1967 she had not really enjoyed performing to live audiences because of the integration chip on her shoulders; but then she realized how prejudiced she had been herself. "I learned to have a ball when I was fifty."

There was considerable press coverage when she agreed to co-star in Universal's Western DEATH OF A GUNFIGHTER (1969). Much was made of the fact that she would play the brothel madam who was the lover-then-wife of the town's marshal (Richard Widmark). The scenario made no reference to the interracial aspect. She sang "Sweet Apple Wine" during the opening/closing credits. In the release print, her role was abbreviated and although (or because) the film was unexploitative, it quickly disappeared from distribution. She continued to appear occasionally in TV specials such as "Harry [Belafonte] and Lena" (ABC, March 22, 1970).

In the troublesome period of 1970–71 her husband Lennie Hayton died (April 24, 1971) of a heart attack; her father passed away; and her son Teddy, aged twenty-nine, with whom she had been reconciled after years of misunderstandings, died from a kidney ailment. "I started to change when everybody left me," she said, "when I found out that the worst had happened to me and I was surviving. I began to think about myself, to look back at what I had been given and what I hadn't had. And I slowly grew into my other self." She moved to a New York City apartment and began concertizing around the country, often co-starring with Count Basie, Alan King, or Tony Bennett. With Bennett she appeared for three weeks at the Minskoff Theatre on Broadway in the fall of 1974. Now at peace with herself and liberated, she confessed, "In my early days I was a sepia Hedy Lamarr. Now I'm black and a woman, singing my own way." In 1978 she made a movie return in Universal's THE WIZ, based on the Broadway hit which was an all-black version of the Judy Garland picture THE WIZARD OF OZ (1939). Looking youthful enough to play the lead herself, she was cast as Glinda the Good Witch to Diana Ross's Dorothy and Michael Jackson's Scarecrow. The film was directed by Sidney Lumet, who was at that time married to Horne's daughter, Gail. Lena sang "Believe in Yourself" with Ross. Made at a cost of $24 million, the overblown musical was not liked and grossed only $13 million domestically.

In 1980 she was named one of the world's ten most beautiful women and after appearing at San Francisco's Fairmont Hotel cabaret in March 1980 she announced her retirement plans. She began a three-month farewell tour that June. However, she had a change of heart and on May 12, 1981, she opened on Broadway in *Lena Horne: The Lady and Her Music*. She performed a host of songs associated with her ("Stormy Weather," "The Lady Is a Tramp," "I Got a Name") and interspersed them with sharp talk and direct reflections on her life. *Newsweek* magazine insisted she was "the most awesome performer to hit Broadway in years." The *New York Times* added, "The lady's range, energy, originality, humor, anger and intelligence are simply not to be believed." For her one-woman show she received a special Tony Award, a Grammy (for the LP album set), and the show was taped for cable TV (and later released on videocassette). *Lena Horne: The Lady and Her Music* ran for 333 performances. It closed on June 30, 1982—her sixty-fifth birthday. She went on tour with the production and performed it in London in the summer of 1984. On December 10 of that year, she was among the five recipients (including Arthur Miller and Isaac Stern) who received the Kennedy Center Honors Award for Lifetime Achievement. In 1985 there was discussion of her doing a TV series to be spun off from the "The Cosby Show," but that did not materialize. She did a benefit concert at Carnegie Hall on May 20, 1986, for the Yale School of Drama and continued to receive artistic and humanitarian awards. (She was given an honorary L.H.D. degree by Howard University in 1979.) Also in 1986 her daughter, Gail, now wed to journalist Kevin Buckley, wrote *The Hornes: An American Family*, which traced the heritage of her family from 1777 to 1986.

To much fanfare, Lena Horne produced a new LP in 1988, *The Men in My Life*, singing solos and duets with the likes of Sammy Davis, Jr. and Joe Williams. She insisted she made the record because "My grandchildren and my daughter hate to see me not working. To get them off my back, I went and did it." The *New York Times* noted of her song style, "she brings an emotional generosity to the material that would have been almost inconceivable until recently from someone who for decades maintained a facade of sophisticated reserve." One of the highlights of the 1989 "Entertaining the Troops," a PBS documentary on World War II, was Lena and Eddie "Rochester" Anderson singing their "Consequences" number from CABIN IN THE COTTON on the black radio show "Jubilee."

Now living in California near Santa Barbara, Lena Horne continues to be a spokesperson for her race and for older people, and an advocate for greater government support for the arts, education, and health care. Examining her past she says now, "I was a guinea pig during much of my career, going where blacks had never been allowed before. . . . I'm really just a piece of Americana when you come down to it." At her age, she insists, "I can do what I damn well please and say what I want. Don't you think I've served enough time?"

## Filmography

The Duke Is Tops [Bronze Venus] (Million Dollar Films, 1938)
Harlem Hot Shot (Metropolitan, 1940)
Boogie Woogie Dream (Soundies, 1942) (s)
Harlem on Parade (Goldberg & Goldberg, 1942)
Panama Hattie (MGM, 1942)
I Dood It [By Hook or by Crook] (MGM, 1943)
Swing Fever (MGM, 1943)
Thousands Cheer (MGM, 1943)
Cabin in the Sky (MGM, 1943)
Stormy Weather (20th–Fox, 1943)

Broadway Rhythm (MGM, 1944)
Two Girls and a Sailor (MGM, 1944)
Ziegfeld Follies of 1946 (MGM, 1946)
Till the Clouds Roll By (MGM, 1946)
Studio Visit (MGM, 1946) (s)
Mantan Messes Up (Toddy Pictures, 1946)
Words and Music (MGM, 1948)
Duchess of Idaho (MGM, 1950)
The Heart of Show Business (Col, 1956) (s)
Meet Me in Las Vegas [Viva Las Vegas!] (MGM, 1956)
Death of a Gunfighter (Univ, 1969)
The Wiz (Univ, 1978)

## Broadway Plays

Dance with Your Gods (1934)
Blackbirds of 1939 (1939)

Jamaica (1957)

## Radio Series

Strictly for Dixie (NBC, ca. 1941)
Jubilee (Synd, ca. 1943–44)

## Album Discography

Cabin in the Sky (Hollywood Soundstage 5003) [ST]
A Date with Lena (Sunbeam 212)
Duchess of Idaho (Titania 508) [ST]
The Essential Lena Horne (Buddah 5669-2)
Fabergé Presents Harry and Lena (RCA PRS-295) [ST/TV] w. Harry Belafonte
Feelin' Good (UA UAL-3433/UAS-6433)
For Someone in Love (Stanyan 10138)
Give the Lady What She Wants (RCA LPM/LSP-1879, RCA Int'l 89459)
Here's Lena Now! (20th Century–Fox 4115)
I Feel So Smoochie (Lion 70050)
It's Love (RCA LPM-1148)
Jamaica (RCA LOC/LSO-1036) [OC]
The Lady and Her Music (Qwest 2QW3597)
Lena, A New Album (RCA BGL1-1799)
Lena and Gabor (Skye 15) w. Gabor Szabo

Lena and Michel (RCA BGL1-1026) w. Michel Legrand
Lena Goes Latin (DRG 510)
Lena Horne (Tops L-1502)
Lena Horne at the Waldorf-Astoria (RCA LOC/LSO-1028)
Lena Horne in Hollywood (UA UAL-3470/UAS-6470)
Lena Horne Live at the Sands (RCA LPM/LSP-2364)
Lena Horne Sings (10" MGM E-545)
Lena Horne Sings Your Requests (Charter 1010)
Lena Likes Latin (Charter 106)
Lena—Lovely and Alive (RCA LPM-2587)
The Men in My Life (Three Cherries TC 44411) w. Sammy Davis, Jr., Joe Williams
Merry (UA UAS-6546)
Nature's Baby (Buddah 5084)

On the Blue Side (RCA LPM/LSP-2465)
Once in a Lifetime (Movietone 71005/72005)
Porgy and Bess (RCA LOP/LSOL-1507) w. Harry Belafonte
Songs by Burke and Van Heusen (RCA LPM/LSP-1895)
Soul (UA UAL-3496/UAS-6496)
Stormy Weather (Sandy Hook 2037, Sountrak 103) [ST]
Stormy Weather (RCA LPM-1375)
Stormy Weather (Stanyan 10126)
Swing Fever (Caliban 6038) [ST]
Swinging Lena Horne (Coronet CXS-CS-165)

This Is Lena Horne (10" RCA LPT-3061)
Thousands Cheer (Amalgamated 232, Hollywood Soundstage 409) [ST]
Till the Clouds Roll By (10" MGM E-501, MGM E-3231, Metro M/S-578, Sountrak 115, Vertinge 2000) [ST]
20 Golden Pieces (Bulldog 2000)
Two Girls and a Sailor (Sound Stage 2307) [ST]
Watch What Happens (Buddah 185)
Words and Music (10" MGM E-505, MGM E-3233, Metro M/S-580) [ST]
Ziegfeld Follies of 1946 (Curtain Calls 100/15-16) [ST]

# BETTY HUTTON

EXUBERANT, A FIRECRACKER, A LIVE WIRE: ALL OF THESE DESCRIBE the dynamo that was Betty Hutton, and yet none of them fully does her justice. For in addition to her mile-a-minute screen persona (which also exemplified her to some degree in real life), Hutton was a seasoned performer who could act and sing and put over a vehicle by the sheer force of her vibrant personality. In the World War II years, her frenetic energy seemed to be a catalyst for the American people in their struggle against the Axis. While she was never a soldier's sex symbol like Betty Grable, Rita Hayworth, or Dorothy Lamour, she certainly appealed to wartime audiences for her looks and talents and, most of all, for her "blonde bombshell" rambunctious screen shenanigans. At one point in the late 1940s she was ranked second only to Judy Garland in her enormous audience appeal. Sadly, Betty Hutton's career began to come apart in the 1950s with a series of bad career moves, several emotional public "retirements" from show business, and the inevitable comebacks. She has spent most of the last two decades as a recluse from the limelight, but always manages to be in the news for one sad event after another.

When Betty Hutton was two years old, her father, a railroad brakeman, deserted his family, which consisted of Betty's mother, Mabel Lum Thornburg, and an older sister, Marion. Betty was born Betty June Thornburg in Battle Creek, Michigan, on February 26, 1921 (a year after her sister). After Percy Thornburg's desertion, Mabel took her two young daughters to Detroit where she got a job in an automobile factory, but made more money operating a bootleg joint. Mrs. Thornburg could play the guitar and she taught Marion and Betty to sing and dance. Betty made her first public singing appearance in her mother's cheap speakeasy at age three standing on a kitchen table. Betty recalled later that they "were so poor, we never had enough to eat. We lived three families in a flat. It was a nightmare." When she was nine years old, Betty happened upon a church where she became inspired by and through religion. It was then that she decided to make something of her life. At age thirteen she got a job as a singer at a Michigan summer resort and then worked with a local band composed of high school students.

When she was fifteen, she saved $200 and went to New York City hoping for a break in show business. However, the trip was a brief, unsuccessful one. Back home she and sister Marion went to a Detroit nightclub where Betty sang a song. Bandleader Vincent Lopez heard her and soon hired the young girl to be a vocalist with his band for $65 weekly. While touring with Lopez, Betty developed her exuberant style of singing and began using the name Betty Darling. However, in 1938, when sister Marion became a vocalist with Glenn Miller, the sisters both began using the surname Hutton. In the autumn of 1938 Betty had her first big professional exposure with Lopez at Billy Rose's Casa Manana Club in Gotham. The next spring she made her recording debut with the bandleader on Bluebird Records with vocals on "Igloo" and "The Jitterbug" and a duet with Sonny Schuyler on "Concert in the Park." She also made her screen debut in the 1939 Vitaphone short VINCENT LOPEZ AND HIS ORCHESTRA and for Vitaphone that year she also appeared with Hal Sherman in ONE FOR THE BOOK and was with Chaz Chase and Hal LeRoy in PUBLIC JITTERBUG #1 (1939). Because of this film and her Bluebird record, Betty was billed as "America's Number One Jitterbug." (Said Betty about this title, "It was just an unfortunate label that was pasted on. I just was a screwball. I sang crazy songs. I did just whatever came to my mind. They didn't know what to call me, so they called me a jitterbug. I don't dance. A jitterbug has to dance.") Also in 1939 she made her first Paramount film, the short THREE KINGS AND A QUEEN. Betty continued to tour with Lopez in vaudeville as well as sing on his NBC radio program. Her contract with the bandsman called for him to have twenty percent of her income in current and all future ventures. It was a clause that was to give Betty future legal headaches.

Early in 1940 Betty Hutton left Vincent Lopez's band and sang and danced to good notice in the revue *Two for the Show* on Broadway. During its run she and Lopez terminated their contract with an out-of-court settlement. Later in the year (opening on October 30, 1940) at $500 weekly, Betty was featured in another Broadway musical, Cole Porter's *Panama Hattie* starring Ethel Merman. (June Allyson was in the chorus and was Betty's understudy.) Again Hutton was a big success and the show's producer, songwriter B. G. "Buddy" DeSylva, hired her for $1,000 a week to appear in his Paramount film musical THE FLEET'S IN (1942). The movie teamed her with Eddie Bracken for the first time. In it she played the part of Dorothy Lamour's hyperactive roommate with the plot centering on sailor William Holden trying to get his way with club singer Dorothy. Betty scored well in the film with the songs "Arthur Murray Taught Me Dancing in a Hurry" and "How to Build a Better Mousetrap." *PM* reported, "[her] facial grimaces, body twists and man-pummeling gymnastics take wonderfully to the screen." Betty was then re-teamed with Eddie Bracken in STAR SPANGLED RHYTHM (1942) as a Paramount Pictures telephone switchboard worker who loves sailor Bracken. The latter's father (Victor Moore) is a studio gateman but has told his son he is a movie executive. By the end of 1942 Betty Hutton was named a star of tomorrow by the *Motion Picture Herald* and she landed a comedy and singing job on radio's "The Bob Hope Show."

Now under contract exclusively with Paramount, the "blitzkrieg bombshell" again appeared with Eddie Bracken in the comedy HAPPY GO LUCKY (1943), and in it she was the hoydenish pal of a golddigger (Mary Martin). The latter is after a rich man (Rudy Vallee) at a Caribbean resort and is being aided by her beachcomber boyfriend (Dick Powell). The film gave Betty the energetic production number "Murder, He Says," which was so popular it became a national catchphrase. Betty then teamed with Bob Hope on celluloid for LET'S FACE IT (1943), the screen version of Cole Porter's Broadway musical comedy, with Hutton running a fat farm and in love with G.I. Hope. She sang "Let's Not

Talk About Love" and solidified her position as one of Paramount's top female box-office attractions.

In 1943 she also became one of the first performers to be signed by Johnny Mercer for the newly formed Capitol Records, singing both energetic novelty tunes like "His Rocking Horse Ran Away" (from her film AND THE ANGELS SING) and "Doin' It the Hard Way" as well as ballads such as "Blue Skies" and "It Had to Be You." In her first nonsinging movie role, Betty scored well in THE MIRACLE OF MORGAN'S CREEK (1944), a comedy now regarded as a classic. She was the fickle girl who convinced her none-too-bright 4-F boyfriend (Eddie Bracken) to marry her so her pregnancy (from a brief one-night marriage when she was intoxicated) will be blessed with respectability. It proved to be one of director Preston Sturges' most satisfying zany screen works. Of AND THE AN-GELS SING (1944), in which she was part of a sister quartette (along with Dorothy Lamour, Diana Lynn, and Mimi Chandler) at odds with a crooked bandleader, James Agee (*The Nation* magazine) praised, "Betty Hutton is almost beyond good and evil, so far as I am concerned." Hutton negotiated a new Paramount contract which paid her $5,000 weekly. She went on a vaudeville tour and appeared on several radio shows, including "The Chase and Sanborn Hour," "Command Performance," and "Mail Call." She closed out 1944 with dual roles as patriotic WAVE sisters in HERE COME THE WAVES with Bing Crosby. Then, at year's end, she embarked on a two-month South Pacific USO tour.

When she returned, Betty was granted the dramatic role she had long wanted, that of Roaring Twenties speakeasy star Texas Guinan in INCENDIARY BLONDE (1945), a title which described the star better than its subject. The film did well and she then sang "The Hard Way" in Paramount's all-star DUFFY'S TAVERN (1945), based on Ed Gardner's pop-ular radio program. THE STORK CLUB (1945) followed, with Betty as a hat-check girl who comes under the benevolent wing of millionaire Barry Fitzgerald after she saves his life, which complicates matters with her bandleader boyfriend (Don DeFore). She sang "I'm a Square in a Social Circle" and then dueted with popular crooner Andy Russell on "If I Had a Dozen Hearts."

By now Betty's studio mentor, B. G. DeSylva, was no longer in charge and Betty's vehicles were variable affairs, usually unworthy of her. CROSS MY HEART (1946) was a mild remake of a Carole Lombard comedy with zany Betty confessing to a murder so her lawyer boyfriend (Sonny Tufts) will gain publicity by proving her innocent. Much better was another biopic, that of Betty playing silent screen serial star Pearl White in THE PERILS OF PAULINE (1947). Among her songs in this film were "Poppa Don't Preach to Me," "I Wish I Didn't Love You So," and "Rumble, Rumble, Rumble," all of which she recorded for Capitol Records. At this point Betty also had a happy domestic life, having wed Ted Briskin, a camera manufacturer, with whom she had two daughters: Candy (born November 23, 1946) and Lindsay (born April 14, 1948). Her return to motion pictures in 1948 was the disastrous fantasy DREAM GIRL, which cast her as a self-centered rich girl who day-dreams about happiness. In contrast to this career setback, she had an extremely successful stand at the London Palladium, earning $17,500 per week.

Back on the screen in 1949, Betty co-starred with Victor Mature in the pleasant farce RED, HOT AND BLUE, which cast her as a stage actress whom a director (Mature) attempts to make a star, while the two become implicated in murder. She also repeated her role in RED, HOT AND BLUE with John Lund on NBC's "Lux Radio Theatre." However, plans to star her in a biography of Theda Bara fell through, as did subsequent projects in which she would play Sophie Tucker, Clara Bow, and Mabel Normand. Having lost the lead in a loanout to Warner Bros. for ROMANCE ON THE HIGH SEAS (1948) due to her second pregnancy, Betty was even more upset to lose the coveted role of Annie Oakley in MGM's screen version of Irving Berlin's ANNIE GET YOUR GUN (1950). The choice part went to Judy Garland, who, however, was forced to withdraw after recording the sound-track. Betty was rushed in to play opposite Howard Keel, as Frank Butler, the sharpshooter Annie loves. She was sensational as Annie and the film made a mint at the box office, with Betty featured on the cover of *Time* magazine and named the year's most popular actress by *Photoplay* magazine. The year 1950 proved to be a good one for Betty as she then teamed with Fred Astaire for LET'S DANCE at Paramount with Hutton as a singer whose husband dies in the war. She makes a show business comeback and meanwhile is attracted to a dancer (Astaire). On radio's "Theatre Guild on the Air" on ABC she starred in "Daisy Mayne" and "Page Miss Glory," the latter with Ronald Reagan. That same year she signed with RCA Victor Records, waxing the LET'S DANCE song "I Can't Stop Thinking About You" and having a top-ten single duet with Perry Como on "A Bushel and a Peck."

Betty Hutton and Fred Astaire in
LET'S DANCE (1950)

In 1951 Hutton and Ted Briskin divorced and for a time she dated actor Robert Sterling, the ex-husband of MGM's Ann Sothern. She returned to the screen in 1952 in Cecil B. De Mille's circus epic THE GREATEST SHOW ON EARTH as a high-wire artist, and the movie made $14 million at the box office. Her next success came with a solid vaudeville engagement, following Judy Garland into the Palace Theatre in New York City. After this engagement she underwent throat surgery (which required her to retrain her voice), and then starred in her third biopic, as vaudevillian Blossom Seeley in SOMEBODY LOVES ME (1952). It was a Technicolor story about the trials and tribulations of Seeley and her husband, Benny Fields (Ralph

Meeker). RCA Victor released the movie's soundtrack and Betty and Gene Barry played the leads in a "Lux Radio Theatre" version.

On March 18, 1952, in Las Vegas, Betty married choreographer Charles O'Curran (her dance director on SOMEBODY LOVES ME). When Paramount balked at her insistence that her husband direct her in her next vehicle (TOPSY AND EVA), she walked out on her contract, which was not scheduled to expire until the end of the year. (Paramount announced it would star Rosemary Clooney in all the planned Hutton vehicles, but that never happened either.) As suddenly as it had begun, her film career had aborted. Betty returned to the London Palladium for a three-week stand and the next year she was performing on the lucrative nightclub circuit. She was back at the Palace Theatre in late 1953 and began making plans for her television debut in the NBC-TV musical special "Satins and Spurs." She returned to Capitol Records, doing an album called *A Square in a Social Circle* and the "Satins and Spurs" soundtrack, which was issued prior to the show's debut on September 12, 1954. The much-touted Max Liebman production cast Betty as a rodeo queen in the Annie Oakley tradition. Despite all the hullabaloo, the program was a disaster and marked the beginning of the end of Betty's career. She was so distraught over its failure that after a good run at Las Vegas's Desert Inn she tearfully announced her retirement.

Early in 1955 Betty and Charles O'Curran were divorced and the next month she wed Capitol Records executive Alan W. Livingston. That summer she had a miscarriage. At year's end she did a poorly received special for NBC-TV (the *New York Times* reported, "She worked much too hard and it showed"). After several false starts, she returned to films in United Artists' SPRING REUNION (1957), a project once planned for Judy Garland. It was a low-key, low-budget entry with lonely spinster Betty falling for Dana Andrews at a high school reunion, while a classmate is murdered. She sang "That Old Feeling" but audiences passed the movie by. Betty Hutton was no longer a marketable screen name.

Before and after the SPRING REUNION failure, Betty guested on NBC-TV's "The Dinah Shore Chevy Show" and did a musical revue in Las Vegas. In mid-1958 Hutton retired again from show business, stating, "I had never given myself the chance to be a housewife." However, a few months later she was reactivating her career, reasoning, "I still had pride enough in myself as a performer not to simply drop out of the business, leaving people asking 'Say, whatever became of Betty Hutton anyhow?'"

In 1959 she starred on CBS-TV in the comedy series "Goldie," which lasted barely one season, and she recorded an album called *Betty Hutton at the Saints and Sinners Ball* for Warner Bros. Then came more club work, more publicized backstage hassles, a divorce (1960) from Alan Livingston, and her fourth marriage (on December 24, 1960) to trumpeter Peter Candoli. In 1962 her mother died in a tragic fire, Betty did a summer tour in *Gypsy,* and, at year's end, she gave birth to her third daughter, Carolyn. Later in the 1960s she toured in *Annie Get Your Gun* and *Gentlemen Prefer Blondes* and was a temporary replacement for Carol Burnett on Broadway in *Fade Out, Fade In* in the summer of 1964. She also did guest spots on TV series such as (ironically) "The Greatest Show on Earth," "Burke's Law," and "Gunsmoke." She and husband Candoli had much-publicized marital problems but were not divorced until 1971. In 1967 the star filed for bankruptcy. She bemoaned, "I've been crucified in this racket, *crucified,* when I only gave out love. I bought houses, Cadillacs, furs, you name it, for people—even churches for my maids. But when the money went, everybody split." Her uncontrolled language forced Betty off a daytime quiz show and she was dropped from two low-budget Westerns being shot at Paramount because she could not handle the quick shooting schedules. She was replaced in RED TOMAHAWK (1967) and BUCKSKIN (1968) by another ex-Paramount star from the 1940s, Joan Caulfield.

After that Betty became a recluse who did not reemerge into the public eye until late in 1971 when she rode in the Hollywood Santa Claus Lane Parade. The occasion brought work offers but nothing gelled for the former star, who admitted she had made and spent over $9 million and was broke. "I don't know the 'in' crowd in Hollywood anymore . . . I don't even have many friends anymore because I backed away from them; when things went wrong for me I didn't want them to have any part of my troubles." She became alienated from her two oldest daughters and had a long, bitter feud with her sister, Marion (who died in 1987), and could obtain work only in small-time summer stock. While on tour in Rhode Island she attempted suicide, but was helped by a Portsmouth priest, Rev. Peter Maguire. On and off for the next several years she worked at his rectory as a cook and housekeeper. In the later 1970s Betty moved back to California, was reconciled with her daughters, and began making sporadic appearances on TV talk shows.

In the fall of 1980 Betty Hutton returned to Broadway in the role of Miss Hannigan in *Annie* and Rex Reed wrote in the New York *Daily News,* "She is a seemingly endless fountain of comic exuberance, a one-woman fireworks display that lights up the stage at the Alvin and leaves the audience cheering." She also made a guest appearance on the PBS television special "Jukebox Saturday Night" singing her old movie hits like "Murder, He Says," "You Can't Get a Man with a Gun," and "His Rocking Horse Ran Away." But once again her show business career drifted away. She returned to Portsmouth, Rhode Island, and eventually enrolled at Salve Regina College in Newport, Rhode Island, where she earned a Master of Arts degree in liberal arts. In 1986 she was made a member of the college's faculty, teaching motion picture and television classes. She was supposed to attend the April 1989 Academy Awards, but illness and insecurity kept her away.

## Filmography

Vincent Lopez and His Orchestra (Vita, 1939) (s)
One for the Book (Vita, 1939) (s)
Headline Bands (Vita, 1939) (s)
Public Jitterbug #1 (Vita, 1939) (s)
Three Kings and a Queen (Par, 1939) (s)
The Fleet's In (Par, 1942)
Star Spangled Rhythm (Par, 1942)

Happy Go Lucky (Par, 1943)
Let's Face It (Par, 1943)
Skirmish on the Home Front (Par, 1943) (s)
The Miracle of Morgan's Creek (Par, 1944)
And the Angels Sing (Par, 1944)
Here Come the Waves (Par, 1944)
Incendiary Blonde (Par, 1945)
Duffy's Tavern (Par, 1945)

Hollywood Victory Caravan (Par, 1945) (s)
The Stork Club (Par, 1945)
Cross My Heart (Par, 1946)
The Perils of Pauline (Par, 1947)
Dream Girl (Par, 1948)
Red, Hot and Blue (Par, 1949)
Annie Get Your Gun (MGM, 1950)

Let's Dance (Par, 1950)
Sailor Beware (Par, 1952)
The Greatest Show on Earth (Par, 1952)
Somebody Loves Me (Par, 1952)
Spring Reunion (UA, 1957)
Jazz Ball (NTA, 1958)

## Broadway Plays

Two for the Show (1940)
Panama Hattie (1940)

Fade Out, Fade in (1964) (replacement)
Annie (1980) (replacement)

## Radio Series

Vincent Lopez and His Orchestra (NBC Blue, 1939)

The Bob Hope Show (NBC, ca. 1942–43)

## TV Series

The Betty Hutton Show [Goldie] (CBS, 1959–60)

## Album Discography

And the Angels Sing/Let's Dance (Caliban 6017) [ST]
Annie Get Your Gun (10" MGM E-509, MGM E-3227, Metro M/S-548) [ST]
Betty Hutton at the Saints and Sinners Ball (WB 1267)
A Blonde Bombshell (AEI 2120)
The Fleet's In (Hollywood Soundstage 405) [ST]
Hutton in Hollywood (Vedette 8702)

Incendiary Blonde (Amalgamated 238) [ST]
Satins and Spurs (10" Cap L-547, MPT 4) [ST/TV]
Somebody Loves Me (10" RCA LPM-3097) [ST]
A Square in a Social Circle (10" Cap H-256, EMI/Pathé 65521)
Star Spangled Rhythm (Curtain Calls 100/20, Sandy Hook 2045) [ST]
Stork Club (Caliban 6020) [ST]

# BURL IVES

ONE OF THE MOST VERSATILE PERFORMERS OF THE TWENTIETH CEN-
tury, Burl Ives is considered a leading folksinger but his appeal has also extended to the
popular and country music fields. In addition to his singing, he has carved for himself a
fine career in acting, one which earned him an Academy Award along with roles in more
than two dozen feature films. He has starred on Broadway and television and is a popular
concert performer. In addition, he has written several books and arranged and popularized
many American folk songs. A big man, standing 6' 2" and weighing 250 pounds, Burl Ives
has loomed large over the American entertainment scene for a half century.

Burl Icle Ivanhoe Ives was born in Jasper County in southern Illinois on June 14,
1909, the son of a tenant farmer who moved with his family frequently. Burl's mother
loved to sing and he and his three sisters and three brothers were all fond of music. At age
four, Ives performed for the first time in public at a reunion for veterans. He attended
school in Hunt City, Illinois, where he learned to play the banjo. At the age of twelve he
performed with great success at a local camp meeting and during high school he played
football. After graduation in 1928 he attended Eastern Illinois State Teachers College
where he continued his avid interest in American folk music.

Foreseeing no future for himself in school, Ives dropped out. "I grabbed my guitar
and hit the road," he was to comment later. He wandered around the country working on
riverboats and obtaining money as a performer when possible but taking any job available
to sustain himself. For a time he played semi-professional football and along the way he
continued collecting folk songs. His interests ranged from not only old English and
Scottish ballads but also to work songs, children's songs and nursery songs, cowboy
ballads, railroad tunes, and other types of melodies of historical importance. He studied
voice with Madame Clara Lyon in Terre Haute, Indiana, and in New York City he
continued his voice training with Ella Toedt. At the same time he also studied acting with
Benno Schneider. In the big city he sang in Greenwich Village cafés and acted in stock
companies, all the while continuing his studies at New York University's School of Music.

In 1938 Burl Ives made his Broadway bow in *I Married an Angel* with Vivienne Segal,
Vera Zorina, and Walter Slezak, and the same year played the tailor in *The Boys from Syr-
acuse* with Eddie Albert and Jimmy Savo. In 1940 he was on Broadway again in *Heavenly
Express* and on the CBS radio series "Forecast." This led to a successful stand at Gotham's
Village Vanguard club and in 1941 he starred in the fifteen-minute CBS radio show "The
Wayfaring Stranger." The show continued into 1942, when Ives was forced to leave it for
military service. As a part of his Army duties he was one of the servicemen cast in the

Broadway production *This Is the Army* (1942). In 1943–44 he was back on CBS radio in a fifteen-minute show. Discharged from the service, he appeared with Alfred Drake in the Broadway production of *Sing Out, Sweet Land!* (1944), a tribute to American folk and popular music, written by Walter Kerr. From 1946 to 1948 he starred on the fifteen-minute Mutual radio program "The Burl Ives Show." The year 1948 also saw the publication of his autobiography, *Wayfaring Stranger*, and the following year he joined in the cast of the Broadway revival of the eighteenth-century comedy *She Stoops to Conquer*.

In 1946 Burl Ives had made his film debut in the outdoor drama SMOKY and in 1948 he had roles in two Westerns, STATION WEST and GREEN GRASS OF WYOMING, as well as a role in the Walt Disney film SO DEAR TO MY HEART. In it he was top-billed as benevolent Uncle Hiram and sang "Lavender Blue" and dueted with Beulah Bondi on "Billy Boy." Said *Variety*, "Ives adds immeasurably as village blacksmith, to the Brown County, Ind. doings." In 1950 he returned to the screen in another Western, SIERRA, starring Audie Murphy.

During World War II, Burl Ives had made recordings for the Office of War Information and after his medical discharge from the service he continued to record for minor commercial labels, introducing the songs "Mule Train" and "Ghost Riders in the Sky"—before they became gold records for Frankie Laine and Vaughn Monroe, respectively. When the demand for folk music increased greatly after the war, Ives was much in demand for personal appearances and in 1950 he filmed ten Snader Telescriptions (short subjects) for television, performing such songs as "John Henry," "On Top of Old Smokey," "Sweet Betsy from Pike," "Hush Little Baby," "The Cowboy's Lament," and "Noah Found Grace in the Eyes of the Lord." In 1953 Ballantine Books published two best-selling paperbacks by the folksinger, *The Burl Ives Songbook* (which contained 115 American folk songs) and *Burl Ives' Sea Songs of Sailing, Whaling and Fishing* (with a total of 68 songs). Commercially he recorded with both Columbia and Decca Records and recorded more than 120 songs for Encyclopedia Britannica Films in its six-album set *Historical America in Song*.

In 1954 Ives played Cap'n Andy in a Broadway revival of *Show Boat* and the next year he won critical acclaim for his performance as domineering Big Daddy in Tennessee Williams' *Cat on a Hot Tin Roof*. Ives was now in demand for dramatic acting roles and he returned to motion pictures as Sam in John Steinbeck's EAST OF EDEN (1955) and in the minor tale of corporate manipulations THE POWER AND THE PRIZE (1956).

Continually active professionally, Burl Ives began his dramatic work on network television in 1957, appearing on the CBS-TV shows "U.S. Steel Hour" and "Playhouse 90," the latter in "The Miracle Worker." In 1958 he repeated his role of the patriarchal Big Daddy in the film version of CAT ON A HOT TIN ROOF. Also that year he won an Academy Award as Best Supporting Actor for his performance in THE BIG COUNTRY, playing the grasping Rufus Hannasy in this sprawling William Wyler–directed Western. That same year he was also impressive as the older man whose young wife (Sophia Loren) is attracted to his son (Anthony Perkins) in Eugene O'Neill's DESIRE UNDER THE ELMS. He then trekked to Florida to film WIND ACROSS THE EVERGLADES (1958). In 1959 he was the brutal outlaw gang leader who takes over a small town in DAY OF THE OUTLAW, and in 1960 he had substantial roles in the comedy OUR MAN IN HAVANA and in the melodrama LET NO MAN WRITE MY EPITAPH.

After a thankless role in THE SPIRAL ROAD (1962), Ives returned to work for Disney in SUMMER MAGIC (1963) with Hayley Mills, based on the old stage favorite *Mother Carey's Chickens*. He was also the jovial genie in THE BRASS BOTTLE (1964); struggled with the other actors in trying to enliven a follow-up to MR. ROBERTS, called ENSIGN PULVER (1964); and provided the songs for MEDITERRANEAN HOLIDAY (1964). In 1966 he was one of the voices in the animated feature THE DAYDREAMER and then starred in a slapped-together science fiction period piece, THOSE FANTASTIC FLYING FOOLS (1967), based on a Jules Verne novel. He was again on Broadway briefly, playing the euthanasia-minded small town physician in *Dr. Cook's Garden* (1967). (In the 1971 telefeature version, Bing Crosby inherited Ives's role.) Ives also played a slave-owning rancher in the violent Western THE McMASTERS (1970) and was in such later features as BAKER'S HAWK (1976—a wholesome family story), JUST YOU AND ME, KID (1979—with George Burns and Brooke Shields), EARTHBOUND (1981—a science fiction tale), and the little-seen racial study WHITE DOG (1982).

Since coming to television in the late 1950s, Burl Ives has been very active in that medium, appearing in such diverse series as "Zane Grey Theatre," "The Name of the Game," "Daniel Boone," "Alias Smith and Jones," "Night Gallery," and "Little House on

Hayley Mills, Burl Ives, and Deborah Walley in SUMMER MAGIC (1963)

the Prairie," and in "Pinocchio" on "Hallmark Hall of Fame." He has also starred in three TV series: "High-Low" (NBC, 1957—a quiz show), "O.K. Crackerby" (ABC, 1965–66—a comedy), and "The Lawyers" (NBC, 1969–72—one of the rotating series on "The Bold Ones"). He has made several telefeatures and was the narrator of "The Ewok Adventure" (1984). He appeared in the miniseries "Captains and the Kings" (1976) and "Roots" (1977—as Justin) and "Poor Little Rich Girl: The Barbara Hutton Story" (1987—as the patriarch Woolworth) as well as in such TV specials as "The Burl Ives Thanksgiving Special," "Rudolph the Red-Nosed Reindeer," and "The First Easter Rabbit."

As a recording artist Burl Ives was most prolific in his work for Decca, having been with that label from the early 1950s until the late 1960s. In the early-to-mid-1960s he had a number of best-selling singles for the label, including "A Little Bitty Tear" in 1961; "Funny Way of Laughin'" (which won him a Grammy Award as Best Country & Western Song), "Mr. In-Between," and "Mary Ann Regrets" in 1962; "This Is All I Ask" in 1963; and "True Love Goes On and On" and "Pearly Shells" in 1964. He also scored with most of these songs on the country charts, along with "Evil Off My Mind" in 1966 and "Lonesome 7-7203" in 1967. His Decca albums were also steady sellers and he had charted LPs for the label with *The Versatile Burl Ives* and *It's Just My Funny Way of Laughin'* in 1962 and *Pearly Shells* in 1965. Since leaving Decca he has recorded for a number of labels, including Bell, Caedmon, United Artists, and Word; for the latter he cut several religious LPs.

In addition to television and recordings—and his role as a very active conservationist—Burl Ives continued to make concert hall appearances throughout the 1970s and into the 1980s. In the fall of 1988 he debuted his one-man show, *The Mystic Trumpeter: Walt Whitman at 70* (which he wrote with his wife, Dorothy, whom he wed in 1971). "Seldom are an actor and the subject of a one-man show so perfectly matched as are Burl Ives and Walt Whitman," observed *Daily Variety*. The reviewer added that the show "looks to be a permanent addition to America's stage literature." Thus at nearly age eighty, Burl Ives set out on a new show business career.

In private life, Ives has a son, Alexander (from his marriage in 1945 to Helen Ehrlich; they were later divorced), and for years kept both a New York apartment and a California ranch. His hobbies have included flying and boating. His versatile show business persona was best summarized in his *Burl Ives Songbook*: "His whole large person and personality radiate with the vigor and warmth that international audiences have come to love. . . ."

## Filmography

Smoky (20th–Fox, 1946)
Green Grass of Wyoming (20th–Fox, 1948)
Station West (RKO, 1948)
So Dear to My Heart (RKO, 1948)
Sierra (Univ, 1950)

East of Eden (WB, 1955)
The Power and the Prize (MGM, 1956)
Desire Under the Elms (Par, 1958)
The Big Country (UA, 1958)
Cat on a Hot Tin Roof (MGM, 1958)

Wind Across the Everglades (UA, 1958)
Day of the Outlaw (UA, 1959)
Let No Man Write My Epitaph (Col, 1960)
Our Man in Havana (Col, 1960)
The Spiral Road (Univ, 1962)
Summer Magic (BV, 1963)
The Brass Bottle (Univ, 1964)
Ensign Pulver (WB, 1964)
Mediterranean Holiday [The Flying Clipper] (Continental, 1964) (songs only)
The Daydreamer (Emb, 1966) (voice only)
Those Fantastic Flying Fools [Rocket to the Moon] (AIP, 1967)
The Sound of Anger (NBC-TV, 12/10/68)

The Whole World Is Watching (NBC-TV, 3/11/69)
The McMasters (Chevron, 1970)
The Man Who Wanted to Live Forever [The Only Way Out Is Dead] (ABC-TV, 12/15/70)
Baker's Hawk (Doty-Dayton, 1976)
The Bermuda Depths (ABC-TV, 1/27/78)
The New Adventures of Heidi (NBC-TV, 12/13/78)
Just You and Me, Kid (Col, 1979)
Earthbound (Taft International, 1981)
White Dog (Par, 1982)
Uphill All the Way (New World, 1985)

## Broadway Plays

I Married an Angel (1938)
The Boys from Syracuse (1938)
Heavenly Express (1940)
This Is the Army (1942)
Sing Out, Sweet Land! (1944)

She Stoops to Conquer (1949) (revival)
Show Boat (1954) (revival)
Cat on a Hot Tin Roof (1955)
Dr. Cook's Garden (1967)

## Radio Series

Forecast (CBS, 1940)
The Wayfaring Stranger [The Burl Ives Show] (CBS, 1941–42)

The Burl Ives Show (CBS, 1942, 1943–44; Mutual, 1946–48)

## TV Series

High-Low (NBC, 1957)
O.K. Crackerby (ABC, 1965–66)

The Lawyers (NBC, 1969–72)

## Album Discography

All-Time Gospel Favorites (Suffolk Marketing)
American Folk Songs (10" Decca DL-5490)
Americana (Album Globe AC-820)
Animal Folk (Disneyland 3920)
Australian Folk Songs (Decca DL-8749)
Ballads (UA UAL-3060/UAS-6060)
Ballads and Folk Songs, Vols. 1–3 (10" Decca DL-5013, 5080, 5093)

The Best of Burl Ives (Decca DX-167/DXS-7167, MCA 4034)
The Best of Burl Ives, Vol. 2 (MCA 4089)
The Best of Burl Ives for Boys and Girls (Decca DL-4390)
Best of Burl's for Boys and Girls (MCA 98)
Big Country Hits (Decca DL-4972/74972)
Big Rock Candy Mountain (Pickwick 3393)

Blue Tail Fly and Other Favorites (Stinson 1)
Burl (Decca DL-4361)
Burl Ives (Camay 3005)
Burl Ives (Coronet CX/CXS-271) w. Chad Willis and the Beachstones
Burl Ives' Coronation Concert (Decca DL-8080)
Burl Ives' Korean Orphan Choir (Word 8140)
Burl Ives Live (Everest FS-340)
Burl Ives Sings (Col CL-980)
Burl Ives Sings for Fun (Decca DL-8248)
Burl Ives Sings Irving Berlin (UA UAL-3117/UAS-6117)
Burl's Broadway (Decca DL-4876/74876)
Burl's Choice (Decca DL-4734/74734)
Captain Burl Ives' Ark (Decca DL-8587)
Cheers (Decca DL-8886/78886)
Children's Favorites (10" Col CL-2570)
Christmas Album (Col CS-9728)
Christmas at the White House (Caedmon TC-1415)
Christmas Day in the Morning (10" Decca DL-5428)
Christmas Eve (Decca DL-8391/78391)
A Day at the Zoo (Disneyland 1347)
The Day Dream (Col OL-6540/OS-2940) [ST]
Down to the Sea in Ships (Decca DL-8245)
The Environment (U.S. Department of the Interior)
Faith and Joy (Word 3259/8140)
Favorites (Sunset 5280)
Folk Lullabies (Disneyland 3924)
Folk Songs (10" Decca DL-5467)
Got the World by the Tail (Har/HS-11275)
Greatest Hits (Decca DL-4850/74850, MCA 114)
Have a Holly Jolly Christmas (Decca DL-4089/74089, MCA 237)
Historical America in Song (Encyclopedia Britannica Films)
How Great Thou Art (Word 8537)
Hugo the Hippo (UA LA-637-G) [ST]
Hymns (10" Col CL-6115)
I Do Believe (World 3391/8391)
In the Quiet of the Night (Decca DL-82470)
It's Cool in the Furnace (Word 8580)
It's Just My Funny Way of Laughin' (Decca DL-4279/74279)

Joy Unspeakable (Word 8391)
Little Red Caboose (Disneyland 1859)
The Little White Duck (Har HL-9507/HS-14507, Col C-33183)
The Lollipop Tree (Har HL-9551/his-14551)
Lonesome Train (Decca DL-9065)
Manhattan Troubadour (UA UAL-3145/UAS-6145)
More Folk Songs (10" Col CL-6144)
My Gal Sal (Decca DL-4606/74606)
Old Time Varieties (Decca DL-8637)
On the Beach at Waikiki (Decca DL-4668/74668)
Paying My Dues Again (MCA 318)
Pearly Shells (Decca DL-4578/74578, MCA 102)
Return of the Wayfaring Stranger (10" Col CL-6058, Col CL-1459)
Rudolph, the Red-Nosed Reindeer (Decca DL-4815/74815, MCA 247) [ST/TV]
Scouting Along with Burl Ives (Col Special Products 3471)
Shall We Gather at the River (Word 3339/8339)
Sing Out, Sweet Land! (Decca DL-8023) [OC]
Singin' Easy (Decca DL-4433/74433)
Softly and Tenderly (Col CS-9925)
Something Special (Decca DL-4789/74789)
Song Book (Coral CB-20029)
Songs for Men (Decca DL-8125)
Songs for Women (Decca DL-8246)
Songs I Sang in Sunday School (Word 8130)
Songs of Ireland (Decca DL-8444)
Songs of the West (Decca DL-4179/74179, MCA 196)
The Special Magic of Burl Ives (Suffolk Marketing/MCA MSM-35043)
Summer Magic (Buena Vista 4025) [ST]
Sweet, Sad and Salty (Decca DL-5028/75028)
Sweeter as the Years Go By (Word 8583)
Time (Bell 6055)
The Times They Are A-Changin' (Col CS-9675)
True Love (Decca DL-4533/74533)
The Versatile Burl Ives (Decca DL-4152/74152)
The Wayfaring Stranger (10" Col CL-6109, Col CL-628/CS-9041)
The Wayfaring Stranger (10" Stinson 1)
The Wild Side of Life (Decca DL-8107)

# GLORIA JEAN

GLORIA JEAN WAS BROUGHT TO HOLLYWOOD BY PRODUCER JOE Pasternak to be groomed as a future Deanna Durbin by Universal Pictures. An immediate success at the studio, she remained there for seven years. Unfortunately, as she grew older her vehicles became more pedestrian. With her combination of fresh looks, a fine singing voice (although she never obtained a recording contract), and sweet personality, Gloria Jean successfully exhibited a picture of American youth popular during the World War II years. Eventually, however, her career faded; she has spent the past quarter of a century attempting to regain a small foothold in the entertainment industry.

Gloria Jean was born in Buffalo, New York, on April 14, 1927, the daughter of Ferman Schoonover, a music store owner, and his wife, Eleanor. She was raised in Scranton, Pennsylvania, along with her three older sisters. As a youngster she exhibited a strong interest in music and her uncle taught her songs and gave her voice lessons. She made her stage debut at age three, billed as Baby Schoonover. At the age of five she had her own radio program in Scranton. The next year she was offered an opportunity to sing with Paul Whiteman's orchestra, but her parents rejected the offer because of the amount of travel it would entail. When she was ten, Gloria went to New York to study opera and it was there that Universal producer Joe Pasternak heard her sing. She was signed to a seven-year contract with the studio. Her entire family eventually moved to Hollywood, where her father later worked in real estate.

Because of her natural abilities and outgoing personality, Gloria Jean was not required to take acting lessons. In 1939 she made her film bow in THE UNDER-PUP in the starring role of a young girl from a poor family who wins a vacation to a summer camp with a group of rich girls. *Variety* bubbled, "youngster has warm poise, winsome person- ality and a screen presence that is remarkable. . . . She also has vocal ability which is demonstrated briefly in several sequences. . . . Gloria Jean is well qualified for starring responsibilities in the future. . . ." Next came the actress's most successful picture, IF I HAD MY WAY (1940) with Bing Crosby. In it she was an orphan who is brought to Gotham by a steelworker-crooner (Crosby), and they become involved in the opening of a nightclub. This movie contained several pleasant songs, including the title number by James V. Monaco and Johnny Burke, and it allowed Gloria full opportunity to both emote and sing in a top-flight production. Her third picture, A LITTLE BIT OF HEAVEN (1940), was equally good. She plays a young singing star who supports her family. When they become snobbish due to her success, she pretends to lose her voice. An interesting plot twist cast several once-famous movie stars (Maurice Costello, Monte Blue, William Desmond, Noah Beery, Charles Ray, Kenneth Harlan) as her "uncles." Gloria recorded the movie's title tune for Decca Records, the company for which she also waxed a trio of songs from THE UNDER-PUP.

Fourteen-year-old Gloria was next matched with W. C. Fields in NEVER GIVE A SUCKER AN EVEN BREAK (1941), an uneven comedy in which she is adopted by con artist Fields after her trapeze artist mother is killed making a circus movie. Although the film was not one of Fields's best outings, he (not Gloria) had the lion's share of screen time. During this period Gloria appeared as guest artist on a number of radio shows including "The Chase and Sanborn Hour," "Screen Actors Guild Theatre," and the programs of Bob Hope and Bing Crosby. In addition, she sang at President Franklin D. Roosevelt's birthday party in 1940.

In 1942, Universal, which was cranking out lots of low-budget musicals, began teaming Gloria Jean with Donald O'Connor in a string of features. Despite the quantity, these pictures were not quality and they marked the beginning of her decline as a screen star. Her first film in this series was WHAT'S COOKIN'? (1942), in which she was fourth-billed, behind The Andrews Sisters, Jane Frazee, and Robert Paige. She was a young singer hoping to get on a big radio show. The picture's emphasis was definitely on the musical numbers featuring The Andrews Sisters, Woody Herman and His Orchestra, and the Jivin' Jacks and Jill. A better showcase for Gloria came with GET HEP TO LOVE (1942), which cast her as a young singer who runs away from her parasitic aunt. She sang "Villanelle,"

Peggy Ryan, Gloria Jean, and Donald O'Connor in
WHEN JOHNNY COMES MARCHING HOME (1942)

"Siboney," "Drink to Me Only with Thine Eyes," and "Sempre Libera" from Verdi's opera *La Traviata*. Her third 1942 release was WHEN JOHNNY COMES MARCHING HOME, which had Jane Frazee as the love interest to soldier Allan Jones, while Gloria romanced Donald O'Connor. The duo then carried on their romantic involvement in IT COMES UP LOVE (1942) with Gloria singing "Love's Old Sweet Song," "Say Si Si," and "What the Rose Said." The peripatetic teenagers were again paired in MISTER BIG (1943), which had them changing a dramatic school's play into a lively musical. (All of the films that the two of them made together were a distillation of the big-budget musicals Judy Garland and Mickey Rooney were making together at MGM.) The final screen teaming of Gloria and O'Connor occurred in MOONLIGHT IN VERMONT (1943), which found Gloria as the Granite State native who heads to Gotham to attend drama school. Her songs were "Something Tells Me," "Be a Good, Good Girl," "Dobbin and a Wagon of Hay," and "Pickin' the Beets." She was outstanding in these tunes, but the melodies were mediocre. By now Universal was ignoring Gloria and focusing instead on its new young musical talent: Susanna Foster and Ann Blyth.

Following a guest bit in Universal's all-star FOLLOW THE BOYS (1944), Gloria had a thankless role in the wacky Olsen and Johnson comedy GHOST CATCHERS (1944). Somewhat better was PARDON MY RHYTHM (1944), in which she was a high school singer who helps her bandleader (Bob Crosby) enter a musical contest. She sang "Do You Believe in Dreams." As 1944 ended, Gloria Jean found herself top-billed in another programmer musical, THE RECKLESS AGE. For a change she played a more mature young woman who leaves the big city for a job in a small town store owned by her grandfather (Henry Stephenson). She closed out the year with a straight dramatic role in DESTINY, a well-directed (by Reginald LeBorg) dual biller about a man (Alan Curtis) wrongly sent to prison. She was cast as the girl who loves him. The film had been conceived originally as an episode of FLESH AND FANTASY (1943), but when that multipart drama was considered overlong, DESTINY was deleted and expanded for a solo outing.

The year 1945 found Gloria closing out her Universal tenure in a trio of programmers, beginning with I'LL REMEMBER APRIL, in which she portrayed the daughter of a wealthy man accused of murder. She sang the film's lovely title song. Kirby Grant was her leading man in this feature as he was again in EASY TO LOOK AT, in which she was seen as a fashion designer accused of selling her firm's designs to a competitor. The film's best number, "Is You Is, or Is You Ain't My Baby?," was sung by the Delta Rhythm Boys. Gloria's final Universal entry was the murder mystery RIVER GANG, about a young woman and her uncle (John Qualen) mixed up in a killing.

Following the expiration of her Universal contract, eighteen-year-old Gloria went on a lengthy personal appearance tour and at her agent's suggestion turned down several lucrative studio offers. She was off the screen for nearly two years, finally returning in COPACABANA (1947), in which she was almost lost amidst the mugging of Groucho Marx and Carmen Miranda, Andy Russell's singing, and romance with Steve Cochran. She had a better role in a lesser film, I SURRENDER DEAR (1948), cast as a band singer in love with her boss (David Street), while in the period piece AN OLD-FASHIONED GIRL (1948) she played a music instructor in Boston during the 1870s. Next she played an advertising agency worker who saves a youth center from being razed by a greedy businessman in MANHATTAN ANGEL (1949). THERE'S A GIRL IN MY HEART (1949) gave her only the second feminine lead, but a chance to sing as the denizen of a theater which is about to be taken over by a crooked politician (Lee Bowman). It was her last film work for six years.

In the early 1950s Gloria again toured the United States, but an appearance at the London Casino was so poorly received (she broke down on stage) that a planned vaudeville tour was cancelled. In Hollywood she got minor work on television and in 1955 she obtained the female lead in a "B" movie for Lippert called AIR STRIKE. However, her role was a background one in the plot of a Navy commander (Richard Denning) working to develop an efficient jet fighter plane. After that, Gloria Jean disappeared from show business, working as a hostess in an Encino (California) restaurant, since her movie money had long since gone to pay back taxes. In the early 1960s Jerry Lewis promised to launch her comeback in his film THE LADIES' MAN (1961), but all she got was a bit assignment. In 1962 she did obtain a starring role in the little-seen comedy THE MADCAPS (LAFFIN' TIME). In 1965 she took a job as a receptionist at Redken Laboratories, a cosmetics firm in Van Nuys, California. She needed the job to support her son, Angelo; she had married in 1962 and was divorced in 1966.

In recent years Gloria Jean has attempted to obtain a Nashville recording contract ("I can still sing," she told an interviewer in 1973) and has made occasional appearances on such shows as Merv Griffin's TV program and Richard Lamparski's "Whatever Became of. . . ?" radio series. "I had a wonderful career, but I want people to know how happy I am today," Gloria Jean recently told the *Los Angeles Times*. "I'm not saying that I'd mind if I got a call from [TV producer] Aaron Spelling or someone like that. I'd be delighted. They use everybody else in town. But it's not the top priority for me."

## Filmography

The Under-Pup (Univ, 1939)
If I Had My Way (Par, 1940)
A Little Bit of Heaven (Univ, 1940)
Winter Serenade (Univ, 1941) (s)
Never Give a Sucker an Even Break (Univ, 1941)
What's Cookin'? [Wake Up and Dream] (Univ, 1942)
Get Hep to Love [She's My Lovely] (Univ, 1942)
When Johnny Comes Marching Home (Univ, 1942)
It Comes Up Love [A Date with an Angel] (Univ, 1942)
Mister Big (Univ, 1943)
Moonlight in Vermont (Univ, 1943)

Follow the Boys (Univ, 1944)
Ghost Catchers (Univ, 1944)
Pardon My Rhythm (Univ, 1944)
The Reckless Age (Univ, 1944)
Destiny (Univ, 1944)
I'll Remember April (Univ, 1945)
Easy to Look At (Univ, 1945)
River Gang [Fairy Tale Murder] (Univ, 1945)
Copacabana (UA, 1947)
I Surrender Dear (Col, 1948)
An Old-Fashioned Girl (Eagle-Lion, 1948)
Manhattan Angel (Col, 1949)
There's a Girl in My Heart (AA, 1949)
Air Strike (Lip, 1955)
The Ladies' Man (Par, 1961)
The Madcaps [Laffin' Time] (Boots and Saddles, 1962)

# AL JOLSON

"THE WORLD'S GREATEST ENTERTAINER," AS AL JOLSON HAS BEEN called, sang for over a half century and endeared himself to millions. Jolson's success encompassed vaudeville, minstrel shows, revues, Broadway, movies, records, radio, and concerts. He probably introduced more popular songs than any other entertainer and he was one of the highest-paid performers of his day. His electric personality and emotional delivery of songs made him a household name. Although he was a Russian Jew, he will be forever thought of as the blackfaced minstrel man singing *con brio* about the Old South. Beneath his show business facade, however, was an extremely complex, egotistical man who could be generous, kind, and considerate and yet also cruel, sadistic, and violent. Although many of his contemporaries disliked him personally, he is one of the few performers to be almost universally lionized by his peers. George Jessel summed it up best by saying, "what a great artist he was!" It was Jolson, though, who had the final word, as usual, when he declared, "I've got so much dough that fourteen guys couldn't spend it in their lifetime. But I'd rather die than quit this business." And that is just what happened.

Al Jolson always claimed he was born May 26, 1886, in St. Petersburg, Russia. His father was a cantor and Al's real name was Asa Yoelson. Because of the anti-Jewish pogroms that persistently swept Russia, the Yoelsons came to the United States when Al was a small boy. They lived in Washington, D.C., where his father planned for him to follow in his footsteps and enter the synagogue as a cantor. Young Al, however, proved to be a problem child, especially with his new-found taste for the popular music of the day. To discipline him, he was placed, for a time, in a Catholic school in Baltimore. However, after being inspired by seeing Fay Templeton perform on the stage and meeting minstrel man Eddie Leonard, Al joined a traveling burlesque company as a comic stooge. He soon graduated to becoming a singer, since his voice had been impressive even as a boy before he left Russia. He made his stage debut on October 16, 1899, at the Herald Square Theatre in New York as one of the young mob in *The Children of the Ghetto*. The next year he teamed with his older brother Harry for a routine called "The Hebrew and the Cadet." In 1901 Al and Harry worked with Joe Palmer in a vaudeville act called Joelson, Palmer, and Joelson. Because the billing was too long for the theater marquee, the "e" was dropped from the brothers' surname, which thus became Jolson. By 1906 Al was working solo in San Francisco, which had just suffered the devastating earthquake. It was there he enjoyed his first real success as a dynamic singer of popular songs. At the time he was still performing without heavy makeup. But on the advice of his dresser, a black man, he began using burnt cork makeup. He found his act was even more enthusiastically received when he worked in blackface with white gloves. (One of Jolson's peers, Eddie Cantor, would have a similar affinity for performing in minstrel blackface.)

In 1909 Al Jolson became a member of Lew Dockstader's Minstrels, the most popular touring minstrel group of the day, and this furthered his success as a singer of "coon songs." In the spring of 1911 he made his Broadway debut playing Erastus Sparkler in *La Belle Paree*. After a good run, he headlined *Vera Violetta* in the fall. It too was a success and in the show he sang "That Haunting Melody," which he recorded for Victor Recordings late in 1911 (it was his recording debut). The show also featured a young Mae West as well as Gaby Deslys, Barney Bernard, Frank Tinney, Jose Collins, and Belle Baker. Both of his Broadway shows had been at New York City's Winter Garden Theatre and there he would remain for the rest of the decade. In 1912 he starred in *The Whirl of Society*, followed by *The Honeymoon Express* in 1913, both with Gaby Deslys. In *Dancing Around* (1914) he sang "It's a Long Way to Tipperary." *Robinson Crusoe, Jr.* debuted early in 1916 with Jolson as its focal point. The show provided him with two big numbers: "Where the Black-Eyed Susans Grow" and "Where Did Robinson Crusoe Go with Friday on Saturday Night?" It was during these shows that Jolson would cause a sensation by interrupting the planned proceedings to devote fifteen to twenty minutes to singing popular songs of the day and telling the enthusiastic audience, "You ain't heard nothin' yet!"

In 1918 Jolson did his final Winter Garden show, *Sinbad*, which had a score by Sigmund Romberg but also additional numbers, some of them co-written by Jolie himself, including "I'll Say She Does." However, his biggest hits in the long-running *Sinbad* were "Swanee," "Rock-a-Bye Your Baby with a Dixie Melody," and "My Mammy." The same year Jolson recorded "Rock-a-Bye Your Baby with a Dixie Melody" and another *Sinbad* song, "Hello Central, Give Me No Man's Land." He had begun recording with Columbia in 1913 and stayed with the label for a decade, lining up a number of best-selling records like "You Made Me Love You," "Sister Susie's Sewing Shirts for Soldiers," "Yaaka Hula Hickey Doola," "Who Played Poker with Pocahontas (When John Smith Went Away)," "Toot Toot Tootsie," and "Avalon."

The Roaring Twenties opened with Al starring in *Bombo* (1921) at his own Jolson's 59th Street Theatre. The show lasted for over two hundred performances and featured such songs as "Who Cares?," "April Showers," "Toot Toot Tootsie," and "California, Here I Come." After its Broadway run, Jolson toured with the production through 1924. In 1925 he was back on Broadway in *Big Boy*, and although it ran for only forty-eight performances, it included several noted Jolson tunes, such as "California, Here I Come," "If You Knew Susie," "Hello, 'Tucky, Hello," and "Miami." The previous year, Jolson had signed with Brunswick Records. In order to attract him, the company had to make him a member of their board of directors and allot him a hefty advance on each of the songs he recorded. The advances were so sizeable that none of his Brunswick records showed a profit for the company until he recorded "Sonny Boy" for them in 1928. Although Jolie had a number of best-sellers for Brunswick, his record sales were easily eclipsed by those of Nick Lucas, who was the label's top record seller from 1926 to 1930.

In 1927 Al Jolson made show business history when he starred in Warner Bros.'

part-talkie feature film THE JAZZ SINGER, doing songs like "My Mammy," "Blue Skies," and "Toot Toot Tootsie." Actually he had made his sound film debut earlier in the year in the short subject AL JOLSON IN A PLANTATION ACT SINGS APRIL SHOWERS, which Vitaphone filmed in New York City in the fall of 1926. It was more or less a screen test for Jolson, who replaced George Jessel in the lead in THE JAZZ SINGER, a film whose story of a young Jewish boy who goes against his cantor father's will and becomes a pop singer obviously paralleled Jolson's own experience. (Jessel had balked at the studio's offer of only $30,000 to recreate his stage role. Eddie Cantor was the next choice but he declined the assignment, thinking it was too identified with Jessel. Jolson accepted the part for $75,000.) *Variety* reported, "Jolson, when singing, is Jolson. There are six instances of this, each running from two to three minutes . . . as soon as he gets under cork the lens picks up that spark of individual personality solely identified with him." The trend-setting feature was such a commercial sensation (grossing over $3.5 million) that Jolson followed it with the even-more-popular (grossing $5.5 million) THE SINGING FOOL for Warners in 1928. It was another part-talkie in which he sang "It All Depends on You," "I'm Sitting on Top of the World," "There's a Rainbow 'Round My Shoulder," "Golden Gate," and "Sonny Boy." The latter tearjerker (sung to little Davey Lee in the movie) sold over three million copies when he recorded it for Brunswick. In fact, Jolson's film work revitalized his record sales as he had several good sellers from his films during this time.

His first all-talkie was SAY IT WITH SONGS (1929) and among his tunes in this overly sentimental drama (with little Davey Lee on hand to milk audience tears) were "Back in Your Own Back Yard," "Used to You," "Little Pal," "One Sweet Kiss," and "I'm in Seventh Heaven." In the summer of 1929 Jolson had an interesting stage "return" when his second wife, Ruby Keeler (he was married to Henrietta Keller from 1906 to 1911), whom he had married the previous year, starred in the Florenz Ziegfeld musical production of *Show Girl* with Nick Lucas, Clayton–Jackson–Durante, and Eddie Foy, Jr. During the show, Jolson, seated in the audience, would rise when Keeler came on stage, and sing the production's chief tune, "Liza," which he also recorded for Brunswick. In 1930 he starred in two additional features for Warners, MAMMY (he made separate trailers for both THE SINGING FOOL and MAMMY to promote the features) and BIG BOY. But by now the public was used to the novelty of sound and were tiring of Jolson's sugary tearjerkers heavily laden with popular songs. Warner Bros. decided that the nearly $1 million they paid Jolson per film was no longer worth it. Meanwhile, the Depression was making inroads into the record industry, and after a 1930 record session with Brunswick in which he recorded songs from MAMMY, he did not record again for nearly three years. His popularity, however, was still so great that in the fall of 1930 he was offered $12,000 per week to headline a vaudeville show at the Palace Theatre in New York City. He declined the offer.

He returned to Broadway in 1931 in *The Wonder Bar* but the show lasted for only eighty-six performances. He had begun being heard on radio in 1929 and after guest appearances on several programs, he starred in his own half-hour series on NBC radio, from November 1932 to February 1933. In the summer of that year he and Paul Whiteman co-hosted "The Kraft Music Hall," a one-hour musical program for NBC which ran for a year. Jolson was earning $5,000 weekly for his radio work. Also in 1933 Jolson returned to films in HALLELUJAH, I'M A BUM for United Artists (as part of an abortive long-term contract), but the innovative musical comedy was unsuccessful, mainly because all of its dialogue was in rhyme. He did record the film's title song and "You Are Too Beautiful," also from the picture, in his last session with Brunswick late in 1932. He would not make another commercial recording for thirteen years.

Plans to star Jolson in a Broadway version of DuBose Heyward's novel *Porgy* did not work out, but he did return to Warner Bros. where his wife, Ruby Keeler, was now a star thanks to her success in 42ND STREET (1932). His initial vehicle back at the studio was a film version of WONDER BAR (1934). It was loaded with diverse studio talent (Kay Francis, Dick Powell, Dolores Del Rio, Ricardo Cortez), and, as the owner of a chic Paris nightclub, Jolson joked, emoted, and had a big production number (in blackface), "Goin' to Heaven on a Mule." The film was popular and Jolson signed a film-a-year contract with the studio, which chose to team him on camera with Keeler in GO INTO YOUR DANCE (1935). It was all too evident on screen that her career was on the rise and his was ebbing. Ironically, the duo starred in a radio adaptation of "Burlesque" on CBS's "Lux Radio

Alice Faye, Tyrone Power, and Al Jolson in ROSE OF WASHINGTON SQUARE (1939)

Theatre" on June 15, 1936, with its storyline of a one-time headliner seeing his career fall apart while his young wife becomes a big success! Warners wanted to rematch Jolson and Keeler, but he refused, instead choosing to do THE SINGING KID (1936). It was a rehash of all that he had done before, looked antiquated, and, even worse, it was a programmer. The picture offered him only one good song, "Here's Looking at You." From December 1936 to December 1939 the singer starred in "The Al Jolson Show" on CBS radio with Martha Raye and Victor Young and His Orchestra. Also in 1939 Jolson and Keeler were divorced; they had one adopted child, Al Jolson, Jr.

He was back on screen in 1939 with three films for 20th Century–Fox, but now he was no longer the top-billed star. In ROSE OF WASHINGTON SQUARE he was featured behind Alice Faye and Tyrone Power, but had a good role (a variation of himself) as a vaudevillian, and the opportunity to reprise "Toot Toot Tootsie," "My Mammy," and "Rock-a-Bye Your Baby with a Dixie Melody." In HOLLYWOOD CAVALCADE he appeared briefly as himself, singing "Kol Nidre" in a recreation of the synagogue sequence from THE JAZZ SINGER. Finally he co-starred with Don Ameche in a biopic of Stephen Foster called SWANEE RIVER in what may have been his finest movie role. He was legendary minstrel man E. P. Christy and had occasion to sing a quartet of Foster favorites, "Oh! Susanna," "De Camptown Races," "My Old Kentucky Home," and "Old Folks at Home." (On April 2, 1945, Jolson reprised the Christy role on "Lux Radio Theatre" with Dennis Morgan now as Stephen Foster.)

The fifty-four-year-old Jolson relaunched his Broadway career in 1940 with a good run of *Hold On to Your Hats* with Martha Raye. During the 1942–43 radio season the star headlined "The Al Jolson Show" on CBS. During World War II he was a tireless entertainer of Allied troops, both at home and abroad. He continued to work on radio, guesting in such series as "Soldiers in Greasepaint," "Philco Radio Hall of Fame," "Your All-Time Hit Parade," and "Let Yourself Go." Late in 1943 he sang "Swanee" as part of an appearance as himself in Warner Bros.' RHAPSODY IN BLUE which was finally released in 1945. In the summer of 1945 he resumed recording when he cut old favorites "April Showers" and "Swanee" for Decca Records.

During his overseas trips to entertain troops, Jolson contracted malaria. Eventually the condition necessitated an operation to remove most of one lung. While recuperating he romanced a young woman named Erle Galbraith and they were married in March 1945. (In 1948 they adopted a son, Asa, Jr.) After recovering, Jolson guested on Milton Berle's radio program and then was hired to sing the songs for the soundtrack of a movie about his life called THE JOLSON STORY (1946). It was made by Columbia Pictures with Larry Parks playing Al. Jolson actually appeared in one scene of the film, a musical number done in blackface with the star on bended knee on the theater rampway. The film's huge success (which netted Jolson several million dollars) revitalized Jolson's career. He began recording again for Decca and several of his old standards became best-sellers again, along with new tunes like "The Anniversary Song," which he co-wrote.

He guest-starred on many radio programs, especially "The Kraft Music Hall" with Bing Crosby. When Crosby left the NBC show in 1947, Jolson was hired to take his place.

He remained with the variety show as its star until the spring of 1949. In 1949 he also did the soundtrack recording of the songs to JOLSON SINGS AGAIN (1949), a biographical sequel to THE JOLSON STORY. Larry Parks again played Al. In addition, Jolson reprised THE JAZZ SINGER on "Lux Radio Theatre" and also portrayed himself when the series adapted "The Jolson Story" and "Jolson Sings Again" to radio.

Al Jolson's health deteriorated in the late 1940s but in 1950 he insisted on a hectic schedule of entertaining troops in Korea in the Far East command. The tour proved too much for him, and a month after he returned home, he died of a heart attack in San Francisco on October 23, 1950. After private financial arrangements were made for his widow and sons, the bulk of his $3 million estate was divided among Catholic, Jewish, and Protestant institutions. At the time RKO had planned to team him with Dinah Shore in a project entitled STARS AND STRIPES FOREVER. Said Eddie Cantor of the late star, "This great personality never learned to live. The moment the curtain came down he died."

## Filmography

Al Jolson in a Plantation Act Sings April Showers (Vita, 1927) (s)
The Jazz Singer (WB, 1927)
The Singing Fool (WB, 1928)
Sonny Boy (WB, 1929)
New York Nights (WB, 1929)
Say It with Songs (WB, 1929)
Screen Snapshots #1 (Col, 1929) (s)
Mammy (WB, 1930)
Big Boy (WB, 1930)
Screen Snapshots #20 (Col, 1930) (s)
Showgirl in Hollywood (FN, 1930)
Hallelujah, I'm a Bum [Hallelujah, I'm a Tramp] (UA, 1933)
Wonder Bar (FN, 1934)
Go into Your Dance [Casino de Paree] (FN, 1935)

Kings of the Turf (Vita, 1935) (s)
The Singing Kid (WB, 1936)
Rose of Washington Square (20th–Fox, 1939)
Hollywood Cavalcade (20th–Fox, 1939)
Swanee River (20th–Fox, 1939)
Cavalcade of the Academy Awards (Vita, 1941) (s)
Show Business at War (20th–Fox, 1943) (s)
Rhapsody in Blue (WB, 1945)
The Jolson Story (Col, 1946)
Screen Snapshots #166 (Col, 1948) (s)
Jolson Sings Again (Col, 1949) (voice only)
Memorial to Al Jolson (Col, 1952) (s) (documentary)
The Great Al Jolson (Col, 1955) (s) (documentary)

## Broadway Plays

The Children of the Ghetto (1899)
La Belle Paree (1911)
Vera Violetta (1911)
The Whirl of Society (1912)
The Honeymoon Express (1913)
Dancing Around (1914)

Robinson Crusoe, Jr. (1916)
Sinbad (1918)
Bombo (1921)
Big Boy (1925)
The Wonder Bar (1931)
Hold On to Your Hats (1940)

## Radio Series

The Al Jolson Show (NBC, 1932–33)
The Kraft Music Hall (NBC, 1933–34)
The Al Jolson Show [The Shell Chateau
  Program] (NBC, 1935–36)

The Al Jolson Show [The Lifebuoy Program]
  (CBS, 1936–39)
The Al Jolson Show (CBS, 1942–43)
The Kraft Music Hall (NBC, 1947–49)

## Album Discography

Al Jolson (10" Decca DL-5316)
Al Jolson and Steve Allen Together (Mark 56
  759)
The Al Jolson Collection (Ronco 5A/5B)
Al Jolson 1885–1950 (Epitaph E-4008)
Al Jolson on Stage (Memory 2575)
Al Jolson on the Air (Sandy Hook 2003)
Al Jolson on the Air, Vols. 1–5 (Totem 1006,
  1012, 1019, 1030, 1040)
Al Jolson Overseas (Decca DL-9070)
Al Jolson with Oscar Levant (Decca DL-9095)
Al Jolson's Scrapbook of Memories (Gemini
  1001)
Among My Souvenirs (Decca DL-9050, MCA
  2064)
The Best of Al Jolson (Decca DX-169/DXS-
  7169, MCA 1000)
The Big Broadcast of 1935 (Kasha King 1935)
  [ST/R]
Bing and Al, Vols. 1–6 (Totem 1003, 1007,
  1013, 1015, 1016, 1017) w. Bing Crosby
Bing Crosby and Al Jolson Duets (Amalgamated
  0003)
Broadway Al (Totem 1010)
Brunswick Rarities (MCA 1560)
Burlesque (Star-Tone 505) [ST/R]
California, Here I Come (Sunbeam 505)
The Early Years (Olympic 7114, Kaola 14126)
An Evening with Al Jolson (ASA 1)
The Famous Al Jolson Show (Memorabilia 701)
The Films of Al Jolson (Golden Legends 2) [ST]
Go into Your Dance/Wonder Bar (Golden
  Legend 200012, Hollywood Soundstage 402,
  Sandy Hook 2030) [ST]
The Greatest of Al Jolson (Col Special Products
  PD-12668, Telehouse 12070)
The Immortal Al Jolson (Decca DL-9063, MCA
  2066)

Immortals—Jolson and Cantor (10" Epic LN-
  1128) w. Eddie Cantor
In the Heart of New York/Say It with Songs
  (Subon 1234) [ST]
The Jazz Singer (Sountrak 102) [ST]
The Jazz Singer (Pelican 125, Radiola 1070)
  [ST/R]
Jolie (Decca DL-9099)
Jolie and Ginger Live (Elgog 887) w. Ginger
  Rogers
Jolie Live in '35 (Amalgamated 124, Sandy
  Hook 2079)
Jolson Rehearses, Reminisces and Rambulates
  (Quango 126)
Jolson Sings (Silver Eagle 1014)
Jolson Sings Again (10" Decca DL-5006)
Jolson Sings Again (Pelican 145) [ST/R]
The Jolson Story (Pelican 129) [ST/R]
The Jolson Story—Outtakes and Alternate
  Takes (Take Two TT-103) [ST]
A Legend Named Jolson (Show Biz 1011)
The Legendary Al Jolson (Col P15530, Murray
  Hill 15528)
The Legends of Al Jolson, Jimmy Durante &
  Eddie Cantor (Ambassador Artists 1003-3)
Let Me Sing and I'm Happy (Ace of Hearts 33)
The Magnificent Al Jolson (Windmill 273)
Mammy (Amalgamated 223) [ST]
The Man and the Legend, Vols. 1–4 (Rhapsody
  1–4)
Memories (Decca DL-9038, MCA 2061)
Old Favorites (10" Decca DL-5080)
Radio Broadcast Follies of 1935 (Amalgamated
  252) [ST/R]
Radio Rarities—You Ain't Heard Nothin' Yet
  (Radiola 3MR1-2)
Rainbow 'Round My Shoulder (Decca DL-
  9036, MCA 2059)

Rock-a-Bye Your Baby (Decca DL-9035, MCA 2058)

Rose of Washington Square (Caliban 60023) [ST]

Say It with Songs (Ace of Hearts 87)

The Singing Fool (Take Two TT-106, Sandy Hook 2107) [ST]

The Singing Kid (Caliban 6013) [ST]

Sitting on Top of the World (Vocalion 3)

Songs He Made Famous (10" Decca DL-5026)

Souvenir Album, Vols. 1–6 (10" Decca DL-5028/31, 5314/15)

Stephen Foster Songs (10" Decca DL-5308)

Steppin' Out (Sunbeam 503)

Swanee River (Totem 1028) [ST/R]

A Tribute to Al Jolson (Audio Rarities 2285)

The Vintage Jolson (Pelican 111)

The Vitaphone Years (A-Jay 3749)

The World's Greatest Entertainer (Decca DL-9074, MCA 1734, MCA 2067)

The World's Greatest Entertainer (Music for Pleasure 5813)

The World's Greatest Entertainer—The Jazz Singer (Halcyon 102)

You Ain't Heard Nothin' Yet (ASV 5038)

You Ain't Heard Nothin' Yet (Decca DL-9037, MCA 1808, MCA 2060)

You Made Me Love You (Decca DL-9034, MCA 2057)

# ALLAN JONES

A HANDSOME TENOR, ALLAN JONES CARVED FOR HIMSELF A WELL-etched career on stage, in films, and in the recording field, as well as on radio. While many today know him best as the father of popular singer Jack Jones, Allan Jones is a multitalented performer whom the great composer Rudolf Friml considered to be his favorite singer. Of course, it was Friml's "The Donkey Serenade" that provided the singer with his biggest record success; for many years, that recording ranked third in sales of all RCA Victor records. Longevity has been the key in keeping Allan Jones before the public in assorted media during the six decades of his professional career.

Of Welsh ancestry, Allan Jones was born near Scranton, Pennsylvania, on October 14, 1907, the son of a coal mine foreman. The boy learned to sing at an early age and did his first public singing in church. When he was sixteen he joined Philadelphia's National Welsh Eisteddfod at the Academy of Music. During high school, Jones worked at odd jobs to earn money, and after graduating from high school he worked as a coal miner to save enough money to study music. In 1926, he obtained a scholarship from Syracuse University and then went to New York University to study voice with Claude Warford. There he was soloist with the University Glee Club and he also performed solos at the University Heights Presbyterian Church. Going to Paris with Claude Warford for further study, Jones took up the study of opera with Felix Leroux of the French National Opera and then moved to London to study oratorio with the noted British conductor Sir Henry Wood. Returning to the United States in 1927, he worked as a professional singer. During this time he became acquainted with famous opera singer Dame Nellie Melba, who became something of a mentor to the young vocalist.

Allan Jones continued to study and perform and in 1929 he wed Marjorie Buel. They had a son, but the marriage was short-lived. Late in the year Jones went back to Paris and the next year sang with the Cannes Opera Company. The year 1931 found him back in the United States performing at Carnegie Hall with the New York Symphony and Philharmonic Orchestras, directed by Walter Damrosch. Later in the year he debuted on Broadway in *Boccaccio* and the next summer he performed in operettas with the St. Louis Municipal Opera Company. In 1933 he toured for the Shuberts in *Blossom Time*, *The Only Girl*, and *The Student Prince*. For the same producers he did a tour of *Bitter Sweet* and in the spring of 1934 he starred in the production on Broadway. The Shuberts, who had him firmly under contract, installed Jones as the star of the Rudolf Friml operetta *Annina* on the road, which was followed by a stint in an aborted presentation of *America Sings*, which played Boston but never opened on Broadway due to a stagehands' strike.

By now, MGM talent scouts had spotted Allan Jones. It required a great deal of negotiation with the Shuberts to get him out of his long-term stage contract. Metro-Goldwyn-Mayer had planned originally to star Jones with Jeanette MacDonald in NAUGHTY MARIETTA, but by the time he could sever his relationship with the Shuberts, the studio had decided to team her with Nelson Eddy. Thus Jones made his delayed film debut in RECKLESS (1935), a Jean Harlow vehicle in which he sang "Everything's Been Done Before." He was the hero in the Marx Brothers' A NIGHT AT THE OPERA (1935) and in it he sang "Alone" and "Cosi Cosa," two songs associated closely with his career. In 1936, Jones supported Jeanette MacDonald and Nelson Eddy in the expansive ROSE MARIE, in which he played opera singer Jeanette's stage co-star. Together they performed the death scene from Charles Gounod's opera *Romeo and Juliet*. Much of Jones's footage, however, ended up on the cutting-room floor. Rumors have it that this was done at the insistence of Eddy, who did not want competition from his handsome rival. Jones also dubbed Dennis Morgan's singing of "A Pretty Girl Is Like a Melody" in THE GREAT ZIEGFELD (1936) and he can be spotted doing a brief song in a crowd sequence in 20th Century–Fox's RAMONA (1936).

Allan Jones's greatest film success came in 1936 when he was loaned to Universal to co-star with Irene Dunne in the expensively produced remake of SHOW BOAT. In it he and Dunne dueted on "Make Believe" and "You Are Love," and on a new song written for the film, "I Have the Room Above." (On June 24, 1940, Jones and Dunne would recreate their roles for CBS's "Lux Radio Theatre of the Air" production of the Jerome Kern–Oscar Hammerstein II musical.) That year also saw Allan Jones marrying actress Irene Hervey (on June 26, 1936); two years later they had a son, John Allan Jones, who grew up to be pop singer Jack Jones.

Now at the height of his screen popularity, Jones returned to MGM as co-star with the Marx Brothers in A DAY AT THE RACES (1937) and then Metro, wanting to test Jeanette MacDonald's appeal *away* from Nelson Eddy, teamed Allan Jones with her in THE FIRE-FLY (1937). This operetta produced his most popular song, Rudolf Friml's "The Donkey Serenade." On January 13, 1938 (the day before the birth of his son), Jones recorded "The Donkey Serenade" and "Giannina Mia" from THE FIREFLY for Victor Records and the recording sold over three million copies. The same day he also waxed "The One I Love" and "Cosi Cosa" for the company, two songs he sang in his final MGM starrer, EVERYBODY SING (1938), which also featured Judy Garland and Fanny Brice.

By now, strong-willed Allan Jones was feuding with MGM chieftain Louis B. Mayer and was forced to sit out the rest of his studio contract. However, he was allowed to host "The Metro–Maxwell House Radio Hour" on NBC and he continued to make lucrative personal appearances. When his MGM contract expired, Jones went to Paramount to headline THE GREAT VICTOR HERBERT (1939), a plodding musical biography which co-starred Mary Martin. The film provided him an opportunity to sing "Sweethearts," "Someday," "Thine Alone," and "I'm Falling in Love with Someone" (all of which he recorded for Victor), but he was overshadowed on screen by Walter Connolly in the title role. For the same studio he appeared in support of Madeleine Carroll and Fred MacMurray in HONEYMOON IN BALI (1939), a vapid comedy which afforded him the occasion to sing the famed tenor aria "O Paradiso" from the opera *L'Africaine*.

In 1940, professionally at loose ends, Allan Jones signed a contract with Universal Pictures. During the next half-dozen years he would star in ten features for this production-line studio, along with two loanouts to Paramount. (Ironically, during this period Nelson Eddy starred at MGM in BITTER SWEET [1940], THE NEW MOON [1940], and THE CHOCOLATE SOLDIER [1941], in all of which Jones had starred on stage.) His Universal tenure began with THE BOYS FROM SYRACUSE (1940), which co-starred his wife, Irene Hervey. In the picture Jones sang "Falling in Love with Love" and "Who Are You?," both of which he recorded for the Victor label. Next he was again supporting a comedy team, this time Bud Abbott and Lou Costello making their screen debut in ONE NIGHT IN THE TROPICS (1940). The low-budget picture did give Jones the chance to sing "Remind Me." Jones returned to Paramount to co-star with Susanna Foster (who had made her screen debut in THE GREAT VICTOR HERBERT) in THE HARD-BOILED CANARY [THERE'S MAGIC IN MUSIC] (1941), a comedy about a burlesque performer who becomes an opera star. He stayed at that studio for TRUE TO THE ARMY (1942), in which he played second fiddle to

Maureen O'Sullivan, Allan Jones, Groucho Marx, Chico Marx, and Harpo Marx in A DAY AT THE RACES (1937)

Judy Canova (as a backwoods girl on the run from gangsters) and to Ann Miller's hoofing.

By now World War II was in progress, and Allan Jones became the first entertainer to volunteer to perform for service personnel and he also cut a number of V-Discs, which were designed for military entertainment use. Back at Universal he starred with Jane Frazee in the quickie MOONLIGHT IN HAVANA (1942) as a baseball player who tries for a singing career. He and Jane Frazee were matched with Gloria Jean and Donald O'Connor for WHEN JOHNNY COMES MARCHING HOME (1942), a drama which featured Phil Spitalny and His All-Girl Orchestra and The Four Step Brothers. The programmer RHYTHM OF THE ISLANDS (1943) found Jones and rotund Andy Devine trying to start a resort on a tropical isle, but the film's sole tune, "I've Set My Mind Up to It," went to Jane Frazee. Jones did get to sing a trio of songs in LARCENY WITH MUSIC (1943) as a singer masquerading as the heir to an estate; Kitty Carlisle co-starred and the low-budget entry featured Alvino Rey and His Orchestra and The King Sisters. This was followed by YOU'RE A LUCKY FELLOW, MR. SMITH (1943) with Jones as a G.I. who marries a young woman (Evelyn Ankers) so she can gain an inheritance. He rounded out the year with a guest cameo in CRAZY HOUSE, featuring the studio's zany comedy team of Olsen and Johnson.

Jones's sole 1944 feature was SING A JINGLE, in which he was a vocalist who goes to work in a manufacturing plant as his contribution to the war effort. That year, however, he returned to network radio starring in "The Allan Jones Show" on CBS; for the same network he and Woody Herman alternated as stars of "The Old Gold Show." He also guest-starred on such series as "The Radio Hall of Fame" and "Music America Loves Best." Back at Universal the star headlined HONEYMOON AHEAD (1945), in which he was a paroled convict singing "Time Will Tell" and "Now and Always," and he closed out his studio contract with THE SENORITA FROM THE WEST (1945) about a girl (Bonita Granville) who wants to be a singer and who becomes involved with Jones, who dubs the radio voice of a noted crooner.

When not making motion pictures, Allan Jones co-starred with Benny Baker, Nanette Fabray, Betty Garrett, and Mary Wickes in the musical comedy *Jackpot* in 1944, which did better business on the road than on Broadway. After the war, he had a successful two-year tour of Great Britain, even giving a command performance for King George VI and the future Queen Elizabeth II, and back in the States in 1947 he and Irene Hervey toured in *State of the Union.* When its run was over Jones worked in vaudeville and then joined *Ed Wynn's Laugh Carnival,* a pre-Broadway show that never made it to Broadway. (Jones sang "The Donkey Serenade," "This Is the Moment," "Begin the Beguine," and the famed tenor aria from the opera *Pagliacci.*) Thereafter, to keep busy professionally he toured in such road shows as *Guys and Dolls,* playing Sky Masterson. His reviews were glowing but Hollywood was no longer interested in him. In 1957 Jones and Irene Hervey were divorced and he soon wed Mary Florsheim Picking, but they were divorced in 1964. By the end of the 1950s, Allan's son, Jack, was beginning his own singing career and the two did some nightclub work together. They would, on occasion, reteam, well into the 1980s. (In April 1989 Jack Jones got a star on the Hollywood Walk of Fame right next to Allan Jones's.)

During the early 1960s, Allan Jones reduced his show business activities, but as the decade progressed he was making personal appearances. In 1962 he recorded his first long-playing album (Victor had reissued his earlier recordings on LPs), called *Allan Jones Sings Only the Greatest,* for the Star label. He also resumed his screen career with character roles. He was the corrupt mayor in Paramount's quickie Western STAGE TO THUNDER ROCK (1964) and a businessman on a holiday in A SWINGIN' SUMMER (1965). He began doing summer theater work in shows such as *How to Succeed in Business Without Really Trying* in 1966, and that year found him in heavy demand for nightclub appearances. In the fall of 1967 the *New York Post* reported that the singer had "only 12 days free in the next 12 months." Regarding his performance at Manhattan's The Living Room at the time, *Variety* noted, "Jones still suggests the robustness and vigor of his voice. There is sufficient power to go the whole route and he does a full turn, asks no quarter and gives out in the best tradition. . . . He does not work as a period piece, but as an entertainer recalling a treasured era, who also gives out with tunes for moderns as well." In 1967 the singer cut another album, the best-selling *Allan Jones Sings for a Man and a Woman* on Scepter Records, and he continued to appear in such varied stage productions as *Silk Stockings, The Happy Time, The Fantasticks,* and *Paint Your Wagon.* When Merv Griffin presented a TV tribute to Rudolf Friml in 1968, Jones appeared and sang several Friml melodies; on the broadcast the composer reaffirmed that Jones was his favorite singer.

In 1971 Jones began performing the role in which he did his best work, that of the aged Don Quixote in the musical *Man of La Mancha,* a show he would do on and off for the next decade. He also appeared in other productions, such as *The Big Show of 1936* (a pre-Broadway nostalgia revue that closed in Philadelphia) and *110 in the Shade.* He guest-starred on such TV programs as "The Steve Allen Show," "Over Easy," "The Mike Douglas Show," and "The Love Boat," the latter in an episode with son Jack (who sang the program's theme song). He also worked the lecture circuit successfully; the Indianapolis *Star* review of his October 1972 performance at Clowes Hall noted: "With a voice strong and steady enough to belie his age by many years, he sang well-remembered melodies from both his pre- and post-retirement days, enchanting audiences with sidelight stories between numbers." In 1976 Jones starred at New York City's Town Hall as well as continued his tours of *Man of La Mancha.*

During the 1970s Jones also found domestic happiness in his marriage to dancer Maria Villavincie, who was many years his junior. In 1971 Jones narrated the Sherpix documentary SUB ROSA RISING and in 1978 (with soprano Patti Stevens) he recorded the album *Allan Jones Sings Friml Favorites,* which was issued by Glendale Records in 1982. "That Allan Jones recorded the Friml 'gems' on disk well into the fifth decade of his career speaks volumes, not only for the lyric beauty and purity of his tenor voice, but as well for the remarkable soundness of his vocal technique," wrote Fred Tyatt on the album's liner notes. It was a fitting tribute to a performer whose career has been so full and productive.

## Filmography

Reckless (MGM, 1935)
A Night at the Opera (MGM, 1935)
The Great Ziegfeld (MGM, 1936) (voice only)
Rose Marie (MGM, 1936)
Ramona (20th–Fox, 1936)
Show Boat (Univ, 1936)
Lest We Forget (WB, 1936) (s)
A Day at the Races (MGM, 1937)
The Firefly (MGM, 1937)
Everybody Sing (MGM, 1938)
Honeymoon in Bali [Husbands or Lovers] (Par, 1939)
The Great Victor Herbert (Par, 1939)
The Boys from Syracuse (Univ, 1940)
One Night in the Tropics (Univ, 1940)
The Hard-Boiled Canary [There's Magic in Music] (Par, 1941)
Moonlight in Havana (Univ, 1942)
True to the Army (Par, 1942)
When Johnny Comes Marching Home (Univ, 1942)
You're a Lucky Fellow, Mr. Smith (Univ, 1943)
Rhythm of the Islands (Univ, 1943)
Larceny with Music (Univ, 1943)
Crazy House (Univ, 1943)
Sing a Jingle [Lucky Days] (Univ, 1944)
Honeymoon Ahead (Univ, 1945)
The Senorita from the West (Univ, 1945)
Stage to Thunder Rock (Par, 1964)
A Swingin' Summer (United Screen Arts, 1965)
Sub Rosa Rising (Sherpix, 1971) (narrator)

## Broadway Plays

Boccaccio (1931)
Bitter Sweet (1934) (revival)
The Chocolate Soldier (1942) (revival)
Jackpot (1944)

## Radio Series

The Metro–Maxwell House Radio Hour (NBC, 1937)
The Allan Jones Show (CBS, 1944–46)
The Old Gold Show (CBS, 1944–46)

## Album Discography

Allan Jones Sings for a Man and a Woman (Scepter 566)
Allan Jones Sings Friml Favorites (Glendale GL-9004) w. Patti Stevens
Allan Jones Sings Only the Greatest (Star 1253)
Allan Jones Sings Show Tunes (Camden CAL-268)
The Best of Allan Jones (RCA International 90065)
The Donkey Serenade (Camden CAL/CAS-2256)
Falling in Love (10" RCA LM-95)
The Firefly (Caliban 6027) [ST]
The Firefly (10" RCA LM-121)
The Great Ziegfeld (CIF 3005) [ST]
It's a Grand Night for Singing (Westwood 505)
Night and Day (RCA LM-1140)
One Night Stand with Woody Herman–Allan Jones (Joyce 1037)
Show Boat (Xeno 251, Vertinge 2004) [ST]
Show Boat (Sunbeam 501) [ST/R]

# SHIRLEY JONES

WHEN SHIRLEY JONES MADE HER SCREEN DEBUT IN OKLAHOMA! IN 1955, Bosley Crowther of the *New York Times* enthused that she was "so full of beauty, sweetness and spirit that a better Laurey cannot be dreamed." Thus, at twenty-one, Shirley Jones found movie stardom. Although her ingenue period in films was brief, the lovely actress not only developed into a seasoned dramatic performer, but she also found success on the musical stage and television. In addition, she had a successful club act with her first husband, Jack Cassidy, and later carved out a new career for herself when she and her stepson, David Cassidy, starred in the popular early 1970s TV sitcom "The Partridge Family." Throughout her movie career, both on film and TV, Shirley Jones has managed to score well in a variety of parts that have demonstrated her acting range. In the 1970s she branched out into assorted show business activities with her second husband, Marty Ingels, although in recent years religion has played an increasingly important role in her life.

The future star was named for Shirley Temple. She was born March 31, 1934, in Smithton, Pennsylvania, the only child of brewery owner Paul Jones and his wife, Marjorie. Shirley had a natural knack for singing which she developed while still very young. By the age of five she was performing church solos. Later she studied voice with Pittsburgh vocal coach Ken Welch. After graduating from South Huntingdon High School in 1952 (as a student she had acted in school plays and had won a stage singing contest), the buxom Shirley won the Miss Pittsburgh contest and placed second for Miss Pennsylvania. She then studied drama at the Pittsburgh Playhouse and made her professional stage debut in *Lady in the Dark* at the Pittsburgh Civic Opera Company, followed by *Call Me Madam.*

In the summer of 1953 Shirley vacationed in New York City and Ken Welch arranged for her to audition there for theatrical agent Gus Schirmer. He was so impressed with her that he, in turn, arranged for her to audition with a casting director for Richard Rodgers and Oscar Hammerstein II. That director took her directly to his bosses, who signed her to a seven-year contract, thus cancelling Shirley's plans to attend Centenary Junior College in Hackettstown, New Jersey. Given vocal and acting lessons, she was placed in the Naval nurse chorus of the long-running *South Pacific* on Broadway and then was given a small role in *Me and Juliet.* When that Rodgers and Hammerstein show went on tour, Shirley assumed the starring role.

In 1954 Shirley went to Hollywood to screen-test for Laurey in Rodgers and Hammerstein's film version of OKLAHOMA! (1955). She made her film debut in the coveted part of the pretty farm girl romanced by a handsome ranchhand (Gordon MacRae). In it she sang "Many a New Day" and "Out of My Dreams" and dueted with MacRae on "The Surrey with the Fringe on Top" and "People Will Say We're in Love." *Variety* endorsed, "This is Miss Jones's first picture, and it is sure to make her a much sought-after star almost overnight." It was logical that this wholesome beauty would be cast in the screen adaptation of Rodgers and Hammerstein's CAROUSEL (1956). When Frank Sinatra walked off the production, Gordon MacRae was brought in to be self-centered carnival barker Billy Bigelow with whom innocent factory worker Julie Jordan (Jones) falls in love. Shirley sang "What's the Use of Wond'rin'" and "You'll Never Walk Alone" and dueted with MacRae on "If I Loved You." Following the making of CAROUSEL Shirley did *Oklahoma!* in Paris and Rome on a good-will tour for the U.S. Department of State. Back home she was a guest on CBS-TV's "Person to Person" and then went to Cambridge, Massachusetts, to appear in *The Beggar's Opera.* There she met actor-singer Jack Cassidy, whom she married on August 5, 1956. That November she appeared as an alcoholic in "The Big Slide" episode of CBS-TV's "Playhouse 90" opposite Red Skelton and on February 19, 1957, was on that network's "U.S. Steel Hour."

For her third film Shirley portrayed a farm girl who helps a juvenile delinquent (Pat Boone) reform as he becomes a silky driver in APRIL LOVE (1957) for 20th Century–Fox. In the feature Shirley reprised a solo on "April Love" and dueted with Boone on "Do It Yourself" and "The Bentonville Fair." By now Shirley was becoming bored with her pristine screen image and, following the birth (September 27, 1958) of her son, Shaun (who later became a TV and singing star in the 1970s), Shirley and her husband undertook a successful nightclub tour. They had worked together the previous spring in stock while Shirley alone had done the CBS-TV production of "The Red Mill" in 1958. Shirley and Cassidy also cut two LP albums for Columbia, *Speaking of Love* and *With Love from Hollywood,* performing show tunes. In 1958, also for Columbia Records, the couple made a studio cast version of *Brigadoon.* After appearing with James Cagney in the labor union expose NEVER STEAL ANYTHING SMALL (1959), an oddball musical comedy/drama, she went to England to co-star with Max Bygraves as the mother of a talking baby in BOBBIKINS (1960).

In post–studio system Hollywood, it was up to performers and their agents to shape careers. Shirley decided on a complete about-face when she played the young woman who turns to prostitution after being violated by an evangelist (Burt Lancaster) in ELMER GANTRY (1960). For her turn-about performance she won the Best Supporting Actress Academy Award. After that, however, she did a summer stock tour of *Oklahoma!* and then provided a guest cameo as a far-out actress in PEPE (1960). Following her work in the John Ford Western TWO RODE TOGETHER (1961), Shirley returned to the musical for the last time when she was seen as Marian, the small town librarian, who finds love with a con man (Robert Preston) in THE MUSIC MAN (1962). In it she did full justice to the haunting "Till There Was You," along with "Goodnight My Someone," "Being in Love," and her duet with Robert Preston on "Goodnight My Someone."

After the highly profitable THE MUSIC MAN, Shirley Jones continued to work in a variety of media, but the success she had enjoyed in her earlier movies would not be repeated. In 1962 her pilot "For the Love of Mike" failed to sell as a CBS-TV series. She continued to make pictures, but none of them were outstanding. By the middle of the 1960s she was no longer considered a major film name. In 1968 Shirley and Jack Cassidy appeared on Broadway in a period musical, *Maggie Flynn*, which had a modest run, and in 1969 she starred in the first of her several made-for-television movies, SILENT NIGHT, LONELY NIGHT. For this drama about two lonely souls (Shirley, Lloyd Bridges) who find love at a remote resort, she was nominated for an Emmy Award.

In the fall of 1970 Shirley starred in the ABC-TV series "The Partridge Family" as Connie Partridge, a widowed mother who forms a successful singing act with her children (David Cassidy, Susan Dey, Danny Bonaduce, Jeremy Gelbwaks [later Brian Forster], Suzanne Crough). The comedy, based on the real-life The Cowsills, was a huge success which ran for four seasons. In addition, The Partridge Family group had several successful single records and albums on the Bell label. Their 1970 single of "I Think I Love You" sold over four million copies and was followed by best-sellers like "Doesn't Somebody Want to Be Wanted," "I'll Meet You Halfway," "I Woke Up in Love This Morning," "It's One of

Shirley Jones and Robert Preston in THE MUSIC MAN (1962)

These Nights," and "Looking Through the Eyes of Love." The act also had nine charted albums for Bell between 1970 and 1973; their first LP, *The Partridge Family Album*, was on the charts for over seventy weeks. Moreover, "The Partridge Family" series was the subject of a massive merchandising campaign, which extended from books to toys. The series, which briefly made a teenage idol of Shirley's stepson, David Cassidy, ran its course and left the network in the summer of 1974. For the public, Shirley was again "Miss Wholesomeness."

In the mid-1970s Shirley and Jack Cassidy were divorced. (He died in a fire on December 12, 1976.) In 1977 she married comic actor–agent Marty Ingels and they became involved in a variety of business projects, including a lucrative talent bureau. During the mid-to-late 1970s she appeared in more TV movies. In 1979 she returned to the big screen for the first time since playing a madam in the Western THE CHEYENNE SOCIAL CLUB (1970). The film was BEYOND THE POSEIDON ADVENTURE (1979), a tepid disaster picture. She attempted a new teleseries with "Shirley" (NBC-TV), but the comedy lasted only three months in the 1979–80 season. Two years later she appeared in the CBS-TV pilot "The Adventures of Pollyanna" but that failed to sell and the following year she was in the pilot for the ABC-TV series "Hotel" (which did sell, but she was not on the program again until a guest appearance early in 1987). She returned to feature films in TANK (1984), opposite James Garner, and the next year starred in the poignant PBS special on Alzheimer's disease, "There Were Times, Dear." In the early to mid-1980s Shirley was a TV and print media spokesperson for the West Coast chain of Ralph's Supermarkets. Early in 1988 she had the running role of love-starved grandmother Kitty Noland in the ABC-TV comedy series "The 'Slap' Maxwell Story."

The year 1988 was extremely productive for Jones as she and Marty Ingels guest-starred on Oprah Winfrey's TV talk show and Shirley was named Woman of the Year by Childhelp USA. She and Ingels were also awarded the National Leukemia Council's first Gift of Life Award for their fifteen years of volunteer work in fighting the disease. In August she closed the thirty-fourth Republican National Convention in New Orleans by singing "America the Beautiful." She also took part in the PBS special "In Performance at the White House" by singing "If I Loved You" and "You'll Never Walk Alone" from *Carousel.* She closed the year by co-hosting a TV special, "Christmas in D.C.," with opera singer Kathleen Battle. She opened 1989 by singing at the Inaugural Ball at the request of President George Bush. She also signed a pact with Diadem Records to record gospel music and she did a sixteen-week tour of *The King and I* with David Carradine. She also made an unsold pilot for a new TV situation comedy series, in which she starred as the owner of a bail bond business.

## Filmography

Oklahoma! (Magna, 1955)
Carousel (20th–Fox, 1956)
April Love (20th–Fox, 1957)
Never Steal Anything Small (Univ, 1959)
Bobbikins (20th–Fox, 1960)
Elmer Gantry (UA, 1960)
Pepe (Col, 1960)
Two Rode Together (Col, 1961)
The Music Man (WB, 1962)
The Courtship of Eddie's Father (MGM, 1963)
A Ticklish Affair (MGM, 1963)
Dark Purpose (Univ, 1964)
Bedtime Story (Univ, 1964)
Fluffy (Univ, 1965)
The Secret of My Success (MGM, 1965)
Silent Night, Lonely Night (NBC-TV, 12/16/69)
The Happy Ending (UA, 1969)

The Cheyenne Social Club (WB, 1970)
But I Don't Want to Get Married (ABC-TV, 10/6/70)
The Girls of Huntingdon House (ABC-TV, 2/14/73)
The Family Nobody Wanted (ABC-TV, 2/19/75)
Winner Take All (NBC-TV, 3/3/75)
The Lives of Jenny Dolan (NBC-TV, 10/27/75)
Yesterday's Child (NBC-TV, 2/3/77)
Who'll Save Our Children? (CBS-TV, 12/16/78)
A Last Cry for Help (ABC-TV, 1/19/79)
Beyond the Poseidon Adventure (20th–Fox, 1979)
The Children of An Lac (CBS-TV, 10/9/80)
Inmates: A Love Story (ABC-TV, 2/13/81)
Tank (Univ, 1984)

## Broadway Plays

South Pacific (1953) (replacement)
Me and Juliet (1953)

Maggie Flynn (1968)

## TV Series

The Partridge Family (ABC, 1970–74)
Shirley (NBC, 1979–80)

The "Slap" Maxwell Story (ABC, 1988)

## Album Discography

April Love (Dot 9000) [ST]
Brigadoon (Col CL-1132, Col OL-7040/OS-2540)
Carousel (Cap W/SW-694) [ST]
Maggie Flynn (RCA LOCD/LSOD-2009) [OC]
The Music Man (WB 1499) [ST]
Oklahoma! (Cap WAO/SWAO-595) [ST]
The Partridge Family Album (Bell 6050)
The Partridge Family at Home with Their Greatest Hits (Bell 1107)
The Partridge Family Bulletin Board (Bell 1137)

The Partridge Family Christmas Carol (Bell 6066)
The Partridge Family Shopping Bag (Bell 6072)
The Partridge Family Sound Magazine (Bell 6064)
The Partridge Family—Up to Date (Bell 6059)
Pepe (Colpix 507) [ST]
Speaking of Love (Col CL-991) w. Jack Cassidy
With Love from Hollywood (Col CL-1255) w. Jack Cassidy
The World of the Partridge Family (Bell 1319)

# HOWARD KEEL

IT IS NOT UNCOMMON FOR PERFORMERS TO HAVE UPS AND DOWNS in their careers. However, it is rare for an entertainer to attain his greatest success after the age of sixty, especially if stardom was initially forthcoming in the performer's early career. But this is just what happened to Howard Keel, who had the biggest boost to his show business standing thanks to the television soap opera "Dallas." From that sprung successful concert tours both here and abroad and, for the first time for the booming baritone of so many MGM musicals of the 1950s, a successful recording career. Furthermore, it is ironic that his TV success was based on his acting ability, whereas previously he had mainly been thought of as the star of glossy screen operettas, a latter-day Nelson Eddy.

Born Harry Clifford Leek on April 13, 1919, in Gillespie, Illinois, he and his young brother moved with their mother to a suburb of San Diego, California, in 1930, following the death of his coal miner father. After graduating from high school he worked at a variety of jobs, including that of an aviation mechanic. He had always enjoyed singing, but never took it seriously until his landlady encouraged him and gave him voice lessons. He got a job as a singing busboy at the Paris Inn Cafe in Los Angeles, but for higher wages accepted a factory job at Douglas Aircraft, studying voice at night. At Douglas he took part in various in-plant shows and there he met singer George Houston who took him on as a pupil at his American Music Theater in Pasadena. Like Keel, Houston was a tall baritone; he had appeared in movies and at the time he met Keel was headlining Producers Releasing Corporation's (PRC) "Lone Rider" Western series. Keel worked in some of the operas staged by Houston but was soon on the road representing Douglas Aircraft across the country and also taking part in talent shows and giving occasional concerts. He auditioned for Oscar Hammerstein II, hoping for a part in the movie STATE FAIR (1945), but instead was cast in the Broadway company of *Carousel.* This was followed by a year's run in the London production of *Oklahoma!* While in England, Keel made his screen debut in THE SMALL VOICE (1948) and was impressive as the oafish criminal who takes refuge in the country home of a married couple (Valerie Hobson, James Donald). By mistake, he was billed as Harold Keel; the film was issued in the United States as HIDEOUT.

Upon his return to the United States, the actor, now calling himself Howard Keel, was hired by MGM for the leading role of the ultra-macho cowboy Frank Butler in the film version of ANNIE GET YOUR GUN (1950) as the result of a screen test he had done earlier for Warner Bros. and his work in THE SMALL VOICE. Despite long delays, resulting from Keel's breaking his leg when a horse fell on him and Judy Garland's being fired and replaced by Betty Hutton, the film was a big success and marked the beginning of the actor's tenure in posh screen musicals. The actor was especially impressive singing "My Defenses Are Down." *Variety* assessed, "Keel's baritone is particularly adaptable to the show tunes and he sounds them out with resonance."

Despite the resounding success of ANNIE GET YOUR GUN, the studio was passing from the control of Louis B. Mayer to Dore Schary, and in the transition little thought was given to the focus of Keel's career. He was shoved into the Esther Williams Technicolor musical PAGAN LOVE SONG (1950), which was set in Tahiti and offered lovely scenery, an empty plot, and lackluster songs. For his third MGM entry, Keel proved he could act in the bright comedy THREE GUYS NAMED MIKE (1951). He was the pilot romancing stewardess Jane Wyman, successfully averting the competition of her other suitors: advertising executive Barry Sullivan and student Van Johnson. That same year he was teamed with Kathryn Grayson for the first time as swaggering Gaylord Ravenal in the third movie edition of SHOW BOAT. They made a pleasing screen couple, but the studio chose next to cast him opposite Esther Williams in the lumbering TEXAS CARNIVAL (1951). In this very busy year he was the narrator of the Clark Gable frontier epic ACROSS THE WIDE MISSOURI and then starred in one of his finest comedies, CALLAWAY WENT THATAWAY, a sharp satire of the "Hopalong Cassidy" craze. He was the has-been Western film star whose movies are

Louis Calhern, Betty Hutton, and Howard Keel in ANNIE GET YOUR GUN (1950)

resurrected by TV, making him much in demand again. The studio rematched him with Kathryn Grayson in a remake of ROBERTA (1935) called LOVELY TO LOOK AT (1952), but it was a pale reincarnation. Keel and Grayson went on a concert tour of South America to promote it and other MGM products.

Upon his return from South America, Howard Keel was shunted to an action programmer, DESPERATE SEARCH (1952), as a pilot searching for two youngsters lost in the Canadian wilderness. His brief singing guest spot in I LOVE MELVIN (1953) ended up on the cutting-room floor. Next, FAST COMPANY (1953) was about a nag that would race to music! Keel was paired with Robert Taylor and Ava Gardner for the big-budget Mexican-set Western RIDE, VAQUERO! (1953). He was the rancher whose wife (Gardner) is more attracted to cowboy Taylor. Like so many other MGM musical stars (e.g., Jane Powell, Kathryn Grayson) in 1953, Keel was loaned to Warner Bros. He was borrowed to co-star in the Western musical CALAMITY JANE opposite Doris Day. It was her movie and her solo "Secret Love" won an Academy Award as Best Song. His final 1953 outing was the lavish production of KISS ME KATE, again with Kathryn Grayson. He was virile, effective, and on the mark in the role of egocentric Petruchio in this 3-D production of Cole Porter's Broadway hit. (At one point MGM considered hiring Laurence Olivier for the male lead and dubbing his singing voice.)

Keel may have insisted the role of the Mountie was "a blithering idiot," but he finally agreed to star in the remake of ROSE MARIE (1954) with Ann Blyth. It was a colorful, but unsatisfying, widescreen entry. His manly interpretation of Captain Mike the Mountie—earlier played by Nelson Eddy—gave the film its only anchor. A happier project was SEVEN BRIDES FOR SEVEN BROTHERS (1954) in which he was the oafish frontiersman who weds Jane Powell. Although the film's songs were mediocre, the production was lavish and the plot entertaining. Following this success, his MGM salary rose to $3,000 weekly. Ironically, he was to do only three more features for the studio.

In the purported screen biography of Sigmund Romberg, DEEP IN MY HEART (1954), Howard Keel made a guest appearance singing "Your Land and My Land" and then he suffered through his third disastrous picture with Esther Williams, JUPITER'S DARLING (1955), which derived from Robert Sherwood's sophisticated Broadway comedy. In this unlavish musical (leftover sets, stock shots from QUO VADIS, etc.) Williams had the title role of the patrician beauty who delays an attack on Rome by romancing Hannibal (Keel). The finale parade of elephants (dyed pastel colors) was the film's sole highlight. Also in 1955 Keel reteamed with Ann Blyth for KISMET. Despite the usual MGM pomp and gloss, and their duet of "Stranger in Paradise," the transplanted Broadway musical was a weak one and the film concluded Keel's studio contract.

By now industry executives had realized that the public was cold toward screen operettas and Howard Keel was too typecast in the genre to succeed as a dramatic actor. Thus he was off the screen for four years doing stage productions, concerts, and nightclub work and performing in Europe, where he remained popular. He served a term as president of the Screen Actors Guild and came to TV in 1957 on "Zane Grey Theatre." He then appeared in such shows as "Tales of Wells Fargo," "Death Valley Days," and

"Run for Your Life." A case of pneumonia prevented him from starring on Broadway as Franklin D. Roosevelt in *Sunrise at Campobello* (Ralph Bellamy took the part). However, on September 19, 1958, he headlined the NBC-TV musical special "Roberta" and that year he also returned to Broadway in a revival of *Carousel.* The 1959 musical *Saratoga* (based on Edna Ferber's *Saratoga Trunk*), which co-starred him with Carol Lawrence, was a flop.

Searching for venues to pursue his craft, Keel returned to pictures in the British-made FLOODS OF FEAR (1959) as an escaped prisoner who becomes a hero during a flood. Back in Hollywood he was commanding as Simon-Peter in Walt Disney's failed biblical opus, THE BIG FISHERMAN (1959). In 1961 he traveled to West Germany for the combat tale ARMORED COMMAND as an Army colonel who foresees the German resistance that became the Battle of the Bulge. Continuing his string of low-budget films, he was in England for the science fiction feature THE DAY OF THE TRIFFIDS (1963) as a temporarily blinded man who regains his sight as the world is invaded by plant-like aliens. Keel wrote much of his own dialogue for the picture which, in recent years, has become a popular TV and videocassette item. While in England he starred in a BBC-TV special of "Kiss Me Kate" with Patricia Morison.

Back home again, Keel starred in the road company of *No Strings* and in 1965 sang the title song for the animated feature film THE MAN FROM BUTTON WILLOW. Keel was then hired by producer A. C. Lyles for a trio of low-budget Paramount Westerns. The gimmick was to pepper the films with former film stars. WACO (1966) matched him with Jane Russell, and for RED TOMAHAWK (1967) he was to be reunited with Betty Hutton (*not* one of his favorite performers). However, she withdrew and was replaced by Joan Caulfield, while Yvonne De Carlo was his vis-à-vis in ARIZONA BUSHWACKERS (1968). Sandwiched between the Lyles mini-features was the John Wayne–Kirk Douglas Western THE WAR WAGON (1967), in which Keel enjoyed his best film assignment in years, that of comical Indian Levi Walking Bear. In 1969 he also made a guest appearance on the CBS-TV program "Here's Lucy."

From the late 1960s until the early 1980s Howard Keel kept active in a variety of show business activities. He and Kathryn Grayson formed a successful club act which debuted in Las Vegas in 1968 and ran throughout the country along with TV appearances and a six-week engagement in Australia. In 1969 he began a ten-month tour in the play *Plaza Suite* and then toured on and off in *Man of La Mancha* for several years. He also did tours of *I Do! I Do!* and *The Unsinkable Molly Brown.* In 1972 he starred in London in an adaptation of Henry James's *The Ambassador,* which he reprised on Broadway later in the year. Keel was frequently reunited with Jane Powell in road shows, including *Seven Brides for Seven Brothers* and *South Pacific.* In 1975 he did a concert tour singing Cole Porter tunes and also appeared at the London Palladium. While in England he and Ethel Merman recorded the score for *Annie Get Your Gun.* In the early 1980s he was on such TV nostalgia-cast programs as "Love Boat" and "Fantasy Island," but real stardom returned in 1981 when he began appearing on the popular CBS-TV prime-time soap opera "Dallas."

Jim Davis, the actor who played Jock Ewing, the patriarch on "Dallas," had died and the producers were seeking a strong, handsome older actor to take his place. Keel began appearing as rancher Clayton Farlow and soon was a show regular. During the 1984–85 season he and Donna Reed (who had temporarily replaced Barbara Bel Geddes) made a particularly attractive TV couple. The success Keel attained from "Dallas" resulted in several SRO tours of England and in 1984 his record album *And I Love You So* became one of the five top-selling LPs in that country, selling over 100,000 copies within a week. When it was issued in the United States as *With Love, Howard Keel,* the album sold so well that a follow-up, *Reminiscing with Howard Keel,* was released. In 1985 he recorded the song "J. R.! Who Do You Think You Are?" for Warner Bros./Lorimar Records' album *Dallas, The Music Story.* Heart surgery in the mid-1980s did not slow Keel down. He continued making successful personal appearances as well as continued his "Dallas" duties as J. R.'s father-in-law. On July 15, 1989, he made his Los Angeles concert debut when he appeared at the Greek Theatre for a one-night performance. The *Los Angeles Times* reported, "Keel's rich bass-baritone cruised easily through [Broadway/film musical] medleys. . . . But his finest moments came during his interpretations of smaller tunes—notably 'Wind Beneath My Wings' . . . and Jacques Brel's 'We Never Learn.' His empathy for the more interior emotions of songs like these suggested that maturity may have endowed Keel with a creative sensitivity to match the sunny glow of his voice."

When not working, Howard Keel likes to golf and fly airplanes. He has been married three times. His first marriage (1943–48) was to actress Rosemary Cooper and in 1950 he wed dancer Helen Anderson; they had three children (Kaija, Kristine, Gunnar) before being divorced in 1970. In 1971 he married former airline stewardess Judy Magamoll. They have a daughter, Leslie, and reside in Sherman Oaks, California.

Looking back on his film career, Keel assesses that the short duration and unevenness of his Hollywood career was due to his independence and his naive refusal to embrace the industry's favorite pastime—studio politics. The veteran of today admits, "As long as I can sing halfway decent, I'd rather sing [than act]. There's nothing like being in good voice, feeling good, having good numbers to do and having a fine orchestra."

## Filmography

The Small Voice [Hideout] (Br, 1948)
Annie Get Your Gun (MGM, 1950)
Pagan Love Song (MGM, 1950)
Three Guys Named Mike (MGM, 1951)
Show Boat (MGM, 1951)
Texas Carnival (MGM, 1951)
Across the Wide Missouri (MGM, 1951)
(narrator)
Callaway Went Thataway [The Star Said No!]
(MGM, 1951)
Lovely to Look At (MGM, 1952)

Desperate Search (MGM, 1952)
I Love Melvin (MGM, 1953) (scene deleted
from release print)
Fast Company (MGM, 1953)
Ride, Vaquero! (MGM, 1953)
Calamity Jane (WB, 1953)
Kiss Me Kate (MGM, 1953)
Rose Marie (MGM, 1954)
Seven Brides for Seven Brothers (MGM, 1954)
Deep in My Heart (MGM, 1954)
Jupiter's Darling (MGM, 1955)

Kismet (MGM, 1955)
Floods of Fear (Univ, 1959)
The Big Fisherman (UA, 1959)
Armored Command (AA, 1961)
The Day of the Triffids (AA, 1963)

The Man from Button Willow (United Screen
    Arts, 1965) (voice only)
Waco (Par, 1966)
Red Tomahawk (Par, 1967)
The War Wagon (Univ, 1967)
Arizona Bushwackers (Par, 1968)

## Broadway Plays

Carousel (1945) (replacement)
Carousel (1958) (revival)

Saratoga (1959)
The Ambassador (1972)

## TV Series

Dallas (CBS, 1981– )

## Album Discography

The Ambassador (RCA SER-5618) [OC]
And I Love You So (Warwick WW-45137)
Annie Get Your Gun (10" MGM E-509, MGM
    E-3227, Metro M/S-548, Sound/Stage 2302)
    [ST]
Annie Get Your Gun (Amalgamated 145, Sandy
    Hook 2053) [ST] w. Judy Garland
Calamity Jane (10" Col CL-6273, Col Special
    Products 19611) [ST]
Deep in My Heart (MGM E-3153) [ST]
General Motors 50th Anniversary Show (RCA
    LOC-1037) [ST/TV]
Kismet (MGM E-3281, Metro M/S-5260) [ST]
Kiss Me Kate (MGM E-3077, Metro M/S-525)
    [ST]
Kiss Me Kate (RCA LOP/LSP-1505) w. Gogi
    Grant, Anne Jeffreys
Lovely to Look At (10" MGM E-150, MGM E-
    3230) [ST]

Oklahoma!/Annie Get Your Gun (Stanyan SR-
    10069)
Pagan Love Song (10" MGM E-534, MGM
    SES-43ST) [ST]
Reminiscing with Howard Keel—His Stage and
    Screen Favorites (Silver Eagle TLS-2259)
Rose Marie (10" MGM E-229, MGM E-3228,
    Metro M/S-616) [ST]
Saratoga (RCA LOC/LSO-1051) [OC]
Seven Brides for Seven Brothers (10" MGM E-
    244, MGM E-3235) [ST]
Show Boat (10" MGM E-559, MGM E-3230,
    Metro M/S-527) [ST]
Show Boat (RCA LOP/LSO-1515) w. Gogi
    Grant, Anne Jeffreys
With Love, Howard Keel—Yesterday, Today
    and Tomorrow (Silver Eagle SE-1026)

# GENE KELLY

TWO MALE DANCERS ARE ASSOCIATED INDELIBLY WITH AMERICAN
screen musicals: dapper Fred Astaire and ingratiating Gene Kelly. Elegant Astaire is forever
aligned with sophistication and romance, as a polished performer who could charm and
woo his partner in the ballroom, park, or skating rink. Convivial Kelly, far more athletic in
his approach, used his masculine Irish good looks to make hoofing more appealing to the
average viewer. He propelled dancing into a fresh dimension where soft shoe, ballet, or
other Terpsichorean activity replaced dialogue and became an integrated part of the
scenario's structure. Like Astaire, Kelly could sing (in a raspy, decent voice) and he
choreographed much of his own screen dancing. But Kelly went several steps further than
Astaire, with whom he co-starred occasionally. Gene became a film producer and director,
doing a better job on those projects (such as SINGIN' IN THE RAIN) where he was in front
of the camera as well. It was always Kelly's ambition "to get rid of the idea that dancing was
not manly and get it across that it is just as manly as any other form of athletics. Being a
dancer is closely allied to being an athlete, and that is the premise on which my whole style
is based. I was always a pretty good athlete." (In fact, he once said, "I never wanted to be a
dancer. . . . I wanted to be a shortstop for the Pittsburgh Pirates.")

Eugene Curran Kelly was born in Pittsburgh, Pennsylvania, on August 23, 1912,
the third of five children of Patrick Joseph and Harriet (Curran) Kelly. His father was a
traveling gramophone salesman; his strong-willed, stagestruck mother encouraged her
children to take lessons in music, dance, and French. Gene and his younger brother Fred
shone at dance, but Gene far preferred sports. He would admit, "I hated dancing. . . . I
thought it was sissy. I bless her now for making me go." Kelly studied journalism at
Pennsylvania State College but when the Depression hit, he quit school and taught
gymnastics at a YMCA camp near Pittsburgh. He and Fred developed a hoofing act—tap
dancing on roller skates—which they displayed at local amateur nights. When he had the
money he returned to his schooling, this time at the University of Pittsburgh, from which
he graduated in 1933 as an economics major. He began law school in the fall of 1933, but
realized dancing was his true career and dropped out of school. During this period, he and
Fred continued their dance teaming and Gene began teaching in the dance school where
he had studied as a child. Each year he would take two weeks of classes at the Chicago
Association of Dancing Masters, where he was later accepted as a member. He developed
his teaching into The Gene Kelly Studio of the Dance, which soon had a branch in
Johnstown, Pennsylvania. It was at this time that Kelly realized, "As much as I loved
classical ballet, I had to face the fact that my style of dancing was more modern." As such,

he rejected an opportunity to join the Ballets Russes de Monte Carlo, which passed through Pittsburgh and was to perform in Chicago.

The Kelly brothers performed their dance routines at local clubs, and during the Chicago World's Fair of 1933–34 they were part of a children's theater unit. They also did nightclub work. Meanwhile, the reputation and fortunes of the Kelly dance studios grew. In the summer of 1935 the Kellys visited California relatives, and while in Los Angeles, Gene was screen-tested (unsuccessfully) at RKO, where Fred Astaire was a dancing star. In the summer of 1937 Gene was offered the chance—so he thought—to choreograph an upcoming Broadway show. When he arrived in New York, he found he was wanted only to appear in one dance number. He chose to return to Pittsburgh. But the next year (in August) he returned to New York, encouraged by his mother not to be so prideful this time around.

He joined the chorus of Cole Porter's *Leave It to Me!*, which opened on November 9, 1938. The show's overnight sensation was Mary Martin, who sang "My Heart Belongs to Daddy" (Gene was one of the chorus boys in this number). Gene quit this production to join the revue *One for the Money* (1939), for which he was paid $115 weekly as one of the six performers who sang, danced, and performed in the skits. When the show went on the road, Gene not only continued to co-star, he also coached the replacements in their routines. In the summer of 1939 he choreographed three shows for the Theatre Guild's straw-hat season in Westport, Connecticut. He was hired for the comedic role of Harry the Hoofer in William Saroyan's Broadway play *The Time of Your Life* (opened October 25, 1939) and played the role for twenty weeks, after which he choreographed Billy Rose's *Diamond Horseshoe Revue* at the New York World's Fair. (Brother Fred took over Kelly's role in *The Time of Your Life* when the show went on the road.) Meanwhile, while dance director for Billy Rose's *Revue* he met a sixteen-year-old dancer named Betsy Blair to whom he was married on September 22, 1941. Their only child, daughter Kerry, would be born in October 1942.

Richard Rodgers had seen Kelly in *The Time of Your Life* and had him audition for *Pal Joey*, which led to Gene's being hired for the lead role. The show opened at the Ethel Barrymore Theater on December 25, 1940, and ran for 374 performances. Gene Kelly was now a star. John Martin (*New York Times*) lauded, "A tap dancer who can characterize his routines and turn them into an integral element of an imaginative theatrical whole would seem to be pretty close, indeed, to unique. . . ." MGM displayed interest in signing him, but when studio head Louis B. Mayer demanded that he be screen-tested (after Kelly had been promised he would not have to be), he refused to proceed. A few months later, movie producer David O. Selznick (Mayer's son-in-law) offered Kelly a screen contract with no test needed. He accepted. Selznick thought Kelly would be ideal for a nonmusical, KEYS OF THE KINGDOM, in which he would play a missionary priest. Selznick abandoned this concept finally (the part was eventually played by Gregory Peck in 1944) and, instead, Kelly was loaned to MGM to co-star with Judy Garland in FOR ME AND MY GAL (1942).

Kelly had played a charismatic heel in *Pal Joey* and his role as an opportunistic 1910s vaudevillian in FOR ME AND MY GAL—originally planned for the film's other star, George

Murphy—was quite similar. Kelly acknowledged later, "I knew nothing about playing to the camera . . . it was Judy who pulled me through." He also analyzed, "In my first picture, I made a startling discovery—things danced on the screen do not look the way they do on the stage. On the stage dancing is three dimensional, but a motion picture is two dimensional."

Selnzick then negotiated a deal with MGM for that studio to take over Gene Kelly's seven-year contract, with Kelly initially receiving $1,000 weekly. Not sure what to do with their new song-and-dance man, Metro ordered Kelly into PILOT NO. 5 (1943), a World War II drama. He was a gloomy Italian-American lieutenant in support of star Franchot Tone. Next came two nondescript musical roles at MGM, and then a role as a belligerent French soldier in THE CROSS OF LORRAINE (1943). Gene was among the many who tested to play the Oriental lead opposite Katharine Hepburn in MGM's DRAGON SEED (1944), but it was another studio that provided his career rescue. Columbia Pictures was shooting a major Rita Hayworth musical, COVER GIRL (1944), and desperately needed a leading man. Initially, studio head Harry Cohn insisted Kelly was wrong for the part: "That tough Irishman with his tough Irish mug! You couldn't put him in the same *frame* as Rita!" But he relented and the film made Kelly a movie star. As the proprietor of a small Brooklyn club he not only got to sing serviceably and dance brilliantly to the Jerome Kern–Ira Gershwin score (including the memorable "Long Ago and Far Away"), but for the unique "Alter Ego" number (in which he danced around and with his own conscience), he and Stanley Donen (whom Kelly met when Donen was a chorus boy on Broadway in *Pal Joey*) took over for choreographer Seymour Felix. Said Kelly of the intricate number, "It was the most difficult thing I've ever done, a technical torture, and I wouldn't want to have to do it again."

After going stridently dramatic in Universal's CHRISTMAS HOLIDAY (1944), a non-musical vehicle for that studio's Deanna Durbin in which he played a charming killer, Kelly returned to MGM where he was allowed to choreograph his next starring vehicle, ANCHORS AWEIGH (1945). His co-stars were Frank Sinatra and Kathryn Grayson. As a sailor on shore leave in Hollywood, Kelly did "The Mexican Hat Dance," shared a soft-shoe routine with Sinatra in "I Begged Her," and in the unique "The King Who Couldn't Dance" mingled with cartoon characters such as Tom and Jerry in a fantasy sequence that cost $100,000. He was nominated for an Academy Award but the Oscar went to Ray Milland for THE LOST WEEKEND. After filming "The Babbitt and The Bromide"—a disappointingly ordinary dance number with Fred Astaire—for THE ZIEGFELD FOLLIES OF 1946, Kelly joined the Navy. He spent most of his time directing propaganda films which, since the war was nearly over, were irrelevant.

Kelly was discharged from the Navy in May 1946 and Metro used him to add box-office appeal to a stalled vehicle for Marie "The Body" McDonald. LIVING IN A BIG WAY (1947) was not salvaged either by Kelly's presence or by the dance routines he and Stanley Donen devised. Cole Porter's THE PIRATE (1948) co-starred him again with Judy Garland and it was directed by her then husband, Vincente Minnelli. It was flamboyant and colorful, but hampered because of Garland's emotional instability. Kelly starred as the flirtatious entertainer Serafin and, with Robert Alton, co-choreographed the athletic "The Pirate Ballet" and the tuneful "Be a Clown." The film was too sophisticated to succeed and Kelly was arch as the clown hero. Like many other MGM contractees tossed into the swashbuckling THE THREE MUSKETEERS (1948), Kelly seemed more foolish than heroic as D'Artagnan, although he considers the lavish film one of his favorite nonmusical projects. He wanted next to do a musical version of *Cyrano de Bergerac*, but instead he choreographed "Slaughter on Tenth Avenue" (by Richard Rodgers) for WORDS AND MUSIC (1948), in which he danced with Vera-Ellen.

Kelly and Sinatra reunited for two additional musicals. Kelly co-wrote and co-choreographed with Stanley Donen TAKE ME OUT TO THE BALL GAME (1949), a period piece in which Esther Williams was the love object and Busby Berkeley was the director (Kelly and Donen actually directed most of the musical scenes). Much more potent was ON THE TOWN (1949), made by the Arthur Freed–MGM musical film unit, with music by Leonard Bernstein. Kelly and Sinatra were again sailors, this time on the loose in New York City. According to Kelly, the film's co-choreographer and co-director along with Donen, "Everything we did in the picture was innovative. . . . The fact that make-believe

Richard Lane, Tom Dugan, Gene Kelly, and Frank Sinatra in
TAKE ME OUT TO THE BALL GAME (1949)

sailors got off a real ship in a real dockyard, and danced through a real New York was a turning-point in itself." ON THE TOWN is Kelly's favorite picture. The film seems dated now, but then it was innovative and trendsetting.

He replaced Robert Taylor in THE BLACK HAND (1950), about the Mafia in turn-of-the-century New York, and the musical SUMMER STOCK (1950) was his final picture with Judy Garland. Much more important were his contributions to AN AMERICAN IN PARIS (1951), directed by Vincente Minnelli. The most celebrated segment of this Technicolor musical is the seventeen-minute ballet sequence set to George Gershwin's music. It cost $450,000 to shoot, with Kelly choreographing it and dancing with Leslie Caron (a Kelly discovery from the Paris ballet). AN AMERICAN IN PARIS won an Oscar as Best Picture of 1951 and Kelly received a special Oscar: "In appreciation of his versatility as an actor, singer, director and dancer, and especially for his brilliant achievement in the art of choreography on film." AN AMERICAN IN PARIS was also a big money-earner. The last Kelly musical of MGM's golden era was SINGIN' IN THE RAIN (1952), which he co-directed and co-choreographed with Donen. It is a classic, with its satirical approach to Hollywood at the time talkies came in. Robust, snappy, and fun, it provided Kelly with his landmark screen moment of dancing jubilantly in the rain.

To take advantage of the new U.S. income tax law which benefited Americans who worked abroad for eighteen months or more, Kelly and his family moved to Europe. Unfortunately, everything soured. THE DEVIL MAKES THREE (1952) was shot in Germany and was a box-office dud. In England he filmed the arty, all-ballet INVITATION TO THE DANCE (which an unhappy MGM did not release until 1955) and continued with CREST OF THE WAVE (1954), a veddy British military comedy that did not appeal to Americans. He was back in Hollywood for a guest stint with brother Fred in DEEP IN MY HEART (1954) and, then, for BRIGADOON (1954). The latter was a widescreen musical which suffered from being too studio-bound (an economy device demanded by new MGM studio boss Dore Schary). Neither Kelly's performance nor his dance staging was inspired.

MGM refused to loan Kelly to Samuel Goldwyn for the role of Sky Masterson in GUYS AND DOLLS (1955—Marlon Brando got the part). Kelly's final picture for the Arthur Freed–MGM unit was IT'S ALWAYS FAIR WEATHER (1955). It also marked the end of his professional association with Stanley Donen, with whom he co-directed and feuded. Moreover, sharing the choreography chores with Michael Kidd was a bad decision. Far more satisfying was the witty and top-drawer LES GIRLS (1957), directed by George Cukor, in which Kelly romanced three leading ladies: Mitzi Gaynor, Kay Kendall, and Taina Elg. It provided him with the type of role he knew best—the *Pal Joey*-type heel. However, it was not big with moviegoers, who wanted more basic fare. He was to do a screen musical in England called GENTLEMAN'S GENTLEMAN but it never materialized. To settle his MGM contract, he directed THE TUNNEL OF LOVE (1958), starring Doris Day and Richard Widmark. There was little that was original about Kelly's direction of this Broadway sex comedy hit.

The late 1950s proved to be a time of transition in Kelly's life. He and his actress wife, Betsy Blair, were divorced in April 1957 and on August 6, 1960, he wed Jeanne

Coyne, a dancer whom he had known since their days at Gene Kelly's dance studio. (They would have a son, Timothy, born in 1962, and a daughter, Bridget, born in 1964.) He stretched hard to play the failed Jewish showman in MARJORIE MORNINGSTAR (1958) opposite Natalie Wood and returned to Broadway to direct the musical *Flower Drum Song* (1959) for Rodgers and Hammerstein. He went dramatic again as the idealistic newspaperman in Stanley Kramer's INHERIT THE WIND (1960), failing to match Spencer Tracy in their dramatic scenes. Also in 1960 he wrote and choreographed the ballet *Pas de Deux*, set to Gershwin's *Piano Concerto in F*, which was presented by the Paris National Opera Ballet. He returned to France to direct the Paris-lensed GIGOT (1962), geared to present Jackie Gleason in a Chaplinesque role as a lovable bum. Kelly and Gleason feuded and the resulting sentimental comedy was unpopular.

Kelly had made his TV bow on the "Schlitz Playhouse of Stars" (CBS-TV, March 1, 1957) in "The Life You Save" and, two years later, he had two television specials: one for "Omnibus" called "Dancing Is a Man's Game" and another in which he danced to a poem written and read by Carl Sandburg. Kelly, unlike Fred Astaire, did not like the small-screen medium—he found it too limiting—but he returned in the fall of 1962 to star in the short-lived series "Going My Way" (ABC-TV), recreating Bing Crosby's film role as the happy-go-lucky priest.

Plans for Kelly to work as producer/director/star for Frank Sinatra's production company in 1963 fell through. Although he was now over fifty, Kelly danced in (and choreographed) a segment of Shirley MacLaine's fitfully entertaining WHAT A WAY TO GO! (1964) and he starred in the well-received "Jack and the Beanstalk" (NBC-TV, 1967) which won an Emmy as Outstanding Children's Program. If anything marked Gene Kelly's screen decline, it was the French-made THE YOUNG GIRLS OF ROCHEFORT (1967), in which he played a dancing American concert pianist. Directed by Jacques Demy, this fiasco emphasized just how much Gene Kelly's success *and* image belonged to the 1940s and 1950s. Kelly was adequate shepherding guest stars through the sex comedy A GUIDE FOR THE MARRIED MAN (1967), but he was overwhelmed by the star (Barbra Streisand) and the expectations for the screen translation of HELLO, DOLLY! (1969). He turned in a very old-fashioned, workmanlike film. The producing studio, 20th Century–Fox, canceled plans for Kelly to direct an adventure musical based on the Tom Swift novels. He also directed the pedestrian Western THE CHEYENNE SOCIAL CLUB (1970). Next he ventured into mounting a traveling children's show, when he directed *Clown Around* in April 1972, starring Ruth Buzzi and Dennis Allen of TV's popular "Laugh-In." The arena show folded in May of that year in San Francisco. He was asked to direct the movie version of CABARET (1972) abroad, but had to turn down the assignment because his wife was dying of leukemia. He did accept a few days' work acting in the romantic comedy 40 CARATS (1973) because he could go to the studio (Columbia) and be home in twenty minutes. Jeanne Kelly died on May 10, 1973, the same year in which his mother passed away.

In 1974 he did a summer stock engagement of the musical *Take Me Along* in Dallas, Texas, playing the role of the ne'er-do-well Sid. Because Gene Kelly sparkled as one of the co-hosts of THAT'S ENTERTAINMENT! (1974), he was asked to co-star in, direct, and choreograph the new bridging sequences with Fred Astaire for THAT'S ENTERTAINMENT, PART 2 (1976). He had a featured dramatic role in VIVA KNIEVEL! (1977) and was drawn out of retirement to co-star as a soured clarinetist in a musical fantasy, XANADU (1980). He and co-star Olivia Newton-John did a brief dance together. The expensive movie was a big flop. He allied with Francis Ford Coppola and was to create an Arthur Freed–type unit for Zoetrope Studios. He worked a bit on ONE FROM THE HEART (1982) but soon ended the relationship with the studio and Coppola. Plans to do a Broadway musical of Louis Armstrong's life did not materialize. He continued to make forays into television. He had hosted the brief-running comedy anthology series "The Funny Side" in 1971 for NBC-TV and starred in and hosted a variety of telespecials including "Gene Kelly: An American in Pasadena" (1978). In 1980 the University of Southern California hosted a tribute to his career and he looked back, saying, "Now that there isn't any studio system, I can see the advantages of it." When his Beverly Hills house burned down in the early 1980s, he lost a lifetime of memorabilia, including his Oscar.

Turning seventy in 1982, he announced he had retired from dancing. "When you get to that age, you can dance, but it's not very exciting. I can't swing from lamp posts anymore." He made occasional acting appearances on TV—"The Love Boat" (1984) and the miniseries "North and South" (1985). Mostly he was on hand to talk about his career (he toured with *An Evening with Gene Kelly*) and to be the focal guest of more retrospectives. Already a recipient of the Kennedy Center Honors, he was the thirteenth recipient of the annual Lifetime Achievement Awards of the American Film Institute on March 7, 1985, where he talked about his career and admitted, "It was a lot of work, but we had fun. We had the best of times. It was because we all thought we were trying to create some sort of magic and joy. If I can make you smile, then I'm very proud to be a song-and-dance man."

For yet another compilation of musical filmmaking, THAT'S DANCING! (1985), he served as executive producer, director, and co-host. It led Hugh Downs of TV's "20/20" to interview Gene Kelly, of whom he said, "He could sing a few bars and dance a little and when he did, time stood still." In December 1988 he was the twenty-fifth recipient of the Screen Actors Guild's Achievement Award "for fostering the finest ideals of the acting profession" and in April 1989 he received the Pied Piper Award from the American Society of Composers, Authors and Publishers (ASCAP) for his contributions to the music industry.

## Filmography

For Me and My Gal [For Me and My Girl] (MGM, 1942)
Pilot No. 5 (MGM, 1943)
Du Barry Was a Lady (MGM, 1943)
Thousands Cheer (MGM, 1943)

The Cross of Lorraine (MGM, 1943)
Cover Girl (Col, 1944) (also co-choreography)
Christmas Holiday (Univ, 1944)
Anchors Aweigh (MGM, 1945) (also choreography)

Ziegfeld Follies of 1946 (MGM, 1946)

Living in a Big Way (MGM, 1947) (also co-choreography)

The Pirate (MGM, 1948) (also co-choreography)

Words and Music (MGM, 1948) (also co-choreography)

The Three Musketeers (MGM, 1948)

Take Me Out to the Ball Game [Everybody's Cheering] (MGM, 1949) (also co-story, co-choreography)

On the Town (MGM, 1949) (also co-director, co-choreography)

The Black Hand (MGM, 1950)

Summer Stock [If You Feel Like Singing] (MGM, 1950)

An American in Paris (MGM, 1951) (also choreography)

It's a Big Country (MGM, 1951)

Singin' in the Rain (MGM, 1952) (also co-director, co-choreography)

The Devil Makes Three (MGM, 1952)

Crest of the Wave [Seagulls over Sorrento) (MGM, 1954)

Brigadoon (MGM, 1954) (also choreography)

Deep in My Heart (MGM, 1954)

It's Always Fair Weather (MGM, 1955) (also co-director, co-choreography)

Invitation to the Dance (MGM, 1955) (also director, screenplay, choreography)

The Happy Road (MGM, 1956) (also producer, director)

Les Girls (MGM, 1957)

Marjorie Morningstar (WB, 1958)

The Tunnel of Love (MGM, 1958) (director only)

Inherit the Wind (UA, 1960)

Let's Make Love (20th–Fox, 1960)

Gigot (20th–Fox, 1962) (director only)

What a Way to Go! (20th–Fox, 1964) (also choreography)

The Young Girls of Rochefort (WB–7 Arts, 1967)

A Guide for the Married Man (20th–Fox, 1967) (director only)

Hello, Dolly! (20th–Fox, 1969) (director only)

The Cheyenne Social Club (NG, 1970) (director only)

40 Carats (Col, 1973)

That's Entertainment! (MGM, 1974) (co-host)

That's Entertainment, Part 2 (MGM, 1976) (co-host) (also director of new sequences)

Viva Knievel! (WB, 1977)

Xanadu (Univ, 1980)

That's Dancing! (MGM, 1985) (co-host) (also executive producer, director)

## Broadway Plays

Leave It to Me! (1938)

One for the Money (1939)

The Time of Your Life (1939)

Pal Joey (1940)

Flower Drum Song (1959) (director only)

## TV Series

Going My Way (ABC, 1962–63)

The Funny Side (NBC, 1971)

## Album Discography

An American in Paris (10" MGM E-93, MGM E-3232, Metro M/S-552) [ST]

Anchors Aweigh (Curtain Calls 100/17) [ST]

Brigadoon (MGM E-3135) [ST]

A Clockwork Orange (WB BS-2573) [ST]

Cover Girl (Curtain Calls 100/24) [ST]

Deep in My Heart (MGM E-3153) [ST]
Du Barry Was a Lady (Titania 509) [ST]
For Me and My Gal (Sountrak 107) [ST]
From Classic MGM Films (MCA 25166) [ST]
Gene Kelly on the Air (Totem 1034)
It's Always Fair Weather (MGM E-3241) [ST]
The King Couldn't Dance (Col J-25)
Les Girls (MGM E-3590) [ST]
The Man Who Came to Dinner (Star-Tone 226) [ST/R]
Nursery Songs and Stories (Col CL-1063, Har HL-9521)
On the Town (Show Biz 5603, Caliban 6023) [ST]
Peter Rabbit/The Pied Piper of Hamelin (Har HL-9527)
Peter Rabbit/When We Were Very Young (10" Col JL-8008)
The Pied Piper of Hamelin/The Shoemaker and the Elves (10" Col JL-8007)
The Pirate (10" MGM E-21, MGM E-3234) [ST]

Les Poupées de Paris (RCA LOC/LSO-1090) [OC]
Singin' in the Rain (10" MGM E-113, MGM E-3236, Metro M/S-599) [ST]
Song and Dance Man (10" MGM E-30)
Song and Dance Man (Stet 15010)
Song and Story Time (Har HL-9529)
The Special Magic of Gene Kelly (MGM 2353-120)
Summer Stock (10" MGM E-519, MGM E-3234) [ST]
Take Me Out to the Ball Game (Curtain Calls 100/18) [ST]
Thousands Cheer (Amalgamated 232, Hollywood Soundstage 409) [ST]
What a Way to Go! (20th Century–Fox 3143) [ST]
Xanadu (MCA 6100) [ST]
Ziegfeld Follies of 1946 (Curtain Calls 100/15-16) [ST]

# KRIS KRISTOFFERSON

KRIS KRISTOFFERSON IS AMONG THE FEW ENTERTAINERS WHO have etched almost separate careers in music and dramatics. This one-time Rhodes scholar is not only a top-notch songwriter and performer, he is also a fine actor who became one of the screen's most popular players in the late 1970s. It is ironic, however, that although he has had best-selling single and album releases, he has rarely sung on film; most of his motion picture appearances have been in solidly dramatic roles. Although Kris Kristoffer-son has been plagued with personal problems several times over the years, he has survived to make new inroads in his show business career. It was Kristofferson, through his songs and personal appearances, who almost singlehandedly ended Nashville's monotonous country sounds of the early 1970s. Yet he is also the actor whom the Foreign Press Association named Best Actor for his performance in the otherwise flat musical A STAR IS BORN (1976). In addition, he has the dubious honor of having starred in one of the biggest box-office fiascoes of all time, the $40 million Western dud HEAVEN'S GATE (1980).

Kristoffer Kristofferson was born in Brownsville, Texas, on June 22, 1936, the son of a two-star Air Force major general who retired to become air operations manager for Armco in Saudi Arabia. As a boy Kris moved often, but the family finally set down roots in California where he developed a liking for country music, particularly that of Hank Williams. While in high school he learned to play the guitar and at Pomona College in Claremont he excelled in both athletics (football, soccer, boxing) and academics. As a writer he won a quartet of *Atlantic Monthly* magazine short story writing contests and he was awarded a Rhodes scholarship to Oxford University in England where he wrote a study of the works of William Blake.

After several of his books were rejected for publication, Kristofferson became disillusioned with academic life and began writing songs. He then started performing in England under the name of Kris Carson and was managed by Tommy Steele's organization. But he failed to make much of an impression. As a result he enlisted in the Army where he served five years, first in West Germany and later going through pilot and parachute-jump training, eventually becoming a helicopter pilot. In 1960 he married Fran Beir and they had two children, Tracy and Kris. Leaving the service in 1965, he got a position teaching English at West Point. However, with his marriage dissolving, he went to Nashville where he met songwriter Marijohn Wilkin and decided to remain in Music City.

The mid- and late 1960s proved rough years for Kristofferson. He worked as a janitor by night at Columbia Records and as a bartender by day at the Tally-Ho Tavern, all the time trying to promote his songs. His pro–Vietnam War balled, "Vietnam Blues," was recorded by Dave Dudley while Roy Drusky waxed "Jody and the Kid," but for the most part Kristofferson made little headway. To make ends meet he was forced to hire out as a pilot flying workers and equipment for Gulf of Mexico oil rigs and as a laborer. Kristofferson was persistent, however, in pushing his material. In the summer of 1969 Roger Miller had a hit record for Smash with his "Me and Bobby McGee," which also became a pop hit for Janis Joplin. Kristofferson made a successful appearance at the Newport Folk Festival in 1969 and Johnny Cash featured him several times on his ABC-TV variety program. In 1970 Cash had a best-selling record for Columbia with Kris's song "Sunday Morning Comin' Down."

By now Kristofferson's career was gaining momentum. He was signed to a record contract by Monument and his songs were popularized by other performers: Ray Price's "For the Good Times" and "I Won't Mention It Again," Sammi Smith's "Help Me Make It Through the Night," Jerry Lee Lewis' "Once More with Feeling," Ronnie Milsap's "Please Don't Tell Me How the Story Ends," and Christy Lane's "One Day at a Time." Kris had a successful engagement at The Troubadour in Los Angeles in the summer of 1970, thereby establishing himself as a nightclub draw. In 1971 he sang (with Rita Coolidge) on the soundtrack of the motion picture THE LAST MOVIE as well as made his film debut in a small role in this Dennis Hopper film. The same year he received critical acclaim for his portrayal of a drug dealer in Columbia's CISCO PIKE, and his songs "Me and Bobby McGee" and "Help Me Make It Through the Night" earned him Grammy nominations, as did "For the Good Times" for Best Country Song.

In the summer of 1973 Kristofferson married Rita Coolidge and that year he had his first really big-selling single for Monument with his song "Why Me," although his earlier recordings of "Loving Her Was Easier" and "Watch Closely" had done well. His albums *The Silver Tongued Devil and I* and *Jesus Was a Capricorn* went on to gold record status. Although he continued to tour, during this period he focused his career primarily on movies. Nevertheless, he netted a Grammy nomination in 1973 for "Why Me" while he and Rita Coolidge won a Grammy for Best Vocal Performance by a Duo for "From the Bottom of the Bottle," a distinction they repeated in 1975 for "Lover Please." On the silver screen he won favorable comments as Susan Anspach's boyfriend in the otherwise poor comedy BLUME IN LOVE (1973). That same year he was straightforward as outlaw William Bonney in PAT GARRETT AND BILLY THE KID, made by filmmaker Sam Peckinpah for MGM. However, it was Bob Dylan, in a guest role in the film, who provided the movie soundtrack singing, *not* Kris. Next he made a guest appearance as a violent biker in the embarrassing adventure BRING ME THE HEAD OF ALFREDO GARCIA (1974). He was paid $150,000 for his brief role.

His sole 1975 film was ALICE DOESN'T LIVE HERE ANYMORE, and in it he offered what is perhaps his best performance to date, as the man who falls in love with a waitress (Ellen Burstyn) who is trying to put her life back together following her husband's death. (*Variety* noted, "Kris Kristofferson brings the film to attention as the man who makes life meaningful for mother and son.") In 1976 he made a trio of feature films, beginning with the violent potboiler VIGILANTE FORCE, as a Vietnam vet who is hired to bring order to a small California town and ends up as its murderous dictator. While the film was exploitative, he gave a shaded performance as the complex central figure. For the British-made THE SAILOR WHO FELL FROM GRACE WITH THE SEA he was cast as a fun-loving sailor who has an affair with a beautiful widow (Sarah Miles). The arty film's production resulted in publicity involving the two lead players' off-screen involvement, and explicit photos from the movie were published in *Playboy* magazine. Next Kristofferson took over for Elvis Presley in the third screen version of A STAR IS BORN, playing an alcoholic rock star who sees his career fade while his wife (Barbra Streisand) rises to stardom. In the indulgent proceedings, Kristofferson performed "Watch Closely Now," "Hellacious Acres," and "Crippled Crow" while he and Streisand (with whom he often feuded during the production) dueted on the film's theme song, "Evergreen," and "Lost Inside of You." With a box-office gross of $37 million, the film gave Kristofferson's screen career the commercial impetus it needed.

But thereafter, his screen career was a mixed bag, heading in no particular direction. In 1977 he and Burt Reynolds teamed as football players who share the same girlfriend (Jill Clayburgh) in the all-too-tepid comedy SEMI-TOUGH (whose soundtrack was made up of Gene Autry recordings). Again for director Sam Peckinpah, he starred as a trucker leading a protest in CONVOY (1978), based on the popular C. W. McCall recording. He played the

Kris Kristofferson and Victoria Principal in VIGILANTE FORCE (1976)

role of Abner Lait in FREEDOM ROAD (1979), also starring Muhammad Ali, which was shown in the United States on television but was screened theatrically in Europe. The year 1980 found Kristofferson toplining the much-maligned HEAVEN'S GATE, a sprawling Western about an educated man (Kris) siding with homesteaders against corrupt railroad bosses. The cinematography was beautiful, but the scenario meandered so persistently and for so long (originally 219 minutes; later cut to 149 minutes) that audiences avoided the picture with a passion during its scant release. Almost as nullifying to his career was his role as a slick banker involved with an oil heiress (Jane Fonda) in the vapid big business expose ROLLOVER (1981).

Although the 1970s found Kris Kristofferson a highly paid movie performer, singer, and songwriter, his personal life was in turmoil. He and Rita Coolidge had a son, Casey, in 1977, but they were divorced in 1979. By then the star had kicked the dependence on alcohol which had plagued him for two decades, and in the early 1980s he stopped using marijuana. He also began touring with Willie Nelson, and in 1981 he made a video, *A Celebration.* In the dwindling record market he had minor successes with "Prove It to You One More Time Again" for Columbia in 1980 and with a couple of other tunes, "Here Comes That Rainbow Again" and "Nobody Loves Anybody Anymore," in 1981—the former for Monument, the latter for Columbia. After a three-year hiatus, he returned to movies in 1984 in the CBS-TV telefeature THE LOST HONOR OF KATHRYN BECK about a woman (Marlo Thomas) who is persecuted because she spent the night with a suspected terrorist (Kristofferson). He was among the many artists (including Johnny Cash, Hank Williams, Jr., Willie Nelson, and Carl Perkins) interviewed for the MGM/UA videocassette *The Other Side of Nashville* (1984). In 1984 he also starred in two Tri-Star features: FLASHPOINT and SONGWRITER. The former is a fairly intriguing mystery in which Texas Rangers Kristofferson and Treat Williams stumble onto money taken in a robbery several years before, while in SONGWRITER he and Willie Nelson teamed as popular singers out to get revenge on a dishonest backer (Richard C. Sarafin). By now, Kristofferson's personal life had become more tranquil with his marriage to attorney Lisa Meyers in 1983.

In 1985 Kristofferson won critical acclaim for his role as an ex-cop just out of prison, who finds love and adventure with a group of youths in the futuristic TROUBLE IN MIND. Then on TV he played a police captain investigating an alleged rape in 1930s Hawaii by four men of mixed Asian heritage in BLOOD & ORCHIDS (1986). That year he also starred in two made-for-television features, THE LAST DAYS OF FRANK AND JESSE JAMES (NBC) and STAGECOACH (CBS). In the first he was cast as the renowned outlaw, with Johnny Cash playing brother Frank; the third version of STAGECOACH—which featured a host of country singers in dramatic roles—had Kristofferson playing The Ringo Kid, the role that brought film stardom to John Wayne in 1939. Neither telefilm was much liked. Also in 1986 he was among those starring in the ABC-TV miniseries "Amerika," as a man leading a rebellion against a supposed Soviet takeover of the United States. In 1987 Kristofferson starred for Home Box Office in a cable TV special, "Welcome Home," which was shot at his Washington, D.C., stage appearance that year. Also for HBO, he starred in the movie THE TRACKER (1988) as an Indian scout who must take along his greenhorn son (Mark Moses) while he attempts to bring in an outlaw (Scott Wilson). More strangely, he turned up as the circus owner in PEE-WEE'S BIG TOP AD-VENTURE (1988), a foolish exploitation of the bizarre Pee-wee Herman. Many noted that Kristofferson, with his snowy white beard, closely resembled the late character actor George "Gabby" Hayes. Thereafter he starred in the science fiction movie MILLENNIUM (1989) and in WELCOME HOME (1989), the latter co-starring Brian Keith and JoBeth Williams.

While Kris Kristofferson remained active as a dramatic actor in the late 1980s, he did not neglect his music. He had a successful album, *Repossessed*, and was professionally reunited with Rita Coolidge on stage in Las Vegas, both in 1987. On stage Kristofferson not only performs his famous songs of the past but also uses his act as a handy forum for compositions about subjects related to his very liberal political viewpoint.

## Filmography

The Last Movie (Univ, 1971)
Cisco Pike (Col, 1971)
Blume in Love (WB, 1973)
Pat Garrett and Billy the Kid (MGM, 1973)
Bring Me the Head of Alfredo Garcia (UA, 1974)
Alice Doesn't Live Here Anymore (WB, 1975)
Vigilante Force (UA, 1976)
The Sailor Who Fell from Grace with the Sea (Avco Emb, 1976)
A Star Is Born (WB, 1976)
Semi-Tough (Par, 1977)
Convoy (UA, 1978)
Freedom Road (NBC-TV, 10/29/79–10/30/79)
Heaven's Gate (UA, 1980)

Rollover (Orion/WB, 1981)
The Lost Honor of Kathryn Beck [Acts of Passion] (CBS-TV, 1/24/84)
Flashpoint (Tri-Star, 1984)
Songwriter (Tri-Star, 1984) (also co-songs)
Trouble in Mind (Alive Films, 1985)
The Last Days of Frank and Jesse James (NBC-TV, 2/16/86)
Blood & Orchids (CBS-TV, 2/23/86–2/24/86)
Stagecoach (CBS-TV, 5/18/86)
The Tracker (Home Box Office [TV], 3/26/88)
Pee-wee's Big Top Adventure (Par, 1988)
Welcome Home (Col, 1989)
Millennium (20th–Fox, 1989)

## TV Series

Amerika (ABC, 2/15/87–2/22/87) (miniseries)

## Album Discography

Border Lord (Monument/Col P-31302)
Breakaway (Monument/Col PZ-033278)
Easter Island (Monument/Col JZ-35310)
Full Moon (A&M 4403) w. Rita Coolidge
Highwayman (Col 40056) w. Willie Nelson, Waylon Jennings, Johnny Cash

Jesus Was a Capricorn (Monument/Col PZ-31909)
Kristofferson (Monument SLP-18139)
Me and Bobby McGee (Monument/Col PZ-30817)
My Songs (Pair PDL-2-1078)

Ned Kelly (UA UAS-5213) [ST]

Repossessed (Mer 830406-1)

Sideshow (Col PZ-32914)

The Silver Tongued Devil and I (Monument/ Col PS-30679)

Songs of Kris Kristofferson (Monument/Col PZ-34687)

Songwriter (Col FC-39531) [ST]

Spooky Lady's Sideshow (Monument KZ-32914)

A Star Is Born (Col JS-34403) [ST]

Surreal Thing (Col PZ-34254)

To the Bone (Col JZ-36885)

Who's to Bless and Who's to Blame (Monument PZ-33379)

Winning Hand (Monument 38389-1) w. Willie Nelson, Dolly Parton, Brenda Lee

# DOROTHY LAMOUR

FOREVER ASSOCIATED WITH EXOTIC SOUTH SEAS SARONG GIRLS, DOrothy Lamour was the queen of jungle movies during the 1930s and 1940s. She grew to hate this stereotype, which limited her growth as an actress (she was a fine comedienne, a competent actress and vocalist). Unfortunately, playing an alluring native in exotic garb remained her screen niche. In the famous "Road" comedy series she made with Bing Crosby and Bob Hope, she definitely played a supporting role in their antic mayhem, and deserved a medal for surviving these lunatic excursions. As for being a pin-up favorite, she ranked behind Betty Grable and Rita Hayworth. Still, the actress has enjoyed a long show business career and while nearly all of her contemporaries are dead or retired, Dorothy Lamour still continues to be in the public eye.

She was born Mary Leta Dorothy Kaumeyer on December 10, 1914, in New Orleans where her father was a waiter and her mother a waitress. After her parents were divorced her mother married a man named Lambour and Dorothy also took that name. (When she went into show business she dropped the "b" from her last name.) She started performing as a child during World War I, selling war stamps and singing patriotic tunes. She planned to be a teacher, but lack of finances forced her to quit school at fourteen and take a business course. She became a secretary. After winning several beauty contests (inspired by her childhood friend Dorothy Dell, who became a movie actress) and becoming Miss New Orleans, 5' 5" Dorothy used her prize money to support herself while working with a stock company. Then, accompanied by her mother, she moved to Chicago where she found employment as a sales clerk at Marshall Field's, the department store. Through a talent night competition at the Hotel Morrisson she came to the attention of orchestra leader Herbie Kaye and after several auditions for him became a vocalist with his group. She went on tour with Kaye and the two fell in love and were married in Waukegan, Illinois, on May 10, 1935.

When they arrived in New York City, Kaye got his pal and former Yale classmate, Rudy Vallee, to promote Dorothy. As a result she was hired as a singer at the Stork Club at $150 weekly. She then teamed briefly with pianists Julius Monk and Joe Lilly for a vaudeville act and then won a spot on NBC radio's "The Dreamer of Songs" program. Dorothy made her film debut in the Vitaphone short THE STARS CAN'T BE WRONG (1936) and then went with the NBC radio show to the West Coast. She was among those who auditioned for, but lost, the role of Julie to Helen Morgan in Universal's SHOW BOAT (1936). However, she also tested at Paramount and was awarded a contract.

She made her feature debut in 1936 in the title role of THE JUNGLE PRINCESS, as a sultry native girl who saves a British hunter (Ray Milland) after he is injured. The two of them battle a crook (Akim Tamiroff) and fall in love. Dorothy's dark beauty, coupled with a tight-fitting sarong, did the unreasonable story justice and she immediately found a place with filmgoers. *Variety* reported, "she lands powerfully in spite of the highly improbable story" and that "many much more seasoned actresses could not have come through on the assignment so impressively." During the picture she sang "Moonlight and Shadows" and early in 1937 she recorded the song with Cy Feuer and his orchestra for Brunswick Records, along with a trio of songs from her second film. An adaptation of the play *Burlesque*, SWING HIGH, SWING LOW (1937) cast her as a vamp dancer attempting to break up singer Carole Lombard and bandsman Fred MacMurray in sultry Panama. Along with other studio contractees she had acting lessons on camera in LAST TRAIN FROM MADRID (1937), a Spanish Civil War programmer; she was Gilbert Roland's mysterious girlfriend. The benefit of the studio system was that a performer could jump from such a "B" picture to an "A" picture like HIGH, WIDE AND HANDSOME (1937), an elaborate musical about Pennsylvania oil-well pioneering in the 1850s. Irene Dunne was the star, with Dorothy subordinate as the immoral honky-tonk torch singer (she warbled "The Things I Want"). Independent filmmaker Sam Goldwyn traded the services of his company's Joel McCrea to borrow Paramount's Dorothy Lamour for his $2 million South Seas idyll THE HURRICANE (1937). This lushly lensed romance tale boasted a spectacular hurricane sequence and Lamour performed her most famous screen song, "The Moon of Manakoora." She closed out 1937 with the "B" picture THRILL OF A LIFETIME as a guest performer singing the title song.

The year 1937 also found Dorothy becoming a regular on NBC radio's "The Chase and Sanborn Hour" where she would remain for two years. During the summer of 1937 she and Don Ameche co-starred in the coffee company's summer program. Meanwhile, her husband and his band were touring, primarily in the Midwest, where they had a big following.

There were plans to include Dorothy in Jack Benny's ARTISTS AND MODELS (1937) and Cecil B. De Mille's THE BUCCANEER (1938). Instead, she began 1938 with THE BIG BROADCAST OF 1938 as the romantic interest, singing "You Took the Words Right Out of My Heart." She recorded this song for Brunswick along with "Thanks for the Memory," which Bob Hope (in his feature film debut) and Shirley Ross dueted in the feature. After the success of THE JUNGLE PRINCESS and THE HURRICANE, it was only a matter of time before Dorothy returned to the tropics and the sarong. She was reteamed with Ray Milland for the Technicolor HER JUNGLE LOVE (1938) as the uninhibited native girl Tura who rescues a British pilot (Milland) after a plane crash. She looked alluring and sang a trio of tunes, including "Lovelight in the Starlight," which she recorded for Brunswick with husband Herbie Kaye and His Orchestra. With Kaye she also recorded "Tonight We Live" and "On a Tropic Night," which she sang in TROPIC HOLIDAY (1938), yet another teaming with Ray Milland—this one set in Mexico. She had a solid dramatic role ("at least she is trying," judged the *New York Times*) in the fishing saga SPAWN OF THE NORTH (1938) as a local gal in love with a fisherman (George Raft). She repeated her role as Nicky Duval on "Lux Radio Theatre."

In 1939, Lamour, tired of being categorized so narrowly in the cinema, kidded her screen image in ST. LOUIS BLUES. She was a stage star who plays saronged characters and who runs away and becomes enamored of a showboat captain (Lloyd Nolan). She sang a quartet of songs that she then recorded for Brunswick Records with Jerry Joyce and His Orchestra (she and Herbie Kaye were separated and would divorce that year). Next Dorothy sang "Strange Enchantment" in the Jack Benny comedy MAN ABOUT TOWN (1939) and then returned to drama—as a Eurasian—for DISPUTED PASSAGE (1939). That year also saw her appearing for a time on Rudy Vallee's radio show.

Dorothy was loaned to 20th Century–Fox to be a gun moll in JOHNNY APOLLO (1940), a part she recreated the next year on "Lux Radio Theatre." Regardless of her preference, it was back to the South Seas and a sarong for Dorothy in TYPHOON (1940), another Technicolor jungle opus, in which she sang (and recorded for Bluebird) "Palms of Paradise." She then began the "Road" pictures with Bing Crosby and Bob Hope. In ROAD TO SINGAPORE (1940) she sang "The Moon and the Willow Tree" and "Too Romantic" (again recording them for Bluebird). She demonstrated that she could match "wits" with

Lynne Overman, Dorothy Lamour, and Ray Milland in HER JUNGLE LOVER (1938)

the frantic shenanigans of Hope and Crosby on any level. She sang (and recorded) the title song in MOON OVER BURMA (1940), in which she was a stranded singer saved by lumbermen Preston Foster and Robert Preston (with whom she had an off-screen romance). Her final 1940 feature, again at 20th Century–Fox, was CHAD HANNA, a period circus drama which cast her as a bareback rider.

By now Paramount was paying Dorothy $5,000 weekly. During the World War II years she would become one of the studio's most valuable properties in a series of topnotch pictures, although she stopped recording until the war's end. In this period she starred in a variety of movies, ranging from the popular "Road" series to a teaming with Bob Hope (her best screen foil) in CAUGHT IN THE DRAFT (1941) and THEY GOT ME COVERED (1943—on loanout to Samuel Goldwyn). There were more sarong efforts, such as ALOMA OF THE SOUTH SEAS (1941), BEYOND THE BLUE HORIZON (1942), and RAINBOW ISLAND (1944), plus high-budgeted musical comedies like THE FLEET'S IN (1942), DIXIE (1943—with Bing Crosby), and RIDING HIGH (1943—with Dick Powell). In several of her films she benefited from good songs, like "Pagan Lullaby" and "Full Moon and Empty Arms" in BEYOND THE BLUE HORIZON and "Constantly" in ROAD TO MOROCCO (1942), while in STAR SPANGLED RHYTHM (1942) she and Paulette Goddard and Veronica Lake teased their screen trademarks with "A Sweater, a Sarong and a Peekaboo Bang." During the war years, Lamour appeared frequently on radio shows like "Lux Radio Theatre" (doing an adaptation of "Dixie"), "Mail Call," and "Palmolive Party" (a Saturday night NBC show she hosted). During one of the many war bond drives she participated in, Lamour auctioned off two of her sarong outfits for $2 million. (One of her original sarongs is now on display at the Smithsonian Institution.)

The World War II years were the apex of Dorothy Lamour's career. Also during that period (on April 7, 1943) she married Captain William Ross Howard II of Baltimore, Maryland. It led the star to admit, "I got serious about my acting for the first time, I can't explain it. I wanted to start all over again on a different basis. Maybe to prove something to somebody." At the end of the war, when her husband returned to Los Angeles and entered the field of advertising, the couple adopted a son, Ridgely, late in 1945.

Per Lamour of the mid-1940s: "Ten years is a long time to be in pictures. But ten years in a sarong is too long. Personally I've had enough." Paramount heeded her feelings: for ROAD TO UTOPIA (1945—completed in May 1944) the setting was the Klondike. In MY FAVORITE BRUNETTE (1947), with Bob Hope as a private eye, she was an heiress in distress. The stars recreated both roles on radio's "Showtime." She was steamy on the prairie with Robert Preston and Alan Ladd in WILD HARVEST (1947) and returned to being exotic in ROAD TO RIO (1947), in which she sang "Experience." In the summer of 1947 she was hostess of the NBC radio show "Front and Center."

In late 1947, like several other Paramount stars (Paulette Goddard, Veronica Lake), she left the studio. Being so typecast in the public's mind and now being in her midthirties, she found it difficult to obtain suitable roles. The vehicles selected for her were creaky melodramas (LULU BELLE, 1948), insipid comedies (THE GIRL FROM MANHATTAN, 1948), or a lumbering murder mystery (THE LUCKY STIFF, 1949). On October 20, 1949,

Dorothy gave birth to a son, Richard, and the family moved to her husband's hometown of Baltimore. In 1950 Lamour had a successful engagement at the London Palladium and in Glasgow, Scotland. She also recorded an LP album for Decca entitled *Favorite Hawaiian Songs*. The next year she appeared in a guest cameo in Bing Crosby's HERE COMES THE GROOM at Paramount and was a substitute hostess on ABC radio's "The Louella Parsons Show." She played Las Vegas in 1951, but no Hollywood offers were forthcoming until Cecil B. De Mille cast her as the aerialist in his circus epic, THE GREATEST SHOW ON EARTH (1952) at Paramount. However, she was subordinate to the three-ring acts and the romancing of Charlton Heston and Betty Hutton. Hope and Crosby were still at Paramount and they had Lamour as a teammate yet again for ROAD TO BALI (1952), which was more labored than funny. Although this was her last screen work for a decade, she made her TV debut with Eddie Cantor on NBC's "The Colgate Comedy Hour" in 1952 and the same year starred in a segment of "Hollywood Opening Night" (NBC). Three years later she appeared on "Damon Runyon Theatre" (CBS) and in 1956 was the subject of a "This Is Your Life" segment. Mostly she concentrated on being a housewife.

In 1956 and 1957 Lamour worked the nightclub circuit and then toured in the comedy *Roger the Sixth*. She was on Broadway for a scant week as Abbe Lane's replacement in *Oh! Captain* before returning to the London Palladium in 1958. She recorded an LP called *The Road to Romance* for the budget Design label. In 1960 she participated on "The Arthur Murray House Party" (NBC-TV) and guested with Bob Hope on one of his NBC network TV specials. In 1961 she was back doing cabaret work, marketing a line of beauty products, and authoring the volume *Road to Beauty*.

There was much publicity when Hope and Crosby announced a new "Road" project—THE ROAD TO HONG KONG (1962) for United Artists—and even more media coverage when it was revealed that Joan Collins and *not* Dorothy Lamour (who was to have a guest cameo) would be the distaff distraction. (It was Crosby who insisted that the far younger Collins have the lead.) After that picture, Dorothy did another Bob Hope NBC-TV special, but Bing Crosby used only pictures of Lamour in his concurrent special. A better film assignment came in the John Wayne vehicle DONOVAN'S REEF (1963), which cast her as a salty Hawaiian Island saloon singer. The same year she toured in *DuBarry Was a Lady* and in 1964 she made two guest shots on ABC-TV's "Burke's Law." She sang as the head saleslady in the teenage science fiction comedy PAJAMA PARTY (1964—looking plump and tired) and in 1966 she entertained troops in Vietnam, where her son Ridgely was stationed. Late in the year she appeared with Bing Crosby on "The Hollywood Palace" (ABC-TV). She embarked on a grueling tour in *Hello, Dolly!* and later starred in the show at the Riviera Hotel in Las Vegas, doing one of the two nightly shows, while Ginger Rogers did the other.

Late in 1967 Lamour guest-starred on "I Spy" (NBC-TV) and the next spring she and her husband bought a Hollywood home. She was reunited with Bing Crosby and Bob Hope on a TV special. In 1971 she and long-time pal Betty Grable dueted in the St. Louis summer theater revue *That's Show Business*. That year she also toured in *Anything Goes*, but rejected several screen bids. One script offered her $120,000 for a few scenes as a madam, but she told the press, "I'm not happy with a lot of dirty movies."

She continued making personal appearances throughout the 1970s, and in 1980 her autobiography, *The Other Side of the Road*, was published. She lamented the fact that neither Crosby nor Hope included her in their lucrative percentage deal with Paramount on the "Road" pictures. In the 1980s the now widowed Dorothy Lamour remained active by touring plus working in such TV shows as "The Love Boat," "Hart to Hart," "Remington Steele," "Crazy Like a Fox," and "Murder, She Wrote."

Bob Hope once quipped of Dorothy Lamour, "She did more for a piece of cloth than any American woman since Betsy Ross." However, Dorothy has admitted the profitable sarong image hurt her badly in the long run. "Nobody has ever wanted to take me seriously or admit I can act." Also, she did not push herself to her own advantage when she was at Paramount. "I just took what they gave me, didn't argue because I didn't want to be put on suspension."

## Filmography

The Stars Can't Be Wrong (Vita, 1936) (s)
The Jungle Princess (Par, 1936)
Swing High, Swing Low (Par, 1937)
High, Wide and Handsome (Par, 1937)
Last Train from Madrid (Par, 1937)
The Hurricane (UA, 1937)
Thrill of a Lifetime (Par, 1937)
Her Jungle Love (Par, 1938)
The Big Broadcast of 1938 (Par, 1938)
Tropic Holiday (Par, 1938)
Spawn of the North (Par, 1938)
St. Louis Blues (Par, 1939)
Man About Town (Par, 1939)
Disputed Passage (Par, 1939)
Typhoon (Par, 1940)
Johnny Apollo (20th–Fox, 1940)
Moon over Burma (Par, 1940)
Road to Singapore (Par, 1940)
Chad Hanna (20th–Fox, 1940)
Aloma of the South Seas (Par, 1941)
Road to Zanzibar (Par, 1941)
Caught in the Draft (Par, 1941)
Beyond the Blue Horizon (Par, 1942)
Road to Morocco (Par, 1942)
The Fleet's In (Par, 1942)
Star Spangled Rhythm (Par, 1942)
They Got Me Covered (RKO, 1943)
Dixie (Par, 1943)
Riding High [Melody Inn] (Par, 1943)

Show Business at War (20th–Fox, 1943) (s)
Rainbow Island (Par, 1944)
And the Angels Sing (Par, 1944)
Road to Utopia (Par, 1945)
Duffy's Tavern (Par, 1945)
A Medal for Benny (Par, 1945)
Masquerade in Mexico (Par, 1945)
My Favorite Brunette (Par, 1947)
Variety Girl (Par, 1947)
Road to Rio (Par, 1947)
Wild Harvest (Par, 1947)
A Miracle Can Happen [On Our Merry Way]
    (UA, 1948)
Lulu Belle (Col, 1948)
The Girl from Manhattan (UA, 1948)
Slightly French (Col, 1948)
Manhandled (Par, 1948)
The Lucky Stiff (UA, 1949)
Here Comes the Groom (Par, 1951)
The Greatest Show on Earth (Par, 1952)
Road to Bali (Par, 1952)
Screen Snapshots #205 (Col, 1952) (s)
The Road to Hong Kong (UA, 1962)
Donovan's Reef (Par, 1963)
Pajama Party (AIP, 1964)
The Phynx (WB, 1970)
Won Ton Ton, the Dog Who Saved Hollywood
    (Par, 1976)
Death at Love House (ABC-TV, 9/3/76)

## Broadway Plays

Oh! Captain (1958) (replacement)

## Radio Series

The Dreamer of Songs (NBC Blue, 1935–36)
The Chase and Sanborn Hour (NBC, 1937–38)
The Rudy Vallee Show (NBC, 1939)

Palmolive Party (NBC, ca. 1944–45)
Front and Center (NBC, 1947)
The Dorothy Lamour Show (NBC, 1948–49)

## Album Discography

And the Angels Sing (Caliban 6017) [ST]
Beyond the Blue Horizon (Caliban 6033) [ST]
Bing Crosby and Bob Hope with Dorothy
    Lamour (Radiola 1044)
Bing Crosby and Dorothy Lamour—Live
    (Amalgamated 237)
Dorothy Lamour (Legends 4)
Favorite Hawaiian Songs (10" Decca DL-5115)
The Fleet's In (Hollywood Soundstage 405)
    [ST]

The Moon of Manakoora (West Coast 14002)
Pajama Party (Buena Vista 3325) [ST]
Riding High (Caliban 6034) [ST]
The Road to Hong Kong (Liberty 16002) [ST]
The Road to Romance (Design 45)
St. Louis Blues (Caliban 6014) [ST]
Star Spangled Rhythm (Curtain Calls 100/20)
    [ST]
Thrill of a Lifetime (Caliban 6046) [ST]
Variety Girl (Caliban 6007) [ST]

# FRANCES LANGFORD

IN THE PRE-ROCK ERA, WHEN VOCALISTS HAD TO HAVE STYLE, PRO-
fessionalism, and personality, above and beyond the miking, to compete for top recognition, Frances Langford was one of the best. With her smoky and sultry contralto voice she
became America's favorite female vocalist in 1938. But there was much more show
business depth to this feisty 5' 2" songstress. During World War II she became known as
the "Sweetheart to the G.I.s" for her years of touring the battlefronts to entertain the
troops. She gained a whole new audience after the war when she revealed her sharp comic
flair in the course of teaming with Don Ameche in "The Bickersons." This domestic
comedy about spatting spouses was a big hit on radio, TV, and recordings. Although she
made over two dozen feature films, and was a frequent television variety performer,
Frances was at her best as a radio and recording artist, shading her lyrical interpretations
with honesty and an easygoing but authoritative sell of the lyrics.

Frances Langford was born in Lakeland, Florida, on April 4, 1913, the daughter of
concert pianist Annie Newbern. She attended Southern College in Florida, majoring in
music and planning a career in opera. All this changed when she had a tonsillectomy in
1930, which altered her soprano voice to contralto. She adjusted her ambitions, and now
focused on popular music. Tampa millionaire and cigar manufacturer Eli Witt heard
Frances perform at an American Legion party and hired her for thirteen weeks to be on his
local radio show at $5 (later $10) per week. Vacationing crooner Rudy Vallee, always on
the lookout for fresh talent, heard Frances singing on the radio and quickly offered her a
guest spot on his network radio show, which was broadcasting some programs from New
Orleans. Thereafter, Vallee continued to take an interest in Frances' career, and when she
moved to New York City he helped to foster show business opportunities for her. She was
hired by Victor Records in 1931, but the singles she waxed for them were not released. By
August 1932 she was recording for Columbia Phonograph Company with such tunes as "I
Can't Believe It's True" and "Having a Good Time, Wish You Were Here." She was heard
on WOR radio (NYC) in the 1932–33 period, made two musical short subjects for
Warner Bros.' Vitaphone release, and had a minor role in the Peter Arno musical *Here Goes
the Bride* (opened November 7, 1933), which lasted only seven performances on Broadway.
More important, all through this period—on radio (singing and doing commercials), on
Broadway, in vaudeville, and in cabaret—she was perfecting her performing skills.

It was during her singing engagement at New York's celebrated Waldorf-Astoria
that Frances was asked to perform at a private party in honor of Cole Porter. Among the
guests attending was Paramount producer Walter Wanger who hired her to sing in motion

pictures—*without* a screen test. Her feature film debut was Paramount's EVERY NIGHT AT EIGHT (1935), a trite but exceedingly engaging rehash about three songsters (Alice Faye, Frances, and Patsy Kelly) aiming to be the singing sensations of the airwaves, with George Raft tossed in as a suave bandleader who romances Langford. *Variety* reported that Langford "gives promise of going places." In this musical, Frances joined in the harmony on several numbers including the title tune, did a torchy rendition of "Then You've Never Had the Blues" (which she co-authored), and made her mark with "I'm in the Mood for Love," which she reprised several times in the film. She recorded four songs from EVERY NIGHT AT EIGHT for Brunswick Records in late July 1935 with Mahlon Merrick's orchestra providing backup.

Now a rising film personality, she was borrowed by MGM for its BROADWAY MELODY OF 1936 (1935) in which she played herself and provided vocals to "You Are My Lucky Star" and "Broadway Rhythm" while Eleanor Powell exhibited spectacular tap dancing. Back at Paramount, Frances was part of the campus romp COLLEGIATE (1936) and sang "You Hit the Spot." For PALM SPRINGS (1936) she sang "I Don't Want to Make History," one of the tunes she recorded under her Decca Records contract, which began in late 1935. In MGM's BORN TO DANCE (1936), a Cole Porter musical designed to showcase Eleanor Powell, Frances was cast as Peppy Turner and vocalized "Swinging the Jinx Away" and "Easy to Love" to support Powell's dancing. Virginia Bruce sang "I've Got You Under My Skin" in the film, but Frances recorded it for Decca and it became a big hit for

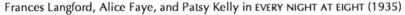

Frances Langford, Alice Faye, and Patsy Kelly in EVERY NIGHT AT EIGHT (1935)

her. As a matter of fact, this song, along with "I'm in the Mood for Love," was most associated with her.

While some performers have an affinity for moviemaking and audiences are drawn to them, Frances continued to be a "film personality," an individual appreciated when on camera, but not missed when she was off screen. She was demoted to Republic Pictures for THE HIT PARADE (1937), a congenial low-budget musical co-starring Phil Regan, and featuring the orchestras of Duke Ellington and Eddie Duchin. *Variety* endorsed, "as the warbling ingenue, [Frances Langford] looks good as photographed and plows into her numbers with authority." Her final film in this period was Warner Bros.' elaborate HOLLYWOOD HOTEL (1937). It was based on the popular CBS network radio variety program (1934–38) originated by columnist Louella Parsons and hosted by Dick Powell. By this time Frances was a regular on this variety radio show. Thus she was spotlighted in the Busby Berkeley–directed film version of HOLLYWOOD HOTEL to sing "Let That Be a Lesson to You" (backed by Benny Goodman's orchestra) and "Silhouetted in the Moonlight" (dueting with Jerry Cooper).

After HOLLYWOOD HOTEL there would be a three-year gap before Frances returned to picturemaking. On June 4, 1938, in Arizona, she married movie actor Jon Hall, who, although on screen since 1935, made his first substantial impression in Samuel Goldwyn's THE HURRICANE (1937), in which his abbreviated native togs vied for attention with Dorothy Lamour's scanty sarong. (Publicity billed handsome Hall as "Goldwyn's Gift to Women.") Frances continued to record for Decca, often backed by such popular musical figures as Victor Young, Jimmy Dorsey, Harry Sosnick, and organist Eddie Dunstedter. (She would stay with this label until 1942.) Having performed regularly on radio with Dick Powell on "Hollywood Hotel," in 1939–40 she was heard on CBS's "The Texaco Star Theatre," co-starring Ken Murray and Kenny Baker. Already in 1938 she had been voted the country's most popular female vocalist and soon became known as the "All-American Girl" of the airwaves.

With America being drawn into World War II, Hollywood increased its output of mind-diverting musicals and Frances found herself in demand again, but still as a featured "film personality." RKO utilized her in support of the radio team of Lum and Abner (in their movie debut) for DREAMING OUT LOUD (1940). In the campus musical TOO MANY GIRLS (1940) she supported Lucille Ball (whose songs were dubbed), Desi Arnaz, and Ann Miller. The situation improved, however, in Republic's THE HIT PARADE OF 1941 (1940), yet another musical about radio station antics. In this film, when the focus was not on the comic shenanigans of Phil Silvers, Patsy Kelly, Hugh Herbert, and Mary Boland, the spotlight was on Frances and Kenny Baker as they dueted "Who Am I?" and on Frances in her solo on "Swing Low, Sweet Rhythm."

With blondes Alice Faye and Betty Grable, the reigning queens of screen musicals, brunette Frances changed hair color to blonde for ALL-AMERICAN CO-ED (1941), a forty-eight-minute streamlined musical comedy produced by Hal Roach for United Artists. She remained a blonde throughout the rest of her career. In SWING IT SOLDIER (1941), a "B" musical from Universal featuring Ken Murray and Skinney Ennis and His Orchestra,

Langford's big screen moment was singing "I'm Gonna Swing My Way to Heaven."

In 1941 Frances was reunited with Dick Powell on the radio series "American Cruise" and then joined Bob Hope's popular NBC comedy/variety radio program. After America entered World War II, she volunteered to join Hope on his many USO tours entertaining the troops in the European and African theaters of war. (Hope would remark, "She knows just how much sex to pour and still be dignified.") It is estimated that Langford logged over 250,000 miles in this period, becoming the most-traveled female of World War II. With her sultry singing voice, her pert figure, and her knack for relating with G.I.s (as she visited hospital wards everywhere), she was quickly labeled the "No. 1 Girl of World War II." (She was also known as "The G.I.'s Nightingale," "The Armed Forces' Sweetheart," and "The Sweetheart of the Fighting Fronts.") Sometimes the treks were dangerous excursions onto the front lines to perform; other times the peril lay in the flights, with long hops from one Allied base to another. ("I've had my share of close calls on these trips," Frances admitted, "but the rewards are worth every nervous twinge.") Once, over Alaska, Langford's plane was having serious engine problems and it seemed the passengers would have to bail out. According to Frances, her concern at the moment was not fear, but how exhilarating it would feel to make a parachute landing! Another time, Langford and Bob Hope's plane was reported missing when they were island-hopping in the Pacific and it was feared they had been lost. Although General Dwight Eisenhower had been opposed to women entertaining in the danger zones, he was won over by Frances' spunk and would later present her with a cherished citation, "To Miss Frances Langford, with appreciation for a grand job in North Africa." Later in the war, Frances would write a syndicated column for the Hearst newspapers entitled "Purple Heart Diary," in which she retold her experiences meeting wounded G.I.s.

Universal may have tossed Frances into such lower-case musicals as MISSISSIPPI GAMBLER (1942) and COWBOY IN MANHATTAN (1943), but Warner Bros. was more gracious to her in YANKEE DOODLE DANDY (1942), for which James Cagney won an Oscar as the zealously patriotic George M. Cohan. Langford was seen to advantage as entertainer Nora Bayes who, among other tunes, sings the flag-raising "Over There" at a bond rally with Cagney. The same studio also used her for THIS IS THE ARMY (1943), based on Irving Berlin's morale-boosting stage musical. For the film—which starred Ronald Reagan, Berlin, Joan Leslie, and Kate Smith—Berlin wrote one new song, "What Does He Look Like?," which was performed by Frances in a café sequence. Then it was back to support-ing-bill fodder at Universal. She was a guest performer, singing "My Melancholy Baby," in FOLLOW THE BAND (1943) and the same year appeared with the Ritz Brothers in NEVER A DULL MOMENT (1943), managing to sing "Sleepy Time Gal" and "My Blue Heaven" amidst the brothers' comic mayhem.

Between USO tours, Frances turned out two weak films in 1944. The first, CAREER GIRL, at poverty-row Producers Releasing Corporation (PRC), was a variation on *Stage Door* and had four undistinguished songs for Kansas City hopeful Langford to sing as she nurtures her Broadway dream. At RKO, in GIRL RUSH, she was the distaff distraction in a period tale featuring the comedy duo of Wally Brown and Alan Carney. Her romantic interest was newcomer Robert Mitchum. In the last of the war years, 1945, she was back at PRC on a showboat in DIXIE JAMBOREE and at RKO for another Brown–Carney musical comedy, RADIO STARS ON PARADE, in which she offered fine versions of "Don't Believe Everything You Dream" and "Couldn't Sleep a Wink Last Night." Paramount's PEOPLE ARE FUNNY (1945) was a double-bill item revolving around the popular radio show. She played herself and her one-time mentor Rudy Vallee was on hand as a stuffy radio show sponsor.

Although the war and her USO foxhole circuit chores were now over, blue-eyed Frances continued to be a spokesperson for the G.I.s, often contributing articles to national magazines on concerns of returning war veterans and what awaited them at home. Her movie assignments remained pedestrian: RKO's THE BAMBOO BLONDE (1946) was a cheap song-and-dance outing vaguely taking advantage of Frances' World War II fame with the G.I.s. She sang to advantage "Dreaming Out Loud." In RKO's economy musical BEAT THE BAND (1947), the highlights were Gene Krupa and his jiving band, with Frances cast as a smalltown girl wanting to break into the show business big time. Even after a dozen years' experience on screen, her dramatics here were weak, but she excelled in her stylish renditions of "I've Got My Fingers Crossed," "I'm in Love," and "Kissin' Well."

If her screen career was stagnating, Frances was excelling on the radio airwaves. On September 8, 1946, she (as Blanche Bickerson) and Don Ameche (as John Bickerson) began a long run on NBC (and later CBS) network radio as the battling love mates in the comedy hit "The Bickersons." The routine had begun as a sketch on an episode of the Charlie McCarthy–Edgar Bergen radio show. Langford was in the headlines in 1948 when she helped authorities corner a salesman attempting to extort money from her. For Walt Disney's musical potpourri MELODY TIME (1948), part live-action, part animation, Frances participated in the "Once upon a Wintertime" animated segment dealing with bickering lovers out ice skating: she was heard singing the Bobby Worth–Ray Gilbert tune. Just as her film career had passed its peak, so had her husband's. Jon Hall had been at his most popular during World War II, teaming with exotic Maria Montez in a series of colorful fantasies at Universal. Now, more portly, he was making action quickies at Columbia Pictures and elsewhere. In 1949 Langford and Hall teamed for their only time on camera in DEPUTY MARSHAL, an overly talky Western from independent Lippert Films. Frances sang "Hideout in Hidden Valley" and "Levis, Plaid Shirt and Spurs."

Still a champion of service veterans, Frances was much in the nation's headlines in May 1950. President Harry S. Truman had announced his decision to relocate a military hospital (for paraplegics) from its Van Nuys, California, base to Long Beach. Frances was the unofficial spokesperson for the G.I.s and met Truman when his train stopped in Coulee City, Washington. When the politician dismissed her abruptly after a ten-second meeting, there was a huge national outcry. Later in the year, Frances was among the many radio/film/recording personalities who turned to television. She and her congenial "Bickersons" co-star, Don Ameche, hosted "Star Time," a variety series featuring music, comedy (including "The Bickersons"), and songs. The show lasted four months, until February 1951. By mid-1951 Frances was making a new film for low-budget picturemaker Sam Katzman, for whom her husband also made movies; PURPLE HEART DIARY (1951) was *supposed* to be the first of a ten-picture pact with the producer, but proved to be the only entry of the deal. The melodrama exploited her World War II efforts as an entertainer/ humanitarian in a contrived biography that blended action, comedy, romance, and, of course, music. Her best numbers were "Hi-Fellow Tourists" and "Bread and Butter Woman." On television, Frances and Don Ameche hosted a variety hour that ran from September 1951 to March 1952 on ABC, and featured Jack Lemmon in a recurring domestic comedy sketch. Later in 1952, Frances flew to Korea to entertain the troops. Late the next year (on December 19, 1953) she guest-starred as herself on an episode ("Honeymooners Christmas Party") of Jackie Gleason's CBS-TV series "The Honeymooners," which is still frequently shown in syndication.

What proved to be her final motion picture appearance was a guest-starring spot in THE GLENN MILLER STORY (1954), in which she appeared, along with the Modernaires and the Glenn Miller Orchestra, entertaining troops overseas during World War II. As always, she was vivacious and stylish in her full-throated song renditions. For years, Langford and Jon Hall had been known as Hollywood's Happy Couple, although their career paths kept them separated much of the time. In the early 1950s they purchased property in Florida, near Lakeland, and she began spending more time there. In April 1954 she and Hall separated and in late August 1955 they were divorced in Titusville, Florida. In the interim, while on a nightclub tour that played Milwaukee, Wisconsin, she met forty-eight-year-old Ralph Evinrude, a marine motor company magnate. On October 6, 1955, they were married aboard his 110-foot yacht (*The Chanticleer*) anchored in Long Island Sound. This was multi-millionaire Evinrude's third marriage; he had two children from his first.

When she married Evinrude, Frances agreed to subordinate her career to their marriage, but in August 1956 she signed with the RKO Unique label to record "When You Speak with Your Eyes" and "Rocking in the Rocket Room." In late 1956, Charles Wick, president of Splendex Enterprises, announced that he would star Frances in a teleseries, as one of the revolving stars of filmed musical short subjects. Neither the series, nor a Broadway musical Wick was going to produce for Frances, materialized. Throughout the decade, Frances, still a languid beauty, continued to appear sporadically on television, often as a guest on one of Bob Hope's network specials. On March 15, 1959, she hosted "Frances Langford Presents" on NBC-TV. It was comprised of two unsold half-hour pilots, featuring songs, dance, and comedy from the likes of Bob Hope, Julie London, Edgar Bergen, and the Four Freshmen. She was back on television with the variety special "The Frances Langford Show" (NBC, May 1, 1960) with Don Ameche, Johnny Mathis, Bob Cummings, and The Three Stooges as her disparate guests.

By the mid-1960s Frances was semi-retired from show business and living on her three-hundred-acre estate in Florida with her husband. She operated "The Outrigger," a club in Stuart where she would perform occasionally. She told the press, "Vaughn Monroe lives down the road, and Perry Como has a house nearby, and they often drop in for a songfest. So I've been able to keep my voice in trim." When the Vietnam War broke out, she volunteered to entertain, going overseas in 1966 both with and without Bob Hope to sing for the servicemen. She said kiddingly, "Oh, I suppose there might be a few of the older officers who will remember me." On May 13, 1967, she and long-standing friend Don Ameche appeared on ABC-TV's "Hollywood Palace" performing one of their classic "Bickersons" skits, which through several record albums have remained audience pleasers.

In the 1970s Frances Langford was out of the limelight until March 1978 when the sixty-four-year-old entertainer underwent successful open-heart surgery at Miami Heart Institute. She and her husband continued their home life in Florida, residing in Jensen Beach, Florida, with a summer retreat at Georgian Bay, and taking frequent trips aboard their yacht, as well as occasionally flying to the Philippines where they owned an engineering plant. Evinrude died in May 1986 and she then sold their Fox Point, Wisconsin, place, preferring to remain full time in Florida.

In the early 1989 PBS-syndicated documentary "Entertaining the Troops," Frances opened the ninety-minute program by singing "It's Been a Long Long Time." She was interviewed about her war efforts (terming her entertaining at the battlefronts as "fun") and later in the show took part in the "Bob Hope Troop Reunion," sitting around a table reminiscing with her World War II co-performers Hope (comedian), Patty Thomas (cheesecake), and Tony Romano (guitarist). Hope remembered the time he got fungus in his feet and Langford got fungus in her ear. Toward the end of these positive and nostalgic tidbits, Frances sang "I'm in the Mood for Love." As always, she was professional and relaxed.

## Filmography

The Subway Symphony (Vita, 1932) (s)
Rambling 'Round Radio Row #5 (Vita, 1933) (s)
Every Night at Eight (Par, 1935)
Broadway Melody of 1936 (MGM, 1935)
Collegiate (Par, 1936)
Palm Springs (Par, 1936)
Born to Dance (MGM, 1936)
The Hit Parade (Rep, 1937)
Hollywood Hotel (WB, 1937)
Dreaming Out Loud (RKO, 1940)
The Hit Parade of 1941 (Rep, 1940)
Too Many Girls (RKO, 1940)
All-American Co-Ed (UA, 1941)
Picture People #4 (RKO, 1941) (s)
Swing It Soldier (Univ, 1941)
Mississippi Gambler (Univ, 1942)
Yankee Doodle Dandy (WB, 1942)
Hedda Hopper's Hollywood #4 (Par, 1942) (s)
Cowboy in Manhattan (Univ, 1943)

Follow the Band (Univ, 1943)
This Is the Army (WB, 1943)
Never a Dull Moment (Univ, 1943)
Career Girl (PRC, 1944)
Memo for Joe (RKO, 1944) (s)
Girl Rush (RKO, 1944)
Dixie Jamboree (PRC, 1945)
Radio Stars on Parade (RKO, 1945)
Tropical Moon (Soundies, 1945) (s)
A Dream Came True (Soundies, 1945) (s)
Some Day When the Clouds Roll By (Soundies, 1945) (s)
People Are Funny (Par, 1945)
The Bamboo Blonde (RKO, 1946)
Beat the Band (RKO, 1947)
Melody Time (RKO, 1948) (voice only)
Deputy Marshal (Lip, 1949)
Purple Heart Diary [No Time for Tears] (Col, 1951) (also story idea)
The Glenn Miller Story (Univ, 1954)

## Broadway Plays

Here Goes the Bride (1933)

## Radio Series

Hollywood Hotel (CBS, ca. 1936–38)
The Texaco Star Theatre (CBS, 1939–40)
American Cruise (NBC, 1941)

The Bob Hope Pepsodent Show (NBC, ca. 1941–45)
The Bickersons (NBC, 1946–47; CBS, 1947–48, 1951)

## TV Series

Star Time (Dumont, 1950–51)

The Frances Langford–Don Ameche Show (ABC, 1951–52)

## Album Discography

The Bickersons (Col CL-1692/CS-8492) w. Don Ameche
The Bickersons (Radiola 1151) w. Don Ameche
The Bickersons Fight Back (Col CL-1883/CS-8683) w. Don Ameche
The Bickersons Rematch (Col G-30523) w. Don Ameche
Born to Dance (CIF 3001) [ST]
Collegiate (Caliban 6042) [ST]
Every Night at Eight (Caliban 6043) [ST]
Hollywood Hotel (EOH 99601, Hollywood Soundstage 5004) [ST]

I Feel a Song Coming On: 1935–37 (Take Two TT 214)
Old Songs for Old Friends (Cap T/ST-1865)
Rainbow Rhapsody (10" Mer MG-25005)
The Return of the Bickersons! (Radiola 3MR-4) w. Don Ameche
This Is the Army (Hollywood Soundstage 408, Sandy Hook 2035) [ST]
Yankee Doodle Dandy (Curtain Calls 100/13) [ST]

# MARIO LANZA

ALTHOUGH MARIO LANZA HAS BEEN DEAD FOR THREE DECADES, HE retains a high degree of popularity, due mainly to his many RCA recordings, which are constantly being re-released. From 1949 to 1959 he was involved in eight feature films which were successful because of his vocalizing. Yet for all his screen success as a powerful if undisciplined tenor, Lanza had a self-destructive streak which eventually cost him his life. Dogged by weight problems (as had been many operatic stars both before and after him) and possessing a temperament to match his poundage, Lanza essentially destroyed himself on a never-ending merry-go-round of drinking, eating, diets, and barbiturates. Despite having earned well over $5 million from his performing, he had little money on hand at the time of his death in 1959.

Mario Lanza's biography would make a good motion picture scenario. He was born in South Philadelphia on January 31, 1921, the son of Antonio and Maria Cocozza. He was christened Alfred Arnold Cocozza and he grew up poor. His father was a disabled World War I veteran and his mother scratched out a living as a seamstress at a local Army quartermasters' depot. As a boy, young Alfred first heard the recordings of Enrico Caruso on a neighbor's phonograph and the famous tenor became the youngster's idol. His sole goal in life was to become a great opera singer like Caruso. While he did poorly in academics and well in sports in school, Alfred (known as Freddie) was able to take voice lessons, straining his mother's meager income.

Two months before he was to graduate from high school he was expelled and he took a job in his grandfather's grocery business. He worked there for three years until Irene Williams, his music instructor, maneuvered him into an audition with the concert manager (William Huff) of the Philadelphia Academy of Music. Huff was impressed with the young man's vocal abilities and arranged an audition with Serge Koussevitzky, conductor of the Boston Symphony Orchestra and head of the Berkshire Music Center in Tanglewood, located in Lenox, Massachusetts. Alfred got a scholarship there and began using the name Mario Lanza, the surname taken from his mother's maiden name.

In the summer of 1942 he made an impressive debut at Tanglewood in *The Merry Wives of Windsor*. Columbia Concerts signed him for a tour, but it never materialized because he was drafted into World War II service the next January. Because of his vocal talents he was assigned to the Army's Special Services and appeared in the service shows *On the Beam* and *Winged Victory*. With the latter production he was on Broadway and went on the West Coast tour, appearing in Los Angeles with the show (but not in the 1944 film version of the play). He did get a break, however, when he sang at a party hosted by actress

Irene Manning. He so impressed her with his singing that she arranged an audition for him with Jack Warner. However, the Warner Bros. studio chief, while liking Lanza's voice, did not feel the soldier (who then weighed over 250 pounds) had a screen future. When he later sang at a party at Frank Sinatra's home, Lanza met agent Art Rush (who managed Roy Rogers and Dale Evans until his death in 1989). Rush thought his singing so good he negotiated a recording contract for the young tenor with RCA Victor. A serious inflammation of the nose resulted in Lanza's being discharged from the Army in early 1945 and he kept active with his concert bookings and recordings. On April 13, 1945, he married Betty Hicks, the sister of an Army friend. His big break came two years later when he sang at the Hollywood Bowl; after seeing him perform, Louis B. Mayer signed Mario Lanza to a seven-year screen contract. He began at $750 a week with his salary to rise to $100,000 a picture.

For his movie debut, Lanza was featured in Joe Pasternak's production of THAT MIDNIGHT KISS (1949). Kathryn Grayson was the heiress who wants to become an opera singer and who falls in love with a singing truck driver (Lanza). During the proceedings he performed operatic arias from Verdi's *Aïda*, Mascagni's *Cavalleria Rusticana*, and Donizetti's *L'Elisir d'Amore*, as well as the contemporary songs "They Won't Believe Me" and "I Know, I Know, I Know." *Variety* assessed his voice as "excellent" and added, "far from resembling the caricatured opera tenor, he's a nice-looking youngster of the 'average American boy' school who will have the femme customers on his side from the start." The movie was a solid box-office success and Lanza caused a sensation in his screen debut.

Louis B. Mayer was so pleased with his new discovery that he gave Lanza a bonus of $10,000 and cast him again with Kathryn Grayson in THE TOAST OF NEW ORLEANS (1950), this time as her co-star. Here he was a singing fisherman who becomes an operatic star and again he sang opera, this time arias from Bizet's *Carmen*, Ponchielli's *La Gioconda*, Verdi's *La Traviata*, and Flotow's *Martha*. However, his best number was his booming rendition of the song "Be My Love," which Nicholas Brodsky had custom-written for Lanza. The song was the highlight of the picture and his RCA Victor recording of it in 1951 remained on the charts for nearly six months. It sold over two million copies, becoming Lanza's best-selling single record.

After making THE TOAST OF NEW ORLEANS, Lanza and Grayson went on a tour around the country to promote the feature. Since Lanza idolized Enrico Caruso, he had long wanted to portray him on film. But there were many delays, some caused by the fact that Louis B. Mayer was being dethroned at the studio. Lanza fumed, "Who the hell do they think can play Caruso, Nelson Eddy? There is nobody but me who can play that role. I am Caruso!" Finally the studio assigned him to the picture, a largely fictional account of the legendary Italian tenor. However, it provided Lanza with a fine showcase for singing traditional Caruso opera favorites, with co-star Ann Blyth performing the new song "The Loveliest Night of the Year." (That number was so popular as a Lanza single for RCA that it almost matched his sales with "Be My Love.")

While THE GREAT CARUSO (1951) was another personal triumph for Lanza, grossing $4.5 million at the box office, it was also the beginning of his career downfall. During its production Lanza became excessively temperamental. After the movie's success, his ego swelled and he became increasingly difficult to work with.

From June 1951 to September 1952 the tenor starred on the weekly CBS radio series "The Mario Lanza Show," sponsored by Coca-Cola. In 1952 he balked at starring in the MGM production of BECAUSE YOU'RE MINE, thinking the vehicle too shabby and that producer Joe Pasternak was betraying him. (He said of the producer, "I make the pictures—I sing—and that bastard thinks it's him.") Lanza was also fuming at the studio for allowing a national magazine to profile him in an unfavorable light; he was upset that Kathryn Grayson had declined to do the new picture, and Doretta Morrow from Broadway substituted. Because of his studio contract, he grudgingly went through with the filming. However, during the shooting, he was very uncooperative, often showing up on the set intoxicated, and he was extremely rude and crude to his co-star. The resultant film was a slim offering. It had Lanza as a drafted opera star falling in love with the sister (Morrow) of his sergeant (James Whitmore). He sang the title tune, "The Song Angels Sing," and "The Lord's Prayer." Once again, because of his personal popularity the movie made money.

Ludwig Donath, Shepard Menken, Mario Lanza, and Ann Blyth
in THE GREAT CARUSO (1951)

For his next showcase MGM assigned Lanza the lead in Sigmund Romberg's classic THE STUDENT PRINCE (1954), but after recording the soundtrack prior to filming, he walked off the film and MGM sued him for $5 million. An agreement was arranged with the new studio regime, headed by Dore Schary. Filming began, but there were more clashes and Lanza walked out again. A final settlement permitted Metro to use his singing voice in the film with rushed-in Edmund Purdom mouthing the words. But after this, Lanza's studio contract was nullified. The star huffed to the press, "My biggest beef with Metro was that the studio wanted to be commercial and I wanted artistic betterment. Put them together—they don't mix. I rebelled because of sincerity to the public and my career."

On October 28, 1954, Lanza made his dramatic television debut in "Lend an Ear," a revue seen on CBS-TV's "Shower of Stars." However, his vocals were dubbed from his own recordings. As a result he lost the lead in Paramount's film of Rudolf Friml's evergreen THE VAGABOND KING (1956) because it was rumored his voice was gone. (The studio instead chose a relative unknown, Oreste, as his budget-saving replacement.) In fact, excessive dieting had made Lanza too weak to vocalize on that TV program. There was more unfavorable publicity when he was booked into the New Frontier Hotel in Las Vegas in 1955 for a week's engagement. He was unable to appear at opening night because a combination of tranquilizers and champagne had felled him. The engagement was cancelled.

Anxious for ways to support his expensive lifestyle, Lanza negotiated a two-picture deal with Warner Bros. at $150,000 per film. The initial vehicle was SERENADE (1956), a project which had sat around for years due to the steamy nature of the James Cain book original. The distilled new version had Lanza being used by an older woman (Joan Fontaine) and his manager (Vincent Price), but loved by a younger woman (Sarita Montiel). Lanza sang the title song and "My Destiny" but SERENADE had fewer opera sequences than usual for a Lanza picture. Although it was modestly successful, Warner Bros. decided to pay off troublesome Lanza rather than make the second picture.

By now Mario Lanza's career was in deep trouble, as was his personal life. With a wife and four children (Colleen, Elisa, Damon, Mark) to support, he had little income apart from his earnings from records. (He was now persona non grata at the studios.) Also, he was coping with eating binges, plus excessive drinking, ballooning his weight to three hundred pounds. All this would be followed by massive rounds of crash dieting and barbiturate abuse. While his RCA soundtrack albums of THE STUDENT PRINCE and SERENADE had sold quite decently, he had no new movie work to generate further soundtrack albums.

After a film layoff of nearly a year, in which he did concerts, he signed a two-picture contract with Italy's Titanus Films. He moved his family to his ancestral homeland, renting the luxurious Rome villa that Benito Mussolini had given to Marshal Badoglio. ("I'm a movie star and I think I should live like one," he reasoned.) His first Italian production, SEVEN HILLS OF ROME (1958), benefited from beautiful locations and a fair plot about a TV star (Lanza) who comes to Rome to find peace and quiet and falls in love with a beautiful young woman (Peggie Castle). He sang the title song, "Lolita," "Come

Dance with Me," "Come Prima," and "Arrivederci Roma." (The latter song brought him back to the singles charts for a six-week run, the first time one of his RCA singles had charted since his 1952 recording of "Because.") Ironically, SEVEN HILLS OF ROME was released in the United States by MGM, which had a distribution arrangement with Titanus. Metro also released FOR THE FIRST TIME (1959), which typecast him as a temperamental opera singer who retreats to Capri where he finds love with a pretty young deaf woman (Johanna von Koszian). Here he performed "Neapolitan Dance," "Mazurka," "The Pineapple Pickers," and "Tarantella." The picture did only average business.

Following the making of FOR THE FIRST TIME, the self-indulgent Lanza's health worsened from his ever-increasing dieting, plus pneumonia and phlebitis. He died on October 7, 1959, when a blood clot in the leg went to his heart and killed him. Following his sudden demise, the RCA soundtrack album of FOR THE FIRST TIME became a bestseller, as did several of his other albums. On March 11, 1960, Betty Lanza, who had been in a deep depression since her husband's death, died of asphyxiation and the Lanza's four children (whom family friend Kathryn Grayson had tended for a spell) became wards of Lanza's parents. Most of his earnings had vanished, but the children had an income from his record royalties of some $100,000 yearly. Only Lanza's daughter Colleen followed in his show business footsteps by becoming a singer.

In the years since his death, the memory of Mario Lanza has been kept alive not only by his films, but by RCA's constant reissuance of his recordings, which to date have sold more than fifty million copies.

## Filmography

That Midnight Kiss (MGM, 1949)
The Toast of New Orleans (MGM, 1950)
The Great Caruso (MGM, 1951)
Because You're Mine (MGM, 1952)
The Student Prince (MGM, 1954) (voice only)

Serenade (WB, 1956)
Seven Hills of Rome (MGM, 1958) (also Italian-
language version: Arrivederci Roma)
For the First Time (MGM, 1959)

## Broadway Plays

Winged Victory (1943) (replacement)

## Radio Series

The Mario Lanza Show (CBS, 1951–52)

## Album Discography

Be My Love (RCA LSC-3289)
Because You're Mine (10" RCA LM-7015) [ST]
The Best of Mario Lanza (RCA LM/LSC-2748)
The Best of Mario Lanza, Vol. 2 (RCA LM/
   LSC-2998)
Carols (RCA LM-2029)
Caruso Favorites (RCA LM/LSC-2393)
Cavalcade of Show Tunes (RCA LM-2090)
Christmas Carols (RCA LM/LSC-2333)
Christmas Hymns and Carols (Camden CAL/
   CAS-777)
Christmas Songs (10" RCA LM-155)
The Desert Song (RCA LM/LSC-2440)
Double Feature: That Midnight Kiss & The
   Toast of New Orleans (RCA LM- 2422)
   [ST]
Favorite Arias (RCA LM/LSC-2932)
For the First Time (RCA LM/LSC-2338) [ST]
The Great Caruso (RCA LM/LSC-1127) [ST]
Greatest Hits from Operettas and Musicals
   (RCA VCS-6192)
If You Are But a Dream (RCA LM/LSC-2790)
I'll See You in My Dreams (RCA LM/LSC-
   2720, RCA International 89060)
I'll Walk with God (RCA LM/LSC-2607)
A Kiss and Other Love Songs (RCA LM-1860)
Lanza on Broadway (RCA LM-2070)
A Legendary Performer (RCA CRL1-1750)
Love Songs and a Neapolitan Serenade (RCA
   LM/LSC-1188)

Magic Mario (RCA LM-1943)
The Magic of Mario Lanza (Heartland Music)
Mario! (RCA LM/LSC-2331)
Mario Lanza (Golden Age of Opera 457)
Mario Lanza (Unique Opera 127)
The Mario Lanza Collection (RCA CRM5-
   4158)
Mario Lanza in Opera (RCA LSC-3101)
Mario Lanza Live (A Touch of Magic 2)
Mario Lanza Memories (RCA LSC-3102)
Mario Lanza on Radio (Radiola 1121)
A Mario Lanza Program (RCA LM/LSC-2454)
Mario Lanza Sings Caruso (RCA ARL1-0314)
Opera's Greatest Hits (RCA VCS-7073)
Pure Gold (RCA ANL1-2874, RCA Interna-
   tional 5005)
Serenade (RCA LM-1996) [ST]
The Seven Hills of Rome (RCA LM-2211) [ST]
Speak to Me of Love (RCA LSC-3103)
The Student Prince (RCA LM-1837, RCA LSC-
   3216) [ST]
The Student Prince (RCA LM/LSC-2339)
That Midnight Kiss (10" RCA LM-86) [ST]
The Toast of New Orleans (10" RCA LM-75,
   Azel 104) [ST]
The Touch of Your Hand (RCA LM-1927)
The Vagabond King (RCA LM/LSC-2509)
You Do Something to Me (Camden CAL/CAS-
   450)
Younger Than Springtime (RCA LSC-3049)

# NICK LUCAS

"I'VE BEEN THE LUCKIEST GUY IN THE WORLD. IF YOU DISC JOCKEYS had been on hand when Nick Lucas first hit his stride, he'd be the biggest name in show business." This statement was made by Bing Crosby at a disc jockey convention in the 1950s and it exemplifies the fact that Nick Lucas, the 5' 8" tenor who could sing in three ranges, was one of the music world's biggest stars in the era *before* radio dictated record-buying tastes. In fact, Nick Lucas was one of the biggest record sellers of the late 1920s and early 1930s (with over eighty-four million records sold) and he was one of vaudeville's top names, at one time earning $3,000 per week with two years' advance bookings. In addition, he scored successes on Broadway, in films, on radio, in nightclubs, and, later, on television. Also a songwriter, Nick Lucas, more than any other twentieth-century musician, is responsible for the popularity of the guitar in modern-day popular music, for he not only had the first custom-made guitar merchandised, but he also composed the first guitar instruction books and had his own line of popular guitar picks. While his motion picture career spanned more than four decades, Nick Lucas focused more on the lucrative field of personal appearances. Nevertheless, he introduced and popularized one of filmdom's most memorable songs, "Tip Toe Through the Tulips."

Born Dominic Antonio Nicholas Lucanese in Newark, New Jersey, on August 22, 1897, the son of Italian immigrants, he was one of nine children. Since his entire family loved music, he started playing the mandolin at age five and then graduated to the guitar. By the time he was nine years old he and his older brother Frank were making extra money for the family by performing at parties, christenings, weddings, and even in saloons or streetcars.

By 1912 brother Frank had gone into vaudeville, and Nick made his recording debut that year making test cylinder pressings for the Edison Company. The next year he graduated from school and took a job in a leather tannery. Music was still his primary interest, though, as he was now adept at not only the mandolin and guitar, but also the banjo. Not long afterward he got a job with a band at a Newark cabaret and in 1917 he married Catherine Cifrodella. They remained together until her death in 1971; they had one daughter, Emily (born in 1918). While appearing at the Iroquois Club in Newark, he was approached about forming a vaudeville act. With friend Ted Fio Rito and three other musicians he formed The Kentucky Five, which toured successfully for six months. After that run he joined Vincent Lopez's orchestra in New York City as a banjo player and in 1919 became a part of the Vernon Country Club Orchestra. He recorded with the group for Columbia and in addition he and brother Frank recorded for Pathé as the Lucas

Ukulele Trio and the Lucas Novelty Quartet. For the same label he recorded with The Don Parker Trio. In 1922 he recorded the first guitar solos ever waxed, his own compositions of "Pickin' the Guitar" and "Teasin' the Frets," for Pathé, and the recording would become a milestone in the history of American guitar music.

Late in 1921 Nick Lucas (as he was now billed) joined Sam Lanin's orchestra; he also recorded with Lanin on Gennett Records as a part of Bailey's Lucky Seven. It was in this period that Lucas replaced the banjo with the guitar as a recording instrument, thus beginning the guitar's popularity as an accompaniment instrument on recordings. He remained with Lanin in New York City for three years and in 1924 relocated to Chicago where he joined the Oriole Terrace Orchestra led by Ted Fio Rito and Danny Russo. Not only was he an instrumentalist with the group but he also began singing with the band, which led to solo appearances with his guitar on radio station WEBH. That Windy City station had exposure across the nation and tremendous amounts of fan mail poured in for Lucas, causing him to be signed as a solo performer by Brunswick Records.

Nick Lucas' initial Brunswick disc was "My Best Girl." It was an immediate hit and he then went out on his own in vaudeville. In the next few years Lucas would become one of the nation's favorite entertainers, both in vaudeville and on records where he was dubbed "The Crooning Troubadour," thus making him the first *official* crooner. Among his hit Brunswick records were "Because They All Love You," "Isn't She the Sweetest Thing?," "Brown Eyes, Why Are You Blue?," "Precious," "In a Little Spanish Town," "Moonbeam, Kiss Her for Me," "My Ohio Home," "I'm Waiting for Ships That Never Come In," "It Must Be Love," and several of his own compositions, including "I've Named My Pillow After You," "I Might Have Known," and "I'm Tired of Everything But You."

Early in 1926 Lucas made his Broadway debut in *Sweetheart Time* popularizing the song "Sleepy Time Gal." In the fall of that year he enjoyed his greatest career success with a three-month stand in London, England, headlining at the Café de Paris where *Variety* noted he was "acclaimed one of the biggest receptions ever given any artist in that establishment." While in London he also appeared at the Palladium, Alhambra Theatre, Kit Kat Klub, Piccadilly Hotel, Coliseum Theatre, and the Victoria Palace, along with giving private recitals for the Prince of Wales and the Queen of Spain.

Following his acclaim abroad, Nick Lucas was in even greater demand in his homeland and for the next several years he toured the Keith–Orpheum vaudeville circuit, commanding up to $3,000 weekly, making him one of the medium's highest-paid star attractions. Because of his record and vaudeville popularity, the demand for six-string guitars increased greatly. The Gibson Guitar Company produced the Nick Lucas Special, from Lucas' own design, which was a perennial favorite well into the late 1930s (today it is manufactured by the Santa Cruz Guitar Company). At the same time he created the first guitar instruction books for Mills Music, eventually authoring a score of guitar method volumes and song folios, making the Nick Lucas Guitar Method one of the best-selling types of guitar instruction formats. In addition, he also lent his name to a brand of guitar picks which, along with his books, remained good sellers over the years.

In the summer of 1929 Nick Lucas returned to Broadway in Florenz Ziegfeld's *Show Girl*, which starred Jimmy Durante. In it Lucas introduced George Gershwin's "Liza" and performed "Singin' in the Rain," which was a big-selling record for him on Brunswick. Earlier in the year Lucas had completed the Technicolor motion picture GOLD DIGGERS OF BROADWAY (1929) for Warner Bros., in which he played entertainer Nick and performed his two most famous songs, "Tip Toe Through the Tulips" and "Painting the Clouds with Sunshine." His Brunswick record of the two tunes sold more than two million copies and the sheet music for the songs topped the best-seller list for over four months. That spring vaudeville audiences voted Nick Lucas the eighth most popular performer in the country and that fall GOLD DIGGERS OF BROADWAY was issued to critical acclaim. *Variety* reported of this entertainer with his striking, dark Italian looks, "there's no voice on the discs like Lucas' for the type of number sung by him." Warner Bros. signed him to appear in its all-star production THE SHOW OF SHOWS (1929) in which he sang "Lady Luck" and "The Only Song I Know" as well as headlined "The Chinese Fantasy" production number with Myrna Loy in which he sang "Li-Po-Li." Again his notices were so good that the studio quickly offered him a seven-year contract, but he turned it down (he was not interested in acting) in favor of the more immediately profitable vaudeville arena. His Brunswick records also continued to be top sellers with such songs as "My Tonia," "Coquette," "Singing a Song to the Stars," "You're Driving Me Crazy," "Lady Play Your Mandolin," and "Running Between the Raindrops."

The two main areas of Nick Lucas' success—vaudeville and recordings—were hit hard by the Depression. However, despite the difficult times, he remained a highly paid headliner in both fields and in the fall of 1931 he came to network radio on NBC with his own program for the Campbell Soup Company at $2,000 per week. Early the next year he began recording for Hit of the Week Records before returning to Brunswick, where he would remain through 1934. Lucas was also the last act to headline the legendary Palace Theatre late in 1932 before it was converted into a movie house. During the mid-1930s Nick Lucas starred on his CBS radio program and he fronted a band, Nick Lucas and His Troubadours.

It was also in the mid-1930s that thirty-seven-year-old Lucas returned to films, where Bing Crosby, Russ Columbo (until his untimely death in 1934), and Dick Powell held sway as the crooning stars of musical feature films. Lucas starred in short subjects for both Universal and Vitaphone (Warner Bros.). In WHAT THIS COUNTRY NEEDS (1934) he performed "Tip Toe Through the Tulips," "How Can You Lose?," and "It Happened in Spain." In NICK LUCAS AND HIS TROUBADOURS (1936) he sang "Tip Toe Through the Tulips," "Goody Goody," and "Sing an Old Fashioned Song," while in VITAPHONE HEADLINERS (1936) he crooned "Broken Hearted Troubadour." From 1936 to 1938 he was the main vocalist with Al Pearce on CBS radio and in 1938 he began working the nightclub circuit before embarking on a world tour. Due to the growing worldwide war fever, his tour ended with a six-month stand in Australia where he not only headlined on the Tivoli circuit but had his own weekday radio program in Melbourne and recorded for Regal Zonophone Records.

Once back in the United States, Lucas made the short films YANKEE DOODLE HOME (1939) and CONGAMANIA (1940) and remained active in club appearances and in the diminished world of vaudeville. In 1944 he was featured in a quartet of shorts (TIP TOE THROUGH THE TULIPS WITH ME; SIDE BY SIDE; GOODNIGHT, WHEREVER YOU ARE; and AN HOUR NEVER PASSES) for Soundies Corporation of America and in 1947 he began a two-year run in *Ken Murray's Blackouts* in Hollywood, which also featured Marie Wilson. When the revue went to Broadway for fifty-nine performances as *Blackouts of 1949*, he was among the star players. Early in 1950 he made his network TV debut on "The Ken Murray Show." During this time he also recorded for Diamond and Capitol Records and in 1951 he made seven musical shorts geared directly for television by Snader Telescriptions. These were "Bela Bimba," "The Sunshine of Your Smile," "Get Out Those Old Records," "Looking at the World Thru Rose Colored Glasses," "Marie Ah Marie," "Mexicali Rose," and "Walking My Baby Back Home." That same year also found him back on network radio as the headliner of ABC's "Saturday Night at the Shamrock." He also returned to movies, appearing as himself in the low-budget Allied Artists musical DISC JOCKEY (1951), which also showcased the likes of Ginny Simms, Tommy Dorsey, Sarah Vaughan, The

Nick Lucas in GOODNIGHT, WHEREVER YOU ARE (1944)

Weavers, Red Nichols, Foy Willing and The Riders of the Purple Sage, and twenty-eight radio disc jockeys from across the country. Nick Lucas sang "Let's Meander Thru the Meadow."

Throughout the 1950s Nick Lucas appeared in clubs across the United States, with lengthy annual stays in Las Vegas, Reno, and Lake Tahoe. He also recorded for Cavalier, Accent, and Crown Records and his 1957 Decca album *Painting the Clouds with Sunshine* sold so well it remained in the company's active catalogue for fifteen years. In 1962 he was a semi-regular on Lawrence Welk's TV variety program and he also appeared on many other network shows including those of Ed Sullivan, Art Linkletter, Liberace, and Kate Smith, and on Patti Page's "The Big Record." During the mid-1960s Lucas began appearing at fairs and fraternal organization shows and in 1966 he starred in the Lake Tahoe production of *Blackouts of 1966.* In the late 1960s, when Tiny Tim repopularized "Tip Toe Through the Tulips," Lucas found himself flooded with job offers. When Tiny Tim was married on Johnny Carson's "The Tonight Show" late in 1969, Nick Lucas sang on the program, the most-watched outing in the show's history.

Lucas returned to feature films in 1974, singing "When You and I Were Seventeen" on the soundtrack of Paramount's elaborate period piece THE GREAT GATSBY. During the same year he crooned "I Wished on the Moon" on the soundtrack of the studio's THE DAY OF THE LOCUST, set in 1930s Hollywood. The next year he performed "I'll See You in My Dreams," "Happy Days Are Here Again," "Ja Da," "Let's Make Hay While the Sun Shines," "Wang Wang Blues," and "My Blue Heaven" on the soundtrack of MGM's HEARTS OF THE WEST starring Jeff Bridges and Andy Griffith. Besides personal appearances, he continued to appear on TV (he was especially popular on Sam Yorty's West Coast program) and to make commercials. He opened the 1980s by appearing on worldwide television in the Tournament of Roses Parade atop a float aptly entitled "Tip Toe Through the Tulips." He remained active on the personal appearance circuit and on TV shows such as those of Merv Griffin and Wally George before succumbing to pneumonia on July 28, 1982, at the age of eighty-four.

One of the best summaries of Nick Lucas' productive career was given in the December 4, 1981, issue of Newark's *Italian Tribune* newspaper: "For sheer musical expertise, and durability, the likes of Nick Lucas, the kid from the streets of Newark, has never been equaled."

## Filmography

Gold Diggers of Broadway (WB, 1929)
The Show of Shows (WB, 1929)
Organloguing the Hits with Nick Lucas (Master Art Products, 1931) (s)
On the Air and Off (Univ, 1933) (s)

What This Country Needs (Vita, 1934) (s)
Nick Lucas and His Troubadours (Vita, 1936) (s)
Vitaphone Headliners (Vita, 1936) (s)
Yankee Doodle Home (Col, 1939) (s)

Congamania (Univ, 1940) (s)
Goodnight, Wherever You Are (Soundies, 1944) (s)
An Hour Never Passes (Soundies, 1944) (s)
Tip Toe Through the Tulips with Me (Soundies, 1944) (s)

Side by Side (Soundies, 1944) (s)
Big Time Revue (WB, 1947) (s)
Disc Jockey (AA, 1951)
The Great Gatsby (Par, 1974) (voice only)
The Day of the Locust (Par, 1974) (voice only)
Hearts of the West (MGM, 1975) (voice only)

## Broadway Plays

Sweetheart Time (1926)
Show Girl (1929)

Blackouts of 1949 (1949)

## Radio Series

The Nick Lucas Show (NBC, 1931–32; CBS, 1934–35)

Al Pearce and His Gang (NBC, 1936–38)
Saturday Night at the Shamrock (ABC, 1951)

## Television Series

The Lawrence Welk Show (ABC, 1962)

## Album Discography

The Day of the Locust (London PS-912) [ST]
An Evening with Nick Lucas (Take Two 1001)
The Great Gatsby (Paramount PAS-2-3001) [ST]
The Nick Lucas Souvenir Album (Accent 5027, Beacon SBEAB-4)

Painting the Clouds with Sunshine (Decca DL-8653)
Rose Colored Glasses (Accent 5043)
The Singing Troubadour (Academy Sound & Vision ASV-5022)
Tip Toe Through the Tulips with Nick Lucas (10" Cavalier 5033, Cavalier CVLP-6007)

# JEANETTE MacDONALD

A BEAUTIFUL, CULTURED RED-HEADED SINGING STAR OF FILMS, stage, and radio, Jeanette MacDonald is mainly remembered today for her eight movie operettas with Nelson Eddy and for resolutely singing "San Francisco" in the 1936 earthquake film epic of the same title. One of the most successful of movie singers and certainly a woman of sturdy determination (she was known as "The Iron Butterfly"), Jeanette MacDonald failed to realize her true goal, that of operatic stardom. Her forte, at least with her adoring and very faithful public, was operettas and there she made her mark in the glossy, luxurious MGM musicals of the 1930s.

Jeanette MacDonald was born June 18, 1903 (her grave marker insists 1907), in Philadelphia, Pennsylvania, the youngest of Daniel and Anne MacDonald's three daughters. Since all three sisters were musically inclined, they were educated in private schools where they learned singing, dancing, and drama. At an early age Jeanette made her stage debut in a children's revue. As a teenager she came to New York City to visit her older sister Blossom (later billed as Marie Blake and Blossom Rock), who was working in the chorus of *The Demi-Tasse Revue,* which was the prologue show for the movie program at the Capitol Theatre. Producer Ned Wayburn hired Jeanette to join the chorine lineup. Next she appeared in the chorus of *The Night Boat* (1920) and supplemented her income with modeling jobs. In 1921 she had roles in two Broadway productions, *Irene* and *Tangerine,* and in 1922 she appeared in *A Fantastic Fricasse.* Her success in that Greenwich Village revue led to a big part in *The Magic Ring* (1923), in which she sang, and in 1925 she was the ingenue in George Gershwin's *Tip Toes.* Her first starring role in a Broadway musical was in the Shubert Brothers' *Bubbling Over* in March 1926. As a Shubert contract star she was in *Yes, Yes Yvette* (1927—in which she got top billing for the first time), *Sunny Days* (1928), *Angela* (1928), and *Boom! Boom!* (1929). Richard Dix saw her on stage and had Paramount Pictures test her for one of his vehicles at the company's Long Island facility. However, her stage contract would not permit her to make films.

In 1929 filmmaker Ernst Lubitsch screened the test footage of Jeanette and, after coming to Chicago to hear her in the touring company of *Boom! Boom!* (to see if she could really sing), he hired her for the leading role in the Paramount musical THE LOVE PARADE (1929) opposite Maurice Chevalier. This sophisticated frou frou cast her as Queen Louise of Sylvania who marries a prince (Chevalier) with a scandalous past. In the film she sang "March of the Grenadier" and "Dream Lover," both of which she recorded for Victor Records late in 1929 in her recording debut. *Variety* enthused of MacDonald, "Her personality, looks and voice make LOVE PARADE all the more a charming, intriguing picture."

---

The *New York Herald Tribune* agreed: "Blessed with a fine voice, a sense of comedy and a definite screen personality, she registers an individual success that makes her future in the new medium an enviable one."

Ensconced in Hollywood with her mother (and still very much in touch with her New York–based stockbroker beau Robert Ritchie) she next co-starred with Dennis King in the color production of Rudolf Friml's THE VAGABOND KING (1930). It was just another of the many ponderous screen operettas in distribution that year, and gave Jeanette no opportunity to display her wit, although she had a big production number ("Only a Rose"). By now Robert Ritchie was in Hollywood full time as her business manager/friend. Eager to maximize MacDonald's availability, Paramount tossed her into the all-star PARAMOUNT ON PARADE (1930), but her rendition (unlike Maurice Chevalier's) of "Sweeping the Clouds Away" was removed from the release print. (However, it was used in the Spanish-language edition, GALAS DE LA PARAMOUNT, for which she was also one of the masters of ceremony.) She worked for Lubitsch again, this time opposite Britisher Jack Buchanan in the polished MONTE CARLO (1930), singing "Beyond the Blue Horizon," which she recorded for Victor. The studio next stuck her with a singing part in the scatterbrained comedy LET'S GO NATIVE (1930). Paramount then ended her contract, feeling that as movie musicals (especially operettas) were becoming moribund, so was Jeanette's usefulness.

She was at United Artists for THE LOTTERY BRIDE (1930), which, despite Rudolf Friml's original score, was embarrassing to all concerned, including Jeanette, who was cast as a Norwegian contestant in a marriage lottery that lands her in Nome, Alaska. The pretentious project at least offered her top billing for the first time. Meanwhile, she made her radio debut at NBC. Next she made a trio of pictures for Fox, which are today both her least-celebrated and least-known screen work. Because the musical film cycle had passed, the Fox entries de-emphasized her singing talents and highlighted her aptitude for ladylike risqué comedy in a drawing-room atmosphere. In fact, most of her singing numbers were deleted from OH, FOR A MAN (1930)—only her aria from *Tristan und Isolde* remained. In the fall of 1931 Jeanette went to London where she recorded four songs for Victor's British label, HMV (His Master's Voice). The trip to London was part of a concert tour undertaken to disprove a French newspaper account that she had been killed in a car crash in France. The tour took her to several European cities, in addition to Paris and London, where she sang at the Dominion Theatre.

Back in Hollywood, Ernst Lubitsch convinced Paramount to reteam Jeanette with Chevalier for ONE HOUR WITH YOU (1932), which George Cukor began as director and Lubitsch completed. MacDonald and Chevalier were a married couple whose harmony is interrupted by another woman (Genevieve Tobin). Jeanette sang the title song and "We Will Always Be Sweethearts." She and Chevalier (who were not fond of one another) also starred in the French-language version, with Lily Damita in the Tobin part. Their next vehicle, LOVE ME TONIGHT (1932), was directed stylishly by Rouben Mamoulian and utilized a Rodgers and Hart score including the popular "Isn't It Romantic?" It presented Chevalier as a French tailor who becomes infatuated with the guest (Jeanette) of a nobleman who cannot pay his bills. With the musical picture definitely out of vogue, Paramount again bid goodbye to MacDonald.

Jeanette went to Europe, ostensibly on a concert tour but actually to cement film offers. She was in London to star in THE QUEEN'S AFFAIR (1933) with Herbert Marshall, but both performers left the project and Anna Neagle took MacDonald's role in that and the next announced project, BITTER SWEET (1933). Meanwhile, on the coast of France, MacDonald had become friendly with MGM star Norma Shearer and her studio executive–husband Irving Thalberg, who was starting his own production unit at the studio and needed a roster of stars. Thalberg acknowledged that screen musicals had come back into fashion (buoyed by Warner Bros.' hit 42ND STREET [1933]), and he courted Jeanette to sign a contract with MGM.

When Jeanette returned to Hollywood, Thalberg and his MGM rival/boss Louis B. Mayer debated and delayed about what project to showcase her in. With her friend Ritchie she began negotiations at United Artists for a project that fell through. Then MGM agreed to star her in I MARRIED AN ANGEL, based on a Rodgers and Hart original, but the musical was too piquant for the industry's Production Code. (The show was transformed into a Broadway musical in 1938 and in 1942 would become a MacDonald–Eddy vehicle.) Instead MacDonald starred in THE CAT AND THE FIDDLE (1934) opposite ex-silent film star Ramon Novarro. Jeanette sang "Tonight Will Teach Me to Forget" and "Try to Forget," but the film lacked a light touch and was only mildly successful. When Grace Moore could not come to terms with MGM, Jeanette replaced her opposite Maurice Chevalier (much to his chagrin) in a remake of THE MERRY WIDOW (1934), staged elaborately by Ernst Lubitsch. She sang "I Love You So" and "Vilia." The expensive, bubbly film was more popular with critics than with the public.

Jeanette had rejected doing NAUGHTY MARIETTA (1935) several times, but now, under a five-year studio pact, she was persuaded to star with a newcomer, Nelson Eddy, in this old-fashioned operetta. MGM reasoned that it would be a change from her cosmopolitan outings with Lubitsch and might make her more popular with grass-roots America. She did "The Italian Street Song" and dueted with Eddy on "Ah, Sweet Mystery of Life." It proved a substantial hit and made her a top industry personality again. The new screen team was reunited (after Grace Moore dropped out) in the even better ROSE MARIE (1936). It provided them with their most famous duet, "Indian Love Call," which sold over one million records when they recorded it for Victor. Jeanette also sang arias from Gounod's opera *Romeo and Juliet* and Puccini's *Tosca* in this tale of an opera singer who falls in love with a persistent Canadian Mountie (Eddy). Despite playing the role of a demanding opera singer, she displayed a winning tongue-in-cheek rapport that made her seem far less lofty to moviegoers. The picture was a top money earner of the year and Jeanette and Nelson Eddy were again hailed as the best screen team since Fred Astaire and Ginger Rogers.

Always a shrewd businesswoman, Jeanette had sold MGM the story of SAN FRAN-CISCO (1936) on the condition that Clark Gable be her co-star. He was uninterested in co-starring with MacDonald (who had a reputation for being a "star" on the set) but she was determined, and Louis B. Mayer supported her choice. In the course of this classic exercise she belted out the title tune, did excerpts from Gounod's *Faust* and Verdi's *Il Trovatore*, and sang "Nearer My God, to Thee." With the addition of the magnetic presence of Gable, reliable Spencer Tracy (as a priest), and a recreation of the Bay City quake, the film was destined for huge box-office results.

By this time Jeanette MacDonald was at the peak of her screen career. The studio dug into the vaults for future MacDonald–Eddy screen teamings. In the schmaltzy MAYTIME (1937), which began production twice due to Irving Thalberg's death in 1936, John Barrymore was her jealous impresario/husband who kills the opera star (Eddy) she loves. She and Eddy provided excerpts from Meyerbeer's grand opera *Les Huguenots* and Herbert Stothart's *Czaritza*, plus giving memorable duets on "Farewell to Dreams," "Will You Remember?," and "Song of Love." It was a sugary success. But there were some roles which even the studio agreed were not right for the MacDonald–Eddy combination. Thus Allan Jones co-starred with Jeanette in THE FIREFLY (1937). In the opinion of many people (including MacDonald), Jones was a more spirited leading man than Eddy. In THE FIRE-FLY he sang "The Donkey Serenade" (which became his trademark song) and Jeanette did

Nelson Eddy and Jeanette MacDonald in MAYTIME (1937)

"Giannina Mia," as she essayed her role as a spy in Napoleonic times. However, the box-office grosses did not match those of the screen teamings of Mac-Donald and Eddy.

On June 17, 1937, Jeanette married actor Gene Raymond in a lavish wedding at the Wilshire Methodist Church in Beverly Hills. (Nelson Eddy sang at the ceremony.) After her marriage she was encouraged in her operatic pursuits by her husband. For a time she studied with the great opera star Lotte Lehmann, and when she recorded "Let Me Always Sing" and "From the Land of the Sky Blue Water" for Victor Records in 1939, Gene Raymond accompanied her on the piano. In 1938 she starred on radio in the CBS program "Vick's Open House" and that year she and Nelson Eddy did the old frontier chestnut GIRL OF THE GOLDEN WEST (1938). She sang "Liebestraum" and "Ave Maria," trying to bolster the lumbering production, which did not show Eddy to advantage. Much more popular was the studio's Technicolor production of SWEETHEARTS (1938), a contemporary story of a married but feuding couple who star in Broadway operettas. The picture was a big moneymaker.

The year 1939 saw both MacDonald and Eddy seeking to test their individual marquee power and to find other movie teammates. These new teamings were also an excellent opportunity for Louis B. Mayer to merchandise his screen team to great profit. But Jeanette's BROADWAY SERENADE (1939) was absurd and had a miscast, nonsinging Lew Ayres as her show business piano-playing husband. By this point Jeanette had fought once too often with studio head Louis B. Mayer and this hurt her future at the studio. Her career began going downhill.

She and Nelson Eddy were back in tandem with NEW MOON, the first of two 1940 releases for the duo. A revamping of the 1931 film with Lawrence Tibbett and Grace Moore, this NEW MOON was set in 1790s New Orleans with newly rich Jeanette attracted to rakish bondsman Eddy. Together they sang "Wanting You," perhaps their most effective duet. Their next outing, BITTER SWEET, was not as good in its contrived account of a music teacher (Eddy) who marries his pupil (Jeanette) and writes an opera for her, only to die in a duel. They dueted "I'll See You Again." The film was abhorred by its author (Noël Coward) and to a great extent ignored by the public; it lost money. Exploiting her off-screen marriage to Gene Raymond, Metro matched her on camera with him in the remake of SMILIN' THROUGH (1941), a lachrymose Technicolor opus. By now Mac-Donald was too mature to play an ingenue and Raymond was even more one-dimensional than critics had accused Nelson Eddy of being on screen. In 1942 MacDonald and Eddy were teamed for the final time on screen in the much-delayed I MARRIED AN ANGEL. As watered down for the movies, it was a failed fantasy about a wealthy banker (Eddy) dreaming he has wed an angel (Jeanette). It went through retakes and re-editing, and the final results were not well received. The same year she had a tongue-in-cheek dramatic role (at which she excelled) in the low-budgeted spy spoof CAIRO, in which she was a film star mixed up in espionage and romance (with Robert Young).

Nelson Eddy engineered his MGM release in 1942, the year Metro terminated Jeanette's studio agreement. She chose to appear in grand opera, making her debut in Charles Gounod's *Romeo and Juliet* in Montreal with tenor Armand Tokatyan as Romeo and a cast which included Ezio Pinza. This was followed by a run of the opera in Chicago and elsewhere in the States, but the rumored debut of Jeanette MacDonald at New York's Metropolitan Opera never occurred. She then appeared in *Faust* with the Chicago Civic Opera Company. Her reviews were mixed, with some critics insisting that her voice was not strong enough for grand opera.

During the World War II years she was a tireless civilian entertainer at USO shows for troops and in 1944 she returned briefly to the screen, playing herself in Universal's FOLLOW THE BOYS, singing "I'll See You in My Dreams" and "Beyond the Blue Horizon."

While recurring news stories insisted that MacDonald and Eddy would be reteamed on screen, nothing came of the rumors. She was a frequent guest on radio's "The Electric Hour" and "Kraft Music Hall," both starring Nelson Eddy. On "Lux Radio Theatre" they did radio versions of "Naughty Marietta," "Maytime," and "Rose Marie" and on December 23, 1948, on NBC's "Camel Screen Guild Theatre," they reprised "Sweethearts." Jeanette had been recording with Victor Records and she would remain with the label until the early 1950s, waxing a variety of songs, ranging from her movie tunes to opera to inspirational numbers.

Producer Joe Pasternak convinced Jeanette to return to MGM for her two final feature films: THREE DARING DAUGHTERS (1948) and THE SUN COMES UP (1949). In the former she sang "You Made Me Love You" while playing the mother (!) of three teenaged girls, while the latter teamed her as a widowed concert singer with Lassie the dog. In the latter she was found doing excerpts from Puccini's evergreen lyric opera *Madama Butterfly* as well as a few folk songs. She looked gorgeous in both features, but chose to make no more pictures.

In 1948 she starred in a very popular Hollywood Bowl concert. In 1951 she and Gene Raymond revived *The Guardsman* on Broadway. They also did occasional tours together. She had the title role of "The Prima Donna" on "Screen Directors Playhouse" (NBC-TV) in 1956 and the next year she was in "Charley's Aunt" on "Playhouse 90" (CBS-TV). The year 1957 also found her doing a nightclub act at the Sahara Hotel in Las Vegas and at the Cocoanut Grove in Los Angeles; the previous year she and Nelson Eddy had been reunited on Gordon MacRae's TV show. (Her voice had shown signs of age, while Eddy's had not.) In 1958 the duo recorded the LP album *Jeanette MacDonald and Nelson Eddy Favorites* for RCA Victor and it proved a good seller, attaining a gold record in 1967. When Louis B. Mayer died in 1957 she sang "Ah, Sweet Mystery of Life" at his funeral.

In her last years Jeanette MacDonald and Gene Raymond lived a quiet, comfortable life in their Bel Air home. They sometimes traveled abroad and later sold their home and moved into a large apartment in Los Angeles. Heart problems plagued Jeanette in her final years and the condition became serious in 1963. She died on July 14, 1965, following open-heart surgery in Houston, Texas. Her husband was at her bedside. At her funeral Nelson Eddy sang "Ah, Sweet Mystery of Life."

In the decades since Jeanette MacDonald starred on screen with and without Nelson Eddy, her movie operettas have been in and out of vogue. To some she became a camp figure, while to others (especially her remarkably devoted fan club) she could do no wrong. Today there is a vast canon of her work available on records and film. These works demonstrate her sharp ability with a comic line, her flair for popularizing highbrow music, and an attractive, vivacious presence which overcame her arch coyness in her later films.

## Filmography

The Love Parade (Par, 1929)*
The Vagabond King (Par, 1930)
Paramount on Parade (Par, 1930)**
Let's Go Native (Par, 1930)
Monte Carlo (Par, 1930)
The Lottery Bride (UA, 1930)
Oh, for a Man (Fox, 1930)
Annabelle's Affairs (Fox, 1931)
Don't Bet on Women (Fox, 1931)
One Hour with You (Par, 1932)*
Love Me Tonight (Par, 1932)*
Hollywood on Parade #7 (Par, 1933) (s)
The Cat and the Fiddle (MGM, 1934)
The Merry Widow (MGM, 1934)*
Naughty Marietta (MGM, 1935)
Rose Marie (MGM, 1936)

San Francisco (MGM, 1936)
The Firefly (MGM, 1937)
Maytime (MGM, 1937)
Girl of the Golden West (MGM, 1938)
Sweethearts (MGM, 1938)
Broadway Serenade (MGM, 1939)
New Moon (MGM, 1940)
Bitter Sweet (MGM, 1940)
Smilin' Through (MGM, 1941)
I Married an Angel (MGM, 1942)
Cairo (MGM, 1942)
Follow the Boys (Univ, 1944)
Three Daring Daughters [The Birds and the Bees] (MGM, 1948)
The Sun Comes Up (MGM, 1949)

*Also starred in the French-language version
**Co-host of Spanish-language version

## Broadway Plays

The Night Boat (1920)
Irene (1921)
Tangerine (1921)
The Magic Ring (1923)
Tip Toes (1925)
Bubbling Over (1926)

Yes, Yes Yvette (1927)
Sunny Days (1928)
Angela (1928)
Boom! Boom! (1929)
The Guardsman (1951) (revival)

## Album Discography

Apple Blossom (Mac/Eddy JN 122) [ST/R] w. Gordon MacRae
Bitter Sweet (Amalgamated 200) [ST/R]
Bitter Sweet (Mac/Eddy JN 117) [ST/R] w. Gordon MacRae
Broadway Serenade (Caliban 6020) [ST]
The Cat and the Fiddle (Caliban 6049) [ST]
Dream Lover (Conifer 133)
The Firefly (Caliban 6027) [ST]
Follow the Boys (Hollywood Soundstage 5012) [ST]
Hollywood Bowl Concert (Mac/Eddy JN 104)
I Married an Angel (Caliban 6004) [ST]
Irene (Mac/Eddy JN 109) [ST/R]
Jeanette MacDonald (Empire 809)

Jeanette MacDonald and Nelson Eddy (Mac/Eddy JN 111)
Jeanette MacDonald and Nelson Eddy (Murray Hill X14078)
Jeanette MacDonald and Nelson Eddy (RCA LPV-526)
Jeanette MacDonald and Nelson Eddy: Christmas Album (Mac/Eddy JN 119)
Jeanette MacDonald and Nelson Eddy: Legendary Performers (RCA CPL1-2468)
Jeanette MacDonald and Nelson Eddy: Patriotic Songs (Mac/Eddy JN 118)
Jeanette MacDonald and Nelson Eddy: Religious Songs (Mac/Eddy JN 127)

Jeanette MacDonald and Nelson Eddy: The Early Years (Mac/Eddy JN 110)

Jeanette MacDonald and Nelson Eddy—Together Again (Sandy Hook 2101)

Jeanette MacDonald and Nelson Eddy Favorites (RCA LPM/LSP-1738, RCA ANL1-1075)

Jeanette MacDonald Favorites (10" RCA LM-73)

Jeanette MacDonald Sings! (Sunbeam 514)

Jeanette MacDonald Sings San Francisco and Other Silver Screen Favorites (RCA International 89059)

Love Me Tonight (Caliban 6047) [ST]

Love Parade/One Hour with You/Love Me Tonight (Ariel CMF 23) [ST]

Maytime (Pelican 121, Sandy Hook 2008) [ST/R]

The Merry Widow (Mac/Eddy JN 120) [ST/R] w. Gordon MacRae

The Merry Widow/The Cat and the Fiddle (Hollywood Soundstage 5015) [ST]

Monte Carlo (Caliban 6037) [ST]

Naughty Marietta (Hollywood Soundstage 413) [ST]

Naughty Marietta (Pelican 117) [ST/R] w. Nelson Eddy

Naughty Marietta (Mac/Eddy JN 115) [ST/R] w. Gordon MacRae

Nelson and the Ladies (Sounds Rare 5002) w. Nelson Eddy

Nelson Eddy and Jeanette MacDonald—America's Singing Sweethearts (RCA/Suffolk Marketing DVM1-0301)

Nelson Eddy on the Air (Totem 1035) w. Nelson Eddy

The Nelson Eddy Show (Mac/Eddy JN 101, JN 102, JN 103, JN 106, JN 107)

New Moon/I Married an Angel (Pelican 103) [ST]

New Moon/Rose Marie (Col Special Products P-13878)

One Hour with You (Caliban 6011) [ST]

Opera and Operetta Favorites (RCA LM-2908)

Operatic Recitals III (Mac/Eddy JN 123) w. Nelson Eddy

Operetta Favorites by Jeanette MacDonald and Nelson Eddy (10" RCA LCT-16)

Romantic Moments (10" RCA LM-62)

Rose Marie (Hollywood Soundstage 414) [ST]

Rose Marie/Naughty Marietta/I Married an Angel/Bitter Sweet (Sandy Hook 3-SH-1) [ST]

Rose Marie/New Moon/Naughty Marietta (Col GB-3)

San Francisco (Caliban 6026) [ST]

San Francisco (Victrola VIC-1515)

Silver Screen Favorites (RCA International 89059)

Smilin' Through (Camden CAL-325)

Smilin' Thru (Mac/Eddy JN 125) [ST/R] w. Brian Aherne

Songs of Faith and Inspiration (Camden CAL-750)

Sweethearts (Pelican 143, Sandy Hook 2025) [ST/R]

Tonight or Never (Mac/Eddy 112) [ST/R] w. Melvyn Douglas, Mary Garden

A Tribute to Jeanette MacDonald (O.A.S.I. 594)

# GORDON MacRAE

POSSESSING AN OUTSTANDING TENOR VOICE, VIRILE GOOD LOOKS, and an easygoing, pleasing personality, Gordon MacRae became one of the more popular of semi-classical singers in the 1950s. He inherited the mantle of King of the Operetta that had once belonged to Nelson Eddy, although he was more active in that entertainment genre on records, radio, and TV than on celluloid. MacRae was a well-rounded entertainer, and was quite successful in all media. However, the heights he might have achieved will never be known due to a long, and for years unknown, battle with alcohol. After finally overcoming his addiction in the mid-1960s, MacRae set out to reestablish his career. He was able to do so, but without attaining the success he had known in the 1940s and 1950s. Like Lillian Roth, MacRae spent his last years as a national spokesman against alcohol abuse, becoming the honorary chairman of the National Council on Alcoholism. Sadly, having overcome one enormous problem, he was struck with cancer of the jaw, which was to kill him eventually. Those close to MacRae have noted that his battle with the disease was just as valiant as had been his earlier conflict.

Gordon MacRae was born on March 12, 1921, in East Orange, New Jersey. He came from a theatrical family; his father, William, was a pioneer radio performer and his mother was a concert pianist. (After his father died, his mother married Philip Osborne and they had a son, Jasper.) Gordon became interested in music at an early age. As a child actor on radio he developed a character called Wee Willie MacRae and later was a juvenile soloist in the touring *The Ray Bolger Revue*. When not performing, MacRae worked as a page at NBC Studios in New York City. At the 1939–40 World's Fair, he won a singing contest which resulted in his performing for two weeks with Harry James and his band. He continued at his NBC job, but in 1940 was hired by orchestra leader Horace Heidt (who had spotted him singing in the NBC lounge) to be a band vocalist. He remained with Heidt for two years, although in 1941 he took a respite to make his stage debut at the Millpond Playhouse in Roslyn (Long Island), New York, followed by a Broadway run as a replacement in the comedy *Junior Miss* (1941).

In the spring of 1942 MacRae was in Hollywood with Heidt's group, and with the orchestra he made his recording debut for Columbia Records, doing the vocals on "Heavenly Highway" and "When Your Lips Met Mine." The previous year (on May 21, 1941) he had married actress Sheila Stevens.

He served in the military during World War II from 1943 to 1945. Returning home from the service, the singer landed his own fifteen-minute radio show each Sunday night on CBS; "The Gordon MacRae Show" lasted one season. In March 1946 he co-starred with Ray Bolger, Arthur Godfrey, and Brenda Forbes in the Broadway musical revue *Three to Make Ready*, which had a 327-performance run; MacRae sang "If It's Love." During this period he also cut a number of records with Walter Gross and His Orchestra for the Musicraft label, including "Prisoner of Love," "They Say It's Wonderful," "Slowly," and "Anybody's Spring." Following his Broadway appearance, the singer returned to network radio during the 1947–48 season with "The Gordon MacRae Show," broadcast by CBS each Monday evening for a half hour.

The year 1948 proved to be a high-water mark in Gordon MacRae's career. He began his six-year association with the popular radio program "The Railroad Hour." He also signed a five-year contract with Warner Bros., which was seeking a successor to Dennis Morgan. Moving to Los Angeles, MacRae hosted "The Railroad Hour" on ABC during the 1948–49 season; the show switched to NBC in 1949 and continued until 1954. Sponsored by American railroads, this popular production presented capsule operettas and dramas hosted by MacRae, who also starred in them with guest stars such as Jane Powell, Betty Garrett, Dorothy Kirsten, Margaret Truman, and Mimi Benzell. He also made guest appearances on other radio series including Perry Como's "The Chesterfield Supper Club," "The Johnson Wax Program," "Navy Star Time," and "Showtime," for which he appeared in "Lady Be Good" with Groucho Marx and "The Red Mill" with Gene Kelly and Lucille Norman.

MacRae, like future screen rival Howard Keel, made his film debut in a dramatic role. In Warner's "B" melodrama THE BIG PUNCH (1948) he was the boxer falsely accused of murder who is aided by a former pugilist (Wayne Morris) turned minister. *Variety* said of MacRae, "He should get along in films, presenting an easy personality and an ability to read lines credibly. He doesn't need vocalizing to sell himself." In 1948 MacRae also signed with Capitol Records, with which he would have a profitable association until well into the 1960s. For Capitol he had a string of moderately good-selling singles plus a host of best-selling record albums that included a range of music. During this period he and his wife had a growing family with children Meredith, Heather, Gordon, and Bruce.

Gordon MacRae's image as the handsome, manly film singer was begun in his second Warner Bros. production, LOOK FOR THE SILVER LINING (1949). This bouncy, colorful biopic of entertainer Marilyn Miller (June Haver—on loan from 20th Century–Fox) gave him occasion to sing several vintage pop songs. Since THE BIG PUNCH had demonstrated that he could easily handle dramatics, he was assigned to BACKFIRE (1950), a taut melodrama with Virginia Mayo, in which he portrayed a man who becomes involved in murder while searching for a missing pal. MacRae's actress wife was also in the cast. He was reteamed with June Haver in another period musical, THE DAUGHTER OF ROSIE O'GRADY (1950), in which he was top restaurateur Tony Pastor. This was followed by an updated remake of *No, No Nanette* called TEA FOR TWO (1950). It was the first of several features he made with the studio's top musical star, Doris Day; their individual wholesomenesses complimented each other. A more rugged role came MacRae's way as a young man falsely accused of murder and jailed by his lawman father (Jack Holt) in the spirited Western RETURN OF THE FRONTIERSMAN (1950). His fifth and final 1950 release was another musical, THE WEST POINT STORY, in which he was a cadet coping with a martinet Broadway director (James Cagney). The latter, in his first dancing role in years, garnered more attention than did co-stars MacRae, Virginia Mayo, or Doris Day.

Following a guest appearance as himself entertaining troops in STARLIFT (1951), MacRae was reunited with Doris Day for ON MOONLIGHT BAY (1951) as a small town lad who falls for the tomboy (Doris Day) next door. Filmed in color and boasting a host of nostalgic period (1915–18) songs, the picture is an adroit piece of Americana. MacRae wanted to do the role of tune composer Gus Kahn in I'LL SEE YOU IN MY DREAMS (1951), but Danny Thomas was given the lead opposite Doris Day. MacRae was a military cadet secretly wed to Phyllis Kirk in ABOUT FACE (1952), a song-and-dance remaking of BROTHER RAT (1938). Because ON MOONLIGHT BAY was so popular, the studio reunited MacRae and Day for a sequel, BY THE LIGHT OF THE SILVERY MOON (1953), with soldier MacRae returning home to face life with bride Day.

This sequel did good box-office business, but MacRae was to make only two more features for the studio, which had become cavalier about its contractee. In THE DESERT SONG (1953) he was the secret leader of the North African "Riffs" who battles a wicked Arab (Steve Cochran) while winning the love of Kathryn Grayson (on loan from MGM). He nicely handled the title song and dueted with Grayson on "One Alone." While this remake of the Sigmund Romberg operetta was pictorially and musically colorful, it was stiff in plot, pleasing 1950s filmgoers little. Ironically, Nelson Eddy, who was MacRae's elder by a decade, would handle the production much better two years later in an NBC-TV special. MacRae's final Warner Bros. feature, THREE SAILORS AND A GIRL (1953), was taken from George S. Kaufman's play *The Butter and Egg Man*. It was about a trio of sailors (MacRae, Gene Nelson, Sam Levene) who use their ship's money to back a musical starring Jane Powell (on loan from MGM), who dueted with MacRae in "Face to Face." The comedy antics of Levene and Jack E. Leonard were the picture's highlights.

Since Warner Bros. and MacRae had lost interest in each other, he negotiated his studio release, which prevented his doing LUCKY ME (1954) with Doris Day. He turned to TV since his radio show (part of a fading medium) also ended in 1954. That year he became the host of NBC-TV's "The Colgate Comedy Hour" and on that program on April 10, 1955, he starred in a production of "Roberta." He hosted the series for one season. More important, in 1955 he achieved his goal of being cast as Curly in the screen version of the Richard Rodgers–Oscar Hammerstein II musical OKLAHOMA! (1955), filmed in an expansive wide-screen process with stereophonic sound. MacRae was the midwestern ranchhand who romanced pretty Laurey (Shirley Jones) but had a rival in nasty Jud (Rod Steiger). MacRae sang "Oh, What a Beautiful Morning" and the title song, and dueted with Jones on "The Surrey with the Fringe on Top" and "People Will Say We're in Love." The screen adaptation was hardly innovative, but it was sufficiently popular to boost MacRae's industry standing. The Capitol soundtrack album remained on the national record charts for more than one hundred weeks.

From March to August 1956 the singer starred in the fifteen-minute NBC-TV series "The Gordon MacRae Show," a live production which took place on a set modeled after the star's own living room. That year, thanks to Frank Sinatra, MacRae had what is perhaps his best-remembered screen part. Sinatra had been hired to star as Billy Bigelow in the musical fantasy CAROUSEL (1956) for 20th Century–Fox. However, he refused to film each scene twice (once for CinemaScope, and then again for normal ratio) and walked off the project. Fox quickly substituted MacRae. He became the swaggering carnival barker who carries out a robbery with unsavory Jigger (Cameron Mitchell) to gain money for his wife (Shirley Jones) and baby. Billy is killed, but fifteen years later he returns from heaven to help his wife and teenaged daughter. MacRae and Jones dueted "If I Loved You" and he performed the famous "Soliloquy," measuring up favorably to John Raitt, who had created the role so indelibly on Broadway. MacRae made CAROUSEL his starring vehicle. Also for 20th Century–Fox, MacRae had his final starring role in a feature film in the entertaining musical THE BEST THINGS IN LIFE ARE FREE (1956), providing a good-natured portrayal of songwriter Buddy DeSylva. During the 1956–57 TV season he hosted the NBC-TV series "Lux Video Theatre" and on the program in 1957 he starred in presentations of "One Sunday Afternoon" and "Eileen." MacRae was to have done *Bells Are Ringing* (1956) on Broadway but could not come to terms, so it was Sydney Chaplin who was cast opposite Judy Holliday in the hit musical.

In the late 1950s, MacRae—who admitted he was "lazy" and worked only to

Gordon MacRae and Shirley Jones in OKLAHOMA! (1955)

support his hobby (gambling)—continued to be active, appearing in top night spots as well as guesting on TV variety shows. (He made an unsold TV pilot called "No Place Like Home.") In 1958 he had a hit single for Capitol with "The Secret." The next year he appeared on several "Voice of Firestone" shows on NBC-TV and late in 1959 he starred in the CBS-TV special "Gift of the Magi." The next year he and wife Sheila (now billed as Sheila MacRae) hosted several segments of CBS-TV's "The Revlon Revue" before embarking on their successful cabaret club act in the early 1960s. By now, MacRae was having personal difficulties due to his long-time drinking problem and in the middle of the decade his marriage ended (just as he began pulling himself together). Following his divorce in April 1967, he wed candy heiress Elizabeth Lambert Schrafft on September 25, 1967, and they later had a daughter, Amanda. He returned to Broadway in 1967, replacing Robert Preston in the hit musical *I Do! I Do!* and in 1968 he was named Star of the Season by the March of Dimes.

During this time MacRae's daughters were also involved in show business, with Meredith MacRae having a hit record ("Image of a Boy") in 1964. In addition, she was a regular on the teleseries "My Three Sons" and "Petticoat Junction" and was featured in the movie NORWOOD (1970). Heather MacRae appeared in such films as EVERYTHING YOU ALWAYS WANTED TO KNOW ABOUT SEX BUT WERE AFRAID TO ASK (1972) and BANG THE DRUM SLOWLY (1973).

In the late 1960s MacRae resumed his club appearances with great success. When he appeared in the St. Regis Hotel's Maisonette Room in New York, Gotham columnist Earl Wilson commented on his "good, rich voice" while Dennis Sheahan (*Women's Wear Daily*) observed, "He is an untiring entertainer who is completely at ease with the audience. He laughs, tells jokes, mingles with guests and he is not beyond poking a little fun at himself." He continued to appear in clubs throughout the country, with long stands in Las Vegas and New York City, and when he appeared at the latter's Plaza Hotel in 1970, *Variety* noted, "With consummate authority spawned in the niteries, legit and major filmusicals, MacRae has the Persian Room customers with him from the start." In the fall of 1974 MacRae resumed his dramatic efforts with a guest appearance on "McCloud" (NBC-TV) and in 1979 he returned to films in the co-starring role of North American Airlines executive Mike Barnes in THE PILOT, whose alcoholic title character was played by Cliff Robertson; Robertson also directed the feature, which received little theatrical release.

Into the 1980s Gordon MacRae continued to be active in clubs and in various stage productions as he settled with his family in Lincoln, Nebraska. In 1982 he suffered a crippling stroke. Following a long and painful battle with cancer of the jaw, he died in Lincoln on January 24, 1986, at the age of sixty-four.

## Filmography

The Big Punch (WB, 1948)
Look for the Silver Lining (WB, 1949)
Backfire (WB, 1950)
The Daughter of Rosie O'Grady (WB, 1950)
Tea for Two (WB, 1950)
Return of the Frontiersman (WB, 1950)
The West Point Story [Fine and Dandy] (WB, 1950)
The Screen Director (Vita, 1951) (s)
Starlift (WB, 1951)
On Moonlight Bay (WB, 1951)
About Face (WB, 1952)

Screen Snapshots #205 (Col, 1952) (s)
By the Light of the Silvery Moon (WB, 1953)
So You Want a Television Set (Vita, 1953) (s)
The Desert Song (WB, 1953)
Three Sailors and a Girl (WB, 1953)
Oklahoma! (Magna, 1955)
The Last Command (Rep, 1955) (voice only)
Carousel (20th–Fox, 1956)
The Best Things in Life Are Free (20th–Fox, 1956)
The Pilot (New Line International, 1979)

## Broadway Plays

Junior Miss (1941) (replacement)
Three to Make Ready (1946)

I Do! I Do! (1967) (replacement)

## Radio Series

The Gordon MacRae Show (CBS, 1945–46)
Skyline Roof (CBS, 1946)
Teentimers Club (NBC, 1947)

The Gordon MacRae Show [Texaco Star Theatre] (CBS, 1947–48)
The Railroad Hour (ABC, 1948–49; NBC, 1949–54)

## TV Series

The Colgate Comedy Hour (NBC, 1954–55)
The Gordon MacRae Show (NBC, 1956)

Lux Video Theatre (NBC, 1956–57)

## Album Discography

Apple Blossom (Mac/Eddy JN 122) [ST/R] w. Jeanette MacDonald
The Best Things in Life Are Free (Cap T-765) [ST]
Bitter Sweet (Mac/Eddy JN 117) [ST/R] w. Jeanette MacDonald
By the Light of the Silvery Moon (10" Cap H-422, Caliban 6019) [ST]
Carousel (Cap W/SW-694) [ST]
Christmas at Boys' Town (Sandcastle SCR-1043) w. The Boys' Town Choir

Cowboy's Lament (Cap T-834, Stetson HAT-3054)
The Desert Song (10" Cap L-351, Cap W/SW-1842, Angel S-37319) w. Dorothy Kirsten, Lucille Norman
The Desert Song (Titania 505) [ST]
The Desert Song/Roberta (Cap T-384)
Gordon MacRae (Galaxy 4805, Rono-lette A5)
Gordon MacRae (10" Royale 18106)
Gordon MacRae and Orchestra (Royale 18155)
Gordon MacRae in Concert (Cap T/ST-980)

Gordon MacRae Sings (10" Cap H-231)

Gordon MacRae Sings (Evon 320)

Gordon MacRae Sings Broadway's Best (Sutton SSU-292)

Gordon MacRae Sings Songs for Lovers (Ember 2007)

Gordon MacRae Sings with Walter Gross' Orchestra (Allegro/Royale 1606)

Hallowed Be Thy Name (Cap T/ST-1466)

Highlights from the World's Greatest Operettas (Cap T-1510)

If She Walked into My Life (Cap T/ST-2578)

Kismet (Cap W/SW-2022, Angel S-37321) w. Dorothy Kirsten

Kiss Me, Kate! (10" Cap H-157) w. Jo Stafford

The Last Command (Citadel CT 7019) [ST]

Look for the Silver Lining (Titania 504) [ST]

Memory Songs (Cap T-428) w. Jo Stafford

The Merry Widow (10" Cap L-335) w. Lucille Norman

The Merry Widow (Mac/Eddy JN 120) [ST/R] w. Jeanette MacDonald

Motion Picture Soundstage (Cap T-875, EMI/ Cap 1183)

Naughty Marietta (10" Cap L-468) w. Marguerite Piazza

Naughty Marietta (Mac/Eddy JN 115) [ST/R] w. Jeanette MacDonald

Naughty Marietta/The Red Mill (Cap T-551)

New Moon (10" Cap H-217) w. Lucille Norman

New Moon (Cap W/SW-1966, Angel S-37320) w. Dorothy Kirsten

Oklahoma! (Cap W/SW-595) [ST]

The Old Rugged Cross (EMI 5798) w. Jo Stafford

On Moonlight Bay (Caliban 6006, Titania 501) [ST]

Only Love (Cap ST-125)

Operetta Favorites (Cap T-681)

Our Love Story (Cap T/ST-1353) w. Sheila MacRae

Prisoner of Love (10" MGM E-104)

The Red Mill (10" Cap L-530) w. Lucille Norman

Roberta (10" Cap L-334) w. Lucille Norman

Romantic Ballads (Cap T-537)

Seasons of Love (Cap T/ST-1146)

Songs for an Evening at Home (Cap T/ST-1251)

South Pacific (10" Cap H-163) w. Margaret Whiting, Peggy Lee

Spotlight on Gordon MacRae (Tiara 7250/520) w. Johnny King

Starlift (Titania 510) [ST]

The Student Prince (10" Cap H-407) w. Dorothy Warenskjold

The Student Prince (Cap W/SW-1841, Angel S-37318) w. Dorothy Kirsten

The Student Prince/The Merry Widow (Cap T-437)

Sunday Evening Songs (10" Cap H-247) w. Jo Stafford

Tea for Two (Caliban 6031) [ST}

There's Peace in the Valley (Cap T/ST-1916) w. Jo Stafford

This Is Gordon MacRae (Cap T-1050)

Three Sailors and a Girl (10" Cap L-485) [ST]

The Vagabond King (10" Cap H-218)

The Vagabond King/New Moon (Cap T-219)

The West Point Story (Titania 501) [ST]

Whispering Hope (Cap T/ST-1696) w. Jo Stafford

Young Man from Boston (No label—MXWR-4546) [ST/TV] w. The Kingston Trio

# MADONNA

THE TOP MEGA-POP STAR TO EMERGE IN THE LATTER 1980s WAS Madonna. As the gum-chewing sex kitten of the rock world, she has produced a slew of recording hits that range, to date, from "Like a Virgin" (1984) to "Like a Prayer" (1989). The determined, 5' 4½" blonde, strutting wantonly on the concert stage, has become an icon of rebellion for her young fans. Her choreographed cavorting has made her the distaff counterpart to Michael Jackson and Prince. In performance she may typically wear black toreador pants, black T-shirt, and black leather jacket. Or her tacky outfit may be a more outrageous variation of a corset ensemble complete with rough boots.

Whether being raunchy or borderline tasteful, Madonna is famous for creating her own high energy. In performance she has learned to blast forth the aggressive lyrics of a controversial song with ease, always intent on being a wild show woman. The public Madonna has delighted in creating a new-generation blonde bombshell image, a pleased successor to past sexpots such as Jean Harlow, Kim Novak, and Marilyn Monroe (her favorite).

As a sign that she is a super attraction, Madonna is a constant headline-creator. Her courtship, marriage, spats, and divorce from actor Sean Penn were constant newsmaking events, as was her later romance with producer/director/actor Warren Beatty. When she starred on Broadway in 1988 in a new work by playwright David Mamet, the critics and her public gave the event dramatic coverage. Her multi-million-dollar spokesperson contract with Pepsi-Cola that same year was the cause of extensive speculation in a variety of diverse arenas: stock market circles, the show business industry, and the tabloids. These events were equalled only by the airing of her controversial "Like a Prayer" video on television in 1989—tied into her Pepsi ad campaign. That sensationalized event and the huge aftermath of controversy over its appropriateness were major newsmakers. Madonna had become the latest Queen of the Media.

Like Elvis Presley thirty years before her, the irrepressible and outlandish Madonna delights her youthful audiences and irks the older generation. The latter do not relate well to her loud, rhythmic messages of independence, assertiveness, and nonestablishment behavior. Also like Presley, Madonna has expanded her activities beyond concertizing and recording. She made a vivid impression in her starring debut in a feature film, DESPERATELY SEEKING SUSAN (1985), displaying a freshness of personality and sensitivity that captivated even the more mainstream viewers. Since then, as one industry wit put it, she has been an actress "desperately seeking a role."

In the United States, where fortune is a key indicator of fame and happiness, *Forbes* magazine in early 1989 listed the five female entertainers who had grossed the largest (estimated) incomes over the previous two years. They were—in order—Madonna, Oprah Winfrey, Whitney Houston, Tina Turner, and Jane Fonda. Madonna headed the list with $46 million for the 1987–88 period.

She was born Madonna Louise Veronica Ciccone on August 16, 1958, in Bay City, Michigan, to Sylvio (Tony) Ciccone and Madonna Ciccone. She was the third child of three girls (she was the eldest) and three boys. Her father, a first-generation Italian-American, was a design engineer for Chrysler/General Motors. Madonna recalls, "I was always precocious as a child. I was just one of those little girls who crawled on everybody's lap. I flirted with everyone. . . . I was aware of my female charm." When Madonna was six, her mother died of breast cancer. Mr. Ciccone moved with his children to Pontiac, Michigan. Some three years later he remarried, to the family's housekeeper. Madonna rebelled at the change in the household. "From that time on I felt like Cinderella with a wicked stepmother. I couldn't wait to escape."

As a youngster with a devout Catholic father, Madonna had decided she would like to become a nun. "I just thought they were so superior." Later, she became "incredibly disenchanted." Looking back on her childhood, she has reflected, "I had a very middle–lower-middle-class sort of upbringing, but I identify with people who have had, at some point in their lives, to struggle to survive. It adds another color to your character." As for her persuasive manner, she says, "From the time that I was very young I just knew that being a girl and being charming in a feminine sort of way could get me a lot of things, and I milked it for everything I could."

In junior high school, Madonna found escape by participating in class plays, but her delight was dance, which became her addiction throughout her teenage years. When she was in the eighth grade, she made a home movie (which she would use years later in her "Like a Prayer" video). In 1972, when she was fourteen, she met Christopher Flynn—some twenty years her senior—who became her dance instructor, mentor, and best friend. He took the adolescent Madonna to Detroit's racy downtown discos, where she developed her skill as an exhibitionist on the dance floor. Despite these distractions, Madonna excelled in academics at Adams High School in Rochester, Michigan, and graduated early, in January 1976. She won a dance scholarship to the University of Michigan, and Flynn joined her there by becoming a dance instructor. After more than a year of college, during which she studied jazz dancing, Madonna dropped out. She had decided, with Flynn's encouragement, to go to New York to make a career for herself in dance.

She arrived in New York in the summer of 1978 with very little money and no clothing besides what she was wearing. She lived in a rundown tenement in the East Village. She worked in a Times Square donut shop for a time, did figure modeling, and in 1979 she made her first movie. The underground opus was called A CERTAIN SACRIFICE, and was created by director/cinematographer Stephen Jon Lewicki and co-producer/co-writer/star Jeremy Pattnosh. The sixty-minute color foray was a crude expedition into soft-core pornography. It featured a few scenes of Madonna topless, and in it the future star participated in a mild "orgy," while being pursued and molested by a young dropout

(Pattnosh) in New York City. The movie would resurface as a video and midnight film in the mid-1980s after Madonna had become a celebrity. When the much-discussed (thought lost) film was shown finally, it was regarded by most as a "so what" item.

In New York, Madonna auditioned for the Alvin Ailey American Dance Theater and won a position with the group's third company. "Everybody was Hispanic or black, and everyone wanted to be a star," she would recall. She left the Ailey company after a few months and began taking dance classes with Pearl Lang, formerly a Martha Graham choreographer. It was not a happy teacher-student relationship. When Madonna met rock musician Dan Gilroy (with whom she had a romance), she became interested in rock 'n' roll music and he taught her to play the guitar, keyboard, and drums. After auditioning for French disco singer Patrick Hernandez, Madonna left for Paris, where she was to be part of his concert show. She did backup singing for him in a few recording sessions. However, her overly independent nature irked Hernandez and his associates, and she was soon jobless.

Back in New York, she became the vocalist/drummer for the rock group Breakfast Club, fronted by Dan Gilroy and his brother. She composed some of their songs while living with the group in an abandoned synagogue in Queens. When that relationship dissolved (she wanted to be their lead singer), she returned to Manhattan and formed her own group with Steve Bray, a songwriter/drummer she had known in her brief college days. Together they started the group known as the Millionaires (a.k.a. Modern Dance, Emmy), with their New Wave rock music heavily influenced by such rock leaders as The Police and the Pretenders. Meanwhile, intent on promoting her solo career, she became a habitue of such trendy rock discos as the Roxy and Danceteria, where she developed a strong liking for rap-dance music rather than the Heavy Metal rock her group preferred. From her notice-causing disco forays, Madonna became friendly with Danceteria deejay Mark Kamins. She provided him with a copy of a demo tape she had made, and her song "Everybody" quickly became a favorite with the disco customers. It was Mark Kamins who introduced Madonna to executives at Sire Records, who signed her to a contract. The label's president, Seymour Stein, would remember his first meeting with the exuberant Madonna: "It hit me right away. I could tell she had the drive to match her talent." It was at this time that Madonna ended her business relationship with her manager, Camille Barbone.

Her first album, *Madonna*, was released in mid-1983, and it took a while for the potpourri of pop disco tunes to catch on. But thanks to her increasingly popular appearances at the Manhattan disco clubs, plus exposure over the airwaves, two selections ("Borderline" and "Lucky Star") from the LP reached the top ten on the charts; "Holiday" topped at number sixteen. The video to "Lucky Star" played on cable television's MTV, which helped to establish Madonna's national image as the pouting, strutting sex kitten whose outfit boasted a provocative bare midriff. (Music videos would play a tremendous role in boosting Madonna's career.) It was her "Like a Virgin" single, with its racy connotations, that made Madonna an acclaimed figure. Released as part of the same-titled album, the song rose to number one in late 1984 and its album, which remained on the charts for fifty-one weeks, also moved into top position. Other cuts ("Material Girl," "Angel," "Dress You Up") from the album scored big and made her an international attraction.

Produced by Jon Peters and Peter Guber and directed by Harold Becker, VISION QUEST (1985) was a ROCKY–like story of a Spokane, Washington, high school wrestler (Matthew Modine) who wants to win the state championship and the love of a twenty-year-old drifter (Linda Fiorentino). It featured a sequence in which the two lead performers dance together at a club. For that scene, Madonna was hired to sing on camera the song "Crazy for You." When released, the picture was considered to have a derivative plot but nicely executed characterizations. More important, the song "Crazy for You" rose to number one on the charts in May 1985, displacing "We Are the World," sung by an all-star charity ensemble. With her offbeat costumes, her unbridled enthusiasm, and her wild dancing, Madonna had become a national craze. Her expressions like "boy toy" (referring to males) became part of her fans' idiom. Her posture as the New Wave 1980s golddigger, bent on outmaneuvering the opposite sex, caused an outcry from feminists worldwide. As had become customary, everything that Madonna, the queen of bimbo rock, did or said or wore caused controversy.

To the surprise of many, Madonna gained critical respect for her first starring role in a feature film. According to the movie's co-producer, Sarah Pillsbury, one of the compelling reasons Madonna was hired for the project was because she represented "a punk Mae West." Said the filmmaker, Madonna was "a total fantasy for both men and women." Made on a $5 million budget by Susan Seidelman, DESPERATELY SEEKING SUSAN (1985) was a wacky screwball comedy told from a woman's point of view. The picture was set in New York City where two disparate types—a bored housewife (Rosanna Arquette) and a trampy, punk drifter (Madonna)—find their lives intertwining in a case of escalating mistaken identities that involves a mobster's murder, a leather jacket (the trademark of Madonna's character), and Arquette's temporary amnesia. *Variety* noted that Madonna "turns in a rounded, interesting performance." The picture grossed $10,937,200 in domestic film rentals and established not only that Madonna possessed a unique screen charisma, but also that she could act. Her single "Into the Groove" was from this picture.

In 1985, Madonna embarked on her cross-country *Like a Virgin* concert tour, an event which gained tremendous momentum as it went with its several truckloads of equipment, scenery, and costumes. Media observers noted quickly that many of the young girls in Madonna's audience (known as "Madonna wanna-be's") came to the concerts dressed like Madonna, complete with scanty outfits, heavily moussed hair, and lots of makeup. When sporting her mod bridal outfit for her "Like a Virgin" number, Madonna was the Queen to her screaming fans.

Madonna had first met actor Sean Penn (the bad boy thespian of the Brat Pack age) on the set while filming her "Material Girl" video. Their first public date was at the New York club Private Eyes in February 1985. They became a much-tracked media couple, and in July 1985, Madonna, rumored to be pregnant, wore black to her bridal shower. On August 16, 1985, Madonna and combative Sean Penn were married on a Malibu,

California, cliff where the eager press buzzed the ceremony in a fleet of helicopters. The couple honeymooned up the coast in Carmel. That September, both *Penthouse* and *Playboy* published artistic nude photo layouts of Madonna taken in 1979, neither of which met with the approval of hot-tempered Penn. That November, while hosting "Saturday Night Live," Madonna insisted again that she was not pregnant.

In 1986, her third album, *True Blue*, became an international success. It was dedicated to Sean Penn, "the coolest guy in the universe." One of the LP's most controversial cuts was "Papa Don't Preach," about a pregnant teenager who intends optimistically to keep her baby. Another cut was "Live to Tell," co-authored by Madonna and Patrick Leonard (who was music director on her *Like a Virgin* tour). It was drawn from the heavy movie drama AT CLOSE RANGE (1986), starring Christopher Walken, Sean Penn, and the latter's brother, Christopher. In the course of the feature film, Madonna was heard singing "Live to Tell," which, like "Papa Don't Preach," rose to number one on the charts. Yet another single from *True Blue*, "Open Your Heart," became a number one tune. It had been conceived originally for Madonna's closest songstress rival, Cyndi Lauper.

Madonna returned to filmmaking with husband Sean Penn in MGM's SHANGHAI SURPRISE (1986), in which she portrayed a quiet Massachusetts missionary in 1937 China. Penn was cast as a sleazy American salesman. In the slight story, both were looking for a missing opium shipment. The media backlash to hot-tempered Penn and Madonna did not help the film when it opened. The expensively mounted feature, with songs by (and sung by) ex-Beatle George Harrison, fizzled. Audiences would not accept the sexy Madonna as a missionary.

In early 1986, Madonna and Penn had purchased an $850,000 Manhattan apartment and, later in the year, between much-publicized public altercations and reconciliations, they appeared at New York's Lincoln Center in a workshop production of David Rabe's play *Goose and Tomtom*. They received the most attention when, walking home one night after a performance, Sean got into a fight with a roving photographer.

Madonna had been scheduled to star in BLIND DATE (1987). However, when Blake Edwards joined the lineup as director and Bruce Willis signed on as co-star, she dropped out. Instead, she appeared in a rather crude neo-screwball comedy, WHO'S THAT GIRL (1987). She was the New York City bimbo who, released after four years in jail, is bent on finding out who framed her for her boyfriend's murder. She is joined on her merry chase by a stuffy yuppie lawyer (Griffin Dunne). He falls in love with the free-spirited waif and, eventually, becomes liberated from his conservatism. Like SHANGHAI SURPRISE, WHO'S THAT GIRL failed to draw Madonna's fans to movie theaters. It was roasted by establishment critics and did badly at the box office. However, the title song (co-written and co-produced by Madonna and Patrick Leonard) rose to number one on the charts in August 1987. Despite her poor track record, moviemakers were still interested in Madonna. Diane Keaton wanted her to star in a remake of THE BLUE ANGEL, which did not materialize.

Meanwhile, Madonna continued to be enormously successful in her recordings and music videos. As such, she embarked on her *Who's That Girl* worldwide concert tour. Her trademark funky dancing was choreographed by Jeffrey Hornaday (of FLASHDANCE fame) and her shows were extravaganzas of mixed media: multiple videos, flashing lights, high-tech accoutrements, and precision dancing. And, of course, Madonna sang her hits in a variety of costumes that highlighted her fame as a punk sex goddess. The *Chicago Tribune* reported when she played Soldier's Field in July 1987: "there are few performers who would be able to carry off many (or any) of Madonna's campy turns with her graceful elan which is, we marvel, a strange combination of self-effacement and grand ego." Madonna's tour took her to Japan (where her popularity outshone that of Bruce Springsteen and Michael Jackson) and to England. In the latter country, her four British dates were estimated to have netted her about $6.4 million.

In June 1987, Sean Penn was sentenced to jail for sixty days for violating his probation. His latest offenses included beating up a movie extra and reckless driving. In mid-September 1987 he was released from jail on a reduced sentence, but by that November the couple (Madonna in particular) were planning to divorce. By December, they had reconciled—temporarily.

When production of Pulitzer Prize–winning playwright David Mamet's play *Speed-the-Plow* was first announced, it was to be off-Broadway. But when Madonna was set to co-star and interest escalated, the vehicle was rescheduled for an on-Broadway showing, and it opened on May 3, 1988, at the Royale Theatre. It was a satirical study of contemporary Hollywood with Madonna cast as a temporary, supposedly naive studio secretary, who becomes the object of lust for sycophant Ron Silver and his boss, Joe

Madonna, John Mills, and Griffin Dunne in WHO'S THAT GIRL (1987)

Mantegna. The play quickly generated a hotly contested debate, not over how good the work was, but over whether or not Madonna could act. Most encouraging was the *New York Times*, which decided, "She delivers the shocking transitions essential to the action and needs only more confidence to relax a bit and fully command her speaking voice." In the dissent were such sources as the *New York Daily News*, which observed, "What's interesting about Madonna is that she misses the musicality of Mamet's writing." The play had amassed a near $1 million advance sale, but did not last a year. Sean Penn, who had not attended her play's opening (he was in Thailand shooting a war film), and Madonna continued their domestic battles, which transferred to the West Coast. In November 1988, Penn was on stage in Los Angeles in *Hurlyburly*. In a turnabout, Madonna showed up for his opening late, accompanied by frequent companion Sandra Bernhard. In this period, Madonna also had a new videocassette in distribution. Of *Ciao: Italia: Live from Italy*, *People* magazine observed, "Madonna shows plenty of warmth—heat, actually—but unhappily slobbers it all over a teen-age dancer in this concert tape."

In January 1989, Madonna filed for divorce from Penn and days later dropped an assault charge against her spouse (he had allegedly bound and beaten her on December 28, 1988). No sooner had the headlines quieted down than Madonna instigated another media frenzy. She had signed a $5 million contract with Pepsi-Cola to star in several commercials for them, which would be tied-in to her new album, *Like a Prayer* (1989), and its title single, for which she made a highly stylized music video. In mid-March 1989, the song debuted on national television (and satellite TV throughout the globe and on MTV the next day) and caused a huge furor among conservative elements who felt the video mocked the Catholic Church. The American Family Association asked the soft drink company to cancel its contract with Madonna, claiming that Madonna was not a proper role model for youth. Quietly the ad was dropped from circulation. However, the album (probably the first to be introduced in a TV commercial) became a number one hit as a hot-selling LP. One of the singles, "Love Song," featured her in duet with Prince. Another single (also made into a music video) from the album was "Express Yourself," which rose high on the charts. In May 1989, the album and single won multi-awards from the Record Industry Association of America for its high sales.

It had been touted that Madonna was to play a concentration camp internee in the film TRIUMPH OF THE SPIRIT, just as earlier she had been one of the contenders to play Eva Peron in the screen version of the musical *Evita*. But Madonna, who had signed a pact with Columbia Pictures (which had right of first refusal on her projects), instead chose to be Breathless Mahoney in Warren Beatty's long-planned feature film DICK TRACY (1990). The $30 million production began filming in February 1989. By then, Madonna, who was scheduled to sing two songs in the picture, had become Beatty's latest liaison. While working on that movie, she prepared her new album, and filmed a video for one of the cuts, "Express Yourself," written by Madonna and Stephen Bray.

In late May 1989, BLOODHOUNDS OF BROADWAY, originally filmed in 1988 for the "American Playhouse" series on PBS and long sitting on the shelf, was screened at the Seattle Film Festival. The movie was based on classic Damon Runyon stories and featured

Madonna, Matt Dillon, Esai Morales, Jennifer Grey, and Rutger Hauer. The episodic film was set on New Year's Eve on Broadway in 1928. Madonna was cast as Hortense Hathaway, the comely showgirl eager for the limelight and for financial security. *Variety* thought she "adeptly played" her role but judged the production a "fluffy little piece" whose commercial prospects "appear dim."

In her rise to fame, Madonna, who seems to have become a bit of everything for everyone, has emerged as the standard bearer for the new wave of mixed music and thought. In response to those who rate her as materialistic, she counters, "There's a difference between being born into money and making money. I've made my money. I'm from a poor background and basically I'm still a working-class girl. I've been known to wash a dish or two, make a bed or two." As for her sex-bent image, she explains, "How can you criticize a woman for having a sexuality when men for years and years have been singing about nothing else? . . . Women have a sexuality that shouldn't be suppressed."

## Filmography

A Certain Sacrifice (Virgin Video, 1979)
Vision Quest (WB, 1985)
Desperately Seeking Susan (Orion, 1985)
At Close Range (Orion, 1986) (voice and co-songs only)

Shanghai Surprise (MGM, 1986)
Who's That Girl (WB, 1987) (also co-songs)
Bloodhounds of Broadway (Col, 1989)
Dick Tracy (BV, 1990)

## Broadway Plays

Speed-the-Plow (1988)

## Album Discography

Like a Prayer (Sire 1-25844)
Like a Virgin (Sire 1-25157)
Madonna (Sire 1-23867)
True Blue (Sire 1-25442)

Vision Quest (Geffen 240063) [ST]
Who's That Girl (Sire 1-25611) [ST]
You Can Dance (Sire 1-25535)

# DEAN MARTIN

BEING THE STRAIGHT MAN/STOOGE TO A PROFESSIONAL PRANK-
ster is never easy, even under the best of circumstances. Sooner or later it is bound to be
ego shattering for the quieter teammate. Moreover, a career can be hampered for years
after such a successful partnership breaks up.

During Dean Martin's working relationship (1946–56) with Jerry Lewis, the lion's
share of attention always went to funny man Lewis. Sleepy-eyed, congenial Martin was
generally dismissed as the better looking of the duo who sang and handled on-camera
romancing with the team's leading ladies. Martin could indeed sing very pleasantly (in the
Perry Como crooner tradition) and he had several singles in the top forty, including his
signature tune, "Everybody Loves Somebody." As a solo performer, he astounded Hollywood continuously with his "hidden" range of talent. He performed in screen drama with
surprising agility. He starred in his own very successful series of James Bond–like movie
spy spoofs (the Matt Helm series). In clubs and on television he was a bon vivant who sang
effortlessly, kidded with his co-workers and the audience, and traded heavily on his image
as the world's greatest lush ("ole red eyes"). However, despite his years of tremendous
success as a single act, most people still think of him in tandem with frantic Jerry Lewis.
Decades after their well-publicized breakup, he remains the ex-partner of the crazy one.

He was born Dino Paul Crocetti in Steubenville, Ohio, on June 17, 1917, son of
immigrant barber Guy Crocetti and his wife, Angela. There was an older boy named Bill
who would be Dean's business manager until Bill's death in 1963. Dino attended Grant
Junior High School and completed the ninth (or tenth) grade of Wells High School. At
that point the sixteen-year-old Dino dropped out of the educational system. "I had a
bicycle and I never missed a meal. But I was just too smart for those teachers in school."
His father gave him $5 to attend barber school, but that did not hold his interest. He tried
a succession of jobs, including drugstore clerk, gas jockey, milkman, coal miner, steel
puddler, and wire bundler. For a time he was a boxer. As Kid Crochet, he was a
welterweight and had three knockouts to his credit. However, when he was floored in a
match, he quit the ring.

Meanwhile, Steubenville was not known as "Little Chicago" for nothing. There
were many distractions in town for the young man including the Rex Smoke Shop, which
was a front for one of the town's more popular gambling centers. He was soon working in
the back room as a chips-and-dice man, earning up to $8 per day plus tips and his
occasional pilfering. ("During the course of a day, I could steal maybe as many as five silver
dollars.")

Besides his gaming activities at the Shop, Dino liked to sing and occasionally entertained his friends there with a song. Bandleader Ernie McKay heard him and offered the young man a job with his group at $50 weekly. Since he was earning $125 a week as a croupier, blackjack dealer, etc., he initially refused. He continued working at the Rex Smoke Shop, with his employers sometimes loaning him out to other gambling establishments in Ohio, Florida, West Virginia, and Washington, D.C. Finally, encouraged by his employers, he accepted the job with McKay and became the band's lead singer.

By the late 1930s Dino Crocetti had changed his name to Dino Martini. However, when people told him he would be confused with the Italian-American singer (and occasional film actor) Nino Martini, he became Dino Martin and then Dean Martin. He was now singing with the Sammy Watkins Band, a group based in Cleveland. In that city on October 2, 1940, at St. Anne's Church, he married Elizabeth MacDonald. (They would have four children: Craig, born in 1942; Claudia, 1944; Gail, 1945; and Deana, 1948.) Hoping to improve his image as a 1940s crooner, Martin had his oversized nose reshaped by plastic surgery. He worked with a succession of bands and then as a single act in clubs where he earned $300 weekly. By 1943 he was performing at the Riobamba Club in New York City at $750 a week, but had yet to make a distinctive impression with the public.

In 1945 Martin came to the attention of MGM, which was considering him for a role in a forthcoming movie musical (TILL THE CLOUDS ROLL BY, 1946). After he was screentested, studio executives wired Martin's agent, "We already have Tony Martin under contract. Why do we want another Italian singer?" (Actually, Tony Martin is Jewish.) It was at about this time that Dean was living with his family at Manhattan's Belmont Plaza Hotel and performing at the Glass Hat Club. Also staying at the hotel and performing at the Glass Hat was nineteen-year-old Jerry Lewis. It became a habit for "big brother" Martin to help out the younger Jerry when audiences grew restless with the latter's fledgling comedy act, while Lewis developed a knack for interrupting Martin's on-stage singing sessions with improvised mayhem. After their "joint" appearance at the Glass Hat, each performer went his separate way, but they stayed in touch. Meanwhile, Martin was recording for Diamond Records.

It was during the week of July 21, 1946, that Martin and Lewis officially became a joint act. Lewis was doing his lip-synching record routine at the Club 500 in Atlantic City and faring badly. He phoned Martin's agent (since his own agent was persona non grata at the club) for advice. (Lewis later insisted he had phoned Martin to tell him of an opening on the club's bill.) In any event, Martin came to Atlantic City and on July 25, 1946, began performing in tandem with Jerry. Soon the impromptu mayhem developed into inspired pandemonium as Lewis would interrupt Martin's singing with braying and screaming. Martin would chase Lewis through and around the audience, and customers would frequently be soaked by streams of seltzer or drinks tossed into their faces. So successful was their improvised routine that the Club 500 held them over for six weeks at $750 weekly.

After months of touring the country's cabaret circuit with increasing success, the duo appeared at New York's Copacabana Club in April 1948 as a backup act to singer/movie actress Vivian Blaine. The team was so popular that Blaine quickly disappeared from the bill and the wacky twosome remained at the Copa for eighteen weeks. Meanwhile, the team appeared at the Roxy Theatre for three weeks of personal appearances, and were now earning a total of $15,000 weekly. When the pair played Slapsie Maxie's Club in Hollywood in the summer of 1948, the engagement proved to be an audition for the film studios, which were already eager to sign this sensational comedy team—the new successors to slapstick kings Bud Abbott and Lou Costello. Producer Hal B. Wallis, operating at Paramount Pictures, signed the team to a five-year, seven-picture contract. The terms called for them to be paid $50,000 per picture (later raised to $75,000 per movie), with the stars producing their own pictures through their York Productions.

Hedging his bets, Wallis first introduced Martin and Lewis to filmgoers in MY FRIEND IRMA (1949), a black-and-white screen translation of a popular radio series and starring that program's wacky blonde star, Marie Wilson. But for critics and moviegoers alike, it was Martin and Lewis who were the film's hits. The comedy established the format that would hold sway throughout their seventeen features together. Lewis would do his juvenile antics, Martin would sing (here: "Just for Fun," "My Own, My Only, My All," and "Here's to Love"), and together they would create mayhem. Said *Variety*, "Martin is a handsome straight man singer. . . . His voice is pleasant and easy, but his nightclub posturing needs toning down for films."

On April 3, 1949, Martin and Lewis debuted in a weekly radio series on NBC, a variety hour that would last through 1953. The next year they were guests on Milton Berle's NBC-TV comedy program and were such audience pleasers that later that year they joined with Abbott and Costello, Eddie Cantor, and Donald O'Connor as rotating hosts (each once monthly) of "The Colgate Comedy Hour" (NBC-TV). For their television appearances Martin and Lewis were initially paid $25,000 per show; because of their popularity, their salary quickly escalated to $75,000 per program. They would remain with the "Comedy Hour" through 1955. In addition, they continued to star on the nightclub circuit to hefty audience response. Meanwhile, Martin, who was in and out of financial difficulty (he had to declare bankruptcy in January 1949), had met Florida beauty queen Jeanne Beiggers. He divorced Elizabeth in August 1949, and on September 1, in Beverly Hills, he married the second Mrs. Martin. Jerry Lewis was his best man. (The new Mr. and Mrs. Martin would parent Dean "Dino" Jr., born in 1951; Ricci, 1953; and Gina, 1956.)

The extremely profitable Martin and Lewis features ran the gamut of Hollywood genres. They were entangled in the military service in AT WAR WITH THE ARMY (1951), SAILOR BEWARE (1951), and JUMPING JACKS (1952). They were involved in show business in THE STOOGE (1952), toyed with the golfing game in THE CADDY (1953—in which Martin sang his hit song "That's Amore"), teased the haunted house genre in SCARED STIFF (1953), went wild under the big top in THREE RING CIRCUS (1954), created lunacy at a Damon Runyonesque racetrack in MONEY FROM HOME (1954—filmed in 3-D), were the worst in the West in PARDNERS (1956), and tore up tinseltown in HOLLYWOOD OR BUST

(1956). By the time of the latter picture, it was no secret to the public that the mutual admiration society between suave Martin and spastic goofball Lewis had run its course. When Martin learned that for their next joint offering, THE DELICATE DELINQUENT (1957), he was to be the friendly local policeman—another stooge—he refused the assignment (which went to Darren McGavin). In short order, he ended their joint moviemaking, which had been netting the team $4 million annually. "I hated being a dumb stooge," Martin explained. "I was happier making $100 a week." The two performers fulfilled a contract at the Copacabana Club in New York, giving their final show on July 25, 1956, ten years to the day of their first professional teaming.

When Martin and Lewis broke up, the industry concluded that Martin was washed up in the business, reasoning that Lewis had been carrying him. After Martin's first disastrous solo picture—MGM's flat romantic comedy TEN THOUSAND BEDROOMS (1957)—the dire predictions seemed to be proved true. Martin took a job in a Pittsburgh nightclub, and after that engagement, he sat in his hotel room with his wife and said, "This is it, baby. I've got nothing else lined up now." The next day he received a call from his agent that he had a role for him (as the result of a talent agency package deal) in 20th Century–Fox's THE YOUNG LIONS (1958). It was the third lead, as a draft dodger, in a

Dean Martin and Nina Foch in YOU'RE NEVER TOO YOUNG (1955)

World War II drama. Because Martin had no track record as a dramatic actor, the assignment paid only $20,000; he had received $250,000 for his role as the prowling playboy in TEN THOUSAND BEDROOMS. Martin took the gamble and amazed everyone by his resilient performance, which compared favorably to those of his two co-stars: Marlon Brando and Montgomery Clift. Later in the year, Martin, who had been a Capitol Records recording artist since 1948, had hit singles with "Angel Baby" and "Volare." (His single "Memories Are Made of This" would be number one on the charts in early 1956.)

As a team, Martin and Lewis had been members of Frank Sinatra's Rat Pack in the 1950s, and as a single, Martin became more closely associated with The Crooner both on and off screen. Together they made SOME CAME RUNNING (1958), in which Martin was cast as the good-hearted gambling pal of ex-G.I. Sinatra. Again Martin received plaudits for his credible, relaxed acting. He went Western in John Wayne's RIO BRAVO (1959), and comedic in WHO WAS THAT LADY? (1960) with the husband-and-wife team of Tony Curtis and Janet Leigh. He made an effective leading man in the movie musical BELLS ARE RINGING (1960) paired with the star of the Broadway original, Judy Holliday. As a charter member of the Rat Pack he frolicked in the group's on-camera clowning in OCEAN'S 11 (1960), SERGEANTS THREE (1962), 4 FOR TEXAS (1963), and ROBIN AND THE SEVEN HOODS (1964). He was teamed with Sinatra (without the Pack) in MARRIAGE ON THE ROCKS (1965) and had a cameo role in Sinatra's comedy COME BLOW YOUR HORN (1963). To outsiders it seemed that in these Rat Pack excursions he was playing the happy stooge again, but this time to kingpin Sinatra. Before Marilyn Monroe was fired from her last feature, SOMETHING'S GOT TO GIVE, in 1962, Dean Martin, who had become an adept screen farceur, was her leading man. When the film was recast with Doris Day (as MOVE OVER, DARLING, 1963), Martin quit the production and was replaced by James Garner.

Along the way in the 1960s, Dean Martin starred in several average Westerns: SERGEANTS THREE (1962), TEXAS ACROSS THE RIVER (1966), ROUGH NIGHT IN JERICHO (1967), FIVE CARD STUD (1968—with Robert Mitchum), BANDOLERO! (1968—with James Stewart), and the much superior sagebrush offering THE SONS OF KATIE ELDER (1965— with John Wayne). But in this decade Martin proved most effective as the freewheeling, girl-chasing, gun-toting, wisecracking Matt Helm, the star of four colorful Columbia pictures: THE SILENCERS (1966), MURDERERS' ROW (1966), THE AMBUSHERS (1967), and THE WRECKING CREW (1968). The popular movie series featured extremely shapely leading ladies (Stella Stevens, Daliah Lavi, Ann-Margret, Camilla Sparv, Senta Berger, Elke Sommer, Sharon Tate, and Nancy Kwan), a flow of gadgets and gimmicks, and, most important, hip Dean Martin as the girlie photographer turned American agent for ICE (Organization for Intelligence and Counter-Espionage). In a period when there were a slew of 007-like spy spoofs, Dean Martin's Matt Helm series was among the top contenders. A fifth entry, THE RAVAGERS, had been planned to start in the fall of 1969 but when its leading lady (Sharon Tate) was murdered that August, production was postponed indefinitely and Martin went on to other projects. The Matt Helm series was shelved, and plans to team him with Sinatra in MATT HELM MEETS TONY ROME were abandoned.

When Frank Sinatra began his Reprise Records in the early 1960s, Sammy Davis, Jr. was the first artist signed; Dean Martin soon followed, in 1962. During the 1960s Martin had a variety of top forty hits, including "Everybody Loves Somebody" (1964), which rose to number one position; "The Door Is Still Open to My Heart" (1964); "You're Nobody Till Somebody Loves You" (1965); "I Will" (1965); "Somewhere There's a Someone" (1966); and "Little Ole Wine Drinker, Me" (1967). Between 1964 and 1969 he had eleven albums in the top forty, including *Dream with Dean* (1964), *Houston* (1965), *Welcome to My World* (1967), and *Gentle on My Mind* (1969).

As a solo act Dean Martin had been an occasional TV performer. He had his own specials in 1958 and 1959, and two in 1960. He had guested as an aging gunslinger on the "Canliss" episode of the Western series "Rawhide" (CBS-TV, October 30, 1964). Then, on September 16, 1965, "The Dean Martin Show" debuted on NBC. Using "Somewhere There's a Someone" as his theme song, he employed a group of curvacious showgirls (The Golddiggers), and traded heavily on his image of being America's favorite drunk (he would sing "Every time it rains, it rains bourbon from heaven. . . ."). As such, he held forth for nine successful seasons. It was an industry wonder that Martin, who abhorred rehearsal, could be so successful in his impromptu hosting of the weekly program. His summer replacement shows fostered the careers of many talents, including Bobby Darin, Charles Nelson Reilly, Lou Rawls, and such country and western talents as Loretta Lynn, Lynn Anderson, and Jerry Reed. In the last season (1973–74) of the variety series he began a celebrity roast segment which became so popular that, later (1974–79), the format (with Martin hosting) was adopted for a series of NBC-TV specials.

In 1970 Martin was the romantic leading man of the hugely commercial disaster epic AIRPORT (1970), and he then made two more Westerns: SOMETHING BIG (1971) and SHOWDOWN (1973—with Rock Hudson). He looked bored and tired in both entries and the films were not successful. He continued to perform in clubs, having become a major staple of Las Vegas, especially at the MGM Grand Hotel. As part of his pact with that entertainment combine, he appeared in MGM's MR. RICCO (1975), a tattered melodrama in which he was a San Francisco attorney caught up in a murder case. It was his last leading role to date in films. In the late 1970s he guested on TV's "Charlie's Angels" (1978), "The Misadventures of Sheriff Lobo" (1979), and "Vega$" (1979) and did occasional specials. In 1972 he and Jeanne were divorced; at the time of the costly settlement, his worth was estimated at $26 million. On April 24, 1973, at his Bel Air, California, home, he married young Hollywood beautician Catherine Mae Hawn. He adopted her daughter (Sasha) by a prior marriage. They were soon involved in separations and reconciliations, but in February 1977 their divorce became final. It has been estimated that Martin's three marriages and divorces cost him approximately $10 million, but that did not stop his much-touted womanizing. Meanwhile, in 1976, during Jerry Lewis' annual Labor Day charity telethon, a relaxed Dean Martin came by the television studio in Las Vegas for a surprise appearance. It was the public ending of a two-decade-long feud.

In the early 1980s Dean Martin had occasional television specials (e.g., "Dean Martin in London," NBC-TV, November 8, 1983) and he returned to filmmaking in the stupid cross-country car chase picture CANNONBALL RUN (1981). That Burt Reynolds "comedy" also featured a cameo by Sammy Davis, Jr. For the sequel, CANNONBALL RUN II (1984), Rat Pack chairman Frank Sinatra made an appearance with Martin and Davis. On March 24, 1985, NBC debuted a new teleseries, "Half Nelson," in a two-hour premiere episode. The show featured Joe Pesci as a pint-sized former New York City undercover cop who is hired by a private security service in Beverly Hills. One of his clients (and later confidant) was series regular Dean Martin. The show, which never garnered good ratings, left the air on May 10, 1985. On March 21, 1987, Martin's actor son, Dean Paul Martin, died at age thirty-five in the crash of his Air National Guard jet plane.

In the late 1980s, Martin, still very much a Las Vegas headliner, agreed to join with Sinatra and Davis in an extensive club tour both in the United States and abroad. After a few initial joint engagements, Dean dropped out (with various causes, including health reasons, being cited) and Liza Minnelli replaced him. On his own, he returned to performing at Bally's in Las Vegas. Now in his seventies, Dean Martin has no retirement plans. "When you quit working, that's when you start dying."

## Filmography

### With Jerry Lewis:

My Friend Irma (Par, 1949)
My Friend Irma Goes West (Par, 1951)
At War with the Army (Par, 1951)
That's My Boy (Par, 1951)
Screen Snapshots #197 (Col, 1951) (s)
Sailor Beware (Par, 1951)
Screen Snapshots #207 (Col, 1952) (s)
The Stooge (Par, 1952)
Jumping Jacks (Par, 1952)
Road to Bali (Par, 1952)
Hollywood Fun Festival (Col, 1952) (s)

Scared Stiff (Par, 1953)
The Caddy (Par, 1953)
Money from Home (Par, 1954)
Living It Up (Par, 1954)
Three Ring Circus (Par, 1954)
You're Never Too Young (Par, 1955)
Artists and Models (Par, 1955)
Hollywood Premiere (Col, 1955) (s)
Pardners (Par, 1956)
Hollywood or Bust (Par, 1956)

### Dean Martin Alone:

Ten Thousand Bedrooms (MGM, 1957)
The Young Lions (20th–Fox, 1958)
Some Came Running (MGM, 1958)
Career (Par, 1959)
Rio Bravo (WB, 1959)
Who Was That Lady? (Col, 1960)
Bells Are Ringing (MGM, 1960)
Pepe (Col, 1960)
Ocean's 11 (WB, 1960)
All in a Night's Work (Par, 1961)
Ada (MGM, 1961)
Sergeants Three (UA, 1962)

The Road to Hong Kong (UA, 1962)
Who's Got the Action? (Par, 1962)
Canzoni nel Mondo [38/24/36] (It, 1962)
Come Blow Your Horn (Par, 1963)
Toys in the Attic (UA, 1963)
Who's Been Sleeping in My Bed? (Par, 1963)
4 for Texas (WB, 1963)
What a Way to Go! (20th–Fox, 1964)
Robin and the Seven Hoods (WB, 1964)
Kiss Me, Stupid (Lopert, 1964)
The Sons of Katie Elder (Par, 1965)
Marriage on the Rocks (WB, 1965)

The Silencers (Col, 1966)
Texas Across the River (Univ, 1966)
Murderers' Row (Col, 1966)
Rough Night in Jericho (Univ, 1967)
The Ambushers (Col, 1967)
Bandolero! (20th–Fox, 1968)
How to Save a Marriage—And Ruin Your Life (Col, 1968)

The Wrecking Crew (Col, 1968)
Five Card Stud (Par, 1968)
Airport (Univ, 1970)
Something Big (NG, 1971)
Showdown (Univ, 1973)
Mr. Ricco (MGM, 1975)
Cannonball Run (20th–Fox, 1981)
Cannonball Run II (WB, 1984)

## Radio Series

The Martin and Lewis Show (NBC, 1949–53)

## TV Series

The Colgate Comedy Hour (NBC, 1950–55)
The Dean Martin Show (NBC, 1965–74)

The Dean Martin Celebrity Roasts (NBC, 1974–79)
Half Nelson (NBC, 1985)

## Album Discography

Bells Are Ringing (Cap W/SW-14350) [ST]
The Best of Dean Martin (Cap T-2604, CAP SM-2601)
The Best of Dean Martin, Vol. 2 (Cap SKAO-140)
The Best of Dean Martin (Silver Eagle)
Cha Cha de Amor (Cap T/ST-1702)
Christmas Album (Reprise 6222)
The Country Side of Dean Martin (Reprise 32432)
The Country Style of Dean Martin (Reprise 6061)
Dean Martin (Pickwick 2051)
Dean Martin and Frank Sinatra (Jocklo International 89315)
The Dean Martin and Jerry Lewis Show (Memorabilia 714)
Dean Martin, Judy Garland & Frank Sinatra (Jocklo International 1007)
Dean Martin Favorites (Cap DT-2941)
Dean Martin Sings (Cap T-401)
Dean Martin Sings, Frank Sinatra Conducts (Cap T/ST-2297, Pickwick 3465)
The Dean Martin TV Show (Reprise 6233)
The Deluxe Set (Cap DT/CL-2815)
Dino (Cap T/ST-1659)

Dino (Reprise 2053)
Dino Latino (Reprise 6054)
The Door Is Still Open to My Heart (Reprise 6140)
Dream with Dean (Reprise 6123)
Everybody Loves Somebody (Reprise 6130)
For the Good Times (Reprise 6428)
French Style (Reprise 6021)
Gentle on My Mind (Reprise 6330)
Greatest (Cap DKAO-378)
Greatest Hits, Vols. 1–2 (Reprise 6301, 6320)
Happiness Is Dean Martin (Reprise 6242)
Happy in Love (Tower T/ST-5036)
Heart-Touching Treasury/Famous Love Songs (Suffolk Marketing)
Hey Brother, Pour the Wine (Cap T/ST-2212)
The Hit Sounds of Dean Martin (Reprise 6213)
Hits Again (Reprise 6146)
Holiday Cheer (Cap T/ST-2343)
Houston (Reprise 6181)
I Can't Give You Anything But Love (Pickwick 3089)
I Have But One Heart (Pickwick 3307)
I Take a Lot of Pride in What I Am (Reprise 6338)
The Lush Years (Tower T/ST-5006)

My Woman, My Woman, My Wife (Reprise 6403)
Pretty Baby (Cap T-849)
Relaxin' (Tower T/DT-5018)
Remember Me, I'm the One Who Loves You (Reprise 6170)
Robin and the Seven Hoods (Reprise 2021) [ST]
The Silencers (Reprise 6211) [ST]
Sleep Warm (Cap T/ST-1150)
Somewhere There's Someone (Reprise 6201)
Southern Style (Cap T/DT-2333)
Summit Meeting at the 500 (Souvenir 247-17)
    w. Frank Sinatra, Sammy Davis, Jr.

Swingin' (Pickwick 2001)
Swingin' Down Yonder (Cap T-1047)
That's Amore (Longines SYS-5235)
This Is Dean Martin (Cap T-1047)
This Time I'm Swingin' (Cap T/ST-1442)
Welcome to My World (Reprise 6250)
Winter Romance (Cap T/ST-1285)
You Can't Win 'Em All (Pickwick 3057)
You Were Made for Love (Pickwick 3175)
Young and Foolish (Pickwick 3136)
You're Nobody Till Somebody Loves You/ Return to Me (Cap ST/BB-523)
You're the Best Thing (Reprise 2174)

# MARY MARTIN

SOMEHOW THE WINNING COMBINATION OF MARY MARTIN'S RICH singing voice, her pleasing looks, and a warm personality never translated properly to the motion picture screen. It remains one of the mysteries of Hollywood history. In her dozen Hollywood features (mostly for Paramount Pictures in the early 1940s) she sang engagingly, acted unself-consciously, and looked attractive. Perhaps audiences sensed that she never enjoyed the slow pace of filmmaking and much preferred to perform for live audiences.

From the late 1930s onwards, Mary Martin appeared on Broadway in an assortment of star roles that quickly made her a rival, with Ethel Merman, for the title of the First Lady of Musical Comedy. She was more dainty than the brassy Merman, but she could be equally feisty (as when she did *her* version of *Annie Get Your Gun*). In an array of long-running Broadway hits (including *South Pacific*, *Peter Pan*, *The Sound of Music*, and *I Do! I Do!*) she displayed a versatility of performance and a clearness of voice that sustained her as a major figure on the New York stage.

She was born Mary Virginia Martin on December 1, 1913, in Weatherford, Texas, the daughter of Preston Martin (an attorney) and Juanita (Presley) Martin (a former violin teacher at the local college). An older child (Geraldine) was eleven at the time of Mary's birth. At the age of five, Mary made her performing debut at an Elks carnival singing "When Apples Grow on Lilac Trees." At her mother's insistence Mary took violin lessons, but much preferred singing and acting. One of her mother's friends was concert singer Helen Cahoon, and she made quite an impression on Mary in choosing a future career. Mary finished high school at age sixteen and was sent to the Ward Belmont Female Academy, a fashionable finishing school in Nashville, Tennessee. However, she dropped out to marry (on November 3, 1930) her high school sweetheart, Benjamin J. Hagman, an accountant. Their child, Lawrence Martin Hagman (who would become the star of TV's "Dallas"), was born on September 21, 1931, in Fort Worth, Texas. When Ben Hagman decided to become an attorney, they moved back to Weatherford, and Juanita Martin took over raising Mary's child. Mary would recall, "I was only seventeen when he was born, so my mother was the mother to both of us."

To help bring income into the household (it was the Depression) and to keep busy (her marriage to Ben Hagman was already foundering), Mary and her friend Mildred Woods opened a dance school in Weatherford, at first using her uncle's grain storage loft as a rehearsal studio. The teachers expanded their circuit and by the time she was nineteen, Mary had three hundred pupils. Meanwhile, she had already made annual treks to Hollywood (financed by her parents) to study dance technique at the Academy run by

Fanchon and Marco. On her second stay in Hollywood, she performed for a week in a stage revue in San Francisco.

By 1936 Mary realized (1) that she wanted to return to Hollywood to try her luck and (2) that her marriage to Ben Hagman was a mistake. By the next year, she and Hagman were divorced and she was in Hollywood, where she won a few jobs singing on radio (but with no pay). Her assortment of agents kept getting her auditions. On one occasion, she was taken to perform for Oscar Hammerstein II, for whom she sang "Oh, Rock It for Me" and then "Indian Love Call," not realizing (she always claimed) that he had written the latter song. Hammerstein was impressed with her presence and promised that some day they would work together. He introduced her to Jerome Kern, who advised her to stop trying to be a prima donna (à la Lily Pons) and to be herself. She auditioned for the film studios, where many saw promise in her but no one offered her a job. Martin remembers she was known as "Audition Mary" in those days.

Although she could not get screen work, Mary had a few assignments dubbing the singing voices of movie stars in films, including Margaret Sullavan and Gypsy Rose Lee. She finally made her screen debut at RKO playing the dance teacher of Danielle Darrieux in THE RAGE OF PARIS (1938). One Sunday night at the Trocadero Club she was part of the "amateur showcase" and sang "Il Bacio," first in a classical mode, then in a swing tempo. In the audience that night was Broadway producer Laurence Schwab, who was so impressed with her lively soprano voice that he signed her for a new Broadway show (*Ring Out the News*) he was planning. She was to receive $150 weekly for a year, $300 if she had a starring part in the show.

By the time she reached New York, Schwab had abandoned the project. Not wanting to pay her salary for nothing, he took her to the Waldorf-Astoria Hotel to meet the collaborators (Bella and Sam Spewack and Cole Porter) on a pending Broadway musical, *Leave It to Me*. She sang four songs for the assemblage, which included three of the show's stars: Sophie Tucker, Victor Moore, and William Gaxton. It was Martin's singing of the naughty "A Weekend in the Life of a Private Secretary" that won her the part of the sultry femme fatale. The show tried out in Boston (where she lost one of her two song numbers because the show's other star, Tamara, objected) and New Haven. *Leave It to Me* bowed on Broadway on November 9, 1938. Within the musical, Mary stopped the show with the song "My Heart Belongs to Daddy," which was full of Cole Porter's typical spicy rhymes. As sung innocently by Martin, the lyrics became all the more enticing. (The number was performed in a Siberian setting with Mary in ermine, fur hat, and gloves— most of which she removed to reveal a more basic outfit. She was lifted by and danced with six Eskimos. One of those chorus boys was Gene Kelly.)

Not only was *Leave It to Me* a big hit, but Mary became the newest toast of Broadway with her risqué number. She was on the cover of *Life* magazine and was the columnists' new darling. During the run of *Leave It to Me*, Mary's father died and the papers were full of "Daddy Girl Sings About Daddy as Daddy Dies." Now the Hollywood studios were interested in her and she signed a contract with Paramount Pictures. She admitted later, "What on earth possessed me to accept it, I don't know. . . . Having been tested and rejected so many times by so many studios, I couldn't wait to get back out there and show them all."

Martin's official screen debut came with THE GREAT VICTOR HERBERT (1939), an elaborate biography of the famous operetta composer, filled with twenty-eight of his songs. In typical Hollywood fashion, Paramount had hired Mary because of her Broadway fame in the revealing "Daddy" strip number. In this movie, however, she was buried beneath period costumes and her individuality was disguised by makeup and hair styles that mimicked the fashion of Claudette Colbert, then the studio's reigning queen. Mary's co-stars were Allan Jones and Walter Connolly (as the turn-of-the-century composer), and the child coloratura Susanna Foster. *Variety* reported, "Although Miss Martin's voice is limited in its range, . . . her trouping stamps her immediately as a capable film artist." Much better was her role in RHYTHM ON THE RIVER (1940), in which she and Bing Crosby were ghost songwriters for Broadway tunesmith Basil Rathbone. The duo finally get their just recognition and find love with each other. In LOVE THY NEIGHBOR (1940) she brightly played Fred Allen's niece and tried to intercede in his long-standing feud with fellow radio star Jack Benny. She reprised "My Heart Belongs to Daddy."

Discouraged by her Hollywood experience, Mary left after her first three pictures to work for producer Laurence Schwab in *Nice Goin'*, a musical based on the hit play *Sailor*

Fred Allen, Mary Martin, and Jack Benny in LOVE THY NEIGHBOR (1940)

*Beware!*, co-starring Bert Wheeler and with songs by Ralph Rainger and Leo Robin. The show opened on October 21, 1939, in New Haven, but closed in Boston on November 4. *Variety* noted of Mary's contributions in her first musical lead, "it is in the dramatic rather than the vocal department that she showed best at the preem." (Paramount Pictures, which had already filmed *Sailor Beware!* as LADY BE CAREFUL in 1936, refilmed it as a musical in 1941—THE FLEET'S IN—starring the studio's sarong queen, Dorothy Lamour, and its newest singing discovery, Betty Hutton.)

Martin returned to Paramount where she co-starred with Don Ameche (borrowed from 20th Century–Fox) and tart-mouthed Oscar Levant in KISS THE BOYS GOODBYE (1941). It was a not-so-bright satire on Hollywood's perennial search for fresh talent à la the search for an actress to play Scarlett O'Hara in GONE WITH THE WIND. Mary was the southern chorus girl (here her slight Texas twang was appropriate) with whom film director Ameche falls in love. The movie's highlight was Mary's singing of "That's How I Got My Start" and Connee Boswell's interpretation of "Sand in My Shoes." Even better was BIRTH OF THE BLUES (1941), which reunited her with one of her favorite performers, Bing Crosby. (She would guest on his radio variety show several times.) The picture was a simplistic rendition of the history of jazz with Crosby as a clarinetist who opens a New Orleans club on Bourbon Street with Mary as his singer. Her solo highlight was a rousing "Wait Till the Sun Shines Nellie," while with Crosby and Jack Teagarden she sang "The Waiter and the Porter and the Upstairs Maid." Her third 1941 film was NEW YORK TOWN, in which she courted wealthy Robert Preston but really loved down-and-out Fred Mac-Murray. Her single song was "Yip I Addy I Ay."

In 1942, Mary's only film release (although she was busy making other pictures) was the studio's all-star salute STAR SPANGLED RHYTHM, in which she teamed with Dick Powell and the Golden Gate Quartet in singing "Hit the Road to Dreamland." The next year she was rematched with Powell in a Technicolor wartime comedy called HAPPY GO LUCKY. She was the ex-cigarette girl from New York who arrives in the Caribbean to make her fortune. Despite the opportunity to marry a wealthy snob (Rudy Vallee), she falls in love with a beachcomber (Powell). While she was bright and chipper, it was Betty Hutton, the studio's "blonde bombshell," who stole the limelight with her snappy rendition of "Murder He Says." On the other hand, Mary showed a delicious sense of screwball comedy in TRUE TO LIFE (1943). In this farce, Franchot Tone and Dick Powell were radio scriptwriters who visit waitress Martin's home to gain fresh material for their radio soap opera. Martin sang "Mr. Bluebird." So ended Mary Martin's movie years, except for guest cameos (as herself) in NIGHT AND DAY (1946—singing "My Heart Belongs to Daddy") and MAIN STREET TO BROADWAY (1953). She would insist later, "My Hollywood period is almost nonexistent in my memory."

Two benefits from her Hollywood years were her friendship with screen star Janet Gaynor and her marriage to Richard Halliday. He had been East Coast story editor for Paramount when she opened on Broadway in *Leave It to Me* but had slept through her "My Heart Belongs to Daddy" number. (He had the flu.) When Paramount considered signing her to a contract, he was against it. About the time she went to California to make

THE GREAT VICTOR HERBERT, he was transferred (against his will) to become Paramount's West Coast story editor. The two met at a party while she was making THE GREAT VICTOR HERBERT, but there was no chemistry. Later, they met again and fell in love. They were married in May 1940. Their daughter, Heller, was born in 1941. In 1942, when she was deciding to quit the movies and return to Broadway, he decided to leave filmmaking and become her manager.

For her stage return, Martin chose *Dancing in the Streets*, which had music by Vernon Duke and lyrics by Howard Dietz. The show opened on March 23, 1943, in Boston and closed there on April 10, never reaching New York City. To accept this musical comedy, she had turned down the lead in *Oklahoma!* Fortunately, at just about this time Marlene Dietrich decided not to make her Broadway bow in the Kurt Weill musical *One Touch of Venus*. Producer Cheryl Crawford offered the role to Mary, who became the heavenly muse who comes to Earth. Her co-star was Kenny Baker and the hit show lasted for 567 performances. After the show closed in New York, it went on tour. It was during this trek that she decided, for the sake of her marriage, that Halliday would be the decisionmaker of the family and that, thereafter, their daughter would always tour with them to keep the family together. (Her son, Larry, had been brought up largely by Mary's mother; when the latter died and Martin took over the upbringing, there were years of friction.) By now the Hallidays had settled into a home in Norwalk, Connecticut.

*Lute Song* (1946) was based on a Chinese play, *Pi-Pa-Ki*, with music by Raymond Scott and lyrics by Bernard Hanighen. Mary was the young Chinese wife who goes in search of her straying husband (Yul Brynner). Her best number was "Mountain High, Valley Low." The show lasted for 142 performances, but this time she did not go on the road with it after Broadway. Instead she sailed for England to star in *Pacific 1860*, more because she adored the musical's author (Noël Coward) than because the period vehicle was right for her. Realizing her error, but already contracted for the show, she went on with the project. The play ran for nine (unhappy for Martin) months in the West End.

While Mary was doing *Lute Song*, another hit show had opened on Broadway, Irving Berlin's *Annie Get Your Gun*. She had not been considered for the part of the rough-and-tumble lead because of her new petite stage image (courtesy of her husband's decisions). However, during Martin's *Pacific 1860* engagement, she was asked to headline the London company of that musical Western. Being homesick, she declined. However, she agreed to star in the U.S. national road company of *Annie Get Your Gun*. Mary's daughter, Heller, played her little sister on stage. The popular tour lasted for eleven months, into late 1948. Martin acknowledges that her happiest moment on the tour was during the dress rehearsal in New York before the company left for its opening engagement in Dallas. Broadway's original musical Annie Oakley, Ethel Merman, was in the second row of the orchestra and gave her enthusiastic approval.

According to Martin she almost rejected the chance to star in *South Pacific*, thinking that Joshua Logan, Richard Rodgers, and Oscar Hammerstein II's idea of a love-struck nurse on a tropical isle during World War II was not a great concept. Fortunately, she changed her mind and when the show opened on Broadway on April 7, 1949, she was

Nurse Nellie Forbush. Her leading man was Metropolitan Opera star Ezio Pinza. For hundreds of Broadway performances she shampooed her close-cropped tresses on stage as she sang "I'm Gonna Wash That Man Right Outa My Hair," dueted with Pinza on "Some Enchanted Evening," and cavorted as she performed "A Cockeyed Optimist," "Wonderful Guy," and "Honey Bun." She went to London (November 1, 1951) to star in the West End production, remaining with it for a year. (As with *One Touch of Venus*—played on the screen in 1948 by Ava Gardner—when *South Pacific* became a film in 1958, Mary Martin was not seriously considered for the role. She was thought too old at forty-five to play the lead.)

Once again back in New York, Martin chose to rest her throat, so for her next vehicle she rejected a musical (Cole Porter's *Kiss Me Kate*) and instead selected the drawing-room comedy *Kind Sir* (1953). The show received no raves ("What a waste of talent!" insisted the *New York Times*), but thanks to its two stars (Martin and Charles Boyer) it lasted for 166 performances. (When it was filmed as INDISCREET in 1958, it starred Ingrid Bergman and Cary Grant.)

Mary Martin had already made an illustrious television bow on "The Ford 50th Anniversary Show" (CBS-TV, June 15, 1953). The program's highlight was the medley of show tunes sung in tandem by Mary Martin and Ethel Merman. It was a video milestone that remains legendary to this day. Then, under her husband's auspices, Mary created another industry stir when on Easter Sunday, March 28, 1954, she appeared in *two* NBC-TV specials telecast live from New York. The first, "Magic with Mary Martin," was geared for a children's audience and featured music by Mary Rodgers (Richard's daughter); the second was "Music with Mary Martin," for adults.

The perennial favorite *Peter Pan* by Sir James M. Barrie had last been revived on Broadway in 1950 with Jean Arthur and Boris Karloff. For the new, musical version (which opened on October 20, 1954), Mary—at age forty-one—was cast as the perpetually youthful male lead with Cyril Ritchard as the dastardly Captain Hook. For 152 performances she flew (thanks to special wiring) and sang "I've Gotta Crow." Her daughter, Heller, was in the cast and joined with her when the show was adapted into a hugely popular TV special (NBC-TV, March 7, 1955), which earned her an Emmy Award. It received such high ratings that it was restaged for a new TV airing in 1956 and then yet another new edition was mounted with Martin on December 8, 1960, this time in color. (The latter, taped while she was doing *The Sound of Music*, is the version which was restored and re-telecast to much fanfare by NBC-TV on March 24, 1989.) By now, it had become customary for the Hallidays, after each stage venture, to take a long, relaxing cruise on a freighter. After *Peter Pan* they booked passage on a freighter bound for South America. They were berthed in Brazil when their friends Janet Gaynor and her husband invited them to their farm retreat in Anapolis (in the state of Golanz). They were so intrigued by the landscape that they bought a farm on a neighboring mountain, eventually acquiring several thousand acres and turning it into a working farm.

After *Peter Pan*, Mary agreed to go abroad on a State Department goodwill tour of Thornton Wilder's comedy *The Skin of Our Teeth*, playing the role of the maid Sabina (originated on Broadway in 1942 by Tallulah Bankhead). The tour opened in Paris, and later Mary recreated the role in a TV special (NBC-TV, September 11, 1955). A month after that special she was reunited with Noël Coward for another television variety outing, "Together with Music" (CBS-TV, October 22, 1955). While these mainstream offerings appealed to Martin's fans, there was an outcry when she appeared as the dicey mistress of a junkyard magnate (Paul Douglas) in the TV adaptation of "Born Yesterday" (NBC-TV, October 28, 1956). Although she was very good in the role, she learned not to stray so far from her image in the future.

In 1957 she did a ten-week West Coast tour of *South Pacific* and *Annie Get Your Gun* and brought the latter to television in a two-hour special on November 27, 1958. Perhaps her greatest triumph was starring as Maria Von Trapp, the Austrian novitiate who, during World War II, falls in love with a widowed baron and his brood of children in *The Sound of Music* (which opened on November 16, 1959). The Richard Rodgers–Oscar Hammerstein II musical, in which she and her husband had a 25 percent investment, ran for 1,443 performances on Broadway. During its run, her husband was hospitalized for alcoholism. For her performance in *The Sound of Music* she was given her fourth Tony Award (having won previously for her general contributions in 1948, for *South Pacific* in 1950, and for *Peter Pan* in 1955) and the best-selling original cast album won a Grammy in 1961. When *The Sound of Music* was brought to the screen in 1965, it was Julie Andrews who inherited the coveted lead role.

In December 1962 Martin was a guest on "The Bing Crosby Christmas Show" (ABC-TV) and the following October she was back on Broadway in a new musical, *Jennie*, based on the life of stage star Laurette Taylor. The show was a failure, closing after only eighty-two performances. In 1965, Martin agreed to star in a State Department tour of *Hello, Dolly!* which played in Vietnam, Japan, and also in parts of the United States. She had another special on NBC-TV (April 3, 1966), "Mary Martin at Eastertime with the Radio City Music Hall." She returned to the Broadway stage in the musical *I Do! I Do!* (May 16, 1966) a two-person show with Robert Preston (her co-leading man from the movie NEW YORK TOWN). The show had a 561-performance run. Although Carol Lawrence succeeded Mary in the Broadway edition, Martin later went on tour with the musical with Preston.

After *I Do! I Do!*, Mary planned a short hiatus, which stretched into several years. In March 1973 her husband died following abdominal surgery and, thereafter, she took a long European trip. As therapy she wrote her sentimental autobiography, *My Heart Belongs to Daddy* (1976), which the *New York Times* thought was gracious but about which it warned: "she maintains her distance." She returned to the stage in *Do You Turn Somersaults* (1977), playing a sixty-year-old woman in an autumnal comedy about a former actress turned circus cashier. Her co-star was Anthony Quayle and the show saw her dancing a Charleston, doing somersaults and singing songs from an upside-down position. She toured with the show on the road for seven months, but it closed after sixteen performances on Broadway.

In 1979 she did a cross-country tour as a designer of linen/performer for the

Fieldcrest Company (the revenue went to charity) and her book *Mary Martin's Needlepoint* was already in its fifteenth edition. She made her telefeature debut in VALENTINE (ABC-TV, December 7, 1979) as a seventy-one-year-old woman having an affair with a man (Jack Albertson) from the same retirement home. She had already begun her co-hosting duty on the "Over Easy" (PBS) talk series aimed at senior citizens, when in September 1982 (in San Francisco, where the show was taped) the taxi she was riding in was hit by a drunken driver. Her fellow passengers included her agent (who was killed), Janet Gaynor (who was severely injured and who died two years later), and Gaynor's husband. Martin suffered a fractured pelvic bone and punctured leg. Doctors thought she would never walk again, but she did. She returned for a time to "Over Easy" and she did a benefit at San Francisco's Davies Symphony Hall for the trauma center (where she had been brought after the accident). For the latter occasion she even flew again briefly as Peter Pan. She guested on "The Love Boat" (1983) and "Hardcastle and McCormick" (1985) and, later in 1985, she was the focus of a tribute at the Shubert Theatre in New York City, a benefit for the Theatre Collection of the Museum of the City of New York.

In 1986, Mary Martin and Carol Channing—two former Dolly Levis of *Hello, Dolly!*—agreed to co-star in *Legends*, a play by James Kirkwood of *A Chorus Line* fame. It was a tale of two former movie greats who agree to do a stage play together to revive their careers, but who hate each other. In the course of the macabre comedy they perform one song together. The show played over 350 performances in a thirty-two-city tour during 1986–87, but never reached Broadway. (James Kirkwood authored a tell-all *Diary of a Mad Playwright: How I Toured with Mary Martin and Carol Channing and Lived to Tell About It*, published in 1989 after his death and revealing the myriad controversies, jealousies, and frustrations that beset the production.)

In August 1988 Mary Martin was part of *Broadway at the Bowl*, a multi-star salute at the Hollywood Bowl. She sang "My Heart Belongs to Daddy," "A Cockeyed Optimist," as well as "Some Enchanted Evening" teamed with Placido Domingo. In early 1989 it was announced that Mary would tour in a musical version of *Our Town* called *Grover's Corners*, but in May of that year she was diagnosed with cancer. Said the feisty star, "I'm fighting this illness. But none of us live forever."

## Filmography

The Rage of Paris (RKO, 1938)
The Great Victor Herbert (Par, 1939)
Rhythm on the River (Par, 1940)
Love Thy Neighbor (Par, 1940)
Kiss the Boys Goodbye (Par, 1941)
Birth of the Blues (Par, 1941)
New York Town (Par, 1941)

Star Spangled Rhythm (Par, 1942)
Happy Go Lucky (Par, 1943)
True to Life (Par, 1943)
Night and Day (WB, 1946)
Main Street to Broadway (MGM, 1953)
Valentine (ABC-TV, 12/7/79)

## Broadway Plays

Leave It to Me (1938)
One Touch of Venus (1943)
Lute Song (1946)
South Pacific (1949)
Kind Sir (1953)

Peter Pan (1954)
The Sound of Music (1959)
Jennie (1963)
I Do! I Do! (1966)
Do You Turn Somersaults (1977)

## TV Series

Over Easy (PBS, 1980–83)

## Album Discography

Annie Get Your Gun (Cap W-913) [ST/TV]
Anything Goes (10" Col ML-2159, 10" Col CL-2582)
Anything Goes/The Bandwagon (Col ML-4751, Col Special Products 4751)
Babes in Arms (Col ML-4488, Col CL-823, Col OL-7070/OS-2570, Col Special Products 2570)
The Bandwagon (10" Col ML-2160)
Bing and Mary—Rhythm on the Radio (Star-Tone 225) w. Bing Crosby
Cinderella/Three to Make Music (RCA LPM/LSP-2012)
The Ford Fiftieth Anniversary Television Show (10" Decca DL-7027) [ST/TV] w. Ethel Merman
Girl Crazy (Col ML-4475, Col CL-822, Col OL-7060/OS-2560, Col Special Products 2560)
The Great Victor Herbert (Caliban 6033) [ST]
Guideposts for Living (Guideposts GP-100) w. Norman Vincent Peale
Happy Go Lucky (Caliban 6021) [ST]
Hello, Dolly! (RCA LOCD/LSOD-2007) [OC]
Hi-Ho (Disneyland 4016)
I Do! I Do! (RCA LOC/LSO-1128) [OC]
Jennie (RCA LOC/LSO-1083) [OC]
Leave It to Me (Smithsonian P-14944) [OC]

Lute Song/On the Town (Decca DL-8030) [OC]
Mary Martin on Broadway (Col Special Products 14282)
Mary Martin Sings for Children (YPR 731)
Mary Martin Sings for You (10" Col ML-2061)
Mary Martin Sings, Richard Rodgers Plays (RCA LPM-1539)
Musical Love Story (Disneyland 3031)
Night and Day (Motion Picture Tracks MPT-6) [ST]
One Touch of Venus (Decca DL-9122/79122) [OC]
Pacific 1860 (Show Biz 5602) [OC]
Peter Pan (RCA LOC/LSO-1019) [OC]
The Sleeping Beauty (Disneyland 3911)
Snow White (Disneyland 4016)
Songs from "The Sound of Music" (Disneyland 1296)
The Sound of Music (Col KOL-5450/KOS-2020, Col S-32601) [OC]
South Pacific (Col OL-4180/OS-2040, Col S-32604) [OC]
Star Spangled Rhythm (Curtain Calls 100/20) [ST]
Together with Music (DRG-21103, Radiola 10136) w. Noël Coward [ST/TV]

# TONY MARTIN

FOR MORE THAN A HALF CENTURY, TONY MARTIN HAS BEEN ONE OF the most accomplished, polished, and best show business singers. His strong yet subtle singing style and beautiful baritone voice have carved out successful careers for him on records, radio, television, and films and as a much-in-demand singer worldwide. For all his success, Tony Martin never truly registered as a movie star, although he appeared, sometimes to advantage, in more than two dozen feature films. His reputation as a show business legend, however, is solid: in Hollywood's Walk of Fame his name appears four times, for records, radio, television, and motion pictures.

The son of Russian Jewish immigrant parents, the future star was born Alvin Morris in Oakland, California, on Christmas Day in 1913. When Al, as the boy was called, was small, his parents were divorced and his mother, Hattie, married a man named Mike Myers, whom the youngster always considered his father. (His real dad committed suicide when Al was a young boy.) Financially, Al's family was poor but it was a close-knit one. He developed a love of music, taking up the saxophone and clarinet. At age twelve he and three other boys formed a group called "The Clarion Four" and a couple of years later he was in a small jazz band, "The Five Red Peppers." After graduating from high school, Al continued to appear with various bands in the Bay area while he attended a Catholic school, St. Mary's College, as a pre-law student. Music was dominant in his life, however, and he joined Tom Coakley's band, recording the song "Here Is My Heart" for Brunswick Records, and then joined Tom Gerun's Orchestra. He sang with this band at the World's Fair in Chicago in 1933 and, returning to the West Coast, he formed Al Morris and His Orchestra. The group was hired for short broadcasts on NBC's Blue Network. Next there was a screen test at MGM, which was not successful, but at that time Nat Goldstone became Al's agent and they remained together for more than three decades.

Although MGM executives were not impressed with twenty-two-year-old Al Morris, the powers that be at RKO Radio were, and he won a contract with that lesser studio, making his film debut in two of the studio's two-reel "Headliner" abbreviated musicals. Believing he was now ready for bigger assignments, the studio cast him in a featured role in their upcoming Fred Astaire musical FOLLOW THE FLEET (1936) and he was assigned to sing a new song, "You and the Night and the Music." Wanting no competition, Astaire took the song for himself, leaving Al with a one-line bit. He fared even worse in his next RKO outing, MUSS 'EM UP (1936), as his part was cut out of the script even before filming started. He wound up on screen only as John Carroll's deceased brother.

With two cinema strikeouts, Al returned to nightclub work, but while singing at

Hollywood's Trocadero Club, he was spotted by 20th Century–Fox chief Darryl F. Zanuck, who signed him for his studio. Bad luck continued to dog Al's film career. The young man (now called Tony Martin because he liked both the name Tony and bandleader Freddy Martin) was cast in the Shirley Temple feature POOR LITTLE RICH GIRL (1936) and sang "When I'm with You." However, when the movie was released, Martin found out that his voice had been dubbed by another singer. His big break, though, came in his next project, SING, BABY, SING (1936), in which he had a featured part singing "When Did You Leave Heaven?," a song he recorded successfully for Decca Records. The star of that picture was popular Alice Faye and after its completion she and Martin began dating. On September 4, 1937, they were married in Yuma, Arizona.

Success came quickly for Tony Martin after he joined 20th Century–Fox in 1936. After playing the boyfriend in the Jones Family series entry BACK TO NATURE (1936), the studio cast him in a number of well-received musicals and comedies, although for a time he was billed as Anthony Martin. Following a decent supporting role in PIGSKIN PARADE (1936), in which he sang "It's Love I'm After," he was given his first starring role, in the minor musical comedy THE HOLY TERROR (1937). Next he and Alice Faye dueted on "Afraid to Dream" in YOU CAN'T HAVE EVERYTHING (1937), and he was the leading man in the Ritz Brothers knockabout comedy KENTUCKY MOONSHINE (1938), after having filled a similar role in Eddie Cantor's ALI BABA GOES TO TOWN (1937). Martin then co-starred again with his wife in the remake of SALLY, IRENE AND MARY (1938) and Fox began giving him dramatic roles, such as the football hero in the prison drama UP THE RIVER (1938) and a boxer in WINNER TAKE ALL (1939). His favorite film assignment was in the 1936 musical drama BANJO ON MY KNEE, which showcased him beautifully as cabaret entertainer Chick Bean, singing "There's Something in the Air," and dueting with star Barbara Stanwyck on "Where the Lazy River Goes By."

In addition to films, Martin continued to branch out in other show business areas. Along with personal appearances, he was briefly on "The Jack Benny Program" on radio before joining "The George Burns and Gracie Allen Show." On radio he also co-starred with André Kostelanetz on CBS's "Tune-Up Time" during the 1939–40 season and in 1940–41 he headlined "The Tony Martin Show" on NBC. Martin also kept up his recording career: he worked for Decca and Brunswick in 1936, he was the vocalist on a number of 1938 records for Brunswick with Ray Noble and His Orchestra, and the same year he cut eight songs for the Vocalion label with Manny Kelin and His Swing-a-Hulas. In 1939 he signed a recording contract with Decca and his first offering, "Begin the Beguine"/"September Song," sold over a million copies, quite a feat since the record industry was still in the Depression doldrums.

After his 20th Century–Fox contract expired in 1940—the same year he and Alice Faye were divorced—Tony Martin freelanced as an actor and starred in the delightful Columbia Pictures musical MUSIC IN MY HEART (1940). The film not only highlighted Rita Hayworth in her first major role (Martin chose her specifically for the part) but also showcased him singing several songs, including "It's a Blue World," which was a best-seller for him on Decca Records. In 1941 he was featured in the posh MGM musical ZIEGFELD

GIRL, singing "You Stepped Out of a Dream" to Lana Turner, Hedy Lamarr, and Judy Garland; this song too was a best-seller for him on Decca. Among his other hit recordings for the label were "Does Your Heart Beat for Me?," "Tonight We Love," "Lilacs in the Rain," "Perfidia," "Fools Rush In," "Don't Take Your Love from Me," "On Miami Shore," and a duet with Frances Langford on "Our Love Affair"/"Two Dreams Met."

In 1942 Tony Martin was enjoying substantial success: he was a multimedia star earning $12,000 per week. But it all ended that year when he joined the Navy and the darkest part of his life began. He was accused falsely of trying to bribe an officer for a commission and was drummed out of the service. Next he joined the Army, where for a time his life was a living hell due to his recent Navy debacle. Finally he was sent to the Far East front, where he participated in a number of bombing missions and acquitted himself with honor, receiving the Bronze Star and the Presidential Unit Citation before being honorably discharged as a sergeant in 1946.

Returning to Hollywood in 1946, Martin not only found himself broke but also the subject of protests because of the 1942 Navy scandal. He was signed to host NBC's "Carnation Contented Hour" but was soon fired due to listener protests, which also led to his losing a major role in a 20th Century–Fox musical. But he remained active in personal appearances and he signed a recording contract with Mercury Records which resulted in the million-selling single "To Each His Own." In 1947 he signed with more powerful RCA Victor Records and in 1948 he was a big success performing at the London Palladium, the highlight being his singing of "Tenement Symphony," which he had introduced in the Marx Brothers feature THE BIG STORE in 1941. Martin would remain with RCA until 1960 and during that time he would have many best-selling records, including eighteen tunes on the *Billboard* charts (such as "I Get Ideas" in 1951 and "It's Better in the Dark" in 1956). His popularity was just as strong abroad, particularly in England and South Africa.

Martin returned to films in 1946 in the MGM musical potpourri TILL THE CLOUDS ROLL BY, singing "All the Things You Are" and, in the *Show Boat* sequence, "Make Believe," and in 1948 he starred in Universal's CASBAH, in which he played amorous thief Pepé Le Moko (a role done previously by Jean Gabin and Charles Boyer). In this picture he sang a quartet of Harold Arlen songs: "For Every Man There's a Woman," "What's Good About Goodbye," "Hooray for Love," and "It Was Written in the Stars." Following off-screen love affairs with Rita Hayworth and Lana Turner, Martin married MGM dancer-actress Cyd Charisse in 1948 and their marriage proved to be one of Hollywood's most durable. Their only child (Cyd had a son, Nicky, from her first marriage), Tony, Jr., was born in 1950.

From the late 1940s well into the early 1960s, Tony Martin was one of the most popular and in-demand singers in the world. He was the first big-name singer to headline in Las Vegas and he was equally popular throughout the country, as well as in London, Paris, Havana, Buenos Aires, and Johannesburg. On television he was extremely successful on NBC's "The Comedy Hour" and for two seasons he headlined his own program, "The Tony Martin Show" (1954–56) on NBC.

For Hollywood, Martin starred with Janet Leigh in the entertaining RKO release TWO TICKETS TO BROADWAY (1951), in which he reprised his hit recording of "There's No Tomorrow," as well as sang "Manhattan" and the prologue to the opera *Pagliacci* (Martin gave serious thought at the time to studying opera). Two years later he played a semi-villainous role when he co-starred with Bob Hope and Rosemary Clooney in the comedy HERE COME THE GIRLS. Also in 1953 he appeared as the other man with Esther Williams and Van Johnson in the vapid musical EASY TO LOVE, the highlight of which was Martin's singing of "That's What a Rainy Day Is For." He also performed a cameo singing "Lover Come Back to Me" in MGM's musical biography of Sigmund Romberg, DEEP IN MY HEART (1954). In 1955 veteran Martin was among those trying to buoy up HIT THE DECK, in which he sang the Vincent Youmans tunes "More Than You Know" and "Keepin' Myself for You." With musical films on the wane and Martin now over forty, he had to stretch for screen assignments. He did a respectable job in the title role of the Western QUINCANNON, FRONTIER SCOUT (1956) and in 1957 he starred in his final film, the British-made musical LET'S BE HAPPY.

Besides his numerous appearances on TV on musical-variety programs and specials, Martin also acted occasionally on TV, on such shows as "Shower of Stars" (1955), "The George Burns Show" (1958), "The Donna Reed Show" (1961), "Death Valley Days" (1963), and "The Name of the Game" (1970). In 1960 Martin left RCA and joined Dot

Tony Martin, Vera-Ellen, and Robert Flemyng in LET'S BE HAPPY (1957)

Records and had several good-selling singles, including "Fly Me to the Moon" and "Convicted." During the rest of the decade he recorded for such labels as Park Avenue, Charter, 20th Century–Fox, Motown, NAN, Dunhill, and Chart. For the latter label he even cut a country music album, *Tony in Nashville*, in 1970. His main source of income, however, still came from personal appearances and throughout the 1960s and 1970s he was much in demand, both as a single and sometimes in tandem with his strikingly attractive and very talented wife, Cyd Charisse. Regarding his solo appearance at New York City's Copacabana in 1967, *Variety* reported, "Tony Martin has been major boxoffice for many years. He remains a superior entertainer. . . ." In the early 1960s the singer was active in the national People-to-People Sports Program and in 1969 baseball commissioner William Eckert authorized him to head the Centennial Baseball Committee to celebrate the sport's 100th anniversary. In 1969 Martin headlined the syndicated TV special "Spotlight on Tony Martin" as well as toured in *Guys and Dolls*, and in 1972 he starred in another syndicated special, "The Tony Martin Show."

In 1975 it was announced that Martin would star as Harry Richman in a musical film of Richman's autobiography, *A Hell of a Life*, for which Martin owned the rights, but American-International Pictures, which announced the project, was sold before it could become a reality. In 1976 Martin and Charisse published their memoirs, *The Two of Us* (also the title of a song he had recorded for Motown in 1966), as told to Dick Kleiner. The performers told their separate stories in alternating chapters. The duo also did a lengthy tour to promote the volume.

Tony Martin continues to make a living singing "the way people used to sing," keeping active well into his seventies, often appearing with his wife. (He and Cyd are renowned for being available to glamourize openings of new clubs, restaurants, etc., in the Los Angeles area.) In the mid-1970s they had a successful British tour and in 1984 Martin repeated as a solo. Most recently, Martin has ventured into a new avenue of show business, as a member of the lecture circuit, nostalgically recounting the early years of his career.

## Filmography

### As Al Morris:

Educating Father (RKO, 1935) (s)
Short Subject (RKO, 1935) (s)
Murder on the Bridle Path (RKO, 1936)

Follow the Fleet (RKO, 1936)
Muss 'Em Up (RKO, 1936)

### As Tony Martin:

Poor Little Rich Girl (20th–Fox, 1936)
Sing, Baby, Sing (20th–Fox, 1936)
Back to Nature (20th–Fox, 1936)
Pigskin Parade (20th–Fox, 1936)
Banjo on My Knee (20th–Fox, 1936)

The Holy Terror (20th–Fox, 1937)
You Can't Have Everything (20th–Fox, 1937)
Life Begins at College (20th–Fox, 1937)
Ali Baba Goes to Town (20th–Fox, 1937)
Kentucky Moonshine (20th–Fox, 1938)

Sally, Irene and Mary (20th–Fox, 1938)
Up the River (20th–Fox, 1938)
Thanks for Everything (20th–Fox, 1938)
Winner Take All (20th–Fox, 1939)
Music in My Heart (Col, 1940)
Ziegfeld Girl (MGM, 1941)
The Big Store (MGM, 1941)
Till the Clouds Roll By (MGM, 1946)
Casbah (UI, 1948)

Two Tickets to Broadway (RKO, 1951)
Here Come the Girls (Par, 1953)
Easy to Love (MGM, 1953)
Deep in My Heart (MGM, 1954)
Hit the Deck (MGM, 1955)
Meet Me in Las Vegas (MGM, 1956)
Quincannon, Frontier Scout (UA, 1956)
Let's Be Happy (AA, 1957)
Party Girl (MGM, 1958) (voice only)

## Radio Series

The Jack Benny Program (NBC, 1937)
The George Burns and Gracie Allen Show
  (NBC, 1937–38)
Tune-Up Time with Tony Martin (CBS, 1939–
  40)

The Tony Martin Show (NBC, 1940–41)
The Carnation Contented Hour (NBC, 1946)
The Tony Martin Show (ABC, 1947–48)

## TV Series

The Tony Martin Show (NBC, 1954–56)

## Album Discography

Casbah (Radiola 1099) [ST/R]
The Days of Wine and Roses (Charter 100)
Deep in My Heart (MGM 3153) [ST]
The Desert Song (10" RCA LPM-3105) w.
  Kathryn Grayson
Dream Music (Mer MG-20079)
Dreamland Rendezvous (10" Mer MG-25122)
Fly Me to the Moon (Dot 3466/25466)
Go South, Young Man (RCA LPM/LSP-1778)
Golden Hits (Mer 20644/60644)
Harold Arlen Songs (10" RCA LPM-3136)
His Greatest Hits (Dot 3360/25360)
Hit the Deck (MGM 3163) [ST]
I Get Ideas (Camden CAL-412)
I'll See You in My Dreams (Applause APLP-
  1003, Diamond 3-82005)
In the Spotlight (Decca DL-8366)
It's Just Love (Wing MGW-12115)
Live at Carnegie Hall (Movietone 71007/72007)
Live at Carnegie Hall (20th Century–Fox 3138)
A Melody by Tony Martin (Coral CB-20019)

Mr. Song Man (Mer MG-20075)
Mr. Song Man (Wing MGW-11203)
A Night at the Copacabana (RCA LPM-01357)
The Night Was Made for Love (RCA LPM-
  1218)
Our Love Affair (Decca DL-8287)
Pigskin Parade (Amalgamated 2312) [ST]
Les Poupées de Paris (RCA LOC/LSO-1090)
  [OC]
Sally, Irene & Mary (Caliban 56031) [ST]
Sing, Baby, Sing (Caliban 6029) [ST]
Songs from the Motion Picture "Gigi" (RCA
  LPM/LSP-1716) w. Gogi Grant
Speak to Me of Love (RCA LPM-1263)
A Stroll Through Melody Lane (Decca DL-
  8286)
Tenement Symphony (RCA International
  90069)
Till the Clouds Roll By (MGM 3231, Metro
  578, Sountrak 115) [ST]
Tonight (Camden CAL-576)

Tony in Nashville (Chart 1029)
Tony Martin (Audio Fidelity 6200)
Tony Martin (MCA 1515)
Tony Martin (10" Mer MG-25036)
Tony Martin (10" Mer MG-25004)
Tony Martin (Vocalion 3610)
Tony Martin at the Desert Inn (RCA LPM/LSP-2146)
Tony Martin at the Plaza (Audio Fidelity 6223)

Tony Martin Sings (10" Decca DL-5189)
Tony Martin Sings of Love (Camden CLA-484)
Two Tickets to Broadway (RCA LPM-39) [ST]
World Wide Favorites (10" RCA LPM-3126)
You and the Night and the Music (10" RCA LPM-3038)
You Can't Have Everything (Titania 508) [ST]
Ziegfeld Girl (CIF 3006) [ST]

# LAURITZ MELCHIOR

IN THE EARLY 1930S HOLLYWOOD DELIGHTED IN THE NOVELTY OF "presenting" Metropolitan Opera stars such as Grace Moore and Lawrence Tibbett in screen vehicles, usually in heavy-handed operettas. The studios enjoyed the prestige of having such vocal luminaries under contract and, it was believed, the public deserved the cultural uplift these renowned stage figures could provide. In the mid-1940s, Joe Pasternak, who had made Deanna Durbin a star at Universal Pictures in the late 1930s, was thriving at MGM, producing a string of colorful, lucrative musical confections. He decided it would be fun for moviegoers (and profitable for him and Metro) if he mixed the likes of classical pianist José Iturbi (or on occasion pop organist Ethel Smith) with such contrasting studio regulars as Esther Williams, Jimmy Durante, Kathryn Grayson, Jane Powell, or Xavier Cugat. One of his more inspired coups was coaxing the Metropolitan Opera's leading Wagnerian tenor, Lauritz Melchior, to appear in four of the studio's Technicolor musical comedies.

Fifty-five-year-old Melchior brought to the screen his massive tenor voice. He also brought his massive girth (240 pounds), which caused one film critic to describe him as Sophie Tucker in a suit. More important, jovial Melchior possessed a delightful sense of theatrics which Pasternak allowed to flourish on camera. For some, Melchior's hamming it up on screen was an insult to his lofty stage reputation. But for most, including the famed, peripatetic singer, it was a grand lark, another profitable forum in which to share his love of music. Moviegoers responded immediately to his zestful personality and the richness of his deep voice. If his acting lacked the finer shadings of that of true actors, that was all right; he obviously was having such a good time in front of the cameras.

Lauritz Lebrecht Hommel Melchior was born in Copenhagen, Denmark, on March 20, 1890, the son of Jorgen Conradt and Julie (Moller) Melchior. From 1896 to 1905 he attended the voice school conducted by his father and grandfather. As a boy soprano at the English church in Copenhagen, he came to the attention of Queen Alexandra. During these early years two individuals greatly influenced Melchior in pursuing his singing career. Because of her disability, his blind sister, Agnes (who later taught at the Royal School for the Blind), was given free box seats under the stage for the Royal Opera. She took her brother along and he would sneak up into the wings to report on the visual goings-on. He soon became the "eyes" for Agnes and the other blind children attending the opera. His other influence was Froeken Kristine Jensen, the housekeeper who brought up the Melchior children after their mother died (when Lauritz was one month old). She not only encouraged her young charge to become a singer, but later she would publish cookbooks to help pay for his singing lessons.

At the age of eighteen, Melchior began seriously to take singing lessons. In 1912 he was accepted by the Royal School of the Opera in Copenhagen where his voice now registered as a baritone. On April 2, 1913, he made his debut—as a baritone—at the Royal Opera in Copenhagen as Silvio in Leoncavallo's *I Pagliacci* and five years later made his bow as a tenor. It had been Mme. Charles Cahier, who worked with Melchior in a traveling opera company, who convinced him that he was actually a "tenor with the lid on." In 1919, Melchior was performing in concert at Queen's Hall in London when British novelist Hugh Walpole was in the audience. The famed writer was impressed and thereafter took a great interest in the singer's career, giving him advice, funds, and encouragement. The two artists became good friends and Walpole dedicated several novels to Melchior, often sending him copies of his manuscripts for criticism. During this period (on July 30, 1920) Melchior was invited by the inventor Marconi to sing on the debut worldwide radio broadcast from the Marconi Experimental Station in Chelmsford, England. His singing partner was Dame Nellie Melba.

It was Walpole who suggested that Melchior go to Germany to study Wagnerian roles. Following his friend's advice, Melchior in 1924 made his debut there as Parsifal and the same year was heard performing Siegmund in Wagner's *Die Walküre*. He made his U.S. debut at the Metropolitan Opera in February 1926 singing the title role in *Tannhäuser*. By now, his first wife, Inger Nathansen, had died. (They had two children, a daughter and a son. The latter, Ib, became a film and television writer/director in the United States.) In 1925 he had married Maria Hacker, a German film actress who specialized in daring screen acrobatics. Their first meeting was most unusual. For one of her movie stunts, she had to make a parachute jump from an airplane. While practicing this routine, she landed in Melchior's garden at his hunting estate at Chossenwitz. Because he was 6' 3" and she was barely 5', he called his wife "kleinchen" (little one). She became his business manager, leading Melchior to say, "I make the noise, she make the business."

The seemingly inexhaustible Melchior performed a wealth of roles (including both Siegmund and Siegfried in entire "Ring" cycles and the role of Tristan in *Tristan und Isolde*) at the Metropolitan Opera, becoming its most famous Wagnerian heldentenor (heroic tenor). By the start of the 1940–41 Met season, he had accumulated a staggering record of Wagnerian performances: 215 Siegfrieds, 171 Tristans, 146 Siegmunds, 109 Tannhäusers, 73 Lohengrins, and 57 Parsifals. But Melchior, not content with just being on the opera stage (both at the Metropolitan and around the world), also performed in concert throughout the United States and in Hawaii. He was heard frequently on radio, and throughout his career made many recordings both in the United States and abroad. When asked how he maintained such a grueling momentum, he responded, "I never strain. I always sing with the interest, never use my principal." Other outlets for his boundless energy were cooking (he was famous for his oxtail soup and smorgasbord), hunting, antique collecting, teaching the therapeutic value of music to the handicapped (at Columbia University's Teachers College), and endless practical jokes. He was given the title "Singer to the Royal Court of Denmark" by the Danish King and his birthland gave him the Knighthood and Silver Cross of Dannebrog as well as the gold medal of "Ingenio et Arti." France bestowed on him the rosette of the Legion of Honor; Bulgaria the Cross for Service to Art; and Germany–Sachen-Coburg-Gotha the Carl Eduard Medal, First Class (for his participation at the Bayreuth Festivals). He had also a Saxonian knighthood and a gold medal from Vassar College for his many services to the arts in the United States.

In 1943, Melchior performed a joking singing commercial (for an imaginary "Pasternak's Pretzels") on Fred Allen's Sunday night CBS network radio show, which producer Joe Pasternak heard. Appreciating the tenor's sense of fun, he began negotiations to bring Melchior to the screen, courtesy of Metro-Goldwyn-Mayer.

Lauritz Melchior made his motion picture debut in THRILL OF A ROMANCE (1945), an Esther Williams vehicle set at a Sierra Nevada mountain lodge where she is about to start her honeymoon. Her stuffy husband is called off to Washington, D.C., before their marriage is consummated, and a romance develops between Williams and a freckle-faced Army major (Van Johnson). Serving as chaperone for this courtship is a girthful cupid named Nils Knudsen (Melchior) who has a penchant for eating and singing. In between Williams' swimming, Johnson's smiling, and the swinging of Tommy Dorsey and His Band, Melchior sang "Please Don't Say No" and a "Serenade" by Franz Schubert. *Variety* endorsed Melchior for "flitting in and out with his bombastic vocal gymnastics dressed up to please the masses."

On February 17, 1946, Melchior celebrated his twentieth year at the Metropolitan Opera, appearing in several sequences from various Wagner operas. Four months later he could be seen on screen in TWO SISTERS FROM BOSTON as Olaf Olstrom, the temperamental Metropolitan Opera tenor. The airy plot finds Kathryn Grayson as a chanteuse (at Jimmy Durante's Bowery saloon) who must pretend to be an opera singer when her stuffy relatives come to New York City. During one of Melchior's arias, Grayson jumps forth from the chorus to join him in song. In more controlled moments, Melchior sang "The Prize Song" from Wagner's *Die Meistersinger,* as well as snatches of a created opera contrived from Liszt and Mendelssohn melodies.

For THIS TIME FOR KEEPS (1947) Melchior was reunited with shapely Esther Williams and he received second billing as Hans Herald, the portly opera star. The setting was Michigan's Mackinac Island where Melchior's rebellious son (Johnnie Johnston), a G.I. who wants a career in swing, not opera, is romancing the star (Williams) of the Aquacaper. For variety there were Xavier Cugat and His Orchestra, razzmatazz Jimmy Durante (delightful in his murderous renditions of "Inka Dinka Doo" and "The Man Who Found the Lost Chord"), Stanley Donen's choreography, and the spectacular Technicolor scenery. Jovial Melchior, who continued to kid his stage image, sang "La Donna e Mobile" from Verdi's *Rigoletto,* "M'Appari" from Flotow's *Martha,* an excerpt from Verdi's *Otello,* and, to further demonstrate his versatility, Cole Porter's "You'd Be So Easy to Love."

For his final MGM foray, Melchior was Olaf Eriksen in LUXURY LINER (1948). He was the opera tenor sailing for a South American tour aboard a vessel skippered by George Brent and bedeviled by Brent's stowaway teenaged daughter (Jane Powell), who insists upon playing matchmaker for her widowed dad. Aboard this "love boat" were Xavier Cugat and His Orchestra (performing "Cugat's Nougat"), the Pied Pipers (harmonizing

"Yes We Have No Bananas"), and classical soprano Marina Koshetz who did a surprisingly comic rendition of Cole Porter's "I've Got You Under My Skin." Melchior was front and center to do a rendition—with Powell—of the Act II duet from Verdi's *Aïda* and to solo "Come Back to Sorrento." He also managed a hearty Danish drinking song, a teasing acknowledgment of his beer-drinking fame.

Melchior, MGM, and filmgoers were all delighted with his movie forays. However, Rudolf Bing, the new manager of the Metropolitan Opera, was not; he had decided to decree a new regime of discipline and decorum for the Metropolitan stars. One of the prime offenders, in Bing's eyes, was Melchior who was too accustomed to setting his own schedule for rehearsals, repertoire, and so on. Bing also thought it improper for a Met luminary to be appearing in Hollywood trifles. After singing *Lohengrin* on February 2, 1950, the peevish Melchior resigned from the company, charging Bing with a lack of "natural courtesy." (Some insist that his contract was not renewed by Bing.) He had given 513 performances in his twenty-year association with the Met.

Undaunted, Melchior continued to perform through concerts, radio, television, clubs, and recordings. He did a personal appearance turn at the Palace Theatre in February 1952 and in 1953 he returned to motion pictures. The project was Paramount's THE STARS ARE SINGING. It was Rosemary Clooney's film debut, and she performed her big 1951 hit "Come on-a My House," among other numbers. Melchior was mirthful Poldi, her Greenwich Village neighbor, who helps to shelter refugee Anna Maria Alberghetti in his digs. Melchior sang "Vesti la Giubba" from Leoncavallo's *I Pagliacci* and the pop tune "Because," and dueted on "My Heart Is Home" with Clooney. The film was not popular and Melchior returned to television guesting (including an appearance on "Arthur Mur-

Marina Koshetz, Lauritz Melchior, George Brent, Frances Gifford, Jane Powell, and Richard Derr in LUXURY LINER (1948)

ray's Dance Party"). He also joined with James McCracken in June 1954 for a run of Guy Lombardo's *Arabian Nights* which played at the Jones Beach Marine Theatre on Long Island.

In the late 1950s Melchior's singing beer commercial was in vogue and in March 1960 he sang Siegmund with the Danish Radio Orchestra to honor his seventieth birthday. In 1963 he starred in a Carnegie Hall concert to commemorate the fiftieth anniversary of his operatic debut. That same year his wife Maria died and in 1964 he wed his secretary, Mary Markan, who was thirty-four years his junior. They divorced two years later.

In 1972, the still tall, imposing (and now white-bearded) Melchior received Germany's top recording award (Deutschen Schallplattenpreises) in recognition of EMI's two-record album *Melchior: The Wagner Tenor of the Century* (1971), composed of singles made between 1926 and 1935. He lived in California in a five-and-a-half-acre mountaintop retreat (which he named The Viking) and devoted much energy to his foundation, which nurtured new generations of heldentenors to handle the great heroic opera roles. He died on March 18, 1973, in Santa Monica, following an emergency gall bladder operation. Interment was in Copenhagen.

## Filmography

Thrill of a Romance (MGM, 1945)
Two Sisters from Boston (MGM, 1946)
This Time for Keeps (MGM, 1947)

Luxury Liner (MGM, 1948)
The Stars Are Singing (Par, 1953)
Glamorous Hollywood (Col, 1958) (s)

## Album Discography

Arabian Nights (Decca DL-9013) [OC]
Fiftieth Anniversary, 1911–61 (American Stereophonic Corp. Asco-121)
Five Duets (RCA LM-2763)
Great Scenes from Wagner: Götterdämmerung (Victrola VIC-1369)
Heldentenor of the Century (RCA CRM3-0308)
The Lauritz Melchior Album (Seraphim 6086)
The Lauritz Melchior Anthology, Vol. 1 (First Recordings) (Danacord DACO-115/116)
The Lauritz Melchior Anthology, Vol. 2 (1923–26) (Danacord DACO-117/118)
The Lauritz Melchior Anthology, Vol. 3 (1928–31) (Danacord DACO-119/120)
The Lauritz Melchior Anthology, Vol. 4 (Part 1) (Danacord DACO-171, 172, 173)

The Lauritz Melchior Anthology, Vol. 4 (Part 2) (Danacord DACO-174, 175, 176)
The Legendary Lauritz Melchior (Odyssey Y-31740)
Lohengrin/Tristan and Isolde (RCA LM-2618)
Melchior: The Wagner Tenor of the Century (EMI)
Melchior in Copenhagen (Danacord DACO-168)
Thrill of a Romance (Camden CAL-424) [ST]
Wagner: Arias (1923–36) (Pearl 228/9)
Wagner: Die Walküre (Act I) (Seraphim 60190)
Wagner/Melchior (Victrola VIC-1500)
Wagner: Siegfried (Abridged) (Electrola/Odeon E-80744/80745)
Die Walküre (RCA LM-2452)

# ETHEL MERMAN

WHEN ETHEL MERMAN SANG, THERE WAS *NEVER* ANY QUESTION WHO it was. She had a unique, brassy voice that may have lacked subtlety but had verve, personality, and volume. She claimed her range extended from G below to C above. As to her singing technique, this very direct, meat-and-potatoes lady once remarked candidly, "I just stand up and holler and hope that my voice holds out." This naturalness was fine with America's great songwriters. George Gershwin told her, "Ethel, don't ever take a music lesson."

Regarding her legendary title as The Belter, composer Irving Berlin warned his confreres, "You better not write a bad lyric for Merman, because people will hear it in the second balcony." Cole Porter insisted (affectionately) that Ethel Merman sounded like a band going by. One Broadway reviewer described the vivacious 5' 6" songstress as "a doll from Astoria [Long Island] with a trumpet in her throat." Another said, "Even before the atomic bomb, there was Ethel Merman. She may never have flattened a playhouse but she has always shaken the rafters and laid an audience low." The "Merm" herself admitted of her lusty vocalizing, "If you hear me, you know who it is. I guess I'm blessed with good lungs."

She was an oversized star on stage and a high-octane gal away from the lights (she loved flea markets, thick steaks, and raunchy jokes and was a stickler for detail). It was this oversized quality that confounded Hollywood. Although she made several feature films, she never became a big movie name. It was not that she was unattractive (she had a pleasing Kewpie doll look) or too mature when she first came to pictures (she was in her early twenties). It was her exultant presentation. No matter how Merman toned down her performance in front of the cameras, it was always too (!) much for closeups. On stage she had two rules about performing. "Why should I get scared, I know my lines" and "I've been told that I'm round-eyed and look surprised. What's wrong with that? Who wants a girl who knows everything?"

If motion pictures kept rejecting her as leading lady material, she was still the First Lady of the American Musical Theater, where she always felt more at home. "Broadway has been very good to me, but I've been very good to Broadway too."

She was born Ethel Agnes Zimmermann on January 16, 1909, in Astoria, Long Island, New York, the daughter of Edward and Agnes Zimmermann. Her father was a bookkeeper. As a child she exhibited vocal talent, sang in amateur talent contests, and appeared in singing entertainments at nearby Army camp shows during World War I. She completed a commercial course at William Cullen Bryant High School (Long Island City) and after graduation began working as a stenographer. It was at the B. K. Vacuum Booster Brake Company in Long Island that she persuaded her millionaire boss, Caleb Bragg, who had many acquaintances in the entertainment industry, to provide her with a letter of introduction to a friend, producer George White. This theatrical producer offered Ethel a job in the chorus line of his current *Scandals*. However, she wanted to sing so she returned to her secretarial job. She continued to sing at every available evening or weekend social function.

It was during her singing engagement at the Little Russia Club on Manhattan's West 57th Street that Ethel came to the attention of theatrical agent Lou Irwin. He signed her to a nine-year contract and soon had her auditioning for Warner Bros. at its Brooklyn studio on Avenue J. She was contracted for six months at $125 per week. She quit her secretarial job, hoping for great things. Instead, her only acting assignment was to wear jungle garb in a studio short subject, THE CAVE CLUB (1930).

Eager to get her singing career moving, she negotiated her release from the contract and was soon appearing with the team of Lou Clayton, Eddie Jackson, and Jimmy Durante at Les Ambassadeurs Club. She sang her numbers and they did their routines. Later, in early 1930, she teamed with piano player Al Siegel and performed in vaudeville. By this time she was singing in Long Island clubs under her new, shortened professional name, Ethel Merman.

It was while she was billed at the Brooklyn Paramount Theatre that Broadway producer Vinton Freedley heard Ethel sing. He had George Gershwin listen to the self-assured miss and Ethel was hired as a rhythm singer for the upcoming *Girl Crazy*. Meanwhile, during play rehearsals, she was appearing at the Palace Theatre in Times Square. With songs by George and Ira Gershwin and Ginger Rogers as its star, *Girl Crazy* opened at the Alvin Theatre on October 14, 1930. Rogers was paid $1,500 a week, Ethel $350 weekly. (Ethel always claimed she never said, in a jealous picque about Rogers, "She's okay, if you like talent.") With her dynamic singing of "I Got Rhythm," Ethel quickly established herself as a major Broadway force. She would recall, "I held a high C note for sixteen bars" and did several encores. "I was nobody before the show opened, and the next day everybody on Broadway knew about me."

*Girl Crazy* ran for 272 performances. During the engagement she sang at the Central Park Casino (after the show) and began making movies again (during the day). This time she was under contract to Paramount Pictures and worked at its Astoria, Long Island, studio. Her first feature—as a last-minute replacement for Ruth Etting—was FOLLOW THE LEADER (1930), a vehicle for stage comedian Ed Wynn which featured Ginger Rogers as the ingenue. Further down in the cast was Merman, who had one song, "Mary." *Variety* noted, "Faulty make-up marked down her true appearance and the recording didn't carry her voice naturally." This lackluster feature film debut was an omen of her screen future. The studio used her thereafter in a series of musical short subjects (such as ROAMING, 1931) and several cartoons (like TIME ON MY HANDS, 1932) for which she provided the singing voice.

On Broadway she was in *George White's Scandals of 1931* (1931), in which she sang

"Life Is Just a Bowl of Cherries." She teamed with Rudy Vallee for an appearance at the New York Paramount in June 1931 and the next month was doing a vaudeville stand at the Palace Theatre. In *Take a Chance* (which began as *Humpty Dumpty*) (1932) she sang "You're an Old Smoothie" and turned the ballad "Eadie Was a Lady" into a boisterous number. The successful show lasted for 243 performances.

After *Take a Chance*, Ethel, accompanied by her mother, went to Hollywood for the first time. Paramount had cast her in WE'RE NOT DRESSING (1934), starring Bing Crosby, Carole Lombard, and George Burns and Gracie Allen. It was all about a cruise ship whose passengers are shipwrecked on a desert isle. Merman was the girlfriend of eccentric Leon Errol and together they sang "It's Just a New Spanish Custom"; the rest of the songs belonged to star Crosby. When Ethel was between Paramount pictures, Samuel Goldwyn borrowed her for KID MILLIONS (1934), his latest Eddie Cantor musical. She was the practical-minded girlfriend of Warren Hymer, both out to grab the $77 million that nebbish Cantor has inherited. She sang "An Earful of Music," and with her energetic, comedic performance, she almost stole the picture from Cantor and newcomers Ann Sothern and George Murphy. One of Ethel's leftover numbers ("It's the Animal in Me"), excised from WE'RE NOT DRESSING, was pulled from the cutting-room floor and used for THE BIG BROADCAST OF 1936 (1935). Paramount clearly did not know what to do with high-voltage Ethel Merman.

With William Gaxton and Victor Moore, she was co-starred on Broadway in Cole Porter's *Anything Goes* (1934), in which she had an abundance of hit songs that became fully associated with her: "I Get a Kick Out of You," "Blow, Gabriel, Blow," and "You're the Top." The *New York Times* applauded her for "the swinging gusto of her platform style." On radio she starred in the variety program "The Ethel Merman Show" over New York City's WABC. Before *Anything Goes* ended its 261-performance run, Merman returned to Hollywood to co-star again with Eddie Cantor in STRIKE ME PINK (1936). When that Samuel Goldwyn picture was delayed, Paramount used her to repeat her stage role in its movie version of ANYTHING GOES (1936). Bing Crosby was the star, and while Ethel repeated some of her stage song numbers, it was his picture all the way. On the other hand, STRIKE ME PINK, which proved to be Cantor's final movie for Goldwyn and which had Sally Eilers as the comedian's leading lady, was really a Merman showcase. She sang three ("First You Have Me High, Then You Have Me Low," "Calabash Pipe," and "Shake It Off with Rhythm") of the four numbers. She was definitely the lively highlight of this meandering production, which boasted a Technicolor finale in an ice cream factory.

On Broadway, Cole Porter's *Red, Hot and Blue!* (1936) provided Merman with such hits as "De-Lovely," "Ridin' High," and "Down in the Depths on the Ninetieth Floor." The production had to deal with the problem of how to give equal billing to co-stars Merman and Jimmy Durante (Bob Hope was featured in the musical) without either's being offended. The final compromise was to have their names intersect in the ads, so neither party would be offended by the other's having "top" billing. Not in the same league with her earlier vehicles, *Red, Hot and Blue!* ran a more modest 183 performances.

Socially Merman was linked with Philadelphia's burgeoning publishing tycoon

Walter Annenberg, but this connection ended when she returned to Hollywood. She now had a one-picture deal (with options) with 20th Century–Fox. There were then three reigning blonde musical stars at that studio: moppet Shirley Temple, singing Alice Faye, and ice-skating Sonja Henie. Realistically, there was no way a dark-haired singing "broad" from Broadway could compete with that trio. However, the lure of a healthy salary (by comparison to her already very healthy Broadway income) bewitched Merman. She was convinced the new studio would showcase (and film) her better than had either Goldwyn or Paramount. She was wrong.

Her first film for Fox, HAPPY LANDING (1938), starred Henie and Don Ameche with Ethel as a distaff second banana. There were ice-skating routines by Henie, tap dancing by the Condos brothers, and Ethel singing "Hot and Happy" and "You Appeal to Me." (Her number "You Are the Music to the Words in My Heart" was cut from the release print.) Her on-screen vis-à-vis was Cesar Romero (whom publicity releases imaginatively insisted she was dating off camera). *Variety* noted of Merman's latest screen appearance that she was "only effective when she's being a tough, acquisitive, etc., or when she's singing rhythm tunes as only she can sing them."

The love triangle of ALEXANDER'S RAGTIME BAND (1938) featured Don Ameche (the composer) and Tyrone Power (the band leader) both in love with a sultry songstress (Alice Faye). Merman was on hand briefly, but nevertheless effectively, as Jerry Allen, the powerful vocalist later hired by Power's band. She sang a lilting medley of Irving Berlin tunes, including "Blue Skies," "Pack Up Your Sins," "Go to the Devil," "We're on Our Way to France," "My Walking Stick," "Everybody Step," and "Heat Wave." For her third 1938 release she was billed *beneath* the zany Ritz Brothers in STRAIGHT, PLACE AND SHOW, a threadbare racetrack story that lacked class or imagination. Ethel's vocal contributions were "With You on My Mind" and "Why Not String Along with Me?" The *New York Times* branded this insipid comedy "one of those pictures produced by the trial and error method—a trial to its audience and an error on the part of the producer." Regarding the end of this phase of her filmmaking career, Merman assessed, "I liked to be in control. You couldn't be in films. And I'd already learned that it was cold down there as the face on the cutting-room floor."

Merman was much more comfortable back in New York where she could perform at clubs and be the toast of the town. She dated Stork Club proprietor Sherman Billingsley and starred in *Stars in Your Eyes* (1939), again teamed with Jimmy Durante. It was a near flop and closed after 127 performances. Much better was *DuBarry Was a Lady* (1939), Cole Porter's follow-up success to *Leave It to Me* (1938), which had made a Broadway star of Mary Martin. In this new musical comedy Ethel was teamed with Bert Lahr and sang "Friendship," "Do I Love You?," and "Well, Did You Evah?" The show featured Benny Baker and Betty Grable and ran for 178 performances. When it was made into a 1943 movie musical by MGM, Lucille Ball inherited Merman's boisterous role.

Even more successful for Merman was Cole Porter's *Panama Hattie* (1940), which gave her a rousing characterization as Hattie Maloney and such infectious numbers as "Let's Be Buddies" and "Make It Another Old-Fashioned, Please." Betty Hutton was the play's ingenue and further down in the cast was June Allyson, who was Hutton's understudy. When *Panama Hattie* became an MGM film in 1942, Ann Sothern was Hattie Maloney. Meanwhile, in 1940 Ethel met and married actor's agent William Smith. They were divorced the next year when he returned to the West Coast to continue working in the film industry. She next married (1941) Robert D. Levitt, a newspaper reporter-turned-publisher for Hearst Publications. Their daughter, Ethel (Jr.), was born in July 1942 and their son, Robert, in August 1945.

Again for Cole Porter, Ethel starred in the splashy wartime musical *Something for the Boys* (1943), in which she sang "Hey, Good Lookin'" and "He's a Right Guy." By the time that musical closed after 422 performances (Vivian Blaine starred in the 1944 movie version), Ethel was enmeshed in her bad luck year of 1944. During that unhappy time, she had a miscarriage, separated and reconciled with her husband, and signed for and dropped out of the stage musical *Sadie Thompson*. (June Havoc took her place and the show closed after thirty-two performances on Broadway.) Much more felicitous was Merman's association with Irving Berlin's *Annie Get Your Gun*, which registered 1,147 performances after its May 16, 1946, opening. Ethel was exuberant as the roisterous Annie Oakley who learns about romance ("They Say It's Wonderful"), courtship ("You Can't Get a Man with a Gun"), and career choices ("There's No Business Like Show Business"). When the hit musical went on the road with a national company, Mary Martin took over the title role; when MGM translated it to the screen in 1950, Betty Hutton was the lead. Meanwhile, in 1949 Ethel Merman had a continuing series over NBC network radio.

Merman made her television bow in a comedy pilot, "Thru the Crystal Ball" (June 20, 1949), and the next year was the hostess with the mostess when she top-billed Irving Berlin's *Call Me Madam* (1950) as an international darling of the political set, à la Perle Mesta. It was a megahit that ran for 644 performances and she won a Tony Award for her lively performance. (She would frequently resurrect the show for stock tour appearances.) For many fans it was a toss-up whether Ethel Merman or Mary Martin was the First Lady of the American Musical Theater, but the two settled for a draw when they teamed to harmonize medleys of their hit show tunes on "The Ford 50th Anniversary Show" (CBS-TV, June 15, 1953). Their sensational pairing was recorded by Decca Records and they would reteam on several occasions in future years for charity events.

In 1952 Merman had divorced Levitt and in March 1953 she married Robert F. Six, president of Continental Airlines, a union which fell apart in the late 1950s and led to a 1960 Mexican divorce. In 1954 Ethel recreated two of her most famous roles when she starred in condensed TV versions of "Anything Goes" (NBC-TV, February 28, 1954) and "Panama Hattie" (CBS-TV, November 10, 1954).

For a change Hollywood used Ethel (at $150,000) to recreate her starring role in CALL ME MADAM (1953), aided on camera by George Sanders, Donald O'Connor, and Vera-Ellen. Because the picture was such a close rendition of the Broadway original, Merman shone as she never had on camera before, delivering one of her zestiest characterizations. The same studio, 20th Century–Fox, also employed Ethel to co-star with Dan Dailey, Donald O'Connor, Mitzi Gaynor, Johnnie Ray, and Marilyn Monroe in the vaudeville saga THERE'S NO BUSINESS LIKE SHOW BUSINESS (1954). The movie was gaudy, in color and in widescreen CinemaScope. Ethel belted forth a host of Irving Berlin numbers. In this film she succeeded in showing the movie colony that they had been wrong to dismiss her as a Broadway oddity in the 1930s. Unfortunately, however, the great age of screen musicals had passed.

The mid-1950s marriage of movie star Grace Kelly to Prince Rainier of Monaco generated a great deal of global publicity. In 1956 Howard Lindsay and Russel Crouse took advantage of that international social event to spawn *Happy Hunting*, a musical comedy starring Merman and Fernando Lamas. During the show's 412-performance run, there was a great deal of publicity about the continuing feud between the two temperamental co-stars. During this time, on television Ethel went dramatic in the "Honest in the Rain" episode (CBS-TV, May 9, 1956) of "U.S. Steel Hour."

If any show is identified completely with Ethel Merman, it is the Jule Styne–Stephen Sondheim musical *Gypsy* (1959). As the stage mother (of stripper Gypsy Rose Lee) to end all stage mothers, she cavorted through the demanding role for almost two years during its 702-performance run. She mesmerized audiences with her vitality, emotional depth, and vocal renditions of such tunes as "Some People," "You'll Never Get Away from Me," her show-stopping "Everything's Coming Up Roses," and her soliloquy, "Rose's Turn." The original cast album became a classic and it won a Grammy Award. When this show went on tour, Ethel went with it. When the Broadway success became a film, however, it was Rosalind Russell, not Ethel Merman, who starred (inadequately) with Natalie Wood in GYPSY (1962). Losing the movie role in GYPSY was one of Merman's saddest professional defeats.

After Mae West and other choices bowed out of James Garner's fluffy screen comedy THE ART OF LOVE (1963), Ethel Merman agreed to substitute. When Stanley Kramer as-

Ethel Merman and George Sanders in CALL ME MADAM (1953)

sembled an all-star comic cast for his cynical IT'S A MAD, MAD, MAD, MAD WORLD (1963), Ethel gamely accepted the role of the archetypical shrewish mother-in-law, standing out strongly in a cast of major comedians. It was during her Hollywood period that she met Oscar-winning actor Ernest Borgnine and, to the amazement of some (and the amusement of others), they were wed on June 26, 1964, only to separate after thirty-eight days of marriage, and to divorce in 1965. In 1966 Irving Berlin persuaded Ethel to revive *Annie Get Your Gun* for the New York stage and he wrote a new song especially for her, "An Old-Fashioned Wedding." The following year (on March 19, 1967) she appeared in a small-screen version of the show on NBC-TV. It was in 1968 that her daughter Ethel (Jr.) died of an overdose of barbiturates and liquor. Some insisted it was suicide.

Producer David Merrick had long wanted Ethel Merman to star in his *Hello, Dolly!* (she had been the original choice for the lead). However, it was not until March 1970 that she agreed to go into the long-running Broadway show for a limited run. For her version, the songs "World Take Me Back" and "Love Look in My Window" (both cut from the original production) were restored to the proceedings. It was Merman who closed the Broadway engagement after its historic 2,844 performances. On April 21, 1972, she received a special Tony Award for her continuing contributions to the musical theater.

In the 1960s Ethel had appeared on television in such campy assignments as "Batman" (1967) and later as a guest star on Marlo Thomas' "That Girl" (1968). In the 1970s she was a frequent guest star on talk shows and on such specials as "Jack Lemmon in 'S Wonderful, 'S Marvelous, 'S Gershwin" (1972), "Ed Sullivan's Broadway" (1973), and "The Ted Knight Musical Comedy Variety Special" (1976). She made an unsold comedy series pilot, "You're Gonna Love It Here," in 1977 and was a guest on "The Love Boat" series in 1979, 1980, and, on their two-hour musical special in 1982, teamed with Ann Miller and Van Johnson. When the disco craze was at its peak in the mid-1970s, she made *The Ethel Merman Disco Album*, showing she had lost little or none of her vibrato. In 1955 her first autobiography, *Who Could Ask for Anything More?* (written with Pete Martin), was published. Her second, *Merman* (written with George Eels), appeared in 1978. She later made a cameo appearance in WON TON TON, THE DOG WHO SAVED HOLLYWOOD (1976) and had a hilarious moment as herself (in pajamas!) in the zany AIRPLANE! (1980).

Unfortunately, her last years were tragic. She suffered from recurrent ailments and "existed" in her midtown Manhattan hotel suite. She was later diagnosed as having a brain tumor and spent her final days incoherent and speechless. She died in her sleep on February 15, 1984, at her apartment, survived by her son. On the evening of that day, theaters on Broadway dimmed their lights at nine p.m. in tribute to one of Broadway's greatest stars. One newspaper obituary stated, "She had a quality that can never again spring spontaneously into being—call it classicism, call it Olympian simplicity, call it God's unattainable socko, but call it Merman."

Just as the equally unique Judy Garland spawned several mimics and impersonators, so has Ethel Merman. Her greatest imitator is Rita McKenzie, who in the late 1980s began mounting a one-woman show entitled *Call Me Ethel!* It has played cabaret and summer stock engagements around the country. Said the *Los Angeles Times,* "McKenzie's nuances, her assertive ruby lips, and that scrunched-up hair style is 'De-Lovely' Merman right down to 'The Animal in Me.'"

## Filmography

The Cave Club (Vita, 1930) (s)
Follow the Leader (Par, 1930)
Devil Sea (Par, 1931) (s)
Old Man Blues (Par, 1931) (s)
Roaming (Par, 1931) (s)
Let Me Call You Sweetheart (Par, 1932) (s) (voice only)
Time on My Hands (Par, 1932) (s) (voice only)
You Try Somebody Else (Par, 1932) (s) (voice only)
Ireno (Par, 1932) (s)
Be Like Me (Par, 1933) (s)
Song Shopping (Par, 1933) (s) (voice only)
We're Not Dressing (Par, 1934)
Kid Millions (UA, 1934)
The Big Broadcast of 1936 (Par, 1935)
Anything Goes (Par, 1936)

Strike Me Pink (UA, 1936)
Happy Landing (20th–Fox, 1938)
Alexander's Ragtime Band (20th–Fox, 1938)
Straight, Place and Show [They're Off] (20th–Fox, 1938)
Stage Door Canteen (UA, 1943)
Call Me Madam (20th–Fox, 1953)
There's No Business Like Show Business (20th–Fox, 1954)
The Art of Love (Univ, 1963)
It's a Mad, Mad, Mad, Mad World (UA, 1963)
Journey Back to Oz [Return to Oz] (Filmation, 1974) (voice only)
Won Ton Ton, the Dog Who Saved Hollywood (Par, 1976)
Airplane! (Par, 1980)

## Broadway Plays

Girl Crazy (1930)
George White's Scandals of 1931 (1931)
Take a Chance (1932)
Anything Goes (1934)
Red, Hot and Blue! (1936)
Stars in Your Eyes (1939)
DuBarry Was a Lady (1939)
Panama Hattie (1940)

Something for the Boys (1943)
Annie Get Your Gun (1946)
Call Me Madam (1950)
Happy Hunting (1956)
Gypsy (1959)
Annie Get Your Gun (1966) (revival)
Hello, Dolly! (1970) (replacement)

## Radio Series

The Ethel Merman Show (WABC, 1935) (local)
The Ethel Merman Show (NBC, 1949)

## Album Discography

Alexander's Ragtime Band (Hollywood Soundstage 406) [ST]

Annie Get Your Gun (Decca DL-8001, Decca DL-9018/79018, MCA 2031) [OC]

Annie Get Your Gun (London XPS-905)

Annie Get Your Gun (RCA LOC/LSO-1123)

Anything Goes (Caliban 6043) [ST]

Anything Goes/Panama Hattie (Larynx 567, Amalgamated 144, Sandy Hooks 2043) [ST/TV]

Call Me Madam (10" Decca DL-5465) [ST]

Call Me Madam (10" Decca DL-5304, Decca DL-8035, Decca DL-9022/89022, MCA 1226, MCA 2055)

The Ethel Merman Disco Album (A&M 4775)

Ethel Merman/Lyda Roberti/Mae West (Col CL-2751, Col Special Products 2751)

Ethel Merman on Stage (X LVA-1004)

Ethel Was a Lady (MCA 1804)

Ethel's Ridin' High (London XPS-909)

The Ford Fiftieth Anniversary Television Show (10" Decca DL-7027) [ST/TV] w. Mary Martin

Gypsy (Col OL-5420/OS-2077, Col S-32607) [OC]

Happy Hunting (RCA LOC-1026) [OC]

Her Greatest Hits (Reprise 6032, Stanyan 10070)

Kid Millions (CIF 3007) [ST]

Lee Wiley and Ethel Merman Sing Cole Porter (JJC 2003)

Memories (Decca DL-9028)

Merman in Las Vegas (Reprise 6062)

Merman in the Movies, 1930–38 (Encore 101)

Merman Sings Merman (London XPS-901)

Musical Autobiography (Decca DX-153)

Les Poupées de Paris (RCA LOC/LSO-1090) [OC]

Red, Hot and Blue/Stars in Your Eyes (AEI 1147) [OC]

Something for the Boys (Sound/Stage 2305) [OC]

Songs She Made Famous (10" Decca DL-5053)

Stage Door Canteen/Hollywood Canteen (Curtain Call 100/11-12) [ST]

Straight, Place and Show (Vertinge 2000) [ST]

There's No Business Like Show Business (Decca DL-8091, MCA 1727) [ST]

Twelve Songs from "Call Me Madam" (MCA 1726) [ST]

The World Is Your Balloon (MCA 1839) w. Jimmy Durante, Ray Bolger

The Young Ethel Merman (JJC 3004)

# BETTE MIDLER

OF ANY ENTERTAINMENT SUPERSTAR WHO HAS EMERGED IN THE LAST
half of the twentieth century, Bette Midler has a life and career filled with the most
intriguing contradictions. She began singing professionally in the chorus of Broadway's
*Fiddler on the Roof* and graduated to showcasing her vocal and comedic talents as a cabaret
performer in a bathhouse catering to homosexuals. Her unconventional stage act was soon
acclaimed for its bizarre mixture of versatile vocals, high camp, and zealous comedy that
leaned to extreme raunch. Bubbly Bette quickly gained fame as "The Divine Miss M." The
racy 5' 1" redhead was renowned as "The Mouth That Launched Sleaze with Ease" and
"The Trash with Flash Lady."

However, beneath Midler's surface glitz and kitsch was an instinctive and intense
dramatic songstress who provided wonderful interpretations of golden oldie songs as well
as new rock numbers. She illustrated the depth of her resourcefulness in her starring movie
role in THE ROSE (1979). Then her career fell apart suddenly. Yet in the mid-1980s
everything again changed for her. She married, had a child, and starred in a string of screen
comedies that did BIG BUSINESS (1988) and made her an OUTRAGEOUS FORTUNE (1987).
She became one of new Hollywood's most bankable stars, whose status was solidified by
BEACHES (1988), a dramatic female buddy picture that she co-produced as well as starred
in. The latter movie provided her with her first number one hit song, "Wind Beneath My
Wings," and a huge-selling sleeper LP album from the film's soundtrack. It seemed a
typically abrupt career turn for the always unpredictable Miss Midler. She soon turned
into a Hollywood establishment figure herself, surprising the entertainment industry yet
again. Go figure it.

She was born in Hawaii on December 1, 1945, the third daughter of Fred Midler
and Ruth (Schindel) Midler who had moved to the islands from New Jersey not long
before. Bette, like her older sisters (Judy and Susan), was named by the star-struck Mrs.
Midler for a movie celebrity, in her case Bette Davis. (Because it was assumed that Davis
pronounced her first name as "Bet," that was how the child was always addressed.) When
Bette was a youngster, the Midlers moved back to Passaic, New Jersey (Mrs. Midler's
home town). However, after a disillusioning six months, they returned to Waikiki
permanently. Fred Midler was a house painter employed frequently by the Navy. As such,
the Midlers had military housing (inexpensive but adequate). Later, when the government
required additional space for military personnel, the Midlers were among those sent to a
housing development. There the Midlers were the only white people in the community's
ethnic mix. The overweight, plain Bette soon convinced the neighborhood children that
she was Portuguese. "It was easier than anything else. Portuguese people were accepted.

Jews were not. I was an alien, a foreigner, even though I was born there." When Bette was six, the Midlers had their first son, Danny, who suffered mental retardation as a result of an ailment in infancy.

Always the outsider at school, Bette found a degree of acceptance by becoming the class comedienne. She won a school talent show singing "Lullaby of Broadway" and that became her standard performance number. When she was twelve, she attended her first theater performance, which convinced her of her love of show business and strengthened her determination to follow it as a career and as an escape from her stifling home life. In her senior year at Radford High, she had the lead in the class production of *When Our Hearts Were Young and Gay*. After graduating in 1963, she spent another summer working in a pineapple factory. That fall she enrolled at the University of Hawaii as a drama major, but soon left. In 1965 Julie Andrews and company were filming HAWAII on location and Bette got an extra's job playing a missionary's seasick wife. When an additional extra's role opened up in the picture, she went to Hollywood for the shoot. It provided her with sufficient funds ($1,000) to try stage work in New York. She had decided she was not conventionally pretty enough to be in the movies. She told her family, "I'm gonna be a star!"

To support herself in Manhattan, Bette held a variety of jobs: as a typist, a hat-check girl, a department store sales clerk, and a go-go dancer in Union City, New Jersey. She won roles in children's theater (usually as a witch) and then was cast in the Tom Eyen play *Miss Nefertiti Regrets* at the Cafe La MaMa. She worked in the Catskill Mountains in *An Evening of Tradition* (based on stories by Paddy Chayevsky and Sholom Aleichem) and sang in showcases. Off-Broadway she was in *Sinderella Revisited*, a Tom Eyen play that was modified into a laundered matinee version for children called *Cinderella Revisited*. After many months of auditioning, in 1966 she was given a chorus part in the hit Broadway musical *Fiddler on the Roof*. She also understudied the role of Tevye's eldest daughter. Later she got to play the part, with Adrienne Barbeau and Tanya Everett as her sisters. Altogether, she was in *Fiddler* for three years. (It was during this period that her oldest sister, Judy, came to New York to see the show and was killed in a freak car accident.)

After this long run in a small part on Broadway at frustratingly low pay, Midler left the musical. She had already begun performing on talent nights at Manhattan clubs. At one of the cabarets, The Improv, the club pianist was Barry Manilow. He and Bette became friendly and he soon became her accompanist. She developed an act which featured nostalgic songs and an eccentric wardrobe which ranged from toreador pants to sequined gowns from past eras. Meanwhile, she joined the cast of the off-Broadway rock musical *Salvation*.

In July 1970, at $50 a weekend, Bette was hired to sing at the Continental Baths, a gay bathhouse on Manhattan's Upper West Side. With Barry Manilow as her accompanist, she began a long-running engagement there, developing her act to include audacious, raunchy comedy and altering her costuming to 1950s flashy trash. When she was a guest on Johnny Carson's "Tonight Show," she told the host, "I'm probably the only female singer in America who sings in a Turkish Bath. It's a health club." On a later Carson appearance, Carson and his entourage (Ed McMahon, Doc Severinsen, and guest Orson

Bean) became her backup singers, The Bang Bangs. By the fall of 1970 Bette was appearing as Jackie Vernon's opening act at Mr. Kelly's Club in Chicago. She sang "Sh-Boom," wore a purple dress, and had a mass of flaming orangish hair. The audience was bewildered by her stream-of-consciousness comedy patter and her outrageousness.

She continued to perform at the Continental Baths, dressing up in crazy outfits and sporting thick platform shoes. (She did a wonderful imitation of Carmen Miranda as well.) In the spring of 1971 she played The Acid Queen and Mrs. Walker for the Seattle Opera Company's production of *Tommy*. She was again at Mr. Kelly's in Chicago, this time the opening act for comedian Mort Sahl. By now her theme song had become "Friends." She was hired to appear at the Downstairs at the Upstairs in New York City. Her two-week engagement turned into a ten-week stand, with celebrities often in the audience. She made one of her final appearances at the Continental Baths in February 1972 and then went on the road. As part of her troupe, she had Barry Manilow as pianist in the small band and a singing trio of backup singers called the Harlettes (originally Melissa Manchester, Merle Miller, and Gail Kantor). She honed her routines, which one critic called "madcap, manic and melodious." She would skitter across the stage in high heels, stop, and say, "I think it's time for a little vulgarity. What do ya say, folks?" Next she would recite with relish one of her outrageous Sophie Tucker jokes and then, with eyes wide and other very expressive facial gestures, she would punctuate audience laughter with, "Ooooh. I didn't say that. I never said. I never said that!"

In April 1972 she was Johnny Carson's opening act at the Sahara Hotel in Las Vegas. She had a successful Carnegie Hall concert and later that summer was performing at the Schaefer Music Festival in Central Park. She had a new manager, Aaron Russo, a battling relationship which also dominated her private life, although he was then married. Her first album—*The Divine Miss M*—was released by Atlantic Records in November 1972. It rose to number nine on the charts. The release contains her campy "Leader of the Pack" and the rhythmic "Chapel of Love." Two singles from the LP became major hits: "Do You Wanna Dance?" and the even more popular "Boogie Woogie Bugle Boy." The latter was her tribute to The Andrews Sisters and the song did much to revive interest in that singing group. Meanwhile, she made a coast-to-coast U.S. tour. In Los Angeles she played at The Troubador. On New Year's Eve, 1972, in New York she appeared at Philharmonic Hall, part of the prestigious Lincoln Center complex.

In 1973 she continued to tour, including a sold-out engagement at the Dorothy Chandler Pavilion in Los Angeles. She was on a Burt Bacharach TV special in February 1973 (ABC) with Peter Ustinov and Stevie Wonder. Her new backup Harlettes were Charlotte Crossley, Sharon Redd, and Robin Grean and the extended tour included Honolulu and the Universal Amphitheatre in Los Angeles. At the latter engagement, Maxene and Patty Andrews (the surviving members of The Andrews Sisters) came on stage to join Bette for "Boogie Woogie Bugle Boy." In December 1973 she began a three-week engagement at New York's Palace Theatre, a near one-woman show in which she sang Kurt Weill's "Surabaya Johnny," "Hello in There," and all her standards, including a production number of "Lullaby of Broadway." She told vulgar jokes, wittily trashed the rich element in the audience, and was a sold-out hit. (A few weeks later, at the nearby

Winter Garden Theatre, Liza Minnelli would have an equally packed engagement, making the two diverse personalities rivals for being the *new* Miss Show Business.) In early 1974 Midler won a Grammy Award as Best New Artist for her debut LP and she was given a special Tony Award (as was Liza Minnelli) for her Broadway concert engagement. She had been named one of the ten worst-dressed women of the year by California designer Mr. Blackwell. He described her as "potluck in a laundromat." It all added to her allure, as did the success of her second album, *Bette Midler* (1973).

In 1974, Bette spent several months in Europe recovering from emotional stress. It was also the year that a low-class religious satire, THE DIVINE MR. J., opened. Bette had played the screen role of a hip Virgin Mary for $250 in 1971, in an amateurish 16mm. production that did not find release until the spring of 1974, when it exploited Midler as its "star" in her film debut. Bette asked fans not to attend the movie, which had a very short run in New York City, with Midler's followers picketing the theater. Later in the year, Bette talked with director Mike Nichols about co-starring with Warren Beatty and Jack Nicholson in THE FORTUNE (1975). However, it was Stockard Channing who won the role in this unsuccessful movie comedy.

Along with Elton John and Flip Wilson, Bette guested on the Cher special on CBS-TV (February 12, 1975). Barry Manilow had already departed by the time Midler opened in the spring of 1975 at New York City's Minskoff Theatre in Bette Midler's *Clams on the Half Shell Revue*. The expensively mounted production featured such outré items as Bette emerging from a huge clam shell as a mermaid, singing in the arms of King Kong, and zipping across the stage in a wheelchair. Her ten-week stand, which included some characterization skits, grossed nearly $2 million. In 1976 she went on *The Depression Show* tour, a condensed version of her *Clams on the Half Shell* production, adding a Statue of Liberty tribute for the bicentennial. When her third album, *Songs for the New Depression*, was released, she called it a "whimsical, reactionary album." Most critics disliked it. It reached only twenty-seventh place on the charts. Her tour played Caesar's Palace in Las Vegas where, as had become a tradition, audiences were not responsive. While in Cleveland her show was taped live for presentation on cable's Home Box Office channel on June 19, 1976. This airing of "The Fabulous Bette Midler Show" allowed home audiences to witness the unexpurgated Bette Midler as network TV censors would never allow her to appear. It was far more engaging than her conventional appearance on a Neil Sedaka television special that September.

Plans for Bette to appear in 1977 with the New York City Ballet in the light opera *The Seven Deadly Sins* did not materialize. By now actor Peter Riegert had replaced Aaron Russo as her steady boyfriend and she appeared, along with Rosemary Clooney, Debbie Reynolds, Bob Hope, Donald O'Connor, and others on Bing Crosby's "A 50th Anniversary Gala" (CBS-TV, March 28, 1977). Her two-record *Live at Last* (live) album contained the song "You're Moving Out Today," written by Carole Bayer Sager, Bruce Roberts, and Bette. As a change of venue and format in late 1977, Bette went on a tour of small clubs throughout the United States. Nevertheless, she remained her usual self-deprecating self ("They were going to star me in a movie called *Close Encounters of the Worst Kind*, but I declined."). She traded insults with the Harlettes and sang her assortment of songs, including heart-felt ballads. Then she starred in her first network special, "Ol' Red Hair Is Back" (NBC-TV, December 8, 1977); although she toned down her act, she was sufficiently unique to gain audience response. However, her fifth album, *Broken Blossom*, released in December 1977, sold poorly.

In 1978 she embarked on an extensive world tour with The New Harlettes (Linda Hart, Katie Sagal, Frannie Eisenberg), which included stopovers in England, Denmark, Sweden, Germany, France, and Australia. By early 1979 Bette had severed her working relationship with Aaron Russo, at about the same time that her mother died of cancer (January 1979). That spring her new album, *Thighs and Whispers*, was released. Years later she would admit, "By that point, I was just grabbing at straws." She would consider the disco novelty number "Nights in Black Leather" as the low point of her recording career. However, another single from the album, "Married Men," reached number forty on the charts, her first single hit in nearly six years. After more playdates (the abbreviated tour was called *Bette! Divine Madness*), Bette Midler made her real feature film debut.

In the 1970s there had been talk of Midler's starring in screen biographies of Sophie Tucker and Texas Guinan, and her manager had turned down roles for her in NASHVILLE (1975), KING KONG (1976), and FOUL PLAY (1978). For Midler, her role as the tragic Janis Joplin–like singer in THE ROSE (1979) was a tour de force. The film was an intense dissection of a rock singer on a self-propelled joyride to self-destruction. *Variety* reported, "It's a tribute to the talent of Midler herself that she makes a basically unsympathetic and unlikable character attractive at all." For her exhaustive and exhausting performance she was Oscar-nominated, but lost the Best Actress award to Sally Field of NORMA RAE. The soundtrack album to THE ROSE reached number twelve on the charts and two Midler singles from the movie, "When a Man Loves a Woman" and "The Rose," were on the top forty charts. She won a Grammy Award for Best Contemporary/Pop Female Solo Vocal for the song "The Rose."

Although THE ROSE would gross over $19 million in domestic film rentals, Bette could not find an appropriate follow-up property. (She would later say of this bleak period, "Once I saw myself on the big screen and had my dream, I was simply lost. There was no new goal.") She took her *Divine Madness* show to Broadway for six weeks in 1980 and for an $850,000 fee recreated it on film (1980) in concert at the Pasadena Civic Auditorium. It was not a box-office bonanza. The *Divine Madness* album reached number thirty-four on the charts and the single "My Mother's Eyes" reached number thirty-nine. Her saucy memoir of her recent European tour, *A View from a Broad*, was published in the spring of 1980. Although the tome was enlivened by a lot of imagined happenings, it was a best-seller.

Much has been written about Bette Midler's JINXED (1982), a trouble-plagued movie which was ridiculed as entertainment and did extremely badly commercially. Co-starring Ken Wahl, it was a black comedy set in and around Lake Tahoe, with Midler as the country singer anxious for the demise of her obnoxious blackjack dealer lover (Rip Torn). The experience left Midler with a nervous breakdown and with no further screen offers. ("That was the first time I realized that I was not as divine as I thought I was.") She went on the road with *De Tour*, which reflected a strong New Wave music influence. But her show still had such rowdy numbers as "Pretty Legs and Great Big Knockers." For her December 31, 1982, appearance at the Universal Amphitheatre, Barry Manilow reunited with her on stage. Her album *No Frills* fared badly but her children's book, *The Saga of Baby Divine* (1983), was number three on the *New York Times* fiction best-seller list. To continue reaching her audience, Bette made the "Beat of Burden" video and single record in January 1984.

In December 1984 in Las Vegas she married Martin von Haselberg, a Los Angeles commodities trader. (He was also a performance artist under the name Harry Kipper.) After nearly three years of no film activity, she returned to picture making. She was to have starred in MY GIRDLE IS KILLING ME, a comedy about a Hollywood star down on her luck. Instead, she was hired for the Paul Mazursky comedy DOWN AND OUT IN BEVERLY HILLS (1986), a wacky comedy based on a French film. She played an intense Beverly Hills housewife who sets a chain of amusing events into motion when she allows a skid-row bum (Nick Nolte) to stay in the guest bedroom of her mansion. The picture grossed $28,277,000 in domestic film rentals and did much to revive the film careers of Richard Dreyfuss (as her on-camera husband) and Midler. Also for Touchstone Pictures and Buena Vista Releasing (both part of the Walt Disney Organization) she starred in the caper comedy RUTHLESS PEOPLE (1986). She was the obnoxiously loud but still good-hearted wife that philandering spouse Danny DeVito refuses to ransom from kidnappers. It successfully exploited Bette's raucous comedy style and the movie grossed $31,443,000 in domestic film rentals. Her first comedy album, *Mud Will Be Flung Tonight*, was released in 1986. In November of that year she gave birth to her first child, Sophie Frederica Alohani von Haselberg. ("She is not named after Sophie Tucker, contrary to what people might think," insisted Midler.) Shortly before her father died in 1986, she and he were reconciled after years of strained relations.

Bette Midler in RUTHLESS PEOPLE (1986)

The R-rated OUTRAGEOUS FORTUNE (1987) paired Midler with Shelley Long as two diverse personalities both in love with a seemingly nice school teacher (Peter Coyote). Its popularity led Touchstone Pictures to sign Midler to a long-term multiple picture deal in which she was to star in three films as well as to develop/produce/star in additional properties. In the comedy BIG BUSINESS (1988), both she and Lily Tomlin played twins, leading to a madcap cascade of slapstick errors. In the full-length animated feature OLIVER & COMPANY (1988), loosely inspired by Charles Dickens' *Oliver Twist*, Bette was the poodle Georgette and sang "Perfect Isn't

Easy." Her March 1988 Home Box Office cable special, "Bette Midler's Mondo Beyon-do," featured her husband, Martin von Haselberg, in one of its more infantile skits. By July 1988, Midler had extended her pact with Touchstone Pictures for four additional films, making her one of the most successful film stars in contemporary Hollywood. Her reputation was capped by her bravura performance in BEACHES (1988), which offered her as CC Bloom, a pop singer whose friendship over the decades with Barbara Hershey forms the film's texture. This mishmash of a movie received very mixed responses, but the reviews for Midler were extremely positive. (*People* magazine stated, "It's hard to think of a more enticing invitation to a movie than these two words: Bette Midler.") The project was packaged by All Girl Productions, a production company she founded with Margaret Jennings South and Bonnie Bruckheimner-Martell. The picture sold $55 million worth of tickets in its first twenty-five weeks of national distribution. The soundtrack album rose to number two on the charts and her hit single from it, "Wind Beneath My Wings," reached number one, displacing Madonna's "Like a Prayer" from the top spot. In early 1989 Midler filmed STELLA, the latest remake of that archetypical tearjerker STELLA DALLAS.

Now at a peak of mainstream popularity, Midler admits, "I do miss singing in front of an audience, but the recording career I can take or leave. Because I haven't had that kind of long, sustained success over years and years, it's not a life-or-death proposition to me."

## Filmography

Hawaii (UA, 1966)
The Divine Mr. J. (National Entertainment, 1974)
The Rose (20th–Fox, 1979)
Divine Madness (WB, 1980)
Jinxed (MGM/UA, 1982)
Down and Out in Beverly Hills (BV, 1986)

Ruthless People (BV, 1986)
Outrageous Fortune (BV, 1987)
Big Business (BV, 1988)
Oliver & Company (BV, 1988) (voice only)
Beaches (BV, 1988) (also co-producer)
Stella (BV, 1989)

## Broadway Plays

Fiddler on the Roof (1966) (replacement)

## Album Discography

Beaches (Atlantic SD-81933) [ST]
Bette Midler (Atlantic SD-7270)
Broken Blossom (Atlantic SD-19151)
Divine Madness (Atlantic SD-16022)
The Divine Miss M (Atlantic QD/SD-7238)
Live at Last (Atlantic SD-9000)
Mud Will Be Flung Tonight (Atlantic 81291)

No Frills (Atlantic 80070)
Oliver & Company (Walt Disney Records 012) [ST]
The Rose (Atlantic SD-16010) [ST]
Songs for the New Depression (Atlantic SD-18155)
Thighs and Whispers (Atlantic SD-16004)

# ANN MILLER

BRASSY, LACQUERED, ROBUST, PERPETUALLY GIRLISH: THESE DESCRIP-
tions cling to Ann Miller, who has tap danced vigorously across stage and screen for six
decades, outlasting most of her performing contemporaries. Despite the insistence by
some that she is high camp, she remains today as professionally enthusiastic as when she
began in the business in the early 1930s. She was a club performer and a contractee at two
lesser studios (RKO and Columbia) before, midway in her screen career, coming to
MGM. She was ready, willing, and able to shine. However, by 1948 Metro was in decline
and there were few musicals being produced on the lot. As always, she made the best of the
situation.

Ann Miller's stocks-in-trade are her fabulous legs (Walter Winchell tagged her
"Legs Miller"), a distinctive terpsichorean strut, a vibrant song style, an extra-wide smile,
and that gushy belief in herself. She is renowned for being charmingly lightheaded. When
learning they were casting *Ari*, the stage version of *Exodus*, she called her agent and said, "If
they're going to do a musical about Ari, I want to play Jackie Onassis." She claims that
once, when she injured her foot and went to the doctor for an X-ray, she was given a form
to complete. "It said 'occupation' and I didn't know whether I should write singer, dancer,
or actress. So I just wrote STAR."

She was born April 12, 1923 (not, she insists, 1919 as her studio biography once
listed it) in Houston, Texas. Her father (John Alfred Collier) was a criminal lawyer. Her
mother (Clara), from whom she inherited her enthusiasm and naiveté, sent the girl to
dancing school at the age of three to cure a case of childhood rickets. She soon was
proficient at "quick-style" dancing numbers and was performing at local functions. At age
ten, she placed first in a Big Brothers personality contest. When Johnnie Lucille (as she was
christened) was eleven, her parents divorced. Clara, who was nearly totally deaf and could
not hold a job, dreamed of making her child a dancing star and the two moved to
Hollywood. After they arrived in Los Angeles, there were occasional dancing engagements
at the Rotary and Lions Clubs. Piano accompanist Harry Fields suggested that under-aged
Johnnie Lucille change her name to Anne (with an "e") Miller. Billed as a "tap dancer with
a new style," she won a talent contest, leading to a two-week engagement at $50 weekly.
With strategic padding to fill out her figure, thirteen-year-old Anne was hired for a brief
chorus job in THE DEVIL ON HORSEBACK (1936), a minor contemporary Western at Grand
National Pictures.

It was later in 1936 that Anne accepted a dancing job at the Bal Tabarin Club in San
Francisco. During her three-week stand there, Lucille Ball (then a blonde actress at RKO)

happened to be in the audience, accompanied by Benny Rubin (then a studio talent scout). Ball thought Miller should be screen-tested. She was, and RKO hired her at $150 weekly. Her new screen name was Ann Miller. She made her debut in NEW FACES OF 1937. She had no dialogue, just tap danced a bit in her inimitable fast style. (There were inevitable comparisons to MGM's reigning tap dancing star, Eleanor Powell, whose style was more athletic and less theatrical.) In the glamour-packed STAGE DOOR (1937) Ann had lines but no dancing, while in RADIO CITY REVELS (1938), which featured Milton Berle, she began to shine. *Variety* enthused of the new dancing personality, "She carries the romantic interest well, is a cute charming personality and has a lot of poise. . . . Miss Miller is a right smart tapster. . . ." She was loaned to Columbia Pictures for the classic YOU CAN'T TAKE IT WITH YOU (1938). Director Frank Capra would recall, "She played Alice's [Jean Arthur] sister, Essie, the awkward Pavlova, played her with the legs of Marlene [Dietrich], the innocence of Pippa, and the brain of a butterfly that flitted on its toes."

Ann and Lucille Ball were window dressing in the Marx Brothers' less-than-hilarious ROOM SERVICE (1938), her seventh and final RKO picture at a weekly salary of $250. She was caught in a career rut and her agents convinced her that she needed a Broadway success to re-establish her movie worth. She left RKO and went to New York to join Willie and Eugene Howard, Ella Logan, and The Three Stooges in *George White's Scandals of 1939*. It opened on August 28, 1939, and closed less than four months later. However, the revue served its attention-getting purpose well. ("Ann is terrific. She's an eye tonic, has loads of style and a personality that whirls with hurricane force across the footlights," wrote Robert Coleman in the *New York Daily Mirror*.) There was renewed studio interest in her. She chose to return to RKO for third billing in TOO MANY GIRLS (1940), starring Lucille Ball and Frances Langford, and introducing Desi Arnaz. In Republic's ambitious Gene Autry Western MELODY RANCH (1940), Ann competed with Champion the horse and the comedy antics of Jimmy Durante.

In 1941 Ann signed a one-picture contract at Columbia. In TIME OUT FOR RHYTHM, she was teamed her with Rudy Vallee. She was given three dance routines, choreographed by LeRoy Prinz, including a prime solo dance number, "A-Twiddlin' My Thumbs." Following on the favorable response to this "nervous A" (her words), movie studio head Harry Cohn signed Ann to a long-term contract. Rita Hayworth may have been the queen of the studio's lavish musicals, but Ann was around to highlight the minor musical quickies for which the lot was famous. After playing in a Western with Glenn Ford, GO WEST, YOUNG LADY (1941), she was loaned to Paramount for two pictures. In the wacky service comedy TRUE TO THE ARMY (1942), she took attention away from co-stars Judy Canova and Allan Jones with her amazingly fast tap dancing. ("Wait until you hear her answer a machine gun with taps," *The Hollywood Reporter* alerted.) When her next picture, PRIORITIES ON PARADE (1942)—about working women in war plants—debuted on Broadway, Ann starred in the stage show at the flagship Paramount Theatre.

Today Ann's REVEILLE WITH BEVERLY (1943), about a female radio disc jockey, is best remembered for a brief appearance by the young Frank Sinatra. But she was very proficient in her obligatory tap dancing routine, "Thumbs Up and V for Victory." In HEY,

ROOKIE (1944) she did her version of a harem dance ("Streamlined Sheik"), while in JAM SESSION (1944) she was outnumbered by six dance bands (including Louis Armstrong's) but tapped her way through the "No Name Jive" number. Costing around $400,000 each, all of Ann Miller's Columbia features made money. They made ample provision for her to dance, and highlighted her gorgeous figure (usually in abbreviated black tights). Her more than competent singing, such as of "You Came Along, Baby" in EADIE WAS A LADY (1945), was often overlooked because of her flashy toe tapping. In EVE KNEW HER APPLES (1945), a poor remake of IT HAPPENED ONE NIGHT, she did not dance at all, but had four pleasing song numbers, including "I'll Remember April."

Columbia was planning finally to star Ann in a major screen musical, the Technicolor THE PETTY GIRL, when she and the studio clashed. She had married millionaire industrialist Reese Llewellyn Milner on February 16, 1946, and he insisted she abandon her movie career. Columbia's Harry Cohn sued her and won a $150,000 judgment. She settled the dispute by starring in THE THRILL OF BRAZIL (1946). She was now pregnant, but according to Ann, her husband in a drunken rage beat her and threw her down the stairs. She lost her baby and broke her back. She and Milner divorced and her studio contract lapsed.

MGM's Louis B. Mayer had long been an admirer of Ann Miller. The two had been on the social scene together before her marriage. He had been particularly impressed by her vivacious performance in EADIE WAS A LADY, playing a Boston co-ed who works as a

Ann Miller in REVEILLE WITH BEVERLY (1943)

burlesque dancer at night. When a leg injury forced Cyd Charisse out of MGM's EASTER PARADE (1948), Mayer arranged for Ann to test for the role of dancing star Nadine Hale who loses Fred Astaire to Judy Garland. It was one of her flashiest and most substantial "other woman" roles and Ann was riveting in her "Shaking the Blues Away" tap number. Her performance was all the more amazing because she still wore a back brace from her recent fall.

MGM signed Ann to a contract to join their musical unit. She insisted later, "I never played politics, I never was a party girl, and I never slept with any of the producers," which may be why the studio never promoted her as a major star. Along with Cyd Charisse and Ricardo Montalban she performed the "Dance of Fury," a much-needed diversion in Frank Sinatra's THE KISSING BANDIT (1948). Then she was among those with the crooner and Gene Kelly in ON THE TOWN (1949), in which Ann was peppery in her "Prehistoric Joe" dance routine. Because MGM was preoccupied with survival, it gave little thought to Ann's career progress. She was wasted in the Red Skelton comedy WATCH THE BIRDIE (1950) but did much better in TEXAS CARNIVAL (1951), with Skelton and Esther Williams—dancing, smiling, and singing. On loan to Howard Hughes' RKO she danced "Let the Worry Bird Worry for You" in TWO TICKETS TO BROADWAY (1951). A scheduled production number, "It Began in Yucatan," was cut when she injured her back during filming. Next, she was once more in tandem with Red Skelton in Metro's LOVELY TO LOOK AT (1952) as showgirl Bubbles Cassidy. In this remake of Jerome Kern's ROBERTA she danced zestfully through "I'll Be Hard to Handle," supported by a male chorus wearing wolf masks.

Her two best MGM assignments were both in 1953. In the overlooked SMALL TOWN GIRL, with Jane Powell and Farley Granger, she is a Broadway star. In this movie she has a fascinating Busby Berkeley–choreographed interlude, "I've Gotta Hear That Beat," in which she taps merrily in the midst of a stage full of protruding musical instruments (and the hands playing them). It was in sharp contrast to her flamenco routine in the picture. By far the best musical she ever appeared in was the movie version of Cole Porter's KISS ME KATE (1953). It was shot in 3-D and she had several show-stopping numbers: "Why Can't You Behave?," "Always True to You Darling, in My Fashion," "Tom, Dick or Harry," and the highly erotic "Too Darn Hot." (*Variety* judged the latter "a spectacular sizzler.") As MGM wound down, so did Ann's movie assignments. She was in two 1956 comedies, the second being a poor remake of THE WOMEN called THE OPPOSITE SEX. Ann inherited the role of the avaricious fortune hunter, played in the 1939 screen original by Paulette Goddard. When Janis Paige was given the role Ann had been promised in SILK STOCKINGS (1957), Ann and MGM ended their relationship.

Now that Ann's screen career was over, she adapted. "I could sing and dance. And I had a very strong mother. That helped a lot. . . . She was there if anything went wrong. She was like my manager, really." In 1958, Miller married Texas oilman William Moss, previously wed to former child star Jane Withers. According to Miller, it was "a disaster that lasted three years." Thirteen days after her divorce in May 1961, she wed Texas oil millionaire Arthur Cameron on the rebound. That marriage was annulled in 1962 and once again she returned to the Beverly Hills mansion she had purchased for her mother.

Ann had made her television debut on NBC on October 6, 1957, on a Bob Hope comedy special. Later there would be guest visits to "The Perry Como Show" (1959), "The Ed Sullivan Show" (1960), and "The Hollywood Palace" (1964). Because of her gushy gusto she was a favorite TV talk show guest. There was occasional club work and she served as "unofficial ambassadress" at Hilton Hotel openings worldwide. She explained of her relationship with hotel tycoon Hilton, "Conrad and I are just good friends. He likes to dance."

When she starred in a Houston, Texas, production of *Can-Can* in early 1969, her career had a great resurgence. It brought her to the attention of the producers of *Mame*, who needed a fresh replacement for the hit musical, now entering its third year on Broadway. She was a far different Mame Dennis than had been Angela Lansbury or her successors, and for the newcomer, Onna White choreographed a special tap sequence interpolated into the "That's How Young I Feel" number. She opened on Broadway on May 26, 1969, to solid reviews and remained with the show until it closed in January 1970.

For many couch potatoes of the younger generation, Ann Miller is best known for starring in an extravagant Heinz soup commercial in 1971. She appeared on a rising, eight-foot-high soup can and tap danced violently to "Let's Face the Gumbo and Dance." Hermes Pan choreographed this unforgettable number. She led a summer tour of *Hello, Dolly!* and later that year (November 15, 1971) she was with Ann-Margret and Fred Gwynne in the NBC production of "Dames at Sea." As temperamental Broadway luminary Mona Kent, she executed a spectacular tap number, "Wall Street." The next summer she toured in *Anything Goes* with Tab Hunter. During the run at the St. Louis Municipal Opera, she was injured on stage (by a steel curtain) and it was feared she would never perform again, but eventually she did (appearing in a tour of *Panama Hattie*). She also authored her autobiography, *Miller's High Life* (1972). "Norma Lee Browning researched the dates and tacked things together, but I wrote most of it in longhand on legal pads. I had a stack of them this big, would you believe?," Ann said.

As a girlfriend of the movie studio president (Art Carney), Ann Miller was one of many former movie stars appearing in the nostalgia fiasco WON TON TON, THE DOG WHO SAVED HOLLYWOOD (1976). She made news as the featured attraction of the million dollar Milliken industrial show in 1978 and 1979 produced at the Waldorf-Astoria's Grand Ballroom. Said one reviewer of her show routine, "Between her extraordinary hair, her gold sequin tights, the 'Ridin' High' music and her tap shoes, there was little more to ask of her." Her tour of *Cactus Flower* (1978–79), into which a tap routine was inserted for her, was followed by her greatest success of recent decades: the starring role in *Sugar Babies*. Originally she wanted Red Skelton or Milton Berle as her co-star, but she "settled" for Mickey Rooney (who in turn thought she was too tall for him). The bawdy burlesque revue had a five-city pre-Broadway tour before it opened at the Mark Hellinger Theatre on October 8, 1979. Filled with ancient routines, decorative chorines, and the very broad mugging of Rooney, it was a surprise hit. The show was given a sharp uplift by Ann's enthusiastic dancing and singing, including a military number she had first done in

REVEILLE WITH BEVERLY and later at MGM in HIT THE DECK (1955). At age fifty-six, Ann could still wow an audience with her tapping, her fine figure, and t-h-a-t hair! Rex Reed (*New York Daily News*) noted, "I loved the fact that Mickey Rooney and Ann Miller have proved, once again, there's nothing like the old pros."

*Sugar Babies* lasted for 1,208 Broadway performances, closing in the late summer of 1982 and then embarking on a lengthy road tour. During this Broadway period, Miller's mother was dying in Los Angeles and Ann commuted every weekend to visit her. (On one of these red-eye flights she lost an uninsured million dollar thirty-carat diamond ring in the rest room.) Ann also joined with Ethel Merman, Carol Channing, Van Johnson, Della Reese, and Cab Calloway in a two-hour "Love Boat" excursion on ABC-TV (February 27, 1982). When *Sugar Babies* reached Los Angeles—again—in early 1984, Ann explained her marathon run in the show: "As you get older you get stronger, it seems. I know that I can dance most of the kids in our show into the ground." (By this point Ann had earned an estimated $2 million from the show.) By September 1985, Ann had played the *Sugar Babies* lead thousands of times. Once a strap on her shoe popped during an intricate dance number. She took off both shoes and danced barefoot. Also in 1985 she donated a pair of her tap shoes (she called them "Moe and Joe") to the Smithsonian Institution. They were displayed next to Ginger Rogers' movie gowns and Irving Berlin's piano.

The *Sugar Babies* saga continued when she and Rooney starred in the London edition (Savoy Theatre, September 20, 1988). The British were more impressed by the leads than by the ragamuffin show itself. "Miss Miller clicketty clicks across the stage with those famous legs in better shape than the Eiffel Tower" (*Daily Express*). The *Daily Telegraph* noted that Ann's "tap-dancing is as innocently delightful, and as energetic, as it was in those MGM musicals of 40 years ago." Because Rooney was homesick, the show closed in early January 1989. Back in California, Miller admitted, "I love Hollywood and honestly, I'm tired of being away from home." In February 1989 she and Mickey Rooney were among the MGM alumni appearing at the televised opening of the Disney-MGM Studios theme park in Florida.

Looking back on her career, Ann Miller reflects, "I worked so hard all my life dancing, that my idea of happiness is to dress up in beads and go out. So I married three playboys who loved to go to parties, but the minute they owned you, they lost interest and the fights started. . . . I'm a survivor. You have to be in this business."

## Filmography

The Devil on Horseback (GN, 1936)
New Faces of 1937 (RKO, 1937)
The Life of the Party (RKO, 1937)
Stage Door (RKO, 1937)
Radio City Revels (RKO, 1938)
Having Wonderful Time (RKO, 1938)
Tarnished Angel (RKO, 1938)

You Can't Take It with You (Col, 1938)
Room Service (RKO, 1938)
Hit Parade of 1941 (Rep, 1940)
Too Many Girls (RKO, 1940)
Melody Ranch (Rep, 1940)
Time Out for Rhythm (Col, 1941)
Go West, Young Lady (Col, 1941)

True to the Army (Par, 1942)
Priorities on Parade (Par, 1942)
Reveille with Beverly (Col, 1943)
What's Buzzin' Cousin? (Col, 1943)
Hey, Rookie (Col, 1944)
Carolina Blues (Col, 1944)
Jam Session (Col, 1944)
Eadie Was a Lady (Col, 1945)
Eve Knew Her Apples (Col, 1945)
The Thrill of Brazil (Col, 1946)
Easter Parade (MGM, 1948)
The Kissing Bandit (MGM, 1948)
On the Town (MGM, 1949)

Watch the Birdie (MGM, 1950)
Two Tickets to Broadway (RKO, 1951)
Texas Carnival (MGM, 1951)
Lovely to Look At (MGM, 1952)
Small Town Girl (MGM, 1953)
Kiss Me Kate (MGM, 1953)
Deep in My Heart (MGM, 1954)
Hit the Deck (MGM, 1955)
The Opposite Sex (MGM, 1956)
The Great American Pastime (MGM, 1956)
Won Ton Ton, the Dog Who Saved Hollywood
   (Par, 1976)

## Broadway Plays

George White's Scandals of 1939 (1939)
Mame (1969) (replacement)

Sugar Babies (1979)

## Album Discography

Dames at Sea (Bell System K-4900) [ST/TV]
Deep in My Heart (MGM E-3153, MGM SES-54ST) [ST]
Easter Parade (10" MGM E-502, MGM E-3227, MGM SES-40ST) [ST]
Hit the Deck (MGM E-3163, MGM SES-43ST) [ST]
Kiss Me Kate (MGM E-3077, Metro M/MS-525, MGM SES-44ST) [ST]

Lovely to Look At (10" MGM E-150, MGM E-3230, MGM SES-50ST) [ST]
On the Town (Show Biz 5603, Caliban 6023) [ST]
Small Town Girl (Scarce Rarities 5503) [ST]
Sugar Babies (Col Special Products BE-8302) [OC]
Two Tickets to Broadway (RCA LPM-39) [ST]

# LIZA MINNELLI

IT IS NOT JUST THAT MOST PEOPLE MISPRONOUNCE AND MISSPELL Liza Minnelli's name. More than that, for much of her early life Liza had to live in the shadow of her illustrious, high-voltage mother, Judy Garland. Then Liza suddenly blossomed forth as a major young performer in the mid-1960s. It surprised everyone, including herself and her (at times envious) mother. At that point, Liza endured the blunted praise of critics and fans alike who insisted they could see the legendary Judy in Minnelli's every mannerism and vocal gesture. In response, Liza insisted dramatically that she was her own person and never, never would she be or become an imitation of her famous (and soon to be late) mother.

But the Liza Minnelli who won an Academy Award, an Emmy, and several Tonys in the early-to-mid 1970s soon proved herself wrong. Like her much-documented mother, Liza became intertwined in a series of romances and marriages that seemed to dissipate the thrust of her career. Like Judy, Liza became dependent upon drink and drugs over the years. (But unlike Garland, she went very public in the mid-1980s when she sought treatment for these addictions.) Like mama, Minnelli has had great career highs and lows. Also like Judy, she has made a cinematic trip over the rainbow into the splendid Land of Oz, albeit in a cartoon feature.

On stage, in cabarets, and on the concert circuit, Liza has long been a consistent major attraction. Her verve, pizazz, and showmanship shine forth wonderfully. However, Liza has never enjoyed a high-level recording career. Especially since the mid-1970s, her albums have had a limited, specialized appeal, prompted more by their subject matter than by her chic song styling. On television, she is at her best as a super-charged guest performer rather than as a sustaining star of her own specials. And on screen, the very talented Liza has never recovered from the career setbacks of three consecutive flops: LUCKY LADY (1976), A MATTER OF TIME (1976), and NEW YORK, NEW YORK (1977).

Liza May Minnelli was born in Hollywood, California, on March 12, 1946. She was the only child of her MGM movie star mother and Garland's second husband, Metro-Goldwyn-Mayer movie director Vincente Minnelli. When Liza was less than three years old, she made her screen debut playing the daughter of Garland and Van Johnson in the closing moments of the MGM musical IN THE GOOD OLD SUMMERTIME (1949).

Years later, Liza would admit, "The kind of childhood I had can make you or break you." She was referring to the fact that her mother was living on an emotional roller coaster, heading for a crash. Before Liza was five, her mother had been hospitalized recurrently for emotional breakdowns. She had been suspended, reinstated, suspended, and then fired from her home-away-from-home, MGM. Garland had attempted suicide, and in 1951 had divorced Vincente Minnelli. The next year Garland married promoter Sid Luft and then embarked on a series of comebacks on stage (at the Palace Theatre) and in films (A STAR IS BORN, 1954). With Luft, Garland would have two more children (Lorna and Joey), and suffer a long string of separations and reconciliations as her career went through several more highs and lows.

Meanwhile, Liza had to cope. "I've had knocks, but I'm not sure it's not better to have them when you're young. At least it teaches you how to handle them when they come later." Because her mother was frequently on concert tours, in debt, in and out of love, or in emotional retreat, much of Liza's youth was spent growing up fast. She was pushed into being her mother's confidante, arbiter, and sidekick, all the while moving from place to place and school to school. Her schooling was haphazard and would encompass educational stays on the West Coast, East Coast, and later in England and Switzerland.

When Garland was headlining her successful Palace Theatre comeback in 1952, Liza came on stage one evening and danced for the audience while "mama" sang "Swanee." But thereafter Liza insisted that she was not interested in show business. However, like Judy, she could and did change her mind. In 1954 Vincente Minnelli used Liza as an extra in his new MGM comedy, THE LONG, LONG TRAILER. She was cast in the scene where Lucille Ball and Desi Arnaz marry. However, before the picture was released, Liza's few screen moments were cut. In 1955 Art Linkletter interviewed her on his TV show. In December 1956, she was on CBS-TV to introduce the network's annual showing of the Garland classic THE WIZARD OF OZ (1939). Her equally awkward co-host was her mother's co-star from that fantasy picture, Bert Lahr. Liza made an appearance on Jack Paar's TV talk show in 1958 and on April 24, 1959, she was on Gene Kelly's CBS-TV special, dancing with him to "For Me and My Gal" (the title tune of one of the several pictures Kelly made with Garland). By the time Liza made an appearance on "Hedda Hopper's Showcase" in January 1960, she was nearly 5' 5" and a very plump 165 pounds.

Throughout 1960 Liza was enrolled at the High School of the Performing Arts in New York City. Her crush on a fellow student—who was moonlighting in the chorus of the Broadway musical *Bye Bye Birdie*—led her to become really enthusiastic about the theater. One of her other friends at school was Marvin Hamlisch, who would later win an Academy Award as a composer. Hamlisch and Liza made a demonstration record, but no record label showed any interest in their talent. By the spring of 1961, Liza had transferred to public high school in Scarsdale, New York, living with one of her father's relatives. Garland would flit in and out of town as the mood hit her. That summer, while Garland was vacationing on Cape Cod (she was among those wanting to be in proximity to President John F. Kennedy's summer White House at Hyannis Port), Liza worked for free as an apprentice at the Cape Cod Melody Tent in Hyannis. The following year at Scarsdale High, Liza starred in a school production of *The Diary of Anne Frank*, and the production was sent on a goodwill tour to Israel, Greece, and Italy during the summer of 1962. Meanwhile, both propelled and repelled by the idea of following in her mother's footsteps, Liza was hired to record the voice of Dorothy in the feature-length cartoon

JOURNEY BACK TO OZ (a.k.a. RETURN TO OZ), which would not be theatrically released until 1974.

After her *Anne Frank* tour, Liza remained in London for schooling and then transferred briefly to the Sorbonne in Paris. But she had decided that she wanted to be in New York City and that she wanted to be in show business. Her mother, busy performing in Las Vegas and coping with an unhappy marriage, reluctantly agreed. At age sixteen Liza embarked on her New York phase, taking acting and speech classes, doing magazine modeling, and surviving. Being Judy Garland's daughter helped Liza get cast in an off-Broadway revival of *Best Foot Forward*, which opened April 2, 1963. She was paid $34 weekly. Shortly before that debut, Garland (who could be a mentor or a monster) arranged with her good friend Jack Paar for Liza to appear again on his TV talk show. Introduced as Dyju Langard, a new Armenian discovery, Liza sang for the television audience. Only later in the program did Paar reveal her identity. Of her *Best Foot Forward* appearance, New York drama critic Walter Kerr wrote, "Liza Minnelli is certainly appealing, and would be even if she wasn't Judy Garland's daughter." Even more encouraging was Liza's being selected as a Promising Newcomer by Daniel Blum's *Theatre World* annual.

Still trailing in her mother's wake, Liza appeared on Garland's CBS-TV variety series. In November 1963, Liza and Judy did several duets together, and Liza was on the program again in December, this time joined by stepsister Lorna and stepbrother Joey. Early the next year Liza was "starred" at the Paper Mill Playhouse in Milburn, New Jersey, in the musical *Carnival!* There was much publicity when a near-hysterical Judy, claiming to be upset by Liza's recent bout of flu, threatened legal action if her daughter endangered her health by performing in the show. To the tune of all this attendant hoopla, Liza went on with the show and the engagement was a success. Later in 1964 Liza played in the comedy *Time Out for Ginger* at the Bucks County Playhouse in New Hope, Pennsylvania, and that summer teamed with Elliott Gould for a tour of *The Fantasticks*. She made her dramatic acting debut on the "Nightingale for Sale" segment (CBS-TV, October 24, 1964) of "Mr. Broadway."

One of the turning points of Liza's career occurred on November 8, 1964. Her mother, having failed with her TV series, was making another return to the London Palladium. In a moment of being friend not foe, she asked Liza to co-star with her for the engagement. Liza was determined to succeed, but was unprepared for her mother's competitiveness on stage. "Working with her was something else. I'll never be afraid to perform with anyone ever again after that terrifying experience." The on-stage duel between two generations of performers was judged a draw by some and an unqualified success for Liza by others. From this English engagement, Liza Minnelli emerged as a full-fledged performing talent whose performances would become more refined as the years passed.

Liza had already been featured on the cast album from *Best Foot Forward*, and in December 1964, Capitol Records (for whom her mother had made several albums in the 1950s) released *Liza! Liza!* The latter album featured the song "Maybe This Time," written by the team of Fred Ebb and John Kander. Ebb, in particular, had already become

Liza's mentor and he did a great deal to groom her professional image. He also favored her trying out for a new musical he and Kander had composed, *Flora, the Red Menace*. Produced by Hal Prince and directed by George Abbott, the show opened on Broadway on May 11, 1965. The musical received mixed reviews, but Liza was praised: "At 19, Liza Minnelli is a star-to-be, a performer of arresting presence who does not merely occupy the stage but fills it" (*Time* magazine). The show folded after eighty-nine performances, but Liza won a Tony Award as Best Actress in a Musical.

In 1965 Liza starred with Vic Damone on TV in the whimsical musical "The Dangerous Christmas of Red Riding Hood" and was a guest on one of Frank Sinatra's TV specials. She debuted at the Plaza Hotel's Persian Room in February 1966, part of a cabaret tour that encompassed London and Los Angeles. More important to her, she auditioned for the role of Sally Bowles in the Broadway musical *Cabaret*. However, a Britisher (Jill Haworth) played the part when the show opened in November 1966 for what would be a 1,166-performance run.

Judy Garland used industry connections to help Liza gain an assignment in the British-filmed CHARLIE BUBBLES (1968). Liza played an American who becomes the secretary and mistress of a quirky writer (Albert Finney). *Variety* was unenthusiastic about her performance in the small role: "Miss Minnelli gets a trifle cloying, but is okay." It was also Garland who introduced Liza to her future husband. In 1965 Judy had hired Australian Peter Allen and his partner Chris Bell to be part of her club act. She thought the talented Allen would make a fine husband for Liza, although the latter had mixed feelings about the idea during the next two years. Nevertheless, on March 3, 1967, they were married in New York City.

Just as Liza had campaigned hard for the stage role in *Cabaret*, she became enamored of the role of the sensitive Pookie Adams in THE STERILE CUCKOO (1969), a film project that Alan J. Pakula had in mind. When he finally received financial backing from Paramount Pictures and agreed to hire her, she turned down the lead in the pending Broadway musical *Promises, Promises* (1969). It is hard to imagine anyone else as the kookie Pookie Adams who finds love with a shy college freshman (Wendell Burton) only to see him outgrow her. So telling was her performance that she was nominated for an Academy Award, but she lost the Best Actress Oscar to Maggie Smith (of THE PRIME OF MISS JEAN BRODIE).

Liza was already in rehearsal for her next film, Otto Preminger's TELL ME THAT YOU LOVE ME, JUNIE MOON (1970), when her mother—now in her fifth marriage—died of an "accidental" overdose of barbiturates in London on June 22, 1969. Liza maturely rose to the occasion, handling all the details of the funeral, which took place amid much hysteria in New York City. For playing the screen role of Junie Moon, the rape victim whose face and arms are scarred by battery acid, Liza was paid $50,000. The oddball film was a box-office flop. Meanwhile, Liza was a hit on the club circuit, especially in Las Vegas. On June 29, 1970, she headlined her own special on NBC-TV. She earned $500,000 that year.

A lot happened to Liza in 1972. She and Peter Allen divorced and she was involved in a highly publicized and media-covered cross-global romance with Desi Arnaz, Jr. (She was twenty-six; he was nineteen.) She also finally got to play in CABARET, starring in the film version, which was shot in Munich. Within the storyline, which focused on the loves and tribulations of an American singer in a decadent club in 1930s Berlin, Liza gave sharp dimension to the role of Sally Bowles. She turned the hit musical's title song into her trademark number, and added the poignant "Maybe This Time" to the roster of songs within this film musical. For her performance she won the Best Actress Oscar. On September 10, 1972, she starred in the TV special "Liza with a 'Z'" and the hour-long show won an Emmy Award. The Columbia LP of that TV special rose to number nineteen on the album charts. (Her 1973 LP, *The Singer*, rose to number thirty-eight on the charts; this was the last time one of her albums made the top forty.)

In the next year, Liza earned as much attention for her international romances as for her performing. She was linked with, among others, Peter Sellers, Edward Albert, Assaf Dayan, and Ben Vereen. Then, in January 1974, she appeared for three sold-out weeks at Manhattan's Winter Garden Theatre in concert, receiving as much attention for lip synching some of her song numbers as for her Bob Fosse–style dance strutting. (She received a special Tony Award for this stage turn.) Her April 30, 1974, special on NBC-TV, "Love from A to Z," teamed her with Charles Aznavour, who had introduced her when she had appeared a few years before in concert at the Olympia Theatre in Paris.

Liza had been one of the co-hosts of the MGM salute THAT'S ENTERTAINMENT! (1974). She had narrated the section focusing on Judy Garland's studio musicals. The producer of that documentary was Jack Haley, Jr., whose father had co-starred with Judy in THE WIZARD OF OZ and PIGSKIN PARADE. On September 15, 1974, Liza and Jack Haley, Jr. were married. The huge wedding reception was hosted by Vincente Minnelli and Sammy Davis, Jr. at Ciro's on the Sunset Strip in Hollywood. The couple would divorce in 1978.

Somehow Liza could not follow up the success of CABARET. She starred in the big-budget musical LUCKY LADY (1976), dealing with rum-running in the 1930s. It also focused on the bizarre ménage à trois of Liza, Burt Reynolds, and Gene Hackman. The gaudy production was a financial bust. Vincente Minnelli had been suffering from poor

Liza Minnelli and Joel Grey in CABARET (1972)

health and an inability to get backing for any new movie projects. As a gesture to the ailing man, she agreed to star in A MATTER OF TIME (1976), a quaint, frequently incoherent fantasy romance that teamed her with Ingrid Bergman and Charles Boyer. It was an arty flop. There was much interest in her next picture, another big musical, this time set in the 1940s big band era: NEW YORK, NEW YORK (1977) co-starred Minnelli with Robert De Niro and was directed in a too meticulous manner by Martin Scorsese. John Kander and Fred Ebb provided the memorable title song for Liza (another of her signature numbers). However, before general release the splashy "Happy Endings" production number was deleted; many said that this cut (later restored for re-issues) was one of the reasons for the picture's failure. (It was all shades of Judy Garland and the editing turmoil surrounding A STAR IS BORN.) The film's failure, in combination with her two previous flops, left Liza without a film career.

For six weeks in the summer of 1975, Liza had taken over the lead role in the Broadway musical *Chicago* (which for years thereafter would be touted as a joint film project for her and Goldie Hawn). On October 29, 1977, *The Act* opened on Broadway, starring Liza. With songs by Kander and Ebb and directed by Martin Scorsese, the musical offered a Las Vegas club star (Liza) performing her act while flashbacks recounted her rocky life and marriage (to Barry Nelson). Said the *New York Times*, "It displays the breathtaking presence of Liza Minnelli, and her command of a force that is the emotional equivalent of what a good coloratura achieves in top form. . . ." The show lasted 233 performances and Liza won another Tony Award. In 1979 she was seen briefly as a temporary replacement—playing Lillian Hellman—in the off-Broadway drama *Are You Now or Have You Ever Been*. In December 1979 Liza wed Mark Gero, a one-time stage manager turned sculptor. He was seven years her junior. Over the next years Liza suffered several miscarriages and her marriage was a very much on-again-off-again proposition.

With club performances and occasional TV outings as her chief venues, Liza had to wait four years before gaining another movie role. ARTHUR (1981) was a starring vehicle for Dudley Moore, who excelled as the drunken, spoiled multi-millionaire who finds true love and redemption with a shoplifting waitress (Liza). The popular movie grossed $42 million in domestic film rentals. While Liza was effective in her performance, the industry did not regard the picture as a "Liza Minnelli picture." (Dudley Moore was the *real* star and the comedy netted John Gielgud a Best Supporting Actor Oscar as Arthur's stuffy butler.) Liza was again in a career slump.

On Broadway Liza was the top-billed draw of *The Rink* (1984), another Kander and Ebb musical, but it was co-lead Chita Rivera (as her mother) who stole the limelight. By the time the unexceptional show closed after 204 performances, Liza had left the cast (she was replaced by Stockard Channing). In July 1984 she entered the Betty Ford Center in Rancho Mirage, California, for treatment of "Valium and alcohol abuse." Accompanied by Lorna Luft and bolstered by another Ford Center alumnus (Elizabeth Taylor), Liza admitted publicly, "I've got a problem and I'm going to deal with it." She was much interviewed then and later and confessed that thereafter she suffered several dependency setbacks.

When not performing in clubs, Liza was back to guest-starring on camera in such passable fare as THE MUPPETS TAKE MANHATTAN (1984). She co-hosted THAT'S DANCING! (1985), a documentary co-produced by her ex-husband (Jack Haley, Jr.) and featuring clips of a plethora of screen song-and-dance talent, including Judy Garland. She made her telefeature debut in A TIME TO LIVE (NBC-TV, October 28, 1985) playing a real-life mother/author whose son (Corey Haim) is combatting muscular dystrophy. The effective drama won a Christopher Award.

Vincente Minnelli died in July 1986, leaving $1 million of his estate to Liza, and the next year she participated in a PBS television tribute entitled "Minnelli on Minnelli." As her mother had done twenty-six years before, Liza played a sold-out (three-week) engagement at Carnegie Hall in May 1987, which brought her rave reviews and led to a new, double LP album set recorded live at the concert. That winter she undertook a five-week European concert tour joined by pianist/singer Michael Feinstein, a good friend on one of whose recent LPs she had sung a duet.

One of the more interesting concepts for a TV special was the ABC-TV offering (on June 7, 1988) "Sam Found Out: A Triple Play." In a trio of playlets (in which she co-starred with Ryan O'Neal, Lou Gossett, Jr., and John Rubinstein), Liza acted out three different premises revolving around what happened after Sam found out. As a showcase for Liza, it was only occasionally successful. But it was far better than her two 1988 pictures. In RENT-A-COP she reteamed with Burt Reynolds, whose cinema track record had floundered as badly as hers. She played a Chicago prostitute who becomes enmeshed in homicide and police corruption. The tacky movie quickly disappeared from theaters. More promising was ARTHUR 2 ON THE ROCKS. But, like most sequels, it could not and did not live up to its predecessor. Liza was as winning as before (her screen character had undergone positive changes), but the plot ploy had worn thin and only the brief reappearance of John Gielgud as the deceased butler/confidant gave the tiresome movie any resonance. Made for $15 million, it grossed only $7.5 million in domestic film rentals.

Decades before, Judy Garland had been a charter member of Frank Sinatra's Rat Pack. Liza and Sinatra had also become pals over the years. In 1988, when Dean Martin dropped out of *The Ultimate Event* tour, headlining Sinatra, Martin, and Sammy Davis, Jr., Liza substituted. She joined her new teammates for a heavy schedule of playdates at home and abroad, climaxed when their sold-out concert tour was taped for a Showtime cable TV special in May 1989. The trio made additional appearances and Liza returned to solo performing on the club circuit. It seems that this is her true métier.

## Filmography

In the Good Old Summertime (MGM, 1949)
Charlie Bubbles (Univ, 1968)
The Sterile Cuckoo (Par, 1969)
Tell Me That You Love Me, Junie Moon (Par, 1970)

Cabaret (AA, 1972)
That's Entertainment! (MGM, 1974) (co-host)
Journey Back to Oz [Return to Oz] (Filmation, 1974) (voice only)
Lucky Lady (20th–Fox, 1976)

A Matter of Time (AIP, 1976)
Silent Movie (20th–Fox, 1976)
New York, New York (UA, 1977)
Arthur (Orion/WB, 1981)
The King of Comedy (20th–Fox, 1983)

The Muppets Take Manhattan (Tri-Star, 1984)
That's Dancing! (MGM, 1985) (co-host)
A Time to Live (NBC-TV, 10/28/85)
Rent-A-Cop (Kings Road Entertainment, 1988)
Arthur 2 on the Rocks (WB, 1988)

## Broadway Plays

Flora, the Red Menace (1964)
Chicago (1975) (replacement)

The Act (1977)
The Rink (1984)

## Album Discography

The Act (DRG 6101) [OC]
Best Foot Forward (Cadence 4012/24102) [OC]
Cabaret (ABC ABCD-752) [ST]
Christmas with Judy (Minerva MIN LP 6JG-XST) w. Judy Garland, Lorna Luft, Jack Jones
Come Saturday Morning (A&M 4164)
The Dangerous Christmas of Red Riding Hood (ABC ABC/ABCS-536) [ST/TV]
Flora, the Red Menace (RCA LOC/LSO-1111) [OC]
Foursider (A&M 3524)
It Amazes Me (Cap T/ST-2271)
Live at the London Palladium (Cap WBO/

SWBO-2295, Cap ST-11191) w. Judy Garland
Live at the Olympia Hall (A&M 4345)
Liza at Carnegie Hall (Telarc DG-15502)
Liza at the Winter Garden (Col TC-32854)
Liza! Liza! (Cap T/ST-2174)
Liza Minnelli (A&M 4141)
Liza with a 'Z' (Col KC-31762) [ST/TV]
Lucky Lady (Arista 4069) [ST]
Maybe This Time (Cap SM-11080)
New Feelin' (A&M 4272)
New York, New York (UA UA-LA750) [ST]
The Singer (Col KC-32149)
There Is a Time (Cap T/ST-2448)
Tropical Nights (Col PC-34887)

# CARMEN MIRANDA

SOUTH-OF-THE-BORDER COUNTRIES HAVE RECURRINGLY SUP-
plied the American entertainment scene with show business personalities. There have been
Dolores Del Rio, Lupe Velez, Maria Montez, and, more recently, Cantinflas. But no one
took the North American continent more by storm than Carmen Miranda. After her
whirlwind arrival on Broadway in 1939, and soon thereafter in the movies, the United
States was never the same.

*Pre*–Carmen Miranda, a banana was a banana and a grape was a grape and they were
meant for eating. But Miranda used fruits interlaced with flowers to assemble wild,
colorful cornucopia hats. They adorned her exotic face, setting off her flashing eyes and
wide mouth as she sang exotically, did the samba, and enchanted the public with her exotic
baiana outfits. She spoke in a wild flurry of broken English and often vocalized in exotic
Portuguese. Her darting, expressive fingers (with those l-o-n-g painted nails and bedecked
with massive costume jewelry) were always flying everywhere, punctuating her volatile
rhythm and directing attention to her multi-hued costumes. She was tagged, appropriately,
the Brazilian Bombshell, and in the World War II era, when the U.S.–South American
"Good Neighbor Policy" was a political expediency, she was the best Goodwill Ambassador the southern continent could have had.

Today, Carmen Miranda is regarded as a delicious show business oddity, a queen of
high camp who is still viewed more as a joke (in the United States) than as an institution
(as she is in her adopted homeland, Brazil). That assessment is shameful, for Carmen was
extremely talented. Moreover, she was a shrewd merchandiser of her flamboyant, oversized
persona, a foreigner who coped very effectively in an era when patronizing Americans
believed that anyone not born in the U.S.A. was to be pitied.

Carmen Miranda was born Maria do Carmo Miranda da Cunha in Marco de
Canavezes, near Lisbon, Portugal, on February 9, 1909. Her parents, José Pinto Cunha
and Maria Emilia (Miranda), moved three months later to Rio de Janeiro, where her father
was a barber. Carmen had three sisters, one older (Olinda) and two younger (Cecilia and
Aurora—the latter of whom also went into show business), and two younger brothers,
Gabriel and Mario.

Even while being schooled at the Convent of Saint Teresenha, Carmen was already
thinking of a show business career. She would recall, "When the sisters asked me to play a
role in the school plays, I always inserted my own lines in the parts I was interpreting and
the sisters didn't like that." Through a childhood acquaintance she obtained a department
store job, but devoted more energy to entertaining her co-workers with songs than to

working. One person who witnessed one of these impromptu performances helped her obtain a weekly singing spot on a local radio station. She kept her show business activities secret because her conservative parents thought such a career unsuitable for their daughter. In 1928 she appeared at the National Institute of Music festival and made a strong impression with both the critics and the public. An executive from the South American division of RCA Records heard Carmen on the radio and she was signed to a recording contract in late 1929. (She later would record in Rio de Janeiro for Brunswick and Odeon.) By 1931 her chief rival in the singing field was the popular Raquel Meller. Already Carmen's family had decided to accede to her wishes for a theatrical career and her father had become her business manager, although Carmen made all her own decisions. She termed her song style *con moviemento*, a quick way of representing her enthusiastic format with its gyrating hips, rolling eyes, and facile hand gestures used to punctuate her rapid-fire words.

Carmen appeared in local Rio nightclubs and in 1930 performed in the revue *Vai Dar o Que Falar* at the João Caetano Theatre in Rio. In 1933, she made her film debut in A VOZ DO CARNAVAL, a semi-documentary of the famed Rio Carnival. She can be spotted in a few sequences, shown singing into a microphone. In the variety musical feature ALÔ, ALÔ BRAZIL (1935), her sister Aurora (already a vocalist) also appeared. They had appeared previously in ESTUDANTES (1934) and would be together once again in ALÔ, ALÔ CARNAVAL (1936). Carmen made her final South American–made film, BANANA DA TERRA, for producer Wallace Downey. It was released by MGM of Brazil in 1939.

By this time Carmen was an extraordinarily well-established recording artist—by 1939 she had made more than three hundred singles—and her cabaret appearances were always very well attended. She had toured South America's leading cities nine times with her act and was already considered a national institution. While playing the Caino Urca in Rio, she was noticed by Claiborne Foster, a former actress and now the wife of Maxwell J. Rice, a Pan-American official based in Brazil. Foster wrote Claude Greneker, press agent to theatrical producer Lee Shubert, that Carmen was a performer worthy of the showman's consideration. On his next trip to Brazil, Shubert saw Carmen perform.

The Broadway impresario offered Carmen a contract to come north, *if* she would learn English. She retorted that "the public likes my songs in Portuguese, and if you want me, it will be on those terms." After further negotiation, Carmen signed a three-year contract with Shubert and headed north by ship, arriving in New York on May 17, 1939. Word of this exotic entertainer had preceded her and the press was on hand to greet the 5' 2" celebrity (she wore very thick platform shoes and high hats to disguise her shortness). She spoke Portuguese, Spanish, and French, but admitted that her (heavily accented) English was limited to saying "money, money, money . . . hot dog. I say yes, no, and I say, money, money, money, and I say turkey sandwich and I say grape juice." Aloysio Oliveria, the lead performer in her Banda da Lua (which she insisted upon bringing north to accompany her numbers in Shubert's shows), served as her interpreter.

Carmen was rushed into rehearsals for *Streets of Paris*, a musical revue that opened in New York on June 19, 1939. She had three solo numbers in the show, including "South

American Way." Said one Broadway critic, "Her face is too heavy to be beautiful, her figure is nothing to write home about and she sings in a foreign language. Yet she is the biggest theatrical sensation of the season." Carmen and *Streets of Paris* were a hit. When not performing on stage at the Broadhurst Theatre, Carmen could be heard on radio variety shows, such as Rudy Vallee's. She also appeared on the roster of the late show at the Waldorf-Astoria's club and played vaudeville engagements.

In 1940 20th Century–Fox was making many musicals. This studio had an affinity for Technicolor productions, and its head, Darryl F. Zanuck, was wise enough to know that fostering Latin American–U.S. friendship would be viewed favorably by the government. Thus it was natural for Carmen and the studio to come together. She signed to make a specialty appearance in DOWN ARGENTINE WAY (1940), a lusciously filmed but frivolous Don Ameche–Betty Grable production. Because Miranda was bound contractually to remain in New York, the studio shot her scenes at the Movietone Studios in Manhattan, while the greater part of the movie, set in Buenos Aires, was lensed in Hollywood. For her contribution, Carmen was paid $20,000 (minus the contractual commission owed to the Shuberts). The *New York Times* noted when the film was released that "Miss Miranda sings 'South American Way' and a few Spanish trifles scorchily, but we don't see enough of her. . . ." 20th Century–Fox was already remedying that. They signed Carmen to a long-term contract, intending to provide the public with many opportunities to witness her enticing "'Souse' American Way."

When Carmen returned to Rio in July 1940, Brazilian President Vargas declared it a national holiday, but Carmen soon learned that the Brazilians were unhappy with her for going Hollywood and for internationalizing a caricature of their native ways. This perception greatly saddened Carmen, who now felt alienated from her beloved homeland. She returned to the States to find the Shuberts uncertain of how next to showcase her. They considered presenting her in a modern version of *Carmen* or teaming her in a revue with Maurice Chevalier. Neither came to be. After conferring with her sister Aurora (now playing nightclub engagements in America) and telling her to turn down a minor MGM contract as well as a bid from the Shuberts, Carmen went to California to appear in THAT NIGHT IN RIO (1941) in support of Alice Faye and Don Ameche. It became evident that Fox, having provided her with an English instructor (named Zacharias Yaconellei), had helped solve her language problem, for her dialogue in this musical was far more intelligible. She had two big numbers: "Chica Chica Boom Chic" and "I Yi Yi Yi," both of which became permanent parts of her repertoire. She was backed by her Bando da Lua, and did the samba. However, some critics insisted that Hollywood was Americanizing her too much. She was now earning $4,000 weekly, which she had to share 50–50 with the Shuberts. She was next teamed on camera with Alice Faye, John Payne, and Cesar Romero in the lush WEEKEND IN HAVANA (1941). As fiery club performer Rosita Rivas, she sang "The Nango" and assorted other tunes and wore an array of attention-grabbing costumes (most of which she designed herself). "Where else," asked the *New York Times*, "can you meet Carmen Miranda wriggling devilishly with harvest baskets on her head, except in whatever capital a Fox musical is set? How Miss Miranda gets around—and all the time standing in one spot!" By now she was grossing $5,000 weekly. On March 23, 1941, she had imprinted her shoe and hand prints at Grauman's Chinese Theatre. She was officially part of Hollywood movie lore.

The Shuberts brought Carmen back to Broadway, teamed with Olsen and Johnson, Ella Logan, the Blackburn Twins, and others in the musical revue *Sons o' Fun* (December 1, 1941). The show was a hodgepodge of slapstick, song, and skits. Richard Watts, Jr. of the *New York Herald-Tribune* concluded, "In her eccentric and highly personalized fashion, Miss Miranda is by way of being an artist and her numbers give the show its one touch of distinction." Her rousing show stopper was "Thank You, North America." On June 1, 1942, she left the production; her Shubert contract had expired. Meanwhile, she continued to record for Decca Records such songs as "Chica Chica Boom Chic," "Tar Doll," "The Tic-Tac of My Heart," "Manuelo," and "Chatanooga Choo Choo."

Carmen was now a full-time Hollywood star. However, off camera, as on screen, she remained an industry enigma. She liked night life, but never drank or smoked, nor was she linked romantically with anyone (there were rumors of a Brazilian lawyer she had left behind in 1939). Her mother and brother Gabriel had moved to California to be with her, her father having died in 1938. If SPRINGTIME IN THE ROCKIES (1942) lacked creative verve with its backstage tale of Betty Grable and John Payne, it boasted Harry James's band and the zesty presence of Carmen, who was developing into a seasoned comedienne. Although Carmen was already mastering English, she wisely retained the illusion of her original accent. On a different note, there had been a rhubarb at Fox when press photographers, taking candids on a set where Carmen was twirling away, revealed in their glossies that she wore (that day) no undergarments beneath her long skirts. The studio had frowned on the "adverse" publicity. This incident would crop up for years thereafter, and was often cited as the reason Fox finally lost interest in her.

Of all Carmen Miranda's feature films—and often it was hard to differentiate one from another—her most memorable was THE GANG'S ALL HERE (1943), which boasted the "new" Carmen, who had had plastic surgery to reshape her nose. It starred Alice Faye, featured Benny Goodman and His Band, and was directed with abandon by Busby Berkeley. Never was the latter more expansive, fluid or erotic than in Carmen's lavish set piece, "The Lady in the Tutti-Frutti Hat." The number showcased Carmen at her most dazzling, dynamic self, despite her top-heavy, fruit-laden chapeau and her having to compete with dancing bananas (phallic imagery much written about in recent decades). But the film, which cast her as Dorita, the Broadway performer who adores but does not win James Ellison (Faye does), emphasized the Achilles' heel in Carmen's career momentum. Hollywood believed moviegoers would not accept her as a leading lady who wins the heart of an American leading man; so she remained a high-energy diversion, always cast as the star's peppery friend or jealous rival. Stuck in such a narrow mold, Carmen was bound to wear out her welcome.

She had three 1944 features. In FOUR JILLS IN A JEEP, a tribute to warfront entertainers, Carmen appeared in a radio broadcast scene singing "Ay Ay Ay." This was her first black-and-white Hollywood feature. She was top-starred in GREENWICH VILLAGE, supported by Don Ameche, William Bendix, and Vivian Blaine. She murdered the English, sang a few numbers, and moved on to SOMETHING FOR THE BOYS, a distillation of Cole Porter's stage musical, which co-starred Vivian Blaine and Perry Como. Carmen offered "Samba Boogie" while running through the plot as Chiquita Hart, whose tooth fillings act as a radio transmitter. Plans for her to star in an original musical, BRAZILIAN BOMBSHELL, did not come to anything.

She was earning more than $200,000 yearly but her star at 20th Century–Fox was dimming. She was to have starred in RIOCABANA but instead was in the black-and-white DOLL FACE (1946), based on a bad Gypsy Rose Lee play, in which Vivian Blaine had the lead. The *New York Herald-Tribune* alerted, "Carmen Miranda does what she always does, only not as well." She was in support of Blaine for the fourth time in IF I'M LUCKY (1946), and the *New York Times* complained that she was just "an animated noise."

World War II was over, public tastes were changing, and Carmen and 20th Century–Fox parted company in January 1946. Her specialized brand of entertainment was no longer required.

She signed a long-term contract with Universal but when that studio merged with International Films to become Universal-International, the new regime had no concrete

Carmen Miranda, Phil Baker, Alice Faye, and Sheila Ryan
in THE GANG'S ALL HERE (1943)

plans for her. Her one film in 1947 was United Artists' COPACABANA, which featured Groucho Marx (*without* his brothers) and Carmen in two roles: as a Latin songstress and as a French harem-veiled thrush wearing a blonde wig. The picture did mild business. She did club work in Florida and then, on March 17, 1947, at the Good Shepherd Church in Beverly Hills, the Catholic Carmen married the Jewish David Sebastian, whose brother-in-law had invested in COPACABANA. Sebastian would become her business manager. In May 1947 Carmen played the actual Copacabana Club in New York; the next year she did cabaret work in Las Vegas and was at the London Palladium in April.

Meanwhile, MGM, which had a far-ranging roster of specialty performers to decorate its musical entries, hired Carmen for two features, both starring Jane Powell and both produced by Joe Pasternak. Miranda was Rosita Conchellas, a dance instructor who accidentally gets Wallace Beery into marital strife, in A DATE WITH JUDY (1948). In this vehicle she worked in tandem with Xavier Cugat and His Orchestra. Her big number was a delightful rendition of "Cuanto la Gusta." For NANCY GOES TO RIO (1950) Carmen ended up supplying local color, sported a blonde hairdo, and performed "Cha Boom Pa Pa."

Amid rumors in 1948 that she was having a baby (she later suffered a miscarriage) and continuing marital problems with her husband, Carmen continued to ply the night-club circuit, earning $7,500 weekly. Later, Paramount used Carmen to enhance their Dean Martin–Jerry Lewis vehicle SCARED STIFF (1953), set in Cuba, but the comedy was weak and Miranda's routines and songs were all too familiar. Also in 1953 she went on a four-month European tour, which concluded with performances in Sweden and Finland. While performing in Cincinnati that October, she collapsed (from recurrent exhaustion) and plans for her to tour several of the Shubert theaters in the United States were dropped. She began suffering from fits of despondency over her diminished career and her long-time rift with her homeland. She underwent electroshock therapy and when that failed to cure her, her physician suggested a return visit to her homeland. Accompanied by her sister Aurora, she arrived in Rio de Janeiro on December 3, 1954, her first visit home in fourteen years. Her acceptance by her fellow country people did much to restore her confidence. She recuperated there until April 4, 1955, when she returned north to rejoin her husband.

In April 1955 Carmen performed at the New Frontier Hotel in Las Vegas and in July enjoyed a highly popular club tour of Cuba. She then returned to Los Angeles to recuperate from a recurring bronchial ailment. She was next scheduled to guest on Jimmy Durante's TV show. On August 4, 1955, while taping a vigorous mambo number with Durante and Eddie Jackson, she fell to one foot during the final sequence and murmured, "I'm all out of breath." That night, after attending a party, she returned home, where she collapsed and died of a heart attack. After Catholic services in Hollywood, her husband and Carmen's mother accompanied the body to Rio for burial at the Cemiterio São João Batista. An estimated one million people lined the streets to bid her farewell. She was buried on August 13, wearing a simple red suit and the red beads of a rosary. Carmen's family directed that the tape of her appearance on the Jimmy Durante show be aired. It was broadcast on October 15, 1955, with the producer substituting a long shot of Carmen's dance finale and omitting her final words.

In 1957 David Sebastian shipped many of Carmen's effects to Rio, where it was hoped that a museum devoted to Miranda's career would be started. Such a shrine did open in 1976 off Flamengo Beach; it is still in operation.

Hollywood was not through with Carmen. In a scene in 20th Century–Fox's BELOVED INFIDEL (1959), Deborah Kerr and Gregory Peck are shown leaving a movie theater that is showing THAT NIGHT IN RIO. In the same studio's MYRA BRECKENRIDGE (1970), there is a clip of Carmen singing "Chica Chica Boom Chic" from THAT NIGHT IN RIO. In MGM's THAT'S ENTERTAINMENT! (1974) there is a bit of Carmen in the ensemble song number from A DATE WITH JUDY. Over the decades there have been several compilation LP albums released both in the United States and in South America of Carmen's many recordings. In 1989, *Brazilian Bombshell*, a biography of Carmen by Martha Gil-Montero, was published and it was also announced that a screen biography of the performer was in the works.

For the record, Carmen Miranda's distinctive personality and headgear were responsible for United Fruit's Chiquita Banana advertisements. Imogene Coca imitated Carmen on stage in *The Straw Hat Revue* (1939) and Cass Daley did her own impersonation of the Miranda mystique in LADIES MAN (1947). However, the two best caricatures of the legendary Miranda have been by Mickey Rooney in BABES ON BROADWAY (1941) and by Milton Berle on his early 1950s teleseries. But none of these parodies could catch the vibrant flavor that was Carmen Miranda.

## Filmography

A Voz do Carnaval (Braz, 1933)
Estudantes (Braz, 1934)
Alô, Alô, Brazil (Braz, 1935)
Alô, Alô Carnaval (Braz, 1936)
Banana da Terra (Braz, 1939)
Down Argentine Way (20th–Fox, 1940)
That Night in Rio (20th–Fox, 1941)
Weekend in Havana (20th–Fox, 1941)
Springtime in the Rockies (20th–Fox, 1942)
The Gang's All Here [The Girls He Left Behind] (20th–Fox, 1943)

Four Jills in a Jeep (20th–Fox, 1944)
Greenwich Village (20th–Fox, 1944)
Something for the Boys (20th–Fox, 1944)
Hollywood on Parade (Col, 1945) (s)
All Star Bond Rally (20th–Fox, 1945) (s)
Doll Face [Come Back to Me] (20th–Fox, 1946)
If I'm Lucky (20th–Fox, 1946)
Copacabana (UA, 1947)
A Date with Judy (MGM, 1948)
Nancy Goes to Rio (MGM, 1950)
Scared Stiff (MGM, 1953)

## Broadway Plays

Streets of Paris (1939)
Sons o' Fun (1941)

## Album Discography

The Brazilian Bombshell (Ace of Hearts 99, Coral 99)

The Brazilian Fireball (World Record Club SH-114)

Carmen Miranda (RCA 1030651/7100651)

Carmen Miranda: A Pequena Notável (RCA Camden CALB-5173)

Carmen Miranda Live—Rare Broadcast Performances (Amalgamated 149)

The Compleat Carmen Miranda (AEI 2101)

Down Argentine Way (Hollywood Soundstage 5012) [ST]

Down Argentine Way/Springtime in the Rockies (Caliban 6003, Hollywood Soundstage 5013) [ST]

The Gang's All Here (CIF 3003) [ST]

Greenwich Village (Caliban 6026) [ST]

Nancy Goes to Rio (10" MGM E-508, MGM SES-53ST) [ST]

Quanto la Gusta (Rio 1900)

Something for the Boys (Caliban 5030) [ST]

South American Way (MCA Coral 8029)

Springtime in the Rockies (Pelican 128) [ST/R]

Weekend in Havana/That Night in Rio (Curtain Calls 100/14) [ST]

# GRACE MOORE

DURING THE MID-1930s, OPERA DIVA GRACE MOORE RETURNED TO moviemaking. In a series of surprisingly successful films she made for Columbia Pictures, she almost singlehandedly brought opera to the masses. Such was her impact on the film industry that she was Oscar-nominated for her performance in ONE NIGHT OF LOVE. Like Lawrence Tibbett and Nelson Eddy, Moore had a varied career that encompassed not only the operatic stage, but also Broadway revues, recordings, radio, and movies. Although her singing career was past its prime when she was killed in an air crash in 1947, this lyrical soprano was then still a potent force in opera. Her popularity abroad equaled or even exceeded that in her homeland; she was given France's Chevalier du Legion d'Honneur in addition to accolades from a dozen other countries.

Mary Willie Grace Moore was born on December 5, 1898, in Nough, Tennessee, the daughter of a clerk/traveling salesman (Richard Lawson Moore) and his wife, Tessie Jane Stokely. (There would be other children: Herbert, Martin, the twins, Estel and Emily, Richard, James, and Anna.) She was five when the family moved to Knoxville and then to the mining town of Jellico. She attended a finishing school (Ward-Belmont College) in Nashville and went to Wilson-Greene Music School in Washington, D.C. From there she went to New York City in 1919 (much against her father's wishes) to pursue a theatrical career. For a six-month period she lost her voice, and required a long rest cure. Returning to voice lessons, she studied under the guidance of Dr. P. Mario Marafioti, a friend of Enrico Caruso. After traveling with a road production, the young singer was spotted in a Greenwich Village club (the Black Cat Cafe) by George M. Cohan, who suggested she try her luck in musical comedy. In 1920 she was signed for a featured spot (singing "Oh Moon of Love") in the revue *Hitchy-Koo of 1920* with Raymond Hitchcock and Julia Sanderson; she was also Sanderson's understudy. The show debuted in Boston at the Colonial Theatre on September 7, 1920, and then moved to Broadway's New Amsterdam Theatre on December 19, 1920, for a seventy-one-performance run. *Town Gossip,* with Grace in the singing lead, closed in Baltimore in September 1921. The revue *Up in the Clouds* (also called *Above the Clouds*) with Skeets Gallagher toured and then came to New York City where it played on the subway circuit.

Intent on gaining admission to the world of opera, Grace realized she must study more. Therefore, she went to France. For the next two years she undertook intensive voice training and worked with the German-American Opera Company in Paris. In France she met Irving Berlin, who suggested she return to Broadway to join in his new *Music Box Revue of 1923.* Thus, in the fall of 1923, she joined with Frank Tinney, the Brox Sisters, and

Robert Benchley for 273 performances of this Irving Berlin show. The next year she starred in Berlin's *Music Box Revue of 1924* with Clark and McCullough, Fanny Brice, Oscar Shaw, the Brox Sisters, and Claire Luce. Among her songs in this production was "What'll I Do?" Despite her growing success on stage, Grace Moore still wanted to sing grand opera and she continued her opera studies. However, she failed two auditions at New York's Metropolitan Opera.

An invitation from opera diva Mary Garden led Grace to the diva's apartment in Monte Carlo where she studied with opera coach Richard Barthelemy. She remained in Europe for the next two years, studying opera under the patronage of Otto Kahn. Returning to the United States once again, she did concert work and then, on February 7, 1928, she made her Metropolitan debut as a soprano in the role of Mimi in *La Bohème*. Because of her Broadway background, Moore's opera bow attracted much attention, including that of the focal figures of the famed Algonquin circle. Among the audience that night were one hundred friends from Tennessee, including its two U.S. Senators. She was to remain at the Metropolitan Opera for nearly two decades (except for three seasons in the mid-1930s) and from 1928 to 1931 she sang the roles of Juliet in Gounod's *Romeo and Juliet*, Micaela in Bizet's *Carmen*, Marguerite in Gounod's *Faust*, and the title role in Massenet's *Manon* before going to Paris in 1929 to appear at the L'Opéra Comique. Her debut role there was again Mimi of *La Bohème*, but she also sang the title role in Gustave Charpentier's *Louise*. (The latter role was generally considered by critics to be her best characterization.)

By now Hollywood was interested in the opera singer. MGM, which had already signed Lawrence Tibbett, contracted her for pictures, assuming that the public would enjoy seeing an opera singer who was not overweight (once she lost a stipulated fifteen pounds) and listening to more high-brow music. It was stipulated that her films would be made during the summer, so she could continue developing her opera career. She made her screen debut in 1930 in A LADY'S MORALS (reviewed as THE SOUL KISS) as the famous Swedish singer Jenny Lind in a contrived plot that had her working for P. T. Barnum (Wallace Beery) and in love with a young composer (Reginald Denny). In the feature she sang "Casta Diva" from Bellini's *Norma* and "Rataplan" from Donizetti's *The Daughter of the Regiment* in addition to such popular numbers as "Is It Destiny?," "I Heard Your Voice," and "Lovely Hour." *Variety* rhapsodized that Moore was "an actress of an indescribable charm, with the added appeal of a voice that registers magically on the mechanical, with a human quality that gives it remarkable appeal." The public was less impressed, preferring more down-to-earth entertainment and heroines who did not display such an apparent air of superiority. (Moore also starred in a French-language version of A LADY'S MORALS called JENNY LIND.) Also in 1930, Moore co-starred with Lawrence Tibbett in Sigmund Romberg's NEW MOON (called PARISIAN BELLE on TV). MGM changed the setting from that of the stage operetta, with Moore as a Slavic princess who is the subject of rivalry between a Russian lieutenant (Tibbett) and his commander (Adolphe Menjou). She sang "Softly As in a Morning Sunrise" and "One Kiss" and dueted with Tibbett on "Wanting You" and "Lover Come Back to Me." *Variety* opined, "There's a doubt as to whether it will be easily digested by the average picturegoer." There were rumors of

Moore's showing temperament on the set, problems with the front office about her dieting, and, worst of all, poor box-office receipts on both pictures. MGM cancelled her contract. Moore returned to Broadway in *The DuBarry* (1932) which had an eighty-seven-performance run. The previous year (on July 15, 1931, in Cannes) she had wed Valentin Parera, a Spanish film actor.

Undaunted by her Hollywood failure, Moore hoped to return to filmmaking in general and to MGM in particular. When that studio began preparations for the film version of Lehár's classic operetta THE MERRY WIDOW, she was very receptive to their bid to star her in the feature. However, problems arose as to whether she or co-lead Maurice Chevalier would have top billing and when the studio favored Chevalier, she left the project (to be replaced by Jeanette MacDonald). Harry Cohn's Columbia Pictures thought he could merchandise the temperamental Ms. Moore for public consumption and hired her for a contract at $25,000 per picture. When Cohn began to have misgivings and indicated that he wanted to end their agreement, she threatened to sue. Instead, he allowed production on ONE NIGHT OF LOVE to proceed, but when he decided to cut the operatic

Lyle Talbot and Grace Moore in ONE NIGHT OF LOVE (1934)

sequences to save costs, she paid for them in exchange for a percentage of the film's profits. Now much glamourised and made more human, she was cast as a promising music student who falls in love with her teacher (Tullio Carminati). He deserts her, but returns in time to make her Metropolitan debut a rousing success. In the film she introduced her most popular number, "Ciribiribin," and also sang the title song, plus several opera arias. She recorded the two pop numbers for Brunswick Records. (She had been recording for nearly a decade, having made her first discs in 1925 for Victor Records with songs from *Music Box Revue of 1924.* In 1927 she had recorded selections from *La Bohème, Carmen,* and Puccini's *Madama Butterfly* for Brunswick and in 1932 she had waxed a trio of songs from *The DuBarry* for Victor, including a duet with Richard Crooks on "Without Your Love.")

The modestly budgeted ONE NIGHT OF LOVE proved to be one of the surprise film successes of 1934, earning Moore an Academy Award nomination as Best Actress (she lost to Claudette Colbert of Columbia's IT HAPPENED ONE NIGHT), as well as garnering Oscars for Best Sound Recording and Best Scoring. It was named one of the ten best films of the year by *Film Daily.* Thanks to ONE NIGHT OF LOVE and IT HAPPENED ONE NIGHT, Columbia Pictures graduated from its near-poverty-row status to become a major Hollywood studio.

Irving Thalberg at MGM was now intent to have her back at the studio for the announced ROSE MARIE (1936) and MAYTIME (1937). However, scheduling problems intervened and Jeanette MacDonald inherited both roles. By then (1936) Thalberg had died and Metro was no longer eager for Moore's services. Meanwhile, Moore made her second Columbia picture. In LOVE ME FOREVER (1935) she portrayed an heiress who loses all her money and becomes a café singer, eventually making a successful debut in grand opera. She sang the title song (also recorded for Decca) and "Whoa!" plus several operatic excerpts. Next came THE KING STEPS OUT (1936), directed by Josef von Sternberg, with Grace as a princess posing as a commoner. She attracts the attention of a handsome young king (Franchot Tone) who requires a bride. She sang "Shall We Remain?," "Stars in My Eyes," "Learn to Lose," and "The End Begins," all of which she recorded for Decca Records. Again there were rumors of conflicts on the set.

Continuing in its attempt to make Grace Moore a more empathetic heroine on screen, Columbia teamed her with Cary Grant in WHEN YOU'RE IN LOVE (1937). She was the Australian opera star who takes part in a marriage of convenience with an artist (Grant) so that she can gain entrance into the United States to sing at a musical festival produced by her uncle (Thomas Mitchell). In this popular musical she sang a variety of songs such as "Siboney," "Minnie the Moocher" (to show how down-to-earth she could be), and "In the Gloaming," plus Schubert's "Serenade" and abbreviated arias from *Madama Butterfly* and *Tosca.* In what proved to be her final Columbia outing, I'LL TAKE ROMANCE (1937), she was the Metropolitan Opera singer who reneges on her promise to sing in Buenos Aires because of a more lucrative offer from Paris. She is kidnapped by an American producer (Melvyn Douglas) who brings her to Rio to fulfill her obligations. Besides arias from *La Traviata,* Flotow's *Martha,* and *Madama Butterfly* (a duet with Frank Forest), she also performed the folk song "She'll Be Comin' 'Round the Mountain."

By now, the popularity of opera in films, which Moore had started with ONE NIGHT OF LOVE, had greatly waned, in part because other studios had diluted the formula: RKO with Lily Pons features, Paramount by the use of contralto Gladys Swarthout, and even Republic in its attempt to make a movie star of Grace Talley. (MGM, by contrast, had found a successful formula with light operettas starring Jeanette MacDonald and Nelson Eddy.) Columbia and Grace Moore ended their partnership.

While making films for Columbia, Grace Moore had made her London operatic debut as Mimi in *La Bohème* on June 6, 1935, at the Covent Garden Opera House. In the United States she became a popular performer on radio. In early 1935 she starred in the radio series "Open House" for a season and from 1936 to 1937 she headlined "General Motors Concert" on NBC on Sundays. From May 1 to June 16 of 1937 she was on the Saturday night CBS program "The Nash Show," and beginning in April 1938 she appeared with André Kostelanetz (who was married to her screen rival, Lily Pons) on CBS's "The Chesterfield Show" on Wednesday nights for three months. She continued to do concerts, perform at the Metropolitan, and make records for Decca and RCA Victor. She was renowned for her high lifestyle: villas in Italy and Cannes and a mansion in Hollywood; lavish party-giving; and traveling with an extensive entourage. Explained Moore of her moviemaking years: "I already had some of the fame, but Hollywood gave me the rich lace trimmings, the royal robes, the furs, the jewels, the international celebrity. . . ."

When no film offers were forthcoming from Hollywood, she went to France in the summer of 1938 to star in what proved to be her final film, the opera LOUISE, directed by Abel Gance. The picture received scattered, unimpressive release in the United States in 1940. (On January 28, 1939, she sang the title role of *Louise* at the Metropolitan.) Meanwhile, the coming of World War II cut Grace Moore off from her lucrative European popularity. She began nurturing new operatic talent, both in sponsorship and through coaching. Her star protégé was Dorothy Kirsten. She continued at the Met and made concert tours across the country. As a goodwill gesture for the State Department, she made a South American tour in 1941. On December 18, 1941, she debuted in the lead of Puccini's *Tosca* at the Metropolitan, later performing the role in Canada and Chicago. During the war she toured with the USO both at home and abroad. Her autobiography, *You're Only Human Once*, was published in 1944.

Following the war's end in 1945, Grace Moore resumed working in Europe (she celebrated the liberation of Paris with a concert at the Paris Opera on July 24, 1945) and in the United States. While on a concert tour, she was killed in an airplane crash over Copenhagen, Denmark, on January 26, 1947. In the years since, her records have continued to be reissued and her (non-MGM) movies retain their appeal to film buffs. In 1953 Kathryn Grayson portrayed Grace Moore in a disappointing feature, SO THIS IS LOVE, released by Warner Bros. It gave little indication that in May 1934 Moore had received the National Service Fellowship (gold) Medal from the Society of Arts and Sciences for "distinctive service in the arts, especially for conspicuous achievement in raising the standard of cinema entertainment."

## Filmography

A Lady's Morals [The Jenny Lind Story, The
    Soul Kiss] (MGM, 1930)*
New Moon [Parisian Belle] (MGM, 1930)
One Night of Love (Col, 1934)
Inside Opera (Col, ca. 1935) (s)

Love Me Forever (Col, 1935)
The King Steps Out (Col, 1936)
I'll Take Romance (Col, 1937)
When You're in Love (Col, 1937)
Louise (Fr, 1940)

*Also French-language version*

## Broadway Plays

Hitchy-Koo of 1920 (1920)
Music Box Revue of 1923 (1923)

Music Box Revue of 1924 (1924)
The DuBarry (1932)

## Radio Series

Open House (NBC, 1935–36)
General Motors Concert (NBC, 1936–37)

The Nash Show (CBS, 1937)
The Chesterfield Show (CBS, 1938)

## Album Discography

The Art of Grace Moore (Camden CAL-519,
    RCA International 90040)
Grace Moore (Empire 801)
Grace Moore in Opera and Song (Rhapsody
    6018)
Grace Moore in Opera and Songs (10" RCA
    LCT-7004)
Grace Moore Sings (Decca DL-9593)
Irving Berlin: 1909–1939 (JJA 19744)

The Memorable Radio Years, 1935–45 (Star-
    Tone 217)
The Music of Broadway (JJA 19779)
One Night of Love (Amalgamated 248) [ST]
Opera and Song (Tap 334)
Parisian Belle [New Moon] (Amalgamated 168,
    Pelican 2020) [ST]
When You're in Love (Caliban 6044) [ST]

# DENNIS MORGAN

DENNIS MORGAN WAS A SOLID UTILITY PERFORMER ON FILM. HE WAS handsome (always with a twinkle in his eyes and a dimpled smile); he had a fine tenor voice; and he had a pleasing disposition on camera. Thus he became an unobtrusive leading man in dozens of feature films in the 1940s and 1950s, eventually developing into one of Warner Bros.' highest-paid stars before the inroads of television ended his movie career. After two false starts at MGM and Paramount in the 1930s, the actor found a niche at Warner Bros. at the end of the decade. For the next thirteen years he became one of Hollywood's most consistent leading men. In many respects his screen career can be compared to that of George Murphy, except that Morgan did not dance like Murphy. On the other hand, Murphy did not make recordings, as Dennis Morgan was to do for both the Columbia and Decca labels. While not an overly memorable movie crooner, Dennis Morgan proved to have the staying power lacking in many of his contemporaries for he could switch from singing roles to dramatics and back again with relative ease.

He was born Stanley Morner on December 10, 1910, in Prentice, Wisconsin. His father was a banker who also owned a number of logging camps. As he was growing up, young Stanley worked for his father (who later became his manager) as a lumberjack, eventually maturing to a solid 6' 2". Because of his hard work at the logging camps, he excelled in such school sports as baseball, football, basketball, and track. After graduating from high school in Marshfield, Wisconsin, he attended Carroll College in Waukesha, Wisconsin. There he continued to participate in sports as well as worked as a radio station disc jockey at WTMJ in Milwaukee for $35 weekly. In addition he took music lessons and became a soloist with the college glee club. After graduation, Morner decided on a musical career—one in opera—and obtained a job with a Chautauqua troupe performing Charles Gounod's *Faust*. After a tour with the group, he landed a job singing on radio in Milwaukee as well as performed as a soloist in various church choirs. From there he worked in vaudeville and then went to Chicago where he studied at the Chicago Musical College and performed at the State Lake Theatre. He negotiated a singing engagement at the Empire Room of the Palmer House. This job led to radio work on NBC as the singing star of the "Silken Strings" program and to the lead in a production of George Frideric Handel's *Xerxes* with a small opera company. It was there that he was heard by opera diva Mary Garden, who recommended him to Metro-Goldwyn-Mayer in Hollywood.

Stanley Morner arrived in Hollywood in 1935 with his wife, Lillian. She had been his high school and college sweetheart, and they married in 1933. (They would have three children: Stanley, James, and Kristin.) Under his own name he had a lead in the independently produced (Academy Pictures) I CONQUER THE SEA (1936). He was the Portuguese harpooner who loses his life at sea. *Variety* noted, "Stanley Morner contributes the best all around performance, though a bit mawkish in early scenes." Then he was at MGM for a year, appearing in small roles in such varied MGM products as SUZY (1936), SONG OF THE CITY (1937), and NAVY BLUE AND GOLD (1937). His best showcase came in THE GREAT ZIEGFELD (1936), singing the song "A Pretty Girl Is Like a Melody." However, after he filmed the sequence, the studio decided they wanted a different voice for the number and dubbed in Allan Jones's singing for the release print.

In 1938 the actor-singer left MGM, where he was not progressing, and went to Paramount where he called himself Richard Stanley, but the best he could get was small parts in three entries, two of them gangster programmers: KING OF ALCATRAZ (1938—as a ship's first mate) and PERSONS IN HIDING (1938). From there he went to Warner Bros. Changing his name again, to Dennis Morgan, he won the unsympathetic lead in a "B" picture called WATERFRONT (1939) as a hot-tempered longshoreman. In 1939 he also played a newlywed husband whose father (Fred Stone) comes to live with him and his new bride (Gloria Dickson) in NO PLACE TO GO. Following this outing he portrayed an interne who tries to save his girlfriend (Rosemary Lane) from a mad scientist (Humphrey Bogart) in THE RETURN OF DR. X. In 1940 Morgan was cast as a member of the famous World War I battalion in THE FIGHTING 69TH and portrayed a pilot in FLIGHT ANGELS, a policeman in TEAR GAS SQUAD, and a mountie after a murderer in the remake of RIVER'S END. That year the studio loaned him to RKO Radio for the role of a wealthy playboy who falls in love with a working-class girl (Ginger Rogers) in KITTY FOYLE. The extremely popular movie netted Rogers an Oscar. It also established Dennis Morgan as a reliable leading man. After that, Warner Bros. kept him on its lot exclusively, using him in a variety of ways: leading man in light comedy, a purveyor of strong dramatic roles, a singer in musical comedies, and the star of an occasional Western. As a result of this versatility, Morgan became one of filmdom's most popular male stars.

After scoring in KITTY FOYLE, Dennis was cast as a husband caught between his wife (Merle Oberon) and a beautiful newspaperwoman (Rita Hayworth) who loves him in the romantic comedy AFFECTIONATELY YOURS (1941). He was one of the notorious Younger Brothers in BAD MEN OF MISSOURI (1941), his first feature with Jane Wyman. The year 1942 found him starring in four solid dramas: IN THIS OUR LIFE as a surgeon who leaves his wife (Olivia de Havilland) for her sister (Bette Davis); as a member of the Royal Canadian Air Force in the Technicolor CAPTAINS OF THE CLOUDS; as a wartime aircraft plant worker in WINGS FOR THE EAGLE, his first screen pairing with both Ann Sheridan and Jack Carson; and, again with Carson, as a vaudevillian in THE HARD WAY. The latter film found Carson marrying pretty Joan Leslie, and all three of them coming under the tyrannical thumb of her ambitious sister (Ida Lupino) with tragic results. Morgan, as an aspiring singer, and Joan Leslie were also paired as lovers in the all-star musical THANK YOUR LUCKY STARS (1943). They sang "Ridin' for a Fall" and "No You, No Me" and Morgan soloed on "Good Night, Good Neighbor."

He was given the lead in the updated version of the operetta THE DESERT SONG

(1943), in which he played Paul Hudson, the secret leader of the North African Riffs, who vies with sinister Bruce Cabot for the affections of beautiful Margot (Irene Manning). In the film he sang the title song, "One Flower Grows Alone in Your Garden," "One Alone," and "The Riff Song," all of which he recorded for Columbia Records. Throughout the mid- and late 1940s, Morgan recorded for Columbia, ranging from songs he sang in his Warner Bros. features to traditional numbers like "The Battle Hymn of the Republic" and "The Lost Chord," which he performed with the Cathedral Choir of the First Presbyterian Church of Hollywood, to albums of Irish songs and Franz Lehár compositions. After leaving Columbia Records, Morgan did not pursue his recording career, although in the 1950s he did wax a single for Decca, "When the Shadows Fall"/"I'll Give You All My Love."

In 1944 the actor was cast in another Warners all-star musical, HOLLYWOOD CANTEEN, in which he and Joe E. Brown dueted on "You Can Always Tell a Yank," and then he was seen in one of his best-remembered film roles, that of composer Jack Norworth to Ann Sheridan's Nora Bayes in SHINE ON HARVEST MOON (1944). It was a spirited, if overlong (111 minutes), period musical which gave him a chance to sing a number of vintage songs including "By the Light of the Silv'ry Moon." *Variety* applauded that Morgan "smacks over his vocal assignments in fine style." For variety, he was cast in the drama THE VERY THOUGHT OF YOU (1944), playing a soldier who returns home from war to face domestic troubles with his wartime bride (Eleanor Parker). He appeared as a wartime flier again in GOD IS MY CO-PILOT (1945) and then switched to a comedy role in CHRISTMAS IN CONNECTICUT (1945). He was the sailor rescued after being marooned on a raft for eighteen days and sent to the home of a writer (Barbara Stanwyck) for the yuletide holidays, with the woman intent on fooling both him and her publisher (Sydney Greenstreet) into believing she has a family. As a seasonal favorite on television, it is one of Morgan's most-shown pictures. On October 10, 1945, Morgan portrayed composer Stephen Foster in "Swanee River," a segment of CBS radio's "Lux Radio Theatre." In this adaptation of the 1939 film (in which Don Ameche had played Foster), Morgan performed several of the composer's songs, although the bulk of them were delivered by Al Jolson, repeating his screen role as E. P. Christy. The following June, Morgan made a guest appearance on Jack Carson's CBS radio show.

During World War II, Morgan's screen career had escalated (along with those of the studio's Errol Flynn and John Garfield) while many leading men were away in military service. Nevertheless, his status continued to improve after the armistice—despite the competition of demobilized movie stars and the changing tastes of moviegoers. At the height of his stardom in the mid- to late 1940s, Morgan, who never had script approval on his vehicles, was receiving a thousand fan letters weekly and had a $6,000 weekly salary. He continued to alternate between drama and musical comedies. In 1946 the studio teamed him with equal workhorse Jack Carson in two lightweight but fun pictures, THE TIME, THE PLACE AND THE GIRL, in which Morgan sang "A Gal in Calico" and "Rainy Night in Rio," and TWO GUYS FROM MILWAUKEE, in which he was a prince who learns about ordinary life from a garrulous cabbie (Carson). ONE MORE TOMORROW (1946—shot in early 1944) was a remake of THE ANIMAL KINGDOM (1932) and he portrayed a rich playboy (one of his frequent screen personae) who becomes smitten with a radical magazine editor (Ann Sheridan); a few years later the film would be used as an example of leftist propaganda that had "infiltrated" Hollywood products.

Another noteworthy musical role came in 1947 when he played Irish entertainer Chauncey Olcott in the biopic MY WILD IRISH ROSE and again he sang a variety of vintage tunes, like "Hush-a-Bye (Wee Rose of Killarney)." The prettified Western CHEYENNE (1947) cast Morgan as a gambler in love with the wife (Jane Wyman) of an outlaw (Bruce Bennett); it was later called THE WYOMING KID. He and Jack Carson reteamed for the comedy TWO GUYS FROM TEXAS (1948) as out-of-work vaudevillians stranded on a Texas ranch. In a memorable scene, the two were caricatured in animated hijinks with Bugs Bunny. It was a pleasing remake of THE COWBOY FROM BROOKLYN (1938) and his next feature, ONE SUNDAY AFTERNOON (1948), was a remake of THE STRAWBERRY BLONDE (1941) with Morgan in James Cagney's old role as a turn-of-the-century dentist who wonders if he married the right girl. He sang the title song plus "Wait 'Til the Sun Shines, Nellie" and "One Little, Sweet Little Girl."

It was back to dramatics for the melodrama TO THE VICTOR (1949), about French wartime collaborators being placed on trial, and he was the object of Jane Wyman's amorous machinations in THE LADY TAKES A SAILOR (1949). The last of his popular

Dennis Morgan, Janis Paige, Dorothy Malone, and Don DeFore in
ONE SUNDAY AFTERNOON (1948)

pairings with Jack Carson was IT'S A GREAT FEELING (1949), which had them playing themselves attempting to wangle backing for a film on the Warners lot—unsuccessfully, until they discover singing waitress Doris Day. Morgan and Day sang "Blame My Absent Minded Heart" while the three stars performed "There's Nothing Rougher Than Love."

By 1950 Dennis Morgan was forty (and noticeably stockier). The competition of TV had severely damaged the studio's economics, and Warner Bros. had a new singing star, Gordon MacRae. But Morgan still had his contract to complete. He was reteamed with Ginger Rogers for PERFECT STRANGERS (1950), in which they were fellow jurors who fall in love. In PRETTY BABY (1950) he was involved with a young woman (Betsy Drake) who becomes a success due to a gimmick, while in RATON PASS (1951)—a rather unsturdy Western—he was a cattle baron who is fleeced by his wife (Patricia Neal) and who gains revenge by aligning homesteaders against her. In his final studio musical, PAINTING THE CLOUDS WITH SUNSHINE (1951), a remake of THE GOLD DIGGERS OF BROADWAY (1929), he was one of three rich men pursued by a trio of Las Vegas husband-hunters. In 1952 he played a rancher forced into a showdown with a gunman (Philip Carey) in the programmer CATTLE TOWN and he completed his Warners contract with the Joan Crawford melodrama (her final for the studio) THIS WOMAN IS DANGEROUS (1952), as a doctor who falls in love with the moll (Crawford) of a gangster (David Brian).

Like many studio stars at this time, Dennis Morgan negotiated a termination of his Warners contract. Instead of opting for a one-time settlement, he asked that payments be made over a ten-year period, thus giving him a healthy income for the next decade. During the next several years he turned to television, appearing on such anthology series as "General Electric Theatre," "Pepsi Cola Playhouse," "Fireside Theatre," "Ford Theatre," "Stage Seven," and a "Best of Broadway" adaptation of "Stage Door." In 1955 he starred in the low-budget Columbia Western THE GUN THAT WON THE WEST as the leader of a cavalry troop that holds off a Sioux attack with new Springfield rifles. For RKO he was in an economy adventure opus, PEARL OF THE SOUTH PACIFIC (1955), in which he and partner David Farrar have Virginia Mayo masquerade as a missionary in order to steal tropical natives' pearls. His final starring picture was a Columbia "B" entry called URANIUM BOOM (1956), in which he and William Talman fight over Patricia Medina and a uranium mine. He then returned to TV for guest roles in "Star Stage," "Telephone Time," and "Alfred Hitchcock Presents," before starring as private investigator Dennis Chase in the 1959 NBC-TV summer replacement series "21 Beacon Street." The show did sufficiently well that ABC-TV reran the episodes in prime time from December 1959 to March 1960. Thereafter, Morgan did guest shots on the TV shows "Saints and Sinners" and "Dick Powell Theatre" in the early 1960s.

After more than two decades in the limelight (but never being part of the Hollywood social scene—he was a happily married family man), Morgan moved from his La Canada home to a Fresno ranch with his wife, Lillian, and enjoyed his well-invested earnings. In 1968 he returned to the screen in ROGUE'S GALLERY as a suspect in a murder case involving a framed private eye (Roger Smith), and he also did a guest shot on the CBS-TV series "Petticoat Junction." Mostly he donated his time as a speaker for the American Cancer

Society. In 1974 he guested on the TV special "Grammy Salutes Oscar," but the next year he rejected a $10,000 per week offer to star in a stage revival of *The Vagabond King*. Looking much older, he showed up in a guest cameo in Paramount's WON TON TON, THE DOG WHO SAVED HOLLYWOOD (1976). His most recent acting appearance was in a guest role on the ABC-TV series "The Love Boat" in 1980.

## Filmography

### As Stanley Morner:

I Conquer the Sea (Academy Pictures, 1936)
Suzy (MGM, 1936)
Piccadilly Jim (MGM, 1936)
Down the Stretch (WB, 1936)
The Great Ziegfeld (MGM, 1936)
Old Hutch (MGM, 1936)
Song of the City (MGM, 1937)
Navy Blue and Gold (MGM, 1937)
Mama Steps Out (MGM, 1937)

### As Richard Stanley:

Men with Wings (Par, 1938)
King of Alcatraz (Par, 1938)
Persons in Hiding (Par, 1938)

### As Dennis Morgan:

Waterfront (WB, 1939)
Ride, Cowboy, Ride (Vita, 1939) (s)
The Return of Dr. X (WB, 1939)
No Place to Go (WB, 1939)
The Singing Dude (Vita, 1940) (s)
Three Cheers for the Irish (WB, 1940)
The Fighting 69th (WB, 1940)
Tear Gas Squad (WB, 1940)
Flight Angels (WB, 1940)
River's End (WB, 1940)
Kitty Foyle (RKO, 1940)
Affectionately Yours (WB, 1941)
Bad Men of Missouri (WB, 1941)
Captains of the Clouds (WB, 1942)
In This Our Life (WB, 1942)
Wings for the Eagle (WB, 1942)
The Hard Way (WB, 1942)
Thank Your Lucky Stars (WB, 1943)
Stars on Horseback (Vita, 1943) (s)
The Desert Song (WB, 1943)
The Shining Future (Vita, 1944) (s)
The Very Thought of You (WB, 1944)
Hollywood Canteen (WB, 1944)
Shine on Harvest Moon (WB, 1944)
God Is My Co-Pilot (WB, 1945)
Movieland Magic (Vita, 1945) (s)
Christmas in Connecticut [Indiscretion] (WB, 1945)
One More Tomorrow (WB, 1946)
Two Guys from Milwaukee [Royal Flush] (WB, 1946)
The Time, the Place and the Girl (WB, 1946)
Cheyenne [The Wyoming Kid] (WB, 1947)
My Wild Irish Rose (WB, 1947)
Always Together (WB, 1947)
Two Guys from Texas [Two Texas Knights] (WB, 1948)
One Sunday Afternoon (WB, 1948)
To the Victor (WB, 1949)
It's a Great Feeling (WB, 1949)
The Lady Takes a Sailor (WB, 1949)
Perfect Strangers [Too Dangerous to Love] (WB, 1950)
Pretty Baby (WB, 1950)
Raton Pass [Canyon Pass] (WB, 1951)
Painting the Clouds with Sunshine (WB, 1951)
This Woman Is Dangerous (WB, 1952)
Cattle Town (WB, 1952)

The Nebraskan (Col, 1953)
The Gun That Won the West (Col, 1955)
Pearl of the South Pacific (RKO, 1955)
Uranium Boom (Col, 1956)

Rogue's Gallery (Par, 1968)
Won Ton Ton, the Dog Who Saved Hollywood
(Par, 1976)

## Radio Series

Silken Strings (NBC Blue, 1933–35)

## TV Series

21 Beacon Street (NBC, 1959)

## Album Discography

Hollywood Canteen (Curtain Calls 100/11-12)
[ST]
It's a Great Feeling (Caliban 6015) [ST]
The Merry Widow (10" Cap ML-2064) w. Risë
Stevens
My Wild Irish Rose and Other Songs (Col ML-
4272)

Painting the Clouds with Sunshine (10" Cap L-
291, Caliban 6012) [ST]
Swanee River (Totem 1028) [ST/R]
Thank Your Lucky Stars (Curtain Calls 100/8)
[ST]
The Time, the Place and the Girl (Titania 511)
[ST]

# HELEN MORGAN

HELEN MORGAN, WITH HER PLAINTIVE VOICE, WILL FOREVER BE THE definitive Torch Singer of the 1920s. Sitting atop a piano and twisting a chiffon scarf, she sang forlorn songs of unrequited love, loneliness, and endless feelings for wayward men. While her career encompassed success in vaudeville, on Broadway, in nightclubs, in motion pictures, and on recordings, Helen Morgan was much like the heroines she sang about. In fact, most of her life was a battle against alcohol abuse. Eventually drink caused her untimely death at just over forty years of age.

She was born Helen Riggins in Danville, Illinois, on August 2, 1900, the daughter of French-Canadian parents. While still in her teens she went to Chicago, where she attended Crane High School. While in school she worked at a variety of jobs, like boxing crackers, as a Marshall Field's department store clerk, and then as a lingerie model—all before starting to sing in honky-tonks, such as the Green Mill Club, in 1918. An attractive young woman, she won several beauty contests and with the prize money she came to New York City. She worked in small cabarets before landing a singing job in Billy Rose's Backstage Club.

In 1920 she was hired to sing in the chorus of Florenz Ziegfeld's Broadway show *Sally*, starring Marilyn Miller. She remained with it during its two-year run before going to Chicago where she had a winning engagement at the Cafe Montmartre. Late in 1922 she returned to Gotham and in the next three years eked out a living singing in small clubs and doing bits in vaudeville and musical revues, including a season of "Grand Guignol" plays in Greenwich Village. She won a small role in *George White's Scandals of 1925* which led to a featured role in *Americana* (1926), in which she sang "Nobody Wants Me." As a result of her popularity in this show, she was used as a front for several popular speakeasies, where she appeared as the star attraction; they included The House of Morgan, Chez Helen Morgan, Helen Morgan's Summer House, and Helen Morgan's 54th Street Club. It was here she developed her famous style of sitting on a piano clutching a scarf and singing sad love songs. It soon made her one of New York's most popular club attractions.

In 1927, often accompanied by Leslie A. "Hutch" Hutchinson, Helen made her recording debut on Brunswick Records and that summer and fall she was performing in London where she also recorded for Brunswick. Returning to the United States, Helen Morgan was cast in her most famous role, that of the beautiful but tragic mulatto Julie in Jerome Kern and Oscar Hammerstein II's celebrated stage musical *Show Boat*, which opened at the Ziegfeld Theatre on December 27, 1927, for a 572-performance run. In the landmark show she sang her two most famous songs, "Bill" and "Can't Help Lovin' Dat

Man," which she recorded for RCA Victor, with whom she would remain until 1934.

By the time *Show Boat* opened, Helen Morgan had also become a headliner in vaudeville, and during the show's run in 1928, she was arrested for Prohibition law violations at one of her speakeasies. Not surprisingly, the event made headlines. In July 1929 she appeared in the cabaret entertainment at the Ziegfeld Roof atop the New Amsterdam Theatre. On September 3, 1929, she opened in another Jerome Kern–Oscar Hammerstein II musical, *Sweet Adeline*, as the young daughter of a beergarden owner who becomes a famous singing star. In it she performed two more of her famous torch songs, "Why Was I Born?" and "Don't Ever Leave Me." The show ran for 234 performances. (When Warner Bros. translated the property to the screen in 1935, Irene Dunne had the lead.)

Universal acquired the screen rights to SHOW BOAT (1929), but chose to revamp the musical numbers in its part-talkie film. Alma Rubens was cast as the trouble-plagued Julie. However, for the New York City showings of the film, an eighteen-minute sound prologue was added, which included Helen Morgan singing "My Bill." Morgan made her own feature film debut that fall to critical acclaim in Rouben Mamoulian's APPLAUSE for Paramount, filmed at its Astoria, Long Island, facility. In this innovative dramatic story, she was superb as aging burlesque queen Kitty Darling who brings her young daughter (Joan Peers) into her show at the behest of her shady comedian lover (Fuller Mellish, Jr.), who has designs on the girl. Helen sang "What Wouldn't I Do for That Man," "Give Your Little Baby Lots of Lovin'," and "I've Got a Feeling I'm Falling." The *New York Times* endorsed that Morgan "does remarkably well" and she "speaks her lines with feeling and she plays her part with ability." Late in 1929 she made a guest appearance in the Paramount musical (also filmed at the Astoria Studio) GLORIFYING THE AMERICAN GIRL. In the big production number she reprised "What Wouldn't I Do for That Man" from APPLAUSE.

In 1930 Helen starred in her third Paramount picture, ROADHOUSE NIGHTS, which cast her as Lola Fagan, a singer who saves her former boyfriend, a newspaper editor (Charles Ruggles), from her gangster employer (Fred Kohler). Outside of Jimmy Durante's antics, the feature had little to offer. Morgan returned to Broadway in the summer of 1931 for *Ziegfeld Follies of 1931*. The show, which ran for 165 performances, also starred Harry Richman, Ruth Etting, Hal LeRoy, Jack Pearl, Buck & Bubbles, and Mitzi Mayfair. By this time Helen's drinking was so out of control that she had to sit on the stage in order to be able to perform. Co-star Ruth Etting later said that Helen Morgan drank to give herself courage because she was petrified of live audiences.

In the early 1930s Helen Morgan continued to star in vaudeville and nightclubs and in 1932 was again playing Julie in *Show Boat* at the Casino Theatre in New York. In 1933 she married Maurice Maschke, Jr., but they were divorced two years later. In 1934 she starred on the CBS radio program "Broadway Melodies." That year she starred in *Memories* at the Biltmore Theatre in Los Angeles and made her first feature films in Hollywood: Fox's MARIE GALANTE and Paramount's YOU BELONG TO ME. In the former she sang "It's Home" and "Song of a Dreamer" and in the latter she warbled "When He

Comes Home to Me." Neither of these (melo)dramas was a starring vehicle for her. In 1935 she made a guest appearance as herself in the Rudy Vallee–Warner Bros. musical SWEET MUSIC singing "I See Two Lovers." She also appeared the same year at Warner Bros.–First National with Al Jolson and Ruby Keeler in GO INTO YOUR DANCE singing "The Little Things You Used to Do." That year she also starred in the RKO production FRANKIE AND JOHNNY, set in the 1890s Bowery, about a good-time gal (Morgan) who is done wrong by her two-timing boyfriend (Chester Morris). In it she sang the title folk ballad, "Give Me a Heart to Sing To" (both recorded for Victor Records), "Rhythm in Your Feet," and "If You Want My Heart." Unfortunately, the picture was so badly received that it gained few showings and RKO soon sold it to fledgling Republic Pictures, which reissued it in 1936.

Helen's final screen appearance was to reprise her role of Julie in Universal's production of SHOW BOAT (1936), starring Irene Dunne and Allan Jones. Again she sang "Bill" and "Can't Help Lovin' Dat Man," as she gave a favorable account of herself in the classic musical. Unfortunately, her drinking had grown worse. It was reported that during filming she would arrive on the set drunk every day and had to be placed under a cold shower and filled with coffee before she could emote before the cameras.

She toured in the musical *George White's Scandals of 1936* and in 1937 she was the

Chester Morris and Helen Morgan in FRANKIE AND JOHNNY (1935)

featured vocalist on Ken Murray's CBS radio program. She returned to England for a tour in 1937. Rudy Vallee reported in his autobiography, *My Time Is Your Time* (1962), that during a performance in London she became ill from excessive drinking and had to be helped off stage. Vallee volunteered to take her place.

Alcohol continued to dominate her life, and after the late 1930s her show business career was an on-again-off-again affair. She stopped recording entirely after a session with Brunswick early in 1935. Because of her drinking problem, she had difficulty obtaining club bookings as the 1930s progressed. In 1941 she married Los Angeles car dealer Lloyd Johnson. By then she had pulled herself together enough to appear in a touring version of the now rather tattered *George White's Scandals* revue. While the show was in Chicago at the State Lake Theatre, she was hospitalized with cirrhosis of the liver. She died on October 8, 1941, in the city where she had begun her career.

In the mid-1950s, interest in Helen Morgan was reactivated, thanks to movie biographies of famous stars who had become alcoholics: Susan Hayward as Lillian Roth in I'LL CRY TOMORROW (1955) and Dorothy Malone as Diana Barrymore in TOO MUCH TOO SOON (1957). On April 16, 1957, Polly Bergen had the title role in the CBS-TV "Playhouse 90" program "Helen Morgan," which recreated the star's life and songs. Bergen also recorded an LP album, *Bergen Sings Morgan*, for Columbia Records. The same year Ann Blyth (to lesser effect than Bergen) portrayed Helen Morgan in the Warner Bros. fictionalized THE HELEN MORGAN STORY. The movie suffered from a cliched scenario but had an excellent music track comprised of Helen's famous torch songs, dubbed by Gogi Grant. RCA issued a best-selling soundtrack album from the otherwise mundane film ("little more than a tuneful soap opera," complained *Variety*).

Today, with cable television and videocassettes resurrecting so many of the early 1930s features and short subjects, viewers have the opportunity to study Helen Morgan. In these offerings she may not be at her peak in looks and presence, but there are always flashes of dramatic poignancy and her song numbers consistently reaffirm her unique song style.

## Filmography

Applause (Par, 1929)
Show Boat Prologue (Univ, 1929) (s)
Glorifying the American Girl (Par, 1929)
Roadhouse Nights (Par, 1930)
The Gigolo Racket (Vita, 1931) (s)
Manhattan Lullaby (Educational, 1933) (s)
The Doctor (Educational, 1934) (s)

Marie Galante (Fox, 1934)
You Belong to Me (Par, 1934)
Sweet Music (WB, 1935)
Go into Your Dance (FN, 1935)
Frankie and Johnny (RKO, 1935)
Show Boat (Univ, 1936)

## Broadway Plays

Sally (1920)
George White's Scandals of 1925 (1925)
Americana (1926)

Show Boat (1927)
Sweet Adeline (1929)
Ziegfeld Follies of 1931 (1931)

## Radio Series

Broadway Melodies (CBS, 1934)
The Ken Murray Show (CBS, 1937)

## Album Discography

Fanny Brice/Helen Morgan (RCA LPV-561)
Go into Your Dance (Golden Legends 2000/2, Hollywood Soundstage 402, Sandy Hook 2030) [ST]
Helen Morgan Sings (Audio Rarities 2330)
The Legacy of a Torch Singer (Take Two TT-220)

Let's Have Fun (Mar-Bren 744, Nostalgia Enterprises 002)
Show Boat (Col Special Products 55)
Show Boat (Vertinge 2004, Xeno 251) [ST]
The Torch Singer and the Mountie (Amalgamated 205) w. Nelson Eddy
Torch Songs (X LVA-1006) w. Fanny Brice

# GEORGE MURPHY

TYPED AS A CONGENIAL SONG-AND-DANCE MAN WHO APPEARED IN scores of films from the early 1930s to the 1950s, blue-eyed George Murphy was always regarded as a dependable player. While his screen image as a clean-cut Irish-American was not charismatic, he could always be relied upon for a workmanlike performance. He was an astute achiever who knew how to keep active in show business, while many of his contemporaries faded. In later years he moved out of one limelight into another—as a major politician. As such, he was one of the first show business celebrities to hold a national office, that of U.S. Senator. He helped to break down the barrier against actors in politics, thus paving the way for fellow Republican Ronald Reagan to ascend to the presidency.

He was born George Lloyd Murphy on July 4, 1902, in New Haven, Connecticut, the son of track coach Michael Charles Murphy (the man who trained the 1912 Olympic team led by Jim Thorpe). When the senior Murphy died in 1913, the family moved to Detroit to be with Mrs. Murphy's family. While a student at the University of Detroit High School, fifteen-year-old George ran away from home to join the Navy, but was soon discharged because of his age. A small sports scholarship got the young man into the Peddie School in Highstown, New Jersey, and then he received a full scholarship to New York's Pawling School. There he took up public speaking, with a speech on Theodore Roosevelt earning him the Chauncey Depew Oratory Award. After graduation in 1921 he went to Yale University to major in engineering. To support himself he worked in the summers as a bouncer at a club, loading coal, and other jobs. He dropped out of Yale in 1924, because of bad grades and an injury received at the coal mine.

That autumn he relocated to New York City, where he became a stock market runner. When he lived in Detroit, Murphy had met Juliette Henkel who was now working in Gotham as dancer Julie Johnson. Since Murphy had natural dancing rhythm, the two formed a duo and worked at parties and clubs before landing a stint with George Olsen and His Orchestra performing the dance craze of the day—the Varsity Drag (which had been introduced in the hit Broadway musical *Good News*). When not working with Olsen, Murphy and Johnson appeared with Emil Coleman's orchestra. When Herbert Morrison, a London producer, came to New York to cast the London edition of *Good News*, he saw the couple dance and signed them to appear in the show. (Murphy and Julie were married on December 28, 1926.)

After the London run, the now celebrated couple returned to the United States where they were signed in 1929 to appear in the Bert Lahr musical *Hold Everything*, replacing Jack Whiting and Betty Compton. They stayed with the show on Broadway for the remainder of its eight-month run and then went on tour, returning for the 1931 Broadway revue *Shoot the Works*. After that stint George went solo, appearing in a supporting role in the long-running George Gershwin musical *Of Thee I Sing* (1931). This was followed by a featured part in Jerome Kern's *Roberta* (1933), whose cast also included Tamara, Bob Hope, and Fred MacMurray. As a result of this performance, Murphy was signed to a Hollywood contract by producer Samuel Goldwyn. He made his movie debut in the Eddie Cantor musical KID MILLIONS (1934) as Ann Sothern's dancing partner, and they dueted "Your Head on My Shoulder."

After his film bow, Murphy signed with Columbia Pictures, but made only a quartet of pictures for that studio, three of them musicals with Nancy Carroll: JEALOUSY (1934), I'LL LOVE YOU ALWAYS (1935), and AFTER THE DANCE (1935). Following THE PUBLIC MENACE (1935) with Jean Arthur, he made WOMAN TRAP (1936) with Gertrude Michael at Paramount and TOP OF THE TOWN (1937) with Doris Nolan at Universal. By now he had negotiated a contract at MGM, where his first outing was WOMEN MEN MARRY (1937), a programmer with Claire Dodd, followed by the murder mystery LONDON BY NIGHT (1937), the first feature in which he obtained top billing. *Variety*

Lana Turner, George Murphy, and Joan Blondell in
TWO GIRLS ON BROADWAY (1940)

reported, "Murphy handles himself very capably, speaks lines well and acquits himself creditably as a romantic lead. . . ."

His first major musical for Metro was BROADWAY MELODY OF 1938 (1937), and it gave him an opportunity to dance, the first man to partner with Eleanor Powell in dance. He was loaned to Universal to join with Alice Faye (also on loanout, from 20th Century–Fox) for YOU'RE A SWEETHEART (1937) and they worked well together. *Variety* commended, "Murphy has acquired a rather pleasing singing voice on top of his dancing skill." Another loanout, to 20th Century–Fox, resulted in one of his best-remembered film assignments, playing opposite Shirley Temple in LITTLE MISS BROADWAY (1938). After this hit MGM found it profitable to loan Murphy out to Universal for a trio of features: LETTER OF IN-TRODUCTION (1938), HOLD THAT CO-ED (1938), and RISKY BUSINESS (1939). He was back on the home lot for BROADWAY MELODY OF 1940 (1940), but in support of two top dancers: Fred Astaire and Eleanor Powell. He was Judy Garland's leading man in LITTLE NELLIE KELLY (1940) and did so nicely as the husband/father that the studio planned to reteam him with Garland in FOR ME AND MY GAL (1942). But by the time that musical went into production, the younger Gene Kelly had been hired by the studio and he was given Murphy's intended role, with Murphy recast as the partner who loses Garland to Kelly.

Several of George Murphy's loanouts were to RKO Radio, which did far better by him than did his home lot. In 1941 RKO starred him in the delightful A GIRL, A GUY AND A GOB as the sailor who vies with a rich young man (Edmond O'Brien) for pretty Lucille Ball. Just as good was RKO's comedy TOM, DICK AND HARRY (1941), with Murphy as one of three men pursuing fickle Ginger Rogers. At the same time, all that his home studio, MGM, offered the actor-hoofer was a co-starring role with Ann Sothern in RINGSIDE MAISIE (1941). RKO provided him with starring assignments in two popular low-budget films, THE MAYOR OF 44TH STREET and THE NAVY COMES THROUGH, both in 1942. He was at United Artists for the musical THE POWERS GIRL (1942) and returned home for the grade "A" film BATAAN (1943), a grimly effective wartime drama in which he demonstrated credible dramatics. The studio continued to prosper by loaning him out. He was at Warner Bros. for Irving Berlin's THIS IS THE ARMY (1943), playing Ronald Reagan's father; he was the World War I veteran who staged a big show for the new war's servicemen.

The seesawing film assignments continued, as did the lack of pattern to his screen career. MGM wasted him as a musical producer feuding with his old-time vaudevillian dad (Charles Winninger) in BROADWAY RHYTHM (1944), a project once planned for Mickey Rooney and Judy Garland. George was with Eddie Cantor in RKO's SHOW BUSINESS (1944), a modest look at the changes in vaudeville over the decades. The highlight was a send-up of grand opera by Murphy, Cantor, Constance Moore, and Joan Davis. Murphy was the ambitious stage producer in RKO's STEP LIVELY (1944), which featured young Frank Sinatra. For the same studio's HAVING WONDERFUL CRIME (1945), a good comedy-mystery, he and Carole Landis were honeymooners mixed up with a detective (Pat O'Brien) in a series of murders. In 1946 MGM again relegated Murphy to a "Maisie" movie with Ann Sothern; this time it was UP GOES MAISIE. For the remainder of his screen career, he would stay at the studio except for a loanout to Columbia for the taut semi-documentary melodrama WALK EAST ON BEACON (1952), which cast him as an FBI agent after foreign spies. Murphy had one of the two (Greta Garbo had the other) MGM contracts which paid him for fifty-two weeks a year, not the standard industry practice of forty weeks.

During the 1940s, several things happened to change George Murphy's life, if not his congenial screen image. In 1940 he campaigned actively for Republican Wendell Willkie for President and gained the close friendship of fellow Republican and MGM chief Louis B. Mayer. From 1940 to 1943 he was vice president of the Screen Actors Guild and he served as its president for two terms beginning in 1944. (He had been one of the Guild's first members in the late 1930s.) In the war years he helped organize entertainment for servicemen through the Hollywood Victory Committee and after the war he and Robert Montgomery formed the Hollywood Republican Committee. In 1948 Murphy attended the Republican National Convention as a delegate for California governor and presidential candidate Earl Warren. In 1950 the Academy of Motion Picture Arts and Sciences gave Murphy a special Oscar for his contributions to the film industry, and in 1952 he was placed in charge of entertainment for the Republican National Convention, a post he held again in 1956 and 1960. From 1953 to 1954 he was chairman of the Republican National Convention. Meanwhile, he and his wife (who had retired from show business) continued a quiet home life with their children: Dennis (born in 1939) and Melissa (born in 1943). Murphy also worked on radio during this time, on such series as the "Kraft Music Hall" and "Suspense." On January 29, 1948, he starred in the "History in the Making" segment of the radio show "Proudly We Hail," sponsored by the U.S. Air Force, and he hosted the summer 1948 NBC radio program "Let's Talk About Holly-wood."

Murphy continued appearing in MGM products, his most notable role being "Pop" among the G.I. ensemble in BATTLEGROUND (1949), a fine World War II drama about the assault on Bastogne. After making TALK ABOUT A STRANGER (1952), which co-starred future first lady Nancy Davis (Reagan), his next film role was in DEEP IN MY HEART (1954), as the master of ceremonies in an aquacade scene featuring swimming star Esther Williams. However, the entire sequence was deleted from the release print. Now retired from acting, Murphy nevertheless remained with MGM in a public relations capacity, promoting the studio in particular and the movie industry in general. He hosted the MGM syndicated radio show "Good News from Hollywood" (1953) and did the same chore on the ABC-TV "MGM Parade" (1955). Although Louis B. Mayer had been ousted as MGM chief in 1951 by Dore Schary and his regime, Murphy continued on good terms with Schary until 1957, when Schary accused him of attempting to aid Mayer in a return to power. Murphy quit his MGM job and became the vice president in charge of public relations for Desilu Studios (owned by Lucille Ball and Desi Arnaz) until 1959. The next year he took over as a director and corporate vice president for the Technicolor Corporation. Also in 1960 (on August 1) he was seen in the CBS-TV comedy pilot "You're Only Young Twice," which failed to sell as a series.

In 1964 George Murphy became the Republican candidate for the U.S. Senate in California and in the general election easily defeated Pierre Salinger, who had briefly held the post following the death of Senator Clair Engle. In 1966 Murphy underwent surgery for throat cancer; although the operation was successful, it lowered his speaking voice to a hoarse whisper, which contributed to his defeat for re-election in 1970. As a campaign tool that year he published his memoirs, *Say . . . Didn't You Used to Be George Murphy?*, a title which kidded his screen image. After leaving the Senate, he became a partner in the public relations firm Washington Consultants, Inc. In 1973 his wife died and he sold their Beverly Hills mansion and moved into an apartment. In 1976 he produced the television special "The All-American Bicentennial Minstrels." Today he makes only rare public appearances, such as when former co-star (and fellow Republican) Shirley Temple was honored at an American Cinema Awards fundraiser in Irvine, California, in 1989.

## Filmography

Kid Millions (UA, 1934)
Jealousy (Col, 1934)
After the Dance (Col, 1935)
The Public Menace (Col, 1935)
I'll Love You Always (Col, 1935)
Woman Trap (Par, 1936)
Top of the Town (Univ, 1937)
Women Men Marry (MGM, 1937)
London by Night (MGM, 1937)
Broadway Melody of 1938 (MGM, 1937)
You're a Sweetheart (Univ, 1937)
Little Miss Broadway (20th–Fox, 1938)
Letter of Introduction (Univ, 1938)
Hold That Co-Ed [Hold That Girl] (Univ, 1938)
Risky Business (Univ, 1939)
Broadway Melody of 1940 (MGM, 1940)
Two Girls on Broadway [Choose Your Partner] (MGM, 1940)
Public Deb No. 1 (20th–Fox, 1940)
Little Nellie Kelly (MGM, 1940)
A Girl, a Guy and a Gob [The Navy Steps Out] (RKO, 1941)
Tom, Dick and Harry (RKO, 1941)
Ringside Maisie [Cash and Carry] (MGM, 1941)
Picture People #10 (RKO, 1941) (s)

Rise and Shine (20th–Fox, 1941)
The Mayor of 44th Street (RKO, 1942)
For Me and My Gal [For Me and My Girl] (MGM, 1942)
The Navy Comes Through (RKO, 1942)
The Powers Girl [Hello! Beautiful] (UA, 1942)
Show Business at War (20th–Fox, 1943) (s)
Bataan (MGM, 1943)
This Is the Army (WB, 1943)
Broadway Rhythm (MGM, 1944)
Show Business (RKO, 1944)
Step Lively (RKO, 1944)
Having Wonderful Crime (RKO, 1945)
Up Goes Maisie [Up She Goes] (MGM, 1946)
The Arnelo Affair (MGM, 1947)
Cynthia [The Rich, Full Life] (MGM, 1947)
Tenth Avenue Angel (MGM, 1948)
The Big City (MGM, 1948)
Border Incident (MGM, 1949)
Battleground (MGM, 1949)
No Questions Asked (MGM, 1951)
It's a Big Country (MGM, 1951)
Walk East on Beacon [The Crime of the Century] (Col, 1952)
Talk About a Stranger (MGM, 1952)
Deep in My Heart (MGM, 1954) (scene deleted from release print)

## Broadway Plays

Hold Everything (1929) (replacement)
Shoot the Works (1931)

Of Thee I Sing (1931)
Roberta (1933)

## Radio Series

Let's Talk About Hollywood (NBC, 1948)
Good News from Hollywood (Synd, ca. 1953)

## TV Series

MGM Parade (ABC, 1955–56)

## Album Discography

Broadway Melody of 1938 (Motion Picture
    Tracks MPT 3) [ST]
Broadway Melody of 1940 (CIF 3002) [ST]
For Me and My Gal (Sountrak STK-107) [ST]
Kid Millions (CIF 3007) [ST]

Show Business (Caliban 6034) [ST]
Step Lively (Hollywood Soundstage 412) [ST]
This Is the Army (Hollywood Soundstage 408,
    Sandy Hook 2035) [ST]
You're a Sweetheart (Scarce Rarities 5502) [ST]

# WILLIE NELSON

ONE OF THE LEADERS IN THE "OUTLAW" MOVEMENT IN COUNTRY
music in the 1970s, Willie Nelson had long established himself as one of the genre's top
songwriters as well as a popular performer and recording artist. His change from the
cleancut singer of the 1960s to the long-haired, bearded troubadour of the next decade led
to a surprising widening of Willie Nelson's popularity. Not only did his hard-core country
fans not desert him, he also found himself a whole new audience with rock fans as well as
urban popular music lovers. By expanding his song repertoire to include pop standards as
well as progressive country and country rock, Nelson became one of the top record sellers
of the 1970s and 1980s, noted for his strong, somewhat raspy singing and his trademark
clipped phrasing. In addition, his wide television exposure led to a lucrative movie career.
During the 1980s he starred in some half-dozen Westerns, making him the premiere
cowboy star of the decade and allowing him to assume John Wayne's mantle as the top star
of this otherwise rather moribund genre.

William Hugh Nelson was born in Abbott, Texas, on April 30, 1933, the son of Ira
and Myrle (Greenhaws) Nelson. He was the younger of two children (his older sister,
Bobbie, has been a member of his touring band for many years), and after his parents
divorced, Willie and his sister were raised by their paternal grandparents. When he was six,
his blacksmith grandfather gave him a guitar. Willie learned to play by ear, mostly from
listening to the "Louisiana Hayride" and the "Grand Ole Opry" programs on radio. While
in high school, he worked as a cotton picker. After graduating in 1949 he worked for a
time as a disc jockey and began his career as a professional singer. In 1950 he joined the Air
Force, but a back injury resulted in his discharge. He attended Baylor University for a
semester and then left, opting instead to sing in local honky-tonks in Waco, Texas. There
he met sixteen-year-old Martha Mathews, a full-blooded Cherokee Indian who was
working as a carhop, and they married. (They would have three children: Lana, Susie, and
Billy.) During the day Nelson had jobs such as selling Bibles, carpet sweepers, and
encyclopedias. He became a disc jockey in San Antonio, working later for other radio
stations in Texas, California, and Oregon until the late 1950s, when he began performing
again on a regular basis. He also started composing songs, and in the early 1960s he moved
to Nashville. By now he was drinking heavily and attempted suicide.

It was meeting performer-songwriter Hank Cochran that led to his contract as a
staff writer for Pamper Music. Ray Price was part-owner of the firm and he hired Nelson as
bass guitarist for his band, the Cherokee Cowboys. Nelson's songs also began selling. (He
had sold his first major composition, "Night Life," for $150 in order to buy a car to get to

Nashville.) Soon, other performers were having hit records with his songs, such as Patsy Cline with "Crazy," Ray Price with "Night Life," Billy Walker with "Funny How Time Slips Away," and Faron Young with the top-selling "Hello Walls." Nelson himself earned a recording contract with Liberty and in 1962 he was on the charts with "Mr. Record Man," "Touch Me," and "There's Gonna Be Love in My House," along with a duet with Shirley Collie on "Willingly" (the two were married in 1963 following Nelson's divorce from his first wife), in turn followed by "You Took My Happy Away" in 1964.

The mid-1960s were successful years for Willie Nelson, with income from his song compositions and from the nightclub and personal appearance work that resulted from his record success, and in 1964 he was made a member of the "Grand Ole Opry." He also signed a contract with RCA Victor and had a string of modest sellers, including "Johnny One Time" and "San Antonio." During the 1966–67 television season he was a regular on the syndicated "The Ernest Tubb Show," often singing the program's weekly spiritual.

Financial setbacks, the loss of his home in a fire, and the breakup of his second marriage, added to his growing dissatisfaction with the slick type of music being produced in Nashville, caused him to leave Music City in the early 1970s. He settled in Austin, Texas, where he became a popular celebrity. It was at this time that he began his annual July 4 picnics in Running Springs, which drew music lovers ranging from hard rockers to hard-core country lovers. Nelson left RCA in 1971 and began singing with Columbia in 1974 as his own producer under his Lone Star Records label. In 1975 his Columbia single of the old Roy Acuff standard "Blue Eyes Crying in the Rain" climbed to number one on the country charts and his album *Red Headed Stranger* also reached first place and broke into the top forty pop album charts as well. Nelson then began a grueling schedule of tours.

In 1973 Nelson had been inducted into the Nashville Songwriters' Hall of Fame and in 1975 he had his first involvement with movies when he was heard singing "Stay All Night, Stay a Little Longer" on the soundtrack of the Roy Rogers feature MACKINTOSH & T.J. After that Nelson had a whole string of hit records, such as "I Love You a Thousand Ways," "Help Me Make It Through the Night," and "Heartbreak Hotel" (with Leon Russell), on his own label, plus hits on RCA, United Artists, and other labels, such as "Crazy Arms," "Sweet Memories," and "There'll Be No Teardrops Tonight." Meanwhile, there were his best-selling albums for Columbia, as well as reissue material, and a series of duet albums with some of his favorite country performers (Webb Pierce, Faron Young, Roger Miller, Hank Snow, and others). He did a group of LPs with Waylon Jennings and their 1976 RCA LP, *Wanted! The Outlaws* with Jessi Colter (Jennings' wife) and Tompall Glaser, is credited with galvanizing the integration of music rebels with traditional country music.

Willie Nelson made his first appearance in a feature film in the Austin-lensed OUTLAW BLUES (1977), about a songwriting ex-con (Peter Fonda) who sets out to get back his filched songs with the aid of a pretty backup singer (Susan Saint James). Nelson's annual July 4 party was documented in 1979 and issued theatrically, and he sang on the soundtrack of VOICES (1979) for United Artists. That year also found him as Robert

Redford's pal in THE ELECTRIC HORSEMAN and his easy, laid-back performance, and his several songs in the film, were about the only things the critics enjoyed in this glossy reworking of LONELY ARE THE BRAVE (1962), now set in Las Vegas. As a result, Nelson landed his first starring film role, in HONEYSUCKLE ROSE (1980)—retitled ON THE ROAD AGAIN for TV—as veteran country singer Buck Bonham. After years of toiling on the road, he is on the threshold of stardom, but forgets his loyal wife (Dyan Cannon) for a fling with his sideman's (Slim Pickens) nubile daughter (Amy Irving). While the film was essentially INTERMEZZO (1939) set in the country, the movie found a ready audience and it made Willie Nelson a commercial film entity. For the singer's fans (many of whom thought the project was semi-biographical), the picture was a treasure trove of Nelson songs, with the star performing favorites like "Whiskey River" and "Uncloudy Day." It also had him doing newer items, like the title tune and "Angel Flying Too Close to the Ground," both of which became chart hits for him on Columbia Records.

In 1981 Nelson and Hank Cochran, who appeared in HONEYSUCKLE ROSE, wrote the songs for the film RUCKUS (1981) and Nelson co-starred in THIEF (1981) as Jailbird Okla, a scruffy convict who is involved with the title character (James Caan). That year also found Nelson continuing his heavy performing schedule, traveling by bus to over 250 road dates a year plus television appearances (from PBS's "Austin City Limits" to guest shots on variety shows and his own cable TV specials). The early 1980s found him with single hits such as "Heartaches of a Fool," "In the Jailhouse Now" (with Webb Pierce),

Willie Nelson in BARBAROSA (1982)

"Midnight Rider," "Faded Love," and "Don't You Ever Get Tired of Hurting Me" (the last two were duets with Ray Price).

During a 1981 tour of Hawaii, Nelson was hospitalized for exhaustion but was soon back starring in his first Western, the highly regarded but poorly distributed BARBAROSA (1982). In this outing he had a straight dramatic role as a famous bandit who befriends a young criminal (Gary Busey) while trying to thwart his rich father-in-law's (Gilbert Roland) attempts to have him killed. Then Willie portrayed an actual person, Red Loon, in the 1982 TV movie COMING OUT OF THE ICE, about Victor Herman (John Savage), a young American sent to a Soviet prison camp in Stalinist Russia. In 1983 he was featured along with Johnny Paycheck, Bo Diddley, and Jerry Garcia in the documentary HELLS ANGELS FOREVER. He and Kris Kristofferson (who toured with Nelson in the late 1980s and whose compositions Nelson recorded on the album *Willie Nelson Sings Kristofferson* in 1979) co-starred in the story of a popular singer (Nelson) who enlists the aid of his ex-partner (Kristofferson) to get even with one of his crooked backers (Richard C. Sarafin) in Tri-Star's SONGWRITER (1984). During this period Nelson organized a series of annual Farm Aid concerts, televised over The Nashville Network, to raise money for financially troubled farmers (he had himself lost money farming while living on a two-hundred-acre farm near Nashville in the late 1960s).

In 1986 Willie Nelson was back on the big screen in RED HEADED STRANGER, whose concept was based on his 1975 record album of the same name. He played a minister in the Old West saddled with an unfaithful wife (Morgan Fairchild) and with the affections of the woman (Katharine Ross) that he learns to love. The movie was his first theatrical release not to make a profit, and since then he has starred only in a quartet of Westerns, all made-for-television productions. He made a guest appearance as an Army general in THE LAST DAYS OF FRANK AND JESSE JAMES (NBC-TV, 1986) and he was in the third film version of STAGECOACH (CBS-TV, 1986). In this poorly received entry, he played Doc Holliday, a strong Indian rights proponent. Then ONCE UPON A TEXAS TRAIN (CBS-TV, 1988) presented him as an old-time outlaw hunted by his long-time adversary (Richard Widmark), an ex-Texas Ranger. Burt Kennedy produced, directed, and wrote this ingratiating tale, as he did Nelson's most recent TV Western outing, WHERE THE HELL'S THAT GOLD? (CBS-TV, 1988). It focused on outlaws (Nelson and Jack Elam) being hunted by both U.S. and Mexican authorities because of their border smuggling activities. He also appeared briefly singing the title song he wrote for the Home Box Office cable feature BAJA OKLAHOMA (1988). On May 20, 1989, he appeared in an NBC-TV special with Dolly Parton and Kenny Rogers, an open-air concert taped at Houston's Johnson Space Center.

Willie Nelson was named the winner of the American Music Awards special Award of Merit in 1989, just one of many prizes and citations he has garnered since the 1970s. Among his accolades are a fistful of Grammys, the Country Music Association's Entertainer of the Year (1979), and many laurels for his various songs. His autobiography, *Willie*, written with Bud Shrake, was published in 1988, and that year also found him involved in a complicated personal scenario when his live-in companion Anne-Marie D'Angelo made him the father of a son on Christmas Day. Early the next year, Nelson's third wife, Connie

(Koepke) Nelson, whom he married in 1972 (and who is the mother of his daughters Paula and Amy), announced she was suing him for divorce.

Despite all his success—and many failures—Willie Nelson continues to do what he does best: travel and sing. At a gig at the Caesar's Palace Circus Maximus Show Room in Las Vegas in 1988, he said, "I haven't changed. I'm doing basically the same thing I've been doing all along. Our music is good, and I think it just took a long time for anyone to hear it. And the people who hear it like it and want to be a part of it."

## Filmography

Mackintosh & T.J. (Univ, 1975) (voice only)
Outlaw Blues (WB, 1977)
Willie Nelson's 4th of July Celebration (Alston/ Zanitsch International, 1979)
Voices (UA, 1979) (voice only)
The Electric Horseman (Col/Univ, 1979)
Honeysuckle Rose [On the Road Again] (WB, 1980) (also songs)
Ruckus [The Loner] (New World, 1981) (co-songs only)
Thief (UA, 1981)
Barbarosa (Univ, 1982)
Coming Out of the Ice (CBS-TV, 5/23/82)
Hells Angels Forever (Marvin Films, 1983)

Welcome Home (Col, 1984) (voice only)
Songwriter (Tri-Star, 1984) (also co-songs)
Red Headed Stranger (Alive Films, 1986)
The Last Days of Frank and Jesse James (NBC-TV, 2/16/86)
Stagecoach (CBS-TV, 5/18/86)
Walking After Midnight (Kay Film, 1988)
Once Upon a Texas Train (CBS-TV, 1/3/88)
Baja Oklahoma (Home Box Office [TV], 2/20/88) (also song)
Where the Hell's That Gold? (CBS-TV, 11/13/88)
Welcome Home (Col, 1989) (voice only)

## TV Series

The Ernest Tubb Show (Synd, 1966–67)

## Album Discography

Alabama (Quicksilver 1013) w. Jerry Lee Lewis
Always on My Mind (Col FC-37951)
And Then I Wrote (Liberty LST-7239) w. Leon Russell
Angel Eyes (Col FC-39363) w. Ray Charles, Jackie King
Bandana Land (H.S.R.D. 181920)
The Best of Willie (RCA AHL1-4420)
The Best of Willie Nelson (Liberty LN-10118)
The Best of Willie Nelson (UA UA-LA086-F)
Both Sides Now (RCA LSP-4294)
Brand on My Heart (Col PC-39977) w. Hank Snow
Broken Promises (Quicksilver 5048)

Charlie's Shoes (Quicksilver DECP-02) w. Billy Walker
City of New Orleans (Col FC-39145)
Columbus Stock Blues and Other Country Favorites (Camden CAS-2444)
Country and Western Classics (Time-Life P3-16946)
Country Classics (Col Special Products P16911)
Country Favorites, Willie Nelson Style (RCA LSP-3528)
Country Willie (UA UA-LA410-E)
Country Willie—His Own Songs (RCA LSP-3418)
Country Winners (Camden ACL1-0326)

Danny Davis, Willie Nelson and the Nashville Brass (RCA AHL1-3549)

Diamonds in the Rough (Delta 1157)

Early Willie (Potomac P7-1000)

The Electric Horseman (Col JS-36327) [ST]

Faces of a Fighter (Lone Star L-4602)

The Family Bible (MCA 3258)

The Family Bible (Songbird 37167)

Funny How Time Slips Away (Col FC-39484) w. Faron Young

The Ghost of the Ghost (Hot Schaltz HS-0052-1)

Good Times (RCA LSP-4057)

Greatest Hits and Some That Will Be (Col KC2-37542)

HBO Presents Willie Nelson & Family (HBO— No Number) [ST/TV]

Hello Walls (Pickwick 3584)

Hello Walls (Sunset 5138)

Here's Willie Nelson (Liberty LST-7308)

Highwayman (Col CK-40056) w. Waylon Jennings, Johnny Cash, Kris Kristofferson

Honeysuckle Rose (Col S2-36752) [ST]

The Hungry Years (Plantation 53)

In the Jailhouse Now (Col PC-38095) w. Webb Pierce

Island in the Sky (Col 40487)

Just Plain Willie—The Unreleased Tapes, Vols. 1–3 (Col P17726-8)

Just Willie (Casino 151)

Laying My Burdens Down (RCA LSP-4404)

The Legend Begins (Takoma 7104)

Live Country Music Concert (RCA LSP-3659)

The Longhorn Jamboree Presents Willie Nelson and Friends (Unk) w. Jerry Lee Lewis, Carl Perkins, David Allan Coe

Love and Pain (Aura/Out of Town Distributors 1003)

Mackintosh & T. J. (RCA APL-1520) [ST]

Make Way for Willie Nelson (RCA LSP-3748)

Me and Paul (Col PCT-40008)

Minstrel Man (RCA AHL1-4045)

Monte Alban Mezcal Proudly Presents Willie Nelson, Country Superstar (RCA/Candlelite DVL1-0446)

My Own Peculiar Way (RCA LSP-4111)

My Own Way (RCA AHL1-4819)

Old Friends (Col PC-38013) w. Roger Miller

Once More with Feeling (RCA DPL1-0496)

One for the Road (Col KC2-36064) w. Leon Russell

Outlaw Reunion, Vols. 1–2 (Aura 1010/11) w. Waylon Jennings

Outlaws (Topline 133) w. David Allan Coe

The Party's Over (RCA LSP-3858)

Phases and Stages (Atlantic SD-7291)

The Poet (Accord 7236)

Poncho and Lefty (Epic FE-37958) w. Merle Haggard

Pretty Paper (Col JC-36189)

Pride Wins Again (Maverick 1004)

The Promiseland (Col JC-36189)

Red Headed Stranger (Col KC-33482)

San Antonio Rose (Col JC-36476) w. Ray Price

Seashores of Old Mexico (Col EK-40293) w. Merle Haggard

Shotgun Willie (Atlantic SD-7762)

Slow Down Old World (Aura/Out of Town Distributors 1002)

Somewhere over the Rainbow (Col FC-36883)

Songwriter (Col FC-39531) [ST]

The Sound in Your Mind (Col KC-34092)

Spotlight on Willie Nelson (Camden ACL1-0705)

Stardust (Col JC-35305)

Sweet Memories (RCA AHL1-3243)

Take It to the Limit (Col FC-38562) w. Waylon Jennings

Texas in My Soul (RCA LSP-3937)

Texas Tornados (Plantation 53) w. Mickey Gilley, Johnny Lee

There'll Be No Teardrops Tonight (UA UA-LA930-H)

To Lefty, from Willie (Col KC-34695)

Together Again (Delta 1139) w. Johnny Bush

Tougher Than Leather (Col QC-338248)

The Troublemaker (Col KC-34112)

20 of the Best (RCA International 89137)

Voices (Planet P-9002) [ST]

Walking the Line (Epic FE-40821) w. Merle Haggard, George Jones

Wanted! The Outlaws (RCA APL1-1321) w. Waylon Jennings, Jessi Colter, Tompall Glaser

Waylon and Willie (RCA AFL1-2686) w. Waylon Jennings

Waylon and Willie II (RCA AHL1-4455) w. Waylon Jennings

What Can You Do to Me Now (RCA APL1-1234)

Wild and Willie (Allegiance 5010)

Willie and Family Live (Col KC2-35642) w. Johnny Paycheck, Emmylou Harris

Willie Before His Time (RCA APL1-2210)

Willie Nelson (Exact 249)

Willie Nelson and David Allan Coe (Plantation 41)

Willie Nelson and Family (RCA LSP-4489)

Willie Nelson and Johnny Lee (Quicksilver 5005)

Willie Nelson Live (RCA APL1-1487)

Willie Nelson, 1961 (Shotgun 1961)

Willie Nelson Sings Kristofferson (Col JC-36188)

Willie or Won't He (Allegiance 5005)

The Willie Way (RCA LSP-4760)

Winning Hand (Monument 38389-1) w. Kris Kristofferson, Dolly Parton, Brenda Lee

Without a Song (Col FC-39110)

The Words Don't Fit the Picture (RCA LSP-4653)

Yesterday's Wine (RCA LSP-4568, RCA AHL1-1102)

# OLIVIA NEWTON-JOHN

IN THE MID-1970s ONE OF THE MOST POPULAR COUNTRY SINGERS IN the United States was *not* from Nashville, but was instead a petite young British woman who had grown up in Australia. To many critics she was bland in her vocal interpretations ("if white bread could sing"), but to her devotees she was sweet in spirit and pure in sound. Within a few years, blonde, blue-eyed Olivia Newton-John crossed over into pop music, emerging with a new, tougher image and a more mainstream sound. In GREASE (1978), co-starred with John Travolta, she demonstrated that she could be more than cotton candy sweet. From that movie musical mega-hit to the embarrassing failure of XANADU (1980)—with Gene Kelly—was a long movie career drop. (Ironically, the XANADU soundtrack album and several of its singles proved that Newton-John still had clout with record buyers.) When another fantasy film (TWO OF A KIND, 1983)—also with John Travolta—was a total box-office dud, Olivia abandoned moviemaking (or vice versa). Meanwhile, she continued experimenting as a songwriter, an ecologist, and, more recently, a very successful businesswoman. Musically, she has now swung from the satirical teasing image of "Let's Get Physical" to the more middle-of-the-road (and recent) "The Rumour," an Elton John tune.

Despite her playing with her innocent image throughout the 1980s, Olivia's pure, dulcet voice, with its childlike overtones, remained intact. Now, in middle age, she has become a pert, safe icon for her middle-aged fans, several restrained leaps from the more current Madonna.

She was born on September 26, 1948, in Cambridge, England, the daughter of Bryn and Irene (Born) Newton-John. There was an older brother (who became a doctor) and an older sister (who became an actress). Her Welsh father had planned to have a career in opera, but instead taught German at King's College, Cambridge University. Her mother was the daughter of Max Born, a Nobel Prize–winning German physicist. When Olivia was five, her father was appointed headmaster of Ormond College in Melbourne and the family migrated to Australia. When she was eleven, her parents divorced and Olivia moved with her mother to an apartment in Melbourne. The teenager was already expressing a strong interest in music, particularly in the singing styles of Tennessee Ernie Ford, Joan Baez, Nina Simone, and Ray Charles. Her mother gave her an acoustic guitar when she was thirteen and this led to her performing in a coffeehouse (owned by her sister and her then-husband) on weekends. Thereafter, with three girlfriends, she formed a singing group, the Sol Four, and they sang traditional jazz material. At fourteen, Olivia (known as "Livvey") won a Hayley Mills look-alike contest and two years later, having appeared on several local television shows (such as "The Go Show"), she won a talent contest. The prize was a trip to England.

She debated for nearly two years before accepting the trip. When she did fly to London, she abandoned further schooling and dropped plans (fostered by her mother) to attend the Royal Academy of Dramatic Arts. She decided to make England her home and became involved with several musical groups. Eventually she came to the attention of American music producer Don Kirschner (who had prefabricated "The Monkees"). He was in the process of creating a new synthetic rock combo. He recalls, "when I heard her sing, I knew we could get a great, sweet sound out of her." The group (three males, one female) was dubbed "Toomorrow" (deliberately misspelled) and in 1970 appeared on film in the science-fiction musical TOOMORROW. With songs by Ritchie Adams and Mark Barkan, the movie failed to arouse much enthusiasm and quickly disappeared. *Variety* noted that "The Toomorrows," cast here as students paying for their education by performing, were "fresh and cleancut, with girl warbler Olivia Newton-John being particularly promising as a screen potential."

After this fiasco, Olivia teamed with fellow Australian Pat Carroll and together the two female singers began playing pub dates and appearing on television. When Carroll's visa expired and she returned to Australia temporarily, Olivia continued on her own as a single performer, which led to her association with the group The Shadows and with singer Cliff Richards. Thus she began appearing on "The Cliff Richards Show" on British television. For a time she dated Bruce Welch, a member of The Shadows, who spun off with other group members into the act Marvin, Welch and Farrar.

Olivia first rose to prominence in the British music industry in 1971 with her middle-of-the-road version of Bob Dylan's "If Not for You" (which that summer rose to number twenty-five on the U.S. singles chart). In 1971 Olivia was created an Officer of the Order of the British Empire, being named Best British Girl Singer. She continued with such British hits as "Banks of the Ohio," "What Is Life," and "Take Me Home, Country Roads," all the time veering further away from folk and closer to country music. Meanwhile, she continued to appear on television and to tour (Britain, Australia, and Japan) with Cliff Richards. Her producer on many of her recordings was guitarist John Farrar (who later married singer Pat Carroll). Newton-John's song "Let Me Be There" was unique on the U.S. record charts by starting on the country charts and then reaching sixth position on the pop charts in early 1974.

Olivia toured in the United States for several months in 1974, including playing (as the opening act) at the Hilton in Las Vegas and Harrah's Club in Lake Tahoe. It was also in 1974 that she was named Female Vocalist of the Year by the Country Music Association (CMA) (as well as by its British counterpart) and won a Grammy for Best Country and Western Female Vocal ("Let Me Be There"). Her CMA win upset many American-bred country singers, including Dolly Parton (who later became a friend), Tammy Wynette, and Johnny Paycheck. (The latter said, when forming the splinter organization, the Association of Country Entertainers, "We don't want somebody out of another field coming in and taking away what we've worked so hard for.") Newton-John did not help matters when, in accepting the CMA award, she remarked ingenuously, "It's probably the first time an English person won an award over Nashville people." Country music purists were even more incensed the next year (1975) when Olivia won two Grammys (Record of the Year, Best Contemporary/Pop Female Solo Vocal) for "I Honestly Love You." By now, Olivia, who had been recording in England with the Pye label, was under contract to MCA Records. "I Honestly Love You" rose to number one on the charts, as did "Have You Never Been Mellow" (written and produced by John Farrar) in 1975. For "Please, Mr. Please" (1975) she received the ASCAP Country Music Award. For the movie drama THE OTHER SIDE OF THE MOUNTAIN (1975) she sang the soundtrack vocal, "Richard's Window."

In October 1975, Olivia Newton-John became a Las Vegas headline act at the Riviera Hotel. The *Los Angeles Times* observed, "Her gentle, whispery vocal tone and sweet, delicate appearance/manner are . . . more important in establishing her appeal on stage than range, dynamics, phrasing and the other technical measure of a singer's talent." Her fifth gold album in a row was *Don't Stop Believin'* (1976), which was deliberately recorded in Nashville (and did a great deal to end the long row over a foreign pop singer's having invaded country turf). She had already appeared on several TV specials, including those of Bob Hope (1974), Perry Como (1975), John Denver (1975), and Glen Campbell (1976) when she hosted her own hour-long variety special. Produced by Lee Kramer, "The Olivia Newton-John Show" (ABC-TV, November 17, 1976) featured such guests as Rock

Olivia Newton-John and John Travolta in GREASE (1978)

Hudson, Ron Howard, Lee Majors, and Nancy Walker. It received sharp raps from reviewers concerning her ability to carry a full show, but the ratings were high and she was back on ABC-TV with another special, "Olivia" (May 17, 1978), with guests ABBA and Andy Gibb.

Such Newton-John songs as "Don't Stop Believin'" (1976) and "Sam" (1977) rose to the top forty (but not on top) on the charts. Increasingly, however, critics insisted that her goody-goody image and overly sweet song delivery were self-defeating. In May 1977 she appeared successfully in concert at the Metropolitan Opera House in New York City, winning over some of her prior detractors. Said the *New York Times*, "Miss Newton-John's soprano isn't as negligible as some think. . . ." She then went on a tour of Great Britain, which included a TV special and an appearance before Queen Elizabeth II.

By late 1977 she announced that she was returning to films in the screen version of the long-running Broadway hit *Grease*. John Travolta had already been signed to play the lead male role of Danny. She claimed she screen-tested for the part of Sandy (who changes from an overly wholesome co-ed into a leather-clad motorcycle-ette to win the love of her beau) because "I didn't want to go into something I couldn't handle or have something to say about. I was playing a naive girl but I didn't want her to be sickly." Released by Paramount Pictures in the summer of 1978, GREASE eventually grossed over $96 million in domestic film rentals. *Variety* opined that "Newton-John registers very impressively— far better than the usual personality casting one has come to expect. . . ." Within this slick satire on the rock 'n' roll era, she soloed "Hopelessly Devoted to You" (which rose to number three on the singles charts) and dueted with John Travolta on "Summer Nights" (which became a number five hit single) and "You're the One That I Want" (written especially for the film by John Farrar and which rose to number one on the charts). All three songs became number one hits on the British singles charts as well. Prior to the summer 1978 phenomenon of the GREASE film and album, Olivia had a well-publicized controversy with MCA Records, claiming they were not promoting her sufficiently, and she sought to end their five-year contract. After GREASE, matters were resolved and she continued recording with the label.

With her image revamped courtesy of GREASE, Olivia pulled further away from her girl-next-door mold with her album *Totally Hot*. It contained the hit song "A Little More Love." She turned down GREASE producer Allan Carr's offer to have her star in the movie musical CAN'T STOP THE MUSIC (1980) but did agree to appear in XANADU (1980), a film musical of high aspirations but little entertainment value. She was a muse who comes to earth and finds herself being courted by a wealthy man (Gene Kelly) and a punk rocker (Michael Beck). The expensive but dreadful production was a financial fiasco. However, the soundtrack music was a big success. "Magic" (written by John Farrar) became a number one hit for her; the title tune peaked in eighth position; and her duet ("Suddenly") with Cliff Richards reached number twenty on the charts. The XANADU soundtrack album went platinum. On April 14, 1980, ABC telecast her latest special, "Olivia Newton-John's Hollywood Nights." Her duet single "I Can't Help It" with Andy Gibb was in the top ten in the spring of 1980.

"I wanted peppy stuff because that's how I'm feeling," insisted Olivia Newton-John when she recorded the hit album *Physical* (1980), which included two top ten songs: "Physical" and "Make a Move on Me." Listeners to the song "Physical" could clearly discern its suggestive lyrics. However, seeing the music video of "Physical" (which won a Grammy as Best Video of the Year) or watching Newton-John perform the rousing, provocative song on her TV special ("Olivia Newton-John: Let's Be Physical," ABC, February 8, 1982) was a far more exciting matter. It proved that the singing star had now become the happy queen of sassy pop tunes. *Billboard* magazine named "Physical" the top single of 1982. Because she could now reach her audiences through TV specials and music videos, she cut down on touring (especially after her controversial concert in Sun City, South Africa, in August 1982), with which she had never been completely comfortable. She concentrated more on her private life, including her love for and care of stray animals. With her long-time friend Pat Carroll she opened the first of the Koala Blue boutiques (selling Australian wares) in Los Angeles. She had ended her romantic relationship of several years with her American businessman manager Lee Kramer and had begun dating Matt Lattanzi, a twenty-two-year-old dancer/extra she had met on the set of XANADU.

Olivia starred in a cable TV special ("Olivia Newton-John in Concert") on Home Box Office on January 23, 1983, mixing her past and present images but getting more intriguing response for her punk persona in such songs as "Heart Attack." Plans for her to co-star with Bryan Brown in D. H. Lawrence's KANGAROO fell apart (Judy Davis starred in the movie project in 1987). Instead, she returned to moviemaking in the disastrous $14 million TWO OF A KIND (1983). It cast her as a would-be actress from Australia who becomes involved with an inventor-turned-robber (John Travolta). Both characters were greedy and not particularly likeable, which made it all the more difficult for four angels from above to use the duo as an example of potential human goodness so that the Supreme Being would not flood the earth. The whimsical production was forced and trite and failed badly at the box office. Nevertheless, the *Two of a Kind* album (for which she co-wrote some of the songs) was popular, and "Twist of Fate" from the film rose to number five on the charts.

On December 12, 1984, Olivia wed Matt Lattanzi at her Malibu home. It was not until the next fall that she returned to the recording limelight with her album *Soul Kiss*, which carried her even further away from her former "Miss Apple Blossom" image. The album (with such songs as "Toughen Up," "Culture Shock," and "The Right Moment") reached only number twenty-nine on the charts and the twenty-minute music video of the album was considered more gross and artificial than playfully shocking. On January 17, 1986, Olivia gave birth to a daughter, Chloe. Having become a mother, she spent most of her time thereafter as a homemaker, although in mid-year she made the video and recorded "The Best of Me" with David Foster. She also opened more branches of the Koala Blue stores. When asked in the summer of 1988 how she kept in shape at age thirty-nine, she replied, "It's called motherhood." Home Box Office promoted "Olivia Newton-John in Australia" (aired July 30, 1988) as a "picture-postcard concept special." In this bicentennial salute to her adopted homeland, she sang several selections from her new album, *The*

*Rumour* (her first since 1985). She was rated cute, but the concept was branded "dorky." As for the album itself, *People* magazine judged it "lively, funny, thoughtful, varied." The title tune was co-written by Elton John, who sang back-up for her; she collaborated on several of the other tunes.

In January 1989, Olivia Newton-John was named celebrity businesswoman of the year by the National Association of Women Business Owners. She and her partners (Pat Carroll Farrar and David Sidell) were operating nine Koala Blue stores with twenty licensed franchisees around the country. Her new business executive status reflected what she had admitted a few years earlier: "I don't have the desire I think a lot of performers feel, to get the applause. It's not life and death to me. I like to sing, and I love doing what I'm doing, but it's not a dire need."

## Filmography

Toomorrow (Br, 1970)
The Other Side of the Mountain [A Window to the Sky] (Univ, 1975) (voice only)

Grease (Par, 1978)
Xanadu (Univ, 1980)
Two of a Kind (20th–Fox, 1983) (also co-songs)

## Album Discography

Clearly (MCA 3015)
Clearly Love (MCA 2148)
Come on Over (MCA 2186, MCA 3016)
Don't Stop Believin' (MCA 2223, MCA 3107)
First Impressions (EMI)
Grease (RSO RS-2-40012) [ST]
Greatest Hits (MCA 3028)
Greatest Hits, Vol. 2 (MCA 5347)
Have You Never Been Mellow (MCA 2133)
If Not for You (Uni 73117)
If You Love Me, Let Me Know (MCA 411, MCA 3013)
Let Me Be There (MCA 389, MCA 3012)
Long Live Love (EMI 3028)

Making a Good Thing Better (MCA 2280, MCA 3018)
Music Makes My Day (Pye 28185)
Never Been Mellow (MCA 3014)
Olivia (Pye 28168)
Olivia Newton-John (Pye 28155)
The Other Side of the Mountain (MCA 2086) [ST]
Physical (MCA 5229)
The Rumour (MCA 53294)
Soul Kiss (MCA 6151)
Toomorrow (RCA CSA-3008) [ST]
Totally Hot (MCA 3067, Mobile 040)
Two of a Kind (MCA 6127) [ST]
Xanadu (MCA 6100) [ST]

# DONALD O'CONNOR

DURING THE WORLD WAR II ERA, DONALD O'CONNOR WAS SO popular that Universal Pictures kept him on the studio payroll even for the two years that he did military service. O'Connor grew up in show business and went from a youth to a young man in front of the movie camera. A multi-talented performer, O'Connor is equally at home with drama, comedy, or music and he was one of filmdom's more energetic and pliable dancers, probably because of his early circus training. O'Connor is mainly associated with motion pictures, in which he passed through four phases: as a child player at Paramount; as the boisterous teenager of many inept Universal musicals of the 1940s; as the human companion to Francis the Talking Mule in that popular if inane series; and as the co-star of the classic SINGIN' IN THE RAIN (1952), made during his brief stay at MGM in the early 1950s. He was also a performer in vaudeville and nightclubs and on television and the stage. Today he is one of the few Universal stars from the 1940s to remain active. His well-rounded career has demonstrated that he is a performer of considerable depth, although his image is that of a song-and-dance man.

Donald David Dixon Ronald O'Connor was born August 28, 1925, in Chicago, the son of John "Chuck" O'Connor and Effie Irene Crane, who were vaudeville performers. With their three older children (John, William, and Arlene) the parents formed "The O'Connor Family," which did an acrobatic act that at times commanded a big salary. When Donald was an infant, his sister was killed by a hit-and-run driver and his father died a few months later. Other family members, including baby Donald, were added to the act, and by the time he was four years old, the boy had his own singing and dancing act. In 1936 he and brothers Jack and Billy appeared in a novelty number in the Warner Bros. film MELODY FOR TWO (1937), and this led to work in Hollywood where Donald was signed by Paramount for the role of the little brother in SING YOU SINNERS (1938). One of the highlights of the musical was his duet with Bing Crosby on the song "Small Fry."

Thanks to his success in SING YOU SINNERS, he was given a Paramount contract and he next starred in SONS OF THE LEGION (1938) as a juvenile delinquent who is helped by the sons of American Legionnaires. He was the impish Huckleberry Finn in TOM SAWYER—DETECTIVE (1938) helping to solve a murder. He was typecast as an orphan in three studio releases: UNMARRIED (1939), NIGHT WORK (1939), and DEATH OF A CHAMPION (1939). He closed out his uneventful, bread-and-butter Paramount contract (at $900 weekly) with the role of the youth who becomes Gary Cooper in the remake of BEAU GESTE (1939). Donald had literally outgrown his studio contract by shooting up ten inches in height and he could no longer be cast as a young boy. As the studio informed him, "You've come into that awkward age. It's tough on kid stars. Some can hold on, but not many, and there just aren't any parts around here for you." Instead, he rejoined his family's vaudeville act and they toured for two years, including an engagement in Australia.

When the family act disbanded in 1941 (Effie retired; Jack became a dance director at Warner Bros.), Donald joined Universal Pictures, where he would remain for nearly fifteen years. His first trio of films at the studio starred The Andrews Sisters, but more important, they teamed him with Peggy Ryan. Eventually she and Donald would become Universal's (budget) answer to MGM's successful duo, Judy Garland (whom Donald had known as Frances Gumm on the vaudeville circuit) and Mickey Rooney. The first film, WHAT'S COOKIN'? (1942), had O'Connor and Ryan as part of a group of entertainers hoping for a radio booking. *Variety* noted, "Young Donald O'Connor . . . catches attention with a standout juvenile performance and displays a clicko screen personality." After doing yeoman duty in GIVE OUT, SISTERS and PRIVATE BUCKAROO (both 1942 and with Peggy Ryan and The Andrews Sisters), things got better for O'Connor in GET HEP TO LOVE (1942). He had second billing as the teenager pursued by star Gloria Jean and rival Peggy Ryan; he and Peggy did a lively jitterbug. He and Ryan were in support of Allan Jones and Gloria Jean in WHEN JOHNNY COMES MARCHING HOME (1943), but in IT COMES UP LOVE (1943) he became Gloria Jean's leading man in a light romance. He and Gloria co-starred again in MISTER BIG (1943) as teenagers who turn their school's pageant into a musical. As always, O'Connor made the most of his screen time, demonstrating a breezy, carefree personality and the ability to break into effortless song, dance, or comedy at the slightest provocation. In TOP MAN (1943) he had top billing for the first time in films, playing a young collegian who becomes the head of the family when his father (Richard Dix) is recalled to active military duty. That year O'Connor was voted a "Star of Tomorrow."

The year 1944 proved to be his busiest at Universal. He and Peggy Ryan executed a jitterbug number in the all-star FOLLOW THE BOYS and in THIS IS THE LIFE he vied with Patric Knowles for Susanna Foster's affections. In THE MERRY MONAHANS, O'Connor and Ryan were siblings whose vaudevillian father (Jack Oakie) is reunited with his ex-love (Rosemary DeCamp), who has a singing daughter (Ann Blyth). Ryan and Blyth were rivals for O'Connor in the musical comedy CHIP OFF THE OLD BLOCK, while he and Peggy were back for a specialty routine, "He Took Her Out for a Sleigh Ride in the Good Old Summertime," in the big-budget musical BOWERY TO BROADWAY. He and Peggy Ryan next starred in PATRICK THE GREAT (1945), which found O'Connor and his father (Donald Cook) seeking the same Broadway role. By the time the picture was released in the spring of 1945, Donald O'Connor was in the Army Air Force. For the next two years he did more than three thousand shows across America, entertaining soldiers for the Special Services. Just prior to enlisting, on February 6, 1944, he had eloped with Gwendolyn Carter (whom he had known while at Paramount) to Tijuana, Mexico. Their daughter, Donna, was born in the summer of 1945.

When Donald O'Connor returned to films in the summer of 1947, Universal was undergoing corporate changes, but the new regime had great use for such a strong utility performer. O'Connor was now an adult and he co-starred with Deanna Durbin in SOMETHING IN THE WIND (1947), in which he used his acrobatic training for a strenuous rendition of "I Love a Mystery." He got mixed up with eccentric Marjorie Main and a town of hillbillies in FEUDIN', FUSSIN', AND A-FIGHTIN' (1948) while performing "Me and My Shadow," and he was a math wizard who joins a carnival in ARE YOU WITH IT? (1948). A bit sturdier was the college comedy YES SIR, THAT'S MY BABY (1949) with O'Connor singing "They've Never Figured Out a Woman" and dueting with Gloria De Haven on the title song and "All Look at Me."

During this period O'Connor made several appearances on Bing Crosby's radio variety show and in 1949 he starred in FRANCIS, a film that was to have a major impact on his career. He played Peter Stirling, an Army lieutenant who becomes involved with the garrulous title character, a talking mule (whose voice was that of Chill Wills). The silly programmer proved so popular that it spawned a 1950s series that rivaled Universal's "Ma and Pa Kettle." O'Connor was to star in a half-dozen of these steady moneymakers. The series revived his sagging career, but he regarded the property as a mixed blessing and referred to the period as "my-mule-and-me era." In 1950 the star headlined the amusing Western satire CURTAIN CALL AT CACTUS CREEK as well as the not-too-funny send-up of buccaneer movies, DOUBLE CROSSBONES, in which he was a falsely accused criminal who becomes a part of Captain Kidd's (Alan Napier) crew. In the fall of 1951 he starred on "The Colgate Comedy Hour" on NBC-TV in a monthly segment ("The Donald O'Connor Show"). The variety show ran for three seasons and in 1953 O'Connor earned an Emmy Award for his work on it.

Donald O'Connor and Gene Kelly in SINGIN' IN THE RAIN (1952)

Despite the inroads TV was making into movie attendance, O'Connor continued to churn out a large number of pictures, such as THE MILKMAN (1950), which teamed him with Jimmy Durante in shenanigans involving murder. In 1952 he went to MGM for the first of two musicals. The best film of his career, SINGIN' IN THE RAIN (1952) focused on the early days of sound musicals, with comedic O'Connor stealing the show (from co-stars Gene Kelly and Debbie Reynolds) with his songs "Make 'Em Laugh" and the energetic "Moses Supposes." (Later he would say, "You know the secret of why Gene Kelly and I looked good together? While most performers turn to the right when dancing, Gene and I both turn to the left.") The second MGM musical, I LOVE MELVIN (1953), top-billed him as a magazine photographer after a pretty starlet (Debbie Reynolds). Made on a limited budget, the feature grossed $4.5 million at the box office. At 20th Century–Fox he co-starred with Ethel Merman in CALL ME MADAM (1953) with him and Ethel dueting on "You're Just in Love." He soloed on Irving Berlin's "What Chance Have I with Love" and he and Vera-Ellen performed "It's a Lovely Day Today."

Thanks to the success of this trio of loanouts, Universal assigned O'Connor to its own musical, WALKING MY BABY BACK HOME (1953), as a G.I. who uses an inheritance to start his own band; he performed the title song and "Rampart Street Parade." Illness caused O'Connor to be replaced by Danny Kaye in Paramount's WHITE CHRISTMAS (1954) starring Bing Crosby, but Donald went back to 20th Century–Fox for THERE'S NO BUSINESS LIKE SHOW BUSINESS (1954). As a member of a show business family, he sang "A Boy Chases a Girl" and romanced Marilyn Monroe. In 1954 he also starred in the bi-weekly half-hour NBC-TV series "The Donald O'Connor Texaco Show," which ran for one season. He concluded his Universal contract with FRANCIS IN THE NAVY (1955). (When O'Connor refused to do yet another Francis film, Mickey Rooney was hired for FRANCIS IN THE HAUNTED HOUSE [1956], which wiped out the series.)

Donald O'Connor and his wife had divorced in 1953 and on October 11, 1956, he wed Gloria Noble. They eventually had three children: Alicia, Donald, and Kevin. The year before his second marriage O'Connor conducted the Los Angeles Philharmonic's world premiere of his symphony "Réflexions d'un Comique" and for the next several seasons he did occasional symphony conducting. In 1956 O'Connor co-starred with Bing Crosby as a television star who does a Broadway show with a has-been (Crosby) in the Paramount musical ANYTHING GOES. (It was O'Connor's last screen musical for, he admitted, he was earning too much money in other mediums to pursue a dying genre any further.) For the same studio he starred in the title role of THE BUSTER KEATON STORY (1957), a disservice to both O'Connor and Keaton. O'Connor then appeared on TV on CBS's "Playhouse 90" and in the "DuPont Show of the Month's" production of "The Red Mill" before starring in his own special on NBC-TV in the fall of 1960. He also worked in nightclubs and in 1960 he became a partner in Reno's Riverside Hotel.

He returned to motion pictures in the title role of the misguided fantasy THE WONDERS OF ALADDIN (1961). In the derivative CRY FOR HAPPY (1961) he and two sailor buddies (Glenn Ford, James Shigeta) made an orphanage out of a geisha house. When he headlined at the Hotel Americana in Gotham in 1963, he received a salary of $12,000 per week, and the next year he toured in the stage musical *Little Me*, which Embassy Pictures planned to (but never did) make as a movie starring O'Connor. Universal was much changed by the time he returned there in 1965 to support Sandra Dee and Bobby Darin in the thin comedy THAT FUNNY FEELING. In 1966 he made a teleseries pilot, "The Hoofer," which did not sell. On "ABC Stage 67" he starred in the original TV musical "Olympus 7-0000" in the fall of 1966. He hosted "The Hollywood Palace" (ABC-TV) a few times and did TV commercials. In 1968 he had a good stint in Las Vegas in a truncated version of *Little Me*, and that fall he starred in a syndicated ninety-minute weekday talk program, "The Donald O'Connor Show," which aired for a season.

During the 1970s, looking bloated, O'Connor remained active, although he was sidelined for a time by a heart attack and bypass surgery. During the decade he appeared on TV in the 1971 NBC special "Li'l Abner" and had guest roles on such series as "The Girl with Something Extra," "Ellery Queen," "The Bionic Woman," "Police Story," and "Hunter." Early in the decade he toured in *Promises, Promises* and in 1976 was on the road in *Where's Charley*. He also headlined *Weekend with Feathers*, which never reached Broadway. That year his daughter Donna made her film bow in ALL THE PRESIDENT'S MEN, whose cast also included Kerry Sherman, Peggy Ryan's daughter. On film he was one of the co-hosts of the MGM musical compilation THAT'S ENTERTAINMENT! (1974) but was represented in its sequel, THAT'S ENTERTAINMENT, PART 2 (1976), only by clips from his films.

In the 1980s O'Connor appeared on such TV fare as "The Music Mart" (a 1980 pilot, which did not sell), "The Love Boat," "Alice," "Fantasy Island," "Simon and Simon," and "Hotel." He returned to films in 1981 at Paramount in the featured role of Evelyn Nesbitt's (Elizabeth McGovern) dance teacher in RAGTIME, and the next year he did a guest bit in the feature PANDEMONIUM. In March 1981 he had a four-performance run on Broadway in *Bring Back Birdie*. It was during this period that he admitted publicly that he had conquered the drinking habit that had plagued him for twenty-five years. He played Cap'n Andy in a 1983 Broadway revival of *Show Boat* that lasted seventy-three performances. His most recent movie appearance was as the Lory Bird on the CBS-TV movie ALICE IN WONDERLAND, late in 1985. On stage he has done a concert/club tour in tandem with Jane Powell and more recently and more frequently with Debbie Reynolds. In early 1989 he became a stage producer when he opened the Donald O'Connor Theatre in Studio City, California, and later that year he toured the country in a cabaret act with Mickey Rooney.

Thanks to his big-budget musicals of the 1950s, Donald O'Connor's reputation as the personification of the agile, comic song-and-dance man will endure. These movies represent only a small part of his musical film output, but his genre outings for Universal in the 1940s pale by comparison. Unlike MGM, which lavished substantial production values and music scores on its Judy Garland–Mickey Rooney offerings, Universal hacked out the Donald O'Connor–Peggy Ryan efforts in quick fashion. Their assembly-line fabrication always showed, but, despite everything, talented Donald O'Connor always sparkled.

## Filmography

Melody for Two (WB, 1937)
Men with Wings (Par, 1938)
Sing You Sinners (Par, 1938)
Sons of the Legion (Par, 1938)
Tom Sawyer—Detective (Par, 1938)
Million Dollar Legs (Par, 1939)
Unmarried [Night Club Hostess] (Par, 1939)
Death of a Champion (Par, 1939)
Night Work (Par, 1939)
On Your Toes (WB, 1939)
Beau Geste (Par, 1939)
What's Cookin'? [Wake Up and Dream] (Univ, 1942)
Get Hep to Love [She's My Lovely!] (Univ, 1942)
Give Out, Sisters (Univ, 1942)
Private Buckaroo (Univ, 1942)
It Comes Up Love [A Date with an Angel] (Univ, 1943)
When Johnny Comes Marching Home (Univ, 1943)
Mister Big (Univ, 1943)
Top Man (Univ, 1943)
Follow the Boys (Univ, 1944)
This Is the Life (Univ, 1944)
The Merry Monahans (Univ, 1944)
Chip Off the Old Block (Univ, 1944)
Bowery to Broadway (Univ, 1944)
Patrick the Great (Univ, 1945)
Something in the Wind (Univ, 1947)

Feudin', Fussin' and A-Fightin' (Univ, 1948)
Are You with It? (Univ, 1948)
Yes Sir, That's My Baby (Univ, 1949)
Francis (Univ, 1949)
Curtain Call at Cactus Creek [Take the Stage] (Univ, 1950)
The Milkman (Univ, 1950)
Double Crossbones (Univ, 1950)
Francis Goes to the Races (Univ, 1951)
Singin' in the Rain (MGM, 1952)
Francis Goes to West Point (Univ, 1952)
I Love Melvin (MGM, 1953)
Call Me Madam (20th–Fox, 1953)
Walking My Baby Back Home (Univ, 1953)
Francis Covers the Big Town (Univ, 1953)
There's No Business Like Show Business (20th–Fox, 1954)
Francis Joins the WACS (Univ, 1954)
Francis in the Navy (Univ, 1955)
Anything Goes (Par, 1956)
The Buster Keaton Story (Par, 1957)
The Wonders of Aladdin (MGM, 1961)
Cry for Happy (Col, 1961)
That Funny Feeling (Univ, 1965)
That's Entertainment! (MGM, 1974) (co-host)
Ragtime (Univ, 1981)
Pandemonium (MGM/UA, 1982)
Alice in Wonderland (CBS-TV, 12/9/85–12/10/85)
A Time to Remember (Filmworld, 1988)

## Broadway Plays

Bring Back Birdie (1981)
Show Boat (1983) (revival)

## TV Series

The Colgate Comedy Hour (NBC, 1951–54)
The Donald O'Connor Texaco Show (NBC, 1954–55)

The Donald O'Connor Show (Synd, 1968–69)

## Album Discography

Anything Goes (Decca DL-8318) [ST]

Bring Back Birdie (Original Cast Records 8132) [OC]

Call Me Madam (10" Decca DL-5465, Stet 15024) [ST]

Donald O'Connor Music (Palette 1021) w. Brussels Symphony

Follow the Boys (Hollywood Soundstage 50120) [ST]

Give Out, Sisters (Vertinge 2004) [ST]

I Love Melvin (10" MGM E-140, MGM SES-52ST) [ST]

Olympus 7-0000 (Command O7) [ST/TV]

Singin' in the Rain (10" MGM E-113, MGM E-3236, Metro M/S-599) [ST]

That Old Song and Dance (Minerva MIN 6JG-FSS) w. Judy Garland

There's No Business Like Show Business (Decca DL-8091, MCA 1727) [ST]

Yes Sir, That's My Baby (Caliban 6019) [ST]

# DOLLY PARTON

FROM A RELATIVELY UNKNOWN COUNTRY MUSIC SINGER, DOLLY Parton evolved into a superstar and first-class performer, not only a top record seller and songwriter, but also a movie star. With her Mae West figure, bubbling personality, and high-pitched singing voice, Dolly has become a national cult figure and, as a consequence, has been the butt of many jokes.

Yet beneath the blonde wig and bizarre costuming is an intelligent, level-headed woman who decided on her career road while as a child. She kept to her goals methodically to become one of today's best-known women in the entertainment arena and to command high salaries for her movie, recording, and nightclub work. With all these varied accomplishments, Dolly Parton's greatest satisfaction derives from her songwriting and from the fact that she is basically a simple person with strong country roots. When she made her career shift in the mid-1970s from country vocalist to pop singer, she told her fans, "I'm not leavin' the country, I'm just takin' it with me where I'm goin'."

The pretty, busty future star was born Dolly Rebecca Parton on January 19, 1946, in the little town of Locust Ridge Hollow, the fourth of twelve children of an east Tennessee dirt farmer (Lee Parton) and his wife (Avie Lee). Dolly later recalled that growing up on a farm was "a great way of life," one which imbued her with a religious outlook and a positive attitude toward the future. Music was an important part of the Partons' life as the family would listen to the "Grand Ole Opry" on radio each week; her father's favorite on the show was Hank Snow. By the time she was five, little Dolly was making up songs and asking her mother to write them down for her. She was playing guitar at age seven and by age ten she was appearing on television in Knoxville with Cas Walker.

At the age of thirteen Dolly cut her first record, "Puggy Love," for a small Louisiana company, and that year she debuted on radio's "Grand Ole Opry." Although she did not like school and was not a good student, she graduated from Sevier County High School in the spring of 1964. She then headed to Nashville, where she stayed with her uncle, songwriter-publisher Bill Owens. Together they composed "Put It Off Until Tomorrow," which was a hit for Bill Phillips on Decca in 1966. Meanwhile, Dolly worked as a waitress. She also performed in Nashville and modeled for a billboard advertisement that inspired the song "Girl on the Billboard" (both Del Reeves and Red Sovine had hit records with this tune). After waxing a few sides for the cut-rate Somerset label (she recorded five Kitty Wells chart songs), Dolly was signed by Monument Records. In 1967 she had country chart singles with "Dumb Blonde," "Something Fishy," and "Why, Why, Why." That same year Norma Jean left as Porter Wagoner's girl singer to get married and Dolly auditioned to become her replacement. For the next half-dozen years she co-starred on "The Porter Wagoner Show," the most popular syndicated country music show, seen in over two hundred markets, in addition to singing with Wagoner's road show. Meanwhile, in 1966, Dolly had married construction contractor Carl Dean, whom she had met when she first arrived in Nashville and had gone immediately to a laundromat.

As a result of being showcased by Porter Wagoner, Dolly Parton was signed by RCA Victor Records, for whom Wagoner had been a big seller for more than a decade. Together they began a series of best-selling duet singles with "The Last Thing on My Mind," late in 1967. Their other hit singles included "Holding On to Nothing" and "Always, Always" in 1968; "Your Love" in 1969; and "Daddy Was an Old Time Preacher Man" and "Tomorrow Is Forever" in 1970. On her own for RCA, Dolly had such hit singles as "In the Good Old Days" and "Daddy Come and Get Me," many of the songs reflecting incidents from her own life. Porter and Parton also recorded several best-selling record albums for RCA. (As a team they won the Country Music Association's Vocal Group of the Year award in 1968, 1970, and 1971.) By 1970 RCA had issued *The Best of Dolly Parton.*

In 1970 Dolly Parton had her first number one country single with "Joshua," followed by "Mule Skinner Blues." In 1972, some of her songs were done on an RCA album by Skeeter Davis called *Skeeter Sings Dolly,* and that year Dolly Parton made her screen debut, in tandem with Porter Wagoner, in the country music feature film THE NASHVILLE SOUND. Dolly continued to have hit records with such songs as "Coat of Many Colors" (an autobiographical song from her childhood about her mother's making her a coat from differently colored pieces of cloth), "My Tennessee Mountain Home," and "Washday Blues." With Porter Wagoner she was successful singing popular tunes such as "Better Move It on Home," "Together Always," and "The Right Combination."

In 1973 Dolly left Porter Wagoner's TV show and touring entourage, although he continued to manage her career and to produce her recordings. She had a best-selling single in 1974 with "Jolene" followed by "I Will Always Love You" and "Love Is Like a Butterfly." The next year brought forth "The Bargain Store" (an autobiographical number) and "We Used To," with "All I Can Do" in 1976. Again with Wagoner she had success with "Say Forever You'll Be Mine" in 1975 and "Is Forever Longer Than Always." In 1975, *Billboard, Cashbox,* and *Record World* magazines named her the top country female vocalist. In 1975 and 1976, Dolly was named the Country Music Association's Singer of the Year.

When she went on her own in 1974, Dolly used the Travelin' Family Band (which included her two brothers, two sisters, an uncle, and a cousin—her younger sister Stella Parton is a noted country singer in her own right). In 1976 she broke all ties with Porter Wagoner, who promptly sued her for $3 million in back fees and royalties; the two were alienated for several years, but the lawsuit was eventually settled out of court.

In 1977, in a move to break into the pop field, she began touring with her Gypsy Fever back-up band, and her RCA album that year, *New Harvest . . . First Gathering,* was a mixture of pop and country tunes. She continued to churn out hit singles ("Heartbreaker," "Light of a Clear Blue Morning," "You're the Only One"). Already she had headlined her own television series, the 1976 syndicated "Dolly." Three years later she signed a multi-million-dollar deal to appear in Las Vegas for six weeks each year. She also signed for her first major film appearance, in the comedy 9 TO 5 (1980), in which she, Jane Fonda, and Lily Tomlin starred as a trio of office workers who take revenge on their chauvinistic boss (Dabney Coleman). For the film, Dolly also composed the title tune, which was a hit record for her on RCA. Of the three female stars of 9 TO 5, she earned the best reviews, thereby launching her career in big-budget feature films. Of her picture-making experience, she recalled, "I never had a bad day on that film. I didn't really have to act. I just played myself, Dolly Parton, as a secretary."

Dolly was a presenter on the Academy Awards telecast in the spring of 1980 and that year she had hit records with "Starting Over Again" and "Old Flames Can't Hold a Candle to You." In 1982 she was named Entertainer of the Year and Female Country Star of the Year by the American Guild of Variety Artists and earned Grammy Awards for the song "9 to 5" for Best Country Female Vocal Performance and Best Country Song.

In 1982 Dolly co-starred with Burt Reynolds in the musical comedy THE BEST LITTLE WHOREHOUSE IN TEXAS as the madame of a brothel that her sheriff-boyfriend (Reynolds) is forced to close. Despite her exuberant efforts, the film was static and stagey and, unlike its stage predecessor, was not the megahit it had been projected to be. (Her

Dolly Parton in 9 TO 5 (1980)

sister Stella toured with the stage production at the time of the film's release). Two years later, after recuperating from stomach surgery, she co-starred with Sylvester Stallone in the unsuccessful RHINESTONE (1984), for which Dolly also composed the songs. In it she was a woman who bets that she can transform anyone into a country music singing star. As luck (and the script) would have it, she picks Gotham cabdriver Stallone. However, there was absolutely no chemistry between these two very different personalities. Thereafter, she took a hiatus from filmmaking to concentrate on her lucrative personal appearances. Her recordings from this period included a duet with Kenny Rogers on "Islands in the Stream," which reached number one on the charts in 1983 and was named Vocal Duet of the Year and Single Record of the Year by the Academy of Country Music.

She made her made-for-television movie debut in A SMOKEY MOUNTAIN CHRIST-MAS (1986), telecast by ABC during the holiday season. She was a country music star in the Tennessee backwoods who shares the yuletide with a woodsman (Lee Majors), several orphans, and a witch (Anita Morris). Dolly composed the half-dozen songs used in this telefeature fantasy. With much fanfare, Dolly returned to television in the fall of 1987 with her own lavish Sunday night series, "Dolly." Budgeted at $44 million, the ABC program featured Dolly's singing, guest stars, and several blackout sketches. However, it failed to generate sufficient ratings, and in mid-season it was moved to Saturdays and the format became more country (one segment even reunited Dolly with Porter Wagoner). Nothing seemed to help, and the show faded after one season.

In 1988 she reached out in many creative and business directions. She won a Country Music Association award in the category of Vocal Event for her album *Trio* with Linda Ronstadt and Emmy Lou Harris. She opened her Smokey Mountains entertainment resort, Dollywood, that year, and, also in 1988, her production company, Sandollar, financed two feature films: JACKNIFE with Robert De Niro and THE WAR AT HOME with Linda Fiorentino. Thereafter, Dolly herself returned to films. She sang the title song (which she composed) for Clint Eastwood's PINK CADILLAC (1989) and starred in the Louisiana-lensed STEEL MAGNOLIAS (1989), which cast her as a small town beauty salon owner sharing her life with friends (played by Shirley MacLaine, Julia Roberts, Sally Field, Daryl Hannah, and Olympia Dukakis). She joined with Willie Nelson and Kenny Rogers in the special "Kenny, Dolly & Willie: Something Inside So Strong" (NBC-TV, May 20, 1989) filmed at Houston's Johnson Space Center. The *Los Angeles Times* commented, "In an array of glitzy outfits, Parton—whose voice and personality, not surprisingly, bring the show alive—looks every bit as marvelous a feat of engineering as the space shuttle seen in the background." Her most recent LP, *White Limozeen* (produced by Ricky Skaggs), debuted in the summer of 1989. It was her most countrified album in years and included her song "Yellow Roses." *People* magazine judged that she "is sounding bright and lively" and said of this newest album from the prolific recording artist, "None of them has been better than this one, which is saying a lot." As to her future plans, Parton projects, "I'd like to do another [TV] series, maybe a sitcom. I'd also like to create my own Broadway show, maybe writing my own life story as a musical, and I'd appear in it on Broadway. I'd also like to get involved with a children's series, and do a line of cosmetics."

## Filmography

The Nashville Sound (John C. Bradford, 1972)
9 to 5 (20th–Fox, 1980) (also song)
The Best Little Whorehouse in Texas (Univ, 1982) (also additional songs)
Rhinestone (20th–Fox, 1984) (also songs)

A Smokey Mountain Christmas (ABC-TV, 12/14/86) (also songs)
Pink Cadillac (WB, 1989) (voice, song only)
Steel Magnolias (Tri-Star, 1989)

## TV Series

The Porter Wagoner Show (Synd, 1967–73)
Dolly (Synd, 1976)

Dolly (ABC, 1987–88)

## Album Discography

All I Can Do (RCA APL1-1665)
Always, Always (RCA LSP-4186)
As Long as I Love (Monument SLP-18136)
The Bargain Store (RCA APL1-0950)
The Best Little Whorehouse in Texas (MCA 6112) [ST]
The Best of Dolly Parton (RCA LSP-4449)
The Best of Dolly Parton, Vol. 2 (RCA APL1-1117)
The Best of Dolly Parton, Vol. 3 (RCA 5706-1-R8)
The Best of Porter Wagoner and Dolly Parton (RCA LSP-4556)
Bubbling Over (RCA APL1-0286)
Burlap and Satin (RCA AHL1-4691)
Coat of Many Colors (RCA LSP-4603)
Country Music (Time-Life STW-107)
Dolly Dolly Dolly (RCA AHL1-3546)
Dolly Parton and George Jones (Starday SLP-429)
Dolly Parton in the Beginning (Monument MG-7623)
Dolly Parton/Kitty Wells (Exact 239)
Dolly Parton Sings (Alshire 5351)
Dolly Parton Sings (RCA LSP-4752)
Dolly Parton Sings Country Oldies (Somerset 29400) w. Faye Tucker
The Fairest of Them All (RCA LSP-4288)
Golden Streets of Glory (RCA LSP-4398)
Great Balls of Fire (RCA AHL1-3361)
The Great Pretender (RCA AHL1-4940)

Greatest Hits (RCA AHL1-4422)
Heartbreak Express (RCA AHL1-4289)
Heartbreaker (RCA AFL1-2797)
Hello, I'm Dolly (Monument SLP-18085)
Hello, I'm Dolly/As Long as I Love (Monument BZ-33876)
Here You Come Again (RCA APL1-2544)
Hits Made Famous by Country Queens Patsy Cline and Kitty Wells (Somerset 19700, Alshire 5131) w. Faye Tucker
I Wish I Felt This Way at Home (Camden ACL1-7002)
In the Good Old Days (RCA LSP-4099, RCA NL-90007)
Jolene (RCA APL1-0473, RCA LSP-4507)
Just Because I'm a Woman (RCA LSP-3040, RCA NL-89853, Camden ACL-7017)
Just Between You and Me (RCA LSP-3926) w. Porter Wagoner
Just the Two of Us (RCA LSP-4039) w. Porter Wagoner
Just the Way I Am (Camden CAS-2583)
Love and Music (RCA APL1-0248) w. Porter Wagoner
Love Is Like a Butterfly (RCA APL1-9712, EMI/Music for Pleasure 5774)
Magic Moments 1964–77 (RCA NL-89620)
Mine (Camden ACL-0307)
My Blue Ridge Mountain Boy (RCA LSP-4188)
My Favorite Song Writer, Porter Wagoner (RCA LSP-4752)

My Tennessee Mountain Home (RCA APL1-0033)

New Harvest . . . First Gathering (RCA APL1-2188)

9 to 5 and Odd Jobs (RCA AAL1-3852, RCA AYL1-4830)

Once More (RCA LSP-4388) w. Porter Wagoner

Once Upon a Christmas (RCA ASL1-5307) w. Kenny Rogers

A Personal Music Dialogue with Dolly Parton (RCA DJL1-0314) w. Mike Harrison

Porter 'n Dolly (RCA APL1-0646) w. Porter Wagoner

Porter Wayne and Dolly Rebecca (RCA AHL1-3700) w. Porter Wagoner

Queen of Country (Quicksilver 5060) w. Donna Fargo

A Real Live Dolly (RCA LSP-4387) w. Porter Wagoner

Rhinestone Cowboy (RCA ABL1-5032) [ST]

Right Combination/Burning the Midnight Oil (RCA LSP-4628) w. Porter Wagoner

Say Forever You'll Be Mine (RCA APL1-1116) w. Porter Wagoner

Together Always (RCA LSP-4761) w. Porter Wagoner

Touch Your Woman (RCA LSP-4686)

Trio (WB 25491) w. Linda Ronstadt, Emmy Lou Harris

Two of a Kind (RCA LSP-4490) w. Porter Wagoner

We Found It (RCA LSP-4841) w. Porter Wagoner

White Limozeen (CBS 44384)

Winning Hand (Monument 38389-1) w. Willie Nelson, Kris Kristofferson, Brenda Lee

The World of Dolly Parton (Monument KZG-31913)

# LILY PONS

LILY PONS WAS ONE OF A NUMBER OF ATTRACTIVE OPERA SINGERS who attempted to carve out Hollywood careers in the 1930s in the wake of Grace Moore's popularity at Columbia Pictures and Jeanette MacDonald's operetta success at Paramount and MGM. Possessing one of the finest coloratura soprano voices ever heard, the petite Lily Pons (she was only slightly over 5 feet tall and weighed about one hundred pounds) was a very attractive personality. Unfortunately, she never found the right screen vehicles to make her a success with moviegoers. While she long remained a favorite on the operatic stage, radio, and recordings, her goal of starring in a serious operatic film never materialized.

She was born Alice Josephine Pons on April 12, 1904 (some sources insist 1898; she claimed 1905), the daughter of a French father and an Italian mother, in Cannes, France. As a child she was musically talented and studied piano at the Conservatoire de Paris, where she graduated with highest honors. As part of the World War I effort, she performed for soldiers in hospitals and at their request also began singing. Deciding she preferred vocalizing to piano playing, Lily began studying voice and found employment as the ingenue in a musical comedy at the Théâtre des Varietés in Paris. In 1923 she married a Dutch lawyer, publisher, and music critic, August Mesritz, who enrolled her with Albert de Gorostiaga for three years of opera vocal study.

In 1928 the singer made her operatic debut in Mulhouse in Alsace singing the title role in Delibes' *Lakmé* and became very popular touring the French provinces. Her attempts to gain employment in Paris opera, however, were futile, although she had learned a dozen coloratura roles. Finally, the husband-wife opera singers Giovanni Zenatello and Maria Gay heard her perform and they recommended her to Giulio Gatti-Casazza, the manager of New York's Metropolitan Opera. Lily came to Gotham to audition for him. However, when the manager met her, he thought she was too petite for opera roles. Pons nevertheless proved her abilities by singing five intricate coloratura arias for him, and she did the same thing for the president of the Metropolitan's board the same day. As a result, she made her Met debut on January 3, 1931, singing one of her favorite operas, Donizetti's popular *Lucia di Lammermoor* (the other was *Lakmé*). Her beginning salary was $450 a week. She caused a sensation in her U.S. debut, leading one New York music critic to observe that she has "a voice of pure and pleasing quality and a technique far above the slovenly average of today." She won a five-year contract with the Met, although she in fact remained with them for a quarter of a century. She also began to sing on radio (she was part of the Met's first commercially sponsored Saturday afternoon broadcast on December 30, 1933), but rejected several film offers. In addition, she sang with various other U.S. opera companies and also made appearances abroad in Buenos Aires and Rio de Janeiro as well as in European cities.

Following Grace Moore's big success in ONE NIGHT OF LOVE in 1934, Pons signed a contract with RKO Radio, which hoped to duplicate Moore's screen success by making popular opera films with Lily. She made her motion picture debut in the starring role of I DREAM TOO MUCH (1935), in which she played an opera singer who is in love with a composer (Henry Fonda—in a very unconvincing performance). Their romance fizzles when she becomes a success while his operas are rejected by the public. The singer saves the day, however, by turning her lover's opera into a hit musical comedy. Lily sang "The Bell Song" from *Lakmé* and "Caro Nome" from Verdi's *Rigoletto* as well as the title song, "I Got Love," and other tunes by Jerome Kern and Dorothy Fields. Although the movie was well mounted, and Pons handled her role well, the movie died at the box office and one unkind critic even dubbed it "I Scream Too Much." (*Variety* was kinder, stating, "Miss Pons is pretty to look at, has charm and personality, a delicious sense of humor besides her magnificent voice.")

Undaunted, RKO, more than a year later, starred Lily Pons in THAT GIRL FROM PARIS (1937), which provided her with her only screen success. It was a tale of a Paris opera diva (Pons) who backs out of marriage and follows American bandleader Gene Raymond

Lily Pons in HITTING A NEW HIGH (1937)

to his homeland. There she involves him and his band in her problems with immigration authorities before the two fall in love. The movie grossed over $1 million at the box office and in it she sang such songs as "Love and Learn," "Seal It with a Kiss," "Moon Face," Panofka's "Tarantella," and "Una Voce Poco Fa" from Rossini's *The Barber of Seville*. Sadly, RKO next cast the comely Lily as Ooga-Hunga, the Bird Girl, in the comedy HITTING A NEW HIGH (1937). She was the opera singer who masquerades in a feathered costume (and talks like a bird!) in order to be sold to the public by a daffy con man (Jack Oakie) as an African missing link. The looney premise sank the film, and not even Lily's singing of "Let's Give Love Another Chance," "This Never Happened Before," "Je Suis Titania" from Thomas' *Mignon*, and "The Nightingale Song" from *Paristys* could save the feature. It ended the star's RKO contract and her Hollywood starring career.

After her movie career came to a halt, Lily Pons continued to star at the Met and to tour. In 1937 she began appearing with orchestra leader André Kostelanetz on the CBS radio program "The Chesterfield Show." She and Kostelanetz fell in love (she had divorced her first husband in 1933) and they were married in 1938, with Geraldine Farrar as her wedding attendant. Lily and Kostelanetz then worked in tandem in concerts, although both continued also to have distinguished separate careers. In 1940 Pons became a United States citizen and during World War II she was an active entertainer of American troops both in the United States and overseas. She also recorded a number of V-Discs for the war effort. Her recording career had begun with Victor Records in the early 1930s, and after she and Kostelanetz were married, they both recorded for Columbia. Among the records Lily Pons made with her husband for Columbia were "A Cupidon"/"A une Fontaine," "The Blue Danube Waltz"/"Estrellita," and "The Last Rose of Summer"/"Les Filles de Cadiz." Her solo Columbia discs ranged from opera works to popular operetta songs like "L'Amour, Toujours, l'Amour," "Kiss Me Again," and "I'll See You Again."

In 1947 Lily Pons made her final screen appearance, in CARNEGIE HALL for United Artists, singing "The Bell Song" from *Lakmé*. The potpourri production also featured such classical music greats as Ezio Pinza, Jan Peerce, Artur Rubinstein, Leopold Stokowski, Jascha Heifetz, Gregor Piatigorsky, Risë Stevens, and Bruno Walter and the New York Philharmonic Orchestra—along with popular acts like Vaughn Monroe and Harry James and His Orchestra. The movie was not a success.

During the 1950s, Lily Pons continued to appear in various operas (such as Verdi's *La Traviata*, Donizetti's *Linda di Chamounix*, Bellini's *La Sonnambula*, and Thomas' *Mignon*) and remained with the Met until 1956. (On January 3 of that year, she had a lavish twenty-fifth anniversary gala at the Met, in which she was joined by Jan Peerce and Robert Merrill for the second act of *Rigoletto*. In addition, she did the Mad Scene from *Lucia di Lammermoor*, and arias from *Mignon*, *Lakmé*, Stravinsky's *Le Rossignol*, and *Linda di Chamounix*.) During the decade she recorded a number of albums for Columbia, including the operas *Lakmé* and *Lucia di Lammermoor* and the operetta *Die Fledermaus* by Johann Strauss, Jr., plus a number of coloratura arias as well as popular and romantic songs and waltzes. She and André Kostelanetz were divorced in 1958, and in 1960 she took up residence in Dallas, Texas. In 1962 she opened the opera season in Fort Worth with *Lucia di Lammermoor.* After that, Lily Pons unofficially retired. She died of cancer on February 13, 1976, survived by a sister. A Maryland town, Lilypond, was named in her honor.

While Lily Pons reached no milestones in her screen career, she was for more than three decades a respected opera singer on stage, radio, and records. In her prime, in the 1930s, it was claimed that for sheer power, her vocal cords were second only to those of Enrico Caruso. Her voice at the time ranged from middle C in the lower register to A above high C. Also, like Grace Moore, she helped to make opera popular with the general non-operagoing public. She made good fan magazine copy with her on-and-off romance (before they married) with André Kostelanetz and her publicized hobbies of walking in the country, reading history and biographies, skating, and collecting antique snuff boxes. Also, she had wide-ranging taste in music. In 1937 she informed an interviewer, "Music is music and jazz is just as much music as is opera, and it is really more fun to sing. . . . I *like* to sing hot songs!"

## Filmography

I Dream Too Much (RKO, 1935)
That Girl from Paris (RKO, 1937)
Hitting a New High (RKO, 1937)

Show Business at War (20th–Fox, 1943) (s)
Carnegie Hall (UA, 1947)

## Radio Series

The Chesterfield Show (CBS, 1937–38)

## Album Discography

Arias (Victrola VIC-1473)
The Art of Lily Pons (Camden CBL-101)
Coloratura Assoluta (Col D3M-34294)
Conversation Piece (Col SL-163)
Five Famous Coloratura Arias (Col ML-4057)
Die Fledermaus (Col SL-108, Odyssey Y2-3266)
I Dream Too Much (Amalgamated 248) [ST]
Lakmé (Operatic Archives 1045)
Lakmé Arias (10" Decca DL-4024)
Lily Pons Favorites (10" Col ML-2138)
Lily Pons Gala (Col ML-5073, Odyssey 32160270)
Lily Pons Sings Debussy (10" Col ML-2135)
Lily Pons Songs (10" Col AL-14)
Lucia di Lammermoor (Col SL-127, Odyssey Y2-32361)

Lucia di Lammermoor (Operatic Archives 1012)
Miss Lily Pons (Caliban 6027)
Mozart Arias (Col ML-4217)
Opera Arias (Odyssey Y-31152)
Operatic Arias/Chansons (Col ML-4300)
Paris (10" Col ML-2020)
A Pons–Kostelanetz Concert (Col ML-4069) w. André Kostelanetz
Popular Concert (10" Col ML-2181)
Repeat Performance (Col ML-4087)
Romances and Songs of the Eighteenth Century (10" Col AAL-53)
Seven Coloratura Arias (10" Col ML-2084)
Waltz Songs (Col ML-4061)

# DICK POWELL

DICK POWELL HAD SEVERAL DISTINCT FILM CAREERS: FIRST AS A 1930s crooner and then as a 1940s tough guy. In the 1950s he branched out into TV where he became a top executive and also a respected film producer and director. Certainly Dick Powell was a hard worker who had the capacity to change with the times. While not exceptionally talented in any given area, his workmanlike activities were always acceptable and he became a wealthy man from his many career avenues.

To moviegoers, however, he will always be the smiling, handsome tenor who romanced Ruby Keeler by a waterfall, while pettin' in the park, by a kissing rock, or in full military uniform strolling down Flirtation Walk. A crooner in the Rudy Vallee tradition, Dick Powell introduced many famous songs. On radio he starred in nine different series and he hosted a trio of his own programs on the small screen. In addition, he was one of the founders of Four Star, one of the most potent of the early TV production organizations. When he died of cancer in 1963, Dick Powell was one of the most highly regarded individuals in the entertainment industry.

Richard Ewing Powell was born on November 14, 1904, in Mountain View, Arkansas, but as a small boy he moved with his family to Little Rock. There he had his first taste of public singing in church choirs, first as a boy soprano and then as a tenor. After high school he went to Little Rock College, where he played clarinet, cornet, and saxophone with a student dance band. He earned extra money by odd jobs such as soda jerk and grocery clerk, as well as being first a line repairman and then a coin-box collector for the local telephone company.

After completing college, Powell married Mildred Maund and they moved to Louisville, Kentucky, where he landed a job with the Royal Peacocks, a touring band for which he was the vocalist. The group disbanded, however, after a murder was committed near the dance hall where they were playing in a small Illinois town. In 1926 he became a banjo player for Charlie Davis' orchestra, which was headquartered in Indianapolis, Indiana. Powell also began singing with the Davis group, and he soon developed a coterie of fans in the area. In late 1927 he traveled to Richmond, Indiana, where he cut his first record, for the Gennett label, but it was never issued. However, he did have a half-dozen takes released on the Vocalion label in 1928 and that year he also performed a trio of vocals with Davis for Brunswick Records.

Dick Powell left Indianapolis in 1930 and got a job in Pittsburgh as the master of ceremonies at the Stanley Theatre, where he played host to, and often performed with, visiting celebrities. He came to the attention of a Warner Bros. talent scout, who signed him to a contract with the intention that he would star in a film called THE CROONER (1932). That part, as it developed, went to David Manners. After providing an off-screen voice in BIG CITY BLUES (1932), he made his on-screen debut in BLESSED EVENT (1932) in a small part. He was impressive singing "How Can You Say No" and "I'm Making Hay in the Moonlight." *Variety* labeled him "very effective" and predicted, "He suggests possibilities especially for cafe and back stage stuff, calling for a singing voice." As a result of the good response, he was cast as the young crooner in the classic 42ND STREET in 1933, his first screen teaming with Ruby Keeler and choreographer Busby Berkeley.

Dick Powell's screen popularity was sealed in 1933 when he starred in GOLD DIGGERS OF 1933 as he and tap-dancing Ruby Keeler performed "Pettin' in the Park" and "Shadow Waltz" while Powell soloed on "I've Got to Sing a Torch Song." For the next three years, Powell and Keeler would be a popular screen pairing, often working with Busby Berkeley in his splashy, kaleidoscopic musical production numbers. In FOOTLIGHT PARADE (1933) he warbled "By a Waterfall" and "Honeymoon Hotel"—numbers filled with lovely chorines and suggestive visuals. In COLLEGE COACH (1933) he sang "Lonely Lane," and he sang the title song in the Warners–N.R.A. short THE ROAD IS OPEN AGAIN (1933). When he appeared in the all-star WONDER BAR (1934) with Al Jolson, Kay Francis, Dolores Del Rio, and Ricardo Cortez, it was Powell alone who survived unscathed, singing "Why Do I Dream Those Dreams?" and "Don't Say Good Night." His warm smile, good looks, and breezy personality fit perfectly the role of a budding radio crooner (allegedly based on Russ Columbo) in 20 MILLION SWEETHEARTS (1934), in which he vocalized "I'll String Along with You."

In that year, Powell appeared with Ruby Keeler in one of the best of the Busby Berkeley production number epics (Ray Enright directed), DAMES (1934). It was another backstage funfare with the crooner this time performing "I Only Have Eyes for You," which has become one of the top standards of all time. His other co-star in that musical was Joan Blondell (whom he married on September 19, 1936, following his divorce from his first wife and her divorce from her cinematographer husband, George Barnes). For a change of pace, Powell was cast as a worker who falls in love with an heiress (Josephine Hutchinson) in Mervyn LeRoy's HAPPINESS AHEAD (1934) and he sang "Pop! Goes Your Heart," "Happiness Ahead," and "Beauty Must Be Loved." With Ruby Keeler he did FLIRTATION WALK (1934) as a wise-mouthed West Point cadet in love with an officer's daughter (Keeler). It was not up to their usual standards, despite the title tune and "Mr. and Mrs. Is the Name."

During this period Dick Powell had become Warner Bros.' answer to Paramount's resident crooner (Bing Crosby). Powell recorded most of his movie songs for Brunswick Records, beginning in 1933, and he would remain with the label before going to Decca late in 1935. There he continued to wax his film tunes, but he also recorded a wide variety of popular numbers. He recorded for the label until 1942. In 1934 he also came to radio, starring in his first series, "The Old Gold Show" on CBS each Wednesday at 10 p.m. with Ted Fio Rito and His Orchestra. In October 1934 he began a four-season association with "Hollywood Hotel," which ran for one hour each Friday on CBS. Regulars on the musical variety shows were Frances Langford, Igor Gorin, and Raymond Paige and His Orchestra.

Dick Powell starred in a half-dozen releases in 1935, the year he was listed as the seventh most popular film star in the United States. The pleasing GOLD DIGGERS OF 1935 (1935) found Powell crooning "I'm Goin' Shoppin' with You" and "The Words Are in My Heart," although Wini Shaw performed the film's most popular number, "Lullaby of Broadway." In BROADWAY GONDOLIER (1935) he had a substantial role as a singer out to land a backer, with such fine songs as "Lonely Gondolier," "Outside of You," "The Rose in Her Hair," and "Lulu's Back in Town." By 1935, Marion Davies, under William Randolph Hearst's auspices, had moved her Cosmopolitan Pictures to Warner Bros. and it was no secret that she was greatly infatuated with Dick Powell. She chose him to co-star with her in the comedy PAGE MISS GLORY (1935). In SHIPMATES FOREVER (1935) he was the unwilling Annapolis cadet who proves his worth by becoming a hero, romancing Ruby Keeler and singing "Don't Give Up the Ship." For the visually spectacular but hard to follow A MIDSUMMER NIGHT'S DREAM (1935), he—like the rest of the studio's stock company—was dragged in to pepper the Shakespearean proceedings; Powell was Lysander. Fox had conceived THANKS A MILLION (1935) as a vehicle for Bing Crosby. When Paramount refused the loanout, Warners agreed to Powell's going over to Fox, where he played a crooner who seeks political office, all with the help of Paul Whiteman, Ann

Ruby Keeler and Dick Powell in DAMES (1934)

Dvorak, and Fred Allen. That musical was very popular, as was Powell's recording of the title tune.

Despite his only average film output for 1936, he was named the sixth most popular film star of the year. He was teamed for the seventh and last time with Ruby Keeler in COLLEEN (1936), a romantic comedy in which Powell sang "An Evening with You." Marion Davies selected him to be with her in HEARTS DIVIDED (1936), a costume romance with Powell as Napoleon's brother Jerome, in love with a Southern girl (Davies) opposed to Bonaparte (Claude Rains). Both Powell and his off-camera wife, Joan Blondell, were wasted in the backstage show business plot of STAGE STRUCK (1936), but they fared better in GOLD DIGGERS OF 1937 (1936), which dealt with showgirls convincing insurance agents to finance their production. He performed "With Plenty of Money and You." He was increasingly doing battle with the studio hierarchy to get a change of pace in his roles. The studio continued to insist that he was doing well in his particular mold.

For his initial 1937 release, he was loaned again to 20th Century–Fox, this time to co-star with Alice Faye and Madeleine Carroll in ON THE AVENUE. He played a stage star and sang several Irving Berlin songs including "I've Got My Love to Keep Me Warm" and "You're Laughing at Me." In the title role of THE SINGING MARINE (1937) he performed "You Can't Run Away from Love," "Cause My Baby Says It's So," "The Singing Marine," and "I Know Now." It was Busby Berkeley who did the geometric production numbers for VARSITY SHOW (1937), with Powell seen as a big-time producer backing a show at his college alma mater and performing "Love Is on the Air Tonight," "You've Got Something There," "Have You Got Any Castles, Baby?," and "Moonlight on the Campus." The popularity of his radio show resulted in his playing a talent scout in HOLLYWOOD HOTEL (1937), directed by Busby Berkeley, and performing "I've Hitched My Wagon to a Star" and "I'm Like a Fish Out of Water."

Dick Powell somewhat kidded his (bland) crooner image in the musical comedy COWBOY FROM BROOKLYN (1938), playing a singer who must prove he is a cowpoke in order to land a radio contract. In it he sang "Ride, Tenderfoot, Ride." For the amusing comedy HARD TO GET (1938) he was the working stiff (a gas station attendant) who romances an heiress (Olivia de Havilland) and sings "You Must Have Been a Beautiful Baby." He refused to join the cast of GARDEN OF THE MOON (1938—John Payne was substituted), but did participate in the mediocre horse-racing comedy GOING PLACES (1938). Louis Armstrong and Maxine Sullivan had the best song, "Jeepers Creepers," in that semi-dud. By now, Powell and Warner Bros. were at loggerheads and he was adamant about not renewing his contract. He closed out his studio association with NAUGHTY BUT NICE (1939; made in 1938) as a stuffed-shirt music professor who accidentally writes a hit song; unfortunately, none of the film's five tunes was memorable. Following the demise of his CBS radio show "Hollywood Hotel" in 1938, he joined the NBC program "Your Hollywood Parade" and in 1939 headlined yet another NBC radio outing, "Tuesday Night Party."

Tired of his movie crooner roles, Dick Powell went to Paramount, where he starred in the funny Preston Sturges picture CHRISTMAS IN JULY (1940) about a poor man who thinks he has won a contest and goes on a big shopping spree. For the same studio he and his wife, Joan Blondell (whom he had coaxed into leaving Warner Bros.), portrayed newlyweds in the tepid comedy I WANT A DIVORCE (1940), and then he made a few features at Universal. He and Joan Blondell were teamed again in MODEL WIFE (1941), as a couple who must keep their nuptials a secret so she will not lose her job. In the Bud Abbott–Lou Costello comedy IN THE NAVY (1941), he was the singing idol who attempts to join the service; he sang "Star Light, Star Bright" and "We're in the Navy." In 1941 Powell also was in two more radio series, NBC's "American Cruise," which reunited him with Frances Langford, and the syndicated mystery comedy "Miss Pinkerton" (based on the Mary Roberts Rinehart character) with Joan Blondell in the title role as a lady detective (a part she had played at Warner Bros. in 1932).

Back at Paramount, he joined Mary Martin and the Golden Gate Quartette for the "Dreamland" number in STAR SPANGLED RHYTHM (1942) and then he played a beachcomber who loves a golddigger (Mary Martin) out to land a rich tycoon (Rudy Vallee) in HAPPY GO LUCKY (1943). In the amusing TRUE TO LIFE (1943), he was a radio script writer who moves in with an "average" family to gain material for his show. After taking a back seat to Dorothy Lamour (as the stripper who puts on a big show to save his silver mine and dude ranch) in RIDING HIGH (1943), Powell rebelled at being stuck in the crooner mold again. He left Paramount.

During the 1943–44 radio season Dick Powell was back on the airwaves, starring in "Campana Serenade," which ran first on NBC from January to August 1943 and then on CBS from September 1943 until February 1944. For United Artists he starred in the amusing fantasy IT HAPPENED TOMORROW (1944) as the confounded newspaper reporter who can predict future headlines. The critics liked the picture better than the public did. At MGM he co-starred with Lucille Ball in the mild musical comedy MEET THE PEOPLE (1944). In the cast was rising starlet June Allyson, whom Powell wed (on August 19, 1945) following his divorce from Joan Blondell. (Blondell would write an unflattering portrait of Powell in her autobiographical novel, *Center Door Fancy*, 1972.)

Dick Powell's fading career took a complete turn when he convinced RKO to allow him to play rugged Philip Marlowe in MURDER, MY SWEET (1944). Much to everyone's surprise, he was perfectly at ease in the role of gumshoe Marlowe. Thereafter, he left behind his image as a crooner for that of tough guy. He landed mature lead roles in *film noir* melodramas like CORNERED (1945), JOHNNY O'CLOCK (1947), PITFALL (1948), and CRY DANGER (1951). Meanwhile, he undertook a Western role in STATION WEST (1948) and that of a mountie in the outdoor romance drama MRS. MIKE (1949). The transformation also extended to radio, where Powell portrayed private eye Richard Rogue in the 1945 ABC series "Rogue's Gallery," which ran on Mutual from 1945 to 1946 and on NBC in the summers of 1946 and 1947. From 1949 to 1952 he had the title role in the radio drama "Richard Diamond, Private Detective," which NBC broadcast during the 1949–50 season and ABC ran from 1951 to 1952; ABC also repeated the NBC shows from 1950 during 1953. Meanwhile, he and his wife had adopted a daughter (Pamela) in 1948 and their son (Richard, Jr.) was born in 1950.

Powell came to television in 1952 as one of the rotating hosts and performers (the others were Charles Boyer, David Niven, and Ida Lupino) on the CBS series "Four Star Playhouse," which ran until 1956. In 1954 he repeated the role of Philip Marlowe in "The Long Goodbye" on "Climax" (CBS-TV), and his Four Star Television company became a leader in the production of TV series. On the movie side of his multi-faceted career, Powell kept active but was far less successful. June Allyson was now a major star and MGM teamed her and Powell in two pedestrian 1950 vehicles: THE REFORMER AND THE RED-HEAD and RIGHT CROSS. He was a detective out to stop the attempted assassination of Abraham Lincoln in THE TALL TARGET (1951), a Hollywood script writer in THE BAD AND THE BEAUTIFUL (1952), and a scripter again in the saucy comedy SUSAN SLEPT HERE (1954), which had him indulging in a May-September romance with Debbie Reynolds. In the interim, he directed *The Caine Mutiny Court-Martial* on Broadway in 1953.

The popular SUSAN SLEPT HERE proved to be his final big-screen acting assignment, as he was now working on the other side of the camera, having directed the melodrama SPLIT SECOND (1953) at RKO. (For a time, Powell's friendship with RKO owner Howard Hughes and his working for that studio led to speculation that he might take over as RKO production chief; he never did.) Thereafter, Powell produced and directed THE CON-QUEROR (1956), YOU CAN'T RUN AWAY FROM IT (1956—starring June Allyson), THE ENEMY BELOW (1957), and THE HUNTERS (1958). From 1956 to 1962 he hosted the popular CBS-TV series "Zane Grey Theater" and acted in fourteen episodes of the program, in addition to making guest appearances on his wife's "The June Allyson Show," "The Tom Ewell Show," and "The Law and Mr. Jones." From 1961 to 1963 he hosted "The Dick Powell Show" on NBC-TV and starred in nine segments of the program, the last telecast December 11, 1962, less than a month before his death.

In the fall of 1962, Dick Powell and June Allyson, who had been estranged for a time before reconciling, went on a press junket to promote various Four Star Television products, and late in the year they were in Cincinnati to appear on Ruth Lyons' "50–50 Club" program on WLWT-TV. Powell had a very sore throat and could scarcely talk while on the show. Doctors told him he had a severe case of hives due to medication he was taking. Back in Hollywood he was diagnosed with throat cancer. He succumbed to the disease on January 2, 1963, leaving a million dollar estate. His son, Dick Powell, Jr., would briefly portray his father in the movie DAY OF THE LOCUST (1975).

## Filmography

Big City Blues (WB, 1932) (voice only)
Blessed Event (WB, 1932)
Too Busy to Work (Fox, 1932)
The King's Vacation (WB, 1933)
42nd Street (WB, 1933)
Gold Diggers of 1933 (WB, 1933)
Footlight Parade (WB, 1933)

College Coach [Football Coach] (WB, 1933)
Convention City (FN, 1933)
The Road Is Open Again (Vita, 1933) (s)
Wonder Bar (FN, 1934)
20 Million Sweethearts (FN, 1934)
Dames (WB, 1934)
Hollywood Newsreel (Vita, 1934) (s)

Happiness Ahead (FN, 1934)
Flirtation Walk (FN, 1934)
Your Sweetheart and Mine (Vita, 1934) (s)
Gold Diggers of 1935 (FN, 1935)
Broadway Gondolier (WB, 1935)
Page Miss Glory (WB, 1935)
Shipmates Forever (FN, 1935)
A Midsummer Night's Dream (WB, 1935)
Thanks a Million (Fox, 1935)
Colleen (WB, 1936)
Screen Snapshots #7 (Col, 1936) (s)
Hearts Divided (FN, 1936)
Gold Diggers of 1937 (WB, 1936)
Stage Struck (FN, 1936)
On the Avenue (20th–Fox, 1937)
The Singing Marine (WB, 1937)
Varsity Show (WB, 1937)
Hollywood Hotel (WB, 1937)
Cowboy from Brooklyn [Romance and Rhythm]
    (WB, 1938)
For Auld Lang Syne (Vita, 1938) (s)
Hard to Get (WB, 1938)
Going Places (WB, 1938)
Naughty But Nice (WB, 1939)
Christmas in July (Par, 1940)
I Want a Divorce (Par, 1940)
Picture People #1 (RKO, 1940) (s)
In the Navy (Univ, 1941)
Model Wife (Univ, 1941)
Star Spangled Rhythm (Par, 1942)
Happy Go Lucky (Par, 1943)

Riding High [Melody Inn] (Par, 1943)
True to Life (Par, 1943)
It Happened Tomorrow (UA, 1944)
Meet the People (MGM, 1944)
Murder, My Sweet [Farewell, My Lovely]
    (RKO, 1944)
Cornered (RKO, 1945)
Johnny O'Clock (RKO, 1947)
Pitfall (UA, 1948)
To the Ends of the Earth (Col, 1948)
Station West (RKO, 1948)
Rogues' Regiment (Univ, 1948)
Mrs. Mike (UA, 1949)
The Reformer and the Redhead (MGM, 1950)
Right Cross (MGM, 1950)
Cry Danger (RKO, 1951)
The Tall Target (MGM, 1951)
You Never Can Tell [You Never Know] (Univ,
    1951)
Callaway Went Thataway (MGM, 1951)
The Bad and the Beautiful (MGM, 1952)
Split Second (RKO, 1953) (director only)
Susan Slept Here (RKO, 1954)
The Conqueror (RKO, 1956) (producer,
    director only)
You Can't Run Away from It (Univ, 1956)
    (producer, director only)
The Enemy Below (20th–Fox, 1957) (producer,
    director only)
The Hunters (20th–Fox, 1958) (producer,
    director only)

## Broadway Plays

The Caine Mutiny Court-Martial (1953)
    (director only)

## Radio Series

The Old Gold Show (CBS, 1934)
Hollywood Hotel (CBS, 1934–38)
Your Hollywood Parade (NBC, 1938)
Tuesday Night Party (NBC, 1939)
American Cruise (NBC, 1941)
Miss Pinkerton (Synd, 1941)

Campana Serenade (NBC, 1943; CBS, 1943–
    44)
Rogue's Gallery (ABC, 1945; Mutual, 1945–46;
    NBC, 1946, 1947)
Richard Diamond, Private Detective (NBC,
    1949–50; ABC, 1951–52)

## TV Series

Four Star Playhouse (CBS, 1952–56)
Dick Powell's Zane Grey Theater (CBS, 1956–62)

The Dick Powell Show (NBC, 1961–63)

## Album Discography

Colleen (Caliban 6007) [ST]
Dames (Caliban 6014) [ST]
Dick Powell–Bing Crosby (Amalgamated 162)
Dick Powell in Hollywood (Col C2L-44)
Dick Powell Live 1934 (Broncoli Gegend 32134)
Dick Powell, 1934–51 (Star-Tone 202)
Dick Powell Presents (Dot 3421/75421)
The Dick Powell Songbook (Decca DL-8837)
Flirtation Walk (Caliban 6042) [ST]
Footlight Parade (Caliban 6045) [ST]
Hollywood Hotel (EOH 99601, Hollywood Soundstage 5004) [ST]
Love Is on the Air Tonight (MCA 1511)
Lullaby of Broadway (ASV 5045)

On the Avenue/Thanks a Million (Sandy Hook 2003) [ST]
Radio Cavalcade of 1936 (Amalgamated 2523) [ST/R]
Rare Recordings (Sandy Hook 2048)
Richard Diamond (Command Performance 6) [ST/R]
Riding High (Caliban 6034) [ST]
Springtime in the Rockies (Pelican 128) [ST/R]
Star Spangled Rhythm (Curtain Calls 100/20, Sandy Hook 2045) [ST]
Thanks a Million/Happy Go Lucky (Caliban 6021) [ST]
20 Million Sweethearts (Amalgamated 223) [ST]
Varsity Show (Vertinge 2001) [ST]
The Wonderful Teens (RPC 105)

# ELEANOR POWELL

MGM'S COMPILATION DOCUMENTARY THAT'S ENTERTAINMENT! (1974) presented a remarkable cornucopia of song-and-dance sequences. Of the talent from the studio's golden past represented in the film clips, none made a greater impression than tap dancing Eleanor Powell in highlights from her several musical features. For the new generation of viewers, the film revealed a dynamic talent in awesome motion; for older filmgoers, it served as a reminder of how exuberantly gifted Eleanor Powell was as a dancer. There have been other female tap dancers on screen: the earlier Ruby Keeler was more breathlessly eager but far less of a dancer; the later Ann Miller was more voluptuously figured and physically dazzling. But 5' 6" Eleanor Powell, the perfectionist, outshone them both as a precision, whirlwind tap dancer: her routines were ambitious and well executed, and always kept moviegoers amazed. Director/choreographer Busby Berkeley would say that she and Fred Astaire were the greatest dancers: "Eleanor Powell's unusual heel and toe tap style was an innovation. She took certain steps and created a broken rhythm. . . . She would take a step that would be good plus another one and she would mix them up."

By Hollywood standards, Eleanor Powell was not strikingly feminine nor was her singing or emoting noteworthy. However, she radiated such a joyous inner glow that audiences overlooked these "deficiencies." Maestro Arturo Toscanini once said, "Three things I will carry through life—the glorious sunset, the splendor of the Grand Canyon and the dancing of Eleanor Powell."

She was born Eleanor Torrey Powell on November 21, 1912, in Springfield, Massachusetts. When she was two, her father left the household. Eleanor was told that he had died, but she much later learned that her parents had divorced. (Her father had contracted a social disease and for a time it was uncertain whether Eleanor, who was born prematurely without fingernails, toenails, or eyebrows, would survive.)

Eleanor's mother held an assortment of jobs (bank teller, waitress, hotel chambermaid) to support the household. At age six, Eleanor began taking lessons from a local dance teacher, Ralph McKernan. Blanche Powell hoped that the lessons would help Eleanor (an introverted only child, very sensitive about being tall for her age) become less shy. The strategy worked.

On a summer visit to Atlantic City in 1925, when she was twelve, Eleanor was spotted on the beach doing acrobatics by showman Gus Edwards, who hired her for his children's revue at the Ritz Grill of the Ambassador Hotel. She received a $7 salary for her two weekly performances. The next summer she returned to the Ambassador Hotel in Atlantic City, this time teamed with Bennie Davis. Both later that year and the following summer she worked at the Silver Slipper Club, soon earning $75 weekly at the swanky supper club.

When Eleanor graduated from high school at age sixteen, Mrs. Powell took her daughter to New York City. It was agreed that if Eleanor did not "make it" in three months, they would return to Springfield and Eleanor would continue her schooling. She found dancing work at Ben Bernie's club, worked in vaudeville, and danced at private parties. She then had minor work in *The Optimists* (1928), a midnight revue produced at the Casino de Paris Club on the Century Theatre Roof.

In the late 1920s, tap dancing was the latest craze on Broadway, and in order to compete at auditions, Eleanor was forced to abandon the ballet and acrobatics she knew, to study the new fad. At Jack Donahue's dance school she learned how to tap. It was he who tied two sandbags to her waist and helped her to perfect those effortless, rapid taps in which her feet seemed never to leave the ground. ("You're a percussion instrument with your feet. You're a musician," he would say later.) Having mastered the tapping technique, she won a specialty assignment on Broadway in the musical *Follow Thru* (1929), starring Jack Haley and Zelma O'Neal. She had a lead in *Fine and Dandy* (1930) and that same year she was at Carnegie Hall with Paul Whiteman's Band doing her tap specialty. On the same bill was Maurice Chevalier making his American "live" debut. More Broadway shows followed, including Florenz Ziegfeld's *Hot-Cha!* (1932) with Buddy Rogers and *George White's Music Hall Varieties* (1932) with Harry Richman and Bert Lahr. Of the latter show, the *New York Times* reported, "There is a large dancing chorus, but among the supporting company it is the lanky Eleanor Powell, an excellent tap dancer, who stands out markedly." Always wanting to improve, Eleanor practiced constantly between Broadway runs. By now, the Dance Masters of America had named her "The World's Greatest Feminine Tap and Rhythm Dancer."

When Fox Films decided to film GEORGE WHITE'S 1935 SCANDALS (1935), starring Alice Faye and James Dunn, showman George White asked Eleanor to come to Hollywood to repeat her tap specialty from the *Music Hall Varieties*. When the film opened, *Variety* reported, "Eleanor Powell, who can tap with the best of them, does just one short number." Fox saw no screen potential in the unglamourous newcomer and she returned to New York. Meanwhile, MGM happened to screen her Fox number and wanted her for a brief specialty role in BROADWAY MELODY OF 1936 (1935) starring Jack Benny. Already hardened to studio politics, Eleanor refused the initially offered role of the switchboard operator (played eventually by Una Merkel). Because studio head Louis B. Mayer was impressed by her talent *and* spunk, he eventually chose to give her the lead opposite handsome newcomer Robert Taylor. She asked for $1,250 for the four weeks' work, which turned into four months on the soundstage. The studio tinted her brunette hair reddish, capped her teeth, hid her freckles with makeup and special lighting, and focused several production numbers around her. As would be her habit throughout her film career, she choreographed her own routines, leaving the chorus movements and other non-Powell dance numbers to the film's dance director. In BROADWAY MELODY OF 1936 she danced with Buddy Ebsen and his sister Vilma in a tenement rooftop number ("Sing Before

Breakfast"), vamped as a French mademoiselle in a blonde wig, and did a cute send-up of Katharine Hepburn à la MORNING GLORY. More important, she tap danced gloriously: both without background music and in such production ensembles as the "Broadway Rhythm" finale (to Frances Langford's singing). Eleanor's singing in BROADWAY MELODY OF 1936, as well as the later BROADWAY MELODY OF 1938 and ROSALIE, was dubbed by Marjorie Lane.

Powell became an "overnight" star because of BROADWAY MELODY OF 1936, but before MGM could use her in further films, she had a Broadway commitment to honor. She joined Beatrice Lillie and Ethel Waters in *At Home Abroad*, which opened in New York in September 1935. While the show was still running, she left due to "exhaustion" and returned to Hollywood, where she had signed a seven-year contract with Metro-Goldwyn-Mayer. Her new screen partner was James Stewart, and the backstage story was the Cole Porter musical BORN TO DANCE (1936). She displayed her rapid-fire tapping in the "Rap-Rap-Tap on Wood" number. For the lavish finale, "Swingin' the Jinx Away," she performed aboard a soundstage-size battleship with hordes of dancing extras, and the added attractions of the Ebsens and Frances Langford. Audiences apparently could not get enough of Eleanor's precision routines, and for BROADWAY MELODY OF 1938 (1937) she was re-matched in love with Robert Taylor and in dance with Buddy Ebsen and George Murphy. The show boasted another "Broadway Rhythm" production spectacle, but straightforward Eleanor was at her best in tux and top hat soloing "Your Broadway and My Broadway." Eager to make the most of Powell's great popularity, the studio cast her with Nelson Eddy (trying his box-office pull *without* screen teammate Jeanette MacDonald) in ROSALIE (1937). It was the ridiculous tale of Powell, as Princess Rosalie of Romanza, attending Vassar College and falling in love with a West Point cadet/football hero (Eddy). The operetta plot creaked, but Powell excelled at tapping (to "I've a Strange New Rhythm in My Heart") in a dorm room sequence. Later, while Eddy boomed out the title song, she performed nimble gymnastics as she rhythm-danced across a progression of huge drums and through a flaming hoop!

There was talk of teaming Powell with Eddie Cantor in a version of Broadway's *Girl Crazy*, but that did not materialize, and it was 1939 before she returned to the screen in HONOLULU, with Robert Young in a dual role and the team of George Burns and Gracie Allen for comic relief. Eleanor was seen to advantage in a hula number and tapping away while skipping rope. She was now earning $125,000 per film.

Eager to team her with a dancer of equal caliber, MGM brought Fred Astaire to the studio for BROADWAY MELODY OF 1940 (1940). Both stars were perfectionists and boasted pleasing personalities, but they lacked screen chemistry together. They danced a duet to Cole Porter's "Begin the Beguine" and she had another elaborate shipboard number, "I Am the Captain," where, as a solo performer, she was far better. The *New York Times* noted of her acting, "the final impression of her characterization continues to be the memory of a professional smile, turned on and off like an essentially unamused neon." Plans to reteam Powell and Astaire were dropped. Astaire would later say of Eleanor that she was the only woman dancer who "put 'em down like a man."

Because she was a stickler for precision and since her numbers required so much intensive rehearsal, Eleanor had settled into a routine of making only one film a year. She was top-billed in LADY BE GOOD (1941) and performed three specialties, including the excellent finale dance to George and Ira Gershwin's "Fascinating Rhythm" (while Connie Russell sang). The number was choreographed by Busby Berkeley with a mass of tuxedoed chorus men and eight grand pianos. Berkeley insisted, "Eleanor was by far the finest female dancer we ever had in films, and a very hard-working perfectionist. . . . I've known very few women that talented and that gracious." However, much of this film's screen story time went to Ann Sothern and Robert Young (as two feuding songwriters) and to Sothern who sang the Oscar-winning song "The Last Time I Saw Paris." Eleanor was caught in nonsense involving World War II enemy agents in SHIP AHOY (1942). Her LADY BE GOOD vis-à-vis, Red Skelton, was now her leading man. Despite the presence of Tommy Dorsey and His Orchestra (which included vocalizing Frank Sinatra), the fare was more slipshod than ship-shape. She and Dan Dailey were scheduled to be in FOR ME AND MY GAL (1942), but it was Judy Garland and Gene Kelly who starred in the musical. With Kelly, Powell practiced routines for what was to have been BROADWAY MELODY OF 1943 but which ended as solo snippets in the all-star THOUSANDS CHEER (1943). For her turn in this vehicle, master of ceremonies Mickey Rooney introduced her as "America's greatest dancer." A few months earlier, the studio had released I DOOD IT (1943), which high-lighted the buffoonery of Red Skelton and reduced Eleanor's role to that of an uncom-fortable secondary lead as the movie star who weds a tailor's assistant. Between Skelton's an-tic comedy routines, Powell did a jump rope number and danced on

Eleanor Powell and Red Skelton in I DOOD IT (1943)

yet another ship set for "Swingin' the Jinx Away," a song/routine repeated almost verbatim from her earlier BORN TO DANCE.

By 1943, MGM had undergone several major talent changes: Jeanette MacDonald, Joan Crawford, and Greta Garbo had all left the studio. And so did Eleanor Powell. Her contract was up and there was no real interest in renewing it. She claimed she was tired of moviemaking. She had been dating her male secretary, Sid Luft (who later wed Judy Garland), but she married (in 1943) rising screen player Glenn Ford. She insisted she wanted to be a housewife. Besides, her husband found it annoying to be known as Mr. Powell. ("He had such an inferiority complex, it was sheer hell," she would admit later. "When we went out together everybody flocked around me. I couldn't see that they were ignoring him, but he thought they were.")

There was an attempt at a screen return in United Artists' SENSATIONS OF 1945 (1944), but the film was a tattered potpourri. (In 1946, MGM released abroad only THE GREAT MORGAN, which used outtakes and edited footage from past MGM productions to create a "new" film; Eleanor was included in a dance sequence.) Thereafter, Eleanor became a mother—a son, Peter, was born in 1945—and threw herself into community service. She taught Sunday School at the Presbyterian Church and later became a scout-master in charge of Boy Scout Troop #17 in Beverly Hills. In the late 1940s, she had a dancing engagement at the London Palladium and turned up as one of the guest stars in Esther Williams' DUCHESS OF IDAHO (1950) at MGM, her alma mater. She did a solo tap routine to a boogie woogie number. She was honored as Woman of the Year and Mother of the Year by assorted civic organizations and even officiated at an Easter Sunrise Service at the Hollywood Bowl. In the fall of 1954 she began participating on the "Faith of Our Children" religious teleseries, writing several scripts and making frequent appearances. For this charitable work, she received the union pay scale of $23.10 an hour. The program would win five Emmy Awards.

Few people in the film business have been held in such high esteem as "Elly" Powell. Thus, although fan magazines continued to publish accounts of her happy marriage to Glenn Ford, it was long known that the union was far from ideal. In May 1959 (on Ford's birthday), she began divorce proceedings. By this point, Ford's career had greatly accelerated, which made the minimal settlement she received all the more unusual. However, she refused to air "dirty linen" in public, although later she admitted, "I sued on grounds of extreme mental cruelty, and that's exactly what I meant." That Christmas she and her son, Peter, were in Las Vegas seeing the acts. Starring performer Pearl Bailey introduced Eleanor from the audience and she got up and danced a few numbers to a big round of applause. Her fourteen-year-old son took sharp notice of her popularity with the audience and began encouraging his mother to return to show business. (He would later have a brief acting career himself.) Eleanor's mother was more blunt. After examining the divorce settlement and the state of her daughter's finances, she concluded, "Elly, you've gotta work!"

Powell went on a strict diet (going from 160 pounds back to her performing 123-pound weight) and began rehearsing with choreographer David Lichine. She opened in

Las Vegas at the Sahara Club on February 28, 1961, with a fifty-minute revue, including film clips and her tap dancing to such songs as "Fascinating Rhythm" and "Life Is Just a Bowl of Cherries." The show was a hit. When she played the Latin Quarter in Manhattan, the *New York Times* announced, "Eleanor Powell has Broadway at her feet once again." She continued with club engagements, appeared on television ("The Perry Como Show" and "The Hollywood Palace"), and gave a command performance for Princess Grace of Monaco. However, by 1964, she decided that her religious activities were far more important than any further rebuilding of her show business career. She became an ordained minister of the Unity Church.

Eleanor Powell was much in the public's mind when THAT'S ENTERTAINMENT! played around the country in 1974, and she was interviewed frequently. Thereafter, however, she returned to private life. She was at Fred Astaire's American Film Institute tribute in March 1981 and that June underwent surgery to remove a malignant tumor. She had a subsequent operation to remove part of her intestine, and on February 11, 1982, she succumbed to cancer.

Eleanor claimed that her philosophy of life was: "What we are is God's gift to us. What we become is our gift to God."

## Filmography

George White's 1935 Scandals (Fox, 1935)
Broadway Melody of 1936 (MGM, 1935)
Born to Dance (MGM, 1936)
Rosalie (MGM, 1937)
Broadway Melody of 1938 (MGM, 1937)
Honolulu (MGM, 1939)
Broadway Melody of 1940 (MGM, 1940)
Lady Be Good (MGM, 1941)
Ship Ahoy (MGM, 1942)

I Dood It [By Hook or by Crook] (MGM, 1943)
Thousands Cheer (MGM, 1943)
Sensations of 1945 (UA, 1944)
The Great Morgan (MGM, 1946) (European release only)
Famous Hollywood Mothers (Col, 1946) (s)
Duchess of Idaho (MGM, 1950)

## Broadway Plays

Follow Thru (1929)
Fine and Dandy (1930)
Hot-Cha! (1932)

George White's Music Hall Varieties (1932)
At Home Abroad (1935)

## TV Series

Faith of Our Children (NBC, 1954–56)

## Album Discography

Born to Dance (CIF 3001) [ST]
Broadway Melody of 1938 (Motion Picture
    Tracks MPT-3) [ST]
Broadway Melody of 1940 (CIF 3002) [ST]
Duchess of Idaho (Titania 508) [ST]

Lady Be Good (Caliban 6010, Hollywood
    Soundstage 5010) [ST]
Ship Ahoy (Hollywood Soundstage 5011) [ST]
Thousands Cheer (Amalgamated 232, Holly-
    wood Soundstage 409) [ST]

# JANE POWELL

ESPECIALLY DURING HOLLYWOOD'S GOLDEN AGE, THE PUBLIC TOOK screen talent for granted. It was expected that movie musical leads could sing, dance, act, be attractive, and live up to their images. With her cultured soprano voice, pert (5' 1"), good-looking, blonde, blue-eyed Jane Powell was everything filmgoers expected in a movie star. Coming ten years after Deanna Durbin, she was the bright successor to that popular screen songstress, playing the same sort of precocious adolescent roles that had endeared Durbin to moviegoers. For a decade (1946–54), her home lot (MGM) employed her in a succession of successful musicals: HOLIDAY IN MEXICO (1946), A DATE WITH JUDY (1948), ROYAL WEDDING (1951), and SEVEN BRIDES FOR SEVEN BROTHERS (1954). In these and other films, Powell was always wholesome, ebullient, and deft. She was quite popular, but still she was taken for granted.

When Hollywood stopped producing lavish musicals in the mid-1950s, she was only in her mid-twenties. However, she had been so typed by her pictures that she struggled for decades (in TV, stock, and cabaret) before reemerging successfully as a Broadway star in *Irene* (1974). And then, being middle-aged, she found it difficult to establish a "new" image to succeed in TV or films.

What gives Jane Powell's career added dimension is the maturing of her personality over the decades, as she adjusted to real-life needs versus her career image. The public was generally unaware of how deeply unhappy she had been conforming to her goody-goody, compliant screen posture. Unlike many of her equally bitter peers (Judy Garland in particular), it took her years to dare to air her frustrations in public. In her 1980s one-woman show, she became very vocal, admitting, "I was always pleasing someone else. My mother, the men I married, the studio. . . . I did what I was told. There were only three things I wanted to do and did—marry, have children, get divorced. Otherwise, it was always someone else who decided for me." Her flinty, honest autobiography, *The Girl Next Door and How She Grew*, was published in 1988. It opens with the statement: "Life is a ladder that we all ascend in a different way. Sometimes we run up too fast and miss a few rungs." It helps to explain much about Jane Powell's extended maturation period.

She was born Suzanne Burce on April 1, 1929, in Portland, Oregon, the daughter of Paul and Eileen Burce. Her father delivered Wonder Bread. The Burces were an unhappily married couple, and Eileen had definitely not wanted a child. (For years Jane Powell would dream of her mother trying to suffocate her, an event she insists may have really occurred.) Mrs. Burce's extreme frustration turned to tunnel-vision ambition when she realized that her daughter had natural talent. She insisted that the little girl take song and dance lessons at the Agnes Peters Dancing School, hoping she might become another Shirley Temple.

When Suzanne was five, she was heard on a local children's radio show, "Stars of Tomorrow." A talent agent convinced Mrs. Burce that Suzanne should be in Oakland, California, and that from that base he could get her into the movies. Thus, the Burces moved to Oakland. However, nothing happened, and when they returned to Portland, Mr. Burce could not regain his position with Wonder Bread. He struggled for years thereafter to find a steady job. Nevertheless, Suzanne's musical lessons continued.

When she was eleven, her vocal teacher introduced her to the local KOIN radio station manager and she soon had her own show, later appearing on an hour-long Sunday evening program. In this period she became Oregon's Victory Girl, singing at World War II bond drive rallies. In June 1943, Suzanne and her parents went to Los Angeles, where Mrs. Burce and Suzanne's manager had arranged for her to be on "Hollywood Showcase: Stars over Hollywood." On this edition of the CBS radio talent program hosted by Janet Gaynor, Suzanne was one of six contestants. With her two-and-a-half-octave range, she won the contest, singing "Il Baccio" from *Carmen*. As a result, she was on the show for a record-breaking six weeks, MGM contacted her for a meeting, and Janet Gaynor arranged for her to be interviewed by film producer David O. Selznick. Both conferences occurred the same day, and MGM offered Suzanne a seven-year contract—without a screen test—starting at $225 weekly and escalating to $1,250 weekly. The Burces urged her to forget about high school back home and to accept the offer. Years later, Jane Powell reflected, "I felt then—and I feel now—that if I hadn't accepted MGM's offer it would have destroyed Mama and Daddy sooner, and would have made their marriage even harder and more unhappy." The Burces moved to Los Angeles, where Paul became a studio union electrician, later opening a donut shop and then a restaurant. The parents would divorce later, each remarrying. Her father would die in 1972 and her relationship with her mother would remain extremely strained.

"In a way, it's easier to be a child performer; you have nothing to unlearn." This according to Jane who, still with no screen test nor any acting lessons, was loaned to United Artists for SONG OF THE OPEN ROAD (1944), in which she shared screen time with W. C. Fields and with the team of Edgar Bergen and Charlie McCarthy. In this musical she played a young movie star named Jane Powell (which became her screen name) who runs away from her studio to join youngsters on a crop-picking trek. She sang four songs, including the classical "Carmena," and *Variety* opined, "Miss Powell has a fine voice . . . and good camera presence." Thereafter she was hired to be dummy Charlie McCarthy's love interest on the Bergen–McCarthy radio program "The Chase and Sanborn Hour." Off camera, she and OPEN ROAD co-player Stan Catron became good friends. She was on loan again to United Artists for DELIGHTFULLY DANGEROUS (1945) as the unsuspecting younger sister of a burlesque star (Constance Moore). The *New York Times* judged her "a shimmering vision of youth in bloom . . . sweet and charming—not the least bit cloying."

Producer Joe Pasternak, who had been Deanna Durbin's mentor at Universal Pictures, had been at MGM since the early 1940s and became a leading booster of Jane's screen progress. (Later, Jane claims, when she learned that he had been making flippant remarks about her virtue, she lost all respect for him.) He cast her in the lead of HOLIDAY

IN MEXICO (1946) as the matchmaking daughter of the American ambassador (Walter Pidgeon). Amid the diverse musical talent (including Ilona Massey and José Iturbi), Jane (blondized by the studio) sang "Ave Maria" and flirted on camera with Roddy McDowall (who became an off-camera friend). She and this Technicolor feature were so successful (she was featured on the cover of *Life* magazine on September 9, 1946) that Powell rene-gotiated her studio contract to a $750 weekly minimum for the next three years, along with bonuses and options. Now seventeen and attending the MGM school, from which she would graduate in 1947, Jane was caught in a social no-person's land: "I'm too young for the old ones, and too old for the young ones." THREE DARING DAUGHTERS (1948), a revamping of Deanna Durbin's THREE SMART GIRLS (1937), not only marked Jeanette MacDonald's screen return, it also showcased Jane as the eldest of MacDonald's three offspring. Jane sang "The Dickey Bird Song." In LUXURY LINER (1948) she was the stowaway daughter of a cruise ship captain (George Brent) and proved she "is as expert a comedienne as a soprano" (*New York Sun*). Off camera, the debonair Brent developed an unrequited crush on the far younger Jane Powell, which he revealed to her only years later. In A DATE WITH JUDY (1948), based on the popular radio show, she shared screen time with Elizabeth Taylor, Wallace Beery, Carmen Miranda, and Xavier Cugat. It was bright, colorful fluff with Jane singing "It's a Most Unusual Day."

Jane Powell, Ann Harding, Debbie Reynolds, Fernando Lamas, Carleton Carpenter, Gary Gray, Phyllis Kirk, and Tommy Rettig in TWO WEEKS WITH LOVE (1950)

By now, MGM had successfully promoted Jane Powell as The Girl Next Door with the high soprano voice. Both characterizations frustrated Jane, who did not feel like the girl next door and who wanted to sing pop. "I loved to sing ballads and the blues, but I rarely got to do them. I hardly ever got a chance to introduce a song, either. I always wanted to have a song on the Hit Parade." To help foster her desire for independence, Jane married Geary Anthony Steffen, Jr. on November 5, 1949, at the Church of the Good Shepherd in Beverly Hills. He was a professional ice skater who was then Sonja Henie's skating partner.

After more than a year off the screen, Jane returned with two 1950 musicals. The first, TWO WEEKS WITH LOVE, was set at a turn-of-the-century Catskills resort where Jane and her younger sister (Debbie Reynolds) seek romance with (respectively) Ricardo Montalban and Carleton Carpenter. Jane sang and danced to "The Oceana Roll" and, in another of the Busby Berkeley–choreographed numbers, had a bizarre Freudian dream sequence in which she wistfully equates wearing a corset (only adult women do that!) with her romantic desire for Montalban. However, it was bubbling Debbie Reynolds who stole the film with her "Aba Daba Honeymoon" duet with Carpenter. The other 1950 musical, NANCY GOES TO RIO, was a Technicolor remake of Deanna Durbin's IT'S A DATE (1940). Jane and her mother (Ann Sothern) are ocean-bound for Rio and become rivals for the same man (Barry Sullivan) *and* the same stage role. Powell's best solo was "Time and Time Again." With Sothern and Louis Calhern she sang and danced to "Shine on Harvest Moon."

When June Allyson became pregnant and Judy Garland became ill, Jane was cast in her first adult role, in ROYAL WEDDING (1951). She played Fred Astaire's sister and dancing partner as they sail to England to perform at the celebrations for Princess Elizabeth's pending marriage. Astaire was nearly thirty years her senior and on the set was pleasant but cool to her. She had only three weeks to learn her routines, including her raucous duet with Astaire, "How Could You Believe Me When I Said I Love You When You Know I've Been a Liar All My Life?" Her solo highlight was "Too Late Now." This movie was her first experience with Arthur Freed's MGM musical unit and was her most prestigious assignment to date. But then it was back to standard form as the studio's petite Miss Fetching. RICH, YOUNG AND PRETTY (1951) provided Vic Damone and Fernando Lamas with their Hollywood debuts and cast Jane as a Texas miss on a Parisian holiday with her dad (Wendell Corey). Powell and Damone, teamed with The Four Freshmen, sang "How Do You Like Your Eggs in the Morning?" Jane had first met Damone when she was seventeen and making a personal appearance at the Capitol Theatre on Broadway.

During the filming of RICH, YOUNG AND PRETTY, Jane was pregnant and gave birth to son Geary Anthony Steffen III ("Jay") on July 21, 1951. She was also pregnant during the making of her next movie, and gave birth to daughter Suzanne Ilene on November 21, 1952. In SMALL TOWN GIRL (1953), a remake of a 1936 Janet Gaynor vehicle, she was again spotless, bubbleheaded, and professional as she sang such tunes as "Small Towns Are Smile Towns." However, the movie's highlights were Busby Berkeley's choreography for Ann Miller's tap number ("I've Gotta Hear That Beat") and Bobby Van's whirlwind dance ("Take Me to Broadway").

MGM loaned Jane to Warner Bros., whose own Girl Next Door—Doris Day—was busy with other movie projects. By this time Jane's marriage to Steffen had soured. While shooting THREE SAILORS AND A GIRL (1953), which paired her on camera with Gordon MacRae, she fell in love with co-player Gene Nelson. He too was married, and their romance put her at loggerheads with MGM, the press, and eventually the public (which was shocked to learn that the off-camera Jane Powell had real emotions). By the start of 1954, the romance had ended. She told the press, "We didn't have a fight. The decision was as much Gene's as it was mine."

The liaison with Nelson almost cost Powell her MGM contract and certainly provided more screen assignments for fellow Metro songsters Ann Blyth and Kathryn Grayson. Powell refused to team with Mario Lanza in THE STUDENT PRINCE but did star in SEVEN BRIDES FOR SEVEN BROTHERS (1954), her most important MGM milestone. It was based loosely on Stephen Vincent Benet's "The Sobbin' Women," and boasted a score by Gene de Paul and Johnny Mercer, Michael Kidd's exceptional choreography, and Stanley Donen's direction. Jane shone as the enforced servant to a gaggle of backwoods brothers, who is tamed and romanced in 1850s Oregon by oafish but virile Howard Keel. She was at her best with "Wonderful, Wonderful Day" and in her ensemble song/dance routine ("June Bride"). Later that year, on November 8, she wed Patrick Nerney, an auto dealer (later turned writer).

Least of anyone, Jane was unaware that the role of Milly in SEVEN BRIDES would be her last superior screen part. She sang the aria "Chacun le Sait" (from Donizetti's opera *The Daughter of the Regiment*) in ATHENA (1954), a satire on Southern California's preoccupation with health fads. After guesting in DEEP IN MY HEART (1954)—performing Sigmund Romberg operetta numbers—she was reunited with Vic Damone, Debbie Reynolds, and Ann Miller in the ambitious but unmemorable musical HIT THE DECK (1955). By now, Jane was revolted at playing empty-headed screen ingenues. She understood how typed she was when the studio chose to borrow Doris Day, instead of using her as promised, for LOVE ME OR LEAVE ME (1955). The executive rationale was that Jane was too refined to play singer Ruth Etting. Other factors added to her professional frustration. "There I was, a grown woman, and my contract wouldn't allow me to do TV appearances and I had to get permission to do a nightclub engagement." She negotiated her studio release, not knowing that (in an economy wave) the studio was about to fire her. Twenty years later she insisted, "I can't even remember what my last film was at MGM. All of my life seems to have happened to somebody else. I just wish I could have been around to enjoy it. None of it sunk in."

Jane was very successful at a Hollywood Bowl concert in front of an audience of twenty thousand, proving she could handle live audiences. On February 1, 1956, she gave birth to daughter Lindsay Averille. Thereafter, when she attempted to resume her film career, she found it extremely difficult to find roles in a Hollywood that no longer required The Girl Next Door. She made three dreadful programmers, including THE FEMALE ANIMAL (1958) at Universal, which cast her as the daughter of predatory Hedy Lamarr. As Powell summed it up, "I didn't quit movies, they quit me." She turned to television, starring in two delightful musical specials: "Ruggles of Red Gap" (NBC, February 3,

1957) and "Meet Me in St. Louis" (CBS, April 26, 1959). She was a recurring regular on TV's "Alcoa/Goodyear Theatre" (1957–58) and began doing summer stock (including *Oklahoma!*) and more cabaret work in New York and Las Vegas. During her summer 1963 run of *The Unsinkable Molly Brown* in Anaheim, California, she set a summer stock theater box-office record. Her popularity led to Jane's preparing a revue, *Just Twenty—Plus Me*, which she hoped to bring to Broadway. It toured Texas but then faded. She did more stock (*My Fair Lady, The Boy Friend, The Sound of Music*). By now Jane had divorced Nerney (on May 8, 1963) and on June 27, 1965, in Sydney, Australia, wed James Fitzgerald, a public relations man who had packaged *Just Twenty—Plus Me*. He became her business manager.

Jane had been suggested for the lead in "The Partridge Family" teleseries (1970–74), which ultimately went to Shirley Jones, and had rejected the idea of following Ruby Keeler into the Broadway (or road) revival of *No, No Nanette*. However, when Debbie Reynolds left the Broadway rebirth of *Irene* in early 1974, Jane replaced her in the sentimental musical. The *New York Post* reported of Jane, "She makes the girl from Ninth Avenue both believable and appealing, and she can play an emotional scene convincingly. Indeed, you might think the part had been created for her." Jane remained with the show for seven months and then went on tour with it. Later (in October 1977), she and Howard Keel, who had toured together in *I Do! I Do!* and *Seven Brides for Seven Brothers*, played in *South Pacific* at the Pantages Theatre in Los Angeles.

Jane and Fitzgerald divorced in 1976 (although he remained her business manager) and on October 21, 1978, she wed David Parlour, a producer/director. They separated a year later and divorced in early 1981 to much publicity about his pricy alimony demands. By then she had resettled herself in Los Angeles, hoping to reestablish her screen/TV career, but she admitted, "the new crop of producers and directors aren't familiar with what I can do unless they're nostalgia buffs." She guested on such teleseries havens for fading stars as "The Love Boat" and "Fantasy Island" and in December 1982 was doing concerts in New Jersey with Vic Damone, with whom she had made four MGM pictures. (A few years earlier, Jane had lost her voice due to tired vocal muscles and for nearly two years could sing only four notes. This was the result of years of improper training from various vocal coaches.)

It was a sharp change of pace when Powell signed for the recurring role of Rebeka Beecham on the soap opera "Loving" (ABC-TV). She was the rich matriarch of the 4-B ranch in Wyoming who meddles in her younger son's (Brian Robert Taylor) life. At this stage, Jane was living in New York and Connecticut with former child actor Dickie Moore, who had been introduced to her in 1982 (by Roddy McDowall) when Moore was researching his book on child stars (*Twinkle Twinkle Little Star—But Don't Have Sex or Take the Car*). In 1987 she was the star of a video (*Jane Powell's Fight Back with Fitness*), an exercise tape for people with arthritis, although she did not herself suffer from the disease. She also continued to tour with the one-woman show *Jane Powell Inside Out—Her Story Live*, in which she recalled her show business career through honest talk and song. She had been encouraged and advised on the project by actress/comedienne Pat Carroll, who had

had success with her own solo stage vehicle, *Gertrude Stein, Gertrude Stein, Gertrude Stein.*

Although she had been quoted as saying, after the fourth of her costly divorces, "No more marriages, no more babies, no more puppies," on May 21, 1988, Powell and Dickie Moore married. Soon she was sharing a concert bill with Donald O'Connor on the road. By mid-year she was promoting her autobiography, which she had begun as a therapeutic diary six years before. Powell said, "The thing I like best about my book is that I don't kill anyone." Said one critic, "Unlike most Hollywood kiss and tell books, it's toughest on the author. Jane Powell doesn't trash anyone, except Jane Powell." She had been back on television as a guest on "Murder, She Wrote" (1987) and in late 1988 began a recurring role as Alan Thicke's widowed mother on "Growing Pains" (ABC-TV), which saw her married to Robert Rockwell (of "Our Miss Brooks") in mid-1989 segments.

Today, Powell claims, "the Girl Next Door has turned into a very happy woman."

## Filmography

Song of the Open Road (UA, 1944)
Delightfully Dangerous (UA, 1945)
Holiday in Mexico (MGM, 1946)
Three Daring Daughters [The Birds and the Bees] (MGM, 1948)
Luxury Liner (MGM, 1948)
A Date with Judy (MGM, 1948)
Two Weeks with Love (MGM, 1950)
Nancy Goes to Rio (MGM, 1950)
Royal Wedding [Wedding Bells] (MGM, 1951)
Rich, Young and Pretty (MGM, 1951)
Small Town Girl (MGM, 1953)

Three Sailors and a Girl (WB, 1953)
Seven Brides for Seven Brothers (MGM, 1954)
Athena (MGM, 1954)
Deep in My Heart (MGM, 1954)
Hit the Deck (MGM, 1955)
The Girl Most Likely (Univ, 1957)
The Female Animal (Univ, 1958)
Enchanted Island (WB, 1958)
Wheeler and Murdoch (ABC-TV, 3/27/72)
The Letters (ABC-TV, 3/6/73)
Mayday at 40,000 Feet (CBS-TV, 11/12/76)

## Broadway Plays

Irene (1974) (revival) (replacement)

## Radio Series

The Chase and Sanborn Hour (NBC, ca. 1944–45)

## TV Series

Alcoa/Goodyear Theatre (NBC, 1957–58)

## *Album Discography*

Alice in Wonderland (Col ML-4148)

Athena (10" Mer MG-25202, Motion Picture Tracks MPT-2) [ST}

Can't We Be Friends? (Verve 2023)

A Date with Jane Powell (10" Col ML-2045)

Deep in My Heart (MGM E-3153, MGM SES-54ST) [ST]

An Evening with Lerner & Loewe (RCA LPM/LSP-6005) w. Robert Merrill, Jan Peerce, Phil Harris

The Girl Most Likely (Cap W-930) [ST]

Great Song Hits from Lerner and Loewe's "Gigi" and "Brigadoon" (RCA LPM/LSP-2275)

Great Song Hits from Lerner and Loewe's "My Fair Lady" and "Paint Your Wagon" (RCA LPM/LSP-2274)

Hansel and Gretel (10" Col ML-2055)

Hit the Deck (MGM E-3163, MGM SES-43ST) [ST]

Jane Powell (Curtain Calls 100/14)

Jane Powell Sings (Lion 70111)

Love to You and Broadway Too (Artco LPE 1103)

Nancy Goes to Rio (10" MGM E-508, MGM SES-53ST) [ST]

Nelson Eddy with Shirley Temple, Jane Powell, Kathryn Grayson, Lois Butler and Norma Nelson (Mac/Eddy JN 128)

Rich, Young and Pretty (10" MGM E-86, MGM E-3236, MGM SES-53ST) [ST]

Romance (10" Col ML-2034)

Royal Wedding (10" MGM E-543, MGM E-3235, MGM SES-53ST) [ST]

Ruggles of Red Gap (Verve 15000, Stet 150007) [ST/TV]

Seven Brides for Seven Brothers (10" MGM E-244, MGM E-3225, MGM SES-41ST) [ST]

Small Town Girl (Scarce Rarities 5503) [ST]

Something Wonderful (MGM E-3451)

Three Sailors and a Girl (10" Cap L-485) [ST]

Two Weeks with Love (10" MGM E-530, MGM E-3233, MGM SES-49ST) [ST]

# ELVIS PRESLEY

ELVIS ARON PRESLEY WAS PERHAPS THE MOST POPULAR ENTERTAINER
ever. He was a superstar for most of his over three decades as a performer. Despite career
swings, he was never out of the limelight. Since his death, his estate has continued to
flourish due to the apparently unceasing demand for anything and everything connected
with the legend that was Elvis Presley.

Presley's voice was strong, versatile, and bluesy in quality. He was an original,
combining country, rhythm-and-blues, and rock 'n' roll music styles. Elvis singlehandedly
changed the texture of popular music with his physical rock 'n' roll style, thus paving the
way for many entertainers who were to follow. A controversial figure, he was either
lionized or despised, with the lionizers vastly outnumbering the despisers. For all of his
immense effect on popular culture, he was a man of many facets. Throughout his career,
and especially in the late 1950s, he was considered the ultimate male sex symbol. On the
other hand, many less liberal groups and individuals pointed to him and his music as the
cause of juvenile delinquency and "deviate" behavior in contemporary youth. His personal
life was never stable; after his death it became known and exploited that he was heavily
dependent on prescription drugs. Yet he was also a religiously devout fundamentalist who
neither drank nor smoked, and who violently opposed the use of drugs for social activities.
And he was a law-and-order advocate. At the same time, Elvis was basically apolitical, and
unlike many of his contemporaries, he never involved himself in social issues or causes.
Elvis' sudden death in 1977 numbed the nation and the world. The entertainer who had
been such a controversial figure during his life suddenly became a no less controversial
legend in death.

Elvis Aron Presley was born on January 8, 1935, in Tupelo, Mississippi, the son of
Vernon Elvis and Gladys (Smith) Presley. His twin brother died at birth. At an early age he
took an interest in singing and began vocalizing in churches. When he was twelve, his
mother bought him a cheap guitar which he learned to play and he became especially
intrigued by country and blues music. In 1948 the Presley family moved to Memphis,
Tennessee, where Vernon worked in a paint factory and Elvis attended Humes High
School. After graduation, he worked at assorted jobs, including theater usher, factory
worker, and truck driver; he planned to become an electrician.

In the summer of 1953, he paid $4 to make a private record for his mother at the
Memphis Recording Service. Its owner, Sam Phillips, also the owner of Sun Records,
eventually heard the disc and was impressed with Elvis' vocalizing, a raw mixture of both
white hillbilly and black blues sounds. The next summer Phillips recorded Elvis singing

"Blue Moon of Kentucky" and "That's All Right, Mama," and the disc ultimately sold some twenty thousand copies. As a result, Presley gave up truck driving and began making personal appearances (along with other Sun recording artists like Carl Perkins and Johnny Cash) as well as appearing on radio's "Louisiana Hayride" and the "Grand Ole Opry." Thanks to his electric vocal style, good looks, and the habit of gyrating while he sang fast numbers, Elvis caused a sensation wherever he appeared. He soon negotiated a tour with Hank Snow, whose manager was Colonel Tom Parker. By 1955, Presley's Sun singles were selling well and Hank Snow and Tom Parker convinced Snow's recording label, RCA, to sign Elvis. The flamboyant Parker became the new star's manager.

In January 1956, RCA issued its first Elvis single (having acquired all his Sun masters for $35,000 and reissued them late in 1955), "Heartbreak Hotel." It instantly went gold. That month Elvis had a sensational success on Tommy and Jimmy Dorsey's CBS-TV program, "Stage Show," and would make five return appearances within the next three months. He also did SRO business at the Frontier Club in Las Vegas in March, and his hot-selling RCA singles included "Hound Dog," "Don't Be Cruel," "Tutti Frutti," "Shake Rattle and Roll," "Love Me Tender," and "Blue Suede Shoes" (which had earlier been popularized on Sun Records by its composer, Carl Perkins). Elvis also continued to appear on national TV, with two guest shots on Milton Berle's NBC variety program, one with Steve Allen on the same network, and three highly publicized appearances (where he was shown only from the waist up to appease censors) on "The Ed Sullivan Show" on CBS. By now Presley was automatic copy for every tabloid and fan magazine in circulation, and thanks to Colonel Parker, an almost endless array of Presley merchandise was on the market for people of all ages, although most of his popularity was with teenaged girls.

It was inevitable that Hollywood, eager to find ways to draw in young audiences, should covet this handsome singing sensation. Colonel Parker arranged several multiple-picture contracts with a variety of studios. Presley made his feature film debut in 20th Century–Fox's LOVE ME TENDER (1956), third billed as Clint Reno, who marries the girlfriend (Debra Paget) of his brother (Richard Egan) when the latter is away fighting with the Rebels during the Civil War. Before the end of this oater, Presley had sung four tunes, been killed, and, at the graveside finale, had his image superimposed on the landscape reprising "Love Me Tender" (which was already a million-seller record). *Variety* noted, "Appraising Presley as an actor, he ain't. . . . The presence of Presley apparently is enough to satisfy the juve set." Elvis displayed a smoky charisma in the role, and thanks to his being in the production, it made a mint. In LOVING YOU (1957) he was a country singer whose press agent (Lizabeth Scott) transforms him into a star.

So strong was Elvis at the box office that when he made JAILHOUSE ROCK (1957), he could command a quarter of a million dollars in salary and one-half of the picture's profits. Many Presley devotees consider JAILHOUSE ROCK to be his finest movie. In it he was a jail inmate who learns to play the guitar and rises to become a rock recording star. Besides the title song, which Elvis performed with an energetic dance number he choreographed, the movie's songs included "Treat Me Nice" and "Don't Leave Me Now." Next he starred in the melodrama KING CREOLE (1958) as a New Orleans club singer who becomes involved with a gangster (Walter Matthau). *Variety* acknowledged, "In all fairness, Presley does show himself to be a surprisingly sympathetic and believable actor on occasion." In addition to the heavy, moody dramatics, which annoyed his light-hearted fans, the movie offered thirteen songs including Elvis performing "King Creole," "Trouble," and "Hard Headed Woman." He was now among the top ten stars at the box office.

In addition to movies and his highly publicized on-again, off-again romances, Presley continued his highly lucrative personal appearances. In 1957, his hit RCA singles included the title songs from JAILHOUSE ROCK and LOVING YOU plus "Teddy Bear," "All Shook Up," "Too Much," and "Don't." That year he also purchased Graceland, a Memphis estate that would be his home base for the remainder of his life. In the spring of 1958, with much fanfare, Elvis was inducted into the U.S. Army and did two years of active duty in West Germany. (He did return home briefly in the summer of 1958 when his mother died of a heart attack.) During his stay in the service, much publicity was garnered from his induction (and the shaving of his famous sideburns) through each step of his military activity. RCA had a reserve of recordings by him, and in 1958 his trio of best-sellers were "Wear My Ring Around Your Neck," "Hard Headed Woman," and "I Got Stung," while in 1959 he was on the charts with "A Fool Such as I" and "A Big Hunk o' Love."

Upon his Army release, Elvis made a guest appearance, for $125,000, on "The Frank Sinatra Timex Show" in May 1960. He went back to Hollywood to star in G.I. BLUES (1960), as a soldier who opens a nightclub and romances a dancer (Juliet Prowse). Among its songs were "Wooden Heart" and "Tonight Is So Right for Love." That year he also was very good as a half-breed in the Western FLAMING STAR. In addition, he had hit records in 1960 with "Stuck on You," "It's Now or Never," and "Are You Lonesome Tonight?," the latter two becoming gold singles.

In 1961 Presley starred in two very popular films, BLUE HAWAII and WILD IN THE COUNTRY. The former provided him with one of his biggest hit records, "Can't Help Falling in Love." He played an ex-soldier who comes to Hawaii to escape from his dominating mother (Angela Lansbury) and finds romance as a tour guide. In WILD IN THE COUNTRY (with a script by Clifford Odets), Elvis was a delinquent who becomes a writer due to guidance from a psychiatrist (Hope Lange). In 1961 he also continued to churn out hit singles such as "Surrender," "I Feel So Bad," "Little Sister," and "Can't Help Falling in Love," and the next year he had hits with "Good Luck Charm," "She's Not You," and "Return to Sender."

Because there were so many Presley screen vehicles in the early 1960s (usually two to three a year), the pictures soon became formularized. It mattered little which studio released the production or who directed or who co-starred. After a while it was difficult for the less ardent fan even to distinguish which song came from which movie. But his followers did not mind. There were three 1962 releases. In FOLLOW THAT DREAM he was the head of a family of homesteaders who fight prejudice in southern Florida, while in KID GALAHAD, a remake of the 1937 film, Presley was a garage mechanic who becomes a boxing champion but prefers the quiet life. The drama had Elvis doing a half-dozen mundane tunes. The third film, GIRLS! GIRLS! GIRLS!, provided him with his hit tune "Return to Sender" in its tale of a club singer (Presley) who is torn between a pretty warbler (Stella Stevens) and an equally attractive wealthy young miss (Laurel Goodwin). Two more Presley musicals were issued in 1963, IT HAPPENED AT THE WORLD'S FAIR and FUN IN ACAPULCO. The first was shot on location at the Seattle World's Fair and cast Elvis as a bush pilot who romances Joan O'Brien; he sang "A World of Our Own," "One Broken Heart for Sale," and "Happy Ending." A scenically splendid outing, FUN IN ACAPULCO had the star dodging his past and working as a lifeguard and singer in the Mexican resort. He performed such forgettable items as "Bossa Nova Baby" and "You Can't Say No in Acapulco." The picture did provide him with one of his most alluring leading ladies, Ursula Andress.

During the mid-1960s, Elvis continued to record for RCA, but his sales had begun to fall off. Nevertheless, he still had hits with numbers like "Blue Christmas," "Tell Me Why," "Guitar Man," and "Let Yourself Go." He continued his film career, but by now his budgets were reduced, although he still received fifty percent of his films' profits. (The tactic of lowering the production costs also lowered his movies' grosses and eventually destroyed his screen career.) In 1964 KISSIN' COUSINS provided two on-camera Elvis Presleys. He was seen as an Air Force officer who is ordered to run country folks off their land so it can be used for a missile base; he also played a local boy who leads the fight against the military. In VIVA LAS VEGAS (1964) he was a sports car racer in the gambling capital's Grand Prix while romancing enticing Ann-Margret. ROUSTABOUT (1964), considered by some to offer the ultimate pre-fabricated Elvis screen characterization, presented him as a cyclist who goes to work for a carnival run by no-nonsense Barbara Stanwyck.

Although his fans had matured and were no longer primarily teenagers (Elvis was now thirty), he continued unabated in

Barbara Stanwyck and Elvis Presley in ROUSTABOUT (1964)

making movies. (The arrival of the Beatles and the "British Invasion" had only a minor effect on Presley's enormous popularity.) GIRL HAPPY (1965) found the star as a singer whom a gangster (Harold J. Stone) hires to watch his nubile daughter (Shelley Fabares) while she vacations in Florida. TICKLE ME (1965) was fluff with Elvis as a bronco rider who works at a dude ranch for women, while HARUM SCARUM (1965) was set in the Middle East with film star Elvis doing battle with an evil sheik (Michael Ansara). His trio of 1966 starrers (FRANKIE AND JOHNNY, PARADISE HAWAIIAN STYLE, and SPINOUT) were no better, with PARADISE HAWAIIAN STYLE being almost a recycling of BLUE HAWAII. The descent continued in 1967 with DOUBLE TROUBLE; EASY COME, EASY GO (the last of nine features for Paramount producer Hal Wallis, who had been with him since LOVING YOU); and CLAMBAKE.

Speculation about Elvis' love life (his extravagant lifestyle was already well documented) had persisted for years. Through publicity fabrication and sometimes reality, he had been linked with such Hollywood actresses as Ann-Margret, Rita Moreno, Natalie Wood, Shelley Fabares, and Suzanna Leigh. However, it was Priscilla Beaulieu whom he married eventually. He had first met her when he was stationed in West Germany; she was the fourteen-year-old daughter of a U.S. Army major based in Frankfurt. She had come to the States, at his invitation, for the Christmas of 1960 and had remained in and around Graceland thereafter, "chaperoned" by Vernon Presley and his new wife (Dee Elliott). In June 1963, she graduated from high school and later took courses at Patricia Stevens Finishing and Career School. During these years, Priscilla's association with Presley had not been much publicized. Therefore, it was a surprise to many when he wed her (amid great hoopla—which did not hurt his slipping movie career) on May 1, 1967, in Las Vegas. Nine months later (on February 1, 1968), their daughter, Lisa Marie, was born. The couple would be divorced in the fall of 1973 and Priscilla Presley, who seemed to grow more attractive as she grew older, began a performing career which included co-starring in the box-office hit THE NAKED GUN (1989). On May 29, 1989, Lisa Marie, married to musician Danny Keough, gave birth to a baby named Danielle.

In 1968, Elvis continued to make features like LIVE A LITTLE, LOVE A LITTLE, which generated some publicity by teaming a past crooner (Rudy Vallee) with a much more contemporary one (Presley). In SPEEDWAY he shared star billing (with Nancy Sinatra) for the first time since his film debut. Far better than any of his three 1968 releases was his December NBC-TV special "Singer Presents Elvis," which did much to reactivate his faltering career. In it he performed his hit single "If I Can Dream." In 1969 he had best-sellers with "How Great Thou Art," "In the Ghetto," "Suspicious Minds," and "Don't Cry Daddy." In the summer of 1969 he made the first of many sold-out appearances in Las Vegas and later in Lake Tahoe. His act was now targeted to an increasingly more mature crowd. That year he ended his sagging movie career with the Western CHARRO! and two sadly inane comedies: THE TROUBLE WITH GIRLS and CHANGE OF HABIT (which included Mary Tyler Moore in its cast).

Few of his fans really mourned the last of his shoddy films as Elvis began his yearly array of concert tours in 1970. He would alternate these engagements with records and his stands in Las Vegas and Lake Tahoe for the rest of his life. Cinematically, two very popular documentaries about him, ELVIS . . . THAT'S THE WAY IT IS (1970) and ELVIS ON TOUR (1972), did well theatrically, and in the spring of 1974 he did a very highly rated TV special for NBC entitled "Elvis: Aloha from Hawaii." The hit records continued with "Kentucky Rain," "The Wonder of You"/"Mama Liked the Roses," "I Really Don't Want to Know," "He Touched Me," "Hurt," and "Moody Blue." His RCA albums had always been best-sellers, many of them having attained gold record status.

In the 1970s, however, it became increasingly difficult to get Elvis into a recording studio, so many of his LPs were taped at his concert appearances. On tour (at $130,000 a night) he was still incredibly popular, and at his December 31, 1975, one-night stand in Detroit he earned a reported $816,000. During the 1970s, however, Elvis began having health problems, due mainly to excess weight and a dependence on prescribed medication. There was talk that he might join with Barbra Streisand in the remake of A STAR IS BORN (1976), but it was Kris Kristofferson who did the musical. On August 16, 1977, Elvis Presley died of a heart attack at his Graceland home, just a few days before he was to embark on yet another tour. His estate was valued at $4.9 million.

Since his passing, Elvis Presley has become more popular than ever. He has been the subject of scores of stage impersonators, books, movies, a TV series, articles, and all types of merchandising, while his records (reissued and repackaged in every conceivable way) have sold in the millions. His films, in revival, on television, and in videocassette/laser disc form, have retained their cult popularity. Of all the movie singers, Elvis alone, through his voice and persona, has remained constantly in the public view. His death only enhanced his popularity as "The King." Now, with the endless rumors that he never really died, he has transcended stardom to become a part of American folklore.

## Filmography

Love Me Tender (20th–Fox, 1956)
Loving You (Par, 1957)
Jailhouse Rock (MGM, 1957)
King Creole (Par, 1958)
G.I. Blues (Par, 1960)
Flaming Star (20th–Fox, 1960)
Wild in the Country (20th–Fox, 1961)
Blue Hawaii (Par, 1961)
Follow That Dream (UA, 1962)
Kid Galahad (UA, 1962)
Girls! Girls! Girls! (Par, 1962)
Fun in Acapulco (Par, 1963)
It Happened at the World's Fair (MGM, 1963)
Kissin' Cousins (MGM, 1964)
Viva Las Vegas (MGM, 1964)
Roustabout (Par, 1964)
Girl Happy (MGM, 1965)
Tickle Me (AA, 1965)

Harum Scarum (MGM, 1965)
Frankie and Johnny (UA, 1966)
Paradise Hawaiian Style (Par, 1966)
Spinout (MGM, 1966)
Easy Come, Easy Go (Par, 1967)
Double Trouble (MGM, 1967)
Clambake (MGM, 1967)
Stay Away, Joe (MGM, 1968)
Live a Little, Love a Little (MGM, 1968)
Speedway (MGM, 1968)
Charro! (NG, 1969)
Change of Habit (Univ, 1969)
The Trouble with Girls (MGM, 1969)
Elvis . . . That's the Way It Is (MGM, 1970)
  (documentary)
Elvis on Tour (MGM, 1972) (documentary)
This Is Elvis (WB, 1981) (documentary)

## Album Discography

Almost in Love (Camden CAS-2440, Pickwick/
  Camden CAS-2440)

Aloha from Hawaii via Satellite (RCA CPD2-
  2642) [ST/TV]

Back in Memphis (RCA LSP-4429)

The Beginning Years (Louisiana Hayride LH-
  3061)

Blue Hawaii (RCA LPM/LSP-2426) [ST]

"Burning Love" and Other Hits from His
  Movies, Vol. 2 (Camden CAS-2595,
  Pickwick/Camden CAS-2595)

A Canadian Tribute (RCA KKL1-7065)

Chicken of the Sea Presents Aloha from Hawaii
  (RCA 213736) [ST/TV]

Clambake (RCA LPM/LSP-3893) [ST]

C'mon Everybody (Camden CAS-2518,
  Pickwick/Camden CAS-2518)

The Complete Sun Sessions (RCA 6414-1)

Country Classics (RCA 233299)

Country Memories (RCA 244069)

A Date with Elvis (RCA LPM-2011)

Double Dynamite (Pickwick DL-2-5001)

Double Trouble (RCA LPM/LSP-3787) [ST]

Elvis (RCA LPM-1382)

Elvis (RCA APL1-0283)

Elvis [The Elvis Commemorative Album] (RCA
  DPL2-0056)

Elvis Aron Presley: 25th Anniversary Limited
  Edition, Vols. 1–8 (RCA CPL8-3699)

Elvis as Recorded at Madison Square Garden
  (RCA LSP-4776, RCA SP33-571)

Elvis as Recorded Live on Stage in Memphis
  (RCA CPL1-0606)

Elvis' Christmas Album (RCA LOC-1035, RCA
  LPM/LSP-1951)

Elvis Country (RCA LSP-4460, RCA International NL-83959)

Elvis for Everyone (RCA LPM/LSP-3450)

Elvis Forever (RCA 7031)

Elvis' Golden Records, Vol. 1 (RCA LPM/LSP-
  1707)

Elvis' Golden Records, Vol. 3 (RCA LPM/LSP-
  2765)

Elvis' Golden Records, Vol. 4 (RCA LSP-3921)

Elvis—HBO Special (RCA Special Products
  0704)

Elvis! His Greatest Hits (RCA/Reader's Digest
  010)

Elvis, His Songs of Faith and Inspiration (RCA
  0728)

Elvis in Concert (RCA APL2-2587)

Elvis in Hollywood (RCA DPL2-0168)

Elvis in Person at the International Hotel, Las
  Vegas (RCA LSP-4428)

Elvis Is Back (RCA LPM/LSP-2231)

Elvis Love Songs (K-Tel 9900)

Elvis Now (RCA LSP-4621)

Elvis Presley (RCA LPM/LSP-1254)

The Elvis Presley Collection (RCA/Candlelite
  Music 0632)

The Elvis Presley Dorsey Shows (Golden
  Archives 56GA/00) w. The Dorsey Brothers

Elvis Presley, Great Hits of 1956–57 (RCA/
  Reader's Digest 072)

Elvis Presley: 1954–61 (Time-Life 106)

The Elvis Presley Story (RCA/Candlelite Music
  0263)

The Elvis Presley Sun Collection (RCA HV-
  1001)

Elvis Sings Country Favorites (RCA/Reader's
  Digest 242)

Elvis Sings "Flaming Star" (Camden CAS-2304,
  Pickwick/Camden CAS-2304)

Elvis Sings for Children and Grownups, Too
  (RCA CPL1-2901)

Elvis Sings Hits from His Movies, Vol. 1
  (Camden CAS-2567, Pickwick/Camden
  CAS-2567)

Elvis Sings Inspirational Favorites (RCA/
  Reader's Digest 181)

Elvis Sings the Wonderful Songs of Christmas
  (RCA LSP-4579)

Elvis . . . That's the Way It Is (RCA LSP-4445)
  [ST]

Elvis Today (RCA APL1-1039)

Elvis' TV Special (RCA LPM-4088) [ST/TV]

The Essential Elvis Presley (RCA International
  PL-89979)

50,000,000 Elvis Fans Can't Be Wrong: Elvis'
  Golden Records, Vol. 2 (RCA LPM/LSP-
  2075)

50 Years 50 Hits (RCA/Suffolk Marketing
  0710)

For LP Fans Only (RCA LPM/LSP-1990)

Forever (RCA International NL-89004-2)

Frankie and Johnny (RCA LPM/LSP-3553, Pickwick ACL-7007) [ST]

From Elvis in Memphis (RCA LSP-4155)

From Elvis Presley Boulevard, Memphis, Tennessee (RCA APL1-1506)

From Elvis with Love (RCA 234340)

From Memphis to Vegas, from Vegas to Memphis (RCA LSP-6020)

Fun in Acapulco (RCA LPM/LSP-2756) [ST]

G.I. Blues (RCA LPM/LSP-2256) [ST]

Girl Happy (RCA LPM/LSP-3338) [ST]

Girls! Girls! Girls! (RCA LPM/LSP-2621) [ST]

A Golden Celebration (RCA 5172)

Good Times (RCA CPL1-0475)

Greatest Hits, Vol. 1 (RCA 2347)

The Greatest Show on Earth (RCA/Candlelite Music 0348)

Harum Scarum (RCA LPM/LSP-3468) [ST]

Having Fun with Elvis on Stage (RCA CPM1-0818)

He Touched Me (RCA LSP-4690)

He Walks Beside Me (RCA AFL1-2772)

His Hand in Mine (RCA LPM/LSP-2328)

I Got Lucky (Camden CAL/CAS-2533, Pickwick/Camden CAS-2533)

Interviews and Memories of the Sun Years (Sun 1001)

It Happened at the World's Fair (RCA LPM/LSP-2697) [ST]

King Creole (RCA LPM/LSP-1884) [ST]

Kissin' Cousins (RCA LPM/LSP-2894) [ST]

Legendary Concert Performances (RCA 244047)

The Legendary Magic (RCA/Candlelite Music 0461)

A Legendary Performer, Vols. 1–4 (RCA CPL1-0341, 1349, 3078, 4848)

The Legendary Recordings (RCA Candlelite Music 0412)

Let's Be Friends (Camden CAS-2408, Pickwick/Camden CAS-2408)

Love Letters from Elvis (RCA LSP-4530)

Loving You (RCA LPM/LSP-1515) [ST]

Mahola from Elvis (Pickwick ACL-7064)

Memories of Elvis (RCA Candlelite Music 0347)

The Memphis Record (RCA 6221-1)

Moody Blue (RCA AFL1-2428)

On Stage: February 1970 (RCA LSP-4362)

The Other Sides: Worldwide Gold Award Hits, Vol. 2 (RCA LPM-6402)

Our Memories of Elvis, Vols. 1–2 (RCA AQL1-3279, AQL1-3448)

Paradise Hawaiian Style (RCA LPM/LSP-3643) [ST]

Pot Luck (RCA LPM/LSP-2523)

Promised Land (RCA APL1-0873)

Pure Gold (RCA ANL1-0971)

Raised on Rock (RCA APL1-0388)

Return of the Rocker (RCA 5600-1)

Rock My Soul [Elvis on Tour] (World [no number]) [ST]

The Rockin' Rebel (Golden Archives GA250)

Roustabout (RCA LPM/LSP-2999) [ST]

Separate Ways (Camden CAS-2611, Pickwick/Camden CAS-2611)

Singer Presents Elvis Singing "Flaming Star" and Others (RCA PRS-279)

Something for Everybody (RCA LPM/LSP-2370)

Songs of Inspiration (RCA/Candlelite Music 0264)

Speedway (RCA LPM/LSP-3989) [ST]

Spinout (RCA LPM/LSP-3702) [ST]

The Sun Sessions (RCA APM1-1675)

This Is Elvis (RCA CPL2-4031)

Top Ten Hits (RCA 6383-1)

Viva Las Vegas (Lucky LR-711) [ST]

Welcome to My World (RCA APL1-2274)

Worldwide 50 Gold Award Hits, Vol. 1 (RCA LPM-6401)

Worldwide Gold Award Hits, Parts 1 and 2 (RCA 213690)

You'll Never Walk Alone (Camden CALX-2472, Pickwick/Camden CAS-2472)

# DEBBIE REYNOLDS

DEBBIE REYNOLDS' LONG AND SUCCESSFUL CAREER HAS BEEN OVER-shadowed by the endless fan magazine publicity generated about her during the 1950s and 1960s. Caught in the triangle when her marriage to Eddie Fisher broke up when he became involved with Elizabeth Taylor, she found herself billed as "the wronged woman." Reams of tabloid and fan magazine copy followed her every move for more than a decade, through her second marriage and two miscarriages. Almost overlooked in all this publicity was that fact that vivacious Debbie Reynolds was a fine, hard-working actress who could also sing and dance. In the past four decades she has proven her worth on screen, stage, TV, and recordings, plus being a highly paid nightclub attraction. From the All-American Girl, Debbie Reynolds emerged as one of filmdom's most solid entertainers.

She was born Mary Frances Reynolds on April 1, 1932, in El Paso, Texas; she had an older brother, Bill. Her parents were poor, for her father was a laborer, and in 1940 the family moved to Burbank, California, where Mr. Reynolds worked for the Southern Pacific railroad as a carpenter. She attended high school in Burbank, where she was an average high school girl who enjoyed sports and was a baton twirler in the school band. At age sixteen she was chosen Miss Burbank of 1948, after doing an imitation of Betty Hutton singing "My Rockin' Horse Ran Away." A talent scout from nearby Warner Bros. signed her for $65 per week and studio head Jack L. Warner changed her first name to Debbie. That year she made her film debut in the Bette Davis–Robert Montgomery comedy JUNE BRIDE in a small role as a teenager, which was followed by a small bit in THE DAUGHTER OF ROSIE O'GRADY (1950) as one of June Haver's sisters. When Warner Bros. dropped her studio option, she signed with MGM, a studio that also had expressed an interest in her when she won the Miss Burbank contest.

At MGM she studied hard with acting, voice, singing, and dancing lessons, deter-mined to make a success of herself at the lot. The work paid off when she was cast as Helen Kane in THREE LITTLE WORDS (1950), with Miss Kane herself doing the soundtrack recording of her famous hit, "I Wanna Be Loved by You." Next she was cast as Jane Powell's irrepressible younger sister in the musical TWO WEEKS WITH LOVE (1950) and she sang "Row, Row, Row" and "Aba Daba Honeymoon," the latter with tall, gawky Carleton Carpenter, with whom she had danced in THREE LITTLE WORDS. Debbie and Carpenter recorded "Aba Daba Honeymoon" for MGM Records; it was her first million-selling single disc. There followed inconsequential supporting parts in MR. IMPERIUM (1951), as Marjorie Main's tomboy niece, and SKIRTS AHOY (1952). However, MGM had great faith in her star potential, and cast Debbie in the important ingenue role in SINGIN' IN THE RAIN

(1952). As the peppy flapper she danced with Gene Kelly and they sang "You Were Meant for Me." Although the part solidified Reynolds' popularity and led to her becoming a star, she reported years later that Kelly drove her so hard during the film's production that she nearly died from extreme exhaustion.

Stardom came for Debbie when she joined with fading Donald O'Connor in the tepid musical I LOVE MELVIN (1953). She gave the picture what little charm it had in her energetic portrayal of a young performer whom a *Look* photographer (O'Connor) promises will be on the cover of the magazine. She was a co-ed in the comedy THE AFFAIRS OF DOBIE GILLIS (1953) and an aspiring musical star in GIVE A GIRL A BREAK (1953). She was loaned to RKO (at a profit to MGM) to star with Dick Powell in the coy sex comedy SUSAN SLEPT HERE (1954). She played a homeless teenager who finds love with an older Hollywood scripter (Powell) who is doing an exposé on juvenile delinquency. Because that film was so popular, MGM gave her a new contract, which brought her earnings up to $3,500 weekly. She had found a nice niche at the studio, somewhere between the wholesomeness of Jane Powell and the glitter of dancer Ann Miller.

Once again she was Jane Powell's sister—but this time her co-star—in the health fad spoof ATHENA (1954), which contained minor but sprightly songs. She was paired off romantically in the film with pop singer Vic Damone, as she would be in her next musical, the colorful production of Vincent Youmans' HIT THE DECK (1955), in which she and Jane Powell were romanced by sailors Damone and Tony Martin. In the comedy THE TENDER TRAP (1955), Debbie was the determined young lady out to snare bachelor Frank Sinatra. By now, Reynolds was extremely well known and popular with the public, due as much to the fan magazine coverage of her extended but fruitless romance with Robert Wagner as to her on-screen assignments. By the time news of Reynolds and Wagner had faded, she had begun a romance with pop singer Eddie Fisher, and they were married on October 21, 1955.

In 1956 she had a fine dramatic part as a Bronx girl in the somber THE CATERED AFFAIR, winning the National Board of Review's Best Supporting Actress nod, and, from the point of view of acting, surprisingly outdistancing co-star Bette Davis, who played her mother. She and husband Eddie Fisher were then teamed (and exploited) for the popular RKO comedy BUNDLE OF JOY (1956), a remake of BACHELOR MOTHER (1939), with Debbie as a salesgirl who finds an abandoned baby that people believe her boyfriend (Fisher) has fathered.

Following a guest bit in MGM's musical MEET ME IN LAS VEGAS (1956), Debbie had the title role in TAMMY AND THE BACHELOR (1957) on loanout to Universal. She was seen as a bayou girl who falls in love with a handsome veteran (Leslie Nielsen). The picture not only proved to be one of the star's most popular vehicles (spawning two sequels with Sandra Dee), it also provided her with her second million-selling single record, "Tammy" for Coral Records. (She would sing the Oscar-nominated song on the March 1958 Academy Awards telecast.) In 1957 she also had another best-selling single for Coral, "A Very Special Love." That song title proved to be prophetic, but not about Debbie's marriage to Eddie Fisher, which had produced two children, Carrie (born in 1956; later the star of the popular STAR WARS trilogy and a best-selling author) and Todd Emmanuel (born in 1958). The boy was named after producer Michael Todd, who had wed Reynolds' friend Elizabeth Taylor (they had graduated together from the MGM School) in 1957. Michael Todd was killed in a 1958 plane crash, and Debbie and Eddie Fisher were experiencing marital problems that year. She eventually discovered that Fisher had become involved with Elizabeth Taylor. Debbie and Fisher divorced, and he and Taylor married in 1959. A few years later, Taylor abandoned him for Richard Burton. All of this provided a goldmine of gossip for the fan magazines and tabloids, and more than a decade passed before the assorted stories surrounding Liz, Debbie, and Eddie faded. Eventually, Reynolds and Taylor patched up their quarrel, both having bad feelings toward their mutual ex-husband.

Reynolds continued in movies, which were more popular than ever thanks to the rash of publicity she was receiving. In THIS HAPPY FEELING (1958) for Universal she was romanced by older actor Curt Jurgens and the younger John Saxon. At MGM, THE MATING GAME (1959) offered her as a tomboy (again) whose farmer father (Paul Douglas) is audited by a tax agent (Tony Randall) who prefers checking the daughter's figure. At 20th Century–Fox she co-starred with Bing Crosby and former beau Robert Wagner in the lame musical SAY ONE FOR ME (1959), which cast her as a showgirl. She completed her MGM contract in 1959 with two middling features opposite Glenn Ford: IT STARTED WITH A KISS had them as an Army couple trying for a happy marriage; THE GAZEBO was a strained mystery comedy about a man and his wife accidentally involved in murder.

Now a freelancer, Reynolds co-starred with Tony Curtis in Paramount's THE RAT RACE (1960) as a would-be show business dancer. The comedy promised far more than it delivered. She also was among those stars contributing guest cameos to Columbia's PEPE (1960). The year 1960 also saw her with a trio of charted records for Dot, "Am I That Easy to Forget," "City Lights," and "Satisfied." At Paramount she played a bride-to-be whose wedding plans are interrupted by the arrival of her estranged father (Fred Astaire) in THE PLEASURE OF HIS COMPANY (1961). The much-touted film was not a box-office bonanza and Debbie, now nearing thirty, was noticeably too mature for the ingenue roles she was still playing. She did better as the resilient frontier widow romanced by Steve Forrest and Andy Griffith in THE SECOND TIME AROUND (1961). Back at MGM she was a spunky (her trademark) pioneer girl in the Cinerama epic HOW THE WEST WAS WON (1962), while Paramount's MY SIX LOVES (1963) cast her as an actress who must decide between her producer (David Janssen) and a minister (Cliff Robertson) as well as shepherd a half-dozen waifs. There was not much box-office interest in this film, but nevertheless Warner Bros. chose her to star in the domestic comedy MARY, MARY (1963). It had been a huge hit on Broadway, but lost a great deal in the transition to screen, with Reynolds comparing unfavorably with the original stage star (Barbara Bel Geddes).

After Doris Day lost out and Shirley MacLaine wanted too much money, Debbie Reynolds was cast in the lead of MGM's THE UNSINKABLE MOLLY BROWN (1964). It was a major part for which she had campaigned long and hard. She was the backwoods girl who wins the man (Harve Presnell) she adores and manages to crash Denver society. *Variety* observed, "She has thrust herself into the role with an enormous amount of verve and vigor." She was Oscar-nominated but lost the Best Actress award to Julie Andrews (MARY POPPINS). It was from the sublime to the ridiculous when Reynolds next starred in the dud comedy GOODBYE CHARLIE (1964), in which she played a beautiful woman with the soul of a murdered man who returns to haunt his best friend (Tony Curtis). The property had been purchased originally as a Marilyn Monroe vehicle. Again at MGM, Debbie was nicely cast in the musical THE SINGING NUN (1966), in which she played the title role of Sister Luc-Gabrielle, but the movie itself was dull and ended the Reynolds upswing begun by THE UNSINKABLE MOLLY BROWN. (Nevertheless, Debbie has stated that it is her favorite picture.) By the time of DIVORCE AMERICAN STYLE (1967) she was no longer playing ingenues; herein she is the wife whose home is breaking up after a lengthy marriage to Dick Van Dyke. She closed out the decade with what seemed a Doris Day reject, HOW SWEET IT IS (1968). Debbie played a married woman who goes on a second honeymoon to Europe with her husband (James Garner) and is attracted to a Frenchman (Maurice Ronet).

In 1969 Debbie Reynolds turned to television, starring in the short-running NBC comedy series "The Debbie Reynolds Show" as well as doing two guest shots on that network's "Bracken's World." In 1971 she returned to films in the fun but tattered gothic horror entry WHAT'S THE MATTER WITH HELEN? She and Shelley Winters played filmland has-beens who open a school for talented children—with tragic results. It was camp, but not in the same league with WHAT EVER HAPPENED TO BABY JANE? (1962).

Debbie had married "wealthy" shoe store tycoon Harry Karl in 1960, and during their problematic marriage had suffered two miscarriages. In 1968 she found out that they were nearly broke and

Debbie Reynolds in THE UNSINKABLE MOLLY BROWN (1964)

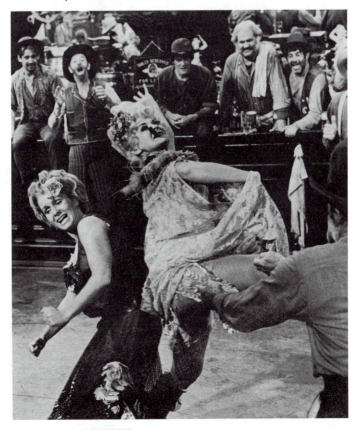

that most of her property had been mortgaged to offset his huge gambling debts. When she divorced Karl in 1974, she discovered she owed millions of dollars and went to work—on an exhausting schedule—to pay off her debts. "It was hard for me to lose my money after I'd worked thirty years to earn it," she said. "The debts took nearly ten years to pay off."

As a result, Debbie made her Broadway debut in 1973 in the musical *Irene*, a revival of the 1919 hit. She broke attendance records with her portrayal of the spunky young woman and sang such songs as "Alice Blue Gown." When she left the New York cast to tour with the production, she was replaced by another ex-MGMer, Jane Powell. Thereafter, Debbie began working in Las Vegas and other resorts with her high-priced nightclub act, and she also started collecting movie memorabilia, especially costumes, for her long-dreamed-of Hollywood Hall of Fame. Throughout the 1970s she worked in nightclubs and on the stage. She played in Australia and at the London Palladium and in 1977 did a West Coast revival of *Annie Get Your Gun.* She was consistently active in the charitable doings of The Thalians. In 1979, *Debbie Does Las Vegas*, a fifty-five-minute video version of her club act, was issued.

In 1980 she returned to TV with a guest role on ABC's "The Love Boat" followed, briefly, in 1981 by her own short-lived comedy series, "Aloha Paradise," for the same network. That year she also cut a record album for AVI Records called *Tammy and Other Songs from the Movies.* Although her own program had only a brief run, Reynolds stayed with TV for guest roles in such series as "Alice," "The Love Boat," and "Jennifer Slept Here." With her zany sense of comedy and her flair for doing celebrity imitations, she was a favorite on the TV talk show circuit. She was briefly a replacement for Lauren Bacall in the Broadway musical *Woman of the Year* (1982). In 1987 she made her telefeature debut starring in SADIE AND SON (CBS-TV) as a dedicated New York City cop who insists that her offspring follow the family tradition. Two years later she was the guest star (as a feisty Broadway/Hollywood song-and-dance star) in THE CASE OF THE MUSICAL MURDER (NBC-TV), a two-hour segment of the ongoing "Perry Mason" TV movie series.

In 1984 Debbie Reynolds married businessman Richard Hamlett. Having already published one autobiography, *If I Knew Then* (1963), she wrote another, *Debbie: My Life* (1988). It told her side of the story of the Eddie Fisher–Elizabeth Taylor affair and recounted other aspects of her career to date. About the memoirs Reynolds recalled, "Writing my book was reliving a nightmare. Many times when I was writing, I would break into tears just recalling the agony I went through."

Like many stars who have reached middle age, Reynolds has expanded in several directions. She established a well-respected dance rehearsal studio in North Hollywood, California (where she now lives modestly), starred in an extremely popular 1983 videocassette exercise tape (*Do It Debbie's Way*), and in the spring of 1989 began a stage tour in *The Unsinkable Molly Brown*, reunited with her film co-star, Harve Presnell. Said the *Los Angeles Times*, "Reynolds still has her knock-about dancing legs, and her raspy voice fills the air like a rusty buzz saw. She lacks a large singing voice, but she can turn a nice plaintive ballad. . . ."

Like many of the characters she plays, Debbie Reynolds seems rambunctious and unsinkable herself.

## Filmography

June Bride (WB, 1948)
The Daughter of Rosie O'Grady (WB, 1950)
Three Little Words (MGM, 1950)
Two Weeks with Love (MGM, 1950)
Mr. Imperium [You Belong to My Heart] (MGM, 1951)
Skirts Ahoy (MGM, 1952)
Singin' in the Rain (MGM, 1952)
I Love Melvin (MGM, 1953)
The Affairs of Dobie Gillis (MGM, 1953)
Give a Girl a Break (MGM, 1953)
Susan Slept Here (RKO, 1954)
Athena (MGM, 1954)
The Tender Trap (MGM, 1955)
Hit the Deck (MGM, 1955)
Bundle of Joy (RKO, 1956)
The Catered Affair [Wedding Breakfast] (MGM, 1956)
Meet Me in Las Vegas (MGM, 1956)
Tammy and the Bachelor [Tammy] (Univ, 1957)
This Happy Feeling (Univ, 1958)

The Mating Game (MGM, 1959)
Say One for Me (20th–Fox, 1959)
It Started with a Kiss (MGM, 1959)
The Gazebo (MGM, 1959)
The Rat Race (Par, 1960)
Pepe (Col, 1960)
The Pleasure of His Company (Par, 1961)
The Second Time Around (20th–Fox, 1961)
How the West Was Won (MGM, 1962)
My Six Loves (Par, 1963)
Mary, Mary (WB, 1963)
Goodbye Charlie (20th–Fox, 1964)
The Unsinkable Molly Brown (MGM, 1964)
The Singing Nun (MGM, 1966)
Divorce American Style (UA, 1967)
How Sweet It Is (National General, 1968)
What's the Matter with Helen? (UA, 1971)
Charlotte's Web (Par, 1973) (voice only)
That's Entertainment! (MGM, 1974) (co-host)
Sadie and Son (CBS-TV, 10/21/87)
Perry Mason: The Case of the Musical Murder (NBC-TV, 4/9/89)

## Broadway Plays

Irene (1973) (revival)
Woman of the Year (1982) (replacement)

## TV Series

The Debbie Reynolds Show (NBC, 1969–70)
Aloha Paradise (ABC, 1981)

## Album Discography

Am I That Easy to Forget (Dot 3295/25295)
And Then I Sang (Pye NSP-184356)
Athena (10" Mer MG-25202, Motion Picture Tracks MPT-2) [ST]

Bundle of Joy (RCA LPM-1399) [ST]
Debbie (Dot 3191/25191, Jasmine 1512)
Fine and Dandy (Dot 3298/25298)
From Debbie with Love (MGM E-3806)

Hit the Deck (MGM E-3163) [ST]

How the West Was Won (MGM 1E/S1E-5) [ST]

I Love Melvin (10" MGM E-190, MGM SES-52ST) [ST]

Irene (Col KS-32266) [OC]

Raise a Ruckus (Metro M/S-535)

Say One for Me (Col CL-1337/CS-8147) [ST]

Singin' in the Rain (10" MGM E-113, MGM E-3236, Metro M/S-599) [ST]

The Singing Nun (MGM 1E/S1E-7) [ST]

Tammy (Dot 3492/25492)

Tammy and Other Songs from the Movies (AVI 6095)

Tammy and the Bachelor (Coral CRL-57159) [ST]

That's Entertainment (GNP AVL-1033)

Two Weeks with Love (10" MGM E-530, MGM E-3236) [ST]

The Unsinkable Molly Brown (MGM E/SE-4232) [ST]

# TEX RITTER

BILLED AS "AMERICA'S MOST BELOVED COWBOY," DEEP, HUSKY-VOICED Tex Ritter was the real McCoy in that he hailed from Texas, grew up and worked on a small ranch, and began a lifelong association with traditional Western music at an early age. While his movies did not have the production values or box-office pull of those of rivals Gene Autry and Roy Rogers, Tex Ritter tried to bring the traditional, true West, especially in music, into his horse operas. As a result, he was in the *Motion Picture Herald*'s poll of top ten money-making Western stars from 1937 through 1941 and again in 1944 and 1945.

Tex Ritter was born on January 12, 1905, on the four-hundred-acre ranch first settled by his great-grandfather Frank Ritter, in Panola County, Texas. He was the son of Jim and Lizzie Ritter. He was christened Maurice Woodward (pronounced Woodard) Ritter and was the youngest of six children; he was named for the family physician, Dr. Woodward. As a boy he was called Woody and he attended school in nearby Murvaul. He participated in high school sports as well as ran a part-time laundry with some of his friends. Always interested in public speaking, young Woody became the county debating champion, and after graduating with honors from South Park High School in Beaumont, he enrolled at the University of Texas in 1922, studying political science. As a teenager, the young man had sung at church and other local functions and he continued to do so in college, where he sang in the glee club. At the university he came under the influence of writer J. Frank Dobie, composer Oscar J. Fox, and folk ballad compiler John A. Lomax. All of these people helped to develop his love of traditional Western music. He also took voice and guitar lessons.

Having graduated, in 1928 he had a summer show on a Houston radio station singing cowboy ballads, and that fall he joined the company of the touring show *Maryland, My Maryland*, which took him to New York City. There he got a bit part in the operetta *The New Moon* as a member of the male chorus. After its run he went to Chicago and enrolled in Northwestern University as a law student. However, by the end of 1930 he was back on the stage as a cowboy (and the understudy to star Franchot Tone) in *Green Grow the Lilacs*, which came to Broadway early in 1931 after brief runs in Philadelphia and Washington, D.C. The play ran for eight weeks on Broadway before having a successful road tour in such cities as St. Louis, Baltimore, and Cleveland.

Following the show's run, Tex (as Ritter was now called) returned to Gotham to get occasional work in coffeehouses and as a lecturer and singer at New York University. In March 1932 he returned to Broadway as Sage Brush Charlie in a revival of *The Roundup* and then began working in local radio in "Lone Star Rangers" and "Maverick Jim." He also landed acting roles in such network series as "Gang Busters," "Eno Crime Club," and "Death Valley Days." In 1932 he originated the role of Buck Mason on the CBS radio series "Bobby Benson and the B-Bar-B Riders" and hosted the local "WHN Barn Dance" show. He soon hosted another WHN program, "Tex Ritter's Campfire," and in 1933 he began a three-year run in the CBS series "Cowboy Tom's Roundup." That year also found him recording for the American Record Company, which issued two discs, "Goodbye Old Paint"/"Rye Whiskey" and "A-Ridin' Old Paint"/"Everyday in the Saddle," on a variety of dime-store labels such as Banner, Conqueror, Oriole, Perfect, Melotone, Romeo, and Vocalion. Ritter's final Broadway appearance occurred late in 1934 when he had two roles in the romance *Mother Lode*, starring Helen Gahagan and her husband, Melvyn Douglas, who also directed.

Tex Ritter's big break came in 1936, when he was spotted on his off hours at a New Jersey dude ranch by film producer Edward Finney, who was seeking a star for a series of "B" Westerns he was about to produce for the new Grand National Pictures. Gene Autry had popularized singing oaters at Republic, and Grand National was looking to duplicate their successful formula. Tex's initial starring Western was the impressive SONG OF THE GRINGO (1936), the first of a dozen features he was to make for Grand National. In this rather austere oater he sang six songs, including "Rye Whiskey" and "Sam Hall," and his film career was well on its way. The *Hollywood Reporter* judged him the "newest bet in prairie warbling." On screen, Ritter comfortably projected the image of a stalwart hero whose penchant for singing traditional Western ballads did not get in the way of the action. After Grand National collapsed in 1938, Ritter and Finney moved to Monogram Pictures, where in the next three years they made twenty additional oaters, whose quality varied greatly. Playing a bit part in SONG OF THE

Tex Ritter in 1938

BUCKAROO (1939) was Dorothy Fay, who was to become Ritter's leading lady in three more Monogram outings: SUNDOWN ON THE PRAIRIE (1939), ROLLIN' WESTWARD (1939), and RAINBOW OVER THE RANGE (1940). She and Tex were married in 1938. While making movies, Tex Ritter recorded with Decca Records between 1935 and 1939, often waxing songs he performed in his films.

After making thirty-two feature Westerns together, Tex and producer Edward Finney parted in 1941. (Tex had earlier been offered Gene Autry's berth at Republic Pictures when that company had contractual problems with Autry, but Ritter declined out of loyalty to Finney and friendship with Autry.) Ritter went to Columbia Pictures where he co-starred with Bill Elliott in eight series Westerns along with co-starring with Charles Starrett in COWBOY CANTEEN (1944). Between the Elliott series and COWBOY CANTEEN, Tex appeared with Johnny Mack Brown in seven oaters at Universal in the 1942–43 season. As in the Elliott features, Ritter provided both music and action in these programmers, but in the 1943 Universal entry FRONTIER BADMEN, he had a straight acting part as Kimball. Universal then signed him to another series, but after headlining ARIZONA TRAIL (1943), MARSHAL OF GUNSMOKE (1944), and OKLAHOMA RAIDERS (1944), Ritter was forced out of the grouping due to an injury (he fell out of his barn loft at home) and was replaced by Russell Hayden, his co-star in MARSHAL OF GUNSMOKE.

Better luck, however, had come Ritter's way in the summer of 1942 when producer Johnny Mercer signed him as the first Western performer for the fledgling Capitol Records label. His initial record for Capitol, "Jingle, Jangle, Jingle," became an immense seller and Ritter was soon the label's hottest property. By early 1945, Tex Ritter had the three most-played jukebox folk records: "I'm Wasting My Tears on You," "There's a New Moon over My Shoulder," and "Jealous Heart."

Tex Ritter's final Western series came in the 1944–45 season when he went to Producers Releasing Corporation (PRC) to replace Jim Newill as one of the leads in "The Texas Rangers" series, co-starring Dave O'Brien and Guy Wilkerson. These eight tattered sagebrushers did little to enhance Ritter's film career, although they did provide him the opportunity to sing on screen such songs as "In Case You Change Your Mind," "Long Time Gone," "Be Honest with Me," and "Too Late to Worry, Too Blue to Cry."

Ritter's next film did not come until 1950, when he made a guest appearance in Lippert's HOLIDAY RHYTHM singing "The Old Chisholm Trail" with The Cass County Boys. In the interim he made personal appearances, guested on radio shows, and continued his streak of best-selling records on Capitol with such tunes as "You Will Have to Pay," "Green Grow the Lilacs," "Boll Weevil," "Blood on the Saddle," "Double Dealin' Darlin'," "Deck of Cards," and "When My Blue Moon Turns to Gold Again." During this period he also recorded children's records and made scores of transcription discs (sold directly to radio stations) for the World Disc and Capitol labels. In 1951 he filmed ten singing shorts for television, produced by Snader Telescriptions.

By the early 1950s, Tex Ritter's career was beginning to flag, but prior to a successful tour of Europe, he recorded the song "High Noon" for Capitol. Its inclusion in the film of the same title in 1952 breathed new life into his career. He sang the theme songs in the features THE MARSHAL'S DAUGHTER (1953), WICHITA (1955), and TROOPER HOOK (1957), and narrated and sang on the soundtrack of THE COWBOY (1954). He was featured as a gunman in APACHE AMBUSH (1955). For Capitol he had best-sellers with "The Bandit," "Remember the Alamo," "The Searchers," and "The Wayward Wind."

On television, he and pals Johnny Bond and Merle Travis headlined the series "Town Hall Party" out of Los Angeles, and it was also heard on NBC radio. The show ran on TV from 1952 to 1961. Ritter also hosted the syndicated series "Ranch Party" from 1957 to 1961. In 1961 he and Jimmy Wakely, Rex Allen, Carl Smith, and Snooky Lanson co-hosted the NBC-TV series "Five Star Jubilee." Ritter also guest-starred on various television programs, such as "Ford Startime Academy Award Show" on NBC, the "Zane Grey Theater" on CBS, and ABC's "The Rebel." However, his hopes of starring in his own TV Western series never came to anything.

In the earlier 1960s, Ritter toured overseas in Europe, the Orient, South Africa, and Vietnam, as well as in Canada. He was very active in the Country Music Association and was elected to the Country Music Hall of Fame. By the mid-1960s, Ritter, who co-owned a musical publishing firm (Vidor Publishing) with Johnny Bond, found himself more often working in Nashville, and in 1965 he moved there permanently. He joined WSM's "Grand Ole Opry" as well as co-hosted that station's all-night country music show with Ralph Emery. Now in his sixties, he returned to films in 1966, starring as a country preacher in THE GIRL FROM TOBACCO ROW for the Ormond Organization and he also portrayed himself in two other features, NASHVILLE REBEL (1966) and WHAT AM I BID? (1967). In the latter, he sang the song "I Never Got to Kiss the Girl," a takeoff on his days as a cowboy film hero. During the decade he continued to record for Capitol, and his best-sellers included "I Dreamed of a Hillbilly Heaven," "Wandrin' Star," and "A Funny Thing Happened on the Way to Miami." The latter was a novelty song about his actual experience as a passenger on a plane being hijacked to Havana. He also guest-starred on Marty Robbins' TV series, "The Drifter."

In 1970 Tex Ritter announced his candidacy for the U.S. Senate from Tennessee as a Republican, but he received only twenty-three percent of the vote and incurred debts that would plague him for the rest of his life. The need for funds forced Ritter to accelerate his activities, but he often found doors closed to him because of his right-wing political leanings. His records, however, continued to sell well. In 1970 he had a hit with "Green Green Valley" on Capitol (by now he had a lifetime contract with the label) and this was followed by "Comin' After Jinny" and "One Night for Willie." However, his 1971 recording of "The Battle Hymn of Lieutenant Calley" was shelved as being too controversial. Ritter made guest appearances as himself in the country music movies THE NASHVILLE STORY (1972) and THE NASHVILLE SOUND (1973). For a time he was considered for the role ultimately played by Ben Johnson in THE LAST PICTURE SHOW (1971).

As the 1970s progressed, Ritter began to enjoy a career resurgence as the demand for personal appearances increased. He continued to appear on the "Grand Ole Opry" as well as guest-starred on such TV shows as "The Jimmy Dean Show" and "Hee Haw." He also lent his name to a series of fast-food restaurants, The Tex Ritter Chuck Wagon, and late in

1973 he was signed to co-star with Burt Reynolds in the upcoming film W. W. AND THE DIXIE DANCE KINGS. As 1974 began, Ritter was preparing to start a college campus tour, following up on the growing success of his latest Capitol single, his recitation of "The Americans." On the morning of January 2, 1974, he went to the Nashville jail to bail out one of his band members, who had been incarcerated for nonpayment of child support. There he suffered a fatal heart attack. He was survived by his wife, Dorothy, and sons John (a TV and film star) and Tom. He was replaced in W. W. AND THE DIXIE DANCE KINGS (1974) by Ned Beatty.

Although he made over seventy films, Tex Ritter never considered himself much of an actor. He felt he was best at singing and songwriting (he wrote over seventy published songs). Today, however, he is largely remembered because of his films and records. He was such an American tradition that his passing was felt deeply, all the way from the President of the United States (he was a personal friend of Richard Nixon) to his millions of fans. In a tribute, a writer for the *London* (England) *Evening Standard* summed it up best: "He epitomized all that was good and right about the West."

## Filmography

Song of the Gringo (GN, 1936)
Headin' for the Rio Grande (GN, 1936)
Arizona Days (GN, 1937)
Trouble in Texas (GN, 1937)
Hittin' the Trail (GN, 1937)
Sing, Cowboy, Sing (GN, 1937)
Riders of the Rockies (GN, 1937)
Tex Rides with the Boy Scouts (GN, 1937)
Mystery of the Hooded Horsemen (GN, 1937)
Frontier Town (GN, 1938)
Rollin' Plains (GN, 1938)
The Utah Trail (GN, 1938)
Starlight over Texas (Mon, 1938)
Where the Buffalo Roam (Mon, 1938)
Song of the Buckaroo (Mon, 1939)
Sundown on the Prairie (Mon, 1939)
Riders of the Frontier (Mon, 1939)
Rollin' Westward (Mon, 1939)
Roll, Wagons, Roll (Mon, 1939)
Down the Wyoming Trail (Mon, 1939)
The Man from Texas (Mon, 1939)
Westbound Stage (Mon, 1939)
Rhythm of the Rio Grande (Mon, 1940)
Pals of the Silver Sage (Mon, 1940)
The Golden Trail (Mon, 1940)
The Cowboy from Sundown (Mon, 1940)
Take Me Back to Oklahoma (Mon, 1940)

Rainbow over the Range (Mon, 1940)
Arizona Frontier (Mon, 1940)
Rollin' Home to Texas (Mon, 1940)
Ridin' the Cherokee Trail (Mon, 1941)
Picture People #8 (RKO, 1941) (s)
The Pioneers (Mon, 1941)
King of Dodge City (Col, 1941)
Roaring Frontiers (Col, 1941)
Lone Star Vigilantes (Col, 1942)
Bullets for Bandits (Col, 1942)
The Devil's Trail (Col, 1942)
North of the Rockies (Col, 1942)
Prairie Gunsmoke (Col, 1942)
Vengeance of the West (Col, 1942)
Deep in the Heart of Texas (Univ, 1942)
Little Joe, the Wrangler (Univ, 1942)
The Old Chisholm Trail (Univ, 1942)
Raiders of San Joaquin (Univ, 1943)
Western Rhythms (Soundies, 1943) (s)
The Lone Star Trail (Univ, 1943)
Tenting Tonight on the Old Camp Ground (Univ, 1943)
Cheyenne Roundup (Univ, 1943)
Frontier Badmen (Univ, 1943)
Arizona Trail (Univ, 1943)
Marshal of Gunsmoke (Univ, 1944)
Oklahoma Raiders (Univ, 1944)

Cowboy Canteen (Col, 1944)
Gangsters of the Frontier (PRC, 1944)
Dead or Alive (PRC, 1944)
The Whispering Skull (PRC, 1944)
Marked for Murder (PRC, 1945)
Enemy of the Law (PRC, 1945)
Three in the Saddle (PRC, 1945)
Frontier Fugitives (PRC, 1945)
Flaming Bullets (PRC, 1945)
Holiday Rhythm (Lip, 1950)
High Noon (UA, 1952) (voice only)
The Marshal's Daughter (UA, 1953) (voice only)
The Cowboy (Lip, 1954) (narrator)
Wichita (AA, 1955) (voice only)

The First Badman (MGM, 1955) (s) (narrator)
Apache Ambush (Col, 1955)
Down Liberty Road (WB, 1956)
Trooper Hook (UA, 1957) (voice only)
What's the Country Coming To? (CMA, 1966) (narrator)
The Girl from Tobacco Row (Ormond Organization, 1966)
Nashville Rebel (AIP, 1966)
Star Route U.S.A. (Medallion, 1966)
What Am I Bid? (Emerson Film, 1967)
The Nashville Story (Donald A. Davis, 1972)
Music City, U.S.A. (International Harvester, 1972) (narrator)
The Nashville Sound (John C. Bradford, 1973)

## Broadway Plays

The New Moon (1928)
Green Grow the Lilacs (1931)

The Roundup (1932) (revival)
Mother Lode (1934)

## Radio Series

Lone Star Rangers (WOR, 1932) (local)
Maverick Jim (WOR, 1932) (local)
Bobby Benson and the B-Bar-B Riders (CBS, 1932–35)
WHN Barn Dance (WHN, 1932) (local)
Tex Ritter's Campfire (WHN, 1932) (local)

Cowboy Tom's Roundup (CBS, 1933–35)
Town Hall Party (NBC, 1952–58)
Grand Ole Opry (WSM, 1965–74) (local)
The Ralph Emery–Tex Ritter Midnight Show (WSM, 1965–70) (local)

## TV Series

Town Hall Party (Synd, 1952–61)
Ranch Party (Synd, 1957–61)

Five Star Jubilee (NBC, 1961)

## Album Discography

An American Legend (Cap SKC-11241)
The Best of Tex Ritter (Cap T/DT-25951)
Blood on the Saddle (Cap T/ST-1292, Cap SM-1292)
A Border Affair (Cap T-1910)
Bump Tiddle Dee Bum Bum (Cap ST-2890)
Chuck Wagon Days (Cap ST-213)

Comin' After Jinny (Cap ST-11503)
Cowboy Favorites (10" Cap H-4004)
Deck of Cards (Camay 30-44)
Fall Away (Cap ST-11351)
The Friendly Voice of Tex Ritter (Cap T/ST-2402)
Greatest Hits by Tex Ritter (Shasta 520)

Green Green Valley (Cap ST-467)
Hank Williams/Tex Ritter (Sunrise Media 3019)
High Noon (Bear Family BFX-15126)
Hillbilly Heaven (Cap T/ST-1623)
Just Beyond the Moon (Cap T/ST-2786)
Lady Killin' Cowboy (Bear Family BFX-15209)
The Lincoln Hymns (Cap W/SW-1562)
Love You as Big as Texas (Pickwick 6075)
My Kinda Songs (Pickwick 2020)
Out of the Past (Album Globe 9023, Quicksilver 5059)
The Phantom Attorney [Marked for Murder] (Amalgamated 226) [ST]
Psalms (Cap T-1100)
The Rare Ones of the Late Tex Ritter (Masterpiece/Cattle 202)
Singin' in the Saddle (Bear Family BFX-15231)
The Singing Cowboy: 30 Early Songs 1935–39 (MCA Coral 7882-D11-12)
Songs from the Western Screen (Cap T-971, Stetson HAT-3041)
Stan Kenton! Tex Ritter! (Cap T/ST-1757)
Starring Tex Ritter (Premier 9023) w. The Rio Grande Valley Boys
Streets of Laredo (Bulldog 1022)
The Supercountrylegendary Tex Ritter (Cap T/ST-2743)
Tennessee Blues (Hilltop 6059)
Tex (Pickwick 6155)
Tex Ritter (Buckboard 1030)
Tex Ritter (Coronet CX-CXS-273)
Tex Ritter (Spino-rama 179) w. Bob Jones
Tex Ritter's Wild West (Cap ST-2974)
These Hands (Cap ECR-8174)
What Am I Bid? (MGM SE-4506) [ST]

# PAUL ROBESON

PAUL ROBESON IS ONE OF THE TWENTIETH CENTURY'S MOST DIS-
tinguished performers, a robust black artist whose long career encompassed the stage,
screen, concerts, and recordings. He was one of the first contemporary singers to put
stirring emotion into his bass-baritone singing, and thereby captured the imagination of
audiences for decades. He was also an extremely controversial figure whose outspoken
rhetoric on social injustice eventually made him anathema in his homeland. In fact, most
of Robeson's creative years were spent abroad, and although he was a film star, only two of
his dozen feature movies were produced in Hollywood. Because of his political leanings,
Robeson was almost excluded from performing in the 1950s and for a time made his home
in the Soviet Union. Ill health eventually ended his performing career and he died in
comparative obscurity. In recent years, there has been renewed interest in Paul Robeson
and his richly varied career.

Paul Leroy Robeson was born on April 9, 1898, in Princeton, New Jersey, the son of
Presbyterian minister (and one-time runaway slave) William Robeson and Maria Louisa
(Bustill) Robeson; he was the last of five children. The boy learned to love music at an early
age in his father's church, and in school he excelled in speaking, debating, and sports. In
1915 he won a full scholarship to Rutgers University, an extraordinary feat for a black at
that time. At the university he played football and was named to the All-American football
team, became a member of Phi Beta Kappa, and excelled in javelin, baseball, and oratory.
He graduated from Rutgers in 1919 as class valedictorian and decided to take up the study
of law. The 6' 3", 215-pound Robeson entered Columbia University Law School in 1920,
and to earn extra money he began singing professionally with The Four Harmony Kings at
the Cotton Club's show *Shuffle Away*, displaying his rich baritone voice.

After appearing in dramatics at the Harlem YMCA, he made his professional acting
debut in *Simon the Cyrenian* at the Lafayette Theatre on Broadway in 1921. That year he
married Eslanda "Essie" Cardozo Goode, who urged him to look for other acting work. In
1922 he appeared in the play *Taboo* opposite Margaret Wycherly. He toured with it under
the title *Voodoo* with Mrs. Patrick Campbell in England and Scotland. Returning home,
he received a law degree from Columbia in 1923. After working briefly in a law firm, in
1924 he accepted the lead roles in two Eugene O'Neill plays for the Provincetown
Theatre, *The Emperor Jones* and *All God's Chillun Got Wings*. Robeson made his film debut
in 1925 in the all-black feature BODY AND SOUL, directed by Oscar Micheaux. After that
he began giving a series of concerts of spiritual music, often in tandem with long-time

friend, pianist, and vocalist Lawrence Brown, who would work with him for the bulk of his career. In the summer of 1925, Robeson (with Brown) made his recording debut doing spirituals for Victor Records, an association that would last for fifteen years, although the bulk of his records would be made in England on Victor's British label, HMV (His Master's Voice).

Having revived his role of Brutus Jones in *The Emperor Jones* at New York's 52nd Street Theatre in February 1925, he went that fall to England to recreate the role on the London stage. Early in 1926 he was back in the United States for a concert tour, followed by a run in *Black Boy* on Broadway that fall, and then by more concerts. In 1927 he was again performing in London's West End in a revival of *Taboo* with Mrs. Patrick Campbell, and on November 2, 1927, his only child, Paul Robeson, Jr., was born. Early in 1928 he had a month's run on Broadway in Gershwin's *Porgy and Bess* as Crown and then sailed again for London to co-star in *Show Boat*, in which he sang his most famous song, "Ole Man River." On March 1, 1928, he recorded the song for Victor with Paul Whiteman and His Orchestra.

When a dispute occurred over a play that Robeson had signed to appear in but did not, he was suspended by Actors' Equity Association and after that he and his family relocated "permanently" to London. In the spring of 1929 he gave concerts in Central Europe, and the next year his wife wrote the book *Paul Robeson, Negro*. The year 1930 also found him appearing in *The Emperor Jones* in Berlin and then doing his most famous stage role, that of Shakespeare's *Othello*, with Peggy Ashcroft as Desdemona. He and his wife also went to Switzerland to star in the motion picture (Robeson's talkie debut) BORDER-LINE (1931), a marital drama. This was followed by a London production of Eugene O'Neill's *The Hairy Ape* in which he was Yank, and thereafter he did concerts in Paris.

In 1932 Robeson returned to America to play Joe in a Broadway revival of *Show Boat* and then did *All God's Chillun Got Wings* in March 1933 in London with Flora Robson. Back in the United States once more, he starred in the film version of THE EMPEROR JONES (1933), which was filmed at Eastern Service Studio on Long Island. Here the actor gave his finest (albeit stagey) film performance as Brutus Jones, an escaped convict who is washed ashore on Haiti and eventually becomes the island's ruler before descending into madness. In the film he sang "Water Boy," "Now Let Me Fly," and "I'm Travelin'." Because of its mostly black cast and its very arty theme, the film did not promise to be a commercial success, despite an "art house" release by United Artists. However, for Robeson as a performer it marked "a personal triumph" (*Variety*).

Back in England, where he had a larger following than in America, Robeson starred in the Alexander Korda movie SANDERS OF THE RIVER (1935), based on some novels by Edgar Wallace. He was cast as Bosambo, a former convict who becomes an African tribal chief. Among his songs in the feature were "Love Song," "Congo Lullaby," "The Canoe Song," and "Killing Song," all recorded for HMV. (As had already become a pattern, he was extremely unhappy with the way the movie was edited and was very vocal in wishing the project shelved.) He then made the first of his many trips to the Soviet Union. While there he met with that country's premiere film director, Sergei Eisenstein, who wanted him to portray Toussaint L'Ouverture in the film BLACK MAJESTY, but the project never materialized.

Returning to London in the spring of 1935, Paul Robeson co-starred with Margaret Webster in the play *Basalik*, followed by *Stevedore*. He returned to the United States for Universal's expansive new version of SHOW BOAT (1936), in which he repeated his acclaimed stage role of Joe the Riverman. In England he recorded "Ole Man River" and "I Still Suits Me" from the film for HMV. He then starred in the British feature SONG OF FREEDOM (1936) as a black man, the last of an African royal family, who is sold into slavery by the Portuguese. Again for HMV, he recorded his quartet of songs from the film: "Sleepy River," "Lonely Road," "The Black Emperor," and "Song of Freedom." In 1936 Robeson also had the starring role of Umbopa in H. Rider Haggard's KING SOLOMON'S MINES (1937), in which he sang "Ho! Ho!" and "Climbing Up," which he recorded for HMV.

A second trip to Russia followed the film's production, and he and his wife decided to send their son to school there in order for him to avoid what they considered racial prejudice in the West. Back in London, Robeson appeared briefly in the play *Toussaint L'Ouverture* and then was cast as a black Marseilles stevedore in the British movie BIG

Ethel Waters, Eddie "Rochester" Anderson, and Paul Robeson in TALES OF MANHATTAN (1942)

FELLA (1937), singing "Lazin'," "Roll Up, Sailorman," and "You Didn't Oughta Do Such Things," all recorded for HMV. In Egypt he starred in the film JERICHO (1937), about an American black who remains in North Africa after World War I; in it he sang "Shortnin' Bread" and "Deep Desert." The movie received some U.S. release as DARK SANDS. Following the making of this picture, Robeson announced that he was retiring from films because the medium did not show his race in a proper light. He went to Spain to entertain Loyalist troops in that country's civil war. Back in London he appeared in the 1938 play *Plant in the Sun*, about labor union activities and strikes.

By this time, most of Paul Robeson's friends were Marxists and he became a proponent of Communist philosophy, although he always denied that he was ever a Communist Party member. He did return to films to portray a noble black coalminer who gives his life for his fellow workers in Wales in PROUD VALLEY (1939). In it he sang "Ebenezer" and "Land of My Fathers," which he recorded for HMV in his last session with the company. This was Robeson's favorite film. (His playing of the noble screen character in PROUD VALLEY established the model for later black movie performers such as Sidney Poitier.) Robeson also narrated the film NATIVE LAND, but it was not issued until 1942.

By December 1939, Robeson was back in the United States, starring on Broadway in the musical drama *John Henry*, and he then gave a concert at the Hollywood Bowl in which he sang "Ballad for Americans," which he recorded for Victor Records. In Chicago he performed an outdoor concert before an audience of 160,000 and he returned to Hollywood for his second and final film in the movie capital, TALES OF MANHATTAN (1942), an episodic film about the ownership of an expensive coat in which he and Ethel Waters appeared as poor southern sharecroppers. He was extremely vocal about his dislike of the film's final format, insisting that it presented a damaging portrayal of blacks. It was Robeson who said once about moviemaking, "The industry is not prepared to permit me to portray the life and express the living interests, hopes and aspirations of the struggling people from whom I come. . . ."

With Count Basie, he recorded the song "King Joe" about Joe Louis for Columbia Records in the fall of 1941, and after the outbreak of World War II, he became a tireless worker for the war effort. In 1942 he did *Othello* on Broadway for 296 performances with Uta Hagen as Desdemona and José Ferrer as Iago, under Margaret Webster's direction. In reviewing his performance, playwright Lawrence Stallings enthusiastically observed, "One can imagine that Shakespeare must have hoped for Robeson." Following the hugely popular New York City run, he toured with the play through the spring of 1945 and then did a series of concerts into the next year.

In 1946 he was elected vice president of the Civil Rights Congress and was involved with the Council on African Affairs; he also informed Congress's Tenney Committee that he was not a Communist. Plans for Robeson to star in FREEDOM ROAD for Jean Renoir in 1947 did not work out. For a time Robeson claimed that he was retiring from concert work, but he returned for an appearance in Jamaica in 1948. But after that he was dropped by his booking agency, Columbia Artists, with whom he had been associated for nearly two decades. That year he campaigned actively for Progressive Party presidential candidate

Henry A. Wallace, the former vice president. When work offers fell off drastically, Robeson went on tour in England, but caused a controversy when he said American blacks would not fight Russians. At home, many of his race were outspoken in opposing his views. He toured Europe and the U.S.S.R. and then came back to Gotham for his son's wedding. He was denounced by witnesses before the House Committee on Un-American Activities (HUAC). Following a bloody riot at a controversial concert to be given by Robeson in Peekskill, New York, in the fall of 1949, the Soviet Union named a mountain in the Urals after him and placed his bust on a high peak.

During the early 1950s, Paul Robeson continued to give concerts and to record for labels like Keynote and Columbia. However, his vocal opposition to U.S. involvement in the Korean conflict led to his passport's being revoked. At that time, he began working on the editorial board of the Harlem *Freedom* newspaper and occasionally he penned an article for it. (His income, which had been $104,000 in 1947, fell to $6,000 in 1952.) In 1952 Russia gave him the Lenin Peace Prize, but his request to travel abroad to perform was denied, although he was allowed to perform in Canada in 1956. That year he was called to testify before HUAC and Robeson took the Fifth Amendment when asked if he was a Communist. In 1958 his autobiography, *Here I Stand*, was published and that year the Supreme Court restored his right to travel abroad. When he performed in New York City in the spring of 1958, *Variety* wrote, "Paul Robeson, now in his 61st year, still is a commanding figure on the stage, a personality of magnetism and authority, able to excite and thrill a vast audience." Later in the year, he entertained in England and Russia, where he met with Soviet Premier Nikita Khrushchev.

In 1959 he portrayed Othello for the last time, at England's Stratford-on-Avon with Mary Ure, but ill health plagued him and he went to live in Russia. Robeson came back to the United States to live in 1963, and two years later he retired due to health problems. His wife, Essie, died that year and Robeson moved to Philadelphia to live with his sister. He remained a recluse (despite a few tributes in later years) until his death there on January 23, 1976, following a stroke. On his tombstone is printed, "The artist must elect to fight for freedom or slavery. I have made my choice. I had no alternative."

In 1978 James Earl Jones portrayed the entertainer in the Broadway show *Paul Robeson*, but Paul Robeson, Jr. protested that the play was "a pernicious perversion of the essence of Paul Robeson." Robeson was also the subject of several books, including *Paul Robeson* (1958) by Marie Seton, Dorothy Butler Gilliam's *Paul Robeson: All-American* (1976), and *Paul Robeson: A Biography* by Martin Bauml Duberman (1988). Since 1980, Bennet Guillory has starred in *Paul Robeson*, a one-character play with music, and in the fall of 1988, Avery Brooks had the title role in the revival of the decade-old *Paul Robeson* play. Over the years there have been several film documentaries about Robeson's controversial life: MY SONG GOES FORTH (1936), SONGS OF THE RIVER (1954), and PAUL ROBESON: PORTRAIT OF AN ARTIST (1979).

Today Paul Robeson's many contributions to culture as a singer and actor are all too easily overlooked by both his political admirers and detractors.

## Filmography

Body and Soul (Micheaux Film Corp, 1925)
Borderline (Kenneth McPherson, 1931)
The Emperor Jones (UA, 1931)
Sanders of the River (Br, 1935)
Show Boat (Univ, 1936)
Song of Freedom (Br, 1936)

Big Fella (Br, 1937)
King Solomon's Mines (Br, 1937)
Jericho [Dark Sands] (Br, 1937)
Proud Valley (Br, 1939)
Native Land (Frontier, 1942) (narrator)
Tales of Manhattan (20th–Fox, 1942)

## Broadway Plays

Simon the Cyrenian (1921)
Taboo (1922)
All God's Chillun Got Wings (1924)
The Emperor Jones (1925) (revival)
Black Boy (1926)

Porgy and Bess (1928) (replacement)
Show Boat (1932) (revival)
John Henry (1939)
Othello (1942) (revival)

## Album Discography

Ballads for Americans (Victrola AVM1-1736) w.
    John Charles Thomas
The Best of Paul Robeson (EMI 5041)
The Best of Paul Robeson (Regal 5193)
The Essential Paul Robeson (Vanguard Twofers
    57-8)
Famous Recordings (Pathé 240647)
Favorite Songs, Vols. 1–2 (Monitor 580/81)
The Golden Age of Paul Robeson (Music for
    Pleasure 5829)
Green Pastures (ASV 5027)
The Incomparable Voice of Paul Robeson (10"
    Odeon 1155)
A Lonesome Road (ASV 5047)
A Man and His Beliefs (Everest 3291)
Othello (Col SLK-153) [OC]
Paul Robeson (Verve 5055/64044)
Paul Robeson (World Record Club SH-123)
Paul Robeson at Carnegie Hall (Vanguard 9051/
    2035)

Paul Robeson in Live Performance (Col M-
    30424)
A Paul Robeson Song Recital (Supraphon
    10062)
Radio Broadcast Follies of 1935 (Amalgamated
    227) [ST/R]
Robeson (Vanguard 9037/2015)
Scandalize My Name (Book-of-the-Month
    Records 30-5647)
Show Boat (Col Special Products 55)
Show Boat (Vertinge 2004, Xeno 251) [ST]
Songs of Freedom (Odyssey 32160268)
Songs of My People (RCA LM-3292)
The Special Magic of Paul Robeson (MGM
    2317-070)
Spirituals and Robeson Recital of Popular
    Favorites (Col ML-4105)
Swing Low, Sweet Chariot (10" Col ML-2038)

# GINGER ROGERS

EARLY IN GINGER ROGERS' EXCEPTIONALLY LONG SHOW BUSINESS career, it would have seemed unlikely that this beautiful blonde, best known as Fred Astaire's dancing partner, would blossom into one of the screen's finest dramatic and comedic actresses. But that is just what occurred. There was little in Ginger Rogers' show business background to suggest that she was a performer of such resources. Yet she has to her credit not only an Oscar as Best Actress but also a string of top-notch pictures in which she gave sparkling performances. Further, she has not only excelled as a dancer and singer, but in addition to her seventy-plus film appearances, she has also triumphed on the stage both in the United States and abroad and has shown that she is more than a competent painter. Most of all, she learned from her mother how to survive professionally.

Today Ginger Rogers is considered to be a glamourous show business legend. Although she is nearing eighty, she has not only retained most of her looks, but, when the occasion merits, still performs. She has kept the enthusiasm and desire that first brought her stardom.

Ginger Rogers was born Virginia Katherine McMath in Independence, Missouri, on July 16, 1911, the daughter of Eddins and Lela Emogene (Owens) McMath; she was their middle child, and the only one of the three to survive. Her parents separated when she was small and she became the object of a custody battle between them. Her father (an electrical engineer) took her away from her mother on two occasions before the courts intervened on Lela's behalf. To support her daughter, Mrs. McMath took all kinds of work, including Hollywood script writing. In 1917 little Virginia was offered a part in a Fox film, but her mother refused to let her work after the first day, thus thwarting her youngster's possible screen career. Later, while a newspaper reporter in Kansas City, Lela married insurance agent John Rogers, who adopted Virginia, whose father had died that year.

During her high school years, after the family moved to Fort Worth, Texas, Virginia took part in school dramatics and took dancing lessons. In 1925 she was good enough to work as a substitute dancer for Eddie Foy when he played a vaudeville engagement in the city. After winning a Charleston contest, Ginger (as she was now called) toured with two other girls in Oklahoma and Texas, billed as "Ginger and Her Redheads." After that she sang in a Galveston café and did a short tour before working in shows in the South and Midwest. By 1928 she was earning $350 a week in vaudeville and that year she married entertainer Jack Pepper. Together they did an act called "Ginger and Pepper," before separating in 1929 (the same year Lela divorced John Rogers).

After working nearly a year in shows in Chicago and St. Louis, Ginger came to New

York City, singing with Paul Ash's orchestra. Although she failed to land a role in the Eddie Cantor show *Whoopee!*, she did appear in the musical comedy *Top Speed*, which opened on Broadway late in 1929. She got good notices doing the song "Hot and Bothered," and this led to a screen test at Paramount at the company's Astoria, Long Island, studio. Prior to this test, while still in vaudeville, Ginger appeared in a quartet of short subjects, including OFFICE BLUES (1930), in which she sang "We Can't Get Along" and "Dear Sir," and the 1930 short CAMPUS SWEETHEARTS with Rudy Vallee. At this time she had a brief romance with Vallee.

In her feature film debut at Paramount, Ginger enacted the role of a Jazz Age flapper in YOUNG MAN OF MANHATTAN (1930). She sang "I've Got 'It' But 'It' Don't Do Me No Good," and in one scene she introduced the catchphrase "Cigarette me, big boy," which became popular thereafter. *Variety* applauded Ginger for her performance, "playing it trimly and without excess." While still in *Top Speed*, she also had roles in Paramount's QUEEN HIGH (1930) and THE SAP FROM SYRACUSE (1930). Then she starred on Broadway, at $1,000 a week, in George and Ira Gershwin's *Girl Crazy* (1930), singing "Embraceable You" and "But Not for Me." It was during this show that she first met Fred Astaire, who helped stage one of her dance numbers.

*Girl Crazy* ran for 272 performances, and during its stand she continued to appear in Paramount movies like FOLLOW THE LEADER (1930), which also featured her *Girl Crazy* co-star Ethel Merman, HONOR AMONG LOVERS (1931), and the short HOLLYWOOD ON PARADE #1 (1932) in which she did a song she had composed, "The Gal Who Used to You." Leaving Paramount, Ginger moved to Los Angeles and signed with Pathé (which had given her a better offer) where she made a trio of films. The best cast her as entertainer Honey in CARNIVAL BOAT (1932), in which she sang "How I Could Go for You."

In 1932 Hollywood, she was named one of the Wampas Baby Stars of the year, and having been dropped by Pathé (which merged into RKO), she worked in a variety of feature films. Her first top-billed role came in the Monogram programmer mystery THE THIRTEENTH GUEST (1932), as a young woman almost murdered for her large inheritance. Just when it seemed that she was destined to play second leads for the remainder of her career, she won the role of wise-cracking Anytime Annie ("the only time she said no, she didn't hear the question") in the classic musical 42ND STREET (1933). She scored even bigger in GOLD DIGGERS OF 1933 (1933), singing "We're in the Money" as the chorine out to land a millionaire. The film was directed by Mervyn LeRoy, whom she had been dating before he married Doris Warner, daughter of one of the Warner brothers.

For RKO she starred in the amusing radio satire PROFESSIONAL SWEETHEART (1933), and no actress has ever looked more fetching in a brief nightie than did Ginger in that production. For the poverty-row outfit Allied, she headlined another old house murder mystery, the taut A SHRIEK IN THE NIGHT (1933), and then worked with Lew Ayres, to whom she was married from 1934 to 1940, in the comedy DON'T BET ON LOVE (1933) at Universal. Following this entry, she was with Jack Oakie in Paramount's SITTING PRETTY (1933).

By now RKO had signed her to a contract, and her big break came when Ginger was teamed with Fred Astaire—as second leads to stars Dolores Del Rio and Gene Raymond—in FLYING DOWN TO RIO (1933). Astaire and Rogers danced "The Carioca" and Ginger sang "Music Makes Me." They caused a sensation and movie patrons demanded another teaming of the dancing duo.

Between her first and second musical with Fred Astaire, Ginger Rogers made a half-dozen pictures, ranging from the nice girl who loses her beau (Joel McCrea) to a rich woman (Marian Nixon) in CHANCE AT HEAVEN (1933) to a free living co-ed in FINISHING SCHOOL (1934), a radio star in 20 MILLION SWEETHEARTS (1934), in which she sang "Out for No Good" and dueted with Dick Powell on "I'll String Along with You," and a chorus girl involved in a love triangle in UPPER WORLD (1934). For the latter film she sang "Shake Your Powder Puff."

Finally, in 1934, RKO paired Fred Astaire and Ginger in their first starring vehicle, THE GAY DIVORCEE, and in it they introduced the popular dance "The Continental" and Ginger sang "Don't Let It Bother You." The film's breezy plot and fine songs, plus the exquisite dancing of Ginger and Fred, made the film very successful and it became the springboard for seven more teamings of the two at RKO. Her sparkling personality did much to lighten Astaire's screen image, and together they were magical. Ginger starred with Francis Lederer in the smooth romantic comedy ROMANCE IN MANHATTAN (1934) as a shop girl who falls in love with an immigrant (Lederer). Irene Dunne was the top star of ROBERTA (1935), but it was Astaire and Rogers who danced to the show's most enduring song, "Smoke Gets in Your Eyes," plus "I Won't Dance" and "Let's Begin."

Unlike Astaire, Rogers smartly chose to work in other screen vehicles outside their dancing forays. She co-starred with William Powell in the mystery-romance STAR OF MIDNIGHT (1935) before starring with Astaire in what may be their most popular vehicle, TOP HAT (1935). They danced beautifully to "Cheek to Cheek," "Isn't This a Lovely Day," and "The Piccolino." Along with "No Strings," which Astaire sang in the feature, Ginger recorded this trio of songs for Decca Records. For the same label she also dueted with Johnny Mercer on "Eeny, Meeny, Miney, Mo." Ginger also starred in RKO's comedy IN PERSON (1935), singing "I Got a New Lease on Life," "Don't Mention Love to Me," and "Out of Sight, Out of Mind." She made guest appearances on Ben Bernie's NBC radio program as well as on CBS's "Shell Chateau" starring Al Jolson. She and Astaire appeared together on Bing Crosby's variety program. Meanwhile, ever-present Lela Rogers continued to manage her daughter's career. At RKO, Lela was kept busy developing new talent; in the 1940s she would write fiction books centered around Ginger's character for Whitman publishers.

Although Ginger wanted to branch out into dramatic roles, RKO instead put her in three consecutive musicals with Fred Astaire. In FOLLOW THE FLEET (1936) she sang "Let Yourself Go" and she and Astaire danced to "Let's Face the Music and Dance." This was followed by SWING TIME (1936), with Ginger performing "A Fine Romance" while she and her co-star danced to "Waltz in Swing Time" and "The Way You Look Tonight" (the song won an Oscar). For the fast-moving SHALL WE DANCE? (1937) Ginger sang "They

All Laughed" and the duo danced to "They Can't Take That Away from Me" and "Let's Call the Whole Thing Off," the latter on roller skates. Rogers demonstrated her abilities as a dramatic actress when, as the apparently brazen actress living at a theatrical boardinghouse, she outshone Katharine Hepburn in STAGE DOOR (1937). Regarding her star quality, *Time* magazine assessed, "Less eccentric than Carole Lombard, less worldly-wise than Myrna Loy, less impudent than Joan Blondell, Ginger Rogers has a careless self-sufficiency they lack."

At $3,000 weekly, she headlined two RKO comedies, HAVING WONDERFUL TIME (1938) and VIVACIOUS LADY (1938). In the latter she sang "You'll Be Reminded of Me." This was followed by her final RKO pictures with Astaire, CAREFREE (1938) and THE STORY OF VERNON AND IRENE CASTLE (1939). The former had her doing "The Yam" with Astaire as well as performing with him on "Change Partners" and "The Night Is Filled with Music" and doing a solo on "I Used to Be Color Blind" (which with "The Yam" she recorded for Bluebird Records). In the latter film the duo played the famous husband-and-wife dance team in a well-executed but not financially successful musical drama. Ginger sang "The Yama Yama Man" and she and Astaire danced to "Only When You're in My Arms," in addition to performing many other ballroom routines.

Fred Astaire, Edward Everett Horton, and Ginger Rogers in SHALL WE DANCE? (1937)

Following her teaming with Astaire, which made her one of the screen's most popular performers, Ginger Rogers starred in two comedies: the zesty BACHELOR MOTHER (1939), as a salesgirl thought to be an unwed mother, and the amusing FIFTH AVENUE GIRL (1939), in which she was hired by a lonely married millionaire (Walter Connolly) to be his companion. (She had initially rejected BACHELOR MOTHER and had gone on suspension for refusing to appear in it; eventually she relented under pressure.) Dramatically, she gave what might well be her best screen performance as the girl from the wrong side of the tracks in PRIMROSE PATH (1940). Although she deserved an Oscar nomination for that film, she was nominated instead for KITTY FOYLE (1940), about the trials and tribulations of a salesgirl. (Rogers seemed to make a specialty of playing working girls.) In a year of heavy competition, she won the Academy Award as Best Actress. Sandwiched between the two dramas was the moderate comedy LUCKY PARTNERS (1940) with Ronald Colman. However, the later TOM, DICK AND HARRY (1941) proved far more inventive.

Her new RKO contract was nonexclusive and she signed for a trio of Paramount Pictures. The first of these, THE MAJOR AND THE MINOR (1942), used her forte of acting the part of a young girl to perfection, while 20th Century–Fox's ROXIE HART (1942) cast her as a gum-chewing babe on trial for murder. She and Henry Fonda were in one of the several episodes of Fox's TALES OF MANHATTAN (1942). She traded looks and quips with Cary Grant in RKO's ONCE UPON A HONEYMOON (1942) and went noble and teary in RKO's TENDER COMRADE (1943), which contained more leftist dialogue than patriotic Ginger liked. While RKO was promoting Ginger Rogers as a major dramatic actress (many of their announced vehicles for her, such as RAIN and SISTER CARRIE, never materialized), she played in a series of overblown projects. The musical LADY IN THE DARK (1944—long in production) was not appreciated, and there seemed something too grand about her movie star characterization in the hubbub of MGM's WEEKEND AT THE WALDORF (1945). During World War II, Rogers made several short films for the war effort and toured with the USO where she met and married (in 1943) Jack Briggs, a twenty-two-year-old Marine, with whom she purchased a ranch in Oregon.

Ginger also remained active in radio. As far back as 1936 she had appeared with Warren William in "The Curtain Rises" on "Lux Radio Theatre," and on October 1, 1939, she starred with Clark Gable and Margaret Lindsay in "Imperfect Lady" on "Gulf Screen Theatre." She repeated her movie roles in "Vivacious Lady" on "Front Line Theatre" in 1943 and "Lady in the Dark" on "Lux Radio Theatre" in 1945, as well as guest-starred on the syndicated show "Command Performance." In 1946 she performed "Kitty Foyle" on "Academy Award Theatre" on CBS.

She earned close to $300,000 in 1946, but after the war, Ginger's film career suffered from her being cast in the inaccurate historical (melo)drama MAGNIFICENT DOLL (1946), although she made a most believable Dolly Madison. She appeared to be straining in the strained comedy IT HAD TO BE YOU (1947). Things were better when, after a two-year layoff, she (replacing Judy Garland) and Fred Astaire teamed for the final time in THE BARKLEYS OF BROADWAY (1949), in which they reprised "They Can't Take That Away from Me." It gave her screen career a new lease on life and she made two modest productions in 1950 at Warner Bros.: STORM WARNINGS and PERFECT STRANGERS. She returned to Broadway in 1951 for a brief run in *Love and Let Love* and on radio she did episodes of "Suspense" and "Cavalcade of America."

Now in her forties, she experienced a career upswing in 1952 when she starred with Cary Grant in the crazy comedy MONKEY BUSINESS and played the ambitious ex-silent movie star in DREAMBOAT, in which she sang "You'll Never Know." Ginger had divorced Jack Briggs in 1949, and in 1953 she wed twenty-five-year-old actor Jacques Bergerac, with whom she co-starred in the British-made TWIST OF FATE (1954). The actress came to TV in 1954 in "Tonight at 8:30" on NBC's "Producer's Showcase," but her screen roles were only average, and THE FIRST TRAVELING SALESLADY (1956), which had been rejected by Mae West, was downright dull. It was one of the last productions made by her old alma mater, RKO. Rogers did more TV work, on "Climax," "The Jack Benny Program," and "Person to Person," and had her own CBS-TV special in 1958. That same year she toured in *Bell, Book and Candle* with William Marshall. She divorced Bergerac in 1958 and married Marshall in 1961 (they were divorced in 1971). Meanwhile, her pre-Broadway show *The Pink Jungle* (1959), about the cosmetics industry, died on the road.

In 1963 Rogers starred in an unsuccessful TV pilot, "A Love Affair Just for Three," and she and Marshall started a film production unit in Jamaica. For that company she starred in the little-seen feature THE CONFESSION in 1964, playing a madam. The next year she received acclaim for her role as the mother (replacing Judy Garland) in the Electronovision version of HARLOW, but it was her last film to date. That year she also played the queen in the CBS-TV special "Cinderella" (with Walter Pidgeon as the king) and replaced Carol Channing in the Broadway production of *Hello, Dolly!* in August 1965. At the time of this stage triumph she said, "I have spent my life doing things created by someone else. There is no stigma in doing something someone else has already done. . . . But then I'm a kid who has turned down more good things than anybody you know." Thereafter, she toured with *Hello, Dolly!* through 1967, but rejected the part of the old-time Broadway star (a role begun by Judy Garland, but finished by Susan Hayward) in VALLEY OF THE DOLLS (1967).

In 1969 she opened in London in *Mame* and played for fifty-six weeks at a salary of $12,000 per week. She then toured the United States in 1971 in *Coco* (which Katharine Hepburn had done on Broadway) and in 1972 signed a seven-year deal to act as a traveling fashion consultant for J. C. Penney stores. In 1973 she appeared with Fred Astaire on a TV tribute to the entertainer. In the mid-1970s she began her successful nightclub act, which was taped for Italian television, and toured in *No, No Nanette* in 1975 and *40 Carats* the next year. In 1977 her mother died. In 1978 she recorded a record album in England for EMI called *Miss Ginger Rogers*, in which she reprised many of the songs associated with her career.

Rogers did guest shots on such TV shows as "Here's Lucy" (1971), "The Love Boat" (1979), "Glitter" (1984), and "Hotel" (1985), and when not on the road with her club act, divided her time between a Palm Springs home and her six-hundred-acre Oregon ranch. In 1988 she sued unsuccessfully the Italian producers of the film GINGER AND FRED for invasion of privacy. Late in the year she returned to TV, looking lovely, as the host of the Disney Channel's seven-part Fred Astaire film festival, "Best of Hollywood." Ginger is still at work on her long-announced autobiography.

Once, the inestimable Ginger was asked what she would prefer to be remembered for. She answered, "I want nothing more than that Ginger Rogers be known as a trailblazer for quality—for all things of the highest levels of goodness, understanding, communication, morality, cleanliness, and consideration."

## Filmography

A Day of a Man of Affairs (RKO, 1929) (s)
Campus Sweethearts (RKO, 1930) (s)
A Night in a Dormitory (Pathé, 1930) (s)
Office Blues (Par, 1930) (s)
Young Man of Manhattan (Par, 1930)
Queen High (Par, 1930)
The Sap from Syracuse [The Sap Abroad] (Par, 1930)
Follow the Leader (Par, 1930)
Honor Among Lovers (Par, 1931)
The Tip Off [Looking for Trouble] (Pathé, 1931)
Suicide Fleet (Pathé, 1931)
Carnival Boat (RKO, 1932)
The Tenderfoot (FN, 1932)
Hat Check Girl [Embassy Girl] (Fox, 1932)
You Said a Mouthful (FN, 1932)
The Thirteenth Guest (Mon, 1932)
Hollywood on Parade #1 (Par, 1932) (s)
Screen Snapshots #12 (Col, 1932) (s)
Broadway Bad [Her Reputation] (Fox, 1933)
Professional Sweetheart [Imaginary Sweetheart] (RKO, 1933)
A Shriek in the Night (Allied, 1933)
Hollywood on Parade #3 (Par, 1933) (s)
42nd Street (WB, 1933)
Gold Diggers of 1933 (WB, 1933)
Don't Bet on Love (Univ, 1933)
Sitting Pretty (Par, 1933)
Flying Down to Rio (RKO, 1933)
Chance at Heaven (RKO, 1933)
Rafter Romance (RKO, 1934)
Finishing School (RKO, 1934)
Change of Heart (Fox, 1934)
20 Million Sweethearts (FN, 1934)
Upper World (WB, 1934)
Hollywood on Parade #13 (Par, 1934) (s)

The Gay Divorcee [The Gay Divorce] (RKO, 1934)
Romance in Manhattan (RKO, 1934)
Top Hat (RKO, 1935)
Roberta (RKO, 1935)
Star of Midnight (RKO, 1935)
In Person (RKO, 1935)
Follow the Fleet (RKO, 1936)
Swing Time (RKO, 1936)
Holiday Greetings (Unk, 1937) (s)
Shall We Dance? (RKO, 1937)
Stage Door (RKO, 1937)
Vivacious Lady (RKO, 1938)
Having Wonderful Time (RKO, 1938)
Carefree (RKO, 1938)
Bachelor Mother (RKO, 1939)
The Story of Vernon and Irene Castle (RKO, 1939)
Fifth Avenue Girl (RKO, 1939)
Lucky Partners (RKO, 1940)
Picture People #1 (RKO, 1940) (s)
Primrose Path (RKO, 1940)
Kitty Foyle (RKO, 1940)
Picture People #10 (RKO, 1941) (s)
Tom, Dick and Harry (RKO, 1941)
Tales of Manhattan (20th–Fox, 1942)
Once upon a Honeymoon (RKO, 1942)
Roxie Hart (20th–Fox, 1942)
Picture People #9 (RKO, 1942) (s)
The Major and the Minor (Par, 1942)
Show Business at War (20th–Fox, 1943) (s)
Tender Comrade (RKO, 1943)
Safeguarding Military Information (Dept. of the Army, 1943) (s)
Battle Stations (20th–Fox, 1944) (s) (narrator)
Lady in the Dark (Par, 1944)
I'll Be Seeing You (UA, 1944)

Ginger Rogers Finds a Bargain (Unk, 1944) (s)
Weekend at the Waldorf (MGM, 1945)
Heartbeat (RKO, 1946)
Magnificent Doll (Univ, 1946)
It Had to Be You (Col, 1947)
The Barkleys of Broadway (MGM, 1949)
Storm Warning (WB, 1950)
Perfect Strangers [Too Dangerous to Love] (WB, 1950)
The Groom Wore Spurs (Univ, 1951)
We're Not Married (20th–Fox, 1952)
Dreamboat (20th–Fox, 1952)

Monkey Business (20th–Fox, 1952)
Forever Female (Par, 1953)
Hollywood's Great Entertainers (Col, 1953) (s)
Black Widow (20th–Fox, 1954)
Twist of Fate [Beautiful Stranger] (UA, 1954)
Tight Spot (Col, 1955)
The First Traveling Saleslady (RKO, 1956)
Teenage Rebel (20th–Fox, 1956)
Oh, Men! Oh, Women! (20th–Fox, 1957)
The Confession [Quick! Let's Get Married] (Golden Eagle, 1964)
Harlow (Magna, 1965)

## Broadway Plays

Top Speed (1929)
Girl Crazy (1930)

Love and Let Love (1951)
Hello, Dolly! (1965) (replacement)

## Album Discography

Alice in Wonderland (10" Decca DL-5040)
The Barkleys of Broadway (MGM SES-51ST, Sountrak 116) [ST]
Cinderella (Col OS-2730165) [ST/TV]
Flying Down to Rio/Carefree (CIF 3004, Sandy Hook 2010) [ST]
Follow the Fleet (Caliban 6024, Sandy Hook 2099, Scarce Rarities 5505) [ST]
The Gay Divorcee/Top Hat (Sountrak 105) [ST]
Ginger Rogers (Curtain Calls 100/21)
Hello, Ginger (Citel 2201)
Jolie and Ginger Live (Elgog 887) w. Al Jolson
Kitty Foyle (Mark 56 675, Nostalgia Lane NLR-1504) [ST/R]
Miss Ginger Rogers (Odeon/EMI 1002)

Rare Recordings (Sandy Hook 2042)
Roberta (Amalgamated 218, CIF 3011, Sandy Hook 2061) [ST]
Roberta/Top Hat (Star-Tone 204) [ST/R]
Shall We Dance?/Swing Time (Sandy Hook 2028, Sountrak 106) [ST]
The Story of Vernon and Irene Castle (Caliban 6000) [ST]
Swing Time/The Gay Divorcee (EMI 101) [ST]
Swing Time/The Gay Divorcee/Top Hat/Shall We Dance? (Pathé 184-95807-08) [ST]
Top Hat/Shall We Dance? (EMI 102) [ST]
Top Hat, White Tie and Golf Shoes (Facit 142) w. Fred Astaire, Bing Crosby
20 Million Sweethearts (Amalgamated 223) [ST]

# ROY ROGERS

FOR MORE THAN A HALF CENTURY, ROY ROGERS, "THE KING OF THE Cowboys," has epitomized the image of the white-hatted hero, astride a majestic horse, righting the wrongs of the West. To some, it is puzzling that his career has survived for so long. However, upon closer examination, it is evident that behind the easygoing exterior is a man of many talents. While his likable, relaxed acting style may belie his thespian abilities, it is obvious that he is a good singer and a charismatic performer. Moreover, he is a competent songwriter (with more than three dozen songs to his credit) and an astute businessman who has amassed a fortune in excess of $50 million. Today, Roy Rogers is content to make only an occasional appearance in the limelight. However, because his films and old TV shows have been revived so successfully on cable television, he is today almost as much of a hero to contemporary youth as he was to their parents and grandparents.

Today, Roy Rogers' birthplace is literally second base for the Cincinnati Reds baseball team in their ballpark. However, on November 5, 1911, it was a boardinghouse, where he was born Leonard Franklin Slye to Andrew and Mattie (Womack) Slye. He was the third of four children; the other three were girls. When Leonard was two, the family moved to a houseboat near Portsmouth on the Ohio River, and five years later to a farm near Duck Run. On the farm the boy developed a lifelong love of horses and, thanks to his family's interest, a love of music. He could play the guitar at age eight and was soon calling square dances, singing in public, and yodeling. In high school, the boy excelled at sports and acting, but dropped out in his junior year to make $35 a week working in a shoe factory. In 1930, the family moved to California to join the Slyes' oldest child, Mary. Leonard worked at odd jobs as a truck driver and a fruit picker.

In Los Angeles, in the summer of 1931, he won a radio amateur contest and obtained a job with an instrumental group called The Rocky Mountaineers. Convincing the group that they needed a singer, he placed a newspaper ad and was very impressed with one of the applicants, Bob Nolan. Soon Slye and Nolan formed a trio with Bill "Slumber" Nichols; they were known as The Singing Rocky Mountaineers. When Nolan left the group in 1932, he was replaced by Tim Spencer, and the new trio then joined another group, The International Cowboys; they toured the Southwest as The O-Bar-O Cowboys. The only substantial thing to come from the trip was Slye's meeting Arlene Wilkens, who would become his second wife.

Back in Los Angeles, the group disbanded, but Slye soon reunited with Spencer and Nolan as The Pioneer Trio. They landed a singing job on Los Angeles radio station KFWB and were so successful that they added to the group fiddle player Hugh Farr and his brother, guitarist Karl Farr. Between 1934, first as The Pioneer Trio and then as The Sons of the Pioneers, they recorded more than eighty radio transcriptions for Standard, with Slye on vocals and guitar. In 1935 they appeared with a group called The Daughters of the Pioneers on the syndicated radio show "The Open Spaces." The group was soon gaining attention by their singing not only of traditional folk and Western tunes, but also of some of Bob Nolan's compositions, such as "Tumbling Tumbleweeds" and "Way Out There."

In 1935, The Sons of the Pioneers made their motion picture debut in the Liberty feature THE OLD HOMESTEAD and the trio was soon performing in a couple of comedy shorts, SLIGHTLY STATIC and WAY UP THAR (both 1935), along with appearing in two Charles Starrett and two Dick Foran "B" Westerns. They also appeared in Paramount's "A" budget feature RHYTHM ON THE RANGE (1936) with Bing Crosby and Frances Farmer. In 1935 the group began recording for Decca Records, and in the summer of 1936 they were a sensation at the Texas Centennial in Dallas. Back in Hollywood, they appeared in two Gene Autry Westerns at Republic: THE BIG SHOW (1936) and THE OLD CORRAL (1936). In 1937 Slye tested for the lead in a series of Westerns at Universal. Although associate producer Paul Malvern wanted him in the part, the assignment went to Bob Baker. Later that year he tested at Republic and won a player's contract. Slye dropped out of the Pioneers, offering old pal Pat Brady as his replacement. Republic changed his name to Dick Weston, and as such he appeared in The Three Mesquiteers series oater WILD HORSE RODEO (1937) and Gene Autry's THE OLD BARN DANCE (1938). When Autry then gave the studio contract troubles, Leonard Slye was groomed as his successor and renamed Roy Rogers (Rogers from Will; Roy because it went well with Rogers) and was handed the lead in UNDER WESTERN STARS (1938), an intended Autry vehicle. The film gave Rogers an opportunity to sing Johnny Marvin's song "Dust," which was nominated for an Academy Award. The film was a huge success and an auspicious starring debut for Roy Rogers. *Variety* reported, "In Roy Rogers producers present a cowboy who looks like a wrangler, is a looker, an actor and a singer . . . he lives up to every expectation, and then some. His appeal to femme mob can also be counted upon."

Meanwhile, Gene Autry soon returned to the Republic fold, but Rogers was kept on as a studio star. However, his vehicles were second best in comparison to Autry's. Mainly Rogers appeared in pseudo-historical dramas or period pieces. For a time, the studio teamed him with pretty Mary Hart for five features, but a much more successful pairing came when veteran character performer George "Gabby" Hayes joined the series in SOUTHWARD HO!, Hart's last entry, in 1939. The cantankerous ("your darn tootin'!") Hayes added zest to the Rogers films and the duo would remain a team for five years.

By 1939, Roy Rogers was ranked as the number three money-making Western star by the *Motion Picture Herald*. By 1941, Rogers had moved into number two position, after Gene Autry. When Autry entered World War II military service in 1942, Rogers became the number one money-making cowboy star, a postion he would hold until the poll's demise in 1954. But though his pictures were top profitmakers for Republic, Rogers himself was poorly paid. His initial starring contract called for him to earn $150 weekly, and by the time his last studio film was made in 1951, the figure had climbed to only $350. So stingy was Republic that the studio would not even hire a secretary to answer the huge volume of fan mail he received. In order to make money, Roy Rogers supplemented his film activity with personal appearances, radio work, and recordings. In 1937 he had cut a few unissued records as Dick Weston for the American Record Company (ARC), the label on which The Sons of the Pioneers recorded at the time. After leaving the Pioneers in 1938, he began recording as Roy Rogers for ARC. He remained with that company until 1940, when he joined Decca, with whom he stayed until 1945, when he joined RCA Victor. Rogers had married Arlene Wilkins in 1936 (an earlier marriage to Lucile Ascolese in 1932 had lasted only a short time); in 1941 they adopted a daughter, Cheryl Darlene, and in 1943 their own daughter, Linda Lou, was born.

Due to Roy Rogers' increasing popularity, his Republic Westerns began to have bigger budgets and better songs. He was even given an important acting role in the studio's lavish historical production DARK COMMAND (1940). In 1943 he made KING OF THE COWBOYS, a fine spy story in a modern Western setting, and the tag stuck. He was soon featured on the cover of *Life* magazine. Unfortunately, Herbert J. Yates, Republic's head,

Roy Rogers in BRAZIL (1944)

chose to turn Rogers' films into lavish musical Westerns, and the gaudily staged production numbers often robbed these later pictures of their needed action. On several occasions, the films' plots came to a halt five minutes before the end in order to insert musical interludes, with Rogers often garbed in outlandish sequined suits. The star, however, retained his traditional, likable persona, and his pictures managed to survive the Yates–*Oklahoma!* phase before they returned to the more standardized, but better and more entertaining, genre plots.

In 1944 Rogers was paired with singer Dale Evans in THE COWBOY AND THE SE-NORITA. The public liked them together, and Dale remained his teammate for three years. In that period, he also performed guest spots in Republic's LAKE PLACID SERENADE (1944) and OUT CALIFORNIA WAY (1946), as well as in Warner Bros.' HOLLYWOOD CANTEEN (1944). In the latter, he introduced "Don't Fence Me In," which was the title of his own 1945 starring movie.

During the World War II years, Roy Rogers devoted much time to entertaining troops and he also appeared in a number of radio shows, such as "Melody Roundup," "Music for Millions," "The Chase and Sanborn Hour," "The RCA Victor Show," "Here's to Veterans," "Command Performance," "G.I. Journal," "The Kraft Music Hall," and many others. In 1944 he began starring on his own "The Roy Rogers Show" on Mutual. In 1946 the program moved to NBC for a season. From 1948 to 1951 it was back on Mutual, and then, from 1951 to 1955, the show was again on NBC. In its early years, the series was a music-variety program with a short Western dramatic story, often with guest villains like Porter Hall, and it featured George "Gabby" Hayes and The Sons of the Pioneers. After she became part of Rogers' feature films, Dale Evans joined the radio show as well, and the musical accompaniment was by Foy Willing and The Riders of the Purple Sage. In its last years, the show was mainly a dramatic one, with a song or two by Rogers and Evans and The Roy Rogers Riders. For most of its long run, the show offered premiums for listeners, mostly toy items endorsed by Rogers. In addition, the character of Roy Rogers was featured in a number of fiction books published by the Whitman Publishing Company from 1945 to 1957. During that time Rogers was also featured by Whitman in a series of children's books and Better Little Books. His character was also adapted for a successful series of comic books. Throughout the 1940s and 1950s, he realized a fortune from the various items he endorsed and promoted.

In 1946, Rogers' wife, Arlene, died after the birth of their son, Dusty, and the heartbroken star was left with three small children to raise. After a time he became involved romantically with Dale Evans and they were married in 1947. They have had a long union, but it has been filled with its share of tragedy: the death of their only natural child, Robin, in 1952, the loss of their nine-year-old adopted daughter, Debbie, in a church bus crash in 1964, and the death of their adopted son, Sandy, in 1966 from alcohol poisoning.

After her marriage to Rogers, Dale Evans left the film series for a time and Jane Frazee took over as his leading lady. In 1948 he and The Sons of the Pioneers, who had appeared in many of his Republic Westerns, did the "Pecos Bill" segment of Walt Disney's MELODY TIME (1948). In their later years, Rogers' series Westerns took on a more austere look, although they were still supplemented by music. In 1951 he made his final series Western, PALS OF THE GOLDEN WEST, and then, in 1952, co-starred with Bob Hope and Jane Russell in Paramount's SON OF PALEFACE.

With the end of his Republic contract, Rogers transferred his character (after a successful court fight to keep his old movies off TV, although the decision was later overturned) to television with "The Roy Rogers Show," which ran on NBC from 1951 to 1957 for nearly one hundred half-hour programs. Dale Evans co-starred, as did Pat Brady and Rogers' beautiful Palomino horse, Trigger (who was in all of Rogers' movies), and the dog Bullet. In 1954 Rogers guest-starred on the "Cavalcade of America" teleseries, and in the 1950s he and Dale often performed on TV variety shows like those of Milton Berle and Perry Como.

During the 1950s Roy Rogers also underwent a conversion to a strong Christian faith and became a follower of Norman Vincent Peale and Billy Graham; this transition was no doubt due in part to the strong religious influence of his wife. During the 1950s Rogers and Evans also kept a busy pace of personal appearances, including rodeos, and overseas tours, such as to England in 1953. After undergoing heart surgery in the late 1950s, however, he began to slow the pace of his professional life. In 1962 he and his wife headlined "The Roy Rogers and Dale Evans Show" on ABC-TV, but the variety program lasted only three months. Three years earlier he had put in a guest appearance in the Bob Hope comedy Western ALIAS JESSE JAMES (1959).

From 1945 to 1952 Rogers had recorded with RCA Victor, often in tandem with Dale, and in the mid-1950s they made numerous children's records for the Golden label. In the late 1950s they cut religious albums for RCA, and in 1962 they did *The Bible Tells Me So* for Capitol, also cutting a Christmas LP for that company in 1967. During the 1960s they raised their large family on a ranch near Chatsworth, California, and continued making personal appearance tours and TV guest shots. Due to his long association with manager Art Rush and wise investments, the Rogerses had become very wealthy. In 1970 he hosted the syndicated TV series "Let's Go Hunting" and that year he recorded again for Capitol, this time coming out with a series of best-selling singles, such as "Money Can't Buy Love" and "Leavenworth," plus three best-selling albums. In 1973 and 1977 the Rogerses cut duet religious albums for Word Records. In 1976 Rogers did an album for 20th Century–Fox Records, which included the most popular recording of his career, "Hoppy, Gene and Me," recorded in 1975. The mid-1970s also found him hosting the syndicated TV show "The Great Movie Cowboys," the opening of the first of nearly two hundred Roy Rogers (fast-food) Restaurants around the country, and his return to feature films in the drama MACKINTOSH AND T.J. in 1975. He won critical kudos for his performance as the aging cowboy who helps a young boy find himself, but this family-oriented picture did not earn wide distribution. In 1980, selections from Rogers and The Sons of the Pioneers were heard on the soundtrack of SMOKEY AND THE BANDIT II.

One of Roy Rogers' pet projects was his career museum, which opened in Apple Valley, California, in 1967 but moved permanently to Victorville in the 1970s. Rogers has devoted a great deal of time to the museum, which houses memorabilia from his and Dale

Evans' careers as well as from Rogers' many and diverse collections (plus Trigger and Bullet, who are stuffed and on display). He has frequently been on hand to visit with the museum's many visitors. He also raises horses, including Trigger's offspring (Trigger died in 1965 at the age of thirty-three). While Rogers concedes that he is a homebody who prefers to leave the family traveling to the more outgoing Dale, he has been quite active in the 1980s, including guesting (in 1983 and 1984) as himself in two action-packed episodes of the TV series "The Fall Guy." In 1984 he and Dale and Roy, Jr. (known as Dusty) cut an album, *Many Happy Trails*, for Teletex Records, and the next year he and Dale began hosting "Happy Trails Theatre" on The Nashville Network. In 1988 Rogers' 1950s TV program resurfaced on the Christian Broadcasting Network's Family Channel with new opening and closing segments filmed by Rogers at his Victorville museum. In 1988 he was inducted into the Country Music Hall of Fame.

The saying "good guys finish last" certainly does not apply to Roy Rogers. For more than half a century, he has kept his popularity intact. Despite all his success, he has never lost touch with himself or the world around him. He would be the last to believe in the glitter and glamour of film stardom, instead appreciating and finding reward in his faith and the joys of living.

## Filmography

### As Leonard Slye:

The Old Homestead (Liberty, 1935)
Slightly Static (MGM, 1935) (s)
Way Up Thar (Educational, 1935) (s)
Radio Scout (Vita, 1935) (s)
The Big Show (Rep, 1936)
Gallant Defender (Col, 1936)
Lonesome Trailer (Vita, 1936) (s)

Song of the Saddle (WB, 1936)
The California Mail (WB, 1936)
Rhythm on the Range (Par, 1936)
The Mysterious Avenger (Col, 1936)
The Old Corral [Texas Serenade] (Rep, 1936)
The Old Wyoming Trail (Col, 1937)
A Feud There Was (Vita, 1938) (s)

### As Dick Weston:

Wild Horse Rodeo (Rep, 1937)
The Old Barn Dance (Rep, 1938)

### As Roy Rogers:

Under Western Stars (Rep, 1938)
Come on Rangers (Rep, 1938)
Shine On Harvest Moon (Rep, 1938)
Billy the Kid Returns (Rep, 1938)
Rough Riders' Roundup (Rep, 1939)
Frontier Pony Express (Rep, 1939)
Southward Ho! (Rep, 1939)
In Old Caliente (Rep, 1939)

The Arizona Kid (Rep, 1939)
Wall Street Cowboy (Rep, 1939)
Saga of Death Valley (Rep, 1939)
Days of Jesse James (Rep, 1939)
Jeepers Creepers [Money Isn't Everything] (Rep, 1939)
Dark Command (Rep, 1940)
The Carson City Kid (Rep, 1940)

627

The Ranger and the Lady (Rep, 1940)
Colorado (Rep, 1940)
Young Buffalo Bill (Rep, 1940)
Rodeo Dough (MGM, 1940) (s)
Young Bill Hickok (Rep, 1940)
Border Legion (Rep, 1940)
Robin Hood of the Pecos (Rep, 1941)
Meet Roy Rogers (Rep, 1941) (s)
In Old Cheyenne (Rep, 1941)
Arkansas Judge [False Witness] (Rep, 1941)
Nevada City (Rep, 1941)
Sheriff of Tombstone (Rep, 1941)
Screen Snapshots #8 (1941) (s)
Picture People #2 (RKO, 1941) (s)
Bad Man of Deadwood (Rep, 1941)
Jesse James at Bay (Rep, 1941)
Picture People #10 (RKO, 1941) (s)
Red River Valley (Rep, 1942)
Man from Cheyenne (Rep, 1942)
South of Santa Fe (Rep, 1942)
Sunset on the Desert (Rep, 1942)
Romance on the Range (Rep, 1942)
Sons of the Pioneers (Rep, 1942)
Sunset Serenade (Rep, 1942)
Heart of the Golden West (Rep, 1942)
Picture People #7 (RKO, 1942) (s)
Ridin' down the Canyon (Rep, 1942)
King of the Cowboys (Rep, 1943)
Idaho (Rep, 1943)
Song of Texas (Rep, 1943)
Silver Spurs (Rep, 1943)
Screen Snapshots #7 (Col, 1943) (s)
Man from Music Mountain (Rep, 1943)
Hands Across the Border (Rep, 1943)
The Cowboy and the Senorita (Rep, 1944)
The Yellow Rose of Texas (Rep, 1944)
Song of Nevada (Rep, 1944)
San Fernando Valley (Rep, 1944)
Lights of Old Santa Fe (Rep, 1944)
Brazil (Rep, 1944)
Hollywood Canteen (WB, 1944)
Lake Placid Serenade (Rep, 1944)
Bells of Rosarita (Rep, 1945)
Utah (Rep, 1945)
Sunset in El Dorado (Rep, 1945)
The Man from Oklahoma (Rep, 1945)

Don't Fence Me In (Rep, 1945)
Along the Navajo Trail (Rep, 1945)
Song of Arizona (Rep, 1946)
Rainbow over Texas (Rep, 1946)
My Pal Trigger (Rep, 1946)
Under Nevada Skies (Rep, 1946)
Roll On Texas Moon (Rep, 1946)
Home in Oklahoma (Rep, 1946)
Out California Way (Rep, 1946)
Heldorado (Rep, 1946)
Hit Parade of 1947 (Rep, 1947)
Apache Rose (Rep, 1947)
Bells of San Angelo (Rep, 1947)
Springtime in the Sierras (Rep, 1947)
On the Old Spanish Trail (Rep, 1947)
Under California Skies (Rep, 1947)
Nighttime in Nevada (Rep, 1948)
Grand Canyon Trail (Rep, 1948)
The Gay Ranchero (Rep, 1948)
The Far Frontier (Rep, 1948)
Eyes of Texas (Rep, 1948)
Melody Time (RKO, 1948) (voice only)
Susanna Pass (Rep, 1949)
Down Dakota Way (Rep, 1949)
The Golden Stallion (Rep, 1949)
Bells of Coronado (Rep, 1949)
Twilight in the Sierras (Rep, 1950)
Trigger, Jr. (Rep, 1950)
Sunset in the West (Rep, 1950)
North of the Great Divide (Rep, 1950)
Trail of Robin Hood (Rep, 1950)
Spoilers of the Plains (Rep, 1951)
Heart of the Rockies (Rep, 1951)
In Old Amarillo (Rep, 1951)
South of Caliente (Rep, 1951)
Pals of the Golden West (Rep, 1951)
Screen Snapshots #205 (Col, 1952) (s)
Son of Paleface (Par, 1952)
Screen Snapshots #24 (Col, 1954) (s)
Alias Jesse James (UA, 1959)
Outdoor Rambling (Dick Chamberlin Productions, 1972) (documentary)
Mackintosh and T. J. (Penland, 1975)
Smokey and the Bandit II (Univ, 1980) (voice only)

## Radio Series

The Open Spaces (Synd, 1935)

The Roy Rogers Show (Mutual, 1944–45; NBC, 1946–47; Mutual, 1948–51; NBC, 1951–55)

## TV Series

The Roy Rogers Show (NBC, 1951–57)

The Roy Rogers and Dale Evans Show (ABC, 1962)

Let's Go Hunting (Synd, 1970)

The Great Movie Cowboys (Synd, 1975)

Happy Trails Theatre (TNN, 1985– )

## Album Discography

The Best of Roy Rogers (Camden ACL1-0953)

The Bible Tells Me So (Cap T/ST-1745, Cap SM-1745) w. Dale Evans

A Child's Introduction to the West (Golden 7) w. Dale Evans

Christmas Is Always (Cap T/ST-2818) w. Dale Evans

The Country Side of Roy Rogers (Cap ST-594, Stetson HAT-3116)

The Country Side of Roy Rogers (EMI/Cap/AXIS ST-26718)

The Good Life (Word 8761) w. Dale Evans

Happy Trails to You (20th Century–Fox 467)

Hollywood Canteen (Curtain Calls 100/11-12) [ST]

Hymns of Faith (10" RCA LPM-3168) w. Dale Evans

In the Sweet By and By (Word 8589) w. Dale Evans

Jesus Loves Me (Bluebird LBY-1022, Camden CAL/CAS-1022, Pickwick/Camden ACL-7021) w. Dale Evans and Family

King of the Cowboys (Amalgamated 177)

Lore of the West (Camden CAL/CAS-1074) w. George "Gabby" Hayes

A Man from Duck Run (Cap ST-785)

Many Happy Trails (Teletex CC-7702) w. Dale Evans, Roy Rogers, Jr.

Pecos Bill (Camden CAL/CAS-1054) w. The Sons of the Pioneers

Peter Cottontail and Friends (Camden CAL/CAS-1097) w. Dale Evans

The Republic Years (Varese Darabonds STV-81212) [ST] w. The Sons of the Pioneers

Roll On Texas Moon (Bear Family BFX-15203)

Roy Rogers (Col FC-38907)

Roy Rogers and the Sons of the Pioneers (Bear Family BFX-15124)

The Roy Rogers Show (Radiola 1032)

The Roy Rogers Souvenir Album (10" RCA LPM-3041)

16 Great Songs of the Old West (Golden 198:7) w. Dale Evans

Smokey and the Bandit II (MCA 927) [ST]

Son of Paleface (Titania 511) [ST]

Sweet Hour of Prayer (RCA LPM-1439, Stetson HAT-3088) w. Dale Evans

Take a Little Love (Cap ST-11020)

## The Sons of the Pioneers (with Len Slye [Roy Rogers]):

Empty Saddles (MCA 1563)

The Legendary Sons of the Pioneers, Vols. 1–2 (Cattle 55, 56; Outlaw 5, 6)

The Original Pioneer Trio Sing Songs of the Hills and Plains (AFM 731)

The Sons of the Pioneers (AFM 721)

The Sons of the Pioneers (Col FC-37439)

# MICKEY ROONEY

> His career is a string of comebacks that would make any Hollywood fight film seem monotonous. . . . The Mickey Rooney story is so improbable that it would make a great movie.
>
> —*New York Times*, 1981

THE IRREPRESSIBLE 5' 3" MICKEY ROONEY HAS MADE, AND BEEN PART of, a tremendous amount of show business history in his seventy years to date. From child movie star in the late 1920s to King of the Box Office in the early 1940s to special Oscar winner in the 1980s, he has appeared in over 140 feature films. He has *also* starred in four teleseries and won an Emmy Award for one of his telefeature performances; been a headliner in vaudeville, nightclubs, and radio; written film music and produced and directed feature pictures; and, on stage, starred in, among other ventures, the enormously successful burlesque revue *Sugar Babies*. Rooney has also been married eight times and divorced seven times, leading him to say, "Alimony is like giving oats to a dead horse." His marital circus has also led him to joke, "I have sat down to many family lives. Family life is a common occurrence for me. I'm the only man who has a marriage license made out 'To Whom It May Concern.'" He also admits, "Had I been brighter, had the ladies been gentler, had the Scotch been weaker, had the gods been kinder, this could have been a one-sentence story: once upon a time Mickey Rooney lived happily ever after."

Mickey Rooney is a Renaissance man for he also paints and is a poet and a novelist. Nowhere have his abundant talents been on better display than in his several late 1930s–early 1940s MGM musicals with Judy Garland. Within these movies (e.g., STRIKE UP THE BAND, 1940), he would sing, dance, play assorted musical instruments, and come up for air long enough to handle dramatic moments and give his layered characterization dimension. Sadly, he has too frequently been a major talent in search of a disaster.

He was born Joe Yule, Jr. on September 23, 1920, in Brooklyn, New York, to Joe and Nell (Carter) Yule, vaudeville performers. He spent his infancy on tour with his show business parents. When he was about fifteen months old, he made his impromptu debut in his parents' act by pantomiming the beating of a kettledrum in the orchestra pit. It brought enthusiastic audience response and he was soon made part of the act. By age two, he was singing "Pal o' My Cradle Days" in the family routine. To avoid being hounded by the Children's Society, the Yules passed their youngster off as a midget (his outfit was a tuxedo, a derby hat, and a big fat rubber cigar). In 1924 the Yules separated and would divorce three years later. Mrs. Yule took her son (known as Sonny) to live with her family in Kansas City and then relocated to Los Angeles, certain that her talented son belonged in pictures. However, Hollywood did not agree, so they returned to Kansas City, only to cross the country yet again with vaudeville friends of Mrs. Yule. For a while in Los Angeles she managed a tourist court and the boy was hired to perform on stage in Will Morrissey's Orange Grove Revue. Finally, after making many rounds of studio casting agents, the boy was hired to play a midget in the short NOT TO BE TRUSTED (1926) and the feature OR-CHIDS AND ERMINE (1927) with Colleen Moore.

Through a friend, Mrs. Yule learned that film producer Larry Darmour was planning a series of short subjects based on the Mickey McGuire character featured in Fontaine Fox's popular cartoon strip. With his blond hair dyed black, the boy auditioned for the role of the impish youth and was hired. From 1927 to 1934 (the period of the talkie transition), he made over sixty of these shorts. For a time he attended Mrs. Lawler's School for Professional Children, where he made friends with the equally young Judy Garland, Richard Quine (an actor and later a director), and Sidney Miller (an actor). On screen he was billed as Mickey McGuire, and Mrs. Yule planned to have his name changed legally. However, Fontaine Fox brought a court action which decided that Joe Yule, Jr. could *not* be Mickey McGuire. When the no-longer-profitable Mickey McGuire series slowed down in 1932, the boy went on an abbreviated vaudeville tour, but it was cancelled for lack of audience appeal (especially since he could not legally do his Mickey McGuire routines on stage).

From infant vaudeville performer to youngster star of movie shorts, the boy was now a nobody at age twelve. He began again almost from the start, making the rounds of casting agents. When he was hired to play an orphan in a racetrack melodrama, FAST COMPANIONS (1932) at Universal, the casting director suggested he change his name to Mickey Rooney. He did, and over the next few years he performed a variety of small on-camera roles, often playing the star as a youngster (which, because of his size, he could do well).

He had made his first MGM picture in 1932 (EMMA with Marie Dressler). In 1934, at the suggestion of interested producer David O. Selznick (the son-in-law of MGM studio head Louis B. Mayer), he was cast as Clark Gable as a young boy in MGM's MANHATTAN MELODRAMA. The response was favorable and the studio signed him to a long-term contract at $150 weekly. His agreement provided for loanouts to other studios. Meanwhile, Austrian film director Max Reinhardt had immigrated to the United States and was planning a spectacular stage rendition of William Shakespeare's *A Midsummer Night's Dream* at the Hollywood Bowl (September 1934). Rooney was cast as the devilish Puck. Both the lavish production and Mickey were hits, and the Shakespearean play was taken on a brief tour to San Francisco, Chicago, and New York. When Warner Bros. filmed the play in 1935, it borrowed Rooney from MGM to recreate his characterization of Puck. (During production, Rooney, frequently his own worst enemy, broke a contractual rule about not playing hazardous sports during filming. He went tobogganing and broke a leg. While he was hospitalized—and the movie continued shooting around him—he discovered the excitement of betting on horse races, which became a long-term addiction.) The film of A MIDSUMMER NIGHT'S DREAM (1935) was too highbrow for much of the public, especially once the novelty of spotting the likes of James Cagney, Joe E. Brown, Dick Powell, and others playing Shakespeare wore off. However, Rooney received solid reviews for his enthusiastic performance as the impish Puck. Wrote one critic, "he is a mischievous and joyous sprite, a snub-nosed elf." (Years later, in the early 1970s, he would play Bottom in a New Jersey stock production of the comedy.)

This screen success should have led immediately to better assignments back at MGM, but it did not. Meanwhile, he attended school on the studio lot, earned his $300 weekly, played sports, and enhanced his reputation as a talented scene-stealer no matter what type of mundane role he was handed. In 1937, MGM casually produced a programmer called A FAMILY AFFAIR, geared as family entertainment to appeal to middle America. Mickey was cast as Andrew Hardy, the good-natured but very human teenaged son of Judge Hardy (Lionel Barrymore). *Variety* reported of this unpretentious entry set in Carvel, U.S.A., "Young Rooney's interpretation is true boy stuff, and good for the best laughs." Because of great public response, a second entry was produced, YOU'RE ONLY YOUNG ONCE (1938), which continued the adventures of high schooler Andy Hardy, his girlfriend Polly Benedict (Ann Rutherford), and his family, which now had Lewis Stone cast as the father. It was not until the fourth entry, LOVE FINDS ANDY HARDY (1938)—which introduced a new girl (Judy Garland) into Andy's life—that MGM realized what a bonanza this property was. From 1937 to 1946 there would be fifteen entries in the series, which served as a training ground for new studio talent (including Judy Garland, Lana Turner, Kathryn Grayson, and Donna Reed). By this time, Rooney's mother had remarried (her ex-bartender husband became an accountant in the MGM payroll department) and Joe Yule, Sr. had resurfaced in his son's life. He had remarried and, now billed as "Mickey Rooney's Father," was playing in a downtown Los Angeles burlesque house. MGM took care of this situation by hiring him as a character actor for studio productions.

Rooney had been paired with Spencer Tracy in the successful CAPTAINS COURA-GEOUS (1937) and they were reteamed for BOYS TOWN (1938). Tracy was the humanitarian Father Edward J. Flannigan, founder of the youth sanctuary in Omaha, Nebraska. Rooney played fourteen-year-old Whitey Marsh, the smart-mouthed pool hall shark who is converted by Tracy's kindness. Tracy won an Academy Award for his superior performance and the equally impressive Rooney, who made nine features in 1938, was given a special Oscar along with Deanna Durbin for "setting a high standard of ability and achievement." By late 1939, Rooney had negotiated a new studio contract that began at $1,000 weekly and, if options were exercised at the end of the third year, would escalate to $3,000 weekly by his seventh year, with $25,000 bonuses for each film made.

For Mickey's friend and co-star Judy Garland, director/choreographer Busby Berkeley was an irritating taskmaster. For Mickey, however, he was a creative force who allowed the young star to display his massive array of musical talent. Rooney and Garland and Berkeley combined to make BABES IN ARMS (1939—for which Rooney was Oscar-nominated),

STRIKE UP THE BAND (1940), BABES ON BROADWAY (1941), and GIRL CRAZY (1943—for which Berkeley was only special choreographer). Most of these joyous musicals utilized the formula of talented youths putting on a "big" show to prove their worth to the older generation. They always allowed Rooney to display his impressive range of singing, dancing, instrument playing, impersonations (he did wonderful impressions of Lionel Barrymore and Carmen Miranda), dramatics, and youthful frolicking. Because he interweaved these musical excursions with more Andy Hardy entries, occasional dramatic appearances (YOUNG TOM EDISON, 1940; MEN OF BOYS TOWN, 1941), personal appearance tours, and radio guesting, Mickey Rooney registered as a leading box-office attraction. He was number one at the box office in 1940, and from 1940 to 1942 was considered the top money-making star in Hollywood. In January 1940, the exceptionally popular Rooney was invited to President Franklin D. Roosevelt's birthday ball at the White House where he played one of his own compositions, a three-part tone poem called "Melodante."

As MGM's most lucrative property, Rooney held sway through four films in 1940, including two Andy Hardy entries. It was while making BABES ON BROADWAY the next year that he met a very beautiful new contractee at the studio. Mickey, the ultimate partygoer/partygiver, was so entranced with Ava Gardner that he pursued her relentlessly until the nineteen-year-old agreed to marry him (they were wed on January 10, 1942). Because no one involved (the studio as well as his relatives) was happy to see him get married (would it ruin his box-office appeal?), there was much pressure on the couple and they were divorced in May 1943. By then, Rooney had starred in THE HUMAN COMEDY (1943), based on the William Saroyan novel about small town America at the start of World War II. For his performance, Rooney received his second Oscar nomination. In the winning NATIONAL VELVET (1944), he was the stable boy who helps a young British girl (Elizabeth Taylor) train her beloved horse to be a jumper in the Grand National.

The studio had fought to have Rooney passed over for military service, but by 1944 he had been inducted into the U.S. Army and sent to Camp Seibert, Alabama, for training. There he met a former Miss Alabama, seventeen-year-old blonde Betty Jane Rase. They were married on September 30, 1944. He soon shipped out for overseas, where he served with the Jeep Theatre. From 1944 to 1946, as part of this entertainment division of the military, he traveled some 150,000 miles (mostly in Europe) entertaining troops. Meanwhile, there had been a much publicized battle with MGM when Rooney's personal corporation pushed the studio into a new contract that guaranteed him $5,000 weekly once he returned from war duty. In the summer of 1946, the demobilized Rooney filmed LOVE LAUGHS AT ANDY HARDY, which tried to parallel reality by having returning G.I. Andy Hardy resume his college education and romance an assortment of co-eds (Bonita Granville, Lina Romay). Rooney was now a mature twenty-six and the country's entertainment interests were changing. The film was not popular. He was the toughie-turned-boxer in KILLER McCOY (1947) and the college graduate son of a New England newspaper publisher (Walter Huston) in the ingratiating but overlooked SUMMER HOLIDAY (1948), and in the embarrassing biopic WORDS AND MUSIC (1948) he struggled with his role as composer Lorenz Hart.

By June 1948, Rooney's life was a mess. His marriage to Betty Jane Rase, which had produced two sons (Mickey, Jr. and Timothy), had concluded in a very costly divorce settlement. His private corporation, thanks to his own ego and a bad partner, had put him deeply in debt, and he had squared off against his one-time mentor, Louis B. Mayer. As a result of the stalemate, he and Metro-Goldwyn-Mayer parted company, which cost Rooney his $5,000 weekly salary and his $49,000 yearly pension (in which he would have been vested in a few years). In fact, the final studio settlement effectively provided that Rooney owed them $500,000.

He played several vaudeville engagements (at $12,000 to $15,000 weekly) in 1948. In 1949 he began dissolving his troublesome partnership, married yet again (this time to sultry actress Martha Vickers), and made the first (THE BIG WHEEL) of two dramas (the other was QUICKSAND, 1950) for United Artists packaged by his own production company. He scrounged around the studios for work, and was considered by most people in the industry to be washed up at age thirty. As part of his latest negotiations with MGM, he returned to the studio, now under a new regime, to make the low-budget THE STRIP (1951), in which he was a jazz drummer accused of murder. Also in 1951 he and his spatting bride, by whom he had son Teddy, were divorced, leading to more alimony payments. He made an unrewarding three-film deal with Columbia Pictures; two of the

Walter Huston, Frank Morgan, Agnes Moorehead, Jackie "Butch" Jenkins, Marilyn Maxwell, Mickey Rooney, and Gloria De Haven in SUMMER HOLIDAY (1948)

projects (SOUND OFF, 1952; ALL ASHORE, 1953) were directed by his boyhood friend Richard Quine. The final MGM settlement required one more film and that programmer—A SLIGHT CASE OF LARCENY (1953)—ended his association with the lot. Meanwhile, in November 1952, he had married statuesque, twenty-three-year-old Elaine Mahnken.

In the mid-1950s, Rooney, who had become a steady drinker and a rather undisciplined performer, seesawed between leads in dreadful minor films (THE ATOMIC KID, 1954) and character roles in major pictures (the helicopter pilot in THE BRIDGES AT TOKO-RI, 1954). He still had enough of a superstar reputation that NBC hired him to star in the television situation comedy series "The Mickey Rooney Show" (1954–55), in which, as a page at NBC Studios in Hollywood, he got into a rash of scrapes. As usual, he was better than his material. When Donald O'Connor refused to film any further misadventures of Francis the Talking Mule, Rooney was hired for FRANCIS IN THE HAUNTED HOUSE (1956), which killed that series. To the total surprise of its producers, Rooney turned in such an amazing performance in the World War II action film THE BOLD AND THE BRAVE (1956) that he was Oscar-nominated as Best Supporting Actor. He had ad-libbed most of the memorable fourteen-minute sequence in which he conducted a crap game during an air raid, determined not to lose his $30,000 pot. The next year on television he displayed his versatility by starring in the specials "Mr. Broadway" (a musical about George M. Cohan) and "Pinocchio." For "The Comedian" episode (CBS-TV, February 14, 1957) of "Playhouse 90" he was Emmy-nominated for essaying the role of an unscrupulous comedian. The next year he was Emmy-nominated again as a desperate gambler in "Eddie" on "Alcoa Theatre" (NBC-TV, November 17, 1958). Also in 1958 he separated from wife number four; they were divorced in 1959 (with more alimony payments due) and he married Barbara Ann Thompson (by whom he would have four children: Kerry, Kyle, Kelly Ann, and Kimmy Sue).

Having starred in a radio version of "The Hardy Family" (Mutual, 1951–52), Rooney had long nurtured plans to play a grown-up Andy Hardy on screen. Joined by his real-life son Teddy, he made ANDY HARDY COMES HOME (1958), a black-and-white "B" entry at MGM which did little business. Two further productions released by that studio (THE BIG OPERATOR, 1959; PLATINUM HIGH SCHOOL, 1960) were exploitative trash. He was Emmy-nominated for playing a lonely longshoreman in the "Somebody's Waiting" episode of "The Dick Powell Show" (NBC-TV, November 7, 1961) and turned in a strong performance as the squealing small-time hoodlum in KING OF THE ROARING 20'S—THE STORY OF ARNOLD ROTHSTEIN (1961). Despite a rash of bad pictures, he consistently proved himself a solid talent. When not working in sporadic movie assignments, the overenergetic performer played club engagements, made an occasional LP album, made race track bets, and continued his fast life. In REQUIEM FOR A HEAVYWEIGHT (1962) he was starkly effective as the trainer of a down-and-out prize fighter (Anthony Quinn), and in the all-star ensemble of IT'S A MAD, MAD, MAD, MAD WORLD (1963) he was teamed with Buddy Hackett as one of the grasping seekers of buried loot.

It was a revelation to the public and to Rooney when he had to declare bankruptcy in 1963, listing himself as $464,914 in debt (after having earned $12 million in show business). That fall he turned up as a guest on the ill-fated "The Judy Garland Show" (CBS-TV), reunited with his old teammate in songs and jokes. In 1964–65 he had a short-lived new comedy series on ABC-TV called "Mickey." In 1965, *I.E., An Autobiography* was published. Years later Rooney admitted it had been ghostwritten by Roger Kahn and that "I didn't say those things. I did it for money—I was broke." With film and TV work scarce, he turned to the stage for a stock theater appearance in *A Funny Thing Happened on the Way to the Forum*. In December 1965 he was separated from wife number five, but the following month, on January 31, her body and that of her boyfriend, Yugoslavian actor Milos Milocevic, were found in the bathroom of Rooney's home. Milocevic had shot her (she and Rooney were planning to reconcile) and then killed himself. A few weeks later, Rooney's mother died of a heart attack.

On September 10, 1966, Rooney married forty-five-year-old Margaret Lang, a friend of his last wife's. This union lasted only a few months. In the late 1960s he was living in Florida. "I was completely escaping into the fact that Mickey Rooney was not in demand." In May 1969 he married wife number seven, Carolyn Hockett, a Miami secretary. They would have two children: Jonell and James (a son from her previous marriage, whom he adopted). He was based in Fort Lauderdale in the early 1970s and had formed a seventeen-piece dance band, which toured in one-night stands. He appeared occasionally in a telefeature, joined with Sammy Davis, Jr. in the variety series "NBC Follies" (1973), and made a rash of character appearances in pictures of assorted quality. He was one of the ex-MGM stars recalled to co-host that studio's nostalgic tribute THAT'S ENTERTAINMENT! (1974). He also played dinner and summer theater and toured in assorted pre-Broadway ventures, including *George M!, Three Goats and a Blanket, Alimony, See How They Run,* and *W. C.* (based on the life of W. C. Fields). He divorced wife number seven in 1974, and four years later married Jan Chamberlin, a country-and-western singer.

Having at long last found a stable domestic life, his career took a turn for the better. He toured as Cap'n Andy in *Show Boat* and continued his filmmaking, including playing Gene Hackman's cellmate in THE DOMINO PRINCIPLE (1977). For his role as the former horse trainer who helps a runaway learn to ride in THE BLACK STALLION (1979), he was Oscar-nominated for Best Supporting Actor. He lost that award, but won the co-lead (opposite Ann Miller) in the burlesque revue *Sugar Babies.* He was the baggy-pants top banana telling mildly raunchy jokes, chasing girls, and performing assorted song-and-dance numbers. The expensively mounted show tried out in Los Angeles in June 1979 and completed a five-city tour before bowing on Broadway on October 8, 1979, where it became a hit. (Said *Time* magazine, "Mickey Rooney has grease paint in his blood and the house in his pocket. . . . He has lungs of iron and feet that skitter like a sandpiper's.") Before the *Sugar Babies* phenomenon, Rooney admitted, "I was the most famous has-been in show business."

Now again much in demand, he starred in telefeatures, including BILL (CBS, December 22, 1981), for which he won an Emmy Award, as an adult with mental retardation who is released to the outside world after forty-four years in an institution. He starred as a retiree who rooms with his college-age grandson in the TV series "One of the Boys," which lasted for a few months on NBC-TV in early 1982. At the Oscarcast in 1983 he was given a Special Academy Award "for fifty years of versatility in a variety of memorable film performances." After 1,208 performances, *Sugar Babies* closed on Broadway and went on assorted road tours. When not involved in that vehicle, Rooney made a sequel to the telefeature BILL entitled BILL: ON HIS OWN (1983) and appeared in such plays as *Go Ahead and Laugh* (a reworking of *Three Goats and a Blanket*) and made yet another tour of *A Funny Thing Happened on the Way to the Forum*, in which he received negative reviews for his unbridled hamming. As he had once (in 1964) opened the Mickey Rooney School of Entertainment and later (in 1970) offered to take over production at MGM and make twenty films for $20 million, so the entrepreneurial Rooney in the mid-1980s became involved in promoting Mickey Rooney lines of yogurt, cosmetics, clothing, and pharmaceuticals. He had a one-man show, *Mickey Rooney Is Mickey Rooney*, was writing his *own* memoirs, and in the fall of 1988 reactivated *Sugar Babies* (again with Ann Miller) for a West End production in London, which closed in January 1989. While in England, he made a new movie (ERIK THE VIKING, 1989) and filmed commercials, and back in the States guested on such TV specials as "The 1989 Miss Hollywood Talent Search." In mid-1989 he reunited with Donald O'Connor for a club tour across the United States.

A few years ago the talented, if undisciplined, Rooney, who had become a born-again Christian, admitted, "I've done an awful lot in my life. . . . I've met the biggest and the lowest. I've been to the highest mountain and the lowest valley. That's good. It makes you feel great when you can get off the canvas . . . and start on the ascent. Everyone in their life has a lot of trouble finding out who they are." More recently he said, "someone once asked me what I want on my epitaph when I pass away. Just two words—'I tried'—and that's what this game is all about, is trying."

## Filmography

Not to Be Trusted (Fox, 1926) (s)
Orchids and Ermine (FN, 1927)
Mickey's Circus (FBO, 1927) (s) (as Mickey Yule)
Mickey's Pals (FBO, 1927) (s)*
Mickey's Battle (FBO, 1927) (s)*
Mickey's Eleven (FBO, 1927) (s)*
Mickey's Parade (FBO, 1928) (s)*
Mickey in School (FBO, 1928) (s)*
Mickey's Nine (FBO, 1928) (s)*
Mickey's Little Eva (FBO, 1928) (s)*
Mickey's Wild West (FBO, 1928) (s)*
Mickey in Love (FBO, 1928) (s)*

Mickey's Triumph (FBO, 1928) (s)*
Mickey's Babies [Baby Show] (FBO, 1928) (s)*
Mickey's Rivals (FBO, 1928) (s)*
Mickey's Athletes (FBO, 1928) (s)*
Mickey's Movies (RKO, 1928) (s)*
Mickey's Big Game Hunt (RKO, 1928) (s)*
Mickey the Detective (RKO, 1928) (s)*
Mickey's Great Idea (RKO, 1929) (s)*
Mickey's Explorers (RKO, 1929) (s)*
Mickey's Menagerie (RKO, 1929) (s)*
Mickey's Surprise (RKO, 1929) (s)*
Mickey's Last Chance (RKO, 1929) (s)*
Mickey's Brown Derby (RKO, 1929) (s)*

*As Mickey "Himself" McGuire

Mickey's Northwest Mounted (RKO, 1929) (s)*

Mickey's Initiation (RKO, 1929) (s)*

Mickey's Mix-Up (RKO, 1929) (s)*

Mickey's Midnight Follies (RKO, 1929) (s)*

Mickey's Big Moment (RKO, 1929) (s)*

Mickey's Champs (RKO, 1930) (s)*

Mickey's Strategy (RKO, 1930) (s)*

Mickey's Master Mind (RKO, 1930) (s)*

Mickey's Luck (RKO, 1930) (s)*

Mickey's Whirlwinds (RKO, 1930) (s)*

Mickey's Warriors (RKO, 1930) (s)*

Mickey the Romeo (RKO, 1930) (s)*

Mickey's Merry Men (RKO, 1930) (s)*

Mickey's Winners (RKO, 1930) (s)*

Mickey's Musketeers (RKO, 1930) (s)*

Mickey's Bargain (RKO, 1930) (s)*

Screen Snapshots (Col, 1930) (s)*

Mickey's Stampede (RKO, 1931) (s)*

Mickey's Crusaders (RKO, 1931) (s)*

Mickey's Rebellion (RKO, 1931) (s)*

Mickey's Diplomacy (RKO, 1931) (s)*

Mickey's Wildcats (RKO, 1931) (s)*

Mickey's Thrill Hunters (RKO, 1931) (s)*

Mickey's Helping Hand (RKO, 1931) (s)*

Mickey's Sideline (RKO, 1931) (s)*

Mickey's Travels (RKO, 1932) (s)*

Mickey's Holiday (RKO, 1932) (s)*

Mickey's Golden Rule (RKO, 1932) (s)*

Mickey's Busy Day (RKO, 1932) (s)*

Mickey's Big Business (RKO, 1932) (s)*

Mickey's Charity (RKO, 1932) (s)*

Sin's Pay Day [Slums of New York] (Mayfair, 1932)*

Fast Companions [Information Kid] (Univ, 1932)

My Pal, the King (Univ, 1932)

The Beast of the City (MGM, 1932)

Emma (MGM, 1932)

High Speed (Col, 1932)

Officer Thirteen (Allied, 1932)*

Mickey's Ape Man (RKO, 1933) (s)*

Mickey's Race (RKO, 1933) (s)**

Mickey's Disguises (RKO, 1933) (s)**

Mickey's Touchdown (Col, 1933) (s)**

Mickey's Covered Wagon (Col, 1933) (s)**

Mickey's Tent Show (Col, 1933) (s)**

Broadway to Hollywood [Ring Up the Curtain] (MGM, 1933)

The Big Cage (Univ, 1933)

The World Changes (FN, 1933)

The Chief [My Old Man's a Fireman] (MGM, 1933)

The Life of Jimmy Dolan [The Kid's Last Fight] (WB, 1933)

The Big Chance (Arthur Greenblatt, 1933)

Mickey's Minstrels (Col, 1934) (s)**

Mickey's Rescue (Col, 1934) (s)**

Mickey's Medicine Man (Col, 1934) (s)**

Beloved (Univ, 1934)

I Like It That Way (Univ, 1934)

Love Birds (Univ, 1934)

Half a Sinner (Univ, 1934)

The Lost Jungle (Mascot, 1934) (serial)

Manhattan Melodrama (MGM, 1934)

Screen Snapshots (Col, 1934) (s)

Upper World (WB, 1934)

Hide-Out (MGM, 1934)

Chained (MGM, 1934)

Blind Date (Col, 1934)

Death on the Diamond (MGM, 1934)

The Country Chairman (Fox, 1935)

Reckless (MGM, 1935)

The Healer [Little Pal] (Mon, 1935)

A Midsummer Night's Dream (WB, 1935)

Ah, Wilderness! (MGM, 1935)

Riff-Raff (MGM, 1935)

Little Lord Fauntleroy (UA, 1936)

Pirate Party on Catalina Isle (MGM, 1936) (s)

The Devil Is a Sissy [The Devil Takes the Count] (MGM, 1936)

Down the Stretch (WB, 1936)

Captains Courageous (MGM, 1937)

Slave Ship (20th–Fox, 1937)

A Family Affair (MGM, 1937)

The Hoosier Schoolboy [Yesterday's Hero] (Mon, 1937)

Live, Love and Learn (MGM, 1937)

Thoroughbreds Don't Cry (MGM, 1937)

You're Only Young Once (MGM, 1938)

---

*As Mickey "Himself" McGuire

**As "Mickey McGuire, now known as Mickey Rooney"

Love Is a Headache (MGM, 1938)

Judge Hardy's Children (MGM, 1938)

Hold That Kiss (MGM, 1938)

Lord Jeff [The Boy from Barnardo's] (MGM, 1938)

Love Finds Andy Hardy (MGM, 1938)

Boys Town (MGM, 1938)

Stablemates (MGM, 1938)

Out West with the Hardys (MGM, 1938)

The Adventures of Huckleberry Finn (MGM, 1939)

The Hardys Ride High (MGM, 1939)

Andy Hardy Gets Spring Fever (MGM, 1939)

Babes in Arms (MGM, 1939)

Judge Hardy and Son (MGM, 1939)

Rodeo Dough (MGM, 1940) (s)

Young Tom Edison (MGM, 1940)

Andy Hardy Meets Debutante (MGM, 1940)

Strike Up the Band (MGM, 1940)

Andy Hardy's Private Secretary (MGM, 1940)

Men of Boys Town (MGM, 1941)

Cavalcade of the Academy Awards (Unk, 1941) (s)

Life Begins for Andy Hardy (MGM, 1941)

Babes on Broadway (MGM, 1941)

Meet the Stars #4 (Rep, 1941) (s)

The Courtship of Andy Hardy (MGM, 1942)

A Yank at Eton (MGM, 1942)

Andy Hardy's Double Life [Andy Hardy Steps Out] (MGM, 1942)

The Human Comedy (MGM, 1943)

Girl Crazy (MGM, 1943)

Show Business at War (20th–Fox, 1943) (s)

Thousands Cheer (MGM, 1943)

National Velvet (MGM, 1944)

Andy Hardy's Blonde Trouble (MGM, 1944)

Love Laughs at Andy Hardy (MGM, 1946)

Killer McCoy (MGM, 1947)

Rough But Hopeful (Unk, 1948) (s)

Summer Holiday (MGM, 1948)

Words and Music (MGM, 1948)

The Big Wheel (UA, 1949)

Quicksand (UA, 1950)

He's a Cockeyed Wonder (Col, 1950)

The Fireball (20th–Fox, 1950)

My Outlaw Brother (Eagle Lion, 1951)

My True Story (Col, 1951) (director only)

The Strip (MGM, 1951)

Sound Off (Col, 1952)

Screen Snapshots #205 (Col, 1952) (s)

All Ashore (Col, 1953)

Off Limits [Military Policemen] (Par, 1953)

A Slight Case of Larceny (MGM, 1953)

Mickey Rooney, Then and Now (Col, 1953) (s)

Drive a Crooked Road (Col, 1954)

The Atomic Kid (Rep, 1954)

The Bridges at Toko-Ri (Par, 1954)

The Twinkle in God's Eye (Rep, 1955) (also producer, song)

The Bold and the Brave (RKO, 1956)

Jaguar (Rep, 1956) (producer only)

Francis in the Haunted House (Univ, 1956)

Magnificent Roughnecks (AA, 1956)

Operation Mad Ball (Col, 1957)

Playtime in Hollywood (Col, 1957) (s)

Baby Face Nelson (UA, 1957)

Andy Hardy Comes Home (MGM, 1958) (also producer)

Glamorous Hollywood (Col, 1958) (s)

A Nice Little Bank That Should Be Robbed (20th–Fox, 1958)

The Last Mile (UA, 1959)

The Big Operator (MGM, 1959)

Platinum High School [Rich, Young and Deadly] (MGM, 1960)

The Private Lives of Adam and Eve (Univ, 1960)

Breakfast at Tiffany's (Par, 1961)

King of the Roaring 20's—The Story of Arnold Rothstein [The Big Payroll] (AA, 1961)

Everything's Ducky (Col, 1961)

Requiem for a Heavyweight [Blood Money] (Col, 1962)

It's a Mad, Mad, Mad, Mad World (UA, 1963)

Secret Invasion (UA, 1964)

How to Stuff a Wild Bikini (AIP, 1965)

24 Hours to Kill (7 Arts, 1965)

Il Diavolo Innamorato [The Devil in Love] (Sp, 1966)

Ambush Bay (UA, 1966)

The Extraordinary Seaman (MGM, 1968)

Skidoo (Par, 1968)

The Comic (Col, 1969)

80 Steps to Jonah (WB–7 Arts, 1969)

The Cockeyed Cowboys of Calico County [A Woman for Charlie] (Univ, 1970)

Hollywood Blue (Blue Light Presentations, 1970) (documentary interviewee)

B. J. Lang Presents (Maron, 1971)
Richard (Billings Associates, 1972)
Pulp (UA, 1972)
Evil Roy Slade (NBC-TV, 2/18/72)
The Godmothers (Michael Viola Films, 1973)
(also screenplay, music)
Ace of Hearts (Panama, 1974)
Thunder Country [Snows in the Everglades]
(Trans-International, 1974)
That's Entertainment! (MGM, 1974) (co-host)
Journey Back to Oz (Filmation, 1974) (voice
only)
Bon Baisers de Hong Kong [From Hong Kong
with Love] (Fr, 1975)
Rachel's Man (Br, 1975)
Find the Lady (Can, 1976)
The Domino Principle [The Domino Killings]
(Avco Emb, 1977)
Pete's Dragon (BV, 1977)

The Magic of Lassie (International Picture
Show, 1978)
The Black Stallion (UA, 1979)
Arabian Adventure (Col, 1979)
My Kidnapper, My Love (NBC-TV, 12/8/80)
The Fox and the Hound (BV, 1981) (voice only)
Odyssey of the Pacific [L'Empereur du Perou/
The Emperor of Peru] (Can/Fr, 1981)
Leave 'em Laughing (CBS-TV, 4/29/81)
Bill (CBS-TV, 12/22/81)
Senior Trip! (CBS-TV, 12/30/81)
Bill: On His Own (CBS-TV, 11/9/83)
It Came upon the Midnight Clear (Synd, 12/15/
84)
The Care Bears Movie (Samuel Goldwyn, 1985)
(voice only)
Lightning—The White Stallion (Cannon, 1986)
The Return of Mickey Spillane's Mike Hammer
(CBS-TV, 4/18/86)
Erik the Viking (Orion, 1989)

## Broadway Plays

A Midsummer Night's Dream (1934) (revival)
Sugar Babies (1979)

## Radio Series

The Hardy Family (Mutual, 1951–52)

## TV Series

The Mickey Rooney Show [Hey, Mulligan!]
(NBC, 1954–55)
Mickey (ABC, 1964–65)

NBC Follies (NBC, 1973)
One of the Boys (NBC, 1982)

## Album Discography

Babes in Arms/Babes on Broadway (Curtain
Calls 100/6-7) [ST]
Baby Face Nelson (Jubilee 2021) [ST]
Crazy Ideas (AVI 6037)
Girl Crazy (10" Decca DL-5412) w. Judy
Garland
How to Stuff a Wild Bikini (Wand 671) [ST]

Lover of the Simple Things (Playback L12332)
Merton of the Movies (Pelican 139 [ST/R]
Mickey Rooney Sings George M. Cohan (RCA
LPM-1520)
Mutual Admiration Society (Minerva MIN 6JG-
FST) w. Judy Garland, Jerry Van Dyke
National Velvet (Aragorn 1004) [ST]

National Velvet (Mar-Bren 747) [ST/R]
Pete's Dragon (Cap SW-11704) [ST]
Pinocchio (Col CL-1055) [ST/TV]
Santa Claus Is Comin' to Town (MGM E/SE-4732) [ST/TV]
Strike Up the Band/Girl Crazy (Curtain Calls 100/9-10) [ST]

Sugar Babies (Col Special Products BE-8302) [OC]
Summer Holiday (Four Jays 602) [ST]
Thousands Cheer (Amalgamated 232, Hollywood Soundstage 409) [ST]
Words and Music (10" MGM E-505, MGM E-3233, Metro M/S-580, MGM SESD-54ST) [ST]

# DIANA ROSS

FEW SINGERS ENJOY A PEAK OF OVERWHELMING POPULARITY once, let alone twice. But willowy, 5' 4" Diana Ross has: first as a member of a very hot singing group (the Supremes), and later as a solo act. As part of the Detroit-based Supremes, she helped to make the "Motown sound" an important part of the 1960s music scene. With their sweet music blend, the Supremes were to that decade what The Andrews Sisters had been to the 1940s. The harmonizing Supremes set many records as disc sellers and became international celebrities.

By 1970, when the exceedingly ambitious Diana left the Supremes, she was a millionaire recording artist (over)eager to branch out on her own. As a solo songstress, she racked up a series of hit singles and albums that rivaled her past chart performance as a Supreme. She continued to refine her act (in recordings, in nightclubs, in concert, and on TV) into a well-accepted combination of flash and class. For many fans, she had become the most stylish interpreter of contemporary pop rock. Paralleling her success as a record seller (she also owned several entertainment corporations), she made three major motion pictures in the 1970s. The most popular of these appearances was her performance as jazz singer Billie Holiday in LADY SINGS THE BLUES (1972). For her first major acting chore, Diana was Oscar-nominated.

By the early 1980s, Diana Ross had broken with Motown Records (to join RCA). After 1981, her albums were still in the top forty, but never in the top ten. In the late 1980s, after toning down her career activity to start a new family, she returned to a heavy performing schedule. It was apparent that she was trying (too) hard to compete with the talents of the new generation—on their level *and* in their forum. Like her peer Barbra Streisand, who passed through a similar period of imitating her successors, Diana Ross has to discover that she can be most successful with today's audiences by remaining her distinctive self.

Like several black singers/actresses before her (including Ethel Waters, Lena Horne, and Diahann Carroll), part of Diana Ross's career drive resulted from a desire to pull herself out of an impoverished childhood. She aimed to create opportunities for herself not then generally available to her race. Because she succeeded so dramatically—first as part of the queen trio of black pop music and then as a solo entertainer—she suffered the backlash of being accused of having forgotten her roots. None of this was helped by her displays of glitz, her interracial marriages, or by the rancor expressed by her former Supremes teammates.

She was born in Detroit, Michigan, on March 26, 1944, the second of six children (three girls, three boys) of brass factory worker Fred Ross and his wife, Ernestine (Earle) Ross. The name on the birth certificate was meant to read Diane, but by mistake it was recorded as Diana. The family lived in a Detroit ghetto where Diana was a tomboy. Looking back, she said, "I suppose life was difficult, but as a child I didn't notice those things." When she was six and her mother was hospitalized with tuberculosis, the children were sent South to live with Ernestine's sister Beatrice in Bessemer, Alabama. While there, Diana sang at the Bessemer Baptist Church where her grandfather was the minister. When Mrs. Ross recovered, the children returned to Detroit (along with Aunt Beatrice) and the family moved into a three-bedroom apartment in a government-subsidized housing project (the Brewster-Douglas) for low-income families. By now, Mr. and Mrs. Ross had separated. When Diana was fourteen, she entered Cass Technical High School where she studied fashion, costume design, and cosmetology. She also had a part-time after-school job as bus girl at Hudson's Department Store cafeteria.

Meanwhile, with friends Florence Ballard and Mary Wilson (and for a time with Betty Travis and later Barbara Martin), Diana had begun singing. First as a lark and then to earn extra money, they performed on streetcorners, at social functions, and wherever else they could, sometimes earning $15 a week. They named themselves the Primettes. Smokey Robinson, a former housing-project neighbor of Diana's, was now recording with his group (the Miracles) for Motown Records. (Berry Gordy, Jr. had recently founded this Detroit company, one of the first black-owned record companies in the United States. In the 1960s it would take black music out of its gospel/ethnic setting and make it universally acceptable and commercial.) Robinson arranged an audition for the Primettes with his label. However, Motown turned the group down, advising them to finish their schooling. At Cass Technical, Diana auditioned for a school musical but was rejected there also. ("You have a nice voice, but it's nothing special," she was told.) Ignoring the rebuffs, the Primettes did a few background vocals for Lu-Pine, another Detroit record company.

Through persistence, the Primettes gained a foothold at Motown Records. Eventually Gordy (for whom Diana once worked for two weeks as a clerical assistant, hoping for a chance to sing) relented. He allowed the group to do background work for the recording sessions of several Motown vocalists (including the Shirelles, Marvin Gaye, Smokey Robinson, and Mary Wells). Finally, in 1961, he was sufficiently impressed with the trio's potential to begin grooming and polishing them for success. He soon changed their name to the Supremes. Their first nine singles (including "I Want a Guy") were all flops, leading other artists at the record company to call the group the "no-hits" Supremes. By this time, the group's lead vocalist had switched from being Florence Ballard to Diana and their numbers exploited Ross's cat-like sexuality and her whispery, coy singing.

In early 1964, the writing team of Brian Holland–Lamont Dozier–Eddie Holland wrote "Where Did Our Love Go" as a number for Motown's The Marvelettes. When that group rejected it, the Supremes, who could not afford to be fussy, recorded the sappy song. At the time of its release in June 1964, the Supremes were on tour (at $500 weekly) with Dick Clark's annual summer show, "Caravan of Stars." By the week of August 22, 1964, the song was number one on the charts; it sold over two million copies. In quick succession came such Supremes hits as "Baby Love," "Come See About Me," "Stop in the Name of Love," "Back in My Arms Again," and "I Hear a Symphony." All of these recordings went gold. Berry Gordy, romantically involved with Diana, temporarily abandoned his duties as head of Motown to become the Supremes' personal manager. It was he who orchestrated their image change into a sharp, commercial package of glitz, glamour, and harmony.

Meanwhile, the group made their motion picture debut. They were part of the singing talent (including Chuck Berry, James Brown and the Flames, Marvin Gaye, Jan and Dean, and The Rolling Stones) who appeared at an October 29, 1964, concert at the Santa Monica Civic Auditorium. It was filmed for release as THE T.A.M.I. SHOW (Teenage Command Performance) in late 1964. That December 24, the Supremes made the first of many appearances on "The Ed Sullivan Show" (CBS-TV), which would help their transition into mainstream performers. By the end of 1965, they had played important club dates in the United States and performed in Europe, and each member of the singing trio (with its already much-imitated choreographed look and harmonized sound) was earning $250,000 a year. The members of the group were already having personality problems with each other, but they were too hot an act to take time to solve their conflicts. Their hit albums in 1965 included *A Bit of Liverpool* and *The Supremes at the Coca* (appearing at the famed Manhattan club in July 1965 was an important career transition for the group). For the surf-and-sand movie BEACH BALL (1965), the Supremes sang two numbers, including the title song, and were seen on screen. By now, according to the music industry and the public, there were two equally distinct and popular sounds: the Liverpool Sound (the Beatles) and the Motown Sound (the Supremes).

"You Can't Hurry Love" and "You Keep Me Hangin' On" were the Supremes' two number one singles of 1966, and their number one album was *The Supremes à Go-Go.* As the group's Mary Wilson described their (Motown) sound, "It has the beat, but not the grinding noise." They were guests on "The Ed Sullivan Show" five times in 1966, and appeared also on "The Sammy Davis, Jr. Show," "The Dean Martin Show," and "The Hollywood Palace." The next year they were heard doing soundtrack vocals for THE HAPPENING and DR. GOLDFOOT AND THE BIKINI MACHINE. "Love Is Here and Now You're Gone" in the spring of 1967 was the last number one single to feature Florence Ballard as a member of the Supremes. By mid-year, Cindy Birdsong (of Patti LaBelle and the Bluebelles) had graduated from being a temporary stand-in for the ailing and unhappy Ballard to becoming a full replacement. (Ballard would become a single act, but by the mid-1970s was at a professional low and on public assistance. She died of a heart attack on February 21, 1976.)

By the fall of 1967, the singing group was known as Diana Ross and the Supremes, and they were making an effort to get away from their overly lavish costumes/makeup/wigs. They also had moved away from the composing team of Holland–Dozier–Holland. On January 12, 1968, Diana Ross and the Supremes (as nuns!) were guest stars on "Tarzan" (NBC-TV). The number one hit, "Love Child," in the winter of 1968, reflected their singing transformation to new composers and production formats. Reaching out for new audiences, they sang in tandem with the Temptations, and in December 1968 they had a number two album with *Diana Ross and the Supremes Join the Temptations* (which included the single "I'm Gonna Make You Love Me"). The singing trio's final number one hit together was "Someday We'll Be Together," which reached the top of the chart during the week of December 28, 1969. A few days earlier, on December 21, they had made their twentieth and final appearance (as a team) on "The Ed Sullivan Show." On January 14, 1970, at the Frontier Hotel in Las Vegas, the group performed their final show together, during which Diana Ross introduced Jean Terrell, her replacement in the Supremes.

Amid much publicity highlighting the "rivalry" between Diana Ross and the competing Supremes, Diana had her first solo hit with "Ain't No Mountain High Enough" (a long narrative talk-song) in the fall of 1970. In January 1971, in Las Vegas, she married twenty-five-year-old white public relations executive Robert Ellis Silberstein. (They would have three daughters: Rhonda, Tracee, and Chudney; they divorced in 1976.) On April 18, 1971, she starred in an hour-long NBC-TV special; her guests included Bill Cosby, Danny Thomas, and The Jackson Five (including young Michael Jackson). On that show she not only sang but also did pantomime impressions of Charlie Chaplin, W. C. Fields, and Harpo Marx, leading *Variety* to judge her "a fresh, pretty, and lively personality" and to praise this added dimension to her act.

On the other hand, there were few plaudits for Paramount's restructuring of Billie Holiday's tragic life in LADY SINGS THE BLUES (1972). Nonetheless, Diana won solid endorsements for her feature film acting debut. It was a calculated gesture by Berry Gordy, still Ross's mentor and this film's producer, to showcase her both as a formidable singer of blues songs and as a dramatic talent. *Variety* noted enthusiastically, "She can make casual chatter come across as genuinely cute without being cutesy, and project subtle irony as well as subtle tragedy." The movie was a big box-office grosser, and Diana was nominated for an Academy Award. (She lost the Best Actress award to Liza Minnelli of CABARET.) The soundtrack album to LADY SINGS THE BLUES—including Ross's interpretations of such Billie Holiday standards as "God Bless the Child" and "Good Morning Heartache"—hit number one. While she continued to play clubs, tour in concert, make guest appearances on television, and record ("Touch Me in the Morning" was a number one hit in 1973), her main career focus was finding another screen property. Along the way, she rejected such projects as a screen version of *No Strings*, an invitation to star in a Broadway musical of SABRINA (1953), and an opportunity to headline a new movie version of BORN YESTERDAY (1950).

Paramount's MAHOGANY (1975) was tailor-made for Ross, casting her as a struggling black fashion designer from the ghetto who becomes world famous. Meanwhile, in the course of its 109 minutes, she becomes involved romantically with a psychotic fashion photographer (Tony Perkins), a wealthy Italian (Jean-Pierre Aumont), and a poor but decent suitor (Billy Dee Williams—her LADY SINGS THE BLUES co-star). For this production Berry Gordy took over from Tony Richardson as director and Diana created the costumes. The critics abhorred the melodrama, and even ardent Ross fans agreed that her soundtrack singing of "Do You Know Where You're Going To" (which became number one on the charts) was the only good thing about this self-indulgent production. The song was Oscar-nominated, and at that year's Academy Awards she sang the hit tune via satellite from Amsterdam (where she was on concert tour). However, "I'm Easy" from NASHVILLE won the Oscar.

In the 1970s, Diana had a checkered recording career, no longer making the top ten—or even top forty—with all her singles and albums. By the middle of the decade, disco (and Donna Summer) were hot, and Ross recorded the disco-beat song "Love Hangover," which was her last number one hit for five years. She continued with television specials (including one in 1977) and remained a top club attraction, traveled the international concert circuit, and appeared in occasional music videos. In 1977 she received a special Tony Award.

If MAHOGANY was a disappointment, the overproduced THE WIZ (1978) was a near disaster. Stephanie Mills had been a joy in the hit stage musical, which used the black idiom to retool the 1939 movie classic THE WIZARD OF OZ. Mills had been just right in recreating Judy Garland's landmark movie success. However, on screen in THE WIZ, Diana Ross (at thirty-four) was far too mature to play the young Harlem schoolteacher whisked off to the magical Emerald City. Much more successful than Diana (who sang such solos as "Can I Go On Not Knowing?" and "Is This What Feeling Gets?") was Michael Jackson as the Scarecrow and especially Lena Horne as Glinda the Good Witch. Made at a cost of $24 million, the musical grossed only $13 million. It effectively ended Ross's picture career. Plans for Ross to star in the life of Josephine Baker, to reteam with Billy Dee Williams in a story of a 1920s New York underworld figure and his lady friend, and to join with Ryan O'Neal (at one point an off-screen boyfriend) in THE BODYGUARD never worked out.

Diana Ross in MAHOGANY (1975)

In 1979 her album *The Boss* (whose title said a great deal about her status at Motown) reached number fourteen position. It seemed that her popularity had peaked, while her performing style and her lifestyle had grown far more opulent and much less accessible. Yet the next year, with her single "Upside Down," she had a number one hit, and its album, *Diana*, reached number two. Her last single hits for the Motown label were both songs recorded for motion pictures. "It's My Turn" was from the 1980 Jill Clayburgh–Michael Douglas comedy and "Endless Love" (Motown's most successful single to that date) was a love duet sung by Ross and Lionel Richie (who wrote the song) for the 1981 romantic drama of the same title.

By the fall of 1981, Diana had left Motown, intent on dramatically asserting her independence. She signed with RCA Victor Records for North America and with EMI/Capitol for the rest of the globe. She already had her own filmmaking company as well as her Diana Ross Enterprises, which included a management firm and a music publishing concern. During the changeover from Motown, none of her albums made the top ten, although the title song (produced by Daryl Hall) from her album *Swept Away* (1984) reached number nineteen and the single "Missing You" (dedicated to Marvin Gaye and produced by Lionel Richie) reached tenth position on the charts. She made additional TV specials. Several of these derived from live concerts, including the July 1983 Central Park charity outing that suffered from a rain-out, many technical problems, and a large financial loss. She continued to star in music videos, including those for "Why Do Fools Fall in Love" (1981), "Work That Body" (1981), "Muscles" (1982—a song written and produced by Michael Jackson), "Pieces of Ice" (1983), and "Swept Away" (1984). Several of her old TV and concert appearances were reassembled for compilation videocassette offerings. Meanwhile, she had set a record by grossing more than $1.7 million during a concert stand at Radio City Music Hall. On record, she could be heard in duet with a variety of performers, including Julio Iglesias and Barry Gibb (of the Bee Gees). She was also part of the all-star ensemble (ranging from Ross to Cyndi Lauper to Stevie Wonder and Bob Dylan) performing the hit song "We Are the World" (1985), with the proceeds from the record and the music video going to the charity U.S.A. for Africa.

The 1980s were a period of transition for Diana Ross. She had a romance with Gene Simmons of the rock group KISS (following his extended relationship with Ross's friend Cher). Diana was reunited with Mary Wilson and Cindy Birdsong for a 1982 NBC-TV special honoring Motown Records and its twenty-five-year history. The show contained the highly publicized moment when Ross seemingly pushed Wilson away from the microphone. That helped to stir up the unending debates about Diana Ross and/versus the Supremes, which had received new fuel from the hit Broadway musical *Dreamgirls* (1981). That show had set forth the lives, music, and frustrations of a Supremes-like black vocal trio. In 1984 Mary Wilson published her autobiography, *Dreamgirl: My Life as a Supreme*, which started a new round of speculation. In May 1985, Diana met Norwegian megamillionaire shipping magnate Arne Naess in the Bahamas, where each was vacationing with their children (he has three from a prior marriage). Five months later they married in a civil ceremony in New York City, but were wed again (in a million dollar wedding) in Switzerland on February 1, 1986. The couple have two sons and the entire family currently resides in a well-fortified mansion in Greenwich, Connecticut.

After nearly three years of professional inactivity, Diana Ross returned to a heavy performing schedule in 1988, at a time when Whitney Houston, Janet Jackson, and Anita Baker—not to mention Madonna and Tiffany—were among the most-in-demand recording artists. In Las Vegas, Ross appeared at Caesar's Palace with a $40 per person minimum (a new high). She was a guest for the second time (March 29, 1989) on a Barbara Walters TV interview special and, in the spring of 1989, had a new album, *Workin' Overtime*, released by Motown Records. (The company had been sold by Berry Gordy, and as an inducement to sign with the restructured label, Diana was made part owner of the firm.) Regarding the album, the *Los Angeles Times* judged, "she seems to be trying too hard to sound contemporary and relevant. . . . Ross should relax and just be herself."

In June 1989, Diana kicked off a national tour with a four-day engagement at Radio City Music Hall. Although the enormously successful concert stand grossed $950,950, the *New York Times* reported, "Compared with singers like Whitney Houston and Anita Baker . . . Miss Ross's thin, slippery voice, with a texture that is two parts honey to one part vinegar, is a modest instrument." When she played Las Vegas later that month (at $450,000 weekly), the *Hollywood Reporter* noted, "On stage, the 45-year-old singer was more animated than usual, and her rapport with the audience was smooth and not contrived." When she reached the West Coast for more playdates, the *Los Angeles Times* recorded, "The fact that this is Ross' first U.S. tour in five years hides some of the familiarity, but over the course of two hours it becomes clear that nothing has really changed. It's the same glamour, glitz, oldies, cornball chatter and endless costume changes."

Ever the demanding perfectionist, Ross has insisted, "No, I'm not secure. I shouldn't be. Being insecure is not necessary, but it makes you better. I'll never be satisfied. I like to win, and I always set my goals for myself." She claims, "I am no different now than in the 1960s," and as for leaving a legacy, "If I raise my children right, that will make a difference in the world."

## Filmography

### With the Supremes:

The T.A.M.I. Show (AIP, 1964)
Beach Ball (Par, 1965)

Dr. Goldfoot and the Bikini Machine (AIP, 1967) (voice only)
The Happening (Col, 1967) (voice only)

### Diana Ross Alone:

Lady Sings the Blues (Par, 1972)
Mahogany (Par, 1975) (also costume designer)
Thank God It's Friday (Col, 1978) (voice only)
The Wiz (Univ, 1978)

It's My Turn (Col, 1980) (voice only)
Endless Love (Univ, 1981) (voice only)
The Land Before Time (Univ, 1988) (voice only)

## Album Discography

### Diana Ross and the Supremes:

Aquarius/Let the Sunshine In (Motown 689)
Baby Love (Pickwick 3393)
A Bit of Liverpool (Motown 623)
Cream of the Crop (Motown 694)
Diana Ross and the Supremes Join the Temptations (Motown 679)
Farewell (Motown 708)
From the Vaults (Motown M5-190)
Greatest Hits, Vols. 1 and 2 (Motown 663)
Greatest Hits, Vol. 3 (Motown 702)
I Hear a Symphony (Motown 643)
It's Happening (MCA MT 734727) w. Neil Diamond
Love Child (Motown 670)
Meet the Supremes (Motown 606)
Merry Christmas (Motown 606)
More Hits by the Supremes (Motown 627)
Motown Superstar Series, Vol. 1 (Motown 5-101)

Reflections (Motown 665)
The Supremes à Go-Go (Motown 649)
The Supremes Anthology (Motown 9-794)
The Supremes at the Copa (Motown 636)
The Supremes Live at the Talk of the Town (Motown 676)
The Supremes Sing and Perform "Funny Girl" (Motown 672)
The Supremes Sing Country and Western and Pop (Motown 625)
The Supremes Sing Holland–Dozier–Holland (Motown 650)
The Supremes Sing Rodgers and Hart ((Motown 659)
T.C.B. (Motown 692) w. the Temptations [ST/TV]
We Remember Sam Cooke (Motown 629)
Where Did Our Love Go? (Motown 621)

### Diana Ross Alone:

All the Greatest Hits (Motown 13-960CE)
Baby It's Me (Motown 890)
The Boss (Motown 923)
Diana! (Motown 7129) [ST/TV]
Diana (Motown 8-936)
Diana and Marvin (Motown 803) w. Marvin Gaye
Diana Ross (Motown 711)
Diana Ross (Motown 861)
Diana's Duets (Motown 214)
Eaten Alive (RCA FL1-5422)
Endless Love (Mer 12001) [ST]
An Evening with Diana Ross (Motown 7-877)
Everything Is Everything (Motown 724)
Greatest Hits (Motown 869)
It's My Turn (Motown M8-847M1) [ST]

Lady Sings the Blues (Motown 758) [ST]
The Land Before Time (MCA 6266) [ST]
The Last Time I Saw Him (Motown 812)
Live! At Caesar's Palace (Motown 801)
Mahogany (Motown 858) [ST]
Red Hot Rhythm and Blues (RCA 6388-1-RS)
Ross (Motown 907)
Surrender (Motown 723)
Swept Away (RCA AFL1-5009)
Thank God It's Friday (Casablanca NBLP-7099-3) [ST]
To Love Again (Motown 951)
Touch Me in the Morning (Motown 772)
Why Do Fools Fall in Love? (RCA AFL1-4153)
The Wiz (MCA 2-14000) [ST]
Workin' Overtime (Motown 6274)

# LILLIAN ROTH

TODAY LILLIAN ROTH IS BEST REMEMBERED FOR HER COURAGEOUS fight with alcohol as detailed in her 1954 best-selling autobiography, *I'll Cry Tomorrow.* The details of the star's tormented private life and addiction to drink have overshadowed the fact that she had an illustrious show business career, dating from her childhood through to the end of her life. Lillian Roth was a vivacious star of vaudeville, Broadway, films, nightclubs, radio, and recordings. She introduced and made famous such songs as "Ain't She Sweet," "When the Red, Red Robin Comes Bob Bob Bobbin' Along," "Eadie Was a Lady," "Sing You Sinners," and "I'd Climb the Highest Mountain." Sadly, Lillian Roth's alcohol abuse nearly killed her and, for a time, destroyed her career and left her destitute. A woman of great fortitude, she rose up against the adversities in her life and, for the most part, conquered her addiction. However, her life did not have a storybook ending, as did her first autobiography. Nevertheless, she remained the person who had fought back to give others the inspiration to take control of their lives again.

Lillian Roth was the oldest daughter of Russian immigrant Arthur Rutstein (who later changed his surname to Roth) and Katie Silverman of Boston, and it was in that city that she was born on December 13, 1910; she was named for Lillian Russell. When she was six, her mother took her and younger sister Ann to Educational Pictures in New York City where Lillian was hired to pose as the company's trademark—the statue of a child holding the lamp of knowledge. Next, Mrs. Roth landed work for her daughters with Samuel Goldwyn, then making pictures in Fort Lee, New Jersey. The girl mainly did bits and extra roles, although Lillian and Ann portrayed the title character's daughters in the quasi-documentary PERSHING'S CRUSADERS (1918).

Meanwhile, Lillian made her Broadway bow on August 13, 1917, in *The Inner Man,* playing Wilton Lackaye's daughter, Flossie. She was such a sensation that she was soon billed as "Broadway's Youngest Star." During the play's run, Lillian was enrolled in the Professional Children's School in Gotham, and her classmates included Milton Berle, Ruby Keeler, Patsy Kelly, Gene Raymond, Helen Chandler, and Penny Singleton. She was Mamie Rennesdale in *Penrod* (1918) and a few months later, in November 1918, played Tyltyl's grandchild in *The Betrothal.* Following these shows, Lillian and her sister were signed by the B. F. Keith circuit to tour in vaudeville, where Lillian was a great success doing impersonations of Ruth Chatterton and John and Lionel Barrymore and introducing such song standards as "When the Red, Red Robin Comes Bob Bob Bobbin' Along" and "Ain't She Sweet." First billed as Lillian Roth and Company, the girls later became The Roth Kids.

They were so popular that they were invited to meet President Woodrow Wilson.

In February 1920, Lillian was back on Broadway as Barbara Armstrong in *Shavings*. Thereafter, Lillian and Ann continued to tour in vaudeville in the early 1920s, and during that time, Lillian attended the Clark School of Concentration. In 1923 (at age thirteen but claiming she was much older), Lillian joined the company of the revue *Artists and Models*, playing with the show both in New York and in Chicago. She then continued as a popular attraction in vaudeville. She was back on Broadway in *Padlocks of 1927* with Texas Guinan. In December 1927, she replaced Winnie Lightner in the Broadway revue *Harry Delmar's Revels* with Frank Fay, Bert Lahr, and Patsy Kelly. In August 1928, she was featured in *Earl Carroll's Vanities of 1928* with W. C. Fields, Ray Dooley, Joe Frisco, Dorothy Knapp, and Vincent Lopez and His Orchestra. She was paid $400 per week for the revue's 203-performance run. During that time, she made a screen test for Fox but was told she had a crooked smile and was unfit for pictures. Next Lillian appeared in Florenz Ziegfeld's *Midnight Frolics* (1929) at the New Amsterdam Theatre Roof for $500 weekly.

By this time talkies had become a Hollywood fixture, and the movie industry was avidly recruiting Broadway/vaudeville personalities who could talk and sing and had some marquee recognition with filmgoers. Lillian made her talking picture debut in the one-reel musical short LILLIAN ROTH AND PIANO BOYS (1929) singing "Ain't She Sweet." She then signed with Paramount and went to Hollywood where she made her feature film debut in Nancy Carroll's ILLUSION, issued in the fall of 1929. Lillian appeared briefly in this society drama as herself, singing "When the Real Thing Comes Your Way." Her first acting role came as Lulu, the bouncey maid to a queen (Jeanette MacDonald) in the Maurice Chevalier vehicle THE LOVE PARADE (1929). The picture had her paired with a valet played by Lupino Lane. Together they provided comic relief and sang such numbers as "Let's Be Common" and "Gossip." Her best screen role, which gained her much critical acclaim, came when she portrayed Huguette, the young French girl who loves and dies for poet François Villon (Dennis King), in the Rudolf Friml operetta THE VAGABOND KING (1930). *Variety*, however, observed, "Miss Roth is a clever girl and a looker, but needs discretion in casting."

In the glut of films (especially musicals) cranked out by Paramount, Lillian was fourth-billed in the musical comedy HONEY, released in the spring of 1930. She played the daughter of a rich woman (Jobyna Howland) who falls in love with a butler (Skeets Gallagher) who turns out to be the owner of the mansion they have rented. The film was mediocre, but it did give Lillian the chance to sing the spirited "Sing You Sinners." She displayed her boundless energy by next co-starring with The Marx Brothers in their crazy comedy ANIMAL CRACKERS (1930), cast as the daughter of a rich hostess (Margaret Dumont) who is in love with a starving artist (Hal Thompson). She sang "Why Am I So Romantic?" Once again her appearance in this film was more a specialty act than an integrated part of the proceedings. In the studio's all-star PARAMOUNT ON PARADE (1930), Lillian and Charles "Buddy" Rogers appeared in the blackout sequence "Love Time" singing "Any Time's the Time to Fall in Love."

Paramount loaned Roth to MGM to play the part of homewrecker Trixie in Cecil B. De Mille's MADAM SATAN (1930). She was very sexy in the role and was the only true asset of this otherwise gaudy and laughable "epic." Lillian returned to Paramount for SEA LEGS (1930), cast as the beautiful daughter of a sea captain (Albert Conti) who is romanced by a shanghaied boxer (Jack Oakie). The film was a dud, and Lillian was increasingly unhappy (as she should have been) with her studio assignments. After being overlooked for the lead in a Maurice Chevalier film and finding out that the studio was making five times as much as she was on her personal appearance junkets for them, she packed up and went back to vaudeville.

Lillian Roth returned to vaudeville at $1,750 a week, and in 1931 she was back on Broadway in *Earl Carroll's Vanities of 1931* with Will Mahoney, Mitchell & Durant, and William Demarest for a 278-performance run. The next year she did another edition, *Earl Carroll's Vanities of 1932*, but the revue ran only 87 performances, with Lillian performing "I Gotta Right to Sing the Blues." That show also featured Helen Broderick, Will Fyffe, and Milton Berle. While in New York in 1932, Lillian made a series of Dave Fleischer cartoons in Paramount's Screen Songs series, in which she sang such numbers as "Down Among the Sugar Cane," "Honeysuckle Rose," and "Let's Fall in Love," and for which she was paid $3,500 each.

Lillian Roth and Kay Johnson in MADAM SATAN (1930)

She returned to feature films for the Warner Bros. women's prison melodrama LADIES THEY TALK ABOUT (1933), singing the song "If I Could Be with You One Hour Tonight." While on the East Coast she joined in the lackluster independent production (for Paramount release) of TAKE A CHANCE (1933), co-starring Cliff Edwards and Charles "Buddy" Rogers in a tale of carnival performers. She sang "Eadie Was a Lady" and "Come Up and See Me Sometime." After LADIES THEY TALK ABOUT, Roth was offered a three-year contract at $1,500 per week by Warner Bros., but she turned it down, preferring to continue working in vaudeville. In the summer and fall of 1934, she starred on her own CBS radio program with Edward Nelle, Jr. She also continued to make film shorts such as RKO's MASKS AND MEMORIES (1934), a frothy featurette in which an old man (Fred Scott) relives his youth at a Mardi Gras with Lillian as the girl he once loved; she sang "Sophisticated Lady," "Mardi Gras," and "I'm All Alone." She was also on Broadway in *Revels of 1935* (1934).

It was during the 1930s that tragedy began to enter Lillian Roth's life, following her first marriage to terminally ill David Lyons. After his death, she started drinking heavily (as much as two quarts of liquor a day for a dozen years), and she went through a series of marriages: to aviator William Scott, Judge Benjamin Shalleck, Eugene Weiner, Edward Goldman, Mark Harris—all ending in divorce. Until the early 1940s, Lillian managed to pull herself together enough to get occasional work in nightclubs and vaudeville, even doing a short tour in 1941. By this time, however, she had made and spent over $1 million and her career was wrecked by alcohol.

When doctors told her that liquor would either kill her or drive her insane, she had herself committed to Bloomingdale's, a Westchester institution, and there she tried to kick the drinking habit for good. She was released in 1946, and long-time friend Milton Berle tried to help her get back into show business. However, she had several more backsliding periods and an attempted suicide before she finally joined Alcoholics Anonymous. It was there that she met Thomas Burt McGuire, who took over the management of her career. They married in 1947, the year Lillian made a successful tour of Australia and New Zealand and began speaking out publicly about her drinking problem. Back in the United States, she had successful cabaret stands at Ciro's in Los Angeles and other night spots, and in 1948 she converted to Catholicism.

In the early 1950s, Ralph Edwards asked Lillian to appear on his NBC-TV program "This Is Your Life" in a tribute to songwriter Nacio Herb Brown and she sang his composition "Take a Chance." Edwards approached Roth about doing her own life story, but she was reluctant. However, in 1953, she finally agreed to do the show, which was so popular and inspirational that it had three airings. As a result of the program, demand for Lillian's services increased dramatically, and with Mike Connolly and Gerold Frank, she wrote her autobiography, *I'll Cry Tomorrow* (1954), which sold over seven million copies and was translated into twenty languages.

The years after the publication of her life story were probably the busiest in Lillian Roth's career. She earned as much as $12,000 per week for personal appearances and received as many as ten thousand letters per week from readers since she had become a symbol for those combatting alcohol addiction. MGM filmed I'LL CRY TOMORROW in 1955 with Susan Hayward, who was Oscar-nominated for her outstanding performance as Lillian. Roth was satisfied with the film, but unhappy that she did not sing on the movie's soundtrack. (She did record the title tune and some of her other favorites for Coral Records.)

Following the release of I'LL CRY TOMORROW, Lillian was more popular than ever with her club act. She guested on such dramatic TV shows as "U.S. Steel Hour," "Matinee Theatre," "Playhouse 90," and "Witness." She played in summer stock, including engagements of *Lady in the Dark*. She recorded two best-selling LP albums (she did not record in her heyday except for an unissued Victor test in 1927) with *I'll Cry Tomorrow* for Epic and *Lillian Roth Sings* for Tops. Both albums had Roth singing songs associated with her career, and the Tops album contained the number "Beyond My Worth" which was also the title of her second—less popular—autobiography, published in 1958.

In 1962, Lillian Roth returned to Broadway in the musical *I Can Get It for You Wholesale*, which had a 301-performance run. Although top-billed, she had only one solo number, "Too Soon," and she participated in four other tunes. The show is best remembered for having introduced Barbra Streisand. In 1963, Lillian's sixteen-year marriage to Burt McGuire ended and she resumed drinking for a time. The next year she headed a successful road company of *Funny Girl* with Anthony George and Marilyn Michaels, playing Fanny Brice's mother. However, rumors of her continued drinking made it difficult to get further work.

In the late 1960s, Lillian moved back to New York City, where she had sporadic bookings with her club act and occasionally appeared on national television programs such as "The Mike Douglas Show." To make ends meet, she accepted various menial labor jobs. She did return to Broadway in 1971 in the musical *70 Girls 70* with Mildred Natwick, Hans Conried, Gil Lamb, and Joey Faye; she had a big production number built around the song "See the Light." After the show's unsuccessful run, it was announced that she would do the Neil Simon comedy *Last of the Red Hot Lovers*, but she was not in the cast when it opened in 1972.

During the mid-1970s, Lillian had a modest revival doing her cabaret act (she did a touching rendition of "Send in the Clowns"), and in 1977 she returned to films in a brief role as a pathologist in the horror film ALICE, SWEET ALICE. Two years later she did a cameo in the feature BOARDWALK, which dealt with the plight of the urban elderly. As the 1970s passed, Lillian Roth's health deteriorated and she entered a New York City nursing home, where she died on May 10, 1980, following a massive stroke and a long illness. There were no immediate survivors.

## Filmography

Pershing's Crusaders (FN, 1918)
Lillian Roth and Piano Boys (Par, 1929) (s)
Lillian Roth and Band (Par, 1929) (s)
Raising the Roof (Par, 1929) (s)
Illusion (Par, 1929)
The Love Parade (Par, 1929)
Meet the Boy Friend (Par, 1930) (s)
The Vagabond King (Par, 1930)
Honey (Par, 1930)
Animal Crackers (Par, 1930)
Paramount on Parade (Par, 1930)
Madam Satan (MGM, 1930)
Sea Legs (Par, 1930)
Puff Your Blues Away (Par, 1931) (s)
Naughty (Par, 1931) (s)

Down Among the Sugar Cane (Par, 1932) (s)
   (voice only)
Honeysuckle Rose (Par, 1932) (s) (voice only)
Let's Fall in Love (Par, 1932) (s) (voice only)
Ladies They Talk About (WB, 1933)
Take a Chance (Par, 1933)
Ain't She Sweet (Par, 1933) (s)
Paramount Pictorial #12 (Par, 1933) (s)
Million Dollar Memory (Educational, 1933) (s)
Story Conference (Vita, 1934) (s)
Masks and Memories (Vita, 1934) (s)
Arcade Varieties (RKO, 1938) (s)
Alice, Sweet Alice [Communion/Holy Terror]
   (AA, 1977)
Boardwalk (Atlantic, 1979)

## Broadway Plays

The Inner Man (1917)
Penrod (1918)
The Betrothal (1918)
Shavings (1920)
Artists and Models (1923)
Padlocks of 1927 (1927)
Harry Delmar's Revels (1927) (replacement)

Earl Carroll's Vanities of 1928 (1928)
Midnight Frolics (1929)
Earl Carroll's Vanities of 1931 (1931)
Earl Carroll's Vanities of 1932 (1932)
Revels of 1935 (1934)
I Can Get It for You Wholesale (1962)
70 Girls 70 (1971)

## Radio Series

The Lillian Roth Show (CBS, 1934)

## Album Discography

Honey (Caliban 6018) [ST]
I Can Get It for You Wholesale (Col KOL-
   5780/KOS-2180, Col Special Products
   2180) [OC]
I'll Cry Tomorrow (Epic LN-3206)

Lillian Roth Recalls the Way We Were!—A
   Musical Autobiography (AEI 1155)
Lillian Roth Sings (Tops L-1567)
Love Parade (Ariel CMF 23) [ST]
Paramount on Parade (Caliban 6044) [ST]
70 Girls 70 (Col S-30589) [OC]

# FRANK SINATRA

NO MATTER HOW ONE REGARDS FRANK SINATRA'S POLITICS, HIS FRE-
quently bizarre choice of associates, or his hot temper—all of which have created sensational
headlines for decades—he remains for many the most enduring show business personality
of the twentieth century. Unlike most big band crooners, who could make the transition
successfully to radio and recordings but *not* to motion pictures, Frank Sinatra has been
highly popular in every performing medium he has tackled. In his prime, his song styling,
with its unique phrasing, was unparalleled. Unlike almost any other performer, and
because he has had such a lengthy singing career, Sinatra has often taken songs he recorded
happily in one era and restyled them with new approaches for presentation to a later
generation. Because his recordings are so vast, rich, and contrasting, there are several radio
stations even today that devote weekly evening sessions to playing his works.

Such is Sinatra's global fame that the various progressions of his show business life
have been catalogued by catchphrases that any hip individual knew could refer only to
Francis Albert Sinatra. Thus he was The Crooner and The Swooner in the 1940s, The
Swinger in the 50s, The Chairman of the Board in the 60s, Ol' Blue Eyes in the 70s, and
just plain The Voice or Frank or Frankie or Sinatra throughout all these decades.

Francis Albert Sinatra was born in Hoboken, New Jersey, on December 12, 1915,
the only child of Anthony Martin and Natalie (Garaventi) Sinatra. Both parents were
Italian-born. Anthony (known as Marty) was a soft-spoken, asthmatic boxer who later
became a member of the Hoboken Fire Department; his wife, Natalie (known as Dolly),
was a gregarious, take-charge sort, renowned as an energetic ward heeler for the Democratic
Party in Hudson County. For a time, the parents ran a saloon called Marty O'Brien's. Of
his streetwise childhood, Sinatra once said, "All I knew was tough kids on street corners,
gang fights, and parents who were too busy trying to make enough money for food, rent,
and clothes."

Sinatra suffered through David E. Rue Junior High, but by the time he entered
Hoboken's Demarest High School, he had developed a hatred of formal education. He
soon quit. By now he had learned to play the ukulele (a gift from his uncle) and was
fascinated with the singing styles of Bing Crosby and Rudy Vallee. He wanted to become
a crooner, but his practical-minded parents (especially his dominating mother) insisted on
something else. Through family connections, he got a menial newspaper job with *The
Jersey Observer*, but this lasted only a short time. Meanwhile, his love of music persisted.
Finally, Mrs. Sinatra financed the purchase of a portable sound system and the young man
began singing with local bands at area roadhouses and nightclubs.

It was Dolly's connections that landed Sinatra a job (first as a driver) with a local singing group, The Three Flashes. When this act made two movie shorts at the Biograph Studios in the Bronx, Dolly insisted that Frank be part of the production. The shorts, THE MINSTREL and THE NIGHT CLUB, were part of a promotional push by talent-finder Major Bowes and were issued together as MAJOR BOWES' THEATRE OF THE AIR, AMATEUR NIGHT in the fall of 1935. Meanwhile, Major Bowes decided to use the group on his weekly radio program, aired from Broadway's Capitol Theatre. The act, now known as The Hoboken Four (to include Sinatra), was heard on the September 8, 1935, broadcast. They won the show's contest that night—singing "Shine"—and went on the road with Bowes and his troupe. While The Hokoken Four was performing on the West Coast, Sinatra became homesick and returned to New Jersey. Thereafter, for the next year and a half, he sang at a north Jersey roadhouse, the Rustic Cabin, earning $15 weekly. On February 4, 1939, having gotten a $10 weekly raise, he married his long-time girlfriend, Nancy Barbato, at Our Lady of Sorrows Church in Jersey City. (They would have three children: Nancy, born in 1940; Franklin Wayne, born in 1944; and Christina, born in 1948.)

Hoping to gain the attention of someone important who could boost his career, Sinatra sang for free on several New York City and New Jersey radio stations, plugging the latest songs of the day. In 1939, Harry James, the lead trumpeter with Benny Goodman's band, broke away from his mentor and began his own group, Harry James and His Music Makers. He heard Sinatra performing on WNEW's "Dance Band Parade" program, which aired from the Rustic Cabin. James hired Sinatra at $75 weekly. He went on the road with the James group, which had Connie Haines as its female vocalist. With the Music Makers he was heard on radio broadcasts as they crisscrossed the country, and with James he made a few singles, including "All or Nothing" for Columbia Records. When James and his musicians played New York City's Roseland, Sinatra received one of his first industry reviews. *Metronome* magazine commended the "pleasing vocals of Frank Sinatra, whose easy phrasing is especially commendable." Sinatra, already aggressive and outspoken, did not feel that James and his troupe were progressing fast enough. When Tommy Dorsey's band offered him $125 weekly, he accepted the deal, agreeing to help James (who tore up Sinatra's contract) to train his replacement, Dick Haymes.

Sinatra would remain with the Dorsey organization for three and a half years. In 1940, Dorsey—with Sinatra as his lead vocalist—was recording for RCA Victor and they had several top ten hits, including "I'll Never Smile Again," "We Three," "Stardust," and "Our Love Affair." It was during this period that Sinatra perfected his effortless song delivery, which seemed unbroken by breathing. He once explained, "I figured if he [Dorsey] could do that phrasing with his horn, I could do it with my voice." On another occasion he said, "I was able to sing six bars, and in some songs eight bars, without taking a visible or audible breath. This gave the melody a flowing, unbroken quality, and that—if anything—is what made me sound different."

When Dorsey went to Hollywood to make movies, Sinatra went with him. In LAS VEGAS NIGHTS (1941) he sang "I'll Never Smile Again" and in SHIP AHOY (1942) he was among those performing "Poor You" and "On Moonlight Bay." By 1942 he was number one in several industry polls of top male vocalists, and in July 1942 he waxed "There Are Such Things" with the Dorsey group. It was to be their final joint recording, for Sinatra soon broke his contract with the bandleader, leading to a bitter feud and a later settlement. Dorsey would later say of Sinatra, "He's the most fascinating man on Earth, but don't put your hand in the cage with him."

It was on December 30, 1942, that Sinatra, now on his own, made his historic appearance—with Benny Goodman and His Orchestra—at New York's Paramount Theatre. Sinatra's publicist hired several teenage girls to be in the audience to start a wave of screaming and swooning and this, along with Sinatra's own charisma and popularity, began an avalanche of squealing audience reaction, especially among the bobby-soxer set. He became known as The Swooner (or The Crooner or The Voice). He was soon the lead singer on CBS network radio's "Your Hit Parade," earning $1,000 a week, and was appearing at Broadway's Riobamba Club. He made several popular return visits to the Paramount Theatre, always attended by hordes of screaming fans. He began recording in mid-1943 with Columbia Records, including such early hits as "You'll Never Know." By this time, he was already becoming famous for his entourage, his hard living, and his passion for the boxing game (he already owned a percentage of a popular fighter).

Sinatra had appeared as a guest performer in the low-budget Ann Miller musical REVEILLE WITH BEVERLY, for Columbia Pictures in 1943. However, it was RKO Pictures which signed the hot singer to a nonexclusive term contract that year. He made his studio bow in HIGHER AND HIGHER (1943), a pleasant but undistinguished musical in which he sang, among other tunes, "I Couldn't Sleep a Wink Last Night" (which became a big hit tune) and "The Music Stopped." Of his acting debut, *Variety* reported, "Though a bit stiff on occasion and not as photogenic as may be desired, he generally handles himself ably. . . ." (The *New York Times* dismissed the film as "Lower and Lower.") RKO's STEP LIVELY (1944), a musical reworking of the Marx Brothers' ROOM SERVICE (1938), cast him as a playwright and paired him with Gloria De Haven and George Murphy. He sang such items as "And Then You Kissed Me" and "As Long as There's Music."

Meanwhile, he performed at the Hollywood Bowl with the Los Angeles Philharmonic Orchestra (August 1943) and debuted (October 1943) at the Wedgewood Room of the Waldorf-Astoria in New York. By the end of 1943 there was no doubt in the polls that Sinatra, famous for singing sentimental ballads of loneliness and lost love, was the top male singer, outdistancing in popularity such rivals as Bing Crosby, Dick Haymes, Perry Como, and Ray Eberle. In short, the skinny beanpole with the big Adam's apple, the trademark bow tie, and the big ears had become the country's number one singing attraction. It was called the age of "Sinatramania."

At the end of 1943, the skinny Sinatra had been classified 1-A by the draft board. When he went through his pre-induction physical in January 1944, it was discovered that he had a punctured eardrum. He was reclassified 4-F. "The Voice" continued to tour the country where he packed them in on every occasion. He had made $25,000 for HIGHER AND HIGHER, $50,000 for STEP LIVELY, and was contracted to be paid $100,000 for his third RKO picture. However, by then, MGM had decided it wanted Sinatra as part of its star stable. It borrowed Frank to join with Gene Kelly in ANCHORS AWEIGH (1945), an in-fectious study of two sailors on leave in Hollywood. The far more experienced dancer Kelly did much to make Sinatra look fluid on screen as the two soft-shoed through the romantic fable. Happier at the more prestigious Metro-Goldwyn-Mayer lot, Sinatra arranged for MGM to share his RKO contract, and the new terms called for him to earn $260,000 a year. To help compensate for his hard-hitting lifestyle and the fact that he was on the homefront while most young men were overseas fighting, he donated his services when he starred in the RKO short subject THE HOUSE I LIVE IN (1945), which preached tolerance. It earned a special Academy Award. His biggest 1945 tunes were "Nancy" (written in honor of his daughter), "I Dream of You," and "Saturday Night." In the fall of 1945 he started a new CBS network radio program, "Songs by Sinatra," which would last two seasons.

In TILL THE CLOUDS ROLL BY (1946), Sinatra climaxed the star-studded proceedings by singing "Ol' Man River." He had a much fuller role in IT HAPPENED IN BROOKLYN (1947), as the ex-G.I. without a family who comes to Brooklyn where he moves in with a school janitor (Jimmy Durante), befriends a British buddy (Peter Lawford), admires a schoolteacher/singer (Kathryn Grayson), and falls in love with an Army nurse (Gloria Grahame) he had met abroad. With Durante, Sinatra performed the duet "The Song's Gotta Come from the Heart," and his solo "Time After Time" became a permanent part of the Sinatra hit catalogue. From this joyous musical, Sinatra returned to RKO to star in a dramatic assignment as a priest in the somber THE MIRACLE OF THE BELLS (1948). The flip was a near flop and certainly did not do for him what GOING MY WAY (1944) or THE BELLS OF ST. MARY'S (1945) had done for his screen crooner rival, Bing Crosby. *Time* magazine decided, "Frank Sinatra, looking rather flea-bitten as the priest, acts properly humble or perhaps ashamed."

The nadir of Sinatra's MGM tenure was THE KISSING BANDIT (1948), in which he played at being the meek young man who must fulfill his father's legacy as a womanizing bandito. Neither Technicolor, nor Ann Miller, Ricardo Montalban, and Cyd Charisse's performing of the "Dance of Fury," nor Kathryn Grayson singing "Love Is Where You Find It" could save this fiasco. Far better were his two 1949 MGM releases. Both TAKE ME OUT TO THE BALL GAME and ON THE TOWN reunited him with singing and dancing star Gene Kelly. Both films presented Sinatra at his relaxed best. He was a baseball player in the former and a sailor in the latter, and in both he romanced rambunctious Betty Garrett. In 1949, his only top ten song was "The Huckle Buck."

By 1950, Sinatra and MGM (which strongly disapproved of the married Sinatra's having such a publicized love life with others) ended their agreement. On Valentine's Day 1950, Sinatra and his wife separated. They were divorced on October 29, 1951, but they have always remained close. On November 7, 1951, he married his long-time romance Ava Gardner, MGM's love goddess. She was already the ex-wife of Mickey Rooney and Artie Shaw. While Ava's career flourished, Sinatra's floundered. He had had an unsuccess-ful two-week engagement at the London Palladium in 1950, his records were not selling (he had no number one hits in the 1950–53 period), and his movies were bombs. He had made his final RKO picture, DOUBLE DYNAMITE (1951), a dud with Groucho Marx and Jane Russell, and then made a semi-autobiographical quickie at Universal, MEET DANNY WILSON (1952), co-starring Shelley Winters. Universal decided against doing further Sinatra vehicles. There were times in this period when the former Crooner was known as The Croaker or Groaner, for he seemed to have a permanent frog in his throat. He was dropped by Columbia Records as well as by his agent, MCA.

Whatever the circumstances surrounding *how* Sinatra acquired the role of Maggio in the (pre)–World War II epic FROM HERE TO ETERNITY (1953), it was the turning point of his career. He campaigned hard for the part, beating out Eli Wallach for the role. Sinatra said later, "I'm no actor, but I know this guy. I went to school with him. I've been beaten up by him. I might have been Maggio." For a fee of $8,000, he played the feisty Italian-American G.I. who is coping with rugged barracks life in pre–Pearl Harbor Hawaii. He gave a surprisingly sensitive dramatic performance and won the Best Supporting Actor Oscar.

It was the start of the new "ring-a-ding-ding" Sinatra. He was now recording for Capitol Records, for whom in 1954 he had two top ten hits: "Three Coins in the Fountain" (he sang the title tune in the 20th Century–Fox film as a favor to his lyricist friend Sammy Cahn) and "Young at Heart." The latter was from his Warner Bros. musical of the same title, co-starring Doris Day. He was troublesome on the set, but gave an excellent account of himself as the unhappy singer who marries Day and nearly wrecks her life before coming to terms with himself after a self-induced car crash. His production company was responsible for SUDDENLY (1954), a dramatically impressive account of an itchy presidential assassin (Sinatra). In

Debbie Reynolds and Frank Sinatra in THE TENDER TRAP (1955)

NOT AS A STRANGER (1955), he supported Robert Mitchum as a wisecracking doctor-to-be. He had a hit album with *Songs for Swingin' Lovers* (1955).

Sinatra returned to MGM in a tailor-made role, as the swinging bachelor in THE TENDER TRAP (1955), with Debbie Reynolds as the spirited young miss who captures the womanizer. Samuel Goldwyn's translation of the Broadway hit GUYS AND DOLLS (1955) into a screen musical was full of surprise casting (especially Marlon Brando), with Sinatra only middling as the Damon Runyonesque Nathan Detroit, a role indelibly handled on stage by Sam Levene. He was considered for the Ensign Pulver role in MISTER ROBERTS (1955) but the part went to Jack Lemmon (who won a Best Supporting Actor Oscar). On the other hand, Frank gave a very strong interpretation of the drug-addicted loser in THE MAN WITH THE GOLDEN ARM (1955—for which he was Oscar-nominated as Best Actor). He went Western again in the unpopular JOHNNY CONCHO (1956—which he financed). Sinatra played second banana to his long-time idol/rival Bing Crosby in the Cole Porter musical HIGH SOCIETY (1956) at his alma mater, MGM. In this superior outing, Crosby wins Grace Kelly's affection and sings "True Love," while magazine writer Sinatra is paired with Celeste Holm and duets with Crosby on "Well, Did You Evah?" In the cameo-studded AROUND THE WORLD IN 80 DAYS (1956), Sinatra appeared as a saloon piano player, paired in the sequence with Marlene Dietrich (a long-time friend and one-time romance). On July 5, 1957, Sinatra and Ava Gardner were divorced, although he remained her benefactor and booster throughout the years.

During the crucial comeback decade of the 1950s, Sinatra was a very active participant on radio and television. On radio he continued with variety-format programs on CBS (1950–51), NBC (1953, 1953–55), and ABC (1956–58) and starred in the detective series "Rocky Fortune" (NBC, 1953–54). On television, where he was never as popular as in other media, he had "The Frank Sinatra Show," which debuted on October 7, 1950, over CBS. It was telecast live from New York and lasted two seasons. However, it could not outdistance the competition ("Your Show of Shows" the first year and Milton Berle's "The Texaco Star Theatre" the second season). He was, to a certain extent, a has-been at the time of the show's departure, but had resurrected his performing career by the time he co-starred with Ethel Merman and Bert Lahr in a condensed version of her stage hit "Anything Goes" (NBC-TV, February 28, 1954). The next year he was the Stage Manager in a musical rendering of "Our Town" (NBC-TV, September 19, 1955). On that network special he sang "Love and Marriage," which rose to number five on the charts.

ABC-TV paid Sinatra $3 million to star in "The Frank Sinatra Show" (1957–58), which featured Nelson Riddle and His Orchestra (with whom Sinatra made many of his finest Capitol recordings). The series fiasco (a very big one) found Sinatra refusing to rehearse, preoccupied with moviemaking and other deal making, and at odds with the format (a mix of variety shows, dramas starring Sinatra, and dramas featuring others). Among his guest stars were Bob Hope, Peggy Lee, and daughter Nancy, who, at age seventeen, made her professional debut on the November 1, 1957, episode. This half-hour Sinatra show folded on June 27, 1958. He concluded the decade with two 1959 ABC-TV specials: the first (October 9) featured Bing Crosby, Dean Martin, Mitzi Gaynor, and Jimmy Durante; the second (December 13) presented Ella Fitzgerald and Juliet Prowse (then one of Sinatra's succession of girlfriends).

The late 1950s was Sinatra's most fertile moviemaking period, although he walked out of CAROUSEL (1956—and was replaced by Gordon MacRae). He was in the foolish period Spanish epic THE PRIDE AND THE PASSION (1957—with Cary Grant and Sophia Loren), for which he was paid $250,000. He then did what he did best—sang—and was strongly dramatic in THE JOKER IS WILD (1957), the story of singer-turned-comedian Joe E. Lewis. That feature produced his hit tune "All the Way." He was the prize heel PAL JOEY (1957) opposite rising Kim Novak and declining Rita Hayworth and got to croon "A Small Hotel," "I Didn't Know What Time It Was," and "The Lady Is a Tramp." He was now in the top ten at the box office. He was very resilient in the gutsy KINGS GO FORTH (1958), a World War II study set in France. It co-featured Tony Curtis and Natalie Wood and dealt with interracial romance and drug addiction. He was very effective as the ex-G.I. writer in SOME CAME RUNNING (1958), which teamed him for the first time with pals Dean Martin and Shirley MacLaine. In A HOLE IN THE HEAD (1959) a very light-hearted Frank Sinatra played father to motherless Eddie Hodges in Miami Beach and sang "High Hopes."

It was in NEVER SO FEW (1959) that Sinatra blatantly used the formula of winging it on camera in an adventure yarn filled with rising new talent (Steve McQueen, Charles Bronson), established personalities (Gina Lollobrigida, Paul Henreid, Brian Donlevy), and old pals (Peter Lawford). Sinatra, acting very much the star, was far from believable as the tough, heavy-drinking American captain who leads a team of guerrillas against the Japanese in World War II Burma. Although CAN-CAN (1960) was a vulgar travesty of the Cole Porter stage hit, it was a major release because it starred Sinatra with Shirley MacLaine, Maurice Chevalier, and Juliet Prowse.

By now the Sinatra Rat Pack (which began with friendships with Humphrey Bogart, Lauren Bacall [who almost became Mrs. Sinatra], and Judy Garland) was legendary. He used his off-camera coterie (especially Dean Martin, Sammy Davis, Jr., and Joey Bishop) to pepper his early 1960s releases: OCEAN'S ELEVEN (1960), SERGEANTS THREE (1962), 4 FOR TEXAS (1963), ROBIN AND THE SEVEN HOODS (1964), and MARRIAGE ON THE ROCKS (1965). In between he was in the fiasco THE DEVIL AT 4 O'CLOCK (1961) with Spencer Tracy, whom he greatly admired, and made the starkly frightening THE MAN-CHURIAN CANDIDATE (1962), a highly regarded, macabre tale of a political assassin. An adaptation of Neil Simon's Broadway hit, COME BLOW YOUR HORN (1963) did nothing to enhance his reputation as a purveyor of the philandering playboy. He played at high adventure in the World War II dramas NONE BUT THE BRAVE (1965—which he co-directed) and VON RYAN'S EXPRESS (1965). He was an American aviator who crashes to his death in CAST A GIANT SHADOW (1966), led a sea heist in ASSAULT ON A QUEEN (1966), and his production company co-financed THE NAKED RUNNER (1967), a spy melodrama focusing on political assassination. Searching for a new screen persona, he turned to playing a detective (the womanizing, boozing, cynical type) in TONY ROME (1967), which spawned a less effective sequel, LADY IN CEMENT (1968). The logical extension was to become a police investigator, which he did in THE DETECTIVE (1968), noted more for its controversial dealing with homosexuality and police corruption than for Sinatra's characterization.

By 1970, Frank Sinatra the legend had gone through many transformations. He was renowned for hob-nobbing with an odd assortment of friends, who ranged from Hollywood celebrities (Rosalind Russell, Claudette Colbert) to sports figures (Joe DiMaggio) to politicians (he was a strong advocate of Franklin D. Roosevelt and later of John F. Kennedy) to underworld associates. He admitted, "I like broads," and that the recurring media accusations of his ties to organized crime were untrue. He retorted, "anyone whose name ends in a vowel gets abused for no reason at all." (Investigative journalist Pete Hamill insisted of Sinatra, "He is the most investigated American performer since John Wilkes Booth, and although he has never been indicted or convicted of any mob-connected crime, the connection is part of the legend.") He was famous for his feuds with the press, for his high-voltage temper, which led to scuffles in clubs across the country, and for his involvement in Las Vegas and Lake Tahoe hotel ownerships. His Hollywood compound boasted a sign that read, "If you haven't been invited, you better have a damn good reason for ringing this bell!"

As the years passed, Frank Sinatra became more isolated from his public. In the 1950s, as The Swinger, he had survived the onslaught of rock 'n' roll and Elvis Presley, and his album *Come Dance with Me!* won a Grammy Award in 1960. However, he could not compete with the British Invasion of the early 1960s led by The Beatles or with the Motown Sound (epitomized by Diana Ross and the Supremes). He formed his own recording company, Reprise Records, which became a part of Warner Bros. when he moved his production company there in 1963. Several of his most popular mid-1960s albums were recorded with Count Basie, including *Frank Sinatra with Count Basie* (1963), *It Might as Well Be Swing* (1964), and *Sinatra at the Sands* (1966). At one point in the mid-1960s, Sinatra was expected to be named the successor to studio head Jack L. Warner, but this never happened. His only number one single hits in the 1960s were "Strangers in the Night" (1966) and his duet with Nancy, Jr. on "Somethin' Stupid" (1967). "That's Life" (1966) was number four on the charts, "Cycles" (1968) was number twenty-three, and "My Way" (1969) was number twenty-seven. Despite falling off the charts, he continued to do sold-out business when he appeared in Las Vegas nightclubs. For his song "It Was a Very Good Year" (1966) and the album *September of My Years* (1966) he was awarded Grammys. The fast-living Sinatra most astounded the media when on July 17, 1966, in Las Vegas he married Mia Farrow, the twenty-one-year-old daughter of actress Maureen O'Sullivan. There were spats from the start, and after she returned from meditation in India with a guru in January 1968, their efforts at reconciliation ended in a final separation and divorce in August 1968. In 1966, 1967, and 1969, Sinatra had several well-regarded TV specials.

Now in his mid-fifties, Sinatra began the new decade with what is considered to be his rock-bottom motion picture, the abysmal Western DIRTY DINGUS MAGEE (1970).

During his late summer 1970 engagement at Caesar's Palace, he had a highly publicized dispute with a casino pit supervisor (surpassing his feud with the Sands Hotel management in 1967) and walked out of his engagement there, later cancelling his performing contract with the hotel. He dropped out of DIRTY HARRY (1971) due to a hand injury, cancelled out of a projected Otto Preminger film, WHERE THE DARK STREETS GO, and discontinued negotiations in 1972 with Paramount to star in the musical THE LITTLE PRINCE. (Richard Kiley did the part in 1974.) In 1971, Sinatra announced his retirement (citing "that need which every thinking man has for a fallow period") and made what was supposed to be his last public performing appearance at the 50th Anniversary charity show of the Motion Picture and Television Relief Fund. During the 1971 Academy Awards presentation, he received the Jean Hersholt Humanitarian Award.

Meanwhile, the former Democrat had turned Republican with his support of Ronald Reagan for Governor of California in 1970. It was in 1972 that Sinatra screamed "Character assassination! I'm no second-class citizen" when a congressional Committee on Crime focused on him, and he later presented the Committee with an $18,750 expense bill. President Nixon said of the now-confirmed Republican in 1973, "Frank Sinatra is . . . the Washington Monument of entertainment." It was Nixon who advised the singer, "You must get out of retirement."

Sinatra returned to recording with *Ol' Blue Eyes Is Back* (1973—which rose to number thirteen on the LP charts), and the TV special "Sinatra—The Main Event" (ABC, October 13, 1974) was a filming of his Madison Square Garden concert. In 1974 he co-hosted MGM's THAT'S ENTERTAINMENT! documentary, and three years later he made his telefeature debut in CONTRACT ON CHERRY STREET (NBC, November 19, 1977) playing a nonestablishment veteran New York police detective. It was not a very imaginative return to filmmaking. He had been off the top forty singles charts since 1969, but returned with his version of "New York, New York" (1980). That same year, his well-regarded three-record album, *Trilogy: Past, Present and Future,* was released by Reprise Records and reached number seventeen on the LP charts. It was his first recording in five years.

His first theatrical feature in a decade was THE FIRST DEADLY SIN (1980), a quickly dismissed detective genre piece set in New York City. It was quirky, badly paced, and wasted Faye Dunaway as his dying wife. His final feature appearance to date was a guest cameo in Burt Reynolds' car chase flop CANNONBALL RUN II (1984). Meanwhile, on July 11, 1976, in Rancho Mirage, California, Sinatra had married Barbara Jane (Blakeley) Marx, the ex-wife of Zeppo Marx (of the Marx Brothers). She was forty-six at the time of her wedding to the sixty-year-old Sinatra. On January 6, 1977, his mother, Dolly Sinatra, was killed in a plane crash, while en route in a chartered craft from Palm Springs to Las Vegas, where her son was performing on stage.

In the 1980s, Sinatra was considered a member of the senior set, but he had become the darling of the Baby Boomers, who found new meaning in his catalogue of recordings, which continue to be steady sellers. He starred in occasional TV specials in the early 1980s and played club and concert dates around the globe, always commanding high ticket prices. In December 1983, he and Dean Martin were in a much publicized brouhaha with a female blackjack dealer at an Atlantic City gambling casino. As a result, Sinatra threatened never to play Atlantic City again, but later recanted his vow. In 1985, Sinatra was given the Medal of Freedom by President Ronald Reagan. That same year he received an honorary degree from Stevens Institute of Technology in Hoboken, New Jersey. In 1985, Nancy Sinatra, Jr. published *Frank Sinatra, My Father,* a laudatory tribute to her famous dad. Not so favorable was Kitty Kelly's explosive exposé, *His Way: The Unauthorized Biography of Frank Sinatra* (1986). Kelly stated that she had interviewed 857 people and that the hardest part of writing her dissecting study was "assuring people they could speak without [fear of] reprisal." The *New York Times* judged it "the most eye-opening celebrity biography of our time."

In September 1986, Sinatra, whose voice had mellowed and then soured with the passing decades, reopened the Chicago Theatre in the Windy City with a series of concerts. He appeared on the February 25, 1987, episode of "Magnum P.I." (CBS-TV) playing a retired Manhattan cop. He had a sold-out eight-performance engagement at Carnegie Hall in September 1987. On March 13, 1988, he kicked off his U.S. concert tour, teamed with Sammy Davis, Jr. and Dean Martin, with Frank Sinatra, Jr. (who has never been able to generate a successful singing/film/recording career) as his band conductor. Martin soon left the tour, to be replaced by Liza Minnelli. The tour continued through the United States and on to Japan and other international destinations. A 1989 performance was filmed for the Showtime cable network as "Frank, Liza & Sammy: The Ultimate Event." In February 1989, he showed up playing himself on an episode of the Tony Danza comedy series "Who's the Boss?" (ABC-TV). He continued to play Las Vegas, made occasional TV commercials (for Las Vegas hotels and beer manufacturers), and developed a line of Italian foods for consumer marketing. Sinatra has also been an active crusader for the newly formed Performers Rights Society of America, seeking to gain compensation for nonsongwriter singers and musicians when their recordings are played on radio or on a jukebox.

At a January 1989 tribute (later televised on ABC), Sinatra was honored with the 30th Annual Will Rogers Memorial Award of the Beverly Hills Chamber of Commerce, in recognition for his having raised nearly $1 billion for various charities. Said presenter Charlton Heston, "A song is really a four-minute play, and has to be interpreted. I don't think there's another living singer that does that better than Frank [Sinatra]. . . . He does what Laurence Olivier does, I can pay no greater tribute."

## Filmography

Major Bowes' Theatre of the Air, Amateur Night
  (RKO, 1935) (s)
Las Vegas Nights (Par, 1941)
Ship Ahoy (MGM, 1942)
Reveille with Beverly (Col, 1943)
Show Business at War (20th–Fox, 1943) (s)

Higher and Higher (RKO, 1943)
The Shining Future (RKO, 1944) (s)
Step Lively (RKO, 1944)
Anchors Aweigh (MGM, 1945)
All Star Bond Rally (20th–Fox, 1945) (s)
The House I Live In (RKO, 1945) (s)

Till the Clouds Roll By (MGM, 1946)
It Happened in Brooklyn (MGM, 1947)
The Miracle of the Bells (RKO, 1948)
The Kissing Bandit (MGM, 1948)
Take Me Out to the Ball Game [Everybody's Cheering] (MGM, 1949)
On the Town (MGM, 1949)
Double Dynamite [On the Double] (RKO, 1951)
Meet Danny Wilson (Univ, 1952)
Screen Snapshots #206 (Col, 1952) (s)
From Here to Eternity (Col, 1953)
Three Coins in the Fountain (20th–Fox, 1953) (voice only)
Suddenly (UA, 1954)
Young at Heart (WB, 1954)
Not as a Stranger (UA, 1955)
The Tender Trap (MGM, 1955)
Guys and Dolls (MGM, 1955)
The Man with the Golden Arm (Col, 1955)
Meet Me in Las Vegas [Viva Las Vegas!] (MGM, 1956)
Johnny Concho (UA, 1956)
High Society (MGM, 1956)
Around the World in 80 Days (UA, 1956)
The Pride and the Passion (UA, 1957)
The Joker Is Wild [All the Way] (Par, 1957)
Pal Joey (Col, 1957)
Kings Go Forth (UA, 1958)
Some Came Running (MGM, 1958)
A Hole in the Head (UA, 1959)

Never So Few (MGM, 1959)
Invitation to Monte Carlo [Love in Monte Carlo] (Valiant Films, 1960) (s)
Can-Can (20th–Fox, 1960)
Ocean's Eleven (WB, 1960)
Pepe (Col, 1960)
The Devil at 4 O'Clock (Col, 1961)
The Road to Hong Kong (UA, 1962)
Sergeants Three (UA, 1962)
The Manchurian Candidate (UA, 1962)
The List of Adrian Messenger (Univ, 1963)
A New Kind of Love (Par, 1963) (voice only)
Come Blow Your Horn (Par, 1963)
4 for Texas (WB, 1963)
Robin and the Seven Hoods (WB, 1964)
None But the Brave (WB, 1965) (also co-director)
Von Ryan's Express (20th–Fox, 1965)
Marriage on the Rocks (WB, 1965)
The Oscar (Par, 1966)
Cast a Giant Shadow (UA, 1966)
Assault on a Queen (Par, 1966)
Tony Rome (20th–Fox, 1967)
The Naked Runner (WB, 1967)
Lady in Cement (20th–Fox, 1968)
The Detective (20th–Fox, 1968)
Dirty Dingus Magee (MGM, 1970)
That's Entertainment! (MGM, 1974) (co-host)
Contract on Cherry Street (NBC-TV, 11/19/77)
The First Deadly Sin (Filmways, 1980)
Cannonball Run II (WB, 1984)

## Radio Series

Dance Band Parade (WNEW, 1939) (local)
Your Hit Parade (CBS, 1943–45)
The Broadway Band Box (CBS, 1943)
The Frank Sinatra Show (CBS, 1944–45)
Songs by Sinatra (CBS, 1945–47)
Light Up Time (NBC, 1949–50)

The Frank Sinatra Show (CBS, 1950–51)
The Frank Sinatra Show (NBC, 1953)
To Be Perfectly Frank (NBC, 1953–55)
Rocky Fortune (NBC, 1953–54)
The Frank Sinatra Show (ABC, 1956–58)

## TV Series

The Frank Sinatra Show (CBS, 1950–52)
The Frank Sinatra Show (ABC, 1957–58)

## Album Discography

Academy Award Winners (Reprise 1011)

Adventures of the Heart (Col CL-953, Cameo 32319)

All Alone (Reprise 1007)

All the Way (Cap W/SW-1538, EMI 260179)

America, I Hear You Singing (Reprise 2020) w. Bing Crosby, Fred Waring

Anchors Aweigh (Curtain Calls 100/17, Sandy Hook 2024) [ST]

Anything Goes (Larynx 567, Amalgamated 144, Sandy Hook 2043) [ST/TV]

The Best of Frank Sinatra (Cap KAO/DKAO-2950)

Best Rarities of Frank Sinatra (Happy Bird B/90100, MB/90100)

Bing Crosby and Frank Sinatra—Live (Amalgamated 148)

The Broadway Band Box (My Way 1004)

The Broadway Kick (Col CL-1297)

Can-Can (Cap W/SW-1301) [ST]

Christmas Album (Cap T/ST-894)

Christmas Album (Reprise 1023)

Christmas Dreaming (Col CL-1032, Col FC-40907)

Christmas Songs (10" Col CL-6019)

Christmas with Sinatra (10" Col CL-2542)

Close to You (Cap W/DW-789)

Close-Up (Cap DWBB-254)

Collectors' Series (Cameron 504)

Columbo, Crosby and Sinatra (10" RCA LPT-5) w. Russ Columbo, Bing Crosby

Come Back to Sorrento (Col CL-1359)

Come Dance with Me! (Cap W/SW-1069, EMI 260080)

Come Fly with Me (Cap W/SW-920, Cap SM-920, EMI 260095)

Come Swing with Me (Cap W/SW-1594, EMI 260180)

Company (Reprise 1033) w. Antonio Carlos Jobim

The Concert Sinatra (Reprise 1009)

The Connoisseurs' Sinatra (Cap T-20734)

Cycles (Reprise 1027)

Dean Martin and Frank Sinatra (Jocklo International 1008)

Dean Martin, Judy Garland and Frank Sinatra (Jocklo International 1007)

Dean Martin Sings—Frank Sinatra Conducts (Cap T/ST-2297, Pickwick 3456)

Dedicated to You (10" Col CL-6096)

The Definitive Sinatra (Chairman 6009)

The Deluxe Set (Cap STFL-2814)

Dick Tracy in B-Flat (Curtain Calls 100/1) [ST/R]

The Dorsey/Sinatra Sessions: 1940–42 (RCA SD-1000) w. Tommy Dorsey

The Early Days (Avenue 1001)

The Early Radio Years (My Way 1004)

The Essential Frank Sinatra (Col S3S-842)

The Fabulous Frankie (10" RCA LPT-3063)

The First Time (Cameron 5001/04)

Forever Frank (Cap T/DT-2602)

Francis A. and Edward K. (Reprise 1024) w. Duke Ellington

Francis Albert Sinatra and Antonio Carlos Jobim (Reprise 1021)

Frank and Nancy (Reprise 1022) w. Nancy Sinatra

Frank Sinatra (Emidisc C-0048-50-701)

Frank Sinatra (Har HS-11390)

Frank Sinatra (Sandy Hook 40)

Frank Sinatra (Vocal Classics 4003)

Frank Sinatra at the Sands (Reprise 2F-1019) w. Count Basie

Frank Sinatra Conducts Music from Pictures and Plays (Reprise 6045)

Frank Sinatra Conducts the Music of Alec Wilder (Col ML-4271, Col CL-884, Odyssey 32160262)

The Frank Sinatra Duets (P. J. International 001)

Frank Sinatra in Hollywood, 1943–49 (Col CL-2913)

Frank Sinatra—1946 (Joyce 6047)

Frank Sinatra—October 30, 1946 (Joyce 6042)

Frank Sinatra on V-Disc, Vols. 1–3 (Joyce 6049, 6051, 6053)

Frank Sinatra Plus Connee Boswell (Joyce 1121)

Frank Sinatra Sings Evergreens (Avenue 1004)

Frank Sinatra Sings Rodgers and Hart (Cap W/DW-1825)

Frank Sinatra Sings the Select Cole Porter (Cap W/SW-2301)

Frank Sinatra Sings the Select Johnny Mercer (Cap W/SW-1948)

Frank Sinatra Sings Van Heusen and Cahn (EMI 2044)

The Frank Sinatra Story in Music (Col C2L-6, Col Special Products 6)

Frank Sinatra with Count Basie (Reprise 1008)

Frankie (Col CL-606)

Frankie and Tommy Dorsey (RCA LPM-1569)

Frankie Boy (P. J. International 002)

Frankly Sentimental (10" Col CL-6059)

Get Happy (10" Col CL-2521)

Great Hits (Cap T/DT-2036)

The Great Years (Cap WCO/SWCO-1762)

The Greatest (Cap DKAO-374)

Greatest Hits (Prestige for Pleasure 4M032-30466)

Greatest Hits (Reprise 1025)

Greatest Hits, Vol. 2 (Col CL-2572/CS-9372)

Greatest Hits, Vol. 2 (Reprise 1034)

Greatest Hits from the Early Years (Col CL-2474/CS-9274)

Greatest Hits—The Early Years (Har HS-30318)

Guys and Dolls (Motion Picture Tracks MPT-1) [ST]

Have Yourself a Merry Little Christmas (Har HS-11200)

Hello, Young Lovers (Col C2-40897)

Here's to the Ladies (Reprise 2259)

High Society (Cap W/SW-750) [ST]

Higher and Higher (Hollywood Soundtrack 411) [ST]

I Remember Tommy (Reprise 1003)

I'll See You in My Dreams (Camden ADL2-0178) w. Tommy Dorsey

I'm Confessin' (Windmill 214)

I'm Gettin' Sentimental over You (Camden CXS-9027) w. Tommy Dorsey

In the Beginning, 1943–51 (Col PG-31358)

In the Wee Small Hours (10" Cap H-1/2-581)

In the Wee Small Hours (Cap W/DW-581, Cap 1008)

It Might as Well Be Swing (Reprise 1012) w. Count Basie

I've Got a Crush on You (10" Col CL-6290)

The Joker Is Wild (Caliban 6024) [ST]

A Jolly Christmas with Frank Sinatra (Cap W/DW-894)

Just One of Those Things (Pickwick/Cap 3457)

L.A. Is My Lady (Qwest 1-25145)

Las Vegas Nights/Ship Ahoy (Caliban 6030) [ST]

Look over My Shoulder (World Record Club TP-81)

Look to Your Heart (Cap W/DW-1164, Cap N-11973)

Love Is a Kick (Col CL-1241)

The Main Event—Live (Reprise 2207)

A Man Alone (Reprise 1030)

A Man and His Music (Reprise 2FS-1016)

Master of Song (Avenue 1012)

Meet Danny Wilson (Caliban 6016) [ST]

Moonlight Sinatra (Reprise 1018)

Movie Songs (Capitol T/DT-2700)

A Musical Montage (Artistry 105)

My Cole Porter (Pickwick 3463)

My Funny Valentine (Cap T/DT-1826)

My Kind of Broadway (Reprise 1015)

My One and Only Love/Sentimental Journey (Cap STBB-724)

My Way (Reprise 1029)

The Nearness of You (Pickwick 3450)

Nevertheless (Pickwick 3456)

Nice 'n Easy (Cap W/SW-1417, Cap SM-1417)

No One Cares (Cap W/SW-1221, Cap SM-1221)

Of Love and Things! (Cap W/SW-1729, Cap SN-16149)

Ol' Blue Eyes Is Back (Reprise 2155)

On the Town (Show Biz 5603, Caliban 6023) [ST]

One More for the Road (Cap ST-11309)

Only the Lonely (Cap W/SW-1053, Cap SM-1053)

Pal Joey (Cap W-912) [ST]

The Paramount Years (Chairman 6011)

Point of No Return (Cap W/SW-1676, Cap SM-1676)

Pure Gold (RCA ANL1-1586)

Put Your Dreams Away (Col CL-1136)

The Rare Recordings (Sandy Hook 2040)

The Rare Sinatra (Cap 24311, M.F.P. 5856)

Reflections (Col CL-1448)

Ring-a-Ding-Ding! (Reprise 1001)

Robin and the Seven Hoods (Reprise 2021) [ST]

The Romantic Sinatra (Avenue 1013)

Romantic Songs from the Early Years (Har HL-7405/HS-11205)

Round One (Cap SABB-11357)

A Salute to Nat (King) Cole (Reprise PRO-212) w. Sammy Davis, Jr.

Screen Sinatra (Cap 50320)

Sentimental Journey (Cap W-90986)

September of My Years (Reprise 1014)

She Shot Me Down (Reprise FS-2305)

Sinatra and Strings (Reprise 1004)

Sinatra and Swingin' Brass (Reprise 1005)

Sinatra at the Sands (Reprise 1019) w. Count Basie

Sinatra—Jobim (Reprise 1028) w. Antonio Carlos Jobim

Sinatra Sings . . . of Love and Things (Cap 1729)

Sinatra Swings (Cap 50320)

Sinatra Swings (Reprise 1022)

Sinatra's Sinatra (Reprise 1010)

Sing and Dance with Sinatra (10" Col CL-6143)

'65 (Reprise 6167)

Softly, as I Leave You (Reprise 1013)

Some Nice Things I've Missed (Reprise 2195)

Someone to Watch over Me (Har HS-11277)

The Song Is You (Avenue 1003)

Songs by Sinatra (10" Col Cl-6087)

Songs for Swingin' Lovers (Cap W/DW-653, Cap SM-653)

Songs for Young Lovers (10" Cap H-488)

Songs for Young Lovers (Cap W/DW-1432, EMI 260074)

Songs from Great Britain (Reprise 1006)

Special (Pickwick 2064)

Strangers in the Night (Reprise 1017)

Summit Meeting at the 500 (Souvenir 247-17) w. Dean Martin, Sammy Davis, Jr.

Swing Easy (10" Cap H-528)

Swing Easy (Cap W/DW-1429)

Swing Easy/Songs for Young Lovers (Cap W-587)

Swingin' Affair (Cap W/DW-803, Cap SM-11502, EMI 260017)

Swinging Sessions!!! (Cap W/SW-1491, Cap SM-1491)

Swinging Sexy Sinatra (EMI/Pathé 51773)

S'Wonderful (Windmill 200)

Take Me Out to the Ballgame (Curtain Calls 100/18) [ST]

Tell Her You Love Her (Cap T/DT-1919)

That Old Feeling (Col CL-902)

That's Life (Reprise 1020)

This Is Sinatra! (Cap T/DT-768, Cap M-11883)

This Is Sinatra, Vols. 1–2 (EMI 1237/38)

This Love of Mine (Pickwick 3458)

This Love of Mine (RCA LPV-583) w. Tommy Dorsey

Through the Years, Vols. 1–6 (Ajazz 506, 508, 514, 519, 522, 525)

To Be Perfectly Frank (Chairman 6010)

The Tommy Dorsey Orchestra with Frank Sinatra (RCA International 43685)

Tone Poems of Color (Cap W-735)

Trilogy: Past, Present and Future (Reprise SFS-2300)

Try a Little Tenderness (Pickwick 3452)

Try a Little Tenderness/Nevertheless (Pickwick/Cap 2021)

Twelve Songs of Christmas (Reprise 6022) w. Bing Crosby, Fred Waring

20 Classic Tracks (MFP 50530)

The V-Disc Years, Vols. 1–2 (My Way 1001/02)

La Voce, un Mito Sinatra, Vols. 1–2 (Castagna 321/22)

The Voice (CBS 3552)

The Voice (Col CL-743)

The Voice of Frank Sinatra (10" Col CL-6001)

The Voice: The Columbia Years: 1943–1952 (Col C6X 40343)

A Warm and Wonderful Christmas Eve (Ho-Ho-Ho 1088) w. Bing Crosby

Watertown (Reprise 1031)

We Three (RCA LPM-1632) w. Tommy Dorsey

What Is This Thing Called Love?/The Night We Called It a Day (Cap STBB-529)

What'll I Do (RCA APL1-0497) w. Tommy Dorsey

Where Are You? (Cap W/SW-855)

Wish You a Merry Christmas (Reprise 1026) w. Nancy Sinatra, Frank Sinatra, Jr.

The World We Knew (Reprise 1022)

Young at Heart (10" Col CL-6339) [ST]

The Young Frank Sinatra (Top Classic Historia H-624)

# KATE SMITH

PERHAPS THE MOST POPULAR FEMALE SINGER IN SHOW BUSINESS
and also one of the most beloved women in American history, Kate Smith entertained
many generations of Americans in her more than fifty years in the limelight. While critics
predicted that a young woman of her girth could never be more than a buffoon, Kate
Smith proved them wrong with her resounding voice, bright smile, and appealing personality. Kate would find great career success on stage, radio, television, personal appearances,
recordings, and, to a far lesser extent, in motion pictures. Her influence in the 1930s and
1940s was such that millions tuned in not only to hear her sing, but also to listen to her
opinions on a variety of topical subjects on her daytime "Kate Smith Speaks" radio
program.

As the years passed, Kate Smith's popularity never dimmed, as she became a part of
Americana; she was once described as "Radio's Own Statue of Liberty." Of all her career
activities, Kate Smith was least pleased with her films, especially her solo starring picture,
HELLO, EVERYBODY (1933). While she made nearly a dozen movie appearances, mostly in
short subjects, Kate Smith is less remembered as an actress than as a radio and television
superstar.

Kathryn Elizabeth Smith was born May 1, 1907, in Greenville, Virginia, the
daughter of William and Charlotte (Hanby) Smith; her sister, Helene, was three years her
senior. Kathryn's father owned the Capitol News Company, an independent news deal-
ership, and since she loved music, her father helped her gain singing and dancing
engagements in Washington, D.C., where the family eventually resided. Although she
became very heavy as a teenager, Kate was an extremely agile dancer. She wanted to pursue
a show business career, but her parents wanted her to be a nurse. Thus, after graduating
from high school in 1925, she entered nurses' training. After a year, she quit and landed a
vaudeville engagement in Washington, D.C. As a result of that assignment, she was
spotted by Broadway producer A. L. "Abe" Erlanger, who hired her to appear in his
upcoming revue *Honeymoon Lane*.

As Tiny Little, Kate made her Broadway bow in the show on September 20, 1926,
at the Knickerbocker Theatre. That year she made her recording debut for Columbia
Records. After a lengthy run on Broadway in *Honeymoon Lane*, Kate toured with the show,
and in 1929, she did a stock company production of *Hit the Deck* and recorded for Columbia's dime store labels. In the spring of 1929, she appeared with Nick Lucas, Ted
Lewis, and Sophie Tucker on NBC's "RKO Radio Hour" and played a successful
engagement at the Palace Theatre. She made her first screen appearance in the Brooklyn-

filmed Vitaphone short KATE SMITH—SONGBIRD OF THE SOUTH (1929), singing "Carolina Moon" and "Bless You Sister."

Early (March 3) in 1930, Kate returned to Broadway in the musical comedy *Flying High*. Although she was a success in the production, she was personally miserable because of the coarse treatment she received from star Bert Lahr and the rest of the cast. (Throughout her career, she had to endure comedians' jokes about her size.) However, it was during that show's run that she met record producer Ted Collins, who took over the management of her career. When the show closed, he convinced Rudy Vallee to give Kate a guest spot on his "The Fleischmann's Hour" radio show. She was so successful that she appeared twice more on the program and then landed a regular spot on Freddy Rich Rhythm King's Monday night CBS broadcast.

In March 1931, the singer was given her own radio show, "Kate Smith Sings," each Tuesday and Thursday at 11:30 p.m. on NBC. It was here that she first used "When the Moon Comes over the Mountain" (for which she wrote the lyrics) as her theme song. While her NBC show was short-lived, on April 26, 1931, she began her "Kate Smith Show" on CBS, three evenings a week at 7 p.m. This program was an immediate success and Kate Smith was soon the most popular female singer on radio, which brought about an increased demand for both her recordings and personal appearances (especially at the Palace Theatre).

There was also a big demand for Kate Smith to make films. In 1932, she appeared in a trio of short subjects. In Vitaphone's RAMBLING 'ROUND RADIO ROW #1, she sang "Whistle and Blow Your Blues Away." In KATE SMITH PRESENTS A MEMORY PROGRAM, she performed "Old Folks at Home," "Grandfather's Clock," "Songs My Mother Taught Me," and "Seeing Nellie Home." In UM & M Pictorial's THE WORLD AT LARGE, she appeared in a segment called "The Radio Star Maker—Ted Collins" and sang "When Work Is Through" and offered a brief rendition of "When the Moon Comes over the Mountain." In this latter short she displayed a relaxed sense of humor that was sadly unexploited in her further movie appearances.

Also in 1932, Kate made her feature film debut as herself in Paramount's THE BIG BROADCAST singing "It Was So Beautiful." By now the singer had signed a long-term contract with Paramount (the home of svelte Claudette Colbert, Marlene Dietrich, and Carole Lombard). In 1932, she went to Hollywood to star in HELLO, EVERYBODY (1933) (which was her familiar radio greeting). In this Fannie Hurst story, she played a farm girl who helps her neighbors save their land from a power company by becoming a big radio star. In the process she loses the man (Randolph Scott) she loves to her sister (Sally Blane). She sang "Moon Song," "Twenty Million People," "Pickaninnies' Heaven," and "My Queen of Lullaby Land," in addition to performing a hot dance to "Dinah." One would have expected Paramount to make an attempt to disguise her figure, but one scene even featured her in a bathing suit, and throughout the story she wore an unflattering hairdo. *Variety* reported diplomatically, "When called upon to emote, Miss Smith was also shrewdly steered, because she's not called on too much or too often." While making the picture in Hollywood, Kate did her radio broadcasts from station KNX on the Paramount lot. However, she was not happy in the movie capital and she and Ted Collins (who had appeared briefly in HELLO, EVERYBODY) cancelled her contract. While at Paramount, Smith also appeared in the studio's short film HOLLYWOOD ON PARADE #11 (1933) singing "Here Lies Love."

Kate Smith left national radio in the fall of 1933 to go on a successful year's vaudeville tour with her Swanee Revue, and then, in the summer of 1934, she returned to CBS radio with "Kate Smith and Her Swanee Music." Over the next few seasons she had several different variety formats on the network, including a 1934–36 afternoon weekly show called "Kate Smith's Matinee Hour." In 1937, she began the very popular "The Kate Smith Hour," which General Foods sponsored through 1945. On this CBS program she not only introduced scores of famous songs (the most notable being Irving Berlin's "God Bless America" in 1938), she also appeared with various guest stars in skits and did many of her own commercials. In 1938, CBS also began broadcasting her weekday noontime series, "Kate Smith Speaks," on which she discussed a variety of topics with Ted Collins. The star also wrote her first autobiography, *Living in a Great Big Way* (1938). When Kate Smith appeared at the White House on June 8, 1939, and sang for the King and Queen of England, President Franklin D. Roosevelt introduced her to the British royalty by saying, "Your Majesties, this is Kate Smith, this is America."

Throughout the 1930s, it was announced at various times that Kate Smith would return to picture making, and 20th Century–Fox even attempted to find a vehicle with which to team her with Shirley Temple. She was spotted briefly at the beginning of that studio's THE GREAT AMERICAN BROADCAST (1941), but it was in footage from a vintage newsreel. It would take World War II to get Kate Smith back on the screen.

No performer was a more tireless worker for the Allied effort during World War II than was Kate Smith, who logged thousands of miles appearing at Army camps for the Office of Defense Transportation in ad-

Kate Smith in THIS IS THE ARMY (1943)

dition to her continuous sale of war bonds. As a result of her efforts, more than $600 million worth of bonds were sold, the highest amount of sales by any one person. In the fall of 1943, she hosted an eighteen-hour war bond drive on radio that resulted in $39 million in sales. As part of the war effort, Kate returned to Hollywood in 1943 and appeared as herself in Warner Bros.' THIS IS THE ARMY, singing "God Bless America." She then starred in the Columbia one-reel short AMERICA SINGS WITH KATE SMITH (1943), in which she performed "We're All Americans," "America, I Love You," "The Marine's Hymn," and "The Caissons Go Rolling Along." (In 1974, this short was incorporated in its entirety into the nostalgia compilation feature THE THREE STOOGES FOLLIES.)

It was during the World War II years that Kate Smith was at the peak of her popularity. Although the Depression had nearly killed the record industry, Kate Smith continued to have good disc sales with such labels as Columbia, Decca, and RCA Victor. During the 1940s, she had many hit records for Columbia, including "The White Cliffs of Dover," "A Nightingale Sang in Berkeley Square," "I Don't Want to Walk Without You," and "The Shrine of St. Cecilia." She is credited with having introduced over six hundred new songs, many of which appeared on the hit parade. (During her career, Kate Smith's picture was featured on more than 270 published song sheets.) In 1947, Kate Smith left CBS and Columbia Records and began broadcasting over the Mutual network and recording for the MGM label. During the late 1940s, it was announced that Kate would portray herself in a biopic about her life, but the project never materialized.

Kate Smith came to television in the fall of 1950 with "The Kate Smith Hour," which was telecast on weekday afternoons on NBC. The show quickly became the most popular daytime program on the air, with an audience equivalent to that of a prime-time show. In addition, Kate continued her radio programs. This proved to be the busiest period of her life professionally. During the 1951–52 season, she also starred in NBC-TV's "The Kate Smith Evening Hour" each Wednesday. Although she ceased her radio shows in 1952 (as the medium was dying), she continued her afternoon TV show until the spring of 1954, when she took a hiatus from performing due to health reasons.

Kate Smith returned to network radio for Mutual during the 1958–59 season with a weekday series, and in 1960 she had a weekly nighttime show on CBS-TV. Basically, however, the star spent the remainder of her career doing personal appearances, television guest shots, and records. During the 1950s, she recorded for the National, Capitol, Kapp, and Tops labels, and in 1960 her second autobiography, *Upon My Lips a Song*, was published. (In 1958, *The Kate Smith Company's Coming Cookbook* had appeared.) One of the highlights of Kate Smith's career was her November 1, 1962, Carnegie Hall concert, which was issued on RCA Records. She signed with the label and over the next six years recorded more than 150 songs for RCA, making this the most prolific recording time of her lengthy career.

In 1962, her mother died. In the spring of 1964, Ted Collins died of a heart attack and that same year she suffered a fall, fracturing her ankle. She did not appear professionally for several months, and during this period she embraced Roman Catholicism. (She would later make a visit to the Vatican and have an audience with the Pope.) In the later 1960s, she became a popular figure on TV variety programs (including those of Sonny and Cher and Dean Martin), boasting a new slimmer look, more contemporary costumes, and an array of flattering wigs. Her RCA albums were best-sellers, including *How Great Thou Art* (1966), which sold extremely well and rose to number thirty-six on the album charts.

In 1969, she starred in the syndicated musical special "The Kate Smith Show," and four years later she headlined another special, "Kate Smith Presents Remembrances and Rock." She played the nightclub circuit briefly and also began doing TV commercials. In 1973, she received a great deal of publicity when the Philadelphia Flyers hockey team won the Stanley Cup and used her recording of "God Bless America" as its good luck charm. During this time, Kate expressed an interest in acting in a TV Western such as "Gunsmoke," although in 1965 she had rejected the role of the Mother Superior in THE SOUND OF MUSIC.

By the mid-1970s, with her voice remarkably intact, Kate Smith's career seemed destined to reach new heights with the nation about to celebrate its Bicentennial. However, late in 1976, she went into a diabetic coma as a result of improper self-medication; she only partially recovered, and was physically unable to resume her singing. The last decade of her life was a nightmare of increasing ill health and family squabbles (with members fighting to gain control of her estate). She returned to the limelight on two occasions in 1982: first when she accepted an Emmy Award for her contributions to television and, later that year, when President Ronald Reagan presented the wheelchair-bound Kate with the Medal of Freedom, the nation's highest civilian honor.

On June 17, 1986, Kate Smith, who had never married, died of heart failure. She was buried in Lake Placid, New York, the resort where she had had a summer retreat for over thirty years.

## Filmography

Kate Smith—Songbird of the South (Vita, 1929) (s)

The Big Broadcast (Par, 1932)

Rambling 'Round Radio Row #1 (Vita, 1932) (s)

Kate Smith Presents a Memory Program (Unk, 1932) (s)

The World at Large (UM & M Pictorial, 1932) (s)

Hello, Everybody (Par, 1933)

Hollywood on Parade #11 (Par, 1933) (s)

The Great American Broadcast (20th–Fox, 1941) [seen only in newsreel footage from the early 1930s]

This Is the Army (WB, 1943)

America Sings with Kate Smith (Col, 1943) (s)

The Three Stooges Follies (Col, 1974) [compilation feature including the short subject *America Sings with Kate Smith*]

## Broadway Plays

Honeymoon Lane (1926)

Flying High (1930)

## Radio Series

Kate Smith Sings (NBC, 1931)
The Kate Smith Show (CBS, 1931–33)
Kate Smith and Her Swanee Music (CBS, 1934–35)
Kate Smith's Matinee Hour (CBS, 1934–36)
Kate Smith's All-Star Revue (CBS, 1935)
Kate Smith's Coffee Time (CBS, 1935–36)
Kate Smith's A & P Bandwagon (CBS, 1936–37)

The Kate Smith Hour (CBS, 1937–45)
Kate Smith Speaks (CBS, 1938–47; Mutual, 1947–51)
Kate Smith Sings (CBS, 1945–47, Mutual, 1947–51)
Kate Smith Calls (ABC, 1949–50)
The Kate Smith Program (NBC, 1951–52)
The Kate Smith Show (Mutual, 1958–59)

## TV Series

The Kate Smith Hour (NBC, 1950–54)
The Kate Smith Evening Hour (NBC, 1951–52)

The Kate Smith Show (CBS, 1960)

## Album Discography

All Time Great Hits by Kate Smith (10"
  National 3002)
America the Beautiful (Metro 606)
America's Favorite (RCA DPL2-0175)
America's Favorite: Kate Smith (Reader's Digest/
  RCA RD-029)
America's Favorites (RCA LPM/LSC-2991) w.
  Arthur Fiedler and The Boston Pops
  Orchestra
The Best of Kate Smith (RCA LPM/LSP-3970)
The Best of Kate Smith—Sacred (RCA LSP-
  4258)
The Big Broadcast (Sountrak 101) [ST]
Christmas with Kate Smith (Tops L-1677/
  Mayfair 9677S, General Electric GEX-1,
  International Award AKX-13, Rondo 1)
Come All Ye Faithful (Pickwick 1002)
The Fabulous Kate (Kapp KL-1082)
The Fabulous Kate Smith (Camden CAS-2439)
The Glorious Voice of Kate Smith (Pickwick
  3055)
God Bless America (Metro 559)
God Bless America (Sunbeam 307)
The Great Kate (Tops L-1672/Mayfair 9672S)
Guideposts to Freedom (Guideposts 102) w.
  Norman Vincent Peale
Hello, Everybody (Book-of-the-Month Records
  91-6666)

Here and Now! (RCA LPM/LSP-3821)
Hootenanny—Folk Songs U.S.A. (Rondo 2004)
How Great Thou Art (RCA LPM/LSP-3445)
I'll Be Seeing You (Sears 431)
The Incomparable Kate Smith (Tee-Vee Records
  1057)
Inspirational Favorites (Reader's Digest/RCA
  RDA-012D)
Johnny Appleseed (MGM CH-102, MGM CH-
  111, Leo the Lion 1034)
Just a Closer Walk with Thee (RCA LPM/LSP-
  3735)
Kate Smith (Cap T-854)
Kate Smith (EMI/Cap/Axis AX-701340)
The Kate Smith Anniversary Album (RCA
  LPM/LSP-3535)
Kate Smith at Carnegie Hall (RCA LPM/LSP-
  2819, Camden CAS-2587)
The Kate Smith Christmas Album (RCA LPM/
  LSP-3607)
Kate Smith—Her Classic CBS Records (CBS
  Special Products P-19451)
Kate Smith—Her Famous RCA Records (RCA
  Special Products DVL1-0752)
Kate Smith on the Air (Sandy Hook 2085)
Kate Smith Sings Folk Songs (Tops L-1706)
Kate Smith Sings God Bless America (Golden
  Age 5037)

Kate Smith Sings God Bless America (Murray Hill M54556)

Kate Smith Sings God Bless America (Tops L-1705, Mayfair 5705S)

Kate Smith Sings Hymns and Spirituals (Tops L-1673, Mayfair 9763S, Rondo 2011)

Kate Smith Today (RCA LPM/LSP-3670)

Kate Smith's Golden Years of Broadcasting (Sunbeam 510)

The Lady and Her Music (Sunbeam KES-1)

A Legendary Performer (RCA CLP1-2661)

May God Be with You (RCA LSP-4031)

Memory Lane (MGM E-3487)

A Merry American Christmas from Kate Smith (Songbird KES-3)

Miss Kate Smith 1926–1931 (Sunbeam MFC-13)

Mr. Pickwick—Happy Birthday to America (Pickwick 5116)

Music, Maestro, Please (Songbird KES-2)

The One and Only Kate Smith (Kapp KL-1496/KS-3496)

Reminiscing with Kate Smith (10" National 3001)

Sincerely, Kate Smith (Sunbeam 516)

Something Special (RCA LPM/LSP-3870)

Songs of Erin (10" Col CL-6031)

Songs of Erin (Har HL-7024) w. Morton Downey

Songs of Stephen Foster (10" MGM E-106)

Songs of the Now Generation (RCA LSP-4105)

Songs to Remember (10" National 3003)

The Sweetest Sounds (RCA LPM/LSP-2921)

This Is the Army (Hollywood Soundstage 408, Sandy Hook 2035) [ST]

A Touch of Magic (RCA LPM/LSP-3308)

TV Curtain Calls (10" Cap H-515)

TV Curtain Calls (10" Cap CLP-048)

TV Curtain Calls (Cap T-515)

TV Curtain Calls (EMI ENC-9598)

The Very Best of Kate Smith (MGM E/SE-4220)

When the Moon Comes over the Mountain (Encore P-14360)

When the Moon Comes over the Mountain (Har HL-7393)

# ANN SOTHERN

WITH HER ABUNDANCE OF TALENT, VERSATILITY, AND BEAUTY, IT IS A
wonder that Ann Sothern was not a greater star in motion pictures. (Granted, being
outspoken and very much her own person did not endear her to industry executives.) She
could sing effectively, dance pleasingly, exude charm as a pert ingenue, and, most
endearingly, could handle light and/or tart comedy with great precision. She passed
through several show business phases, as well as studios, before arriving at MGM in 1939.
At that time she was considered washed up in films, and the project was a throwaway semi-
programmer called MAISIE. However, it proved so popular that Metro signed Ann to a
long-term contract that extended throughout the 1940s. Unfortunately for Ann, she was
so appreciated as the hard-boiled but lovable chorine Maisie Ravier that the studio
hamstrung her to that profitable budget series. Occasionally, this overqualified backup star
would be assigned to major MGM productions. Whether they were musicals (LADY BE
GOOD, 1941; PANAMA HATTIE, 1942) or drama (CRY HAVOC, 1943), she demonstrated
repeatedly that the studio was stifling her career for the sake of the MAISIE bonanza.

In the mid-1950s, Ann made a tremendous comeback in another medium. As
television's "Private Secretary," she played Susie McNamera, a refined but close cousin to
her memorable Maisie. The series made her a household name and wealthy. That teleseries
is still in syndication and is her keynote to enduring fame. But there would be more
professional rebirths for Ann: as a character star of films and the stage in the 1960s and
1970s, and competing so competently for audience attention in THE WHALES OF AUGUST
(1987) against Bette Davis and Lillian Gish that she was Oscar-nominated as Best
Supporting Actress.

Harriette Arlene Lake was born on January 22, 1909 (some sources list 1910), in
Valley City, North Dakota. She insists she never really saw her birthplace because her
mother (concert singer Annette Yde-Lake) was merely passing through town. Her father
(Walter J. Lake) was a traveling actor (he has also been described variously as a meat
salesman, an importer, and a produce broker). The Lakes would have two more daughters:
Marion, who would work later as a secretary for her movie star sister and then as an
assistant to "Dear Abby"; and Bonnie, who became a songstress (with the bands of Artie
Shaw and her husband, Jack Jenney) and songwriter. Harriette's paternal grandfather was
Simon Lake, who invented the modern submarine; her maternal grandfather was Hans
Nilson, the Danish concert violinist.

Because her mother traveled so much, Harriette had a nomadic childhood, with
years spent in Michigan, Iowa, and Minnesota. For a time she studied piano at the

McPhail School for Music in Minneapolis where her mother was an instructor, and one of Harriette's classical compositions (written at the age of thirteen) was performed by the Minneapolis Symphony. The Lakes divorced in 1927, and while Annette relocated to California to work as a vocal coach at Warner Bros., Walter moved his import/export firm to Seattle, Washington. Harriette stayed with her father while attending the University of Washington, but after a year she abandoned her schooling. She had become a movie player.

While visiting her mother in Los Angeles in 1929, Harriette won a role in the film musical THE SHOW OF SHOWS, a revue produced at Warner Bros. In the segment "Meet My Sister," featuring several real-life sisters (e.g., Loretta Young and Sally Blane), Harriette was cast as Marion Byron's sibling and wore a native Italian costume. Also for Warner Bros. she appeared in the Dolores Costello melodrama HEARTS IN EXILE (1929) and the Joe E. Brown musical comedy HOLD EVERYTHING (1930). But she made no lasting impression at the studio and moved on. At MGM, producer Paul Bern showed a passing interest in her. She was tested and signed to a studio contract. But the petite (5' 1") brunette was wasted on publicity photo sessions and brief walk-ons. She had a bit in Buster Keaton's comedy DOUGHBOYS (1930). Meanwhile, Florenz Ziegfeld was in Hollywood working on the screen version of Eddie Cantor's WHOOPEE! (1930). Ziegfeld met Harriette at a party, where she sang for the theater impresario. He was impressed enough to offer her a Broadway part, and since MGM had dropped her option, she accepted the New York job. (Some sources cite BROADWAY NIGHTS [1927] and WHOOPEE! [1930] as picture credits for Harriette Lake.)

Back East, she was cast in the Marilyn Miller stage musical *Smiles*, which featured Fred and Adele Astaire. However, during the Boston tryout, Miller demanded that Harriette, who had three well-received song numbers, be dropped from the production. Despite this setback, Harriette was signed for the Broadway cast of the Richard Rodgers–Lorenz Hart musical *America's Sweetheart*, which opened on February 10, 1931. With Jack Whiting she introduced the song "I've Got Five Dollars." *Time* magazine decided she was a "lovely synthesis, one part Ginger Rogers, one part Ethel Merman." In October 1931, Harriette opened in the musical *Everybody's Welcome*. Thereafter, she toured for seven months with the national company of the Pulitzer Prize–winning *Of Thee I Sing* and was back in New York in June 1933 as a replacement for Lois Moran in the Broadway edition of that show. However, a sudden heat wave closed most New York theaters for the summer and she was unemployed after a week.

Harriette made another attempt at a film career. She was in the "Shanghai Lil" production number of FOOTLIGHT PARADE (1933) and was in a brief beach scene in BROADWAY THRU A KEYHOLE (1933). Her co-player in that sequence was would-be starlet Lucille Ball and the two became long-standing friends. Then redheaded Ann came to the attention of Columbia Pictures mogul Harry Cohn, who decided she could play the circus sideshow attendant who poses as a blonde Scandinavian film actress in LET'S FALL IN LOVE (1934). It was Cohn who changed her name to Ann Sothern. This modest musical, with a Harold Arlen score, was a success and Columbia signed Ann to a long-term contract. In typical industry fashion, Cohn wasted Ann in a succession of "B" pictures. She did much better on loanout. For Paramount, she was romanced by radio crooner Lanny Ross in MELODY IN SPRING (1934), and Samuel Goldwyn used her in Eddie Cantor's KID MILLIONS (1934). In the latter, she was teamed with George Murphy and they sang "Your Head on My Shoulder." For producer Darryl F. Zanuck, Ann was Maurice Chevalier's tempestuous chorine mistress in FOLIES BERGERE (1935). *Variety* reported, "She sings and dances with Chevalier and makes a definite sock impression." Another undistinguished backstage musical, HOORAY FOR LOVE (1935) cast Ann as a stage songstress, but it represented two firsts. It was her first picture at RKO and it was the first of several screen teamings with pleasant (but all too bland) Gene Raymond. Only three of her five 1935 releases were for her home lot.

Having made fifteen films in less than three years (during which time she experimented with her screen look and hair color—finally settling on being a honey blonde), Ann decided that she loathed her assembly-line picture-making at Columbia, especially playing empty-headed ingenues. She reasoned, "character parts are what I want to play most of all. I'd trade a 'pretty girl' role any day in the week for that of an old hag, if the hag was a real character." Some reports claim she asked for her Columbia release in 1936; others state that she was dropped in an economy wave. Whatever the circumstances, Ann signed with RKO. However, that studio also considered her a utilitarian asset to be shoved into middling stories and, even worse (by Ann's standards), to be reteamed with Gene Raymond. She was with him in a quartet of undistinguished romantic comedies: WALKING ON AIR (1936), THE SMARTEST GIRL IN TOWN (1936), THERE GOES MY GIRL (1937), and SHE'S GOT EVERYTHING (1938). Occasionally she was on loanout, such as going to 20th Century–Fox to co-star with Don Ameche in FIFTY ROADS TO TOWN (1937). *Variety* noted, "Miss Sothern has an abundance of good looks, has made progress and now qualifies for good comedy leads."

On September 27, 1936, Ann married actor/bandleader Roger Pryor at the Hollywood Congregational Church. The son of orchestra leader Arthur Pryor, he had been married previously and had a daughter. He and Ann had first met in Chicago in 1932 when she was in *Of Thee I Sing* and he was acting in *Blessed Event*. They had renewed their friendship during the making of THE GIRL FRIEND (1935) at Columbia. Now, happily married, she was even less enthusiastic about making further junk films. Stating, "I will never play another sweet leading role on the screen as long as I live," she negotiated the end of her seven-year RKO contract, which was paying her $50,000 yearly. At liberty, she frequently traveled with Roger and his band, sometimes performing as vocalist.

Producer Walter Wanger hired Ann for TRADE WINDS (1938), which starred Wanger's wife, Joan Bennett, and Fredric March. As the wayward stenographer with a dumb mouth and a heart of gold, Ann stole the notices. She was now asked to play opposite Bing Crosby in EAST SIDE OF HEAVEN (1939), but declined because she had commitments to perform with Pryor's band. The film part went to Joan Blondell and Ann was again on the sidelines. Fortunately, MGM producer J. Walter Ruben had appreciated Ann's performance in TRADE WINDS and suggested her for the lead in MAISIE (1939), a project initially bought for the late Jean Harlow. The part called for Ann to be Maisie Ravier, a sassy Brooklyn chorus girl who discovers adventure and romance as she passes from gig to gig. Sothern commented later, "I took it because by now I knew that any girl in Hollywood who thinks she is going on and on playing ingenues or pretty romantic parts is in for the surprise of her life."

The film was enormously popular and MGM signed Ann to a long-term contract. It led to her playing in nine additional MAISIE pictures as well as starring in a radio version of the property. According to Ann, "Every Maisie film cost under $500,000 and made two to three times that back. Sure, I felt she was a millstone around my neck at times. I'd tell Mr. Mayer to give me a musical and I'd do another Maisie. We'd bargain in that way." Along the way she played variations of the dumb blonde in JOE AND ETHEL TURP CALL ON THE PRESIDENT (1939—which was considered as a potential new series but fell flat at the box office), FAST AND FURIOUS (1939), BROTHER ORCHID (1940—on loan to Warner Bros.), and DULCY (1940). One role she avoided was that of Kitty in Vivien Leigh's WATERLOO BRIDGE (1940). Ann scheduled an appendectomy and Virginia Field took the part.

Then there were the Sothern musicals. "People never think of me as a singer," she said in retrospect. "Few of them know I introduced 'The Last Time I Saw Paris.'" The picture was LADY BE GOOD (1940) and her co-stars were Eleanor Powell, Robert Young,

Ann Sothern and Rita Johnson in CONGO MAISIE (1940)

and Red Skelton. The memorable tune went on to win an Oscar for Best Song of 1941. Sothern inherited Ethel Merman's brassy stage role in Cole Porter's PANAMA HATTIE (1942), providing her own interpretation of "Make It Another Old Fashioned Please," "I've Still Got My Health," and "Let's Be Buddies." Much to her displeasure, the vehicle had been much altered (to provide for the mugging of Red Skelton and others), leaving Ann disgruntled throughout production. After disastrous previews and while Ann was already making her next MAISIE picture, PANAMA HATTIE went through $300,000 of additional shooting with Vincente Minnelli staging the new musical interludes. The restructured PANAMA HATTIE grossed over $4 million at the box office.

Also in 1942—in May—Ann filed for divorce from Roger Pryor, claiming that his infatuation with flying (and disappearing for a week at a time) was the cause of "great and grievous cruelty." On May 23, 1943, a few days after her divorce had become final, she married MGM actor Robert Sterling, whom she had met during the shooting of RINGSIDE MAISIE (1941). He was more than seven years her junior. Later, when Ann became pregnant (daughter Patricia Ann was born on December 10, 1944), she had to relinquish the role of the vixenish Em in MEET ME IN ST. LOUIS (1944), which went instead to Angela Lansbury. Ann claimed she wanted more children and hoped to leave picture making to devote herself to being a full-time wife and mother. However, in 1946, with Sterling now demobilized from military service, he and Ann separated in the first of several breakups and reconciliations, finally divorcing on March 8, 1949.

MGM did not renew Ann's contract and she made the overlooked vaudeville musical APRIL SHOWERS (1948) with Dennis Morgan at Warner Bros. She returned to MGM to guest briefly in WORDS AND MUSIC (1948), singing the wistful "Where's That Rainbow." She photographed attractively in color. Her best dramatic assignment was in Joseph L. Mankiewicz's A LETTER TO THREE WIVES (1949), in which she was teamed with Linda Darnell and Jeanne Crain, but THE JUDGE STEPS OUT (1949) at RKO was a comedy dud. For MGM she was a murderess in SHADOW ON THE WALL (1950) and the studio cast her as Jane Powell's chic stage star mother in NANCY GOES TO RIO (1950). This role should have heralded a new start for Ann, but she contracted infectious hepatitis. She became so sensitive to light and sound that for the next two years she was confined to her house, often in a dark, deadly silent room. It was during this period that, encouraged by actor friend Richard Egan, she converted to Catholicism.

She went to Broadway for her show business return with *Faithfully Yours* in October 1951. It was a formula comedy that flopped after sixty-eight performances. Her first film in three years was THE BLUE GARDENIA (1953), supporting Anne Baxter as a wisecracking friend. Since her movie career seemed over, Ann tried television. Her dramatic debut was on "Schlitz Playhouse of Stars" (CBS, February 1, 1952). She thought of bringing MAISIE to TV as a series but MGM would not relinquish the rights, so she settled on "Private Secretary," which bowed on CBS on February 1, 1953. As the meddlesome, stylish secretary, Susie McNamera, who constantly interferes in the hectic life of her boss (Don Porter), she and the show were a huge hit and it had a four-season run. To prove her versatility, she starred in a color special of the musical "Lady in the Dark" (NBC-TV,

September 24, 1954). That same year she made her nightclub debut in Las Vegas and later appeared at the Chez Paree in Chicago. When asked about her workaholic nature, she replied, "I leave the house early in the morning and I bring home the bacon late at night and the servants think I'm crazy to work so hard."

In 1957, Ann and her "Private Secretary" producer (Jack Chertok) had a contractual disagreement. The series was cancelled, although for a time June Allyson was among those considered to replace Ann in it. Meanwhile, Ann teamed (CBS, November 6, 1957) with pal Lucille Ball on one of the latter's TV hour versions of "I Love Lucy." In addition, Sothern became involved with a cattle ranch (which her father ran), a music publishing business, and a Sewing Center in Sun Valley, Idaho (where she had a home). On October 6, 1958, she starred in a new comedy series on CBS-TV called "The Ann Sothern Show" which, in midstream, brought in Don Porter to make it an even closer copy of her past hit series.

In 1961, Sothern moved to New York where daughter Tisha was attending school. (Tisha later became an actress whose career was interrupted in 1976 by cancer, from which she recovered.) Ann made a pilot ("Atta Boy, Mama") for a TV series that did not sell. In 1963, she toured in *God Bless Our Bank*, which did not reach Broadway. She again tried movies, this time as a character actress (for which her maturity and her added weight qualified her). She was blowsy and effective in a quartet of features, the best being the thriller LADY IN A CAGE (1964), starring Olivia de Havilland. Meanwhile, she provided the off-screen voice in "My Mother the Car," a 1965–66 NBC-TV series that was regarded at the time as trash and is now considered nostalgic camp. She made several appearances on Lucille Ball's comedy series "The Lucy Show," but refused a regular role, not wanting to be committed for a long run. There was more summer stock (*The Solid Gold Cadillac*, *The Glass Menagerie*) and an engagement in the musical *Mame* in Hawaii. (She had turned down offers to be one of the Broadway replacements in both *Gypsy* and *Mame*.)

While appearing at a dinner theater in Jacksonville, Florida, in 1973, Ann was injured by a piece of falling scenery. The accident fractured a lumbar vertebra and damaged the nerves in her legs. She was told she would never walk again, but later was able to get around with the use of a cane. Her few film appearances in the later 1970s were mostly trash, including CRAZY MAMA (1975), in which daughter Tisha appeared. She made a cameo appearance in the poor television remake of A LETTER TO THREE WIVES (NBC, December 16, 1985), sharply playing the role handled by Connie Gilchrist in the original. In the much-publicized geriatric study THE WHALES OF AUGUST (1987), Ann received outstanding reviews, but lost the Best Supporting Actress Oscar to Olympia Dukakis (of MOONSTRUCK).

Ann has lived in Ketchum, Idaho, since 1984. In 1987, an album of her compositions was recorded. Although several publishers have expressed interest, she has declined to write her autobiography.

## Filmography

### As Harriette Lake:

The Show of Shows (WB, 1929)
Hearts in Exile (WB, 1929)
Doughboys [Forward March] (MGM, 1930)

Hold Everything (WB, 1930)
Broadway Thru a Keyhole (UA, 1933)
Footlight Parade (FN, 1933)

### As Ann Sothern:

Let's Fall in Love (Col, 1934)
Melody in Spring (Par, 1934)
The Party's Over (Col, 1934)
The Hell Cat (Col, 1934)
Blind Date (Col, 1934)
Kid Millions (UA, 1934)
Folies Bergere (UA, 1935)
Eight Bells (Col, 1935)
Hooray for Love (RKO, 1935)
The Girl Friend (Col, 1935)
Grand Exit (Col, 1935)
You May Be Next! [Panic on the Air] (Col, 1936)
Hell-Ship Morgan (Col, 1936)
Don't Gamble with Love (Col, 1936)
My American Wife (Par, 1936)
Walking on Air (RKO, 1936)
The Smartest Girl in Town (RKO, 1936)
Dangerous Number (MGM, 1937)
Fifty Roads to Town (20th–Fox, 1937)
Ali Baba Goes to Town (20th–Fox, 1937)
There Goes My Girl (RKO, 1937)
Super Sleuth (RKO, 1937)
There Goes the Groom (RKO, 1937)
Danger—Love at Work (20th–Fox, 1937)
She's Got Everything (RKO, 1938)
Trade Winds (UA, 1938)
Maisie (MGM, 1939)
Elsa Maxwell's Hotel for Women [Hotel for Women] (20th–Fox, 1939)
Fast and Furious (MGM, 1939)
Joe and Ethel Turp Call on the President [A Call on the President] (MGM, 1939)
Congo Maisie (MGM, 1940)
Brother Orchid (WB, 1940)
Gold Rush Maisie (MGM, 1940)
Dulcy (MGM, 1940)
Maisie Was a Lady (MGM, 1941)
Lady Be Good (MGM, 1941)

Ringside Maisie (MGM, 1941)
Maisie Gets Her Man [She Gets Her Man] (MGM, 1942)
Panama Hattie (MGM, 1942)
You John Jones (MGM, 1942) (s)
Three Hearts for Julia (MGM, 1943)
Swing Shift Maisie [The Girl in Overalls] (MGM, 1943)
Thousands Cheer (MGM, 1943)
Cry Havoc (MGM, 1943)
Maisie Goes to Reno [You Can't Do That to Me] (MGM, 1944)
Up Goes Maisie [Up She Goes] (MGM, 1946)
Undercover Maisie [Undercover Girl] (MGM, 1947)
April Showers (WB, 1948)
Words and Music (MGM, 1948)
The Judge Steps Out [Indian Summer] (RKO, 1949)
A Letter to Three Wives (20th–Fox, 1949)
Nancy Goes to Rio (MGM, 1950)
Shadow on the Wall (MGM, 1950)
The Blue Gardenia (WB, 1953)
The Best Man (UA, 1964)
Lady in a Cage (Par, 1964)
Sylvia (Par, 1965)
Chubasco (WB–7 Arts, 1967)
The Outsider (NBC-TV, 11/21/67)
Congratulations, It's a Boy (ABC-TV, 9/21/71)
A Death of Innocence (CBS-TV, 11/26/71)
The Weekend Nun (ABC-TV, 12/20/72)
The Killing Kind (Media Trend, 1973)
The Great Man's Whiskers (NBC-TV, 2/13/73)
The Golden Needles (AIP, 1974)
Crazy Mama (New World, 1975)
The Manitou (Avco Emb, 1978)
The Little Dragons (Aurora, 1980) (voice only)
A Letter to Three Wives (NBC-TV, 12/16/85)
The Whales of August (Alive Films, 1987)

## Broadway Plays

America's Sweetheart (1931)
Everybody's Welcome (1932)

Of Thee I Sing (1933) (replacement)
Faithfully Yours (1951)

## Radio Series

Maisie (CBS, 1945–47; Mutual, 1949–52)

## TV Series

Private Secretary (CBS, 1953–57)
The Ann Sothern Show (CBS, 1958–61)

My Mother the Car (NBC, 1965–66) (voice
   only)

## Album Discography

Ann Sothern and the Broadway Blues (Tiara
   7531/531)
It's Ann Sothern Time (Craftsmen C-8061)
Kid Millions (CIF 3007, Sandy Hook 2039)
   [ST]
Lady Be Good (Caliban 6010, Hollywood
   Soundstage 5010) [ST]
Lady in the Dark (RCA LM-1882) [ST/TV]
Nancy Goes to Rio (10" MGM E-508, MGM
   SES-53ST) [ST]

Red Dust (Pelican 106) [ST/R]
Song Stylings Featuring Ann Sothern (Sutton
   SSU-317)
Sothern Exposure (Tops L-1611, Zenith 1611)
Thousands Cheer (Cheerio 5000, Hollywood
   Soundstage 409) [ST]
Words and Music (10" MGM E-505, MGM E-
   3233, MGM E-3771, Metro M/S-580,
   MGM SES-54ST) [ST]

# BARBRA STREISAND

AS AN ENDURING SUPERSTAR, MANY SIDES OF BARBRA STREISAND
have been visible. Perhaps none of her other several career levels has been as engaging as
when she was blossoming in the early 1960s. It was in this period that she postured as a
beatnik, surmounted her unique profile, and sang gorgeously, with a vocal richness and
range that paralleled her dramatic song styling. Whether on stage, in concert, or on
television, she was spontaneous, frank, and vivacious, always creating an immediate
rapport with her audience (who responded in enthusiastic kind). She was indeed an
original, and was beloved as such.

Flashing ahead, Barbra became an Oscar-winning movie megastar and the new
Streisand became far less accessible with her elaborate Malibu compound. It seems to
many people that her increasingly lavish lifestyle and her growing insistence upon total
control over her every activity have isolated her from the mainstream. She has become a
demanding perfectionist too frequently at odds with the entertainment industry. Yet her
enormous popularity with audiences (now growing middle-aged) remains virtually intact.

Barbra Streisand has long been a consistently strong record seller. Over the decades,
she has stretched her vocal style—shrewdly for the most part—to compete with changing
musical tastes and new rivals. Despite being an overpowering individualist, in the mid-
1970s she began recording occasional duets with the likes of Donna Summer, Neil
Diamond, Barry Gibb, and, more recently, with TV hunk and then-boyfriend Don
Johnson. However, in the last decade, when she returned to her roots in the ungimmicky
*The Broadway Album* (1985), she enjoyed her first number one album in several years.

Although to date she has appeared on screen in only fourteen features, Streisand has
acted in a wide range of screen fare. Whatever one's personal feelings about La Streisand
may be, she is never less than fascinating on camera. Her film canon includes several
translated-from-Broadway musicals, highlighted by her screen debut in FUNNY GIRL
(1968). She has gone from sexy comedy (THE OWL AND THE PUSSYCAT, 1970) to slapstick
farce (FOR PETE'S SAKE, 1974). She has done a feminist fantasy (UP THE SANDBOX, 1972)
and glossy romance (THE WAY WE WERE, 1973). If her all-consuming project YENTL
(1983) (for which she was also producer, director, and co-scenarist) was indulgent and
derivative, her NUTS (1987) was raw drama filled with restraint and intense histrionics.

She was born Barbara Joan Streisand on April 24, 1942, in Brooklyn, New York, to
Emanuel and Diana Streisand. There was another child, Sheldon, born eight years earlier.
Mr. Streisand was a teacher of English and psychology, with a Ph.D. from Columbia
University. When Barbara was fifteen months old, her father died of a cerebral hemor-

rhage. Mrs. Streisand returned to working as a bookkeeper and the family survived—barely. "We were poor, but not *poor* poor," Streisand would say later. "We just never had anything." To escape her lackluster existence, Barbara immersed herself in the fantasy world of the movies she saw every Saturday afternoon; she pictured herself as an adored, pretty movie star. "My mother says I had lipstick smeared on my face and was acting on a dresser when I was two. . . . Maybe that was the first time I actually acted." When Barbara was seven her mother remarried, to Louis Kind, a used-car salesman. (They would have a daughter, Rosalind, and would later separate.)

At age fourteen, Barbara took a subway to Times Square and paid $1.75 for a balcony seat to see *The Diary of Anne Frank*. This performance confirmed her determination to go on the stage. She spent the next school vacation working as a summer stock apprentice at the Malden Bridge Playhouse in Malden, New York. She was so intent on becoming a star that she ignored her mother's practical suggestion that she study stenography and typing in school. After Barbara graduated from Erasmus Hall High School in 1959 (with a very high academic average), she moved into Manhattan.

She would admit that as a teenager, "I was a real ugly kid. . . . I dressed wild to show I didn't care." In New York City, she supported herself as a theater usher and as a switchboard operator. She took occasional acting lessons from Eli Rill and Allan Miller. The nonconformist Barbara acted like a kook and refused the advice of various friends to be more conventional, to have her prominent nose surgically altered, and to discard her Brooklyn accent. One affectation to which she did agree was changing her name from Barbara to Barbra. In the spring of 1961 she entered a talent contest at The Lion's Head, a Greenwich Village bar. She won the $50 prize singing "A Sleepin' Bee" and performed at the club for a week. Her repertoire included such songs as "Who's Afraid of the Big Bad Wolf." She was next hired for the Bon Soir Club on West 8th Street, on the same bill with female impersonator Lynn Carter. She remained there for eleven weeks, performing such numbers as "Cry Me a River." She began making TV talk show appearances, including a stint on "PM East," hosted by Mike Wallace. She was quickly gaining a reputation as a kooky girl who sang wonderfully. On October 21, 1961, she debuted on stage in the off-Broadway revue *Another Evening with Harry Stoones*. Others in the cast included Dom De Luise and Diana Sands. Barbra performed in several skits and had a few songs to sing, including "Value." Unfortunately, the show closed after one night. Barbra moved on to the Blue Angel, a club that showcased rising new talent.

At the Blue Angel, she was spotted by Broadway producer David Merrick, who auditioned and hired her for his upcoming musical *I Can Get It for You Wholesale*. The show, starring Lillian Roth, Sheree North, and Elliott Gould, opened on March 22, 1962. Ever the exotic, Barbra's program biography stated, "Born in Madagascar, reared in Rangoon. . . ." The show received mixed reviews, but there was almost unanimous praise for Streisand as the bizarre, unbeloved Yetta Tessye Marmelstein in her beehive hairdo, a Brooklyn secretary in search of love and fulfillment. Much of her one big number, "Miss Marmelstein," was sung cavorting on a secretarial chair. For her show-stopping performance, she was nominated for a Tony Award and named Best Supporting Actress in a

Musical by the New York Drama Critics Circle. During the show's run (it closed on December 9, 1962), she joined in recording the original cast album for Columbia Records, which soon signed her to a contract. Also during *Wholesale*, Barbra, who lived in a tiny, stinking apartment over a Third Avenue fish shop, began dating the musical's co-star, Elliott Gould.

In February 1963, her first solo album, the eclectic *The Barbra Streisand Album* (which included her extremely popular interpretation of "Happy Days Are Here Again"), was released. It rose to number eight on the charts, proving that she had audience appeal beyond New York City. For the LP, she won her first Grammy Award. She began touring nightclubs from coast to coast, now earning $7,000 weekly. In Los Angeles she appeared at the Hollywood Bowl and the Cocoanut Grove Club where Judy Garland asked her to guest on her CBS-TV variety show, along with Ethel Merman. On the Sunday night program, Garland teased, "You're so good I hate you." Streisand retorted teasingly, "You're so good, I've hated you for years." In September 1963, Barbra had married Elliott Gould in Carson City, Nevada, and they honeymooned in Las Vegas. That same month her latest LP, *The Second Barbra Streisand Album*, was released and rose to number two on the charts.

The great comedienne Fanny Brice had died in 1951, and since then many people had talked of producing a stage musical based on her life. Finally, movie producer Ray Stark (Brice's son-in-law) brought it to reality with *Funny Girl*. Anne Bancroft was cast in the leading role. However, when she could not handle the range of vocals required by the new Jule Styne–Bob Merrill score, she left and Streisand, who in many ways resembled the comedic Brice, was hired. There were many production delays before the show opened on March 26, 1964. Walter Kerr (in the *New York Herald-Tribune*) concluded, "Everyone knew Barbra Streisand would be a star and so she is." The original cast album became a top ten LP and two singles from the show, "Second Hand Rose" and the even-more-popular "People," became hits for Barbra. In addition, she appeared on the covers of *Time* and *Life* magazines. Suddenly, Streisand was in and so was her look. It was an amazing transformation. Only a few seasons before she was being chastised for her aggressively slovenly look, her too small chest, her too wide hips, her too closely set eyes, her lumpy figure, and her "infamous" nose. Some less kind critics insisted that her proboscis caused her to look like "a furious hamster," an "amiable anteater," or a "ferret." Now the refined Barbra Streisand look was the latest fad: her page boy hairdo, her Cleopatra eye makeup, her thrift shop outfits, her extended fingernails. On Christmas Day 1965, Streisand left the still-running *Funny Girl* to star in the London production, which opened at the Prince of Wales Theatre on April 13, 1966. She was a sensation abroad during her fourteen-week run and was named Best Foreign Actress by the London Drama Critics. It was her last role, to date, on the stage.

Because of the impending birth of her first child (Jason Emanuel, born on December 29, 1966), Barbra cancelled a concert tour scheduled for late 1966. However, she could still be seen on TV. Her first special, part of a multi-million-dollar pact with CBS, was "My Name Is Barbra" (April 28, 1965). There were moments of sophistication, childhood fantasy, and pure entertainment. *Variety*, in its review, said, "Her self-confidence, especially for her years and for one so recently come to stardom, is astounding, and she carries it well." The special won her an Emmy Award, and the soundtrack album rose to number two on the charts. Her next special, "Color Me Barbra" (CBS-TV, March 30, 1966), was filmed as a three-act entertainment: one segment was shot at the Philadelphia Museum of Art, another as a circus interlude, and the third as a concert performance. That soundtrack album rose to the number three spot. On October 11, 1967, she would star in "The Belle of 14th Street" special, this time with guest stars (including Jason Robards and John Bubbles). On September 16, 1968, CBS telecast "A Happening in Central Park," which consisted of highlights from her live June 17, 1968, concert in the Manhattan park. (The 1968 live album reached only number thirty on the charts.)

Streisand also continued to record independently of her TV specials and shows. Her *Je M'Appelle Barbra* (1966) was a departure from her previous solo LPs, containing French songs sung both in French and English. It also contained her first musical composition, "Ma Première Chanson." Her 1967 *A Christmas Album* proved that a Jewish performer could have a hit Yuletide record. By the end of the decade, with *What About Today?* (1969), Streisand had abandoned the nostalgic songs of her earlier albums. She chose to

Barbra Streisand in HELLO, DOLLY! (1969)

record the compositions of such contemporary composers as Jimmy Webb, John Lennon and Paul McCartney, and Paul Simon.

It was inevitable that Streisand (despite her special looks) would make motion pictures and that when *Funny Girl* became a movie she would star in it. For $200,000 she headlined the movie version of FUNNY GIRL (1968), with Omar Sharif as her gambler husband, Nicky Arnstein. The expensive production was directed by veteran William Wyler. There was talk of Streisand's acting the "star" during filming—even bulldozing Wyler—but the end result was commercially sound. *Variety* noted, "Miss Streisand's basic Grecian-profiled personality has not been photographically camouflaged. . . ." The film went on to gross $26,325,000 in domestic film rentals and Barbra co-won an Oscar, tying with Katharine Hepburn (for THE LION IN WINTER). When Streisand accepted her Oscar at the telecast ceremonies, she was her nonconventional self, picking up the trophy and saying "Hello, gorgeous!" (the first words she had uttered in the film).

In 1969, for $750,000 plus a percentage of the profits, Barbra starred in HELLO, DOLLY! The film was directed in an old-fashioned way by Gene Kelly and co-starred Walter Matthau, with whom Streisand continuously feuded. Matthau called her "a complete megalomaniac" and reminded his vis-à-vis of what had befallen an earlier self-possessed musical star queen named Betty Hutton. The overproduced musical was not well received. However, based on Streisand's marquee value it drew audiences, but not enough to offset its exorbitant $22 million cost. Streisand's oversized caricature of a mature matchmaker was an inappropriate mixture of Mae West, Fanny Brice, and Vivien Leigh. Likewise, for ON A CLEAR DAY YOU CAN SEE FOREVER (1970), her third consecutive movie derived from a Broadway musical, Streisand brought in the audiences. However, the confused fantasy and the lack of chemistry between her and Yves Montand were all too apparent, even to her most devoted fans.

By 1969, Streisand and Elliott Gould were divorced and she was linked romantically with a range of celebrities, from Omar Sharif to Canadian Prime Minister Pierre Trudeau. As a diversion from her big-budgeted musicals, Streisand appeared in THE OWL AND THE PUSSYCAT (1970), an intentionally small-scale comedy based on a Broadway play. The scenario was an extended verbal battle of wits between a would-be writer (George Segal) and a zany prostitute (Streisand) and showed that Barbra could succeed in a nonsinging role.

A wild comedy set in San Francisco, WHAT'S UP DOC? (1972) was reminiscent of the 1930s screwball comedies made by directors such as Preston Sturges and Howard Hawks, and teamed Streisand most effectively with Ryan O'Neal, who would become an off-screen pal. Her next vehicle, in a sharp change of pace, was UP THE SANDBOX (1972), in which she was a pregnant Manhattan housewife who already has two children. Frustrated in her desire to be liberated, she has a series of fantasies. Judith Crist (*New York* magazine) observed of the star in this feminist comedy, "She has the class to be herself, and the impudent music of her speaking voice is proof that she knows it." However, the film, made as part of her association with First Artists Productions, was not popular.

She made her first TV special in five years with "Barbra Streisand . . . and Other

Musical Instruments" (CBS, November 2, 1973) and on the big screen was paired with Robert Redford in a lavish romantic idyll about a bright New York Jewish girl who marries a handsome WASP (screen)writer with resultant conflicts over priorities, politics, and intellectualism. The tearjerker THE WAY WE WERE (1973) grossed $22,457,000 in domestic film rentals and its theme song, "Memories," was Streisand's first number one hit. She was Oscar-nominated, but lost the Best Actress Award to Glenda Jackson of A TOUCH OF CLASS. Having made the foolish FOR PETE'S SAKE (1974), Streisand was next seen in FUNNY LADY (1975), a long-expected sequel to FUNNY GIRL. It was implausible and plastic in its attempt to ape its predecessor. It grossed $19,313,000 in domestic film rentals.

In 1974, Streisand had met hair stylist Jon Peters (who then owned twenty-three beauty salons) on the set of one of her pictures. He was ending his marriage to actress Lesley Ann Warren. He and Streisand became a romantic team and he was soon serving as her producer. He produced her album *ButterFly* (1984) and served as producer (she was executive producer) on the contemporary musical remake of A STAR IS BORN (1976). The expensive production went through an assortment of talent who came and went as well as excessive on-location live concertizing to gain needed footage for its story of a declining rock star (Kris Kristofferson) loved by a rising rock songstress (Streisand). At one point, it was rumored that Peters would direct the film, and many acknowledged Streisand as the unofficial helmer on the production (Frank Pierson was the credited director). The movie was detested by critics (Rex Reed labeled it "The Worst Movie of the Year"). However, it grossed over $33 million in domestic film rentals. The theme song, "Evergreen," which Streisand co-wrote with Paul Williams, became a number one hit, and it won an Academy Award as Best Song. (The song and Streisand each won Grammy Awards.)

When Jon Peters produced EYES OF LAURA MARS (1978), a thriller starring Faye Dunaway, Barbra sang the film's theme song ("Prisoner"), which rose to number twenty-one on the charts. Even more popular was her duet with Neil Diamond on "You Don't Bring Me Flowers" (1978), which rose to number one. She and Diamond sang the song on the 1980 Grammy Awards telecast. More in the contemporary idiom was her duet with disco queen Donna Summer on "No More Tears (Enough Is Enough)" (1979). It was her fourth song to reach number one. Collaborating with Barry Gibb (of the Bee Gees) led to the *Guilty* album (1980)—which rose to number one—and to such high-ranking album cuts as "Woman in Love," which was a duet between Gibb and Streisand. As the decade ended, so did Streisand's appeal to rock/pop audiences.

Streisand had been off the screen for three years when she reunited with Ryan O'Neal for THE MAIN EVENT (1979), a goofy comedy set in the boxing milieu. It was filled with sappy shenanigans but the song "The Main Event/Fight" was a hit tune. In ALL NIGHT LONG (1981), Barbra was a last-minute replacement for Lisa Eichhorn in the story of a manager (Gene Hackman) of an all-night drug store who becomes obsessed with his neighbor's wife (Streisand). It was decidedly offbeat to cast Barbra as a sexy suburban housewife.

For years Barbra Streisand had been fixated on the idea of doing a screen version of Isaac Bashevis Singer's story "Yentl, the Yeshiva Boy." She saw the production as a means to become closer to (or to come to terms with) her late father's heritage. However, she feared making a career commitment to such an uncommercial project: in turn-of-the-century Russia, a young girl wants to gain scholarly knowledge by attending the Yeshiva (which is only open to men), so she masquerades as a boy. Over the years, Streisand's obsession with the project had made her the butt of industry jokes. Determined to film the story, she finally took complete control (and responsibility) as the musical's producer, director, co-scenarist, and star. Filmed in London and Czechoslovakia, with Mandy Patinkin as the handsome fellow scholar she loves and Amy Irving as the young woman she must marry to carry on her masquerade, YENTL was released in November 1983. The 134-minute film received mixed press and audience reaction, many agreeing that too much of Streisand was *not* a good thing. The picture grossed a relatively flat $19,680,127 in domestic film rentals. Although the film won several Golden Globe Awards and was on several critics' "Top Ten" lists, Streisand herself received no Academy Award nominations, which many considered a deliberate snub to her. Of the many, many musical numbers in YENTL, Streisand's "The Way He Makes Me Feel" received the most air play and rose to number forty on the charts. Meanwhile, the lengthy making of YENTL helped to end (1983) her relationship with Jon Peters, who had become a highly successful full-time film producer (and who is now a studio head).

In 1984, Streisand made her first music video, "Left in the Dark," which co-starred Kris Kristofferson as a bartender, while she was a cabaret singer. Her album *Emotion* (1984) was intended to make Streisand, then forty-two, ultra-contemporary in the Cyndi Lauper mold. It did not work. The next year she released *The Broadway Album*, which brought her back to the forefront as a recording artist. The Grammy-winning disc contained fourteen of her favorite Broadway show tunes and it engendered a Home Box Office cable TV special (1986) entitled "'Putting It Together'—The Making of The Broadway Album."

It was four years before Streisand, very sensitive to the negative response of the industry to her overdominant role in the making of YENTL, returned to feature filmmaking. She produced and starred in (and wrote the music for) a screen version of a 1980 drama, NUTS (1987). She played a high-priced New York City call girl involved in the homicide of a client (Leslie Nielsen). Her family attempts to have her committed to a mental institution rather than have her go on trial for murder and ruin the family image. A public defender (Richard Dreyfuss) is assigned to handle Streisand's sanity hearing, during which she reveals a past sexual relationship with her stepfather (Karl Malden). As the eccentric, intellectual New York call girl, Streisand gave a relatively unmannered performance. Many thought her showcasing role was calculated to win her another Academy Award. (She was not even nominated, in the year that saw Cher win for MOONSTRUCK.) The movie grossed only $14.1 million in domestic film rentals. Earlier in 1987 she had starred in the Home Box Office cable TV special "Barbra Streisand: One Voice."

Off screen, Streisand gained tremendous media coverage for her relationship with Don Johnson, the star of TV's "Miami Vice." He had been married three times (one of his wives was actress Melanie Griffith), had a son by actress Patti D'Arbanville, and at age thirty-seven had a million-selling LP album with *Heartbeat* (1987). The contrast between free-living Johnson and overly self-protective Barbra intrigued the paparazzi, and also brought Streisand to the attention of the younger generation. There was talk of joint picture making (which never occurred) and joint harmonizing (which did). On her fall 1988 album, *Till I Loved You*—considered a very "high concept" romantic album by the industry—she and Johnson dueted on the title song. By the time the LP was released, she and the actor had parted company, and he later remarried Melanie Griffith. The *New York Times* ranked the new Streisand album as "a collection of Rodeo Drive musical baubles" and wondered, "Imagine what Ms. Streisand would do with a pop song cycle about love that matched her dramatic reach." In late summer 1989, Streisand, who had been a long-time contender to play the lead role in the screen adaptation of the musical *Evita*, was set to begin filming PRINCE OF TIDES, based on the stage drama about a southern man's odyssey through his troubled past. She would not only direct, but also play the role of Dr. Lowenstein, a New York psychiatrist.

## Filmography

Funny Girl (Col, 1968)
Hello, Dolly! (20th–Fox, 1969)
On a Clear Day You Can See Forever (Par, 1970)
The Owl and the Pussycat (Col, 1970)
What's Up Doc? (WB, 1972)
Up the Sandbox (NG, 1972)
The Way We Were (Par, 1973)
For Pete's Sake (WB, 1974)

Funny Lady (Col, 1975)
A Star Is Born (WB, 1976) (also co-producer, co-song)
Eyes of Laura Mars (Col, 1978) (voice only)
The Main Event (WB, 1979)
All Night Long (Univ 1981)
Yentl (MGM/UA, 1983) (also producer, director, co-screenplay)
Nuts (WB, 1987) (also producer, music)

## Broadway Plays

I Can Get It for You Wholesale (1962)
Funny Girl (1964)

## Album Discography

Barbra Joan Streisand (Col KC-030792)
The Barbra Streisand Album (Col CL-2007/CS-8807)
The Broadway Album (Col OC-40092)
ButterFly (Col PC-3305)
A Christmas Album (Col CL-2757/CS-9557)
Classical Barbra (Col M-33452)
Color Me Barbra (Col CL-2478/CS-9278)
Emotion (Col OC-39480)

Eyes of Laura Mars (Col JS-35487) [ST]
Funny Girl (Cap VAS/SVAS-2059) [OC]
Funny Girl (Col BOS-3220) [ST]
Funny Lady (Arista 9004) [ST]
Greatest Hits (Col KCS-9968)
Greatest Hits, Vol. 2 (Col FC-35679)
Guilty (Col FC-36750)
A Happening in Central Park (Col CS-9710)
Harold Sings Arlen (With Friend) (Col OL-6520/OS-2920)

Hello, Dolly! (20th Century–Fox DTCS-5103, 20th Century–Fox 102) [ST]

I Can Get It for You Wholesale (Col KOL-5780/KOS-2180, Col Special Products 2180) [OC]

Je M'Appelle Barbra (Col CL-2547/CS-9347)

Lazy Afternoon (Col PC-33815)

The Legendary Barbra Streisand (Col CL-1779)

Live in Concert at the Forum (Col KC-3176)

The Main Event (Col JS-36115) [ST]

Memories (Col TC-37678)

My Name Is Barbra (Col CL-2336/CS-9136)

My Name Is Barbra, Two . . . (Col CL-2409/CS-9209)

On a Clear Day You Can See Forever (Col S-30086) [ST]

The Owl and the Pussycat (Col S-30401) [ST]

People (Col CL-2215/CS-9015)

Pins and Needles (Col OS/AOS-2210) [OC]

The Second Barbra Streisand Album (Col CL-2054/CS-8854)

Simply Streisand (Col CL-2682/CS-9482)

Songbird (Col KC-30378)

A Star Is Born (Col JS-34403) [ST]

Stony End (Col KC-30378)

Streisand Superman (Col JC-34830)

The Third Barbra Streisand Album (Col CL-2154/CS-8954)

Till I Loved You (Col OC-40880-S1)

The Way We Were (Col KS-32830) [ST]

The Way We Were (Col PC-32801)

Wet (Col FC-36258)

What About Today? (Col CS-9816)

Yentl (Col JS-39152) [ST]

# SHIRLEY TEMPLE

MARY PICKFORD WAS DUBBED "AMERICA'S SWEETHEART" IN THE silent movie era, but the title passed to Shirley Temple during the Depression. To this day she is still considered the nation's most precious (and precocious) little girl, although she is well past sixty and has not been involved in show business for nearly three decades.

The appeal of Shirley Temple is a fairly simple one. She was a talented, attractive, and very ingratiating little lady whose ringlet curls and cherub demeanor, as well as her cheerful smile and optimistic attitude, made millions forget temporarily the woes of the Depression. Through the magic of film, the little girl Shirley Temple has endured, and her appeal to each new generation remains consistently strong. Although she had an average post-moppet movie career and became a wife and mother and grandmother—and eventually a highly regarded diplomat—Shirley Temple will forever remain in the minds of her public as that sweet child who brought so much happiness at a time when it was needed so badly.

She was born Shirley Jane Temple on April 23, 1928, in Santa Monica, California. She was the third child (preceded by brothers Jack in 1916 and George in 1920) of bank teller George Temple and his wife, Gertrude (Craiger) Temple. When Shirley was three, her very ambitious mother had the child take dancing lessons. Director Charles Lamont from the poverty-row Educational Pictures hired the tyke (at $10 a day) to appear in his series of "Baby Burlesks," one-reel comedies that were spoofs of current major films with small children coyly enacting the adult roles. Shirley made her motion picture debut in the first of the series, WAR BABIES (1932), a take-off on WHAT PRICE GLORY? (1926), and the first words she spoke on screen were in French, "Mais oui, mon cher!" Over the next several months she made seven more of these hastily assembled mini-productions. The little lady sang her first screen song, "She's Only a Bird in a Gilded Cage," in GLAD RAGS TO RICHES (1933) and did imitations of Mae West and Marlene Dietrich in KID 'N' HOLLYWOOD (1933). Shirley made her first feature picture, THE RED-HAIRED ALIBI, for Capitol Films in 1932 in a tiny role, and she then supported Andy Clyde in his series comedy DORA'S DUNKIN' DONUTS (1933) and had parts in a trio of Educational's "Frolics of Youth" series shorts. Mrs. Temple attempted to have Shirley cast as a regular in Hal Roach's popular "Our Gang" comedies, but she was unsuccessful.

More film work for the child came as the offspring of a hillbilly family in TO THE LAST MAN (1933), as a store nursery charge in OUT ALL NIGHT (1933), and in small child roles in CAROLINA (1934), NOW I'LL TELL (1934), MANDALAY (1934), and the musical short NEW DEAL RHYTHM (1934). By this time, both Paramount and Fox were interested in Shirley Temple and each came up with feature projects for her. At Fox she stole the show in the all-star musical STAND UP AND CHEER (1934) when she appeared with James Dunn and Patricia White and sang and danced "Baby Take a Bow." *Variety* reported, "She's a cinch female Jackie Cooper and Jackie Coogan in one, excepting in a more jovial being. She's the unofficial star of this Fox musical." At Paramount she portrayed a youngster adopted by a race track denizen (Adolphe Menjou) whose heart she softens in the Damon Runyon tale LITTLE MISS MARKER (1934). *Variety* was quick to note, "the child is the greater part of the show and proves again that she can act in spite of her immature years." Fox was the studio, however, to realize Shirley's screen potential, and she was signed to a seven-year contract there, starting at $150 weekly.

Following a small role in CHANGE OF HEART (1934), Fox toplined Shirley Temple in BABY TAKE A BOW in 1934, which in many ways set the pattern for her subsequent screen career. Its story was syrupy melodrama lightened by music and by Shirley's sweet personality. She played a little girl whose ex-convict dad (James Dunn) is suspected of having stolen a priceless pearl. She and Dunn dueted the pleasing "On Accounta I Love You." As part of a two-picture deal made earlier in the year by Mrs. Temple, Shirley returned to Paramount for the tearjerker NOW AND FOREVER (1934) as the daughter of two classy thieves (Gary Cooper and Carole Lombard). Even in competition with two such formidable screen personalities, Shirley easily stole the limelight. By now she was earning over $1,250 weekly. Late in 1934, Fox issued BRIGHT EYES, which proved to be one of Shirley's most popular efforts. In it she sang her most famous song, "On the Good Ship Lollipop" (which composer Richard Whiting had written for his daughter, Margaret). In addition, the film had Shirley involved in a custody battle and coping with bratty Jane Withers.

BRIGHT EYES was a smash hit. Soon the country (and the world) were deluged with all kinds of Shirley Temple merchandise, ranging from dolls, books, and clothing to the emulation of her hair style. There was even a nonalcoholic drink named in her honor. Millions of willing and unwilling little girls had their dress styles and looks patterned after Shirley, who was the role model many parents looked to in raising their offspring. By the end of 1934, Shirley Temple was fast rising to the top of the list of Hollywood's biggest box-office attractions. The next year she would be presented with a special Academy Award. (The award was bestowed because she "brought more happiness to millions of children and millions of grownups than any child of her years in the history of the world.")

Shirley Temple starred in a quartet of big moneymakers for Fox in 1935, beginning with THE LITTLE COLONEL, based on the Annie Fellows Johnston novel. The film had Shirley softening the heart of her stubborn Confederate grandfather (Lionel Barrymore), whose daughter (Evelyn Venable) had married a Yankee (John Lodge). It was the first of her screen teamings with dance great Bill "Bojangles" Robinson, and the finale was filmed in color. Next came one of her very best properties, CURLY TOP, in which she and Rochelle Hudson played orphaned sisters taken in by wealthy John Boles because he had fallen under Shirley's spell. Before long, she has played cupid for her sister and Boles. Few can forget the scene in which Shirley perched on a piano as Boles sang the title song to her, although the movie also provided the child with two fine numbers: "Animal Crackers in My Soup" and "When I Grow Up." The first of Shirley's features to be distributed by the new Darryl F. Zanuck regime at 20th Century–Fox was THE LITTLEST REBEL. Shirley breathed new life into this old stage vehicle about a child caught up in the Civil War, trying to save her Confederate father (John Boles) from a Union officer (Jack Holt) determined to capture him. Shirley sang "Polly Wolly Doodle," she and Bill Robinson did a memorable staircase tap dance, and she won accolades for the scene in which she shares an apple with Abraham Lincoln (Frank McGlynn, Sr.).

In 1936, Shirley turned out another quartet of successful pictures, beginning with CAPTAIN JANUARY, in which she was a shipwreck victim adopted by two old lighthouse keepers (Guy Kibbee, Slim Summerville). Here Shirley sang "At the Codfish Ball," "The Right Somebody to Love," "Early Bird," and even an aria from the opera *Lucia di Lammermoor*. She also performed a hula with Buddy Ebsen. In POOR LITTLE RICH GIRL, Shirley is a lonely child who becomes friendly with vaudevillians Alice Faye and Jack Haley while trying to marry off her dad (Michael Whalen) to an advertising executive (Gloria Stuart). By now, 20th Century–Fox was loading Shirley's vehicles with songs, and this one

Shirley Temple and Bill "Bojangles" Robinson in THE LITTLEST REBEL (1935)

had a bountiful harvest with "When I'm with You," "Oh! My Goodness," "You Gotta Eat Your Spinach," "But Definitely," and "Military Man." In DIMPLES, as a poor child trying to revitalize her fallen guardian (Frank Morgan), Shirley performed "Picture Me Without You," "Hey, What Did the Blue Jay Say?," and "When Somebody Loves Somebody" and enacted the part of Little Eva in an adaptation of *Uncle Tom's Cabin*. Her final 1936 star vehicle, issued for the Christmas trade, was STOWAWAY, which had her as the orphaned child of missionaries killed in China. She hides on a ship and tries to arrange a romance between a playboy (Robert Young) and a pretty passenger (Alice Faye). Shirley did imitations (Eddie Cantor, Bing Crosby, and Al Jolson) and sang "Goodnight, My Love" (which became closely associated with Alice Faye, who also did it in the film) and "That's What I Want for Christmas." By now Shirley had displaced Janet Gaynor as the blonde queen of 20th Century–Fox, as later, in turn, Alice Faye, Sonja Henie, Betty Grable, and Marilyn Monroe would hold that distinction.

Rudyard Kipling's story *Wee Willie Winkie* (with a sex change made to accommodate the star) was the basis for WEE WILLIE WINKIE, the first of two 1937 Temple starrers. Here she played the adopted mascot of a British colonial regiment in India. This movie is the star's personal favorite of her forty-two feature films. She especially liked working with co-star Victor McLaglen and director John Ford. Her holiday offering for 1937 was a fine version of HEIDI with Shirley as the nineteenth-century Swiss miss who is taken from her loving grandfather (Jean Hersholt) to live with cruel Mary Nash.

Allan Dwan handled the directorial chores on HEIDI as he was to do with REBECCA OF SUNNYBROOK FARM, the first of a trio of 1938 releases for Shirley. This one had her playing cupid for Randolph Scott and Gloria Stuart, dancing (once again with Bill "Bojangles" Robinson), and performing "An Old Straw Hat" and "Come and Get Your Happiness," all the while becoming a singing star on radio. Shirley was now ten years old, and no matter how the studio tried to disguise it, she was fast maturing. She returned to the musical format with LITTLE MISS BROADWAY, in which she again was orphaned and was adopted by a former stage dancer (George Murphy); they dueted on "We Should Get Together" while Shirley soloed with "Be Optimistic," "Sing Me an Old Fashioned Song," and "How Can I Thank You?" The *New York Herald-Tribune* cautioned, "We have seen all of Miss Temple's tricks and pirouettes so many times that they are apt to seem a bit monotonous in so dull a framework as this." Shirley closed out the year with one of her lesser vehicles, JUST AROUND THE CORNER, which found her as the daughter of an impoverished man (Charles Farrell). Shirley takes it upon herself to persuade self-centered tycoon (Claude Gillingwater) to give him work. She and Bill Robinson dueted on "I Love to Walk in the Rain," and Shirley sang the pleasant "This Is a Happy Little Ditty." Around this time, MGM wanted to star Temple in its THE WIZARD OF OZ (1939), but the part went eventually to Judy Garland, while 20th never found the proper script for a promised screen pairing of Shirley with Kate Smith. At this juncture, Shirley was earning $100,000 per film.

To shore up what seemed to be her slipping box-office appeal, 20th Century–Fox gave Shirley a posh Technicolor production, THE LITTLE PRINCESS (1939), which cast her as a waif in nineteenth-century England searching for her lost father and even meeting Queen Victoria (Beryl Mercer). She was reunited with Randolph Scott for the Sepiatone Western SUSANNAH OF THE MOUNTIES (1939), in which she survived a wagon train massacre and was adopted by the Mounties; she sang "I'll Teach You to Waltz."

In 1940, Shirley, who was now earning close to $300,000 per film, starred in the lavish (and costly) Technicolor fantasy feature THE BLUE BIRD, about a little girl's search for happiness; she sang "Lay-De-O." Even in its edited version for general distribution, the picture was heavy-handed and dull. It was Temple's first box-office dud. She closed out her 20th Century–Fox contract with YOUNG PEOPLE (1940), as an orphaned young lady who is raised by vaudevillians Jack Oakie and Charlotte Greenwood. It used footage from STAND UP AND CHEER and CURLY TOP, and Shirley dueted with Oakie and Greenwood on "Tra-La-La."

During her Fox tenure, Shirley had earned some $3 million (which was carefully invested by her banker father) and her films made more than $25 million for the studio. As part of her contract settlement, Mrs. Temple (long the bane of the studio hierarchy) reportedly negotiated a $300,000 payment. When she left Fox, the studio—in typical Hollywood tradition—mouthed platitudes, gave her a few old costumes and her rehearsal piano, and promptly went about its business. According to her YOUNG PEOPLE co-star Jack Oakie, she "received a chill from the studio to go down in movie history."

Shirley enrolled in the Westlake School for Girls, allegedly in retirement. However, on October 14, 1940, she repeated her role from "The Littlest Rebel" on a segment of the CBS program "Lux Radio Theatre" with Claude Rains and Preston Foster. Early in 1941, she signed a contract with MGM for $2,500 a week. But that studio had Judy Garland and Mickey Rooney and the only project to materialize for Shirley was the disappointing KATHLEEN (1941). She played a lonely girl who attempts to bring romance to her father (Herbert Marshall) and Laraine Day. She sang "Around the Corner," but in the release print her voice was dubbed! Her 1941 quartet of radio specials called "Shirley Temple Time" were more satisfactory, and from March to September 1942 she had the title role in the Wednesday night CBS radio comedy "Junior Miss." A 1942 issue of *Life* magazine labeled Shirley a has-been.

Like most ex-child stars, Shirley Temple had a difficult time getting cast in pictures as she matured. For producer Edward Small she had the title role in the 1942 comedy MISS ANNIE ROONEY. She did a jitterbug and received her first screen kiss, from another ex-child star, Dickie Moore. Hollywood in general lost interest in the teenaged Shirley, but producer David O. Selznick thought she had potential as an adult performer and he signed her to a seven-year contract. She made her "comeback" in his extravagant domestic wartime epic SINCE YOU WENT AWAY (1944), in which she played the younger daughter of Claudette Colbert. She was just fine, but the role was that of a stereotypical young adolescent and she could only be so cute. After that, her screen roles were a mixed lot. They ranged from the aborted Selznick project of LITTLE WOMEN to playing teenagers with crushes on older men in I'LL BE SEEING YOU (1944) and THE BACHELOR AND THE BOBBY-SOXER (1947). In a continuing series of loanouts she had grown-up roles in outings such as

HONEYMOON (1947), MR. BELVEDERE GOES TO COLLEGE (1949), for which she returned to her old studio, 20th Century–Fox, and THE STORY OF SEABISCUIT (1949). She played fickle Corliss Archer in two middling comedies, KISS AND TELL (1945) and A KISS FOR CORLISS (1949).

On September 19, 1945, amid much publicity, she married former serviceman John Agar (who suddenly decided to become an actor), and they had a child, Linda Susan, in 1948. Shirley and Agar also did two movies together, FORT APACHE (1948), which reunited her with director John Ford, and ADVENTURE IN BALTIMORE (1949). They were divorced in late 1949. She told the press, "One of the mistakes I made was always acting the happy wife in public. I felt the responsibility of being Shirley Temple. . . . You see, no publicity campaign or even a studio genius made me a star. The public did it. I felt a responsibility to them." On December 16, 1950, she married Charles Black, a TV executive who claimed never to have seen a Shirley Temple movie before that time. They had two children: Charles (born in 1952, at whose birth Shirley nearly died from pleurisy and a blood clot after the delivery) and Lori (born in 1954).

When, in early 1958, Shirley Temple decided to return to show business, she paused to reminisce about her famous childhood. "I have no sad memories. I never had to work very hard. We all just seemed to play games." Her vehicle was the NBC-TV series "Shirley Temple's Storybook," which debuted on January 12, 1958, and for which she was hostess and sometimes episode star. The series lasted till late 1958. In the fall of 1960, she returned with "The Shirley Temple Theatre," for the same network, which ran for a season. At this time she also recorded *Bambi* and *Dumbo* for RCA Victor. (She was not allowed to make commercial recordings while at Fox, although songs from her film soundtracks have been used to make up several record albums.) She made occasional guest appearances on such programs as "The Red Skelton Show" and "Sing Along with Mitch." In 1965, she filmed the unsuccessful TV pilot "Go Fight City Hall."

From 1964 to 1966, she was a member of the board of the San Francisco Film Festival, but withdrew over a dispute as to the advisability of screening Mai Zetterling's NIGHT GAMES, which Temple insisted was pornographic. Shirley Temple Black ran for Congress in California in a special 1967 election as a Republican, but she was defeated. In August 1968, she was among those trapped in Prague during the Russian invasion of that city. She had flown to Czechoslovakia to attend the International Federation of Multiple Sclerosis Societies seminars. (Her brother George suffered from the disease.) In 1969, President Richard Nixon named her as a delegate to the United Nations. Three years later, she became a Special Assistant to the Chairman of the President's Council on the Environment. Also that year, she underwent a radical mastectomy. In 1974, she became U.S. Ambassador to Ghana, and in 1976, she was named Chief of Protocol for the State Department. In 1988 she wrote her autobiography, *Child Star*. In mid-1989 she was selected by President George Bush as the new U.S. Ambassador to Czechoslovakia, and in August 1989, she arrived in Prague to assume her duties.

For Shirley Temple, the past is past. "I class myself with Rin Tin Tin. At the end of the Depression people were perhaps looking for something to cheer themselves up. They fell in love with a dog and a little girl. It won't happen again." For her, today is important. She once said, "The trick to getting older is to keep busy. In this day a woman any age has to find something she is really for—or against—and then work at it. If you are not involved, the alternative is corrosive apathy."

## Filmography

War Babies (Educational, 1932) (s)
The Runt Page (Univ, 1932) (s)
Pie-Covered Wagon (Educational, 1932) (s)
Kid's Last Fight (Educational, 1932) (s)
The Red-Haired Alibi (Capitol Film Exchange, 1932)
Merrily Yours (Educational, 1932) (s)
Polly-Tix in Washington (Educational, 1933) (s)
Kid 'n' Hollywood (Educational, 1933) (s)
Glad Rags to Riches (Educational, 1933) (s)
Out All Night (Univ, 1933)
Dora's Dunkin' Donuts (Educational, 1933) (s)
Managed Money (Educational, 1933) (s)
What to Do? (Educational, 1933) (s)
To the Last Man (Par, 1933)
As the Earth Turns (WB, 1933)
Pardon My Pups (Educational, 1934) (s)
Mandalay (WB, 1934)
New Deal Rhythm (Par, 1934) (s)
Carolina (Fox, 1934)
Stand Up and Cheer (Fox, 1934)
Now I'll Tell [When New York Sleeps] (Fox, 1934)
Change of Heart (Fox, 1934)
Little Miss Marker [Girl in Pawn] (Par, 1934)
Baby Take a Bow (Fox, 1934)
Now and Forever (Par, 1934)
Bright Eyes (Fox, 1934)
The Little Colonel (Fox, 1935)
Our Little Girl (Fox, 1935)
Curly Top (Fox, 1935)
The Littlest Rebel (20th–Fox, 1935)
Our Girl Shirley (Astor, 1935) (s)
Captain January (20th–Fox, 1936)

Dimples (20th–Fox, 1936)
Poor Little Rich Girl (20th–Fox, 1936)
Stowaway (20th–Fox, 1936)
Wee Willie Winkie (20th–Fox, 1937)
Heidi (20th–Fox, 1937)
Ali Baba Goes to Town (20th–Fox, 1937) (clip only)
Rebecca of Sunnybrook Farm (20th–Fox, 1938)
Little Miss Broadway (20th–Fox, 1938)
Just Around the Corner (20th–Fox, 1938)
The World Is Ours (20th–Fox, 1938) (s)
The Little Princess (20th–Fox, 1939)
Susannah of the Mounties (20th–Fox, 1939)
The Blue Bird (20th–Fox, 1940)
Young People (20th–Fox, 1940)
Kathleen (MGM, 1941)
Miss Annie Rooney (UA, 1942)
Since You Went Away (UA, 1944)
I'll Be Seeing You (UA, 1944)
Kiss and Tell (Col, 1945)
Honeymoon [Two Men and a Girl] (RKO, 1947)
The Bachelor and the Bobby-Soxer [Bachelor Knight] (RKO, 1947)
That Hagen Girl (WB, 1947)
Fort Apache (RKO, 1948)
Mr. Belvedere Goes to College (20th–Fox, 1949)
Adventure in Baltimore [Bachelor Bait] (RKO, 1949)
The Story of Seabiscuit [Pride of Kentucky] (WB, 1949)
A Kiss for Corliss (UA, 1949)

## Radio Series

Junior Miss (CBS, 1942)

## TV Series

Shirley Temple's Storybook (NBC, 1958)
The Shirley Temple Theatre (NBC, 1960–61)

## Album Discography

Bambi (Camden CAL-1012)
The Best of Shirley Temple, Vols. 1–2 (20th
  Century–Fox 3102, 3172)
The Complete Shirley Temple Songbook (20th
  Century–Fox 103-2)
Curtain Call (Movietone 71012)
Dumbo (Camden CAL-1026)
Little Miss Shirley Temple (Pickwick 3177)
Little Miss Wonderful (20th Century–Fox
  3045)

The Littlest Rebel (Radiola MR-116) [ST/R]
Nelson Eddy with Shirley Temple, Jane Powell,
  Kathryn Grayson, Lois Butler, and Norma
  Nelson (Mac/Eddy JN 128)
On the Good Ship Lollipop (Movietone 71001)
On the Good Ship Lollipop (Murray Hill
  S5610X)
Remember Shirley (20th Century–Fox 906)
Shirley Temple—Original Film Soundtracks
  (20th Century–Fox 1003)

# LAWRENCE TIBBETT

FOR MANY YEARS, OPERA AND POPULAR MUSIC WERE WIDELY DIVERSE and performers of one did not trespass on the other. Opera was considered the music of the elite, while popular music suited the masses. Lawrence Tibbett, more than any other performer in his time, helped to tear down this barrier in his presentation not only of opera but also of Tin Pan Alley songs, black spirituals, and cowboy ballads. In addition, the 6' 1¹/₂" handsome baritone was a decent actor who scored well in a half dozen movies in addition to achieving success on the concert stage, records, and radio, as well as at the Metropolitan Opera and on Broadway.

Lawrence Tibbett's father was a deputy sheriff in Kern County, California, and Lawrence was born November 19, 1896, in Bakersfield. He took to music at an early age, and in 1902 he made his singing debut in the choir of the Methodist Church in Bakersfield. The next year, his lawman father was killed in a shootout with cattle rustlers and Lawrence moved with his mother to Los Angeles, where he attended school, but spent summers on the family ranch back in Bakersfield. In school he participated in plays and the glee club, and after graduation, he became an actor with various Los Angeles stock companies and studied acting with Basil Ruysdael. Next he landed a job with the touring Shakespearean stock company of Tyrone Power (Sr.). However, his acting career was interrupted by Navy service during World War I. After the war, he returned to the stage and also studied voice, singing with a light opera company.

In 1923, Lawrence Tibbett sang Amonasro in Verdi's *Aïda* at the Hollywood Bowl. His reception was so good that he went to New York City, where he took further operatic lessons while singing in a church choir. Frank La Forge, Tibbett's voice coach, was so impressed with him that he arranged an audition for the young man at the Metropolitan. Tibbett was rejected, but he continued studying and a few months later was successful in his second tryout. He won a twenty-two-week contract with the Met at a salary of $60 per week. On November 23, 1923, he made an inconspicuous debut at the Metropolitan in *Boris Godunov* as a monk and a week later he sang Valentin in Gounod's *Faust*. (Tibbett's surname originally had only one final "t," but the printer of the opera's programs misspelled his name and the new spelling stuck.)

Tibbett's big break came in 1925 when he sang Ford in Verdi's last opera, *Falstaff,* and literally stopped the show, receiving a fifteen-minute ovation. From that point on, the Met gave him leading roles and in the next two decades he performed over six dozen different baritone roles. He was also instrumental in the staging of American operas at the Metropolitan, and during his first decade with the organization he appeared in every

English-language opera introduced there, including *The King's Henchman* by Deems Taylor in 1927. Opera critics and audiences agreed that Tibbett was not only one of the finest baritones on the operatic stage, but also its finest actor.

Tibbett's continued success at the Met coincided with the arrival of talking pictures and Hollywood's need for both singers and actors who could adapt to sound. Tibbett fit the bill on both counts, and Metro-Goldwyn-Mayer, which also brought Met diva Grace Moore into its fold, signed him to star in its Technicolor production of THE ROGUE SONG (1930), based on Franz Lehár's 1910 operetta *Zigeunerliebe* (*Gypsy Love*). Under Lionel Barrymore's direction, Tibbett was cast as the singing bandit Yegor, who steals from the rich Cossacks oppressing his Caucasian Mountains people. However, he falls in love with the beautiful Princess Vera (Catherine Dale Owen), the sister of the Cossack commander. For comic relief, Stan Laurel and Oliver Hardy were added to the film's cast. His next film, THE ROGUE SONG, provided Tibbett with a rousing swashbuckling role and several fine numbers, including "The White Dove," "The Rogue Song," and "When I'm Looking at You." The production was issued early in 1930 and *Photoplay* magazine noted enthusiastically, "Lawrence Tibbett, grand opera star, flashes across the phonoplay horizon, an inimitable and dashing personality . . . this operetta is roistering, brilliant and dramatic— a feast for the eye and ear." For his performance, Lawrence Tibbett was nominated for an Academy Award, but lost the Best Actor Oscar to George Arliss of DISRAELI. (Sadly, THE ROGUE SONG no longer exists except for brief footage and the soundtrack, which has been issued on Pelican Records.) Tibbett also recorded the film's songs for Victor Records early in 1930. (He would also record his songs from his other MGM movies for Victor.) He had been recording with the label since the late 1920s and would remain with it well into the 1940s, recording both opera and popular music, the latter ranging from folk songs like "De Glory Road" and "Battle Hymn of the Republic" to George Gershwin's *Porgy and Bess* score.

"The first American baritone of talking pictures" (as MGM billed him) was next assigned to the studio's production of the Sigmund Romberg operetta NEW MOON (1930) with Grace Moore. She had fared poorly in her screen debut (A LADY'S MORALS, 1930), and MGM hoped that Tibbett would help to humanize her lofty screen image. The NEW MOON setting (far different than that of the later Jeanette MacDonald–Nelson Eddy movie version) was the wilds of Russia, with Tibbett as the dashing Russian lieutenant in love with a beautiful princess (Grace Moore). The picture offered him the opportunity to perform duets with Moore on "Lover Come Back to Me" and "Wanting You." If THE ROGUE SONG had displayed Tibbett at his dramatic best, NEW MOON weighed him down. Moreover, Grace Moore's overly theatrical performance did not help matters. *Variety* warned, "Old style three cornered musical romance with the accent on the music. There's a doubt as to whether it will be easily digested by the average picturegoer." The film did modest box-office business.

While MGM would soon give up on Grace Moore, the studio had more faith in Tibbett's screen potential. Deciding that he needed a new down-to-earth screen image, MGM next presented him in THE PRODIGAL, a.k.a. THE SOUTHERNER (1931). The film was a modern updating of the biblical tale of the Prodigal Son with Tibbett cast as a hobo, tramping around the countryside with Cliff Edwards and Roland Young, and eventually returning home to get a hero's welcome. The musical offered him the songs "Life Is a Dream" and "Without a Song." Compared to his earlier forays, this production gave him much more realistic dialogue to speak, but still the public was not enthusiastic about his screen persona. The hastily assembled CUBAN LOVE SONG (1931) proved to be his final MGM feature. He played a Marine in love with a Cuban girl (Lupe Velez). He later goes to France and marries unhappily, only to return to Cuba to find that the girl he loves has died, but has left him a son. Tibbett sang "From the Halls of Montezuma," "Tramps at Sea," "The Peanut Vendor," and "Cuban Love Song." To inject some life into the film, Jimmy Durante was thrown in as comic relief. By now, *Variety* was referring to the opera star's presence in a picture as "the Tibbett drawback," and the movie was a failure. MGM and Tibbett called it quits.

Following his disappointing foray into motion pictures, Lawrence Tibbett returned to the Metropolitan to sing the lead in Deems Taylor's *Peter Ibbetson* in 1931, and the next year he made his network radio debut on NBC. From 1933 to 1934 he was a regular on that network's "Voice of Firestone" series, and from 1934 to 1935 he starred on "The Packard Show" on the NBC Blue network. He also continued to headline at the Met with the first U.S. production of Verdi's *Simon Boccanegra* in 1932, Louis Gruenberg's *The Emperor Jones* in 1933, and Howard Hanson's *Merry Mount* in 1934 (the latter two being

Lupe Velez and Lawrence Tibbett in CUBAN LOVE SONG (1931)

American operas given their world premieres at the Met).

Hollywood rediscovered Grace Moore in 1934 with Columbia's hugely popular ONE NIGHT OF LOVE. The film's success created fresh interest in opera stars, and Lawrence Tibbett was summoned back to Hollywood. Fox Films hired him to star in the expensive production METROPOLITAN (1935), a backstage story that displayed him rising from extra to star and romancing Virginia Bruce. He had the opportunity to sing one of his most requested ballads, Rudyard Kipling's "On the Road to Mandalay." The film also gave him a chance to sing complete arias, instead of excerpts. But METROPOLITAN was considered stuffy and stilted by a bored public. Studio head Darryl F. Zanuck wanted to settle Tibbett's $200,000 contract, but Tibbett refused. The studio (now restructured as 20th Century–Fox) shoved him into a "B" production directed by Otto Preminger. In UNDER YOUR SPELL (1937), he was a difficult-to-get-along-with opera singer who escapes the public eye by going to New Mexico and finding romance with a pretty socialite (Wendy Barrie). The modest movie was a flop.

From 1936 to 1938, Tibbett appeared with André Kostelanetz on "The Chesterfield Show" on CBS radio, and he continued appearing at the Met and doing concerts. During the mid-1930s, critics acclaimed him as the leading male singer on radio. (He was one of the founders of the American Federation of Radio Artists.) In London in 1937, he sang the title role in the world premiere of Eugene Goossens' opera *Don Juan de Manera.* In 1940, he underwent throat surgery that left his voice with a husky timber, in contrast to its former lyric quality. Nevertheless, most critics still agreed that he had one of the finest voices of his time. In the 1942 season, he appeared with Donald Voorhees on "The Bell Telephone Hour" on NBC radio. In 1945, he surprised the music world by replacing Frank Sinatra on that network's very popular "Your Hit Parade" for a seven-month period.

Tibbett continued his Metropolitan appearances, and in 1950, he sang in that company's premiere of *Khovanshchina* by Mussorgsky. In the same year he made his Broadway debut in *The Barrier,* a drama which lasted only four performances. Also as a dramatic actor he came to television in 1951, appearing in the "Close Harmony" episode of NBC's "Armstrong Circle Theatre."

In addition to his performances at the Met, Tibbett sang opera with other companies throughout the country. Between 1927 and 1949, he worked for nine seasons at the San Francisco Opera Company; in 1949, he opened the season as Scarpia in Verdi's *Tosca* and then sang both Dapertutto and Dr. Miracle in Offenbach's *Tales of Hoffmann.*

Just as Lauritz Melchior had come into conflict with Rudolf Bing, the dictatorial new director of the Metropolitan, for his various nonoperatic activities, so did Tibbett. Thus, after 1950, he did not again work at the Met. In the mid-1950s, Tibbett was recording both opera and popular ballads for the Record Corporation of America. When Ezio Pinza became ill, Tibbett replaced him in the Broadway musical *Fanny* in 1956. He remained active until his death on July 15, 1960, after undergoing neurosurgery.

In addition to his career successes, Lawrence Tibbett had a rewarding personal life. He had wed Grace Mackay Smith in 1919, and they had two sons, Lawrence, Jr. and Richard. The boys appeared as extras in his films (Lawrence also appeared in the 1948

Western EL PASO) and traveled with him on his tours, along with his long-time accompanist, Stewart Willie. In 1931, he and Grace were divorced and he later married Jane Maston Bugard, the daughter of a New York banker, by whom he had one son (Michael).

Tibbett was the first opera singer to be given the gold medal of the American Academy of Arts and Letters for displaying excellence in diction. In 1937, the King of Sweden bestowed the Letteris et Artibus medal on the famed opera star.

## Filmography

The Rogue Song (MGM, 1930)
New Moon [Parisian Belle] (MGM, 1930)
The Prodigal [The Southerner/The Wandering Son] (MGM, 1931)

Cuban Love Song (MGM, 1931)
Metropolitan (20th–Fox, 1935)
Under Your Spell (20th–Fox, 1937)

## Broadway Plays

The Barrier (1950)
Fanny (1956) (replacement)

## Radio Series

Voice of Firestone (NBC, 1933–34)
The Packard Show (NBC Blue, 1934–35)
The Chesterfield Show (CBS, 1936–38)

The Bell Telephone Hour (NBC, 1942)
Your Hit Parade (NBC, 1945)

## Album Discography

The Art of Lawrence Tibbett (Victrola 1340)
The Crucifixion (Camden CAL-235, Victrola 1403) w. Richard Crooks
Great Actor-Baritone-Opera Arias (Pearl 257/258)
Home on the Range (Halo 50266, Ultraphonic 50266)
Lawrence Tibbett (Allegro/Royale 1627)
Lawrence Tibbett (Empire 804)
Lawrence Tibbett (Glendale 8001)
Lawrence Tibbett, Vols. 1–2 (Rococo 5266, 5324)

Lawrence Tibbett Program (Camden CAL-168)
Lawrence Tibbett Sings (10" Royale 18171, Hudson 224)
Operatic Arias (Camden CAL-171)
Otello (Excerpts) (RCA Victrola Bic-1185)
Parisian Belle [New Moon] (Amalgamated 168) [ST]
Porgy and Bess (Camden CAL-500) w. Helen Jepson
The Rogue Song (Pelican 2019) [ST]
La Traviata (Pearl 235/236)
A Tribute to Lawrence Tibbett (O.A.S.I. 586)

# SOPHIE TUCKER

SELF-PROCLAIMED AS "THE LAST OF THE RED HOT MAMAS," SOPHIE Tucker was a show business legend for six decades in many arenas: vaudeville, stage, radio, records, motion pictures, and TV. She deftly integrated her real-life personality with her persona as an entertainer to create a larger-than-life character. Sophie Tucker was of the old school of singing. She could toss out a song to a vast audience long before the microphone came along. She was equally at home with love songs, sentimental tunes, and bawdy ballads. As she grew older, and heavier, she more frequently than not kidded her own image and love-making prowess. As the years passed, so did her voice. Thus, in later years, she talked a song, rather than sang it. However, she never lost her command of the public. When she died in 1966, she was still very much in demand as an entertainer.

Sadly, Sophie Tucker's movie career was not extensive. Her type of act was suitable for talking pictures, but when talkies came into vogue, she was simply too old to qualify as a leading lady. Thus, she made only sporadic movie appearances.

Sophie Tucker was born in Poland on January 13, 1884 (some sources say 1888 and list Boston as her city of birth), as her family was migrating from Russia to the United States. Her father, whose original surname was Kalish, had deserted from the Russian military and had changed his name to Abuza. At the age of three months, Sophie arrived in the United States and settled with her parents in Hartford, Connecticut, where they opened a restaurant. As a youngster she worked in the family business as a waitress and began singing for customers. As a teenager she entered many amateur contests. It was during this period that she was briefly married to Louis Tuck, whose last name she lengthened for her stage name of Sophie Tucker. (She would later be married to Frank Westphal and then to Albert Lackerman.)

When Willie and Eugene Howard appeared in New Haven in 1906, Sophie told Willie she wanted to be a professional entertainer and he gave her a letter of introduction to Harry Von Tilzer, the composer of such standards as "I Want a Girl Just Like the Girl Who Married Dear Old Dad" and "In the Evening by the Moonlight." Although Von Tilzer could not help Sophie, she managed to get a job at the Cafe Monopol in Gotham, where she sang, cooked, and washed dishes. Soon she was performing in blackface and was billed as "The World-Renowned Coon Shouter." She sang at the German Village Cafe, made her vaudeville debut, and appeared at Tony Pastor's 14th Street Theatre. Next came work in cabarets in New York City as well as a tour in burlesque on the Manchester and Hills circuit. During this trek, producer Marc Klaw saw her act and signed Sophie to appear in the Broadway revue *Ziegfeld Follies of 1909*. It opened at the Jardin de Paris on

June 14, 1909, and featured Nora Bayes, Jack Norworth, Eva Tanguay, Billie Reeves, and Mae Murray. Sophie appeared only in a jungle comedy skit; because of enmity between her and Nora Bayes, all but one of Tucker's songs were cut from the production.

Following her tepid Broadway debut, Sophie Tucker returned to vaudeville, where she had the good fortune to have her career guided by William Morris. In 1909, she scored a success in Chicago at the American Music Hall, and slowly her fame as a vaudeville performer began. Over the next several years, she strode the boards from city to city and town to town. In 1910, she made her recording debut for Edison, cutting a number of cylinders in the next two years, including "Some of These Days," the song that became her trademark. She came upon this Sheldon Brooks song by accident around 1911 when, as a favor to her maid, she listened to the tune which Brooks (then a porter) had composed. "I knew that 'Some of These Days' was the song for me," she said later. "It has been ever since and always will be."

As the years went by, Sophie's fame and size grew. She was a top vaudeville headliner and was especially popular at the important Palace Theatre in New York City. By the late teens, her act included a male backup group, "The Kings of Syncopation," and she is credited (along with Gilda Gray and Mae West) with having introduced during this period the famous dance The Shimmy. (It was Gilda Gray whom Sophie replaced in the Broadway show *Shubert Gaieties of 1919* when it played Boston.) By now Sophie was also a headliner in the finer night spots of New York City, and at Reisenwebers she introduced another of her trademark songs, "A Good Man Is Hard to Find."

In the fall of 1919, she appeared with McIntyre and Heath, Lou Clayton, and Gilda Gray in the Broadway revue *Hello, Alexander* and then returned to vaudeville where she was more popular than ever. In 1922, her act included two piano players, Ted Shapiro and Jack Carrol; Shapiro, who composed "If I Had You," would remain with Tucker for the rest of her career. That year also found her working for Okeh Records, and in the next half-dozen years she would wax a number of songs for the label, many from her vaudeville act, such as "Pick Me Up and Lay Me Down in Dear Old Dixieland," "You've Got to See Your Mama Every Night," "My Pet," and "There'll Be Some Changes Made." Sophie was popular not only in the United States, she also had a strong following in England, where she first appeared in 1922 at the London Hippodrome in *Round in Fifty*. Over the next four decades, she would make many return engagements to England, appearing on stage, making records, and even doing a movie there.

By the mid-1920s, Sophie Tucker was one of the best-known and most popular stars in the entertainment world. She also operated a Gotham nitery called Sophie Tucker's Playground. She headlined *Earl Carroll's Vanities of 1924* (1924) on Broadway, and by 1928 her vaudeville act included not only a half-dozen Tivoli Girls but also her son, Bert. In the spring of 1929, RKO conducted a radio contest to determine who were the most popular vaudeville headliners, with patrons voting at all Keith Theatres. Tieing for first place were Sophie Tucker and Belle Baker, followed by Van & Schenck, Rudy Vallee, Fred Waring's Pennsylvanians, Vincent Lopez, Ted Lewis, Nick Lucas, Leatrice Joy, and Ben Bernie. As a result, Sophie, along with six others in the poll, headlined an NBC radio program. While appearing at the Orpheum Theatre in Los Angeles, Sophie, Nick Lucas, and Ted Lewis did a remote radio broadcast from Los Angeles station KFI on April 2, 1929, heard over the NBC network.

While in Los Angeles, Sophie Tucker was signed by Warner Bros. (at the personal invitation of Harry Warner) to make her feature film debut in HONKY TONK (1929). She was cast as a cabaret singer who does not want her grown daughter (Lila Lee) to know what she does for a living. The movie was a potboiler, but it gave Tucker a chance to belt out such songs as "I'm the Last of the Red Hot Mamas," "I'm Doin' What I'm Doin' for Love," "He's a Good Man to Have Around," "I'm Feathering a Nest for a Little Bluebird," and "I Don't Want to Get Thin." She recorded these tunes for Victor Records. Although HONKY TONK made money (sound was still a novelty as was her screen debut), it did not establish her as a screen star, especially as movie musicals were soon to be out of vogue. In London in 1930, Sophie appeared with Vivian Ellis in the musical *Follow a Star*, in which she sang "I Never Can Think of the Words." (While she was a favorite in England, a previous foray onto the Continent in 1928 had proven unsuccessful. In Paris she was booed off the stage for singing one of her most popular numbers, the ethnic "My Yiddishe Mama," which she had recorded for Columbia in England that year in both English and Yiddish.)

As the 1930s progressed, Sophie Tucker was no longer an innovator on stage. She

Judy Garland and Sophie Tucker in BROADWAY MELODY OF 1938 (1937)

now relied primarily on old favorites, newer risqué songs, and the kidding of her image as a "big fat mama." In 1934, she was a headliner at the London Palladium's Royal Variety Performance. While in England she made a feature film called GAY LOVE (1934), portraying herself in a story of a singer (Florence Desmond) who loves a nobleman (Ivor McLaren) but learns that he is engaged to her sister (Enid-Stamp Taylor). In April 1935, she was elected Honorary President of the American Federation of Actors.

In 1937, without much fanfare, Sophie was featured in matronly roles in two MGM musicals, BROADWAY MELODY OF 1938 and THOROUGHBREDS DON'T CRY. In the former she played Judy Garland's mom and sang "Your Broadway and My Broadway," while in the latter (the first feature to team Judy Garland and Mickey Rooney) she had a dramatic role in a horse-racing drama. Late in 1938, she was back on Broadway in *Leave It to Me* with Victor Moore, William Gaxton, Mary Martin, Tamara, George Tobias, and Gene Kelly, for a run of 291 performances, singing Cole Porter's "Most Gentlemen Don't Like Love." It was Mary Martin who was the hit of the musical with her provocative rendition of "My Heart Belongs to Daddy." (Martin has always credited Tucker with helping her to style her presentation of that career-establishing number.)

During this period, Sophie Tucker was also active on radio, guesting on such programs as Rudy Vallee's "The Fleischmann's Hour," and during the 1938–39 season, with her own fifteen-minute CBS series, "Sophie Tucker and Her Show." In the summer of 1940, she teamed with Harry Richman, with whom she would work on and off for the next fourteen years. She also paired with Joe E. Lewis to headline at Ben Marden's Riviera Club on Broadway. In 1941, she had her final New York stage outing in *The High Kickers* with George Jessel; it ran for 191 performances with Sophie singing "You're on My Mind." During the 1940s, she did USO tour work and made a guest appearance in Universal's all-star movie FOLLOW THE BOYS (1944) singing "Some of These Days." She also made a similar cameo appearance in the United Artists musical SENSATIONS OF 1945 (1944). This was a potpourri of talent that included Eleanor Powell, W. C. Fields, and Tucker, with Sophie philosophizing in her song "You Can't Sew a Button on a Heart."

In the late 1940s and into the 1950s, Sophie Tucker recorded for Mercury Records, cutting a series of albums that featured somewhat risqué songs such as "I'm Living Alone and I Like It," "Vitamins, Hormones and Pills," "I'm the 3-D Mama with the Big Wide Screen," "There's No Business Like That Matrimonial Business," "The Middle Age Mambo," and "I May Be Getting Older Every Day But I'm Getting Younger Every Night." She continued to tour regularly, now mainly working in nightclubs, and she guested on radio shows like those of The Andrews Sisters and on "Saturday Night at the Shamrock."

In the 1950s, poured into outlandish spangled gowns, Sophie became a television fixture by appearing frequently on the variety programs of Jimmy Durante and Ed Sullivan. In 1957, she appeared briefly as herself in THE JOKER IS WILD, the Joe E. Lewis biopic starring Frank Sinatra. By the 1960s, her voice was nearly gone and she mostly talked her songs—filling her numbers with dramatic gestures and fluttering her trademark chiffon scarf. There was much publicity when Steve Allen wrote the songs for *Sophie*, a

Broadway musical supposedly based on the life of Sophie Tucker. It opened at the Winter Garden Theatre on April 15, 1963 (with Sophie in attendance). However, the book was specious, the songs derivative, and Libi Staiger had too much to contend with to be either convincing or entertaining as the "Red Hot Mama."

In the mid-1960s, Tucker undertook a long and profitable tour teamed with Ted Lewis and George Jessel. Early in 1966, she signed for a four-week stand at the Latin Quarter in New York City, but appeared for only two nights before she entered Mount Sinai Hospital for treatment of an intestinal inflammation. She then returned to her New York City apartment, where she died on February 9, 1966, of a chronic lung ailment and kidney failure. Even in death Sophie Tucker drew a crowd. Her funeral was attended by over three thousand mourners. In her memory, the Teamsters Union hearse drivers, who were on strike, did not picket during her funeral.

Sophie Tucker's appeal was universal and enduring and resulted in a love affair between herself and the public. "When I walk past, total strangers get up and want to kiss me," she once said. "And I love them all."

## Filmography

Honky Tonk (WB, 1929)
Little Red Hot Schoolhouse (Stanley Distributing Co., 1932) (s)
Gay Love (Br, 1934)
Broadway Highlights #1 (Par, 1935) (s)
Broadway Melody of 1938 (MGM, 1937)

Thoroughbreds Don't Cry (MGM, 1937)
Follow the Boys (Univ, 1944)
Sensations of 1945 (UA, 1944)
The Joker Is Wild [All the Way] (Par, 1957)
The Heart of Show Business (Col, 1957) (s)

## Broadway Plays

Ziegfeld Follies of 1909 (1909)
Hello, Alexander (1919)
Earl Carroll's Vanities of 1924 (1924)

Leave It to Me (1938)
The High Kickers (1941)

## Radio Series

Sophie Tucker and Her Show (CBS, 1938–39)

## Album Discography

Bigger and Better Than Ever (Mer MG-20267, Wing 12176)
Broadway Melody of 1938 (Motion Picture Tracks MPT-3) [ST]

Cabaret Days (Mer MG-20046, Wing 12213/16213)
A Collection of Songs (Mer MG-20025)
Famous Songs (10" Decca DL-5371)

Follow a Star (ASV 5046)

Follow the Boys (Hollywood Soundstage 5012) [ST]

Golden Jubilee (Mer MG-20049)

The Great Sophie Tucker (Decca DL-8355)

Harry Richman & Sophie Tucker—His Broadway and Hers (Monmouth/Evergreen 7048)

Her Latest and Greatest Spicy Songs (Mer MG-20073, Wing 12167)

The Last of the Red Hot Mamas—Sophie Tucker's Greatest Hits (Col CL-2604)

A Pair of Red Hot Mamas (Take Two TT-208) w. Belle Baker

The Red Hot Mama Abroad (Take Two TT-221)

Some of These Days (Pelican 133, Westwood 503)

Some of These Days (World Record Club SH-234)

Sophie Tucker (Decca DL-4942/7442)

Sophie Tucker in Person (Mer MG-20567/SR-60227)

Sophie Tucker's Greatest Hits (MCA 263, MCA 32318)

The Spice of Life (Mer MG-230126, Wing 2235/16215)

Ted Lewis–Sophie Tucker Live (Amalgamated 246)

# RUDY VALLEE

RUDY VALLEE WAS AMERICA'S FIRST SINGING SENSATION, THE IDOL OF millions of women in the late 1920s and well into the next decade. His image as the romantic crooner with a megaphone would never leave him, despite his well-rounded career encompassing all aspects of show business and despite his accomplishments as a musician and composer. It was Rudy Vallee who singlehandedly developed the radio variety-show format, which carried over to television. He was also considered one of the greatest talent makers of his time, with scores of performers owing their breakthrough success in show business to Rudy Vallee.

His career spanned seven decades. Although his greatest triumphs came at the start of the Depression, he was able to change and adapt to the times and to achieve success in each decade thereafter. In his later years, Rudy Vallee said he would make headlines until the day he died. He was absolutely right.

He was born Hubert Prior Vallee in Island Pond, Vermont, on July 28, 1901, the second of three children. His father, Charles Alphonse Vallee, was a druggist of French descent, while his mother was Anglo-Irish. As a boy, he showed a talent for music, first on the drums and later on the clarinet. He was also an avid worker, and often assisted his druggist father in his business in Westbrook, Maine, where the family moved when he was small. At the age of seventeen, he worked in the town's theater as usher, janitor, and projectionist. After high school he obtained a similar job in Portland, where he purchased his first saxophone. He became a student of the recordings of saxophonist Rudy Wiedoeft, who later became his mentor. When Vallee entered the University of Maine in 1920, his devotion to Wiedoeft's records earned him the nickname Rudy, which he retained for the rest of his life.

By now, Vallee was earning extra money playing the saxophone with various bands, and he often journeyed to New York City or Boston to pick up such work, occasionally singing with one of the groups. Because he possessed a relatively soft voice, he used a megaphone to amplify his singing, and the small megaphone became his trademark. In 1921, he made his first private recording with the saxophone and the next year he did an unissued session for Edison; that same year he transferred to Yale University. From September 1924 to July 1925, he was an instrumentalist with the Savoy Havana Band in London and with that group he recorded for Columbia and HMV (His Master's Voice) records. He also participated in recording sessions with Beatrice Lillie and Gertrude Lawrence. Upon his return to America in 1926, he resumed his Yale studies, but also continued his musical activities and led the Yale football band. He graduated from Yale in

1928 with a degree in Spanish and plans to move to Argentina to raise cattle. However, he was also involved with the Yale Collegians band and had recorded for Edison and Vocalion records. In the summer of 1928, he became the band's leader and the group began cutting records for Columbia's dime store labels (Harmony, Diva, Velvet Tone, Clarion) as well as appearing in Gotham night spots and on radio.

The big break came for Rudy Vallee and his band when they began appearing at the Heigh-Ho Club in New York City and a local station broadcast their performances. Vallee would open each show by saying "Heigh-Ho Everybody," which became not only one of his trademarks, but also a national catchphrase, still in vogue. Within weeks, the radio station was swamped with fan letters for Rudy and his band and their recordings began to sell well. Vallee also became a big success in vaudeville, quickly becoming one of the top stars of the medium. As a result, he signed with RCA Victor Records, and with his Connecticut Yankees (as the band was now called), he cut his first RCA record in 1929, the best-selling "Deep Night," a song Vallee co-wrote. He also began making short subjects, including RADIO RHYTHM (1929) and CAMPUS SWEETHEARTS (1930), the latter with Ginger Rogers.

In the summer of 1929, Rudy Vallee and his band journeyed to Hollywood to make their first feature, RKO's THE VAGABOND LOVER (1929). In it he portrayed a young singer who impersonates his idol, gets into hot water, and finds romance with Sally Blane. Vallee was an anemic actor, but he excelled in singing songs like "I'm Just a Vagabond Lover," "If You Were the Only Girl in the World," "A Little Kiss Each Morning," and "I'll Be Reminded of You." The movie, which brought Marie Dressler back to prominence, was a money maker. In later years, however, Vallee kidded the movie by insisting that it was shown only to captive audiences in prisons and comfort stations! That same year Vallee also made a guest appearance in Paramount's GLORIFYING THE AMERICAN GIRL (1929) singing "I'm Just a Vagabond Lover."

In the fall of 1929, Vallee began starring on the NBC radio program "The Fleischmann's Hour" for Standard Brands. At first the show was a typical musical program featuring Rudy, his band, and guest performers. By 1932, however, he had altered the format, making it radio's first variety show. The format included not only the star's vocalizing, but also a well-rounded hour of entertainment—ranging from portions of the latest Broadway plays to the introduction of new music (such as George Gershwin playing his own works) and of new talent, many of whom were discovered by Vallee's talent agency. Among those whose careers he fostered were Kate Smith, Alice Faye, Edgar Bergen, Dorothy Lamour, Red Skelton, Bob Hope, Dolores Gray, and the radio character "Henry Aldrich."

The period 1929 to 1931 saw Vallee's greatest show business success. In addition to his popular weekly radio program, and other broadcasts during the week on NBC, his sold-out appearances at Brooklyn's Paramount Theatre literally caused mob scenes as women clamored to see their idol. His RCA Victor records were big sellers, including "Coquette," "Honey," "I'm Just a Vagabond Lover," "My Time Is Your Time" (which became his radio theme song), "Miss You," "Gypsy Dream Rose," "Lonely Troubador," and "Baby, Oh Where Can You Be?" Unfortunately for Vallee, he emerged on the scene at a time when the combination of the Depression and the popularity of radio nearly killed the record industry. More than 120 million records had been sold in the United States in 1927, but in 1930 less than ten percent of that number were sold, although his recording that year of the "Maine Stein Song" for Victor did sell over one million platters. Even so, he still had hits like "Betty Coed," "You're Driving Me Crazy," "Pardon Me Pretty Baby," and "When Yuba Plays the Rhumba on the Tuba."

In 1931, Vallee made his Broadway debut in the revue *George White's Scandals of 1931*, singing "This Is the Missus," "My Song," and "The Thrill Is Gone," all recorded for Victor along with another of the show's songs, "Life Is Just a Bowl of Cherries." The *Scandals* had a successful Broadway run followed by a lengthy tour, and during this time he continued to make film shorts. In 1933, he had a guest appearance in the W. C. Fields movie INTERNATIONAL HOUSE (1933), singing "Thank Heaven for You." In 1934, he starred in GEORGE WHITE'S SCANDALS (1934) for Fox, and for Warner Bros. he headlined SWEET MUSIC (1935), in which he sang several songs including his popular version of "There's a Tavern in the Town," which had been a best-selling disc for him.

During this time, Rudy Vallee operated a talent agency and owned two music publishing firms. In addition to performing, he also composed many popular songs such as "I'm Still Caring," "Don't Play with Fire," and "Oh, Ma-Ma (The Butcher Boy)." It was during this time that his turbulent divorce proceedings from Fay Webb (whom he had wed in 1931) made headlines before he won a divorce decree in 1936. (His first marriage, in 1928, to tea heiress Leonie Cauchois had been annulled the same year.)

He returned to Broadway for *George White's Scandals of 1936* (1936), but left the production after a falling-out with producer George White. Thereafter, he toured England successfully in 1937 and, while there, recorded "Vieni, Vieni" and "The Whiffenpoof Song" for English Columbia. Both songs became big sellers for him in the United States when he waxed them later that year for RCA Victor. Between 1931 and 1937, Vallee also recorded for Hit-of-the-Week, Columbia, Bluebird, and dime store labels like Meltone, Perfect, and Conqueror. From 1936 to 1939, his successful radio show was redubbed "The Royal Gelatin Hour." He starred for Warner Bros. in the lackluster GOLD DIGGERS IN PARIS (1938). At 20th Century–Fox he was in SECOND FIDDLE (1939), an appropriate title as that was his role, since Sonja Henie and Tyrone Power were the stars. His quartet of Irving Berlin songs in that movie, which he recorded for Decca, were mediocre.

Now in his forties and past the peak of his popularity, Rudy appeared in two 1941 programmers, Columbia's TIME OUT FOR RHYTHM and Universal's TOO MANY BLONDES. In the latter he sang "The Man on the Flying Trapeze," a number he had revived successfully in the 1930s. Director Preston Sturges then cast Vallee as the stuffy millionaire in the hilarious comedy THE PALM BEACH STORY (1942), and the major production breathed new life into his waning screen career. He sang "Good Night, Sweetheart" (a song he first popularized on radio in 1931) in the picture, but he also created the definitive character of the pince-nez wearing, self-centered stuffed shirt. It was a characterization he was to reuse in a series of movies throughout the 1940s. For his superb performance in THE PALM BEACH

STORY, he was named one of the year's best actors by the National Film Board of Review.

Vallee's initial NBC radio series had ended its decade-long run in the fall of 1939. However, the next spring he was back on the air for the network in "The Sealtest Hour," which, for a time, co-starred John Barrymore, in a sprightly mixture of comedy and song. The show ran until the summer of 1943, when Vallee enlisted in World War II service and was made the director of the U.S. Coast Guard Band, a post he held until 1945. He appeared in the Paramount comedy HAPPY GO LUCKY (1943—starring Dick Powell, Mary Martin, and Betty Hutton) and married actress Jane Greer in 1943. She was nineteen and he was forty-two and the marriage lasted less than a year.

Upon the completion of his war service, Vallee was back on NBC radio with "The Drene Show," a variety outing that ran for two seasons. He played his stuffy rich man character in a rash of comedy features, including MAN ALIVE (1945), THE FABULOUS SUZANNE (1946), THE BACHELOR AND THE BOBBY-SOXER (1947), MY DEAR SECRETARY (1948), and as late as 1954 in Marjorie Main's RICOCHET ROMANCE. He won critical acclaim for his performance as the doctor in Irene Dunne's I REMEMBER MAMA (1948) and as the race-track denizen in SO THIS IS NEW YORK (1948). During the 1947–48 season he starred in "The Philip Morris Show" on NBC radio.

Vallee's recordings were no longer major items in the late 1940s, although his eleven-year-old RCA recording of "As Time Goes By" had done well in 1942–43 because

Helen Walker and Rudy Vallee in PEOPLE ARE FUNNY (1946)

of the song's use in the movie CASABLANCA (1942). Nonetheless, Vallee continued to make occasional recordings. In the late 1940s, he began working the nightclub circuit with great success and would do so for the rest of his career. In 1951, he hosted a radio program on station WOR in New York City, which was broadcast nationally by Mutual. In 1955, he co-starred with Jane Russell and Jeanne Crain in GENTLEMEN MARRY BRUNETTES, singing "Have You Met Miss Jones" and "I Wanna Be Loved by You." Two years later he appeared as himself in THE HELEN MORGAN STORY (1957) performing "My Time Is Your Time."

During the 1950s, Rudy Vallee began appearing on TV, having turned down an offer to take over Ed Sullivan's TV spot after debuting on the program in 1949. He made guest appearances on such shows as "The Eddie Cantor Comedy Theatre," "December Bride," "The Lucy-Desi Comedy Hour," "Kraft Theatre," and the NBC-TV special "Hansel and Gretel" in 1958. On "Matinee Theatre" he starred in "Jenny Kissed Me," a play in which he toured on and off well into the 1970s. From February to August 1955, he starred on CBS radio as the host of the "Kraft Music Hall." By this time, when not touring, Vallee resided in a mansion called Silver Tip in the Hollywood Hills with his fourth wife, Eleanor (Norris) Vallee, who was thirty years his junior.

In 1961, he returned to Broadway in the Pulitzer Prize–winning musical comedy *How to Succeed in Business Without Really Trying*, and he stayed with the hit show for three years. During that time he hosted two CBS-TV runs of the variety show "On Broadway Tonight" and was himself a guest on many variety programs, like those of Perry Como and Johnny Carson. He repeated his role of the philandering business executive in the 1967 movie HOW TO SUCCEED IN BUSINESS WITHOUT REALLY TRYING. He next worked with Elvis Presley in LIVE A LITTLE, LOVE A LITTLE (1968).

Vallee kept busy on TV, guesting on such shows as "Batman," "Death Valley Days," and "Here's Lucy," as well as continuing on the cabaret circuit. In the mid-1960s, he had a popular album (*The Funny Side of Rudy Vallee*) on Jubilee Records, which captured the comedy portion of his club act. In 1967, his Diva LP (*Hi Ho, Everybody*), which contained his rendition of the pop hit "Winchester Cathedral," sold well. His 1929 recording of "Deep Night" was used as the theme song of the film BONNIE AND CLYDE (1967) while he himself sang "I Can't Give You Anything But Love" for THE GRISSOM GANG (1971). Also in 1971, he was appointed to the Los Angeles Board of Traffic Commissioners.

In the 1970s, he did the pantomime role of King Septimus in the play *Once upon a Mattress* in stock, and in 1975 he revived his role in *How to Succeed in Business Without Really Trying*. That year also found him honored as the Man of the Year by the state of Maine. Ever active, Vallee toured in the nostalgic revue *The Big Broadcast of 1976* and worked on television in such shows as "Night Gallery," "Alias Smith and Jones," "Ellery Queen" and "CHiPs." In 1975, his third autobiography, *Let the Chips Fall* (which was issued in paperback the next year as *Rudy Vallee Kisses and Tells*), was published. It had been preceded by *Vagabond Dreams Come True* (1930) and *My Time Is Your Time* (1962).

The 1980s found Rudy Vallee maintaining a strong professional schedule with personal and TV appearances. In 1985, he appeared with Linda Nardini in the rock video

"Girls Talk," and early in 1986 he recorded the song "Junior Movie Star." After that he suffered a fall in his home, was operated on for throat cancer, and suffered a mild stroke. He recovered sufficiently to return home, but he died there on July 3, 1986, while watching the unveiling of the restored Statue of Liberty on TV.

Since his death, a movie about his career has been announced, as has the publication of his fourth autobiography, about the several women in his life. In the late 1980s, an auction was held to sell off much of the memorabilia he collected over the decades.

## Filmography

Radio Rhythm (Par, 1929) (s)
Rudy Vallee and His Connecticut Yankees (Vita, 1929) (s)
The Vagabond Lover (RKO, 1929)
Glorifying the American Girl (Par, 1929)
Campus Sweethearts (RKO, 1930) (s)
The Stein Song (Par, 1930) (s) (voice only)
Betty Coed (Par, 1930) (s) (voice only)
Kitty from Kansas City (Par, 1930) (s) (voice only)
Musical Justice (Par, 1931) (s)
Paramount Pictorial #7 (Par, 1931) (s)
Knowmore College (Par, 1932) (s)
Musical Doctor (Par, 1932) (s)
Rudy Vallee Melodies (Par, 1932) (s)
International House (Par, 1933)
George White's Scandals (Fox, 1934)
Sweet Music (WB, 1935)
The Great Megaphone Mystery (Vita, 1935) (s)
A Trip Thru a Hollywood Studio (Vita, 1935) (s)
For Auld Lang Syne (Vita, 1938) (s)
Gold Diggers in Paris [The Gay Imposters] (WB, 1938)
Lydia (Soundies, 1939) (s)
Second Fiddle (20th-Fox, 1939)
Picture People #3 (RKO, 1940) (s)
Picture People #4 (RKO, 1941) (s)
Picture People #5 (RKO, 1941) (s)
Screen Snapshots #9 (Col, 1941) (s)
Time Out for Rhythm (Col, 1941)
Too Many Blondes (Univ, 1941)
Hedda Hopper's Hollywood (Par, 1942) (s)
The Palm Beach Story (Par, 1942)
Happy Go Lucky (Par, 1943)
Rudy Vallee's Coast Guard Band (Vita, 1944) (s)

U.S. Coast Guard Band (Vita, 1944) (s)
It's in the Bag (UA, 1945)
Man Alive (RKO, 1945)
Screen Snapshots (Col, 1945) (s)
People Are Funny (Par, 1946)
The Fabulous Suzanne (Rep, 1946)
The Sin of Harold Diddlebock [Mad Wednesday] (RKO, 1947)
The Bachelor and the Bobby-Soxer [Bachelor Knight] (RKO, 1947)
I Remember Mama (RKO, 1948)
So This Is New York (UA, 1948)
My Dear Secretary (UA, 1948)
Unfaithfully Yours (20th-Fox, 1948)
Mother Is a Freshman [Mother Knows Best] (20th-Fox, 1949)
The Beautiful Blonde from Bashful Bend (20th-Fox, 1949)
Father Was a Fullback (20th-Fox, 1949)
The Admiral Was a Lady (UA, 1950)
Ricochet Romance (Univ, 1954)
Gentlemen Marry Brunettes (UA, 1955)
The Helen Morgan Story [Both Ends of the Candle] (WB, 1957)
Jazzball (NTA, 1958)
How to Succeed in Business Without Really Trying (UA, 1967)
The Night They Raided Minsky's (UA, 1968) (narrator only)
Live a Little, Love a Little (MGM, 1968)
The Phynx (WB, 1970)
The Grissom Gang (Cinerama, 1971) (voice only)
Sunburst (Cinema Financial, 1975)
Won Ton Ton, the Dog Who Saved Hollywood (Par, 1976)
The Perfect Woman (Gold Key, 1981)

## Broadway Plays

George White's Scandals of 1931 (1931)
George White's Scandals of 1936 (1936)

How to Succeed in Business Without Really Trying (1961)

## Radio Series

The Fleischmann's Hour (NBC, 1929–36)
The Royal Gelatin Hour (NBC, 1936–39)
The Sealtest Hour (NBC, 1940–43)
The Drene Program (NBC, 1945–47)

The Philip Morris Show (NBC, 1947–48)
The Rudy Vallee Show (Mutual, 1951)
Kraft Music Hall (CBS, 1955)

## TV Series

On Broadway Tonight (CBS, 1964, 1965)
Matinee at the Bijou (PBS, 1980–85) (voice only)

## Album Discography

The Best of Rudy Vallee (RCA LSP-3816, Camden CDN-170, RCA International 1343)
An Evening with Rudy Vallee (Mark 56 681)
An Evening with Rudy Vallee at the San Francisco Press Club (Private Label—No Number)
The Fleischmann's Hour (Mark 56 613)
The Funny Side of Rudy Vallee (Jubilee 2051)
Gentlemen Marry Brunettes (Coral CRL-57013) [ST]
The Greatest Vaudeo-Doe-R of All Time (Pickwick 3063)
Hansel and Gretel (MGM E-3690) [ST/TV]
Heigh Ho, Everybody (Olympic 7128)
Heigh Ho, Everybody, This Is Rudy Vallee (ASV 5009)
Hi Ho, Everybody (Viva V36005, Dot V6005)
How to Succeed in Business Without Really Trying (RCA LOC/LSO-1066) [OC]

How to Succeed in Business Without Really Trying (UA UAL-4152/UAS- 5151) [ST]
Is This Your Rudy Vallee? (Crown CLP-5204)
The Kid from Maine (Unique 116)
Let's Do It (Regent 6029)
The Night They Raided Minsky's (UA UAS-5191) [ST]
Rudy Vallee and His Connecticut Yankees (Halcyon 105)
Rudy Vallee and His Connecticut Yankees (Sunbeam 515)
Rudy Vallee and His Famous World War II Coast Guard Band (Mark 56 714)
Rudy Vallee on the Air (Totem 1027)
Rudy Vallee Reads Fairy Tales (Treasure 407)
Rudy Vallee's Drinking Songs (10" Storyville 315)
Songs of a Vagabond Lover (10" Cap H-550)
Stein Songs (Decca DL-4242/74242)
The Young Rudy Vallee (RCA LPM-2507)

# JIMMY WAKELY

JIMMY WAKELY HAD A VERY DIVERSIFIED SHOW BUSINESS CAREER, ranging from stardom in radio, movies, records, TV, and personal appearances to composing and producing records. He emerged from the Dust Bowl of Oklahoma in the 1940s to become one of the country's top recording artists, and for six years he headlined his own series of Western feature films for Monogram Pictures. He was also one of network radio's last big stars and through the years he performed at some of the country's top nightclubs. Unlike most motion picture cowboy stars, Jimmy Wakely was not totally typed as a country-western singer. He was equally at ease with pop songs and campfire ballads. While he was weakest as an actor, and is not highly regarded as a "B" Western star, Jimmy Wakely was definitely one of the finest vocalists ever to sing in Hollywood films.

Jimmy Wakely was born on February 16, 1914, in Mineola, Arkansas, one of four children (he had two brothers, John and Fletch, and a sister, Effie) of a farm family. When he was three, the family moved to Octavia, Oklahoma, and the next year they settled in Ida (later called Battiest), Oklahoma. Life was hard, and Wakely would reflect later, "I never witnessed as much ignorance per square acre" as he did there. When he was thirteen, the Wakely family moved again, this time to the western part of the state to pick cotton. After a time they settled near Cowen. When the Depression hit, life became even worse and the family returned to Battiest where they accepted any type of work. During his teen years, Jimmy Wakely took a liking to the music of Jimmie Rodgers and he learned to play the guitar and piano.

The family next moved to Rosedale, where he met Inez Harvey, the sister of one of his high school pals. After graduating from high school, Wakely operated a filling station. He and Inez began dating and they were married on December 13, 1935. They moved to Oklahoma City, where their first child, Deanna, was born. They later had three more children (John, Carol, and Linda Lee). Soon, Wakely began getting radio jobs as a pianist for various local bands. For station KTOK he became a singing cowboy and then he and Inez worked with a traveling medicine show. After that they went back to Oklahoma City, where Wakely became part of a trio called The Bell Boys on radio station WKY. He refined the act into a cowboy singing trio which was soon composed of himself, Johnny Bond, and Scotty Harrel. The Bell Boys became very popular on radio and supplemented their income by making personal appearances.

When Gene Autry arrived in Oklahoma City to promote one of his films late in 1938, the trio auditioned for him and Autry offered them a job on his CBS network radio show "Melody Ranch." The next spring, Wakely, Johnny Bond, and Dick Rinehart

(Scotty Harrel elected to remain behind) moved their families to California where they made transcription records for Standard and did nightclub work. Wakely also landed a recording contract with Decca Records, and his initial solo record was Johnny Bond's composition "Cimarron." The group, now calling themselves The Jimmy Wakely Trio, also got their first movie job, singing Bob Nolan's "The Song of the Bandit" in the Roy Rogers starring vehicle SAGA OF DEATH VALLEY, issued by Republic Pictures late in 1939.

The Jimmy Wakely Trio then settled into a comfortable pattern of appearing in "B" Westerns singing a song or two, recording both as a group and as individuals (Johnny Bond and Dick Rinehart both signed with Columbia Records), and making personal appearances, besides working with Gene Autry on "Melody Ranch." On film, the trio appeared in movies with such Western stars as Don "Red" Barry, The Range Busters (Ray "Crash" Corrigan, John King, and Max Terhune), and William Boyd. After making two features at Universal in 1940 with Johnny Mack Brown, Wakely's group was signed to appear in a series of seven horse operas co-starring Brown and Tex Ritter. They also worked in non-Western movies such as Universal's GIVE US WINGS (1940)—with the Dead End Kids—in which they performed "On a Blue Ridge Mountain Trail," and SIX LESSONS FROM MADAME LA ZONGA (1941), wherein they not only sang Wakely's song "I'm a Rootin' Tootin' Cowboy" but also had their first screen acting roles. In the 1942 Universal short RAINBOW RHYTHM, the trio (to which Scotty Harrel had returned to replace Dick Rinehart) sang "Deep in the Heart of Texas," and they did a half-dozen numbers in STRICTLY IN THE GROOVE (1942).

It was in 1943 that the Jimmy Wakely Trio moved to Columbia Pictures, where they appeared in films with Charles Starrett, singing such songs as "I'll Never Let You Go Little Darlin'" (written by Wakely, from ROBIN HOOD OF THE RANGE, 1943). During the making of the Starrett series, the members of the trio went their separate ways. In COWBOY IN THE CLOUDS (1943), Wakely not only sang the title song but also had a featured part. At PRC (Producers Releasing Corporation) he sang "Don't Ever Let Me Down Little Darlin'" in I'M FROM ARKANSAS (1944), and through Phil Isley, movie star Jennifer Jones's brother, he landed a contract with Monogram Pictures to headline a series of "B" Westerns. At this time, Wakely's Decca records were also selling well with tunes like "Cattle Call," "I Wonder Where You Are Tonight," written by Johnny Bond, "Be Honest with Me," "I'll Never Let You Go," "After Tomorrow," "Don't Bite the Hand That's Feeding You," "Fort Worth Jail," "Be My Darlin'," and "I'm Sending You Red Roses."

From 1944 to 1949, Jimmy Wakely starred in twenty-eight Westerns for Monogram. Along with Johnny Mack Brown, he became the studio's top series grosser. His initial screen project there was SONG OF THE RANGE in 1944, which, in many ways, set the pattern for his subsequent features. He played a cowboy who helps a Western movie star (Dennis Moore) clear himself of a murder charge. Wakely handled the singing chores well enough, but he possessed a bland screen personality and the bulk of the dramatics was fortunately carried by the more capable Moore. Lee "Lasses" White, an old-time minstrel performer, provided the comic relief in the film as he would do in eleven more Wakely entries well into 1947, before being replaced as the comic sidekick by Dub Taylor.

Fortunately, the Wakely productions had solid directors (Lambert Hillyer, Christy Cabanne, Howard Bretherton, Thomas Carr, Ford Beebe, Oliver Drake) and fair scripts, and Jimmy Wakely provided many of the movie songs. The profitable installments were budgeted at around $30,000 to $40,000 each, and in the first group of films Wakely patterned his screen persona after Gene Autry, even to wearing fancy cowboy clothes and doing quite a few musical numbers in each picture. Later, the economy-minded Monogram producers gave the films a more arid look, drastically cutting the song content, and thus robbing the offerings of what little entertainment value the earlier entries had. A future Monogram cowboy star, Whip Wilson, was introduced in SILVER TRAILS (1948) and a very young Polly Bergen (then billed as Polly Burgin) appeared in ACROSS THE RIO GRANDE (1949). No doubt adding to the popularity of the Wakely films was the fact that after World War II he signed with Capitol Records, where he had a string of hit recordings. He was also active in personal appearances, often touring with his movies, and he guested on such radio shows as "Command Performance," "All-Star Western Theatre," "Melody Roundup," and "Here's to Veterans."

When Wakely's Monogram contract expired in 1949, the thirty-five-year-old performer did not renew it. He believed he had nowhere left to go as a movie cowboy star, particularly with the competition from television already cutting into the output of budget Westerns. Another factor influencing his decision was that his recordings were selling

Kay Morley, Jimmy Wakely, Stanley Ellison, Arthur Smith, and Rivers Lewis
in SIX GUN SERENADE (1947)

briskly. That year he and Margaret Whiting became the first country-western and pop performers to team on record with the Capitol single "Slippin' Around," which sold over three million records. They followed it with a sequel, "I'll Never Slip Around Again," which sold over 800,000 platters, and in 1950 they had a hit with "Silver Bells." Wakely's other hit records for Capitol included "Peter Cottontail," "My Heart Cries for You," "Each Step of the Way," "Won't You Ride in My Little Red Wagon," "Pale Moon," "I Love You So Much It Hurts," "Sweethearts on Parade," and the Eddie Dean composition "One Has My Name, the Other Has My Heart," which was a big seller for Wakely in 1950. In both 1949 and 1950, he was number one in Cashbox magazine's poll of "Best Western Recording Artists," and in 1950, he placed high on both *Billboard*'s "Top Artists on Juke Boxes" in the folk singer category (he was third, behind Eddy Arnold and Hank Williams) and "Top Male Singers on Juke Boxes," where he came in behind Perry Como and Frankie Laine, but ahead of Bing Crosby.

During the 1950s, Jimmy Wakely headlined top night spots in Las Vegas, Reno, Hollywood, and elsewhere. He continued his successful association with Capitol Records through the middle of the decade, and guest-starred on radio shows like "The Spade Cooley Show" (Wakely once hired Cooley to play the fiddle in his band) and "Country Hoedown." From 1953 to 1958, he starred in the CBS radio series "The Jimmy Wakely Show." Later in the decade, he returned to Decca Records for a series of albums and singles, and in 1959, he cut an LP for Tops Records. From March to September 1961, he was one of the rotating hosts of the half-hour NBC-TV series "Five Star Jubilee." Also hosting the program were Tex Ritter, Rex Allen, Snooky Lanson, and Carl Smith; the show was telecast from Springfield, Missouri. In the 1950s, Wakely also appeared occasionally in films, mostly associated with music. In 1953, he guest-starred in Ken Murray's THE MARSHAL'S DAUGHTER and also sang the title song, and the next year he appeared in ARROW IN THE DUST, performing his composition "The Weary Stranger." He sang the title song for THE SILVER STAR (1955), and his song "Cowboy" was used in the 1957 Western SLIM CARTER. His final movie assignment was performing the main song for the 1959 feature MONEY, WOMEN AND GUNS; it was another of his songs, "Lonely Is the Hunter."

In the 1960s, Jimmy Wakely continued to keep active with personal appearances, sometimes with his children John (who recorded for Decca Records) and Linda Lee, making records for the Decca and Dot labels. He was also busy with his music publishing firm and his own record company, Shasta Records. In the late 1960s, he began an association with the American Forces Radio Network, and in the 1970s, he found time to be an active guest star at Western film buff conventions. In the 1970s, his Shasta Records business accelerated: he not only released albums of his own songs, both newly recorded and from his old CBS radio show, but he also produced LPs by such singers as Eddie Dean, Merle Travis, Johnny Bond, Tex Williams, and Smokey Rodgers. Wakely also produced several LPs for the MCR label. In the late 1970s, before the fall of the Shah of Iran, he hosted a one-hour daily program called "Jimmy Wakely and Friends" for Radio Iran.

Jimmy Wakely's health began to deteriorate in the early 1980s, although he continued to record for Shasta and to make personal appearances. He died of heart failure at the age of sixty-eight in Mission Hills, California, on September 23, 1982. Before his death he had completed most of his autobiography, *The Jimmy Wakely Story*, which was finished by his widow but has yet to be published. Shasta Records is still in operation.

## Filmography

Saga of Death Valley (Rep, 1939)
Twilight on the Trail (Par, 1940)
The Tulsa Kid (Rep, 1940)
Pony Post (Univ, 1940)
Give Us Wings (Univ, 1940)
Texas Terrors (Univ, 1940)
Trailing Double Trouble (Mon, 1940)
Bury Me Not on the Lone Prairie (Univ, 1941)
Six Lessons from Madame La Zonga (Univ, 1941)
Stick to Your Guns (Par, 1941)
Heart of the Rio Grande (Rep, 1942)
Deep in the Heart of Texas (Univ, 1942)
Little Joe the Wrangler (Univ, 1942)
Raiders of San Joaquin (Univ, 1942)
Strictly in the Groove (Univ, 1942)
Rainbow Rhythm (Univ, 1942) (s)
Robin Hood of the Range (Col, 1943)
Tenting Tonight on the Old Camp Ground (Univ, 1943)
Cheyenne Roundup (Univ, 1943)
The Lone Star Trail (Univ, 1943)
Cowboy in the Clouds (Col, 1943)
Old Chisholm Trail (Rep, 1943)
Cowboy from Lonesome River (Col, 1944)
I'm from Arkansas (PRC, 1944)
Song of the Range (Mon, 1944)
Springtime in Texas (Mon, 1945)
Lonesome Trail (Mon, 1945)
Saddle Serenade (Mon, 1945)
Riders of the Dawn (Mon, 1945)

Moon over Montana (Mon, 1946)
West of the Alamo (Mon, 1946)
Trail to Mexico (Mon, 1946)
Song of the Sierras (Mon, 1946)
Rainbow over the Rockies (Mon, 1947)
Six Gun Serenade (Mon, 1947)
Song of the Wasteland (Mon, 1947)
Ridin' down the Trail (Mon, 1947)
Song of the Drifter (Mon, 1948)
Oklahoma Blues (Mon, 1948)
Partners of the Sunset (Mon, 1948)
Range Renegades (Mon, 1948)
Silver Trails (Mon, 1948)
The Rangers Ride (Mon, 1948)
Outlaw Brand (Mon, 1948)
Courtin' Trouble (Mon, 1948)
Cowboy Cavalier (Mon, 1948)
Gun Runner (Mon, 1949)
Gun Law Justice (Mon, 1949)
Across the Rio Grande (Mon, 1949)
Brand of Fear (Mon, 1949)
Roaring Westward (Mon, 1949)
Lawless Code (Mon, 1949)
The Marshal's Daughter (UA, 1953)
Arrow in the Dust (AA, 1954) (also song)
The Silver Star (Lip, 1955) (voice only)
The James Dean Story (WB, 1957)
Slim Carter (Univ, 1957) (song only)
Money, Women and Guns (Univ, 1959) (voice only)

## Radio Series

Melody Ranch (CBS, 1939–43)
The Jimmy Wakely Show (CBS, 1953–58)

## TV Series

Five Star Jubilee (NBC, 1961)

## Album Discography

Big Country Songs (Vocalion 73904, MCA VL7-3904)
Blue Shadows (Coral CB-20033)
Christmas on the Range (10" Cap H-9004)
Christmas with Jimmy Wakely (Dot DLP-25754)
Country Million Sellers (Shasta 501)
A Cowboy Serenade (Tops L-1601)
Early Transcriptions (Danny/Cattle 7803)
Enter and Rest and Pray (Decca DL-8680)
The Gentle Touch (Shasta 521) w. Linda Lee Wakely
Heartaches (Decca DL-75077)
Here's Jimmy Wakely (Vocalion 73857)
I'll Never Slip Around Again (Hilltop 6053) w. Margaret Whiting
The James Dean Story (Coral CRL-57094) [ST]
Jimmy Wakely (MCR 1254)
Jimmy Wakely and Russ Morgan (Shasta 518)
Jimmy Wakely Country (Shasta 528)

The Jimmy Wakely Family Show (Shasta 512)
Jimmy Wakely on Stage (Shasta 515)
Jimmy Wakely Sings (Shasta 505)
Lonesome Guitar Man (Album Globe 9028)
Merry Christmas (Shasta 502)
Now and Then (Decca DL-75192)
An Old Fashioned Christmas (Shasta 533)
Precious Memories (Shasta 532)
Reflections (Shasta 527)
Santa Fe Trail (Decca DL-8409, Stetson HAT-3012)
Show Me the Way (Vocalion 73855)
The Singing Cowboy (Shasta 522)
Slippin' Around (Dot 3711/25711)
Songs of the West (10" Cap H-4008)
A Tribute to Bob Wills (MCR 1250)
The Wakely Way with Country Hits (Shasta 514)
Western Swing and Pretty Things (Shasta 526)

# ETHEL WATERS

"WHOEVER TEACHES THE FISH TO SWIM AND THE BIRDS TO FLY taught me to sing. I can't remember having a lesson," Ethel Waters once said. Despite this lack of formal vocal training, her singing was melodious, with a distinctive tone and vibrato often lacking in the rough-hewn blues singers of her day. It was mostly due to her smooth singing style that Ethel Waters was able to break away from the ethnic entertainment circuit and make a name for herself in nightclubs, vaudeville, recordings, Broadway, radio, movies, and later television. Like most non-white people in the early twentieth century, Ethel suffered from prejudice, but she was (mostly) philosophical about it. "I've never been sorry I'm colored. Suffering isn't prejudice. Just because a person is white doesn't mean he doesn't have trouble too." Although she reached great heights in her career and had many successes not then often accorded to members of her race, Ethel Waters was not a happy woman until she turned fully to religion in the late 1950s. "When I had everything, I had nothing," she reasoned. "Now I have nothing, but I have everything."

Ethel Waters was born October 31, 1896 (not 1900 as is often reported), in Chester, Pennsylvania, the daughter of unwed thirteen-year-old Louise Anderson and John Waters; she had been conceived at knife point. The infant was raised by her grandmother, Sally Anderson, but she had a vagabond life in the slums of Chester and Philadelphia, where her grandmother worked as a maid. Often Ethel lacked for food and even shelter as she was growing up. Although she had little formal education, she was highly intelligent and found some solace from her hard life at a Catholic school and a Methodist church. When she was thirteen, she married Buddy Purnsley, a brutal man ten years her senior. Ethel managed to get menial jobs, and she also began to practice dancing and singing, which she found were outlets for her feelings and an escape from her tawdry environment. (At one point while growing up in the red-light district where her grandmother lived, she ran errands for whores and pimps.)

When she was fifteen, Ethel was given the chance to sing at a Philadelphia club on her birthday; she was such a success that she was hired on the spot and billed as Sweet Mama Stringbean. (She was very thin in those days.) She was the first woman to gain W. C. Handy's permission to perform his "St. Louis Blues," and she was a big success with it when she sang it in Baltimore with the Hill Sisters. She later toured with the sisters and then signed with Theatre Owners Booking Association (TOBA), which booked acts for the black club circuit.

By 1921, Ethel Waters was recording for the Black Swan label, which was aimed at the ethnic market, and her discs included good sellers like "Down Home Blues," "Jazzin' Babies Blues," "Memphis Man," and "All the Time." She also became a popular attraction in such Harlem clubs as Edmond Johnson's Cellar and the Cotton Club, and became famous for her sexy performance with its bumps and grinds. In 1925, she replaced Florence Mills as the stellar attraction at the Plantation Club, and there she introduced "Dinah," which she recorded successfully for Columbia Records. (She remained with that label for nearly a decade.)

She made her Broadway debut in Donald Heywood's *Africana* in the summer of 1927; it ran for seventy-two performances. After years of toiling in blacks-only vaudeville houses, she made her debut at the Palace Theatre in New York City in the fall of 1927 performing "I Don't Care" and "Shake That Thing." A road tour with *Africana* followed, and then she returned to vaudeville. At the time, many of Ethel's songs were considered risqué, as were many blues numbers, but her records for Columbia sold quite well, as evidenced by such sellers as "Sweet Georgia Brown," "Am I Blue?," "Memories of You," and "Harlem on My Mind." She also did such double-entendre tunes as "My Handy Man" and "Long Lean Lanky Mama." Frequently there was a strain of belligerent weariness to her numbers, a result of her hard childhood.

In the rush to turn out musical features in 1929–30, Hollywood eagerly signed all types of singers, from opera singers like Grace Moore to blues interpreters like Ethel Waters. She made her screen debut in the Warner Bros. Technicolor feature ON WITH THE SHOW (1929), exuberantly singing two of her most popular numbers, "Am I Blue?" and "Birmingham Bertha." She appeared as herself in this backstage story, and her spicy songs were spliced into the proceedings.

With no place for a black star in 1930 Hollywood, she returned to Broadway for the Lew Leslie production of *Blackbirds of 1930*, with songs by Eubie Blake and Andy Razaf. Despite her songs ("You're Lucky to Me" and "Memories of You"), the revue folded after only twenty-six performances in the fall of that year. The next spring she had a slightly better run with eighty performances as the star of *Rhapsody in Black* (1931), in which she performed "You Can't Stop Me from Lovin' You," "Till the Real Thing Comes Along," and "I'm Feelin' Blue." Ethel introduced the Harold Arlen song "Stormy Weather" at the Cotton Club in 1933 and recorded it for Brunswick Records. When Irving Berlin heard her fine rendition of the song, he hired her to appear in the Broadway production of *As Thousands Cheer* (1933), in which she sang "Suppertime," "Heat Wave," and "Harlem on My Mind." This was the first time a black performer had appeared on Broadway with an otherwise all-white cast. The revue ran for four hundred performances.

In 1933, Ethel was in the (Brooklyn studio filmed) Vitaphone movie short RUFUS JONES FOR PRESIDENT, playing the mother of a little boy (Sammy Davis, Jr.) who dreams he becomes President of the United States. The next year she was in the RKO short BUBBLING OVER, in which she sang "That's Why Darkies Were Born." Meanwhile, she had starred on CBS radio's "American Revue" each Sunday. In 1934, she was also featured in the Universal movie GIFT OF GAB, singing "I Ain't Gonna Sin No More." It was a slapdash potpourri that showcased an assortment of entertainers (mostly doing specialties) including Gene Austin and the Mills Brothers, as well as a radio playlet starring Boris Karloff, Bela Lugosi, and Paul Lukas. Hollywood clearly did not know what to do with Ethel Waters, who was now starting to look a bit matronly.

In the fall of 1935, she was back on Broadway appearing with Beatrice Lillie, Eleanor Powell, and Eddie Foy, Jr. in the Howard Dietz–Arthur Schwartz revue *At Home Abroad*, which had a 198-performance run. During this time, Ethel, long since divorced from her first husband, married bandleader Eddie Mallory, and she toured with him until 1939 in her vaudeville production of *Swing, Harlem, Swing*. In 1938, she gave a concert at Carnegie Hall, and in the late 1930s, she was heard on radio from the Cotton Club, backed by the Dorsey Brothers' orchestra.

The year 1939 found Ethel Waters starring on Broadway in the dramatic play *Mamba's Daughters* in the role of Hagar, and she won critical acclaim for her acting. It was the first time a black woman had starred in a dramatic work on the Great White Way. After that show's success, Ethel starred for 156 successful performances in the Broadway musical fantasy *Cabin in the Sky* (1940), with Todd Duncan, Dooley Wilson, and Rex Ingram. She sang "Cabin in the Sky" and "Taking a Chance on Love," which she recorded for the Liberty Music Shop record label.

Now in her forties and no longer svelte, Ethel returned to Hollywood. For 20th Century–Fox in the episodic TALES OF MANHATTAN (1942), she and Paul Robeson played poor sharecroppers who come into possession of an expensive coat. At MGM, Lena Horne (in some ways a successor to Waters as a song stylist) had refused to play the stereotypical role of a maid in CAIRO (1942), but Ethel agreed to the supporting part. The "B" spy spoof starred Jeanette MacDonald, with Waters cast as her domestic helper, Cleo. Ethel sang "Buds Won't Bloom," but there was little she could do with her pigeonholed role. However, she had agreed to it as part of a deal with the studio to recreate her role in CABIN IN THE SKY (1943). In addition to her two songs from the stage show, she introduced a new tune written especially for the film, "Happiness Is a Thing Called Joe," and she had a surprisingly agile jitterbug number in a club scene. *Variety* acknowledged of Waters, "Her sincerity, compassion, personal warmth and dramatic skill, plus her unique talent as a singer make her performance as Petunia an overpowering accomplishment." However, there had been problems during the making of CABIN IN THE SKY with Waters feuding with Lena Horne and being outspokenly unhappy with the MGM hierarchy. In an era when there were few roles, if any, for black stars, she sealed her fate by being "troublesome." Despite having purchased a Hollywood home, she returned to New York.

In 1943, she was back on Broadway in the show *Laugh Time*, a short-lived musical with Bert Wheeler, Frank Fay, and Buck & Bubbles. While in Gotham she made a guest appearance in the film STAGE DOOR CANTEEN (1943) performing "Quicksands" with Count Basie and His Orchestra. Between engagements during the war years, Ethel entertained soldiers with the USO.

During the later 1940s, Ethel Waters received no film or stage offers, although she continued to work in nightclubs. In 1948–49, she toured with Fletcher Henderson as her pianist. When 20th Century–Fox decided to film the controversial PINKY (1949), the story of a black girl (played by Caucasian Jeanne Crain) who passes for white, Ethel was hired to play her grandmother. She was nominated for an Oscar, but lost the Supporting Actress Award to Mercedes McCambridge of ALL THE KING'S MEN. The next year she returned to Broadway in *The Member of the Wedding,* as the understanding housekeeper Berenice Sadie Brown, and she was given the New York Drama Critics Award as best actress. In the otherwise dramatic play by Carson McCullers, she sang her favorite spiritual, "His Eye Is on the Sparrow," which she used as the title of her best-selling autobiography in 1951.

As a result of the success of *The Member of the Wedding,* she was signed to star in the title role of the ABC-TV series "Beulah" as a wise domestic (the part had been played on radio by *actor* Marlin Hurt) and she stayed with the popular comedy program for two seasons (1950–52) before being replaced by Louise Beavers. Butterfly McQueen was cast as her lightheaded girlfriend Oriole, and Percy Harris was her aimless boyfriend Bill. She left the hit series so she could repeat her role in the Columbia film version of THE MEMBER OF THE WEDDING (1952). She gave a fine performance and should have received an Oscar nomination.

Following these successes, Ethel's career fell apart, and tax problems and poor investments left her broke. Matters were not helped by the fact that she had put on a great deal of weight. At one time she weighed nearly 350 pounds. About the only work she could get was occasional club dates with accompanist Reginald Beane. She had infrequent guest spots on TV shows like "Favorite Playhouse," "Climax," "G.E. Theatre," "Playwright '56," and "Matinee Theatre" in rather demeaning acting chores, considering her former star status. In 1956, she appeared on the

Jeanne Crain and Ethel Waters in PINKY (1949)

· "Break the $250,000 Bank" quiz show, seeking money to pay her back taxes.

It was in 1957 that matters changed dramatically for Ethel Waters when she accepted an invitation to sing at a Billy Graham crusade at Madison Square Garden. The event changed her life. She returned to the religious teachings of her childhood and thereby found inner peace and happiness. She became a close friend and associate of the evangelist and would be associated with his crusades, both in the United States and abroad, for the remainder of her career.

Soon after she began working with Graham, Ethel started making albums of spirituals for Word Records. She also performed concerts in churches, as well as at religious conventions and Youth for Christ meetings. She also continued her one-woman show, which she took to Broadway as *At Home with Ethel Waters* in 1953 and *An Evening with Ethel Waters* in 1959. She also revived *The Member of the Wedding* on several occasions in stock. Occasional TV guest spots on shows like "Whirlybirds," "Route 66," and "Great Adventures" were also forthcoming, but did little to showcase the white-haired lady's talents. Ethel also turned to composing music, including religious numbers such as "Partners with God."

She appeared in the religious film THE HEART IS A REBEL for World Wide Pictures in 1956. The film dealt with greed in a Madison Avenue advertising agency, and Waters played a nurse and sang "His Eye Is on the Sparrow." She made her final theatrical film, THE SOUND AND THE FURY (1959), playing the family maid. Especially when compared to the performances in mixed acting styles by Joanne Woodward, Margaret Leighton, and Yul Brynner (in a toupee!), her performance exceeded the limits of her one-dimensional role as a matriarch. She returned to TV in 1967 in the unsuccessful comedy pilot "Professor Hubert Abernathy" for CBS-TV and later had guest roles in the "Daniel Boone" and "Owen Marshall, Counselor at Law" TV series.

In 1971, she was honored at a testimonial dinner in Los Angeles, and the next year she wrote her second autobiography, *To Me It's Wonderful.* In 1974, Ethel underwent an operation for cataracts and she recuperated at Billy Graham's home in Charlotte, North Carolina. (Some years before, she had sold her Los Angeles home and had moved into an apartment in the same city.) In 1976, she was featured, in clips from CABIN IN THE SKY, in the MGM documentary THAT'S ENTERTAINMENT, PART 2 and appeared on Mike Douglas' TV show. She also lost over one hundred pounds, getting down to a weight of 130. Ethel Waters continued to sing at Billy Graham Crusades into 1976, but that year she was hospitalized with cancer. Her condition deteriorated and she died September 1, 1976, and was buried in Forest Lawn Cemetery.

## Filmography

On with the Show (WB, 1929)
Rufus Jones for President (Vita, 1933) (s)
Gift of Gab (Univ, 1934)
Bubbling Over (RKO, 1934) (s)
Tales of Manhattan (20th–Fox, 1942)
Cairo (MGM, 1942)
Hot Frogs (Soundies, 1942) (s) (voice only)
The Voice That Thrilled the World (WB, 1943)
    (s) (clips from On with the Show)
Cabin in the Sky (MGM, 1943)

Stage Door Canteen (UA, 1943)
Pinky (20th–Fox, 1949)
The Negro in Entertainment (Pennsylvania
    Dept. of Public Instruction, 1950) (s)
The Member of the Wedding (Col, 1952)
The Heart Is a Rebel (World Wide, 1956)
The Sound and the Fury (20th–Fox, 1959)
Harlem in the Twenties (Encyclopedia Britanni-
    ca Educational Corp., 1971) (s)

## Broadway Plays

Africana (1927)
Blackbirds of 1930 (1930)
Rhapsody in Black (1931)
As Thousands Cheer (1933)
At Home Abroad (1935)

Mamba's Daughters (1939)
Cabin in the Sky (1940)
Laugh Time (1943)
Blue Holiday (1945)
The Member of the Wedding (1950)

## Radio Series

American Revue (CBS, 1933–34)

## TV Series

Beulah (ABC, 1950–52)

## Album Discography

Blackbirds of 1928 (Col OL-6770, Sutton SSU-
    270) [OC]
Cabin in the Sky (Hollywood Soundstage 5003)
    [ST]
The Complete Bluebird Sessions 1938–39
    (Rosetta 1314)
Complete Decca Recordings (Swingtime 1031)
Ethel Waters (10" Remington 1025)
Ethel Waters (Continental 5084)
Ethel Waters Live (Amalgamated 199)
Ethel Waters 1946–47 (Glendale 9011)
Ethel Waters on Stage and Screen, 1925–40
    (Col CL-2792, Col Special Products 2792)

Ethel Waters on the Air (Totem 1041)
Ethel Waters Reminisces (Word 3173/8107)
Ethel Waters Sings Her Best (10" Jay 3010)
Ethel Waters—Vault Originals (X LVA-1009)
The Greatest Years (Col PG-31571)
Harlem Lullaby (HEP 1-006)
His Eye Is on the Sparrow (Word 3100/8044)
Jazzin' Babies Blues (Biograph 12026)
Miss Ethel Waters in Person (Monmouth/
    Evergreen 6812)
Oh, Daddy (Biograph 12022)
Stage Door Canteen (Curtain Calls 100/11-12)
    [ST]

# MAE WEST

WITHOUT DOUBT, ONE OF THE MOST UNIQUE FABRICATIONS OF the twentieth century was the show business phenomenon known as Mae West. She was assertive in an age when women were supposed to be submissive; she was openly bawdy when decorum was the order of the day. With her buxom hour-glass figure and her lascivious frame of reference, she shocked, intrigued, captivated, and amused many generations of fans. For over seven (!) decades, she was an active performer, shrewdly promoting what she knew and understood best—Miss Mae West.

If Mae West was a vaudeville oddity and then a spicy treat on Broadway, she was a sensation in her initial Hollywood feature films. On screen, she appreciated that virtue is its own reward, but doesn't sell tickets at the box office. She proved to be the salvation of the near-bankrupt Paramount Pictures, insisting, "Why should I go good when I'm packing them in because I'm bad?" In her ribald screen characterizations, her philosophy was "Let both the men and the women wonder. The men for what they think they haven't got and the women for what they know they haven't got." Most admirably of all, she never allowed her oversized personality (and ego) to be diminished by the filmmaking production line. She always retained her iconoclastic self-identity, living up to her battle cry when she first arrived in Hollywood in 1932: "I'm not a little girl from a little town making good in a big town. I'm a big girl from a big town making good in a little town."

Generations have celebrated the wit and wisdom of Mae West and have acknowledged her as one of the most engaging forerunners of women's liberation. She has also been well applauded as an icon of the anti-censorship movement. (She is the one who said, "Sex and I have a lot in common. I don't want to take any credit for inventing it, but I may say—in my own modest way, and in a manner of speaking—that I have rediscovered it.") But not to be overlooked is her ability as a noteworthy song stylist, whether captivating a stage audience with an explicit tune while dancing a shimmy or, much more recently, offering her own bold (albeit nasal) interpretations of such rock 'n' roll classics as "Great Balls of Fire" or such West-ian Christmas salutes as "Santa, Bring My Baby Back to Me."

She was born Mary Jane West on August 17, 1892 (sources range in date from 1887 to 1893) in Brooklyn, New York, the daughter of John Patrick West (a prizefighter) and German immigrant Matilda Delker Doelger (a corset designer). Later, two other children would be born to the Wests: Mildred (Beverly) and John Patrick II. From an early age, Mae (as she became known) was drawn to show business and away from the classroom. At age five, she sang "Ring Out, Wild Bells" at a church social and soon was taking dance classes at "Professor" Watts Academy. At age six, she made her stage debut at Brooklyn's

Royal Theatre, doing a song and dance for its amateur night. Next she was part of the Hal Clarendon Stock Company, based at Brooklyn's Gotham Theatre, and remained there four years. She graduated to becoming a strong woman in a Coney Island acrobatic act, and by the age of fifteen she was touring in vaudeville with William Hogan, playing Huck Finn's girlfriend.

Years later, the ever audacious Mae revealed that she had lost her virginity at the age of thirteen to her twenty-one-year-old music teacher, adding, "I've never been without a man for more than a week since I was thirteen years old." On April 11, 1911, she wed jazz singer Frank Wallace in Milwaukee, Wisconsin. Several months later, Mae—having second thoughts about being tied down by matrimony—separated from him. They divorced in 1943, after he made headlines by detailing his union to the sex symbol. She never remarried.

It was also in 1911 (on September 22) that Mae made her Broadway bow in *A la Broadway* at the Folies Bergere dinner theater. She quickly developed a reputation in vaudeville and theater as being a risqué entertainer who was very avant-garde. As later in her career, audiences and critics alike were unsure whether to regard Mae's posturing as a sex symbol seriously or as an entertaining come-on. By 1913, she and her sister, Beverly, were appearing in a vaudeville act at the Fifth Avenue Theatre and Mae (alone) continued to tour vaudeville as a headliner on the Loew's circuit. There she was known as "The Baby Vamp." Comedian Ed Wynn may have been the star of the Arthur Hammerstein musical *Sometime* (1918), but Mae was the sensation of this Broadway musical with her interpretive dancing of "The Shimmy" and her singing of "Any Kind of Man" and "All I Want Is Just a Little Lovin'." The show lasted 283 performances. In 1920, Mae *almost* made her screen debut when she tested for the lead opposite Jack Dempsey in the Pathé serial DAREDEVIL JACK.

More vaudeville followed, and in 1926 she gave Broadway a jolt when she starred in *Sex*, a notoriously open-minded and sexy play. It ran for 375 performances before pressure groups had the play closed and West arrested. She was sentenced to ten days in jail at Blackwell's Island and was fined $500. When she was released after eight days, she noted, "The warden was very nice. He used to take me out driving every night." Undaunted, the ribald Mae produced *The Drag*, with an all-gay cast, which tried out in Paterson, New Jersey, in early 1927 but never opened in Manhattan.

She wrote and starred in *The Wicked Age* (1927), yet that show lasted only nineteen performances. But then she wrote *Diamond Lil* (which opened on April 9, 1928), a lewd tale of a prowling golddigger. West's three risqué songs became part of her permanent repertoire: "A Guy That Takes His Time," "Easy Rider," and "Frankie and Johnny." As Mae described the 1890s vamp she was playing, "I'm her and she's me and we're each other." The memorable production ran for 323 performances. However, its follow-up, *Pleasure Man* (1928)—whose cast included female impersonators—folded quickly. Mae toured in *Diamond Lil* and was back on the New York stage in *The Constant Sinner* (1931).

Meanwhile, one of Mae's colorful show business friends, formerly an underworld underling, had made a successful transition to moviemaking. George Raft was under

Paramount contract and it was he who suggested that West would be an ideal asset for his next picture, NIGHT AFTER NIGHT (1932). Suffering financially from the Depression, the desperate studio agreed to contract her at $5,000 weekly with a ten-week minimum. West soon coerced the studio into allowing her to customize her tepid scenes. Thus, at age forty, she made her bow on camera as the diamond-clad Maude Triplett. From the start, her trademarks were fully in place: swaying hips (because she was short, she wore thick platform heels, and it was impossible to stride in these lifts), rolling eyes, and well-punctuated "aaahhss." Her repertoire of naughty witticisms immediately made her the darling of agog filmgoers and the bane of reactionary forces such as the Hearst newspapers (they denounced her as a "menace to the sacred institution of the American family"). Mae was fourth-billed in NIGHT AFTER NIGHT, but Paramount offered her top billing and over $100,000 to star in another movie for them. She decreed that a picture version of *Diamond Lil* be the vehicle and charged the studio an additional $25,000 for creating its screenplay. She picked a studio contractee, Cary Grant, as her leading man, and the movie—retitled SHE DONE HIM WRONG—premiered in February 1933. The movie was a box-office bonanza, grossing ten times its cost (in the United States alone), and Paramount breathed a financial sigh of relief.

For her next vehicle, Paramount marched her into I'M NO ANGEL (1933), in which she sashayed as the liontamer Tira who tolerates no doubles in the cage or in the boudoir. She toyed with her leading man (Cary Grant), exchanged bon mots democratically with her black maids (Libby Taylor, Gertrude Howard), sang "They Call Me Sister Honky Tonk," and tossed off such quips as "When I'm good, I'm very good, but when I'm bad, I'm better." By now, Mae was ranked number eight among the top ten box-office stars and Paramount renegotiated her contract: $100,000 per film plus an additional $100,000 for writing its scenario.

Most moviegoers were captivated by Mae's unique screen presence and her knack of removing the screen heroine from her pedestal and putting her in face-to-face confrontation with the opposite sex. However, such groups as the Catholic Legion of Decency denounced her as obscene. The concerned studio changed the title of her next feature from "It Ain't No Sin" to BELLE OF THE NINETIES (1934). This was another period costume outing, with Roger Pryor and Johnny Mack Brown as her co-stars. In this vehicle, Mae's Ruby Carter informed filmgoers, "A man in the house is worth two in the street." Displaying her affinity for ethnic music, West included Duke Ellington and His Orchestra in this New Orleans tale, and she sang "Troubled Waters."

In GOIN' TO TOWN (1935), Mae was adventuress Cleo Borden and the ads proclaimed "Mae West goes modern with seven leading men! . . . Mae's a streamlined gal now—it increases her speed and cuts down resistance." Along the road to riches and emotional satisfaction, she performed the aria "My Heart at Thy Sweet Voice" from the opera *Samson and Delilah*. If the public was surprised by her vocal virtuosity, she was not. The ever-confident star told the press about the operatic sequence and its heroine, "I have a lot of respect for that dame. There's one lady barber that made good." While the bloom of novelty might have been off Mae's shocking screen persona, the queen of screen wisecracks nevertheless earned $480,833 that year.

"I'm an Occidental Woman in an Oriental Mood for Love," crooned Mae in KLONDIKE ANNIE (1936) before fate and the plot transplanted her from San Francisco to the frozen north where she posed as a missionary soul saver. In the icy land, she delivered the song "It's Better to Give Than to Receive," and when not courting Victor McLaglen, she was found advising, "Any time you take religion as a joke, the laugh's on you." In GO WEST, YOUNG MAN (1936), she was very up to date as the Gloria Swanson–type movie star Mavis Arden, who prefers love with rustic Randolph Scott to screen fame. However, as a concession to censorship, Mae was very sedate (by Westian standards) in this mild comedy/drama.

In 1937, Paramount underwent further corporate changes and the new regime looked askance at Mae West's brand of screen entertainment, especially since the outcry against her "vulgarism" was increasingly pronounced and more organized. Her final picture for the studio, EVERY DAY'S A HOLIDAY, was made in 1937 but not released until 1938. She was Peaches O'Day, an old-fashioned con artist, who masquerades as Mademoiselle Fifi in turn-of-the-century New York. Mae struggled valiantly with the tedious plot involving politics and impersonation, but the film's meager highlight belonged to jubilant Louis Armstrong in the parade finale.

On December 12, 1937, Mae's controversial status reached a new peak when she appeared on NBC radio's "Chase and Sanborn Hour," starring Edgar Bergen and Charlie McCarthy. In the "Garden of Eden" skit, in which Don Ameche was Adam and the dummy was the snake, Mae purred, "Would you, honey, like to try this apple sometime?" That and other suggestive lines led to a censorial brouhaha that kept Mae West off the airwaves for twelve years. (She would return to radio as a guest on Perry Como's "Chesterfield Supper Club" in 1949.) Adding to her professional problems, in a 1938 *Motion Picture Herald* poll, Mae, along with such personalities as Marlene Dietrich, Katharine Hepburn, and Fred Astaire, was listed as box-office poison.

Undaunted, she returned to the stage with a personal appearance act. It was not until 1940 that she reappeared on screen, this time for Universal Pictures and paired with another Paramount Pictures exile, W. C. Fields. The two comedic institutions wrote their own material, were tremendously wary of each other, and suffered each other's ego with ill grace. However, the results were classic. In MY LITTLE CHICKADEE, she traipsed as Flower Belle Lee and he snarled as Cuthbert J. Twillie. The disparate duo ended up tied together in matrimony in the Old West. She sang "Willie of the Valley," exchanged quips with the bulbous-nosed Fields, and invited him (and the audience) to "Come on up and see me sometime." Nevertheless, it was three years before she returned to the screen, in Columbia Pictures' THE HEAT'S ON (1943) with Victor Moore and Xavier Cugat and His Orchestra. It was low-budget claptrap, and despite her contemporary costumes and hairdo, she seemed out of date and overweight.

Mae had long nurtured the hope of starring in a film about the great Catherine, queen of Russia. Instead, she played the role on Broadway, in *Catherine Was Great* (1944). West's approach to history was revealed in her famous curtain speech: "Catherine was a great empress. She also had 300 lovers. I did the best I could in a couple of hours." The play ran for 191 performances and then she took it on tour. She played summer stock in 1946 with the sex comedy *Ring Twice Tonight* and then brought *Diamond Lil* to England in 1947. For the next four years she toured with this vehicle, including two return engagements on Broadway. She played stock again in 1952 with *Come on Up . . . Ring Twice* and two years later made her Las Vegas cabaret debut at the Sahara Hotel. She opened the highly publicized act by singing "I Wanna Do All Day What I Do All Night" and had a chorus line of nine musclemen. Among the beefcake were Mickey Hargitay (who later wed Jayne Mansfield) and Paul Novak, West's longtime companion. The act was a sensation and was brought to New York's Latin Quarter and, the next year, to Chicago's Chez Paree. She returned to stock in 1956, and on the March 26, 1958, Academy Awards telecast she created a sensation singing "Baby, It's Cold Outside" with Rock Hudson. The interlude stopped the show. She taped an interview for CBS-TV's "Person to Person" in October 1959, but her double-entendre responses frightened the censors and the program was not aired. But she was seen swapping repartee with a talking horse in a 1964 segment of the TV sitcom "Mr. Ed."

In July 1961, she starred in her new play, *Sextette*, at the Edgewater Beach Playhouse

Mae West and Victor Moore in THE HEAT'S ON (1943)

in Chicago. Her co-star was Jack LaRue, who had played in Mae's original stage production of *Diamond Lil.* Repeatedly, over the years, there were many movie offers, which Mae rejected as unsuitable. Finally, at age seventy-eight, she made her comeback. She accepted a starring part in Gore Vidal's MYRA BRECKENRIDGE (1970). Raquel Welch was nominally the lead of this bizarre sex comedy, but Mae, who received $350,000 for ten days of work and for writing her own scenes, stole the limelight. As talent agent Letitia Van Allen she sang "Hard to Handle" and "You Gotta Taste All the Fruit," wiggled her hips, batted her eyes, and tossed off Westian remarks that amazed even the post-hippie generation. However, the film was a flop.

In her mid-eighties, Mae continued onward. She authored (some insist it was ghostwritten) *Mae West on Sex, Health, and ESP* (1975). Her novel, *Pleasure Man,* was published in 1976. (An update of her memoirs, *Goodness Had Nothing to Do with It,* had been published in 1970.) She was a guest interviewee on Dick Cavett's CBS-TV special (April 5, 1976) dealing with Hollywood. On the show she sang "Frankie and Johnny" and "After You've Gone." And she made another movie. She was paid $250,000, plus a percentage of the profits, for the screen version of SEXTETTE, which did not find release (and then only spottily) until 1978. One of the film's musical numbers featured West singing "Happy Birthday 21." On May 13, 1977, the be-wigged Mae was given *After Dark* magazine's Ruby Award. The citation read, "Always up, always funny, always glamorous, Mae West is undisputedly one of the most important women of the century."

She suffered a stroke in July 1980, and on November 23, 1980, at age eighty-eight, she died peacefully in a chair in her living room of "natural causes." She was survived by her sister, Beverly, with whom she long had feuded.

In a final analysis, this sultry star best summed up her career: "Every studio wanted a Mae West, they never found one 'cause my technique's my own—it can't be copied."

## Filmography

Night After Night (Par, 1932) (also additional dialogue)

Hollywood on Parade #A2 (Par, 1932) (s)

She Done Him Wrong (Par, 1933) (also original play)

I'm No Angel (Par, 1933) (also story, screenplay)

Belle of the Nineties (Par, 1934) (also story, screenplay)

Goin' to Town (Par, 1935) (also screenplay)

Klondike Annie (Par, 1936) (also original play, screenplay)

Go West, Young Man (Par, 1936) (also screenplay)

Every Day's a Holiday (Par, 1938) (also story, screenplay)

My Little Chickadee (Univ, 1940) (also co-screenplay)

The Heat's On [Tropicana] (Col, 1943)

Myra Breckinridge (20th–Fox, 1970)

Sextette (Crown–International, 1978) (also original play)

## Broadway Plays

A la Broadway (1911)
Vera Violetta (1911)
A Winsome Widow (1912)
Sometime (1918)
The Mimic World of 1921 (1921)
Sex (1926) (also script)
The Wicked Age (1927) (also script)
Diamond Lil (1928) (also script)

Pleasure Man (1928) (script and co-direction only)
The Constant Sinner (1931) (also original novel, script)
Catherine Was Great (1944) (also script)
Diamond Lil (1949) (revival) (also script)
Diamond Lil (1951) (revival) (also script)

## Album Discography

Ethel Merman/Lyda Roberti/Mae West (Col CL-2751, Col Special Products 2751)
The Fabulous Mae West (Decca DL-9016/ 79016, MCA 2053)
Great Balls of Fire (MGM SE-4869)
Mae West (MCA 1530)
Mae West and Her Guys (Caliban 6036)
Mae West on the Air (Sandy Hook 2098)
Mae West on the Chase and Sanborn Hour (Radiola MR-1126)
Mae West—Original Radio Broadcasts (Mark 56 643)

Mae West—Original Voice Tracks from Her Greatest Movies (Decca DL-79176)
The Queen of Sex (Rosetta C-1315)
Under the Mistletoe with Mae West (Round RS100)
W. C. Fields and Mae West (Proscenium 22, American 120)
W. C. Fields and Mae West—Side by Side (Har HS-11405)
Way Out West (Tower T/ST-5026)
Wild Christmas [Mae in December] (Dagonet DG-4)

# GENERAL INDEX

Boldface page references at the end of entries indicate photographs. Titles of films and made-for-television movies are in italics; radio and television titles are in quotation marks; titles of books and stage productions are in italics and are indicated as such in parentheses.

# SONG AND ALBUM INDEX

Songs titles are in quotation marks, album titles in italics.